Nafisa P8B

McGraw-Hill Ryerson

Principles of Mathematics 9

Authors

Chris Dearling
B.Sc., M.Sc.
Burlington, Ontario

Wayne Erdman
B.Math., B.Ed.
Toronto District School Board

Fred Ferneyhough
B.Math.
Peel District School Board

Brian McCudden
M.A., M.Ed., Ph.D.
Toronto, Ontario

Fran McLaren
B.Sc., B.Ed.
Upper Grand District
School Board

Roland W. Meisel
B.Sc., B.Ed., M.Sc.
Port Colborne, Ontario

Jacob Speijer
B.Eng., M.Sc.Ed., P.Eng.
District School Board of Niagara

Assessment Consultants

Chris Dearling

Brian McCudden

Technology Consultant

Roland W. Meisel

Literacy Consultant

Barbara Canton
Limestone District School Board

Advisors

Derrick Driscoll
Thames Valley District
School Board

Jeff Irvine
Peel District School Board

Tess Miller
Queen's University
Kingston, Ontario

Larry Romano
Toronto Catholic District
School Board

Carol Shiffman
Peel District School Board

Toronto Montréal Boston Burr Ridge, IL Dubuque, IA Madison, WI New York
San Francisco St. Louis Bangkok Bogotá Caracas Kuala Lumpur Lisbon London
Madrid Mexico City Milan New Delhi Santiago Seoul Singapore Sydney Taipei

The McGraw·Hill Companies

COPIES OF THIS BOOK MAY BE OBTAINED BY CONTACTING:

McGraw-Hill Ryerson Ltd.

WEB SITE:
http://www.mcgrawhill.ca

E-MAIL:
orders@mcgrawhill.ca

TOLL-FREE FAX:
1-800-463-5885

TOLL-FREE CALL:
1-800-565-5758

OR BY MAILING YOUR ORDER TO:
McGraw-Hill Ryerson
Order Department
300 Water Street
Whitby, ON L1N 9B6

Please quote the ISBN and title when placing your order.

McGraw-Hill Ryerson
Principles of Mathematics 9

ISBN 0-07-097319-9

http://www.mcgrawhill.ca

1 2 3 4 5 6 7 8 9 0 TCP 0 9 8 7 6

Printed and bound in Canada

PUBLISHER: Linda Allison
PROJECT MANAGERS: Maggie Cheverie, Janice Dyer
DEVELOPMENTAL EDITORS: Julia Cochrane, Jackie Lacoursiere, David Peebles
MANAGER, EDITORIAL SERVICES: Crystal Shortt
SENIOR SUPERVISING EDITOR: Kristi Moreau
COPY EDITORS: Julia Cochrane, Linda Jenkins, Red Pen Services
PHOTO RESEARCH/PERMISSION: Jean Ford, Linda Tanaka
PHOTO RESEARCH/SET-UP PHOTOGAPHY: Roland W. Meisel
EDITORIAL ASSISTANT: Erin Hartley
EDITORIAL COORDINATOR: Valerie Janicki
ASSISTANT PROJECT COORDINATOR: Janie Reeson
MANAGER PRODUCTION SERVICES: Yolanda Pigden
PRODUCTION COORDINATOR: Sheryl MacAdam
COVER DESIGN: Pronk & Associates
INTERIOR DESIGN: Pronk & Associates
ELECTRONIC PAGE MAKE-UP: Tom Dart, Greg Duhaney, and Kim Hutchinson/
First Folio Resource Group, Inc.
COVER IMAGE: Paul Rapson/Science Photo Library

Acknowledgements

REVIEWERS OF *PRINCIPLES OF MATHEMATICS 9*

The publishers, authors, and editors of *McGraw-Hill Ryerson Principles of Mathematics 9*, wish to extend their sincere thanks to the students, teachers, consultants, and reviewers who contributed their time, energy, and expertise to the creation of this textbook. We are grateful for their thoughtful comments and suggestions. This feedback has been invaluable in ensuring that the text and related teacher's resource meet the needs of students and teachers. We would also like to extend special thanks to the students of Harold M. Brathwaite Secondary School, Brampton, who participated in set-up photography sessions for some of the visuals in this text.

Flanny Alamparambil
York Catholic District School Board

Dan Bruni
York Catholic District School Board

I. Charlton
Thames Valley District School Board

Sandra Connolly
Peterborough Victoria Northumberland and Clarington Catholic District School Board

Bibiana Couto
Peel District School Board

Mary Ellen Diamond
Niagara Catholic District School Board

Emidio DiAntonio
Dufferin Peel Catholic District School Board

John DiVizio
Durham Catholic District School Board

Sandy Hawthorn
Grand Erie District School Board

Beverly A. Hitchman
Upper Grand District School Board

Mike Jacobs
Durham Catholic District School Board

Nina Jaiswal
Peel District School Board

Estella Jones
Hamilton-Wentworth District School Board

Alan Jones
Peel District School Board

David Lovisa
York Region District School Board

Teresa Marques
Dufferin Peel Catholic District School Board

Gordana Milenkovich
Peel District School Board

Sharon Morris
Thames Valley District School Board

Robert O'Connell
Toronto District School Board

Terry Paradellis
Toronto District School Board

Richard Poremba
Brant Haldimand Norfolk Catholic District School Board

Clyde Ramlochan
Toronto District School Board

Sharon Ramlochan
Toronto District School Board

John Santarelli
Hamilton-Wentworth Catholic District School Board

Robert Slemon
Toronto District School Board

Carol Sproule
Ottawa Carleton District School Board

Michelle St. Pierre
Simcoe County District School Board

Tara Townes
Waterloo Catholic District School Board

Angela Van Kralingen
Niagara Catholic District School Board

Robert F. K. Wong
Grand Erie District School Board

Contents

Chapter 3

Chapter 4

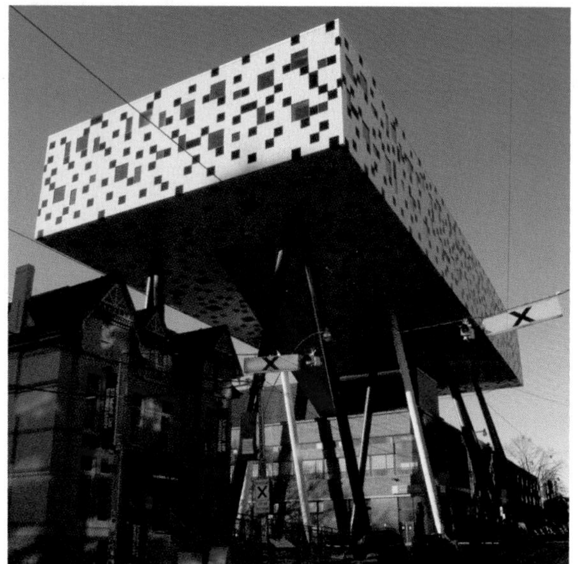

Chapter 5

Chapter 6

Chapter 7

Chapter 8

Chapter 9

A Tour of Your Textbook

Chapter Opener

- This two-page spread introduces what you will learn in the chapter.
- The specific curriculum expectations that the chapter covers are listed.
- The mathematical terms that are introduced and defined in the chapter are listed.
- The chapter problem is introduced. Questions related to the chapter problem occur in the Connect and Apply sections of the exercises throughout the chapter and are identified by a **Chapter Problem** descriptor.

2

Relations

This chapter introduces methods for analysing relationships between variables. These relationships occur in many areas, including business, science, sports, and the arts. Analysing these relationships helps you understand trends and make accurate predictions.

Chapter Problem

A coach is selecting students to compete in the high jump event for the school's track and field team. What factors should the coach consider? Explain your thinking.

You will be designing an experiment to test how these factors affect an athlete's performance in the high jump.

Get Ready

Examples and practise questions review key skills from previous mathematics courses that are needed for success with the new concepts of the chapter.

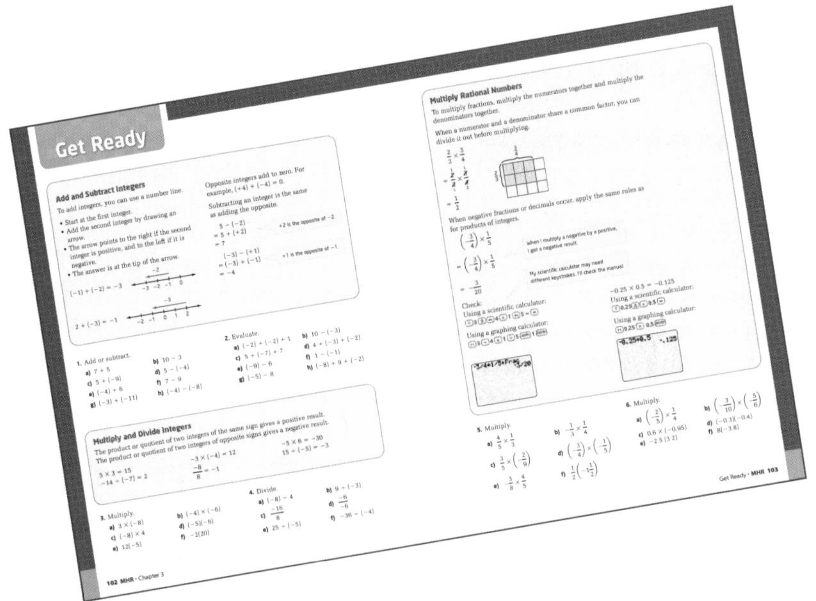

Get Ready

Add and Subtract Integers

Multiply and Divide Integers

Multiply Rational Numbers

Numbered Sections

Lesson Opener

Many lessons start with a photograph and short description of a real-world setting to which the mathematical concepts relate.

Investigate

These are step-by-step activities, leading you to build your own understanding of the new concepts of the lesson. Many of these activities can best be done by working in pairs or small groups to share ideas.

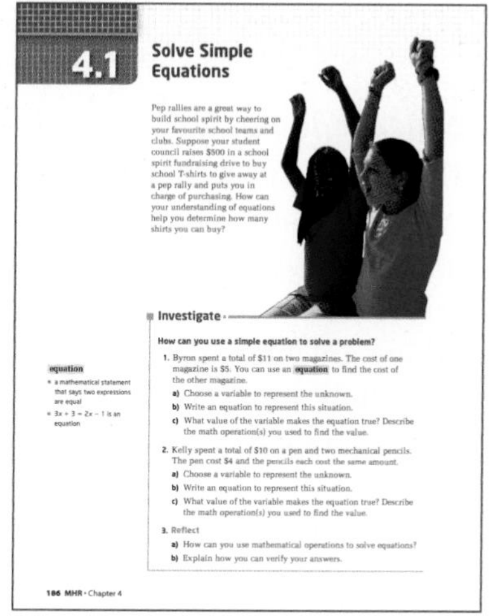

4.1 Solve Simple Equations

Pep rallies are a great way to build school spirit by cheering on your favourite school teams and clubs. Suppose your student council raises $500 in a school spirit fundraising drive to buy school T-shirts to give away at a pep rally and puts you in charge of purchasing. How can your understanding of equations help you determine how many shirts you can buy?

Investigate

How can you use a simple equation to solve a problem?

1. Byron spent a total of $11 on two magazines. The cost of one magazine is $5. You can use an **equation** to find the cost of the other magazine.
   a) Choose a variable to represent the unknown.
   b) Write an equation to represent this situation.
   c) What value of the variable makes the equation true? Describe the math operation(s) you used to find the value.
2. Kelly spent a total of $10 on a pen and two mechanical pencils. The pen cost $4 and the pencils each cost the same amount.
   a) Choose a variable to represent the unknown.
   b) Write an equation to represent this situation.
   c) What value of the variable makes the equation true? Describe the math operation(s) you used to find the value.
3. Reflect
   a) How can you use mathematical operations to solve equations?
   b) Explain how you can verify your answers.

equation
- a mathematical statement that says two expressions are equal
- $3x + 3 = 2x - 1$ is an equation

186 MHR • Chapter 4

Examples

- Worked examples provide model solutions that show how the new concepts are used.
- The examples and their worked solutions include several tools to help you understand the work.
  - Notes in a thought bubble help you to think through the steps.
  - Sometimes different methods of solving the same problem are shown. One way may make more sense to you than the others.
- You can refer to these examples as you work on the exercises.

Key Concepts

This feature summarizes the concepts learned in the lesson. You can refer to this summary when you are studying or doing homework.

Communicate Your Understanding

These questions allow you to reflect on the concepts of the section. By discussing these questions in a group, you can see whether you understand the main points and are ready to start the exercises.

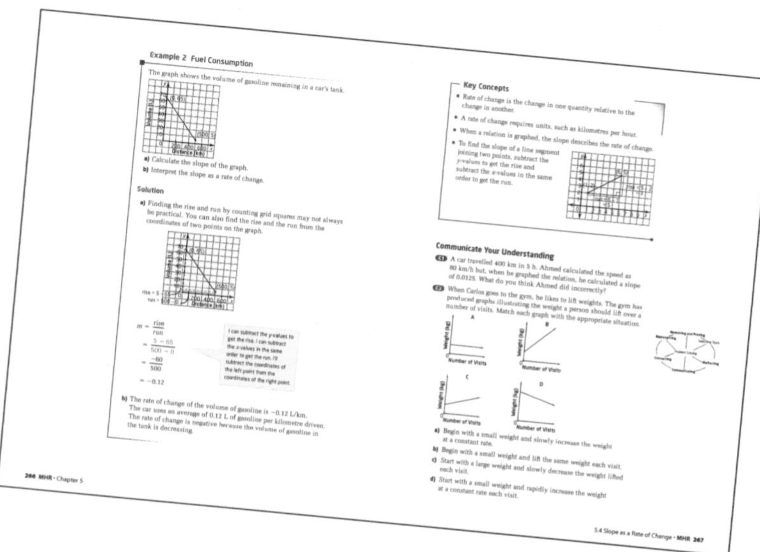

Example 2 Fuel Consumption

The graph shows the volume of gasoline remaining in a car's tank.

a) Calculate the slope of the graph.
b) Interpret the slope as a rate of change.

Solution

a) Finding the rise and run by counting grid squares may not always be practical. You can also find the rise and the run from the coordinates of two points on the graph.

$$m = \frac{\text{rise}}{\text{run}} = \frac{5 - 65}{500 - 0} = \frac{-60}{500} = -0.12$$

I can subtract the y-values to get the rise. I can subtract the x-values in the same order to get the run. I'll subtract the coordinates of the left point from the coordinates of the right point.

b) The rate of change of the volume of gasoline is −0.12 L/km. The car uses an average of 0.12 L of gasoline per kilometre driven. The rate of change is negative because the volume of gasoline in the tank is decreasing.

266 MHR • Chapter 5

Key Concepts
- Rate of change is the change in one quantity relative to the change in another.
- A rate of change requires units, such as kilometres per hour.
- When a relation is graphed, the slope describes the rate of change.
- To find the slope of a line segment joining two points, subtract the y-values to get the rise and subtract the x-values in the same order to get the run.

Communicate Your Understanding

C1 A car travelled 400 km in 5 h. Ahmed calculated the speed as 80 km/h but, when he graphed the relation, he calculated a slope of 0.0125. What do you think Ahmed did incorrectly?

C2 When Carlos goes to the gym, he likes to lift weights. The gym has produced graphs illustrating the weight a person should lift over a number of visits. Match each graph with the appropriate situation.

a) Begin with a small weight and slowly increase the weight at a constant rate.
b) Begin with a small weight and lift the same weight each visit.
c) Start with a large weight and slowly decrease the weight lifted each visit.
d) Start with a small weight and rapidly increase the weight at a constant rate each visit.

5.4 Slope as a Rate of Change • MHR 267

Exercises

Practise

- These questions provide an opportunity to practise your knowledge and understanding of the new concept.
- To help you, questions are referenced to the worked examples.

Connect and Apply

- These questions allow you to use what you have learned to solve problems and make connections among concepts. In answering these questions you will be integrating your skills with many of the math processes.
- There are many opportunities to use technology. If specific tools or materials are needed, they are noted and the question has a **Use Technology** descriptor.

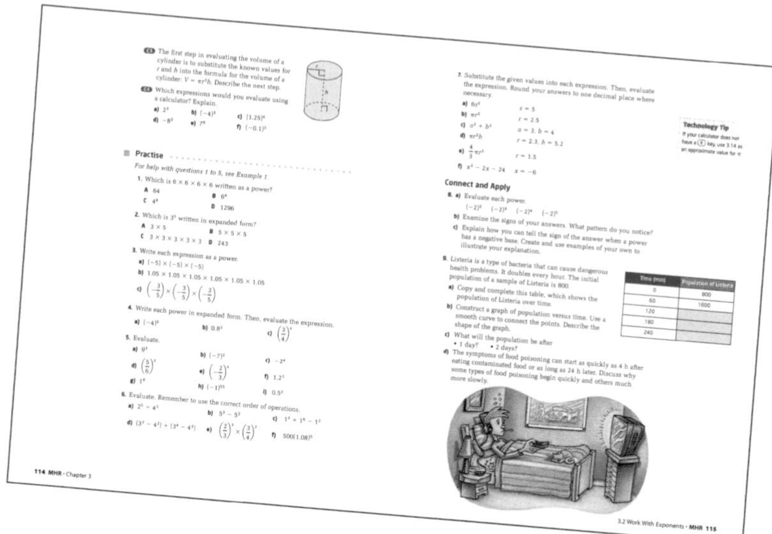

Extend

- These are more challenging and thought-provoking questions.
- Most sections conclude with a few **Math Contest** questions.

Technology

Scientific calculators are useful for many sections. Keystroke sequences are provided for techniques that may be new to you.

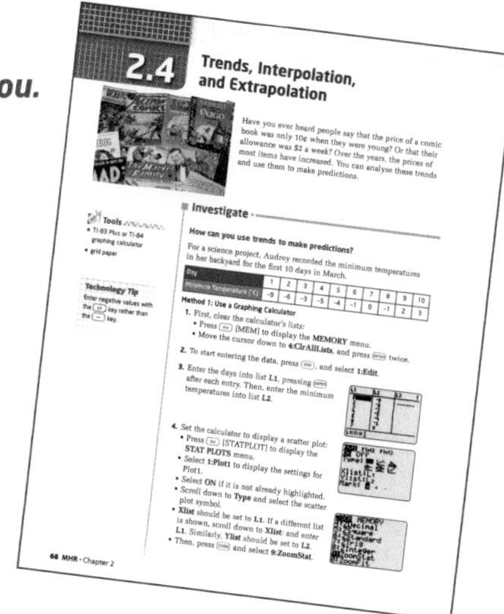
2.4 Trends, Interpolation, and Extrapolation

Investigate

How can you use trends to make predictions?

- A TI-83 Plus or TI-84 Plus graphing calculator is useful for some sections, particularly for graphing relations.

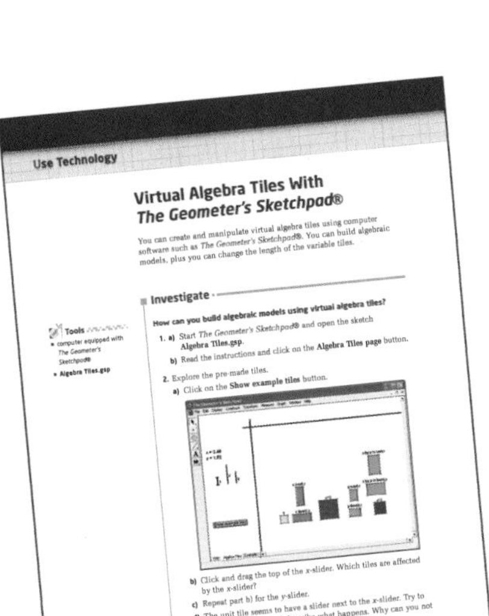
Use Technology

Virtual Algebra Tiles With The Geometer's Sketchpad®

Investigate

How can you build algebraic models using virtual algebra tiles?

- *The Geometer's Sketchpad®* is used in several sections for investigating concepts related to relations, measurement, and geometry. Alternative steps for doing investigations using pencil and paper are provided if you do not have access to this computer software.

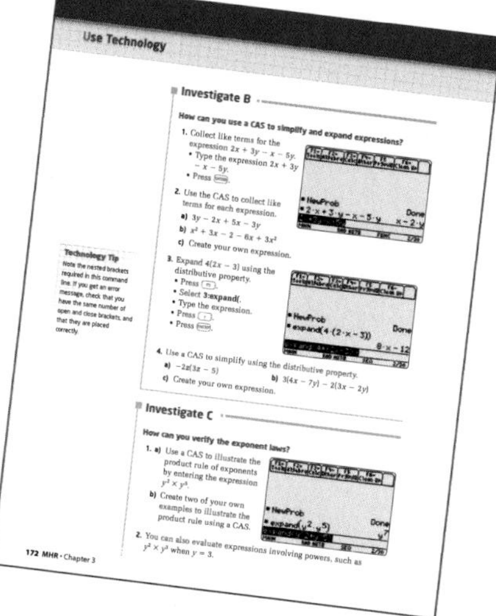
Use Technology

Investigate B

How can you use a CAS to simplify and expand expressions?

Investigate C

How can you verify the exponent laws?

- Some sections show you how to use a Computer Algebra System as an alternative way to solve algebraic problems. This text used the TI-89 calculator.

- The **Technology Appendix**, on pages 524–537, provides detailed help for some basic functions of *The Geometer's Sketchpad®* and the TI-83 Plus or TI-84 Plus graphing calculator. These pages will be particularly helpful to if you have not used these tools before.

Technology Tip

This margin feature points out helpful hints or alternative strategies for working with graphing calculators or *The Geometer's Sketchpad®*.

Assessment

Communicate Your Understanding

- These questions provide an opportunity to assess your understanding of the concepts before proceeding to use your skills in the Practise, Connect and Apply, and Extend questions.
- Through this discussion, you can identify any concepts or areas you need to study further.

Special Connect and Apply questions:

- Some questions are related to the chapter problem.
- **Achievement Check** The last Connect and Apply question of some sections provides an opportunity to demonstrate your knowledge and understanding, and your ability to apply, think about and communicate what you have learned. Achievement Check questions occur every two or three sections and are designed to assess learning of the key concepts in those few sections.

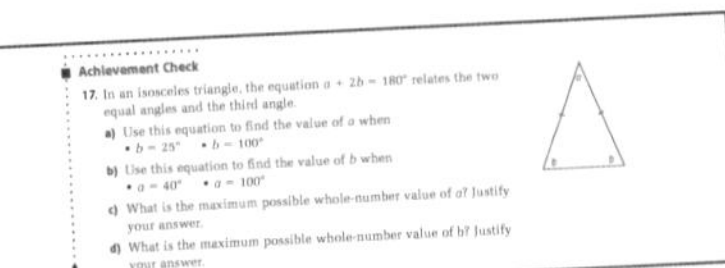
Achievement Check

Practice Test

Each chapter, except Chapter 1, ends with a practice test. The test has three styles of question: multiple choice, short response, and extended response. Practising these types of questions will help you prepare for provincial testing.

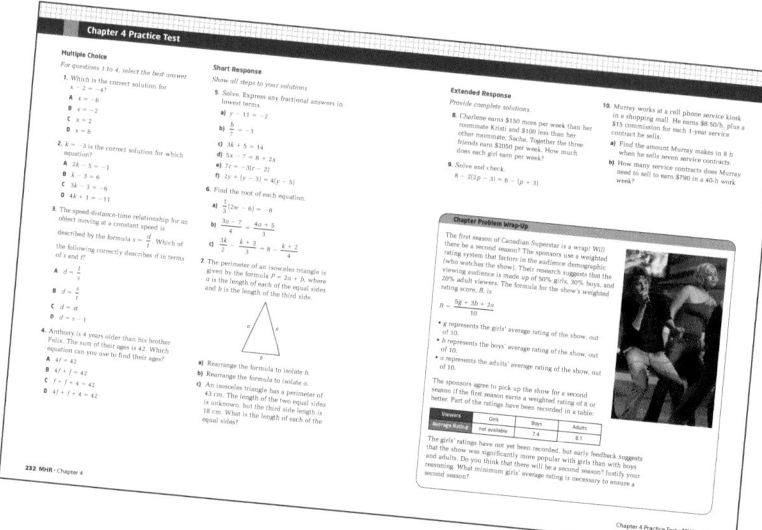
Chapter 4 Practice Test

Chapter Problem Wrap-Up

This summary problem occurs at the end of the practice test. The chapter problem may be assigned as a project.

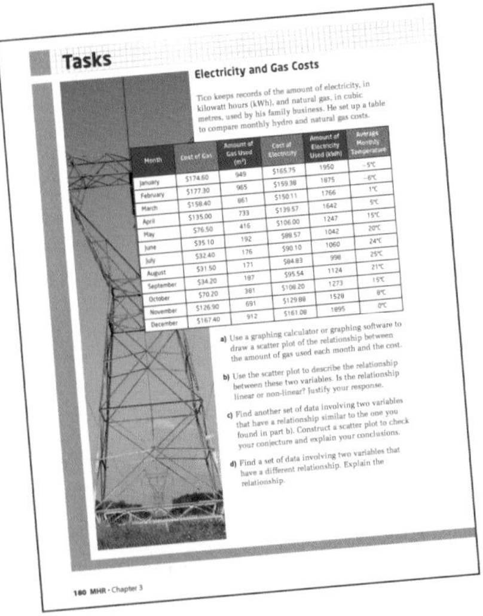
Tasks

Electricity and Gas Costs

Tasks

- Tasks are presented at the end of Chapters 3, 6, and 9. These problems require you to use several concepts from the preceding chapters. Each task has multi-part questions and may take about 20 min to complete.

Chapter Review

- This feature appears at the end of each chapter.
- By working through these questions, you will identify areas where you may need more review or study before doing the practice test.

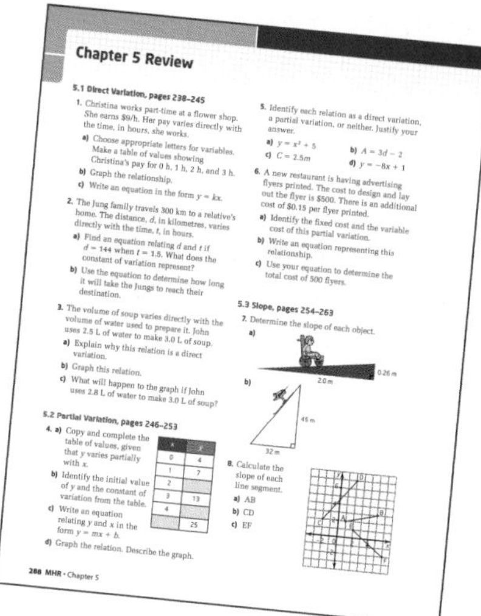

Chapter 5 Review

5.1 Direct Variation, pages 238–245

1. Christina works part-time at a flower shop. She earns $9/h. Her pay varies directly with the time, in hours, she works.
   a) Choose appropriate letters for variables. Make a table of values showing Christina's pay for 0 h, 1 h, 2 h, and 3 h.
   b) Graph the relationship.
   c) Write an equation in the form $y = kx$.
2. The Jung family travels 300 km to a relative's home. The distance, d, in kilometres, varies directly with the time, t, in hours.
   a) Find an equation relating d and t if $d = 144$ when $t = 1.5$. What does the constant of variation represent?
   b) Use the equation to determine how long it will take the Jungs to reach their destination.
3. The volume of soup varies directly with the volume of water used to prepare it. John uses 2.5 L of water to make 3.0 L of soup.
   a) Explain why this relation is a direct variation.
   b) Graph this relation.
   c) What will happen to the graph if John uses 2.8 L of water to make 3.0 L of soup?

5.2 Partial Variation, pages 246–253

4. a) Copy and complete the table of values, given that y varies partially with x.
   b) Identify the initial value of y and the constant of variation from the table.
   c) Write an equation relating y and x in the form $y = mx + b$.
   d) Graph the relation. Describe the graph.

x	y
0	4
1	7
2	
3	13
4	
	25

5. Identify each relation as a direct variation, a partial variation, or neither. Justify your answer.
   a) $y = x^2 + 5$
   b) $A = 3d - 2$
   c) $C = 2.5m$
   d) $y = -8x + 1$
6. A new restaurant is having advertising flyers printed. The cost to design and lay out the flyer is $500. There is an additional cost of $0.15 per flyer printed.
   a) Identify the fixed cost and the variable cost of this partial variation.
   b) Write an equation representing this relationship.
   c) Use your equation to determine the total cost of 500 flyers.

5.3 Slope, pages 254–263

7. Determine the slope of each object.
   a) 0.26 m, 2.0 m
   b) 45 m, 32 m
8. Calculate the slope of each line segment.
   a) AB
   b) CD
   c) EF

288 MHR • Chapter 5

Cumulative Review

- A cumulative review occurs at the end of Chapters 3, 6, and 9. These questions allow you to review concepts you learned in the chapters since the last cumulative review. They also help to prepare you for the Tasks that follow.

Other Features

Chapter 1 The Mathematical Process

The first chapter presents an introduction to the seven mathematical processes that are integral to learning mathematics.

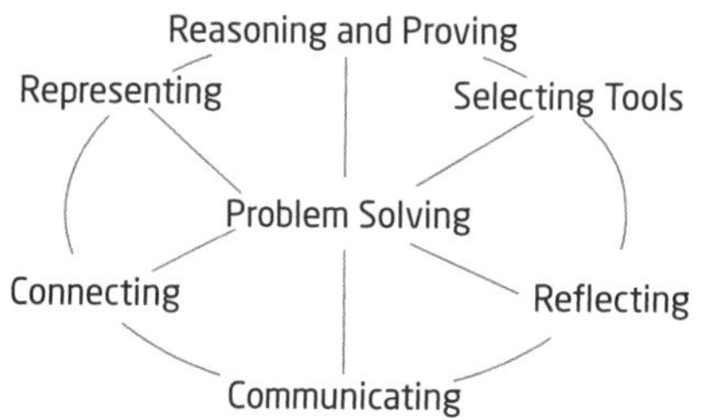

Each section of Chapter 1 focuses on one of the mathematical processes but naturally involves other processes. The processes are interconnected and are used throughout the rest of the course. Some examples and exercises are flagged with a math processes graphic to show or remind you which of the processes are involved in solving the problem.

Literacy Connections

This margin feature provides tips to help you read and interpret items in math.

Literacy Connections

Rectangular prism is the mathematical name for a box.

Making Connections

This margin feature points out some of the connections between topics in the course.

Making Connections

You will explore measurement relationships in greater depth in Chapter 8: Measurement and Chapter 9: Optimization.

Internet Links

WWW This logo is shown beside questions in which it is suggested that you use the Internet to help solve the problem or to research or collect information. Some direct links are provided on our Web site *www.school.mcgrawhill.ca/links/principles9*.

Did You Know?

This feature appears in the margin of some pages. It provides interesting facts related to the topics.

Did You Know?

Your school can get free access to data from Statistics Canada through its educational Web resource, Σ -STAT.

CHAPTER

1

Mathematical Processes

The mathematical process has many components. These components help you to organize your thoughts, solve problems effectively, and communicate your understanding.

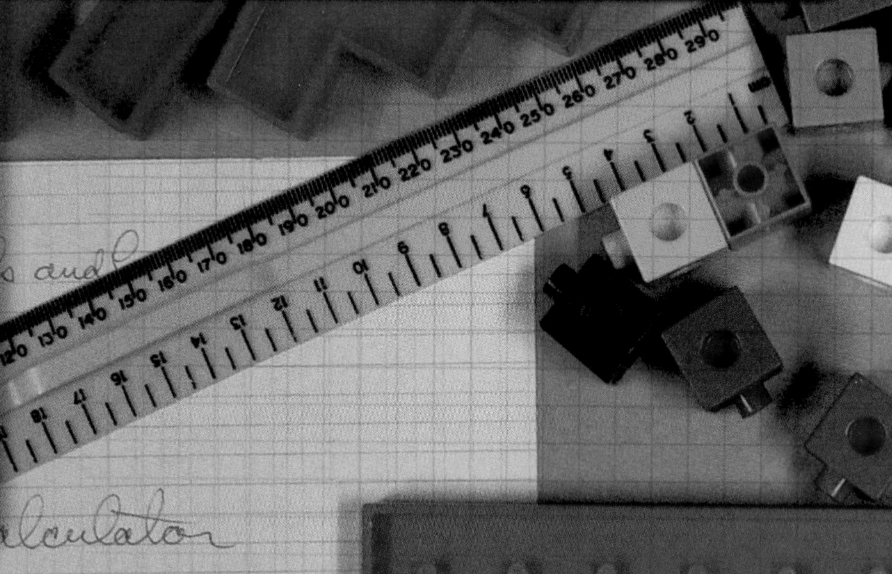

Mathematical Processes

- Problem Solving
- Reasoning and Proving
- Reflecting
- Selecting Tools and Computational Strategies
- Connecting
- Representing
- Communicating

Number Sense and Algebra

- Simplify numerical expressions involving integers and rational numbers.
- Solve problems requiring the manipulation of expressions arising from applications of percent, ratio, rate, and proportion.

Vocabulary

natural number
prime number
perfect square
vertex
pentomino
rational number
conjecture
mean
counter-example

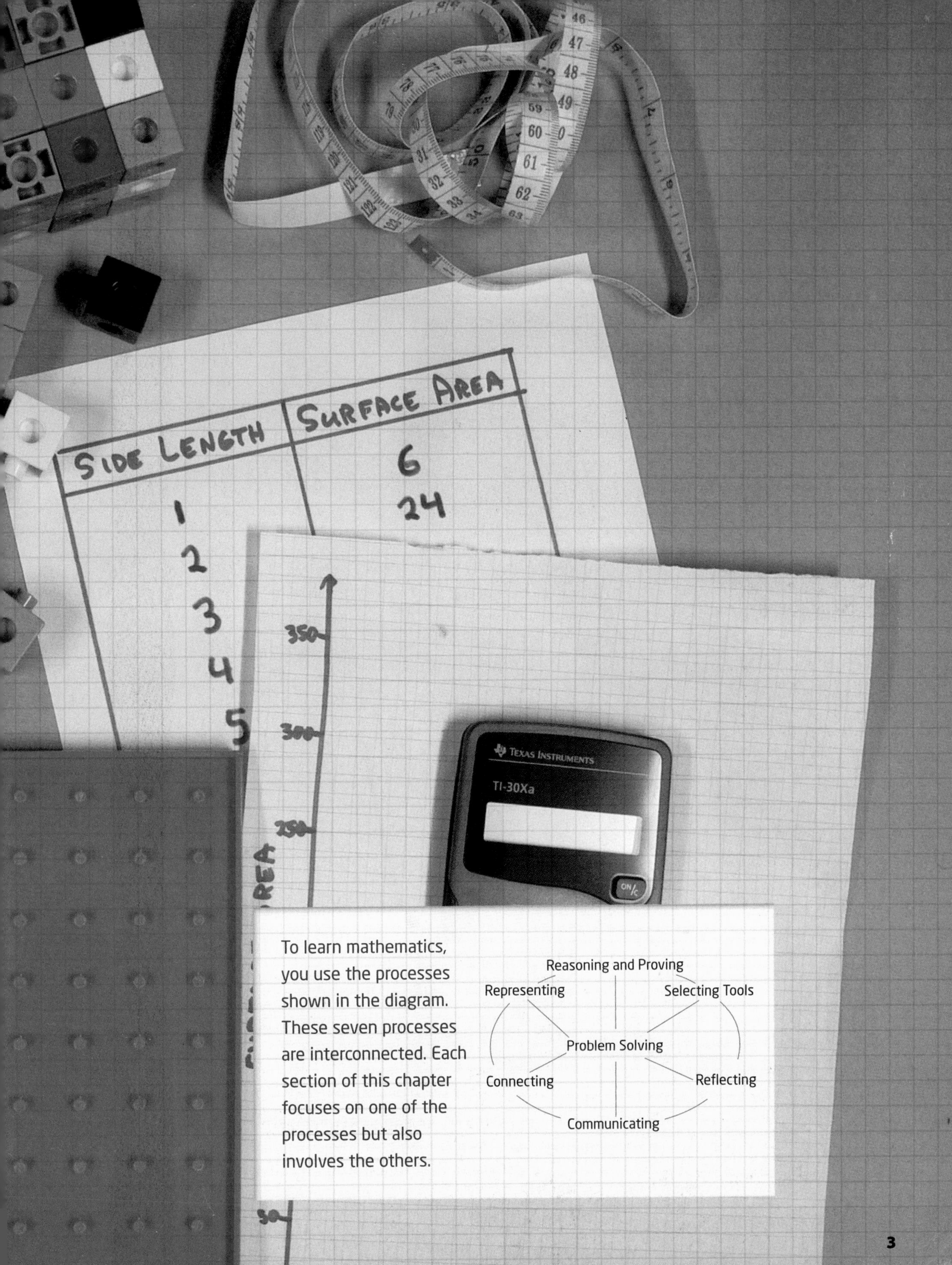

To learn mathematics, you use the processes shown in the diagram. These seven processes are interconnected. Each section of this chapter focuses on one of the processes but also involves the others.

Get Ready

Operations With Fractions

Fractions can be added or subtracted easily if they have the same **denominator**.

For example, $\frac{2}{5} + \frac{1}{5} = \frac{3}{5}$.

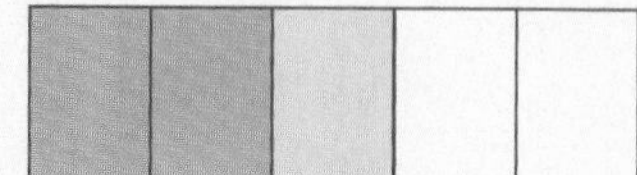

To add or subtract fractions with different denominators, the first step is to find the **lowest common denominator**.

For example,

$$\begin{aligned}\frac{3}{4} + \frac{1}{2} &= \frac{3}{4} + \frac{1 \times 2}{2 \times 2}\\ &= \frac{3}{4} + \frac{2}{4}\\ &= \frac{5}{4} \text{ or } 1\frac{1}{4}\end{aligned}$$

$$\begin{aligned}\frac{3}{4} - \frac{1}{3} &= \frac{3 \times 3}{4 \times 3} - \frac{1 \times 4}{3 \times 4}\\ &= \frac{9}{12} - \frac{4}{12}\\ &= \frac{5}{12}\end{aligned}$$

To multiply fractions, divide the numerator and the denominator by any common factors. Any mixed numbers should first be converted to improper fractions. To divide by a fraction, multiply by its **reciprocal**.

$$\begin{aligned}\frac{8}{9} \times \frac{3}{4} &= \frac{\overset{2}{\cancel{8}}}{\underset{3}{\cancel{9}}} \times \frac{\overset{1}{\cancel{3}}}{\underset{1}{\cancel{4}}}\\ &= \frac{2}{3} \times \frac{1}{1}\\ &= \frac{2}{3}\end{aligned}$$

$$\begin{aligned}3\frac{1}{2} \div \frac{6}{7} &= \frac{7}{2} \div \frac{6}{7}\\ &= \frac{7}{2} \times \frac{7}{6}\\ &= \frac{49}{12}\\ &= 4\frac{1}{12}\end{aligned}$$

The reciprocal of $\frac{6}{7}$ is $\frac{7}{6}$.

$12\overline{)49}$ = 4 R 1

1. Find each sum or difference. Express your answers in **lowest terms**.

a) $\frac{3}{10} + \frac{9}{10}$

b) $\frac{3}{8} + \frac{1}{4}$

c) $\frac{5}{6} - \frac{2}{5}$

d) $1\frac{7}{9} - \frac{2}{5}$

Literacy Connections

Refer to the Glossary, pages 582 to 591, to find the definition of **boldface** words.

2. Find each product or quotient. Express your answers in lowest terms.

a) $\frac{5}{12} \times \frac{3}{10}$

b) $\left(\frac{3}{4} \div \frac{2}{3}\right)$

c) $2\frac{7}{8} \times 6\frac{1}{2}$

d) $\frac{2}{9} \div 2\frac{2}{7}$

3. Five friends shared two pizzas. Fran ate $\frac{1}{3}$ of a pizza, Abdul ate $\frac{3}{8}$ of a pizza, Hannah ate $\frac{1}{4}$ of a pizza, and Siva ate $\frac{1}{2}$ of a pizza. What fraction of the pizza remains for Brad?

Operations With Integers

An **integer** number line and integer chips are tools that can help you understand operations with integers. You may also think in terms of profit and loss.

Add Integers:

$-2 + 5 = 3$ $\qquad$ $2 + (-6) = -4$

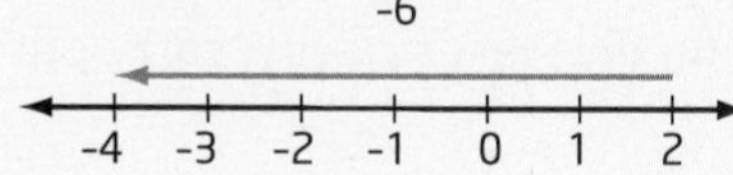

Subtract Integers:

$-4 - 9 = -4 + (-9)$
$= -13$

$3 - 10 = 3 + (-10)$
$= -7$

$-2 - (-4) = -2 + 4$
$= 2$

Multiply or Divide Integers:

$9 \times (-5) = -45$ $\qquad$ $-6 \times (-7) = 42$ $\qquad$ $20 \div (-4) = -5$ $\qquad$ $-16 \div (-2) = 8$

4. Perform each integer operation.

a) $13 + (-5)$
b) $-7 + 2$
c) $-8 + (-15)$
d) $7 - 11$
e) $2 - 16$
f) $8 - (-7)$
g) $-5 - (-9)$
h) $100 \times (-4)$
i) -7×7
j) $-3 \times (-14)$
k) $42 \div (-6)$
l) $-28 \div 7$

5. Evaluate.

a) $-16 \times 6 \div (-2)$
b) $-3 + 5 \times (-1)$
c) $-15 + (-12) - 4 - (-8)$

6. A small business lost \$6200 in its first year, lost \$2150 in its second year, and earned \$4780 in its third year. Overall, in the 3-year period, how much did the business earn or lose?

Order of Operations

$$\begin{aligned} & 2(15 - 18) \\ &= 2(-3) \\ &= -6 \end{aligned}$$

$$\begin{aligned} & 7 - 3(4^2 + 10) \\ &= 7 - 3(16 + 10) \\ &= 7 - 3(26) \\ &= 7 - 78 \\ &= -71 \end{aligned}$$

B Brackets
E Exponents
D } Division and
M } Multiplication, in order from left to right
A } Addition and
S } Subtraction, in order from left to right

7. Evaluate.

a) $-3(9 + 11)$
b) $2 + 3(10 - 4)^2$
c) $(7 - 15) \div (4 + 4)$
d) $-5(-3) + (-8)(10)$
e) $[2 - (6 + 3)^2]^2$
f) $-15 + 8 \times 7 - 32 \div 16$

8. Scientific calculators are programmed to follow the order of operations. Check your answers to question 7 using a scientific calculator.

9. At a collectors' fair, Jason sold six sports cards at \$56 each and bought eight sports cards at \$43 each. What was Jason's net profit or loss?

10. Create a problem that involves at least three different operations. Exchange problems with a classmate.

1.1 Focus on Problem Solving

Understand the Problem
Choose a Strategy
Carry Out the Strategy
Reflect

When you solve problems in mathematics, or in other subjects, a specific process helps you to organize your thoughts. This way, you can clearly understand the problem, devise a strategy, carry out the strategy, and reflect on the results.

Consider the following strategies when you are developing mathematical solutions to problems. You may use other strategies too.

- Make an Organized List
- Look for a Pattern
- Work Backward
- Draw a Diagram
- Select a Tool
- Use Systematic Trial
- Use Logic or Reasoning

Investigate

How can a pattern help you solve a problem?

Part A: Make an organized list or table

Pennies are laid out in a triangular pattern as shown. How many pennies do you need to form a triangle with 10 pennies in its base?

Understand the Problem

1. Read the problem above. Read it again. Express it in your own words.

Choose a Strategy

2. A possible strategy is to identify and continue the pattern started in the diagram. Copy the diagram into your notebook.

Carry Out the Strategy

3. Extend the pattern. Describe how the pattern develops. Use your description to extend it to a triangle with a base of 10 pennies. Record your numbers in a table with the following headings.

Diagram Number	Number of Pennies

Reflect

4. Explain how you used the pattern to solve the problem. Can you find another pattern that could help you solve this problem?

Part B: Use Logic or Reasoning

In the grid, each letter represents a different **natural number** from 1 to 9. Use the clues to find the value of each letter.

- A, C, and G are **prime numbers**.
- A and I are both greater than 5.
- I is a multiple of H.
- B is $\frac{1}{2}$ of F, which is $\frac{1}{3}$ of E.
- C is greater than F.

A	B	C
D	E	F
G	H	I

natural number

- a number in the sequence 1, 2, 3, 4, ….

prime number

- a number with exactly two factors—itself and 1

Understand the Problem

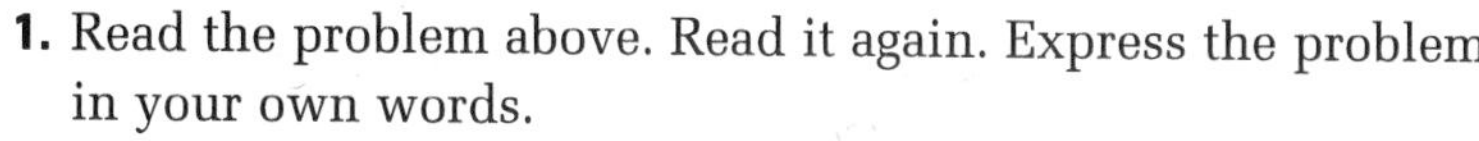

1. Read the problem above. Read it again. Express the problem in your own words.

Choose a Strategy

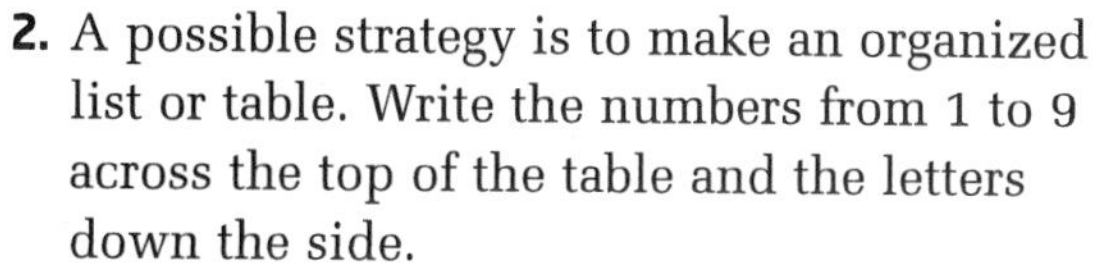

2. A possible strategy is to make an organized list or table. Write the numbers from 1 to 9 across the top of the table and the letters down the side.

	1	2	3	…
A				
B				
…				

Carry Out the Strategy

3. Analyse the information given.

a) Use the clues to mark Xs in the table for values that each letter cannot be. For example, A, C, and G are prime numbers, so they cannot be 1, 4, 6, 8, or 9.

b) Put a check mark in your table as you confirm values of letters.

Reflect

4. Verify that your results hold in the original grid.

Key Concepts

- Making an organized list or chart is a strategy that helps you to organize your thoughts and to see the information in an organized way.
- Identifying and describing a pattern is a strategy that can be used when a sequence of operations or diagrams occurs.
- When solving a problem, you will often use more than one strategy. Here are some problem solving strategies:
  - Draw a diagram.
  - Work backward.
  - Make a model.
  - Make an organized list.
  - Look for a pattern.
  - Find needed information.
  - Act it out.
  - Use systematic trial.
  - Use a formula.
  - Solve a similar but simpler problem.

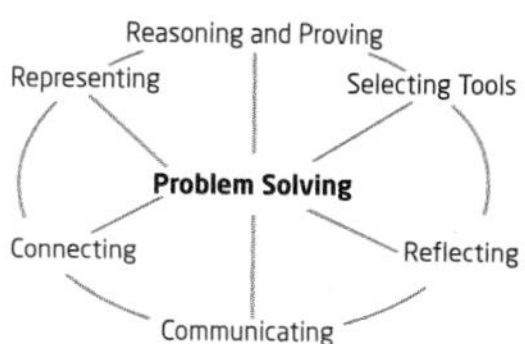

Communicate Your Understanding

C1 In the Investigate, Part A, the strategy recommended was to use an organized list.

a) Which other strategies did you use?

b) How could you answer the problem using a different strategy?

C2 In the Investigate, Part B, the strategy recommended was to make an organized list or chart. Which other strategies did you use?

Practise

1. Continue each pattern for three more terms. Describe how to find successive terms.

a) 1, 3, 5, 7, 9
b) 4, 17, 30, 43
c) 2, 4, 8, 16
d) 1, 1, 2, 3, 5, 8

2. You have two quarters, a dime, and a nickel. How many different sums of money can you make?

3. a) Copy and complete these products.

$1 \times 1 = ?$
$11 \times 11 = ?$
$111 \times 111 = ?$
$1111 \times 1111 = ?$

b) Describe the pattern in the answers.

c) Use the pattern to predict the product 111 111 111 × 111 111 111.

4. a) Evaluate each product.

$11 \times 37 = ?$
$22 \times 37 = ?$
$33 \times 37 = ?$

b) Continue and identify a pattern in the results.

c) Use the pattern to evaluate 99 × 37.

Connect and Apply

In each problem, write one or two sentences to describe your strategy. Then, carry out your strategy.

5. a) Express the fractions $\frac{1}{9}, \frac{2}{9}, \frac{3}{9}$, and so on as decimals. Describe the pattern.

b) How does the pattern change if the denominator is 99?

c) What if the denominator is 99 999?

6. A Sudoku is a Japanese number puzzle that follows a simple set of rules. Each three by three square, each row, and each column must contain each of the numerals 1 through 9 only once. Here is a Sudoku that is almost completed. What must the missing digits be?

4	8	9	5	3	2	6	1	7
2	6	1	8	7	9	5	4	3
7	5	3	4	1	6	9	8	2
6	7	8		4		1	5	9
1	3	2	9		8	4	7	6
5	9	4		6		2	3	8
8	2	5	7	9	4	3	6	1
9	4	6	3	8	1	7	2	5
3	1	7	6	2	5	8	9	4

7. Gina was born on September 15, 1997. Sam was born on January 23, 1994.

   a) How many years, months, and days old is each of them on January 1, 2020?

   b) Describe a method of determining anyone's age in years, months, and days.

8. In the opening round of a chess tournament, players must play each other only once. How many matches are necessary in the opening round for a tournament that is set up for

   a) 2 players? **b)** 3 players?

   c) 4 players? **d)** 10 players?

9. How many **perfect squares** divide evenly into 8820?

perfect square

- a number that can be expressed as the product of two identical factors
- 36 is a perfect square, since $36 = 6 \times 6$

Extend

10. In the following sum, each letter represents a different digit. F is half of C and R = 7. Find the value of each letter.

$$\begin{array}{r} \text{EAT} \\ +\text{FREE} \\ \hline \text{CAKE} \end{array}$$

11. In the grid, each letter represents a different natural number from 1 to 16. The sum of the numbers in each row, column, and diagonal is 34. Use these clues to find the value of each letter.
    - B, C, N, and R are greater than 12.
    - H and D are perfect squares.
    - R is double the value of J, which is double the value of D.
    - Q is one third of F, which is half of E. G is 7 times A.
    - P is less than or equal to 4.

A	B	C	D
E	F	G	H
J	K	L	M
N	P	Q	R

1.2 Focus on Communicating

Number	1	2	3	4	5	6	7	8	9
Greek	α	β	γ	δ	ϵ	ς	ζ	η	θ
Roman	I	II	III	IV	V	VI	VII	VIII	IX
Chinese (ancient)	—	=	≡	≣	⧖	∧	+	)(	[illegible]
Chinese (modern)	一	二	三	四	五	六	七	八	九

People have been communicating for thousands of years—that includes communicating mathematically. We currently represent numbers using the numerals 0, 1, 2, and so on. Ancient civilizations used different symbols to represent numbers.

Did You Know?

The numerals, 1, 2, 3, ... , 9, that we use are known as the Hindu-Arabic system. They were probably developed in India. They have been found on a Hindu plate dated 595. The symbols came to the Western world via Arabia.

Investigate

How can you represent numbers with ancient symbols?

About 5000 years ago, the ancient Egyptians used symbols to represent numbers.

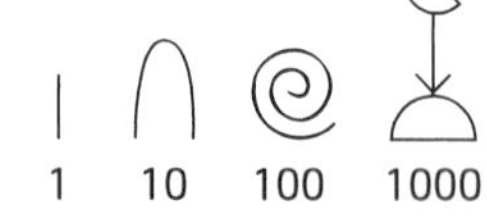

1. How would the Egyptians represent the numbers 13, 126, and 1291?

2. The Egyptians also used fractions, placing the numeral symbols under the symbol ⬭.

   They represented $\frac{1}{2}$ as ⬭ over ||.

   a) How would the Egyptians represent $\frac{1}{10}$?

   b) Describe two ways in which the Egyptians might have represented the fraction $\frac{2}{3}$.

3. Describe any similarities between the Egyptian number system and the ancient Chinese number system in the table above.

4. **Reflect** Is our number system more like the Egyptian or the Chinese system? In what way?

Example Use a Diagram to Communicate

How does the diagram illustrate a relationship between the areas of squares on the sides of a right triangle?

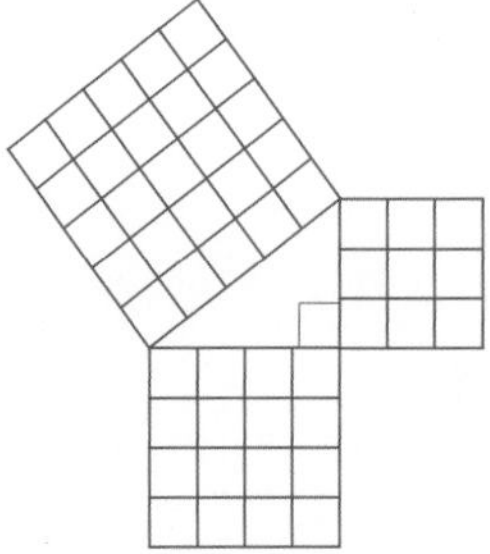

Solution

The triangle is right angled, with a square placed on each side.

The sum of the areas of the two smaller squares is

$$3^2 + 4^2 = 9 + 16$$
$$= 25$$

The area of the square on the hypotenuse is 25, or 5^2.

This shows that the area of the square on the hypotenuse equals the sum of the areas of the squares on the other two sides. This is the Pythagorean relationship.

Key Concepts

- It is important to be able to communicate clearly in mathematics. Communication can take the form of words, diagrams, and symbols.
- Use mathematical vocabulary when explaining your strategies.
- Use correct mathematical form when using symbols and simplifying expressions.
- Draw neat, fully labelled diagrams to illustrate a situation.

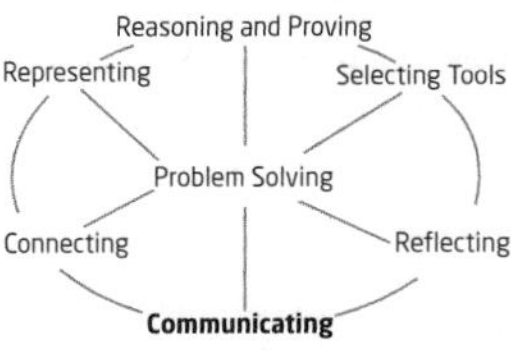

Communicate Your Understanding

C1 The ancient Maya from Central America used symbols to represent numbers as shown.

4 8 17

a) Describe the meaning of each symbol.

b) Represent the numbers 10 and 27 using Mayan symbols.

C2 Describe how to determine the pattern in the sequence 13, 15, 18, 22, ... What are the next two terms?

C3 To calculate 8% of 120, Greg wrote

$8\% \times 120 = .08 \times 120 = 9.6$

a) There are two things that Greg should do to rewrite his work in better mathematical form. What are they?

b) Give two reasons why it is a good idea to use correct mathematical form.

Practise

1. Describe the pattern in each sequence. Give the next two terms.

   a) 15, 10, 5

   b) −6, −10, −14

   c) $\frac{1}{4}, \frac{1}{2}, \frac{3}{4}$

   d) $\frac{12}{5}, 2, \frac{8}{5}$

   e) 3, −6, 12, −24

   f) −96, −48, −24

   g) 100, 80, 65, 55

   h) 3, 3, 6, 18, 72

   i) 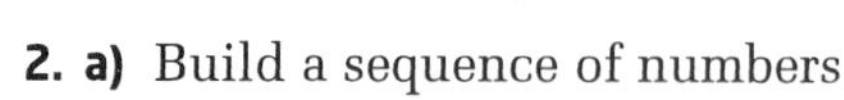

   j)

2. a) Build a sequence of numbers.

   b) Describe the process you used to build the sequence.

   c) Trade your sequence with a classmate. Find the pattern.

Connect and Apply

Making Connections

You worked with the formula for the area of a circle in grade 8. $A = \pi r^2$.

3. Refer to the Example. Is there a relationship between the areas of semicircles placed on each side of a right triangle? Use the diagram to help you explain your answer.

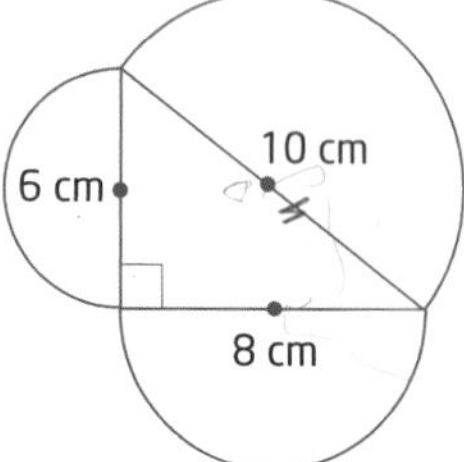

4. A light is attached to the circumference of a wheel. As the wheel rolls along the road, which of the following diagrams represents the path of the light? Explain your reasoning.

A

B 

C 

5. a) Explain how the time zone map uses integers to determine the time in another time zone.

   b) If it is 3:00 P.M. in Toronto, what time is it in Halifax?

   c) If it is 2:30 A.M. in Vancouver, what time is it in Winnipeg?

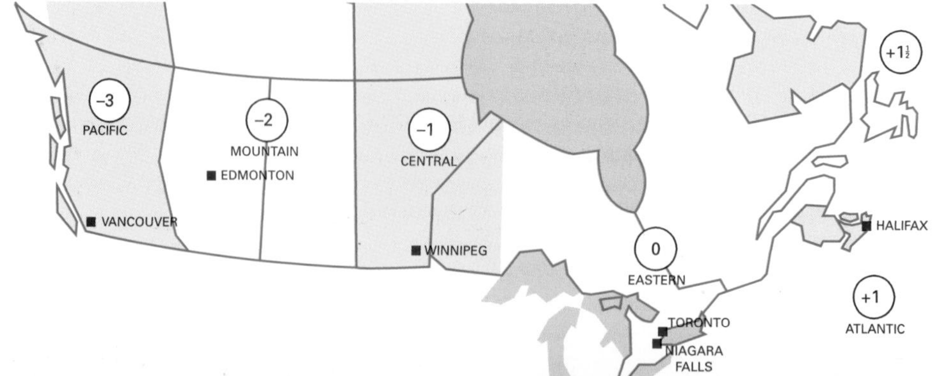

6. The diagram illustrates the meaning of fractions.

a) Explain how to use the diagram to illustrate which is greater, $\frac{3}{7}$ or $\frac{4}{8}$.

b) How could you use the diagram to illustrate how to add $\frac{1}{2} + \frac{1}{3}$? Explain.

c) How many rows would you need to illustrate $\frac{1}{3} + \frac{1}{4}$? Explain.

d) Describe a pattern or trend in the dark blue bars.

7. **a)** Explain how the diagram illustrates the fact that $\frac{2}{3} \times \frac{3}{4} = \frac{1}{2}$.

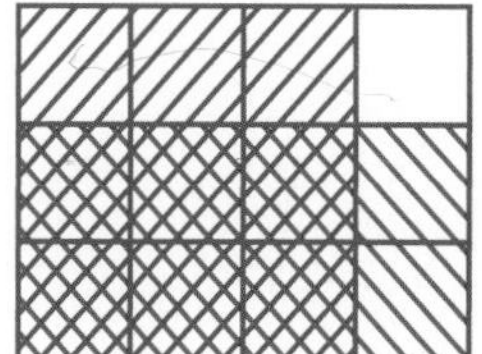

b) What product is modelled by the number line diagram?

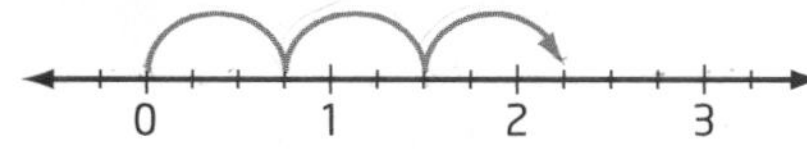

8. The diagrams illustrate a rule for adding odd numbers.

a) Describe the rule.

b) Verify your rule for the fifth and sixth diagrams.

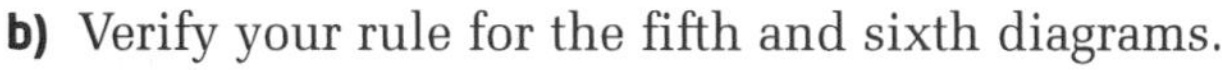

c) Use your rule to find the sum of the odd numbers from 1 to 99.

d) Use your rule to find the sum of the odd numbers from 150 to 600.

Extend

9. Each three by three square, each row, and each column must contain each of the numerals 1 through 9 only once. Copy and complete this Sudoku puzzle. Describe the problem solving process that you used.

		9		7	8			2
	7	5				3		1
8		3			1		7	
	6			2		8		4
	3	8	1		4		6	7
9		2			7		3	5
		1		3	2	5		6
	5	4			6	9		8
	8			4	5		1	

10. In a factory, there are 10 assembly points equally spaced along a 9-m section of an assembly line. A supply bin is to be located 5 m away from the assembly line. Where is the best location for the supply bin so that the workers will have to go the least distance to get their supplies? Justify your solution.

1.3 Focus on Connecting

Situations in real life often involve problems that you can solve using mathematical processes. You can make connecting mathematics to real life easier by drawing a diagram to illustrate the situation. You can then use the diagram to help you solve the problem. You can also use other strategies, such as making an organized list or looking for a pattern.

Often, in solving problems, you need to make connections among different areas of mathematics. For example, to find the amount of paint needed, you would use measurement, geometry, and number skills.

Investigate

How can you connect different representations of a problem?

A Superball is dropped from a height of 160 cm. When it lands on the ground, it bounces to a height that is 75% of the previous height. What is the total distance travelled by the ball at the moment it bounces for the fifth time?

Understand the Problem

1. Read the problem above. Read it again. Express the problem in your own words.

Choose a Strategy

2. A good strategy is to draw a diagram to illustrate the bouncing of the ball. What will your diagram look like? What labels will you put on your diagram? What calculations will you need to do?

Carry Out the Strategy

3. Draw a diagram representing the path of the bouncing ball. Label the diagram with the appropriate measurements. Do you need to show all five bounces? Why?

Reflect

4. Does your answer seem reasonable? If you are not sure, what should you do?

Example 1 Number of Point Totals

The Aces hockey team has played five games. A win is worth 2 points, a tie is worth 1 point, and a loss is worth 0 points. Determine the number of different point totals the Aces could have after five games.

Solution

Make an organized list to help with the solution.

Wins	Losses	Ties	Total Points
5	0	0	10
4	1	0	8
4	0	1	9
3	2	0	6
3	1	1	7
3	0	2	8
2	3	0	4
2	2	1	5
2	1	2	6
2	0	3	7
1	4	0	2
1	3	1	3
1	2	2	3
1	1	3	5
1	0	4	6
0	5	0	0
0	4	1	1
0	3	2	2
0	2	3	3
0	1	4	4
0	0	5	5

Each win is worth 2 points. $5 \times 2 = 10$.

There are 11 possible point totals—between 0 and 10 points.

How many hockey pucks are there in Canada?
Many problems, like this one, do not have exact answers.

A **Fermi problem** is one that uses estimation in its solution. It is solved by asking appropriate questions, whose answers lead to the next stage in the solution. Making connections and using various mathematical skills are important aspects of the solution.

Did You Know?

Fermi problems are named after Enrico Fermi (1901–1954). He was a well-respected Italian physicist who liked to pose these problems. See Example 2 on the next page.

Example 2 Jelly Beans in a Jar

How many jelly beans will fill a 4-L jar?

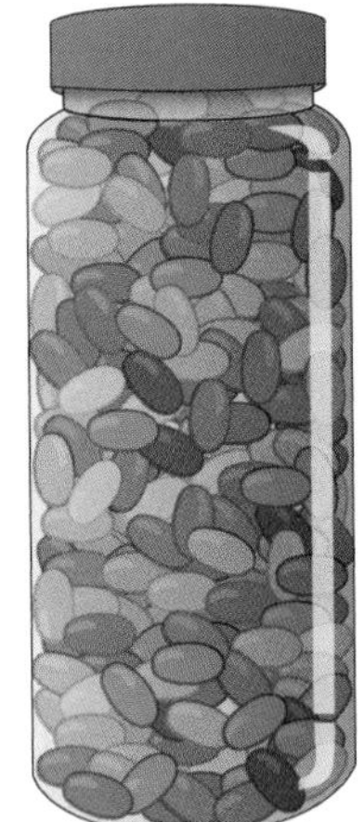

Solution

Understand the Problem

I need to figure out the size of a jelly bean, then how many fit into 4 L. I will need to account for space between the beans.

Choose a Strategy

Use estimation and make assumptions.
What shape is a jelly bean?
It is roughly the shape of a cylinder.
It is about 1.5 cm long and about 0.5 cm in radius.

I need to make some assumptions about the shape and size of a jelly bean.

Carry Out the Strategy

Find the approximate volume of a jelly bean.

$$V = \pi r^2 h$$
$$= \pi(0.5)^2(1.5)$$
$$\doteq 1.2$$

I need to use the formula for the volume of a cylinder.

The volume of a jelly bean is about 1.2 cm^3.

What is the volume of the jar in cubic centimetres?

$1 \text{ L} = 1000 \text{ cm}^3$
$4 \text{ L} = 4000 \text{ cm}^3$

Adjust for the space between the jelly beans.

Air might take up about 10% of the volume. So, only 90% of the jar's volume will be jelly beans.

10% is a reasonable guess for the amount of air.

$$90\% \text{ of } 4000 = 0.9 \times 4000$$
$$= 3600$$

Now, I need to use my skills with percent.

Number of jelly beans = volume ÷ volume of a jelly bean
= 3600 ÷ 1.2
= 3000

About 3000 jelly beans will fill a 4-L jar.

Reflect

A 4-L jar is pretty large. I could test the answer by seeing how many jelly beans fit into a 250-mL cup, then multiplying the count by 16 (because 16 × 250 mL = 4000 mL or 4 L).

Key Concepts

- You can make connections that relate math to other areas of study and of daily life.
- You can also make connections between areas of mathematics, such as geometry and number sense.

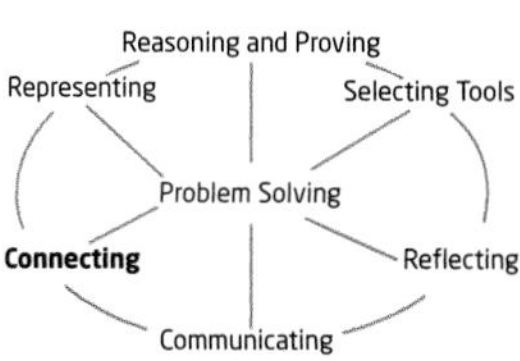

Communicate Your Understanding

C1 Using the Investigate as a reference, explain how drawing a diagram is different from drawing a picture.

C2 How many people are sitting down in your school at this moment? What information will you need to find or estimate to solve this Fermi problem?

Practise

For help with question 1, see the Investigate.

1. A bird flew 800 m in one direction. It turned around and flew half as far back. Then, it turned around and again flew half as far back. The bird continued this pattern for a total of six flights.

a) Draw a diagram illustrating this situation.

b) What was the total distance the bird flew?

c) How far from its starting point did the bird end up?

For help with question 2, see Example 1.

2. Raoul has four Canadian coins in his pocket. The coins are quarters, dimes, or nickels. What are the possible total values of the coins?

For help with questions 3 and 4, see Example 2.

3. How many hockey pucks would fit inside your classroom? Explain your reasoning.

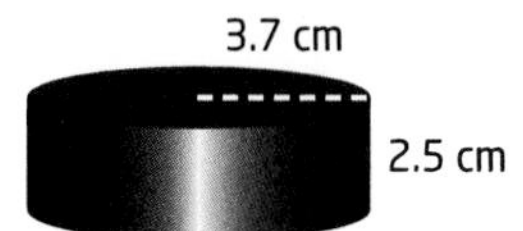

4. The tires on Honi's bike are guaranteed to last 2000 km. She uses her bike mostly to ride to school, which is 8 km from her home. How many years can she expect the tires to last? Explain your reasoning.

Connect and Apply

In each problem, write a sentence to describe your strategy. Then, carry out your strategy.

5. Five friends ate a 12-slice pizza. Samir ate three times as many slices as Joe. Joe ate half as many slices as Emily. Kendra and Fong together ate half a pizza. Kendra ate one third as many slices as Samir. Fong ate the most slices. What fraction of a pizza did each person eat?

6. How many triangles of all sizes are there in the diagram?

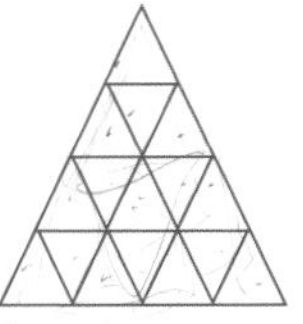

7. If each square on the grid measures 0.5 cm by 0.5 cm, what is the approximate area of the arrow?

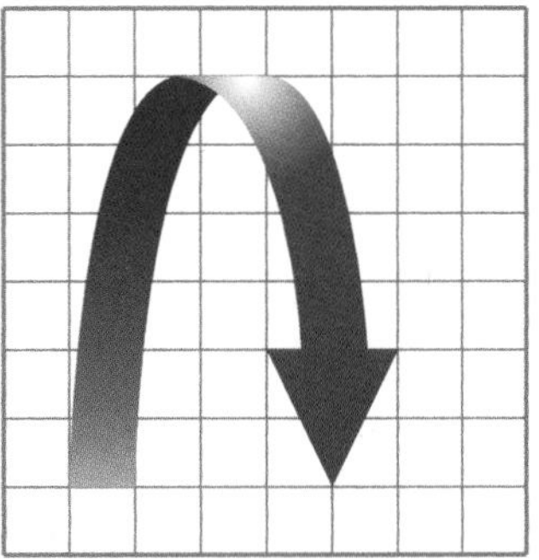

8. A snail begins climbing a pipe from a point 20 m below the ground. Each day, the snail climbs 4 m and slides back 3 m. How long will it take to reach the top of the pipe, which is 7 m above the ground?

9. How many times does a cat's heart beat in a lifetime?

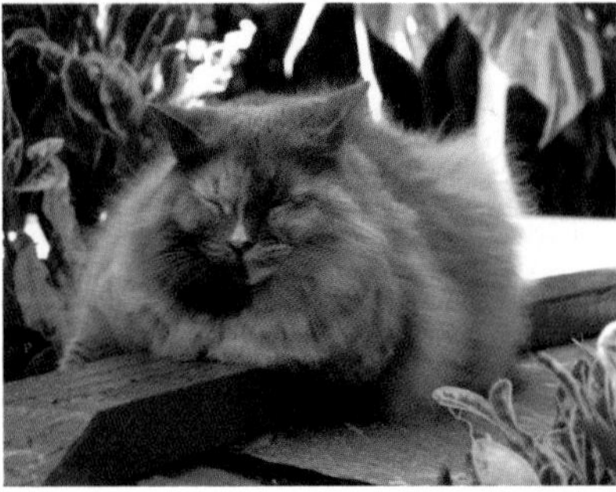

Extend

10. Each three by three square, each row, and each column must contain each of the numerals 1 through 9 only once. Copy and complete this Sudoku puzzle.

	6		7		3			4
2		7	6		4		9	
4		5		2		6		
1	7			8				
			9		1			
				3			6	8
		3		4		8		6
	1		5		6	3		9
6			3		8		2	

11. Design your own geometry problem in which a diagram would be useful to help solve the problem.

12. A polygon has 20 sides. How many diagonals does it have?

1.4 Focus on Representing

Mathematics can be used to represent situations using diagrams, numbers, graphs, algebra, calculator applications, and computer software. In this section, you will develop ideas on how to represent both mathematical and real-life situations.

Investigate

How can you represent a situation numerically?

When Kevin was scuba diving, he entered a shipwreck and immediately dove down 6 m, came up 5 m, dove down 9 m, and then dove a further 2 m, to finish at 32 m below the surface of the water. What was Kevin's depth when he entered the shipwreck?

Understand the Problem

1. Read the problem above. Read it again. Express the problem in your own words.

Choose a Strategy

2. An effective strategy is to represent Kevin's movements as integers on a labelled diagram. Then, work backward from Kevin's finishing position.

Carry Out the Strategy

3. Start at the finishing level and record Kevin's previous steps in reverse.

Reflect

4. Verify that your results hold for Kevin's dive.

Example Represent a Situation Using a Diagram

Eight friends arrive at a party. Each person shakes hands with each other person once. How many handshakes occur?

Solution

Illustrate the handshakes using a diagram. Place the eight letters from A to H in a circular pattern. Draw seven green line segments from person A to all the other friends, B to H.

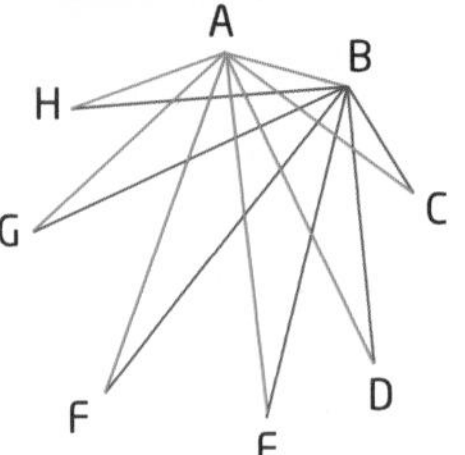

Continue by drawing six blue line segments from B to the remaining friends, C to H. Continue the pattern. Find the total number of line segments.

$7 + 6 + 5 + 4 + 3 + 2 + 1 = 28$

There are 28 handshakes among eight friends.

Reasoning and Proving
Representing
Selecting Tools
Problem Solving
Connecting
Reflecting
Communicating

Key Concepts

- A mathematical situation can be represented in many ways, including numerically, graphically, algebraically, and with a diagram.
- Drawing a diagram can be a useful strategy to help visualize the situation.
- Representing data numerically can help you see a pattern or a relationship between numbers.

Communicate Your Understanding

C1 In the Investigate, you used the working backward strategy. Describe another strategy that you could use to determine Kevin's depth when he entered the shipwreck.

C2 In a walk-a-thon, Ginny is 5 m behind Alice, who is 8 m ahead of Barbara. Sarah is 4 m ahead of Alice and 10 m ahead of both Ruth and Denise. What is the distance between the first and last of the girls? Describe how you would solve this problem.

Practise

For help with question 1, see the Investigate.

1. On a treasure hunt, players are instructed to go 2 km north, then 5 km east, then 4 km south, then 3 km west, and finally 2 km north. Where is the treasure relative to the starting point?

For help with questions 2 to 4, see the Example.

2. The top floor of an apartment building has eight apartments. Each of the other floors below it has $1\frac{1}{2}$ times as many apartments as the floor above. Use a diagram and a numeric representation to help determine the maximum number of floors that this building can have.

3. Seven friends have initials O, P, Q, R, S, T, and U. Each must have a telephone conversation with friends whose initials are within two letters of their own. Use a diagram and a numeric representation to determine how many telephone conversations will occur.

4. A direct road needs to be built between each pair of the six towns shown. How many roads need to be built?

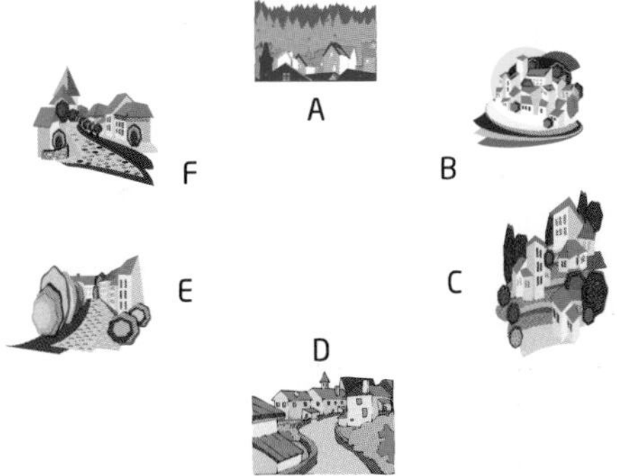

Connect and Apply

5. Plot each set of points on a grid. Describe the pattern and plot the next three points.
   a) A(2, 3), B(5, 4), C(8, 5)
   b) P(1, 6), Q(−4, 4), R(−9, 2)
   c) G(3, 3), H(0, 0), I(−3, −3)

6. Use a diagram to show which fraction is greater. Describe the pattern in the two fractions being compared. Make a general statement about the pattern and which fraction is greater.
   a) $\frac{1}{2}$ or $\frac{2}{3}$
   b) $\frac{2}{3}$ or $\frac{3}{4}$
   c) $\frac{3}{4}$ or $\frac{4}{5}$
   d) $\frac{4}{5}$ or $\frac{5}{6}$

7. A bicycle gear ratio compares the number of teeth on the driver cog to the number of teeth on the driving cog. The driver cog on a bicycle has 30 teeth and the driving cog has 20 teeth.

a) If the driver cog rotates three turns, how many turns does the driving cog make?

b) If the driver cog makes a half turn, how many turns does the driving cog make?

c) How many turns of the driver cog are required for the driving cog to turn five times?

d) On a different bicycle, the driver cog has 24 teeth and the driving cog has 40 teeth. If the driver cog makes a half turn, how many turns does the driving cog make?

vertex (pl vertices)

- a point at which two sides meet

8. The points A(1, 2) and B(−3, −2) are two **vertices** of a square. Find all possible locations of the other two vertices.

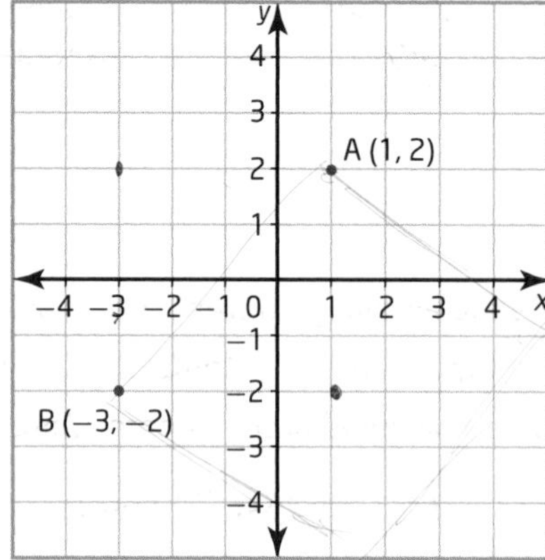

Extend

9. The points C(−7, −3) and D(−1, −3) are two vertices of right △CDE. Find all possible locations of the third vertex so that the area of the triangle is 15 square units.

10. Use question 7 as a reference. How would you determine the resulting number of turns of the driving cog if another, middle, cog is added?

1.5 Focus on Selecting Tools and Computational Strategies

When solving problems, it is important to select appropriate tools. You may be able to solve some problems using pencil and paper, while for others you may need a calculator. Sometimes it helps to use manipulatives such as linking cubes or integer chips, while other situations are best tackled using a graph. Quite often, you may find you need several tools. In other situations, you might start with one tool, then find you need another tool to help find the answer.

Investigate

Tools

- square tiles
- linking squares
- grid paper

pentomino

- a shape made of five unit squares
- each square shares at least one side with another square

Which tool(s) can you use to solve a problem?

A: Create shapes with square tiles

Five square tiles are to be used to make different shapes. Sides must align exactly. These shapes are called **pentominos**. Shapes that can be rotated or flipped to form each other are considered the same. For example, the following two are considered the same.

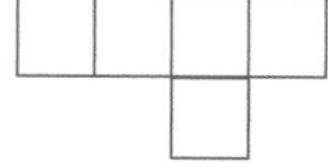

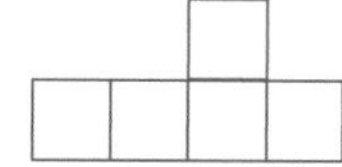

1. **a)** Make as many different pentominos as you can.
   b) Compare your pentominos with a classmate's.
   c) How many different pentominos are possible?

2. **Reflect** Which tool(s) did you use? Were they effective? Explain.

B: Sums of cubes

Select an appropriate tool to solve the following problem.

1. **a)** Find the sum of the cubes of the first two natural numbers: $1^3 + 2^3 = ?$
   b) Find the sum of the cubes of the first three natural numbers: $1^3 + 2^3 + 3^3 = ?$
   c) Continue extending these sums and investigate the pattern in the results. Describe the pattern in your own words.

2. **a)** **Reflect** Verify that your pattern is correct.
   b) Use your pattern to find the sum of the cubes of the first 15 natural numbers.

3. **Reflect** Which tool(s) did you use? Were they effective? Explain.

rational numbers

- numbers that can be expressed as the quotient of two integers, where the divisor is not zero
- $\frac{3}{5}$, 0.25, $-1\frac{3}{4}$, and -3 are rational numbers

Example Computational Strategy, Operations With Rational Numbers

Add or subtract each pair of **rational numbers**, as indicated.

a) $\frac{3}{8} + \left(-\frac{1}{8}\right)$ **b)** $-\frac{1}{2} + \left(-\frac{2}{3}\right)$ **c)** $-\frac{3}{5} - \left(-\frac{1}{4}\right)$

Solution

The strategy for adding and subtracting rational numbers is to connect your skills with fractions and integers.

a) $\frac{3}{8} + \left(-\frac{1}{8}\right)$

The denominators are the same, so I can add the numerators. $3 + (-1) = 2$

$= \frac{2}{8}$

This fraction isn't in lowest terms. I can divide the numerator and the denominator by 2.

$= \frac{1}{4}$

b) $-\frac{1}{2} + \left(-\frac{2}{3}\right)$

The denominators are different, so I need to find a common denominator.

$= -\frac{3}{6} + \left(-\frac{4}{6}\right)$

$= -\frac{7}{6}$ Add the numerators.

$= -1\frac{1}{6}$ Change to a mixed number.

c) $-\frac{3}{5} - \left(-\frac{1}{4}\right)$

$= -\frac{3}{5} + \frac{1}{4}$ Change subtracting to adding the opposite.

$= -\frac{12}{20} + \frac{5}{20}$ Find the common denominator.

$= -\frac{7}{20}$ Add the numerators.

Key Concepts

- Tools such as calculators, physical models, graph paper, and computers can help you solve problems.
- Choosing the best tool for a given situation can make you a more efficient problem solver. For example,
  - adding 10 and 20 on a scientific calculator would take longer than finding the sum mentally
  - using a 30-cm ruler to measure the length of a soccer field would take longer than using a trundle wheel
- A variety of computational strategies need to be considered when investigating mathematical ideas and solving problems.

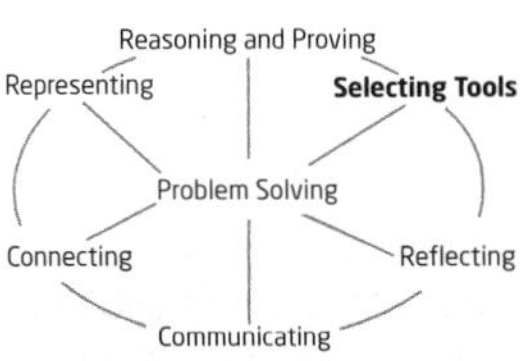

Communicate Your Understanding

C1 A Fermi problem asks how many times a truck wheel turns in driving along the 401 highway from Windsor to London. What tools would you use to solve this problem?

C2 Ted used a calculator to evaluate the expression $\frac{5}{9} + \frac{2}{3} - \frac{1}{8}$ in the following way:

$$\frac{5}{9} + \frac{2}{3} - \frac{1}{8}$$
$$= 0.6 + 0.7 - 0.1$$
$$= 1.2$$

Explain what Ted's error was and how he could have used his calculator more appropriately.

Practise

1. a) Explain how the diagram illustrates the fact that $12 \div 4 = 3$.

b) Draw a diagram to illustrate that $12 \div 3 = 4$.

c) Draw a diagram to illustrate that $12 \div 2 = 6$.

d) Continue the pattern. How do these models show that $12 \div 0$ is not defined?

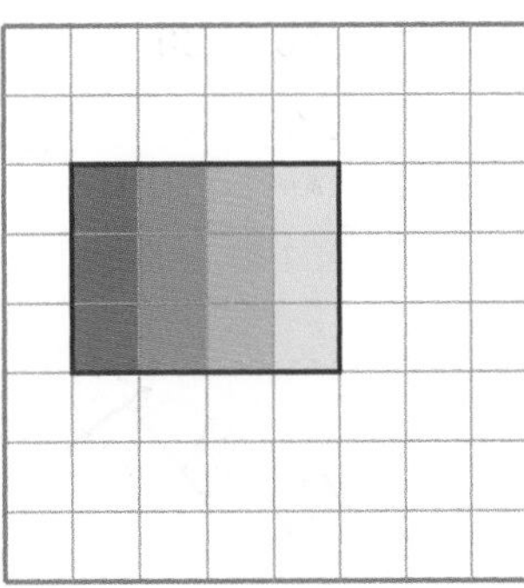

2. a) Explain how the diagram illustrates the fact that $3 \times \left(-\frac{2}{3}\right) = -2$

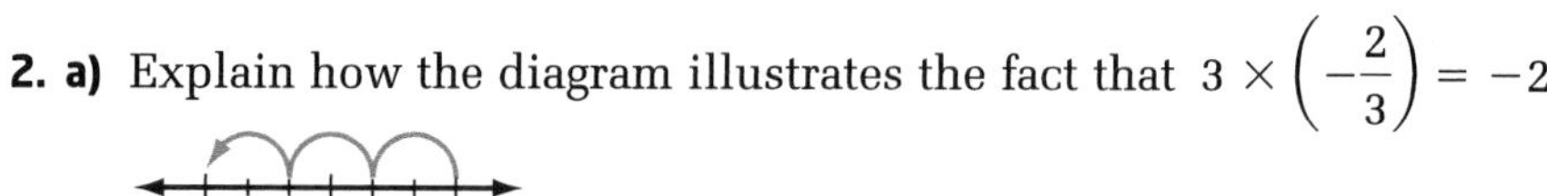

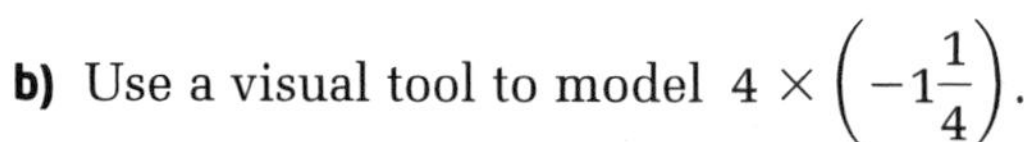

b) Use a visual tool to model $4 \times \left(-1\frac{1}{4}\right)$.

3. a) Four views of a cube are shown. What letter belongs on the blank face, and which way should the letter face?

b) What tool did you use to help solve this problem? Was it effective?

c) Make up your own similar problem, using numbers instead of letters. Have a classmate solve the problem.

4. What tools would you use to find the average cost of admission to a movie in your area?

5. Describe when it would be appropriate to use each tool to solve a mathematical problem. Give examples.

a) a calculator

b) grid paper

c) a physical model

d) a computer

6. The number 90 224 199 is the fifth power of what number? Which tool did you use?

7. Use an appropriate tool and strategy to find the two missing values in each sequence.

a) 15, 9, 3, … , ■, ■, −69

b) 5, 15, 45, … , ■, ■, 10 935

c) −1024, 512, −256, … , ■, ■, −1

d) −5, −8, −11, … , ■, ■, −164

e) 3, −6, 12, … , ■, ■, −24 576

f) −400, −376, −352, … , ■, ■, 80

8. Use appropriate tools and strategies to find the next three terms in each sequence.

a) 240, 120, 40, 10, 2

b) $0, -\frac{1}{3}, -\frac{2}{3}, -1$

c) $\frac{3}{4}, \frac{1}{2}, \frac{1}{4}$

d) $\frac{2}{3}, \frac{7}{12}, \frac{1}{2}, \frac{5}{12}$

9. Find each sum.

a) $-\frac{1}{2} + \left(-\frac{1}{2}\right)$ **b)** $-\frac{2}{3} + \left(-\frac{3}{4}\right)$

c) $\frac{1}{7} + \left(-\frac{2}{5}\right)$ **d)** $-\frac{2}{3} + \frac{3}{8}$

10. Find each difference.

a) $\frac{3}{8} - \frac{5}{6}$ **b)** $\frac{1}{2} - \frac{2}{3}$

c) $\left(-\frac{1}{4}\right) - \frac{1}{6}$ **d)** $\left(-\frac{4}{5}\right) - \left(-\frac{3}{10}\right)$

Connect and Apply

11. The Example demonstrated how to add and subtract rational numbers. Describe how to multiply and divide rational numbers. Provide examples.

12. Evaluate.

a) $-\frac{5}{6} \times \frac{3}{10}$ **b)** $\left(-\frac{1}{7}\right) \times \left(-\frac{3}{5}\right)$

c) $\left(-\frac{1}{8}\right) \times \frac{6}{11}$ **d)** $\frac{7}{8} \div \left(-\frac{5}{6}\right)$

e) $\left(-\frac{5}{12}\right) \div \left(-\frac{3}{8}\right)$ **f)** $\left(-4\frac{2}{5}\right) \div 1\frac{4}{7}$

13. A sheet of paper is 0.08 mm thick.

a) How many times do you think you can fold a sheet of paper in half?

b) If you fold it in half, how thick are the two layers?

c) If you could fold it in half again and again, a total of 20 times, how thick would the layers be? Are you surprised at the answer? Why?

d) Find out for yourself how many times you can fold a piece of paper in half. Explain the results.

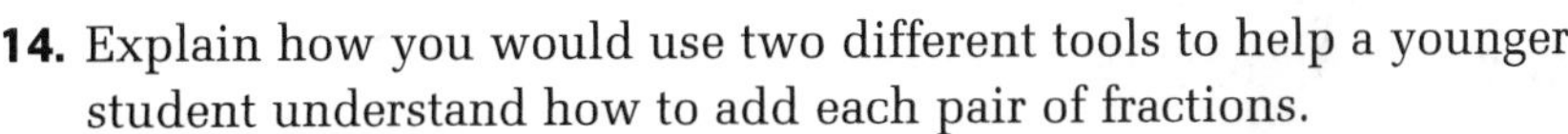

14. Explain how you would use two different tools to help a younger student understand how to add each pair of fractions.

a) $\frac{1}{2} + \frac{1}{4}$ **b)** $\frac{2}{3} + \frac{4}{5}$

15. Use a geoboard or centimetre dot paper to find how many different rectangles with a perimeter of 20 cm and whole-number side lengths can be made. Find the area of each rectangle. Record your results in a table.

Length (cm)	Width (cm)	Perimeter (cm)	Area (cm²)
		20	

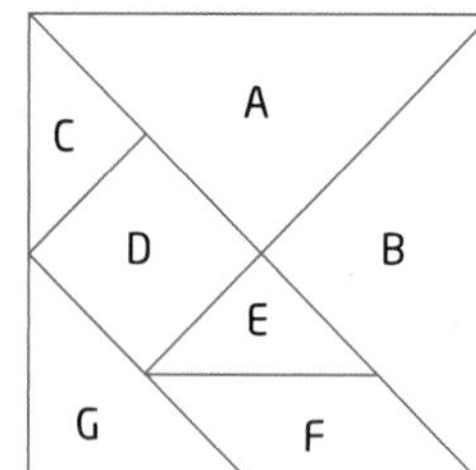

16. This is a tangram, which is a very old puzzle that originated in ancient China.

    a) Determine the fraction of the whole square that each labelled shape represents.

    b) What fraction of the whole square does each of the following represent? Illustrate your answer using pieces of the tangram and using operations with fractions.

    i) A + B **ii)** C + G **iii)** D + E

    iv) F − E **v)** $\frac{1}{4}$A **vi)** $\frac{1}{2}$D − F

17. Use the tangram in question 16.

    a) Write piece F as the sum of two or more smaller pieces.

    b) Write piece B as the sum of two or more smaller pieces.

18. Use an appropriate tool to help determine the thousandth term in the sequence 45, 41, 37, 33, … .

19. Use an appropriate tool to help determine which term in the sequence 100, 93, 86, … is −600.

20. How many cups of water would fill up a bathtub? Explain your reasoning.

Extend

21. If you fold a piece of string in half, in half again, and so on, up to n folds, and then cut it through the middle with a pair of scissors, how many pieces of string will you have?

    a) Develop a solution. Explain your reasoning.

    b) Use a model to verify your solution.

22. A rope winds around a cylindrical tube a total of four times. The tube has a circumference of 10 m and a height of 24 m. How long is the rope?

1.6 Focus on Reasoning and Proving

People need to use their reasoning skills to make mathematical observations (such as those from patterns), to justify conclusions, and to use mathematics to plan and support solutions to problems.

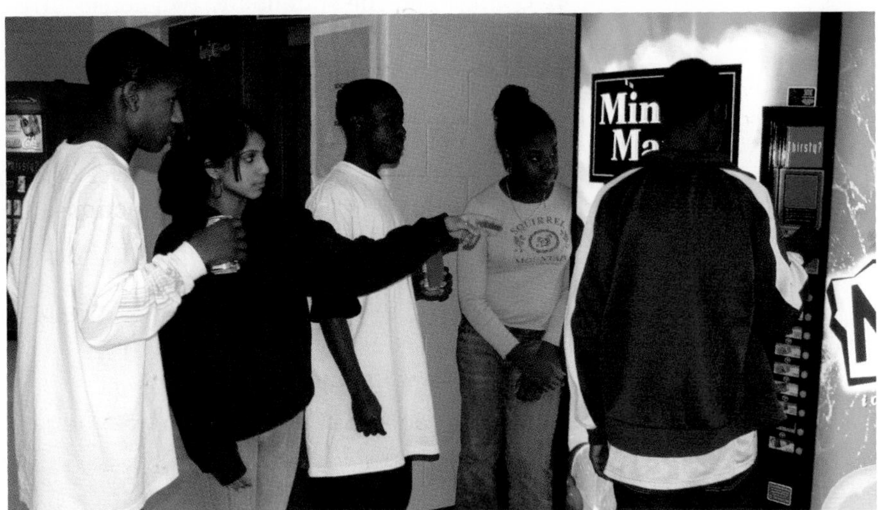

Investigate

How can you apply reasoning skills to solve a problem?

A vending machine has 90 coins in its coin-collecting slots. There are one third as many dimes as quarters and half as many dimes as nickels. How much money is in the machine?

Understand the Problem

1. Read the problem above. Read it again. Express it in your own words.

Choose a Strategy

2. A possible strategy is to guess the answer, check to see if it works, and then revise the guess if necessary. What type of number must the number of nickels be? What type of number must the number of quarters be?

Carry Out the Strategy

3. Make your first guess. If it is incorrect, read the clues again and use reasoning skills to decide what needs changing. Continue until you are successful.

4. Check that your answer works for each clue. Is another answer possible?

Reflect

5. **Reflect** Was this the appropriate strategy for this problem? Explain.

conjecture

- a general conclusion drawn from a number of individual facts
- it may or may not be true

You may be asked to prove a mathematical **conjecture**. This means that you need to provide mathematical evidence that a statement is true.

Example Prove a Conjecture

Conjecture: The sum of any two consecutive whole numbers is an odd number.

a) Give three examples of the conjecture.

b) Prove that the conjecture is true.

Solution

a) $1 + 2 = 3$
$2 + 3 = 5$
$3 + 4 = 7$

In these examples, the sum of two consecutive whole numbers is an odd number.

b) Let n represent a whole number.
Then, $n + 1$ represents the next consecutive whole number.
The sum of these two consecutive numbers is
$n + n + 1$
$= 2n + 1$
Since $2n$ means 2 times any whole number, this is always an even number. When you add 1 to an even number, you get the next odd number.
So, the conjecture is true.

Key Concepts

- You can use reasoning to determine which mathematical process is best in a given situation.
- Many simple problems can be solved using reasoning by systematic trial, especially if you have not yet learned other mathematical methods.
- To prove a mathematical conjecture, you need to justify your conclusion by using a well-organized mathematical argument.

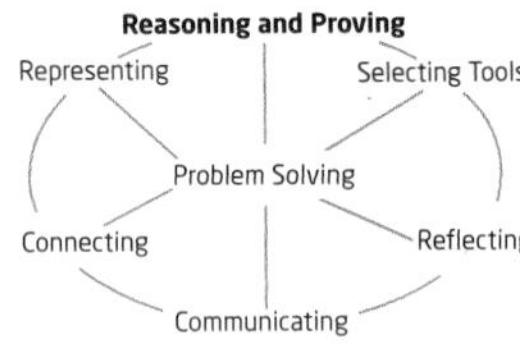

Communicate Your Understanding

C1 Jay's method for solving the problem "Which power of -2 is closest to -300?" is shown.

$(-2)^5 = -32$
$(-2)^6 = 64$
$(-2)^7 = -128 \quad \Rightarrow \quad -300 - (-512) = 212$
$(-2)^8 = 256 \quad \Rightarrow \quad -300 - (-128) = -172$
$(-2)^9 = -512$

The power of -2 that is closest to -300 is $(-2)^7$.

a) Describe Jay's strategy.

b) Do you think this was the most efficient strategy? Explain.

C2 **a)** Estimate the measure of each of the equal angles in the following triangles.

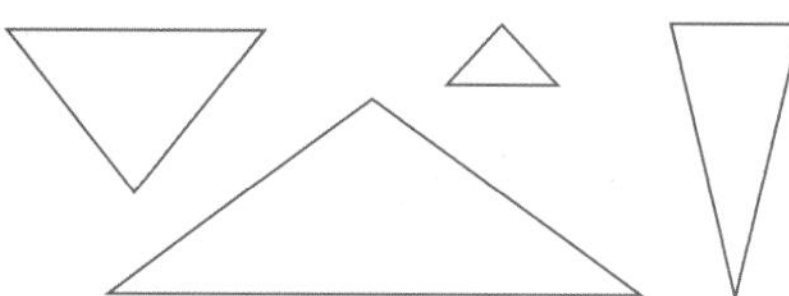

b) In each case, is your estimate greater than or less than 90°?

c) Do your results prove that the equal angles of an isosceles triangle are acute? Explain.

Practise

For help with questions 1 and 2, see the Investigate.

1. Copy the diagram. Place one of the numbers from 1 to 6 in each circle so that the sum of the three numbers on each side is the same.

2. Copy the diagram. Place one of the integers from -6 to 5 in each circle so that the sum of the three numbers on each side is the same.

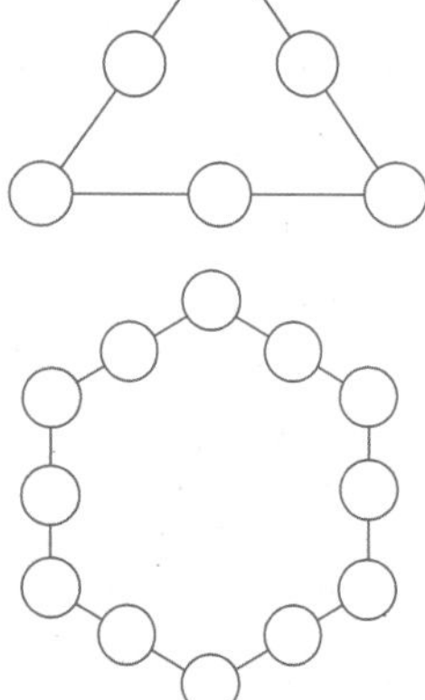

For help with questions 3 and 4, see the Example.

3. Prove that the sum of three consecutive whole numbers is divisible by 3.

4. Prove that a newspaper always has an even number of pages.

Connect and Apply

In each problem, write one or two sentences to describe your strategy. Then, carry out your strategy and justify your solution. Reflect and decide if your strategy was an appropriate one.

5. Paul claims that you only need seven coins to be able to make any amount of money up to 50¢. Show that Paul is correct.

6. Copy the numbers in the order shown. Replace each ■ with some of the symbols +, −, ×, ÷, ( ), and = to make true statements.

a) 5 ■ 2 ■ 8 ■ 3 ■ 15

b) 25 ■ 5 ■ 11 ■ 25 ■ 9

c) $\frac{1}{2}$ ■ $\frac{1}{3}$ ■ $\frac{11}{12}$ ■ $\frac{1}{12}$

d) $\frac{2}{3}$ ■ $\frac{1}{8}$ ■ $\left(-\frac{1}{12}\right)$

mean

- the sum of the values in a set of data, divided by the number of values in the set

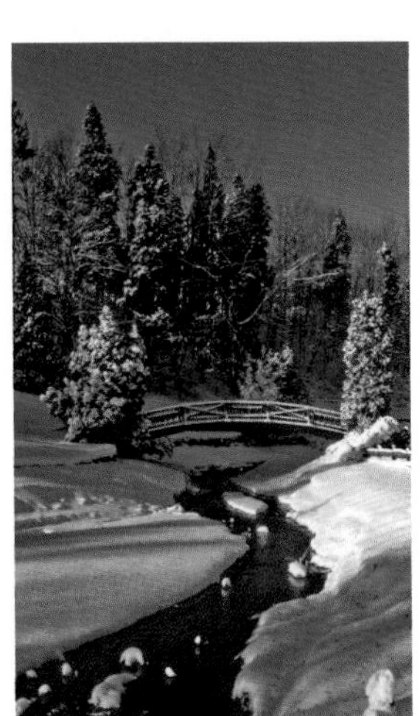

7. The **mean** low temperature between January 1 and January 30 was −5°C.

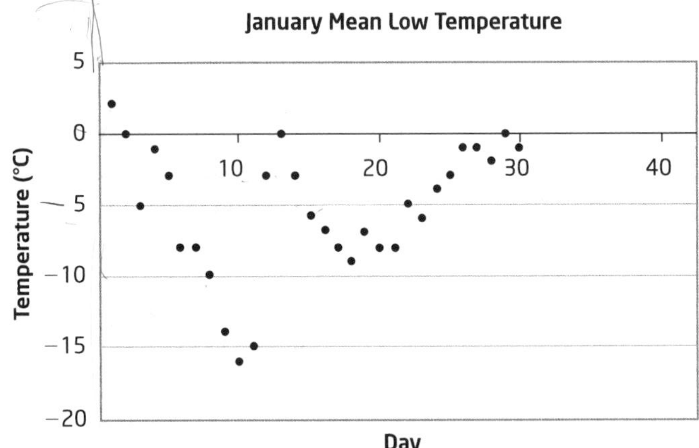

a) What would the temperature need to be on January 31 to lower the mean temperature to −6°C?

b) What would the temperature need to be on January 31 to raise the mean temperature to −4.5°C?

counter-example

- an example that proves that a conjecture is false

8. Give a **counter-example** to prove each statement false.

a) All prime numbers are odd.

b) The sum of any two integers is always negative.

c) All fractions are less than 1.

d) All quadrilaterals are rectangles.

9. In the game of chess, a knight can move two spaces forward or backward and one space left or right, or two spaces left or right and one space forward or backward. Copy the small board shown. Can a knight eventually land on any square on the board?

10. Although most masses are measured in kilograms or grams in Canada, cheese is often bought by the pound. Three quarters of a pound and three quarters of a block of cheese balance with an entire block of cheese. What is the mass of the block of cheese, in pounds?

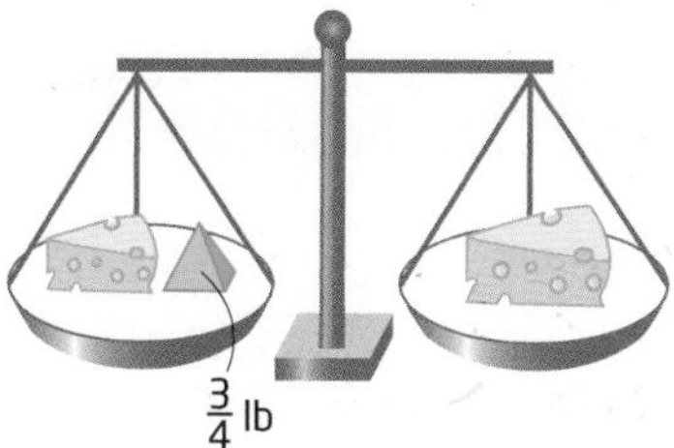

11. The integer −5 can be expressed as a difference of squares.

$$\begin{aligned} &2^2 - 3^2 \\ &= 4 - 9 \\ &= -5 \end{aligned}$$

How many integers between −1 and −10 can be expressed as a difference of squares of whole numbers?

12. Sam went on four rides a total of eight times at the fair. Roller Magic costs \$3.25, Death Drop costs \$3.75, The Amazing Loop costs \$4.00, and Fire Pit costs \$4.50. Sam says he went on one ride more than three times. He spent a total of \$33.00. How many times did Sam go on each ride?

13. How many floor tiles are there on the floors in your school?

Extend

14. Each three by three square, each row, and each column must contain each of the numerals 1 through 9 only once. Copy and complete this Sudoku puzzle.

		1	6	9		8		2
		7	5					
	9		2	4			7	
	2	5						
	1		8	5	9		2	
						9	5	
	7			1	5		9	
					3	2		
3		9		2	6	4		

15. What is the mass of a school bus with 45 student passengers?

16. For the sequence 1, −2, −2, 3, 3, 3, −4, −4, −4, −4, 5, 5, 5, 5, 5, … ,

a) what is the 50th term?

b) what is the 100th term?

c) what is the sum of the first 50 terms?

d) what is the sum of the first 100 terms?

1.7 Focus on Reflecting

When you solve a problem, you need to regularly check and re-check your thought processes.

- Is your strategy the best one?
- Are you checking to make sure you are not making any errors?
- Have you considered alternative strategies or the use of different tools?
- Does your answer make sense?
- Can you verify that your solution is correct?

Reflecting on your processes will make you a better problem solver.

Investigate

Tools
- paper strips
- tape
- pencil

How can the process of reflecting help you solve problems?

A: Möbius strip

How can a sheet of paper have only one side?

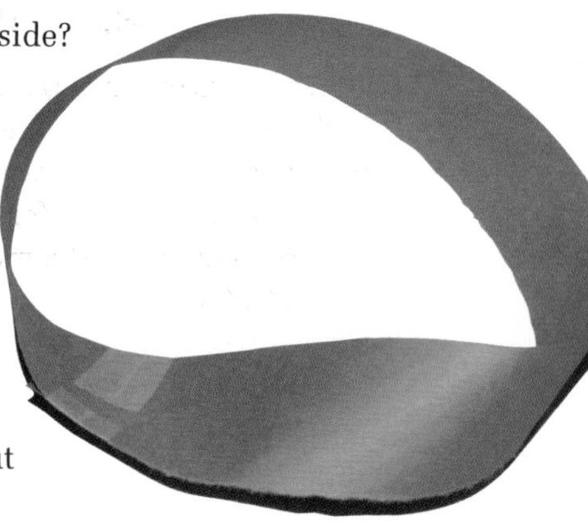

1. Cut a strip of paper about 4 cm wide and 28 cm long. Twist it a half turn and tape the ends together. This is called a Möbius strip.
2. Draw a line along one face of the paper without lifting your pencil. Describe what happened.
3. Predict what would happen if you cut all the way along this line.
4. Test your hypothesis. What happened? Explain.
5. Make another Möbius strip. This time, draw two lines, each one-third of the distance from each edge. Then, cut along the two lines.
6. **Reflect** What happened? Can you explain why the result was different?

B: Strategies

How many numbers between 1 and 100 are divisible by 7?

1. Devise two strategies that would be efficient in solving this problem.
2. Solve the problem in two ways, using both strategies.
3. **Reflect** Explain which strategy was more effective.

Key Concepts

- As you solve a problem, indicate, in words or symbols, what your strategy is, so you can evaluate it later on.
- Reflect back to evaluate the effectiveness of your strategies and to verify that your solution is correct.
- If you determine that the solution was incorrect, check to see if your steps were done correctly, or try a different strategy.

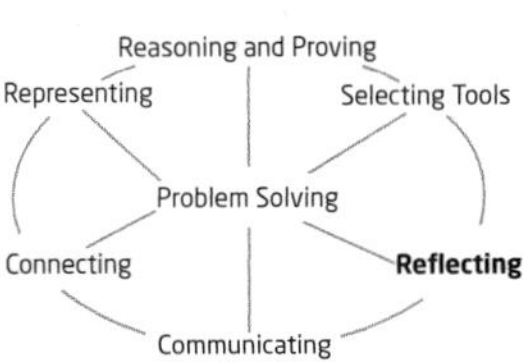

Communicate Your Understanding

C1 To answer the problem, "Find five odd numbers that add up to 55," Ben used the strategy of systematic trial.

a) Ben's first trial was $3 + 5 + 7 + 9 + 11 = 35$. What might his next trial be? Why?

b) Do you think that systematic trial is a good strategy for this problem? Explain.

C2 A triangle has sides of length 3 cm, 5 cm, and 7 cm. Describe how you can verify whether this is a right triangle.

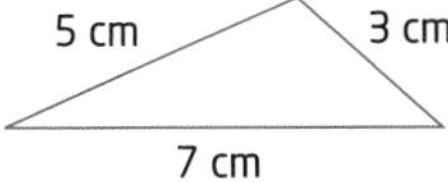

C3 Using the drive-through one night at a local coffee shop, Tara ordered a large coffee and a muffin. The drive-through attendant told her that her total was \$19.38. Tara argued with the attendant that it is not possible for the total to be \$19.38 when she only ordered a coffee and a muffin. The attendant insisted the total was \$19.38.

a) Explain what the drive-through attendant should have done when Tara questioned the total.

b) Discuss what the drive-through attendant might have done wrong.

Practise

For help with question 1, see the Investigate, Part A.

1. To create a double Möbius strip, place two strips of paper together, one on top of the other. Twist them a half-turn and tape them together, end to end, at both the top and bottom. Then, cut the strip down the middle. Describe the results and explain why it happened.

2. If you multiply a number by -7, and then add 12, the result is -380. What is the number?

3. Half of a number, decreased by $\frac{3}{4}$, gives $\frac{7}{12}$. What is the number?

4. What strategies did you use in questions 2 and 3? How effective were they?

5. What is the least number divisible by all of the integers 1 through 9? Explain your strategy and whether it was effective.

Connect and Apply

6. a) Using only the integers -3, -2, -1, 0, 1, 2, and 3, find all solutions to $X + Y + Z = -5$. You may repeat numbers.
   b) What strategy did you use? Was it effective? Explain.

7. a) Multiply $1 \times 2 \times 3 \times 4$.
   b) Calculate $5^2 - 1$.
   c) Multiply $2 \times 3 \times 4 \times 5$.
   d) Calculate $11^2 - 1$.
   e) Multiply $4 \times 5 \times 6 \times 7$.
   f) Calculate $29^2 - 1$.
   g) Describe a rule that this pattern seems to illustrate.
   h) Verify your rule by trying it with two more examples.
   i) Did your examples work? If not, try to develop a different rule and verify it.

Literacy Connections

A pixel is a single grid point on a computer or TV screen. Many screens are 640 pixels across and 480 pixels high.

8. In a video game, a character has been programmed to start at 60 pixels to the left of centre. The character moves 90 pixels to the right, then 75 pixels to the left, then 60 pixels to the right, and so on.
   a) The character disappears when it lands on zero, the centre. After how many moves will this occur?
   b) Verify that your answer is correct.

9. How many numbers between 1 and 100 are divisible by either 2 or 3? Explain your strategy and verify that it works.

10. A recipe calls for 1 kg of flour, 500 mL of milk, 2 eggs, and 125 g of sugar. To triple the recipe, Karen calculated that she needed 3 kg of flour, 15 L of milk, 6 eggs, and 3.75 kg of sugar.
    a) Without calculating the correct amounts, find Karen's errors, and describe the clues to her errors.
    b) Verify that your discoveries are correct.

Extend

11. How many square metres of pizza are ordered in Ontario in a year?

12. In a magic square, the rows, columns, and diagonals each add to the same sum.
    a) Construct a magic square using these numbers:
       i) 1, 2, 3, 4, 5, 6, 7, 8, 9
       ii) $-4, -3, -2, -1, 0, 1, 2, 3, 4$
    b) Describe the strategies that you used.

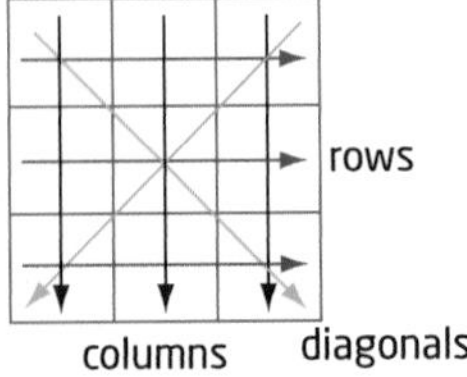

Chapter 1 Review

For each question, try to use the most appropriate tools, computational methods, and problem solving strategies. Provide complete justification for each solution.

1. Continue each pattern for three more terms. Describe how to find successive terms.

a) 12, 9, 6, 3 **b)** 7, 14, 28

c) 5, 6, 8, 11 **d)** 3, −1, −6, −12

2. A fence will be built to enclose a 100-m by 70-m field. It will need a post at each corner and one every 5 m. How many posts are needed?

3. An archery target has points as shown.

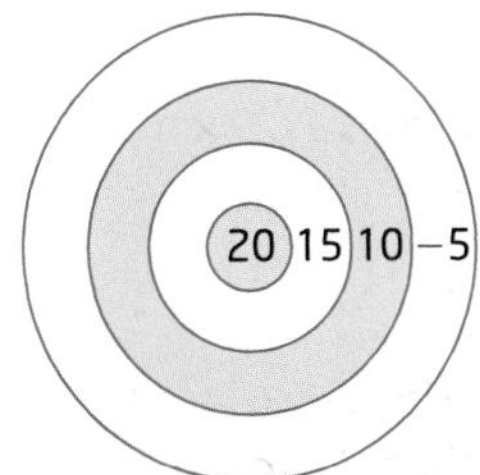

a) Describe a strategy to determine how many different scores are possible with three arrows.

b) Use your strategy to find the different possible scores.

4. Three houses, A, B, and C, are to be connected to hydro, cable TV, and telephone wires, labelled as P, Q, and R, without the wires crossing each other. Can this be done? If yes, show the solution. If not, explain why.

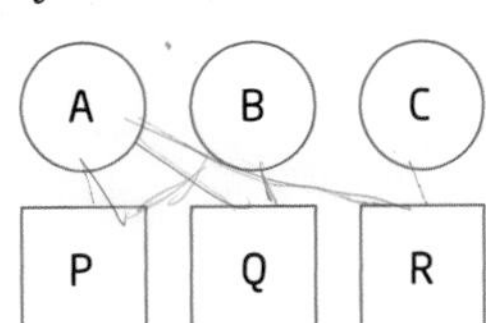

5. Plot the points E(4, 5), F(7, 0), and G(1, −4). Find all locations of the point H so that EFGH is a parallelogram.

6. How many squares of all sizes are there in this diagram? What strategy did you use?

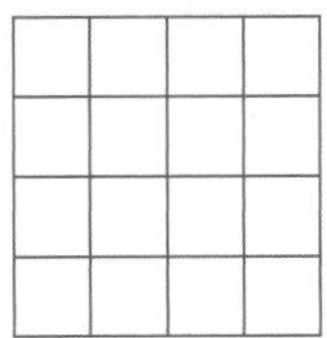

7. Dave is meeting his friends at 7:30 P.M. The average speed of the bus is 28 km/h, and he needs to travel 20 km. When should he catch the bus? Describe your strategy and whether it was appropriate.

8. a) A rectangular yard measures 8 m by 6 m. What happens to the area if each dimension is doubled?

b) Use an appropriate tool to illustrate what happens to the area of any rectangle when its dimensions are doubled.

9. What power of 7 is 40 353 607? Describe your strategy.

10. Find three consecutive integers that have a sum of −402. Describe your strategy.

11. Evaluate.

a) $\frac{2}{5} + \left(-\frac{3}{7}\right)$ **b)** $-\frac{2}{9} - \left(-\frac{1}{6}\right)$

c) $-\frac{2}{3} \times \frac{1}{4}$ **d)** $\frac{7}{12} \div \left(-1\frac{3}{4}\right)$

12. Using only fractions between −1 and 1, find three different solutions to

$A + B + C = -\frac{7}{12}$.

13. A bracelet is to be made from 2 red and 5 blue beads. How many different bracelets can be made? Describe your strategy.

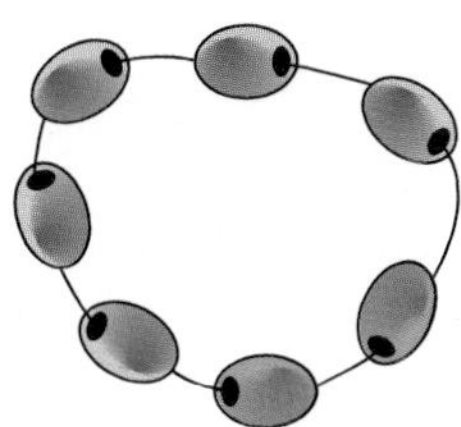

CHAPTER

2

Relations

This chapter introduces methods for analysing relationships between variables. These relationships occur in many areas, including business, science, sports, and the arts. Analysing these relationships helps you understand trends and make accurate predictions.

Linear Relations

- Interpret the meanings of points on scatter plots and graphs.
- Pose problems, identify variables, and formulate hypotheses about relationships between two variables.
- Design and carry out an investigation or experiment involving relationships between two variables.
- Describe trends and relationships observed in data, make inferences from data, compare the inferences with hypotheses, and explain any differences between them.
- Construct graphs, using a variety of tools.
- Construct tables of values, scatter plots, and lines or curves of best fit.
- Determine values of a linear relation by interpolating or extrapolating from the graph of the relation.
- Describe a situation that corresponds to a graph of a relationship between two variables.
- Determine a line of best fit for a scatter plot, using an informal process.
- Determine other representations of a linear relation, given one representation.

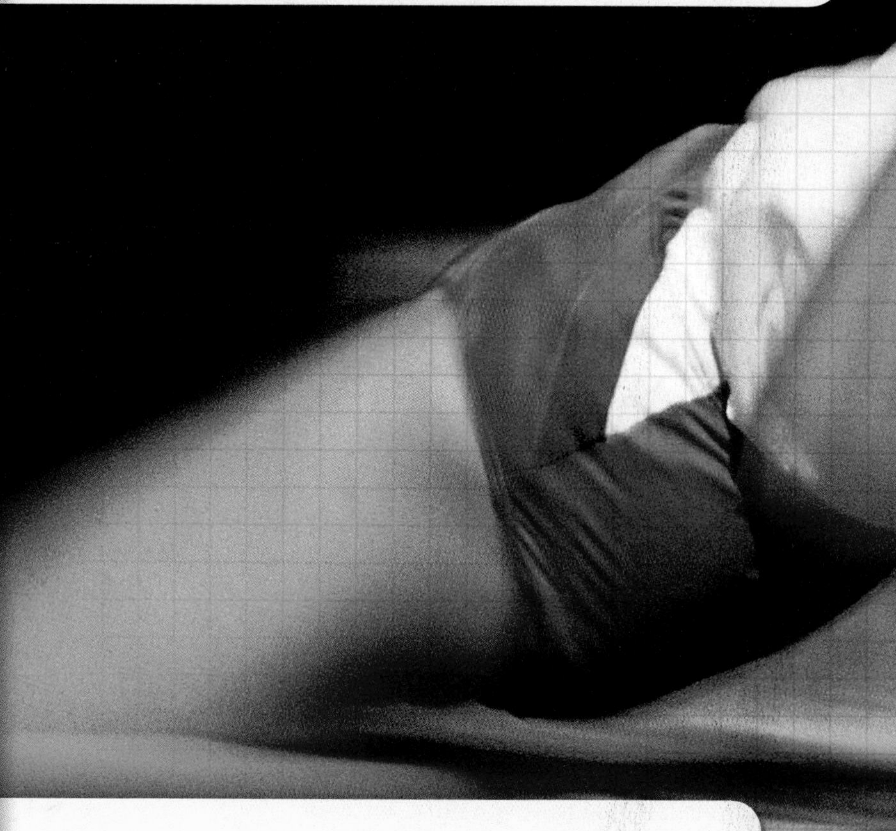

Vocabulary

hypothesis
statistics
primary data
secondary data
sample
population
census
random sample
simple random sampling
systematic random sampling
stratified random sampling
non-random sampling
bias
inference
dependent variable
independent variable
outlier
interpolate
extrapolate
linear relation
line of best fit
curve of best fit
distance-time graph

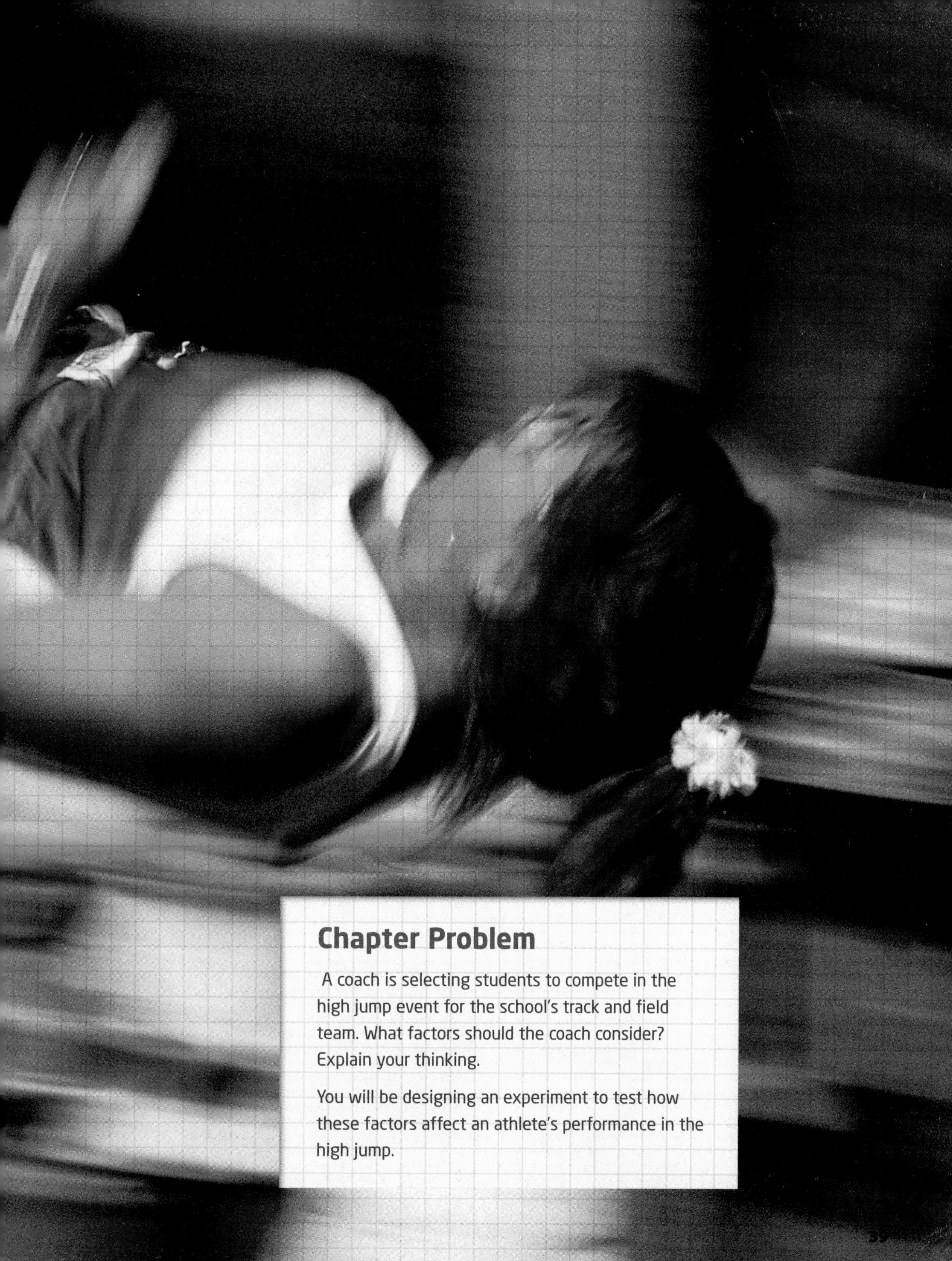

Chapter Problem

A coach is selecting students to compete in the high jump event for the school's track and field team. What factors should the coach consider? Explain your thinking.

You will be designing an experiment to test how these factors affect an athlete's performance in the high jump.

Get Ready

Bar Graphs

This bar graph shows the number of tickets sold during one week at the Main Street Cinema.

The graph shows that the cinema sold the fewest tickets on Monday and the most on Saturday. The attendance increases from Monday to Saturday but drops on Sunday.

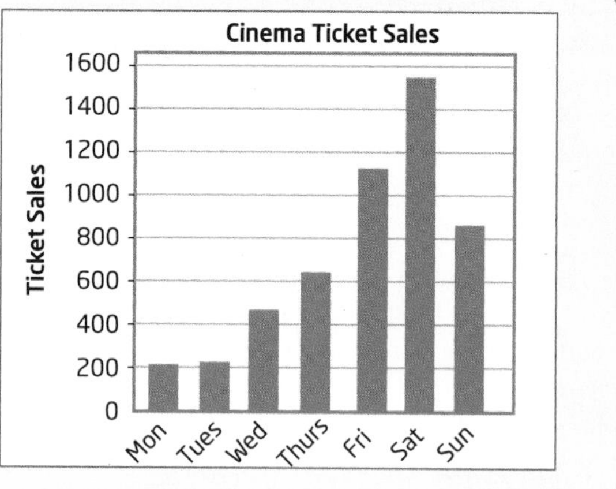

1. This graph shows data from a survey taken by Statistics Canada.
   a) What do the heights of the bars represent?
   b) Which province has the greatest unemployment rate?
   c) In what region did people have the best chance of finding work in 2003? Why?

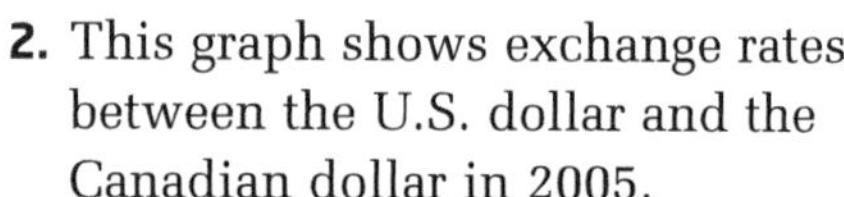
Adapted from Statistics Canada, CANSIM database, Table 109-5204, accessed via http://estat.statcan.ca, February 2006.

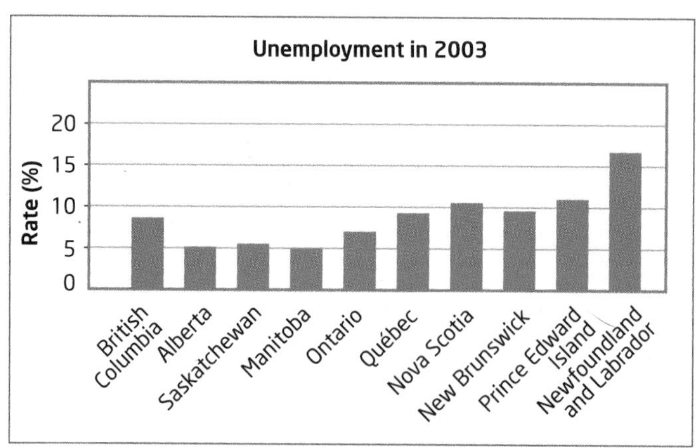

2. This graph shows exchange rates between the U.S. dollar and the Canadian dollar in 2005.
   a) What is the lowest value of the U.S. dollar shown on the graph?
   b) When was the value of the U.S. dollar the greatest compared to the Canadian dollar?
   c) Describe any pattern you see in the graph.

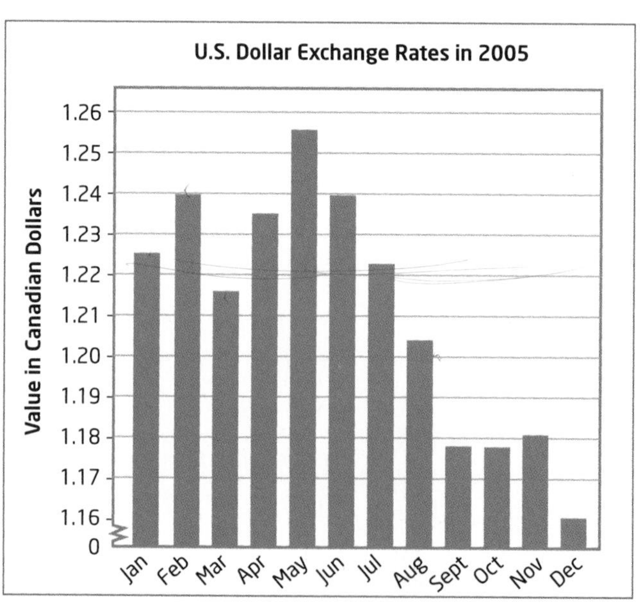

Scatter Plots

Here are the ages and annual incomes of 11 members of a family.

Age (years)	25	28	32	32	33	45	47	53	54	59	60
Income (thousands of dollars)	35	75	34	37	36	44	60	51	58	68	72

You can use a **scatter plot** to display data involving two variables.

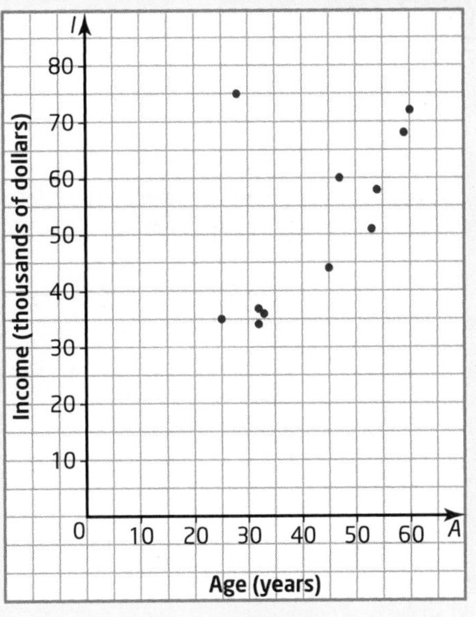

3. Every hour for 7 h, a biology student counted the number of larvae that hatched from a batch of fruit fly eggs. Here are the student's data.

Time (h)	0	1	2	3	4	5	6
Number of Larvae	5	10	21	43	82	168	320

a) Make a scatter plot of the data. Put time on the *x*-axis and the number of larvae on the *y*-axis. Label the axes, and include a title for the scatter plot.

b) Estimate the number of larvae hatched after 4.5 h.

4. This table shows the mean air pressure at various altitudes.

Altitude (km)	0	5	10	15	20	25	30
Air Pressure (kPa)	101.3	54.0	26.0	12.0	5.5	2.5	1.2

a) Make a scatter plot of the data. Put altitude on the *x*-axis and air pressure on the *y*-axis. Label the axes, and include a title for the scatter plot.

b) Estimate the air pressure at an altitude of 18 km.

Rates

A **rate** compares quantities that are measured in different units.

A rate of 348 km in 4.0 h is equivalent to a **unit rate** of $\frac{348 \text{ km}}{4.0 \text{ h}} = 87$ km/h.

5. Calculate each unit rate.

a) A printer prints 42 pages in 6 min.

b) Dog food costs $15 for a 5-kg bag.

c) A car travelled 880 km in 11 h.

6. Calculate each unit rate.

a) A breakfast cereal costs $4.19 for 750 g.

b) A recipe calls for 500 mL of flour to make 24 bran muffins.

c) Jessie ran 5000 m in 38.6 min.

2.1 Hypotheses and Sources of Data

hypothesis

- a theory or statement that is either true or false

statistics

- numerical data, or the collection, organization, and analysis of numerical data

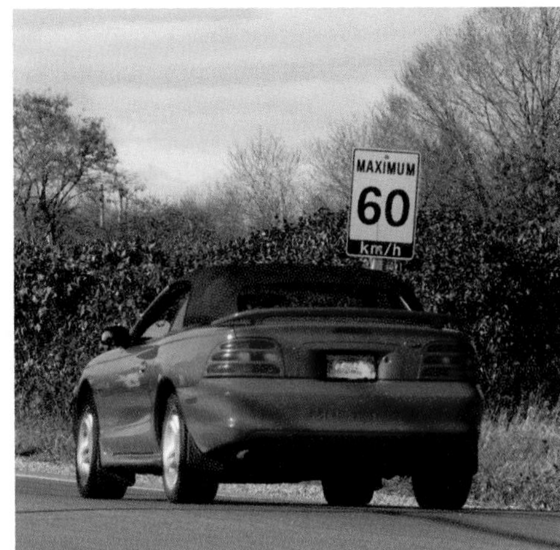

Some people think that drivers of red cars are more likely than other drivers to have an accident. How can you tell if this opinion is valid? First, write a **hypothesis** that clearly states what you want to prove or disprove. You can use **statistics** to test whether the hypothesis is likely to be true.

For example, you could start with the hypothesis that the accident rate for red cars is higher than that for other cars. You could then use data from accident reports or insurance claims to see if your hypothesis is correct. Often, it is not practical to collect enough data to determine for certain whether a hypothesis is true.

Investigate

How do you state a hypothesis?

1. Write a hypothesis for each question.
   - **a)** What percent of students in your school will get a driver's licence this year?
   - **b)** Is television advertising more effective than newspaper advertising?
   - **c)** Do people consider price or brand more important when buying toothpaste?
   - **d)** Do boys and girls have different study habits?
   - **e)** How often do people use the phonebook?
   - **f)** Which sport do teenagers like the most?
2. Do all hypotheses have to include numbers? How could you classify different types of hypotheses?
3. **Reflect** What information would you need to test each hypothesis in step 1?

All hypotheses are either true or false. If a hypothesis is false, then its opposite must be true.

Example 1 State a Hypothesis and Its Opposite

Write a hypothesis about a relationship between the variables in each pair. Then, give the opposite hypothesis.

a) a driver's age and the risk of having an accident

b) attendance at school and marks

c) the heights of boys and the heights of girls

Solution

There are many possible hypotheses. Here is one example for each pair of variables.

a) *Hypothesis:* As drivers age, their risk of having an accident increases.
Opposite: As drivers age, their risk of having an accident does not increase. You can state the opposite another way: As drivers age, their risk of having an accident either decreases or stays the same.

b) *Hypothesis:* Students' marks decrease as they miss more classes.
Opposite: Students' marks do not decrease as they miss more classes.

c) *Hypothesis:* On average, boys and girls of the same age are the same height.
Opposite: On average, boys and girls of the same age are not the same height.

Data Sources

Often, you need data to test a hypothesis. Researchers must decide whether to collect new data or use data that other people have already collected. **Primary data** come from experiments and surveys done by the researchers. Researchers can find **secondary data** in sources such as publications, the Internet, and surveys done by Statistics Canada.

primary data

- original data that a researcher gathers specifically for a particular experiment or survey

secondary data

- data that someone else has already gathered for some other purpose

Example 2 Identify Primary and Secondary Data

Explain whether each set of data is primary or secondary. What are the advantages and any disadvantages of each person's choice of data source?

a) Daniel telephoned 100 families in his town to ask them how many pets they have.

b) Cathy used data from Statistics Canada to determine the proportion of households in Canada that have at least one car.

c) Anja found a Web site with the results from a survey on the spending habits of teenagers across Canada.

d) Tomas checked the Web sites of 24 stores for the price of the latest Harry Potter DVD.

Solution

a) The telephone interviews produce primary data because Daniel performed the survey himself. The telephone survey is easy to do, but time-consuming. Data on pets in his town are unlikely to be available from a secondary source.

b) Cathy is using a secondary source since Statistics Canada gathered the survey data. Statistics Canada is an excellent source because it collects data from a huge number of families all across Canada. Cathy could never gather that much data by herself.

Did You Know?

Your school can get free access to data from Statistics Canada through its educational Web resource, Σ -STAT.

c) The Web site is a secondary source since Anja did not collect the survey data herself. The Web site is a convenient way to get survey results. It might take Anja a lot of time and expense to gather similar data herself. However, data on Web sites are not always reliable. Anja should check who did the survey and whether the results are complete and accurate. When a business or organization does a survey, they sometimes publish only data that are favourable to them.

d) Tomas used the Web sites as a way to survey the prices that the video stores charged for the DVD. So, Tomas collected primary data from the Internet. This method was probably faster and cheaper than phoning all the video stores.

Key Concepts

- A hypothesis is a statement that can be tested to determine if it is likely to be true.
- Primary data are new information collected by a researcher.
- Secondary data are existing data that were gathered for some other purpose.

Communicate Your Understanding

C1 **a)** Give an example of a hypothesis that involves numbers.

b) Give an example of a hypothesis that does not involve numbers.

c) Describe how you could test each hypothesis.

C2 Is it always better to use primary data when testing a hypothesis? Explain why or why not.

Practise

For help with questions 1 and 2, see Example 1.

1. State the opposite of each hypothesis.

a) Most people's favourite number is 7.

b) Adults spend more time listening to classical music than to rap.

c) In Ontario, more teenagers join soccer teams than hockey teams.

d) Chocolate is not the most popular flavour of ice cream.

2. State a hypothesis about a relationship between each pair of variables. Then, state the opposite of each hypothesis.

a) a student's age and time spent doing homework

b) a mother's height and the height of her children

c) temperature and crime rates

d) the cost of gasoline and the number of people using public transit

For help with questions 3 and 4, see Example 2.

3. Which of the following data are primary and which are secondary? Explain.

a) An office manager hands out a questionnaire to see if employees want to work earlier hours during the summer.

b) A student finds data on Internet use in a report published by Statistics Canada.

c) A researcher collects information about how far people travel on public transit by talking to passengers on the buses.

d) A researcher downloads data about the length of rides taken on public transit from a transit authority's Web site.

4. Identify each data source as primary or secondary. State one advantage of each source of data.

a) A researcher interviewed 100 students about their study habits.

b) A sporting goods company searched on the Internet for data on how Canadians spend their leisure time.

c) A manufacturer surveyed 1000 recent customers about possible changes to a product.

d) A student found advertisements in out-of-town newspapers at a library to check admission prices at theatres across the country.

Connect and Apply

5. a) Make a hypothesis about whether the students in your class prefer cats or dogs as pets.

b) Describe how you could test your hypothesis. Explain whether you would use primary or secondary data.

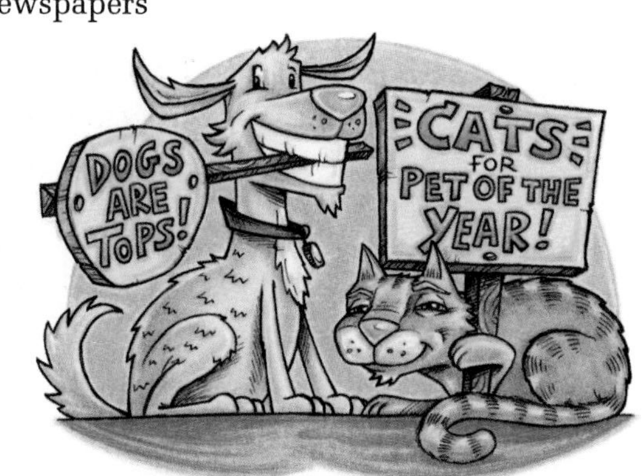

6. Steve prepared the following table using data volunteered by eight male students in his science class.

Name	Eye Colour	Height (cm)
Josanth	brown	167
Fred	green	181
Graham	green	185
Cho	brown	171
Seth	blue	154
Jamal	green	183
Juan	brown	160
Cameron	blue	173

   a) Is Steve using primary or secondary data? Explain.

   b) Make two hypotheses based on these data.

   c) How could you test your hypotheses?

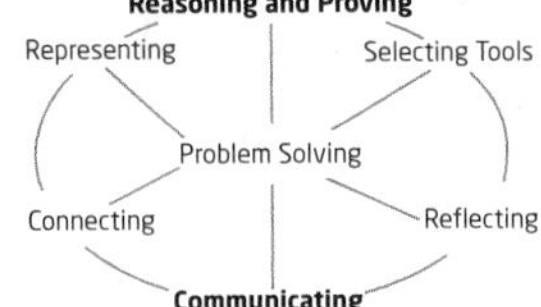

7. **a)** Make a hypothesis about the number of phone calls Canadians make.

   b) Describe how you could use primary data to test your hypothesis.

   c) Describe how you could use secondary data to test your hypothesis.

   d) Which set of data is more likely to give accurate results?

8. **Chapter Problem** A coach is selecting students to compete in the high jump for the school's track and field team.

   a) Make a hypothesis about a physical characteristic that could help an athlete do well in the high jump.

   b) What data would you need to test your hypothesis? Would you use primary or secondary data? Explain why.

9. **a)** Make a hypothesis about the relationship between the speed of a computer and its price.

   b) **Use Technology** Use an Internet search engine to collect data about computer prices. Compare the results when you use the key words "computer stores," "computer memory," and "computer prices."

   c) Did you conduct primary or secondary research? Explain.

   d) Describe another method for gathering data about computer speeds and prices.

10. **Use Technology**

   a) Make a hypothesis about how much milk a cow produces in a day. Then, use an Internet search engine to find data to test your hypothesis.

   b) Make a hypothesis about how much hay a cow eats in a day. Then, use data from the Internet to test your hypothesis.

   c) Did you gather primary or secondary data in parts a) and b)? Explain.

Achievement Check

11. This table shows the number of fish that entrants in a fishing derby caught.

Number of Fish	Number of Entrants
0	20
1	12
2	12
3	7
4	3
5	0
6	1

Before the fishing derby began, Heather predicted that most entrants would not catch any fish. George predicted that most entrants would catch either one or two fish.

a) Is Heather's hypothesis true? Explain.

b) Is George's hypothesis true? Explain.

c) Write the opposite of Heather's hypothesis and of George's hypothesis.

d) Can the opposite of Heather's hypothesis and the opposite of George's hypothesis both be true? Explain your reasoning.

e) George found the results of the derby in a local newspaper. Are these data primary or secondary? Explain.

f) Modify Heather's prediction and George's prediction to make new hypotheses that are true.

Extend

12. a) Make a hypothesis about the relationship between the latitude of a city and the mean of its daily maximum temperatures in January.

b) Use data from an atlas or an online source to test your hypothesis.

13. a) Make a hypothesis about how the difference between the Olympic records for men and women in the marathon has changed over the years.

b) Use the Internet or other sources to collect data to test your hypothesis.

c) Explain how the data you found prove or disprove your hypothesis.

14. Math Contest The mean of a list of n numbers is 6. When the number 17 is added to the list, the mean becomes 7. What is the value of n?

Did You Know?

The coldest temperature ever recorded in North America was − 63°C at Snag, Yukon on February 3, 1947.

2.2 Sampling Principles

Do radio call-in shows accurately reflect the opinions of all their listeners? Are these listeners likely to have the same opinions as people who do not listen to the program? How can you reduce the chances of inaccurate results from a survey?

Investigate

How can you choose participants for a survey?

A sportswear manufacturer is thinking of hiring a world-champion speed skater to help promote its products. Since the company wants someone who will appeal to teenagers, it surveyed 200 teenagers for their opinions about the speed skater.

sample

- any group of people or items selected from a population

1. Which of these **samples** is likely to accurately reflect the opinions of teenagers in the whole country? Explain.
   a) 200 students at a school near the company's office
   b) 200 teenagers selected from across Canada
   c) the first 200 teenagers willing to answer a questionnaire at a shopping mall
   d) 10 teenagers from each of 20 schools chosen from across Canada

population

- the whole group of people or items being studied

2. **Reflect** How could you select a sample so that it properly represents the whole **population**?

census

- a survey of all members of a population

The population depends on what you are trying to measure or study. If you are studying the music preferences of teenagers in your school, the population is all the teenagers in the school. It is often not practical to survey all members of a large population. So, instead of doing a **census**, you survey a sample of the population.

Example 1 Identify the Population

Identify the population in each situation. Then, indicate whether each researcher should survey a sample of the population or do a census. Explain your reasoning.

a) A teacher wishes to know how early his students wake up in the morning.

b) The principal of a school with 2100 students wants to find out how much homework her students have each day.

c) A clothing store needs to find out whether its customers are happy with its service.

d) A newspaper wants to know the public's opinion of a federal political party.

e) A polling firm wants to know how people will vote in the next federal election.

Solution

a) The population is the students in the teacher's class. He should do a census since the population is small and easy to survey.

b) The population is the students in the school. The principal should use a sample, since the school population is quite large and all students in any particular class may have the same amount of homework for that subject.

c) The population is the store's customers. A random sample is probably best because it could be difficult and time-consuming to reach all of the store's customers.

d) The population is everyone in Canada. The newspaper will have to use a sample since it is next to impossible to get the opinion of every person in Canada.

e) The population is every person who can vote in the next federal election. Again, a census is not practical. It will take far less time and expense to interview a sample of voters from across the country.

You can never be completely certain that a sample is representative of the population. However, a **random sample** usually gives reasonably accurate results. You can use several different methods to select a random sample.

random sample

- a sample in which all members of a population have an equal chance of being chosen

Example 2 Choose a Random Sample

A principal of a school with 1600 students wants to know whether they favour introducing school uniforms. Describe three methods he could use to select a random sample of 200 students.

Solution

1. The principal takes an alphabetical list of all the students at the school and numbers the names in sequence. He then uses a graphing calculator or a spreadsheet to generate 200 random numbers between 1 and 1600. He selects the names on the list that correspond to these numbers. This method is an example of **simple random sampling**.

2. The principal finds a starting point on the list of students by picking a single random number between 1 and 1600. To get a random sample with 200 students, he then selects every eighth name before and after the starting point. This method is an example of **systematic random sampling**.

3. The principal uses lists of the students in each grade. He then randomly selects the same fraction of students from the list for each grade. Since he wants a sample of 200 students out of a total of 1600, he needs to choose $\frac{200}{1600} = \frac{1}{8}$ of the students in each grade. Thus, if there are 480 students in grade 9, he would randomly select $\frac{1}{8} \times 480 = 60$ of these grade 9 students to be part of the sample. This method is an example of **stratified random sampling**.

simple random sampling

- choosing a specific number of members randomly from the entire population

systematic random sampling

- choosing members of a population at fixed intervals from a randomly selected member

stratified random sampling

- dividing a population into distinct groups and then choosing the same fraction of members from each group

non-random sampling

- using a method that is not random to choose a sample from a population

bias

- error resulting from choosing a sample that does not represent the whole population

Sometimes people use samples that are not randomly chosen. **Non-random sampling** can be cheaper or more convenient than random sampling, but the results are less likely to be accurate. Samples that are not random may tend to choose a certain type of member from the population. As a result of this **bias**, the sample does not properly represent the whole population.

Example 3 Identify Sampling Techniques

Identify the type of sampling in each situation. Explain any bias that the samples could have.

a) The personnel department sends questionnaires to 75 employees randomly selected from a list of everyone working for the company.

b) A computer randomly chooses one name from an alphabetical list of a store's customers and then also selects every 25th person listed before and after that name.

c) The president of a restaurant chain interviews employees at one branch.

d) The student council of a school randomly selects a number of students from each class. This number is proportional to the size of the class.

Solution

a) simple random sampling

b) systematic random sampling

c) non-random sampling: This sample could be biased since the employees of one branch may not be representative of the employees of the whole chain.

d) stratified random sampling

Key Concepts

- A population is the entire group of people or items that is being studied.
- A sample is any part of the population.
- A random sampling technique ensures that all members of a population are equally likely to be selected. As a result, a random sample is likely to be representative of the whole population.
- Sampling methods include simple random, systematic random, stratified random, and non-random sampling.
- Bias can make the results of a survey inaccurate.

Communicate Your Understanding

C1 The city council is considering building a new library. Your councillor surveys 75 people in your neighbourhood to see if they approve of this expense. Is this survey a good method for judging how the citizens of the city feel about the project? Use the words "population" and "sample" in your explanation.

C2 **a)** Describe two ways you could select a random sample to estimate how many of the students in your school have access to the Internet at home.

b) Describe a survey method that is unlikely to give an accurate estimate.

Practise

For help with questions 1 and 2, see Example 1.

1. Identify the population in each situation.

a) Generally, girls learn to walk before boys do.

b) The mean mark on yesterday's test was 72%.

c) As cars age, their repair costs increase.

d) Most food stores charge more for cream than for milk.

2. Describe the data required to answer each question. Explain whether you would use a census or a sample to collect each set of data.

a) Do girls learn to walk before boys do?

b) Is the mean mark on a test greater than 75%?

c) Is the mean annual salary of employees in Canada less than $50 000?

d) How are a person's height and age related?

e) What is the most common make of car in your school's parking lot?

f) What is the most common colour among the cars that drive by your school?

For help with question 3, see Example 2.

3. Describe how you could choose a random sample to determine each of the following.

a) the type of coffee preferred by customers of a local cafe

b) Ontario teenagers' favourite magazines

c) political parties supported by bilingual Canadians

d) countries of origin for immigrants to Canada

For help with question 4, see Example 3.

4. Identify the type of sample in each situation. Comment on any possible bias in these samples.

a) A career studies class interviews University of Waterloo graduates to learn about career choices for university graduates.

b) A town council randomly selects phone numbers from a town directory to survey citizens' opinions on a new park.

c) Moviegoers leaving a cinema are interviewed to find out how people spend their free time.

d) Every fifth person entering the cafeteria is asked to fill out a questionnaire about the menu.

Connect and Apply

5. List three ways you could divide the students in your school into groups for selecting a stratified random sample.

6. A government agency wants to survey Ontario farmers.

a) Identify the population.

b) Suggest a stratified random sampling technique that the agency could use.

7. A company wants to select 50 of its 325 employees for a survey.

a) Identify the population.

b) Describe a systematic random sampling technique that the company could use.

8. The physical education department wants to survey the members of school teams.

a) Identify the population.

b) Describe a method of randomly selecting 15% of the members of the teams.

9. This table lists the enrolment at a high school.

Grade	Number of Students
9	330
10	308
11	295
12	283

The school administration wants to interview a random sample of 150 students, stratified by grade. How many students should the administration select from each grade?

Did You Know?

Births in Canada peaked at 405 486 in 1990. As a result, total enrolment is high schools is now declining.

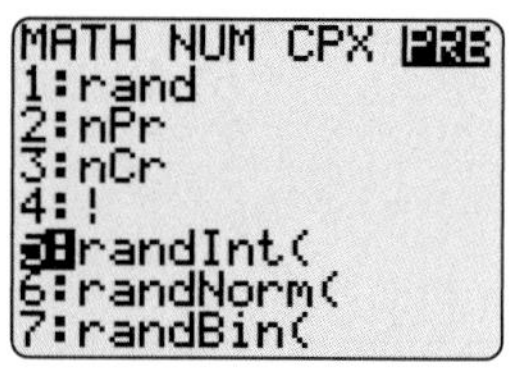

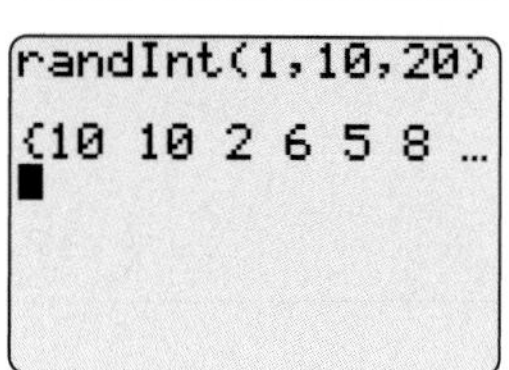

10. Use Technology Use this method to generate random integers with a TI-83 Plus or TI-84 graphing calculator.

- Press (MATH). Cursor over to display the **PRB** menu.
- Move the cursor down to **5:randInt(**, and press (ENTER).
- Press **1** (,) **10** (,) **20** ()) (ENTER).

The calculator will display 20 randomly selected integers between 1 and 10, inclusive.

a) What command would you enter to produce a list of 25 random integers between 12 and 36?

b) How could you use a graphing calculator to randomly select 40 house numbers between 1 and 500?

c) What command would you enter to randomly select 75 house numbers between 100 and 1000?

11. A survey selects five students from each grade at 100 high schools across Ontario.

a) Explain why this sample is not completely random.

b) How does this sampling method bias the results of the survey?

12. Identify the population for each of the following. Then, describe how you could select an appropriate sample of each population.

a) the popularity of various kinds of music in your school

b) the popularity of various kinds of music in your community

c) the effectiveness of a national campaign to convince people between the ages of 18 and 30 not to smoke

d) the spending habits of senior citizens in Ontario

e) the quality of printing from various computer printers on sale in Canada

f) the mean cost of gasoline in your community

13. In a *voluntary sample*, people choose to answer the survey, rather than being selected by the person doing the survey. For example, a Web site could ask people browsing the site to fill out an online survey form. Discuss whether this voluntary sample accurately represents a population.

14. Even in the 1920s, polling companies conducted surveys by calling people randomly selected from telephone directories.

a) Explain why using this sampling method in the 1920s would not produce a representative sample of the opinions of everyone in the country.

b) Describe two ways in which a telephone survey today could be biased.

15. Design and conduct a survey to determine how much exercise students get. Present your results in a table and a graph. Explain your choice of sampling technique.

16. Design and conduct a survey to determine
- the percent of students in your school who buy lunch in the school's cafeteria
- the reasons for their choice

Present your data in a table and a bar graph. Explain your choice of sampling technique.

Extend

17. Bias can occur in a survey if it uses non-random sampling. Describe two other ways a survey can become biased.

18. To make sure that the Asian long-horned beetle is not infesting trees in a large downtown park, the city's forester decides to inspect 10% of the trees. Describe how the forester could choose which trees to inspect using

a) simple random sampling

b) stratified random sampling

c) systematic random sampling

d) non-random sampling

Which would be the best method to use? Explain your reasoning.

Did You Know?

The Asian long-horned beetle, *Anoplophora glabripennis* is called long-horned because it has two long antennae.

19. Survey companies often use *convenience samples* because they are easy to do. Interviewing shoppers at a mall is one example of a convenience sample.

a) Work with a partner to list two more examples of convenience samples.

b) Debate the statement "Convenience samples are true random samples." One partner argues for the statement, while the other argues against it. Debate for a maximum of 5 min. Then, decide if the statement is correct.

20. **Math Contest** How many odd three-digit numbers can be made by choosing from the digits 1, 2, 3, 4, 5, 6, and 7 if each number must contain three different digits?

2.3

Use Scatter Plots to Analyse Data

Doctors and dieticians often tell people to "eat smart." By choosing your food carefully, you can get the nutrients that your body needs while avoiding the less healthy types of fats and carbohydrates. You can use graphs to analyse the relationship between these nutrients and the energy content of common fast foods.

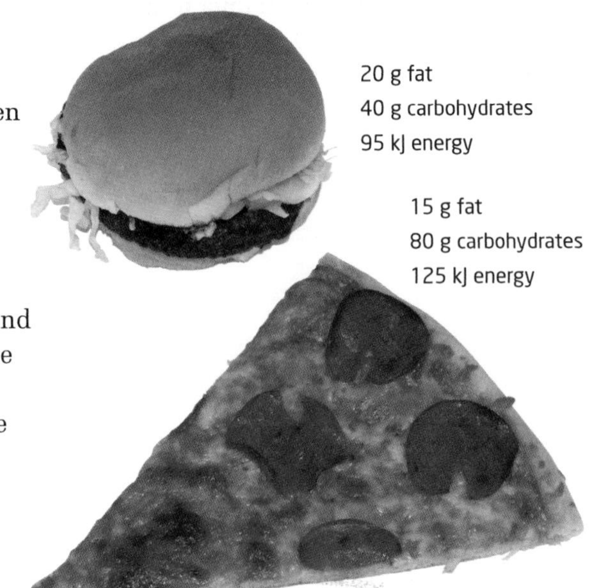

Investigate A

Tools

- TI-83 Plus or TI-84 graphing calculator
- grid paper

How can you use a scatter plot to analyse data?

In a science fiction movie, Martians land on Earth. The scientists in the movie notice that the Martians have small hands and thin arms. The scientists measure the left forearm and left handspan of a sample of 10 Martians. The table lists these data.

Name of Martian	Left Forearm Length (cm)	Left Handspan (cm)
Enyaw	23.1	14.6
Yaj	27.3	17.2
Adnil	21.0	11.5
Sset	21.5	12.4
Nairb	26.8	15.0
Eiggam	20.2	11.1
Derf	24.4	13.2
Sirhc	23.1	15.8
Narf	24.6	17.0
Yllor	22.1	12.7

The following steps outline how to use a graphing calculator to organize and display the data.

1. First, clear any old data from the calculator's lists:
   - Press (2nd) [MEM] to display the **MEMORY** menu.
   - Move the cursor down to **4:ClrAllLists**, and press (ENTER) twice.

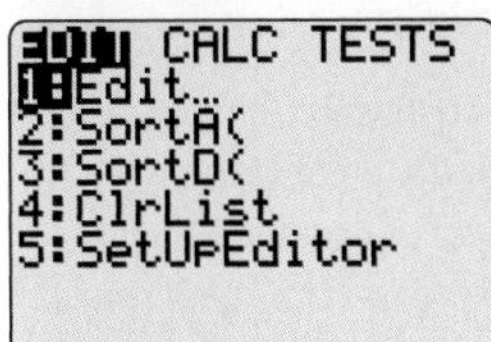

2. To start entering a table of data, press (STAT). Then, select **1:Edit** by pressing either **1** or (ENTER).

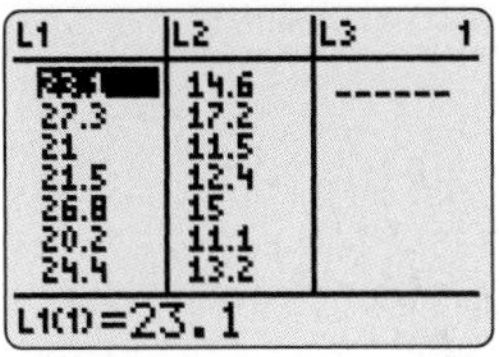

3. Enter the data for left forearm length into list **L1**, pressing (ENTER) after each entry. Similarly, enter the data for left handspan into list **L2**.

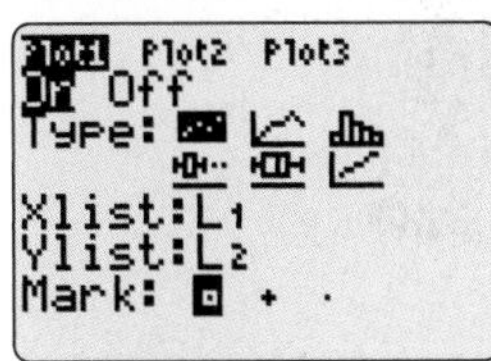

4. Now, set the calculator to display a scatter plot of the data:
   - Press (2nd) [STATPLOT] to display the **STAT PLOTS** menu.
   - Select **1:Plot1** to display the settings for Plot 1.
   - Select **ON** if it is not already highlighted.
   - Scroll down to **Type** and select the scatter plot symbol.
   - **Xlist** should be set to **L1**. If a different list is already selected, scroll down to **Xlist**: and enter **L1**. Similarly, **Ylist** should be set to **L2**.
   - Then, press (ZOOM) and select **9:ZoomStat**.

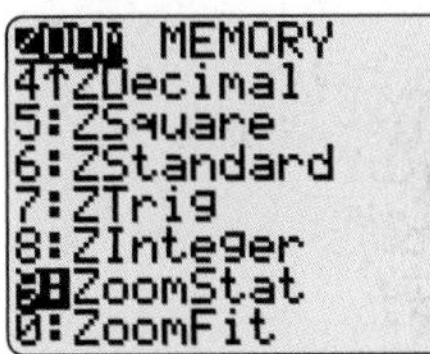

5. What does the horizontal axis of the scatter plot represent? What does the vertical axis represent?
6. Copy the scatter plot onto a sheet of graph paper. Label your graph properly.
7. **Reflect** Describe the relationship between a Martian's left forearm length and left handspan.
8. Derf's ordered pair on the graph is (24.4, 13.2). Describe the meaning of this ordered pair. How does this ordered pair differ from the rest of the data?
9. **Reflect** What could cause the data for Derf to differ from the pattern of the other data?

Technology Tip

Pressing the (ENTER) key is like saying "Please do this." It tells the calculator to carry out the command displayed on the screen.

You can select a menu option either by pressing the number for the option or by moving the cursor to the option and pressing (ENTER).

Investigate B

How do you conduct an experiment?

Is there a relationship between a human's forearm length and handspan? To answer this question, you need to collect and analyse data.

1. ***Objective:*** Outline the purpose of your experiment.
2. ***Hypothesis:*** Make a hypothesis based on the objective. Do you think a person's forearm length and handspan are related? If so, what pattern do you expect the data to have?
3. ***Procedure:*** Measure your own forearm length and handspan. Then, gather more data from nine classmates. Record these data in a table similar to the one for the Martian data.
4. ***Observations:*** Make a scatter plot of your data. Describe any pattern you see in the data.
5. ***Conclusion:*** Make an **inference** based on your observations. Does this inference support your hypothesis? Explain.
6. ***Evaluation:*** Did the experiment meet its objective? How could you improve the experiment?
7. **Reflect** How could you compare the relationship between a Martian's forearm length and handspan that you found in Investigate A to the relationship between a human's forearm length and handspan?

Literacy Connections

Your forearm is the part of your arm from your elbow to your wrist.

Your handspan is the distance from the tip of your thumb to the tip of your little finger when your fingers are spread out.

inference

- conclusion based on reasoning and data

If you have a set of measurements of one variable, you can calculate statistics for that variable, such as the mean and the median. When you have data for two variables, you can look for a relationship between the two variables. Often, you use the data to determine whether the value of the **dependent variable** changes when the value of the **independent variable** changes.

dependent variable

- a variable that is affected by some other variable

independent variable

- a variable that affects the value of another variable

Example 1 Identify Related Variables

Identify the independent and dependent variable in each situation.

a) Does the outdoor temperature affect the amount of fuel needed to heat a house?

b) Is there a relationship between people's ages and their heights?

c) Does the amount of rain in a region depend on its latitude?

Solution

a) Since you want to know whether the outdoor temperature affects the amount of fuel required for heating, the independent variable is the outdoor temperature and the dependent variable is the amount of fuel required.

b) The independent variable is age and the dependent variable is height.

c) The dependent variable is the amount of rain and the independent variable is the latitude. Note that the latitude might not actually affect the amount of rain. However, to analyse the data, you treat latitude as the independent variable and the amount of rain as the dependent variable.

Often, a **scatter plot** can help you see if there is a relationship between two variables. On such graphs, the horizontal axis usually represents the independent variable, while the vertical axis represents the dependent variable. A measurement of the independent variable and the corresponding measurement of the dependent variable make up an ordered pair, (x, y), which appears as a point on the scatter plot.

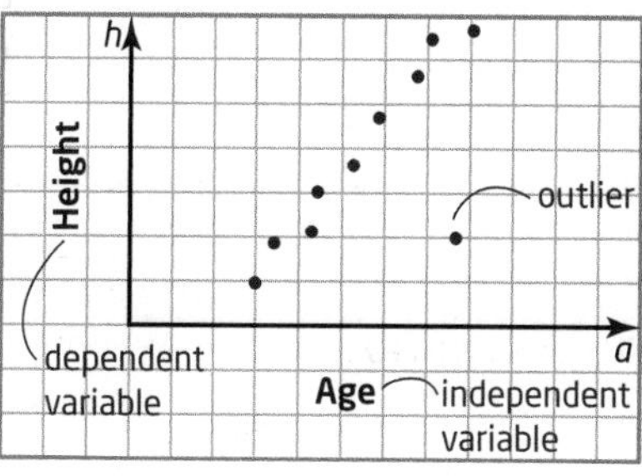

An **outlier** is a point separated from the main body of data on a graph. Sometimes, an outlier results from a measurement error or from some factor that affects only a few of the observed values for a variable. If you can show that an outlier is inaccurate or unrepresentative, you can leave it out of your calculations. Otherwise, you should include the outlier in the data set.

outlier

- measurement that differs significantly from the rest of the data

Example 2 Draw a Scatter Plot

A skateboarder starts from various points along a steep ramp and practises coasting to the bottom. This table lists the skateboarder's initial height above the bottom of the ramp and his speed at the bottom of the ramp.

Initial Height (m)	2.0	2.7	3.4	3.8	4.0	4.5	4.7	5.0
Speed (m/s)	4.4	5.2	5.8	6.1	4.5	6.5	6.6	6.9

a) Identify the independent variable and the dependent variable. Explain your reasoning.

b) Make a scatter plot of the data.

c) Describe the relationship between the variables.

d) Identify any outliers. What might cause an outlier in the data?

Solution

a) The skateboarder's speed at the bottom of the ramp depends on how high up the ramp he starts. So, the independent variable is the initial height, and the dependent variable is the skateboarder's speed at the bottom of the ramp.

b) Method 1: Use Pencil and Paper

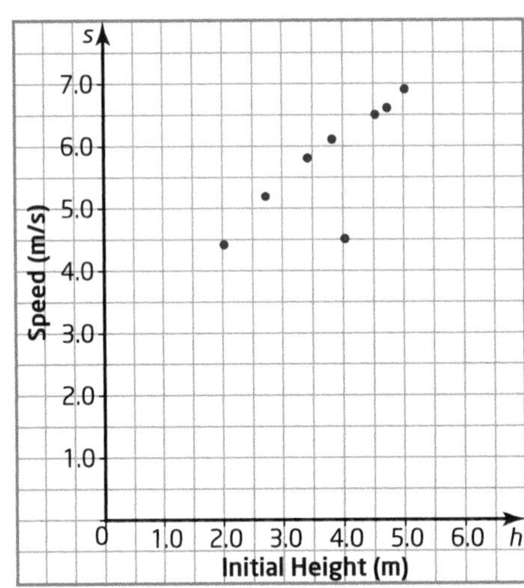

Method 2: Use *Fathom*™

Click on the case table icon and drag it onto the desktop.

Click on <**new**> in the first column, and enter "InitialHeight." Click on <**new**> in the second column, and enter "Speed."

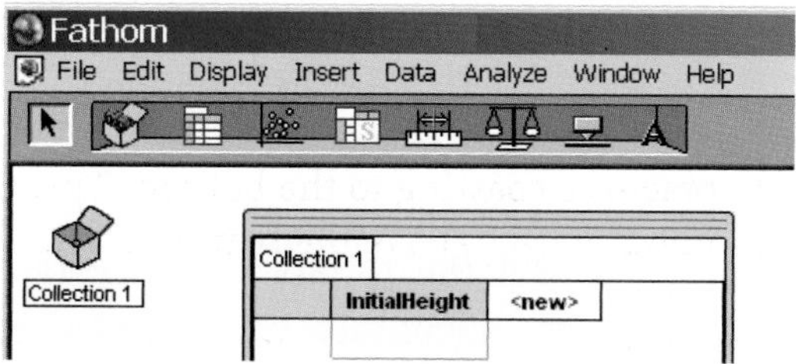

Enter the data in the case table.

Click on the graph icon and drag it onto the desktop.

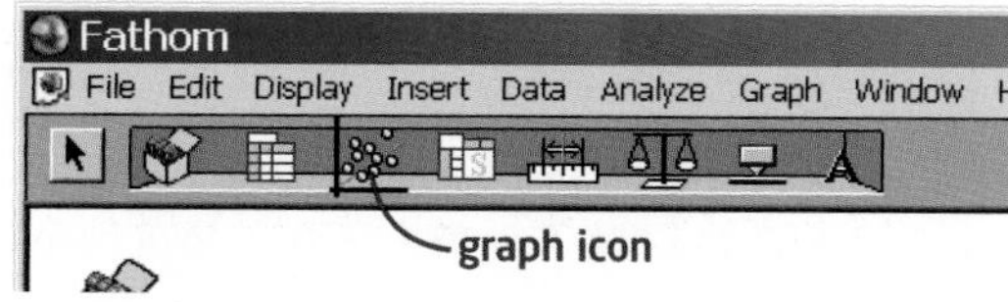

Drag the "InitialHeight" heading to the horizontal axis.

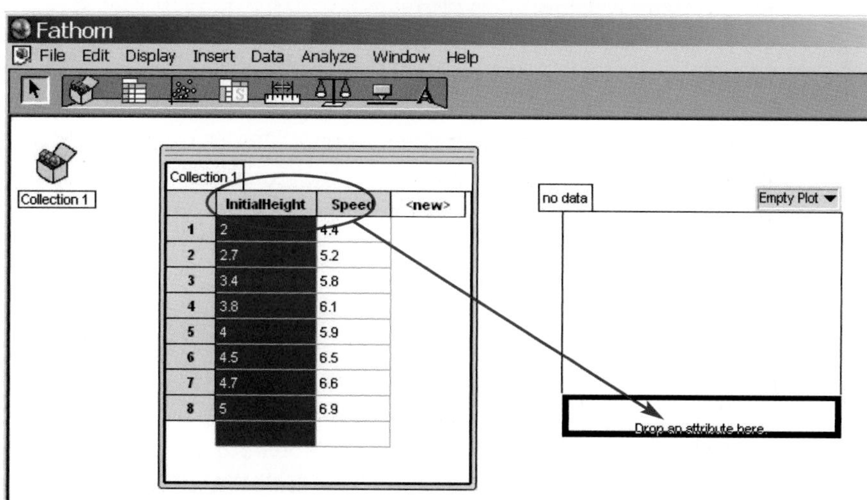

Technology Tip

You can use **Ctrl-Z** to undo an action. This shortcut works in many programs.

Drag the "Speed" heading to the vertical axis. *Fathom*™ then generates the scatter plot automatically.

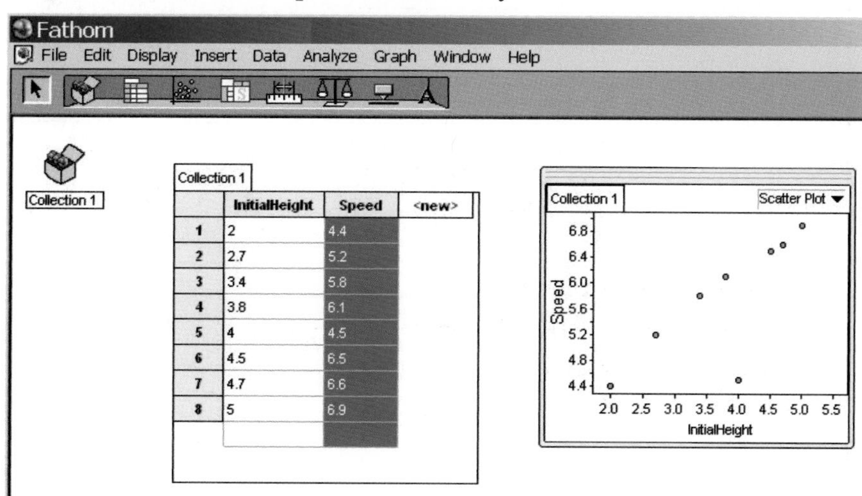

Technology Tip

You can delete the legend box from your graph.

In Quattro® Pro, click on the graph, then click **Chart** on the toolbar. Select **Legend**, click on the image of a graph without a legend, and click OK.

In Excel, right-click on the graph, select Chart Options, click the **Legend** tab, and uncheck the **Show Legend** box.

Method 3: Use a Spreadsheet

Enter the data in the first two columns of the spreadsheet. Then, select these data.

In Corel® Quattro® Pro, click **Insert/Chart**. Then, click **Next**. Uncheck the **3D** box. For chart type, click on **Scatter**, and select the **no line** option. Click **Next** again.
Enter the title for your graph and the labels for the axes. Click **Finish**. Then, move the cursor to where you want the graph to appear, and click to place it.

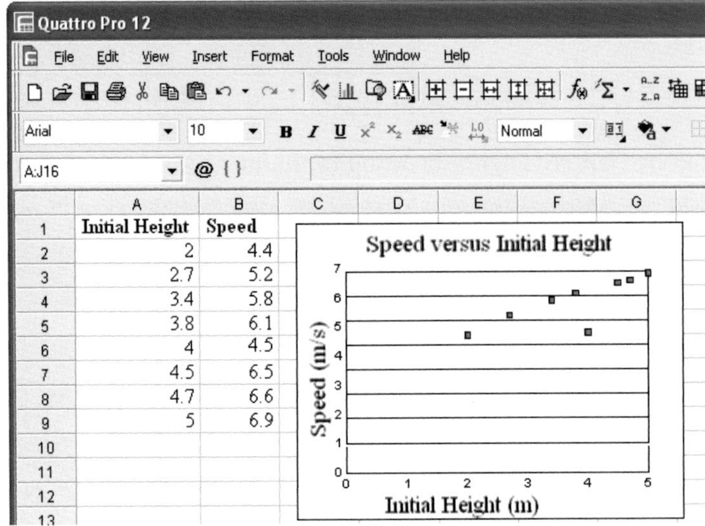

In Microsoft® Excel, click **Insert/Chart**. Under Chart type, click on **XY (Scatter)**, and click the **Next** button twice.
Enter the title for your graph and the labels for the axes.
Click the **Next** button again, and then click **Finish**.

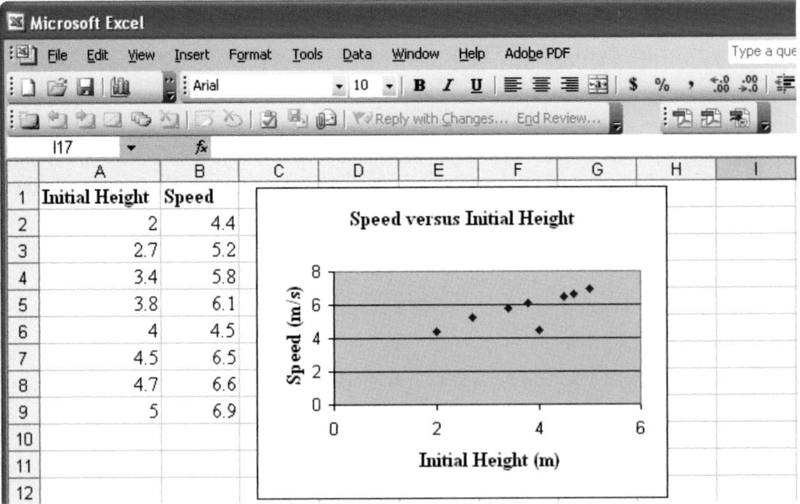

You can make your graph easier to read by enlarging it. Click on the graph, then drag a side or corner.

You can also adjust the scale of the axes.

- In Quattro® Pro, click on the axis to select it, then right-click. Select **Axis Properties**, click on the **Scale** tab, and enter the settings you want.
- In Excel, right-click on the axis and select **Format Axis**. Then, click on the **Scale** tab and enter the settings you want.

c) As the initial height increases, the skateboarder's speed at the bottom of the ramp increases. The pattern of the data points is a curve rather than a straight line.

d) The ordered pair (4.0, 4.5) is an outlier because it is separated from the rest of the data. The speed is less than you would expect from looking at the rest of the data. The skateboarder could have dragged his foot or started at an angle that slowed him down.

Key Concepts

- Scatter plots can help you see relationships between variables.
- Graphing calculators, spreadsheets, and statistics software can plot graphs of data.
- When the value of the independent variable changes, the value of the dependent variable may also change.
- An outlier is separate from the main body of data. You can discard an outlier only if you know that it not representative of the relationship between the variables.

Communicate Your Understanding

C1 Explain how a scatter plot can show that two variables are related.

C2 Which statement is true? Why?

A You should discard all outliers since they do not follow the pattern of the rest of the data.

B You should not discard an outlier unless you can show that it does not accurately represent the relationship between the variables.

Practise

For help with question 1, see Example 1.

1. Identify the independent and the dependent variable in each pair.

a) blood pressure and physical fitness

b) income and level of education

c) load in an airplane and length of runway needed for takeoff

For help with questions 2 and 3, see Example 2.

2. This scatter plot compares the body lengths and wingspans of 11 birds of prey.

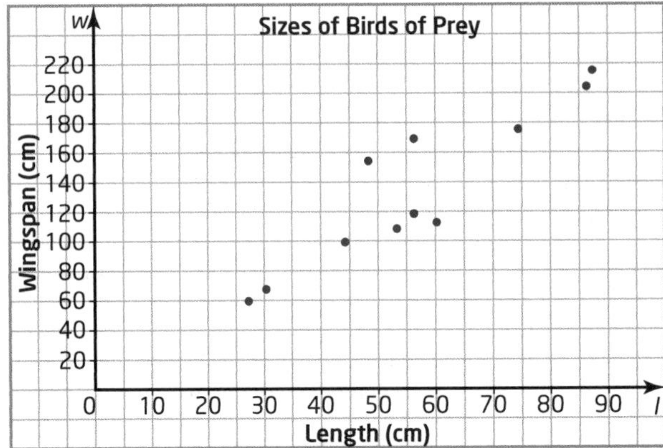

a) How would you change the graph to show wingspan as the independent variable?

b) Describe the relationship between length and wingspan of the birds of prey.

3. This table shows the numbers of days absent from science class and the report card marks for 15 students.

a) Identify the independent variable and the dependent variable. Explain your reasoning.

b) Make a scatter plot of the data.

c) Describe the relationship between a student's marks and attendance.

d) Are there any outliers? If so, explain how they differ from the rest of the data.

Number of Days Absent	Mark (%)
2	81
0	73
12	50
7	63
1	77
22	38
10	44
3	95
3	56
4	71
8	67
0	78
9	61
15	40

Connect and Apply

In these questions, you can draw the scatter plots by hand or produce them with a graphing calculator, Fathom™, *or a spreadsheet.*

4. This table lists the data from an experiment to measure how high a ball bounces after being dropped from six different heights.

Initial Height (m)	Bounce Height (m)
1.00	0.62
1.50	0.91
2.00	1.18
2.50	1.51
3.00	1.80
3.50	2.08

a) Identify the independent variable and the dependent variable. Explain your reasoning.

b) Make a scatter plot of the data.

c) Describe the relationship between the initial height of the ball and its bounce height.

d) If the data included the ordered pair (4.00, 1.62), would you consider it to be an outlier? Would you discard this ordered pair from the data set? Explain your reasoning.

5. This table shows the distance it took a car to stop when travelling at various speeds.

Speed (km/h)	40	50	60	70	80	90	100	120	140	160
Stopping Distance (m)	12	14	21	35	41	51	62	84	122	159

a) Make a scatter plot of these data.

b) Describe the relationship between the speed of a car and its stopping distance.

c) An additional measurement produces the ordered pair (85, 46). Explain the meaning of this pair. Is it an outlier? Explain why or why not.

Literacy Connections

Shoulder width is the distance from the outside of one shoulder to the outside of the other.

6. a) Make a hypothesis about the relationship between a person's height and shoulder width.

b) Design and carry out an experiment to investigate the relationship. What conclusions can you make from the data you collected?

c) Compare your hypothesis with the results of your experiment.

d) How could you improve your experiment?

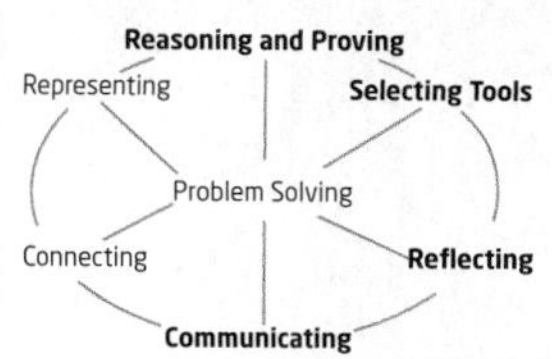

7. **Chapter Problem** In Section 2.1, question 8, you made a hypothesis about a physical characteristic that could help an athlete do well in the high jump.

a) Outline an experiment to examine the relationship between this physical characteristic and the height a person can jump. Describe how you could collect the data.

b) Identify the independent and the dependent variable in your experiment.

c) Describe how you could use a scatter plot to analyse the data. What pattern would you see in the scatter plot if your hypothesis were true?

8. This table shows the fat and energy content in typical servings of fast food.

Item	Serving Size (g)	Fat (g)	Energy (kJ)
Harvey's Original Hamburger	157	20	410
Harvey's Veggie Burger	142	9	317
Mr. Submarine Small Assorted Sub	179	6	280
Mr. Submarine Small Vegetarian Sub	117	3	180
Pizza Pizza Pepperoni Slice (walk-in)	277	19	630
Pizza Pizza Vegetarian Slice (walk-in)	326	14	580
KFC Chicken Breast	161	19	380
KFC Popcorn Chicken	114	21	380
Swiss Chalet Quarter Chicken Breast	159	12	300
Swiss Chalet Garden Salad (no dressing)	162	0	30
Swiss Chalet Caesar Salad	170	32	360

a) Calculate the amount of fat, in milligrams, per gram of each item. Round to the nearest milligram. Then, calculate the energy content per gram of each item. List the results of your calculations in a table.

b) Make a scatter plot of the two sets of data you calculated in part a). Would you put the fat per gram or the energy per gram on the horizontal axis? Why?

c) Identify and explain any outliers. Should they be removed from the data set? Explain.

d) Describe what you can learn from the scatter plot.

Extend

9. The costume designers for a science-fiction movie decide to make the Martians' heights about 6 times their neck circumferences. North Americans' heights are about 4.5 times their neck circumferences. Draw a graph of both relationships on the same grid.

10. This table lists the number of times at bat and the numbers of doubles, home runs, and strikeouts for starting first basemen in American League baseball during the 2004 season.

Player	At Bats	Doubles	Home Runs	Strikeouts
B. Broussard	418	28	17	95
C. Delgado	458	26	32	115
D. Erstad	495	29	7	74
J. Giambi	264	9	12	62
K. Harvey	456	20	13	89
S. Hatteberg	550	30	15	48
P. Konerko	563	22	41	107
T. Martinez	458	20	23	72
D. Mientkiewicz	391	24	6	56
J. Morneau	280	17	19	54
J. Olerud	425	20	9	61
R. Palmero	550	29	23	61
C. Pena	481	22	27	146
M. Sweeney	411	23	22	44
M. Teixeira	545	34	38	117

a) Make a scatter plot of doubles per at bat versus home runs per at bat.

b) Make a scatter plot of doubles per at bat versus strikeouts per at bat.

c) Make a scatter plot of home runs per at bat versus strikeouts per at bat.

d) Do any of the scatter plots show a relationship between the variables?

11. Math Contest Each of the letters in the expression $\frac{a}{b} + \frac{c}{d} + \frac{e}{f}$ represents a different integer from 1 to 6 inclusive. Find the smallest possible value for $\frac{a}{b} + \frac{c}{d} + \frac{e}{f}$.

Did You Know?

The earliest known baseball game in Canada took place in Beachville, Ontario on June 14, 1838.

2.4 Trends, Interpolation, and Extrapolation

Have you ever heard people say that the price of a comic book was only 10¢ when they were young? Or that their allowance was $2 a week? Over the years, the prices of most items have increased. You can analyse these trends and use them to make predictions.

Investigate

Tools

- TI-83 Plus or TI-84 graphing calculator
- grid paper

Technology Tip

Enter negative values with the (−) key rather than the − key.

How can you use trends to make predictions?

For a science project, Audrey recorded the minimum temperatures in her backyard for the first 10 days in March.

Day	1	2	3	4	5	6	7	8	9	10
Minimum Temperature (°C)	−9	−6	−3	−5	−4	−1	0	−1	2	3

Method 1: Use a Graphing Calculator

1. First, clear the calculator's lists:
   - Press 2nd [MEM] to display the **MEMORY** menu.
   - Move the cursor down to **4:ClrAllLists**, and press ENTER twice.

2. To start entering the data, press STAT, and select **1:Edit**.

3. Enter the days into list **L1**, pressing ENTER after each entry. Then, enter the minimum temperatures into list **L2**.

L1 | L2 | L3 1
1 | −9 | ------
2 | −6 |
3 | −3 |
4 | −5 |
5 | −4 |
6 | −1 |
7 | 0 |
L1(1)=1

4. Set the calculator to display a scatter plot:
   - Press 2nd [STATPLOT] to display the **STAT PLOTS** menu.
   - Select **1:Plot1** to display the settings for Plot1.
   - Select **ON** if it is not already highlighted.
   - Scroll down to **Type** and select the scatter plot symbol.
   - **Xlist** should be set to **L1**. If a different list is shown, scroll down to **Xlist**: and enter **L1**. Similarly, **Ylist** should be set to **L2**.
   - Then, press ZOOM and select **9:ZoomStat**.

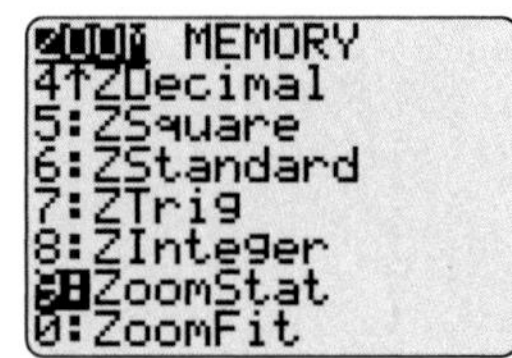

5. What does the horizontal axis of the scatter plot graph represent? What does the vertical axis represent?

6. Copy the scatter plot onto a sheet of graph paper. Label your graph completely.

7. Describe any trend you see in the temperatures on your graph.

8. **Reflect** Can you use a trend in the data to predict the minimum temperatures on March 11 and 12? Explain. Describe how you could estimate what the minimum temperature was on February 26.

Method 2: Use *Fathom*™

1. Click on the case table icon and drag it onto the desktop.

2. Click on <**new**> at the top of the first column. Enter the heading "Day," then press ENTER. Enter the heading "MinTemp" in the second column. Then, enter the data in the appropriate cells.

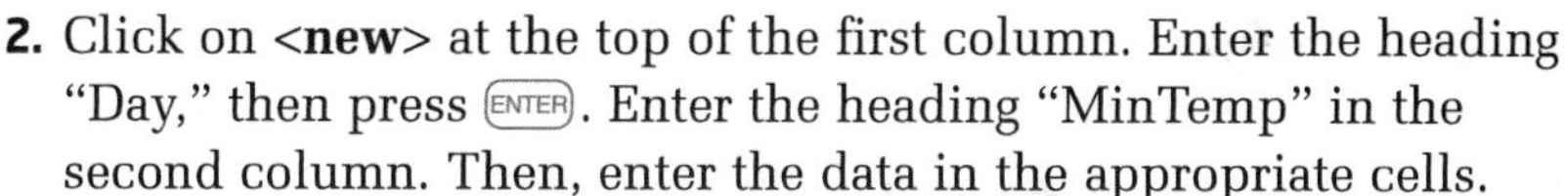

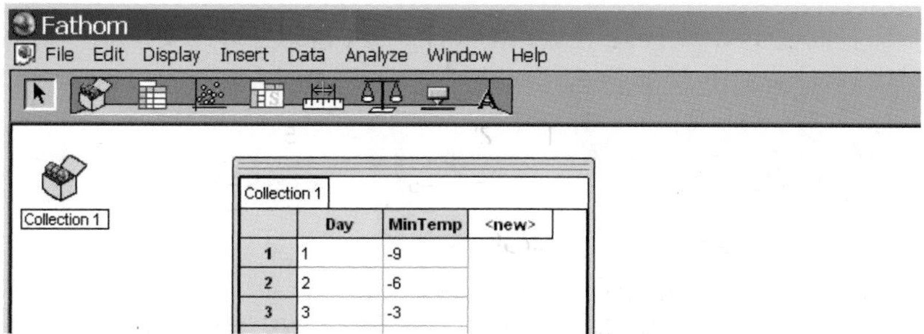

3. Click on the graph icon and drag it onto the desktop.
Drag the "Day" heading to the horizontal axis.
Then, drag the "MinTemp" heading to the vertical axis.
You will see a scatter plot in the graph window.

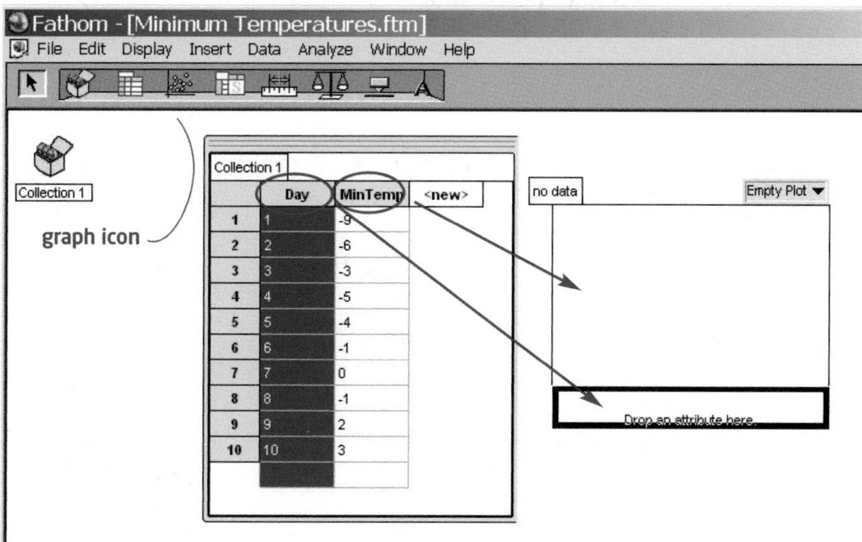

4. What does the horizontal axis of the scatter plot represent? What does the vertical axis represent?

5. Print the scatter plot. Then, add a title and proper labels to the axes on the printout.

6. Describe any trend you see in the temperatures on your graph.

7. **Reflect** Can you use a trend in the data to predict the minimum temperatures on March 11 and 12? Explain. Describe how you could estimate what the minimum temperature was on February 26.

Graphs can help you recognize trends in a set of data. If you find a trend, you can use it to predict values of the variables.

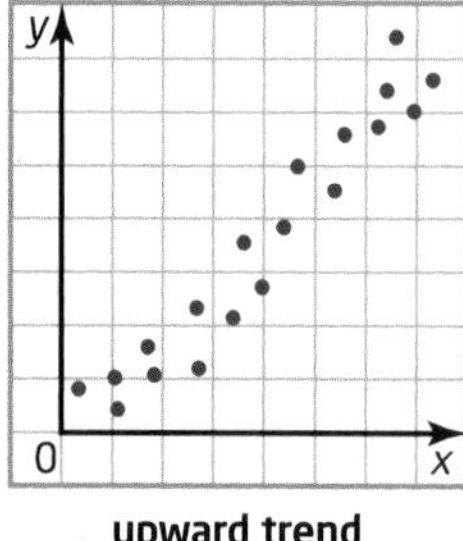

upward trend

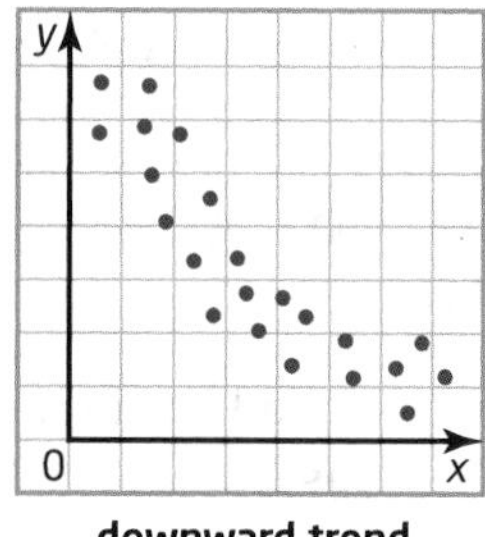

downward trend

Literacy Connections

A fiscal year is a 12-month period used for accounting. The federal government and many businesses have a fiscal year that ends on March 31.

Did You Know?

Severe acute respiratory syndrome (SARS) is a serious illness caused by a virus. An outbreak of SARS spread from China to North America, South America, and Europe in the spring of 2003. However, this outbreak was contained, and only a few isolated cases have appeared since.

Example Use a Graph to Make Predictions

This table shows the number of paid admissions to movies in Canada for 12-month periods (fiscal years) ending on March 31.

Fiscal Year	1994	1995	1996	1997	1998	1999	2000	2001	2002	2003
Attendance (millions)	83.8	87.3	91.3	99.1	111.6	119.3	119.3	no data	125.4	119.6

a) Graph the data.

b) Describe any trends in movie attendance from 1994 to 2004.

c) Statistics Canada did not survey movie attendance for the period from April 2001 to March 2002. Estimate the movie attendance during this period.

d) Predict the number of paid admissions to movies in Canada for the 12-month period ending in March 2006.

e) The SARS outbreak in Canada occurred in the spring and summer of 2003. Would you change your prediction for 2005–2006 based on this additional information?

Solution

a) The movie admissions are given for 1-year intervals. A bar graph is a good way to display data for intervals.

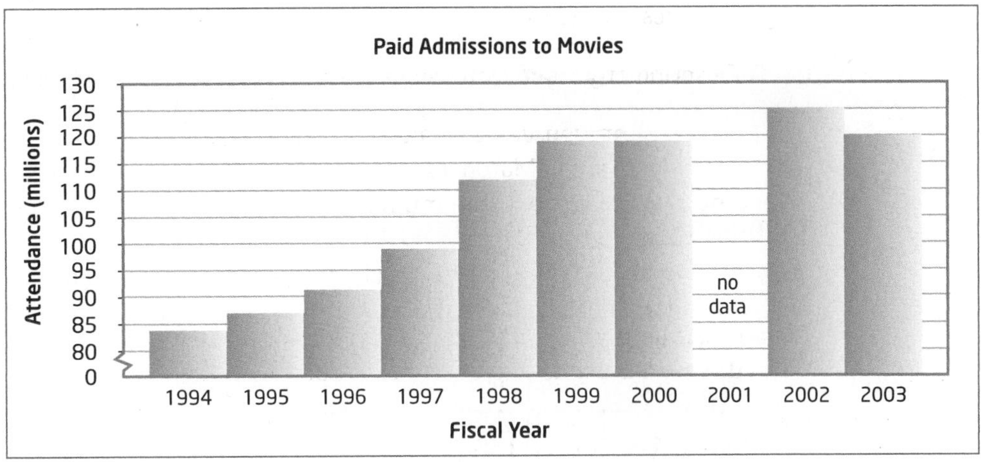

Adapted from Statistics Canada, "Movie theatres and drive-ins: data tables," Catalogue 87F0009XIE, 2003/2004, 2002/2003, 2000/2001, and from Statistics Canada, Motion Picture Theatres Survey, various years.

b) The attendance at movies increased by almost half from 1994 to 2000, but after 2000 there was little increase overall.

c) You can **interpolate** an estimate of attendance at movies in the 2001–2002 period. A reasonable estimate is the mean of the numbers for 2000–2001 and 2002–2003, or about 122 million.

d) You can **extrapolate** the trend in the data. Since there was only a small overall increase since 2000, a reasonable estimate for the 2005–2006 period is 120 million paid admissions.

interpolate

- estimate a value between two measurements in a set of data

extrapolate

- estimate a value beyond the range of a set of data

e) During the SARS outbreak, many people avoided crowds, especially in Toronto and Vancouver. The SARS outbreak likely caused a drop in movie attendance during the 2003–2004 period. So, the number of paid admissions during this period may not reflect the overall trend in movie attendance. If you leave out this outlier, then a reasonable prediction is that movie attendance will increase at the same rate as it did from 2000 to 2003. This trend gives an estimate of about 131 million paid admissions in the 2005–2006 period.

Key Concepts

- A pattern in the graph of a set of data often indicates a trend.
- You can interpolate values between those in a set of data.
- You can extrapolate trends to predict values outside the range of a set of data.

Communicate Your Understanding

C1 Amy collected the following data on the sales of cell phones at her store. What type of graph should she use to display these data? Explain.

Year	2000	2001	2002	2003	2004	2005
Number Sold	2451	3010	3559	4925	4388	6052

C2 The national fertility rate is the mean number of children born of women between the ages of 15 and 49 in Canada. This graph shows Canadian fertility rates since 1950.

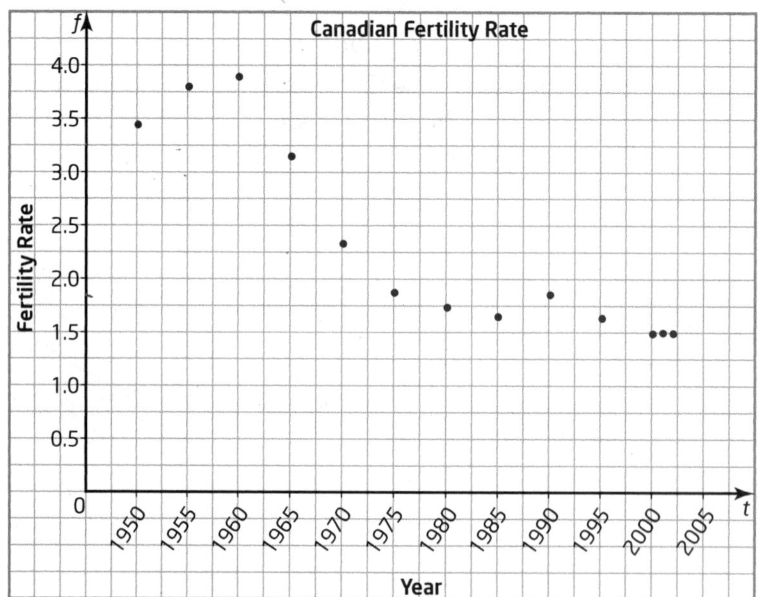

Adapted from Statistics Canada, Vitial Statistics, Birth Database, various years

A newspaper reporter predicted, "If the trend continues, there will be no children born in 2030."

a) Has the reporter interpreted the graph correctly? Explain.

b) What fertility rate would you predict for 2030? Explain how you made your estimate.

Did You Know?

National surveys by Statistics Canada require processing huge amounts of data. Often, the results of these surveys are not available until several years after the data were collected.

Practise

For help with questions 1 and 2, see the Example.

1. This table shows the mean monthly rent for a two-bedroom apartment in Guelph, Ontario, from 1996 to 2003.

Year	1996	1997	1998	1999	2000	2001	2002	2003
Rent ($)	658	678	686	702	736	764	801	823

Adapted from CMHC Rental Market Reports, 1996–2003

a) Make a bar graph of the data.

b) Describe the trend in rents.

c) Predict the mean rent for a two-bedroom apartment in Guelph in 2010.

2. This table lists the estimated population of the world over the last 1000 years.

Year	1000	1250	1500	1750	1800	1850	1900	1950	2000
Population (millions)	310	400	500	790	980	1260	1650	2520	6060

a) Make a scatter plot of the data.

b) Describe the trend in world population growth.

c) The United Nations predicts that the world population will stabilize at about 10 billion people around the year 2200. Does this prediction follow the trend shown in your graph? Explain.

Connect and Apply

3. This table shows the height of a bean plant during the first 2 weeks after it germinated.

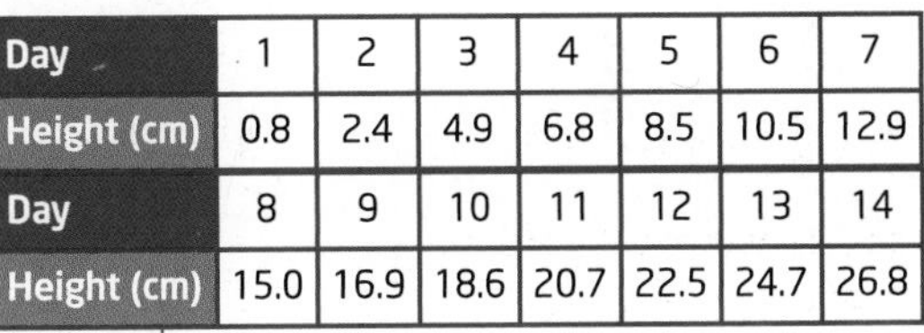

Day	1	2	3	4	5	6	7
Height (cm)	0.8	2.4	4.9	6.8	8.5	10.5	12.9
Day	8	9	10	11	12	13	14
Height (cm)	15.0	16.9	18.6	20.7	22.5	24.7	26.8

a) Make a scatter plot of the data.

b) Describe the growth trend of the bean plant during the 2 weeks.

c) Predict what will happen to the trend in future weeks. Explain your reasoning.

4. This table shows the approximate mean retail price for 4 L of milk in southern Ontario since 1980.

Year	1980	1985	1990	1995	2000	2005
Price ($)	1.87	2.85	3.30	3.56	3.82	4.70

a) Graph the data.

b) Describe the trend in milk prices.

c) Estimate the cost of 4 L of milk in 1998.

d) Predict when the price of 4 L of milk will reach $6.00. What assumption did you make for this prediction?

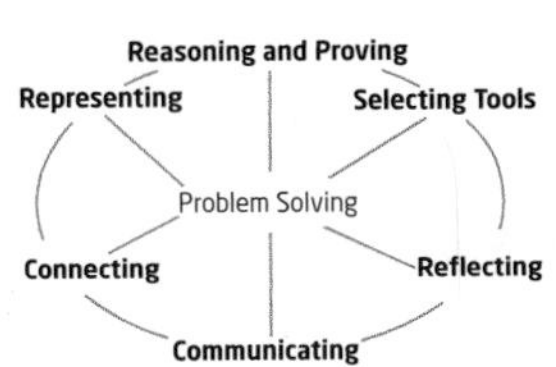

5. This table summarizes the results of a survey of charitable donations by Canadians.

Age Group	Donor Rate (%)	Mean Amount per Donor ($)
15–19	58	114
20–24	70	122
25–34	77	229
35–44	85	242
45–54	83	338
55–64	81	316
65–74	80	294
75+	72	330

a) Make a bar graph of the data for the donor rates of the age groups. Describe the trend in this graph.

b) Make a bar graph of the data for mean donations by the age groups. Describe the trend in this graph.

c) Compare the trends in the two graphs.

6. This table summarizes data about Internet use in Canada.

Households Using the Internet (%)			
Year	**Canada**	**Ontario**	**Saskatchewan**
1998	22.6	25.5	18.2
1999	28.7	32.0	23.6
2000	40.1	44.1	32.5
2001	48.7	53.4	40.2
2002	51.4	57.7	46.0
2003	54.5	59.7	50.6

Adapted from Statistics Canada CANSIM Database, Table 358-0002, http://estat.statcan.ca/cgi-win/CNSMCGI.EXE?CANSIMFILE=EStat\English\CII_1_E.htm, November 2005

a) Use a graph to compare the trend in Internet use in Canada with the trends in Ontario and Saskatchewan.

b) Statistics Canada stopped this survey of Internet use after 2003. Estimate the percent of Canadian households that used the Internet in 2005. List any assumptions that you make.

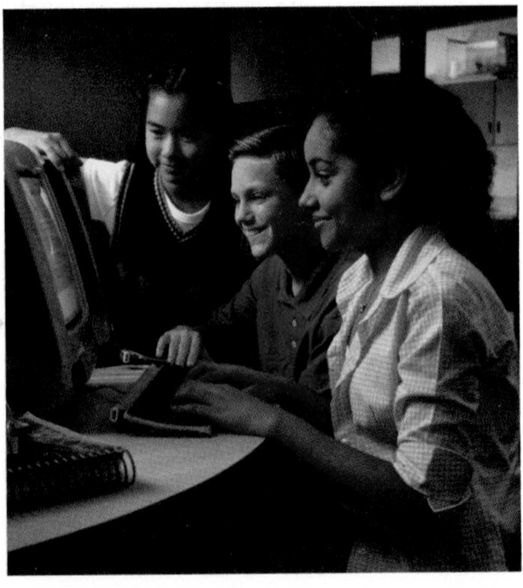

7. The table shows the number of music singles, cassettes, and CDs sold in Canada between 1998 and 2004.

Sales of Recorded Music in Canada (millions of units)			
Year	Singles	Cassettes	CDs
1998	0.9	8.4	57.7
1999	0.8	5.7	58.4
2000	0.5	2.8	57.3
2001	0.5	1.4	54.0
2002	0.6	1.0	50.9
2003	0.8	0.3	49.0
2004	0.5	< 0.1	51.3

a) Use graphs to help you describe the trends in the sales of each type of recording.

b) Predict the sales of each type of recording in 2005.

c) Use data from the Internet to check if your predictions were correct. Did any of the trends change in 2005?

Go to www.mcgrawhill.ca/links/principles9 and follow the links to learn more about the sales of recordings in Canada.

Achievement Check

8. This table shows the time it takes a skateboarder to reach the bottom of a ramp when starting from various points along the ramp.

Initial Height (m)	Descent Time (s)
2.0	1.4
2.7	1.9
3.4	2.5
3.8	2.7
4.0	2.8
4.5	2.2
4.7	3.0
5.0	3.1

a) Identify the independent variable and the dependent variable. Explain your reasoning.

b) Make a scatter plot of the data.

c) Describe the relationship between the variables.

d) Identify any outliers. Explain whether you would include any of these outliers in the data set.

e) Estimate the time it would take the skateboarder to reach the bottom of the ramp from a starting height of 3.6 m. Explain how you made your estimate.

Extend

Making Connections

To earn a highschool diploma, you must do 40 h of volunteer community service. See your guidance teacher for details.

9. This table shows some of the results of a survey of volunteer work by Canadians.

	Volunteer Rate		Mean Hours per Volunteer	
Age Group	**Canada (%)**	**Ontario (%)**	**Canada**	**Ontario**
15–24	29	28	130	150
25–34	24	19	131	149
35–44	30	29	153	163
45–54	30	31	158	151
55–64	28	28	181	157
65+	18	17	269	261

a) Compare the relationship between age and volunteerism for Ontario residents with the relationship for all Canadians.

b) Which age group in Ontario has the greatest volunteer rate? Suggest why this age group volunteers more than others.

c) Describe the relationship between age and hours volunteered across Canada. Suggest a reason for this relationship.

WWW Go to www.mcgrawhill.ca/links/principles9 and follow the links to learn more information about *Limits to Growth*.

10. The Club of Rome is a group of scientists, teachers, economists, and others who study world issues. In 1972, this group published a book called *Limits to Growth*. Use the Internet or a library to find one of the predictions made in this book. Describe the prediction. Discuss whether it is correct and how it relates to the topics in this section.

11. Math Contest At noon a group of boys and girl are in the cafeteria. When 15 girls leave, the ratio of boys to girls becomes 2:1. Then, 45 boys leave. There are now 5 girls for each boy. The number of girls in the group at noon was

A 29

B 40

C 43

D 50

12. Math Contest Find the greatest number of Saturdays that can occur in the first 100 days of a year. Justify your answer.

2.5 Linear and Non-Linear Relations

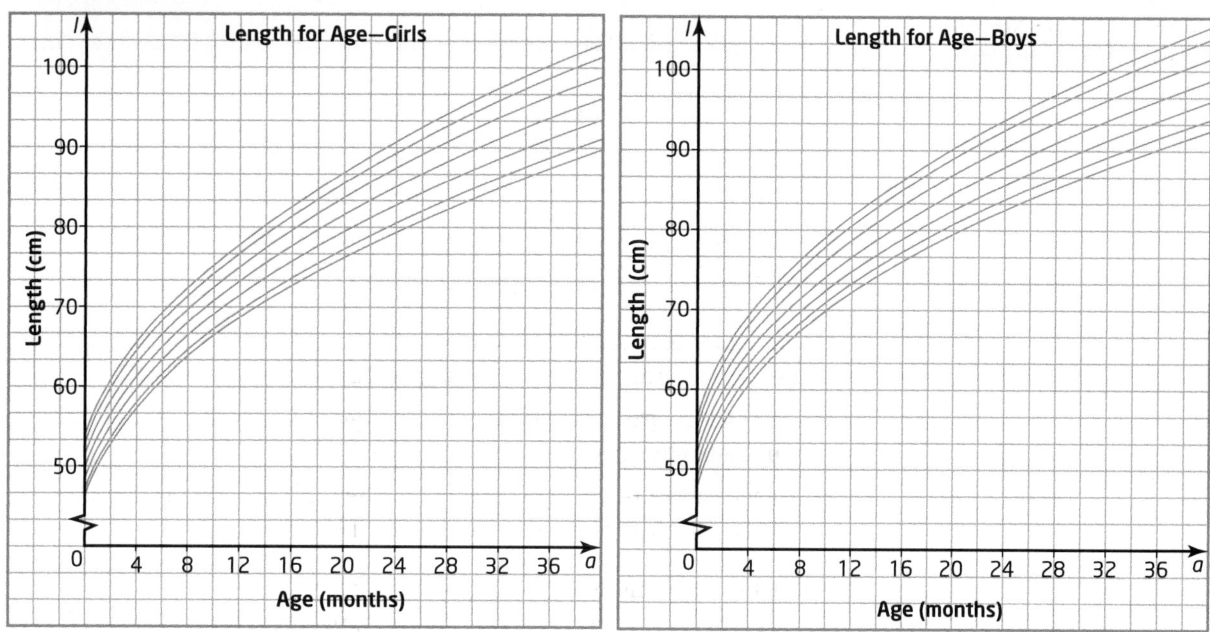

These graphs are called growth charts. Doctors use them to help judge the health of young children. The graphs show the normal range of lengths for boys and girls from birth to age 3.

Investigate

How do linear and non-linear graphs compare?

Use the growth charts to answer the following questions.

1. What is the same about the growth of young girls and the growth of young boys?
2. How does the growth of young girls differ from that of young boys?
3. A graph of a **linear relation** forms a straight line. For what age range does the growth of girls and boys appear to be linear?
4. For what age range does the growth of girls and boys appear to be non-linear?
5. **Reflect** How do changes in non-linear graphs differ from changes in linear graphs?

linear relation

- a relation between two variables that forms a straight line when graphed

Often, you can use a linear relation to model the data on a scatter plot. This linear relation corresponds to a **line of best fit**. Lines of best fit pass through or close to as many points as possible. Any points that are not on the line of best fit should be distributed evenly above and below it. A line of best fit can help you make interpolations and extrapolations.

line of best fit

- a straight line that comes closest to the points on a scatter plot

Many non-linear relations can be modelled with a **curve of best fit**. You can draw curves of best fit using the same method as for a line of best fit. A curve of best fit should pass through or close to as many points as possible, and any points that are not on the curve should be distributed evenly above and below it.

curve of best fit

- a curve that comes closest to the points on a scatter plot of a non-linear relation

Example 1 Use a Line of Best Fit

The gymnophthalmid lizard lives in the Amazon rainforest. Recent research found that this lizard keeps its body temperature close to the temperature of its surroundings. The table lists data from this research.

Surrounding Temperature (°C)	25.0	24.8	27.9	30.3	28.2	24.8	25.6	29.9	25.5	28.4	28.5	28.0	27.9
Lizard's Body Temperature (°C)	26.2	28.2	29.7	30.3	29.8	28.3	27.6	30.8	29.5	30.0	28.8	28.7	29.0

a) Graph the data.

b) How are the two variables related? Is this relationship linear or non-linear? Explain.

c) Draw a line of best fit.

d) Estimate the lizard's body temperature if the surrounding temperature is 26°C.

e) Estimate the lizard's temperature if the surrounding temperature is 35°C.

Solution

a) Plot the data using a scatter plot.

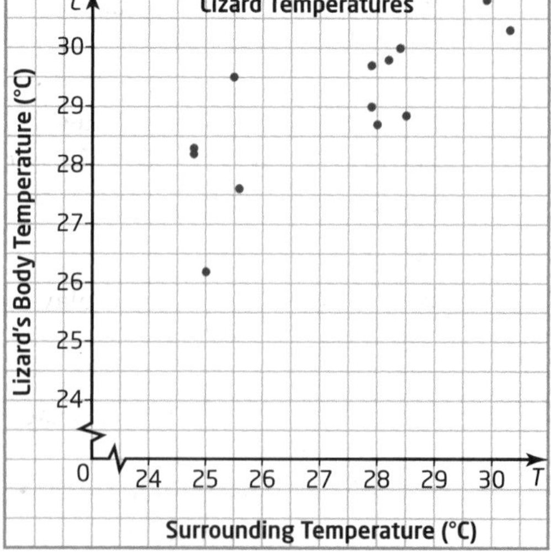

b) The data points show a clear trend. As the surrounding temperature increases, so does the lizard's body temperature. You can classify the relationship as linear since the data points lie close to a straight line. Although the relationship is not perfectly linear, a linear relation is a good model for the data.

c) Method 1: Use Pencil and Paper

Draw a straight line as close as possible to the points on the graph.

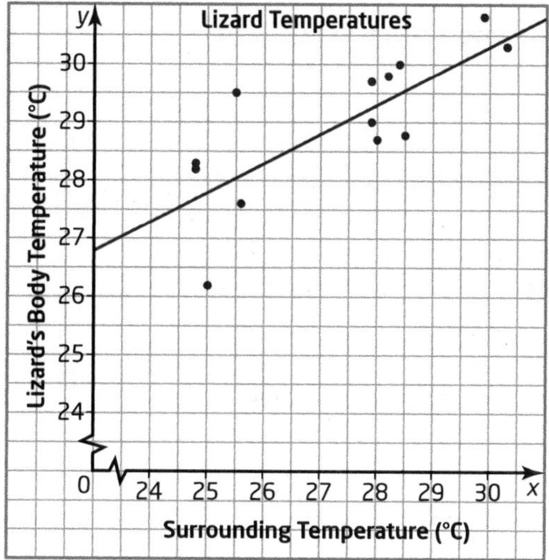

Method 2: Use a Graphing Calculator

Clear all the calculator's lists.
Press STAT and select **1:Edit**.
Enter the surrounding temperatures in list **L1** and the lizard's body temperatures in list **L2**.

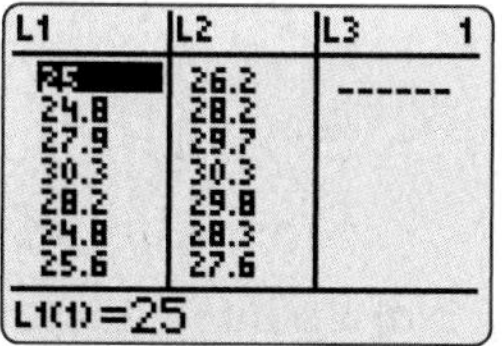

Display the scatter plot:

- Press 2nd [STAT PLOT] to display the **STAT PLOTS** menu.
- Select **1:Plot1** to display the settings for Plot1.
- Select **On** and the scatter plot symbol if they are not already highlighted.
- Make sure that **Xlist** is set to **L1** and **Ylist** is set to **L2**.
- Press ZOOM and select **9:ZoomStat**.

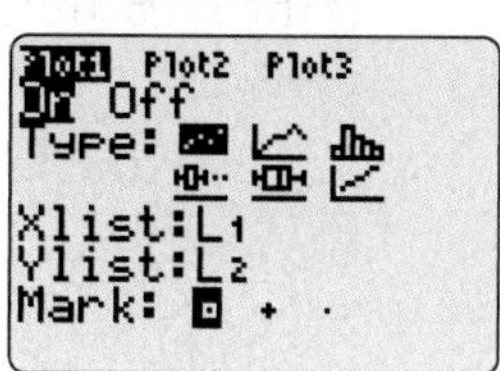

Add the line of best fit:

- Press STAT, cursor over to display the **CALC** menu, and select **4:LinReg(ax + b)**.
- Press VARS, and cursor over to display the **Y-VARS** menu.
- Select **1:FUNCTION**; then, select **1:Y1**.
- Press ENTER to get to the LinReg screen, and press GRAPH.

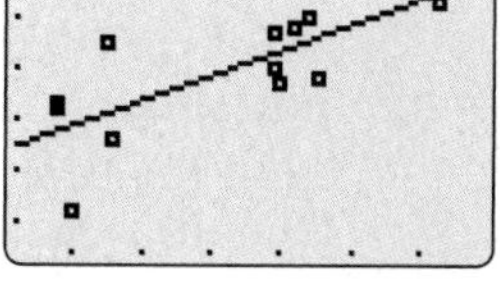

Method 3: Use *Fathom*™

Drag the case table icon onto the desktop.
Enter the headings "SurroundTemp" and "LizardTemp" at the top of the first two columns.
Enter the data into the case table.

Drag the graph icon onto the desktop.
Drag the "SurroundTemp" heading to the horizontal axis and the "LizardTemp" heading to the vertical axis.
To add a line of best fit, click on **Graph**, and choose **Least Squares Line**.

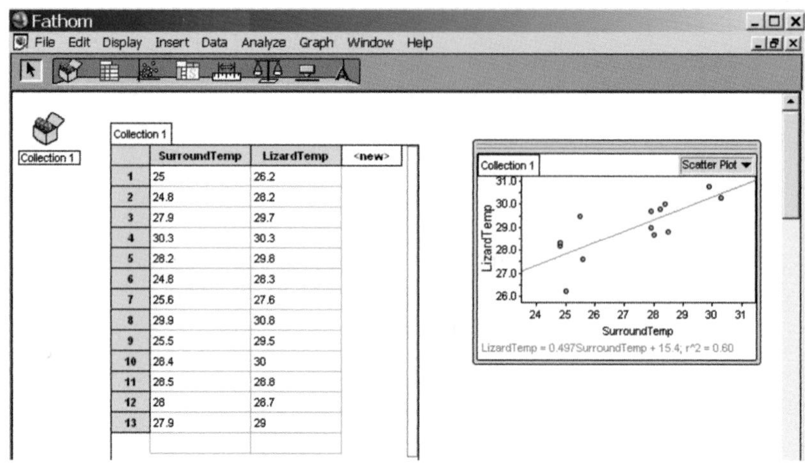

Method 4: Use a Spreadsheet

Enter the data in the first two columns of a spreadsheet. Then, select these data.

In Corel® Quattro® Pro, click **Insert/Chart**. Click **Next**.
Uncheck the **3D** box. For chart type, click on **Scatter**, and select the **no line** option. Click **Next** again.
Enter the title for your graph and the labels for the axes.
Click **Finish**.
Then, move the cursor to where you want the graph to appear and click to place it.
To add a line of best fit, select the scatter plot. Right-click on the data points, and select **Series Properties**. Then, click on the **Trendline** tab and select **Linear fit**.

In Microsoft® Excel, click **Insert/Chart**.
Under Chart type, click on **XY (Scatter)**, and click the **Next** button twice.
Enter the title for your graph and the labels for the axes.
Click the **Next** button again; then, click **Finish**.
To add a line of best fit, click on **Chart** and select **Add Trendline**.
In the dialogue box for **Type**, choose **Linear**, and click **OK**.

Technology Tip

Ctrl-Z will undo an action in either Corel® Quattro® Pro or Microsoft® Excel. For example, you can use **Ctrl-Z** to restore something you deleted by mistake.

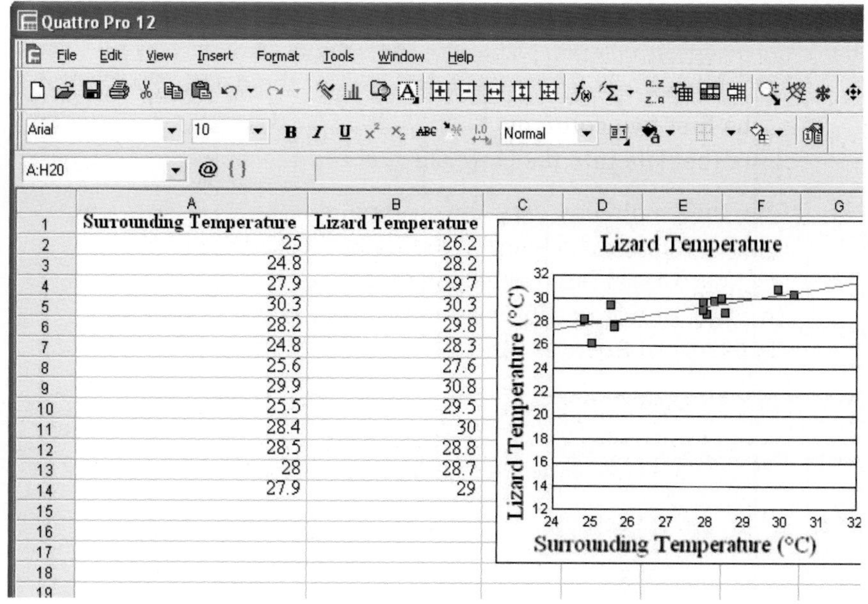

	A	B
1	Surrounding Temperature	Lizard Temperature
2	25	26.2
3	24.8	28.2
4	27.9	29.7
5	30.3	30.3
6	28.2	29.8
7	24.8	28.3
8	25.6	27.6
9	29.9	30.8
10	25.5	29.5
11	28.4	30
12	28.5	28.8
13	28	28.7
14	27.9	29

d) Interpolate using a line of best fit. Read up from 26°C on the horizontal axis to the line of best fit. Then, read across to find that the lizard's body temperature is about 28°C.

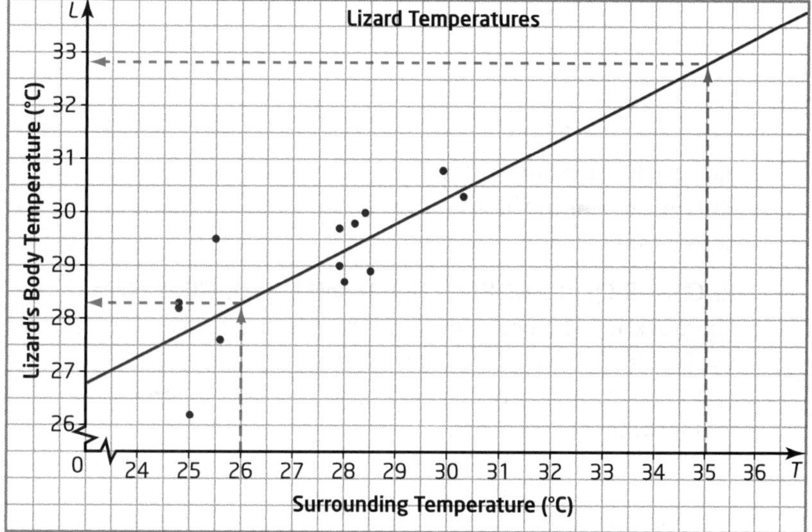

e) Extrapolate using a line of best fit. Extend the line far enough that you can read up to it from 35°C on the horizontal axis. Then, read across to the vertical axis to find the corresponding body temperature of the lizard. The temperature of the lizard will be about 33°C when the surrounding temperature is 35°C. This estimate is reasonable only if the relationship between the two temperatures is still linear at temperatures greater than those in the set of data.

Example 2 Decide Whether a Line of Best Fit Is Appropriate

Why is a line of best fit not a good model for the data in each graph?

a)

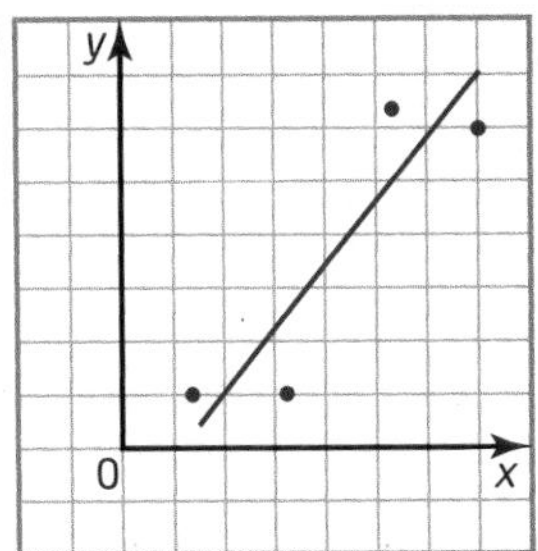

b)

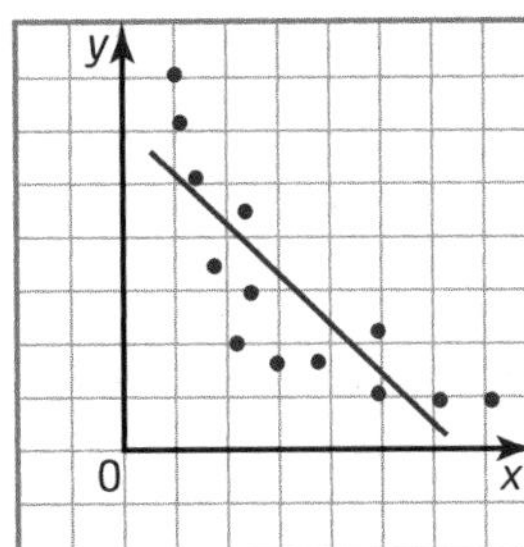

c)

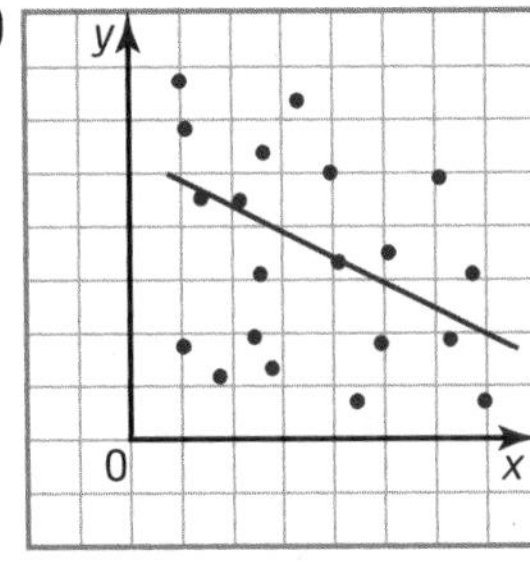

Solution

a) There are not enough data points to determine the relationship between the variables.

b) The data points tend to follow a curve rather than a straight line. The middle points are all below the line and the points near the ends are mostly above the line. The relation is non-linear. A curve of best fit is a better model for these data.

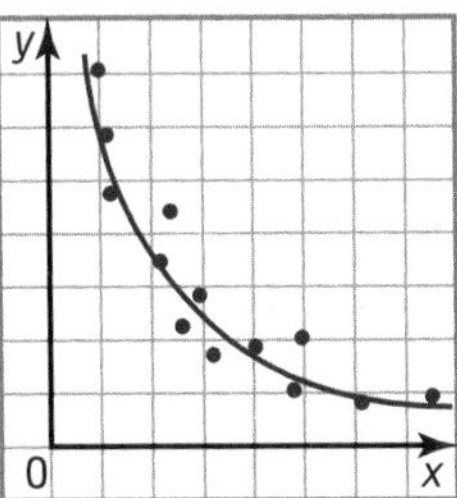

c) The points have no apparent pattern.

Key Concepts

- Data that form a relatively straight line on a scatter plot indicate a linear relationship between the variables.
- A line of best fit can model a linear relationship, but is usually a poor model for a non-linear relationship.
- You can use a line or curve of best fit to interpolate values within a data set.
- You can extrapolate values beyond the range of a set of data by extending a line or curve of best fit.

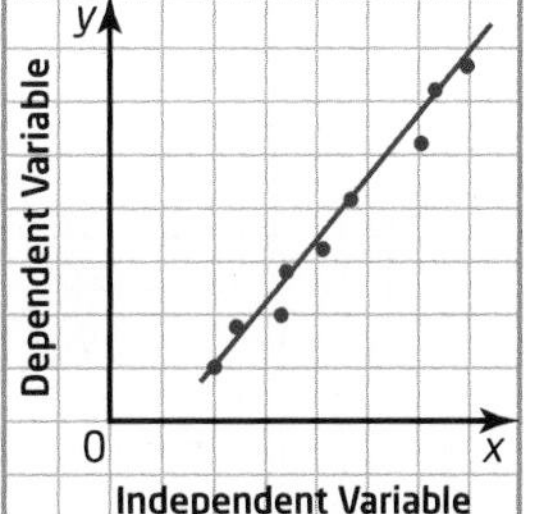

Communicate Your Understanding

C1 Which of these scatter plots shows a linear relationship? Explain.

a)

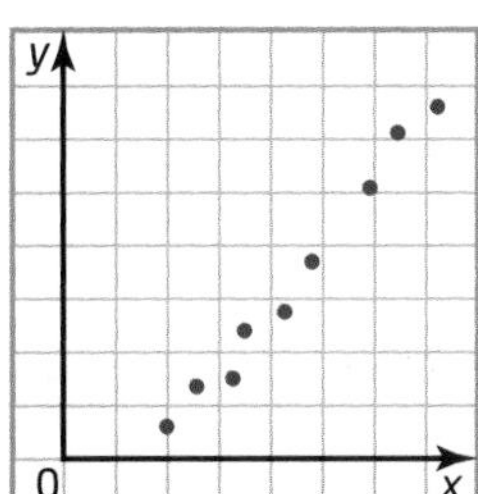

b)

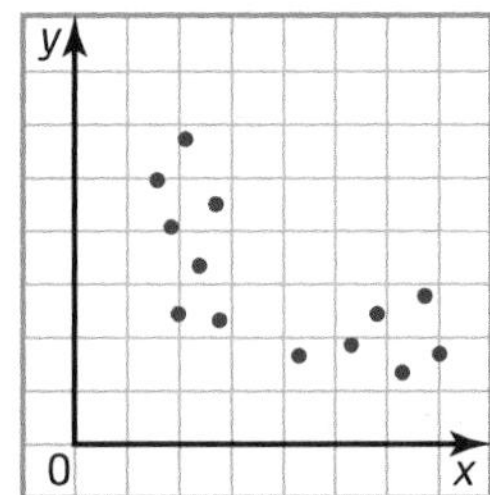

C2 Can you draw a line of best fit that does not pass through any of the data points? Explain your answer. Give an example if possible.

Practise

1. Does each graph show a linear relationship? Explain.

a)

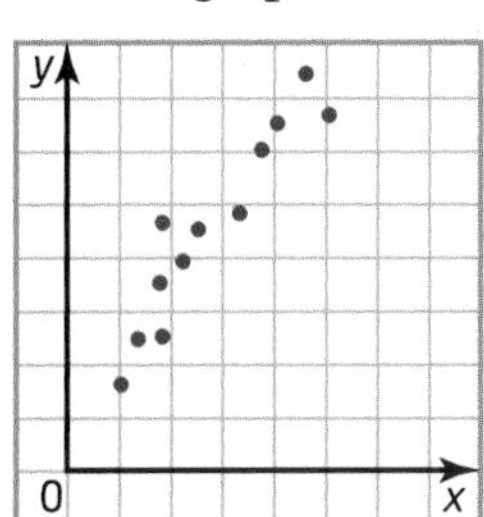

b)

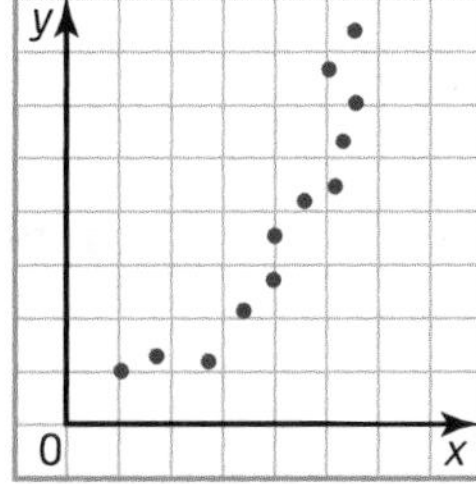

2. Does each set of points have a linear relationship? Justify your answer.

a) (−6, −4), (−5, −2), (−4, 0), (−3, 2), (−2, 4), (−1, 6), (0, 8), (1, 10), (2, 12), (3, 14)

b) (0, 0), (1, 1), (2, 4), (3, 9), (4, 16), (5, 25), (6, 36)

For help with questions 3 and 4, see Example 2.

3. State whether each of these lines of best fit is a good model for the data. Justify your answers.

a)

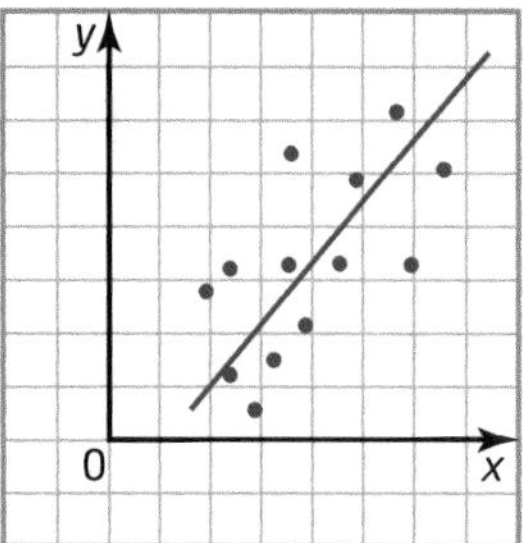

b)

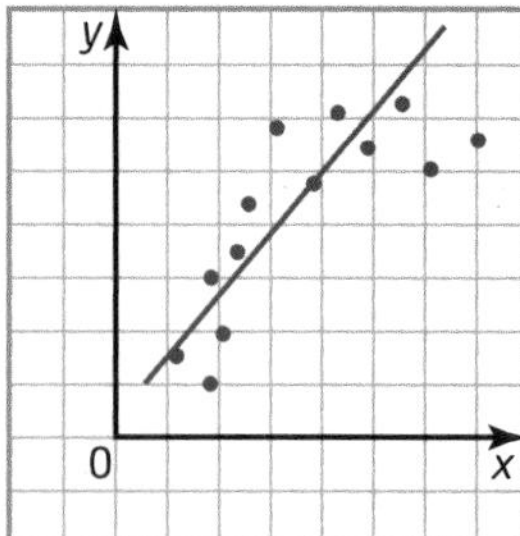

c)

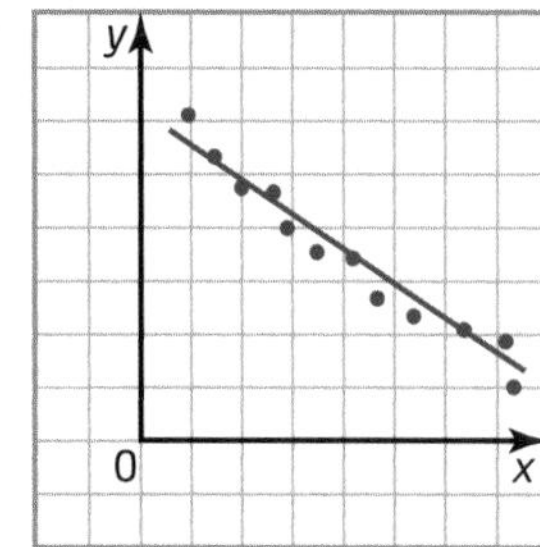

d)

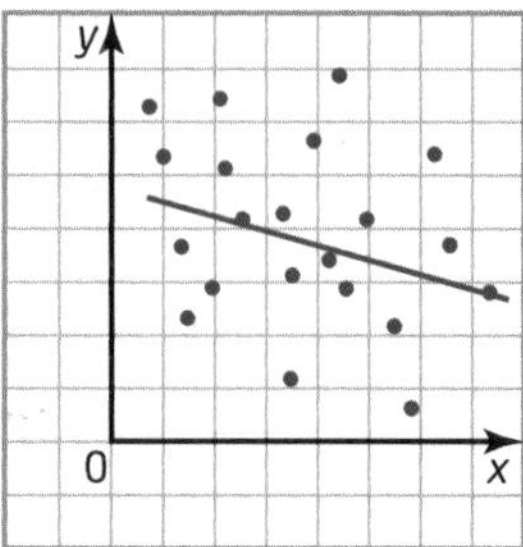

e)

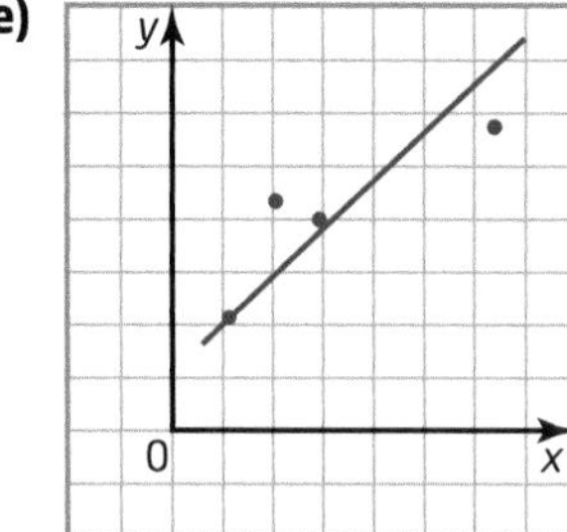

4. Plot each set of points on a grid. If your plot shows a linear relationship, draw a line of best fit. If the relation appears non-linear, sketch a curve of best fit.

a)

x	1	2	7	4	9	3	6	2
y	-2	0	12	5	20	3	11	1

b)

Time (s)	40	32	55	18	66	43	37
Score	7	9.5	6	10	4	6	7.5

c) $(-5, 3)$, $(6, 1)$, $(2, 2)$, $(-3, 0)$, $(-1, 2)$, $(9, 10)$, $(8, 4)$, $(0, 1)$, $(7, 5)$, $(-4, 1)$

Connect and Apply

5. A weather balloon recorded the air temperature at various altitudes.

Altitude (m)	500	800	1000	1500	1700	2100
Temperature (°C)	16.2	14.5	13.1	11.2	9.8	8.1

   a) Make a scatter plot of the data.

   b) Describe the relation and draw a line or curve of best fit.

   c) Use your line or curve of best fit to estimate the temperature at an altitude of 600 m.

   d) Estimate the temperature at 2500 m.

Did You Know?

About 1800 weather balloons are launched every day to measure conditions high in the atmosphere.

6. Farmers have found that the spacing between plants affects the crop yield. This table lists data for canola.

   a) Make a scatter plot of the data.

   b) Describe any trends you see in the scatter plot. What type of relation do these trends indicate?

   c) Is a line of best fit a good model for the data? Explain why or why not.

   d) Suggest two factors that could affect the relation between planting density and crop yields for canola.

Density (plants/m^2)	Plants With Good Yield (%)
20	57.0
40	85.0
60	91.5
80	94.0
100	95.5
120	96.5
140	96.0
160	95.5
180	95.0
200	94.5
300	91.5
400	86.5
500	85.0

7. **a)** This table lists the speed of a skydiver during the first 4 s of free fall. Plot the data on a grid with time from 0 s to 12 s on the horizontal axis and speed from 0 m/s to 100 m/s on the vertical axis.

Time (s)	0	1	2	3	4
Speed (m/s)	0	6	12	18	23

   b) Extrapolate to estimate the skydiver's speed after 12 s of free fall.

   c) This table gives the skydiver's speed for the next 8 s of free fall. Add these data to the graph you made in part a).

Time (s)	5	6	7	8	9	10	11	12
Speed (m/s)	28	33	37	40	42	43	43	43

   d) Describe the trend in the enlarged set of data. What causes this trend?

   e) Explain why extrapolations can be inaccurate.

Did You Know?

Leonardo da Vinci drew designs for a parachute around 1492. However, the first known parachute jump was made by Faust Vrancic in 1617.

8. Conduct an experiment to investigate how a person's heart rate changes immediately after exercise. Work with a partner.

a) ***Objective:*** Describe the purpose of your experiment.

b) ***Hypothesis:*** Make a hypothesis about the trend in a person's heart rate after exercise.

c) ***Procedure:*** One partner runs on the spot for 2 min while the other partner keeps track of the time. Then, the runner counts his or her pulse over 10-s intervals for a total of 80 s. The other partner records the data in a table.

d) ***Observations:*** Graph your measurements. Draw a line or a curve of best fit. Compare your graph with those drawn by your classmates. Do you see any pattern in the way your heart rates slow down?

e) ***Conclusion:*** What inference can you make from the data? Do your observations support your hypothesis?

f) ***Evaluation:*** Did the experiment meet its objective? Could there be any errors in your data? How could you improve the experiment?

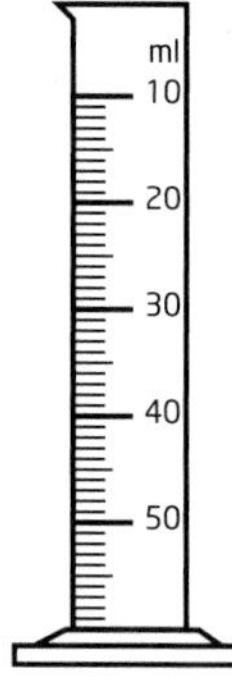

9. Design and carry out an experiment to see if there is a linear relation between the height of water in a graduated cylinder and the number of pennies dropped into the water. Write a report on your experiment. This report should include

a) the objective of the experiment

b) your hypothesis

c) a description of your procedure

d) your observations

e) your conclusions

f) an evaluation of the experiment

Achievement Check

10. This table shows a series of measurements of water temperature at various depths below a research ship.

Depth (m)	100	200	300	400	500	800	1000	1200
Temperature (°C)	19.4	19.0	18.1	17.5	16.0	9.7	6.2	6.0

a) Make a scatter plot of the data.

b) Draw a line or curve of best fit.

c) Describe the relationship between the variables.

d) Estimate the water temperature at a depth of 700 m.

e) Extrapolate to estimate the temperature at a depth of 1600 m.

f) Which of your two estimates is likely to be more accurate? Explain your reasoning.

Extend

11. Consider each set of data. How can you tell whether the relation between the variables in each pair is linear without graphing the data?

a)

t	-2	-1	0	1	2	3	4	5
d	-9	-4	1	6	11	16	21	26

b)

t	-3	-2	-1	0	1	2
h	5	0	-3	-4	-3	0

12. Gayle recorded the distances she drove and the readings of the fuel gauge in her truck.

Distance Travelled (km)	Fuel Gauge Reading (eighths)
0	8 (full)
105	7
205	6
300	5
395	4
460	3
525	2
580	1
625	0

If the truck's fuel efficiency was constant, what can you conclude about the relation between the fuel gauge reading and the amount of fuel left in the tank? Explain your reasoning.

13. Math Contest If n is positive, which of the following expressions always has a value less than 1?

A $\frac{1}{n}$ **B** $\frac{1-n}{n}$

C $\frac{1+n}{n}$ **D** $\frac{n}{n+1}$

14. Math Contest Determine the number of even three-digit numbers that can be made by choosing from the digits 1, 2, 3, 4, 5, and 6 if each number must contain three different digits.

2.6 Distance-Time Graphs

Radar antennas on ships send out pulses of radio waves. By measuring the pulses that reflect back from objects, such as other ships, a radar system can determine the location of the objects. Sonic rangefinders work in a similar way. These devices send out pulses of sound waves. By measuring the time it takes a pulse to reflect back from an object, the rangefinder can calculate the distance to the object.

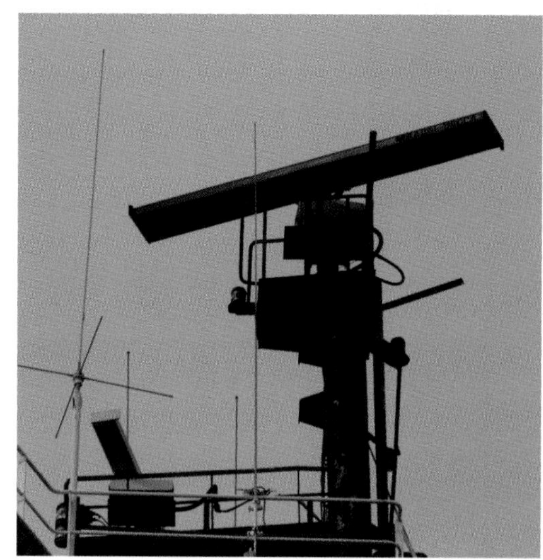

Investigate A

Tools

- TI-83 Plus or TI-84 graphing calculator
- CBR™ (**c**alculator-**b**ased **r**angefinder)
- link cable

How can you make distance-time graphs with a rangefinder?

Work with a partner. There are several different models of rangefinders. Your teacher will tell you if the model you have requires any changes to the directions below.

1. Connect the CBR™ to a graphing calculator.

2. Set the calculator to record data from the CBR™:
- Press (APPS), select **CBL/CBR**, and press (ENTER).
- Select **3:RANGER**, press (ENTER), and select **1:SETUP/SAMPLE**.
- Make sure that your settings match those shown here. With these settings, the rangefinder will record distances in metres for a period of 4 s.
- Move the cursor up to **START NOW** at the top of the screen, and press (ENTER).

```
MAIN MENU      ▶START NOW

 REALTIME:  NO
  TIME(S):  4
  DISPLAY:  DIST
 BEGIN ON:  [ENTER]
SMOOTHING:  NONE
    UNITS:  METERS
```

3. Stand about 3 m from a wall, and hold the rangefinder with its sensor pointed at the wall. Press (ENTER) and walk slowly toward the wall for about 2 s. Pause for a moment; then, back away from the wall, slowly at first, but steadily faster for the remaining 2 s. Keep the sensor pointed at the wall as you walk. You will hear a clicking sound from the CBR™ as it measures distances.

4. When the measurements are complete, a **distance-time graph** will appear on the calculator's screen. If you are not satisfied with your graph, press (ENTER), and select **5:REPEAT SAMPLE**. Then, repeat step 3.

5. What does the horizontal axis of the graph represent? What does the vertical axis represent? Which variable is independent? Explain.

6. **a)** Describe the graph of your motion toward the wall.
   b) Describe the graph of your motion away from the wall.
   c) Describe the graph when you are standing still.
   d) Which parts of your graph are straight? Which part is curved? How does the motion represented by a straight part of your graph differ from the motion represented by the curved part?

7. Match each of the following distance-time graphs by pointing the CBR™ at a wall and walking toward or away from the wall. Describe how you moved to match each graph.

a)

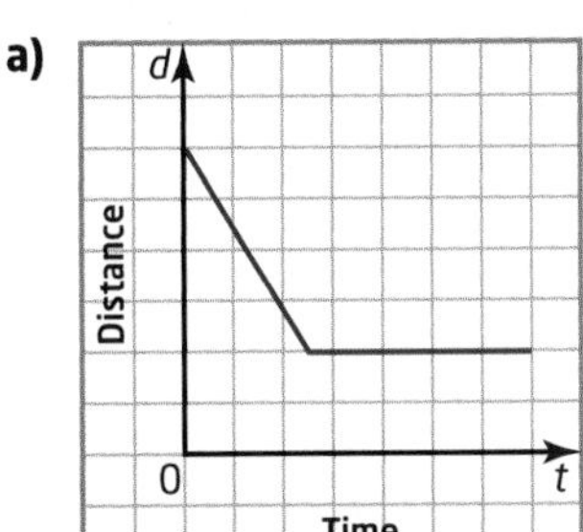

b)

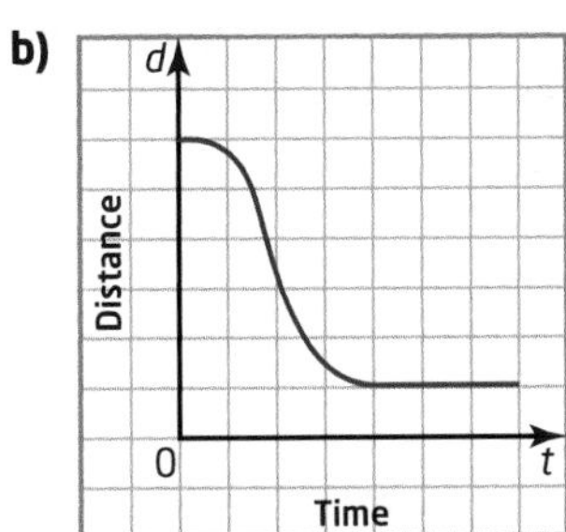

8. **Reflect** Summarize how different kinds of motion appear on a distance-time graph.

distance-time graph

- a graph that shows how distance varies with time

Investigate B

How can you graph the motion of a falling object?

Work with a partner to produce a distance-time graph for a falling ball.

1. Connect the CBR™ to a graphing calculator.

2. Set the calculator to record data from the CBR™:
   - Press (APPS), select **CBL/CBR**, and press (ENTER).
   - Select **3:RANGER**, press (ENTER), and select **1:SETUP/SAMPLE**.
   - Make sure that your settings match those shown here. With these settings, the rangefinder will record distances in metres for a period of 1 s.
   - Move the cursor up to **START NOW** at the top of the screen, and press (ENTER).

Tools

- TI-83 Plus or TI-84 graphing calculator
- CBR™ (calculator-based rangefinder)
- link cable
- large ball (such as a basketball or volleyball)

```
MAIN MENU      ▶START NOW

REALTIME:   NO
 TIME(S):   1
 DISPLAY:   DIST
BEGIN ON:   [ENTER]
SMOOTHING:  NONE
   UNITS:   METERS
```

3. One partner holds the CBR™ steady about 2.0 m above the floor and points the sensor downward. The other partner holds the ball 0.5 m directly below the CBR™. Press ENTER and immediately release the ball. Let the ball bounce.

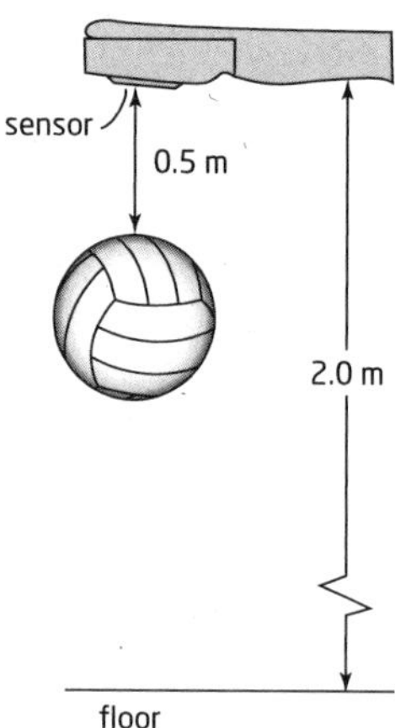

4. When the measurements are complete, a distance-time graph will appear on the calculator's screen. If you are not satisfied with your graph, press ENTER, and select **5:REPEAT SAMPLE**. Then, repeat step 3.

5. What does the horizontal axis of the graph represent? What does the vertical axis represent?

6. How you can identify the point on the graph where the ball hit the floor?

7. Use the **TRACE** feature to find the coordinates of this point. Press TRACE, and use the arrow keys to move the cursor along the graph to the point where the ball hit the floor. What do the coordinates of this point represent?

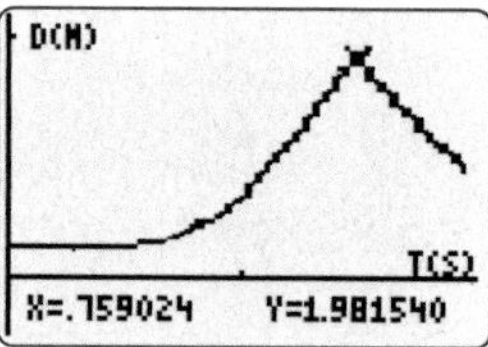

8. **Reflect** Is the relation between distance and time linear from the time you released the ball until it reached the floor? Explain how you can tell from the distance-time graph. What can you conclude about the speed of the ball?

Key Concepts

- A distance-time graph shows an object's distance from a fixed point over a period of time.
- On these graphs, a rising line shows that the distance increases as time increases. A falling line shows a decrease with time, and a horizontal line shows that the distance remains constant.

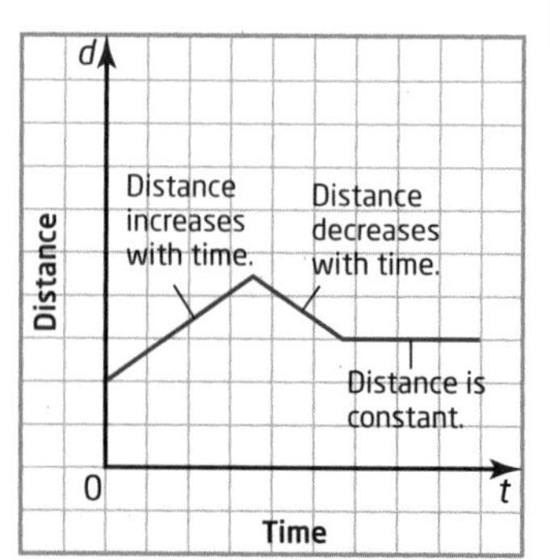

Communicate Your Understanding

C1 State which phrase best describes each segment of this distance-time graph. Justify your answer.

a) no movement

b) fastest movement

c) slowest movement

d) backward movement

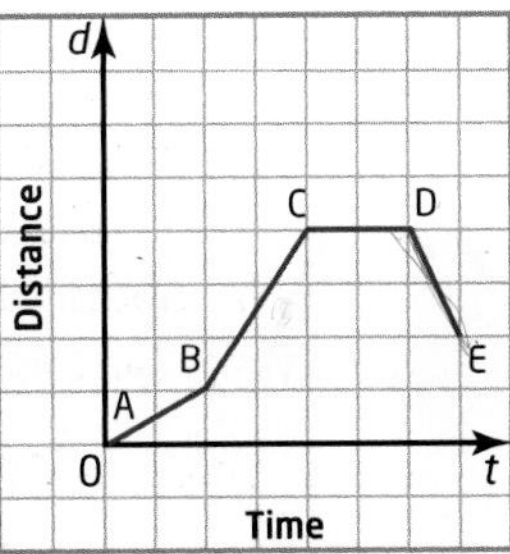

C2 These graphs show a person's distance from a wall. Describe the motion shown in the first graph. Then, explain how the motion in each of the other two graphs differs from that shown in the first graph.

a)

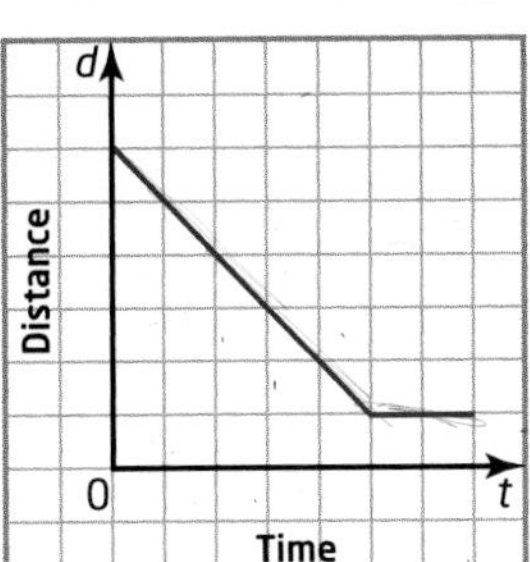

b)

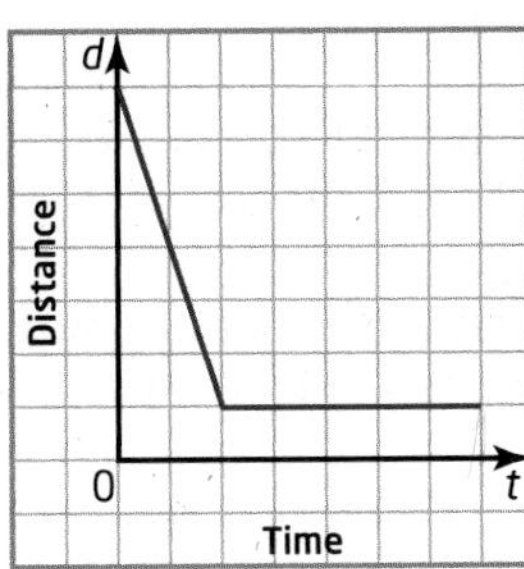

c)

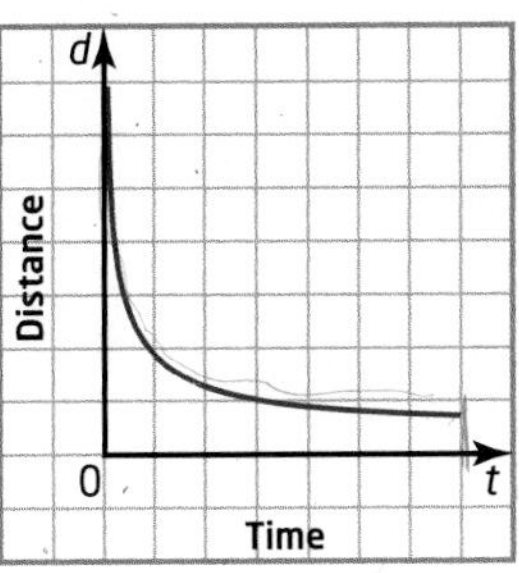

Practise

1. Describe the motion shown in each distance-time graph. Write a few sentences describing a situation that could be represented by each graph.

a)

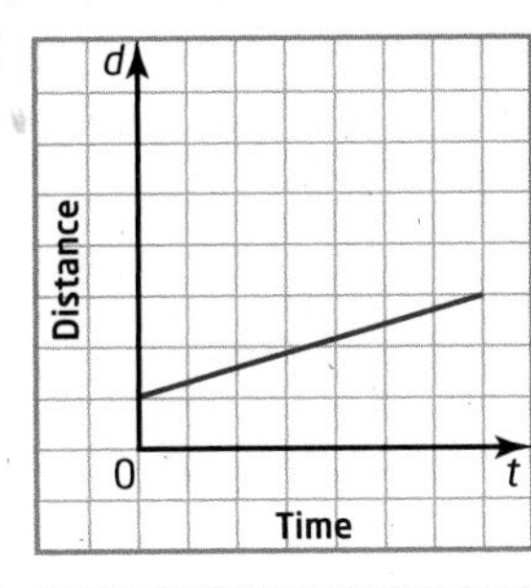

b)

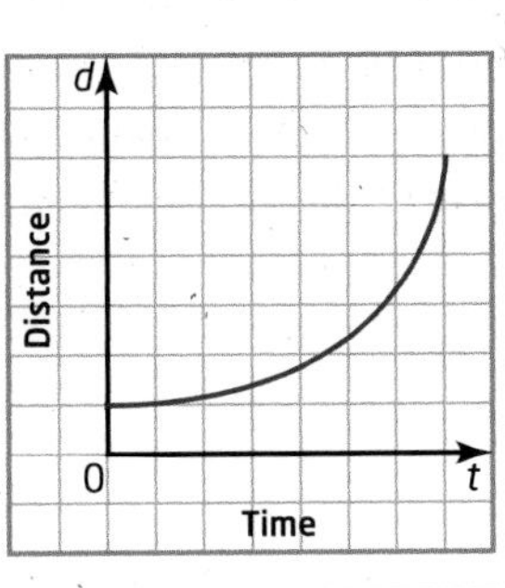

c)

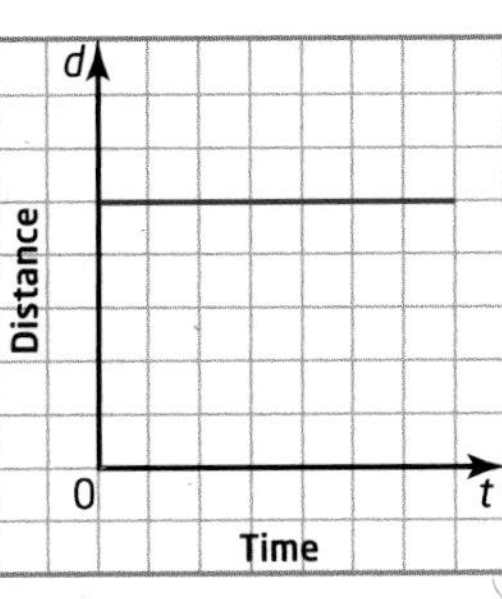

d)

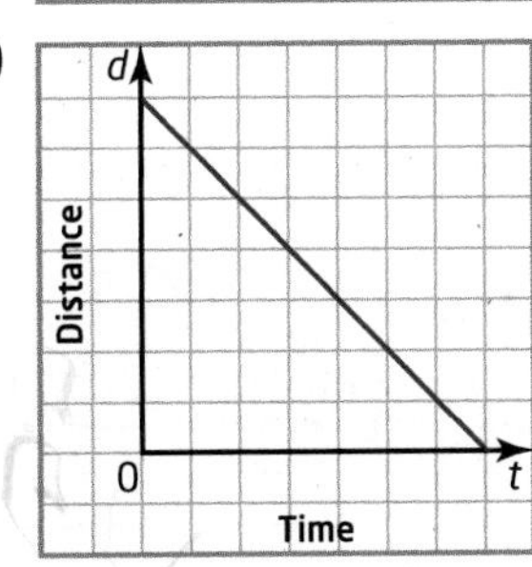

e)

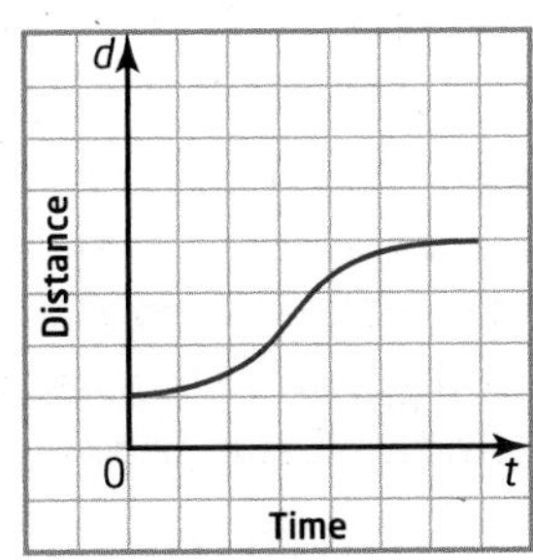

f)

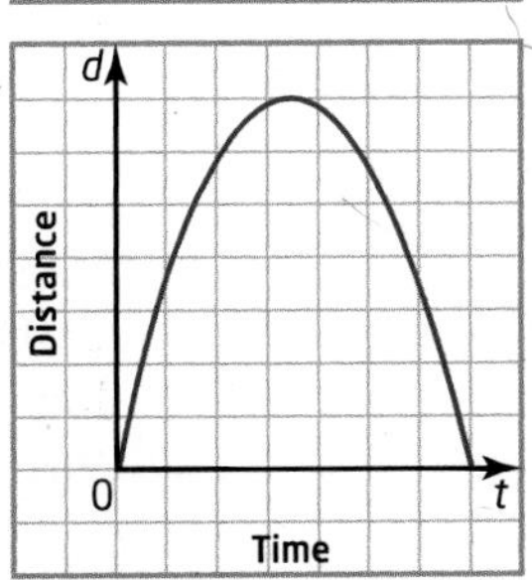

2. Which of the graphs in question 1 show linear relations between distance and time? Justify your answer.

Connect and Apply

3. A canoeist starts from a dock and paddles to the end of a lake and back. This graph shows the canoeist's distance from the dock during this trip.

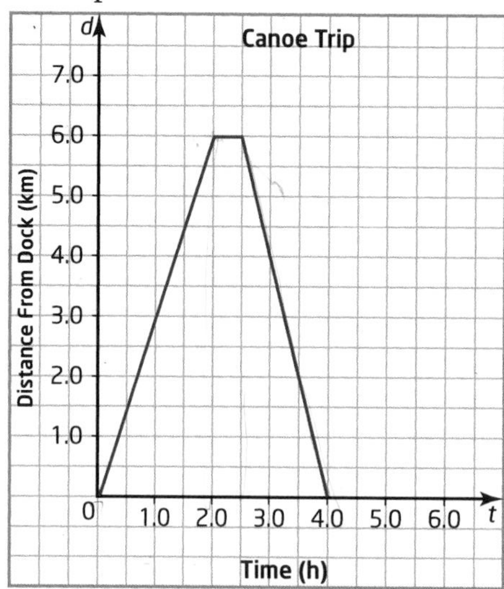

a) How long did this trip take?

b) How far is it to the end of the lake?

c) What does the flat portion of the graph represent?

d) Was the canoeist travelling faster on the way out or on the way back?

4. This graph shows how far a cyclist has travelled from her starting point. Describe the cyclist's motion in a few sentences.

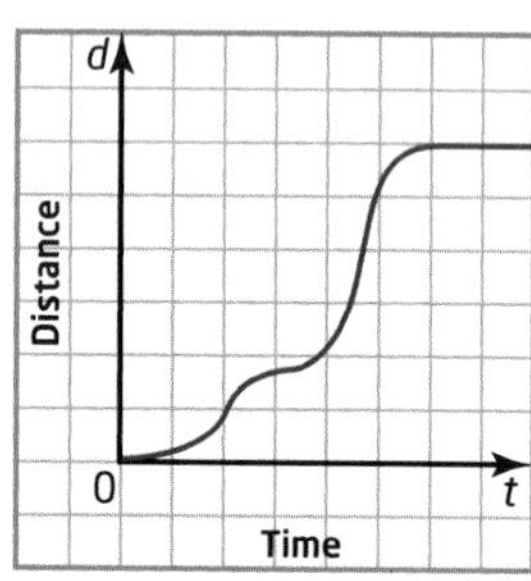

5. a) You are holding a rangefinder pointed at a nearby wall. Describe how you would move in order to match this graph.

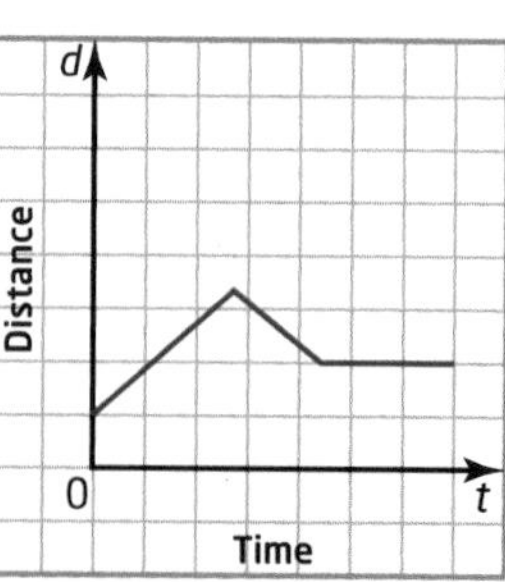

b) How would the distance-time graph change if you walked faster?

c) How would the graph change if you walked slower?

d) How would the graph change if you stopped sooner?

e) If a rangefinder and graphing calculator are available, use them to check your answers to parts b), c), and d).

6. a) Sketch your own distance-time graph.

b) Describe the motion shown in your graph.

c) If a rangefinder and graphing calculator are available, use them to check your answer to part b).

7. Draw a distance-time graph for this situation:

A student leaves home, walking at a steady pace. He slows down, then stops for a few seconds to mail a letter. He turns around and runs home at a constant speed.

8. Sketch a distance-time graph for a car that slowly speeds up after stopping at a traffic light.

9. Water is flowing at a constant rate into each pail. The pails have the same height and the same base. Draw a graph showing the depth of the water in each pail during the time it takes to fill the pails.

a)

b)

10. Use Technology Carry out this activity with a small group.

a) Connect a CBR™ to a graphing calculator.

b) Press (APPS), select **CBL/CBR**, and press (ENTER). Then, select **3:RANGER**, press (ENTER), and select **3:APPLICATIONS**. Select **1:METERS** and then **1:DIST MATCH**.

c) Follow the instructions on the screen. Have each member of the group try to match a different distance-time graph.

d) Write a brief summary of what you learned about distance-time graphs.

Technology Tip

CLR/CBR may appear anywhere on the **APPLICATIONS** menu. If **CBL/CBR** is not among the first seven items, scroll down to see the rest of the list.

Extend

11. a) Find the speed of the canoeist in question 3 during each of the three segments of the trip.

b) Draw a speed-time graph for the canoeist's trip.

c) How is the speed of the canoeist related to the shape of the distance-time graph?

d) What does negative speed represent in this situation?

12. **Use Technology** Work with a partner to investigate the motion of a bouncing ball. Use a large ball, such as a basketball or a volleyball.

a) Connect a CBR™ to a graphing calculator. Clear all lists.

b) Press (APPS), select **CBL/CBR**, and press (ENTER). Then, select **3:RANGER**, press (ENTER), and select **3:APPLICATIONS**. Select **METERS** and then **BALL BOUNCE**.

APPLICATIONS
1:DIST MATCH
2:VEL MATCH
3:BALL BOUNCE
4:MAIN MENU

c) Follow the instructions on the screen. Hold the CBR™ up high with the sensor pointed down. Drop the ball from a point about 0.5 m directly below the CBR™. Press the trigger on the CBR™ the moment the ball first hits the floor. Allow the ball to bounce at least five times.

d) When the measurements are complete, a graph will appear on the calculator's screen. What does the horizontal axis of this graph represent? What does the vertical axis represent?

e) Is there a linear relation between these two variables? Explain.

f) Use the **TRACE** function to find the maximum height the ball reaches on each bounce. Move the cursor to the top of the curve representing each bounce. Record the coordinates of these points in a table under the headings "Time" and "Bounce Height."

g) Enter the times into list **L3** and the bounce heights into **L4**.

h) To plot these coordinates, Press (2nd) [STAT PLOT] and select **2:Plot2**. Select **On** and the line graph icon. Enter L3 for **Xlist** and L4 for **Ylist**. Then, press (GRAPH).

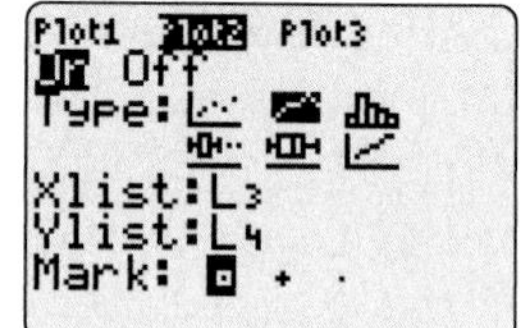

i) Is there a linear relation between time and bounce height? Explain.

13. **Use Technology** Carry out this activity with a small group.

a) Connect a CBR™ to a graphing calculator.

b) Press (APPS), select **CBL/CBR**, and press (ENTER). Then, select **3:RANGER**, press (ENTER), and select **3:APPLICATIONS**. Select **1:METERS** and then **2:VEL MATCH**.

c) Follow the instructions on the screen. Have each member of the group try to match a different speed-time graph.

d) Write a brief summary of what you learned about speed-time graphs.

14. **Math Contest** In 2005, Shaheen's age on her birthday was equal to the sum of the digits of the year she was born. In what year was Shaheen born?

Chapter 2 Review

2.1 Hypotheses and Sources of Data, pages 42–47

1. State a hypothesis about a relationship between each pair of variables. Then, state the opposite hypothesis.

a) the temperature in a town during the summer and the volume of water used by the town's residents

b) a person's height and marks in mathematics

2. State whether each data source is primary or secondary. Then, discuss whether the source is a good choice.

a) To determine the number of each size of school uniform to buy, a principal surveyed 200 of the school's students by telephone.

b) To check trends in house prices across Canada, a real-estate agent found a database on the Internet.

c) To find data on the sizes of bears in British Columbia, a student used an encyclopedia.

d) To choose music for a school dance, the dance committee checked a list of the top-selling CDs in Canada in a music magazine.

2.2 Sampling Principles, pages 48–55

3. You want to survey students' opinions about the extracurricular activities at your school.

a) Identify the population.

b) Describe how you could use a stratified random sample for your survey.

4. An airline wants to determine how its passengers feel about paying extra for in-flight meals.

a) Identify the population.

b) Describe how the airline could use a systematic random sample for its survey.

5. Identify the population in each situation and describe the sampling technique you would use.

a) A department store wishes to know how far away its customers live.

b) The Ontario government wants to find out the incomes of people who camp in provincial parks.

c) Your school librarian needs to find out how to improve lunchtime services for students.

2.3 Use Scatter Plots to Analyse Data, pages 56–67

6. This table shows the heights and shoe sizes of ten grade-9 boys.

Height (cm)	Shoe Size
157	7
168	8.5
162	8
151	6.5
186	12
180	11
167	12
159	9
168	9.5
181	10

a) Make a scatter plot of the data.

b) Describe the relationship between a student's height and shoe size.

c) Identify any outliers. Should you discard the outliers? Explain.

7. This table shows the length of ten ferries and the number of cars each one can carry.

a) Make a scatter plot of the data.

b) Describe the relationship between the length of a ferry and its capacity.

c) Identify any outliers. What could cause these outliers?

Length (m)	Capacity (cars)
34.1	16
167.2	600
27.4	11
22.9	12
115.5	205
100.0	150
15.2	4
51.2	35
75.8	100
110.8	80

2.4 Trends, Interpolation, and Extrapolation, pages 68–76

8. This table shows the population of Canada from 1861 to 2001.

a) Make a scatter plot of the data.

b) Describe the trend in the population.

c) Estimate the population during Canada's centennial year, 1967.

d) Predict Canada's population in 2021.

Year	Population (millions)
1861	3.2
1871	3.7
1881	4.3
1891	4.8
1901	5.4
1911	7.2
1921	8.8
1931	10.4
1941	11.5
1951	13.6
1961	18.2
1971	21.6
1981	24.8
1991	28.0
2001	31.0

Adapted from Statistics Canada, Web site, http://www40.statcan.ca/l01/cst01/demo03.htm, November 2005

9. This table lists the winning heights in the high jump for men and women at the Olympics from 1928 to 2004.

Winning Heights in Olympic High Jump

Year	Men (m)	Women (m)
1928	1.94	1.59
1932	1.97	1.66
1936	2.03	1.60
1948	1.98	1.68
1952	2.04	1.67
1956	2.12	1.76
1960	2.16	1.85
1964	2.18	1.90
1968	2.24	1.82
1972	2.23	1.92
1976	2.25	1.93
1980	2.36	1.97
1984	2.35	2.02
1988	2.38	2.03
1992	2.34	2.02
1996	2.39	2.05
2000	2.35	2.01
2004	2.36	2.06

a) Graph the data. Use one colour for the men's data and another for the women's data.

b) Compare the trends in the men's and women's results.

c) Identify any outliers.

d) Predict the winning heights in the men's and women's high jump at the 2012 Olympics. Explain your reasoning.

2.5 Linear and Non-Linear Relations, pages 77–87

10. Graph each set of points on a grid. Then, draw a line of best fit. Is a line of best fit a good model for each set of data? Explain.

a)

x	y
4	-8
8	-14
-2	7
6	-11
0	1
-5	15
-2	5
3	-5
10	-17
7	-11
-3	8

b)

Time (days)	Height (cm)
0	0.4
1	1.7
2	3.5
3	4.4
4	5.1
5	5.4
6	5.7
7	5.9

11. Two ships are travelling on parallel courses that are 10 km apart. This table shows the distance between the two ships over a 12-h period.

a) Make a scatter plot of the data.

b) Describe the relationship and draw a line of best fit.

c) Identify any outliers.

d) Estimate when the ships will be closest to each other.

Time (h)	Separation (km)
0	575.5
1	534.3
2	501.5
3	447.2
4	412.1
5	379.1
6	330.6
7	299.0
8	255.8
9	210.6
10	177.2
11	134.1
12	95.3

2.6 Distance-Time Graphs, pages 88–94

12. Describe a situation that corresponds to each distance-time graph.

a)

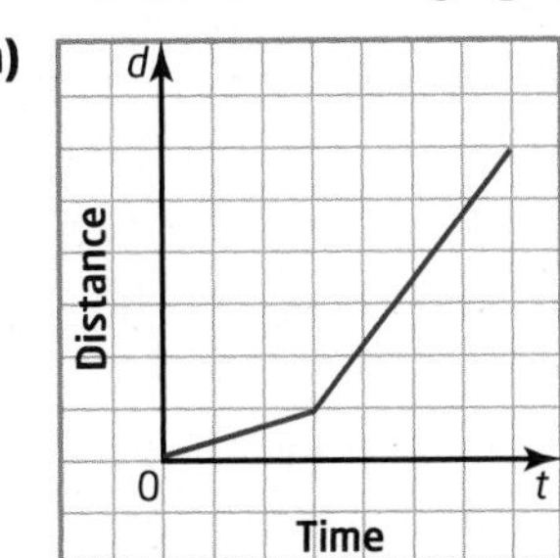

b)

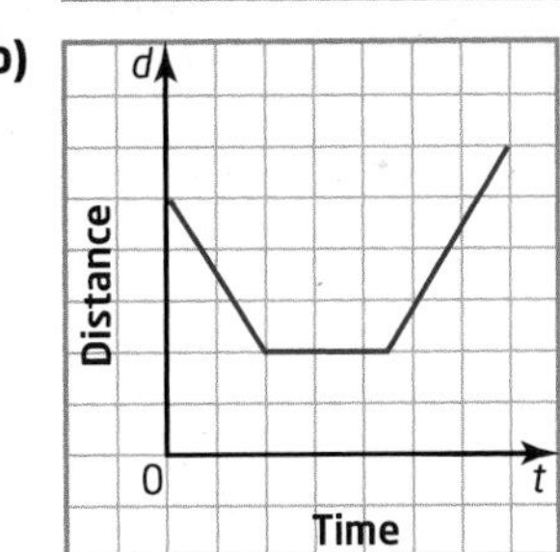

c)

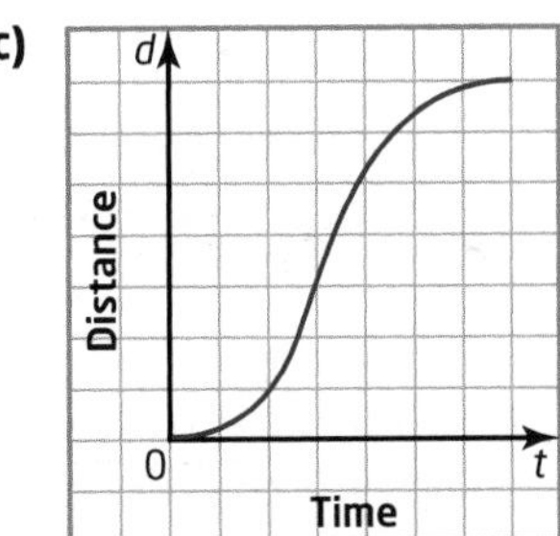

13. Draw a distance-time graph to represent each situation.

a) A worker with a wheelbarrow filled with bricks starts at a point 50 m from the entrance to a construction site. The worker pushes the wheelbarrow away from the entrance at a speed of 1 m/s for 10 s, stops for 5 s to unload, and then moves back toward the entrance at a speed of 2 m/s for 20 s.

b) A stone dropped from a height of 10 m steadily increases in speed until it hits the ground after about 1.4 s.

Chapter 2 Practice Test

Multiple Choice

For questions 1 to 4, select the best answer.

1. Which of the following is a primary data source?

A finding a list of the year's top-grossing films in the newspaper

B having 20 of your friends ask their family members for their favourite colour

C getting information on the world's longest rivers from an atlas

D using the Internet to find the results of the latest Paralympic Games

2. Which of the following is not an example of random sampling?

A using a random-number generator to select 10% of the players in each division of a provincial soccer league

B selecting every 10th person on a list, beginning with the name corresponding to a randomly generated number between 1 and 10, inclusive

C standing on a street corner and asking every 10th person who goes by for their opinions

D writing names on slips of paper and picking 10% of the slips out of a box after shaking the box thoroughly

3. Estimating values beyond the known data for a relation is

A extrapolation

B interpolation

C a line of best fit

D discarding outliers

4. The final step in an experiment is the

A procedure

B conclusion

C evaluation

D hypothesis

Short Response

Show all steps to your solutions.

5. Write the opposite of each hypothesis.

a) Caffeine can affect your sleep.

b) The more you study, the worse you do on tests.

c) At least half of the students in your school have a part-time job.

d) Cell phone use has more than doubled in the past 2 years.

6. A school board wishes to survey a representative sample of its teachers.

a) Identify the population.

b) Describe a suitable stratified random sample for this survey.

c) Describe a suitable systematic random sample.

d) Give an example of a non-random sample.

e) Explain why the non-random sample might not be representative of the population.

7. Make a scatter plot of each set of data. Draw a line or curve of best fit. State whether each scatter plot shows a linear or non-linear relationship. Justify your answer.

a)

Time (s)	Mass (g)
0	106.1
0.5	51.4
1.0	28.9
1.5	13.5
2.0	5.8
2.5	3.7
3.0	1.6
3.5	0.9
4.0	0.4

b)

Time (h)	Distance (km)
2	7.0
1	7.0
2	9.5
0	4.0
7	16.5
4	11.0
1	6.0
2	9.0
6	19.0

8. Briefly describe the motion represented by each section of this distance-time graph.

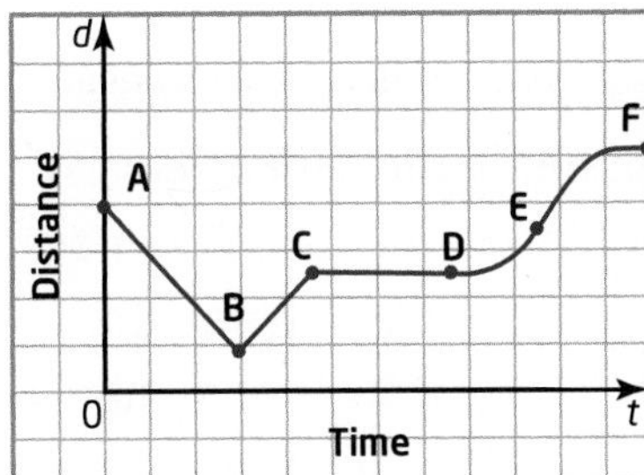

Extended Response

Provide complete solutions.

9. Outline an experiment to investigate the relationship between the distance a person stands from a ceiling light and the length of the person's shadow. Your outline should include

a) a hypothesis

b) a procedure for gathering data

c) a description of how you will analyse the data

d) an explanation of how you can tell if the data show a linear relation

10. After landing on Mars, a spacecraft shoots out a probe to take measurements away from any possible contamination at the landing site. This table shows the probe's height during the first 4 s of its flight.

Time (s)	Height (m)
0	1.0
0.5	5.5
1.0	9.2
1.5	11.8
2.0	13.6
2.5	21.4
3.0	14.4
3.5	13.3
4.0	11.4

a) Make a scatter plot of the data. Label your graph.

b) Describe the relationship between time and the height of the probe.

c) Identify any outliers. What could cause such outliers?

d) Draw a line or a curve of best fit, excluding any outliers.

e) Estimate the probe's height after 5 s.

Chapter Problem Wrap-Up

In Section 2.3, question 7, you outlined an experiment to examine the relationship between a physical characteristic and performance in the high jump.

a) Carry out the experiment. Did you have to make any changes to the procedure you described in Section 2.3? Explain.

b) Draw a scatter plot of the data. Does this scatter plot suggest a linear or a non-linear relationship? Explain.

c) Draw a line or a curve of best fit. Comment on the accuracy of this line or curve of best fit.

d) Compare the results of the experiment with your hypothesis. What conclusion can you make?

CHAPTER

3

Polynomials

As science becomes more complex, it becomes more important to communicate mathematical ideas clearly. Imagine if Einstein always had to write out his famous equation $E = mc^2$ as "energy equals mass times the square of the speed of light." Using letters or symbols to represent unknown amounts is called algebra. Algebra is a basic building block of advanced mathematical and scientific thinking. How can you use algebra to communicate your mathematical ideas?

Number Sense and Algebra

- Substitute into and evaluate algebraic expressions involving exponents.
- Describe the relationship between the algebraic and geometric representations of a single-variable term up to degree three.
- Derive, through the investigation and examination of patterns, the exponent rules for multiplying and dividing monomials, and apply these rules in expressions involving one and two variables with positive exponents.
- Relate understanding of inverse operations to squaring and taking the square root.
- Extend the multiplication rule to derive and understand the power of a power rule, and apply it to simplify expressions involving one and two variables with positive exponents.
- Add and subtract polynomials with up to two variables.
- Multiply a polynomial by a monomial involving the same variable.
- Expand and simplify polynomial expressions involving one variable.

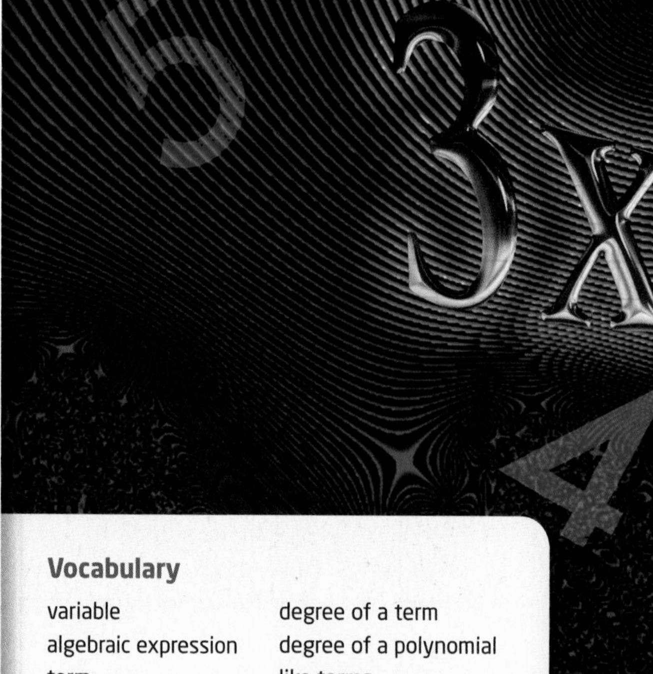

Vocabulary

variable
algebraic expression
term
polynomial
degree of a term
degree of a polynomial
like terms
distributive property

Chapter Problem

Alysia has selected the letter E to design the logo for her school team, the Eagles.

The design will be used to make different-sized crests for clothing such as jackets, sweaters, and baseball caps. How can Alysia make sure that, when the crest is made larger or smaller, the proportions do not change?

Get Ready

Add and Subtract Integers

To add integers, you can use a number line.

- Start at the first integer.
- Add the second integer by drawing an arrow.
- The arrow points to the right if the second integer is positive, and to the left if it is negative.
- The answer is at the tip of the arrow.

$(-1) + (-2) = -3$

$2 + (-3) = -1$

Opposite integers add to zero. For example, $(+4) + (-4) = 0$.

Subtracting an integer is the same as adding the opposite.

$$\begin{aligned} &5 - (-2) \\ &= 5 + (+2) \\ &= 7 \end{aligned}$$

+2 is the opposite of −2.

$$\begin{aligned} &(-3) - (+1) \\ &= (-3) + (-1) \\ &= -4 \end{aligned}$$

+1 is the opposite of −1.

1. Add or subtract.

a) $7 + 5$ **b)** $10 - 3$
c) $5 + (-9)$ **d)** $5 - (-4)$
e) $(-4) + 6$ **f)** $7 - 9$
g) $(-3) + (-11)$ **h)** $(-4) - (-8)$

2. Evaluate.

a) $(-2) + (-2) + 1$ **b)** $10 - (-3)$
c) $5 + (-7) + 7$ **d)** $4 + (-3) + (-2)$
e) $(-9) - 6$ **f)** $1 - (-1)$
g) $(-5) - 8$ **h)** $(-8) + 9 + (-2)$

Multiply and Divide Integers

The product or quotient of two integers of the same sign gives a positive result.
The product or quotient of two integers of opposite signs gives a negative result.

$5 \times 3 = 15$ $-3 \times (-4) = 12$ $-5 \times 6 = -30$

$-14 \div (-7) = 2$ $\frac{-8}{8} = -1$ $15 \div (-5) = -3$

3. Multiply.

a) $3 \times (-8)$ **b)** $(-4) \times (-6)$
c) $(-8) \times 4$ **d)** $(-5)(-6)$
e) $12(-5)$ **f)** $-2(20)$

4. Divide.

a) $(-8) \div 4$ **b)** $9 \div (-3)$
c) $\frac{-16}{8}$ **d)** $\frac{-6}{-6}$
e) $25 \div (-5)$ **f)** $-36 \div (-4)$

Multiply Rational Numbers

To multiply fractions, multiply the numerators together and multiply the denominators together.

When a numerator and a denominator share a common factor, you can divide it out before multiplying.

$$\frac{2}{3} \times \frac{3}{4}$$

$$= \frac{\overset{1}{\cancel{2}}}{\underset{1}{\cancel{3}}} \times \frac{\overset{1}{\cancel{3}}}{\underset{2}{\cancel{4}}}$$

$$= \frac{1}{2}$$

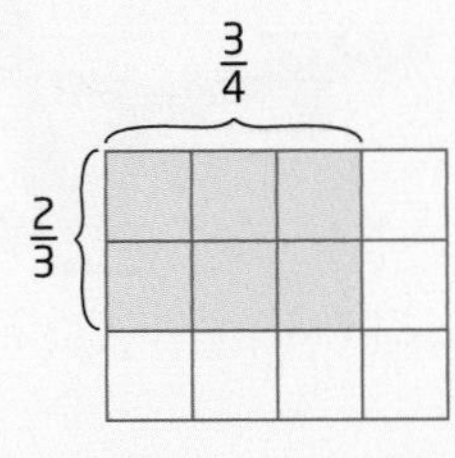

When negative fractions or decimals occur, apply the same rules as for products of integers.

$$\left(-\frac{3}{4}\right) \times \frac{1}{5}$$

$$= \left(-\frac{3}{4}\right) \times \frac{1}{5}$$

When I multiply a negative by a positive, I get a negative result.

$$= -\frac{3}{20}$$

My scientific calculator may need different keystrokes. I'll check the manual.

Check:

Using a scientific calculator:

C 3 ± a b/c 4 × 1 a b/c 5 = =

Using a graphing calculator:

(–) 3 ÷ 4 × 1 ÷ 5 MATH 1 ENTER

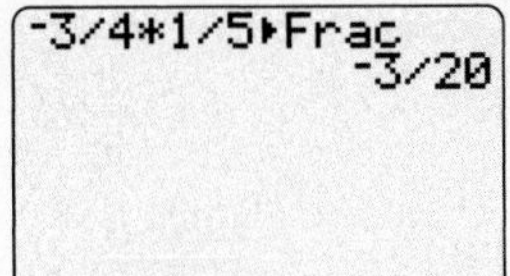

$-0.25 \times 0.5 = -0.125$

Using a scientific calculator:

C 0.25 ± × 0.5 =

Using a graphing calculator:

(–) 0.25 × 0.5 ENTER

-0.25*0.5
-.125

5. Multiply.

a) $\frac{4}{5} \times \frac{1}{3}$

b) $-\frac{1}{3} \times \frac{1}{4}$

c) $\frac{3}{5} \times \left(-\frac{2}{9}\right)$

d) $\left(-\frac{3}{4}\right) \times \left(-\frac{1}{5}\right)$

e) $-\frac{3}{8} \times \frac{4}{5}$

f) $\frac{1}{2}\left(-1\frac{1}{2}\right)$

6. Multiply.

a) $\left(-\frac{2}{5}\right) \times \frac{1}{4}$

b) $\left(-\frac{3}{10}\right) \times \left(-\frac{5}{6}\right)$

c) $0.6 \times (-0.95)$

d) $(-0.3)(-0.4)$

e) $-2.5\ (3.2)$

f) $8(-3.8)$

3.1 Build Algebraic Models Using Concrete Materials

Petra likes to run at the track to keep in shape. This year, to motivate herself, she will record her training progress visually. What are some ways that she can do this?

Investigate

Tools
- algebra tiles
- linking cubes

How can you model length, area, and volume using concrete materials?

Part A: Model Length

Petra's running record for the first 2 weeks of the year is shown below. Petra used algebra tiles to model each distance. She used the side length of a **unit tile** to represent 1 km.

Algebra tiles are tools that can be used to model measured quantities.

A unit tile is a square tile that measures 1 unit by 1 unit. It can be used as a counter.

■ unit tile

In this book, positive algebra tiles are green and negative algebra tiles are white.

What other concrete materials could I use to represent one unit?

On July 14, Petra ran 4 km.

Date	Distance (km)	Progress
January 1	1	■
January 3	2	■■
January 6	2	■■
January 8	3	■■■
January 10	3	■■■
January 14	4	■■■■

A tile model is a good way of tracking Petra's progress visually.

One weekend, Petra cross-country skiied around a lake three times. She did not know the distance around the lake, so she used a **variable**, x, to represent it.

variable

- a quantity whose value can change (or vary)
- usually represented by a letter

An **x-tile** is a rectangular tile that is used to represent the variable x. It has the same width as the side length of a unit tile. You can use an x-tile to describe any unknown value.

The total distance can be modelled using three x-tiles:

This means that on the weekend, Petra skiied a total of $3x$ kilometres, where x is the distance around the lake.

1. Use tiles to represent each length.

a) 6 km

b) an unknown distance

c) an unknown distance and back

d) 3 km plus an unknown distance

2. Use tiles to model each **algebraic expression**.

a) 7 **b)** $4x$ **c)** $x + 3$ **d)** $3x + 2$

algebraic expression

- a mathematical phrase made up of numbers and variables, connected by addition or subtraction operators
- can be used to model real-life situations
- $2x + 3$ is an algebraic expression

3. Write an algebraic expression for each model.

a) 

b)

c) 

d) 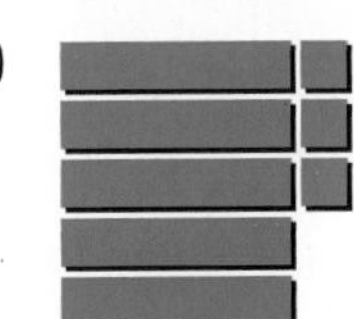

4. Create an algebraic expression of your own and build a tile model to represent it. Record the expression and the model.

Literacy Connections

Expressions are sometimes confused with equations. For example, $2x + 3$ is an expression, but $2x + 3 = 1$ is an equation. Equations contain an equal sign, expressions do not.

Part B: Model Area

You can use an **x^2-tile** to represent an unknown area, measured in square units, if you let the side length of each tile represent x units. Note that the side length of an x^2-tile is equal to the length of an x-tile.

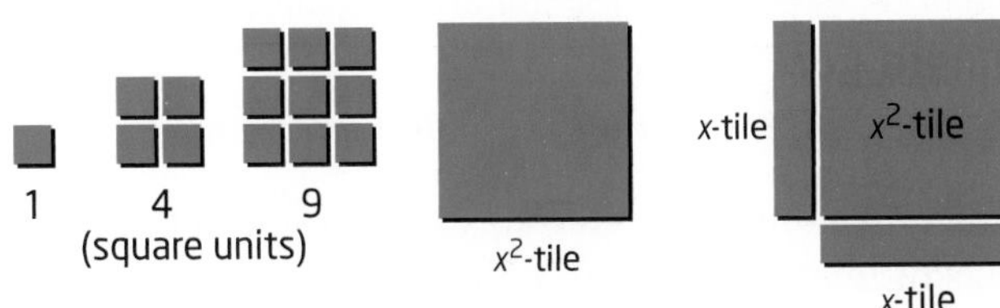

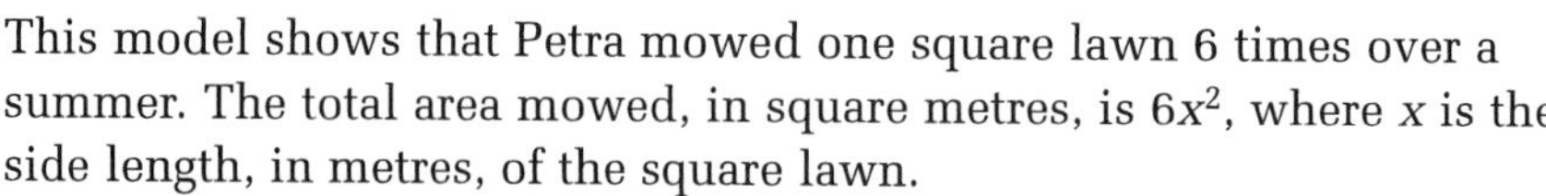

This model shows that Petra mowed one square lawn 6 times over a summer. The total area mowed, in square metres, is $6x^2$, where x is the side length, in metres, of the square lawn.

5. Use algebra tiles to represent each area.
   a) 16 square units
   b) 25 square units
   c) $3x^2$
   d) $5x^2$

6. Use algebra tiles to represent each expression.
   a) $x^2 + 2$
   b) $2x^2 + x$
   c) $x^2 + 3x + 2$
   d) $3x^2 + 5x + 1$

Part C: Model Volume

7. A cube is a rectangular prism with length, width, and height all equal.
   a) Use linking cubes to build a model of a cube that has a side length of 3 cm. Sketch your model.
   b) What is the volume, in cubic centimetres, of this cube?
   c) Express the volume of the cube as a power.

8. Repeat step 7 for a cube with a side length of 5 cm.

9. Describe other concrete materials you could use to build an algebraic model of volume.

10. Suppose you do not know the side length of a cube. You can use the variable x to represent the side length.
    a) Sketch the cube and label its length, width, and height.
    b) Write an algebraic expression for the area of one face of the cube.
    c) Write an algebraic expression for the volume of the cube.

11. **Reflect** Describe how concrete materials can be used to build algebraic models of length, area, and volume. Use words, expressions, and diagrams to support your explanation.

Key Concepts

- Concrete materials, such as algebra tiles and linking cubes, can be used to build algebraic models.
- You can build length models with algebra tiles.
- You can build area models with algebra tiles.
- You can build volume models with linking cubes.

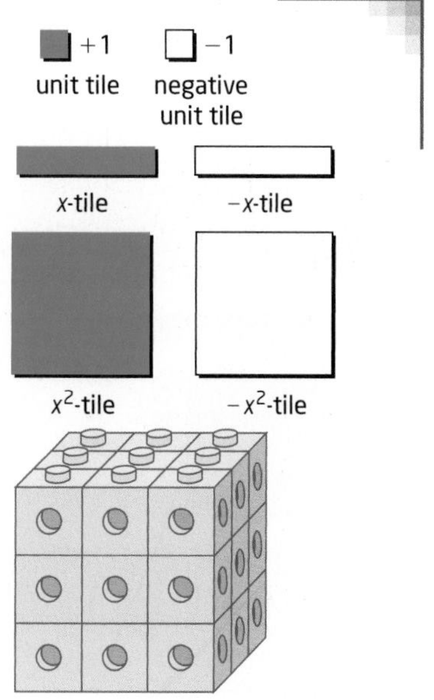

Communicate Your Understanding

C1 State the length and width of each.

a) a unit tile

b) an x-tile

c) an x^2-tile

C2 **a)** How are the length and width of a unit tile and an x-tile related?

b) How are the length and width of an x-tile and an x^2-tile related?

C3 **a)** Suggest two other objects that could be used to model length.

b) Suggest two other objects that could be used to model area.

c) For your answers to parts a) and b), identify any advantages or disadvantages of each object.

C4 Explain how concrete materials can be used to model each type of measurement. Include a diagram to support each explanation.

a) length **b)** area **c)** volume

Practise

1. Which expression is represented by the algebra tile model?

A $4x^2 + 2x - 5$ **B** $-4x^2 - 2x - 5$

C $4x^2 - 2x - 5$ **D** $4x^2 + 2x + 5$

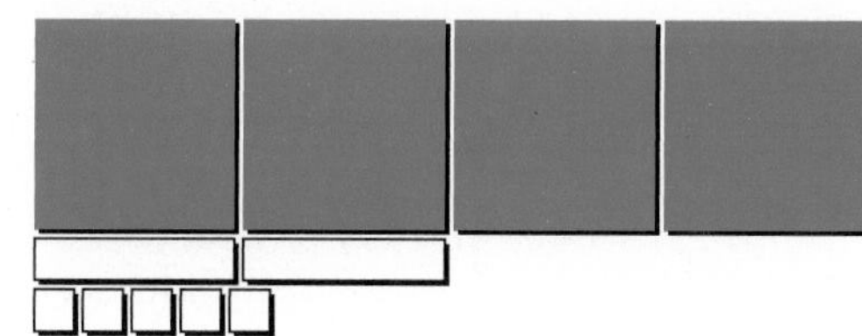

Did You Know?

The Greek mathematician Diophantus (about 250-275) was the first person to use a letter to represent an unknown.

2. Use tiles to model each algebraic expression.

a) $x^2 + 3x$

b) $2x^2 + 5$

c) $3x^2 + x + 2$

d) $x^2 + 2x + 4$

3. Write the algebraic expression represented by each model.

a) 

b) 

c) 

d) 

Connect and Apply

4. Each unit tile represents 1 km that Miko rode her bicycle. Find each distance.

a) 

b) 

c) 

d)

5. Create an algebraic expression of your own, using x^2-tiles, x-tiles, and unit tiles, and build a tile model to represent it. Record the expression and the model.

6. a) Build a volume model to represent a cube with length, width, and height all equal to 4 cm. Sketch the model and label the length, width, and height.

b) What is the volume? Write this as a power.

c) Write an expression for the area of one face as a power. Evaluate the area of one face.

7. A cube has a volume of 216 cm^3.

   a) What side length of the cube would give this volume?

   b) Determine the area of one face of the cube.

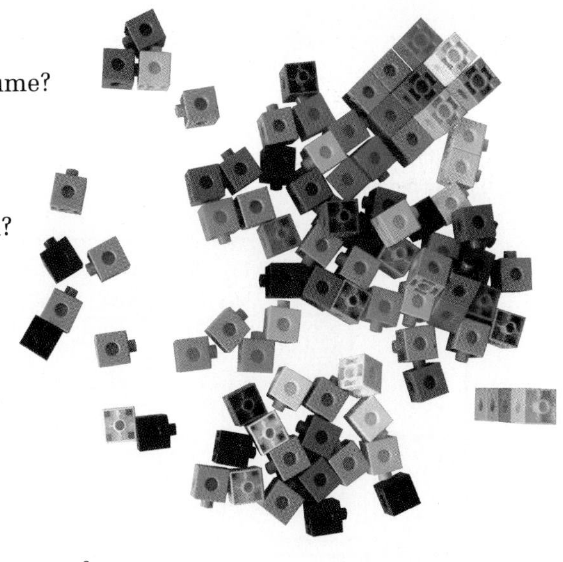

8. The area of one face of a cube is 49 m^2.

   a) What side length of the cube would give this area?

   b) Determine the volume of the cube.

Extend

9. Build an area model using tiles that have length and width as indicated.

   a) length = $x + 3$, width = x

   b) length = $x + 4$, width = $x + 1$

10. A cube has a volume of 8 cm^3. Find the total surface area of all six faces.

11. **Math Contest** Mersenne numbers are numbers of the form $2^n - 1$. Father Marin Mersenne (1588–1648) was especially interested in prime numbers of this form. One conjecture about Mersenne numbers is that numbers of the form $2^p - 1$ are prime if p is prime. Investigate this conjecture and write a brief report of your findings.

12. **Math Contest** Find the smallest possible value of $a^b + c^d + e^f$ if a, b, c, d, e, and f are all different and are chosen from the values 1, 2, 3, 4, 5, and 6.

13. **Math Contest** When $30^{40} \times 40^{30}$ is written in expanded form, the number of zeros at the end of the number is

    A 30

    B 40

    C 70

    D 120

    E 1200

14. **Math Contest** Fermat numbers are numbers of the form $2^{2^n} + 1$. Pierre de Fermat (1601–1665) conjectured that all numbers of this form are primes. Investigate this conjecture. Write a brief report of your findings.

3.2 Work With Exponents

One day, Sammy decided to try a new place for lunch.
BARNEY'S BURGERS
NOW OPEN
You've got to try the new Barney's Burgers. Can you say "Yum!"
All right!
But I'm a vegetarian.
No Problem! They have Veggie Burgers too!
Let's go tomorrow!
The next day...
YOU HAVE TO TRY BARNEY'S!
Before long, word got around about Barney's Burgers...
... and business is booming!
NOW HIRING!

Suppose the trend in the cartoon continues: every day each new customer tells two new friends at school about the Barney Burger. How many new customers will Barney get each day?

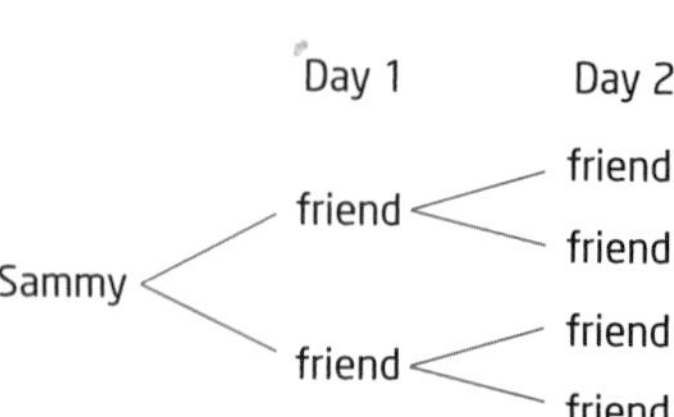

Investigate

How can you use exponential models to describe growth patterns?

1. Copy and complete the table. In the last column, write the number of new customers as a power of 2.

New Customers After Sammy Tells His Two Friends

Day	New Customers	Expanded Form	Power
1	2	2	2^1
2	4	2×2	2^2
3			
4			

2. Barney's is open 7 days a week. Use this model to determine how many new customers Barney should expect on Day 7. Explain how you found your answer.

3. Use this model to determine how many new customers Barney should expect on Day 14. Is this answer realistic? Why or why not?

4. Estimate the number of students at your school. How long would it take for everyone at your school to find out about Barney's? Describe how you found your answer, and identify any assumptions you made.

5. Suppose that each new customer told three friends about Barney's, instead of two, and that this trend continued.

   Use exponents to help explain your answers to the following.

   a) How many new customers should Barney expect after 2 days?

   b) How many new customers should Barney expect after 4 days?

   c) How much more quickly would word reach all the students at your school? Explain.

6. **Reflect** Explain how exponents are useful in describing growth patterns.

A **power** is a product of identical factors and consists of two parts: a **base** and an **exponent**.

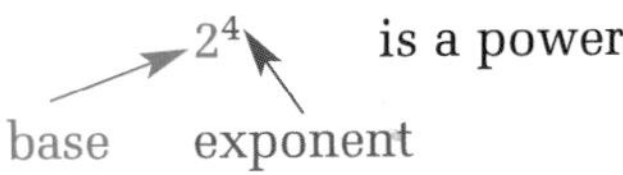

The base is the identical factor, and the exponent tells how many factors there are.

$$2^4 = 2 \times 2 \times 2 \times 2$$

exponential form expanded form

Powers are useful for expressing repeated multiplication.

Example 1 Evaluate Powers

Write in expanded form, and then evaluate.

a) 2^5 **b)** $(-3)^3$ **c)** $(-3)^4$

d) -3^4 **e)** 3.5^3 **f)** $\left(\frac{2}{3}\right)^3$

Solution

a) $2^5 = 2 \times 2 \times 2 \times 2 \times 2$
$= 32$

b) $(-3)^3 = (-3) \times (-3) \times (-3)$
$= -27$

There is an odd number of negative factors. The answer is negative.

c) $(-3)^4 = (-3) \times (-3) \times (-3) \times (-3)$
$= 81$

There is an even number of negative factors. The answer is positive.

d) $-3^4 = -(3 \times 3 \times 3 \times 3)$
$= -81$

The base of this power is 3, not −3. The negative sign in front makes the result negative.

e) $3.5^3 = 3.5 \times 3.5 \times 3.5$
$= 42.875$

C 3.5 y^x 3 =

f) $\left(\frac{2}{3}\right)^3 = \left(\frac{2}{3}\right)\left(\frac{2}{3}\right)\left(\frac{2}{3}\right)$
$= \frac{2 \times 2 \times 2}{3 \times 3 \times 3}$
$= \frac{8}{27}$

To multiply fractions, I multiply numerators together and multiply denominators together.

Example 2 Apply Exponents to Solve Problems

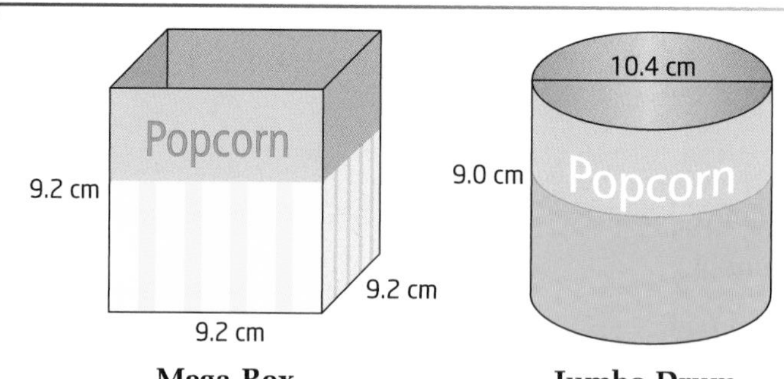

Which container holds more popcorn? How much more? Assume that each container is filled just to the top. Round your answer to the nearest cubic centimetre.

Solution

Mega-Box

Reasoning and Proving
Representing
Selecting Tools
Problem Solving
Connecting
Reflecting
Communicating

The Mega-Box is in the shape of a cube. Apply the formula for the volume of a cube.

$V = s^3$ **s is the side length of the cube.**
$= 9.2^3$ C 9.2 y^x 3 =
$= 778.688$

The Mega-Box holds about 779 cm^3 of popcorn.

Jumbo Drum

The Jumbo Drum is in the shape of a cylinder. Apply the formula for the volume of a cylinder.

$V = \pi r^2 h$ **r is the radius of the base and h is the height of the cylinder.**
$= \pi(5.2)^2(9.0)$ **The radius is half the diameter: 10.4 ÷ 2 = 5.2**
$\doteq 764.54$ C π × 5.2 x^2 × 9 =

The Jumbo Drum holds about 765 cm^3 of popcorn.

The Mega-Box holds 14 cm^3 more popcorn than the Jumbo Drum.

779 − 765 = 14

Key Concepts

- Powers are a useful way to express repeated multiplication. For example,
  $4 \times 4 \times 4 = 4^3$
- A power consists of a base and an exponent, e.g., 4^3.
  - The base is the identical factor.
  - The exponent tells how many factors there are.
- Powers sometimes appear in formulas. When evaluating expressions involving powers, follow the correct order of operations.

Communicate Your Understanding

C1 Identify the base and the exponent of each power.

a) 3^4 **b)** $\left(\frac{1}{2}\right)^4$ **c)** $(-2)^6$ **d)** -2^6 **e)** 1.2^2

C2 **a)** Evaluate each power in question 1.

b) Explain why the answers to parts c) and d) are different.

C3 The first step in evaluating the volume of a cylinder is to substitute the known values for r and h into the formula for the volume of a cylinder: $V = \pi r^2 h$. Describe the next step.

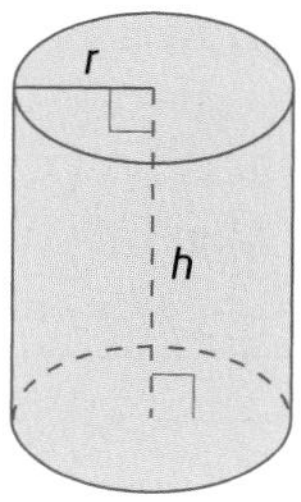

C4 Which expressions would you evaluate using a calculator? Explain.

a) 2^3 **b)** $(-4)^2$ **c)** $(1.25)^4$

d) -8^2 **e)** 7^6 **f)** $(-0.1)^3$

Practise

For help with questions 1 to 5, see Example 1.

1. Which is $6 \times 6 \times 6 \times 6$ written as a power?

A 64 **B** 6^4

C 4^6 **D** 1296

2. Which is 3^5 written in expanded form?

A 3×5 **B** $5 \times 5 \times 5$

C $3 \times 3 \times 3 \times 3 \times 3$ **D** 243

3. Write each expression as a power.

a) $(-5) \times (-5) \times (-5)$

b) $1.05 \times 1.05 \times 1.05 \times 1.05 \times 1.05 \times 1.05$

c) $\left(-\frac{3}{5}\right) \times \left(-\frac{3}{5}\right) \times \left(-\frac{3}{5}\right)$

4. Write each power in expanded form. Then, evaluate the expression.

a) $(-4)^3$ **b)** 0.8^2 **c)** $\left(\frac{3}{4}\right)^4$

5. Evaluate.

a) 9^3 **b)** $(-7)^2$ **c)** -2^4

d) $\left(\frac{5}{6}\right)^3$ **e)** $\left(-\frac{2}{3}\right)^4$ **f)** 1.2^2

g) 1^8 **h)** $(-1)^{55}$ **i)** 0.5^3

6. Evaluate. Remember to use the correct order of operations.

a) $2^5 \div 4^2$ **b)** $5^3 - 5^2$ **c)** $1^3 + 1^6 - 1^2$

d) $(3^2 - 4^2) + (3^4 - 4^3)$ **e)** $\left(\frac{2}{3}\right)^3 \times \left(\frac{3}{4}\right)^2$ **f)** $500(1.08)^5$

7. Substitute the given values into each expression. Then, evaluate the expression. Round your answers to one decimal place where necessary.

a) $6s^2$ $s = 5$

b) πr^2 $r = 2.5$

c) $a^2 + b^2$ $a = 3, b = 4$

d) $\pi r^2 h$ $r = 2.3, h = 5.2$

e) $\frac{4}{3}\pi r^3$ $r = 1.5$

f) $x^2 - 2x - 24$ $x = -6$

Technology Tip

If your calculator does not have a (π) key, use 3.14 as an approximate value for π.

Connect and Apply

8. a) Evaluate each power.

$(-2)^2$ $(-2)^3$ $(-2)^4$ $(-2)^5$

b) Examine the signs of your answers. What pattern do you notice?

c) Explain how you can tell the sign of the answer when a power has a negative base. Create and use examples of your own to illustrate your explanation.

9. Listeria is a type of bacteria that can cause dangerous health problems. It doubles every hour. The initial population of a sample of Listeria is 800.

a) Copy and complete this table, which shows the population of Listeria over time.

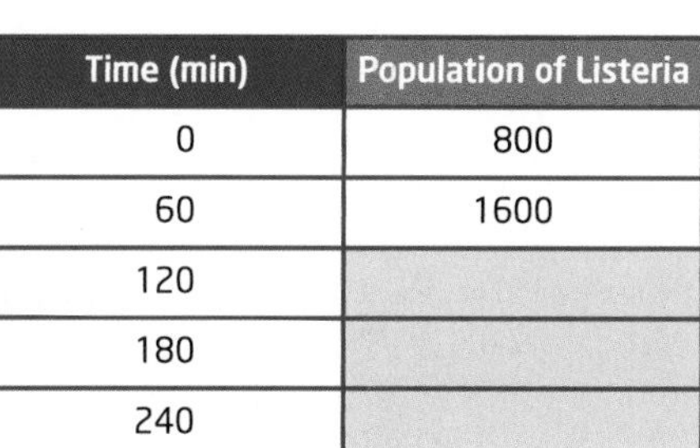

Time (min)	Population of Listeria
0	800
60	1600
120	
180	
240	

b) Construct a graph of population versus time. Use a smooth curve to connect the points. Describe the shape of the graph.

c) What will the population be after
- 1 day?
- 2 days?

d) The symptoms of food poisoning can start as quickly as 4 h after eating contaminated food or as long as 24 h later. Discuss why some types of food poisoning begin quickly and others much more slowly.

Did You Know?

Food and water contaminated with E. coli (escherichia coli) can be very dangerous, but infections are easily treatable with certain antibiotics.

10. E. coli is a type of bacteria that lives in our intestines and is necessary for digestion. It doubles in population every 20 min. The initial population is 10.

a) Copy and complete the table. Refer to your table from question 9 to complete the second column.

Time (min)	Population of Listeria	Population of E. Coli
0		
20		
40		
60		
80		
100		
120		

b) When will the population of E. coli overtake the population of Listeria?

c) What population will the two cultures have when they are equal?

11. The durations (lengths of time) of musical notes are related by powers of $\frac{1}{2}$, beginning with a whole note. Copy and complete the table.

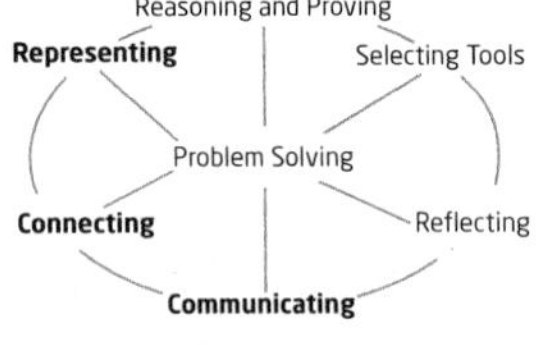

Note	Symbol	Duration (in beats)	Power Form
whole	𝅝	1	
half	𝅗𝅥	$\frac{1}{2}$	$\left(\frac{1}{2}\right)^1$
quarter	♩	$\frac{1}{4}$	$\left(\frac{1}{2}\right)^2$
eighth	♪		
sixteenth	𝅘𝅥𝅯		
thirty-second	𝅘𝅥𝅰		

12. Refer to question 11. Look at the pattern in the last column. Extend this pattern backward to write the power form for a whole note. Does this answer make sense? Use a calculator to evaluate this power. Describe what you observe.

13. Chapter Problem Alysia has selected the letter E to design the logo for her school team, the Eagles.

The design will be used to make different-sized crests for clothing such as jackets, sweaters, and baseball caps. The height of the crest is twice the width. How can Alysia make sure that, when the crest is made larger or smaller, the proportions will not change?

a) Find an expression for the area of the crest in terms of the width.

b) Determine the area of a crest with a width of 8 cm.

c) Determine the height of a crest with an area of 72 cm^2.

14. Uranium is a radioactive material that emits energy when it changes into another substance. Uranium comes in different forms, called isotopes. One isotope, U-235, has a half-life of 23 min, which means that it takes 23 min for a sample to decay to half its original amount.

a) Suppose you started with a 100-mg sample of U-235. Copy and complete the table.

Number of Half-Life Periods	Time (min)	Amount of U-235 Remaining (mg)	Expression
0	0	100	
1	23	50	$100\left(\frac{1}{2}\right)^1$
2	46		$100\left(\frac{1}{2}\right)^2$
3			
4			

b) Construct a graph of the amount, in milligrams, of U-235 remaining versus time, in minutes. Describe the shape of the graph.

c) Approximately how much U-235 will remain after 2 h?

d) How long will it take until only 1 mg of U-235 remains?

e) Use the pattern in the table to write an expression, using powers of $\frac{1}{2}$, for the original amount of U-235. Does this make sense?

Did You Know?

Uranium is used as a fuel source in nuclear fission reactors, which provide 48% of Ontario's electrical power.

CANDU (**Can**ada **D**euterium **U**ranium) reactors are among the safest nuclear power generators in the world.

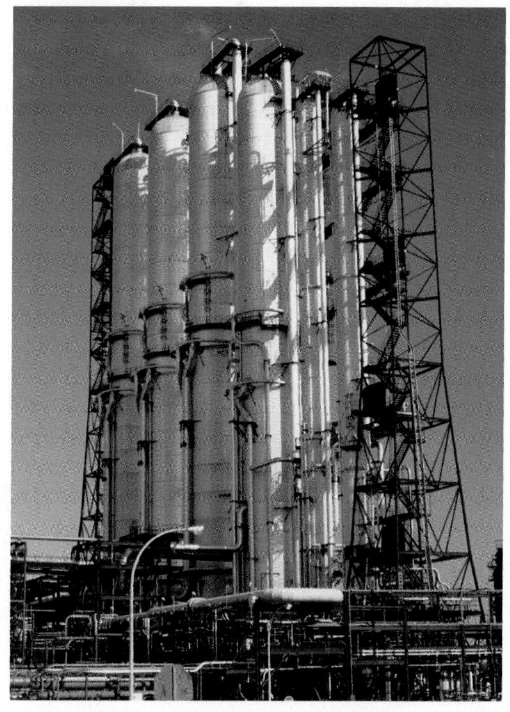

Literacy Connections

Scientific notation is a convenient way to write very large or very small numbers. In scientific notation, the value is expressed as the product of a number between 1 and 10 and a power of 10.

For example,

$56\ 000\ 000\ 000 = 5.6 \times 10^{10}$

$0.000\ 342 = 3.42 \times 10^{-4}$

Scientific calculators express numbers in scientific notation when there are too many digits for the display. Multiply 1234 by 1000. Repeat until the output appears in scientific notation.

You can enter a number in scientific notation into a scientific calculator.

For example, to enter 5.6×10^{10}, press

C 5.6 EE 10 =

To enter 3.42×10^{-4}, press

C 3.42 EE 4 ± =

Not all calculators show scientific notation, or let you enter such numbers, in exactly the same way. Experiment or refer to the user's manual for your calculator.

Extend

15. Uranium-233 is another isotope that is used in nuclear power generation. 1 kg of U-233 can provide about the same amount of electrical power as 3 000 000 kg of coal. This number can be written in **scientific notation** as 3×10^6.

a) Another isotope of uranium, U-238, has a half-life of 4 500 000 000 years. Write this number in scientific notation.

b) What is the half-life of U-238, in seconds? Write your answer in scientific notation.

c) The number 6.022×10^{23} is a very important number in chemistry. It is called "one mole." One mole is the amount of a substance that contains as many atoms, molecules, ions, or other elementary units as the number of atoms in 12 g of carbon-12. Carbon-12 is the basic building block of living things. Write one mole in standard notation.

d) Describe any advantages you see to using scientific notation.

16. Refer to the cartoon at the beginning of the section. Suppose that every new customer returns to Barney's every day for lunch, in addition to recruiting two new customers.

a) How many customers in total will Barney have

- 2 days after Sammy's first visit?
- 5 days after Sammy's first visit?

b) On which day will Barney's reach 500 new customers for lunch?

c) Write an expression that gives the total number of new lunch customers n days after Sammy's first visit.

d) Describe any assumptions you must make in finding your answers.

17. Math Contest Determine the last digit of the number 3^{1234} when written in expanded form. Justify your answer.

18. Math Contest If $3^x = 729$, the value of x is

A 3 **B** 5 **C** 6 **D** 7 **E** 8

19. Math Contest Numbers are called perfect powers if they can be written in the form x^y for positive integer values of x and y. Find all perfect powers less than 1000.

20. Math Contest x^x is always greater than y^y as long as $x > y$. For what whole-number values of x and y is $x^y > y^x$? Justify your answer.

3.3 Discover the Exponent Laws

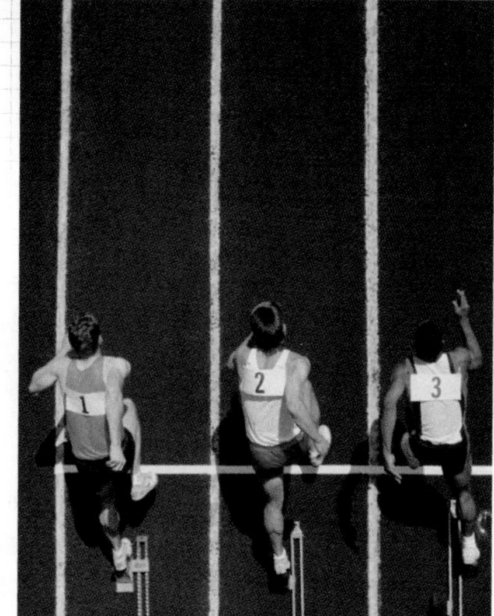

The 100-m dash is one of the most exciting events in track and field. If you ran this race, how many centimetres would you run? How many millimetres is this?

Investigate A

How can you simplify expressions involving products and quotients of powers?

Part A: Patterns Involving Powers of 10

In the metric system, length measures are related by powers of 10. For example, there are 10 mm in 1 cm. This makes it easy to convert one unit of length to another. Note that hectometres and decametres are uncommon units.

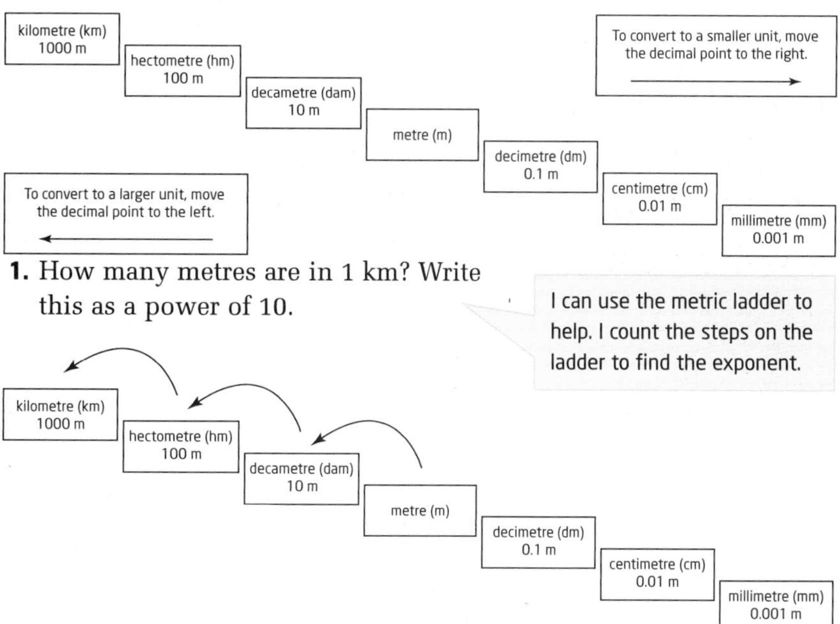

1. How many metres are in 1 km? Write this as a power of 10.

I can use the metric ladder to help. I count the steps on the ladder to find the exponent.

2. Copy and complete the table.

Unit	Number of these in 1 m	Power of 10
decimetre	10	10^1
centimetre	100	
millimetre		

Did You Know?

A Canadian named Donovan Bailey set the men's world record for the 100-m dash at the 1996 Olympics. He ran the race in 9.84 s, and was considered at that time to be the world's fastest human.

3. a) Multiply the number of centimetres in 1 m by the number of metres in 1 km. What does this answer give you?

   b) Write the product in part a) using powers of 10. Write the answer as a power of 10.

4. Repeat step 3 for millimetres instead of centimetres.

5. **Reflect** Look at the exponents in the powers of 10 in your answers to steps 3b) and 4b). Describe how these numbers are related.

Part B: Products of Powers

How can you simplify expressions containing products of powers with the same base?

6. Copy and complete the table, including an example of your own.

Quotient	Expanded Form	Single Power
$3^2 \times 3^4$	$(3 \times 3) \times (3 \times 3 \times 3 \times 3)$	3^6
$4^3 \times 4^3$		
$6^4 \times 6^1$		
$2^4 \times 2^2 \times 2^3$		
$k^3 \times k^5$		
Create your own example		

7. What do you notice about the bases of the powers in each product in the first column?

8. Look at the exponents in the first column for each product. How does the sum of the exponents compare to the exponent in the last column?

9. **Reflect** Explain how you can write a product of powers using a single power. Use your example to illustrate your explanation.

10. Write a rule for finding the product of powers by copying and completing the equation $x^a \times x^b = \blacksquare$.

Part C: Quotients of Powers

How can you simplify expressions containing quotients of powers with the same base?

11. Copy and complete the table, including an example of your own.

I can reduce common factors.

Quotient	Expanded Form	Single Power
$5^5 \div 5^3$	$\frac{5 \times 5 \times \cancel{5} \times \cancel{5} \times \cancel{5}}{\cancel{5} \times \cancel{5} \times \cancel{5}}$	5^2
$7^4 \div 7^1$		
$10^6 \div 10^4$		
$2^7 \div 2^6$		
$p^8 \div p^5$		
Create your own example		

12. What do you notice about the bases of the powers in each quotient in the first column?

13. Look at the exponents in the first column for each quotient. How do they relate to the exponent of the single power in the last column?

14. **Reflect** Explain how you can write a quotient of powers using a single power. Use your example to illustrate your explanation.

15. Write a rule for finding the quotient of powers by copying and completing the equation $x^a \div x^b = \blacksquare$.

The patterns in the activity above illustrate two **exponent laws**. The exponent laws are a set of rules that allow you to simplify expressions involving powers with *the same base*.

Product Rule

When multiplying powers with *the same base*, add the exponents to write the product as a single power:
$x^a \times x^b = x^{a+b}$

Quotient Rule

When dividing powers with *the same base*, subtract the exponents to write the quotient as a single power:
$x^a \div x^b = x^{a-b}$

Example 1 Apply the Product Rule

Write each product as a single power. Then, evaluate the power.

a) $3^2 \times 3^3$

b) $5^2 \times 5 \times 5^2$

c) $(-2)^4 \times (-2)^3$

d) $\left(\frac{1}{2}\right)^3 \times \left(\frac{1}{2}\right)^2$

e) $0.1^4 \times 0.1^2$

Solution

a) $3^2 \times 3^3$
$= 3^{2+3}$
$= 3^5$
$= 243$

The bases are the same, so I can add the exponents.

C 3 y^x 5 =

b) $5^2 \times 5 \times 5^2$
$= 5^2 \times 5^1 \times 5^2$
$= 5^5$
$= 3125$

When no exponent appears, I know that it is 1.

$5^2 \times 5 \times 5^2 = 5^2 \times 5^1 \times 5^2$

Now, I can add the exponents: $2 + 1 + 2 = 5$

c) $(-2)^4 \times (-2)^3$
$= (-2)^{4+3}$
$= (-2)^7$
$= -128$

d) $\left(\frac{1}{2}\right)^3 \times \left(\frac{1}{2}\right)^2$

$= \left(\frac{1}{2}\right)^{3+2}$

$= \left(\frac{1}{2}\right)^5$

$= \left(\frac{1}{2}\right) \times \left(\frac{1}{2}\right) \times \left(\frac{1}{2}\right) \times \left(\frac{1}{2}\right) \times \left(\frac{1}{2}\right)$

$= \frac{1 \times 1 \times 1 \times 1 \times 1}{2 \times 2 \times 2 \times 2 \times 2}$

$= \frac{1}{32}$

e) $0.1^4 \times 0.1^2$
$= 0.1^{4+2}$
$= 0.1^6$
$= 0.000\ 001$

To find the sixth power of 0.1, I need to multiply 0.1 by itself six times. In the product, there will be six digits after the decimal point.

Example 2 Apply the Quotient Rule

Write each product as a single power. Then, evaluate the power.

a) $8^7 \div 8^5$

b) $4^7 \div 4 \div 4^3$

c) $\frac{(-0.5)^6}{(-0.5)^3}$

d) $\frac{\left(\frac{3}{4}\right)^3 \times \left(\frac{3}{4}\right)^2}{\left(\frac{3}{4}\right)^5}$

Solution

a) $8^7 \div 8^5$
$= 8^{7-5}$
$= 8^2$
$= 64$

The bases are the same, so I can subtract the exponents.

b) $4^7 \div 4 \div 4^3$

$= 4^7 \div 4^1 \div 4^3$

$= 4^{7-1} \div 4^3$

$= 4^6 \div 4^3$

$= 4^{6-3}$

$= 4^3$

$= 64$

Divide in order from left to right.

c) $\dfrac{(-0.5)^6}{(-0.5)^3}$

$= (-0.5)^{6-3}$

$= (-0.5)^3$

$= -0.125$

d) $\dfrac{\left(\frac{3}{4}\right)^3 \times \left(\frac{3}{4}\right)^2}{\left(\frac{3}{4}\right)^5}$

$= \dfrac{\left(\frac{3}{4}\right)^{3+2}}{\left(\frac{3}{4}\right)^5}$

$= \dfrac{\left(\frac{3}{4}\right)^5}{\left(\frac{3}{4}\right)^5}$

$= 1$

Apply the product rule first to simplify the numerator.

Anything divided by itself equals 1.

What if I use the quotient rule?

$\dfrac{\left(\frac{3}{4}\right)^5}{\left(\frac{3}{4}\right)^5} = \left(\frac{3}{4}\right)^{5-5}$

$= \left(\frac{3}{4}\right)^0$

I know the answer is 1.
I wonder if an exponent of 0 always gives an answer of 1?

Investigate B

How can you simplify expressions involving powers of powers?

1. Copy and complete the table, including an example of your own.

Power of a Power	Expanded Form	Single Power
$(2^2)^3$	$(2^2) \times (2^2) \times (2^2)$ $= (2 \times 2) \times (2 \times 2) \times (2 \times 2)$	2^6
$(5^3)^4$		
$(10^4)^2$		
Create your own example		

2. Look at the exponents in the first column for each case. How do they relate to the exponent of the single power in the last column?

3. **Reflect** Explain how you can write a power of a power using a single power. Use your example to illustrate your explanation.

4. Write a rule for finding the power of a power by copying and completing the equation $(x^a)^b = \blacksquare$.

The patterns in Investigate B illustrate another exponent law.

Power of a Power Rule

A power of a power can be written as a single power by multiplying the exponents.

$(x^a)^b = x^{a \times b}$

Example 3 Apply the Power of a Power Rule

Write each as a single power. Then, evaluate the power.

a) $(3^2)^4$

b) $[(-2)^3]^4$

c) $\left[\left(\frac{2}{3}\right)^2\right]^2$

d) $(0.2^3)^2$

Solution

a) $(3^2)^4 = 3^{2 \times 4}$
$= 3^8$
$= 6561$

b) $[(-2)^3]^4 = (-2)^{3 \times 4}$
$= (-2)^{12}$
$= 4096$

c) $\left[\left(\frac{2}{3}\right)^2\right]^2 = \left(\frac{2}{3}\right)^{2 \times 2}$
$= \left(\frac{2}{3}\right)^4$
$= \frac{2}{3} \times \frac{2}{3} \times \frac{2}{3} \times \frac{2}{3}$
$= \frac{16}{81}$

d) $(0.2^3)^2 = 0.2^{3 \times 2}$
$= 0.2^6$
$= 0.000\ 064$

Example 4 Simplify Algebraic Expressions

Simplify each algebraic expression by applying the exponent laws.

a) $y^3 \times y^5$

b) $6p^7 \div 3p^3$

c) $a^2b^3 \times a^6b^4$

d) $\dfrac{-2uv^3 \times 8u^2v^2}{(4uv^2)^2}$

Solution

a) $y^3 \times y^5 = y^{3+5}$ **Apply the product rule.**

$= y^8$

b) $6p^7 \div 3p^3 = 2p^{7-3}$ **Divide the numeric factors, 6 ÷ 3 = 2.**

$= 2p^4$

c) $a^2b^3 \times a^6b^1 = a^8b^4$

Exponent laws only apply to powers with the same base.
- First, I add exponents of *a*: $a^{2+6} = a^8$
- Then, I add exponents of *b*: $b^{3+1} = b^4$

d) $\dfrac{-2uv^3 \times 8u^2v^2}{(4uv^2)^2}$ **Simplify numerator and denominator first. The exponent in the denominator applies to all the factors inside the brackets.**

$= \dfrac{(-2) \times 8 \times u \times u^2 \times v^3 \times v^2}{4^2u^2(v^2)^2}$

$= \dfrac{-16 \times u^{1+2} \times v^{3+2}}{16u^2v^{2\times 2}}$

$= \dfrac{-16u^3v^5}{16u^2v^4}$ **Divide.**

$= -u^{3-2}v^{5-4}$

$= -uv$

Key Concepts

- The exponent laws are a way to simplify expressions involving powers with the same base.
- When multiplying powers with the same base, add the exponents: $x^a \times x^b = x^{a+b}$
- When dividing powers with the same base, subtract the exponents: $x^a \div x^b = x^{a-b}$
- When finding the power of a power, multiply the exponents: $(x^a)^b = x^{a \times b}$

Communicate Your Understanding

C1 Identify which exponent law you can apply to simplify each expression. If no exponent law can be used, explain why not.

a) $6^3 \div 6^2$

b) $(m^2)^3$

c) $3^4 \times 4^3$

d) $a^2b \times a^3b^4$

e) $\dfrac{p^3q^2}{pq}$

f) $\dfrac{u^4v^5}{w^2x^3}$

C2 Create an example involving powers where you can

a) add exponents

b) multiply exponents

c) subtract exponents

C3 Look at part d) of Example 4. Suppose that $u = 3$ and $v = -2$:

Original expression	Simplified expression
$\dfrac{-2uv^3 \times 8u^2v^2}{(4uv^2)^2}$	$-uv$

a) Which expression would you rather substitute into to evaluate the expression, and why?

b) What is the value of the expression after substituting the given values?

Practise

For help with questions 1 and 2, see Example 1.

1. Which is $7^3 \times 7^2$ expressed as a single power?

A 7^6 **B** 7^5

C 7^9 **D** 49^6

2. Apply the product rule to write each as a single power. Then, evaluate the expression.

a) $3^4 \times 3^7$ **b)** $2^4 \times 2 \times 2^3$

c) $(-1)^5 \times (-1)^6$ **d)** $\left(\dfrac{2}{5}\right)^3 \times \left(\dfrac{2}{5}\right)^3$

For help with questions 3 and 4, see Example 2.

3. Which is $11^7 \div 11^5$ expressed as a single power?

A 11^{12} **B** $11^{1.4}$ **C** 1^2 **D** 11^2

4. Apply the quotient rule to write each as a single power. Then, evaluate the expression.

a) $12^8 \div 12^2$ **b)** $(-6)^5 \div (-6)^2 \div (-6)^2$

c) $\left(-\frac{3}{4}\right)^4 \div \left(-\frac{3}{4}\right)$ **d)** $\frac{0.1^6 \div 0.1^4}{0.1^2}$

For help with questions 5 and 6, see Example 3.

5. Which is $(5^4)^2$ expressed as a single power?

A 5^8 **B** 5^6

C 25^6 **D** 25^8

6. Apply the power of a power rule to write each as a single power. Then, evaluate the expression.

a) $(4^2)^2$ **b)** $[(-3)^3]^2$

c) $[(-0.1)^4]^2$ **d)** $\left[\left(\frac{3}{2}\right)^3\right]^2$

7. Simplify using the exponent laws. Then, evaluate.

a) $5^2 \times 5^3 \div 5^4$ **b)** $3^7 \div 3^5 \times 3$

c) $\frac{(0.5^3)^4}{0.5^6 \times 0.5^4}$ **d)** $(-2)^4 \times (-2)^5 \div [(-2)^3]^3$

For help with questions 8 and 9, see Example 4.

8. Simplify.

a) $y^4 \times y^2$ **b)** $m^8 \div m^5$ **c)** $k^2 \times k^3 \times k^5$

d) $(c^3)^4$ **e)** $a^2b^2 \times a^3b$ **f)** $(2uv^2)^3$

g) $m^2n \times mn^2$ **h)** $h^2k^3 \div hk$ **i)** $(-a^3b)^2$

Connect and Apply

9. Simplify.

a) $12k^2m^8 \div 4km^5$ **b)** $-8a^5 \times (2a^3)^2$ **c)** $(-x^2)^3 \times (3x^2)^2$

d) $\frac{4d^4w^3 \times 6dw^4}{3d^3w \times 8dw^2}$ **e)** $\frac{3f^4g^3 \times 8fg^4}{(6f^2g^3)^2}$ **f)** $(3a^2b)^2 \div (ab)^2$

g) $\frac{5c^3d \times 4c^2d^2}{(2c^2d)^2}$ **h)** $\frac{(3xy^2)^3 \times (-4x^2y)}{(2x^2y^2)^2}$ **i)** $\frac{30g^2h \times (2gh)^2}{5gh^2 \times 6gh}$

Did You Know?

The notation that we use for powers, with a raised number for the exponent, was invented by Réné Descartes (1596-1650). Descartes used this notation in his text Géométrie, published in 1637. In this famous text, Descartes connected algebra and geometry, starting the branch of mathematics called Cartesian geometry.

10. Consider the expression $\dfrac{5xy^2 \times 2x^2y}{(2xy)^2}$.

a) Substitute $x = 3$ and $y = -1$ into the expression. Then, evaluate the expression.

b) Simplify the original expression using the exponent laws. Then, substitute the given values and evaluate the expression.

c) Describe the advantages and disadvantages of each method.

Literacy Connections

Rectangular prism is the mathematical name for a box.

11. A crawlspace in a space station has the shape of a rectangular prism. It is about 100 cm high, 10 m wide, and 1 km long. What is the volume enclosed by the crawlspace?

12. The probability of tossing heads with a standard coin is $\frac{1}{2}$, because it is one of two possible outcomes. The probability of tossing three heads in a row is $\left(\frac{1}{2}\right)^3$ or $\frac{1}{8}$.

a) What is the probability of tossing
- six heads in a row?
- 12 heads in a row?

b) Write each answer in part a) as a power of a power.

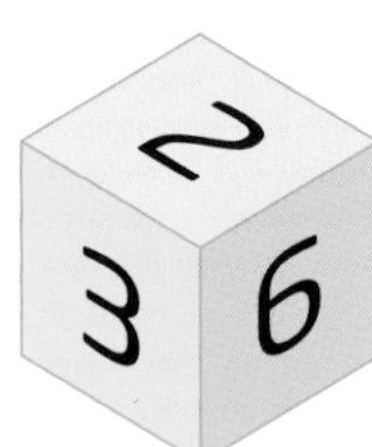

13. a) What is the probability of rolling a 6 with a standard number cube?

b) What is the probability of rolling four 6s in a row?

c) What is the probability of rolling a perfect square with a number cube?

d) What is the probability of rolling eight perfect squares in a row?

e) Write each answer in parts b) and d) as a power of a power.

Achievement Check

14. Consider the expression $\dfrac{-3m^2n \times 4m^3n^2}{(2m^2n)^2 \times 3mn}$.

a) Substitute $m = 4$ and $n = -3$ into the expression and evaluate it.

b) Simplify the original expression using the exponent laws.

c) Substitute $m = 4$ and $n = -3$ into the simplified expression and evaluate it.

d) What did you notice? What are the advantages and disadvantages of the two methods?

e) Josie made two errors in copying the above expression. She wrote $\dfrac{-3m^2n \times 4mn^2}{(2mn)^2 \times 3mn}$, but she still got the correct answer. Explain how this is possible.

Extend

15. You can multiply and divide numbers in scientific notation by applying the exponent laws. For example,

$$(3 \times 10^5) \times (2 \times 10^4)$$
$$= 3 \times 2 \times 10^5 \times 10^4$$
$$= 6 \times 10^9$$

$$(9 \times 10^8) \div (3 \times 10^5)$$
$$= \frac{9 \times 10^8}{3 \times 10^5}$$
$$= \frac{\overset{3}{\cancel{9}} \times 10^8}{\underset{1}{\cancel{3}} \times 10^5}$$
$$= 3 \times 10^3$$

Evaluate each of the following. Express each answer in scientific notation and then in standard notation.

a) $4 \times 10^2 \times 2 \times 10^3$ **b)** $1.5 \times 10^4 \times 6 \times 10^6$

c) $(8 \times 10^7) \div (2 \times 10^5)$ **d)** $(3.9 \times 10^{12}) \div (3 \times 10^8)$

16. a) Predict the screen output of your scientific or graphing calculator when you enter the following calculation: $(3 \times 10^5) \div (2 \times 10^6)$.

b) Is the answer what you predicted? Explain the answer that the calculator has provided.

17. a) Predict the screen output of your scientific or graphing calculator when you enter the following calculation: $(3 \times 10^{18}) \div (6 \times 10^2)$.

b) Is the answer what you predicted? Explain the answer that the calculator has provided.

18. a) Evaluate $(2 \times 10^5)^3$. Express your answer in both scientific and standard notation.

b) Explain how you can evaluate a power of a number expressed in scientific notation. Create an example of your own to help illustrate your explanation.

19. Math Contest Copy and complete the table to make the square a multiplicative magic square (the product of every row, column, and diagonal is equal).

$a^{19}b^{16}$		$a^{15}b^{12}$
a^9b^6	$a^{13}b^{10}$	
	$a^{21}b^{18}$	a^7b^4

20. Math Contest If $x = \frac{1}{9}$, place the following values in order from least to greatest:

$x, x^2, x^3, \sqrt{x}, \frac{1}{x}$

3.4 Communicate With Algebra

You have seen how algebra tiles can be used to model algebraic expressions.

The model below shows that Petra mowed a square lawn of unknown area once a week for 4 weeks.

The algebraic representation is $4x^2$. Look at each part of this expression. What does the 4 represent? What does the x^2 represent?

term

- an expression formed by the product of numbers and/or variables

The expression $4x^2$ is called a **term**. A term consists of two parts:

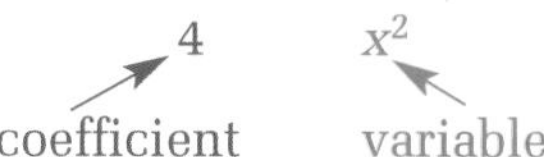

When you represent an algebraic expression using algebra tiles, the variable in the expression tells you which type of tile to use. To represent x^2, use an x^2-tile.

x^2-tile

The number of tiles corresponds to the coefficient. Since the expression is $4x^2$, there are four x^2-tiles.

Example 1 Identify Coefficients and Variables

Identify the coefficient and the variable of each term.

a) Jim earns \$7 per hour at his part-time job. If he works for x hours, his earnings, in dollars, are $7x$.

b) The depth, in metres, of a falling stone in a well after t seconds is $-4.9t^2$.

c) The area of a triangle with base b and height h is $\frac{1}{2}bh$.

d) The area of a square with side length k is k^2.

e) Amir walks 6 blocks to school.

Solution

	Expression	Coefficient	Variable	Comments
a)	$7x$	7	x	
b)	$-4.9t^2$	-4.9	t^2	The negative sign is included with the coefficient.
c)	$\frac{1}{2}bh$	$\frac{1}{2}$	bh	The variable can consist of more than one letter or symbol.
d)	k^2	1	k^2	When the coefficient is not shown, it is 1.
e)	6	6	none	A term with no variable is called a **constant term**, or simply a **constant**.

Literacy Connections

The **coefficient** is also called the **numerical coefficient**. It is a number only.

The **variable** is also called the **literal coefficient**. It consists of one or more variables and their exponents, if they exist.

Exponents on the variables belong to the literal coefficient, because they represent a product of variables: $x^2 = x \times x$.

A **polynomial** can be classified by the number of terms it has.

Type of Polynomial	Number of Terms	Examples
monomial	1	$x, 3y, -4a^2, 5$
binomial	2	$2x - 3, ab + 2a, 0.4x^2 - x$
trinomial	3	$2x^2 + 3x - 1, a + 2b - c$

polynomial

- an algebraic expression consisting of one or more terms connected by addition or subtraction operators

Literacy Connections

The prefixes of the polynomial names have the following meanings:

- *mono* means 1
- *bi* means 2
- *tri* means 3

Example 2 Classify Polynomials by Name

Classify each polynomial by the number of terms it has.

a) $3x^2 + 2x$ **b)** $-2m$ **c)** $4x^2 - 3xy + y^2$ **d)** $a - 2b + c - 3$

Solution

	Polynomial	Number of Terms	Type of Polynomial
a)	$3x^2 + 2x$	2	binomial
b)	$-2m$	1	monomial
c)	$4x^2 - 3xy + y^2$	3	trinomial
d)	$a - 2b + c - 3$	4	four-term polynomial

$3x^2 + 2x$ has two terms, $3x^2$ and $2x$.

I can find the number of terms by looking for the addition and subtraction operators that separate the terms:
$4x^2 - 3xy + y^2$

Two operators separate the three terms in this trinomial.

Example 3 Classify Terms by Degree

degree of a term

- the sum of the exponents on the variables in a term

Find the **degree of each term**.

a) x^2 **b)** $3y^4$ **c)** $0.7u$

d) $-2a^2b$ **e)** $\frac{2}{3}xy$ **f)** -5

Solution

Look at the exponents of the variables. Add them if there is more than one.

Remember, when no exponent appears on a variable, the value of the exponent is 1. For example, $4u = 4u^1$.

If the term has no variable at all, then the degree is 0.

	Term	Sum of Exponents	Degree
a)	x^2	2	2
b)	$3y^4$	4	4
c)	$0.7u^1$	1	1
d)	$-2a^2b^1$	$2 + 1 = 3$	3
e)	$\frac{2}{3}x^1y^1$	$1 + 1 = 2$	2
f)	-5	0	0

Example 4 Classify Polynomials by Degree

degree of a polynomial

- the degree of the highest-degree term

Find the **degree of each polynomial**.

a) $x + 3$

b) $5x^2 - 2x$

c) $3y^3 + 0.2y - 1$

d) $7x^2y^4 + x^6y$

Solution

The degree of the first term is 1. The degree of the second term is 0. The highest degree is 1.

The degree of the first term is 2 + 4. The degree of the second term is 6 + 1.

	Polynomial	Term With Highest Degree	Degree of Term in Column 2	Degree of Polynomial
a)	$x + 3$	x	1	first
b)	$5x^2 - 2x$	$5x^2$	2	second
c)	$3y^3 + 0.2y - 1$	$3y^3$	3	third
d)	$7x^2y^4 + x^6y$	x^6y	7	seventh

Example 5 Use an Algebraic Model to Solve a Problem

Cheryl works part-time as a ski instructor. She earns $125 for the season, plus $20 for each children's lesson and $30 for each adult lesson that she gives.

a) Write an expression that describes Cheryl's total earnings for the season. Identify the variable and the coefficient of each term and explain what they mean.

b) One winter, Cheryl gave eight children's lessons and six adult lessons. What were her total earnings?

Solution

a) Cheryl's total earnings can be described by the polynomial expression $20c + 30a + 125$.

Term	Variable	Meaning of Coefficient
$20c$	c represents the number of children's lessons.	20 represents the earnings per children's lesson.
$30a$	a represents the number of adult lessons.	30 represents the earnings per adult lesson.
125	There is no variable.	Cheryl has fixed earnings of $125 per season.

b) Substitute $c = 8$ and $a = 6$, and evaluate the expression.

$$\begin{aligned} & 20c + 30a + 125 \\ &= 20(8) + 30(6) + 125 \\ &= 160 + 180 + 125 \\ &= 465 \end{aligned}$$

Cheryl's total earnings for this season were $465.

Key Concepts

- Algebraic expressions can be used to communicate mathematical ideas.
- A term is the product of a coefficient and variable part.
- A polynomial can be a single term or a combination of terms using addition or subtraction operators.
- A polynomials can be classified
  - by the number of terms it has
  - by its degree

Communicate Your Understanding

C1 Create two examples of each.

a) monomial
b) binomial
c) trinomial
d) four-term polynomial

C2 Julio says that the term x^2 has a coefficient of 2 and a variable x. Is Julio correct? Explain.

C3 **a)** Are these expressions equivalent? Explain.

$2w + 1t$ $\quad$ $2w + t$

b) Are these expressions equivalent? Explain.

$3x + 1$ $\quad$ $3x$

c) Explain when you must write the number 1, and when you do not need to.

Practise

For help with question 1, see Example 1.

1. Identify the coefficient and the variable part of each term.

a) $2y$
b) $-3x$
c) mn
d) $\frac{1}{2}x^2$
e) $-w^2$
f) $-0.4gh^3$

For help with questions 2 and 3, see Example 2.

2. $7x^2 + 3xy + 4y^2$ is a

A monomial
B binomial
C trinomial
D term

3. Classify each polynomial by the number of terms.

a) $-2x$
b) $6y^2 + 2y - 1$
c) $a - \frac{1}{2}b$
d) $3u^2 - uv + 2v^2$
e) $3k^2 - \frac{1}{2}k$
f) $m + 0.2n - 0.3 + mn$

For help with questions 4 and 5, see Example 3.

4. The degree of $4u - 5u^2 + 9$ is

A 1
B 2
C 3
D 0

5. State the degree of each term.

a) $5x^2$
b) $-6y$
c) -3
d) u^2v^4
e) $\frac{1}{3}x^2y^3$
f) $0.2a^2b$

For help with question 6, see Example 4.

6. State the degree of each polynomial.

a) $3x - 4$ **b)** $y^2 + 3y - 1$ **c)** $m - 2m^3$

d) $a^3b^2 - 8a^2b^5$ **e)** $2x^2y^4 - \frac{2}{5}xy^3$

For help with questions 7 and 8, see Example 4.

7. In a TV trivia show, a contestant receives 500 points for a correct answer and loses 200 points for an incorrect answer. Let c represent the number of correct answers and i represent the number of incorrect answers. Which expression describes a contestant's total points?

A $500c + 200i$ **B** $500c - 200i$

C $500i + 200c$ **D** $500i - 200c$

8. A hockey team earns 2 points for a win and 1 point for a tie. Let w represent the number of wins and t represent the number of ties.

a) Which expression can be used to describe the total points?

A $2w + 1$ **B** $w + t$ **C** $2w + 1t$ **D** $2w + t$

b) Is there more than one correct answer? Justify your answer.

9. Substitute the given values and evaluate each expression.

a) $3x + 5$ $x = 2$

b) $4y + 4$ $y = -2$

c) $a^2 + 2b - 7$ $a = 4, b = 1$

d) $2m^2 - 3n + 8$ $m = -2, n = 5$

Connect and Apply

10. The students at Prince Albert Public School sell magazine subscriptions to raise money. The school receives 37% of the money paid for the subscriptions.

a) Choose a variable to represent the money paid for the subscriptions.

b) Using your variable from part a), write an expression for the amount of money the school will receive.

c) Tyler sold one magazine subscription to his aunt for \$25.99. Calculate the amount the school receives on this sale.

d) The sum of all the subscription orders was \$4257.49. Use your formula to calculate how much the school will receive for this fundraiser.

11. Meredith has a summer job at a fitness club. She earns a $5 bonus for each student membership and a $7 bonus for each adult membership she sells.

a) Write a polynomial expression that describes Meredith's total bonus.

b) Identify the variable and the coefficient of each term and explain what they mean.

c) How much will Meredith's bonus be if she sells 12 student memberships and 10 adult memberships?

12. An arena charges $25 for gold seats, $18 for red seats, and $15 for blue seats.

a) Write an expression that describes the total earnings from seat sales.

b) Identify the variable and the coefficient of each term and explain what they mean.

c) How much will the arena earn if it sells 100 gold seats, 200 blue seats, and 250 red seats?

13. On a multiple-choice test, you earn 2 points for each correct answer and lose 1 point for each incorrect answer.

a) Write an expression for a student's total score.

b) Maria answered 15 questions correctly and 3 incorrectly. Find Maria's total score.

14. **a)** Describe a situation that can be modelled by an algebraic expression.

b) Select variables and write the expression.

c) Illustrate your expression using algebra tiles or a diagram.

15. Write a response to this e-mail from a classmate.

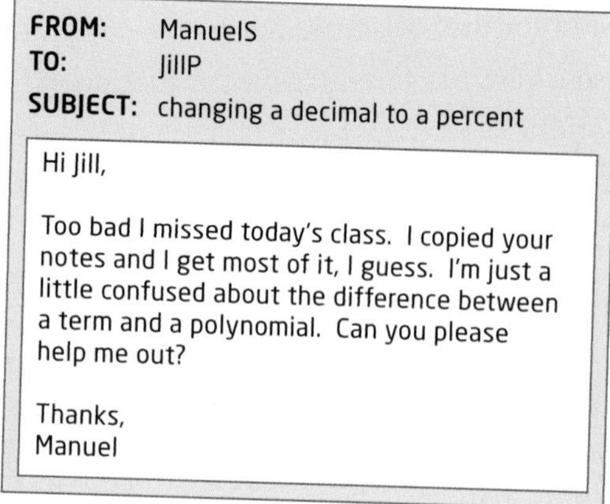
FROM: ManuelS
TO: JillP
SUBJECT: changing a decimal to a percent

Hi Jill,

Too bad I missed today's class. I copied your notes and I get most of it, I guess. I'm just a little confused about the difference between a term and a polynomial. Can you please help me out?

Thanks,
Manuel

16. Chapter Problem Alysia is designing a logo for her school team, the Eagles. The design will be used to make different-sized crests for clothing such as jackets, sweaters, and baseball caps. How can Alysia make sure that, when the crest is made larger or smaller, the shape will not change?

The height will always be double the width.

a) If w represents the width, what expression represents the height?

b) How high will a crest that is 5 cm wide be?

c) How wide will a crest that is 25 cm high be?

Achievement Check

17. In a soccer league, teams receive 3 points for a win, 2 points for a loss, and 1 point for a tie.

a) Write an algebraic expression to represent a team's total points.

b) What variables did you choose? Identify what each variable represents.

c) The Falcons' record for the season was 5 wins, 2 losses, and 3 ties. Use your expression to find the Falcons' total points.

d) The 10-game season ended with the Falcons tied for second place with the same number of points as the Eagles. The Eagles had a different record than the Falcons. How is this possible?

Extend

18. Alberto is training for a triathlon, where athletes swim, cycle, and run. During his training program, he has found that he can swim at 1.2 km/h, cycle at 25 km/h, and run at 10 km/h. To estimate his time for an upcoming race, Alberto rearranges the formula distance = speed × time to find that: time = $\frac{\text{distance}}{\text{speed}}$.

a) Choose a variable to represent the distance travelled for each part of the race. For example, choose s for the swim.

b) Copy and complete the table. The first row is done for you.

Part of the Race	Speed (km/h)	Distance (km)	Time (h)
swim	1.2	s	$\frac{s}{1.2}$
cycle			
run			

c) Write a trinomial to model Alberto's total time.

d) A triathlon is advertised in Kingston. Participants have to swim 1.5 km, cycle 40 km, and run 10 km. Using your expression from part c), calculate how long it will take Alberto to finish the race.

e) Is your answer a reasonable estimate of Alberto's triathlon time? Explain.

I can use the formula $\text{time} = \frac{\text{distance}}{\text{speed}}$ to calculate Ashleigh's travel time.

19. Ashleigh can walk 2 m/s and swim 1 m/s. What is the quickest way for Ashleigh to get from one corner of her pool to the opposite corner?

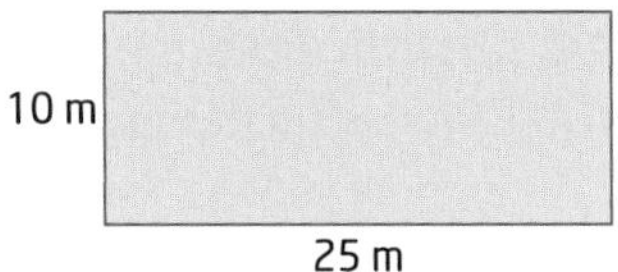

a) Predict whether it is faster for Ashleigh to walk or swim.

b) Ashleigh can walk at a speed of 2 m/s. The time, in seconds, for Ashleigh to walk is $\frac{w}{2}$, where w is the distance, in metres, she walks. Use this relationship to find the travel time if Ashleigh walks around the pool.

Path 1: Walk the entire distance.

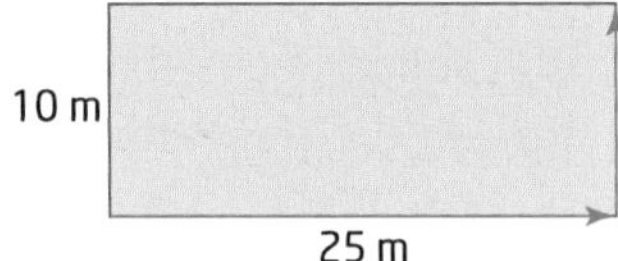

c) Write a similar expression to represent the time taken for Ashleigh to swim a distance s. Her swimming speed is 1 m/s. Use this relationship to find the travel time if Ashleigh swims straight across.

Path 2: Swim the entire distance.

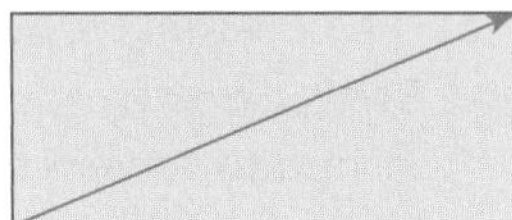

d) Which route is faster, and by how much?

20. Refer to question 19.

a) Do you think it will be faster for Ashleigh to walk half the length and then swim? Explain your reasoning.

Path 3: Walk half the length, then swim.

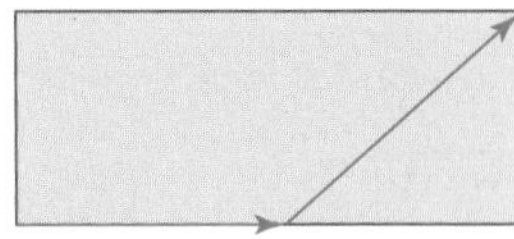

b) Find the travel time for this path. Compare this with your answers to question 19.

c) Do you think this is the fastest possible path? Find the fastest path and the minimum time required to cross the pool, corner to opposite corner. Describe how you solved this.

Did You Know?

Sixteen year-old Marilyn Bell of Toronto was the first person to swim across Lake Ontario. In September 1954 Marilyn swam from Youngstown, NY, to the CNE grounds in Toronto. The 51.5 km distance took her 21 h.

21. Some algebraic expressions involve more than one variable. You can model these using an expanded set of algebra tiles.

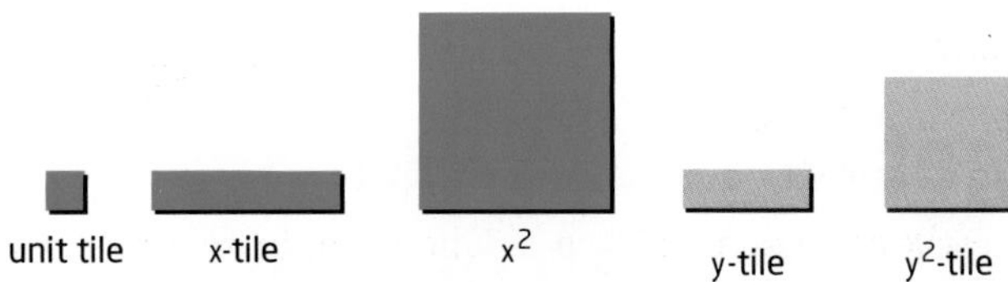

Fly By Night Aero Insurance company charges \$500 for liability, plus 10% of the value of the plane, plus \$300 per seat. Let v represent the value of the plane and s represent the number of seats. The cost of the insurance is modelled by $C = 500 + 0.1v + 300s$. A four-seat Piper Cherokee valued at \$30 000 would cost $500 + 0.1(30\ 000) + 300(4)$ or \$4700 per year to insure.

a) Explain how you would use tiles to represent $0.1v$.

b) Explain how you would use tiles to represent $300s$.

c) Build an algebraic model to describe the cost for airplane insurance for the Piper Cherokee, using algebra tiles, diagrams, or virtual algebra tiles.

d) Find the cost of insurance for a 50-seat plane, valued at \$500 000.

22. Math Contest If $3m + 5 = 23$ and $2n - 7 = 21$, the value of $3m + 2n$ is

A 20 **B** 44 **C** 46 **D** 54 **E** 56

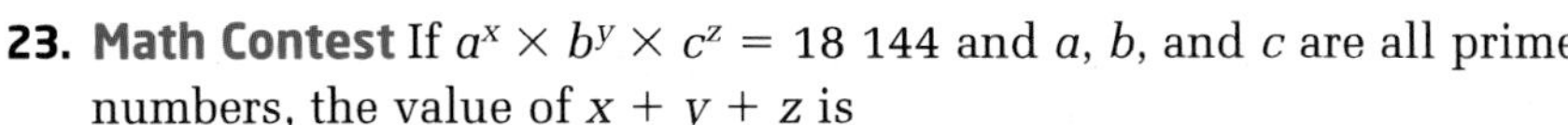

23. Math Contest If $a^x \times b^y \times c^z = 18\ 144$ and a, b, and c are all prime numbers, the value of $x + y + z$ is

A 7 **B** 10 **C** 11 **D** 12 **E** 20

24. Math Contest Find value(s) of m for which $\left(\frac{1}{2}\right)^{2m} = \left(\frac{1}{4}\right)^{m}$. Is there more than one possible value of m? Explain.

Virtual Algebra Tiles With *The Geometer's Sketchpad®*

You can create and manipulate virtual algebra tiles using computer software such as *The Geometer's Sketchpad®*. You can build algebraic models, plus you can change the length of the variable tiles.

Investigate

Tools

- computer equipped with *The Geometer's Sketchpad®*
- **Algebra Tiles.gsp**

How can you build algebraic models using virtual algebra tiles?

1. a) Start *The Geometer's Sketchpad®* and open the sketch **Algebra Tiles.gsp**.
   b) Read the instructions and click on the **Algebra Tiles page** button.
2. Explore the pre-made tiles.
   a) Click on the **Show example tiles** button.

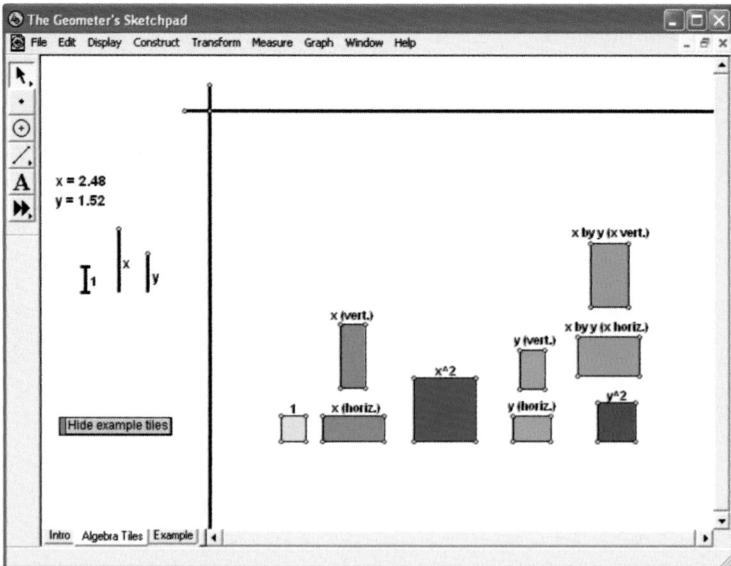

   b) Click and drag the top of the x-slider. Which tiles are affected by the x-slider?
   c) Repeat part b) for the y-slider.
   d) The unit tile seems to have a slider next to the x-slider. Try to change its length, and describe what happens. Why can you not change the dimensions of the unit tile?

For the rest of this activity, you will work only with

- unit tiles

- x-tiles (horizontal and vertical)

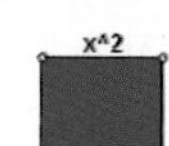

- x^2-tiles

3. Clear the workspace and bring out only the algebra tiles you need:
- Click on **Hide example tiles**.
- Click and hold the **Custom Tool** icon at the left side of the screen.

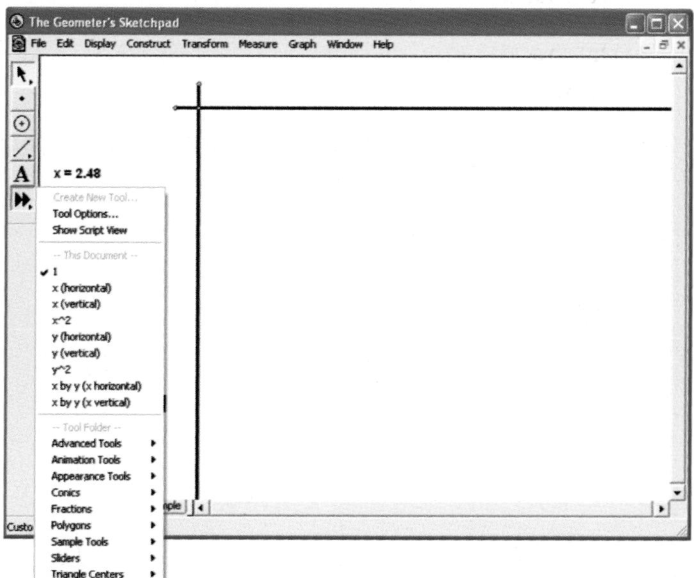

- Select **1** (the unit tile) and place a unit tile somewhere on the workspace.
- Click and hold the **Custom Tool** again and select **x (horizontal)** and place a tile on the workspace.
- Repeat for the **x (vertical)** and **x^2** (x^2) tiles.

Technology Tip

If you do not see the list of tools when you click on the **Custom Tool** icon, try holding the left mouse button for a couple of seconds, and they will appear.

Technology Tip

You can add more tiles by using the **Custom Tool** or by using the **Copy** and **Paste** commands in the **Edit** menu. To copy an entire tile, use the **Selection Arrow Tool** to click and drag a dashed box around the tile you want to copy. Then, paste it and move it wherever you like.

Once you have all four tiles, choose the **Selection Arrow Tool** and click somewhere in the white space to deselect the last object you created.

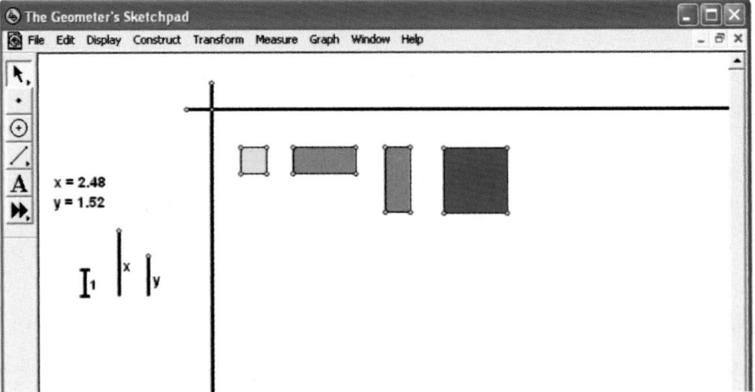

4. Explore the relationships between the tiles. Arrange the tiles as shown, by clicking and dragging them one at a time.

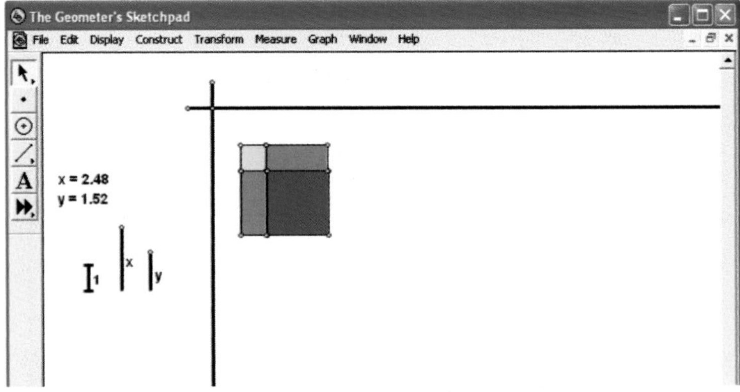

a) Move the x-slider and describe what happens to the length and width of each tile.

Tile	Length (changes/does not change)	Width (changes/does not change)
unit		
x (horizontal)		
x (vertical)		
x^2		

b) Describe how the length of the x-tile is related to the length and width of the x^2-tile. Why is this so?

c) Describe how the width of the x-tile is related to the length and width of the unit tile. Why is this so?

5. a) Why is it that you can change the length of an x-tile, but not a unit tile?

b) What advantage does this give to virtual algebra tiles over physical algebra tiles?

6. Build each algebraic model using virtual algebra tiles.

a) $3x + 2$ **b)** $x^2 + 2x + 5$

7. Build each algebraic model and try to put the parts together to form a rectangle. You may have to change horizontal x-tiles to vertical ones, or vice versa. Once you have built the rectangle, write expressions for its length and width. The first one is shown as an example.

a) $x^2 + 5x + 6$

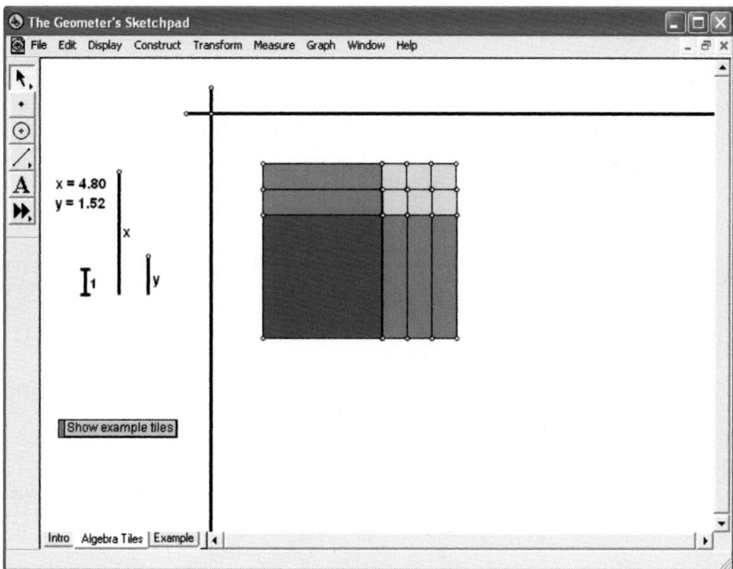

The length is $x + 3$ and the width is $x + 2$.

Now try these.

b) $x^2 + 2x + 1$

c) $x^2 + 7x + 12$

8. a) Create your own example like the ones in step 7. Not all expressions will work. Make sure that you can create a rectangle to model your expression.

b) Trade expressions with a classmate and try to build each other's algebraic models.

9. Describe at least one advantage and one disadvantage of using virtual algebra tiles to build algebraic models.

3.5 Collect Like Terms

Recreational vehicles can be a lot of fun. However, they sometimes require costly repairs. Suppose you are faced with a repair bill involving parts and labour charges. How can you use algebra to simplify the information?

Example 1 Build and Simplify an Algebra Tile Model

Crystal bought a used personal watercraft with her summer earnings. Unfortunately, it needs some repairs before she can use it.

Item	Cost for Parts($)	Labour (h)
Alternator	200	4
Fuel Pump	100	3

a) Model each repair using algebra tiles and write an expression to describe it.

b) Find a simplified expression for both repairs.

c) Calculate the total repair cost if the mechanic charges \$50/h for labour.

Solution

a) Let each unit tile represent \$100 and each x-tile represent an hour's labour charge.

Alternator

$200 + 4x$ expresses the cost to repair the alternator.

Fuel Pump

$100 + 3x$ expresses the cost to repair the fuel pump.

b) Find a **simplified** expression for both repairs by adding these expressions.

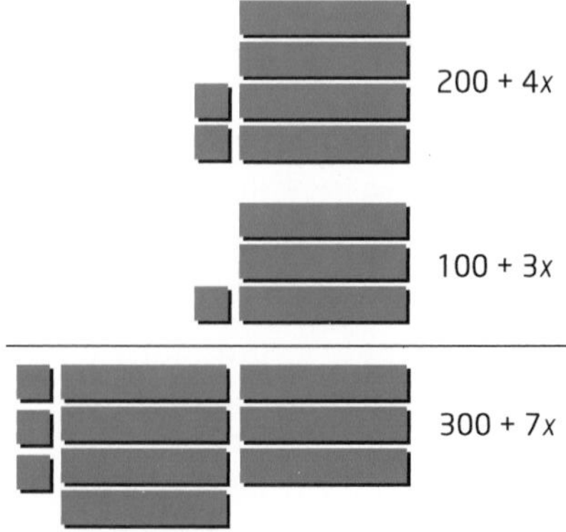

Making Connections

You will study relations such as this in **5.2 Partial Variation**.

Literacy Connections

To **simplify** an expression is to find an equivalent, simpler, and shorter expression.

Original expression:
$200 + 4x + 100 + 3x$

Simplified expression:
$300 + 7x$

c) The mechanic charges \$50/h. Substitute 50 into the expression and evaluate it.

$$\begin{aligned} & 300 + 7x \\ &= 300 + 7(50) \\ &= 300 + 350 \\ &= 650 \end{aligned}$$

The total repair cost for Crystal's personal watercraft is \$650.

In Example 1 you added fixed costs—the cost of the parts:
$200 + 100 = 300$

You also added variable costs—the cost of the labour:
$4x + 3x = 7x$

When you add all the fixed costs, or add all the variable costs, you are adding **like terms**.

like terms

- terms that have identical variables

Example 2 Identify Like and Unlike Terms

Identify the like terms in each group.

a) $2x$, 2, $5x$, $3xy$, $3x$

b) $4a^2$, $2a$, $-a^2$, a^3, a^2b

c) $3u^2$, $-4uv$, 6, $2u^2$, $\frac{1}{2}v$, -5

Solution

a) Like terms have identical variable parts.

$2x$, 2, $5x$, $3xy$, $3x$

$2x$, $5x$, and $3x$ all have x as the variable. They are like terms.

$2x$ and 2 are unlike terms because the second term has no variable.

$2x$ and $3xy$ are unlike terms because the second term includes a y.

b) $4a^2$, $2a$, $-a^2$, a^3, a^2b

$4a^2$ and $-a^2$ have identical variables: a^2. They are like terms. The other terms all have different variables.

The exponents on all variables must be identical for terms to be like.

c) $3u^2$, $-4uv$, 6, $2u^2$, $\frac{1}{2}v$, -5

$3u^2$ and $2u^2$ are like terms.
6 and -5 are also like terms.

$\frac{1}{2}v$ and $-4uv$ are unlike any of the other terms.

To simplify a polynomial expression, add or subtract like terms.

Example 3 Add Like Terms

Add.

a) $4x + 3x$

b) $4x + 3 + 2x + 5$

Solution

a) $4x + 3x$
$= 7x$

b) $4x + 3 + 2x + 5$
$= 4x + 2x + 3 + 5$
$= 6x + 8$
$= 6x + 8$

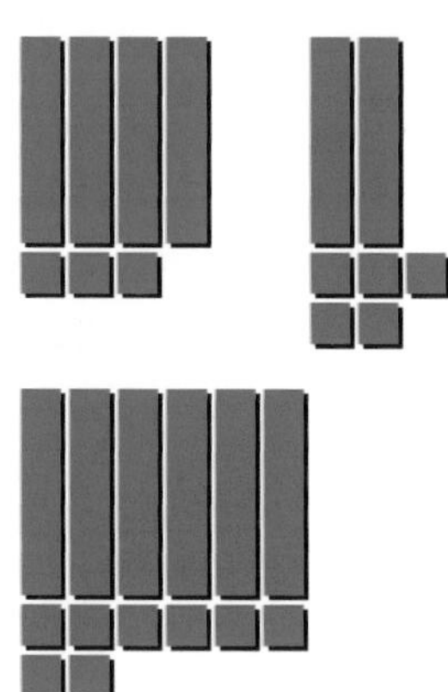

Example 4 Subtract Like Terms

Subtract.

a) $8x - 3x$

b) $2x - 5x$

Solution

a) $8x - 3x$

Method 1: Take Away

Start with 8 x-tiles. Remove 3 of them.

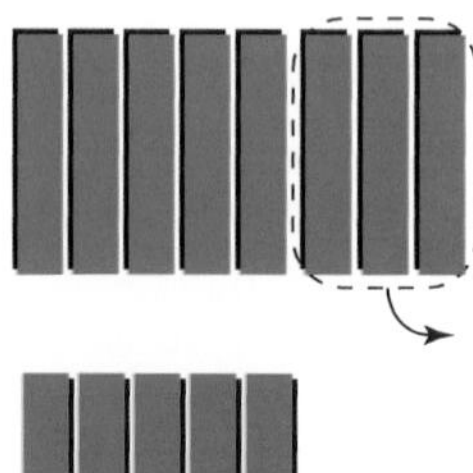

$8x - 3x$
$= 5x$

Method 2: Add the Opposite

Start with 8 x-tiles. Add 3 negative x-tiles.

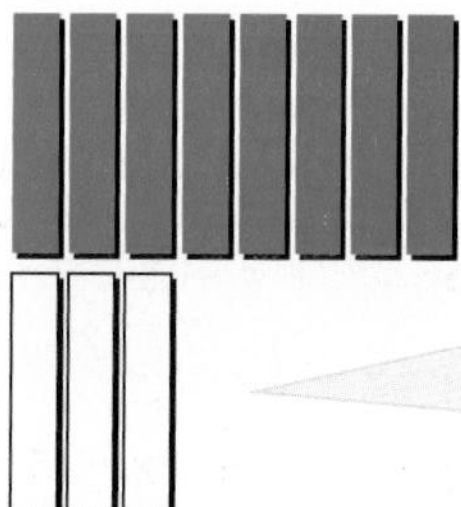

I use a different colour of tile to represent negative values.

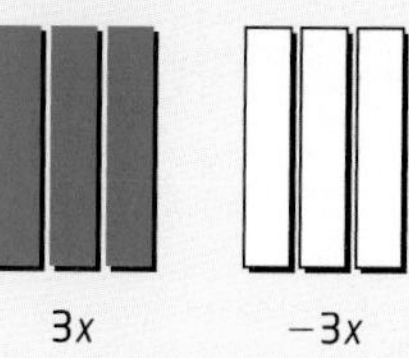

Remove 3 zero pairs.

$3x$ and $-3x$ are opposites. Their sum is 0, leaving $5x$ as the result.

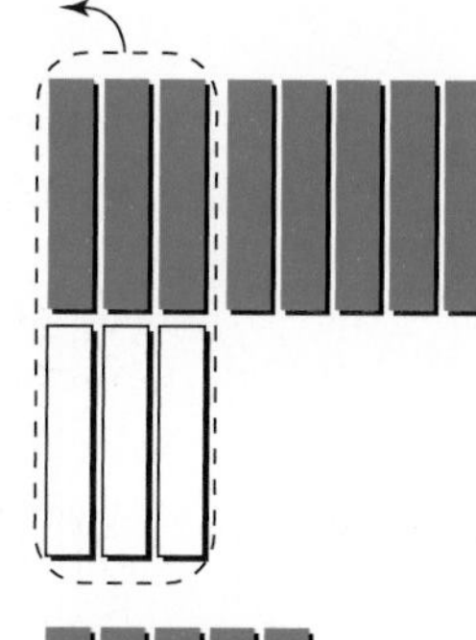

$8x - 3x$
$= 5x$

b) Start with $2x$-tiles.

You cannot remove 5 x-tiles, because there are only 2 of them. You must add 5 $-x$-tiles.

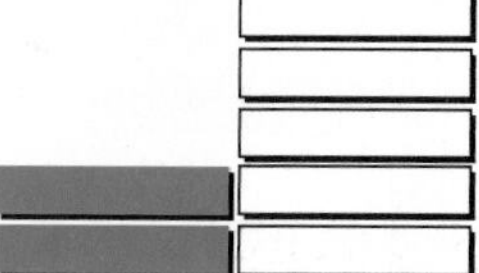

Remove 2 zero pairs.

$2x - 5x$
$= -3x$

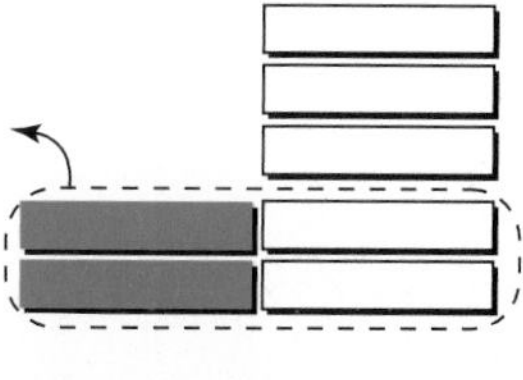

Adding and subtracting to simplify algebraic expressions is called **collecting like terms.**

Example 5 Collect Like Terms With Concrete Materials

Use algebra tiles to simplify each expression.

a) $5k - 3k - 6 + 3$

b) $3c^2 + c - 2 - 5c - 4c^2$

Solution

a) $5k - 3k - 6 + 3$

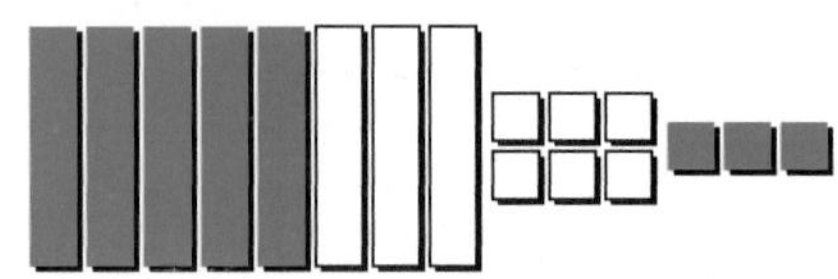

$= 5k - 3k - 6 + 3$

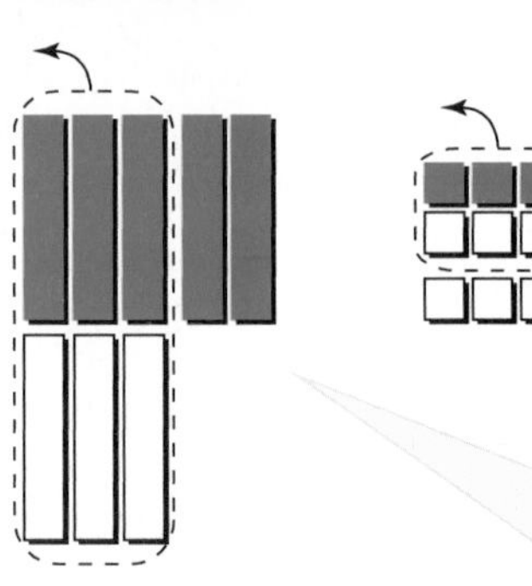

I can rearrange the tiles to group zero pairs, then remove them.

$= 2k - 3$

b) $3c^2 + c - 2 - 5c - 4c^2$

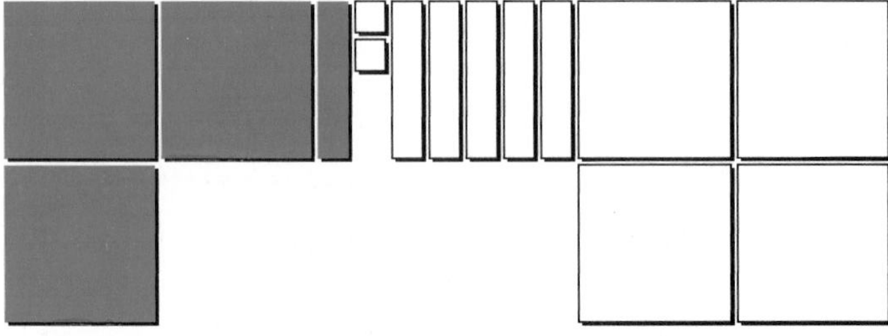

Rearrange the tiles to group like terms.

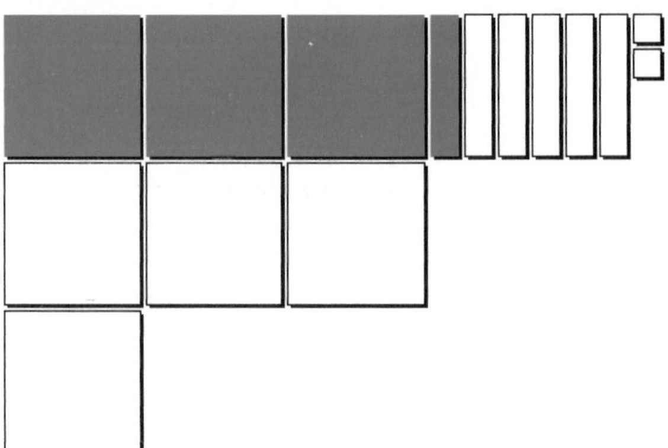

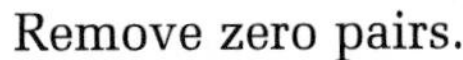

Remove zero pairs.

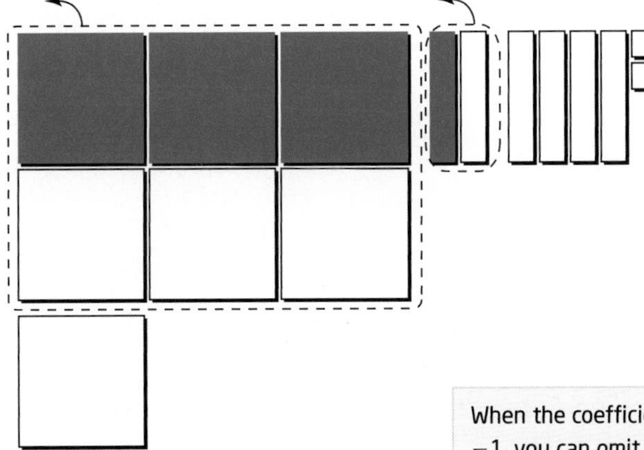

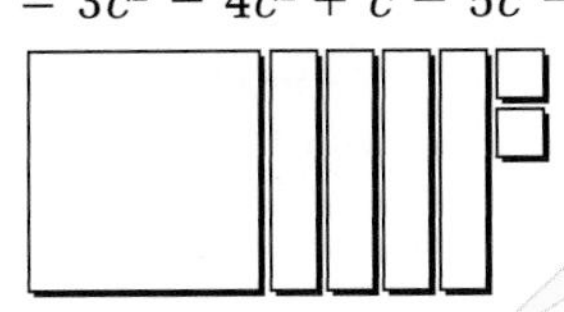

$= 3c^2 - 4c^2 + c - 5c - 2$

When the coefficient is 1 or −1, you can omit the 1. But you must keep the minus sign.

$3c^2 - 4c^2 = -1c^2$
$= -c^2$

Algebraic expressions are usually written in order of degree, with the greatest-degree term first and the least-degree term last.

$= -c^2 - 4c - 2$

Example 6: Collect Like Terms Without Concrete Materials

Simplify.

a) $6x + 4 + 8x + 3$

b) $2b - b + 7 - 8$

c) $3r^2 + 2 - 6r + 9r - 3r^2$

d) $0.5m - 4.5n + 0.7m + 4.5n - 1.5$

Solution

When collecting like terms,
- group or identify like terms
- add or subtract like terms only
- apply integer rules to the coefficients of like terms
- do not change the variable parts

a) $6x + 4 + 8x + 3$

Identify like terms first. $6x$ and $8x$ are like terms. 4 and 3 are also like terms.

Method 1: Align Like Terms Vertically

$$\begin{array}{r} 6x + 4 \\ \underline{+\ 8x + 3} \\ 14x + 7 \end{array}$$

Method 2: Collect Like Terms

$6x + 4 + 8x + 3$
$= 6x + 8x + 4 + 3$ **Once you have had some practice, you may be able to skip this step.**
$= 14x + 7$

Literacy Connections

When reading coefficients, always include the sign on the left. For example, the coefficient of $-b$ is -1. Then, add the coefficients of like terms using integer rules. It is important that when you collect terms, you include the sign to the left of them:

$2b - b \underline{+ 7} \underline{- 8}$

b) $2b - b + 7 - 8$

$2b$ and $-b$ are like terms. 7 and -8 are also like terms.

Method 1: Align Like Terms Vertically

$$\begin{array}{r} 2b + 7 \\ \underline{+ -b - 8} \\ b - 1 \end{array}$$

Apply integer rules to the coefficients of like terms:
$2 + (-1) = 1$
$7 + (-8) = -1$

Method 2: Collect Like Terms

$$\begin{aligned} & 2b - b + 7 - 8 \\ &= b - 1 \end{aligned}$$

c)
$$\begin{aligned} & 3r^2 + 2 - 6r + 9r - 3r^2 \\ &= 3r^2 - 3r^2 - 6r + 9r + 2 \\ &= 3r + 2 \end{aligned}$$

d)
$$\begin{aligned} & 0.5m - 4.5n + 0.7m + 4.5n - 1.5 \\ &= 0.5m + 0.7m - 4.5n + 4.5n - 1.5 \\ &= 1.2m - 1.5 \end{aligned}$$

$-4.5n$ and $4.5n$ are opposites. They add to 0.

Key Concepts

- Like terms have identical variables.
- You can simplify a polynomial by adding or subtracting like terms. This is called collecting like terms.
- It is helpful to think of only adding terms. When a subtraction sign appears, think of adding a negative term.

Communicate Your Understanding

C1 **a)** Explain what is meant by *like terms* and *unlike terms*.

b) Provide two examples of each.

C2 Explain why the two sides are not equal.

a) $2x + x + 3x \neq 5x$

b) $y + y + y \neq y^3$

c) $-5m + 2m \neq 3m$

d) $-2x - 2x \neq 0$

e) $x + x \neq x^2$

f) $3ab - 2b \neq a$

Practise

For help with questions 1 to 4, see Example 2.

1. Which polynomial contains no like terms?

A $2x + 5 - 3x + 2xy$ **B** $3x^2 + 3xy + 3$

C $4 - 9x + 9y + 3$ **D** $-4a^3 + 5b - 2a^2 + 7b$

2. Classify each pair of terms as either like or unlike.

a) $2x$ and $-5x$ **b)** $3y$ and $3z$ **c)** $-x^2$ and $\frac{1}{2}x^2$

d) $4a^2$ and $3a^3$ **e)** $2ab$ and $3a^2$ **f)** $5x^2y$ and $-2xy^2$

g) $3uv$ and $2vu$ **h)** $9p^2q^3$ and $-4q^3p^2$

3. Copy the two columns of terms into your notebook. Connect each term in the first column with the like term in the second column.

$3x^2$	$-4xy$
$-x$	y^2
xy	$\frac{1}{2}y$
$2y^2$	$7x$
$5x^2y$	$4x^2$
$-7y$	$3x^2y$

4. Write two like terms for each.

a) $5m$ **b)** $-x$ **c)** $2y^2$ **d)** $3ab$

For help with question 5, see Example 3.

5. Simplify where possible. If it is not possible to simplify, explain why.

a) $3x + 6x$ **b)** $2m + 5n$

c) $5h + 8h + 2h$ **d)** $7u + 4u + u$

For help with question 6, see Example 4.

6. Simplify. If it is not possible to simplify, explain why.

a) $4k - 2k$ **b)** $8n - n$

c) $3z - 7z$ **d)** $p - 6$

For help with questions 7 to 9, see Example 5.

7. Simplify by collecting like terms.

a) $3x + 5 + 2x + 1$ **b)** $3 + 7y + 8 + y$

c) $2k + 3m + 4m + 6k$ **d)** $7u + v + v + u$

e) $8n + 5 - 3n - 2$ **f)** $4p + 7q - 3q - p$

Making Connections

Algebraic expressions are used in work with spreadsheets. You use formulas in cells to tell the computer to make specified calculations. For example, the formula in cell D2 might be 2 × B2 +2 × C2. You will have the opportunity to apply this connection in Chapter 9 Optimizing Measurement.

8. Simplify.

a) $3x - 8 - 4x + 3$

b) $y - 9 - 7 - 6y$

c) $2x^2 + 7x + 4x^2 + x$

d) $7m + 6m^2 - 2m + m^2$

e) $3k - 5 + 8 - k + 1 - 4k$

f) $-3u + 2 - u^2 - 5 + 3u + 2u^2 - 3$

9. Simplify.

a) $2a^2 - 3ab - 6 + 4b^2 + 7 + 5ab - 3b - 2a^2$

b) $3mn + 6m^2 - n^2 + 3 - m^2 - 3mn + 2n^2 - 4$

Connect and Apply

10. Claudette, Johanna, and Ming all have summer jobs at a clothing store. They earn \$7/h, plus a bonus every week that depends on how well they do that week. The table shows how many hours they work and their bonuses one week this summer.

Employee	Number of Hours	Bonus
Claudette	20	\$100
Johanna	25	\$125
Ming	27	\$110

a) Using t to represent the time, in hours, write a binomial to represent the amount each student makes that week.

b) Substitute the time, in hours, into each expression, and find how much each student makes.

c) The three students decide to put their earnings for that week together to go for an end-of-summer trip. Write a binomial to represent the total amount they earn that week.

d) Substitute the total number of hours and find the total amount the students make that week. Compare your answer with what you found in part b).

11. Yannick simplified the following expression:

$$3x + 4 + 6x$$
$$= 13x$$

a) Describe the error Yannick made.

b) How can you convince Yannick that these two expressions are not equal?

c) Simplify the expression properly. How can you convince Yannick that your answer is correct?

12. The length of a rectangular field is three times its width.

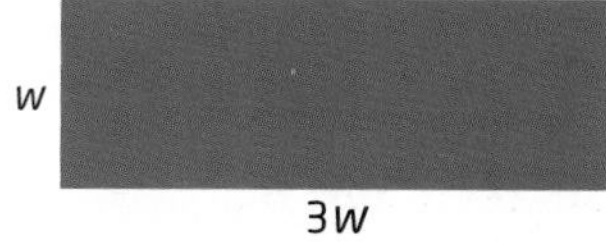

a) Write an expression for the perimeter of the field.

b) Find the perimeter if the field is 300 m wide.

c) Find the length and width of the field if the perimeter is 1600 m.

13. Use algebra tiles, virtual algebra tiles, or a diagram to model and simplify each expression.

a) $3x + 1 + 5x + 4$

b) $4y + 3 - y - 2$

c) $x + 5y + 8 - x - 2y + 2$

14. Chapter Problem The white bars from the right of the crest into the centre run halfway across the width.

a) Find an expression for the
- perimeter
- total length of white trim needed

b) What length of trim will be needed for a crest that is 10 cm wide?

Extend

15. a) An equilateral triangle has an unknown side length, x. Write a simplified expression for its perimeter.

b) A right isosceles triangle has two sides equal to x. Which triangle, the equilateral triangle in part a) or the right isosceles triangle, has the greater perimeter? Use algebraic reasoning to justify your answer.

16. Which triangle in question 15 has the greater area? Use algebraic reasoning to justify your answer.

17. Math Contest What is the value of the 100th term in the sequence $3x + 2y, 5x^2 + 5y^3, 7x^3 + 8y^5, \ldots$?

A $199x^{100} + 296y^{197}$

B $200x^{100} + 300y^{199}$

C $200x^{100} + 300y^{197}$

D $201x^{100} + 299y^{199}$

E $203x^{100} + 299y^{199}$

18. Math Contest The last digit of the number 2^{2020} when written in expanded form is

A 2 **B** 4 **C** 6

D 8 **E** 0

3.6 Add and Subtract Polynomials

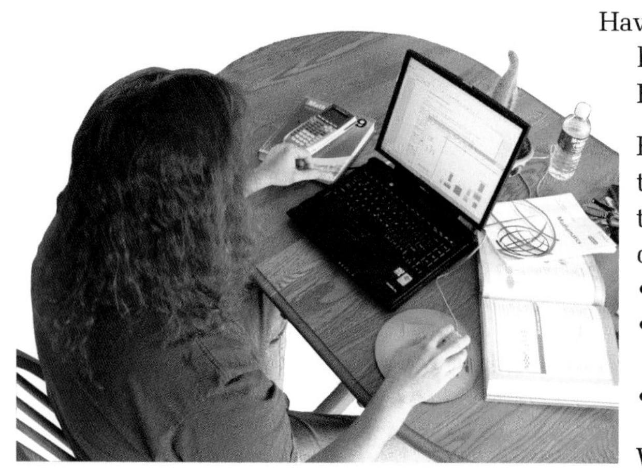

Have you ever wondered about who writes textbooks like this one? When do they write these books? How do they get paid?

Experienced mathematics teachers write most math textbooks. They usually write when they are not teaching. They are paid in different ways, depending on their contracts:

- a fixed amount, or flat rate
- a royalty, which depends on the number of books sold
- a combination of fixed amount plus royalty

Why do you think that they are paid in these ways?

Example 1 Add Polynomials

Simplify each expression.

a) $(4x + 3) + (7x + 2)$

b) $(2p - 2) + (4p - 7)$

c) $(0.5v^2 + 2v) + (-2.4v^2 - 3v)$

Solution

a)
$$\begin{aligned} & (4x + 3) + (7x + 2) \\ &= 4x + 3 + 7x + 2 \\ &= 4x + 7x + 3 + 2 \\ &= 11x + 5 \end{aligned}$$

First, remove the brackets, and then collect like terms.

I can rearrange terms to group like terms.

b)
$$\begin{aligned} & (2p - 2) + (4p - 7) \\ &= 2p - 2 + 4p - 7 \\ &= 2p + 4p - 2 - 7 \\ &= 6p - 9 \end{aligned}$$

I use integer rules to collect like terms.

c) Method 1: Remove Brackets and Collect Like Terms

$$\begin{aligned} & (0.5v^2 + 2v) + (-2.4v^2 - 3v) \\ &= 0.5v^2 + 2v - 2.4v^2 - 3v \\ &= 0.5v^2 - 2.4v^2 + 2v - 3v \\ &= -1.9v^2 - v \end{aligned}$$

Apply the integer rules when you remove brackets.

Method 2: Write the Addition Vertically

$$\begin{array}{r} 0.5v^2 + 2v \\ + \ -2.4v^2 - 3v \\ \hline -1.9v^2 - v \end{array}$$

Add the numerical coefficients of the like terms vertically. $0.5 + (-2.4) = -1.9$ and $2 + (-3) = -1$.

$(0.5v^2 + 2v) + (-2.4v^2 - 3v) = -1.9v^2 - v$

Example 2 Opposite Polynomials

State the opposite of each expression.

a) 7 **b)** $-2x$ **c)** $4x + 1$

d) $5y - 2$ **e)** $x^2 - 3x + 7$

Solution

Opposites add to give 0.

a) The opposite of 7 is −7.

b) The opposite of $-2x$ is $2x$.

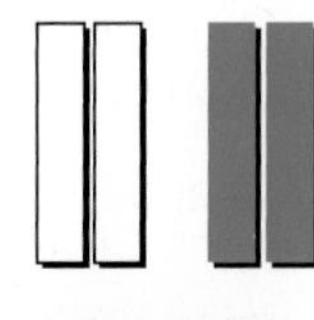

c) To find the opposite of a polynomial, find the opposite of each term.

The opposite of $4x + 1$ is $-4x - 1$.

d) The opposite of $5y - 2$ is $-5y + 2$.

e) The opposite of $x^2 - 3x + 7$ is $-x^2 + 3x - 7$.

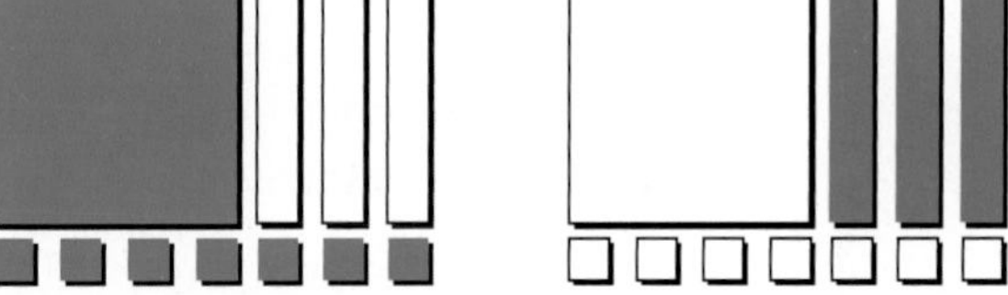

Example 3 Subtract Polynomials

Simplify.

a) $(3y + 5) - (7y - 4)$ **b)** $(a^2 - 2a + 1) - (-a^2 - 2a - 5)$

Solution

a)
$$
\begin{aligned}
&(3y + 5) - (7y - 4) \\
&= (3y + 5) + (-7y + 4) \\
&= 3y + 5 - 7y + 4 \\
&= 3y - 7y + 5 + 4 \\
&= -4y + 9
\end{aligned}
$$

To subtract a polynomial, add its opposite.

The opposite of $7y - 4$ is $-7y + 4$.

b)
$$
\begin{aligned}
&(a^2 - 2a + 1) - (-a^2 - 2a - 5) \\
&= (a^2 - 2a + 1) + (a^2 + 2a + 5) \\
&= a^2 - 2a + 1 + a^2 + 2a + 5 \\
&= 2a^2 + 6
\end{aligned}
$$

$-2a$ and $2a$ are opposites. They add to give 0. There is no a term in the final expression.

Example 4 Apply an Algebraic Model to Solve a Problem

Four authors team up to write a textbook. The publisher negotiates the following contracts with them.

Author	Fixed Rate ($)	Royalty ($ per n books sold)
Lita	2000	–
Jamal	1000	$2n$
Vera	1500	n
Fleming	–	$3n$

a) Write a simplified expression for the total payout to the authors.

b) Determine the total amount paid to the authors for 1200 books sold.

Solution

a) Write an expression for the total amount paid to each author. Then, add these expressions.

Lita: 2000
Jamal: $1000 + 2n$
Vera: $1500 + n$
Fleming: $3n$

Total payout:

$$\begin{aligned} & 2000 + (1000 + 2n) + (1500 + n) + 3n \\ &= 2000 + 1000 + 2n + 1500 + n + 3n \\ &= 4500 + 6n \end{aligned}$$

The publisher will pay $4500 + 6n$ to the authors, where n is the number of books sold.

b) Substitute $n = 1200$ and evaluate the expression.

$$\begin{aligned} & 4500 + 6n \\ &= 4500 + 6(1200) \\ &= 4500 + 7200 \\ &= 11\ 700 \end{aligned}$$

If 1200 books are sold, the publisher will pay $11 700 to the authors.

Key Concepts

- To add polynomials, remove brackets and collect like terms.
- To subtract a polynomial, add the opposite polynomial.

Communicate Your Understanding

C1 **a)** Describe the process of adding one polynomial to another. Use an example to support your explanation.

b) Describe the process of subtracting one polynomial from another. Use an example to support your explanation.

C2 Each of the following solutions contains an error. Describe the error and suggest how it should be corrected.

a) $(2x - 3) + (6x - 2)$
$= 2x - 3 + 6x - 2$
$= 8x - 1$

b) $(4y - 7) - (2y - 5)$
$= 4y - 7 - 2y - 5$
$= 2y - 12$

Practise

For help with questions 1 and 2, see Example 1.

1. $(2x - 7) + (3x + 8)$ simplified is

A $5x - 15$ **B** $5x - 1$ **C** $5x + 1$ **D** $6x - 56$

2. Simplify by removing brackets and collecting like terms.

a) $(3x + 4) + (7x + 5)$
b) $(y + 2) + (3 + 6y)$
c) $(4m - 1) + (3m - 8)$
d) $(5 - 3d) + (d - 6)$
e) $(4k - 3) + (5 + k) + (5k + 3)$
f) $(6r - 1) + (3r + 2) + (-6r - 1)$

For help with questions 3 and 4, see Examples 2 and 3.

3. $(3x - 5) - (x - 4)$ simplified is

A $2x - 1$ **B** $2x + 1$ **C** $2x - 9$ **D** $2x + 9$

4. Simplify by adding the opposite polynomial.

a) $(2x + 3) - (x + 6)$
b) $(8s + 5) - (s + 5)$
c) $(6m + 4) - (2m + 1)$
d) $(4v - 9) - (8 - 3v)$
e) $(9 - 6w) - (-6w - 8)$
f) $(5h + 9) - (-5h + 6)$

5. Simplify.

a) $(7x - 9) + (x - 4)$
b) $(3y + 8) + (-y - 5)$
c) $(8c - 6) - (c + 7)$
d) $(k + 2) - (3k - 2)$
e) $(3p^2 - 8p + 1) + (9p^2 + 4p - 1)$
f) $(5xy^2 + 6x - 7y) - (3xy^2 - 6x + 7y)$
g) $(4x - 3) + (x + 8) - (2x - 5)$
h) $(2uv^2 - 3v) - (v + 3u) + (4uv^2 - 9u)$

8x−

Connect and Apply

For help with questions 6 and 7, see Example 4.

6. A group of musicians who made a CD are paid according to the following breakdown, where n is the number of CDs sold.

Musician	Fixed Rate ($)	Royalty ($ for n CDs sold)
Ling	2000	$0.1n$
Fredrick	–	$0.3n$
Nigel	1500	$0.2n$
Tulia	5000	–

a) Find a simplified expression for the total amount paid to the group.

b) The table shows sales achievement levels for the Canadian recording industry.

Status	Number of CDs Sold
Gold	50 000
Platinum	100 000
Diamond	1 000 000

Find the total amount paid to the group if their CD
- sells 100 copies
- reaches gold status
- reaches diamond status

c) Which musician makes the most money at each level in the table in part b)?

d) Describe the advantages and disadvantages of being paid
- by a fixed rate
- by royalty
- by a combination of fixed rate and royalty

Use mathematical reasoning to support your answers.

7. A women's basketball team gives players a bonus of $100 on top of their base salary for every 3-point basket. Data for some of the team's players are given.

Player	Base Salary ($1000s)	3-Point Baskets
Gomez	50	25
Henreid	40	20
Jones	100	44

a) Find a simplified expression for the total earnings for these three players.

b) Find the total earnings for these players.

8. Use algebra tiles, virtual algebra tiles, or a diagram to model and simplify each expression.

a) $(2x + 5) + (3x + 2)$

b) $(y^2 + 3y + 1) + (y^2 + 2y + 2)$

c) $(2x^2 + 3x + 4y^2) + (2x^2 + x + 2y^2)$

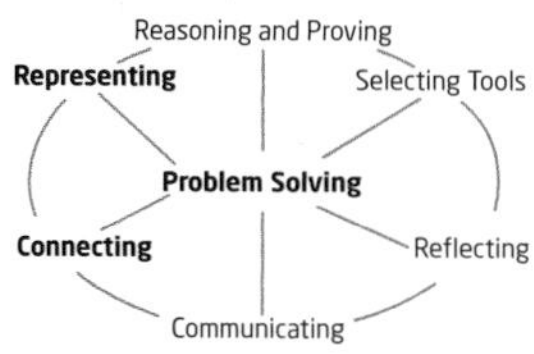

9. A swimming pool manufacturer installs rectangular pools whose length is twice the width, plus 5 m.

a) Draw a diagram of the pool and label the width and length with algebraic expressions.

b) The entire outer edge of the pool must be fitted with coping, which is a cap used to join the wall of the pool and the deck. Find a simplified algebraic expression that describes the total length of coping needed.

c) How much coping is required if the width of the pool is 6 m?

10. Refer to question 9.

a) Predict how the amount of coping will change if you double the width of the pool.

b) Calculate the new amount required and compare this with your prediction. Explain the results.

Extend

11. Refer to question 9. If you use the same expressions for the length and width of the pool as in question 9, do the proportions of the pool change when you change the width? Describe the relationships between width, length, and perimeter as you change the width. Use diagrams, words, and algebraic expressions to support your explanations.

12. Math Contest

a) Copy and complete the addition cascade.

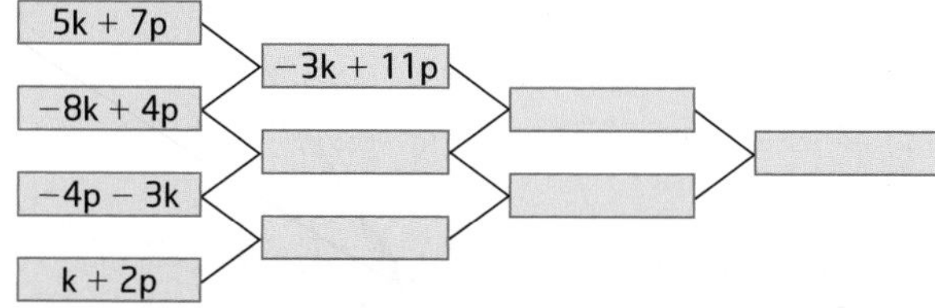

b) Build your own addition cascade. Have another student complete it, and then verify each other's work.

3.7 The Distributive Property

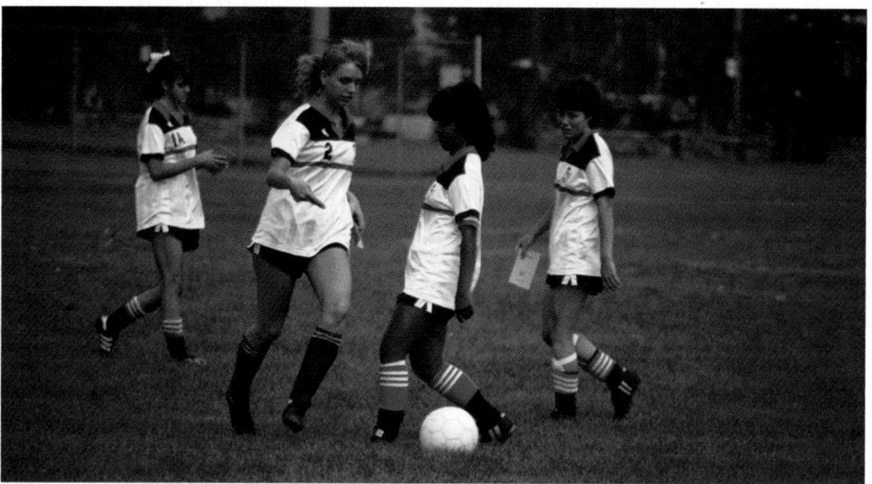

Any successful sports team must practise. Often a practice begins with a warm-up. Suppose the coach tells her players to run the perimeter of the field. How can you use algebra to write an expression for the total distance? Is there more than one way to do this?

James claims, "I can calculate the perimeter of the field by using the formula $P = 2(l + w)$."

Sylvie replies, "That's not right, James. The correct formula is $P = 2l + 2w$."

Who is correct, James or Sylvie? Can they both be right?

Investigate

- algebra tiles

How can you simplify algebraic expressions involving multiplication?

The area of a rectangle can be expressed as the product of its width and length:

$A = w \times l$

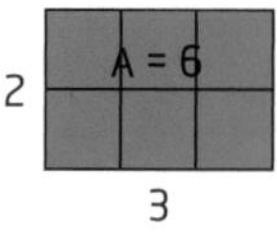

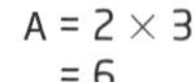

A = 2 × 3
= 6

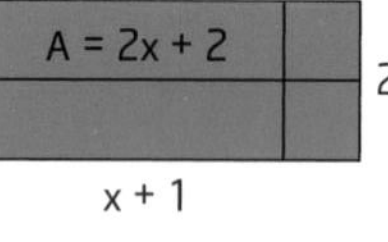

A = 2(x + 1)
= 2x + 2

The dimensions of algebra tiles:

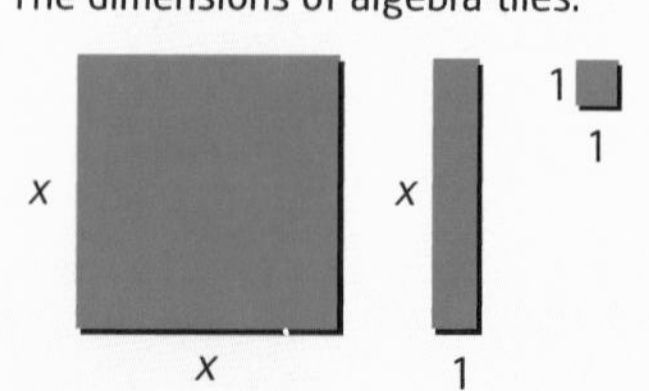

1. Copy and complete the table. Use algebra tiles to help.

Rectangle	Width	Length	Area	Equation $w \times l = A$
	2	$x + 1$	$2x + 2$	$2 \times (x + 1) = 2x + 2$
	x		$x^2 + 2x$	
	$2x$	$2x + 3$		
Create your own				

2. Look at the last column. Describe how you can start with the expression on the left side of the equation and get the expression on the right side.

3. Use the technique from step 2 to multiply the following.

a) $4(x + 3)$

b) $x(2x + 7)$

c) $3x(x + 2)$

4. **Reflect** Create an example and use it to explain how you can multiply a monomial by a polynomial.

Suppose that you have three dimes and three nickels.

The total amount can be expressed different ways:

$$\begin{aligned} & 3(10) + 3(5) \\ &= 30 + 15 \\ &= 45 \end{aligned}$$

$$\begin{aligned} & 3(10 + 5) \\ &= 3(15) \\ &= 45 \end{aligned}$$

Whether you use $3(10) + 3(5)$ or $3(10 + 5)$, the result is 45¢. What does this tell you about these two numeric expressions?

Some algebraic expressions cannot be simplified using the second method. Reflect on the situations when you cannot simplify an expression. Suppose you add two nickels to a pile of nickels. The value of the nickels can be modelled by $5(x + 2)$, where x is the number of nickels in the original pile.

$5(x + 2)$

You cannot add $x + 2$ because they are not like terms. However, you can multiply the 5 by both terms in the binomial:

$$\begin{aligned} & 5(x + 2) \\ &= 5(x) + 5(2) \\ &= 5x + 10 \end{aligned}$$

This is called the **distributive property**.

distributive property

- $a(x + y) = ax + ay$

Example 1 Apply the Distributive Property

Expand.

a) $3(x + 2)$

b) $-5(4m - 3)$

c) $(2y + 5)(-4)$

d) $2(5a^2 - 7a + 2)$

Literacy Connections

When you apply the distributive property, you are **expanding** an expression.

Solution

a)
$$\begin{aligned} & 3(x + 2) \\ &= 3(x) + 3(2) \\ &= 3x + 6 \end{aligned}$$

To apply the distributive property, I need to multiply both terms in the brackets by 3.

b) Method 1: Show the Distributive Step

$-5(4m - 3)$
$= -5(4m + (-3))$
$= (-5)(4m) + (-5)(-3)$ **Remember to keep the negative sign when you are distributing.**
$= -20m + 15$

When I distribute a negative term, I must follow the integer rules for multiplication.

Method 2: Apply the Distributive Step Mentally

$-5(4m - 3)$
$= -20m + 15$

$(-5) \times 4m = -20m$
$(-5) \times (-3) = 15$

c) The monomial is usually written before the polynomial, but sometimes it appears after. Apply the distributive property in the same way.

$(2y + 5)(-4)$
$= 2y(-4) + 5(-4)$
$= -8y + (-20)$
$= -8y - 20$

d) You can also apply the distributive property to trinomials.

$2(5a^2 - 7a + 2)$
$= 10a^2 - 14a + 4$

The distributive property can be applied to polynomials with any number of terms.

Example 2 Distribute Variables

Simplify using the distributive property.

a) $x(x - 3)$ **b)** $p(p^2 - 2p + 1)$

Solution

a) $x(x - 3)$
$= x(x) + x(-3)$
$= x^2 - 3x$

To multiply variables, I need to use the exponent laws. The product rule is $x^a \times x^b = x^{a + b}$.

b) $p(p^2 - 2p + 1)$
$= p^3 - 2p^2 + p$

I need to use the product rule.
$p \times p^2 = p^{(1 + 2)}$
$= p^3$

The distributive property allows you to simplify complicated expressions.

Example 3 Expand and Simplify Expressions

Expand and simplify.

a) $-4(x + 3) + 2(2x - 1)$

b) $3m(m - 5) - (2m^2 - m)$

c) $\frac{1}{2}(2w - 6) - \frac{2}{3}(9w - 6)$

Solution

a)

$$
\begin{aligned}
&-4(x + 3) + 2(2x - 1) \\
&= -4(x) - 4(3) + 2(2x) + 2(-1) \\
&= -4x - 12 + 4x - 2 \\
&= -4x + 4x - 12 - 2 \\
&= -14
\end{aligned}
$$

Apply the distributive property first to remove brackets. Then, collect like terms.

b) Method 1: Add the Opposite Polynomial

$$
\begin{aligned}
&3m(m - 5) - (2m^2 - m) \\
&= 3m(m - 5) + (-2m^2 + m) \\
&= 3m^2 - 15m - 2m^2 + m \\
&= 3m^2 - 2m^2 - 15m + m \\
&= m^2 - 14m
\end{aligned}
$$

$-2m^2 + m$ is the opposite of $2m^2 - m$.

Method 2: Distribute −1

$$
\begin{aligned}
&3m(m - 5) - (2m^2 - m) \\
&= 3m(m - 5) + (-1)(2m^2 - m) \\
&= 3m^2 - 15m - 2m^2 + m \\
&= m^2 - 14m
\end{aligned}
$$

Multiplying a polynomial by −1 produces the opposite polynomial: $(-1)(2m^2 - m) = -2m^2 + m$

c)

$$
\begin{aligned}
&\frac{1}{2}(2w - 6) - \frac{2}{3}(9w - 6) \\
&= \frac{1}{\cancel{2}_1}(\cancel{2}^1w) + \frac{1}{\cancel{2}_1}(\cancel{-6}^{-3}) - \frac{2}{\cancel{3}_1}(\cancel{9}^3w) - \frac{2}{\cancel{3}_1}(\cancel{-6}^{-2}) \\
&= 1(1w) + 1(-3) - 2(3w) - 2(-2) \\
&= w - 3 - 6w + 4 \\
&= -5w + 1
\end{aligned}
$$

Example 4 Nested Brackets

Expand and simplify.

$3[2 + 5(2k - 1)]$

Solution

When simplifying expressions involving nested brackets, begin with the inner brackets and work your way outward.

$$\begin{aligned} &3[2 + 5(2k - 1)] \\ &= 3(2 + 10k - 5) \\ &= 3(10k - 3) \\ &= 30k - 9 \end{aligned}$$

Simplify the inner brackets before distributing the 3.

Key Concepts

- The distributive property allows you to expand algebraic expressions:
  $a(x + y) = ax + ay$
  - When distributing, multiply the monomial by each term in the polynomial.
  - Multiply numerical coefficients.
  - Apply exponent laws to variables.

Literacy Connections

When you *distribute* a handout in class, you give one copy to each student. Similarly, when you use the distributive property, the term in front of the brackets is multiplied by, or given to, each term inside the brackets..

Communicate Your Understanding

C1 Consider the expression $3(x + 5)$. Why do you need to use the distributive property? Why can you not just add the terms in the brackets first?

C2 Explain the distributive property. Create an example to support your explanation.

C3 Dmitri simplified the following expression, as shown:

$$\begin{aligned} &3x(x + 2) \\ &= 3x + 2x \\ &= 5x \end{aligned}$$

a) Explain the errors in Dmitri's solution and how to correct them.

b) How can you prove that Dmitri's answer is not correct?

C4 Explain why the following simplification is incorrect.

$$\begin{aligned} &(x^2 - 3x + 1)(-5) \\ &= x^2 - 3x - 4 \end{aligned}$$

C5 Describe the steps you must follow to simplify the expression $3[x + 2(x - 1)]$.

Practise

For help with questions 1 to 3, see Example 1.

1. Which expression shows $-3(x + 5)$ expanded?

A $-3x + 15$ **B** $-3x + 5$

C $-3x - 8$ **D** $-3x - 15$

2. Use algebra tiles, virtual algebra tiles, or a diagram to model and simplify each expression.

a) $2(x + 3)$ **b)** $x(x + 4)$

c) $3(x + 1) + 2(x + 5)$

3. Expand, using the distributive property.

a) $4(x + 2)$ **b)** $5(k - 3)$

c) $-2(y + 1)$ **d)** $-8(2 - d)$

e) $5(2t - 3)$ **f)** $-(4y - 5)$

For questions 4 and 5, see Example 2.

4. Expand.

a) $y(y - 4)$ **b)** $r(r + 5)$

c) $x(2x - 5)$ **d)** $q(-4q + 8)$

e) $z(-3z + 2)$ **f)** $m(-m - 5)$

5. Expand.

a) $2b(3b - 5)$ **b)** $3v(8v + 7)$

c) $-4w(3w - 1)$ **d)** $-6m(-m - 5)$

e) $2q(-4q + 3)$ **f)** $-3d(-d + 2)$

6. Expand using the distributive property.

a) $(n - 5) \times 4$ **b)** $(2p + 4) \times 9$

c) $(7m + 6) \times (-4)$ **d)** $(7 + c)(3c)$

e) $(3 - 6w)(-2)$ **f)** $(4k + 7)(-3k)$

7. Expand.

a) $2(a^2 + 5a + 3)$ **b)** $-3(2n^2 - 8n + 5)$

c) $4k(k^2 + k - 3)$ **d)** $-5h(3h^2 - 7h - 2)$

e) $(x^2 - 5x + 2)(-3)$ **f)** $(2y^2 + 3y - 1)(4y)$

For help with question 8, see Example 3.

8. Expand and simplify.

a) $3(x + 2) + 4(x - 5)$ **b)** $-4(y + 1) + 2(2y - 3)$

c) $2(u + v) - 3(u - v)$ **d)** $4(w - 2) - 2(2w + 7)$

e) $-3(a + b) - 2(a - b)$ **f)** $2(p - q) + 2(-p + q)$

For help with question 9, see Example 4.

9. Expand and simplify.

a) $3[x + 2(x - 4)]$ **b)** $5[2(y - 1) - 3]$

c) $3[2k - (2 + k)]$ **d)** $4[-3(r - 5) + 2r]$

e) $2[-h - 2(h - 1)]$ **f)** $-3[2(p + 2) - 3p]$

Connect and Apply

10. A computer repair technician charges \$50 per visit plus \$30/h for house calls.

a) Write an algebraic expression that describes the service charge for one household visit.

b) Use your expression to find the total service charge for a 2.5-h repair job.

c) Suppose all charges are doubled for evenings, weekends, and holidays. Write a simplified expression for these service charges.

d) Use your simplified expression from part c) to calculate the cost for a 2.5-h repair job on a holiday. Does this answer make sense? Explain.

11. Who is right? Use examples to explain your answer.

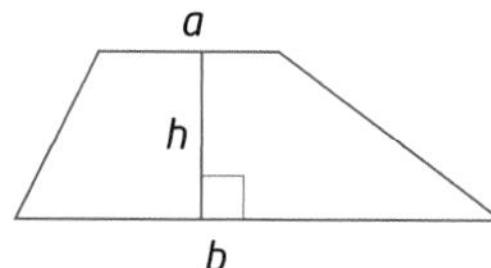

12. The formula for the area of a trapezoid is

$$A = \frac{1}{2}(a + b)h$$

Apply the distributive property twice to write this formula in another way.

13. A garden has dimensions as shown.

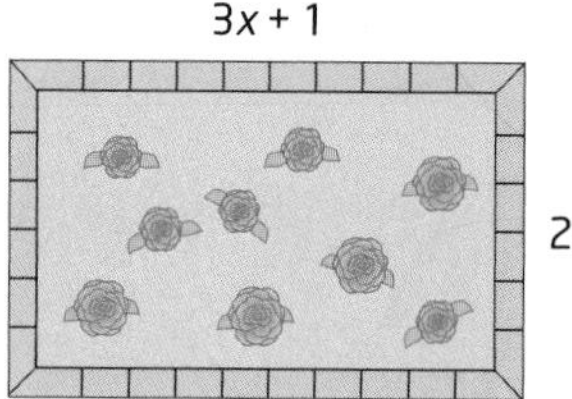

a) Find a simplified expression for the perimeter.

b) Find a simplified expression for the area.

c) Repeat parts a) and b) if both the length and width are tripled.

d) Has this tripled the perimeter? Justify your answer.

e) Has this tripled the area? Justify your answer.

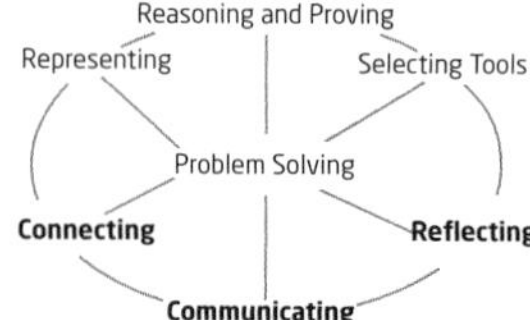

14. Is the distributive property true for numerical expressions (expressions without variables)? Make a prediction. Then, create some numerical expressions and explore this. Describe any conclusions that you reach.

15. Expand and simplify.

a) $2(x - 3) + 3(x + 5)$

b) $3(k - 4) - 2(k + 1)$

c) $0.2p(p - 5) + 0.4p(3p - 2)$

d) $-4h(h + 2) + h(2h - 3)$

e) $5j(j - 3) - (2j^2 - 3j)$

f) $-0.7w(2w - 3) - 0.6w(w + 3)$

g) $3(y - 2) - 2(4 - 2y) + (6 - 7y)$

h) $4k(k - 3) - 2(k^2 - 3k + 4) - (k^2 - 5)$

16. Expand and simplify.

a) $\frac{1}{3}(3a + 2) + \frac{1}{4}(4a - 2)$

b) $\frac{1}{2}(x - 2y) + \frac{1}{3}(3y - 2x)$

c) $\frac{2}{3}(3m - 2) - \frac{3}{4}(8m - 2)$

d) $-\frac{1}{4}(4u - 3v) - \frac{3}{5}(6u - 10v)$

Achievement Check

17. a) Find a simplified expression for the perimeter of each figure. Use algebra tiles if you wish.

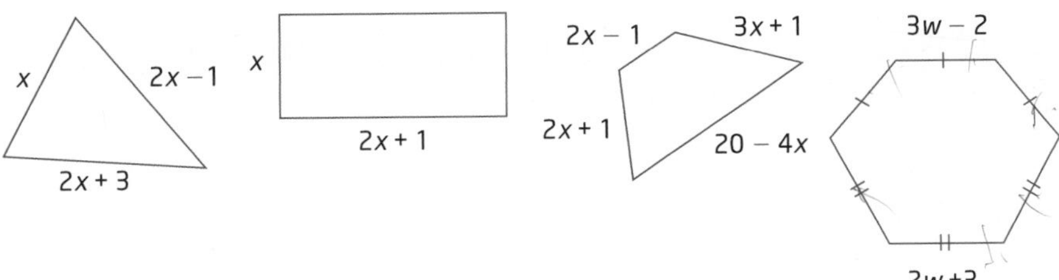

b) A rectangle has length $2x - 1$ and width $8 - 2x$. What is unusual about the perimeter?

c) For what value of x is the rectangle in part b) also a square?

Extend

18. Expand and simplify.

a) $2m[m - 3(m + 2)]$

b) $-3p[2p(p + 4) + p^2]$

c) $2[3 + 2(x - 6)] + 3[-2(x - 5) + 8]$

d) $-3[2 - (y - 5)] - 4[3(y + 1) - (6 - y)(-2)]$

19. How do you distribute a binomial? Consider the following product of two binomials:

$(x + 3)(2x - 2)$

Distribute the $(x + 3)$ to each term in the second binomial to form an expression consisting of two products:

$(x + 3)(2x) + (x + 3)(-2)$

a) Simplify this expression. Check to see that your result appears to be equivalent to the original expression, by substituting values into both expressions.

b) Make up your own question similar to this and simplify it.

c) Can you see an easier way to expand the product of two binomials? Find and explain an easier method.

Making Connections

You will multiply binomials in grade 10 and beyond as a method of simplifying polynomial expressions.

20. Expand and simplify. Check to see if your result is correct. If you need a hint, look at the method from question 19.

$(k + 1)(k^2 - 2k - 1)$

21. Math Contest If $\left(\frac{1}{2}\right)^x = 0.015\ 625$, determine the value of x.

Computer Algebra Systems

A computer algebra system (CAS) is a type of calculator or computer software that can perform algebraic functions. They are sometimes called symbolic manipulators. You can investigate many of the skills that you have learned in this chapter using CAS systems.

Tools

- TI-89 calculators

Technology Tip

Before you start doing calculations, clear the calculator's memory.

Press [2nd] [F1] for [F6] to display the **Clean Up** menu.

Select **2:NewProb**. Press [ENTER].

Technology Tip

Note that you use a different button for leading negative signs [(–)], as in the −5 in question 2 part c), than the subtraction button [–].

Investigate A

How can you learn about a CAS?

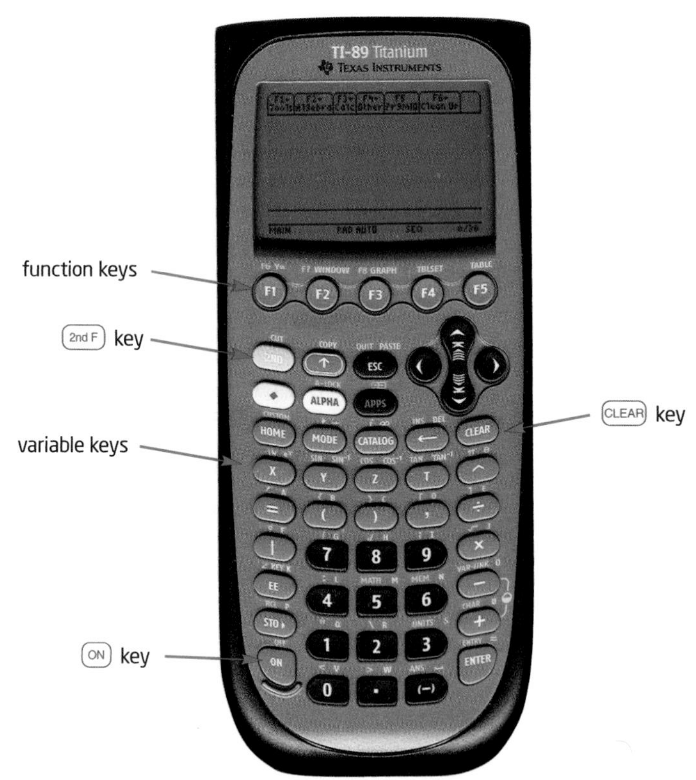

1. Press the [ON] key to turn the calculator on. If you do not see the Home screen, as shown, press the [HOME] key.

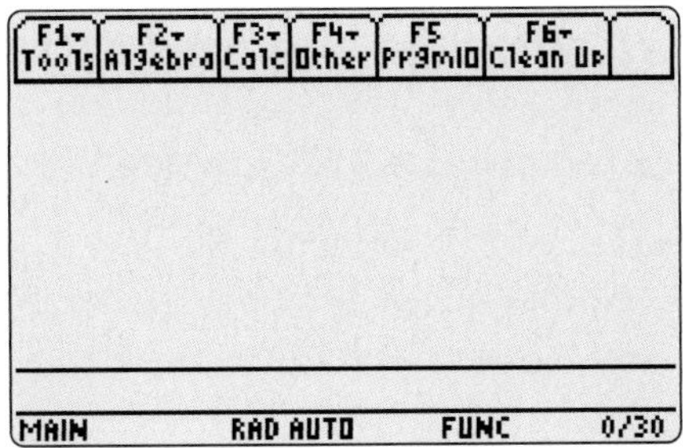

2. Perform some basic calculations to get familiar with the keyboard and display. Follow the keystrokes shown.

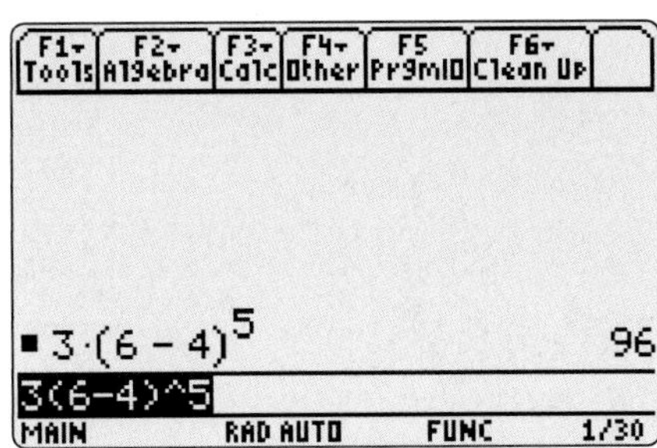

   a) $3(6 - 4)^5$

   3 [×] [(] 6 [−] 4 [)] [^] 5 [ENTER]

   b) $\pi\,(2.5)^2$

   [2nd] [^] [×] 2.5 [^] 2 [ENTER]

   c) $-5 - \sqrt{9}$

3. Explore the Function keys at the top of the keypad.

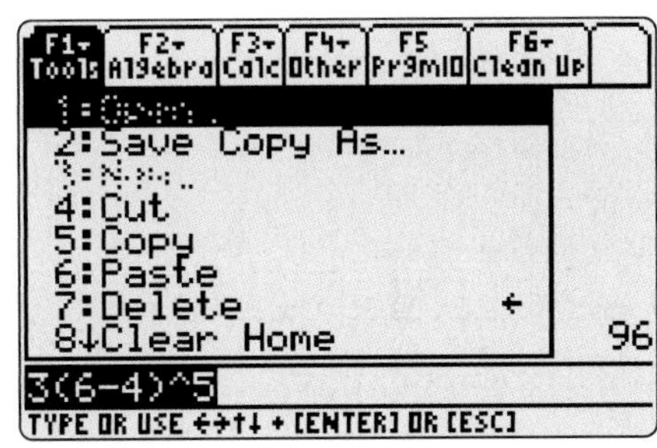

   a) Press [F1] to see the TI-89 **Tools** menu. Identify at least three commands that you recognize from working on a computer. Use the up and down cursor keys to see more commands.

   b) Press [F2] to see the algebra functions that the TI-89 can perform. Identify two commands that you recognize from this chapter and two that you do not recognize.

   c) You can also use the left and right cursor keys to see the different function menus. Scroll over to see the menus of **F3** and **F4**. You will learn about these functions in future mathematics courses.

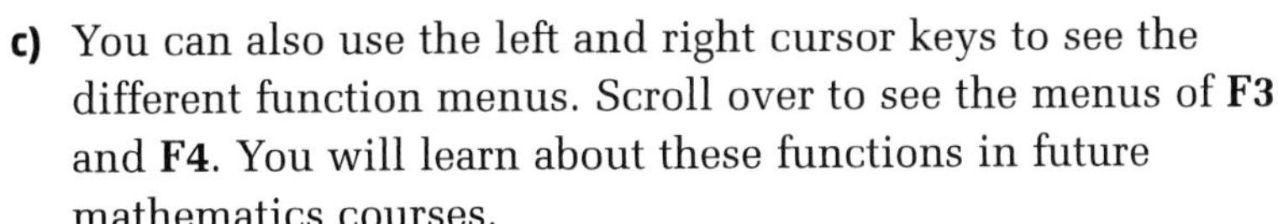

   d) Clean up the home screen:
   - Press [2nd] [F6] to display the **Clean Up** menu.
   - Select **2:NewProb**.
   - Press [ENTER].

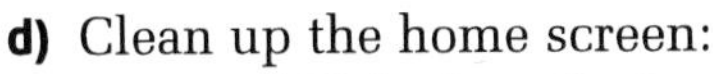

Investigate B

How can you use a CAS to simplify and expand expressions?

1. Collect like terms for the expression $2x + 3y - x - 5y$.
   - Type the expression $2x + 3y - x - 5y$.
   - Press ENTER.

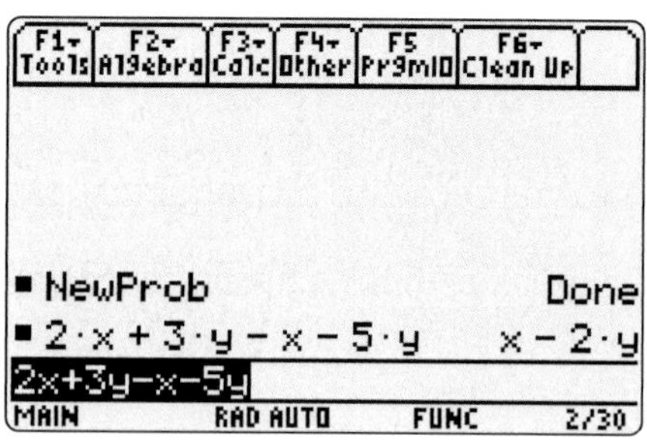

2. Use the CAS to collect like terms for each expression.
   a) $3y - 2x + 5x - 3y$
   b) $x^2 + 3x - 2 - 6x + 3x^2$
   c) Create your own expression.

3. Expand $4(2x - 3)$ using the distributive property.
   - Press F2.
   - Select **3:expand(**.
   - Type the expression.
   - Press).
   - Press ENTER.

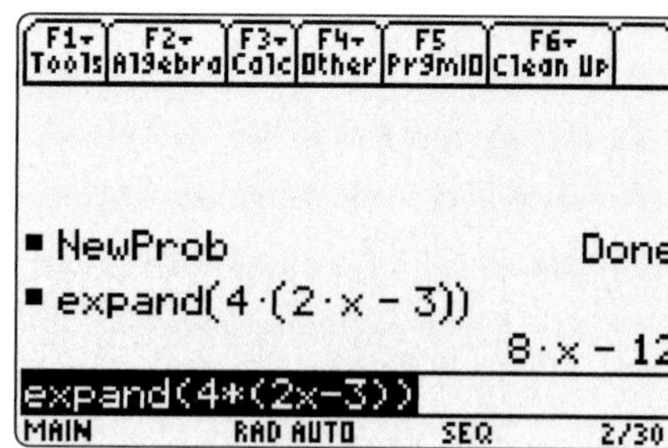

Technology Tip

Note the nested brackets required in this command line. If you get an error message, check that you have the same number of open and close brackets, and that they are placed correctly.

4. Use a CAS to simplify using the distributive property.
   a) $-2z(3z - 5)$
   b) $3(4x - 7y) - 2(3x - 2y)$
   c) Create your own expression.

Investigate C

How can you verify the exponent laws?

1. a) Use a CAS to illustrate the product rule of exponents by entering the expression $y^2 \times y^5$.
   b) Create two of your own examples to illustrate the product rule using a CAS.

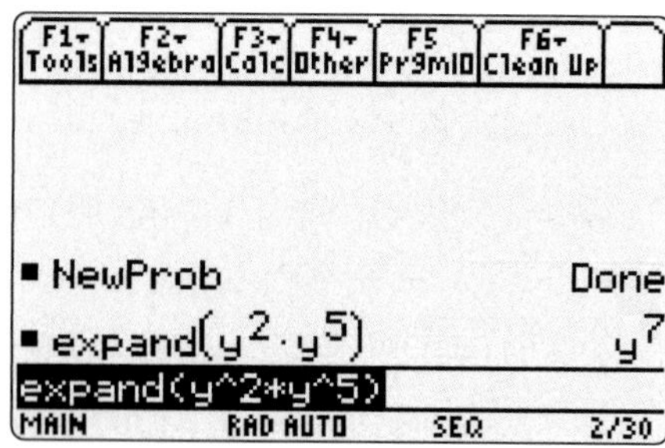

2. You can also evaluate expressions involving powers, such as $y^2 \times y^3$ when $y = 3$.

Press Y ^ 2 × Y ^ 3 | Y = 3.

Use this feature to evaluate

a) $y^3 \times y^4$ when $y = 4$

b) $\dfrac{z^8}{z^5}$ when $z = -5$

c) $\dfrac{x^4 \times x^7}{x^5}$ when $x = \dfrac{2}{3}$

3. Design your own method for verifying either the quotient rule or the power of a power rule for exponents. Describe your steps, keystrokes, and screen outputs.

Investigate D

How can you explore an unknown function?

Many of the functions of the CAS will be unknown to you at this level. Several of them you will learn about in future mathematics courses, but in this section you will have the opportunity to experiment and learn a little about some of these "mystery" functions.

1. a) Clear the home screen. Press 2nd F1 for [F6] to display the **Clean Up** menu. Select **2:NewProb** and press ENTER.

b) Use the **Expand** command to simplify the expression $3(x + 4)$.

c) Factor the result:

- Press F2.
- Select **2:Factor(**.
- Type $3x + 12$.
- Press).
- Press ENTER.

What does the **Factor** function do?

d) Write down the result. What do you notice?

2. Repeat step 1 for each expression.

a) $y(2y - 3)$

b) $5z(2z - 1)$

Making Connections

You will learn about factoring in grade 10.

3. Explain what the **Factor** command seems to do. How does it seem to be related to the **Expand** command?

4. a) Repeat step 1 for the expression $2(2x + 6)$.

b) Is the factored result what you expected? Explain.

c) Create a few examples of your own. Describe what you discover.

5. Explore some of the unknown features of the TI-89. Try to figure out what one of them does. Write a brief report of your findings.

Chapter 3 Review

3.1 Build Algebraic Models Using Concrete Materials, pages 104–109

1. Use algebra tiles to build a model for each situation. Write an algebraic expression to represent the model.
   a) Jeanne ran 4 km.
   b) Klaus drove an unknown distance, twice.
   c) Evelyn ran 3 km plus an unknown distance.
   d) Suki painted her house with two coats of paint.

2. **a)** Build a volume model to represent a cube with side length 3 cm. Sketch the model and label the length, width, and height.
   b) What is the volume of the cube? Write this as a power.
   c) Write an expression for the area of one face of the cube as a power. Evaluate the area of one face.

3.2 Work With Exponents, pages 110–118

3. Evaluate.
   a) 4^5
   b) $(-3)^4$
   c) $\left(\frac{2}{5}\right)^3$
   d) 1.05^8

4. $100 is put into a bank account that pays interest so that the amount in the account grows according to the expression $100(1.06)^n$, where n is the number of years. Find the amount in the account after
   a) 5 years
   b) 10 years

5. Find the annual interest rate of the account in question 4.

6. The half-life of carbon-14 (C-14) is 5700 years.
   a) Copy and complete the table for a 50-g sample of C-14.

Number of Half-Life Periods	Years	Amount of C-14 Remaining (g)	Expression
0	0	50	
1	5 700	25	$50\left(\frac{1}{2}\right)^1$
2	11 400		$50\left(\frac{1}{2}\right)^2$
3			
4			

   b) Construct a graph of the amount of C-14 remaining versus time, in years. Describe the shape of the graph.
   c) Approximately how much C-14 will remain after 20 000 years?
   d) How long will it take until only 1 g of C-14 remains?

Did You Know?

Carbon dating is a method of determining the age of fossilized creatures, such as dinosaur remains.

Scientists compare the ratio of two carbon isotopes in the sample: C-14, which is radioactive, and C-12, which is stable. Because everything on Earth has about the same ratio of C-14 to C-12 at any given time, measuring this ratio tells when the creature lived.

3.3 Discover the Exponent Laws, pages 119–129

7. Write as a single power. Then, evaluate the expression.
   a) $2^3 \times 2^2 \times 2^4$
   b) $6^7 \div 6^2 \div 6^3$
   c) $[(-4)^2]^3$
   d) $\frac{7^4 \times 7^5}{(7^4)^2}$

8. Simplify.

a) $\frac{n^5 \times n^3}{n^4}$

b) $cd^3 \times c^4d^2$

c) $\frac{2ab^2 \times 3a^3b^3}{(4ab^2)^2}$

3.4 Communicate With Algebra, pages 130–139

9. Identify the coefficient and the variable part of each term.

a) $5y$

b) uv

c) $\frac{1}{2}ab^2$

d) $-de^2f$

e) 8

10. Classify each polynomial by the number of terms.

a) $x^2 + 3x - 5$

b) $24xy$

c) $a + 2b - c + 3$

d) $-\frac{2}{3}$

e) $16u^2 - 7v^2$

11. In a hockey tournament, teams are awarded 3 points for a win, 2 points for an overtime win, and 1 point for an overtime loss.

a) Write an expression that describes the number of points a team has.

b) Use your expression to find the number of points earned by a team that has 4 wins, 1 overtime win, and 2 overtime losses.

12. State the degree of each term.

a) $3x^2$

b) $6n^4$

c) 17

d) abc^2

13. State the degree of each polynomial.

a) $3y - 5$

b) $2d^2 - d$

c) $3w - 6w^2 + 4$

d) $3x^3 - 5x^2 + x$

3.5 Collect Like Terms, pages 144–153

14. Identify the like terms in each set.

a) $2p, 3q, -2, p, 3q^2$

b) $5x^2, 5x, x^5, -5x^2, 3x^2$

15. Simplify by collecting like terms.

a) $4x - 3 + 6x + 5$

b) $7k + 5m - k - 6m$

c) $6a^2 - 5a + 3 - 3a^2 + 5a - 4$

d) $3x^2 - 4xy + 5y^2 - 6 + 3x^2 + 4xy - 2$

3.6 Add and Subtract Polynomials, pages 154–159

16. Simplify.

a) $(4x + 3) + (3x - 2)$

b) $(5k - 2) + (3k - 5)$

c) $(6u + 1) - (2u + 5)$

d) $(y^2 - 3y) - (2y^2 - 5y)$

e) $(2a^2 - 4a - 2) - (a^2 - 4a + 2)$

f) $(3v - 2) - (v - 3) + (2v - 7)$

17. A rectangular window frame has dimensions expressed by $3x$ and $2x - 5$. Find a simplified expression for its perimeter.

3.7 The Distributive Property, pages 160–169

18. Expand.

a) $3(y - 7)$

b) $-2(x + 3)$

c) $m(5m - 3)$

d) $-4k(2k + 6)$

e) $-5(p^2 + 3p - 1)$

f) $4b(b^2 - 2b + 5)$

19. Expand and simplify.

a) $2(q - 5) + 4(3q + 2)$

b) $5x(2x - 4) - 3(2x^2 + 8)$

c) $-3(2m - 6) - (8 - 6m)$

d) $4(2d - 5) + 3(d^2 - 3d) - 2d(d + 1)$

20. Simplify.

a) $2[4 + 3(x - 5)]$

b) $-3[9 - 2(k + 3) + 5k]$

Chapter 3 Practice Test

Multiple Choice

For questions 1 to 9, select the correct answer.

1. What is the value of $\left(\frac{1}{3}\right)^3$?

A 1 **B** $\frac{1}{3}$

C $\frac{1}{9}$ **D** $\frac{1}{27}$

2. What is the simplified form of the expression $w^2 \times w^4 \times w$?

A w^6 **B** w^7

C w^8 **D** w^9

3. What does $\frac{4^5}{4^3}$ equal?

A 4 **B** 8

C 16 **D** 32

4. What does $(2^3)^2$ equal?

A 10 **B** 12

C 32 **D** 64

5. Which of the following shows three like terms?

A $3x$ $2x$ $-x^2$

B $4a$ $4b$ $4c$

C $3y$ $-y$ $8y$

D $3m^2n$ $2mn^2$ $4mn$

6. $2k^2 - 3k$ is a

A monomial **B** binomial

C trinomial **D** term

7. What is the degree of $2u^3v$?

A 1 **B** 2

C 3 **D** 4

8. $3x - 5 + 2x + 3$ can be simplified to

A $3x$ **B** $5x - 2$

C $x - 2$ **D** $5x + 2$

9. What does $-2m(3m - 1)$ simplify to?

A $-6m^2 + 2m$ **B** $-6m^2 - 1$

C $6m^2 - 2m$ **D** $-6m^2 - 2m$

Short Response

Show all steps in your solutions.

10. Write as a single power. Then, evaluate.

a) $(-2)^2 \times (-2)^3 \times (-2)$

b) $\frac{3^5 \times 3^3}{(3^2)^3}$

11. Simplify.

a) $k^2n^3 \times kn^4$

b) $-6p^5 \div 3p^2$

c) $(-3g^2h)^3$

12. Simplify.

a) $(5x - 3) + (2x + 7)$

b) $(3u - 4) - (5u - 1)$

13. Expand and simplify.

a) $3(y + 4) + 6(y - 2)$

b) $-4(6b - 3) - (3b + 5)$

14. James and Sylvie need to paint the line around the outside of a soccer field. To know how much paint to buy, they must find the perimeter of the field.

James claims, "I can calculate the perimeter of the field by using the formula $P = 2(l + w)$."

Sylvie replies, "That's not right, James. The correct formula is $P = 2l + 2w$."

a) Who is correct? Is it possible for both to be right? Provide evidence to support your answer.

b) Find two other ways to write a valid formula for the perimeter of a rectangle and explain why they work.

c) Even though the students accurately calculated the perimeter, they ran out of paint. Discuss possible reasons for this situation.

Extended Response

Provide complete solutions.

15. Vanessa, the student council president, needed to get a message to the whole school, but she did not have time to e-mail every student. So she set up an e-mail tree. She sent the message to her two vice-presidents, and asked them each to forward it to two students. Suppose that this pattern is repeated and assume that no one receives the e-mail more than once.

a) How many people will receive the e-mail on the seventh mailing?

b) On which mailing will the e-mail be sent to at least 500 people? Explain how you found this answer.

c) At this point, how many people would have received the e-mail, in total?

d) There are 500 students in the school. How many mailings would it take to reach all the students?

16. Three authors team up to write a children's book. The publisher pays them according to the following contracts.

Author	Fixed Rate ($)	Royalty ($ for n books sold)
Latoya	3000	–
Sven	1500	$2n$
Michelle	1000	$3n$

a) Find a simplified expression that represents the total that the publisher must pay the writing team.

b) Determine the total payout if the book sells

- 200 copies
- 5000 copies

17. Suppose you place a penny on the first square of a checkerboard.

Now, suppose you double the amount and place this on the second square. If you repeat this for the entire board, how much will be on the

a) 64th square?

b) entire board?

Chapter Problem Wrap-Up

a) Design a logo for your school team, or a team of your choice. You can pick your favourite professional team and create a new logo for them, or make up your own fantasy team. Your design should include one or more polygons.

b) Use one or more variables to represent the dimensions in your design and label them on your design.

c) Find a simplified expression for the perimeter of your logo.

d) Find a simplified expression for the area of your logo.

e) Create two problems involving your logo. Solve the problems.

f) Trade problems with a classmate. Solve each other's problems and check your solutions.

Chapters 1 to 3 Review

Chapter 1 Mathematical Processes

1. Find the next three terms in each sequence. Describe how to find successive terms.
   a) 1, 2, 4, 7
   b) 1, 4, 9, 16
   c) 17, 12, 7, 2
   d) 2, 6, 12, 20

2. Use the clues to find the value of E. Describe your strategy.
   $A \times B = 80$
   $A \times C = 200$
   $B \times D = 36$
   $D \times E = 18$
   $C = 100$

3. You have three \$5 bills, a \$10 bill, and two \$20 bills. How many different sums of money can you make?

4. The area of this figure is 400 cm^2. What is its perimeter?

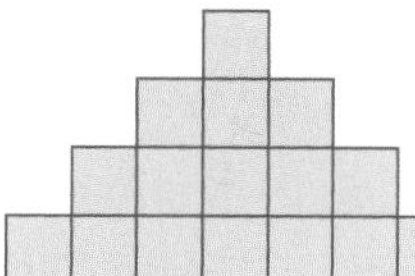

5. Evaluate.
   a) $\frac{2}{3} - \frac{3}{4} \times \frac{1}{2}$
   b) $\left(\frac{2}{3} - \frac{3}{4}\right) \times \frac{1}{2}$
   c) $\frac{3}{4} - \frac{2}{3} \times \frac{1}{2}$
   d) $\left(\frac{3}{4} - \frac{2}{3}\right) \times \frac{1}{2}$

6. The daily high temperatures during one week in February were −6°C, 2°C, −8°C, −5°C, 4°C, 1°C, and −9°C. What was the mean high temperature that week?

7. A number is considered a perfect number if its factors (not including itself) add up to the number. For example, 6 is a perfect number because 1, 2, and 3 are factors of 6 and $1 + 2 + 3 = 6$. Find the next perfect number. Describe the strategy that you used.

8. How many breaths do you take in 1 year? Describe your strategy.

9. Can you find five odd numbers that add up to 50? What about six numbers? Explain.

10. Give a counter-example to prove that each statement is false.
    a) The sum of two square numbers is always a square number.
    b) The sum of two acute angles is an obtuse angle.
    c) The sum of two prime numbers is a prime number.

Chapter 2 Relations

11. **a)** Make a hypothesis about the percent of students in your school that have computers in their home.
    b) Describe how you could collect data to test your hypothesis. Is this primary or secondary data?

12. Describe how you could choose a random sample to determine
    a) the favourite TV show of grade 9 girls
    b) the percent of students in your school who have their own cell phone

13. The table shows the heights and shoe sizes of 10 grade 9 girls.
    a) Make a scatter plot of the data.
    b) Describe the relationship between a student's height and her shoe size.
    c) Identify any outliers. Should you discard them? Explain.

Height (cm)	Shoe Size
157	5.5
153	5
165	8
160	6
175	9
162	7
164	6.5
155	7
168	7.5
162	7

14. A store has 30 female employees and 20 male employees. The manager wants to select 10 employees to help choose a new uniform.

a) Identify the population.

b) Describe how the manager can choose a stratified random sample.

15. The table shows the numbers of storeys and heights of six Canadian buildings.

Building	Number of Storeys	Height (m)
First Canadian Place, Toronto	72	290
Manulife Place, Toronto	36	146
Petro-Canada Centre, West Tower, Calgary	52	210
Place de Ville, Ottawa	29	112
Royal Centre Tower, Vancouver	36	140
Toronto Dominion Centre, Winnipeg	33	126

a) Graph the data.

b) Draw a line of best fit.

c) Describe the relationship between the number of storeys and the height of the building.

d) Use your graph to predict the height of a new 40-storey office tower.

16. Claire is training for a half-marathon. The graph shows how her distance from home changed with time on a 14-km run. Write a description of her run.

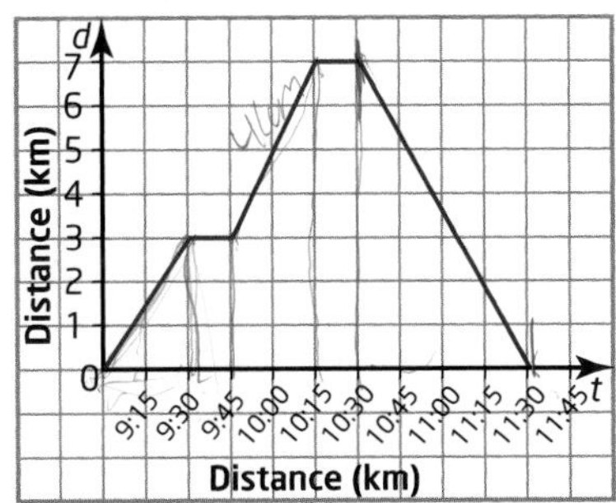

Chapter 3 Polynomials

17. The area of one face of a cube is 64 cm^2.

a) What is the side length of the cube?

b) Determine the volume of the cube.

18. Evaluate.

a) $3^2 + 2^3$ **b)** $5^2 - 6^2 \div 2^2$

c) $(4^3 - 3^3) + (2^5 \div 4^2)$ **d)** $\left(\frac{3}{5}\right)^2 \div \frac{9}{10}$

19. Simplify.

a) $n^2 \times n^3$ **b)** $d^8 \div d^2$

c) $(a^3)^4$ **d)** $3m^2n \times 4mn^3$

e) $24k^5q^3 \div (2k^2q)^2$

20. In a quiz show, contestants receive 10 points for each correct answer but lose 5 points for each incorrect answer.

a) Write an expression for a contestant's total score.

b) Theo answered 12 questions correctly and 5 questions incorrectly. Find his total score.

21. Simplify.

a) $5m + 8 - 3m - 10$

b) $3x^2 + 6x - 3 - x^2 - 5x - 1$

c) $(h + 5) - (3h - 8)$

d) $(4t + 5w) + (t - 2w) - (3t + 4w)$

22. Expand and simplify.

a) $5(x + 3)$ **b)** $k(2k - 1)$

c) $4(3y + 2) + 3(2y - 7)$

d) $\frac{2}{3}(3a + 1) + \frac{1}{2}(4a - 1)$

23. **a)** Find a simplifed expression for the perimeter of the triangle.

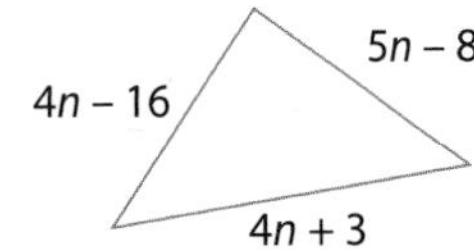

b) Determine the perimeter when $n = 5$.

Electricity and Gas Costs

Tico keeps records of the amount of electricity, in kilowatt hours (kWh), and natural gas, in cubic metres, used by his family business. He set up a table to compare monthly hydro and natural gas costs.

Month	Cost of Gas	Amount of Gas Used (m^3)	Cost of Electricity	Amount of Electricity Used (kWh)	Average Monthly Temperature
January	$174.60	949	$165.75	1950	−5°C
February	$177.30	965	$159.38	1875	−6°C
March	$158.40	861	$150.11	1766	1°C
April	$135.00	733	$139.57	1642	5°C
May	$76.50	416	$106.00	1247	15°C
June	$35.10	192	$88.57	1042	20°C
July	$32.40	176	$90.10	1060	24°C
August	$31.50	171	$84.83	998	25°C
September	$34.20	187	$95.54	1124	21°C
October	$70.20	381	$108.20	1273	15°C
November	$126.90	691	$129.88	1528	8°C
December	$167.40	912	$161.08	1895	0°C

a) Use a graphing calculator or graphing software to draw a scatter plot of the relationship between the amount of gas used each month and the cost.

b) Use the scatter plot to describe the relationship between these two variables. Is the relationship linear or non-linear? Justify your response.

c) Find another set of data involving two variables that have a relationship similar to the one you found in part b). Construct a scatter plot to check your conjecture and explain your conclusions.

d) Find a set of data involving two variables that have a different relationship. Explain the relationship.

Perimeters and Areas

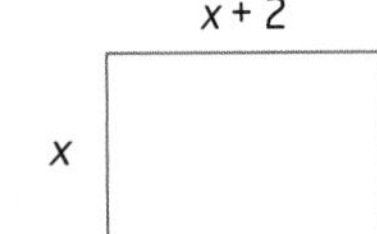

a) Write an expression, in simplified form, for the perimeter of this rectangle.

b) Write an expression for the area of the rectangle.

c) Suppose 16 of these rectangles are put together to form a larger rectangle. Show all the possible ways of combining them. Write an expression for the perimeter in each case.

d) For each of the values $x = 1$, $x = 2$, and $x = 3$, which combination of small rectangles from part c) has the least perimeter? Is this more than one combination? Justify your answer.

e) Find the area of each combined rectangle in part c).

Mind Reader

Part 1

Aidan's cousin Heather found this Mind Reader challenge in a games magazine. She asked Aidan to explain how it works.

- Think of a number.
- Add 20.
- Multiply the answer by 5.
- Double the result.
- Subtract 200.
- Divide by the number you picked.

The answer will always be the same. What is it?

a) Heather thought of the number 5. Show how the steps work for this number.

b) Explain how this challenge works, using words, numbers, and/or symbols.

Part 2

Aidan found another Mind Reader in the magazine. It involves a person's birth date. In this challenge, 15 April 1993 is written numerically as 150493.

- Write down the day of the month that you were born.
- Multiply the number by 5.
- Add 4.
- Multiply by 20.
- Add the number of the month you were born.
- Multiply by 100.
- Add the last two digits of the year you were born.
- Subtract 8000.

a) What is the result? What does it mean?

b) Explain, using symbols, how this Mind Reader works.

CHAPTER

4 Equations

Organizing an event, such as a party for a few friends or a dance for the entire school, can involve algebra. You might use algebraic expressions and equations to determine how much money you can spend on food, decorations, and entertainment. If the event involves ticket sales, your knowledge of algebra can help you determine what the price of a ticket should be.

In this chapter, you will solve a variety of equations, rearrange formulas, and solve problems using algebraic modelling.

Number Sense and Algebra

- Solve first-degree equations using a variety of tools and strategies.
- Rearrange formulas involving variables in the first degree.
- Solve problems that can be modelled with first-degree equations, and compare algebraic methods to other solution methods.
- Relate understanding of inverse operations to squaring and taking the square root, and apply inverse operations to simplify expressions and solve equations.

Vocabulary

equation
solution
root
constant term
formula

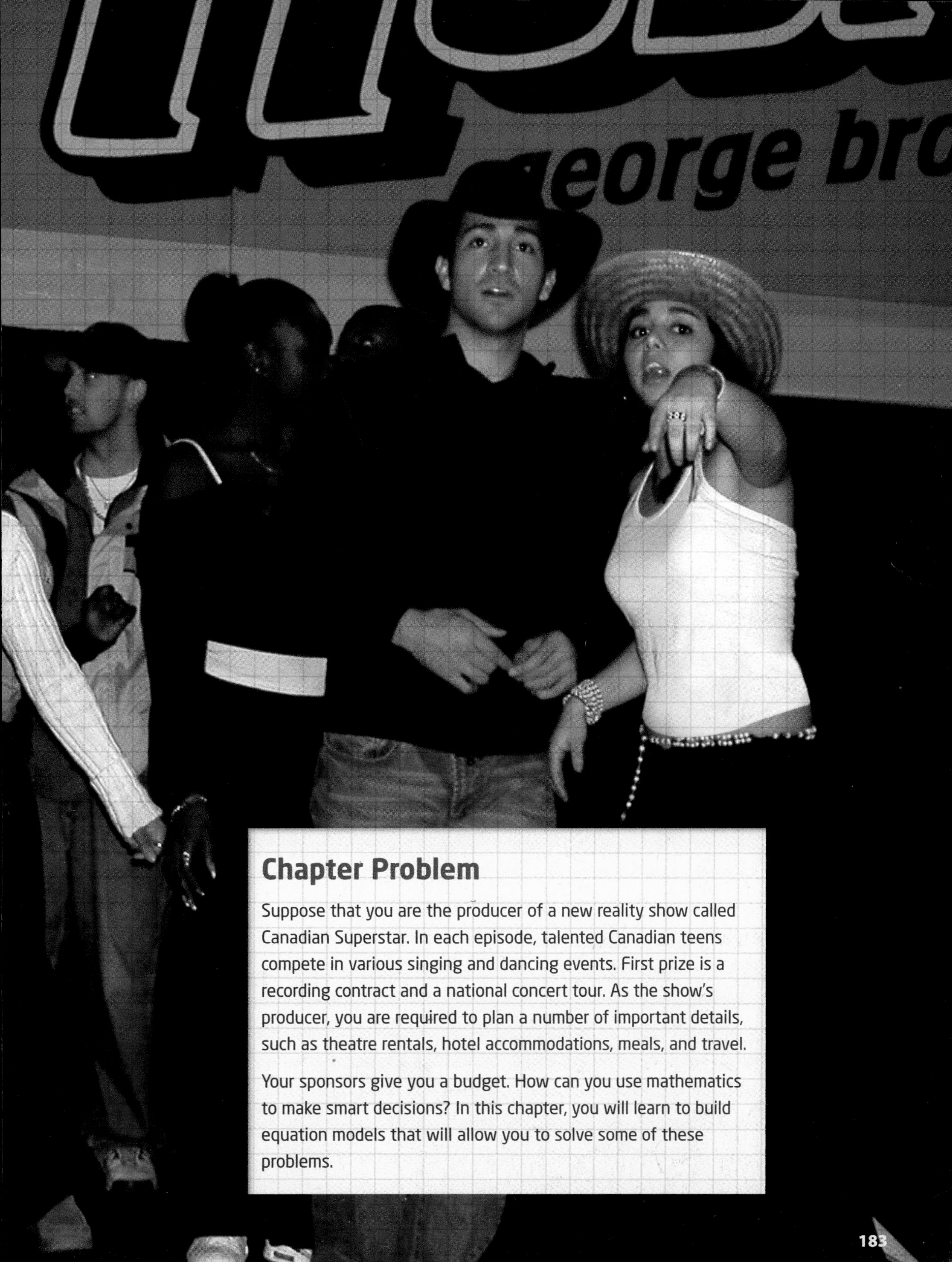

Chapter Problem

Suppose that you are the producer of a new reality show called Canadian Superstar. In each episode, talented Canadian teens compete in various singing and dancing events. First prize is a recording contract and a national concert tour. As the show's producer, you are required to plan a number of important details, such as theatre rentals, hotel accommodations, meals, and travel.

Your sponsors give you a budget. How can you use mathematics to make smart decisions? In this chapter, you will learn to build equation models that will allow you to solve some of these problems.

Get Ready

Collect Like Terms

To collect like terms, add the numerical coefficients.
The variable part of the terms does not change.

$4x + 2x - 5x$	$5y - 3y + y$	$4k + 2 - k - 8$
$= x$	$= 3y$	$= 3k - 6$

1. Simplify.

a) $6x + 5x - 3x$ **b)** $2y - 5y + 7y$

c) $8m - 5m + m$ **d)** $-3n + 10n - 2n$

2. Simplify.

a) $5v + 2 - 4 - v$ **b)** $6 - 2x - 3 + 9x$

c) $-7y + 6 + 4y - 2$ **d)** $3k - 8 - 5k + 5$

Distributive Property

To multiply a binomial by a constant, use the distributive property.
Multiply each term inside the brackets by the constant.

$-2(3f - 5)$
$= -6f + 10$

$3(u - 2) - 4(2u - 7)$
$= 3u - 6 - 8u + 28$ **Collect like terms.**
$= -5u + 22$

3. Simplify.

a) $4(2k - 9)$

b) $-2(5m + 6)$

c) $3(6x + 1)$

d) $-7(y - 2)$

4. Simplify.

a) $2(2x - 5) + 3(x + 9)$

b) $-4(y + 1) + 6(5y - 2)$

c) $3(7n - 1) - (2n - 3)$

d) $-5(k + 2) - 3(2k - 3)$

Geometric Relationships

In earlier grades, you studied the following geometric relationships.

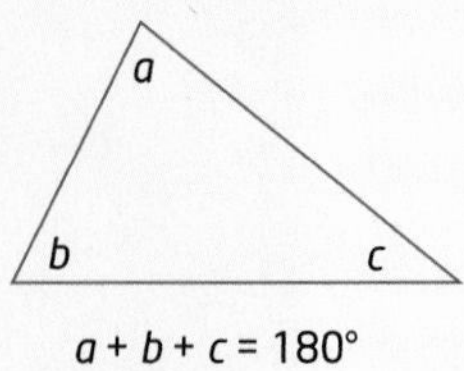

a + b + c = 180°

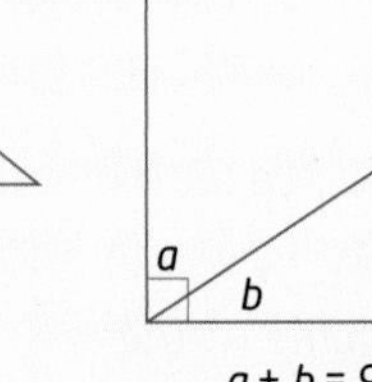

a + b = 90°

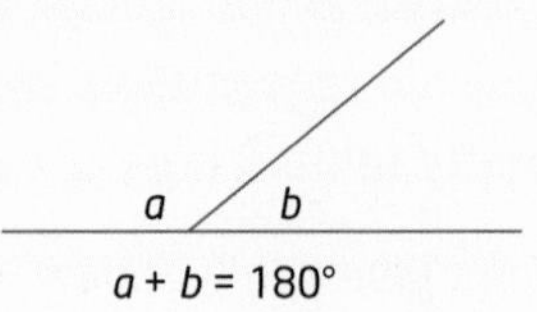

a + b = 180°

5. Find the measure of each unknown angle.

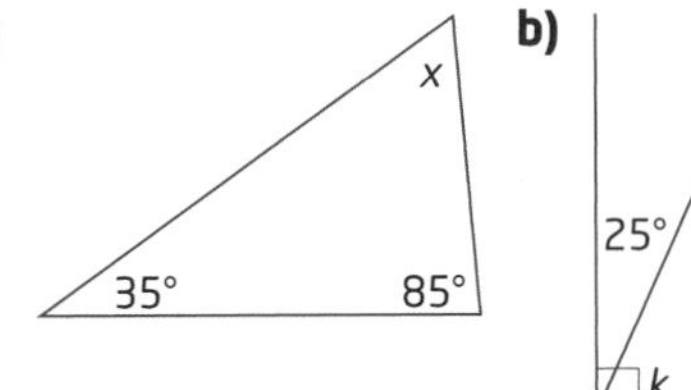

6. Find the measure of each unknown angle.

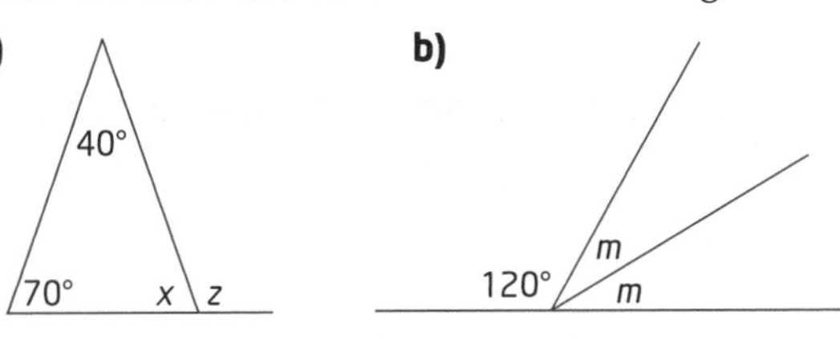

Lowest Common Denominator

The lowest common denominator (LCD) is the lowest common multiple of the denominators of two or more fractions. You can find the LCD using multiples or prime factors.

Find the LCD for $\frac{1}{6}$ and $\frac{1}{8}$.

Method 1: Use Multiples

List the multiples of 6 and 8 until you reach a common value.

6, 12, 18, (24)
8, 16, (24)

The LCD for $\frac{1}{6}$ and $\frac{1}{8}$ is 24.

Method 2: Use Prime Factors

$6 = 2 \times 3$
$8 = 2 \times 2 \times 2$

The LCD will have all the prime factors of each number.

Start with the factors of the first number. Add any missing factors from the next number.

$\text{LCD} = 2 \times 3 \times 2 \times 2$
$= 24$

I need both factors of 6: 2×3

For the factors of 8, I need to include two more factors of 2.

The LCD is 24.

7. Find the LCD for each pair of fractions.

a) $\frac{1}{5}, \frac{1}{8}$ b) $\frac{1}{6}, \frac{1}{9}$

8. Find the LCD for each set of fractions.

a) $\frac{1}{2}, \frac{1}{3}, \frac{1}{4}$ b) $\frac{1}{4}, \frac{1}{9}, \frac{1}{12}$

9. Evaluate.

a) $\frac{3}{4} + \frac{7}{12}$ b) $\frac{7}{8} - \frac{1}{2}$

10. Evaluate.

a) $\frac{5}{8} + \frac{2}{3}$ b) $\frac{11}{12} - \frac{1}{10}$

4.1 Solve Simple Equations

Pep rallies are a great way to build school spirit by cheering on your favourite school teams and clubs. Suppose your student council raises \$500 in a school spirit fundraising drive to buy school T-shirts to give away at a pep rally and puts you in charge of purchasing. How can your understanding of equations help you determine how many shirts you can buy?

equation

- a mathematical statement that says two expressions are equal
- $3x + 3 = 2x - 1$ is an equation

Investigate

How can you use a simple equation to solve a problem?

1. Byron spent a total of \$11 on two magazines. The cost of one magazine is \$5. You can use an **equation** to find the cost of the other magazine.
   a) Choose a variable to represent the unknown.
   b) Write an equation to represent this situation.
   c) What value of the variable makes the equation true? Describe the math operation(s) you used to find the value.

2. Kelly spent a total of \$10 on a pen and two mechanical pencils. The pen cost \$4 and the pencils each cost the same amount.
   a) Choose a variable to represent the unknown.
   b) Write an equation to represent this situation.
   c) What value of the variable makes the equation true? Describe the math operation(s) you used to find the value.

3. **Reflect**
   a) How can you use mathematical operations to solve equations?
   b) Explain how you can verify your answers.

Example 1 Solve Equations Involving Adding and Subtracting

Solve each equation.

a) $x + 4 = 13$

b) $x - 8 = 2$

c) $-4 + x = -1$

To solve an equation means to find the value of the variable that makes the statement true.

Solution

a) Method 1: Inspection

Sometimes you can solve an equation by inspection, which means just looking at it and applying number sense.

$$x + 4 = 13$$
$$x = 9$$

A number plus 4 gives 13. The number must be 9.

The **solution** is $x = 9$.

solution

- the value of the variable that makes an equation true

Method 2: Balance Method

Think of an equation as being like a balance, with the equal sign representing the centre. You can use algebra tiles to represent the quantity on each side.

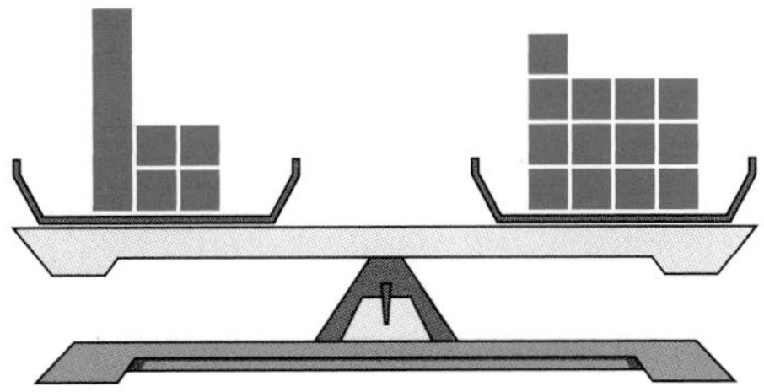

To find what x equals, remove 4 unit tiles. You must do this to both sides to keep the equation balanced.

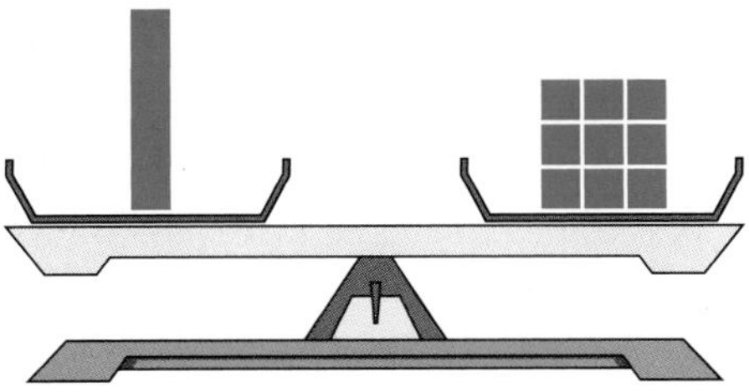

The solution is $x = 9$.

Go to www.mcgrawhill.ca/links/principles9 and follow the links to find a Web site that provides an interactive model of the balance method for solving equations.

Method 3: Use the Opposite Operation

An equation is still true if you apply identical operations to both sides.

$$x + 4 = 13$$
$$x + 4 - 4 = 13 - 4$$
$$x = 9$$

If I subtract 4 on the left, I'll be left with just x, because $+ 4 - 4$ makes zero. That means I'll need to subtract 4 on the right, too.

The solution is $x = 9$.

Literacy Connections

Follow these guidelines to communicate your solution effectively:

- Show all steps clearly.
- Use one equal sign per line.

b) Method 1: Inspection

$$x - 8 = 2$$
$$x = 10$$

A number minus 8 gives 2. The number must be 10.

The solution is $x = 10$.

Method 2: Balance Method

There are eight negative unit tiles on the left that need to be removed. You cannot do this immediately because there are none on the right side.

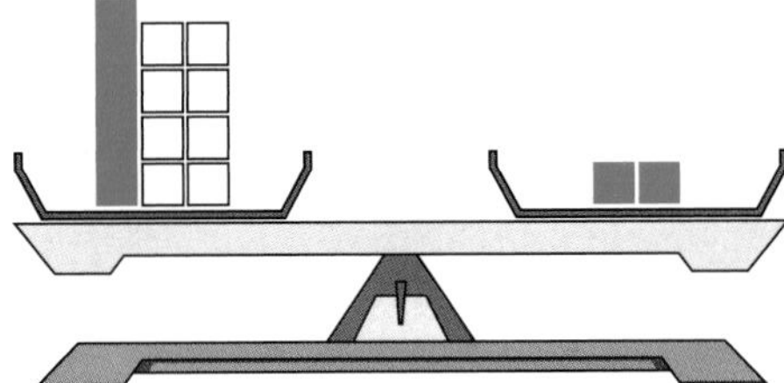

Add eight zero pairs to the right side first.

Now remove eight negative unit tiles from each side to solve for the unknown.

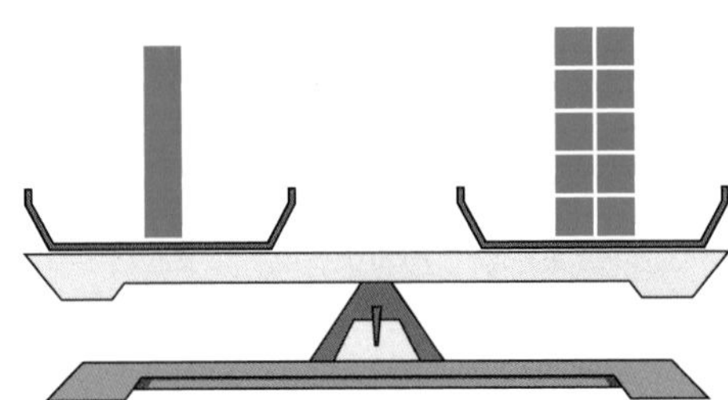

The solution is $x = 10$.

Method 3: Use the Opposite Operation

$$x - 8 = 2$$
$$x - 8 + 8 = 2 + 8$$
$$x = 10$$

I need to add 8 to both sides.

The solution is $x = 10$.

c) Solving equations by inspection is efficient if the numbers are easy to work with. Otherwise, it is better to apply opposite operations. When applying opposite operations, you are isolating the variable.

$$-4 + x = -1$$
$$-4 + 4 + x = -1 + 4$$
$$x = 3$$

I need to add 4 to both sides to get x by itself.

The solution is $x = 3$.

Literacy Connections

To isolate the variable means to express an equation so that the variable appears alone on one side of the equation. For example,

$$-4 + x = -1$$
$$-4 + 4 + x = -1 + 4$$
$$x = 3$$

The variable x has been isolated on the left side of the equation.

Example 2 Solve Equations Involving Multiplying and Dividing

Solve each equation.

a) $3y = 18$ **b)** $\frac{n}{3} = -4$ **c)** $-v = 9$

Solution

a) Method 1: Balance Method

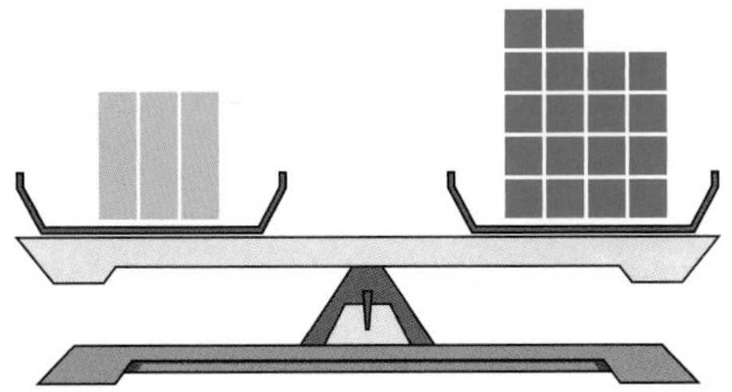

Divide both sides into three equal groups.

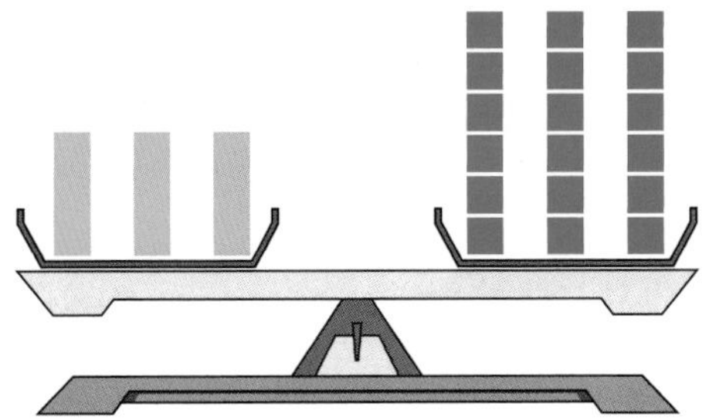

The solution is $y = 6$.

Method 2: Use the Opposite Operation

$$3y = 18$$
$$\frac{3y}{3} = \frac{18}{3}$$
$$y = 6$$

3 times a number gives 18. I can divide both sides of the equation by 3 to find the unknown.

b) Use the Opposite Operation

$$\frac{n}{3} = -4$$
$$\overset{1}{\cancel{3}} \times \frac{n}{\underset{1}{\cancel{3}}} = 3 \times (-4)$$
$$n = -12$$

n divided by 3 gives −4. To find the number, I need to undo the division. The opposite of dividing is multiplying. I need to multiply both sides by 3.

c) Use the Opposite Operation

$$-v = 9$$
$$\frac{-v}{-1} = \frac{9}{-1}$$
$$v = -9$$

−*v* means the same as −1*v*. To undo multiplication by −1, I need to divide by −1.

root (of an equation)

- the value of the variable that makes an equation true
- the same as the solution of an equation

Literacy Connections

Finding the root of an equation means the same thing as solving an equation. For example:

$9 - x = 2$

The root of this equation is 7 because it makes the statement true: $9 - 7 = 2$.

Example 3 Solve a Two-Step Equation

Find the **root** of the equation and check the solution.

$5x + 25 = 500$

Solution

Method 1: Use Opposite Operations, Pencil and Paper

Isolate the variable term first.

$$5x + 25 = 500$$

$$5x + 25 - 25 = 500 - 25 \quad \text{Subtract 25 from both sides.}$$

$$5x = 475$$

$$\frac{5x}{5} = \frac{475}{5} \quad \text{Divide both sides by 5.}$$

$$x = 95$$

The root of the equation is $x = 95$.

Check if this answer is correct by substituting $x = 95$. Evaluate the left side (L.S.) and the right side (R.S.) of the equation. Both sides of the equation must have the same value.

$$\begin{aligned} \text{L.S.} &= 5x + 25 \\ &= 5(95) + 25 \\ &= 475 + 25 \\ &= 500 \end{aligned} \qquad \text{R.S.} = 500$$

$$\text{L.S.} = \text{R.S.}$$

Therefore, $x = 95$ is correct.

The root is 95.

When $x = 95$, L.S. = 500 and R.S. = 500.

To check a solution, I must make sure that the left side and the right side have the same value.

Method 2: Use Opposite Operations, Computer Algebra System (TI-89)

In the Home screen, type the equation $5x + 25 = 500$.
Then, press ENTER.
Notice that the equation has been repeated in the command line.

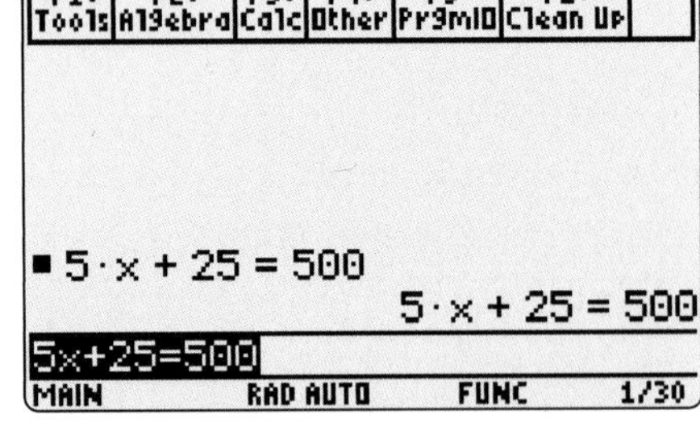

Isolate the variable term first.
Press the left cursor key.
Insert a bracket before the 5.
Cursor right, and place another bracket after the 500.
Then, subtract 25.
Press ENTER.

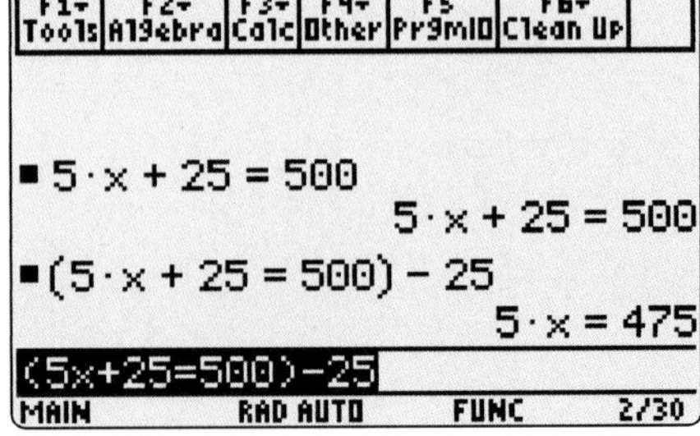

I am subtracting, so I use the subtract key, not the negative key.

Copy and paste the new equation onto the command line:

- Use the up cursor key to highlight the new equation.
- Press ◆ ↑ for [COPY].
- Use the down cursor key to return to the command line.
- Press ◆ ESC for [PASTE].

F1 Tools | F2 Algebra | F3 Calc | F4 Other | F5 PrgmIO | F6 Clean Up

■ 5·x + 25 = 500   5·x + 25 = 500

■ (5·x + 25 = 500) − 25   5·x = 475

5*x=475

MAIN   RAD AUTO   FUNC   2/30

Instead of copying and pasting, I could retype the equation in the command line.

Put brackets around the equation and divide by 5. The brackets are needed for a Computer Algebra System (CAS) to understand where the equation begins and ends.

- Press ENTER.

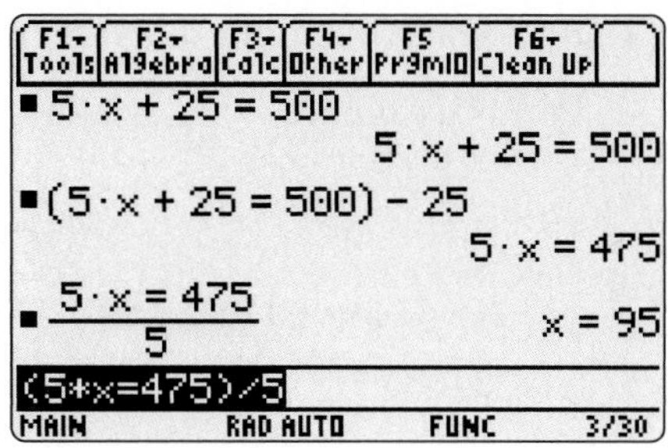

The solution is $x = 95$.

Technology Tip

When you use a CAS to solve an equation step by step, the equation should look simpler after each step. If it does not, check that you have performed the correct step. You may need to backtrack and correct your error. A CAS makes this easy, using the COPY and PASTE commands.

Check if this solution is correct by substituting $x = 95$ into the equation. The CAS result will be either true or false. Press the following:

(5 × X + 25 = 500
| X = 95) ENTER

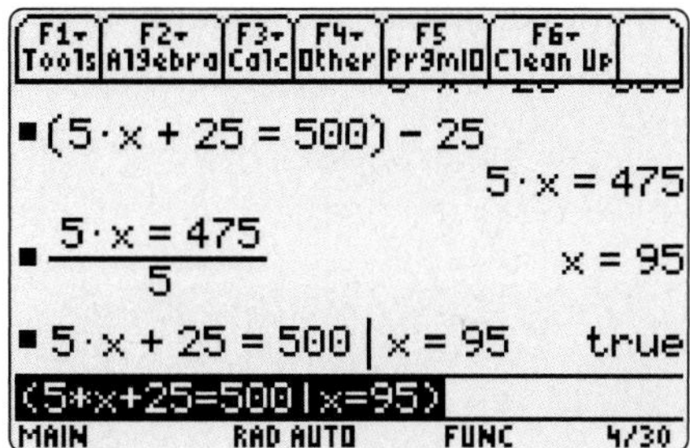

The *true* result verifies that $x = 95$ is a correct solution.

Example 4 Modelling With Equations

A student council has raised \$500 in a school spirit fundraising drive. The council decides to use the funds to buy school T-shirts to give away at a pep rally. If the T-shirts cost \$6 each, how many can the student council buy?

Solution

Use n to represent the number of T-shirts the student council can buy.

$$6n = 500$$

$$\frac{6n}{6} = \frac{500}{6} \quad \text{Divide both sides by 6.}$$

$$n = 83.\overline{3}$$

\$6 times the number of T-shirts, *n*, must give \$500. I can solve this equation for *n*.

Since you cannot buy part of a T-shirt, round to 83. The student council can buy 83 T-shirts.

Key Concepts

- To solve an equation means to find the value of the variable that makes the statement true. This is also called finding the root of the equation.
- To solve a one-step equation, isolate the variable by performing the opposite operation.
- In a two-step equation, there is more than one term on one side, so isolate the variable term first by adding or subtracting. Then, divide by the coefficient of the variable term.

  For example:

  $$2x - 7 = 9$$

  $$2x - 7 + 7 = 9 + 7$$ **Add or subtract to isolate the variable term. BEDMAS**

  $$2x = 16$$

  $$\frac{2x}{2} = \frac{16}{2}$$ **Multiply or divide to solve for the variable. BEDMAS**

  $$x = 8$$

This is like applying BEDMAS in reverse.

- Check a solution to an equation by substituting the root into the left side and the right side of the equation. Both sides must be equal.

  For the example above:
  Substitute $x = 8$.

  L.S. $= 2(8) - 7$ R.S. $= 9$
  $= 16 - 7$
  $= 9$

  L.S. = R.S.

Communicate Your Understanding

C1 Describe the first step you would take to solve each equation.

a) $k - 5 = -11$ **b)** $3m = 18$

c) $\frac{x}{5} = -4$ **d)** $5n + 75 = 225$

C2 Which is the correct solution to $2x + 5 = 21$? Explain how you can tell without solving the equation.

A $x = 7$ **B** $x = 8$ **C** $x = 9$

C3 A high school football team has raised \$1000 to spend on team jackets. The cost is \$50 per jacket. Which equation can be used to solve for the number of jackets the team can buy? Explain.

A $50 = 1000n$ **B** $50n = 1000$ **C** $1000n = 50n$

Practise

For help with questions 1 to 3, see Example 1.

1. Solve by inspection.

a) $x - 5 = 4$ **b)** $m + 8 = 11$

c) $y - 3 = 0$ **d)** $h + 2 = 6$

2. Solve using the balance method.

a) $x + 5 = 12$ **b)** $x - 6 = 7$

c) $y + 3 = 10$ **d)** $y - 4 = 2$

3. Solve using opposite operations.

a) $x + 7 = 12$ **b)** $n - 8 = 11$

c) $-5 + y = -2$ **d)** $-9 + h = -6$

For help with questions 4 and 5, see Example 2.

4. Solve using the balance method.

a) $3x = 12$ **b)** $5y = 20$

c) $\frac{n}{3} = 8$ **d)** $-2k = 16$

5. Solve using opposite operations.

a) $4z = -24$ **b)** $\frac{h}{-5} = -6$

c) $-6c = -42$ **d)** $-9u = 45$

For help with questions 6 and 7, see Example 3.

6. Find the root of each equation using paper and pencil. Apply opposite operations. Check each root.

a) $7x - 4 = 10$ **b)** $7k + 2 = 16$

c) $-p + 7 = 0$ **d)** $-12g - 33 = 0$

7. Use a CAS to solve. Apply opposite operations. Check each solution.

a) $k - 4 = -9$ **b)** $6x = -30$

c) $\frac{q}{7} = 2$ **d)** $2y - 7 = 9$

e) $-3w - 1 = 14$ **f)** $2q - 9 = -13$

8. Solve using the method of your choice. Check your answers.

a) $p + 9 = -2$ **b)** $-5x = 35$

c) $\frac{u}{4} = -8$ **d)** $6r + 3 = 33$

e) $10c - 6 = -16$ **f)** $-3v + 6 = -9$

For help with questions 9 and 10, see Example 4.

9. At a bake sale, pies cost $7 each. One customer buys $84 worth of pies.

a) Write an equation to model the number of pies the customer bought.

b) Solve the equation.

10. A hockey team has $700 to buy new jerseys. Ice-wear, a jersey supplier, charges $50 per jersey. How many new jerseys can the team buy?

a) Write an equation that models the number of jerseys the team can afford.

b) Solve the equation. Write a conclusion to the problem.

Connect and Apply

11. Copy the following solution. Write a short explanation beside each step. The first step has been done for you.

Step	*Explanation*
$3x - 8 = 7$	
$3x - 8 + 8 = 7 + 8$	**Add 8 to both sides.**
$3x = 15$	
$\frac{3x}{3} = \frac{15}{3}$	
$x = 5$	

12. Solve each equation. Express fraction answers in lowest terms. Check each solution.

a) $2k - 7 = -8$ **b)** $3x + 8 = 2$

c) $4m - 6 = 12$ **d)** $-9u + 8 = 23$

13. Solve each equation. Express fraction answers in lowest terms.

a) $8r - \frac{3}{2} = -15$ **b)** $-10h - 6 = -\frac{2}{5}$

14. Chapter Problem Your first task as producer of Canadian Superstar is to rent a theatre for the first event, a singing competition. Rental includes lunch and snacks for the competitors. Details for the two best choices are shown:

Royal James Hall	***Broadway Nights***
$50 per person	$1000 plus $30 per person

You have $2000 in your budget for this event. You would like to begin the competition with as many contestants as you can afford.

a) Write an equation to model the cost for renting Royal James Hall. Solve the equation.

b) The cost for renting Broadway Nights can be modelled by the equation $C = 1000 + 30n$.
Explain why this equation correctly gives the cost, C, in dollars, for n contestants.

c) Use the total amount budgeted ($C = 2000$) to solve this equation for n.

d) Which hall should you rent? Explain.

15. A hockey team has $700 to buy new jerseys. In question 10, you found how many jerseys the team could buy from Ice-wear. Another jersey supplier, Rink Rat, sells jerseys for $40 each plus a $75 logo design fee.

a) Write an equation that models the number of jerseys the team can afford.

b) Solve the equation.

c) From which supplier should the team buy their jerseys? Explain.

d) What other factors might influence this decision?

16. Marcel has $40 to spend on amusement park rides. Tickets cost $1.50 without a special membership pass, or $1.25 with a membership pass. A membership pass costs $5.00. Should Marcel buy a membership pass? Use mathematical reasoning to justify your answer.

Achievement Check

17. In an isosceles triangle, the equation $a + 2b = 180°$ relates the two equal angles and the third angle.

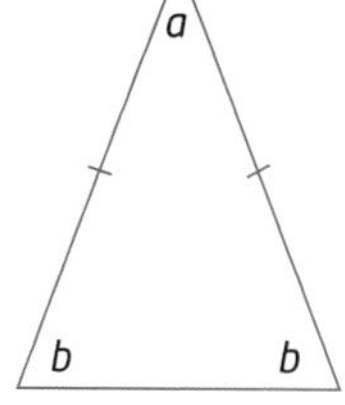

a) Use this equation to find the value of a when
- $b = 25°$
- $b = 100°$

b) Use this equation to find the value of b when
- $a = 40°$
- $a = 100°$

c) What is the maximum possible whole-number value of a? Justify your answer.

d) What is the maximum possible whole-number value of b? Justify your answer.

Extend

18. Justine's mother is building an ultralight airplane. The fuel tank is made of plastic and has a mass of 5000 g. Each litre of gasoline has a mass of 840 g. The total mass of the fuel plus the tank cannot exceed 21 800 g.

a) Write an equation that models the number of litres of gasoline that the tank may hold.

b) Solve the equation to determine the number of litres of fuel in a full tank.

19. Refer to question 14.

a) Would you change your decision if your budget were doubled for this event? Explain.

b) Is there a budget value for which it does not matter which hall you rent? If so, find the value.

20. **Math Contest** If m and n are positive integers and $m + n = 6$, which is a possible value for $3m - 2n$?

A 4 **B** -4 **C** 0 **D** 2 **E** -2

4.2 Solve Multi-Step Equations

Look at the shapes in the bridge. The beams that form the triangular structures are called trusses. These are very useful in engineering and architecture, because they add strength and stability to structures such as bridges and buildings.

Where else are you likely to find triangles in common settings? How can equations be used to describe geometric relationships and to solve problems?

Investigate

How can you use equations to model and solve problems?

These two triangles have the same perimeter.

$2x$, 3, $3x$

x, $x + 3$, $x + 4$

You can use the equation $5x + 3 = 3x + 7$ to model the situation and find the side lengths of the two triangles.

Making Connections

Perimeter is the distance around the outside of a shape. Think how each side of this equation was found.

1. Solve the equation by isolating the variable on the left side of the equation. Explain your steps in words and algebraic symbols.

2. Solve the equation by isolating the variable on the right side of the equation. Explain your steps in words and algebraic symbols.

3. **Reflect**

a) Compare your results from steps 1 and 2.

b) Explain how you can collect like terms to solve equations with the variable on both sides.

4. Describe how you would use the solution to the equation to find the side lengths of each triangle.

Example 1 Solve Equations by Collecting Like Terms

Solve.

a) $3x + 2 = 2x - 4$ **b)** $7 - 2k = 8 - 5k$ **c)** $5 - 3m = -2 - 2m$

Solution

To solve an equation involving several terms, collect variable terms on one side of the equation and **constant terms** on the other.

a)

$$3x + 2 = 2x - 4$$
$$3x + 2 - 2x = 2x - 4 - 2x$$
$$x + 2 = -4$$
$$x + 2 - 2 = -4 - 2$$
$$x = -6$$

The variable terms are $3x$ and $2x$. I'll collect these on the left side by subtracting $2x$ from each side.

The constant terms are 2 and –4. I'll collect these on the right side by subtracting 2 from each side.

b) You can collect variable terms and constant terms in one step.

Method 1: Pencil and Paper

$$7 - 2k = 8 - 5k$$
$$7 - 2k + 5k - 7 = 8 - 5k + 5k - 7$$
$$-2k + 5k = 8 - 7$$
$$3k = 1$$
$$\frac{3k}{3} = \frac{1}{3}$$ **Divide both sides by 3.**
$$k = \frac{1}{3}$$

I'll collect variable terms on the left side by adding $5k$ to both sides.

I'll collect constant terms on the right side by subtracting 7 from both sides.

Method 2: Computer Algebra System (CAS)

In the Home screen, type the equation $7 - 2k = 8 - 5k$.
Press ENTER.

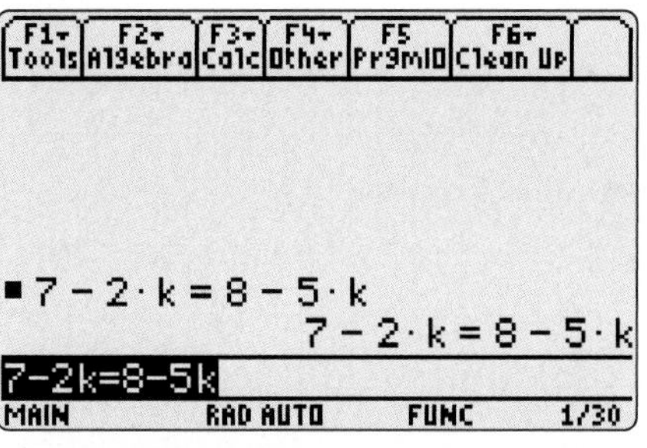

To collect variable terms on the left side and constant terms on the right, add $5k$ and subtract 7:
- Put brackets around the equation.
- Type $+ 5k - 7$.
- Press ENTER.

F1 Tools F2 Algebra F3 Calc F4 Other F5 PrgmIO F6 Clean Up
7 - 2·k = 8 - 5·k
7 - 2·k = 8 - 5·k
(7 - 2·k = 8 - 5·k) + 5·k - 7
3·k = 1
(3·k = 1)/3
k = 1/3
(3*k=1)/3
MAIN RAD AUTO FUNC 3/30

Making Connections

You learned how to collect like terms in Chapter 3.

constant term

- a term that does not include a variable
- in $2x + 5$, the constant term is 5

Literacy Connections

A constant term is called constant because its value does not change.

Technology Tip

Use the **ALPHA** key to enter variables other than **X**, **Y**, **Z**, or **T**. For example, to enter the variable k, press ALPHA EE for [K].

COPY and PASTE the resulting equation in the command line.
Put brackets around the equation.
Divide by 3 to find the solution.

$$k = \frac{1}{3}$$

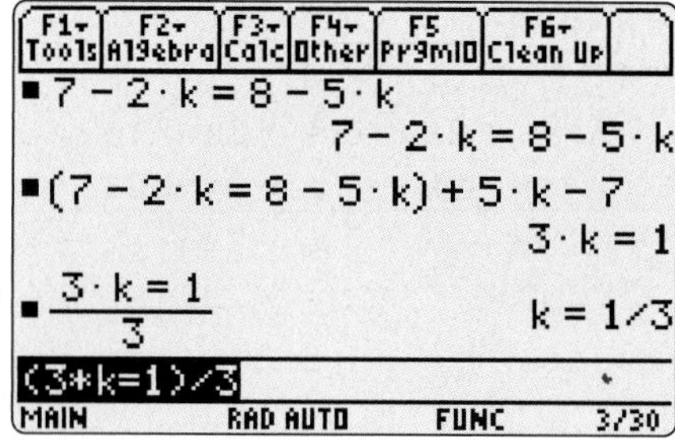

c) When you solve an equation, it does not matter which side you isolate the variable on.

Method 1: Isolate *m* on the Left Side

$$5 - 3m = -2 - 2m$$

$$5 - 3m + 2m - 5 = -2 - 2m + 2m - 5$$ Add $2m$ to both sides and subtract 5 from both sides.

$$-3m + 2m = -2 - 5$$

$$-m = -7$$

$$\frac{-m}{-1} = \frac{-7}{-1}$$ Divide both sides by -1.

m

Method 2: Isolate *m* on the Right Side

$$5 - 3m = -2 - 2m$$

$$5 - 3m + 3m + 2 = -2 - 2m + 3m + 2$$ Add $3m$ and add 2 to both sides.

$$5 + 2 = -2m + 3m$$

$$7 = m$$

Both methods give the solution, $m = 7$. In this case, isolating the variable on the right side saves a step.

Example 2 Solve Equations With Brackets

a) Solve. $5(y - 3) - (y - 2) = 19$

b) Solve and check. $2(x - 3) = -3(x + 5) - 6$

Solution

a) Expand to remove the brackets. Then, collect like terms.

$$5(y - 3) - (y - 2) = 19$$

$$5(y - 3) - 1(y - 2) = 19$$ Apply the distributive property to remove brackets.

$$5y - 15 - y + 2 = 19$$

$$4y - 13 = 19$$

$$4y - 13 + 13 = 19 + 13$$ Add 13 to both sides.

$$4y = 32$$

$$\frac{4y}{4} = \frac{32}{4}$$ Divide both sides by 4.

$$y = 8$$

b)

$$
\begin{aligned}
2(x - 3) &= -3(x + 5) - 6 && \text{Apply the distributive property to remove brackets.}\\
2x - 6 &= -3x - 15 - 6\\
2x - 6 &= -3x - 21\\
2x - 6 + 6 &= -3x - 21 + 6 && \text{Add 6 to both sides.}\\
2x &= -3x - 15\\
2x + 3x &= -3x - 15 + 3x && \text{Add 3x to both sides.}\\
5x &= -15\\
\frac{5x}{5} &= \frac{-15}{5} && \text{Divide both sides by 5.}\\
x &= -3
\end{aligned}
$$

Check by substituting $x = -3$ into each side of the equation. Both sides must have the same value for this solution to be correct.

$$
\begin{aligned}
\text{L.S.} &= 2(x - 3) & \text{R.S.} &= -3(x + 5) - 6\\
&= 2[(-3) - 3] & &= -3[(-3) + 5] - 6\\
&= 2(-6) & &= -3(2) - 6\\
&= -12 & &= -6 - 6\\
& & &= -12
\end{aligned}
$$

L.S. = R.S.

Since L.S. = R.S., $x = -3$ is the solution, or root, of the equation.

Literacy Connections

Follow these guidelines when checking a solution (root):

- Use nested brackets when substituting, where necessary. For example: $2(x - 3)$ when $x = -3$ $= 2[(-3) - 3]$
- Follow the correct order of operations. Use BEDMAS to help you remember the order.
- Remember the rules for integer operations.

Example 3 Use an Equation to Model a Geometric Relationship

A triangle has angle measures that are related as follows:

- the largest angle is triple the smallest angle
- the middle angle is double the smallest angle

Find the measures of the angles.

Solution

Let x represent the smallest angle. The other angles are double and triple this value: $2x$ and $3x$.

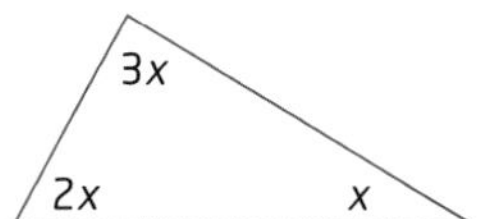

The sum of the three interior angles of a triangle is 180°.

$$
\begin{aligned}
x + 2x + 3x &= 180^\circ\\
6x &= 180^\circ\\
\frac{6x}{6} &= \frac{180^\circ}{6} && \text{Divide both sides by 6.}\\
x &= 30^\circ
\end{aligned}
$$

Have I answered the question? I have only found x, which is the smallest angle. I still need to find the other two angles.

$$
\begin{aligned}
&2x & &3x\\
&= 2(30^\circ) & &= 3(30^\circ)\\
&= 60^\circ & &= 90^\circ
\end{aligned}
$$

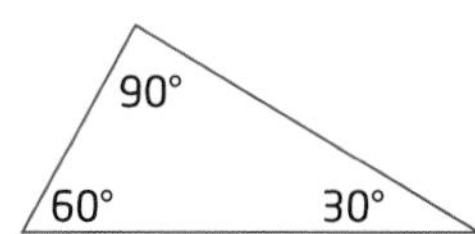

The three angles are 30°, 60°, and 90°.

Key Concepts

- To solve an equation involving multiple terms, collect variable terms on one side of the equation and constant terms on the other.
- To solve an equation involving brackets, you may need to expand the brackets first.
- Check a solution by substituting the root into the left side and right side of the original equation. Both sides must have the same value.

Communicate Your Understanding

C1 Describe the first step you would take to solve each equation.

a) $2x + 7 = 4x - 9$

b) $13 = -8 + 3m$

c) $3(k - 2) = 2(k + 8)$

C2 $p = -2$ is the correct solution to which equation? Explain how you can tell without solving the equations.

A $6p - 5 = 8p - 9$

B $4(p - 1) = -7(p + 4)$

C $3(p - 1) = -6 - (p + 5)$

Practise

For help with questions 1 to 3, see Example 1.

1. Solve using pencil and paper.

a) $3 + 4m + 5m = 21$ **b)** $16y - 8 - 9y = 27$

c) $46 = 2 - 8w - 3w$ **d)** $3d + 4 - 9d + 12 = 0$

2. Solve using pencil and paper.

a) $5x + 9 = 3x + 7$ **b)** $-2u - 8 = 5u - 1$

c) $4y - 13 = -6y + 7$ **d)** $7 - 5m = -2 - 2m$

3. Solve using a CAS. Use at least two steps.

a) $0 = 14 - x + 6x - 9$ **b)** $11 - n + 3 = 3n + 3n$

c) $4t - 5 = 2t + 5$ **d)** $6k - 3 - 2k = k - 3$

For help with questions 4 and 5, see Example 2.

4. Find the root of each equation using pencil and paper.

a) $2(x - 2) = 4x - 2$ **b)** $4c + 3 = 3(c - 4)$

c) $6p + 4(8 - p) = 22$ **d)** $k = 2(11 - k) + 14$

5. Find the root of each equation using pencil and paper. Check each solution.

a) $2(x - 3) + 3(x - 2) = 18$ **b)** $4(y - 1) - (y - 5) = 10$

c) $2(c + 2) = 5(c + 1) - 7$ **d)** $3(t - 4) = -2(t + 3) + 14$

For help with questions 6 and 7, see Example 3.

6. Two or more angles are supplementary if their sum is 180°.

a) An angle is twice the size of its supplement. Set up and solve an equation to find the measures of the two angles.

b) An angle is five times the value of its supplement. Find the measures of the two angles.

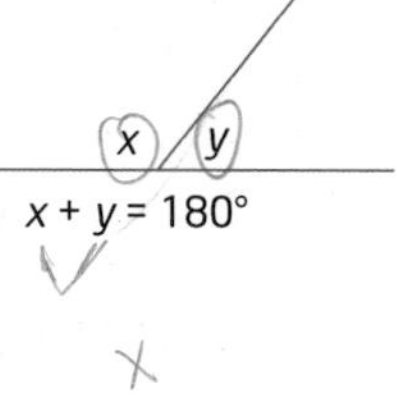

Making Connections

You will study geometric relationships in more depth in Chapter 7: Geometric Relations.

7. Two or more angles are complementary if their sum is 90°.

Three angles are complementary. One angle is double the smallest angle. The largest angle is triple the smallest angle. Find the measures of the three angles.

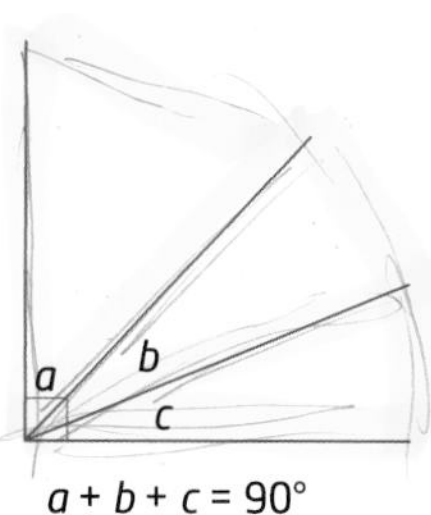

Connect and Apply

8. The following shows that $x = -3$ is the correct solution to the equation $2(x + 4) + 5 = 6 - (x + 2)$. Copy this check and explain each step. The first step has been done for you.

Step	***Explanation***
L.S. $= 2[(-3) + 4] + 5$	**Substitute the root into the left side.**
$= 2(1) + 5$	
$= 2 + 5$	
$= 7$	
R.S. $= 6 - [(-3) + 2]$	
$= 6 - (-1)$	
$= 6 + 1$	
$= 7$	
L.S. = R.S.	
Therefore, $x = -3$ is correct.	

9. Solve each equation. Express fraction answers in lowest terms. Check each solution.

a) $3x - 8 = 7x + 10$ **b)** $3 + 10i = 4i - 18$

c) $-4(u + 6) = 2(3u - 4)$ **d)** $4(k - 3) = 2 - (2k - 6)$

e) $3(p + 7) - (4p - 1) = -5(2p - 3) + 1$

f) $8 - (3w - 2) = -5(w - 3) - (4w - 3)$

10. Find the root, to one decimal place. Check each answer.

a) $3.2x - 7.4 = 2.1x + 1.5$

b) $3(2.5d - 1.1) = 2(5.2 - 3.3d)$

11. How does a Computer Algebra System handle complicated equations? Refer to Example 2, part a):

$5(y - 3) - (y - 2) = 19$

a) Enter this equation into the Home screen and press ENTER.

b) Write down the screen output.

c) Explain what the CAS did to the equation.

d) Use the CAS to finish solving the equation.

12. Use a CAS to find the root of each equation.

a) $(5q - 2) + (3 - 4q) = 4$

b) $17 = (6u + 7) - (3u - 10)$

Reasoning and Proving
Representing
Selecting Tools
Problem Solving
Connecting
Reflecting
Communicating

13. One type of truss design commonly used to build bridges is known as the Warren truss pattern. This features a series of equilateral or isosceles triangles.

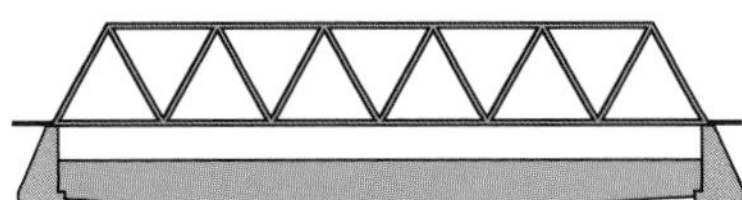

An isosceles triangle and an equilateral triangle have the same perimeter. Find the side lengths of each triangle.

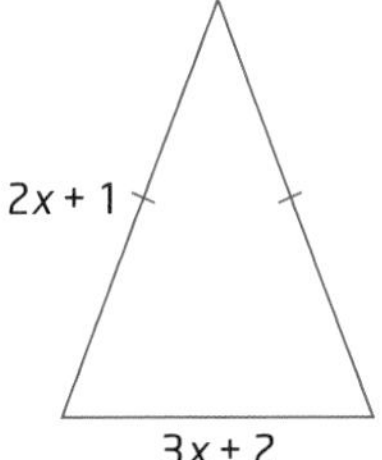

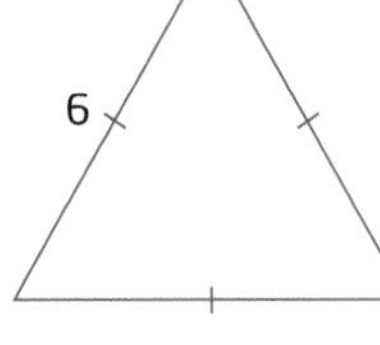

Literacy Connections

An isosceles triangle has two equal sides and two equal angles.

14. A family of isosceles triangles has the property that the two equal angles are each half the value of the third angle. Find the measures of the angles.

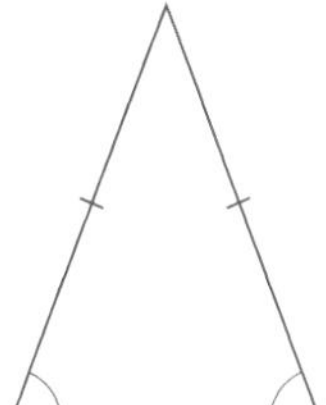

Extend

15. A family of right isosceles triangles has side lengths in the approximate ratio 1:1:1.4. A triangle belonging to this family has a perimeter of 50 cm.

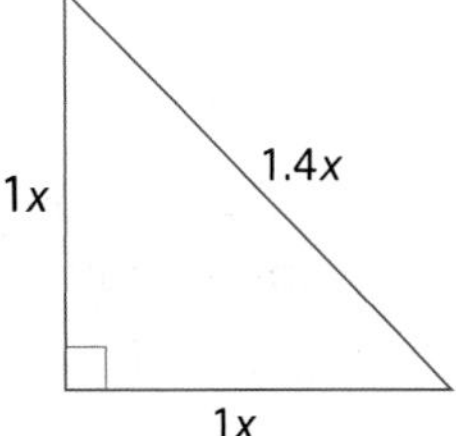

a) Find the length of each side, to the nearest tenth of a centimetre.

b) Explain how you solved this.

16. A family of right triangles has side lengths in the approximate ratio 1:1.7:2. One triangle belonging to this family has a perimeter of 100 cm. Find its area, to the nearest square centimetre.

17. Solve each equation. Express fraction answers in lowest terms.

a) $\frac{1}{2}(x + 6) = 4(x - 2)$

b) $\frac{1}{3}k + \frac{1}{2} = \frac{1}{4}k$

18. Math Contest Solve. Check your solutions.

a) $x(x - 12) = 30 + x(x + 3)$

b) $14 - x(x + 3) = 2x - x(x - 6) + 8$

19. Math Contest If $x = -4$ and $y = 3$ satisfy the equation $3x^2 + ky^2 = 24$, then which is the value of k?

A $\frac{1}{2}$ **B** $-\frac{1}{2}$ **C** 8 **D** $\frac{8}{3}$ **E** $-\frac{8}{3}$

20. Math Contest How many possible values of x make the triangle isosceles?

A 0

B 1

C 2

D 3

E more than 3

3x − 4
5x − 8
x + 6

21. Math Contest Is there a value of x that makes this triangle equilateral? Explain your decision.

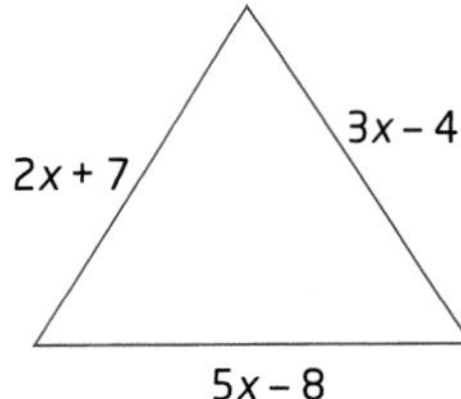

4.3 Solve Equations Involving Fractions

Rock gardens are a fascinating tradition of the Japanese culture. Their beauty is a result of a careful combination of natural landscape and artistic design. The peaceful atmosphere of a Japanese rock garden can provide moments of quiet reflection, contemplation, and appreciation of the simple beauties in life. How can mathematics be used in the design of a rock garden?

Investigate

What techniques can you use to solve equations involving fractions?

Kumiko is designing a rock garden in the shape of a trapezoid. She decides that the garden should have a front width of 8 m and a depth of 5 m. The area must be 50 m² to fit her design. How wide should Kumiko's garden be at the back?

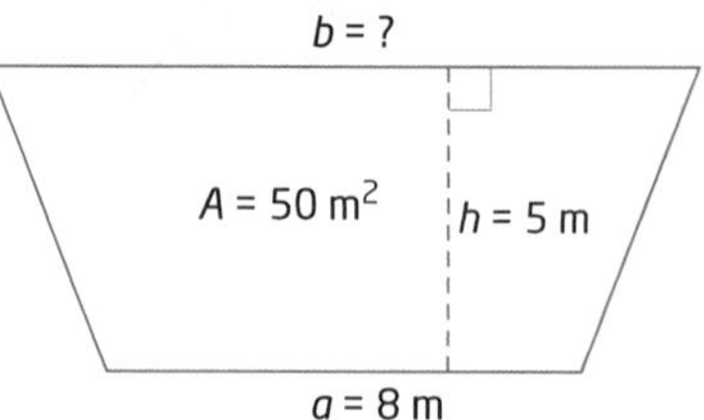

1. The formula for the area of a trapezoid is $A = \frac{(a + b)h}{2}$. Substitute the known values into this formula.

2. Find the value of the unknown, b.

3. **Reflect** Describe any difficulties you encountered in solving this equation. What can you do to make it easier to solve equations involving fractions?

Example 1 Solve Equations Involving One Fraction

Solve.

a) $6 = \frac{1}{3}(8 + x)$ **b)** $\frac{3(y - 5)}{4} = 7$

Solution

When solving an equation involving fractions, it is helpful to multiply both sides by the same value to eliminate the fractions.

a)

$$\begin{aligned} 6 &= \frac{1}{3}(8 + x) \\ 3 \times 6 &= 3 \times \frac{1}{3}(8 + x) \\ 18 &= 8 + x \\ 18 - 8 &= 8 + x - 8 \\ 10 &= x \end{aligned}$$

Instead of distributing a fraction to remove brackets, multiply both sides of the equation by 3 to eliminate the fraction on the right side.

Subtract 8 from both sides.

b) Method 1: Pencil and Paper

$$\begin{aligned} \frac{3(y - 5)}{4} &= 7 \\ 4 \times \frac{3(y - 5)}{4} &= 4 \times 7 \\ 3(y - 5) &= 28 \\ 3y - 15 &= 28 \\ 3y - 15 + 15 &= 28 + 15 \\ 3y &= 43 \\ \frac{3y}{3} &= \frac{43}{3} \\ y &= \frac{43}{3} \end{aligned}$$

Multiply both sides of the equation by 4 to eliminate the fraction.

Apply the distributive property to remove brackets.

Add 15 to both sides.

Divide both sides by 3.

Method 2: Computer Algebra System (CAS)

In the Home screen, enter the equation $\frac{3(y - 5)}{4} = 7$.

Multiply by 4 to eliminate the fraction.

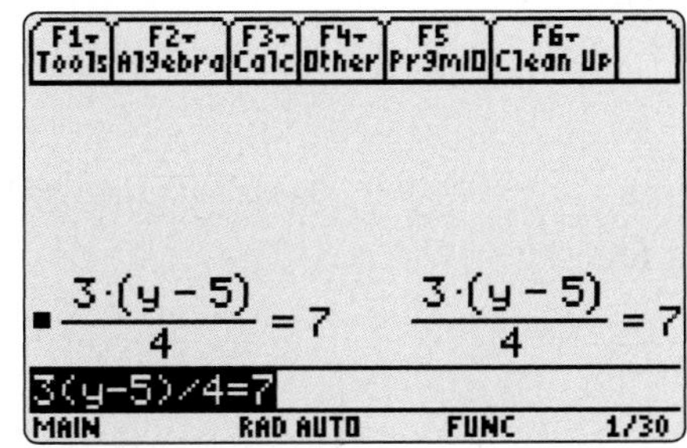

You can distribute the 3, or you can simply divide both sides by 3 to remove the brackets.

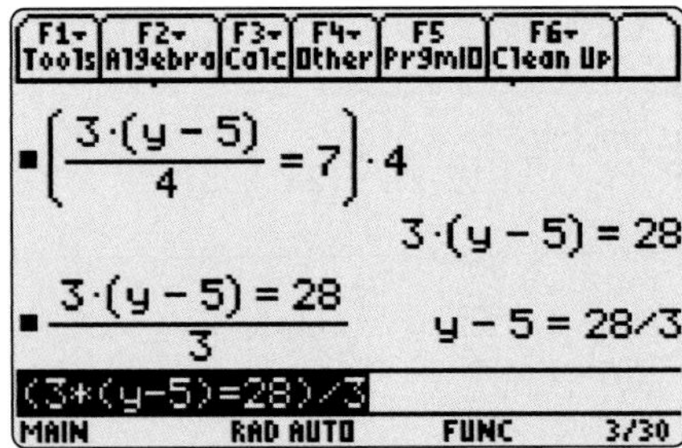

This produces an unpleasant fraction on the right side. However, a CAS has no difficulty working with fractions. Finish the solution by adding 5 to both sides.

F1 Tools F2 Algebra F3 Calc F4 Other F5 PrgmIO F6 Clean Up
■ $\left(\frac{\ldots}{4}=7\right)\cdot 4$
$3\cdot(y-5)=28$
■ $\frac{3\cdot(y-5)=28}{3}$
$y-5=28/3$
■ $(y-5=28/3)+5$
$y=43/3$
(y-5=28/3)+5
MAIN RAD AUTO FUNC 4/30

The solution is $y = \frac{43}{3}$.

Example 2 Solve Equations With More Than One Fraction

a) Solve $\frac{k+2}{3} = \frac{k-4}{5}$.

b) Solve and check $\frac{1}{3}(2x-5) = \frac{3}{4}(x-2)$.

Solution

a)

$$\frac{k+2}{3} = \frac{k-4}{5}$$

To find the LCD for $\frac{1}{3}$ and $\frac{1}{5}$, I'll count by 3s and 5s.
3 6 9 12 (15)
5 10 (15)
The LCD is 15.

$$\overset{5}{\cancel{15}} \times \frac{k+2}{\underset{1}{\cancel{3}}} = \overset{3}{\cancel{15}} \times \frac{k-4}{\underset{1}{\cancel{5}}}$$

Multiply both sides by the lowest common denominator to eliminate both fractions.

$$5(k+2) = 3(k-4)$$
$$5k + 10 = 3k - 12$$

Apply the distributive property to remove brackets.

$$5k + 10 - 3k - 10 = 3k - 12 - 3k - 10$$
$$2k = -22$$

Subtract 3*k* and 10 from both sides.

$$\frac{2k}{2} = \frac{-22}{2}$$

Divide both sides by 2.

$$k = -11$$

b)

$$\frac{1}{3}(2x - 5) = \frac{3}{4}(x - 2)$$

$$12 \times \frac{1}{3}(2x - 5) = 12 \times \frac{3}{4}(x - 2)$$

Multiply both sides by the lowest common denominator to eliminate both fractions.

I'll use prime factors to find the LCD.

3 = 3   4 = 2 × 2

The LCD is 3 × 2 × 2, or 12.

$$\frac{\overset{4}{\cancel{12}}}{1} \times \frac{1}{\underset{1}{\cancel{3}}}(2x - 5) = \frac{\overset{3}{\cancel{12}}}{1} \times \frac{3}{\underset{1}{\cancel{4}}}(x - 2)$$

$$4(2x - 5) = 9(x - 2)$$

$$8x - 20 = 9x - 18$$

Apply the distributive property to remove brackets.

$$8x - 20 - 8x + 18 = 9x - 18 - 8x + 18$$

$$-2 = x$$

Subtract $8x$ from both sides and add 18 to both sides.

Check:

$$\begin{aligned} \text{L.S.} &= \frac{1}{3}(2x - 5) \\ &= \frac{1}{3}[2(-2) - 5] \\ &= \frac{1}{3}(-4 - 5) \\ &= \frac{1}{3}(-9) \\ &= -3 \end{aligned} \qquad \begin{aligned} \text{R.S.} &= \frac{3}{4}(x - 2) \\ &= \frac{3}{4}[(-2) - 2] \\ &= \frac{3}{4}(-4) \\ &= -3 \end{aligned}$$

Substitute $x = -2$ into the left side and right side of the original equation.

L.S. = R.S.

Since L.S. = R.S., $x = -2$ is the root of this equation.

Key Concepts

- You can simplify equations involving one fraction by multiplying both sides by the denominator of the fraction.
- When eliminating more than one fraction, find the lowest common denominator and multiply all terms on both sides of the equation by this value.

Communicate Your Understanding

C1 Explain the first step you would take to solve each equation.

a) $\frac{1}{4}(x - 3) = 5$ **b)** $5 - k = \frac{2}{3}$

C2 Without solving, identify which of these equations has the solution $k = 2$.

A $\frac{2}{3}(5 - k) = 2$ **B** $k - 1 = \frac{3}{4}$ **C** $-3 = \frac{k - 17}{5}$

C3 By what value should you multiply both sides of each equation to eliminate all fractions? Explain.

a) $\frac{x + 1}{5} = \frac{x}{6}$ **b)** $\frac{y + 2}{9} = \frac{y - 3}{3}$

Practise

For help with questions 1 and 2, see Example 1.

1. Solve using pencil and paper.

a) $\frac{1}{3}(x - 2) = 5$

b) $4 = -\frac{2}{3}(p - 2)$

c) $\frac{m + 4}{3} = 7$

d) $-14 = \frac{2(h - 3)}{5}$

2. Solve using a CAS. Use at least two steps.

a) $\frac{y - 4}{5} = -6$

b) $\frac{1}{4}(u - 5) = -2$

c) $3 = \frac{2}{5}(n + 7)$

d) $16 = \frac{3(v + 7)}{2}$

For help with questions 3 and 4, see Example 2.

3. Find the root of each equation. Check your answers.

a) $\frac{m - 3}{4} = \frac{m + 1}{3}$

b) $\frac{w - 1}{4} = \frac{w + 2}{3}$

c) $\frac{1}{4}(x - 3) = \frac{1}{3}(x - 2)$

d) $\frac{1}{5}(y - 3) = \frac{1}{6}(y + 4)$

4. Find the root of each equation. Use a CAS to check your answers.

a) $\frac{2}{3}(5n - 1) = -\frac{3}{5}(n + 2)$

b) $-\frac{3}{4}(d + 3) = \frac{4}{5}(3d - 2)$

c) $\frac{3c - 2}{5} = \frac{2c - 1}{3}$

d) $\frac{5 - 2a}{4} = \frac{6 - a}{5}$

Connect and Apply

5. A trapezoidal backyard has an area of 100 m^2. The front and back widths are 8 m and 12 m, as shown.

What is the length of the yard from front to back?

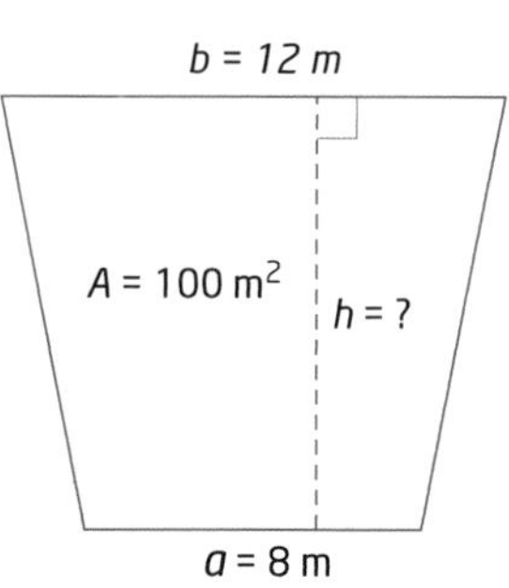

6. Each of the following solutions contains an error. Identify the error and describe how to correct it.

a)

$$\begin{aligned} \frac{x-3}{5} &= \frac{x+1}{4} \\ 5(x-3) &= 4(x+1) \\ 5x - 15 &= 4x + 4 \\ 5x - 15 - 4x + 15 &= 4x + 4 - 4x + 15 \\ x &= 19 \end{aligned}$$

b)

$$\begin{aligned} \frac{1}{3}(3y-2) &= \frac{1}{4}(y+3) \\ 12 \times \frac{1}{3}(3y-2) &= 12 \times \frac{1}{4}(y+3) \\ 3y - 2 &= y + 3 \\ 3y - 2 - y + 2 &= y + 3 - y + 2 \\ 2y &= 5 \\ \frac{2y}{2} &= \frac{5}{2} \\ y &= \frac{5}{2} \end{aligned}$$

7. The equation $C = \frac{5}{9}(F - 32)$ allows you to convert between Celsius and Fahrenheit temperatures. C is the temperature in degrees Celsius (°C) and F is the temperature in degrees Fahrenheit (°F).

a) A U.S. weather station predicts that the overnight low temperature will reach 25°F. What is this in degrees Celsius?

b) Room temperature is approximately 20°C. What is this equivalent to in degrees Fahrenheit?

Did You Know?

The Celsius scale is based on two key properties of water. Under normal conditions, water freezes at 0°C and boils at 100°C. Splitting the temperature difference between these two points into 100 equal intervals produces the Celsius scale.

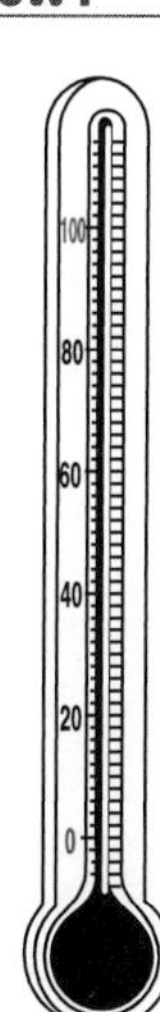

8. Find the height of a triangle with base 10 cm and area 50 cm^2.

9. A garden is in the shape of a right triangle. The base of the triangle is 12 m, and the garden covers an area of 30 m^2. What length of fence is needed to surround the garden?

Achievement Check

10. A backyard has a perimeter of 144 m.

a) If the backyard is square, what are the dimensions?

b) If the backyard is rectangular, and the length is three times the width, what are the dimensions?

c) If the backyard is a triangle, as shown, write an algebraic expression for the perimeter and find its dimensions.

d) Which of the three backyard designs has the greatest area? Which has the least?

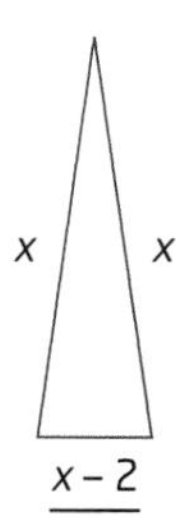

Extend

11. Solve.

a) $\frac{3p}{4} + \frac{p - 5}{3} = \frac{1}{2}$

b) $\frac{u - 3}{4} - 2 = \frac{3u}{2} + \frac{2u + 1}{5}$

12. Fahad called Sara over. "I'm stuck on this question about equations," he said.

"Where did you get it from?" asked Sara.

"From my older brother's book," Fahad told her. "It asks you to find the roots of $x(x - 5) = 0$. I know how to solve equations, but this one is different."

Sara said "I know! The answer is $x = 0$! If I substitute 0, it works!"

"Great!" said Fahad. "But the book says there are two roots."

"Well," said Sara, "if $a \times b = 0$, then either $a = 0$ or $b = 0$."

"I've got it!" said Fahad. "The other solution is $x = 5$, because it makes the value of the second bracket zero."

"Excellent!" said Sara.

Solve these questions from Fahad's brother's book.

a) $(x - 3)(x - 7) = 0$ (2 roots)

b) $x(x - 4)(x + 2) = 0$ (3 roots)

13. Math Contest Diophantus of Alexandria was born around the year 200. He is known as the Father of Arithmetic. A puzzle about Diophantus is as follows:

"His boyhood lasted one sixth of his life. He married after one seventh more. His beard grew after one twelfth more and his son was born 5 years later. The son lived to half his father's final age, and the father died 4 years after the son."

How old was Diophantus when he died?

4.4 Modelling With Formulas

The CN Tower, in downtown Toronto, is the world's tallest freestanding structure. It was built in the 1970s as a giant radio antenna. Every year, thousands of tourists enjoy a thrilling ride to the top and a breathtaking view. Have you ever been up the CN Tower? How far can you see?

Investigate

How can you use formulas to solve problems?

formula

- describes an algebraic relationship between two or more variables

Have you ever seen a ship disappear over the horizon? This happens because of the curvature of Earth. The higher you are above the surface of Earth, the farther away the horizon appears. The relationship between how high you are and how far you can see is given by the **formula**

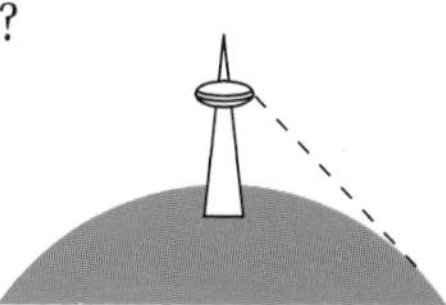

$d = 2\sqrt{3.2h}$

where h is your height, in metres, above ground and d is the distance, in kilometres, to the horizon. Use this relationship to answer the following.

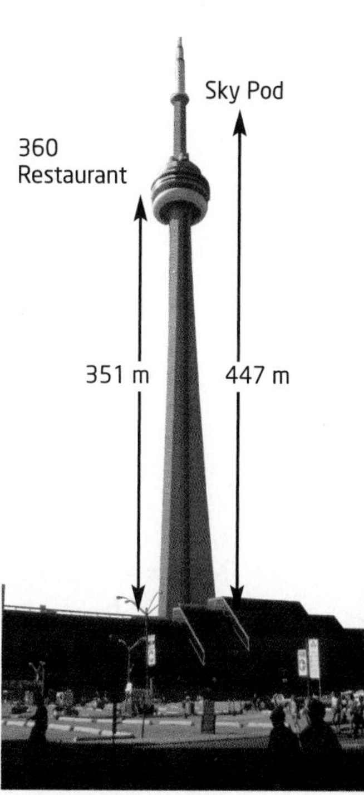

1. How far can you see from each? Round your answers to the nearest kilometre.

a) the 360 Restaurant

b) the Sky Pod observation deck

2. a) How high would you have to go for the horizon to appear to be 100 km away? Round your answer to the nearest metre.

b) Explain how you found your answer.

3. Reflect Explain how you can use formulas in different ways to solve problems. Think of other formulas that you have used before. Use one of them to illustrate your explanation.

Example 1 Rearrange a Formula in One Step

Making Connections

You will explore geometric relationships in greater depth in Chapter 7: Geometric Relations.

a) In geometry, an exterior angle of a triangle is equal to the sum of the two opposite interior angles:
$d = a + b$

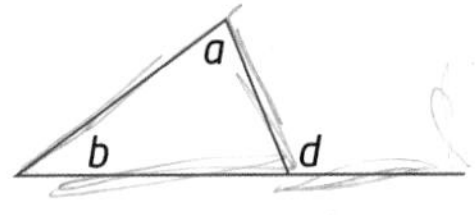

Rearrange this formula to express a in terms of b and d.

b) The circumference of a circle, in terms of its radius, is given by the formula $C = 2\pi r$. Rearrange this formula to isolate r.

c) The area, A, of a square is related to its side length, l, by the formula $A = l^2$. Find the length, to the nearest tenth of a centimetre, of a side of a square with area 32 cm^2.

Solution

a) $d = a + b$

This formula expresses d in terms of a and b. To express a in terms of b and d, subtract b from both sides of the equation.

$$d - b = a + b - b$$
$$d - b = a$$
$$\text{or } a = d - b$$

b) $C = 2\pi r$

$$\frac{C}{2\pi} = \frac{\cancel{2\pi} r}{\cancel{2\pi}}$$
$$\frac{C}{2\pi} = r$$
$$\text{or } r = \frac{C}{2\pi}$$

This formula has C isolated. To isolate r, I need to divide both sides of the equation by 2π.

c) $A = l^2$

The formula gives A in terms of l. You can also use it to find l if you are given A.

Method 1: Substitute, Then Rearrange

Substitute $A = 32$.

$$32 = l^2$$
$$\sqrt{32} = l$$
$$5.66 \doteq l$$

The square of a number gives 32. To find the number, I need to take the square root. I'll use a calculator.

The side length of the square is 5.7 cm, to the nearest tenth of a centimetre.

Technology Tip

Calculators vary. The key sequence may be different on your calculator. Check using a value you know, such as $\sqrt{25} = 5$.

Method 2: Rearrange, Then Substitute

Rearrange the formula to express l in terms of A.

$A = l^2$ **Take the square root of both sides.**

$\sqrt{A} = l$

or $l = \sqrt{A}$

Substitute $A = 32$.

$l = \sqrt{32}$

$\doteq 5.66$

The side length is 5.7 cm, to the nearest tenth of a centimetre.

These two methods each take about the same amount of time and effort. However, by rearranging the formula before substituting, you get a new formula, $l = \sqrt{A}$, that you can use again, if needed.

Example 2 Rearrange a Formula in More Than One Step

The equation of a line relates y to x, m, and b: $y = mx + b$
Rearrange this equation to express x in terms of y, m, and b.

Making Connections

In Chapter 6: Analyse Linear Relations you will learn the significance of *m* and *b* in the $y = mx + b$ form of a linear equation.

Solution

To rearrange a formula in terms of an unknown variable,
- isolate the term that contains the unknown variable
- isolate the unknown variable

Method 1: Use Opposite Operations, Pencil and Paper

$y = mx + b$

$y - b = mx + b - b$ **Subtract *b* from both sides to isolate the term containing *x*.**

$y - b = mx$

$\frac{y - b}{m} = \frac{mx}{m}$ **Divide both sides by *m* to isolate *x*.**

$\frac{y - b}{m} = x$

or $x = \frac{y - b}{m}$

Method 2: Use Opposite Operations, Computer Algebra System (CAS)

In the Home screen, type the formula $y = mx + b$. Make sure that you use a multiplication sign between m and x, or the CAS will consider mx as a single variable.

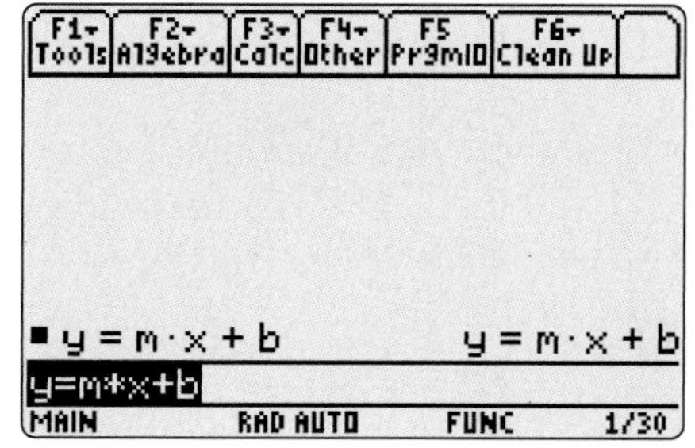

Subtract b to isolate the term containing x.

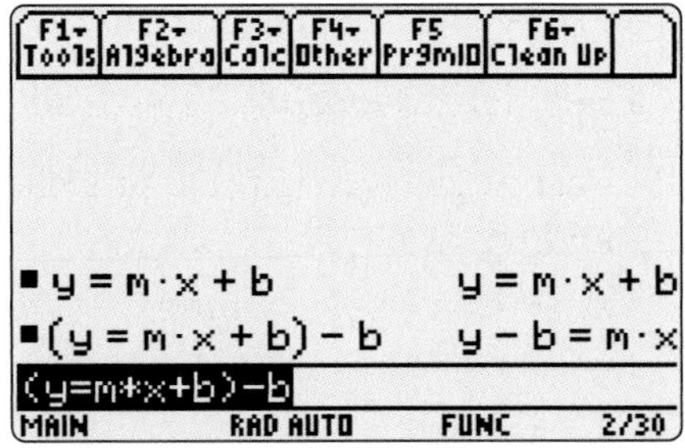

Divide by m to isolate x.

$$\frac{y-b}{m} = x$$

$$\text{or } x = \frac{y-b}{m}$$

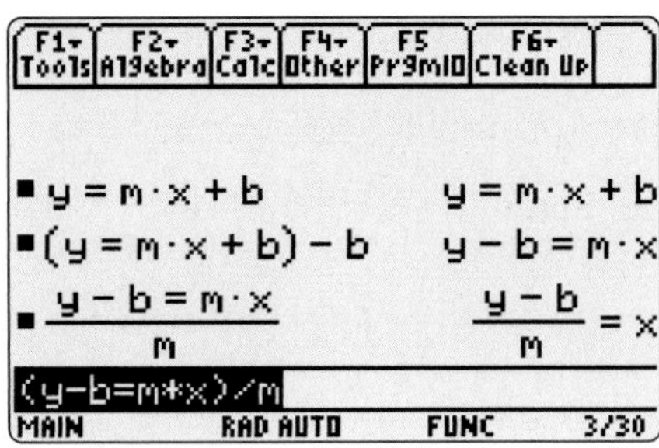

Key Concepts

- Formulas can be rearranged to isolate different variables.
- To rearrange a formula in terms of a variable,
  - isolate the term that contains the variable
  - isolate the variable

Communicate Your Understanding

C1 Describe the first step you would take to isolate the variable indicated for each equation.

a) $v = \frac{d}{t}$ for d (speed)

b) $y = mx + b$ for m (linear relations)

c) $A = \pi r^2$ for r (area of a circle)

C2 Describe any advantages to rearranging a formula before substituting values.

C3 The formula for the perimeter of a rectangle can be expressed in more than one way. One way is $P = 2(l + w)$. Discuss how you could manipulate this equation to isolate l. Write down the steps and include an explanation of each step. Is there more than one way to do this? Explain.

Practise

For help with question 1, see Example 1.

1. Rearrange each formula to isolate the variable indicated using pencil and paper.

a) $P = 4s$	for s	(perimeter of a square)
b) $A = P + I$	for P	(investments)
c) $C = 2\pi r$	for r	(circumference of a circle)
d) $y = mx + b$	for b	(linear relations)

For help with question 2, see Example 2.

2. Rearrange each formula to isolate the variable indicated.

a) $d = mt + b$	for m	(distance-time relationships)
b) $P = 2l + 2w$	for w	(perimeter of a rectangle)
c) $a = \frac{v}{t}$	for v	(acceleration)
d) $v = \frac{d}{t}$	for t	(speed)
e) $A = \pi r^2$	for r	(area of a circle)
f) $P = I^2R$	for I	(electrical power)

Connect and Apply

3. You can use the formula $C = 2.5I$ to obtain an approximate value for converting a length, I, in inches to a length, C, in centimetres.
   a) Use the formula to find the number of centimetres in
   - 6 inches
   - 3 feet (1 foot = 12 inches)

   b) Rearrange the formula to express I in terms of C.
   c) How many inches are in
   - 75 cm?
   - 1 m?

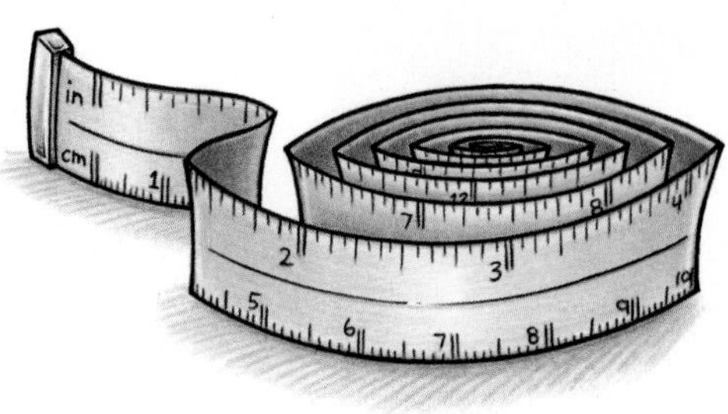

4. Refer to question 3.
   a) Plot a graph of $C = 2.5I$, either by hand or using technology such as a graphing calculator or graphing software.
   b) Is the graph linear or non-linear? Explain.
   c) Use the graph to find
   - the number of centimetres in 8 inches
   - the number of inches in 35 cm

Making Connections

You learned about linear and non-linear relations in Chapter 2: Relations.

5. Refer to questions 3 and 4. Describe one advantage and one disadvantage of using
   a) the equation model **b)** the graphical model

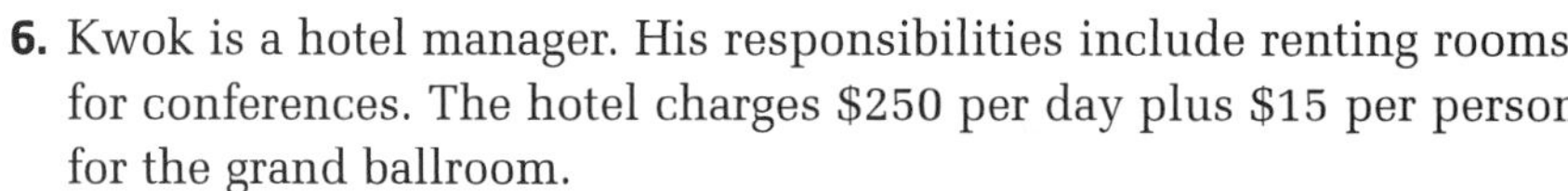

6. Kwok is a hotel manager. His responsibilities include renting rooms for conferences. The hotel charges \$250 per day plus \$15 per person for the grand ballroom.
   a) Create a formula that relates the cost, C, in dollars, of renting the ballroom to the number of people, n.
   b) How much should Kwok charge to rent the hall for
   - 50 people?
   - 100 people?

   c) Rearrange your formula to express n in terms of C.
   d) How many people could attend a wedding reception if the wedding planners have a budget of
   - \$4000?
   - \$2000?

   e) In part d), is it better to substitute into the original equation or the rearranged equation? Explain.
   f) Is the relationship between cost and number of guests linear or non-linear? Explain how you can tell.

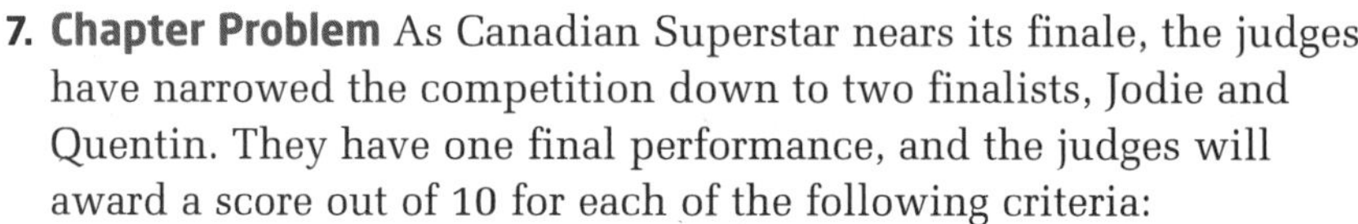

7. **Chapter Problem** As Canadian Superstar nears its finale, the judges have narrowed the competition down to two finalists, Jodie and Quentin. They have one final performance, and the judges will award a score out of 10 for each of the following criteria:
   - vocal performance, v
   - movement, m
   - stage presence, p

   The formula $S = 7v + 5m + 3p$ will be used to determine each competitor's overall score, S.
   a) After Jodie's performance, the judges awarded her scores of 9 for vocal performance, 7 for movement, and 7 for stage presence. What is Jodie's overall score?
   b) It is Quentin's turn. Quentin thinks he can match Jodie on vocal performance, but will likely score only a 6 on movement. Can Quentin win the competition? If so, what is the minimum score he must obtain for stage presence?

8. The area, A, of a square is related to its perimeter, P, by the formula
$$A = \frac{P^2}{16}$$
   a) Rearrange this formula to express P in terms of A.
   b) Find the perimeter of a square with area
   - 25 cm^2
   - 50 cm^2

9. Refer to question 8.

a) Solve this problem using a graphing calculator or graphing software, by entering the equation shown.

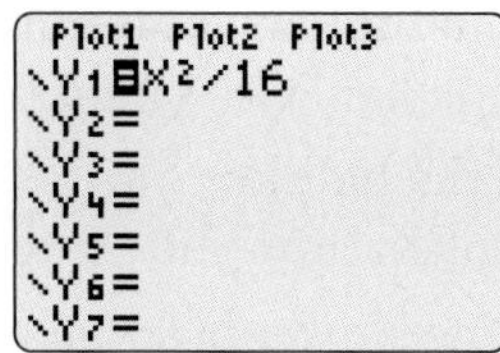

b) Is this a linear or non-linear relation? Explain how you know.

c) Describe two advantages of using an algebraic model to solve this problem.

d) Describe two advantages of using a graphical model to solve this problem.

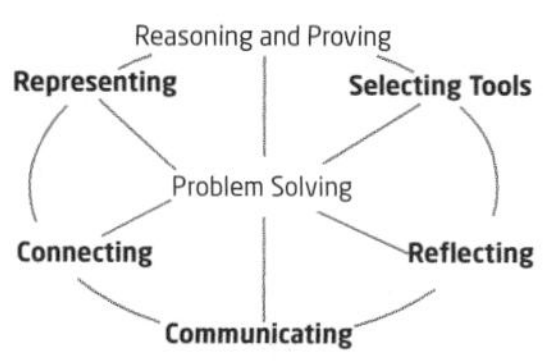

10. The kinetic energy (energy due to motion) of an object depends on its mass and how fast it is moving:

$$E = \frac{1}{2}mv^2$$

In this formula,

- E is the kinetic energy, in joules
- m is the mass, in kilograms
- v is the speed, in metres per second

The following steps show how the formula can be rearranged to express v in terms of E and m. Copy these steps into your notebook and write a short explanation beside each one. Some hints are provided for you.

Step	***Explanation***
$E = \frac{1}{2}mv^2$	**Start with the original formula.**
$2E = mv^2$	**____________ both sides of the equation by ______.**
$\frac{2E}{m} = \frac{mv^2}{m}$	
$\frac{2E}{m} = v^2$	
$\sqrt{\frac{2E}{m}} = \sqrt{v^2}$	**Take the __________ __________ of both sides.**
$\sqrt{\frac{2E}{m}} = v$	

Did You Know?

The formula in question 10 will remind you of Albert Einstein's famous equation $E = mc^2$. In 1905, while he was studying for his Ph.D. at the University of Zurich in Switzerland, Einstein published several papers which revolutionized scientific ideas. Included in these publications was his discovery that Energy = mass × (speed of light)^2. This property has had huge implications in many fields. In medicine, it is the basis on which modern diagnostic imaging scanners work.

11. Use the formula in question 10 to solve this problem.

    Two koala bears, Rocco and Biff, are wrestling in a meadow, when suddenly they notice a nice clump of eucalyptus fall to the ground. Both bears bolt for the tasty treat at the same time. Rocco's mass is 5 kg and he has 4.2 J of kinetic energy. Biff is half a kilogram heavier than Rocco, but has 1 J more of kinetic energy.

    a) Who will reach the eucalyptus first? Explain how you know.

    b) How much more kinetic energy would the slower bear have to exert for the two bears to reach the eucalyptus at the same time?

12. Sometimes the same formula can have many different forms. $PV = nRT$ is a useful formula in chemistry. It relates the characteristics of a gas:

Variable	Characteristic
P	pressure
V	volume
R	universal gas constant
n	number of moles, or how much gas there is
T	temperature

a) Rearrange this formula to isolate each variable. The first one is done for you as an example:

$$PV = nRT$$

$$\frac{PV}{V} = \frac{nRT}{V}$$

$$P = \frac{nRT}{V}$$ The formula is rearranged to isolate pressure, P.

b) Explain when these forms may be more useful than the form $PV = nRT$.

Extend

Making Connections

You will explore measurement relationships in greater depth in Chapter 8: Measurement and Chapter 9: Optimization.

13. The area, A, of a square is related to its side length, l, by the formula $A = l^2$.

    a) Express l in terms of A.

    b) Graph both formulas using a graphing calculator or graphing software.

    c) How are the graphs similar?

    d) How are they different?

14. The volume, V, of a cube is related to its side length, l, by the formula $V = l^3$.

    a) Rearrange the formula to express l in terms of V.

    b) Graph both formulas and comment on any similarities or differences you see.

15. The distance an accelerating object travels is related to its initial speed, v, its rate of acceleration, a, and time, t:

$$d = vt + \frac{1}{2}at^2$$

a) Rearrange this formula to isolate v.

b) An object travels 30 m while accelerating at a rate of 6 m/s^2 for 3 s. What was its initial speed?

16. Refer to the formula in question 15.

a) Rearrange the formula to isolate a.

b) What acceleration would be required for the object in question 15 part b) to have travelled twice the distance in the same time interval?

17. Math Contest The formula for keyboarding speed (s) is $s = \frac{w - 10e}{t}$, where e is the number of errors, w is the number of words typed, and t is the time, in minutes. Solve the formula for e and find the number of errors made by Saher, who typed 400 words in 5 min, and had a keyboarding speed of 70 words per minute.

18. Math Contest The period (time for one complete swing back and forth) p, in seconds, of a pendulum is related to its length, L, in metres, by the formula $p = 2\pi\sqrt{\frac{L}{g}}$, where $g = 9.8$ m/s^2 is a constant. Solve this formula for L, and find the length needed for the pendulum to have a period of 1 s.

19. Math Contest The escape velocity (speed needed to escape a planet's gravitational field), in metres per second, is given by $v = \sqrt{\frac{2GM}{r}}$.

$M = 5.98 \times 10^{24}$ kg is the mass of the Earth,
$G = 0.000\,000\,000\,066\,73$ (a constant), and r is the radius of the orbit. The average radius of Earth is 6.38×10^6 m.

a) Find the escape velocity for an Earth satellite in kilometres per second.

b) Solve the formula for M.

c) Find the mass of the planet Mars. Mars has a diameter of 6794 km. A Martian satellite requires an escape velocity of 5 km/s.

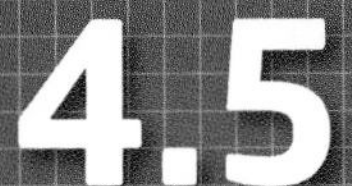

4.5 Modelling With Algebra

Algebra is an efficient way to express mathematical ideas. Algebraic modelling is one of many ways to solve a problem. The best method often depends on the type of problem and the preference of the problem solver.

Investigate

How can you use algebraic modelling to solve problems?

1. Work with a partner or in a small group. One person will be the magician, and the others will be the audience. Have all students close their textbooks except the magician.

Magician's Instructions to the Audience

2. Tell the audience to pick a number from 1 to 10 and write it down so everyone but the magician can see it. Instruct the audience to carry out the following arithmetic steps, out of view of the magician.
   - **a)** Take the number and double it.
   - **b)** Add 50.
   - **c)** Triple the result.
   - **d)** Subtract 100.
   - **e)** Divide this value in half.
   - **f)** Write down the final result and show it to the magician. Show *only* the final result.

Magician's Secret Steps to Find the Number

3. Look at the result. Announce the following: "I will now use the magic of algebra to determine your number!" Add a magic word or phrase if you like. Try not to let the audience know that you are doing the following calculations mentally.
   - **a)** Subtract 25 from the number you see.
   - **b)** Divide by 3. The result is the number the audience picked.
   - **c)** Announce the number to the amazement of your audience. Take a bow!

4. Repeat the magic trick with a different number.

Time to Reveal the Secret

5. Everyone in the group should now open their books and look at all of the instructions. As a group, discuss how you think this magic trick works.

6. Reflect

a) Is this trick really magic? Explain.

b) Will this trick work for numbers greater than 10? What about negative numbers? Explain.

c) How can you use algebra to create a magic trick of your own?

Example 1 Apply Algebraic Modelling to a Payroll Problem

Mr. Skyvington operates a variety store with his two sons, Jerry and Koko.

- Jerry makes twice as much as Koko, who only works part-time.
- Mr. Skyvington makes $200 per week more than Jerry.
- The total weekly payroll is $1450.

How much does each family member earn per week?

Solution

Use algebra to model and solve the problem.

Write an expression that describes each person's earnings. Let k represent Koko's earnings.

Worker	Expression	Explanation
Koko	k	Koko's earnings are unknown.
Jerry	$2k$	Jerry makes twice as much as Koko.
Mr. Skyvington	$2k + 200$	Mr. Skyvington earns $200 more than Jerry.
Total	$1450	

Use a table to organize your thinking.

Write an equation that relates these expressions to the total payroll.

$$\underbrace{k}_{\text{Koko's earnings}} + \underbrace{2k}_{\text{Jerry's earnings}} + \underbrace{2k + 200}_{\text{Mr. Skyvington's earnings}} = \underbrace{1450}_{\text{Total payroll}}$$

Solve the equation for k.

$$k + 2k + 2k + 200 = 1450$$
$$5k + 200 = 1450$$
$$5k + 200 - 200 = 1450 - 200$$ **Subtract 200 from both sides.**
$$5k = 1250$$
$$\frac{5k}{5} = \frac{1250}{5}$$ **Divide both sides by 5.**
$$k = 250$$

I can check to see if these answers add to give the correct total:

Koko:	$250
Jerry:	$500
Mr. Skyvington:	$700
Total	$1450

The three wages add to the correct total.

The solution $k = 250$ means that Koko earns $250 per week. Substitute into the other expressions to find how much Jerry and Mr. Skyvington earn.

Jerry:

$$2k$$
$$= 2(250)$$
$$= 500$$

Jerry earns $500 per week.

Mr. Skyvington:

$$2k + 200$$
$$= 2(250) + 200$$
$$= 500 + 200$$
$$= 700$$

Mr. Skyvington earns $700 per week.

Example 2 Apply Algebraic Modelling to an Earnings Problem

Uma works at a ballpark, selling peanuts. She is paid $6/h plus a 50¢ commission for every bag of peanuts she sells.

a) Find Uma's earnings if she sells 42 bags of peanuts during a 4-h shift.

b) How many bags of peanuts must she sell to earn $100 in 7 h?

Solution

a) Uma is paid in two ways:

- for the length of time she works (hourly wage)
- for the number of bags of peanuts she sells (commission)

Write an expression for each. Then, write a formula that models Uma's total earnings.

Earnings	Variable	Expression	Explanation
Hourly Wage	h	$6h$	Uma makes $6/h.
Commission	p	$0.5p$	Uma earns 50¢ per bag of peanuts.
Total Earnings	E	$6h + 0.5p$	Add wage and commission to get total earnings.

The following formula describes Uma's earnings:

$E = 6h + 0.5p$

Substitute $h = 4$ and $p = 42$ to find Uma's total earnings.

$$E = 6(4) + 0.5(42)$$
$$= 24 + 21$$
$$= 45$$

Uma earns $45 if she sells 42 bags of peanuts in 4 h.

b) To find the number of bags of peanuts Uma must sell to make $100 in 7 h, rearrange the formula to express p in terms of E and h.

$$E = 6h + 0.5p$$
$$E - 6h = 6h + 0.5p - 6h$$ **Subtract 6*h* from both sides.**
$$E - 6h = 0.5p$$

Literacy Connections

A wage is a payment that depends on the length of time worked. A commission is a payment based on the number of items sold or a percent of total sales.

Method 1: Divide by 0.5

$$E - 6h = 0.5p$$
$$\frac{E - 6h}{0.5} = \frac{0.5p}{0.5}$$
$$\frac{E - 6h}{0.5} = p$$
$$\text{or } p = \frac{E - 6h}{0.5}$$

Substitute $E = 100$ and $h = 7$.

$$p = \frac{100 - 6(7)}{0.5}$$
$$= \frac{100 - 42}{0.5}$$
$$= \frac{58}{0.5}$$
$$= 116$$

Method 2: Multiply by 2

$$E - 6h = 0.5p$$
$$2(E - 6h) = 2(0.5)p$$
$$2(E - 6h) = p$$
$$\text{or } p = 2(E - 6h)$$

Substitute $E = 100$ and $h = 7$.

$$p = 2[(100) - 6(7)]$$
$$= 2(100 - 42)$$
$$= 2(58)$$
$$= 116$$

I can also solve for p by multiplying by 2, because 0.5 is $\frac{1}{2}$. $2 \times 0.5p = p$

Uma must sell 116 bags of peanuts to earn $100 in a 7-h shift.

Compare these two equations: $p = \frac{E - 6h}{0.5}$ and $p = 2(E - 6h)$.

These are equivalent equations. Why do you think the second equation may be a little easier to use?

Example 3 Compare Algebraic Modelling With Other Strategies

Tan is designing a Japanese rock garden in the shape of a right triangle so that the second-shortest side is twice the length of the shortest side. The area of the garden must be 30 m^2. What are the three side lengths of Tan's garden, to the nearest tenth?

Solution

Method 1: Algebraic Model

The garden is in the shape of a right triangle. The second-shortest side is twice the length of the shortest side.

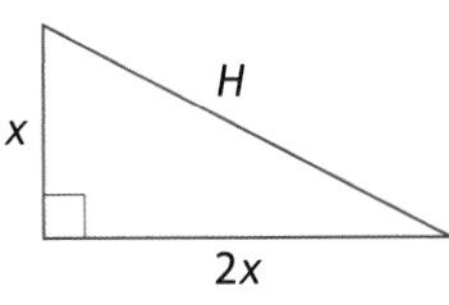

Let x represent the shortest side and $2x$ the second-shortest side.

Let H represent the hypotenuse.

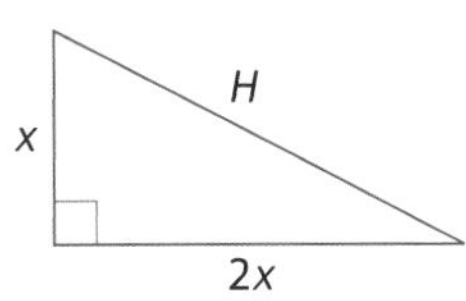

Apply the formula for the area of a triangle.

$$A = \frac{1}{2}bh$$

$$30 = \frac{1}{2}(2x)(x)$$ **Substitute $b = 2x$ and $h = x$.**

$$30 = \frac{1}{2}(2x^2)$$

$$30 = x^2$$

$$\sqrt{30} = \sqrt{x^2}$$ **Take the square root of both sides.**

$$5.48 \doteq x$$

The length of the shortest side is 5.5 m, to the nearest tenth. Double this to find the length of the second-shortest side.

$$2x$$
$$= 2(5.5)$$
$$= 11$$

The two shorter sides are 5.5 m and 11 m. Apply the Pythagorean theorem to find the hypotenuse.

$$H^2 = 5.5^2 + 11^2$$
$$H^2 = 30.25 + 121$$
$$H^2 = 151.25$$
$$\sqrt{H^2} = \sqrt{151.25}$$ **Take the square root of both sides.**
$$H \doteq 12.3$$

The algebraic model shows how measurement, algebra, and the Pythagorean Theorem are all connected. That's cool!

The three side lengths of Tan's garden are 5.5 m, 11 m, and 12.3 m.

Method 2: Construct a Graphical Model With *The Geometer's Sketchpad*®

Open a new sketch and construct a right triangle that meets the requirements.

• Construct a horizontal line segment AB.

Technology Tip

Hold the Shift key down while you drag to make vertical and horizontal line segments.

Remember to deselect before making new selections. You can deselect by clicking anywhere in the white space with the **Selection Arrow Tool**.

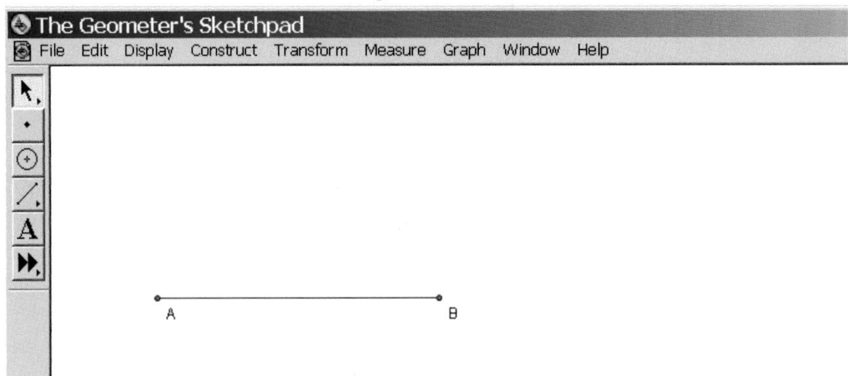

• Select point A. From the **Transform** menu, choose **Mark Center**.
• Select line segment AB and point B. From the **Transform** menu, choose **Dilate**. Dilate the segment in the ratio 1:2. Click on **Dilate**.

- Select AB′. From the **Transform** menu, choose **Rotate**. Rotate the segment and point by 90°. Click on **Rotate**.
- Construct a segment that connects B and B″.

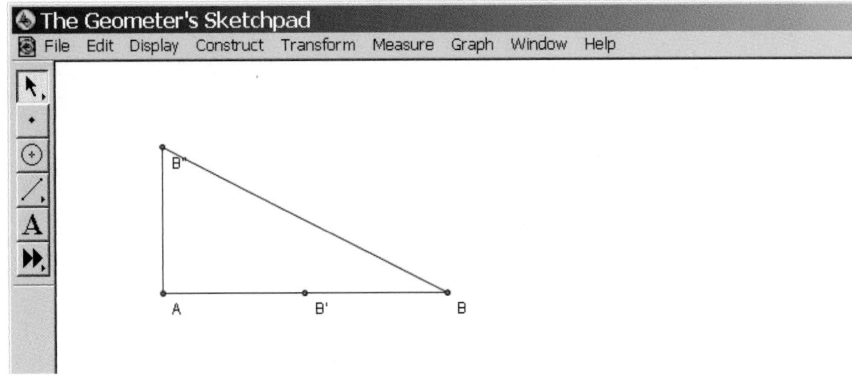

Measure the lengths of the three sides and verify that the two shorter sides are in the ratio 1:2.

- Select the three sides and, from the **Measure** menu, choose **Length**.
- From the **Measure** menu, choose **Calculate**. Divide the longer measure by the shorter measure.

Next, measure the area of the triangle.

- Select the three vertices, and from the **Construct** menu, choose **Triangle Interior**.
- From the **Measure** menu, choose **Area**.

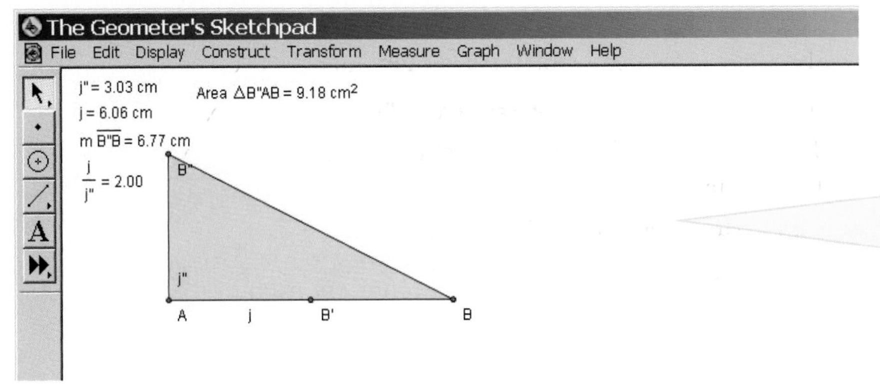

Once I set up a geometric model with *The Geometer's Sketchpad®*, I can explore all kinds of relationships. I wonder how perimeter and area are related in this type of triangle.

- Adjust the size of the triangle so that its area is as close to 30 cm^2 as possible. Select and drag any of the vertices. Verify that the triangle has the following properties:
  - it is a right triangle
  - the second-shortest side is twice the length of the shortest side

The lengths of the three sides give the dimensions of Tan's garden. The measures are in centimetres in the sketch, but Tan's garden is measured in metres. The lengths of the three sides of Tan's garden are 5.5 m, 11 m, and 12 m.

Key Concepts

- Algebraic modelling is one method that can be used to describe mathematical situations and solve problems.
- Many problems can be solved using more than one method.

Communicate Your Understanding

C1 Rufio is 5 years older than his sister, Hanna. The sum of their ages is 37. Which equation can you use to find their ages? Explain why.

A $5h = 37$ **B** $h + 5h = 37$

C $h + 5 = 37$ **D** $h + (h + 5) = 37$

C2 One summer, Brittany had a paper route and a babysitting job. She made twice as much money babysitting as she did delivering papers. Altogether she made \$800 that summer. Which equation can you use to find how much Brittany earned delivering papers? Explain.

A $2p = 800$ **B** $p + 2p = 800$

C $p + 2 = 800$ **D** $p + (p + 2) = 800$

C3 Asraf sells computers. He is paid \$12/h, plus a 10% commission on sales. Which expression describes Asraf's total earnings? Explain.

A $12h + 0.1$ **B** $12 + 0.1s$

C $12h + 0.1s$ **D** $12h + 10s$

Practise

For help with questions 1 to 5, see Examples 1 and 2.

1. Write an algebraic expression to represent each description.
   a) triple a number
   b) four more than a number
   c) half a number
   d) five less than double a number

2. Write an equation to represent each sentence. Explain your choice of variable and what it represents in each case.
   a) four times a number is 112
   b) a perimeter increased by 12 is 56
   c) five more than triple a number is 29
   d) the sum of two consecutive integers is 63

Literacy Connections

Consecutive means one after the other. For example:
- 3, 4, and 5 are consecutive integers
- q, r, and s are consecutive letters

3. Solve each equation in question 2, and explain what the answer means.

4. Estaban is 6 years older than his brother Raoul. The sum of their ages is 38. How old are the brothers?

5. Two friends enter a trivia challenge as a team. Fayth scored 200 more points than Jamal. As a team, they collected a total of 2250 points. How many points did each friend earn?

Connect and Apply

6. Natalie, Chantal, and Samara play together as a forward line on a hockey team. At the end of the season, Chantal had scored eight more goals than Natalie, while Samara had scored twice as many goals as Natalie. The three girls scored a total of 52 goals. How many goals did each girl score?

7. Kyle sells used cars. He is paid \$14/hour plus an 8% commission on sales. What dollar amount of car sales must Kyle make to earn \$1200 in a 38-h work week?

8. **Chapter Problem** At the season finale, you present the winner of Canadian Superstar with a recording-and-tour contract. The contract states that the winner will be paid \$5000 per month while on tour plus \$2 per CD sold.
   a) Write an equation that relates total earnings in terms of the number of months, m, on tour and the number, n, of CDs sold.
   b) How much will the winner earn after the first month if 500 CDs are sold?
   c) Suppose after the third month on tour the new recording artist has earned a total of \$74 000. How many CDs were sold?
   d) In Canada, a record album or CD achieves gold status once it sells 50 000 units. How much will the artist make if the CD goes gold after 6 months of touring?

Did You Know?

In March 2003, *Dark Side of the Moon*, by Pink Floyd, achieved double diamond status in Canada for selling over 2 000 000 units.

9. The sum of three consecutive integers is 54. Find the numbers.

10. The sum of two consecutive even integers is -134. Find the numbers.

11. A circular garden has a diameter of 12 m. By how much should the diameter be increased to triple the area of the garden?

12. Refer to question 11.
   a) Solve the problem using a different method.
   b) Compare the two methods. Identify at least one advantage and one disadvantage of each approach.

11
19 41
22

13. The length of Laurie's rectangular swimming pool is triple its width. The pool covers an area of 192 m^2.

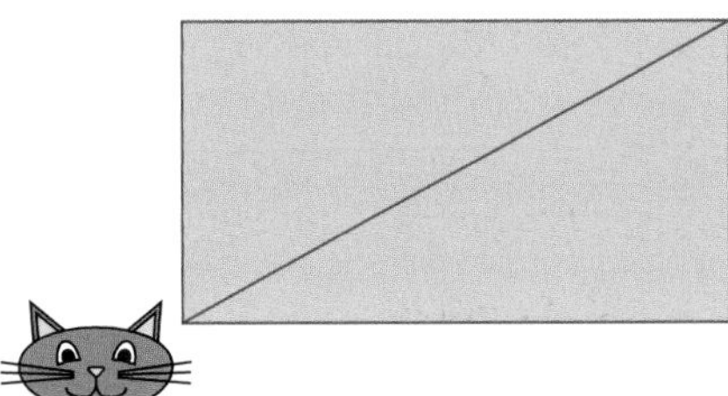

a) If Laurie swims across the diagonal and back, how far does she travel?

b) At the same time Laurie starts swimming, her cat walks one lap around the edge of the pool. Laurie can swim $\frac{3}{4}$ as fast as her cat can walk. Who will return to the starting point first? Justify your answer.

14. Refer to the magic trick in the Investigate. Create a magic trick of your own. Try your trick out on a friend or family member.

Achievement Check

15. Paloma works part-time, 4 h per day, selling fitness club memberships. She is paid \$9/h, plus a \$12 commission for each 1-year membership she sells.

a) Write an algebraic expression that describes Paloma's total earnings.

b) Find the amount Paloma makes in 8 h when she sells seven memberships.

c) How many memberships does Paloma need to sell to earn \$600 in a 24-h workweek?

d) Paloma notices that her sales have a pattern: for the first 12 h of the week she sells an average of two memberships per hour and for the last 12 h of the week she sells an average of three memberships per hour. Use an organized method (e.g., chart, graph, equations) to determine when Paloma will reach a special \$900 earnings goal.

Extend

16. A checkerboard has 64 congruent squares. Suppose a checkerboard has a diagonal length of 40 cm. Find the area of each square on the board.

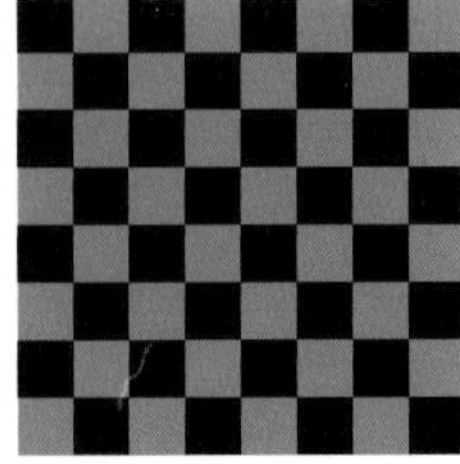

17. Johnny is directly in front of Dougie, who is playing goalie, as shown.

Johnny is 2.8 m from both goal posts. He is also three times as far from Dougie as Dougie is from either post.

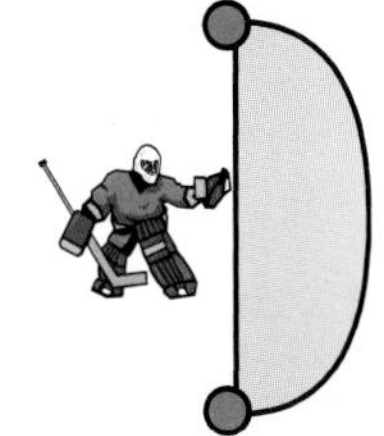

a) How wide is the net?

b) Describe how you solved this problem.

c) Discuss any assumptions you had to make.

18. Johannes Kepler (1571–1630) was a German astronomer who noticed a pattern in the orbits of planets. The table shows data for the planets known when Kepler was alive.

Planet	Radius of Orbit (AU)*	Period of Orbit (Earth Days)
Mercury	0.389	87.77
Venus	0.724	224.70
Earth	1.0	365.25
Mars	1.524	686.98
Jupiter	5.200	4332.62
Saturn	9.150	10759.20

**AU, or astronomical unit, is the mean distance from Earth to the Sun, 1.49×10^8 km.*

a) Kepler conjectured that the square of the period divided by the cube of the radius is a constant. Copy the table. Add another column and compute the value of the square of the period divided by the cube of the radius for each planet. Then, find the mean of these values to find Kepler's constant.

b) Write a formula for the relationship that Kepler found. This is called Kepler's Third Law.

c) In 1781, William Herschel discovered the planet Uranus, which has a period of 30 588.70 days. Use Kepler's Third Law to determine the radius of Uranus's orbit.

d) In 1846, the planet Neptune was discovered. Neptune's orbital radius is 30 AU. Use Kepler's Third Law to find the orbital period of Neptune.

e) The planet Pluto has an orbital radius of 39.5 AU and a period of 90 588 days. Does Pluto satisfy Kepler's Third Law? Explain.

f) Investigate Kepler's other two laws of planetary motion. Write a brief report of your findings.

19. Math Contest The mass of a banana plus its peel is 360 g. The mass of the banana is four times the mass of the peel. What is the mass of the peel?

20. Math Contest Given that $y = 4x + 1$ and $z = 5x - 3$, and the value of z is 7, what is the value of y?

A -2 **B** -9 **C** 2 **D** 9 **E** 29

Chapter 4 Review

4.1 Solve Simple Equations, pages 186–195

1. Solve using pencil and paper.

a) $8 + m = -2$

b) $k - 7 = -11$

c) $3x = 18$

d) $\frac{h}{5} = -4$

2. Find the root of each equation using pencil and paper. Check each answer.

a) $2y - 7 = 13$

b) $4 + 5v = -21$

c) $9 - 2x = -1$

d) $-3s - 6 = 9$

3. Find the root of each equation using a Computer Algebra System. Check each answer.

a) $3n + 8 = 20$

b) $9 - 4r = -27$

c) $5x - 2 = 18$

d) $-7y - 6 = -20$

4. Cindy has \$2.50 to spend on milk and candy. The milk costs \$0.70. Her favourite candies cost \$0.12 each.

a) Write an equation that models the number of candies that Cindy can afford.

b) Solve the equation.

4.2 Solve Multi-Step Equations, pages 196–203

5. Solve using pencil and paper.

a) $3 + 2m + 6m = 19$

b) $7w - 4 + w + 12 = 0$

c) $3x + 7 = 2x - 3$

d) $5w - 6 = -4w + 3$

6. Solve using a Computer Algebra System.

a) $5 + 4y = 2y + 9$

b) $7 + 3k - 2 = 4k$

c) $2w - 9 + 5w + 2 = 0$

d) $-5 + 7n = 9n + 11$

7. Find the root of each equation using pencil and paper. Check each solution.

a) $4 - (3p - 2) = p - 10$

b) $3 + (h - 2) = 5 + 3h$

c) $2(n - 8) = -4(2n - 1)$

d) $3(2k - 5) - k = 4 - (3k + 7)$

8. A triangle has angle measures that are related as follows:

- the largest angle is eight times the smallest angle
- the middle angle is triple the smallest angle

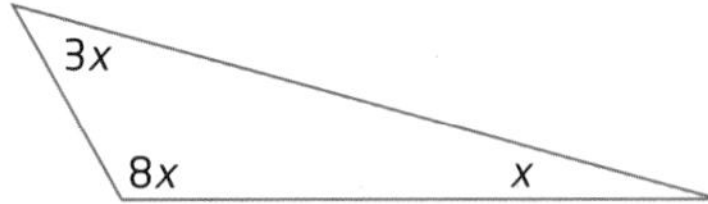

Find the measures of the angles.

4.3 Solve Equations Involving Fractions, pages 204–210

9. Find the root of each equation using pencil and paper. Check each solution.

a) $\frac{1}{3}(x - 1) = 4$

b) $\frac{b - 4}{3} = -5$

c) $3 = \frac{3}{4}(p - 1)$

d) $-3 = \frac{5x + 4}{7}$

10. Find the root of each equation using a Computer Algebra System. Check each root.

a) $7 = \frac{6q + 8}{4}$

b) $\frac{1}{2}(u - 5) = 2u + 5$

11. Find the solution to each equation.

a) $\frac{y - 8}{3} = \frac{y + 4}{2}$

b) $\frac{2}{3}(w - 5) = \frac{3}{4}(w + 2)$

c) $\frac{c + 3}{4} = \frac{c - 5}{6}$

d) $\frac{2}{5}(x + 3) = \frac{1}{2}(x - 5)$

4.4 Modelling With Formulas, pages 211–219

12. Rearrange each formula to isolate the variable indicated.

a) $P = a + b + c$ for a (perimeter of a triangle)

b) $C = \pi d$ for d (circumference of a circle)

c) $a = \frac{F}{m}$ for F (force)

d) $d = mt + b$ for t (distance-time relationships)

13. The power, P, in an electric circuit is related to the current, I, and resistance, R, by the formula $P = I^2R$.

a) Find the power, in watts (W), when the current is 0.5 A (amperes) and the resistance is 600 Ω (ohms).

b) What is the resistance of a circuit that uses 500 W of power with a current of 2 A?

c) The resistance in a circuit is 4 Ω. The same circuit uses 100 W of power. Find the current in the circuit.

4.5 Modelling With Algebra, pages 220–229

14. The total of three sisters' ages is 39. Dina is half as old as Michelle and 3 years younger than Juliette. How old are the sisters?

15. Sven sells hamburgers at a ballpark. He earns $7.50/h, plus $0.40 for each hamburger he sells.

a) How much will Sven earn in a 3-h shift if he sells 24 hamburgers?

b) How many hamburgers must Sven sell to earn $100 in a 6.5-h shift?

16. Hitori's rock garden is in the shape of a trapezoid. The garden has an area of 60 m^2 and a depth of 8 m. The front width is double the back width.

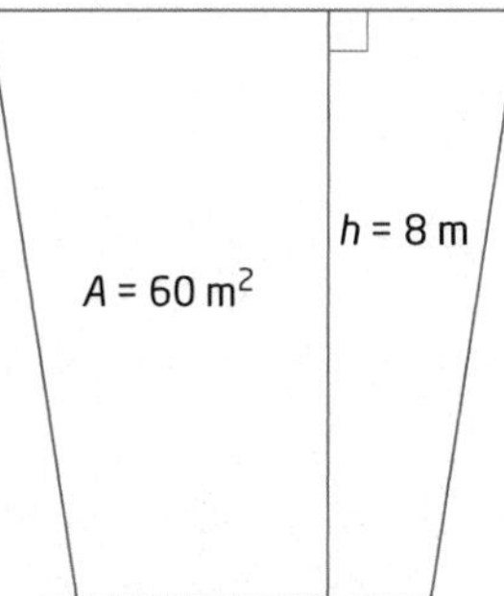

Without changing the front or back widths, by how much must Hitori increase the depth of his garden to double its area?

17. Refer to question 16.

a) Solve this problem using a different method.

b) Compare the methods. Describe at least one advantage and one disadvantage of each approach.

Chapter 4 Practice Test

Multiple Choice

For questions 1 to 4, select the best answer.

1. Which is the correct solution for $x - 2 = -4$?

A $x = -6$

B $x = -2$

C $x = 2$

D $x = 6$

2. $k = -3$ is the correct solution for which equation?

A $2k - 5 = -1$

B $k - 3 = 6$

C $3k - 3 = -6$

D $4k + 1 = -11$

3. The speed-distance-time relationship for an object moving at a constant speed is described by the formula $s = \frac{d}{t}$. Which of the following correctly describes d in terms of s and t?

A $d = \frac{t}{s}$

B $d = \frac{s}{t}$

C $d = st$

D $d = s - t$

4. Anthony is 4 years older than his brother Felix. The sum of their ages is 42. Which equation can you use to find their ages?

A $4f = 42$

B $4f + f = 42$

C $f + f + 4 = 42$

D $4f + f + 4 = 42$

Short Response

Show all steps to your solutions.

5. Solve. Express any fractional answers in lowest terms.

a) $y - 11 = -2$

b) $\frac{h}{7} = -3$

c) $3k + 5 = 14$

d) $5x - 7 = 8 + 2x$

e) $7r = -3(r - 2)$

f) $2y + (y - 3) = 4(y - 5)$

6. Find the root of each equation.

a) $\frac{1}{3}(2w - 6) = -8$

b) $\frac{3a - 7}{4} = \frac{4a + 5}{3}$

c) $\frac{3k}{2} - \frac{k + 3}{3} = 8 - \frac{k + 2}{4}$

7. The perimeter of an isosceles triangle is given by the formula $P = 2a + b$, where a is the length of each of the equal sides and b is the length of the third side.

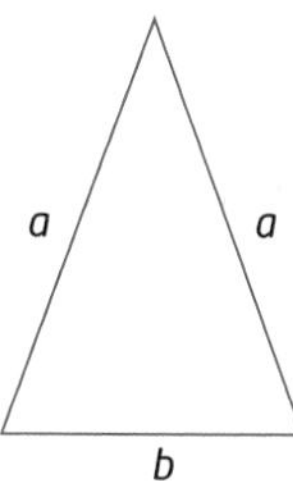

a) Rearrange the formula to isolate b.

b) Rearrange the formula to isolate a.

c) An isosceles triangle has a perimeter of 43 cm. The length of the two equal sides is unknown, but the third side length is 18 cm. What is the length of each of the equal sides?

Extended Response

Provide complete solutions.

8. Charlene earns \$150 more per week than her roommate Kristi and \$100 less than her other roommate, Sacha. Together the three friends earn \$2050 per week. How much does each girl earn per week?

9. Solve and check.

$8 - 2(2p - 3) = 6 - (p + 3)$

10. Murray works at a cell phone service kiosk in a shopping mall. He earns \$8.50/h, plus a \$15 commission for each 1-year service contract he sells.

a) Find the amount Murray makes in 8 h when he sells seven service contracts.

b) How many service contracts does Murray need to sell to earn \$790 in a 40-h work week?

Chapter Problem Wrap-Up

The first season of Canadian Superstar is a wrap! Will there be a second season? The sponsors use a weighted rating system that factors in the audience demographic (who watches the show). Their research suggests that the viewing audience is made up of 50% girls, 30% boys, and 20% adult viewers. The formula for the show's weighted rating score, R, is

$$R = \frac{5g + 3b + 2a}{10}$$

- g represents the girls' average rating of the show, out of 10.
- b represents the boys' average rating of the show, out of 10.
- a represents the adults' average rating of the show, out of 10.

The sponsors agree to pick up the show for a second season if the first season earns a weighted rating of 8 or better. Part of the ratings have been recorded in a table:

Viewers	Girls	Boys	Adults
Average Rating	not available	7.4	8.1

The girls' ratings have not yet been recorded, but early feedback suggests that the show was significantly more popular with girls than with boys and adults. Do you think that there will be a second season? Justify your reasoning. What minimum girls' average rating is necessary to ensure a second season?

CHAPTER

5

Modelling With Graphs

Linear Relations

- Construct tables of values, graphs, and equations.
- Identify, through investigation, some properties of linear relations, and apply these properties to determine whether a relation is linear or non-linear.
- Compare the properties of direct variation and partial variation in applications, and identify the initial value.
- Determine values of a linear relation by using a table of values and by using the equation of the relation.
- Determine other representations of a linear relation, given one representation.
- Describe the effects on a linear graph and make the corresponding changes to the linear equation when the conditions of the situation they represent are varied.

Analytic Geometry

- Determine, through investigation, various formulas for the slope of a line segment or a line, and use the formulas to determine the slope of a line segment or a line.
- Determine, through investigation, connections among the representations of a constant rate of change of a linear relation.

There are many types of puzzles—logic puzzles, word puzzles, number puzzles, mechanical puzzles, and puzzles based on diagrams. Puzzles may be solved by methods such as guessing, trial and error, and analysing data. The solution to a puzzle may rely on patterns and relations. Being able to represent data in a variety of ways is a useful skill in puzzle solving. In this chapter, you will investigate graphs and data and develop equations that represent relations between two variables. You will also analyse and interpret data so that you can make conclusions and extensions.

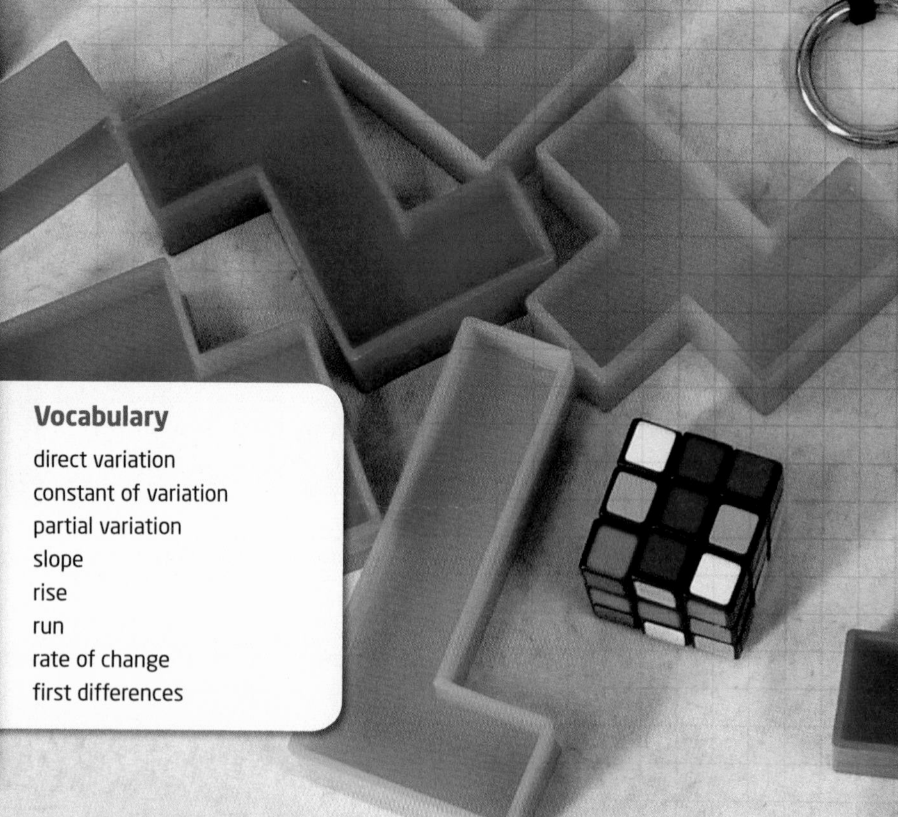

Vocabulary

direct variation
constant of variation
partial variation
slope
rise
run
rate of change
first differences

Chapter Problem

Toothpick patterns are popular puzzles. How does each pattern relate to the number of toothpicks? In this chapter, you will develop equations to represent relationships like these.

Get Ready

Rational Numbers

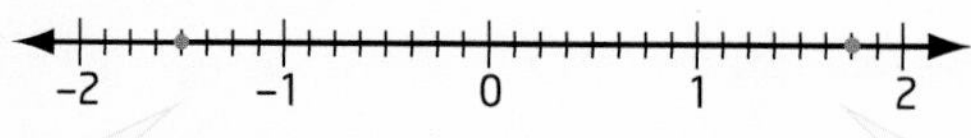

This dot is at $-1\frac{1}{2}$. I could also name this point $-\frac{3}{2}$ or -1.5.

This dot is at $1\frac{3}{4}$. I could also name this point $\frac{7}{4}$ or 1.75.

$-1\frac{1}{2}$, $-\frac{3}{2}$, $\frac{-3}{2}$, $\frac{3}{-2}$, and -1.5 are equivalent rational numbers.

Often, rational numbers can be simplified, or expressed in lowest terms.

$$-\frac{9}{6} = -\frac{9 \div 3}{6 \div 3} = -\frac{3}{2}$$

1. In each part, decide which rational number is not equivalent to the others.

a) $\frac{3}{4}$, 0.75, $\frac{-3}{4}$, $\frac{-3}{-4}$

b) -2.5, $-2\frac{1}{2}$, $\frac{-5}{2}$, $\frac{5}{2}$

c) -0.5, $\frac{1}{-2}$, $\frac{-1}{-2}$, $\frac{-1}{2}$

2. Express each rational number in decimal form.

a) $\frac{2}{5}$ **b)** $-\frac{7}{10}$ **c)** $\frac{-35}{40}$ **d)** $\frac{-12}{5}$

3. Express each rational number in lowest terms.

a) $-\frac{3}{9}$ **b)** $\frac{-15}{10}$ **c)** $\frac{-12}{-48}$ **d)** $\frac{30}{-12}$

Ratio and Proportion

The body of a 50-kg woman contains about 25 kg of water. The body of an 80-kg man contains about 48 kg of water.

Person	Ratio of Water to Mass	Ratio in Simplest Form	Ratio in Fraction Form
50-kg woman	25:50	1:2	$\frac{25}{50} = \frac{1}{2}$
80-kg man	48:80	3:5	$\frac{48}{80} = \frac{3}{5}$

Find the mass of water in the bodies of a 60-kg woman and a 60-kg man.

Woman: $\frac{1}{2} \times 60 = 30$

Man: $\frac{3}{5} \times 60 = 36$

The body of a 60-kg woman contains 30 kg of water, and the body of a 60-kg man contains 36 kg of water.

4. Write a ratio to compare each quantity to its total. Express each ratio in simplest form.
   a) 5 kg of potassium in 20 kg of fertilizer
   b) 12 g of fat in 96 g of meat
   c) 12 L of water in 14 L of juice
   d) 40 mL of chlorine in 850 mL of solution

5. Seven out of ten people prefer Fresh toothpaste. How many would prefer Fresh in a group of 120 people?

6. To convert from centimetres to inches, you can use the fact that a 30-cm ruler is just over 12 inches long. A person is 160 cm tall. What is the person's approximate height, in inches?

Percents

Over the track and field season, the height Fred cleared in the high jump increased from 1.81 m to 1.96 m. He was hoping to have a 20% increase in height.

$$\begin{aligned}\text{Height increase} &= 1.96 - 1.81\\ &= 0.15\end{aligned}$$

$$\begin{aligned}\text{Percent increase} &= \frac{\text{height increase}}{\text{original height}} \times 100\%\\ &= \frac{0.15}{1.81} \times 100\%\\ &\doteq 8.3\%\end{aligned}$$

Fred increased his jump height by about 8.3%.

For a 20% increase, multiply by 20% or 0.2, and then add the result to the original height.

$0.20 \times 1.81 = 0.362$

$1.81 + 0.362 = 2.172$

Fred would have to clear about 2.17 m to increase his jump height by 20%.

7. The table lists the number of days with rain during July in four Canadian cities. For each city, express the number of rainy days as a percent of the 31 days in July. Round to one decimal place.

Location	Number of Days With Rain
Toronto, ON	10
Vancouver, BC	7
Charlottetown, PE	12
St. John's, NL	14

8. The three key elements in lawn fertilizer are expressed as a ratio of their percents of the total mass. For example, in 20:4:8 fertilizer, 20% is nitrogen, 4% is phosphorus, and 8% is potassium.

   Calculate the mass of each element in each bag of fertilizer.
   a) 10-kg bag of 20:4:8 fertilizer
   b) 25-kg bag of 21:7:7 fertilizer
   c) 50-kg bag of 15:5:3 fertilizer
   d) 20-kg bag of 10:6:4 fertilizer

5.1 Direct Variation

The distance that a person can jog is related to time. If you are jogging at a constant speed of 100 m/min, how far can you jog in 10 min? in 1 h?

Investigate

Tools
- grid paper

Making Connections

You learned about independent and dependent variables in Chapter 2: Relations.

What is the relationship between distance and time?

1. Susan can jog at a steady pace of 150 m/min for the first hour.
   a) Create a table showing the distance that Susan jogs in 0 min, 1 min, 2 min, and so on up to 10 min.
   b) Identify the **independent variable** and the **dependent variable**. Graph this relationship.
   c) Describe the shape of the graph. Where does it intersect the vertical axis?
   d) Write an equation to find the distance, d, in metres, that Susan jogs in t minutes.
   e) Use the equation to determine the distance that Susan can jog in 40 min.
   f) Consider the distance Susan jogged in 2 min. What happens to the distance when the time is doubled? What happens to the distance when the time is tripled?

2. Trish's steady jogging pace is 175 m/min. Repeat step 1 using Trish's speed.

3. **Reflect** Describe how to develop an equation for distance when you know the average speed.

The relationship between distance and time is an example of a **direct variation**. For example, the table shows distances travelled in various time periods at a constant speed of 10 m/s.

Time (s)	Distance (m)
1	10
2	20
3	30
4	40
5	50

When time is multiplied by a specific number, distance is also multiplied by the same number. Another way to describe this direct variation is to say that distance *varies directly* with time.

direct variation

- a relationship between two variables in which one variable is a constant multiple of the other

In a direct variation, the ratio of corresponding values of the variables does not change. So, if d is distance and t is time, then $\frac{d}{t} = k$, where k is called the **constant of variation**. Multiplying both sides of the equation by t gives $d = kt$.

For the data in the table, $\frac{d}{t} = 10$, or $d = 10t$. The constant of variation is 10.

constant of variation

- in a direct variation, the ratio of corresponding values of the variables, often represented by k, or the constant multiple by which one variable is multiplied
- if d varies directly as t, then the constant of variation, k, is given by $k = \frac{d}{t}$ or $d = kt$

Example 1 Algebraic Direct Variation

The Fredrick family travels 250 km to a relative's home. The distance, d, in kilometres, varies directly with the time, t, in hours.

a) Find the equation relating d and t if $d = 43$ when $t = 0.5$. What does the constant of variation represent?

b) Use the equation to determine how long it will take the Fredricks to reach their destination.

Solution

a) Since d varies directly with t, the equation has the form $d = kt$.

To find k, substitute the given values into $k = \frac{d}{t}$.

$$k = \frac{43}{0.5}$$
$$= 86$$

The constant of variation represents the constant average speed, 86 km/h. The equation relating d to t is $d = 86t$.

b) Substitute $d = 250$.

$$250 = 86t$$
$$\frac{250}{86} = t \quad \text{Divide both sides by 86.}$$
$$2.9 \doteq t$$

It will take the Fredricks about 2.9 h to reach their destination.

Example 2 Hourly Rate of Pay

Amir works part-time at a local bookstore. He earns \$7.50/h.

a) Describe the relationship between his pay, in dollars, and the time, in hours, he works.

b) Illustrate the relationship graphically and represent it with an equation.

c) One week, Amir works 9 h. Find his pay for that week.

Solution

a) To get Amir's pay, multiply the time worked, in hours, by \$7.50. This means that Amir's pay, P, in dollars, varies directly with the time, t, in hours worked.

b) Method 1: Pencil and Paper

Time Worked, t (h)	Pay, P (\$)
0	0
2	15
4	30
6	45
8	60
10	75

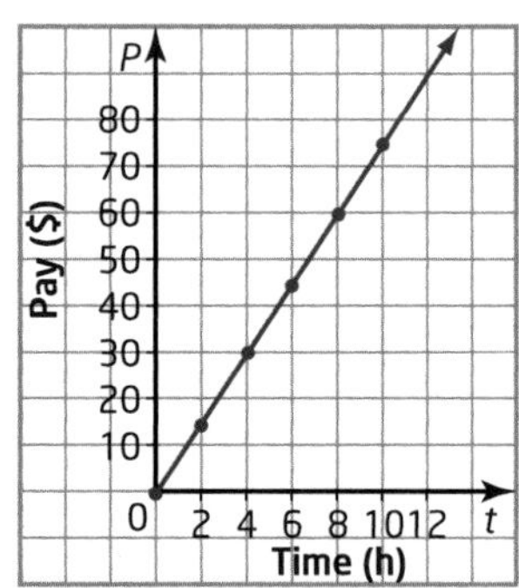

This direct variation can be modelled by the equation $P = 7.50t$, where $k = 7.50$ is the constant of variation.

Method 2: Use a Graphing Calculator

Use the data from the table in **Method 1**.

- To clear all lists, press (2nd) [MEM] to display the **MEMORY** menu, select **4:ClrAllLists**, and press (ENTER).
- To enter the data into the lists, press (STAT) and select **1:Edit**. Under list **L1**, enter the values for time worked, in hours. Under list **L2**, enter the values for pay, in dollars.
- To display the scatter plot, set up Plot1 as shown. Press (ZOOM) and select **9:ZoomStat**.

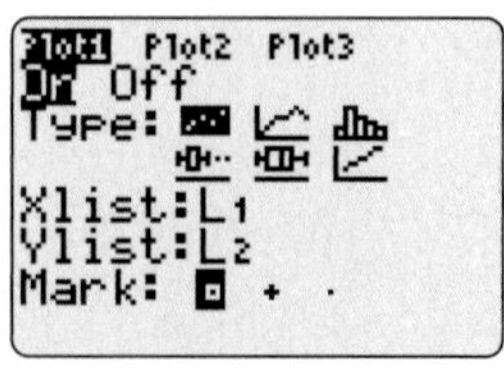

Draw the line of best fit.

- Press (STAT), cursor over to display the **CALC** menu, and then select **4:LinReg(ax+b)**. Enter **L1**, a comma, **L2**, and another comma. Then, press (VARS), cursor over to display the **Y-VARS** menu, then select **1:FUNCTION**, and then **1:Y1**. Press (ENTER), and then press (GRAPH).

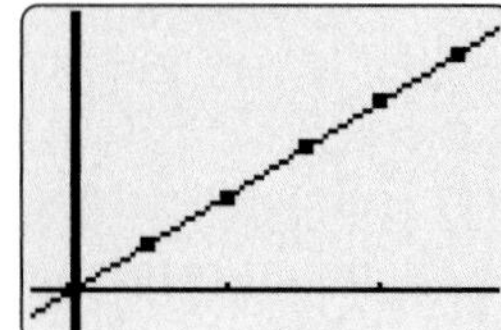

- Press (Y=) to see the equation representing the relationship between the time, in hours, worked and Amir's pay, in dollars.
  Y1 = 7.50X

Method 3: Use *Fathom*™

From the **Tool shelf**, click and drag the **Case Table** icon into the workspace. Name two attributes Time and Pay. Enter the data from the table in **Method 1** into the appropriate cells.

From the **Tool shelf**, click and drag the **New Graph** icon into the workspace. Drag the Time attribute to the horizontal axis and the Pay attribute to the vertical axis. You will see a scatter plot of the data.

From the **Graph** menu, select **Least-Squares Line.**
The equation representing the relationship between the time worked and Amir's pay will be indicated in the space below the graph.

Pay = 7.50Time

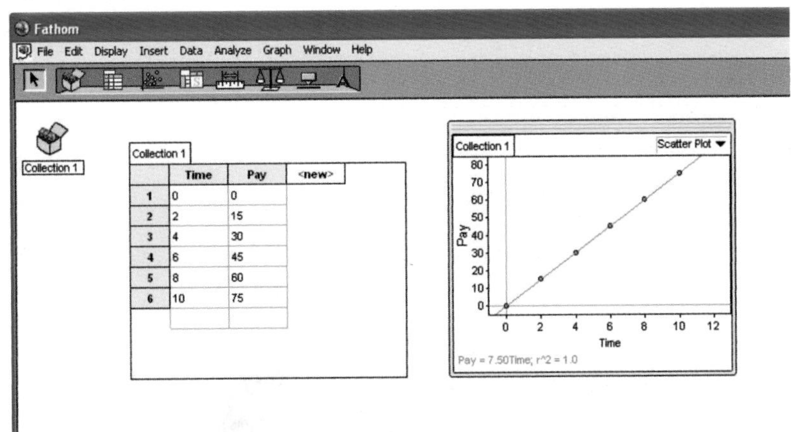

c) Interpolate from the graph. Read up from 9 h on the horizontal axis to the line. Then, read across to find that Amir's pay is about $68.

You can also use the equation. Substitute $t = 9$ into $P = 7.50t$.

$$P = 7.50(9)$$
$$= 67.50$$

Amir's pay for 9 h is $67.50.

In this case, if I use the graph, I only get an approximate answer, but if I use the equation, I get an exact answer.

Key Concepts

- Direct variation occurs when the dependent variable varies by the same factor as the independent variable.
- Direct variation can be defined algebraically as $\frac{y}{x} = k$ or $y = kx$, where k is the constant of variation.
- The graph of a direct variation is a straight line that passes through the origin.

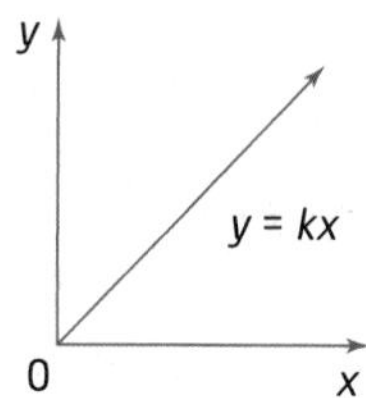

Communicate Your Understanding

C1 Consider the two equations $A = 2C + 5$ and $A = 2C$. Which is an example of a direct variation? Explain.

C2 Consider the graphs of $d = 2t$ and $d = 3t$.

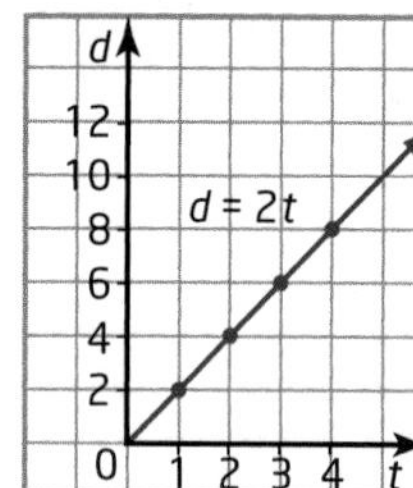

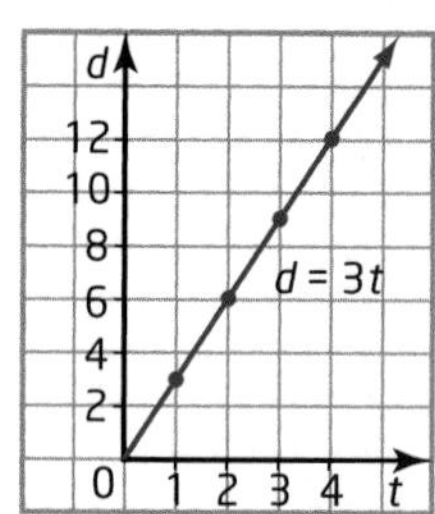

a) Describe the similarities.

b) Describe the differences. Explain why these differences occur.

Practise

For help with questions 1 and 2, see Example 1.

1. Determine the constant of variation for each direct variation.

a) The distance travelled by a bus varies directly with time. The bus travels 240 km in 3 h.

b) The total cost varies directly with the number of books bought. Five books cost \$35.

c) The volume of water varies directly with time. A swimming pool contains 500 L of water after 5 min.

2. The cost, C, in dollars, of building a concrete sidewalk varies directly with its length, s, in metres.

   a) Find an equation relating C and s if a 200-m sidewalk costs \$4500.

   b) What does the constant of variation represent?

   c) Use the equation to determine the cost of a 700-m sidewalk.

For help with questions 3 to 5, see Example 2.

3. Passent's pay varies directly with the time, in hours, she works. She earns \$8/h.

   a) Choose appropriate letters for variables. Make a table of values showing Passent's pay for 0 h, 1 h, 2 h, and 3 h.

   b) Graph the relationship.

   c) Write an equation in the form $y = kx$.

4. The total cost of apples varies directly with the mass, in kilograms, bought. Apples cost \$1.50/kg.

   a) Choose appropriate letters for variables. Make a table of values showing the cost of 0 kg, 1 kg, 2 kg, and 3 kg of apples.

   b) Graph the relationship.

   c) Write an equation in the form $y = kx$.

5. A parking garage charges \$2.75/h for parking.

   a) Describe the relationship between the cost of parking and the time, in hours, parked.

   b) Illustrate the relationship graphically and represent it with an equation.

   c) Use your graph to estimate the cost for 7 h of parking.

   d) Use your equation to determine the exact cost for 7 h of parking.

Connect and Apply

6. The cost of oranges varies directly with the total mass bought. 2 kg of oranges costs \$4.50.

   a) Describe the relationship in words.

   b) Write an equation relating the cost and the mass of the oranges. What does the constant of variation represent?

   c) What is the cost of 30 kg of oranges?

7. To raise money for a local charity, students organized a wake-a-thon where they attempted to stay awake for 24 h. At this event, the amount of money raised varied directly with the time, in hours, a participant stayed awake. Tania raised $50 by staying awake for 16 h.

   a) Graph this direct variation for times from 0 h to 16 h, using pencil and paper or technology.

   b) Write an equation relating the money Tania raised and the amount of time, in hours, she stayed awake.

   c) How much would she have raised by staying awake for 24 h?

8. At his summer job, Sam's regular wage is $9.50/h. For any overtime, Sam earns 1.5 times his regular wage.

   a) Write an equation representing Sam's regular pay.

   b) Write a separate equation representing Sam's overtime pay.

   c) Sam gets a raise to $10/h. How does this change affect the equations?

9. At a bulk store, 0.5 kg of sugar costs $1.29.

   a) Explain why this relationship is considered a direct variation.

   b) Graph this relationship, using pencil and paper or technology.

   c) What would happen to the graph if the price increased to $1.49 for 0.5 kg?

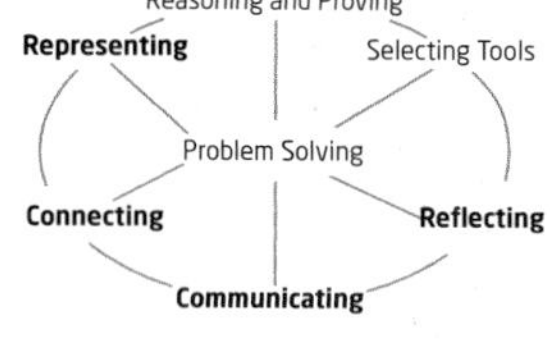

10. Describe a situation that could be illustrated by each graph.

   a)

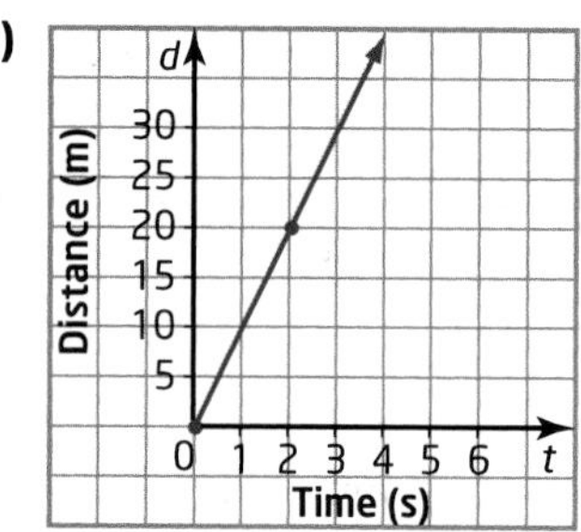

   b)

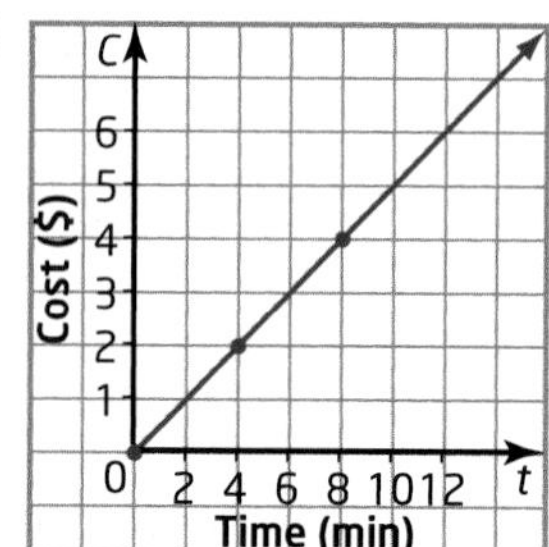

11. A bat uses sound waves to avoid flying into objects. A sound wave travels at 342 m/s. The times for sound waves to reach several objects and return to the bat are shown in the table. Set up an equation to determine the distance from the bat to the object. Then, copy and complete the table.

Object	Time (s)	Distance (m)
Tree	0.1	
House	0.25	
Cliff wall	0.04	

12. The volume of water in a swimming pool varies directly with time. 500 L of water is in the pool after 4 min.

a) Write an equation relating the volume of water and time. What does the constant of variation represent?

b) Graph this relationship using pencil and paper or technology.

c) What volume of water is in the swimming pool after 20 min?

d) How long will it take to fill a swimming pool that holds 115 000 L of water?

e) Describe the changes to the equation and graph if only 400 L of water is in the pool after 4 min.

13. The freezing point of water varies directly with the salt content of the water. Fresh water (no salt content) freezes at a temperature of 0°C. Ocean water has a salt content of 3.5% and freezes at −2°C.

a) Which is the independent variable? Why?

b) Write an equation relating the freezing point of water and the salt content.

c) At what temperature will water with a salt content of 1% freeze?

d) What is the salt content of water that freezes at −3°C?

Extend

14. To convert from kilometres to miles, multiply by 0.62. Write an equation to convert miles to kilometres.

15. Determine the set of ordered pairs that lists the diameter and circumference of four different coins: a penny, a nickel, a dime, and a quarter. Does the circumference vary directly with the diameter? Explain.

16. **Math Contest** From a bag of disks numbered 1 through 100, one disk is chosen. What is the probability that the number on the disk contains a 3? Justify your answer.

17. **Math Contest** The digits 2, 3, 4, 5, and 6 are used to create five-digit odd numbers, with no digit being repeated in any number. Determine the difference between the greatest and least of these numbers.

5.2 Partial Variation

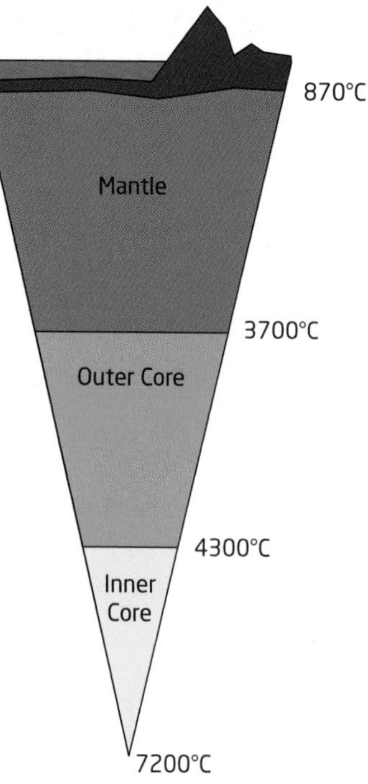

Earth is made up of several distinct layers. Beneath the oceans, the outermost layer, or crust, is 5 km to 12 km thick. Below the continents, Earth's crust is 25 km to 90 km thick. The mantle is about 2750 km thick. The outer core is about 2260 km thick, while the inner core has a thickness of about 1228 km. The deeper layers are hotter and denser because the temperature and pressure inside Earth increase with depth.

Investigate

Tools
- grid paper

What is the relationship between temperature and depth?

The temperature of Earth's crust increases by about 145°C for every kilometre below the oceans. The temperature increases by about 21.75°C for every kilometre below the continents.

1. Starting at a temperature of 10°C at the surface of Earth's crust, make a table showing the depth and temperature of Earth's crust under the ocean and under the continents, at depths between 0 km and 5 km.

Depth (km)	Temperature Under Oceans (°C)	Temperature Under Continents (°C)

2. a) Plot temperature versus depth for your data under the oceans.
   b) On the same grid, plot temperature versus depth for your data under the continents.
3. Compare and contrast the two graphs.
4. How do these graphs differ from those you made for direct variation in Section 5.1?

5. Consider the equation $T = 145d + 10$, where T represents the temperature, in degrees Celsius, under the oceans and d represents the depth, in kilometres.

   a) Substitute $d = 1$ and calculate T. Repeat for $d = 2, 3, 4, 5$. Compare the results with those you obtained in step 1.

   b) Explain why this equation works.

   c) Write a similar equation relating the temperature under the continents with depth.

6. **Reflect** Describe the parts of each equation and how they relate to the data in your table and graph.

The graph illustrates the total cost, C, in dollars, of a taxi fare for a distance, d, in kilometres.

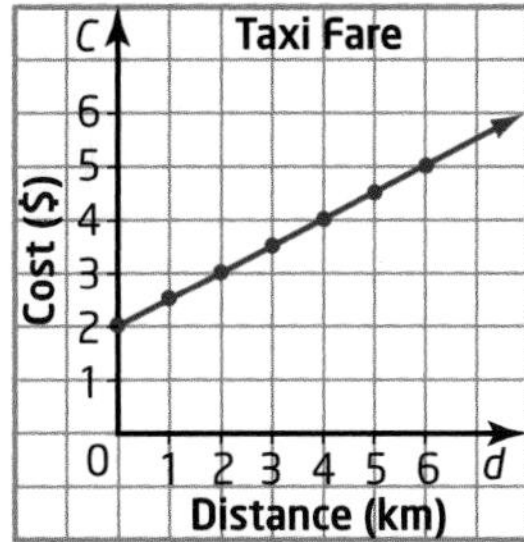

The fixed cost of $2 represents the initial meter fare. The distance travelled by taxi changes, or is *variable*, depending on the passenger's destination. For this reason, the variable cost is $0.50 times the distance.

$$C = 2 + 0.5d$$

fixed cost ↗ ↖ variable cost

The graph is a straight line, but it does not show a direct variation because the line does not pass through the origin. This type of relationship is called a **partial variation**. Another way to describe this partial variation is to say that "*C varies partially* with *d*."

partial variation

- a relationship between two variables in which the dependent variable is the sum of a constant number and a constant multiple of the independent variable

In general, if y varies partially with x, the equation is of the form $y = mx + b$, where m and b are constants, and

- m represents the constant of variation
- b represents the fixed, or initial, value of y

Example 1 Graph a Partial Variation

a) Copy and complete the table of values given that y varies partially with x.

b) Identify the initial value of y and the constant of variation from the completed table. Write an equation relating y and x in the form $y = mx + b$.

c) Graph this relation.

d) Describe the graph.

x	y
0	6
1	9
2	
3	15
4	
	27

Solution

a) As x changes from 0 to 1, y changes from 6 to 9. Therefore, y increases by 3 as x increases by 1.

x	y
0	6
1	9
2	12
3	15
4	18
7	27

The pattern of increasing the y-values by 3 checks for the other values that were given.

b) The initial value of y occurs when $x = 0$. The initial value of y is 6. As x increases by 1, y increases by 3. So, the constant of variation is 3.

Use $b = 6$ and $m = 3$ to obtain the equation $y = 3x + 6$.

c)

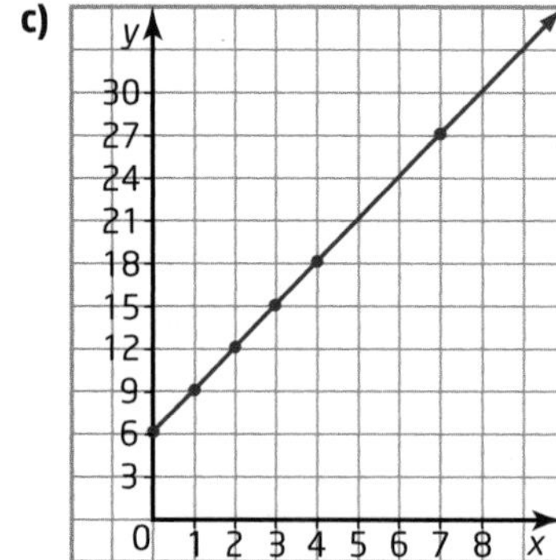

d) The graph is a straight line that intersects the y-axis at the point (0, 6). The y-values increase by 3 as the x-values increase by 1.

Example 2 School Awards Banquet

A school is planning an awards banquet. The cost of renting the banquet facility and hiring serving staff is \$675. There is an additional cost of \$12 per person for the meal.

a) Identify the fixed cost and the variable cost of this partial variation.

b) Write an equation to represent this relationship.

c) Use your equation to determine the total cost if 500 people attend the banquet.

Solution

a) The fixed cost is \$675. The variable cost is \$12 times the number of people.

b) Let C represent the total cost, in dollars. Let n represent the number of people attending.
Multiply the number of people by 12 and add 675.
$C = 12n + 675$

c) Substitute $n = 500$.

$$C = 12(500) + 675$$
$$= 6675$$

The total cost for 500 people is \$6675.

Key Concepts

- A partial variation has an equation of the form $y = mx + b$, where b represents the fixed, or initial, value of y and m represents the constant of variation.
- The graph of a partial variation is a straight line that does not pass through the origin.

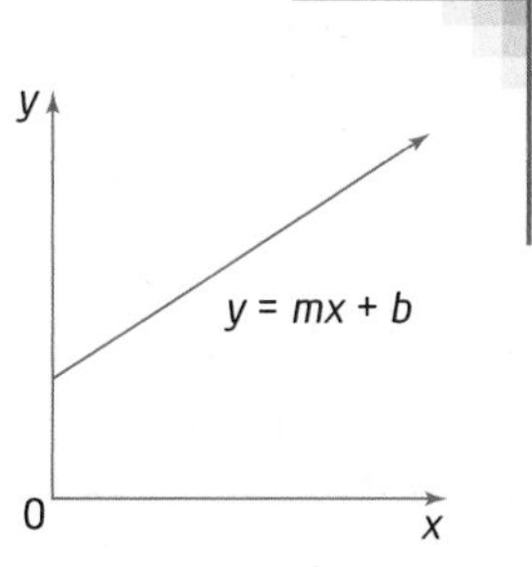

Communicate Your Understanding

C1 Classify each graph as a direct variation, a partial variation, or neither. Justify your answer.

a) 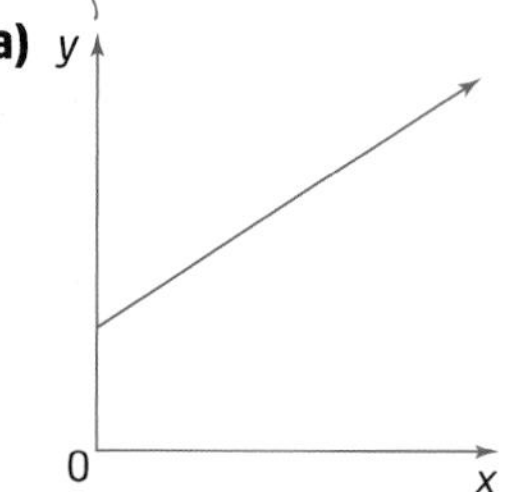

b) 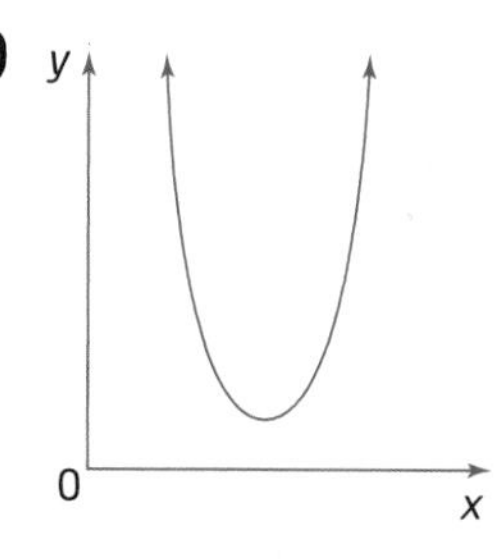

c) 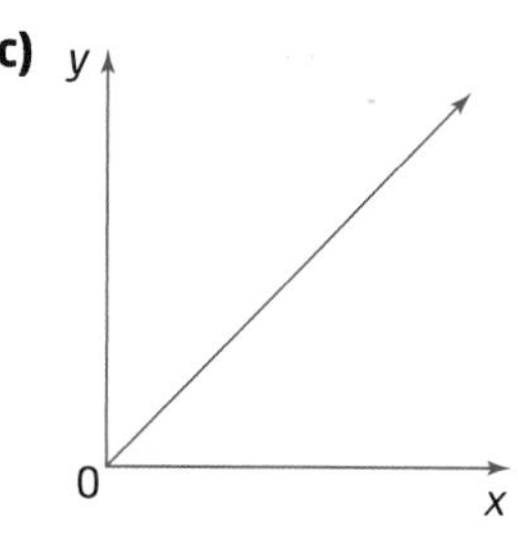

C2 The cost to repair a television set is made up of a service charge of \$50, which covers the travel time and gas for the repairperson, plus \$40/h. Describe the steps involved in developing a partial variation equation that relates the cost and the time required to complete the repairs.

C3 The table models a partial variation. Discuss how you can use the table to find m and b in the equation $y = mx + b$.

x	y
0	10
1	14
2	18
3	22
4	26

Practise

1. Identify each relation as a direct variation, a partial variation, or neither. Justify your answer.

a) $y = 3x$ **b)** $y = 2x + 1$

c) $C = 20n + 500$ **d)** $d = 5t$

For help with questions 2 and 3, see Example 1.

2. a) Copy and complete the table of values given that y varies partially with x.

b) Identify the initial value of y and the constant of variation from the table.

c) Write an equation relating y and x in the form $y = mx + b$.

d) Graph the relation.

e) Describe the graph.

x	y
0	5
1	10
2	
3	20
4	
	40

3. a) Copy and complete the table of values given that y varies partially with x.

b) Identify the initial value of y and the constant of variation from the table.

c) Write an equation relating y and x in the form $y = mx + b$.

d) Graph the relation.

e) Describe the graph.

x	y
0	−2
1	3
2	
3	13
4	
	33

For help with questions 4 and 5, see Example 2.

4. A small pizza costs $7.00 plus $1.50 per topping.

a) Identify the fixed cost and the variable cost of this partial variation.

b) Determine the equation relating the cost, C, in dollars, and the number of toppings, n.

c) Use the equation to determine the cost of a small pizza with five toppings.

5. A class is planning a field trip to an art gallery. The cost of renting a bus is $250. There is an additional cost of $4 per student for the entrance fee.

a) Identify the fixed cost and the variable cost of this partial variation.

b) Write an equation relating the cost, C, in dollars, and the number of students, n.

c) Use your equation to determine the total cost if 25 students attend.

Connect and Apply

6. A fitness club offers two types of monthly memberships:

- membership A: $4 per visit
- membership B: a flat fee of $12 plus $2 per visit

a) Graph both relations for 0 to 10 visits.

b) Classify each relation as a direct variation or a partial variation.

c) Write an equation relating the cost and the number of visits.

d) Compare the monthly membership costs. When is membership A cheaper than membership B? When is membership B cheaper than membership A?

7. The table shows the amount a printing company charges for advertising flyers.

Number of Flyers, n	Cost, C (\$)
0	100
100	120
200	140
300	160

a) Identify the fixed cost this company charges for producing the flyers. What do you think this amount might represent?

b) Determine the variable cost for producing one flyer. Explain how you found this.

c) Write an equation representing the price for the flyers.

d) What is the cost to produce 1000 flyers?

e) How many flyers can be produced for \$280?

8. **Chapter Problem** Toothpick patterns are popular puzzles. Here is an example of a toothpick pattern.

Diagram 1 **Diagram 2** **Diagram 3**

a) Write an equation relating the diagram number and the number of toothpicks. Is this a partial variation? Explain.

b) Use your equation to determine the number of toothpicks in Diagram 20.

Did You Know?

Scuba divers will ascend slowly to the surface to avoid decompression sickness, or the bends. After deep or long dives, a scuba diver needs to undergo decompression by returning to the surface slowly and in stages.

9. At the surface of a lake, a scuba diver experiences 102.4 kPa (kilopascal) of pressure. As the diver descends, the pressure increases by 101.3 kPa for every 10 m.

a) Write an equation that relates the pressure experienced by a diver and the depth that the diver has descended.

b) Divers must be aware of nitrogen narcosis, which occurs when too much nitrogen dissolves in the blood. Narcosis becomes possible when the diver is exposed to a pressure of about 400 kPa. At what depth does the danger from narcosis begin?

10. Describe a situation that might lead to this graph.

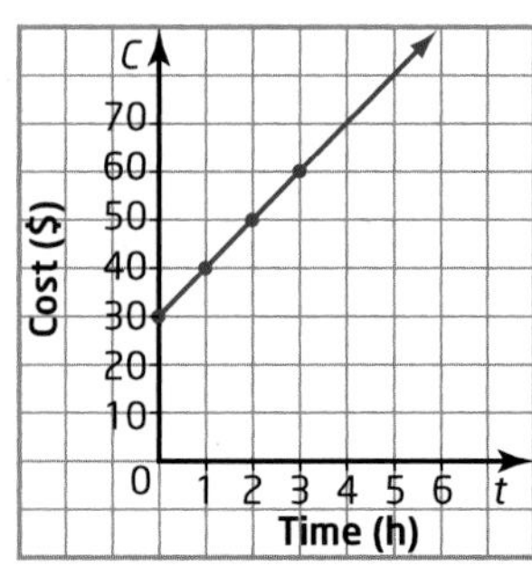

11. At 12:05 P.M., a parachutist was 8000 m above the ground. At 12:06 P.M., the parachutist was 7750 m above the ground. At 12:07 P.M., the parachutist was 7500 m above the ground.

a) Graph this relation.

b) Find the average rate of descent, in metres per minute.

c) Write an equation for this relation.

Achievement Check

12. A theatre company produced the musical *Cats*. The company had to pay a royalty fee of \$1250 plus \$325 per performance. The same theatre company also presented the musical production of *Fame* in the same year. For the production of *Fame*, they had to pay a royalty fee of \$1400 plus \$250 per performance.

a) Write an equation that relates the total royalties and the number of performances for each musical.

b) Graph the two relations on the same grid.

c) When does the company pay the same royalty fee for the two productions?

d) Why do you think the creators of these musicals would set royalties in the form of a partial variation instead of a direct variation?

Extend

13. In Earth's atmosphere, the speed of sound can be approximated using partial variation. The speed of sound is approximately 331 m/s at 0°C and approximately 343 m/s at 20°C.

a) What is the approximate speed of sound at

i) 30°C? **ii)** −30°C?

b) Jenny yells out "Hello" in a canyon when the air temperature is −10°C. It takes 1.4 s to hear her echo. How far away is the wall of the canyon?

14. A battery was recharged, remained fully charged, and then slowly lost its charge, as shown in the table.

Time (h)	0	5	10	15	20	25	30	35	40	45	50	55	60
Charge (%)	92	94	96	98	100	100	100	100	95	90	85	80	75

a) Graph the battery's charge over time.

b) Determine an appropriate set of equations for the charge of the battery.

c) What was the remaining charge after

i) 12 h? **ii)** 26 h? **iii)** 71 h?

5.3 Slope

Good skiers enjoy skiing on hills with a greater **slope** because they can go faster. Ski runs are rated on a variety of factors, including the slope, or steepness. The steeper the ski run, the more challenging it is.

slope

- a measure of the steepness of a line
- calculated as $\frac{\text{rise}}{\text{run}}$

Investigate A

How can you determine the steepness of a hill?

The diagrams represent ski hills.

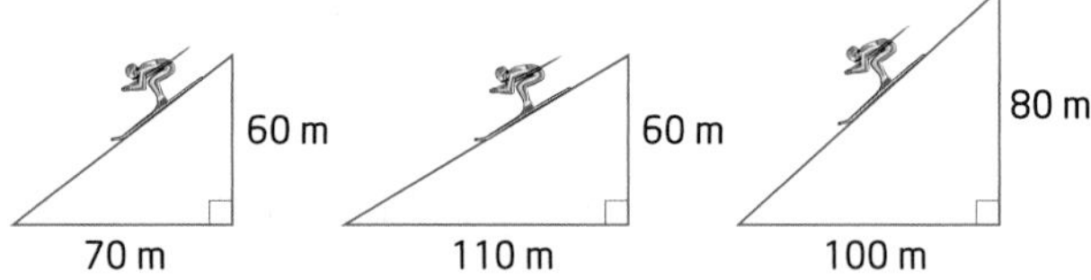

1. Rank the hills in order of their steepness, from least to greatest.
2. A hill rises 2 m over a horizontal run of 8 m. A second hill rises 4 m over a horizontal run of 10 m. Which is the steeper hill? Explain.
3. **Reflect** Describe your technique for determining steepness.

Investigate B

Tools

- grid paper

How can you determine the slope of any line segment?

The steepness of a line segment is measured by its slope. The slope is the ratio of the **rise** to the **run** and is often represented by the letter m.

rise

- the vertical distance between two points

run

- the horizontal distance between two points

$$m = \frac{\text{rise}}{\text{run}}$$

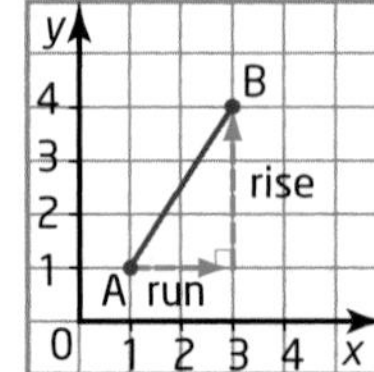

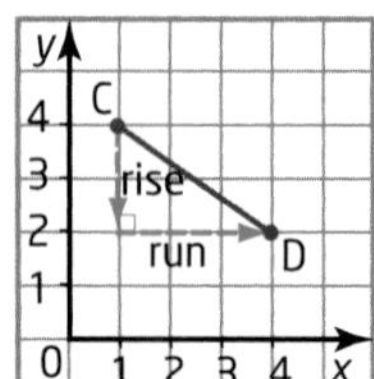

When you are looking at a graph on a Cartesian grid, read from left to right. A line segment rising from left to right has a positive slope. A line segment falling from left to right has a negative slope.

1. Consider the graph of line segment AB.
   a) Is the slope positive or negative? Explain how you know.
   b) Determine the rise and run by counting grid units.
   c) Determine the slope of the line segment AB using $m = \frac{\text{rise}}{\text{run}}$.
2. Consider the graph of line segment CD.
   a) Is the slope positive or negative? Explain how you know.
   b) Determine the rise and run by counting of grid units.
   c) Determine the slope of the line segment CD using $m = \frac{\text{rise}}{\text{run}}$.
3. a) On a piece of grid paper, set up coordinate axes. Plot the points A(1, 1) and D(5, 1). Join the points to form line segment AD.
   b) Determine the rise and the run.
   c) Describe what happens when you calculate the slope of a horizontal line segment.
4. a) On the same set of axes, plot the point E(1, 5). Join points to form line segment AE.
   b) Determine the rise and the run.
   c) Do you think it is possible to calculate the slope of a vertical line segment? Justify your answer.
5. **Reflect** Describe how you can find the slope of any line segment.

Example 1 Slope of a Loading Dock

The ramp at a loading dock rises 2.50 m over a run of 4.00 m.

a) Calculate the slope of the ramp.

b) Explain the meaning of the slope.

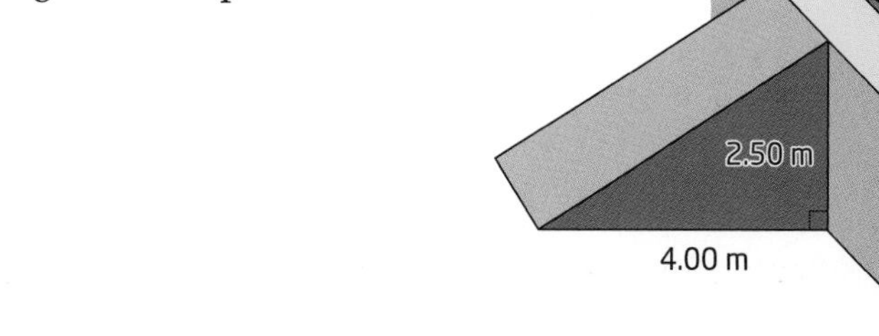

Solution

a)
$$m = \frac{\text{rise}}{\text{run}} = \frac{2.50}{4.00} = 0.625$$

The slope of the ramp is 0.625.

b) The ramp rises 0.625 m vertically for every 1 m run horizontally.

Example 2 Slope of Line Segments

Calculate the slope of each line segment, where possible. Describe the direction and how it relates to the slope.

a) AB

b) CD

c) EF

d) GH

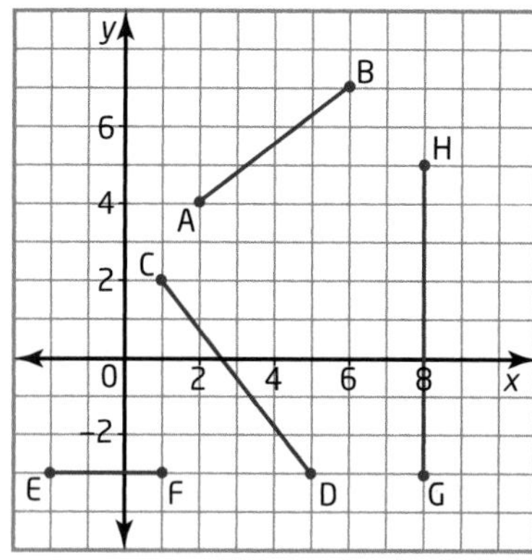

Solution

a) Count the number of grid units to find the rise and the run.

$$m = \frac{\text{rise}}{\text{run}}$$
$$= \frac{3}{4}$$

The slope of AB is $\frac{3}{4}$. The direction is up 3 units as you go to the right 4 units.

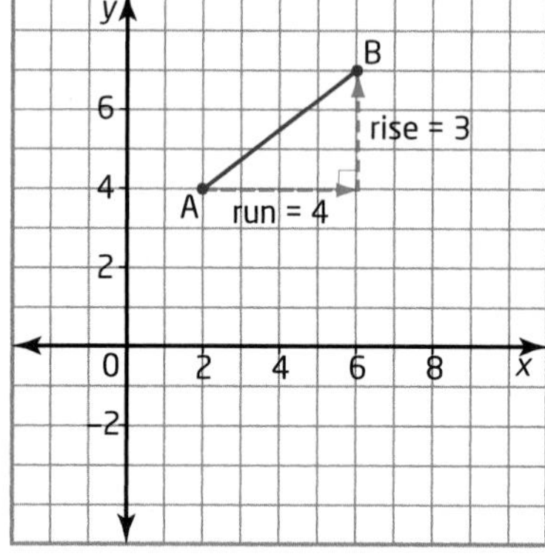

The rise tells me if the direction is up or down. The run tells me if the direction is right or left. So, a rise of 3 means go up 3, and a run of 4 means go right 4.

b) $m = \frac{\text{rise}}{\text{run}}$

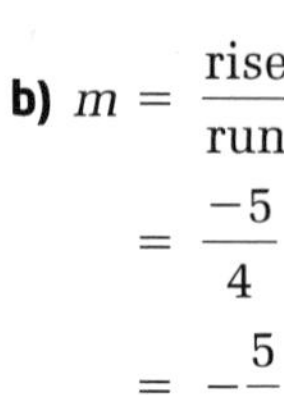

$$= \frac{-5}{4}$$
$$= -\frac{5}{4}$$

The slope of CD is $-\frac{5}{4}$. The direction is down 5 units as you go to the right 4 units. This is why it is negative.

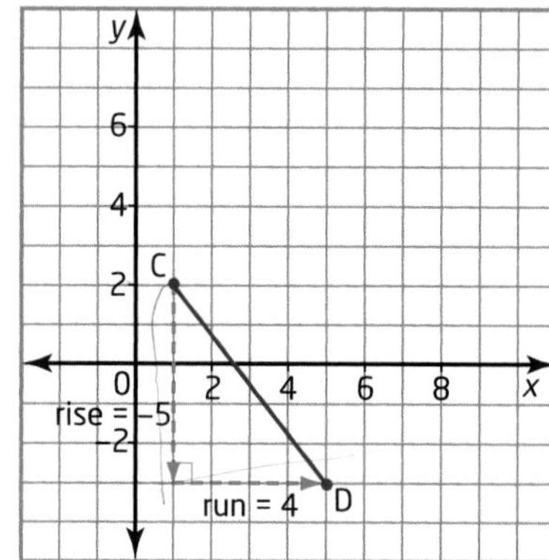

A rise of −5 means go down 5, and a run of 4 means go right 4.

c) EF is a horizontal line segment. This line segment has no rise.

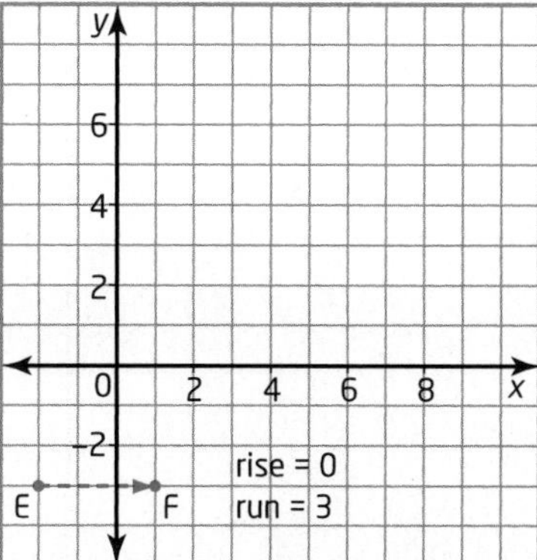

$$m = \frac{\text{rise}}{\text{run}}$$
$$= \frac{0}{3}$$
$$= 0$$

The slope of EF is 0. EF does not have an up or down direction. It is flat. The rise is 0 for a run of 3.

d) GH is a vertical line segment. This line segment has no run.

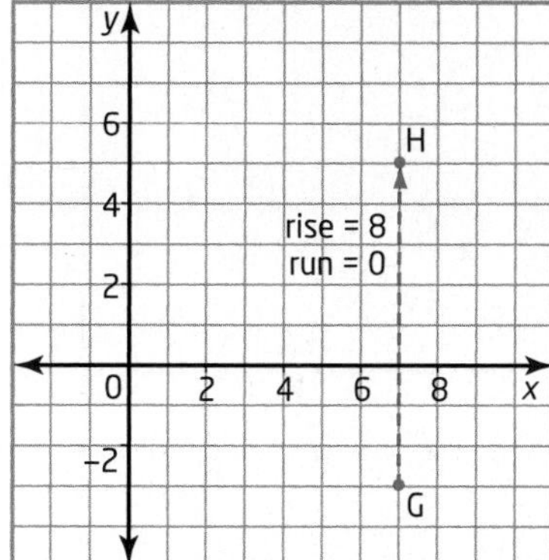

$$m = \frac{\text{rise}}{\text{run}}$$
$$= \frac{8}{0}$$

Since division by zero is undefined, the slope of GH is undefined. EF does not have a left or right direction. The run is 0 for a rise of 8.

Example 3 Use the Slope to Find a Point

A line segment has one endpoint, A(4, 7), and slope of $-\frac{5}{3}$. Find the coordinates of another possible endpoint, B.

Solution

Method 1: Draw a Graph

Plot the point A(4, 7).

Use the slope $-\frac{5}{3}$ to find another point.

Another possible endpoint is B(7, 2).

Since $-\frac{5}{3} = \frac{-5}{3} = \frac{\text{rise}}{\text{run}}$, I will go to the right 3 and down 5.

There is an infinite number of solutions. What if I had used a rise of 5 and a run of −3? or 10 and −6? or −10 and 6?

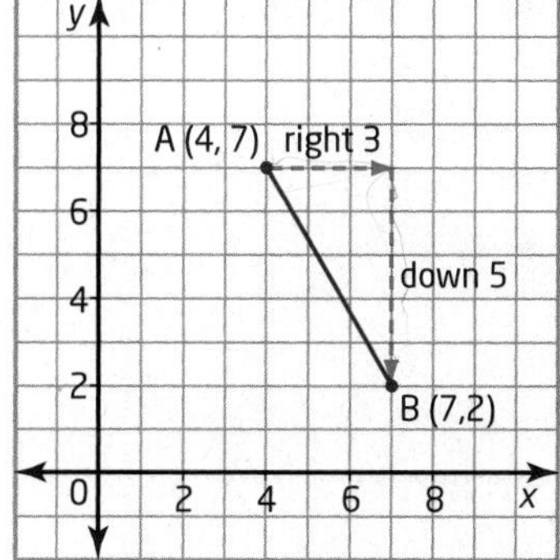

Method 2: Use the Coordinates

The run is 3 and the rise is -5. Add these values to the x- and y-coordinates, respectively, of point A.

$(4 + 3, 7 + (-5)) = (7, 2)$

Another possible endpoint is B(7, 2).

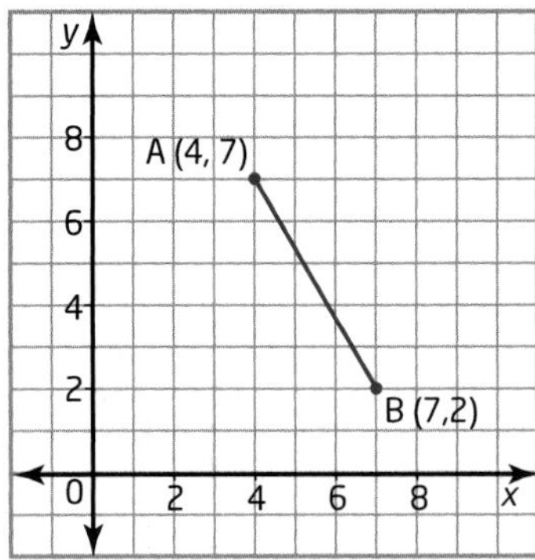

Key Concepts

- The slope, m, is a measure of the steepness of a line segment. It is calculated as $m = \frac{\text{rise}}{\text{run}}$.
- A line segment rising from left to right has a positive slope.
- A line segment falling from left to right has a negative slope.

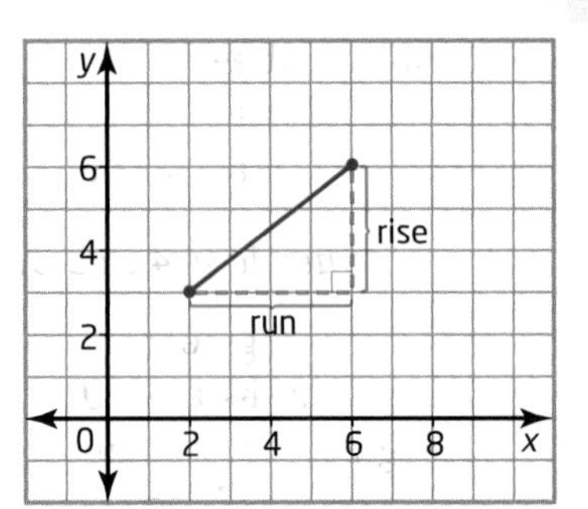

Communicate Your Understanding

C1 Kelly looked at this line segment and concluded that the slope had to be negative because the coordinates of the points contained negative numbers. Is her reasoning correct? Explain.

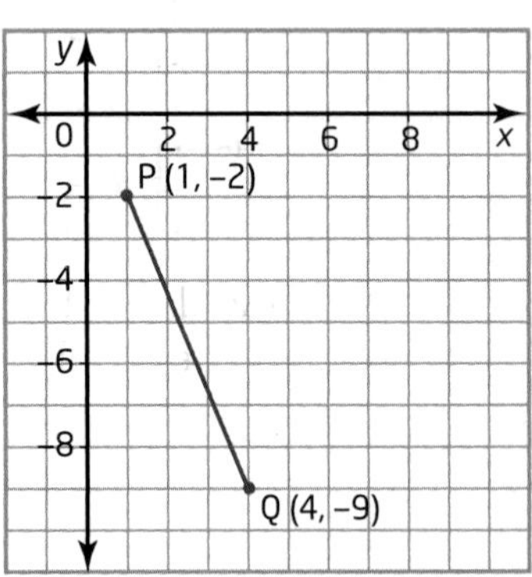

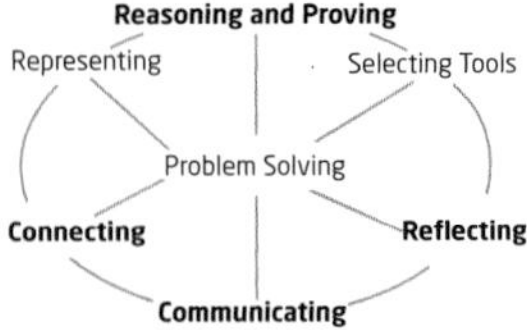

C2 A ramp rises 2 m over a run of 5 m.

a) How would you change the rise to make the slope steeper?

b) How would you change the run to make the slope steeper?

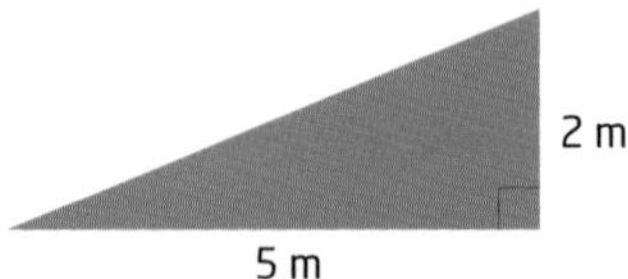

Practise

For help with questions 1 to 3, see Example 1.

1. Determine the slope of each object.

a) 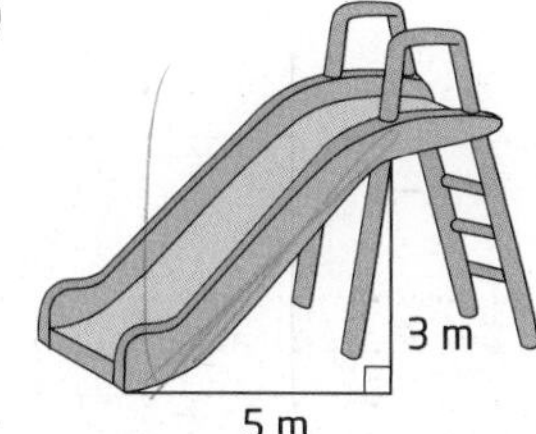

b) 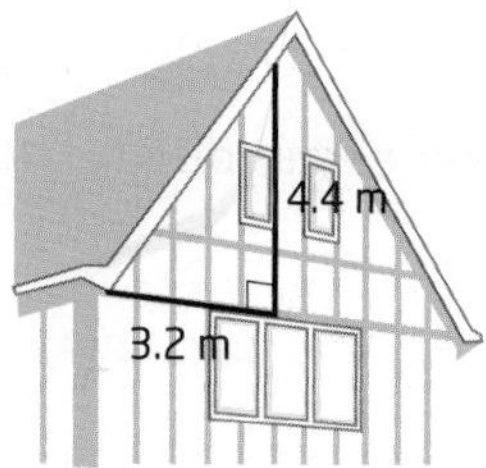

2. A section of road is built with a vertical rise of 2.5 m over a horizontal run of 152 m. Find the slope, to the nearest hundredth.

3. To be safe, a wheelchair ramp needs to have a slope no greater than 0.08. Does a wheelchair ramp with a vertical rise of 1.4 m along a horizontal run of 8 m satisfy the safety regulation?

For help with questions 4 and 5, see Example 2.

4. For each line segment,
   - count grid units to find the rise
   - count grid units to find the run
   - determine the slope

a) 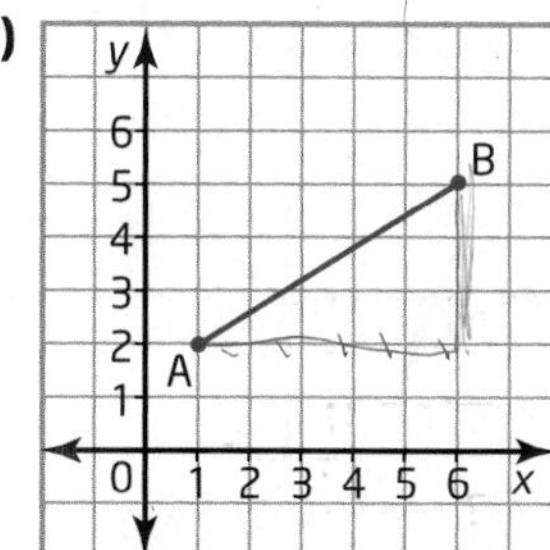

b) 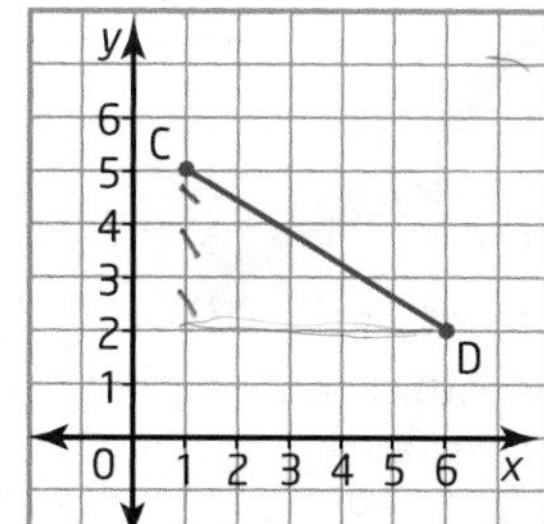

5. Calculate the slope of each line segment, where possible.

a) AB
b) CD
c) EF
d) GH
e) IJ
f) KL

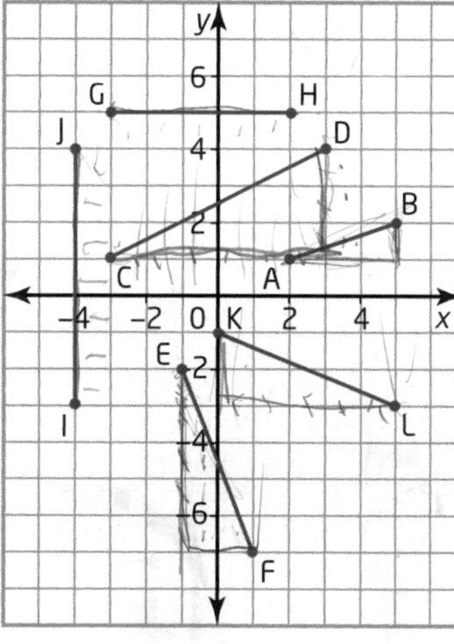

For help with questions 6 and 7, see Example 3.

6. A line segment has one endpoint of A(3, 1).

a) Plot the point A on a grid.

b) Use the slope $\frac{3}{2}$ to locate another possible endpoint B. What are the coordinates of point B?

7. A line segment has one endpoint of A(6, −2) and slope of $-\frac{3}{4}$. Find the coordinates of another possible endpoint B by adding the appropriate values to the coordinates of point A.

Connect and Apply

8. For safety reasons, a staircase should have a slope of between 0.58 and 0.70. Determine whether each staircase is within the safe range.

a)

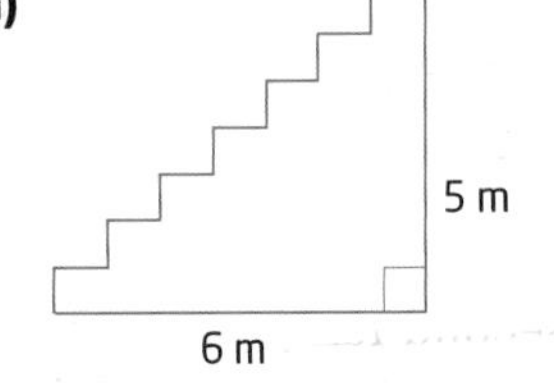

b)

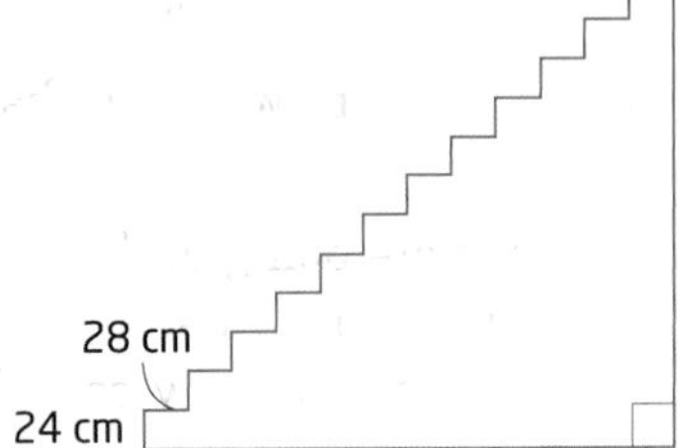

9. Given a point A(−2, 5), find the coordinates of a point B so that the line segment AB has each slope.

a) $\frac{2}{3}$ **b)** $-\frac{2}{3}$ **c)** 4

d) −3 **e)** 0 **f)** undefined

10. A ramp needs to have a slope of $\frac{3}{5}$. Determine the length of each vertical brace.

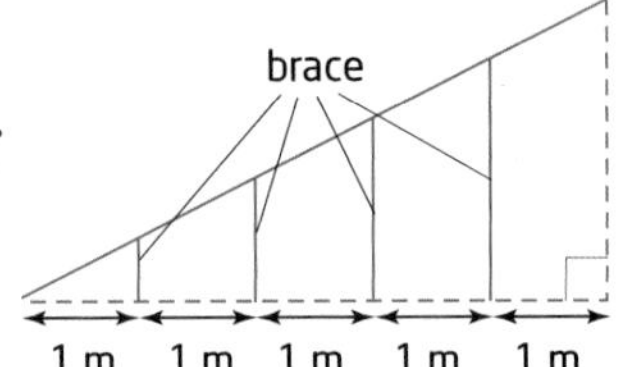

Did You Know?

Saint John, New Brunswick has the steepest main street in Canada. King Street has an 8% grade.

11. Slopes of roads are called grades and are expressed as percents.

a) Calculate the grade of a road that rises 21 m over a run of 500 m.

b) For a road to have a grade of 3%, how far does it have to rise over a run of 600 m?

12. Roofers call the slope of a roof its pitch. Roofs have different pitch classifications, which indicate how safe they are for roofers to walk on. They are classified as shown in this table.

Classification	Pitch
Shallow	$m \le \frac{3}{12}$
Medium	$\frac{3}{12} < m \le \frac{6}{12}$
Steep	$m > \frac{6}{12}$

a) Classify each roof by its pitch.

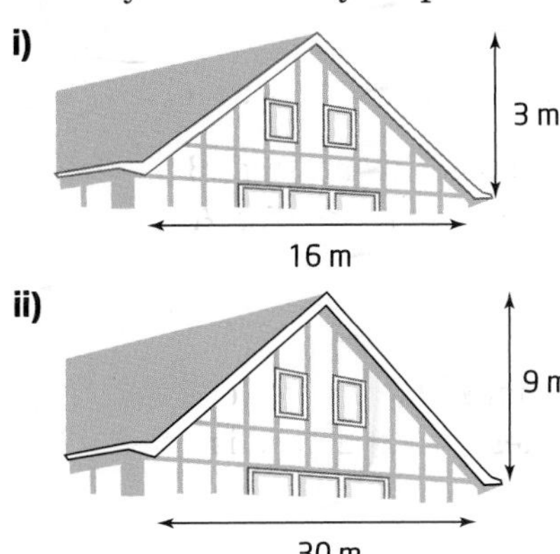

b) A roof is 10 m wide and has a pitch of $\frac{5}{12}$. Find the height.

13. Two ramps are being built with the same slope. The first ramp is twice the height of the second ramp. Does the first ramp have to be twice as long as the second ramp? Explain.

14. A steel beam goes between the tops of two buildings that are 7 m apart. One building is 41 m tall. The other is 52 m tall. What is the slope of the beam?

15. For safety reasons, an extension ladder should have a slope of between 6.3 and 9.5 when it is placed against a wall. If a ladder reaches 8 m up a wall, what are the maximum and minimum distances from the foot of the ladder to the wall?

16. The Great Pyramid of Cheops has a height of about 147 m and a base width of about 230 m. How does its slope compare to a standard staircase with slope 0.7?

17. In 1967, Montreal hosted Expo 67, an international fair, to celebrate Canada's 100th birthday. Canada's pavilion was an upside-down pyramid called Katimavik, which means *meeting place* in Inuktitut, the language of the Inuit. The base width is about 55 m and the height is about 18 m. Calculate the slope of the sides. Compare the slope of the sides to the slope of the Great Pyramid of Cheops, which you found in question 16.

Extend

18. A cross-country ski area classifies its courses based on the range of slopes. If the slopes are less than 0.09, the course is classified as easy. For slopes between 0.09 and 0.18, the course is intermediate. For slopes greater than 0.18, the course is difficult. For a ski hill 10 m tall, what range of horizontal runs is appropriate for each classification?

19. A hiking trail has been cut diagonally along the side of a hill, as shown. What is the slope of the trail?

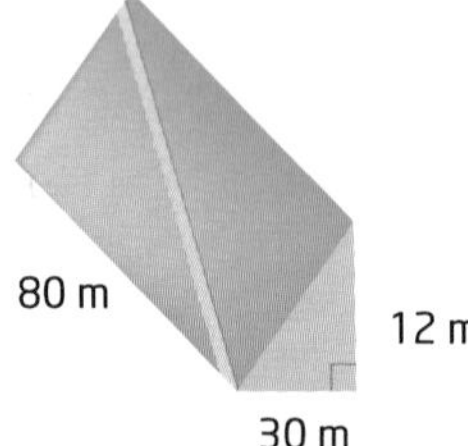

20. A regular hexagon has six sides of equal length. One is drawn on a grid as shown. Determine the slope of the line segment from the centre to the vertex indicated. Explain your reasoning.

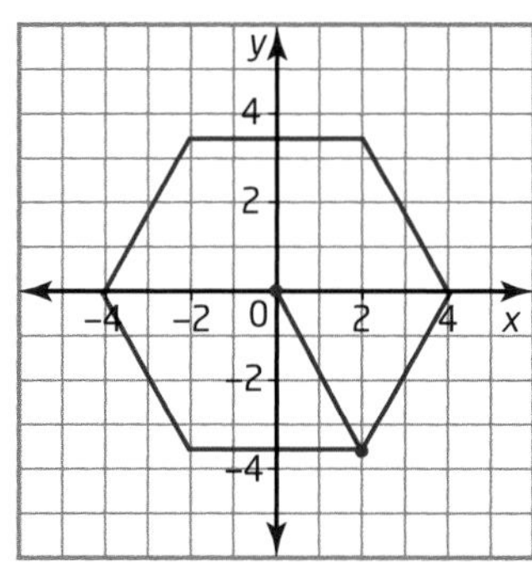

21. How safe are the stairs around your home? To answer this question, carry out the following investigation.

a) For different sets of stairs around your home, measure the tread width and riser height. Try to get measurements for several sets of stairs. Record your measurements in a table, and compute the slope for each set of stairs. Draw conclusions about which set of stairs is the least safe in your home.

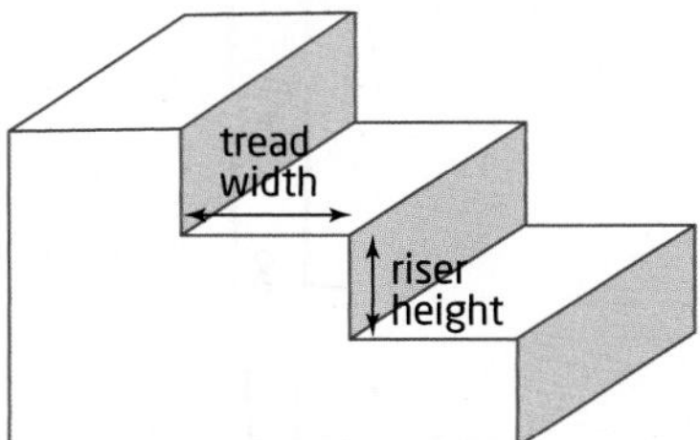

b) Collect data from at least five classmates. Construct a scatter plot of the data, and draw a line of best fit. Analyse your results and write a report on your findings.

22. Math Contest Railroad trains cannot go up tracks with a grade (slope) greater than 7%. To go over hills steeper than this, the railroad company builds *switchbacks*. How many switchbacks are needed to get to the top of a hill that is 250 m high? Assume that the maximum length of the run is 1 km. Explain your solution.

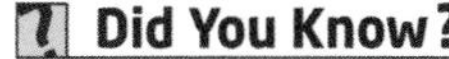

Did You Know?

The steepest railroad in the world is in the Blue Mountains of New South Wales, Australia.

The maximum gradient is 122%.

23. Math Contest The area of the shaded region is 12 square units. What is the slope of the line through AB?

A $\frac{3}{2}$

B $-\frac{3}{2}$

C 4

D $\frac{2}{3}$

E $-\frac{2}{3}$

y
B
A (−6, 0)
x

5.4 Slope as a Rate of Change

Asafa Powell of Jamaica set the men's 100-m world record in Athens, Greece, on June 14, 2005. He ran 100 m in 9.77 s. His average speed can be found by dividing the distance by his time.

$$\text{Average speed} = \frac{100}{9.77}$$
$$\doteq 10.2$$

Asafa's average speed was about 10.2 m/s. This means that, on average, he covered a distance of 10.2 m per second of the race. Speed is an example of a **rate of change**, because it is a rate that refers to the change in distance relative to the change in time.

rate of change

- a change in one quantity relative to the change in another quantity

Investigate

How can you find a rate of change from a graph?

The graph shows the average distance, in metres, that each animal or person can run in 10 s.

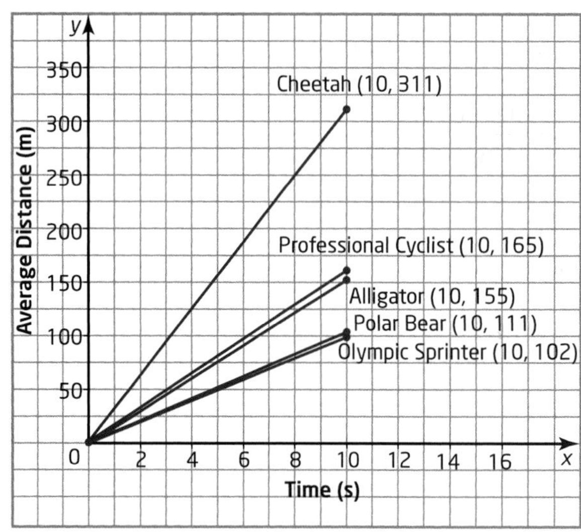

1. What do you think is meant by average distance?

2. Visually compare the steepness of each graph. Determine the slope of each graph. Rank the slopes from least to greatest.

3. Calculate the speed of each animal or person as $\frac{\text{distance}}{\text{time}}$. Rank the speeds from least to greatest.

4. **Reflect** Describe how the rate of change relates to the graph of a relation.

Example 1 Speed

Sarah is on the soccer team and runs every morning before school. One day, she ran 5 km in 20 min.

a) Calculate the rate of change of Sarah's distance from her starting point.

b) Graph Sarah's distance as it relates to time.

c) Explain the meaning of the rate of change and how it relates to the graph.

Solution

a) The rate of change is the distance travelled over the elapsed time.

$$\text{rate of change} = \frac{\text{change in distance}}{\text{change in time}}$$
$$= \frac{5}{20}$$
$$= 0.25$$

The rate of change is 0.25 km/min.

b)

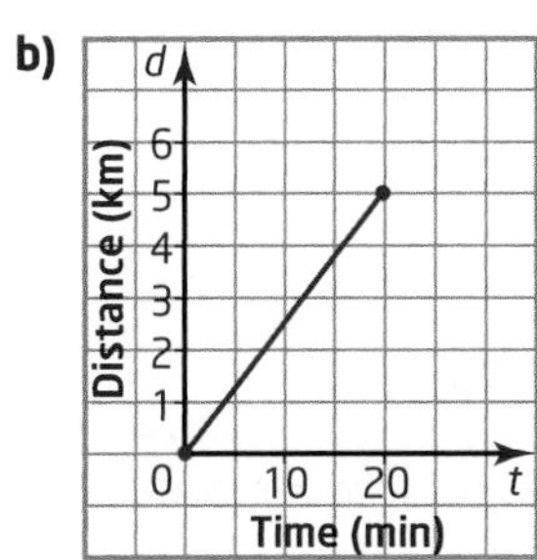

c) The rate of change is Sarah's average running speed. It is also the slope of the graph.

Example 2 Fuel Consumption

The graph shows the volume of gasoline remaining in a car's tank.

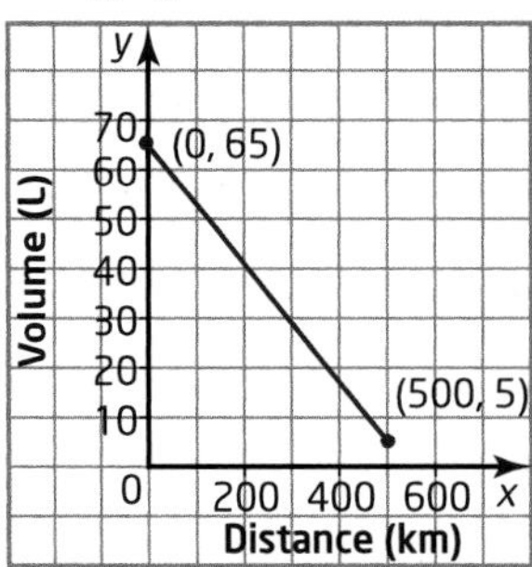

a) Calculate the slope of the graph.

b) Interpret the slope as a rate of change.

Solution

a) Finding the rise and run by counting grid squares may not always be practical. You can also find the rise and the run from the coordinates of two points on the graph.

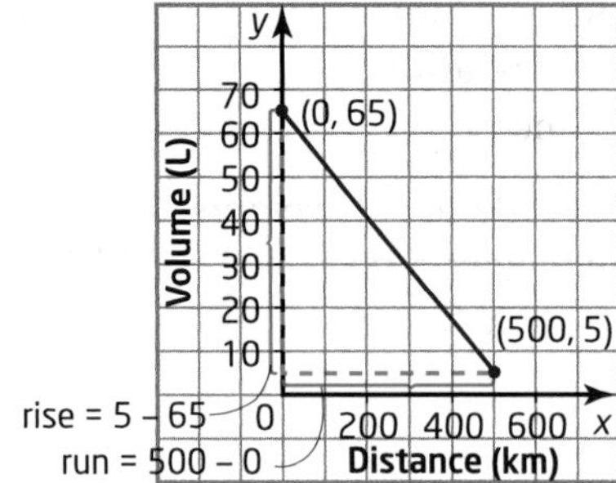

$$
\begin{aligned}
m &= \frac{\text{rise}}{\text{run}} \\
&= \frac{5 - 65}{500 - 0} \\
&= \frac{-60}{500} \\
&= -0.12
\end{aligned}
$$

I can subtract the y-values to get the rise. I can subtract the x-values in the same order to get the run. I'll subtract the coordinates of the left point from the coordinates of the right point.

b) The rate of change of the volume of gasoline is -0.12 L/km. The car uses an average of 0.12 L of gasoline per kilometre driven. The rate of change is negative because the volume of gasoline in the tank is decreasing.

Key Concepts

- Rate of change is the change in one quantity relative to the change in another.
- A rate of change requires units, such as kilometres per hour.
- When a relation is graphed, the slope describes the rate of change.
- To find the slope of a line segment joining two points, subtract the y-values to get the rise and subtract the x-values in the same order to get the run.

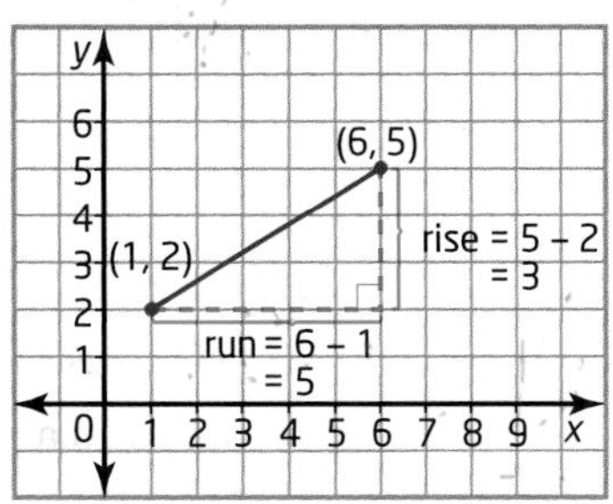

Communicate Your Understanding

C1 A car travelled 400 km in 5 h. Ahmed calculated the speed as 80 km/h but, when he graphed the relation, he calculated a slope of 0.0125. What do you think Ahmed did incorrectly?

C2 When Carlos goes to the gym, he likes to lift weights. The gym has produced graphs illustrating the weight a person should lift over a number of visits. Match each graph with the appropriate situation.

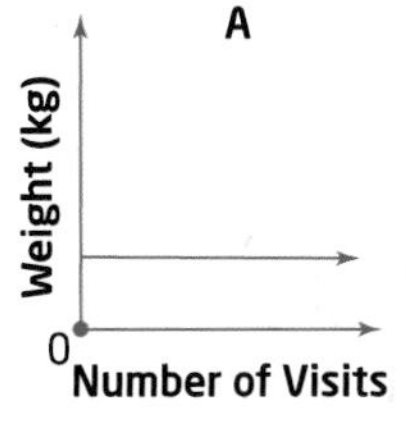

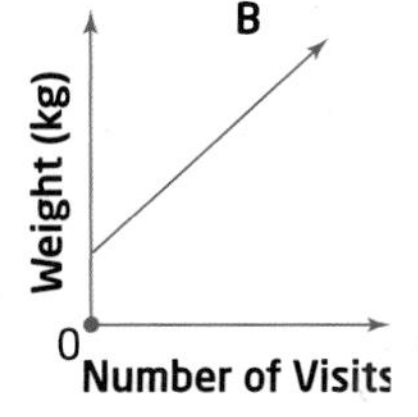

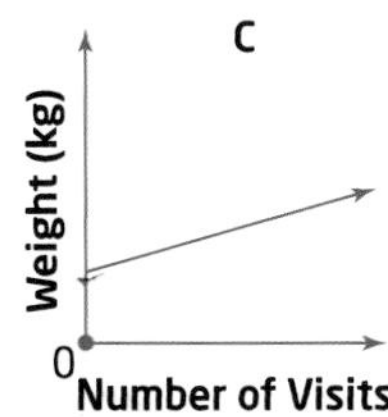

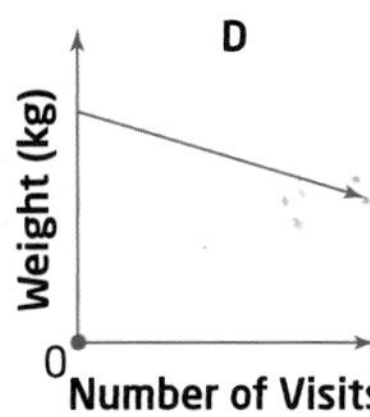

a) Begin with a small weight and slowly increase the weight at a constant rate.

b) Begin with a small weight and lift the same weight each visit.

c) Start with a large weight and slowly decrease the weight lifted each visit.

d) Start with a small weight and rapidly increase the weight at a constant rate each visit.

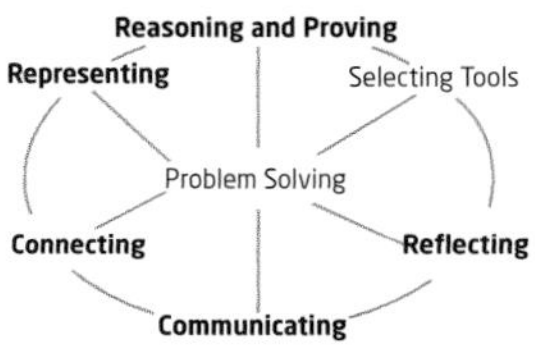

Practise

For help with questions 1 to 3, see Example 1.

1. The average adult breathes in about 37 L of air every 5 min. What is the rate of change of volume of air?

2. A teenager's heart pumps an average of 7200 L of blood every 24 h. What is the rate of change of volume of blood?

3. A hummingbird can flap its wings an average of 1800 times every 30 s. What is the rate of change of wing flaps?

For help with questions 4 and 5, see Example 2.

4. The graph shows the height above the ground of a rock climber over time.
   - **a)** Calculate the slope of the graph.
   - **b)** Interpret the slope as a rate of change.

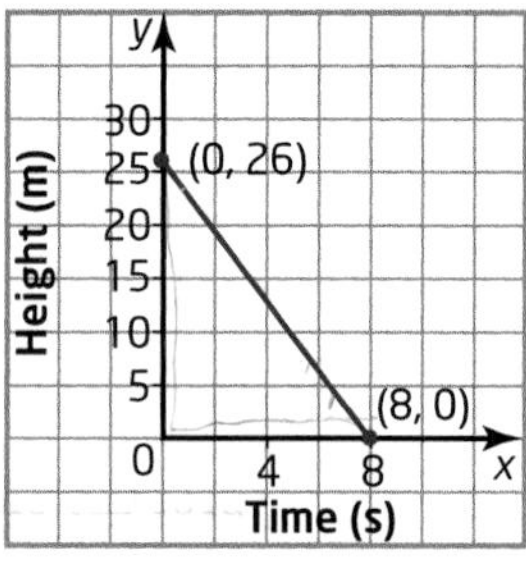

5. The graph shows the relationship between temperature and altitude.
   - **a)** Calculate the slope of the graph.
   - **b)** Interpret the slope as a rate of change.

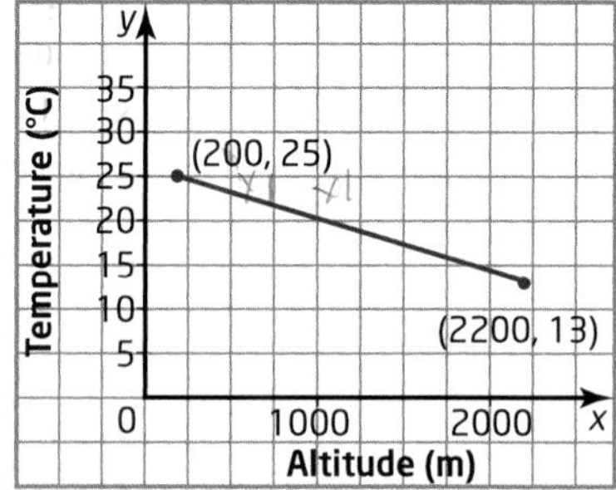

Connect and Apply

6. The price of a loaf of bread increased from $1.45 in 2003 to $1.78 in 2006. What is the average price increase per year?

7. The graph shows the height of a plant over a 2-month growth period. Calculate the rate of change per day.

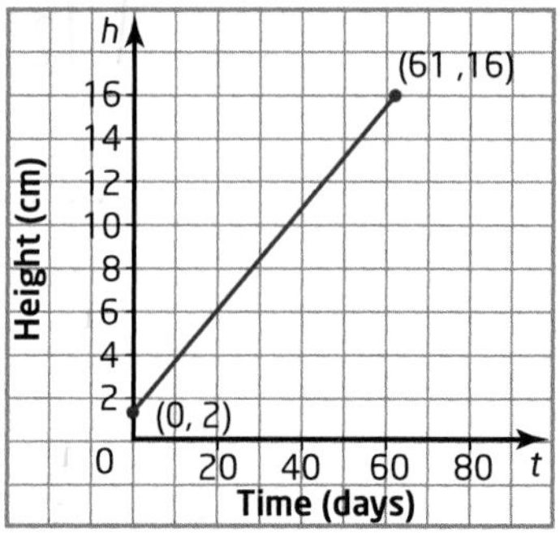

8. The table shows the approximate number of downloads of a freeware program on the Internet over a 2-month period.

a) Graph the data.

b) Calculate the slope and describe it as a rate of change.

c) Do you think this is a popular piece of software? Why or why not?

Date	Downloads
Sept 3	52 000
Sept 10	70 000
Sept 17	88 000
Sept 24	106 000
Oct 1	124 000
Oct 8	142 000
Oct 15	160 000
Oct 22	178 000
Oct 29	196 000
Nov 5	214 000

9. Chapter Problem

a) Plot a graph relating the number of toothpicks to the diagram number.

b) Calculate the slope of the line through these points.

c) Interpret the slope as a rate of change.

Diagram 1 Diagram 2 Diagram 3

10. From age 12 to 16, girls grow at an average of 8.5 cm/year, while boys grow at an average of 9.5 cm/year. Helen and John are both 12 years old. Helen is 150 cm tall and John is 146 cm tall. Graph their heights on the same grid. When can they expect their heights to be the same?

11. A fire hose can deliver water at a maximum rate of 500 L/min.

a) Plot a graph showing the maximum volume of water that a fire hose can pour onto a fire in time spans of up to 30 min.

b) Suppose two fire hoses are used. How will this affect the slope of the graph?

12. The table shows the minimum volume of water needed to fight a typical fire in rooms of various sizes.

Floor Area (m^2)	Minimum Volume of Water (L)
25	39
50	78
75	117

a) Graph the data in the table.

b) Calculate the rate of change.

c) If a fire truck is pumping water at a rate of 200 L/min, how long will it take to put out a fire in a room with a floor area of 140 m^2?

13. A large party balloon is being filled with helium at a constant rate. After 8 s, there is 2.5 L of helium in the balloon.

a) Graph this relation.

b) The balloon will burst if there is more than 10 L of helium in it. How long will it take to fill the balloon with that much helium? Mark this point on your graph.

Reasoning and Proving
Representing
Selecting Tools
Problem Solving
Connecting
Reflecting
Communicating

14. The distance-time graph shows two cars that are travelling at the same time.

a) Which car has the greater speed, and by how much?

b) What does the point of intersection of the two lines represent?

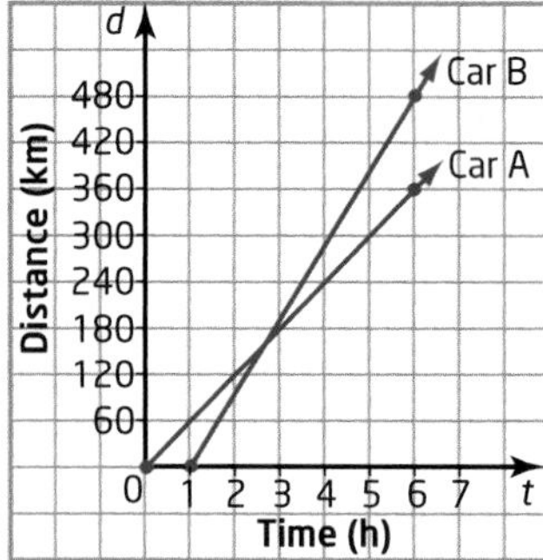

15. The table shows the number of people who have a university degree in Canada.

Year	Number of People With Degrees (millions)
1990	2.3
1995	3.0
2000	3.7
2005	4.7

a) Graph the data with a broken-line graph.

b) When was the rate of change relatively constant?

c) When was the rate of change different? How was it different?

16. A scuba tank holds 2.6 m^3 of compressed air. A diver at a shallow depth uses about 0.002 m^3 per breath and takes about 15 breaths per minute.

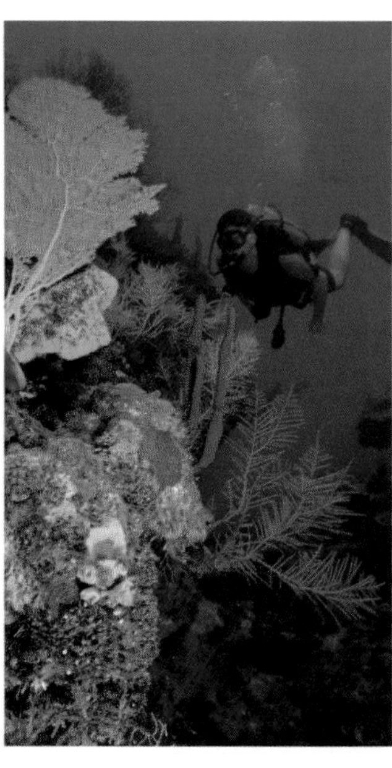

a) How much air will the diver use in 1 min?

b) How long will the air in the tank last at this rate?

c) At a depth of 10 m, the diver is breathing compressed air at 0.004 m^3 per breath. How long will the air last at this depth?

d) At the maximum depth recommended for sport diving, a diver is breathing air at a rate of 0.01 m^3 per breath. How long will the air last at this depth?

17. The table shows the number of people in Canada employed in the tourism industry by year.

a) Is the rate of change constant over the 10-year period?

b) Are the rates of change large or small relative to the total number of jobs? Explain.

Year	Jobs (thousands)
1995	38.8
1996	37.4
1997	37.5
1998	37.9
1999	39.9
2000	41.8
2001	41.7
2002	42.0
2003	41.6
2004	43.1

Achievement Check

18. The fuel efficiency of cars is stated in litres per 100 km. Kim's car has a fuel efficiency of 8 L/100 km. The fuel tank on Kim's car holds 32 L.

a) Graph the relationship between the amount of gasoline remaining in the car's tank and the distance Kim drives. Assume that she started with a full tank.

b) Find the slope of the graph. What does this slope represent?

c) Kim's car uses 25% more gas when she drives in the city. Redraw the graph. Find and interpret the slope for driving in the city.

Extend

19. A store is holding a special clearance sale on a $200 coat. Initially, there is a discount of 5%. Every 2 h, an additional 5% is taken off the latest price.

a) Make a table showing the price over the 16 h the sale is in effect.

b) Graph the price over the 16 h of the sale.

c) Explain the shape of the graph.

20. A cell phone company does not have a monthly fee but charges by the minute. The graph shows the monthly cost of phone calls based on the number of minutes talked.

Describe this cell phone company's rate plan.

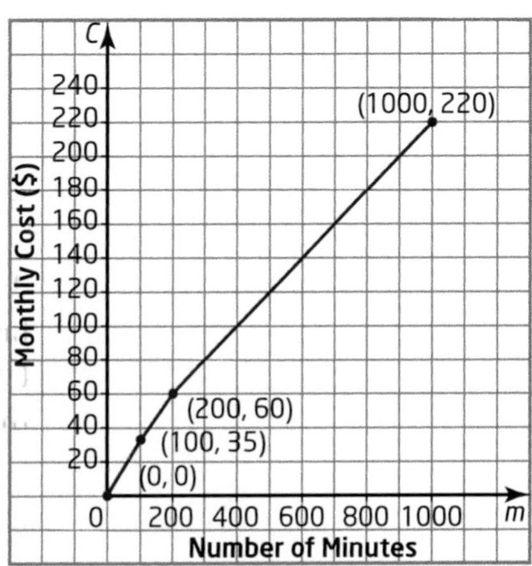

5.5 First Differences

Immediately after jumping from an airplane, a skydiver falls toward Earth with increasing speed. How can you tell if the speed is increasing linearly or non-linearly over time?

In Chapter 2: Relations, you learned how to identify linear and non-linear relations through graphing. In this section, you will learn how to use tables of values to identify the type of relation.

Investigate

Tools

- grid paper

How can you use a table of values to determine if a relation is linear or non-linear?

Method 1: Use Pencil and Paper

1. Consider the relation $y = 3x$.

a) Copy and complete the table of values.

b) Graph the relation.

c) Classify the relation as linear or non-linear.

x	y
0	0
1	3
2	
3	
4	

2. a) Describe the pattern in the x-values.

b) Add a third column to your table to record the change in y. Calculate each entry by subtracting consecutive values of y. The values in the third column are called **first differences**.

first differences

- differences between consecutive y-values in tables of values with evenly spaced x-values

x	y	First Differences
0	0	
1	3	3
2		
3		
4		

$3 - 0 = 3$

c) What do you notice about the values in the third column?

3. Repeat steps 1 and 2 for each relation using a table of values with the x-values shown.

a) $y = -2x + 7$

b) $y = x^2$

c) $y = 2^x$

x	y
0	
1	
2	
3	
4	

4. Consider your results for the four relations. Make an observation regarding linear relations and first differences.

5. Use first differences to determine which of these relations are linear and which are non-linear.

a)

x	y
0	7
1	3
2	-1
3	-5
4	-9

b)

x	y
0	-3
2	-1
4	3
6	9
8	17

c)

x	y
-4	-10
-1	-5
2	0
5	5
8	10

6. **Reflect** Write a rule for using first differences to determine whether a relation is linear or non-linear.

7. **Reflect** Describe how you can tell if the equation of a relation represents a linear relation.

Method 2: Use Technology

Tools

- graphing calculator

1. Create a table of values for $y = 3x$ using five values for x: 0, 1, 2, 3, 4, 5.
   - To clear all lists, press (2nd) [MEM] to display the **MEMORY** menu, select **4:ClrAllLists**, and press (ENTER).
   - To enter the data into the lists, press (STAT) and select **1:Edit**. Under list **L1**, enter the x-values.
   - To generate the y-values, scroll over to list **L2**, then up to the L2 heading. Type the expression for y, substituting the list L1 for x. Press 3 (×) (2nd) [L1] (ENTER).

2. Graph the relation. Is it linear?
   - Press (2nd) [STATPLOT] to display the **STAT PLOTS** menu. Select **1:Plot1**.
   - Press (ENTER) to select **On**.
   - For **Type**:, select line graph.
   - Ensure that **Xlist**: is set to **L1** and **Ylist**: is set to **L2**.
   - Press (ZOOM) and select **9:ZoomStat**.

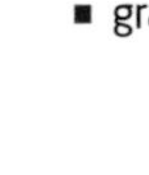

3. **a)** Describe the pattern in the x-values displayed in list **L1**.

b) Find the differences between successive y-values.

- To find the first differences, scroll over and up to the **L3** heading.
- Press (2nd) [LIST] to display the **LIST MATH** menu.
- From the **OPS** menu, select **7:ΔList(**.
- Then, press (2nd) [L2] ( )) (ENTER).

L1	L2	L3 3
0	0	------
1	3	
2	6	
3	9	
4	12	
5	15	

L3 =ΔList(L2)

c) What do you notice about the values in list **L3**?

4. Repeat steps 1 to 3 for each relation.

a) $y = -2x + 7$

b) $y = x^2$

c) $y = 2^x$

5. Consider your results in steps 2 and 3 for the four relations. Make an observation about linear relations and first differences.

6. Use first differences to determine which of these relations are linear and which are non-linear.

a)

x	y
0	7
1	3
2	−1
3	−5
4	−9

b)

x	y
0	−3
2	−1
4	3
6	9
8	17

c)

x	y
−4	−10
−1	−5
2	0
5	5
8	10

7. **Reflect** Write a rule for using first differences to determine whether a relation is linear or non-linear.

8. **Reflect** Describe how you can tell if the equation of a relation represents a linear relation.

Key Concepts

- To work with first differences, the values of x (independent variable) must change by a constant amount.
- To find first differences, subtract consecutive values of y (dependent variable).

x	y	First Differences
0	0	
1	2	2
2	4	2
3	6	2
4	8	2

$2 - 0 = 2$
$4 - 2 = 2$
$6 - 4 = 2$
$8 - 6 = 2$

- If the first differences of a relation are constant, the relation is linear.
- If the first differences of a relation are not constant, the relation is non-linear.

Communicate Your Understanding

C1 For each table of values, decide whether it is possible to use first differences to determine whether the relation is linear or non-linear. Explain your decision.

a)

x	y
0	7
1	10
2	13
3	16

b)

x	y
0	7
1	10
3	16
6	25

C2 Jacob's rate of pay is \$9.50/h. If you made a table of values of Jacob's earnings, how would his hourly wage relate to the first differences?

Practise

1. Look at each equation. Predict whether it represents a linear relation or a non-linear relation. Use a graphing calculator to confirm your answers.

a) $y = 5x + 6$ **b)** $y = -3x - 2$

c) $y = 4x^2 + 1$ **d)** $y = 10^x$

e) $y = -\frac{4}{3}x + \frac{1}{2}$ **f)** $y = \frac{6}{x}$

2. Copy each table and include a third column to record first differences. Classify each relation as linear or non-linear.

a)

x	y
0	5
1	6
2	8
3	12

b)

x	y
3	–4
4	–1
5	2
6	5

c)

x	y
–1	1
0	0
1	1
2	4

d)

x	y
–5	8
–3	4
–1	0
1	–4

3. Each table shows the speed of a skydiver before the parachute opens. Without graphing, determine whether the relation is linear or non-linear.

a) There is no air resistance.

Time (s)	Speed (m/s)
0	0
1	9.8
2	19.6
3	29.4
4	39.2
5	49.0

b) There is air resistance.

Time (s)	Speed (m/s)
0	0
1	9.6
2	16.6
3	23.1
4	30.8
5	34.2

Connect and Apply

4. Use first differences to determine which relations are linear and which are non-linear. Write an equation representing each linear relation. Extrapolate the relation to predict the outcome for the seventh step.

a)

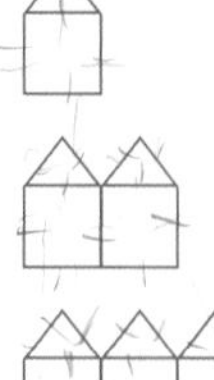

Number of Houses	Number of Segments
1	
2	
3	
4	

b)

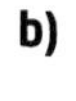

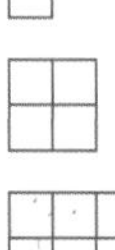

Base Side Length	Total Number of Tiles
1	
2	
3	
4	

5. Use first differences to determine which relations are linear and which are non-linear. Write an equation representing each linear relation. Extrapolate the relation to predict the outcome for the seventh step.

a) 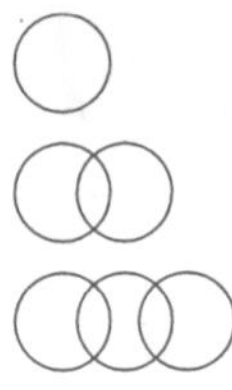

Number of Circles	Number of Intersection Points
1	
2	
3	
4	

b) 

Number of Sides	Number of Diagonals
4	
5	
6	
7	

6. Chapter Problem A pattern is made from toothpicks as shown.

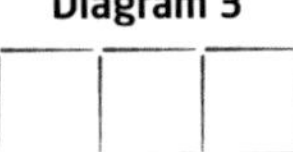

a) Create a table comparing the diagram number to the number of toothpicks.

b) Use first differences to show that the pattern is a linear relation.

c) Write an equation for the relation.

d) Extrapolate the relation to predict the outcome for the 10th step.

7. A rectangular piece of cardboard is 16 cm wide. It is dipped in water and is wet from the bottom up.

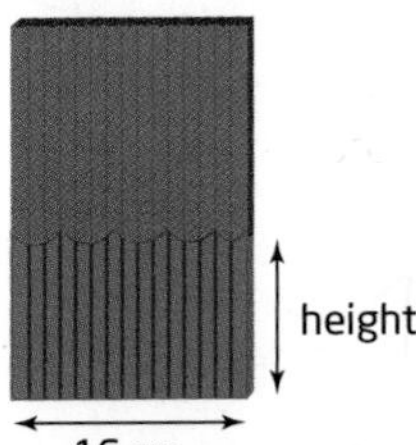

a) Create a table comparing the height of the wet cardboard to its area as the height increases from 0 cm to 10 cm.

b) Use first differences to determine whether the relation is linear.

c) What is the area of wet cardboard if the height is 50 cm?

Extend

8. The triangle's base is twice its height. The triangle is painted from the bottom up.

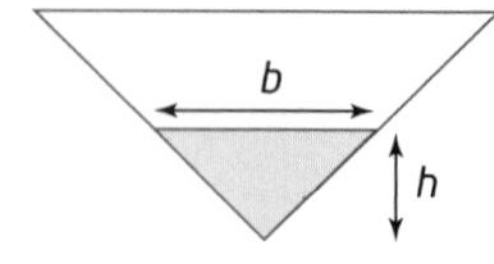

a) Create a table comparing the height of the painted portion to its area as the height increases.

b) Use first differences to determine whether the relation is linear.

9. A class conducted an experiment to see how high a ball would bounce from various heights. The results of one group's experiment are shown in the table.

Drop Height (cm)	50	100	150	200	250	300
Bounce Height (cm)	41	82	125	166	208	254

Provide two or more pieces of evidence to show whether this relationship is linear or non-linear.

10. The first few figures in a pattern are shown.

Figure 1 Figure 2 Figure 3 Figure 4

a) Copy and complete the table.

Figure Number	Number of Circles in Pattern
1	1
2	3
3	
4	
5	
6	
7	
8	

b) **Use Technology** A graphing calculator can be used to compute first differences. Follow the steps below.

- Enter the values from column 1 (Figure Number) in list **L1**.
- Enter the values from column 2 (Number of Circles in Pattern) in list **L2**.
- Place the cursor on **L3** using the cursor keys.
- Press (2nd) [LIST]. From the **OPS** menu, select **7:ΔList(**. Press (2nd) [L2] ( )) (ENTER).

What information is in **L3**? Use this information to create a non-linear equation for this pattern.

5.6 Connecting Variation, Slope, and First Differences

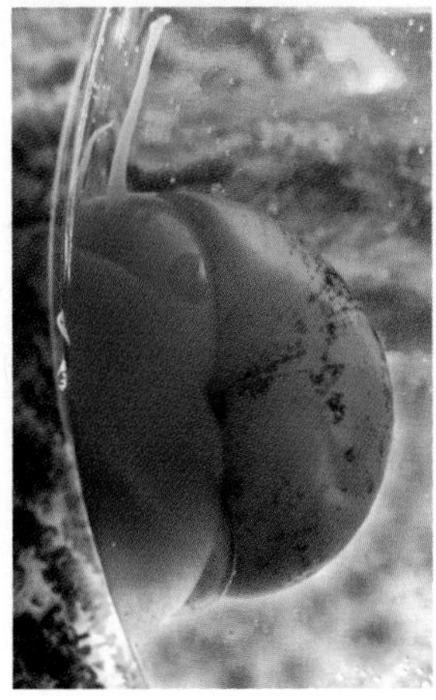

You have learned to identify a linear relation from its graph, equation, and table of values. For example, from the graph of a linear relation, you can tell if it is a direct variation or a partial variation and calculate its slope. In addition, you can identify a linear relation from its table of values by calculating first differences.

Consider the distance travelled by a snail over time. Is the graph of this relationship linear? How could you find the slope?

In this section, you will learn how variation, slope, and first differences are connected.

Investigate

- grid paper

How are variation, slope, and first differences connected?

The table shows the height, compared to the ground, of a snail as it crawls up a pipe.

Time, t (min)	Height, h (m)
0	−3
3	1
6	5
9	9
12	13

1. Graph the relation. Is this a direct variation or a partial variation?

2. Describe the pattern in the t-values. Use first differences to confirm that the relation is linear.

3. Calculate the slope.

4. How does the slope relate to the first differences and the pattern in the t-values?

5. What is the initial value of the height?

6. Write an equation of the line.

7. **Reflect** Describe how first differences, slope, and partial variation are related.

The slope of a linear relation remains constant. The first differences also remain constant when the changes in the x-values are constant.

The slope, m, of a line can be calculated by dividing the change in y by the change in x.

$$m = \frac{\text{rise}}{\text{run}}$$
$$= \frac{\text{change in } y}{\text{change in } x}$$
$$= \frac{y_2 - y_1}{x_2 - x_1}$$

This is sometimes abbreviated as $\frac{\Delta y}{\Delta x}$, which is read as "delta y over delta x." The Greek letter delta is the symbol for *change in*.

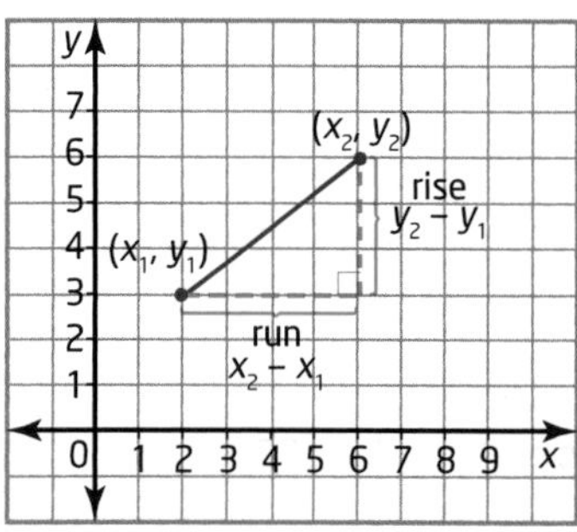

The equation of a line has the form $y = mx + b$, where m represents the slope and b represents the vertical intercept, or the value of the dependent variable where the line intersects the vertical axis.

Example 1 Fuel Consumption

The graph shows the relationship between the volume of gasoline remaining in a car's fuel tank and the distance driven.

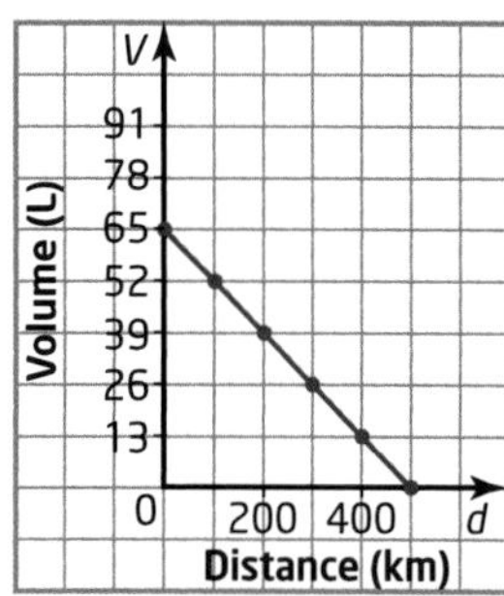

a) Calculate the slope and describe its meaning.

b) Determine the vertical intercept.

c) Write an equation for this relation.

Solution

a) Use the first two points on the line to calculate the slope.

Use $(x_1, y_1) = (0, 65)$ and $(x_2, y_2) = (100, 52)$.

$$m = \frac{y_2 - y_1}{x_2 - x_1}$$
$$= \frac{52 - 65}{100 - 0}$$
$$= \frac{-13}{100}$$
$$= -\frac{13}{100}$$

Since the slope of a linear relation is constant, I can use any pair of points and the slope will be the same.

The rate of change of the volume of fuel in the tank is $-\frac{13}{100}$ L/km.

The car uses an average of 13 L of gasoline per 100 km driven. This is a negative quantity because the volume of gasoline is decreasing.

b) The vertical intercept is the value of V when $d = 0$. From the graph, $V = 65$ when $d = 0$. Therefore, $b = 65$.

c) This is a partial variation, so its equation has the form $V = md + b$. The equation of this relation is $V = -\frac{13}{100}d + 65$.

Example 2 Slope and the Constant of Variation

Make a table of values and graph the relation $y = 2x - 5$. Draw a right triangle on your graph to find the slope.

Solution

x	y
1	-3
2	-1
3	1
4	3

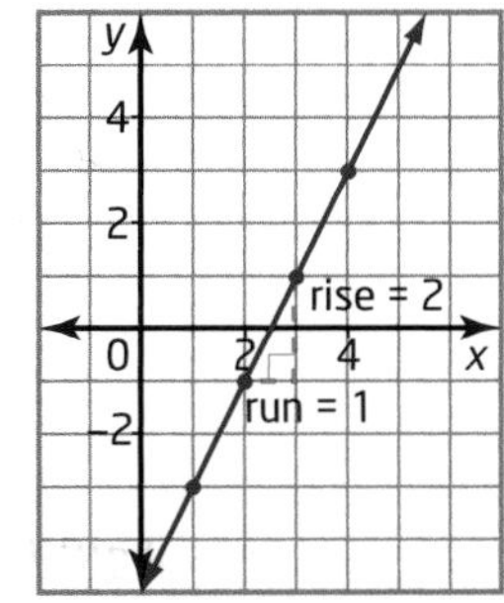

$$m = \frac{\text{rise}}{\text{run}}$$
$$= \frac{2}{1}$$
$$= 2$$

The slope is the same as the constant of variation in the equation $y = 2x - 5$.

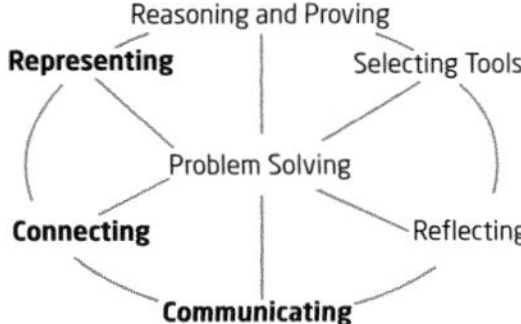

The Rule of Four

A relation can be represented in a variety of ways so that it can be looked at from different points of view. A mathematical relation can be described in four ways:

- using words
- using a diagram or a graph
- using numbers
- using an equation

Example 3 Slope and the Equation of a Relation

Jacques earns \$25 per day plus \$9 per 100 flyers for delivering advertising flyers. This is an example of using words to describe a relation. Use the rule of four to describe this relation in three other ways.

Solution

Using numbers: Create a table showing Jacques's earnings for various numbers of flyers.

Number of Flyers, F	Earnings, E (\$)
0	25
100	34
200	43
300	52

Using a graph: Graph this relation.

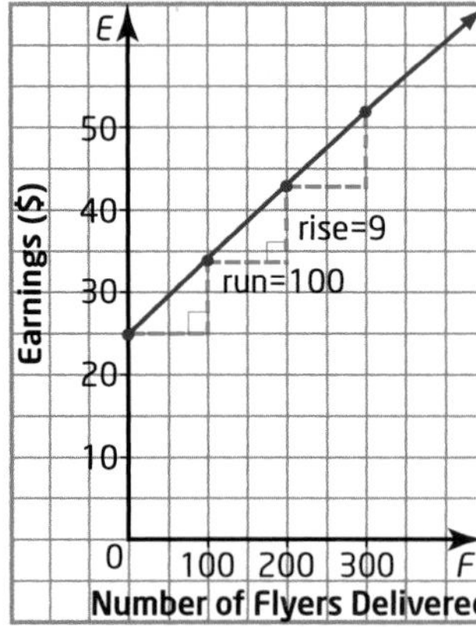

The graph is a straight line that does not pass through (0, 0). This is a partial variation.

Between any pair of points, there is a rise of 9 for a run of 100. The graph intersects the vertical axis at $E = 25$.

Using an equation:

The relation is linear with $m = \frac{9}{100}$ and an initial value of 25.

This is a partial variation. The equation representing this relation is $E = \frac{9}{100}F + 25$, where E is Jacques's earnings, in dollars, and F is the number of flyers delivered. The slope represents Jacques's rate of pay in relation to the number of flyers delivered.

Looking at the table, the F-values change by a constant amount of 100 and the E-values change by a constant amount of 9.

$$m = \frac{\text{change in } E}{\text{change in } F}$$
$$= \frac{9}{100}$$

The initial value of E is 25.

Key Concepts

- Finite differences and the pattern in the x-values can be used to find the slope of a linear relation.
- The constant of variation is also the slope of a linear relation.
- A constant, or average, rate of change can be interpreted as the slope of a relation.
- Slope can be symbolized as $m = \frac{\Delta y}{\Delta x}$, where Δ represents *change in*, or $m = \frac{y_2 - y_1}{x_2 - x_1}$.

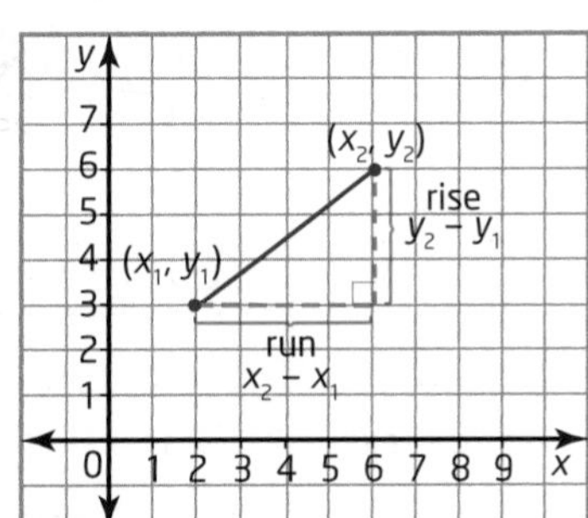

- A line has an equation of the form $y = mx + b$, where m represents the slope and b represents the vertical intercept.
- The Rule of Four can be used to represent a relation in four ways:
  - using words
  - using a diagram or a graph
  - using numbers
  - using an equation

Communicate Your Understanding

C1 The constant of variation and the slope of a relation are the same. Explain why this is true.

C2 Describe the different ways you can find the slope of a linear relation.

C3 How can you find the slope of this line? Explain.

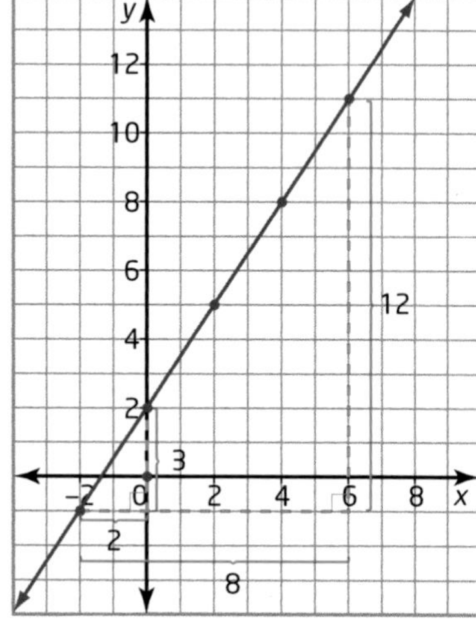

Practise

For help with questions 1 and 2, see Example 1.

1. a) Calculate the slope.

b) Determine the vertical intercept.

c) Write an equation for the relation.

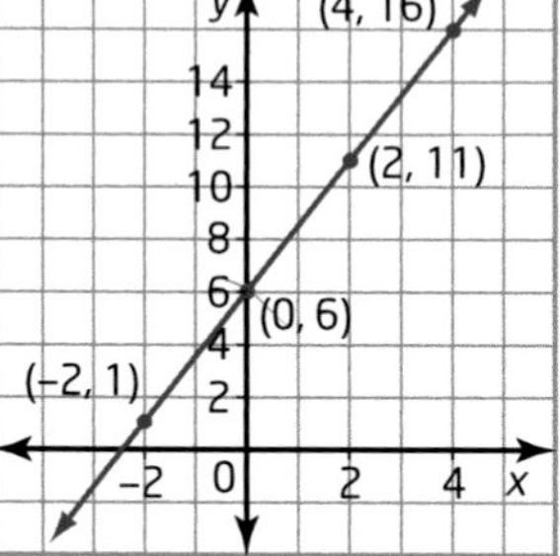

2. a) Calculate the slope.

b) Determine the vertical intercept.

c) Write an equation for the relation.

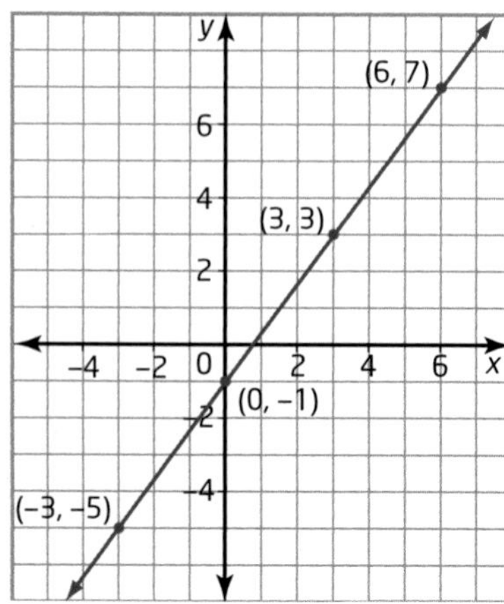

For help with question 3, see Example 2.

3. Make a table of values and graph each relation. Draw a right triangle on your graph to find the slope.

a) $y = 2x + 1$

b) $y = -3x + 4$

c) $y = -\frac{3}{2}x$

d) $y = 0.5x + 0.2$

For help with questions 4 to 6, see Example 3.

4. Use the rule of four to represent this relation in three other ways.

a) Use a graph.

b) Use words.

c) Use an equation.

x	y
0	2
1	5
2	8
3	11
4	14

5. Use the rule of four to represent this relation in three other ways.

a) Use a graph.

b) Use words.

c) Use an equation.

x	y
-6	1
-4	6
-2	11
0	16
2	21

6. A house painter charges $400 plus $200 per room to paint the interior of a house. Represent the relation using numbers, a graph, and an equation.

Connect and Apply

7. The cost of a taxi ride is $5.00 plus $0.75 for every 0.5 km.

a) Graph this relation.

b) Identify the slope and the vertical intercept of the line. What do they represent?

c) Is this a direct or a partial variation? Explain.

d) Write an equation relating the cost and the distance travelled.

8. The table shows how the depth of a scuba diver changes with time. Complete the rule of four for the relation by representing it using words, a graph, and an equation.

Time (s)	Depth (m)
0	-50
5	-45
10	-40
15	-35
20	-30

9. y varies directly with x. When $x = 4$, $y = 9$.

a) Find the slope and the vertical intercept of the line.

b) Write an equation for this relation.

c) Graph this relation.

10. y varies partially with x. When $x = 0$, $y = 5$, and when $x = 6$, $y = 8$.

a) Find the slope and the vertical intercept of the line.

b) Write an equation for this relation.

c) Graph this relation.

11. Complete the rule of four for this relation by representing it numerically, in words, and with an equation.

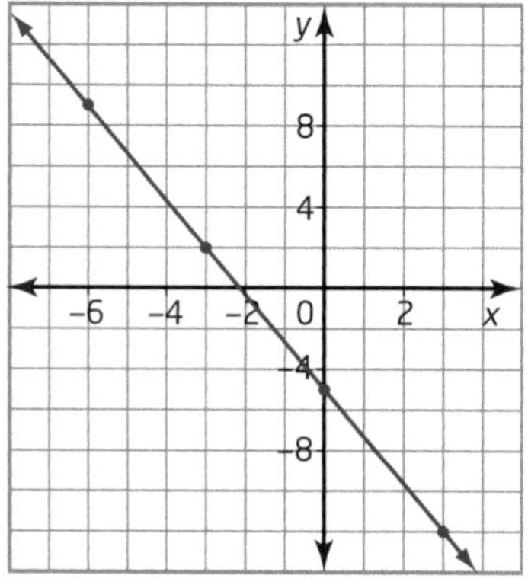

12. Complete the rule of four for the relation $y = 4x - 3$ by representing it numerically, graphically, and in words.

13. A swimming pool is being drained. The table shows the volume of water, in kilolitres, remaining after an elapsed time, in minutes.

Time (min)	0	40	120	180
Volume of Water (kL)	50	40	20	5

a) Confirm that this relation is linear.

b) Graph this relation.

c) Find the slope of the graph as both a fraction and a decimal. Is the slope constant? What does the slope represent?

d) Write an equation for the volume of water in terms of the time.

e) Use your graph or equation to find the volume of water after 60 min.

Achievement Check

14. A company tests the heavy-duty elastic bands it makes by measuring how much they stretch when supporting various masses. This table shows the results of tests on one of the elastic bands.

Mass (kg)	0	2	4	6	8
Length (cm)	6.2	9.6	13.0	16.4	19.8

a) Graph the relation between mass and length.

b) What does the point (0, 6.2) represent?

c) Find the slope of the graph. Is it constant? What does it represent?

d) Write an equation for the length in terms of the mass.

e) Predict how long the elastic band will be when it is supporting a 10-kg mass.

f) If the length for an 8-kg mass were 19.0 cm, how would the answer to part e) change?

Extend

15. This table shows the recommended dosage for a particular drug, based on the patient's mass.

Mass (kg)	Dosage (mg)
40	30
50	35
60	40
70	45
80	50
90	55
100	60
110	65
120	70

a) Write an equation relating the dosage and the mass of the patient.

b) The maximum dosage is 110% of the recommended dosage. Write an equation relating the maximum dosage and the patient's mass.

c) Graph both relations. Compare the graphs.

16. A salesperson's monthly sales and pay for a 4-month period are shown in the table. Determine the salesperson's base salary and percent commission on sales. Describe any assumptions you had to make.

Sales ($)	Salary ($)
15 000	1300
28 000	1560
34 000	1680
17 500	1350

Chapter 5 Review

5.1 Direct Variation, pages 238–245

1. Christina works part-time at a flower shop. She earns \$9/h. Her pay varies directly with the time, in hours, she works.

a) Choose appropriate letters for variables. Make a table of values showing Christina's pay for 0 h, 1 h, 2 h, and 3 h.

b) Graph the relationship.

c) Write an equation in the form $y = kx$.

2. The Jung family travels 300 km to a relative's home. The distance, d, in kilometres, varies directly with the time, t, in hours.

a) Find an equation relating d and t if $d = 144$ when $t = 1.5$. What does the constant of variation represent?

b) Use the equation to determine how long it will take the Jungs to reach their destination.

3. The volume of soup varies directly with the volume of water used to prepare it. John uses 2.5 L of water to make 3.0 L of soup.

a) Explain why this relation is a direct variation.

b) Graph this relation.

c) What will happen to the graph if John uses 2.8 L of water to make 3.0 L of soup?

5.2 Partial Variation, pages 246–253

4. a) Copy and complete the table of values, given that y varies partially with x.

x	y
0	4
1	7
2	
3	13
4	
	25

b) Identify the initial value of y and the constant of variation from the table.

c) Write an equation relating y and x in the form $y = mx + b$.

d) Graph the relation. Describe the graph.

5. Identify each relation as a direct variation, a partial variation, or neither. Justify your answer.

a) $y = x^2 + 5$

b) $A = 3d - 2$

c) $C = 2.5m$

d) $y = -8x + 1$

6. A new restaurant is having advertising flyers printed. The cost to design and lay out the flyer is \$500. There is an additional cost of \$0.15 per flyer printed.

a) Identify the fixed cost and the variable cost of this partial variation.

b) Write an equation representing this relationship.

c) Use your equation to determine the total cost of 500 flyers.

5.3 Slope, pages 254–263

7. Determine the slope of each object.

a)

b)

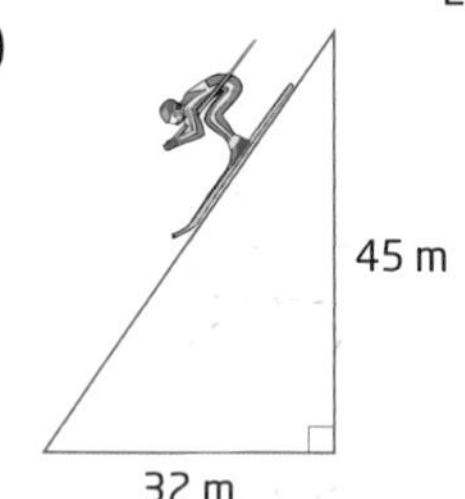

8. Calculate the slope of each line segment.

a) AB

b) CD

c) EF

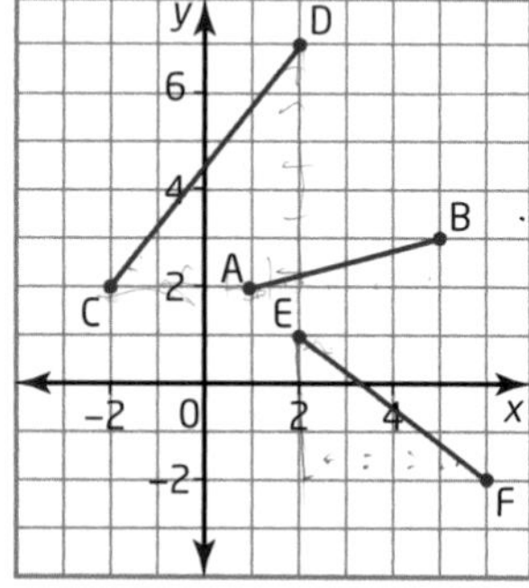

9\. a) Draw an example of a line segment with an endpoint (3, 5) and a slope of 0.

b) Draw an example of a line segment with an endpoint (−4, 1) and an undefined slope.

10\. A ladder reaches 2 m up a wall. The foot of the ladder is 0.4 m from the wall. For safety reasons, the slope should be between 6.3 and 9.5. Is this ladder within the safe range?

5.4 Slope as a Rate of Change, pages 264–271

11\. The graph shows the average amount of food energy used by a 50-kg person while taking part in various activities.

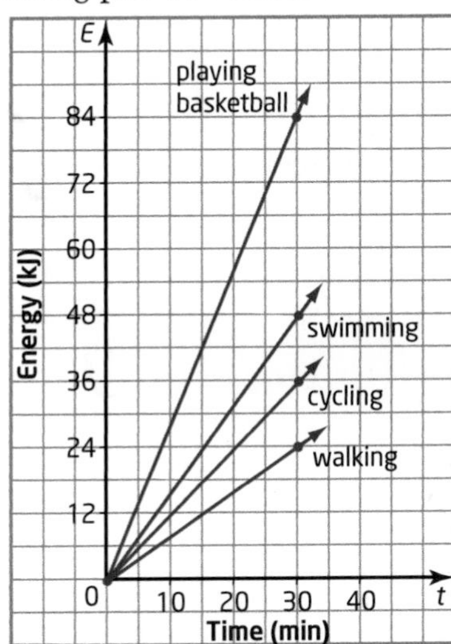

Describe the slope of each activity as a rate of change.

12\. The hair on your head grows at a constant rate. The longest strands of Samira's hair were 45 cm long on her 12th birthday. She decided not to cut her hair for 5 years and the longest strands grew to 106 cm. Graph the length of Samira's hair over the 5-year period. What is the slope of the graph? Express it as a rate of change.

5.5 First Differences, pages 272–278

13\. Use first differences to determine whether each relation is linear or non-linear.

a)

x	y
0	4
1	11
2	18
3	25
4	32

b)

t	d
−1	21
0	13
1	9
2	7
3	6

14\. Each tile measures 2 cm by 2 cm. Use first differences to determine whether the relationship between the length of the row of tiles and its area is linear or non-linear.

5.6 Connecting Variation, Slope, and First Differences, pages 279–287

15\. a) Confirm that this relation is linear.

b) Calculate the slope.

c) Write an equation for the relation.

d) Graph the relation.

x	y
0	2
1	5
2	8
3	11
4	14

16\. The table shows the mass of propane fuel remaining in a barbecue tank.

Time (h)	0	1	2	3	4	5
Mass (kg)	9.0	8.6	8.2	7.8	7.4	7.0

a) Confirm that this relation is linear.

b) Graph this relation.

c) Find the slope and the vertical intercept of the graph. What do they represent?

d) Write an equation for the mass of propane fuel in terms of the time.

Chapter 5 Practice Test

Multiple Choice

For questions 1 to 5, select the best answer.

1. Which of the following is an example of a partial variation?

A $M = 9N$

B $p = 3^q$

C $k = 9h - 7$

D $y = 4x^2$

2. The distance travelled by a car in a given time varies directly with its speed. A car travelled 150 km in 1.5 h. What is the constant of variation?

A 100

B 0.01

C 15

D 375

3. What is the slope of this roof?

A 3

B 12

C 0.75

D 0.5

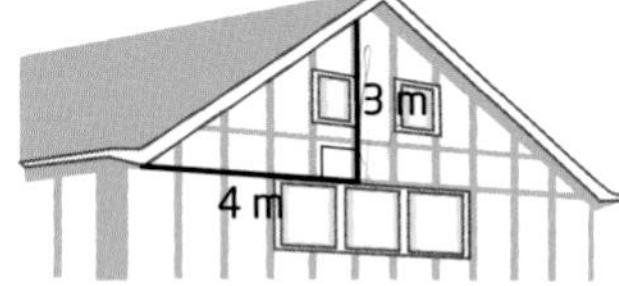

4. Which statement is false?

A The slope of a linear relation also represents a constant rate of change.

B Slope can be calculated as $\frac{\text{rise}}{\text{run}}$.

C Non-linear relations have constant first differences.

D In the equation $y = mx + b$, the slope is represented by m.

5. The cost of gasoline varies directly with the volume purchased. 50 L of gasoline costs \$43.50. Which of the following relates the cost, C, and the volume of gasoline, G?

A $C = 0.87G + 43.50$

B $C = 1.15G$

C $C = 1.15G + 50$

D $C = 0.87G$

Short Response

Show all steps to your solutions

6. a) Calculate the slope.

b) Determine the vertical intercept.

c) Write an equation for the relation.

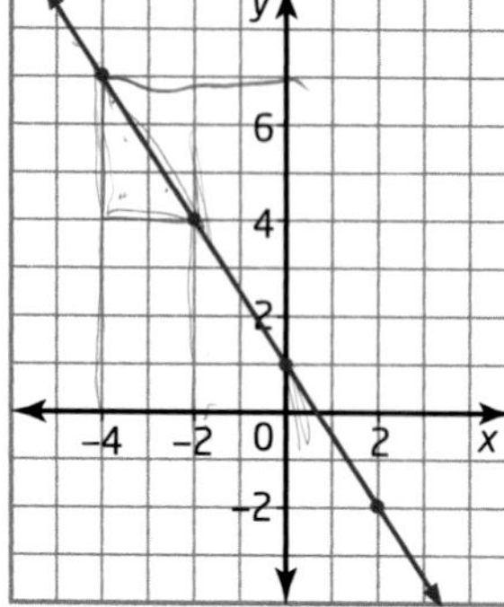

7. The time between seeing a lightning flash and hearing the thunder it creates varies directly with how far away the lightning is. The thunder from a lightning flash 685 m away was heard after 2.0 s.

a) Determine an equation relating the time before hearing the thunder and the distance from the lightning flash.

b) Graph this relationship.

8. When water freezes, its volume increases, as shown in the table.

Liquid Volume of Water (L)	Frozen Volume of Water (L)
5	5.45
10	10.90
15	16.35
20	21.80

Without graphing, determine whether the relation is linear or non-linear. Justify your answer.

9. The price charged to repair a computer is \$60, plus \$50/h.

a) Write an equation representing this relationship.

b) What is the total cost of a repair that takes 3.5 h?

c) How would the equation change if the hourly cost changed to \$45?

Extended Response

Provide complete solutions.

10. This graph shows the cost of producing 1000 copies of a school yearbook as it relates to the number of pages in the yearbook.

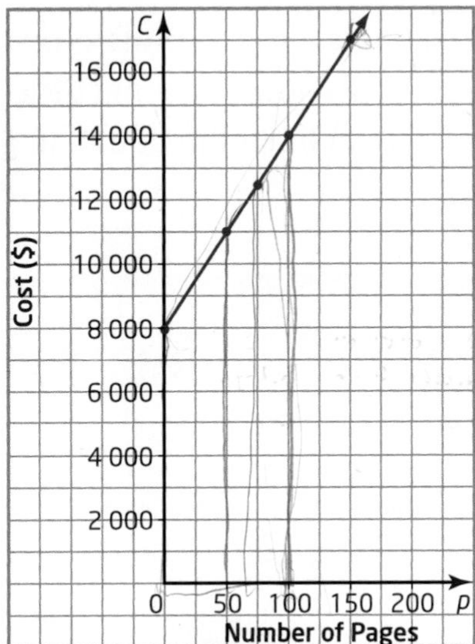

a) Calculate the rate of change. How does it relate to the graph?

b) Write an equation for this relationship.

c) Describe how the equation and graph would change if the base cost changed to $9000.

d) Producing 2000 copies of the yearbook would increase the cost per page by 8%, with no change in the base cost. Determine the equation for the cost of producing 2000 copies of this yearbook as it relates to the number of pages.

Chapter Problem Wrap-Up

Consider the relationship between the number of closed regions and the number of toothpicks in the patterns. Decide whether each toothpick pattern is linear or non-linear. Justify your answer. If the pattern is linear, state the rate of change and develop an equation for the relationship. If the pattern is non-linear, describe how to adjust the diagrams to make a linear pattern, and write an equation to define the relationship.

Pattern A

Pattern B

CHAPTER

6

Analyse Linear Relations

In this chapter, you will look more closely at the equation for a linear relation. You will learn how to connect the equation to the graph and how to build the equation given a few facts about the line.

Analytic Geometry

- Determine, through investigation, the characteristics that distinguish the equation of a straight line from the equations of non-linear relations.
- Identify, through investigation, the equation of a line in any of the forms $y = mx + b$, $Ax = By + C = 0$, $x = a$, $y = b$.
- Express the equation of a line in the form $y = mx + b$, given the form $Ax + By + C = 0$.
- Identify, through investigation with technology, the geometric significance of m and b in the equation $y = mx + b$.
- Identify, through investigation, properties of the slopes of lines and line segments, using graphing technology to facilitate investigations, where appropriate.
- Graph lines by hand, using a variety of techniques.
- Determine the equation of a line from information about the line.
- Describe the meaning of the slope and y-intercept for a linear relation arising from a realistic situation and describe a situation that could be modelled by a given linear equation.
- Identify and explain any restrictions on the variables in a linear relation arising from a realistic situation.
- Determine graphically the point of intersection of two linear relations, and interpret the intersection point in the context of an application.

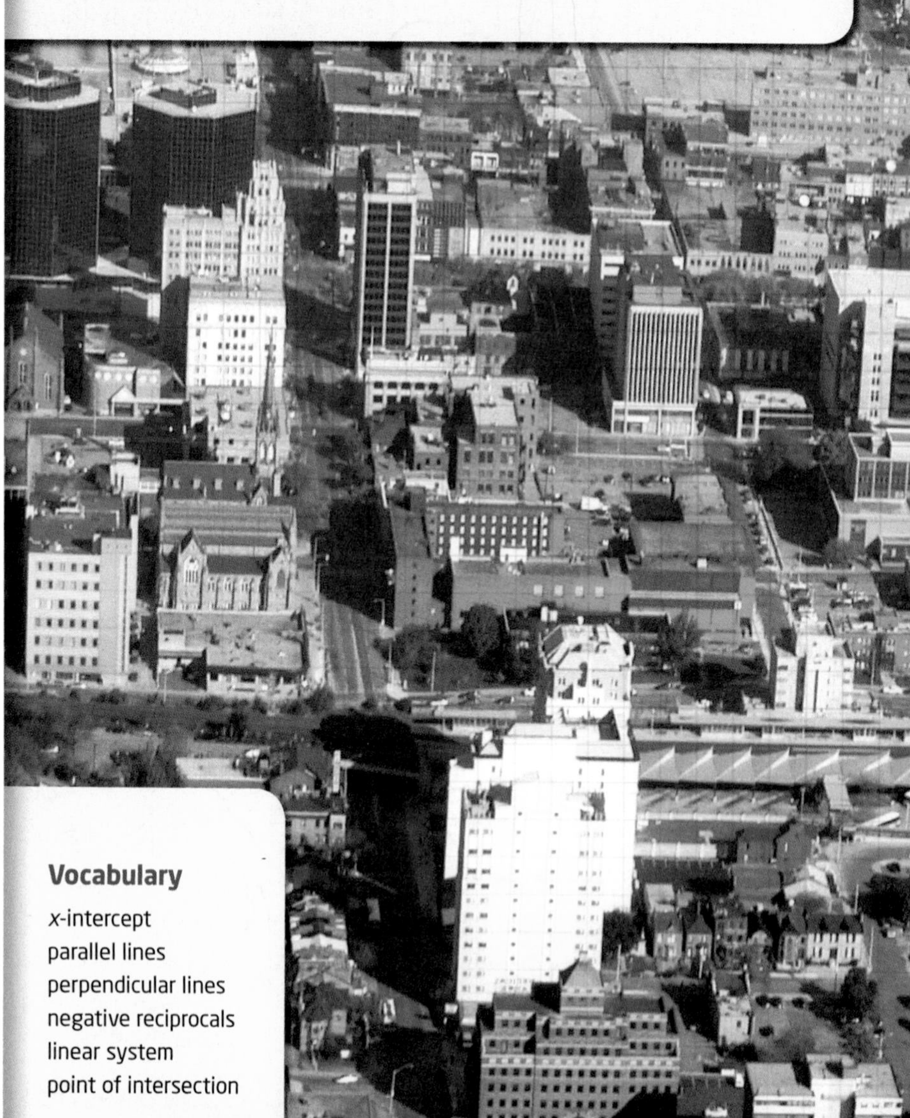

Vocabulary

x-intercept
parallel lines
perpendicular lines
negative reciprocals
linear system
point of intersection

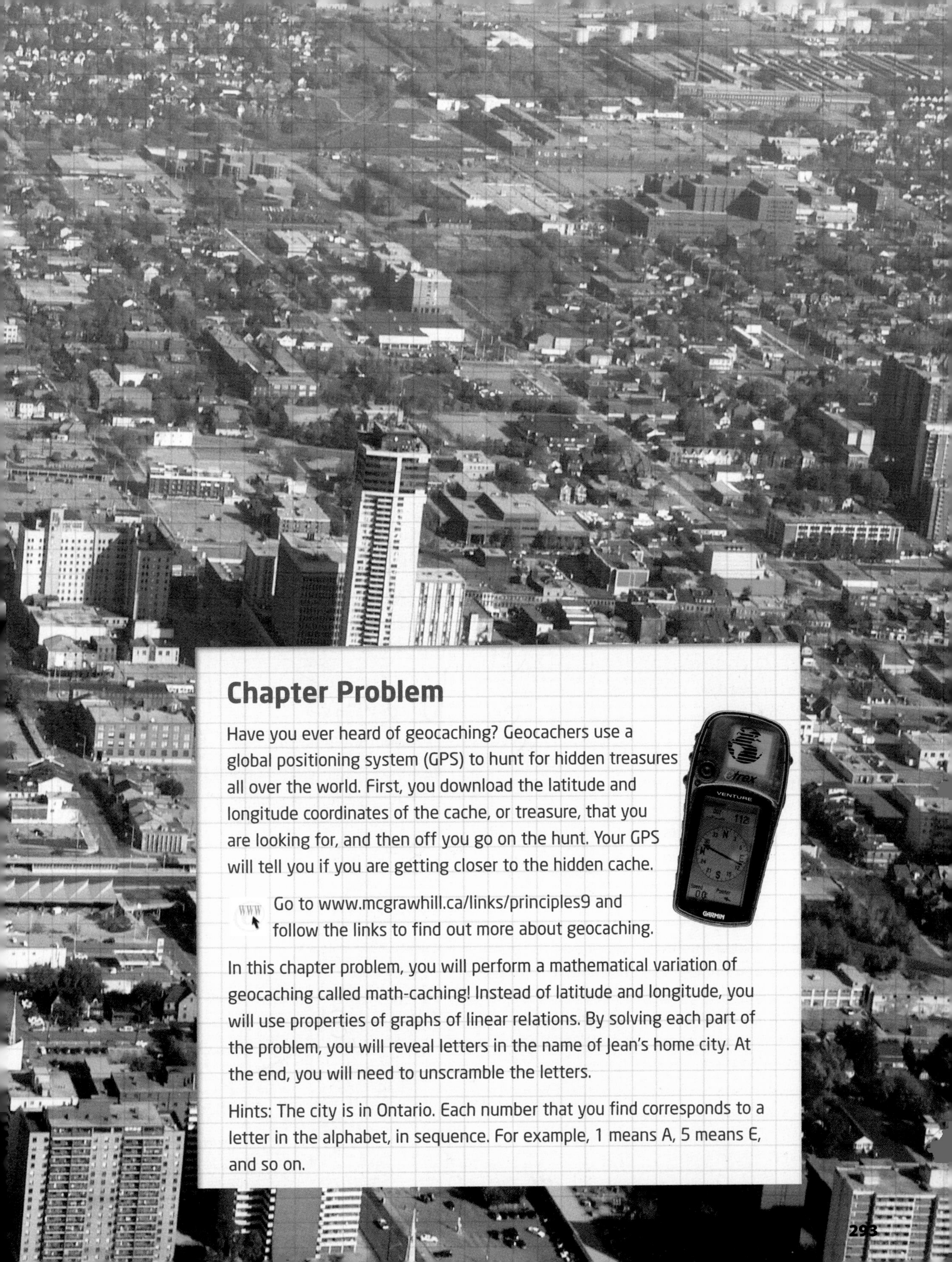

Chapter Problem

Have you ever heard of geocaching? Geocachers use a global positioning system (GPS) to hunt for hidden treasures all over the world. First, you download the latitude and longitude coordinates of the cache, or treasure, that you are looking for, and then off you go on the hunt. Your GPS will tell you if you are getting closer to the hidden cache.

Go to www.mcgrawhill.ca/links/principles9 and follow the links to find out more about geocaching.

In this chapter problem, you will perform a mathematical variation of geocaching called math-caching! Instead of latitude and longitude, you will use properties of graphs of linear relations. By solving each part of the problem, you will reveal letters in the name of Jean's home city. At the end, you will need to unscramble the letters.

Hints: The city is in Ontario. Each number that you find corresponds to a letter in the alphabet, in sequence. For example, 1 means A, 5 means E, and so on.

Get Ready

Linear Relations

Two variables share a linear relationship if a graph of their data forms a straight line. For example, the relationship between earnings and time worked can be linear.

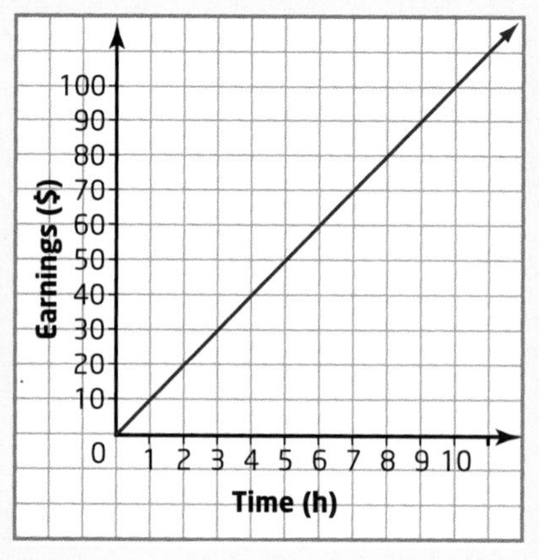

1. a) Use the graph of earnings versus time worked. Copy and complete the table.

Time Worked (h)	Earnings ($)
3	
	50
6	
	90

b) Identify the coordinates where the graph crosses the vertical axis. Explain the significance of this point.

2. Carlo makes house calls to repair home computers. The following is a partial list of his repair charges.

Labour (h)	Repair Cost ($)
1	100
2	140
3	180

a) Graph the relation.

b) What is the repair cost for a 5-h job?

c) Identify the coordinates of the point where the graph crosses the vertical axis. Explain the significance of this point.

Line of Best Fit

Sometimes a relationship is not perfectly linear. When this happens, a line of best fit can be drawn that passes as closely as possible to as many points as possible. For example, the graph shows how a person's distance from a sensor changes with time.

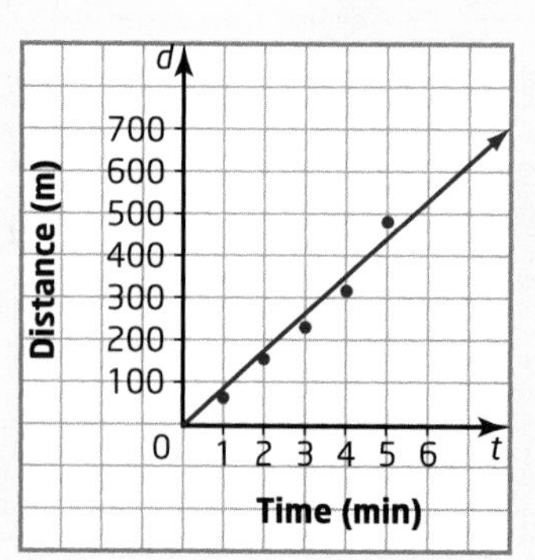

Refer to the graph of distance versus time to answer questions 3 and 4.

3. Estimate the distance travelled after each time.

a) 2.5 min

b) 6 min

4. Estimate how long it took to travel each distance.

a) 200 m

b) 600 m

5. The table shows the number of goals scored and the salaries for some professional hockey forwards.

Number of Goals	Salary ($millions)
35	1.2
27	1.0
20	0.8
42	1.6
12	0.5

a) Graph the relation. Draw a line of best fit.

b) Based on the trend, how much should a player be paid who scores
- 30 goals?
- 50 goals?

c) Based on the trend, how many goals would you expect a player earning each salary to score?
- $1.4 million
- $2 million

Slope

The slope of a line illustrates the rate of change of one variable compared to the other.

Slope, m, is defined as

$$m = \frac{\text{rise}}{\text{run}} \text{ or } m = \frac{\Delta y}{\Delta x}$$

Δy means the change in y, or $y_2 - y_1$.

$$m = \frac{y_2 - y_1}{x_2 - x_1}$$

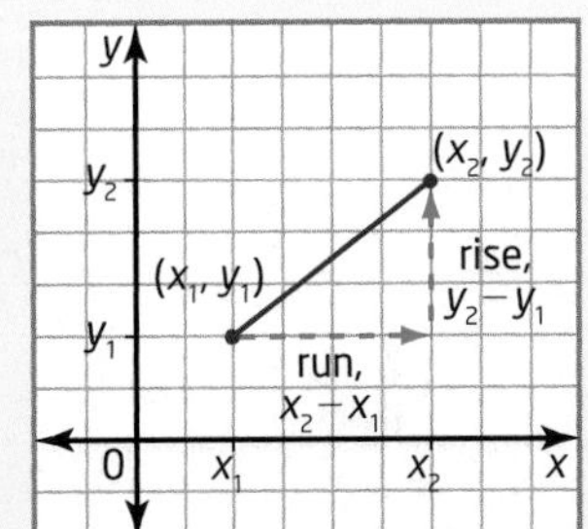

6. Find the slope of each line.

a)

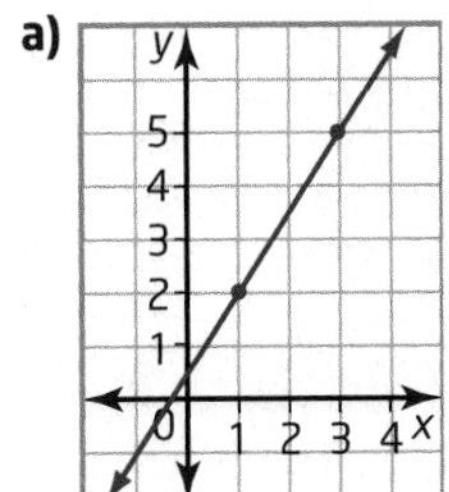

b)

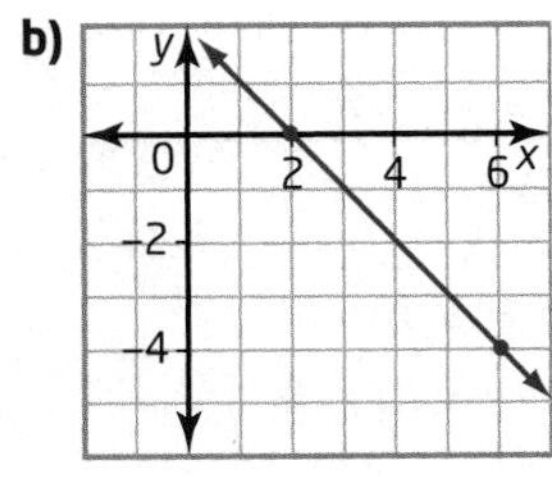

7. The shown data are collected for a car.

Time (h)	Distance (km)
0	0
1	60
2	100
3	165
4	205

a) Graph this relation and draw a line of best fit.

b) Choose two points on the line of best fit and identify their coordinates.

c) Use these points to find the slope of the line of best fit. Explain what the slope means.

6.1 The Equation of a Line in Slope y-Intercept Form: $y = mx + b$

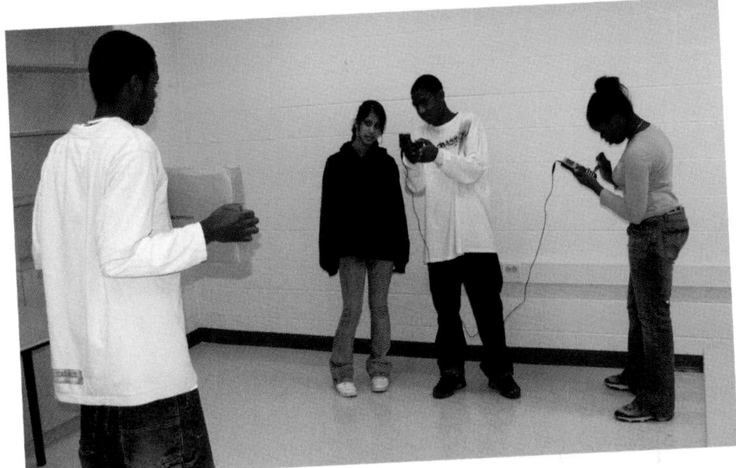

In Chapter 2: Relations, you discovered that when a person walks at a constant speed in front of a motion sensor, a straight line is produced. What information can this line tell you about the person's motion? How can you use algebra to describe and analyse a distance-time graph?

Investigate

Tools

- TI-84 or TI-83+ graphing calculator
- CBR™ motion sensor
- masking tape
- metre stick
- stopwatch or watch that measures seconds

How can you use an equation to describe a person's motion?

1. Find a clear location where you have plenty of room to move, such as a hallway. Carefully measure 1-m intervals and mark with masking tape, up to 6 m.

2. Set up for data collection:

a) One person will be the walker. Have the walker practise walking at a constant speed of 1 m/s. Use a stopwatch to practise. Then, get ready at the 1-m mark.

b) Connect the CBR™ to the calculator. Turn the calculator on and load the Ranger program.

- Press (APPS).
- Select **2:CBL/CBR**.
- Press (ENTER).
- Select **3:RANGER**.
- Press (ENTER).
- Select **1:SETUP/SAMPLE**.

```
MAIN MENU      ▸START NOW

 REALTIME:  yes
  TIME(S):  15
  DISPLAY:  DIST
 BEGIN ON:  [ENTER]
SMOOTHING:  NONE
    UNITS:  METERS
```

Make sure that your settings match those shown here. With these settings, the CBR™ will record distances in metres for a period of 15 s. Move the cursor up to **START NOW** at the top of the screen.

c) Set the CBR™ so that it is 1 m from, and pointing toward, the walker.

3. Press (ENTER). You should hear a ticking sound from the CBR™. Have the walker start walking away from the CBR™ at a slow steady pace of 1 m/s. A graph will begin to form on the calculator screen.

4. a) Use the blue cursor keys to trace along the graph. You will see the coordinates of each data point appear at the bottom of the screen.

   b) The left-most point is the y-intercept, usually labelled with the letter b. Write down the coordinates of this point. What do you notice about this point? Why might this value not be exactly what you expect?

   c) Pick any two points along the linear part of the graph (try to use two points that are not close together) and write down their coordinates. Use these points to calculate the slope of the line using the slope formula $m = \frac{y_2 - y_1}{x_2 - x_1}$. Compare the slope to the speed of the walker and describe what you notice.

5. a) Substitute the values of b and m that you found in step 4 into the equation $y = mx + b$.

   b) This equation describes where the walker is, y, at any time, x. Trace along the graph and pick any point to test the equation.
   - Substitute the value of the x-coordinate into the equation you found in part a).
   - Calculate the value of y.
   - Compare this to the actual y-coordinate of that point.
   - Explain why these points may not be exactly the same.

   c) Repeat part b) for another point on the graph.

6. a) Now, collect a new set of motion data.
   - Press (ENTER) and select **3:REPEAT SAMPLE**.
   - Have your partner pick a different starting point and walking speed (take note of these values).
   - Press (ENTER) and have your partner begin walking.

   b) Repeat steps 4 and 5 for your new graph.

7. **Reflect** Describe how an equation of the form $y = mx + b$ can be used to describe a person's motion. What do the values of m and b describe in this case?

Technology Tip

You may need a few practice attempts to get a feel for the correct speed. Try to get a graph that is fairly linear. If you are unsatisfied with your graph, you can collect a new set of data after the CBR™ has stopped ticking:
- Press (ENTER).

Select 3:REPEAT SAMPLE.

Example 1 Identify the Slope and the y-Intercept

Identify the slope and the y-intercept of each linear relation. Use these values to write the equation of the line.

a) 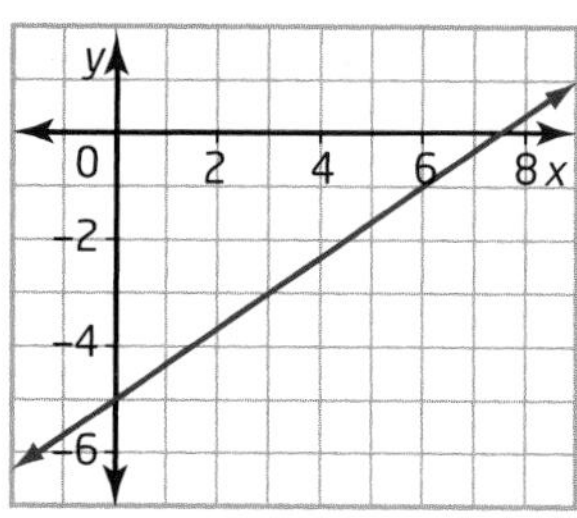

b) 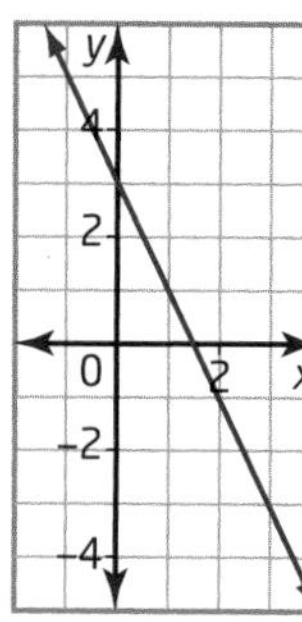

c) 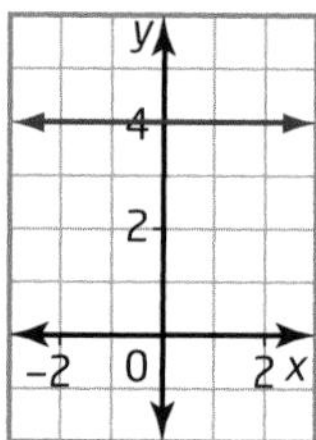

d) 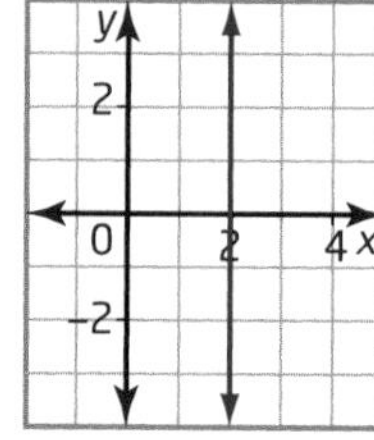

Solution

To find the slope, use two points on the graph.

a)
$$m = \frac{y_2 - y_1}{x_2 - x_1}$$ **Apply the slope formula.**

$$= \frac{-1 - (-5)}{6 - 0}$$

$$= \frac{-1 + 5}{6}$$ **Take care with operations with integers.**

$$= \frac{4}{6}$$

$$= \frac{2}{3}$$ **Express fraction answers in lowest terms.**

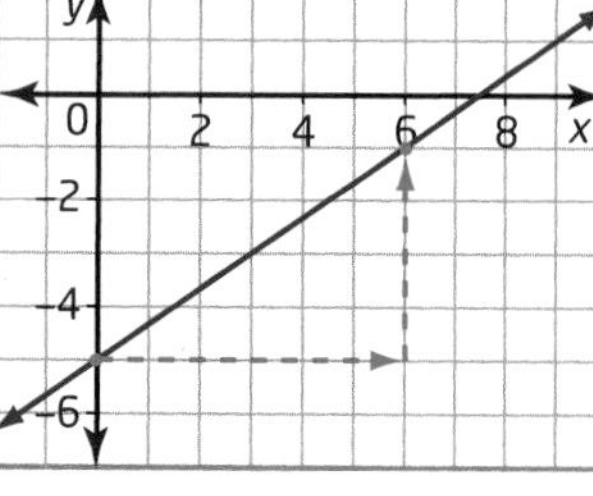

The slope is $\frac{2}{3}$.

From the graph, you can see that the y-intercept is -5.

So, $m = \frac{2}{3}$ and $b = -5$. Substitute these values into the equation $y = mx + b$.

$$y = \frac{2}{3}x + (-5)$$

The equation of the line is $y = \frac{2}{3}x - 5$.

b) $m = \dfrac{-3 - 3}{3 - 0}$

$= \dfrac{-6}{3}$

$= -2$

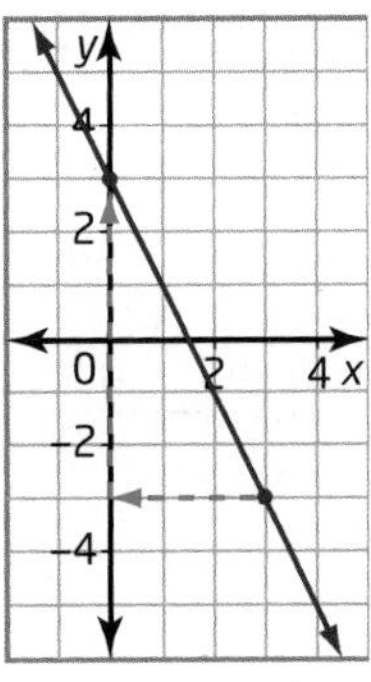

The slope is -2.
The y-intercept is 3. So, $m = -2$ and $b = 3$.
$y = -2x + 3$
The equation of the line is $y = -2x + 3$.

c) $m = \dfrac{4 - 4}{2 - 0}$

$= \dfrac{0}{2}$

$= 0$

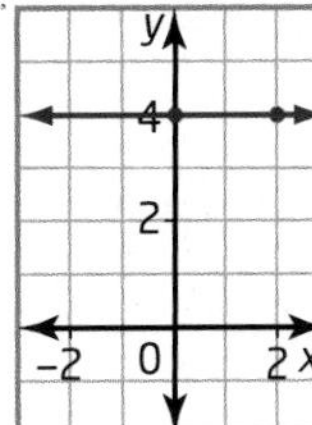

The slope is zero.
The y-intercept is 4.

$y = 0x + 4$

The equation of the line is
$y = 4$.

This equation means that for any point on this line, the y-coordinate is always 4, no matter what the x-coordinate is.

This is a horizontal line. It has no rise.

$m = \dfrac{\text{rise}}{\text{run}}$ ← zero

Zero divided by any value for the run gives zero. So, the slope of any horizontal line is zero.

d) $m = \dfrac{1 - 0}{0 - 0}$

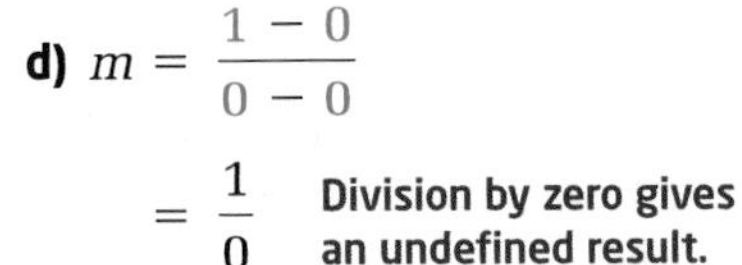

$= \dfrac{1}{0}$ **Division by zero gives an undefined result.**

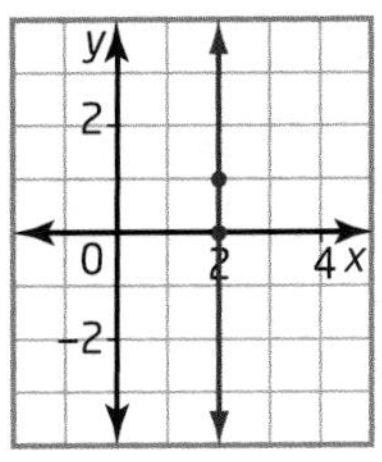

The slope is undefined.
There is no y-intercept.
A vertical line cannot be expressed in the form $y = mx + b$.

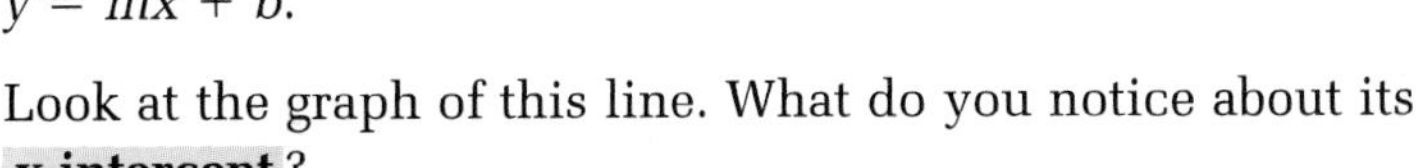

Look at the graph of this line. What do you notice about its **x-intercept**?

The equation for this line is $x = 2$.

This means that for any point on this line, the x-coordinate is always 2, no matter what the y-coordinate is.

x-intercept

- the x-coordinate of the point where a line crosses the x-axis

Example 2 Graph a Line, Given *m* and *b*

The slope and the y-intercept are given. In each case, write the equation of the line and graph the line.

a) $m = \frac{3}{4}$, $b = -2$

b) $m = -3$, $b = 0$

c) $m = -\frac{1}{2}$, $b = 5$

d) $m = 0$, $b = 6$

Solution

a) Substitute the slope and the y-intercept into the equation $y = mx + b$.

$$y = \frac{3}{4}x + (-2)$$

The equation of the line is $y = \frac{3}{4}x - 2$.

To graph this line, begin by plotting the y-intercept, $(0, -2)$.
Then, use the slope to locate other points on the line.

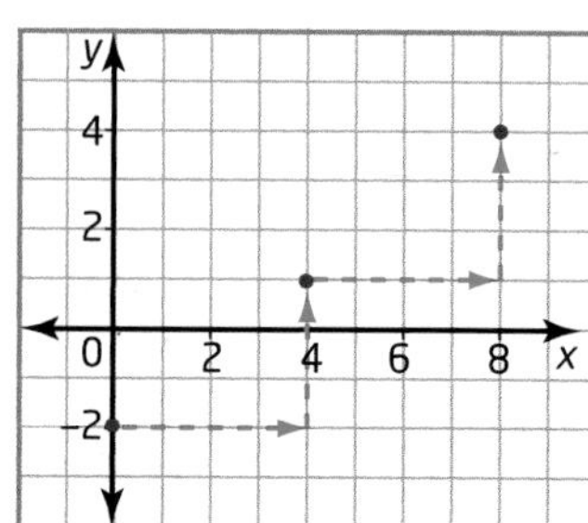

The slope is $\frac{3}{4}$. Starting at $(0, -2)$, I move 4 to the right and up 3 to find another point on the line. I can repeat this to find other points on the line.

Once you have located two or three points, draw and label the line.

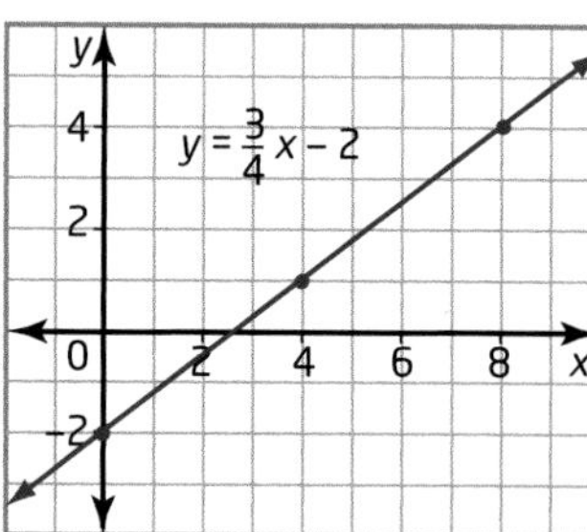

b) $y = -3 + 0$
$y = -3x$

The y-intercept is 0.

Start at the origin, and use $m = \frac{-3}{1}$ to find other points on the line.

Using the slope in the form $\frac{-3}{1}$ helps me to think of "rising −3" (or actually "falling 3") and then "running 1."

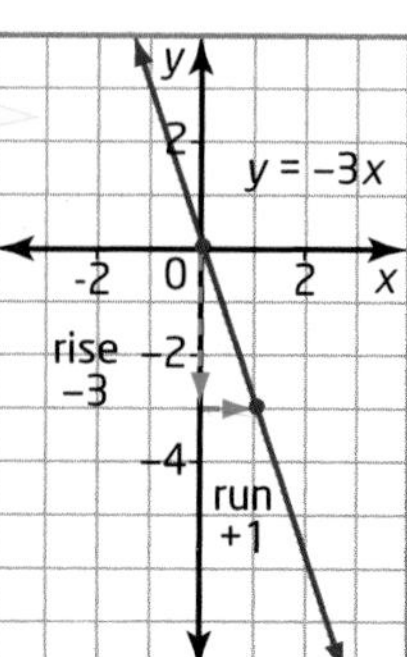

c) $y = -\frac{1}{2}x + 5$

The y-intercept is 5. The slope is $-\frac{1}{2}$.

Method 1: Let $m = \frac{-1}{2}$.

Start at (0, 5). Go down 1 and right 2 to find other points on the line.

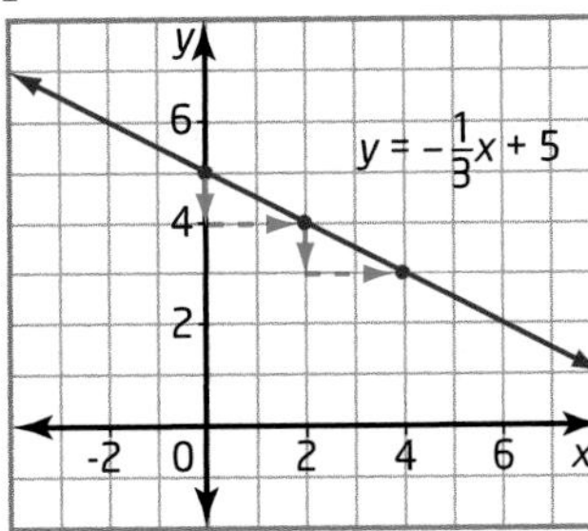

Method 2: Let $m = \frac{1}{-2}$.

Start at (0, 5). Go up 1 and left 2 to find other points on the line.

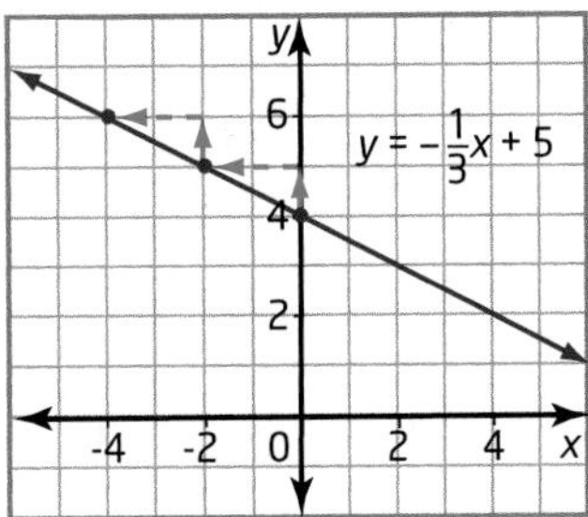

Compare these two methods. Notice that they produce the same line.

d) The slope is zero. This is a horizontal line with equation $y = 6$. All points on this line have a y-coordinate of 6.

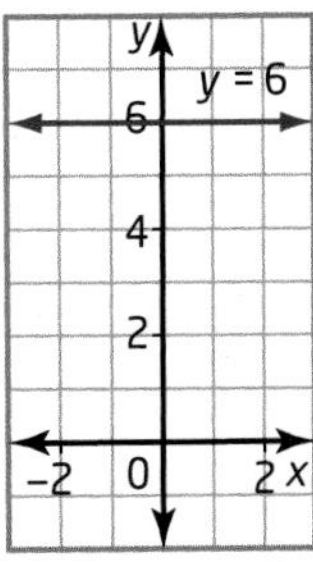

Example 3 Interpret a Linear Relation

Identify the slope and the vertical intercept of each linear relation and explain what they mean. Write an equation to describe the relationship.

a)

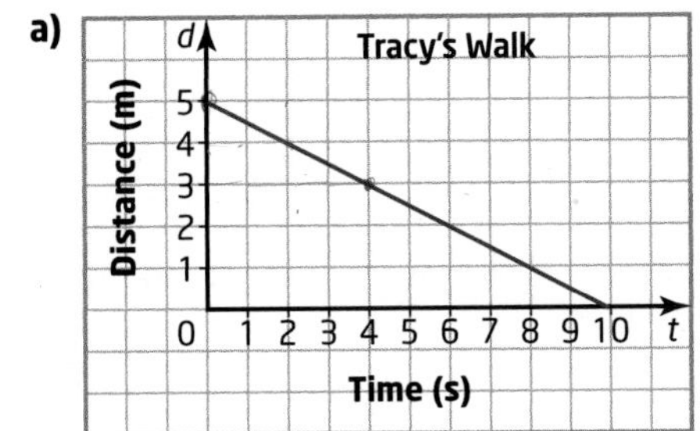

b)

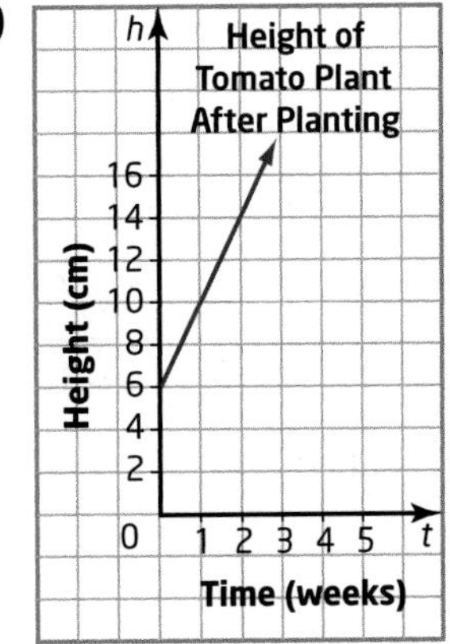

Solution

a)

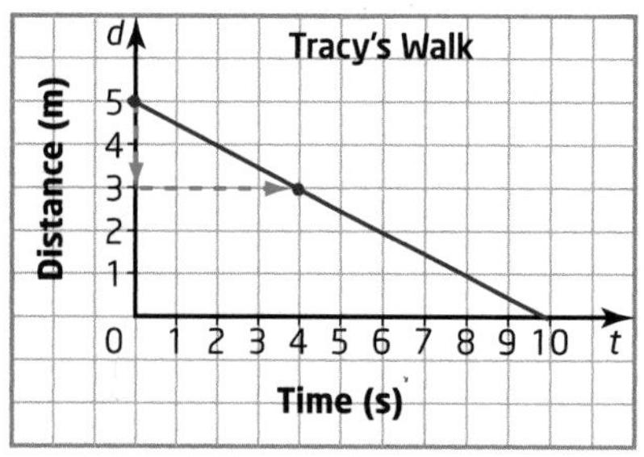

$$\text{slope} = \frac{-2}{4}$$
$$= -0.5$$

This is a distance-time graph. The d-intercept is 5, which means that Tracy began walking at a distance of 5 m from the sensor.

The slope is -0.5, which represents the change in distance over the change in time. The negative value means that the distance is decreasing. This means that Tracy's speed was 0.5 m/s toward the sensor.

The equation describing this relationship is $d = -0.5t + 5$.

b)

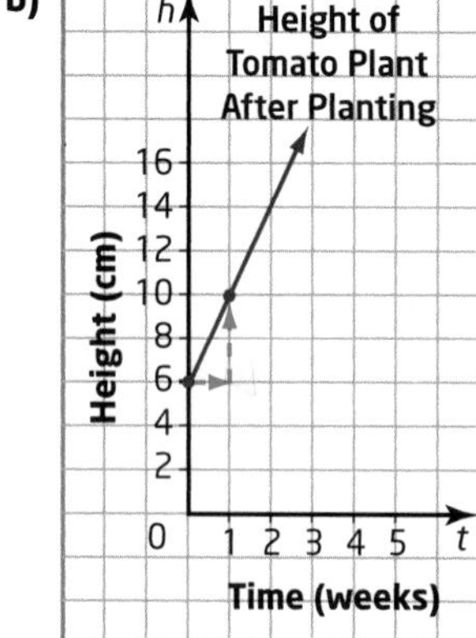

$$\text{slope} = \frac{4}{1}$$
$$= 4$$

This is a graph of the height of a tomato plant versus time. The h-intercept is 6, which means that the tomato plant was 6 cm tall when it was planted in the garden.

The slope is 4, which represents the change in height over the change in time. This means that the tomato plant grew at a rate of 4 cm per week.

The equation describing this relationship is $h = 4t + 6$.

Key Concepts

- The equation of a line can be written in slope y-intercept form: $y = mx + b$, where
  - m is the slope of the line
  - b is the y-intercept of the line

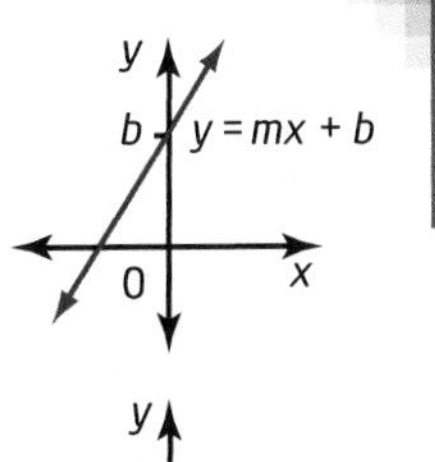

- A horizontal line is written in the form $y = b$, where b is the y-intercept. The slope of a horizontal line is zero.

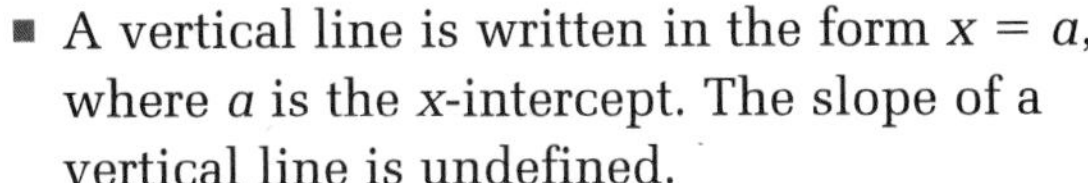

- A vertical line is written in the form $x = a$, where a is the x-intercept. The slope of a vertical line is undefined.

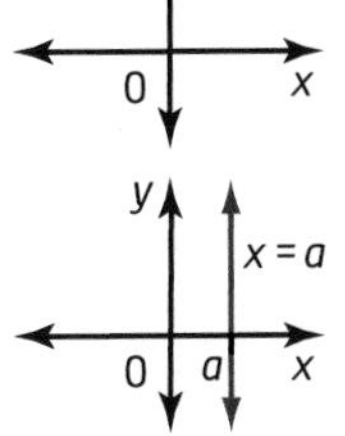

Communicate Your Understanding

C1 The equations of four lines are given:

$y = 2x - 3$ $y = 6$ $y = -x + 4$ $x = -3$

Which of these represents

a) a vertical line?

b) a horizontal line?

c) a line that slopes upward to the right?

d) a line that slopes downward to the right?

Explain each answer you chose.

C2 A line has a y-intercept of 2 and a slope of $\frac{3}{5}$. Explain how you can use this information to graph the line.

C3 The distance-time graph for a person walking in front of a motion sensor is shown.

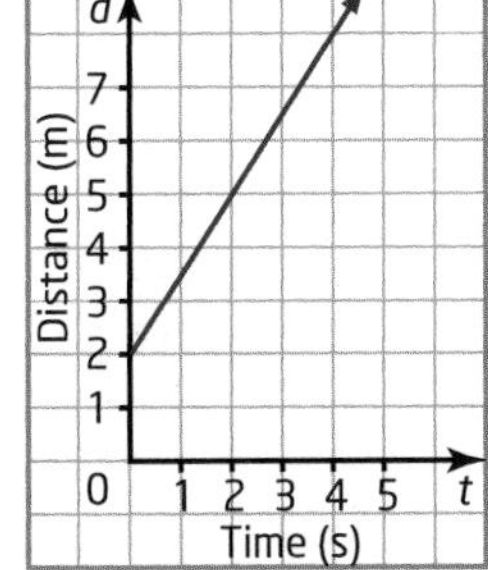

a) At what distance did this person begin walking? How do you know?

b) Was the person walking toward or away from the sensor? Explain how you know.

c) How fast was the person walking?

d) Write an equation in the form $d = mt + b$ to describe the person's motion.

C4 Refer to Example 3, part b).

a) Does the graph to the left of the h-axis have meaning?

b) What would this portion of the graph represent?

c) What is the significance of the h-intercept?

Practise

For help with questions 1 to 4, see Example 1.

1. Identify the slope and the y-intercept of each line. Organize your answers in a table like the one shown.

Equation	Slope	y-intercept

a) $y = 4x + 1$ 

b) $y = \frac{2}{3}x + 3$

c) $y = x - 2$

d) $y = -\frac{2}{3}x$

e) $y = 3$

f) $y = -x - \frac{1}{2}$

2. Find the slope and the y-intercept of each line.

a) 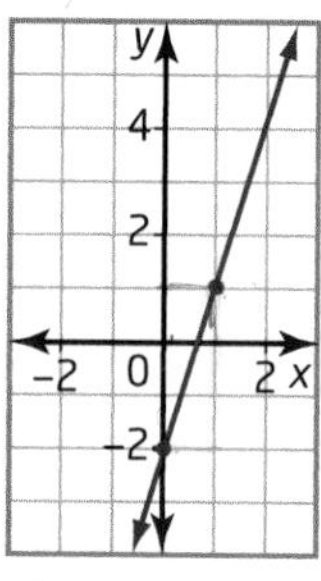

b) 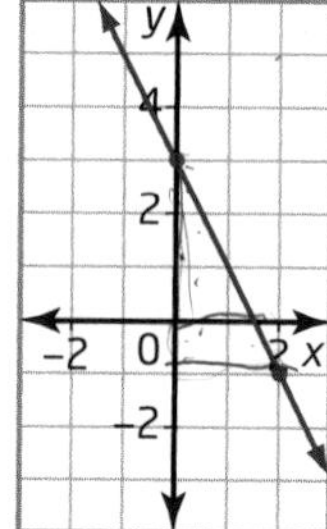

c) 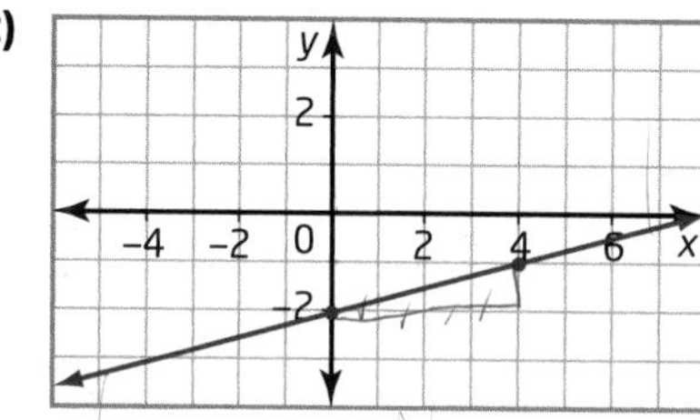

d) 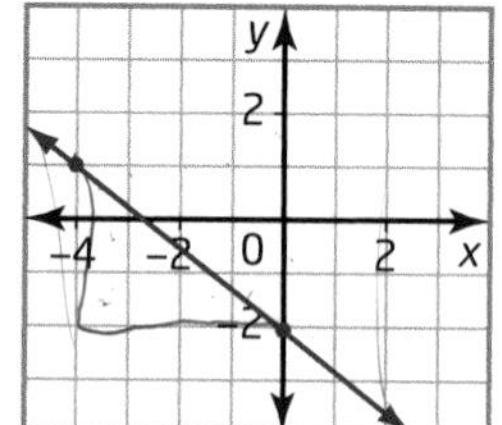

3. Write the equation of each line in question 2.

4. Write the equation of each line. State its slope and y-intercept, if they exist.

a) 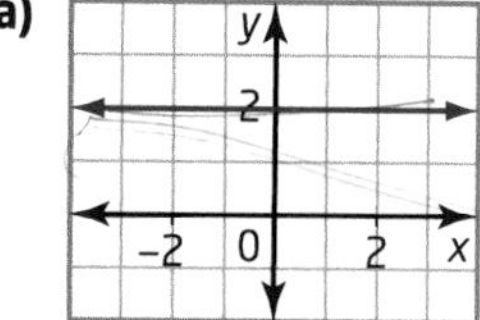

b) 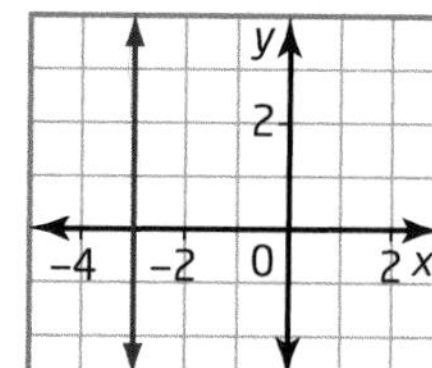

c) 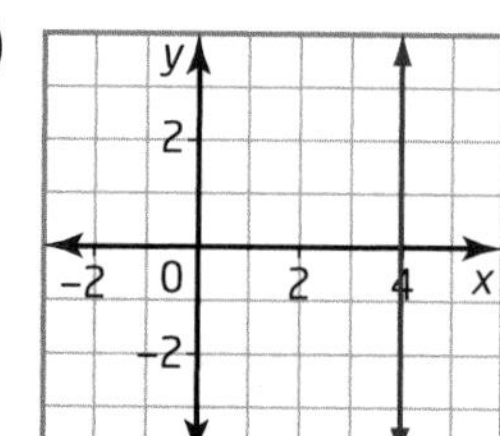

d) 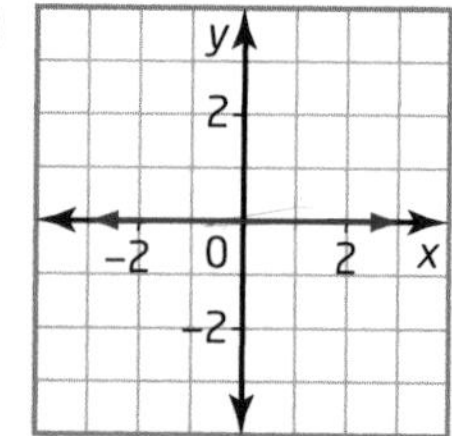

5. The line in question 4, part d), has a special name. What is it?

For help with questions 6 to 8, see Example 2.

6. The slope and the y-intercept are given. Write the equation and graph each line.

	Slope	y-intercept
a)	$\frac{2}{3}$	3
b)	$-\frac{3}{5}$	1
c)	−2	0
d)	$\frac{4}{3}$	−4
e)	0	−4

7. State the slope and the y-intercept of each line, if they exist. Graph each line.

a) $y = -5$

b) $x = 1$

c) $y = \frac{7}{2}$

d) $x = -2.5$

Connect and Apply

8. The distance-time graph of a person walking in front of a motion sensor is shown.

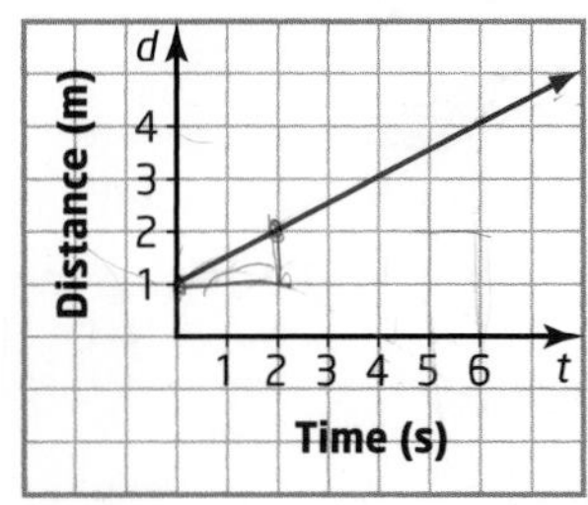

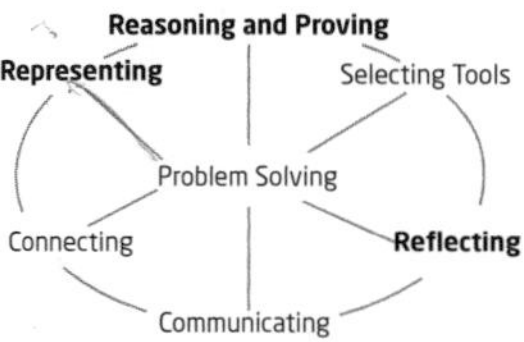

a) How far from the sensor did the person begin walking?

b) How fast did the person walk?

c) Did the person walk away from or toward the sensor? Explain.

9. Sketch a distance-time graph for each walker for the first 4 s.

a) Eleanor started at a distance of 2 m and walked away from the sensor at a constant speed of 1 m/s.

b) Pierre began walking toward the sensor at a constant speed of 0.5 m/s from an initial distance of 5 m.

c) Jesse stood at a distance of 2.5 m from the sensor and did not move.

d) Cassandra started at 1 m from the sensor and walked away from it at a constant speed of 1 m/s for 3 s. Then, she turned around and walked, at the same speed, toward the sensor for 1 s.

For help with question 10, see Example 3.

10. Identify the slope and the vertical intercept of each linear relation and explain what they represent. Write an equation to describe the relationship.

a)

Shannon's Walk

Distance (m)

Time (s)

b)

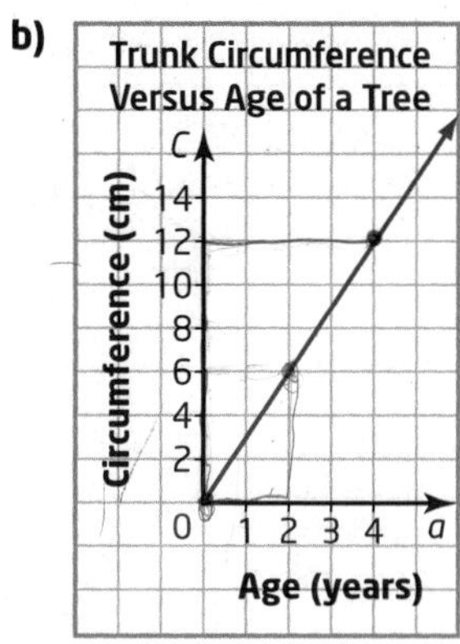

11. Chapter Problem Jean grew up in this city in Ontario. In one part of it, there is a very steep slope. Two of the letters in the name of this city can be found by determining the slope and the y-intercept of the graph shown.

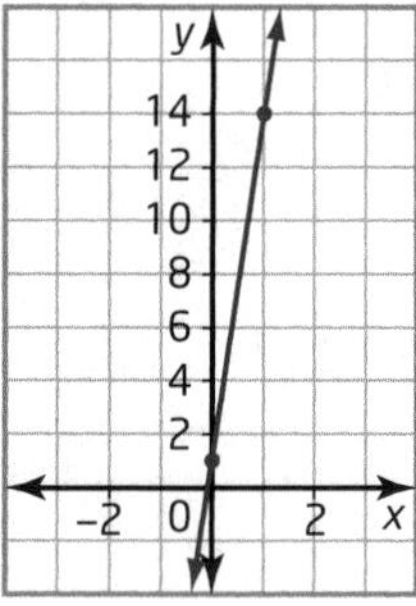

Reasoning and Proving

Representing

Selecting Tools

Problem Solving

Connecting

Reflecting

Communicating

12. Yuri tries hard not to be late for class, but sometimes he does not quite make it on time. Class begins at 8:30 A.M. The distance-time graph shows his progress from home to school one morning.

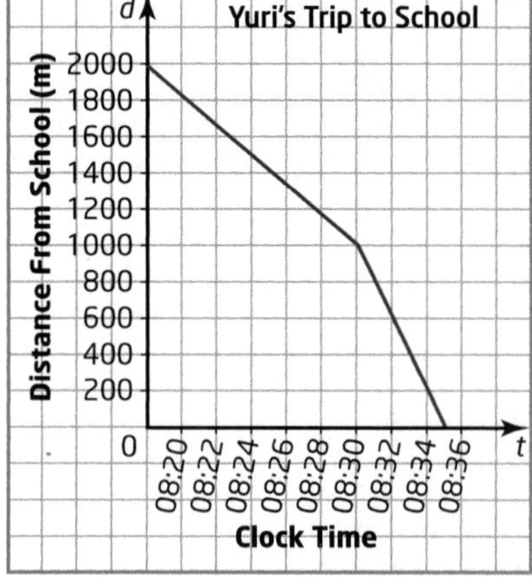

Write a story about Yuri's trip to school. Include the speed, distance, and time in your story.

13. Refer to question 12. How would the graph change if Yuri left 10 min earlier? How would this change affect the outcome of your story?

Extend

14. Two koala bears, Rocco and Biff, are playing near a stream. Suddenly they both realize that it is dinner-time and begin to race to their eucalyptus tree home. Their distance-time graphs are shown:

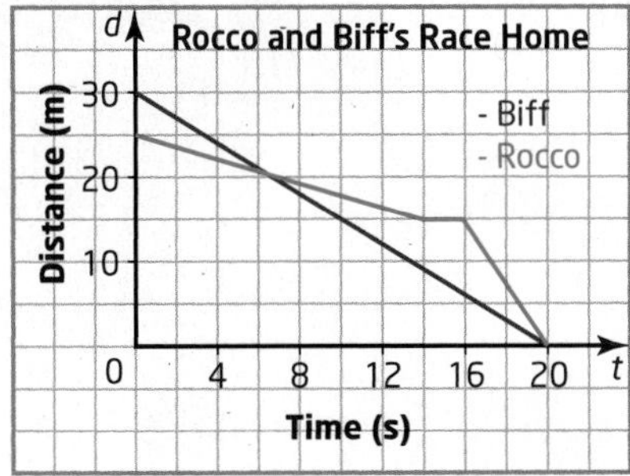

Rocco starts from the stream, which is 30 m from home. Biff is a few metres from Rocco when he starts. Describe this race. In your description, be sure to mention speed, distance, and time.

15. The x-intercept is the x-coordinate of the point where a graph crosses the x-axis.

a) What is the value of the y-coordinate for any x-intercept? Use a diagram to explain your answer.

b) Find the x-intercept of each line.

- $y = 3x - 6$
- $y = \frac{2}{3}x + 5$

16. Math Contest

a) Find a number that leaves a remainder of 1 when divided by 2, a remainder of 2 when divided by 3, and a remainder of 3 when divided by 4.

b) Find at least five other numbers that satisfy the conditions in part a).

c) Describe a pattern or formula that can be used to find more numbers that satisfy the conditions in part a).

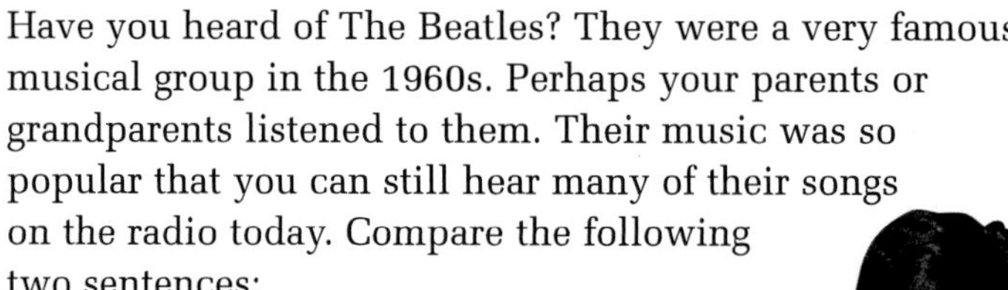

6.2 The Equation of a Line in Standard Form: $Ax + By + C = 0$

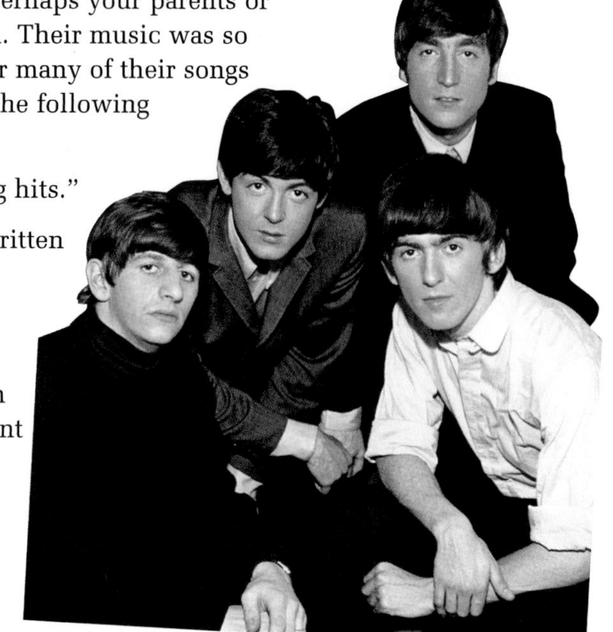

Have you heard of The Beatles? They were a very famous musical group in the 1960s. Perhaps your parents or grandparents listened to them. Their music was so popular that you can still hear many of their songs on the radio today. Compare the following two sentences:

"The Beatles wrote several big hits."

"A number of big hits were written by The Beatles."

These two sentences mean basically the same thing, but the way they are written, each sentence has a slightly different emphasis. Which sentence places greater emphasis on

- The Beatles as a group?
- the songs that they wrote?

Literacy Connections

In mathematics, you can also express values and equations that mean the same thing in different ways. Here are four ways to represent one quarter:

$\frac{1}{4}$, $\frac{3}{12}$, 0.25, 25%

Depending on the application, one form may be preferable to the others.

Investigate

Tools

- grid paper

How can you write the equation of a line using different forms?

1. Consider the following equation that relates x and y:
   $3x - 4y + 8 = 0$
   Do you think a graph of this relationship will be linear or non-linear? Explain why you think so.

2. You can find the y-intercept of any graph by substituting $x = 0$ into the equation and solving the resulting equation for y. Find the y-intercept of this graph.

3. Find the coordinates of two other points that are on the graph. *Hint*: If a point is on the graph, then its coordinates must satisfy the equation (make the equation true).

4. Plot all three points, including the y-intercept. Do they line up? If yes, draw a straight line through them. If no, check your calculations.

5. Use two points on the graph to find the slope of the line.

6. Use the slope and the y-intercept to write the equation of this line in the form $y = mx + b$.

7. **Reflect** Compare the equation you wrote in step 6 to the original equation in step 1. What can you tell about how these equations are related?

The **standard form** of the equation of a line is $Ax + By + C = 0$, where A, B, and C are integers and A and B are not both zero. You can convert an equation from standard form to slope y-intercept form by performing some algebraic manipulation.

In standard form, the coefficient of the x-term is always positive. If the coefficient of the x-term is negative, you can multiply both sides by -1 to express the equation in standard form. For example,
$-3x + 4y - 7 = 0$ is not in standard form.
$(-1)(-3x + 4y - 7) = (-1)(0)$
gives $3x - 4y + 7 = 0$, which is in standard form.

Example 1 Change From Standard Form to Slope y-Intercept Form

Express each equation in the form $y = mx + b$ and identify its slope and y-intercept.

a) $x + y - 3 = 0$ **b)** $x + 2y - 4 = 0$ **c)** $6x - 3y - 15 = 0$

Solution

a) Isolate the y-term on one side of the equation.

$$x + y - 3 = 0$$
Subtract x from both sides and add 3 to both sides.
$$y = -x + 3$$

The slope is -1 and the y-intercept is 3.

b) Begin by isolating the term containing y. Then, divide by the coefficient of the y-term.

$$x + 2y - 4 = 0$$
Subtract x from both sides and add 4 to both sides.
$$2y = -x + 4$$
$$\frac{\overset{1}{\cancel{2}}y}{\underset{1}{\cancel{2}}} = \frac{-x + 4}{2}$$
Divide both sides by 2.
$$y = \frac{-1x}{2} + \frac{4}{2}$$
Divide each term on the right side by 2.
$$y = -\frac{1}{2}x + 2$$

The slope is $-\frac{1}{2}$ and the y-intercept is 2.

c) $6x - 3y - 15 = 0$

$$-3y = -6x + 15 \quad \text{Isolate the } y\text{-term.}$$

$$\frac{\overset{1}{\cancel{-3}}y}{\underset{1}{\cancel{-3}}} = \frac{-6x + 15}{-3} \quad \text{Divide both sides by } -3.$$

$$y = \frac{-6x}{-3} + \frac{15}{-3}$$

$$y = 2x + (-5)$$

$$y = 2x - 5$$

The slope is 2 and the y-intercept is -5.

Example 2 Identify Fixed and Variable Costs in a Partial Variation

The Celebrations Banquet Hall uses the equation $25n - C + 1250 = 0$ to determine the cost for a hall rental, where C represents the cost, in dollars, which depends on n, the number of people attending.

a) Express the equation in slope y-intercept form: $C = mn + b$.

b) Identify the fixed and variable costs.

c) Illustrate the relation graphically using a graphing calculator.

d) What is the rental cost if 100 people attend a soccer banquet?

Solution

a) Method 1: Isolate *C* on the Left Side.

$$25n - C + 1250 = 0 \quad \text{Subtract } 25n \text{ and } 1250 \text{ from both sides.}$$

$$-C = -25n - 1250 \quad \text{Divide both sides by } -1.$$

$$\frac{-C}{-1} = \frac{-25n}{-1} + \frac{-1250}{-1}$$

$$C = 25n + 1250$$

Dividing all terms by -1 changes the signs of all the terms.

Method 2: Isolate *C* on the Right Side.

$$25n - C + 1250 = 0 \quad \text{Add } C \text{ to both sides.}$$

$$25n + 1250 = C$$

or $C = 25n + 1250$

This equation is the in slope y-intercept form.

Making Connections

You studied partial variation in Chapter 5: Modelling With Graphs.

How can you identify the fixed part and the variable part?

b) This is a partial variation. The fixed cost is \$1250. The variable cost is \$25 per person attending.

c) To illustrate this graphically on a graphing calculator do the following:

- Press (Y=). Enter **25** (X,T,θ,n) (+) **1250**.
- Note that the graphing calculator uses x and y instead of n and C.

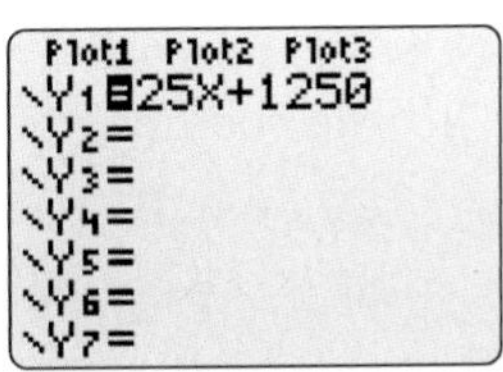

- Press (WINDOW). Use the settings shown.

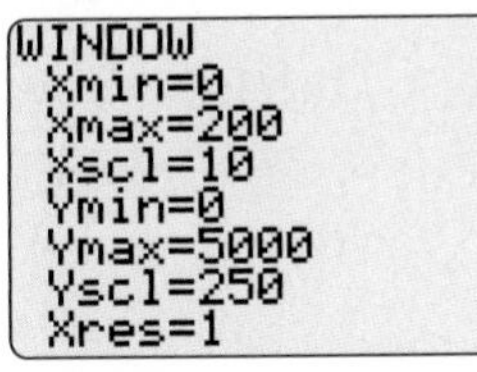

- Press (GRAPH) to see the linear relation.

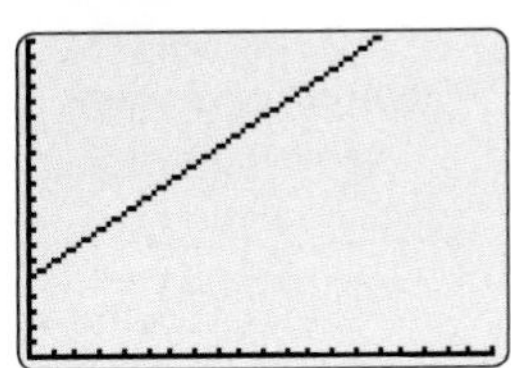

Technology Tip

Before graphing, ensure that all STATPLOTs are turned off. Press (2nd) [STATPLOT]. Select **4:Plots Off.** Press (ENTER).

I don't need to consider negative values. The cost starts at \$1250 and goes up by \$25 per person. I'll graph from 0 up to 200 people and set the vertical scale to \$5000. If that doesn't give enough information, I can change the window settings.

d) To find the cost for 100 attendees, use either the equation or the graphical model.

Method 1: Use the Equation

Substitute $n = 100$ into the equation $C = 25n + 1250$ and solve for C.

$$C = 25(100) + 1250$$
$$= 2500 + 1250$$
$$= 3750$$

Method 2: Use the Graph

Press (TRACE).
Type 100, and then press (ENTER).

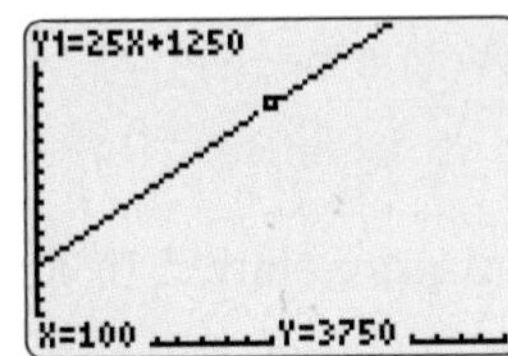

When $x = 100$, $y = 3750$.

It would cost \$3750 to rent the banquet hall for 100 people.

Key Concepts

- The equation of a line can be expressed in different ways:
  - standard form: $Ax + By + C = 0$
  - slope y-intercept form: $y = mx + b$
- You can convert an equation in standard form to slope y-intercept form by rearranging the equation.

Communicate Your Understanding

C1 The following equations are expressed in standard form. Identify the coefficients A, B, and C in each.

a) $2x + 3y + 6 = 0$

b) $5x - 2y - 1 = 0$

c) $x - y = 0$

C2 The steps show how to convert an equation in standard form to slope y-intercept form. Explain each step.

Step	***Explanation***
$5x - 4y - 20 = 0$	**Start with the equation in standard form.**
$-4y = -5x + 20$	
$\frac{-4y}{-4} = \frac{-5x + 20}{-4}$	
$y = \frac{5}{4}x - 5$	

Practise

For help with questions 1 to 3, see Example 1.

1. Express each equation in the form $y = mx + b$.

a) $x + y - 3 = 0$ **b)** $2x + 3y + 6 = 0$

c) $x - 4y + 12 = 0$ **d)** $3x + 2y - 5 = 0$

2. For each linear relation in question 1,

- identify the slope and the y-intercept
- use this information to graph the line

3. Identify the slope and the y-intercept of each line.

a) $x + 3y - 3 = 0$ **b)** $2x - 5y + 8 = 0$

Connect and Apply

4. Refer to Example 2. The Easy Event banquet hall charges according to the equation $40n - C + 250 = 0$.

a) Express the equation in slope y-intercept form: $C = mn + b$.

b) Identify the fixed and variable costs.

c) Illustrate the relation graphically.

d) What is the rental cost if 100 people attend a soccer banquet?

e) Is this a better deal than Celebrations? Explain.

5. How does your answer to question 4, part e), change if only 50 people attend? Explain.

6. **Chapter Problem** There are a lot of factories in the Jean's home city. The equation $n - E + 15 = 0$ describes how much a worker might earn, E, in dollars per hour, according to the number of years experience, n.

   Find the hourly earnings of a beginning factory worker, and of a worker with 5 years of experience, and you will have two more letters in the name of this city.

7. The equation $9C - 5F + 160 = 0$ describes the relationship between temperature, C, in degrees Celsius, and temperature, F, in degrees Fahrenheit.

   a) Express this equation in the form $C = mF + b$.

   b) Graph this relation.

   c) Identify the slope and the C-intercept and explain what they mean.

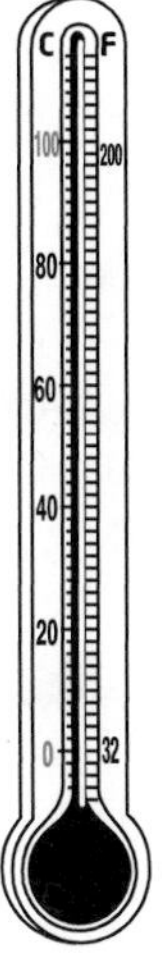

8. Refer to question 7.

   a) Express the equation in the form $F = mC + b$.

   b) Graph this relation.

   c) Identify the slope and the F-intercept and explain what they mean.

9. Compare the two relations from questions 7 and 8.

   a) Describe how their graphs are
   - similar
   - different

   b) How are the slopes of the two graphs related?

Achievement Check

10. The Knights Banquet Hall uses the equation $25n - C + 1250 = 0$ to determine the cost for a hall rental.

    The Legions Banquet Hall uses the equation $30n + 995 - C = 0$ to determine the cost for their hall rental.

    In each case, C represents the cost, in dollars, which depends on n, the number of people attending.

    a) Express each equation in slope y-intercept form: $C = mn + b$.

    b) Identify the fixed and variable costs for each hall.

    c) What is the cost at each hall for a graduation banquet for 45 people?

    d) Which hall offers the better price? Comment on whether your conclusion changes if a few more people wish to attend.

Extend

11. You can change an equation from slope y-intercept form to standard form by rearranging terms in the equation. Rearrange each of the following equations into standard form, $Ax + By + C = 0$, and identify the coefficients A, B, and C.

Hint: In standard form, the coefficient of the x-term is always positive and there are no fractions.

a) $y = -2x + 7$ **b)** $y = x - 3$ **c)** $y = \frac{3}{4}x - 2$

Technology Tip

Clear the calculator first. Press (2nd)(F1) for [F6] to display the **Clean Up** menu. Select 2: **New Prob.** Press (ENTER).

12. You can use a computer algebra system (CAS) to change an equation from standard form to slope y-intercept form. Use a CAS to change the equation $2x + 3y - 5 = 0$ to slope y-intercept form.

a) Enter the equation $2x + 3y - 5 = 0$ and press (ENTER).

F1 Tools | F2 Algebra | F3 Calc | F4 Other | F5 PrgmIO | F6 Clean Up

■ 2·x + 3·y − 5 = 0
2·x + 3·y − 5 = 0
2x+3y-5=0
MAIN RAD AUTO FUNC 1/30

b) Subtract $2x$ from both sides and then add 5 to both sides. Remember to press (ENTER) after each command.

Put brackets around the entire equation and subtract $2x$.

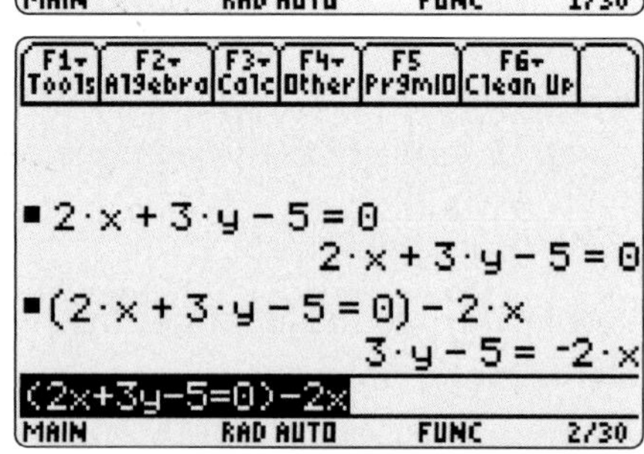

Use the cursor keys, [COPY], and [PASTE] to enter the new equation. Put brackets around it and add 5.

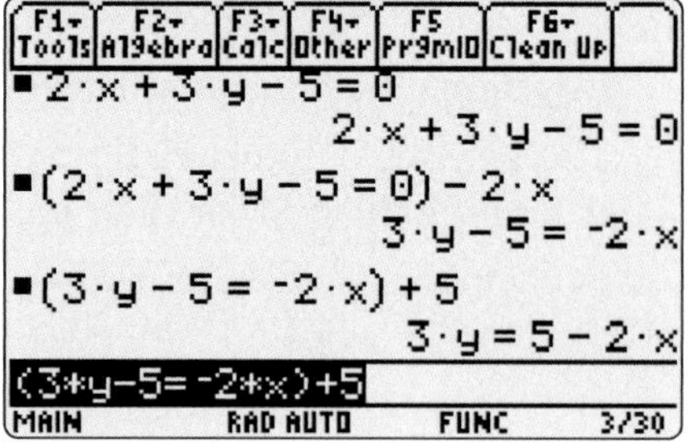

c) Divide both sides by 3.

d) Has the CAS put the equation into slope y-intercept form? Explain.

e) Complete the steps to put the equation into slope y-intercept form.

f) Express each equation in slope y-intercept form using a CAS.

- $3x + y - 8 = 0$
- $4x - 5y + 20 = 0$

6.3 Graph a Line Using Intercepts

Joanne loves reading. She has \$48 to spend at her favourite used book store. She likes comic books, which cost \$4 each, and novels, which cost \$6 each. What combinations of comic books and novels can Joanne buy?

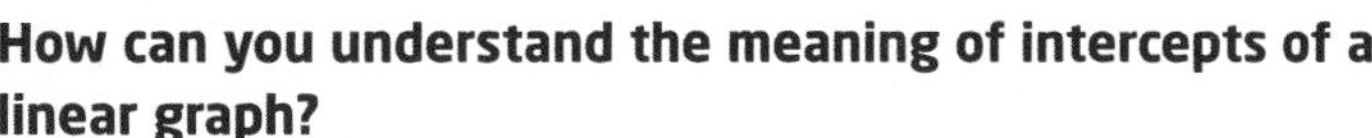

Investigate

Tools
- grid paper

How can you understand the meaning of intercepts of a linear graph?

Refer to the information above.

1. If Joanne buys only comic books, and no novels, how many can she buy?

2. If Joanne buys only novels, and no comic books, how many can she buy?

3. Let x be the number of comic books. Let y be the number of novels. Write each combination in steps 1 and 2 as an ordered pair (x, y).

4. Plot the ordered pairs from step 3 on a graph. Join the points with a straight line.

5. a) If Joanne buys a combination of comic books and used novels, what combinations can she buy?

b) Explain how you found these combinations.

6. **Reflect** Look at your graph.

a) Explain how you can use the graph to discover combinations that work.

b) You must be careful when using a linear model. In this situation, the point $\left(\frac{3}{2}, 7\right)$ has no meaning, even though it is on the line. Why not? *Hint*: What does x represent?

c) Identify two other points that are on the line, but have no meaning. Explain why they have no meaning.

Lines can be written in many forms.

$y = -\frac{2}{3}x + 8$ **Slope *y*-intercept form.**

$2x + 3y - 24 = 0$ **Standard form.**

Both of these equations describe the same line. You could also express this line in another way: $2x + 3y = 24$.

Although this form has no special name, it is useful for graphing purposes.

Example 1 Calculate Intercepts

The following equation can be used to model the situation described in the Investigate:

$$\underset{\$4 \times (\text{number of comic books})}{4x} + \underset{\$6 \times (\text{number of novels})}{6y} = \underset{\text{Total spent}}{48}$$

a) Determine the *x*- and *y*-intercepts of the equation $4x + 6y = 48$.

b) Use the intercepts to graph the line.

Solution

a) Find the *x*-intercept.

At the *x*-intercept, the value of *y* is 0.

$4x + 6(0) = 48$

$4x = 48$ **Solve for x.**

$\frac{4x}{4} = \frac{48}{4}$

$x = 12$

The *x*-intercept is 12.
The point (12, 0) is on the line.

Find the *y*-intercept.

At the *y*-intercept, the value of *x* is 0.

$4(0) + 6y = 48$

$6y = 48$ **Solve for *y*.**

$\frac{6y}{6} = \frac{48}{6}$

$y = 8$

The *y*-intercept is 8.
The point (0, 8) is on the line.

b) Plot the intercepts to graph this relation.

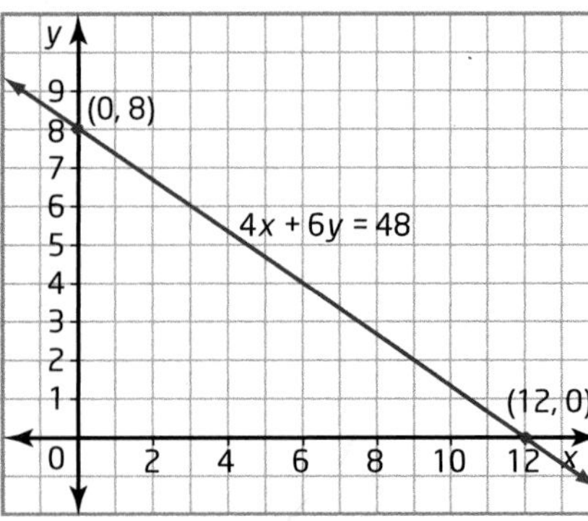

You can use this graph to find other points that satisfy the equation, such as (3, 6), (6, 4), and (9, 2).

Reflect

Be careful when using a linear model. In this example, the point $\left(11, \frac{2}{3}\right)$ is on the line, but has no meaning. Why not? *Hint*: What does *y* represent?

Example 2 Use Intercepts to Graph a Line

For each linear relation, determine the x- and y-intercepts and graph the line.

a) $2x - y = 7$ **b)** $3x - 5y + 15 = 0$

Solution

a) Find the x-intercept.
Substitute $y = 0$.

$$2x - 0 = 7$$
$$2x = 7 \quad \text{Solve for } x.$$
$$\frac{2x}{2} = \frac{7}{2}$$
$$x = \frac{7}{2}$$

The x-intercept is $\frac{7}{2}$ or 3.5.

The point (3.5, 0) is on the line.

Find the y-intercept.
Substitute $x = 0$.

$$2(0) - y = 7$$
$$-y = 7 \quad \text{Solve for } y.$$
$$\frac{-y}{-1} = \frac{7}{-1}$$
$$y = -7$$

The y-intercept is -7.
The point $(0, -7)$ is on the line.

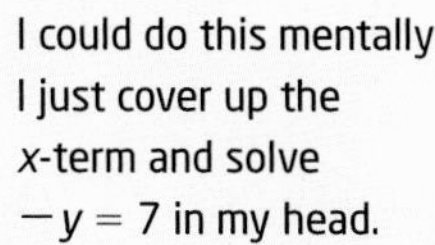

Plot the intercepts.
Draw a line through the intercepts.
Label the line with the equation.

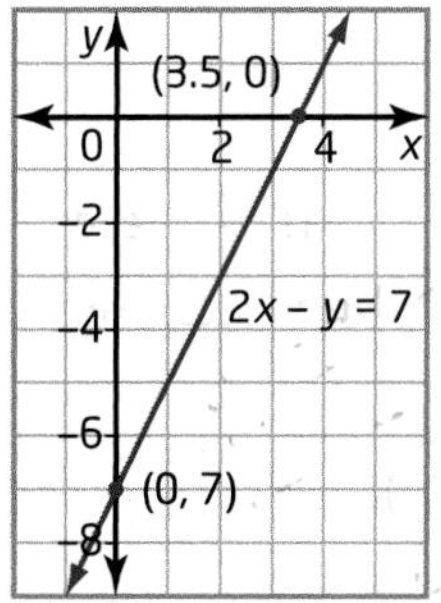

b) $3x - 5y + 15 = 0$

Find the x-intercept.
Substitute $y = 0$.

$$3x - 5(0) + 15 = 0$$
$$3x + 15 = 0$$
$$3x = -15$$
$$x = -5$$

The x-intercept is -5.
The point $(-5, 0)$ is on the line.

Find the y-intercept.
Substitute $x = 0$.

$$3(0) - 5y + 15 = 0$$
$$-5y + 15 = 0$$
$$-5y = -15$$
$$y = 3$$

The y-intercept is 3.
The point (0, 3) is on the line.

Plot the intercepts.
Draw a line through the intercepts.
Label the line with the equation.

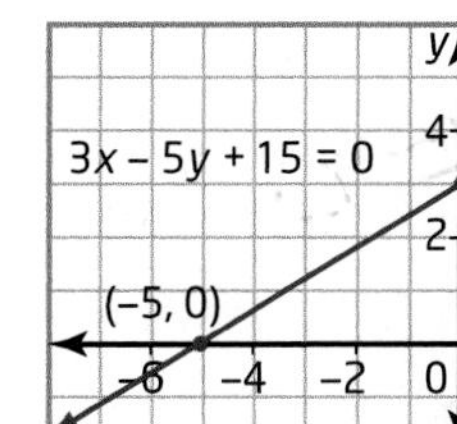

Example 3 Find the Slope Using the Intercepts

Determine the slope of the line whose x-intercept is -4 and y-intercept is -6.

Solution

Reasoning and Proving
Representing
Selecting Tools
Problem Solving
Connecting
Reflecting
Communicating

Method 1: Apply Algebraic Reasoning

The points $(-4, 0)$ and $(0, -6)$ are on the line. Substitute these into the slope formula.

$$\begin{aligned} m &= \frac{y_2 - y_1}{x_2 - x_1} \\ &= \frac{-6 - 0}{0 - (-4)} \\ &= \frac{-6}{4} \\ &= -\frac{3}{2} \end{aligned}$$

The slope of the line is $-\frac{3}{2}$.

Method 2: Apply Geometric Reasoning

Graph the line by plotting the intercepts. Read the rise and the run from the graph.

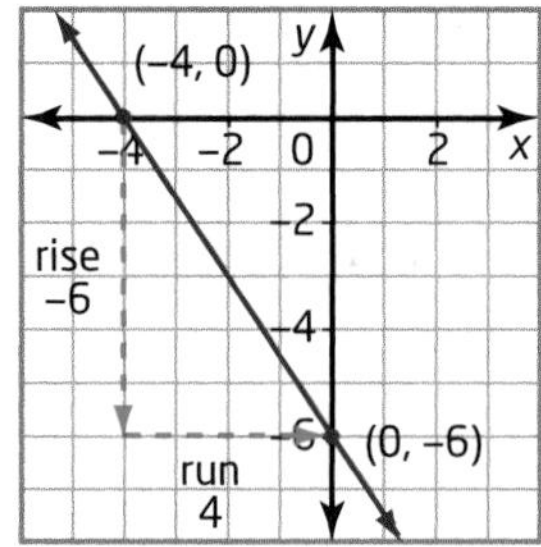

I go down 6 units to move from the first point, $(-4, 0)$, to the second point, $(0, -6)$, so the rise is -6. The run is 4.

$$\begin{aligned} m &= \frac{\text{rise}}{\text{run}} \\ &= \frac{-6}{4} \\ &= -\frac{3}{2} \end{aligned}$$

Key Concepts

- The x-intercept is the x-coordinate of the point where a line crosses the x-axis. At this point, $y = 0$.

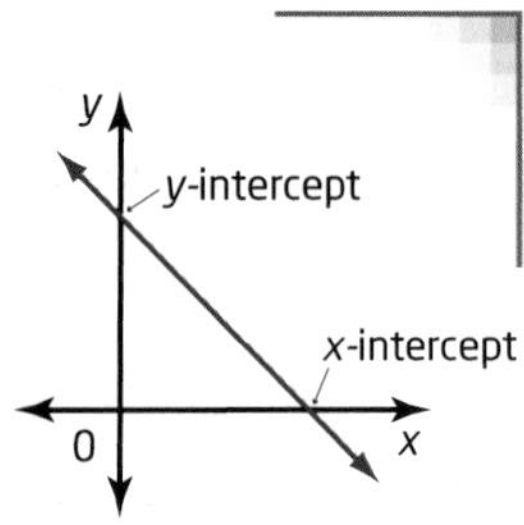

- The y-intercept is the y-coordinate of the point where a line crosses the y-axis. At this point, $x = 0$.
- For some equations, it is easy to graph a line using intercepts. For example, for $3x + 2y = 6$:
  - When $x = 0$, $y = 3$.
  - When $y = 0$, $x = 2$
  - Plot the two intercepts and draw a line through them.

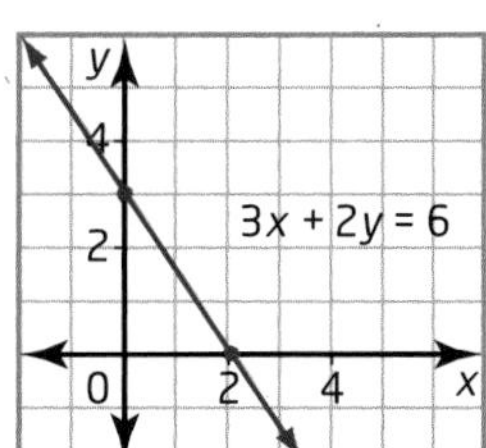

Communicate Your Understanding

C1 A line has an x-intercept of 3 and a y-intercept of -4. Use the intercepts to state the coordinates of two points on this line.

C2 **a)** Is it possible for a line to have no y-intercept? Explain.

b) Give an example of a line that has no y-intercept. Write the equation and sketch its graph.

C3 A line has a y-intercept of -2, but has no x-intercept. Describe this line in words, and sketch its graph.

Practise

1. Identify the x- and y-intercepts of each graph, if they exist.

a)

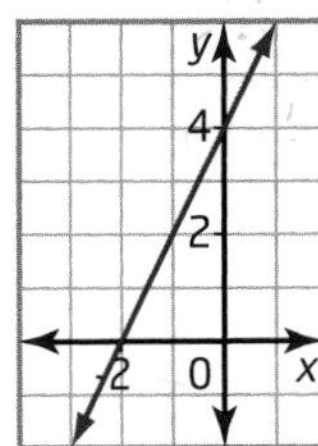

b)

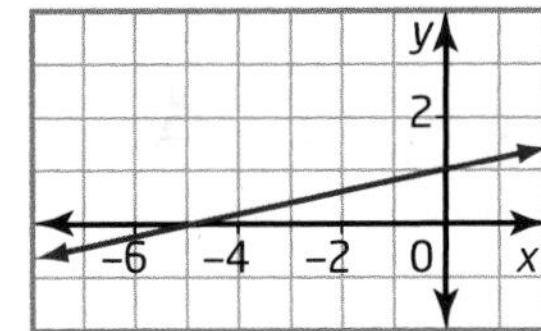

c)

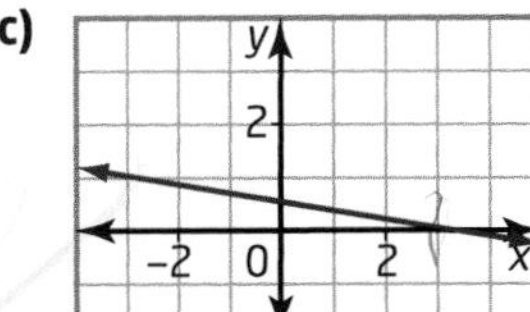

d)

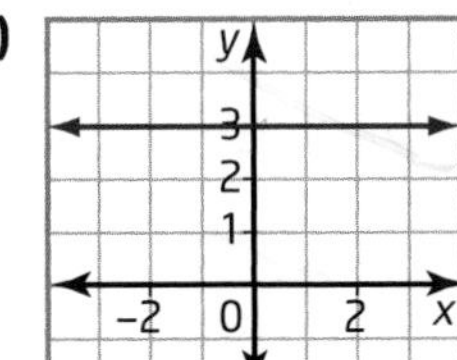

e)

For help with questions 2 and 3, see Example 1.

2. For each part, plot the intercepts and graph the line.

	x-intercept	y-intercept
a)	2	5
b)	−3	3
c)	1.5	−4
d)	none	6
e)	4	none

3. Determine the x- and y-intercepts and use them to graph each line.

a) $2x + 3y = 12$ **b)** $3x + y = 6$

c) $x - 4y = 4$ **d)** $-5x + 2y = 10$

e) $4x = 12$ **f)** $3y = -9$

g) $4x + 2y = 6$ **h)** $x - 3y = 5$

Connect and Apply

For help with question 4, see Example 2.

4. Draw a graph and determine the slope of each line using the rise and run from the graph.

	x-intercept	y-intercept
a)	5	-5
b)	-2	3
c)	3	none
d)	2.5	-4

For help with question 5, see Example 3.

5. Find the slope of each line, given the x- and y-intercepts, using the slope formula.

	x-intercept	y-intercept
a)	6	5
b)	3	-4
c)	-6	3
d)	none	$\frac{1}{2}$

6. The distance-time graph shows Carlo's motion in front of a motion sensor.

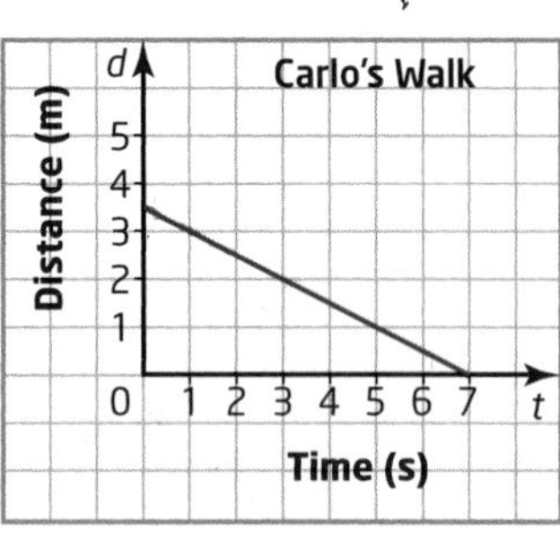

a) Identify the d-intercept and explain what it means.

b) Identify the t-intercept and explain what it means.

c) Describe the instructions you would give to a person walking in front of a motion sensor to reproduce this graph.

7. Consider the line $x + 4y = -4$. To graph this line, you could

- determine the x- and y-intercepts
- create a table of values
- use the equation to find the coordinates of three points on the line

Which method of graphing do you prefer in this case? Explain.

8. A candle burns at a constant rate of 2.5 cm/h. The candle is 15 cm tall when it is first lit.

a) Set up a graph of length, l, in centimetres, versus time, t, in hours, and plot the l-intercept.

b) Should the slope of this linear relation be positive or negative? Explain.

c) Graph the line.

d) What is the length of the candle after
- 3 h?
- 4.5 h?

e) Identify the t-intercept and explain what it means.

f) Explain why this graph has no meaning below the t-axis.

9. Explain and use sketches to support your answers to each question.

a) Is it possible for a line to have no x-intercept?

b) Is it possible for a line to have more than one x-intercept?

c) Is it possible for a line to have no x-intercept and no y-intercept?

10. **Use Technology** Use *The Geometer's Sketchpad®* to model and explore in more depth the problem posed in the Investigate.

a) Construct a geometric model for the problem.
- Open *The Geometer's Sketchpad®* and begin a new sketch.
- From the **Graph** menu, choose **Show Grid**.
- Select the x-axis and, from the **Construct** menu, choose **Point On Axis**. Click and drag the point until it is at (12, 0).
- Construct a point on the y-axis and move it to (0, 8).
- Select the two intercept points and, from the **Construct** menu, choose **Line**.

b) Explore the effects on the linear model when the intercepts change. What happens to the slope of the line in each situation?
- The x-intercept is increased.
- The x-intercept is decreased.
- The y-intercept is increased.
- The y-intercept is decreased.

c) Suppose that the price of comic books goes up. What effect will this have on the linear model? What impact will this have on Joanne's buying power? Explain your reasoning.

d) Suppose that the store has a 50% off sale on novels. Repeat part c) for this scenario.

11. When you buy a computer, its value depreciates (becomes less) over time. The graph illustrates the value of a computer from the time it was bought.

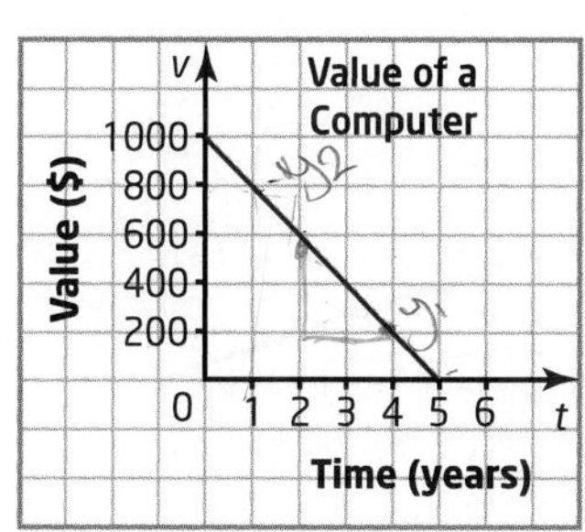

a) How much did the computer originally cost?

b) After what period of time does the computer no longer have any value?

c) What is the slope of this graph and what does it mean?

Extend

12. Refer to question 11. Sometimes depreciation is calculated differently. Suppose that each year, the computer's value becomes 50% of its previous year's value.

a) Construct a table of values of the computer's value versus time for the first 5 years after the date of purchase.

b) Graph this relation. Is it linear or non-linear? Explain.

c) After how many years will the computer be worth
- less than 10% of its original value?
- zero?

d) Does the t-intercept exist? If yes, what is it? If no, why not?

e) Compare this graph with the one in question 11. Under which system does the computer's value depreciate faster? Explain.

Making Connections

The graph in question 13 illustrates a special type of non-linear relationship called a *quadratic relation*. You will study these in depth in grade 10.

13. a) How many x-intercepts does this graph have? What are they?

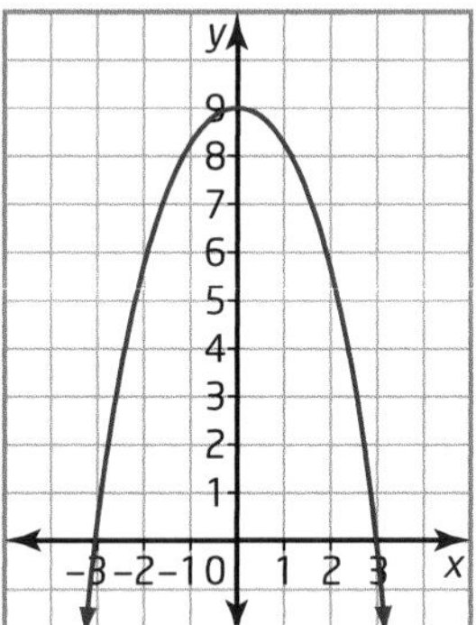

b) How many y-intercepts does this graph have? What are they?

c) Sketch the graph of a relation that has two y-intercepts.

d) Sketch the graph of a relation that has three x-intercepts.

e) Sketch the graph of a relation that has two x-intercepts and two y-intercepts.

14. Math Contest The ordered pair (x, y) locates a point on a plane. The ordered triple (x, y, z) can be used to locate a point in three-dimensional space. For example, to locate the point A(2, 3, 4), start at the origin, (0, 0, 0), move 2 units right, 3 units up, and 4 units out of the page. Describe how to locate the points B(5, −3, 1) and C(−2, 0, 4). If you were to join the three points, what would the shape of the resulting figure be?

15. Math Contest Start with the equation $6x - 2y - 18 = 0$. Write this equation in the form $y = m(x - a)$. What information does the value of a give you about the graph of this line? Repeat this investigation using any other line written in standard form. Draw conclusions about the form $y = m(x - a)$.

Use *The Geometer's Sketchpad*® to Explore Parallel and Perpendicular Lines

The geometric properties of parallel and perpendicular lines make them very useful in mathematics. How can you recognize whether two equations represent parallel or perpendicular lines?

Tools

- *The Geometer's Sketchpad*®
- protractor

Investigate

How are the slopes of parallel and perpendicular lines related?

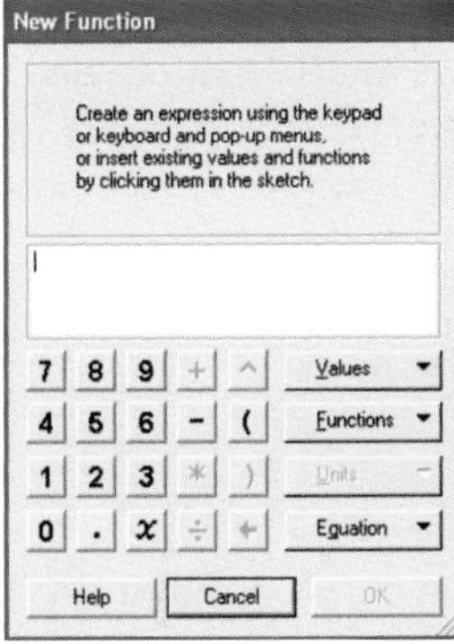

1. Graph the line $y = 2x + 3$ using *The Geometer's Sketchpad*®.
   - Open *The Geometer's Sketchpad*® and begin a new sketch.
   - From the **Graph** menu, choose **Show Grid**.
   - From the **Graph** menu, choose **New Function**. A function calculator screen will appear.
   - Click on $2 * x + 3$.
   - Click on **OK**.
   - From the **Graph** menu, choose **Plot Function**. The line $y = 2x + 3$ should appear.

Technology Tip

A *parameter* is a variable that is assigned a specific value. By setting the slope as a parameter, you can change its value either by hand or automatically and immediately see the effect on the line.

2. Set a **parameter** for the slope of a new line.
   - Deselect by clicking somewhere in the white space.
   - From the **Graph** menu, choose **New Parameter**. A dialogue box with the heading **New Parameter** will appear.
   - Type *m* in the **Name** field. Click on **OK**. Leave the **Value** set at 1.0. A parameter measure, *m*, will appear near the left side of the screen. You will use this in the next step.

Literacy Connections

The Geometer's Sketchpad® uses a special notation called *function notation*. In function notation, you replace y with $f(x)$.

Regular notation:

$y = 2x + 3$

Function notation:

$f(x) = 2x + 3$

To read function notation aloud, you say "f of x equals..." or "f at x equals...." You can also use other letters, such as $g(x)$ and $h(x)$. This is useful when you are working with more than one equation at a time.

3. a) Graph a line $y = mx + 2$ with a moveable slope.

- Deselect by clicking in the white space.
- From the **Graph** menu, choose **New Function**.
- When the dialogue box appears, click on the parameter measure m.
- Click on $* \ x + 2$
- Click on **OK**.
- From the **Graph** menu, choose **Plot Function**. The line $y = x + 2$ will appear.

b) Why did a line with a slope of 1 appear? *Hint:* Think about how you set the parameter.

4. Change the slope of $y = mx + 2$ automatically.

- Deselect.
- Right click on the parameter measure m.
- Select **Animate Parameter**.
- Watch the line and the value of m. Describe what happens.

5. Explore the **Motion Controller**. When you click on **Animate Parameter**, a **Motion Controller** dialogue box appears. Experiment with the different controls. Write a brief explanation of what each command does.

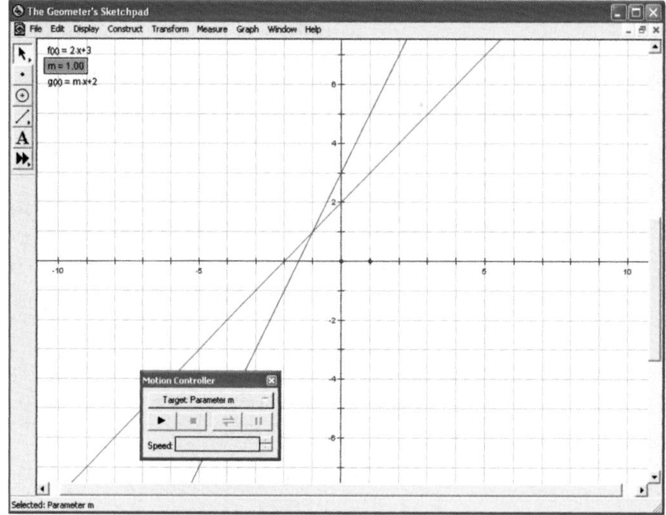

6. Change the slope of $y = mx + 2$ by hand.
   - Stop the **Motion Controller** and close its window.
   - With the parameter measure m still selected, type the + sign on the keyboard several times. Describe what happens to the line and the slope. Repeat for the − sign.

7. a) Try to find the value that makes the line $y = mx + 2$ parallel to $y = 2x + 3$. To set a precise value, do the following:
   - Right click on the parameter measure m.
   - Choose **Edit Parameter**. An **Edit Parameter Definition** dialogue box will appear.
   - Type in a value. Are the lines parallel? If not, repeat the above step until they are.

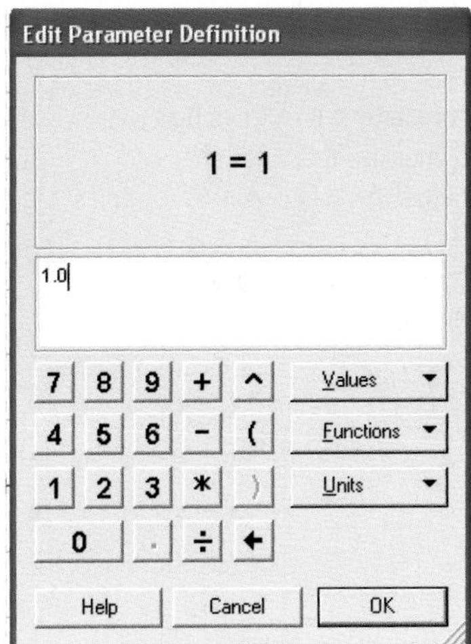

   b) For what value of m is the line $y = mx + 2$ parallel to the line $y = 2x + 3$?

8. Find the value of m that makes $y = mx + 2$ perpendicular to $y = 2x + 3$. You can use a protractor to measure the angle of intersection of the two lines.

9. Find the slopes of lines that are parallel and perpendicular to each line given. Organize your results in a table like this.

Given Line	Slope of Given Line	Slope of Parallel Line	Slope of Perpendicular Line
$y = -x + 2$			
$y = \frac{2}{3}x - 4$			
line of your choice			

10. **Reflect** Look at your results.
   a) Describe how the slopes of parallel lines are related.
   b) Describe how the slopes of perpendicular lines are related. *Hint:* Explore the products of the slopes of perpendicular lines.

6.4 Parallel and Perpendicular Lines

parallel lines

- lines that run in the same direction and never cross

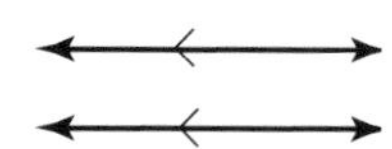

- matching arrow symbols indicate that lines are parallel

perpendicular lines

- lines that intersect at right angles

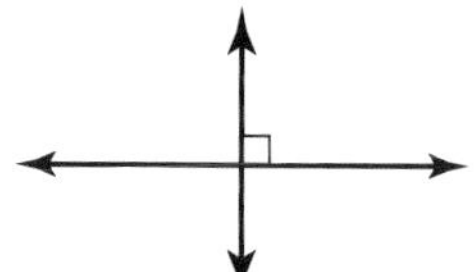

- a small box at the intersection indicates a 90° angle

 **Tools** 

- grid paper
- protractor
- graphing calculator

Parallel and **perpendicular lines** appear all the time in the world around you. Think of streets, wallpaper, railway tracks, and skyscrapers. Look around your classroom. Where can you see examples of

- parallel lines?
- perpendicular lines?

Investigate

How are the slopes of parallel and perpendicular lines related?

1. Graph each set of lines on the same grid.

a) $y = 2x - 3$

$y = 2x + 1$

$y = 2x - 2$

b) $y = -\frac{1}{2}x + 4$

$y = -\frac{1}{2}x + 2$

$y = -\frac{1}{2}x - 1$

2. How are the lines in each set in step 1 related geometrically? How are the equations related?

3. Graph each pair of lines on the same grid. Use the same scale on both axes. If you are using a graphing calculator, press ZOOM and select **5:ZSquare**.

a) $y = 2x + 3$

$y = -\frac{1}{2}x + 1$

b) $y = -\frac{2}{3}x + 3$

$y = \frac{3}{2}x - 4$

c) $y = -x + 1$

$y = x - 3$

4. How are the lines in each set in step 3 related geometrically? How are the equations related?

5. Reflect

a) How can you tell whether lines are parallel from their equations?

b) How can you tell whether lines are perpendicular from their equations?

Example Slopes of Parallel and Perpendicular Lines

a) The equation of a line is $y = 3x - 4$. Give the slope of a parallel line.

b) The equation of a line is $y = \frac{3}{5}x + 2$. Give the slope of a perpendicular line.

Solution

a) The line $y = 3x - 4$ has slope 3.
A parallel line will have the same slope, 3.

b) The line $y = \frac{3}{5}x + 2$ has slope $\frac{3}{5}$.

A perpendicular line will have slope $-\frac{5}{3}$.

To find the perpendicular slope, I turn the fraction upside down and use the opposite sign.

Key Concepts

- The slopes of parallel lines are the same.

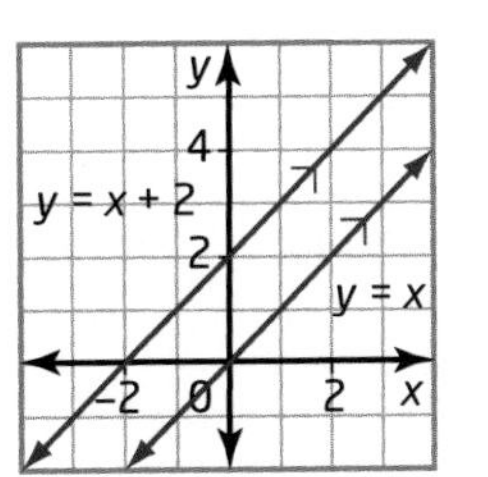

- The slopes of perpendicular lines are **negative reciprocals**.

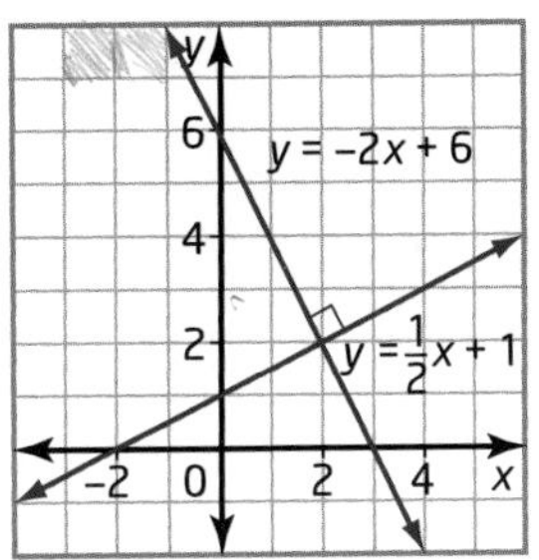

negative reciprocals
- two numbers whose product is −1

Communicate Your Understanding

C1 Which lines are parallel? Explain how you know.

A $y = \frac{3}{4}x + 1$ **B** $y = 3x + 4$

C $y = \frac{3}{4}x$ **D** $y = \frac{4}{3}x + 1$

C2 Which lines are perpendicular? Explain how you know.

A $y = 3x + 2$ **B** $y = -\frac{1}{3}x - 5$

C $y = \frac{1}{3}x + 3$ **D** $y = -3x - 1$

Practise

1. Graph each pair of lines on the same coordinate grid. Find their slopes and conclude whether the lines are parallel, perpendicular, or neither.

a) $y = \frac{1}{4}x - 2$ $\quad y = \frac{1}{4}x + 3$

b) $y = 2x + 5$ $\quad 4x - 2y + 6 = 0$

c) $x + y = 4$ $\quad y = x - 3$

d) $y = \frac{1}{2}x - 4$ $\quad x - 2y + 1 = 0$

2. Graph each pair of lines on the same coordinate grid. Find their slopes and conclude whether the lines are parallel, perpendicular, or neither.

a) $y = 3$ $\quad x = -2$

b) $y = -4$ $\quad y = x$

c) $x = 5$ $\quad x = 0$

d) $y = x + 1$ $\quad y = -x$

Connect and Apply

3. The slopes of two lines are given. Conclude whether the lines are parallel, perpendicular, or neither. Justify your answers.

a) $m = \frac{2}{3}, m = \frac{4}{6}$

b) $m = \frac{3}{4}, m = -\frac{4}{3}$

c) $m = 2, m = -2$

d) $m = 1, m = -1$

e) $m = \frac{1}{5}, m = 0.2$

f) $m = 2\frac{1}{4}, m = -\frac{4}{9}$

For help with questions 4 and 5, see the Example.

4. What is the slope of a line that is parallel to each line?

a) $y = \frac{3}{5}x - 2$

b) $y = -x + 7$

c) $2x - y + 3 = 0$

d) $4x + 3y = 12$

e) $y = 2$

f) $x = -5$

5. For each line in question 4, give the slope of a perpendicular line.

6. Write the equations of two lines that are parallel to the line $3x - 6y - 5 = 0$.

7. Write the equations of two lines that are perpendicular to the line $4x + y - 2 = 0$.

8. A triangle has vertices A(1, 2), B(3, 8), and C(6, 7).

a) Plot these points and draw the triangle.

b) Does this appear to be a right triangle? Explain.

c) Find the slopes of the line segments that form this triangle.

d) Explain how the slopes can be used to conclude whether or not this is a right triangle. Is it?

9. Determine whether or not the following sets of points form right triangles. Justify your answers with mathematical reasoning.

a) A(1, 1), B(−2, 5), C(3, −2)

b) P(2, 4), Q(−2, 2), R(5, −2)

10. △KLM has vertices K(−2, 3) and L(−6, −2).

a) Find the coordinates of M such that △KLM is a right triangle.

b) Is there more than one solution? Explain.

Achievement Check

11. a) Using intercepts, graph the three lines $4x + y - 8 = 0$, $2x - y - 4 = 0$, and $x + 2y - 16 = 0$ on the same coordinate grid.

b) The three lines form a triangle. Does this triangle appear to be a right triangle?

c) Using slopes, explain how you can be sure of your conclusion in part b).

d) Give the equations for three different lines that do form a right triangle.

Extend

12. a) Graph this pair of lines and identify their *x*- and *y*-intercepts.

$2x + 5y = 10$ $\qquad$ $2x + 5y = -10$

b) Repeat part a) for this pair of lines.

$3x + 4y = 12$ $\qquad$ $3x + 4y = -12$

c) Describe how you can use intercepts to quickly find a line that is parallel to a given line. Create an example of your own to support your explanation.

13. a) Graph this pair of lines and identify their *x*- and *y*-intercepts.

$3x + 5y = 15$ $\qquad$ $5x - 3y = -15$

b) Repeat part a) for this pair of lines.

$2x + 7y = 14$ $\qquad$ $7x - 2y = -14$

c) Describe how you can use intercepts to quickly find a line that is perpendicular to a given line. Create an example of your own to support your explanation.

14. Math Contest A and k are one-digit numbers. Given two lines, $Ax - 3y + 15 = 0$ and $y = kx + 7$, determine the number of pairs of values for A and k for which the two lines are

a) parallel

b) perpendicular

c) coincident (the same line)

6.5 Find an Equation for a Line Given the Slope and a Point

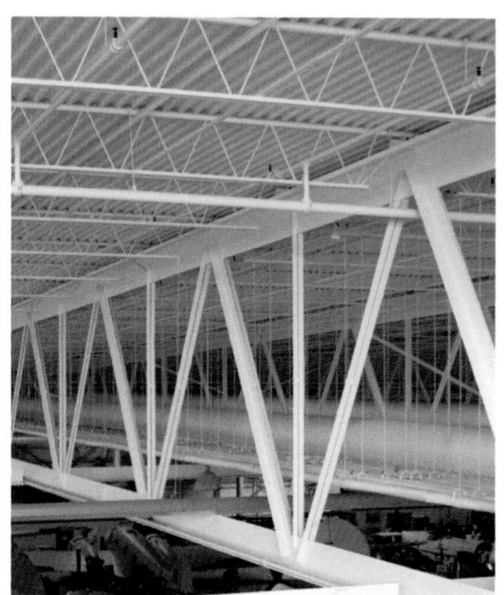

The slope of a line gives its direction. For any given slope value, there are many possible lines. This family of lines has a slope of $\frac{1}{2}$. How many different lines share the same slope? How do you know? What additional information would you need in order to pinpoint a specific line?

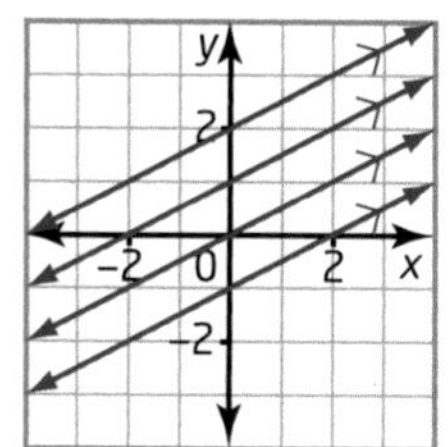

Suppose that you know that a line with a slope of $\frac{1}{2}$ passes through the point (1, 5). There is only one line that does this. In fact, if you know the slope and any point on a line, you can identify its equation.

Example 1 Find the Equation of a Line Given Its Slope and a Point

a) Find the equation of a line with a slope of $\frac{1}{2}$ that passes through (1, 5).

b) Graph the line.

Solution

a) Substitute $x = 1$, $y = 5$, and $m = \frac{1}{2}$ into the slope and y-intercept form of the equation of a line, and solve for b.

$$y = mx + b$$
$$5 = \frac{1}{2}(1) + b$$
$$5 = \frac{1}{2} + b$$
$$5 - \frac{1}{2} = b$$
$$4\frac{1}{2} = b$$

I can write the equation of a line once I know its slope and y-intercept.

I'm given the slope, so $m = \frac{1}{2}$. I don't know the y-intercept, but I'm given the point (1, 5). So, I know that when $x = 1$, $y = 5$.

The y-intercept is $4\frac{1}{2}$ or $\frac{9}{2}$.

Substitute the values of m and b into $y = mx + b$ to write the equation of the line.

$$y = \frac{1}{2}x + \frac{9}{2}$$

The equation of the line is $y = \frac{1}{2}x + \frac{9}{2}$.

b) The y-intercept is $\frac{9}{2}$, or 4.5.
Plot this point and the given point (1, 5) to graph the line.

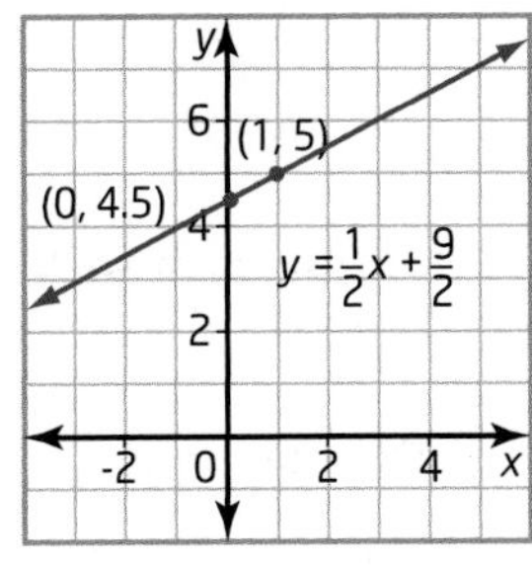

Example 2 Find the Equation of a Partial Variation

Gina knows that it costs $25 to take a taxi to work, which is 10 km from her home. She forgets what the fixed cost is, but remembers that the variable cost is $2/km. Her friend lives 12 km from Gina's home. Gina has $60 to spend on the weekend. Can she afford a round trip to see her friend?

a) Find the fixed cost and write the equation that relates the cost, in dollars, of a trip to the distance, in kilometres.

b) Graph the linear relation.

c) Find the cost of a 12-km trip. Can Gina, who has $60 to spend, afford a round trip of this distance?

Solution

a) This is an example of a partial variation. A graph of cost, C, in dollars, versus distance, d, in kilometres, will produce a straight line.

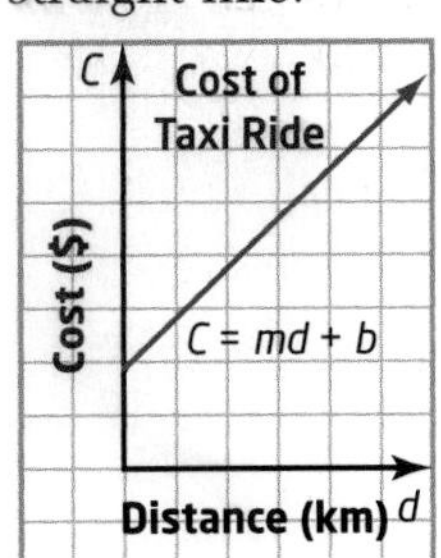

The variable cost is \$2/km, which represents the slope of the line. The fixed cost is unknown, but it is equal to the vertical intercept. You also know that (10, 25) is on the line.

To find the fixed cost, substitute $d = 10$, $C = 25$, and $m = 2$ into $C = md + b$ and solve for b.

$$C = md + b$$
$$25 = 2(10) + b$$
$$25 = 20 + b$$
$$25 - 20 = b$$
$$5 = b$$

The vertical intercept is 5. This means that the fixed cost is \$5. To write the equation of the line, substitute m and b into $C = md + b$.

$C = 2n + 5$

The equation $C = 2n + 5$ gives the cost, C, in dollars, for a trip d kilometres long.

b) You can use the vertical intercept and the slope to graph this relation. Plot the point (0, 5). Then, go up 2 and right 1 to find other points.

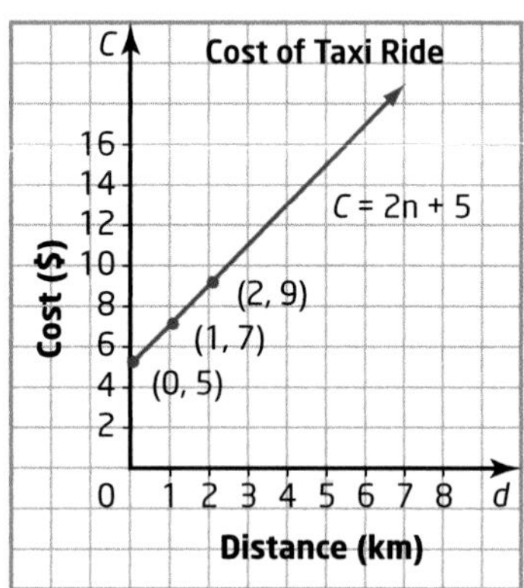

c) To find the cost of a 12-km trip, you can use the graph or the equation.

Method 1: Use the Graph

Extend the graph until you can read the value of C when $d = 12$.

The cost of a 12-km trip is \$29.

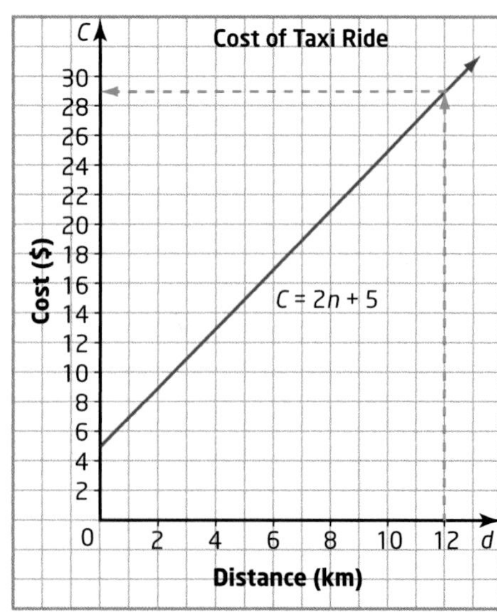

Method 2: Use the Equation

Substitute $d = 12$ into the equation relating cost and distance, and solve for C.

$$
\begin{aligned}
C &= 2n + 5 \\
&= 2(12) + 5 \\
&= 24 + 5 \\
&= 29
\end{aligned}
$$

The cost of a 12-km trip is \$29.

A round trip would cost $2 \times \$29$, or \$58. Since Gina has \$60 to spend, she can afford to see her friend.

Sometimes the properties of parallel and perpendicular lines are useful in finding the equation of a line.

Recall from Section 6.4 that parallel lines have the same slope.

For example, $y = 3x + 2$ and $y = 3x - 1$ are parallel lines.
In both cases, $m = 3$.

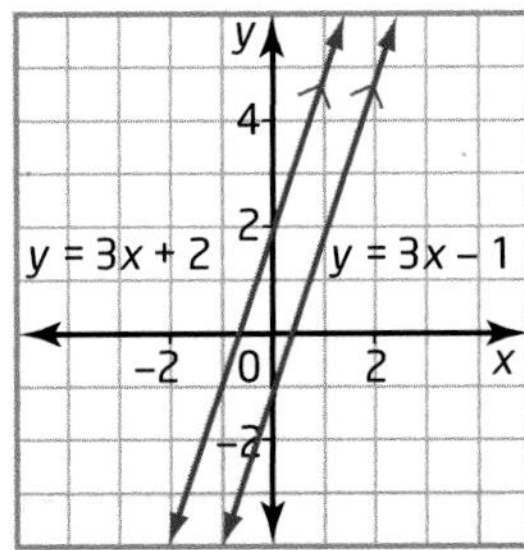

Perpendicular lines have slopes that are negative reciprocals.
The product of the slopes of perpendicular lines equals -1.

For example, $y = \frac{3}{4}x + 2$ and $y = -\frac{4}{3}x + 2$ are perpendicular lines.

$$\left(\frac{3}{4}\right) \times \left(-\frac{4}{3}\right) = -1$$

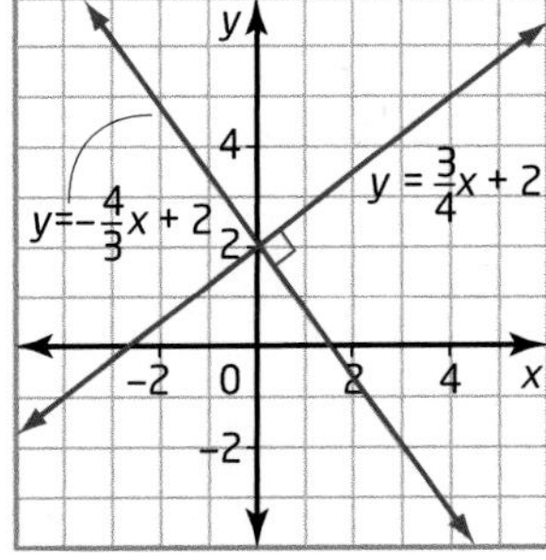

Literacy Connections

Negative reciprocals are pairs of numbers that are related in two ways. The negative part means that they are opposite in sign. The reciprocal part means that, when expressed as a proper or improper fraction, the numerator of one is the denominator of the other, and vice versa.
For example:

$\frac{5}{3}$ and $-\frac{3}{5}$ 1 and -1

$\frac{1}{2}$ and -2 $\frac{2}{3}$ and -1.5

Example 3 Find Equations of Lines Parallel or Perpendicular to Given Lines

Find the equation of a line

a) parallel to $x - y - 12 = 0$ that passes through $(2, -5)$

b) perpendicular to $y = 4x + 5$ that passes through the origin

Solution

a) The unknown line is parallel to $x - y - 12 = 0$, so it must have the same slope as this line. To find the slope, rearrange the equation to express it in slope y-intercept form.

$$x - y - 12 = 0 \qquad \text{Add } y \text{ to both sides.}$$
$$x - 12 = y$$
$$\text{or } y = x - 12$$

The slope of this line, and any line parallel to it, is 1. Substitute $m = 1$ and the known point, $(2, -5)$, into $y = mx + b$ and solve for b.

$$y = mx + b$$
$$-5 = 1(2) + b$$
$$-5 = 2 + b$$
$$-5 - 2 = b$$
$$-7 = b$$

Substitute m and b into $y = mx + b$ to write the equation of the line.

$y = 1x + (-7)$

The equation of the line is $y = x - 7$.

b) The unknown line is perpendicular to $y = 4x + 5$. That means that their slopes are negative reciprocals.

slope of given line: $m = 4$ or $\frac{4}{1}$

negative reciprocal: $-\frac{1}{4}$

The slope of the unknown line is $-\frac{1}{4}$. Use this to find the equation of the line.

The unknown line passes through the origin, which means that its y-intercept is 0. Substitute $m = -\frac{1}{4}$ and $b = 0$ into $y = mx + b$.

$$y = -\frac{1}{4}x + 0$$

$$y = -\frac{1}{4}x$$

The equation of the line is $y = -\frac{1}{4}x$.

Key Concepts

- You can find the equation of a line if you know its slope and one point on the line.
  - Substitute the given slope for m and the coordinates of the given point into the equation $y = mx + b$ and solve for b.
  - Write the equation by substituting the values for m and b into $y = mx + b$.

Communicate Your Understanding

C1 A line has a slope of 3 and passes through the point (2, 1). Explain each step in finding the equation of this line.

Step	*Explanation*
$y = mx + b$	Start with the slope y-intercept form of the equation of a line.
$1 = 3(2) + b$	
$1 = 6 + b$	
$1 - 6 = b$	
$-5 = b$	

The equation of the line is $y = 3x - 5$.

C2 What is the slope of a line that is perpendicular to a line with each slope?

a) $\frac{3}{5}$ **b)** $-\frac{1}{4}$ **c)** 5 **d)** -3.5

Practise

For help with questions 1 and 2, see Example 1.

1. Find the equation of a line with the given slope and passing through the given point, P.

a) $m = 1$, P(3, 5)

b) $m = -3$, P(0, −4)

c) $m = \frac{2}{3}$, P(−2, 6)

d) $m = -\frac{1}{2}$, P(5, −2)

e) $m = -\frac{4}{5}$, P(0, 0)

f) $m = 2$, $P\left(\frac{1}{2}, \frac{3}{4}\right)$

2. Find the equation of a line

a) with a slope of -3, passing through the origin

b) parallel to $y = \frac{2}{3}x + 5$, passing through $(4, -5)$

c) parallel to the x-axis, passing through $(3, -6)$

d) perpendicular to $y = -\frac{2}{5}x + 4$, passing through the origin

e) perpendicular to $x = -2$, passing through the point $(1, -3)$

f) perpendicular to $y = 4x - 3$, passing through the point $(-2, 7)$

Connect and Apply

For help with questions 3 and 4, see Example 2.

3. In Niagara-on-the-Lake, you can ride a horse-drawn carriage for a fixed price plus a variable amount that depends on the length of the trip. The variable cost is \$10/km and a 2.5-km trip costs \$40.

a) Determine the equation relating cost, C, in dollars, and distance, d, in kilometres.

b) Use your equation to find the cost of a 6.5-km ride.

c) Graph this relation.

d) Use the graph to find the cost of a 6.5-km ride.

Making Connections

You learned about first differences and their relationship with slope in 5.6 Connecting Variation, Slope, and First Differences.

4. Refer to question 3.

a) Copy and complete the table to solve the problem using a third method. Explain this method.

Distance (km)	Cost (\$)	First Differences
2.5	40	
3.5	50	10
4.5		
5.5		
6.5		

b) Use all three methods (equation, graph, table) to determine how far you could travel in the horse-drawn carriage for \$100.

c) Use each method to determine the cost of a 5.8-km ride.

d) Describe at least one advantage and one disadvantage to each method of solution.

For help with questions 5 and 6, see Example 3.

5. Find an equation for the line parallel to $2x - 3y + 6 = 0$, with the same y-intercept as $y = 7x - 1$.

6. Find an equation for the line perpendicular to $4x - 5y = 20$ and sharing the same y-intercept.

7. Chapter Problem Jean's home city is one of the best designed in North America for traffic flow, Traffic lights are carefully programmed to keep cars moving. Some lanes on one-way streets change direction depending on the time of day. To find two more letters in the name of this city, find the x- and y-intercepts of the line that is perpendicular to $y = \frac{9}{8}x + 1$ and passes through the point $(18, -8)$.

8. Aki has been driving at an average speed of 80 km/h toward Ottawa for 3 h, when he sees the sign shown.

Ottawa 300 km

The equation relating distance and time is of the form $d = mt + b$.

a) What does the ordered pair (3, 300) mean?

b) The slope is $m = -80$. What does this value represent? Why is it negative?

c) Determine the value of b.

d) Write an equation relating distance and time.

e) Graph the relation. What is the meaning of the d-intercept?

f) How long will the trip to Ottawa take, in total?

g) Has Aki reached the halfway point of his trip yet? Explain.

9. Use Technology You can use *The Geometer's Sketchpad®* to solve the taxi problem in Example 2.

a) Follow these steps:
- Open a new sketch and display the grid.
- Create a new parameter and call it b.
- Create a new function and define it as $f(x) = 2x + b$.
- Plot the point (10, 25). Click and drag the two control points near the origin to adjust the scales and the position of the origin so that you can see this point.
- Manipulate the parameter b until the line passes through the point (10, 25).

b) Explain how this method works.

10. Use Technology A city taxi charges \$2.50/km plus a fixed cost. A 6-km taxi ride costs \$22. Use *The Geometer's Sketchpad®* to find

a) the fixed cost

b) the equation relating cost, C, in dollars, and distance, d, in kilometres

c) Find the equation using another method to check your results.

Extend

11. Refer to question 8. Suppose that, when Aki sees the sign, he increases his driving speed to 100 km/h.

a) Construct a graph to model Aki's trip.

b) How would your answers to parts f) and g) change?

c) Explain how you solved this problem.

6.6 Find an Equation for a Line Given Two Points

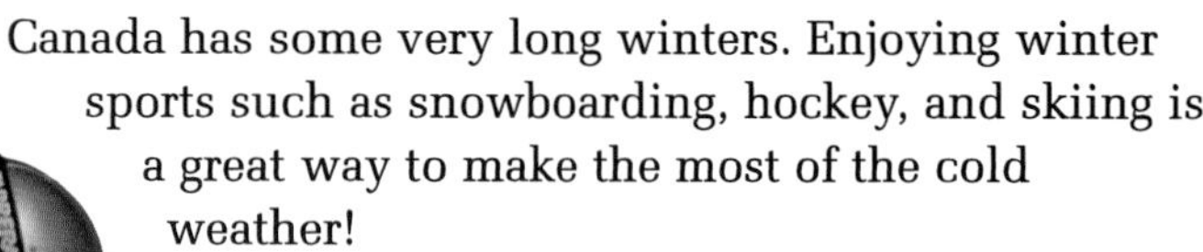

Canada has some very long winters. Enjoying winter sports such as snowboarding, hockey, and skiing is a great way to make the most of the cold weather!

A ski resort rents snowboards by the day. There is a flat insurance cost, plus a daily rental fee. Two friends, Josh and Kylie, have used the rental service before. They compare costs.

Josh: "For 3 days, the snowboard rental cost me \$85."

Kylie: "I rented a board for a full week, and it cost me \$165."

How much are the insurance cost and the daily rental fee? If you have \$120, can you afford to go snowboarding for 5 days?

Tools
- grid paper
- ruler

Making Connections

You studied direct and partial variations in Chapter 5: Modelling With Graphs. Is this a direct or a partial variation? How do you know?

Investigate

How can you construct a linear model if you know two points of information?

See the information above about renting a snowboard.

1. **a)** On grid paper, draw and label two sets of axes with
   - cost, C, in dollars, on the vertical axis
   - time, d, in days, on the horizontal axis

   b) Add appropriate scales to your axes to fit the data in the introduction.

2. **a)** Plot the points (3, 85) and (7, 165) and explain what they mean.

   b) Draw a line through these points. Extend the line so that it crosses the vertical axis.

3. **a)** Find the slope of this line and explain what it means.

   b) Find the C-intercept and explain what it means in terms of renting a snowboard.

4. Write the equation of the line in the form $C = md + b$, where m is the slope and b is the C-intercept.

5. **a)** Use the graph to find the cost of renting a snowboard for 5 days.
   b) Use your equation from step 4 to find the cost of renting a snowboard for 5 days.
   c) Are these answers the same? Explain.

6. **Reflect** Is it possible to find an equation for this line without graphing it? Explain.

Linear models can be useful for making predictions in many situations involving direct and partial variation. If you know two points of information, you can find an equation for the line.

Step 1. Find the slope. Substitute the two known points into the slope formula: $m = \dfrac{y_2 - y_1}{x_2 - x_1}$.

Step 2. Find the y-intercept. Substitute the slope and one of the two points into $y = mx + b$. Solve for b.

Step 3. Write the equation. Substitute the slope and y-intercept into $y = mx + b$.

Example Find an Equation for a Line, Given Two Points

a) A line passes through (1, 2) and (5, 10). Find an equation for the line.

b) A line passes through (−3, −2) and (6, −8). Find an equation for the line.

Solution

a) *Step 1.* Find the slope.

Substitute (1, 2) and (5, 10) into the slope formula: $m = \dfrac{y_2 - y_1}{x_2 - x_1}$.

$$m = \frac{10 - 2}{5 - 1}$$
$$= \frac{8}{4} \text{ or } 2$$

The slope is 2.

Step 2. Find the y-intercept.

Substitute $m = 2$ and one of the points, say (1, 2), into $y = mx + b$.

$2 = 2(1) + b$
$2 = 2 + b$
$0 = b$

The y-intercept is 0.

Step 3. Write the equation.

Substitute $m = 2$ and $b = 0$ into $y = mx + b$.

$$\begin{aligned} y &= (2)x + (0) \\ &= 2x + 0 \\ &= 2x \end{aligned}$$

The equation of the line passing through (1, 2) and (5, 10) is $y = 2x$.

b) *Step 1.* Find the slope.

Substitute (−3, −2) and (6, −8) into the slope formula.

$$\begin{aligned} m &= \frac{y_2 - y_1}{x_2 - x_1} \\ &= \frac{-8 - (-2)}{6 - (-3)} \\ &= \frac{-8 + 2}{6 + 3} \\ &= \frac{-6}{9} \\ &= -\frac{2}{3} \end{aligned}$$

Simplify integer calculations.

The slope is $-\frac{2}{3}$.

Step 2. Find the *y*-intercept.

Substitute $m = -\frac{2}{3}$ and one of the points, say (6, −8), into $y = mx + b$.

$$-8 = \left(-\frac{2}{\cancel{3}_1}\right)(\cancel{6}^2) + b$$

$$\begin{aligned} -8 &= -4 + b \\ -8 + 4 &= b \\ -4 &= b \end{aligned}$$

The *y*-intercept is −4.

Step 3. Write the equation.

$y = mx + b$

$y = -\frac{2}{3}x + (-4)$ **Substitute $m = -\frac{2}{3}$ and $b = -4$.**

The equation of the line is $y = -\frac{2}{3}x - 4$.

Key Concepts

- You can find an equation for a line if you know two points on the line. To find the equation,
  - find the slope by substituting the two points into the slope formula: $m = \dfrac{y_2 - y_1}{x_2 - x_1}$
  - find the y-intercept by substituting the slope and one of the points into $y = mx + b$, and then solve for b
  - write the equation by substituting m and b into $y = mx + b$

Communicate Your Understanding

C1 Explain how you can find an equation for a line if you are given

a) the slope and the y-intercept

b) the slope and a point on the line

c) two points on the line

C2 Create an example of each type in question C1 to illustrate your explanation.

C3 Suppose that you know two points on a line: (1, 2) and (−3, −2).

a) Once you have found the slope, investigate whether it matters which point you substitute into $y = mx + b$.

b) Which point would you prefer to use, and why?

C4 The graph illustrates a walker's movement in front of a motion sensor. Answer true or false to the following statements, and explain your answers.

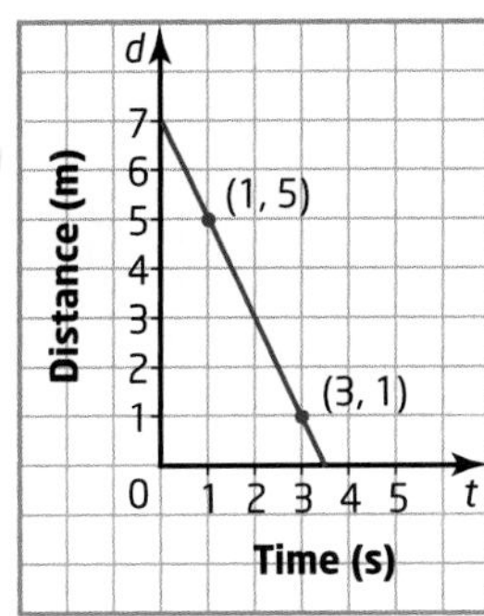

a) The walker started at a distance of 1 m from the sensor.

b) After 3 s, the walker was 1 m from the sensor.

c) The walker's speed was 2 m/s toward the sensor.

C5 The method you follow to write an equation for a line differs depending on the information you are given. Summarize the steps you would use to write the equation of a line given the following information:

a) two points on the line

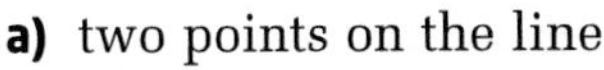

b) one point on the line and its y-intercept

c) the x- and y-intercepts

Practise

For help with questions 1 to 4, see Example 1.

1. Find an equation for the line passing through each pair of points.

a) P(2, 3) and Q(5, 6) **b)** A(4, −1) and B(0, 5)

c) U(−3, 4) and V(−2, −6) **d)** $L\left(\frac{1}{2}, 0\right)$ and $M\left(\frac{7}{2}, -5\right)$

2. Find an equation for each line.

a)

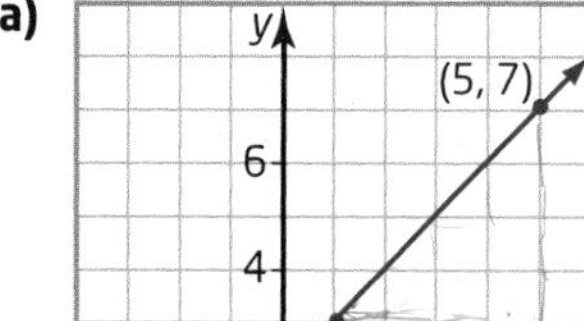

b)

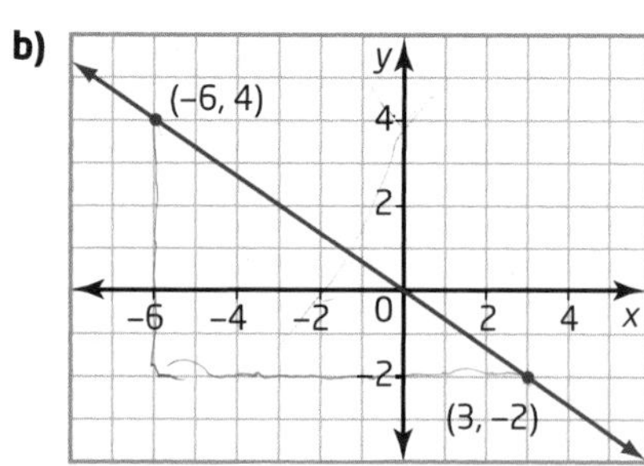

3. a) Find an equation for the line with an *x*-intercept of 4 and a *y*-intercept of −2.

b) Find an equation for the line whose *x*- and *y*-intercepts are both −5.

4. Find the equation of a line passing through each pair of points.

a) M(0, 3) and N(5, 3) **b)** K(−2, 6) and L(−2, −4)

Connect and Apply

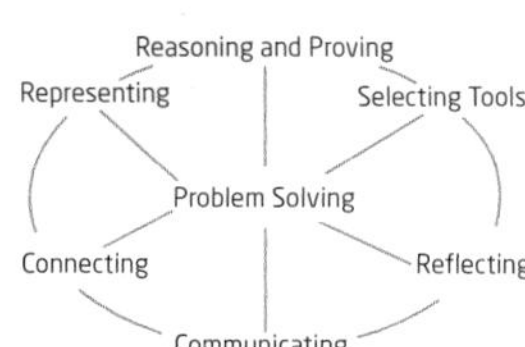

5. A bowling alley has a fixed base cost and charges a variable per game rate. It costs \$20.50 for five games and \$28.50 for nine games.

a) What is the variable cost?

b) Find an equation for the line relating cost, *C*, in dollars, and number of games, *g*, in the form $C = mg + b$.

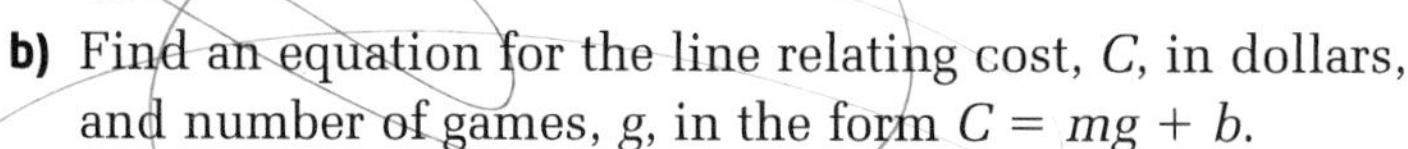

c) Graph this linear relation.

d) What is the *C*-intercept? What does it mean?

e) Use the graph to find the cost of 20 games.

f) Use the equation to find the cost of 20 games.

g) Describe one advantage and one disadvantage of using
- the graph
- the equation

6. Fiona is walking at a constant speed in front of a motion sensor. After 2 s, she is 1.5 m from the sensor. 2 s later, she is 4.5 m from the sensor.

a) Is Fiona moving toward or away from the sensor? Explain how you know.

b) How fast is Fiona walking?

c) Find the equation that describes Fiona's motion in the form $d = mt + b$.

d) What is the *d*-intercept? What does it mean?

7. Workers at a laboratory get the same raise each year. Colette, who has been working at the lab for 5 years, earns \$17.25/h. Lee, who has been working at the lab for 1 year, earns \$14.25/h. The equation relating wage and number of years worked is of the form $w = mn + b$, where w is the hourly wage and n is the number of years worked.

   a) (5, 17.25) and (1, 14.25) are two points on the line. Explain why.

   b) Find the slope and the w-intercept of this line, and explain what they mean.

   c) Write the equation of the line.

   d) Maria has been working at the lab for 7 years. Determine her hourly wage.

   e) What wage does this linear model predict for a worker who has been with the lab for 25 years? Does this seem reasonable? Explain. How might the store modify the raise policy?

8. Anil's family is driving home to Toronto. Anil hopes that they will make it back in time to see the hockey game on television. While travelling at a fairly constant speed, he observes two signs along the trip.

   a) How fast is Anil's family travelling?

   b) Find a linear equation that relates distance from home, in kilometres, to time travelled, in hours.

   c) The game starts at 7:45 P.M. Will they make it back to Toronto in time? If yes, how much spare time will Anil have to make it to the TV? If not, how late will he be? What assumptions must you make?

At 4:30 P.M.:

Toronto 240 km

At 7:00 P.M.:

Toronto 40 km

Extend

9. Two students are walking at constant speeds in front of two motion sensors.
   - Lucas starts at a distance of 6 m and, after 10 s, he is 1 m away from his sensor.
   - Myrna starts at a distance of 2 m and, after 8 s, she is 6 m from her sensor.

   a) Find a distance-time equation for each walker.

   b) At what time were they at the same distance from their sensors?

   c) At what distance did this occur?

   d) Explain how you solved parts b) and c).

10. Refer to question 9.

   a) Graph both linear relations on the same grid.

   b) Identify the point where the two lines cross. This is called the point of intersection. What are the coordinates of this point?

   c) Compare this point to your answers to question 9, parts b) and c). Explain what you notice.

6.7 Linear Systems

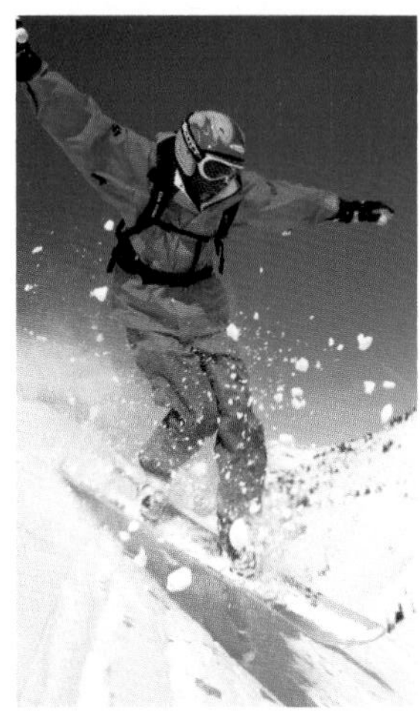

Mike wants to join a ski club for the winter season. He is considering the two options shown.

Which payment option should Mike choose?

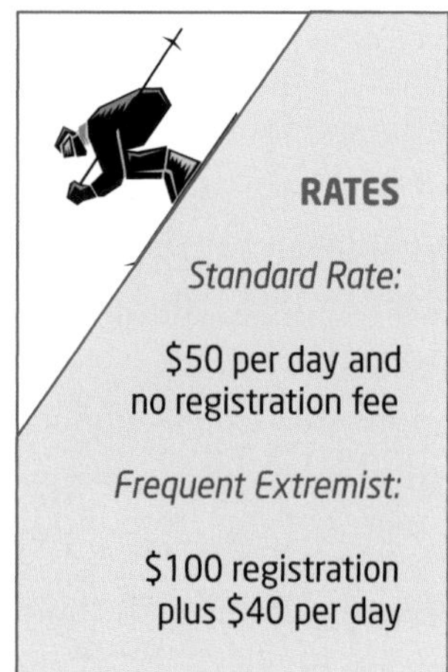

Investigate

Tools
- grid paper
- ruler

How can you use a linear system to solve problems?

Refer to the information above.

1. a) Write an equation that relates the total cost, C, in dollars, and the number of days, n, that Mike goes skiing if he chooses the Standard Rate.

b) Is this a direct or a partial variation? Explain how you know.

2. Repeat step 1 for the Frequent Extremist option.

3. Graph both linear relations on the same grid. Use two different colours, one for each line. Clearly label each line with its equation. This combined graph illustrates a **linear system**.

linear system
- a set of two or more linear equations that are considered simultaneously (at the same time)

point of intersection
- the point where two or more lines cross

4. a) Look at the point where the two lines cross. This is called the **point of intersection**. What is the value of n at this point?

b) Look to the left of the point of intersection. Which plan is cheaper? Explain how you know.

c) Look to the right of the point of intersection. Which plan is cheaper? Explain how you know.

d) Find the cost of both plans at the point of intersection. What does this mean?

5. Reflect Is one of the two payment options clearly better than the other? Explain what additional information a skier or snowboarder needs to know to choose between the two.

A solution to a linear system of two equations is a point or set of points that satisfy both equations. There are three different types of solutions:

- two parallel lines

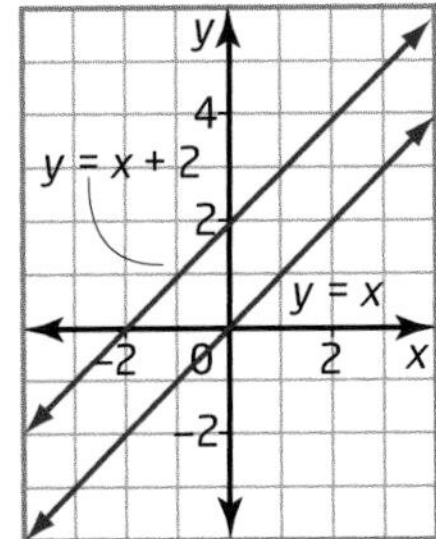

These lines never cross. There is no point that satisfies both equations. There is no solution.

- two non-parallel lines

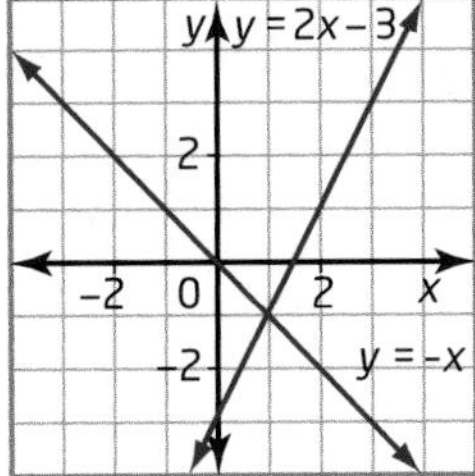

These lines intersect at one point: (1, −1). This is the only point that satisfies both equations. There is one solution.

- two identical lines

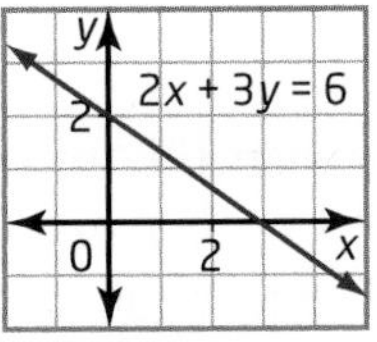

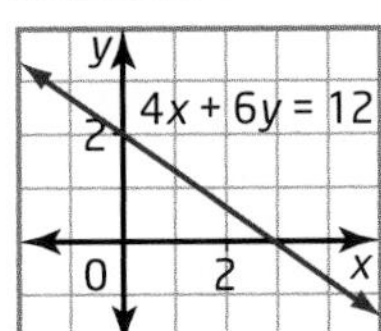

Although the equations look different, they describe the same line. All points on one line satisfy the equation of the other. There is an infinite number of solutions.

Example 1 Solve a Linear System Graphically

a) Graph the following lines on the same grid and identify the coordinates of the point of intersection.

$y = \frac{1}{2}x - 3$ and $x + y = -6$

b) Verify that your solution satisfies both equations.

Solution

a) The first equation is in slope y-intercept form: $y = \frac{1}{2}x - 3$.

The slope is $\frac{1}{2}$ and the y-intercept is -3. Use this information to graph the line.

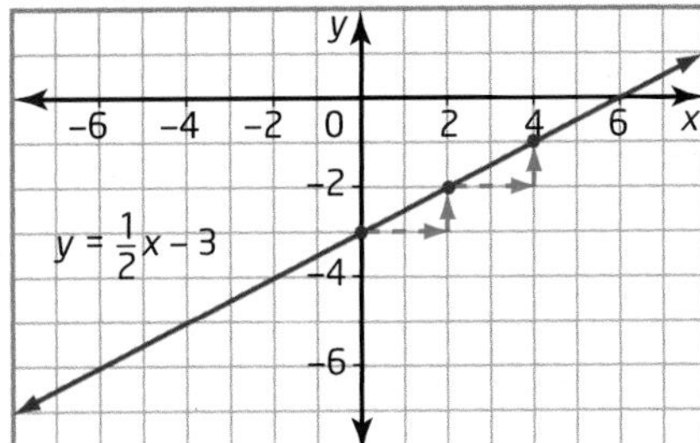

The form of the second equation makes it easy to determine its x- and y-intercepts and then use them to graph the line.

Find the x-intercept.
Substitute $y = 0$.

$$\begin{aligned} x + y &= -6 \\ x + (0) &= -6 \\ x &= -6 \end{aligned}$$

The x-intercept is -6.

Find the y-intercept
Substitute $x = 0$.

$$\begin{aligned} x + y &= -6 \\ (0) + y &= -6 \\ y &= -6 \end{aligned}$$

The y-intercept is -6.

Use the intercepts to graph this line on the same grid as the first line.

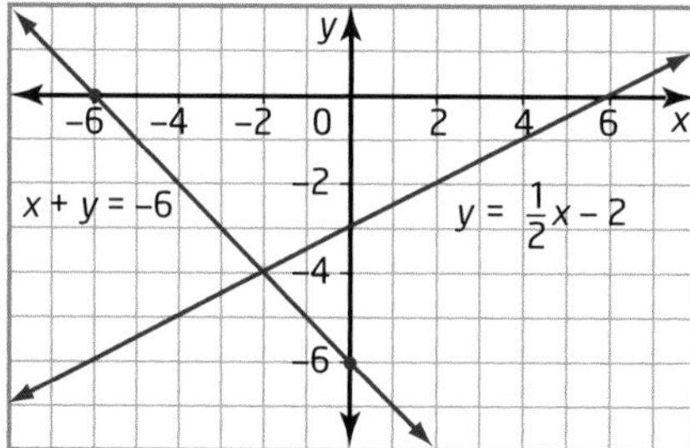

The two lines intersect at the point $(-2, -4)$. This is the solution to this linear system.

b) To verify the solution, $(-2, -4)$, substitute the coordinates into both equations and check that they hold true. Use the left side/right side (L.S./R.S.) method.

Check: $y = \frac{1}{2}x - 3$

$$\begin{aligned} \text{L.S.} &= y \\ &= -4 \end{aligned} \qquad \begin{aligned} \text{R.S.} &= \frac{1}{2}x - 3 \\ &= \frac{1}{2}(-2) - 3 \\ &= -1 - 3 \\ &= -4 \end{aligned}$$

L.S. = R.S.

Therefore, the point $(-2, -4)$ satisfies the equation $y = \frac{1}{2}x - 3$.

Check: $x + y = -6$

$$\begin{aligned} \text{L.S.} &= x - y \\ &= (-2) + (-4) \\ &= -6 \end{aligned} \qquad \text{R.S.} = -6$$

L.S. = R.S.

Therefore, the point $(-2, -4)$ satisfies the equation $x + y = -6$.

The point $(-2, -4)$ satisfies both equations. $(-2, -4)$ is the correct solution to the linear system.

Example 2 Solve a Linear System Using a Graphing Calculator

A couple has budgeted \$5000 for their wedding reception. Which hotel offers the better deal, and under what conditions?

Waverly Inn	Hotel Niagara
\$200 plus \$40 per guest	\$1000 plus \$30 per guest

Solution

Write an equation to model each cost, C, in dollars, as it relates to the number of guests, n.

Waverly Inn: $C = 40n + 200$
Hotel Niagara: $C = 30n + 1000$

Graph the linear system using a graphing calculator:

Enter each equation using Y=.
Use x and y instead of n and C.

```
Plot1 Plot2 Plot3
\Y1=40X+200
\Y2=30X+1000
\Y3=
\Y4=
\Y5=
\Y6=
\Y7=
```

Press WINDOW and enter the settings shown.

```
WINDOW
 Xmin=0
 Xmax=200
 Xscl=10
 Ymin=0
 Ymax=5000
 Yscl=250
 Xres=1
```

I only need to consider positive values. I'll start both axes at zero. A wedding might have about 200 guests or less, and the cost should be no greater than about \$5000. I'll try these as the x- and y-scale settings.

Press GRAPH to see the linear system.

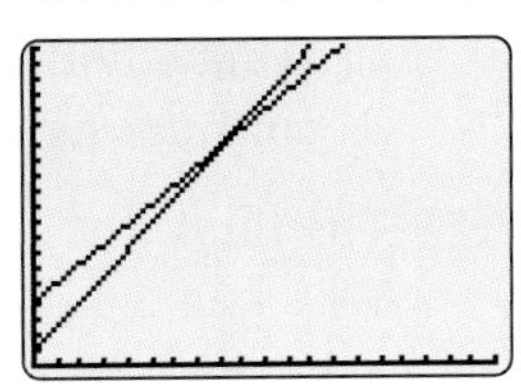

Press TRACE to read coordinates from one of the lines. Use the up and down cursor keys to switch from one line to the other.

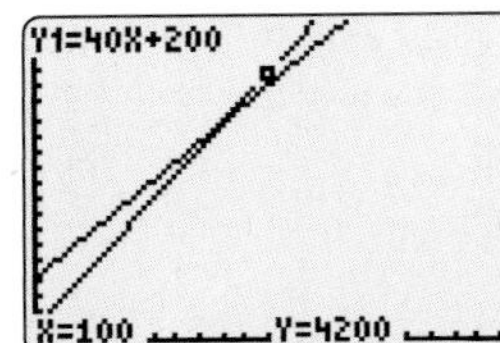

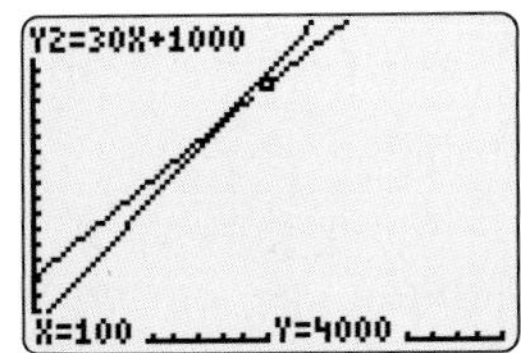

Use the left and right cursor keys to move along the graphs.
To accurately find the intersection point,

- press 2nd [CALC]
- select **5:intersect**

The calculator will prompt you three times: for the first curve, the second curve, and a guess for the intersection point. Press ENTER three times to respond.

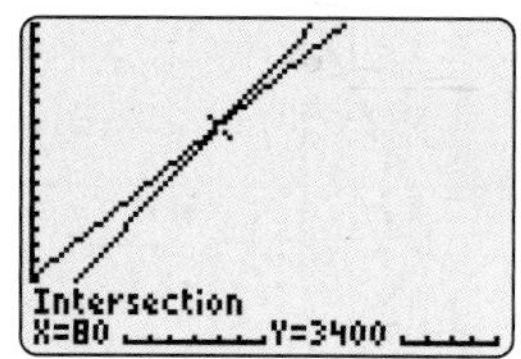

The two lines intersect at the point (80, 3400). At this point, Y1 and Y2 are equal. This means that if exactly 80 guests attend, the cost is the same at either hotel: $3400.

For $n < 80$ (less than 80 guests), Y1 is below Y2. This means that the cost at Waverly Inn is less than the cost at Hotel Niagara.

For $n > 80$ (more than 80 guests), the situation is reversed: Y2 is below Y1. In this case, Hotel Niagara is cheaper.

Key Concepts

- A linear system is two or more linear equations considered together.
- The solution of a linear system of two equations is the point at which their graphs intersect. The coordinates of a solution must satisfy both equations.

Communicate Your Understanding

C1 Refer to Example 2.

a) Which hotel costs less if 50 guests attend? How much less is it?

b) Which hotel costs less if 100 guests attend? How much less is it?

c) What advice would you give to a friend or relative that is considering holding a wedding at one of the two hotels?

C2 The lines $y = x - 2$ and $x + y = 6$ intersect at a point. Which is the point of intersection? Explain how you know.

A (3, 5) **B** (3, 3) **C** (2, 4) **D** (4, 2)

C3 Describe the steps you would use to find the solution to a linear system if you were given the two equations.

Practise

For help with questions 1 and 2, see Example 1.

1. Give the coordinates of the point of intersection of each linear system.

a)

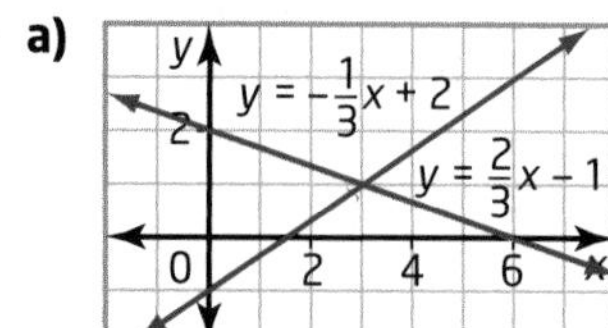

b)

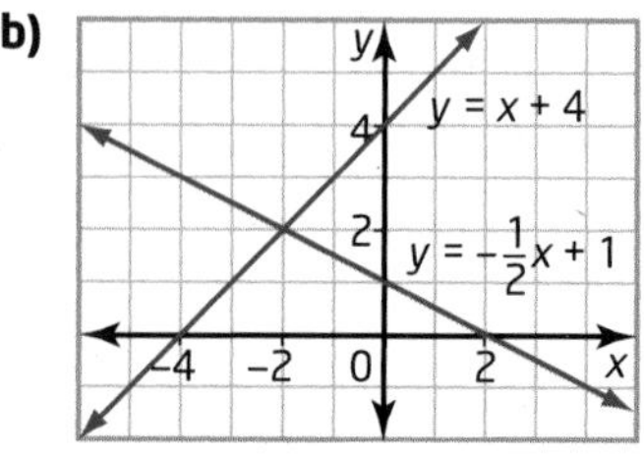

2. Solve each linear system. Verify each solution by substituting the coordinates of your solution into both equations.

a) $y = -x$ and $y = x - 6$

b) $x - y = 8$ and $x + 2y = 2$

c) $x + 2y = 7$ and $y = 4x - 10$

d) $y = -\frac{1}{2}x + \frac{9}{2}$ and $y = 3x - 6$

Connect and Apply

It is recommended that you use a graphing calculator or graphing software for some of these questions. See the Investigate to answer questions 3 to 5.

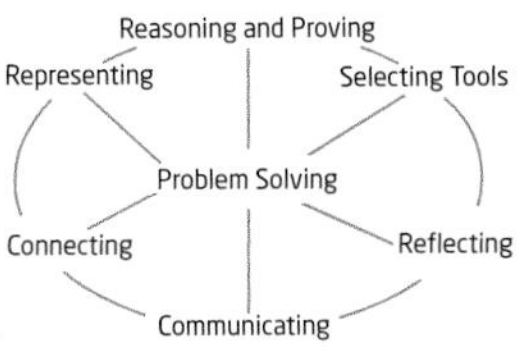

3. Suppose Mike went skiing six times over the winter season.

a) How much would it cost him
- under the Standard Rate option?
- under the Frequent Extremist option?

b) Which option should Mike choose in this case? Explain.

4. Suppose Mike went skiing 20 times over the winter season. Repeat question 3 for this scenario.

5. Is there a scenario in which it does not matter which option Mike chooses? If so, describe it, referring to the graph.

6. See Example 2. Suppose Hotel Niagara offers a special. Explain how this special may affect the couple's decision.

7. The Friendship Trail is a multi-use recreational trail that runs from Port Colborne to Fort Erie, a distance of 25 km. At 2 P.M., Debbie starts rollerblading from Port Colborne at 10 km/h. At the same time, Ken starts bicycling from Fort Erie at 20 km/h. When will they meet each other? How far from Fort Erie will they be at this time?

8. **Chapter Problem** An interesting, but unusual, feature of Jean's hometown is that two major east-west streets run parallel most of the time, but actually cross each other twice! How is this possible? Graph the following linear system and find the intersection point to discover the final two letters in the name of this city.

$x - y + 2 = 0$
$7x - 6y = 0$

9. Cersei and her brother Tyrion decide to race home. Cersei is a faster runner than Tyrion, so she gives him a head start. Their distance-time graphs are shown.

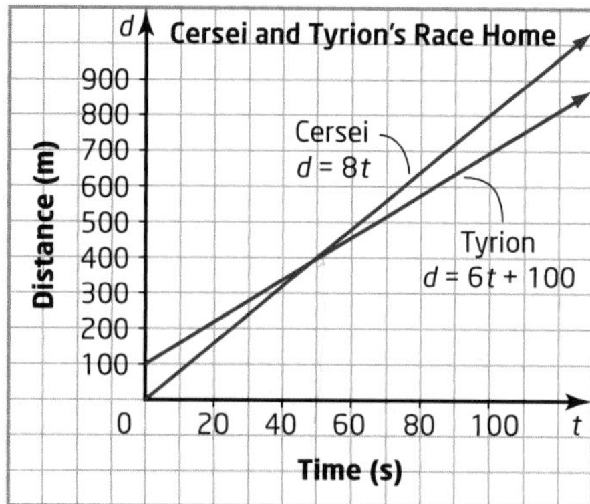

a) How much of a head start did Tyrion get?

b) How fast does Cersei run?

c) How fast does Tyrion run?

d) For what length of race will each runner win? For what length of race will they tie?

e) Explain the significance of the solution of this linear system.

10. Refer to question 9. How do your answers to part d) change if Tyrion's head start is

a) doubled?

b) cut in half?

Achievement Check

11. A recording artist is offered two deals for her fourth CD release:

- Royalty only: \$1 per CD sold
- Partial royalty: \$2000 plus \$0.50 per CD sold

a) Graph both linear relations on the same grid.

b) Find the solution to the linear system and explain what it means.

c) Sales figures for the artist's first three CDs are shown.

CD	Copies Sold
1	1500
2	3500
3	6000

Which deal do you think the artist should choose? Explain your reasoning.

Extend

12. Systems of equations can involve non-linear relations. Consider the population growth patterns of two towns since the turn of the century.

- Numberton has been growing steadily by 1000 every year, from an initial population of 25 000.
- Decimalville has been growing by 10% of its previous year's population every year, from an initial population of 15 000.

a) Copy and complete the table of values up to 15 years. Round to the nearest whole number if necessary.

Year	Numberton's Population	Decimalville's Population
0	25 000	15 000
1	26 000	16 500
2	27 000	18 150
3		

b) Graph population versus years for the towns on the same grid.

c) Classify each relation as linear or non-linear.

d) Identify the solution of this system, and explain what it means.

13. Math Contest Which is the point of intersection for the linear system $3x + 5y = 2$ and $x - 3y = 10$?

A $(4, 2)$

B $(4, -2)$

C $(-4, 2)$

D $(-4, -2)$

E $(2, -2)$

14. Math Contest Find the equation of the line that passes through the point of intersection of $-2x + 4y = 14$ and $5x - 3y = -14$, and that is perpendicular to $4x - 6y + 12 = 0$.

15. Math Contest

a) Find the point of intersection of the lines $3x + 5y = 7$ and $2x + 4y = 6$.

b) Now, find the point of intersection of $x + 5y = 9$ and $5x + 3y = 1$.

c) Investigate the point of intersection of the lines $ax + by = c$ and $dx + ey = f$, where a, b, c and d, e, f are both arithmetic sequences (an arithmetic sequence is a sequence with constant first differences). Write a summary of your findings.

Chapter 6 Review

6.1 The Equation of a Line in Slope y-Intercept Form: $y = mx + b$, pages 296–307

1. Identify the slope and the y-intercept of each line.

a)

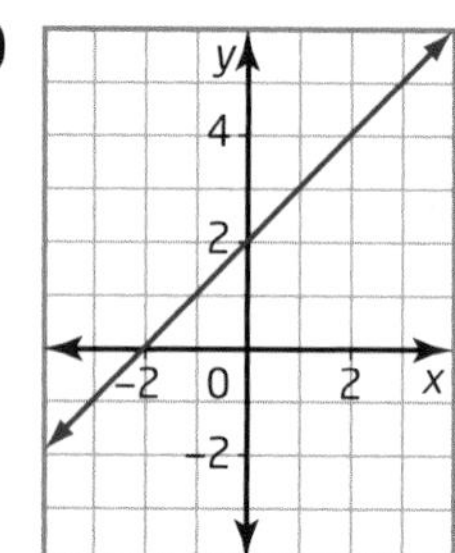

b)

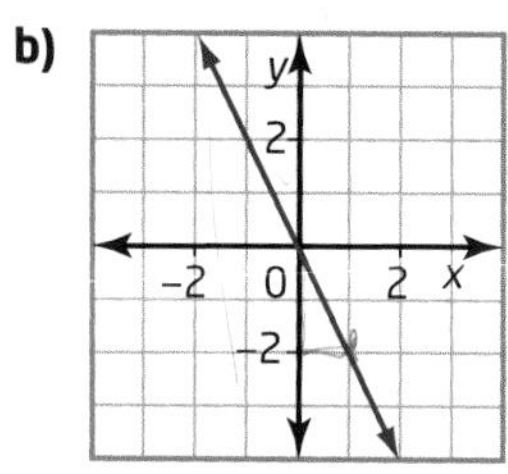

2. Identify the slope and the y-intercept of each line.

a) $y = -3x + 2$ **b)** $y = \frac{3}{5}x - 1$

3. Write the equation of a line with the given slope and y-intercept. Then, graph the line.

a) $m = -2, b = 3$

b) $m = \frac{2}{3}, b = -4$

c) $m = 0, b = 2$

4. The distance-time graph illustrates a person's movements in front of a motion sensor.

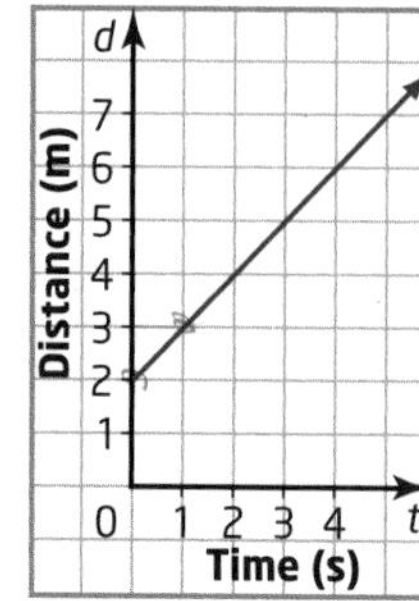

a) Identify the slope and the d-intercept. Explain what they mean.

b) Write an equation in the form $d = mt + b$ that describes the walker's motion.

6.2 The Equation of a Line in Standard Form: $Ax + By + C = 0$, pages 308–314

5. Rewrite each equation in the form $y = mx + b$.

a) $2x + y - 6 = 0$

b) $3x + 5y + 15 = 0$

6. A plumber charges according to the equation $60n - C + 90 = 0$, where C is the total charge, in dollars, for a house call, and n is the time, in hours, the job takes.

a) Rearrange the equation to express it in the form $C = mn + b$.

b) Identify the slope and the C-intercept and explain what they mean.

c) Graph the relation.

d) What would a 3-h house call cost?

6.3 Graph a Line Using Intercepts, pages 315–322

7. Determine the x- and y-intercepts of each line. Then, graph the line.

a) $3x - 4y = 12$

b) $6x - y = 9$

8. Cindy is at a baseball game with her younger brother, Mike. She has \$18 to spend on hamburgers and pop. Hamburgers cost \$3 each and pop cost \$2 each.

a) If Cindy buys only hamburgers, how many can she buy?

b) If she buys only pop, how many can she buy?

c) The equation $2x + 3y = 18$ can be used to model this problem. Graph this line. What other combinations can Cindy buy?

6.4 Parallel and Perpendicular Lines, pages 326–329

9. Explain how the slopes of parallel lines are related. Create an example to support your explanation.

10. Explain how the slopes of perpendicular lines are related. Create an example to support your explanation.

6.5 Find an Equation for a Line Given the Slope and a Point, pages 330–337

11. Find an equation for a line with a slope of $\frac{2}{3}$, passing through $(1, -4)$.

12. Find an equation for a line parallel to $3x - 4y = 12$, with an x-intercept of 6.

13. Find an equation for a line perpendicular to $y = 2x - 3$, passing through the origin.

14. An airplane must always carry a minimum amount of fuel, above what is needed for the flight. Seth's plane burns fuel at a constant rate of 32 L/h. For a 2-h flight, Seth has to carry 88 L of fuel.

a) What is the minimum amount of extra fuel that Seth must carry in his plane at all times?

b) Write an equation that relates the amount of fuel, in litres, required versus the trip length, in hours.

c) The fuel tank in Seth's plane has a capacity of 160 L. How long can he fly before having to refuel?

d) If Seth tunes up his plane, the fuel burn rate reduces to 24 L/h. How does this change your answers to parts b) and c)?

6.6 Find the Equation of a Line Given Two Points, pages 338–343

15. Find an equation for a line passing through $(-2, 5)$ and $(3, -5)$.

16. Claudia is walking at a constant speed in front of a motion sensor. After 1 s, she is 2.5 m from the sensor. 2 s later, she is 4.0 m from the sensor.

a) Find the equation in the form $d = mt + b$ that describes her motion.

b) Determine the slope and the d-intercept and explain what they mean.

c) How far will Claudia be from the sensor 5 s after she begins walking?

6.7 Linear Systems, pages 344–351

17. a) Solve the following linear system:

$$y = \frac{1}{3}x - 2$$

$$y = -x - 6$$

b) Check that the solution is correct by substituting into both equations.

18. Two tutors charge according to the following equations, relating the tutoring charge, C, in dollars, to the time, t, in hours:

- Mr. Wellington: $C = 40t$
- Ms. Tenshu: $C = 35t + 20$

a) Solve the linear system and explain what the solution means.

b) Under what conditions should a student hire either tutor? Explain any assumptions you must make.

Chapter 6 Practice Test

Multiple Choice

For questions 1 to 5, select the best answer.

1. Which are the slope and the y-intercept of the line $y = -3x - 1$?

A $m = 3, b = 1$

B $m = -3, b = 1$

C $m = -3, b = -1$

D $m = \frac{1}{3}, b = -1$

2. What are the x- and y-intercepts of the line?

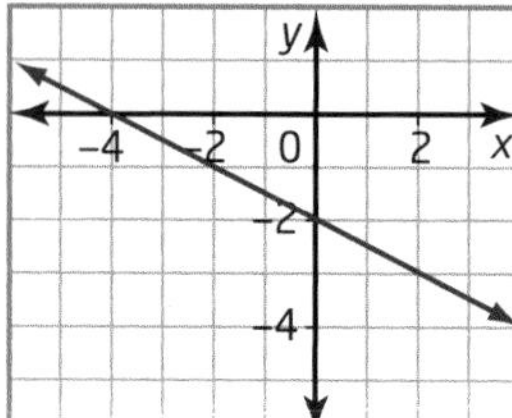

A x-intercept $= 2$, y-intercept $= 4$

B x-intercept $= -2$, y-intercept $= -4$

C x-intercept $= -4$, y-intercept $= 2$

D x-intercept $= -4$, y-intercept $= -2$

3. Which line is parallel to the line $y = \frac{1}{5}x - 1$?

A $y = -\frac{1}{5}x - 1$ **B** $y = \frac{1}{5}x + 3$

C $y = 5x + 1$ **D** $y = -5x - 4$

4. Which line is perpendicular to the line $y = \frac{3}{2}x - 1$?

A $y = \frac{2}{3}x + 1$ **B** $y = -\frac{2}{3}x + 4$

C $y = \frac{3}{2}x - 3$ **D** $y = -\frac{3}{2}x - 1$

5. Which is a solution to the linear system?

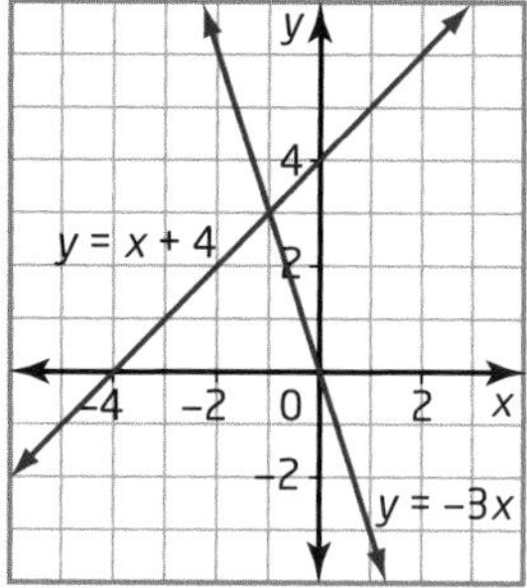

A $(-1, 3)$

B $(-4, 0)$

C $(0, 4)$

D $(3, -1)$

Short Response

Show all steps in your solutions.

6. The distance-time graph of a person walking at a constant speed in front of a motion sensor is shown.

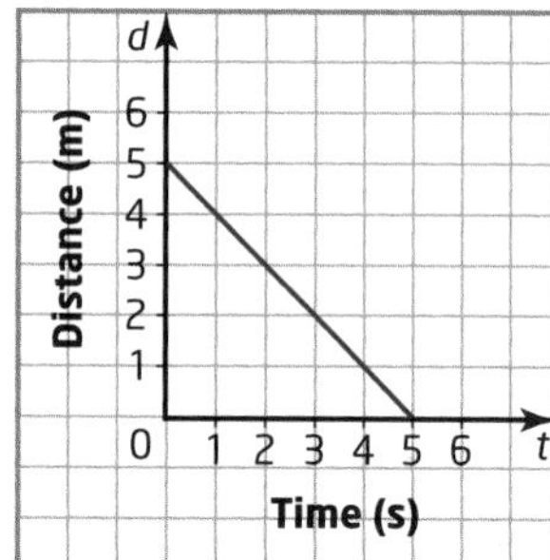

a) How far from the motion sensor was the person when she began walking?

b) Was she moving toward or away from the sensor? Explain how you know.

c) How fast was she walking?

d) Write an equation that describes this distance-time relationship.

7. a) What are the x- and y-intercepts of the line $3x - y = 6$?

b) Use this information to graph the line.

8. An electrician charges according to the equation $75n - C + 60 = 0$, where C is the total charge, in dollars, for a house call, and n is the time, in hours, the job takes.

a) Rearrange this equation to express it in the form $C = mn + b$.

b) Identify the slope and the C-intercept and explain what they mean.

c) Graph the relation.

d) What would a 2-h house call cost?

9. Find an equation for a line with a slope of $\frac{2}{3}$ that passes through the point (4, −1).

10. Find an equation for a line passing through the points (−3, −4) and (6, 8).

11. You can use the formula $L = 3.8G$ to obtain an approximate value for converting a volume in U.S. gallons, G, to a volume in litres, L.

a) Use the formula to find the number of litres in
- 0.5 gallons
- 1 pint (1 pint = 0.125 gallons)

b) Rearrange the formula to express G in terms of L.

c) How many gallons are in
- 4 L?
- 250 mL?

Extended Response

Provide complete solutions.

12. Find an equation for a line that is perpendicular to $2x - 3y + 6 = 0$ and has the same x-intercept as $3x + 7y + 9 = 0$.

13. A video rental company has two monthly plans:
- Plan A: $40 for unlimited rentals
- Plan B: $10 plus $3 per video

a) Graph this linear system and find the solution.

b) Explain the conditions under which each plan is better.

14. Tess is flying an airplane from Wainfleet to her cottage at a constant speed. She takes off at noon and passes St. Catharines at 12:15. Tess knows that St. Catharines is 40 km from Wainfleet.

a) How fast is Tess's airplane flying, in kilometres per hour?

b) Write an equation relating distance travelled to flight time.

c) Assuming Tess continues on a straight path, at what time will she arrive at her cottage, which is 360 km due north of St. Catharines?

Chapter Problem Wrap-Up

By now you should have all eight letters in the name of Jean's home city. All you need to do is unscramble them.

Create a problem like this one based on the name of your city or town. Or, if you prefer, pick a city or town of a friend or relative. Then, trade problems with a classmate and try to discover each other's mystery location. Happy math-caching!

Chapters 4 to 6 Review

Chapter 4 Equations

1. Solve each equation.

a) $x - 2 = -5$ **b)** $\frac{y}{6} = -7$

c) $9 + w = 13$ **d)** $8s = 32$

e) $4n + 9 = 25$ **f)** $16 - 5r = -14$

2. Find the root of each equation. Check each root.

a) $5x - 8 = 2x + 7$

b) $-2y - 7 = 4y + 11$

c) $4(3w + 2) = w - 14$

d) $3 - 2(s - 1) = 13 + 6s$

e) $2(n + 9) = -6(2n - 5) + 8$

f) $5(4k - 3) - 5k = 10 + 2(3k + 1)$

3. An isosceles triangle and a square have the same perimeter. Find the side lengths of the triangle.

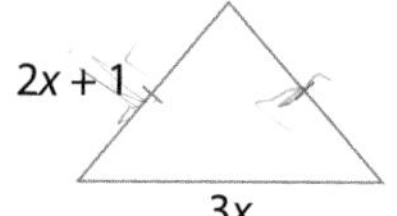

4. Find the solution to each equation. Check each solution.

a) $\frac{x + 6}{5} = -2$ **b)** $6 = \frac{2}{5}(n - 1)$

c) $\frac{y + 3}{2} = \frac{y - 4}{3}$

d) $\frac{1}{4}(k - 3) = \frac{1}{5}(k + 1)$

5. Rearrange each formula to isolate the variable indicated.

a) $A = P + I$, for P (investments)

b) $d = 2r$, for r (diameter of a circle)

c) $v = u + at$, for a (velocity)

d) $P = 2(l + w)$, for l (perimeter of a rectangle)

6. International basketball competitions are played on a rectangular court where the length is 2 m less than twice the width.

a) If the perimeter of the court is 86 m, what are the dimensions of the court?

b) Solve this problem using a different method.

c) Compare the methods. Describe one advantage and one disadvantage of each approach.

Chapter 5 Modelling With Graphs

7. Natalie's pay varies directly with the time she works. She earns $45 for 5 h.

a) Describe the relationship in words.

b) Write an equation relating her pay and the time worked. What does the constant of variation represent?

c) How much will Natalie earn for 9 h worked?

8. The table shows the cost, C, in dollars, to rent a car for a day and drive a distance, d, in kilometres.

Distance, d (km)	Cost, C ($)
0	50
100	65
200	80
300	95
400	110

a) What is the fixed cost?

b) What is the variable cost? Explain how you found this.

c) Write an equation relating C and d.

d) What is the cost of renting a car for a day and driving 750 km?

9. Find the slope of each line segment.

a) AB **b)** CD
c) EF **d)** GH

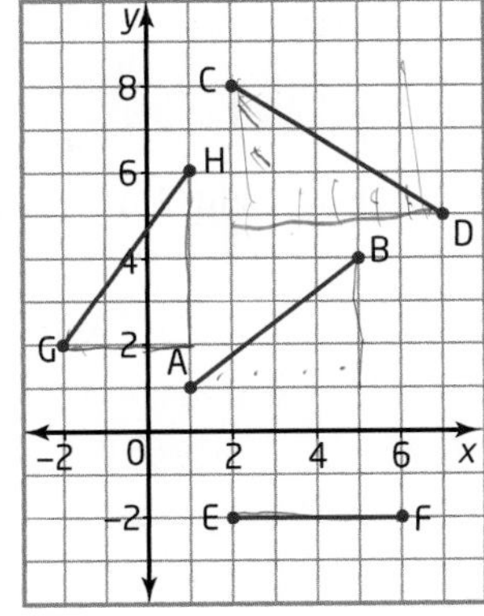

10. A racehorse can run 6 km in 5 min.

a) Calculate the rate of change of the horse's distance.

b) Graph the horse's distance as it relates to time.

c) Explain the meaning of the rate of change and how it relates to the graph.

11. Copy each table and include a third column to record first differences. Classify each relation as linear or non-linear.

a)

x	y
0	5
1	7
2	9
3	11
4	13

b)

x	y
0	-4
2	-2
4	2
6	8
8	16

12. Use the rule of four to represent this relation in three other ways.

x	y
0	4
5	8
10	12
15	16
20	20

a) Use a graph.

b) Use words.

c) Use an equation.

Chapter 6 Analyse Linear Relations

13. For each line,
- identify the slope and the y-intercept
- write the equation of the line in slope y-intercept form

a)

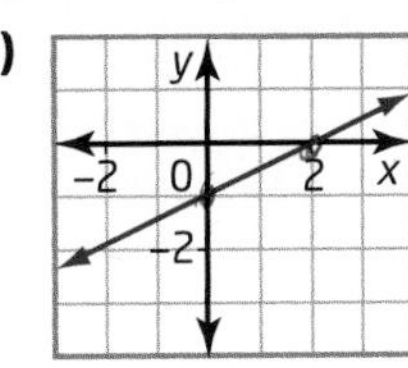

b)

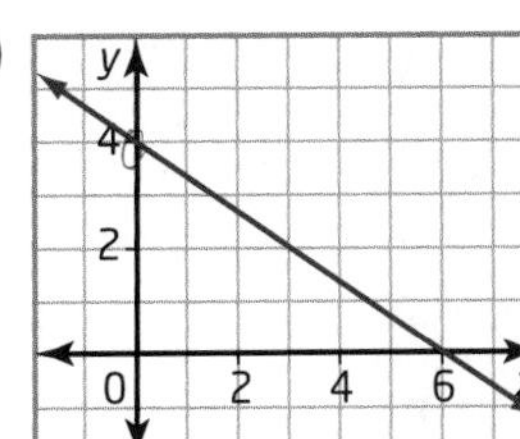

14. a) Rearrange $3x - 4y + 8 = 0$ into the form $y = mx + b$.

b) Identify the slope and the y-intercept.

c) Use this information to graph the line.

15. For each linear relation, determine the x- and y-intercepts and graph the line.

a) $3x - y = 6$ **b)** $-2x + 5y = 15$

16. Classify each pair of lines as parallel, perpendicular, or neither. Justify your answers.

a) $y = 2x + 5$ $\quad y = -\frac{1}{2}x - 2$

b) $y = -3x + 2$ $\quad y = -3x - 8$

c) $y = \frac{3}{4}x + 2$ $\quad y = \frac{4}{3}x - 2$

d) $y = 3$ $\quad x = -2$

17. Find an equation for the line passing through each pair of points.

a) A(3, 2) and B(6, 3)

b) C(−2, 3) and D(1, −3)

18. An online music download site offers two monthly plans:
- Plan A: \$10 plus \$1 per download
- Plan B: \$1.50 per download

a) Graph this linear system and find the solution.

b) Explain the conditions under which each plan is better.

Tasks

Salary and Commission

Part A

Carmella works 37.5 h per week for Century Home selling electronics equipment. She earns a base salary of \$12/h and receives a commission of 5¢ for every dollar of sales she makes.

a) What is Carmella's weekly base salary?

b) Copy and complete the table showing weekly sales, commission, and total salary.

Weekly Sales (\$)	Commission (\$)	Total Salary (\$)
0	0	
1000	50	
2000		
3000		
4000		

c) Graph Carmella's total salary, T, versus her weekly sales, S. What type of relation is this?

d) What is the equation of the relation?

e) What is the slope of the relation? What does the slope represent?

f) What is the T-intercept of the relation? What does it represent?

Part B

Carmella's friends Maria and Sam work for two other electronics equipment stores, Better Purchase and Transistor City. They also work 37.5 h per week. Maria earns \$8/h with 10% commission. Sam earns \$18/h with no commission.

a) One week, Carmella and Sam earned the same total salary. Determine each person's total sales and salary.

b) Another week, Sam earned more than Carmella but less than Maria. What could each person's total sales have been?

c) Each of the three friends sells about \$5000 worth of equipment each week. Which person seems to have the best-paid job? Justify your answer mathematically.

Cod Fish Catches

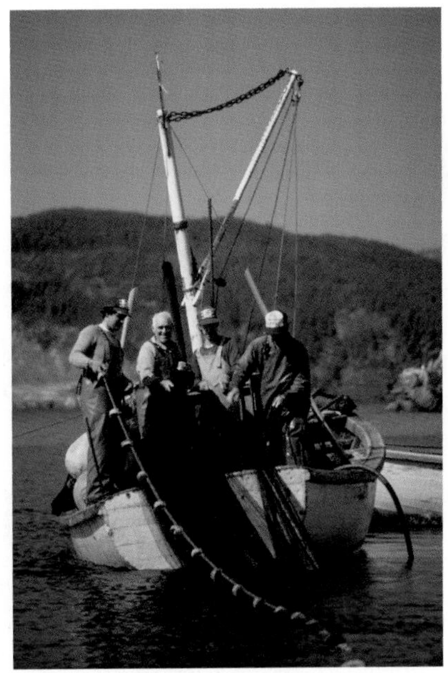

The Grand Banks, off the east coast of Canada, was the best cod-fishing area in the world. Cod was the favourite fish to catch because of its taste, abundance, and predictable life cycle. Cod was frequently used for making fish and chips, a very popular meal in Europe and Canada. Overfishing by Canadian and international fleets devastated the cod stocks, so the Canadian government closed the cod-fishing industry. Unfortunately, the closure has not yet resulted in a significant increase in cod stocks.

The tables show the amount of cod, in millions of kilograms, that was caught by Canadians during two time periods of the last century.

Year	Amount of Cod Fished (millions of kg)
1950	114
1951	103
1952	283
1953	241
1954	291
1955	263
1956	297

Year	Amount of Cod Fished (millions of kg)
1969	114
1970	220
1971	204
1972	183
1973	148
1974	131
1975	120

a) Graph each set of data.

b) Describe the shapes of the graphs and discuss possible reasons why each graph has this shape.

c) Research and discuss why there was a huge increase in the amount of cod caught in the years 1952 to 1956.

d) What happened to the amount of cod from 1969 to 1975? Justify your answer using mathematical terminology.

e) Draw a line of best fit for each set of data. What does the slope of the graph represent in each case?

CHAPTER

7

Geometric Relationships

These two radar towers contain a variety of geometric shapes. In this chapter, you will explore some of the relationships of common geometric shapes. You will also learn to apply the properties of these shapes to solve problems in design and construction.

Measurement and Geometry

- Determine and describe the properties and relationships of the interior and exterior angles of triangles, quadrilaterals, and other polygons, and apply the results.
- Determine and describe properties of polygons, and apply the results in problem solving.
- Pose questions about geometric relationships, investigate them, and present findings.
- Illustrate a statement about a geometric property by demonstrating the statement with multiple examples, or use a counter-example to disprove the statement.

Vocabulary

polygon
vertex
interior angle
exterior angle
ray
equiangular
adjacent
supplementary
transversal
congruent
convex polygon
concave polygon
pentagon
hexagon
heptagon
octagon
regular polygon
midpoint
median
bisect
right bisector
centroid
similar

Chapter Problem

Suppose you have a triangle cut out of cardboard. If you try to hold up the triangle using one finger, it will probably slip off. However, every object has a point where the weight balances on all sides. Describe how you can find this point on a flat triangular object.

Get Ready

Classify Triangles

Triangles can be classified using their side lengths or their angle measures.

scalene triangle
- no equal sides
- no equal angles

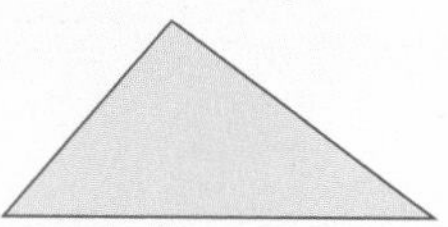

isosceles triangle
- two equal sides
- two equal angles

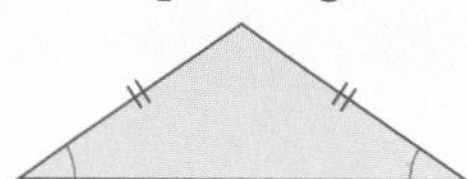

equilateral triangle
- three equal sides
- three equal angles

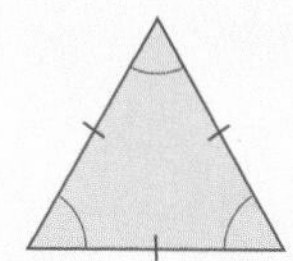

acute triangle
- three acute angles (less than 90°)

right triangle
- one right angle (90°)

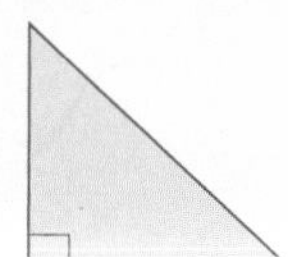

obtuse triangle
- one obtuse angle (between 90° and 180°)

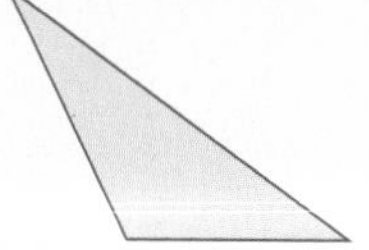

1. Classify each triangle using its side lengths.

a)

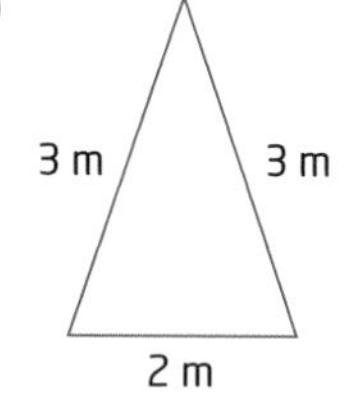

b)

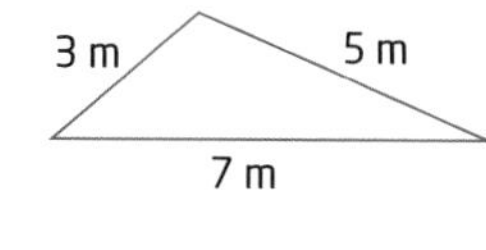

2. Classify each triangle in two ways using its angle measures.

a)

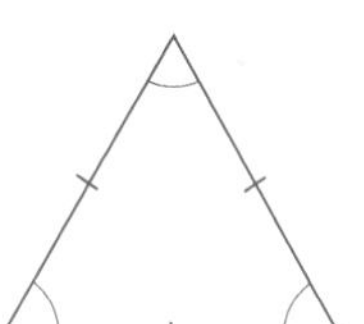

b)

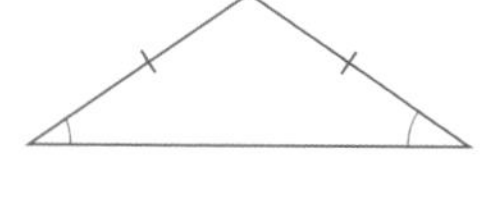

Classify Polygons

A **polygon** is a closed figure formed by three or more line segments.

A **regular polygon** has all sides equal and all angles equal.

Some quadrilaterals have special names. A regular quadrilateral is a **square**. An irregular quadrilateral may be a **rectangle**, a **rhombus**, a **parallelogram**, or a **trapezoid**.

Number of Sides	Name
3	triangle
4	quadrilateral
5	pentagon
6	hexagon

square

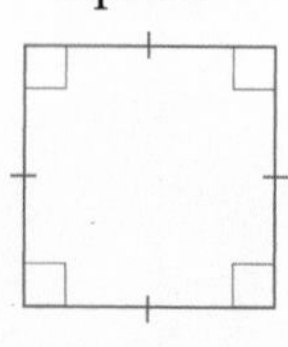

rhombus

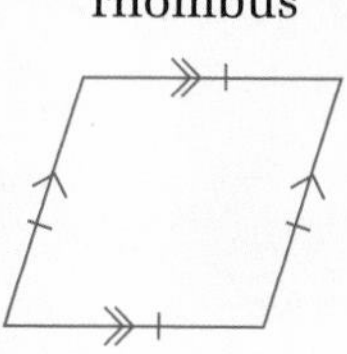

rectangle

parallelogram

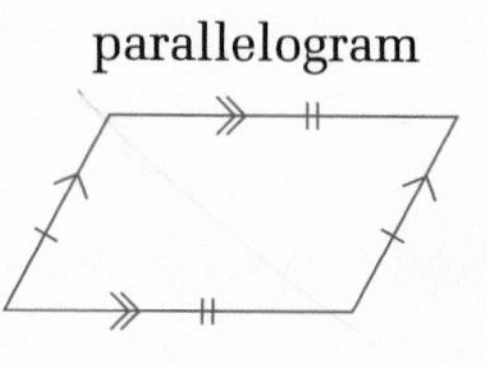

trapezoid

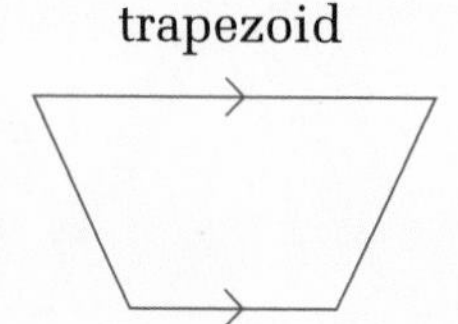

3. Classify each polygon according to its number of sides and whether it is regular or irregular.

a) 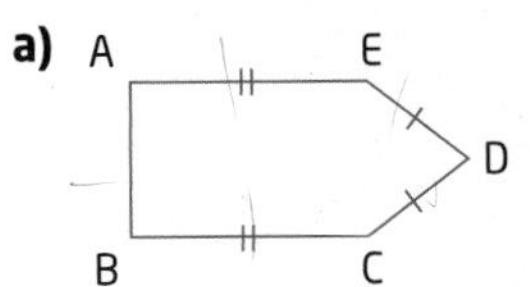

b) 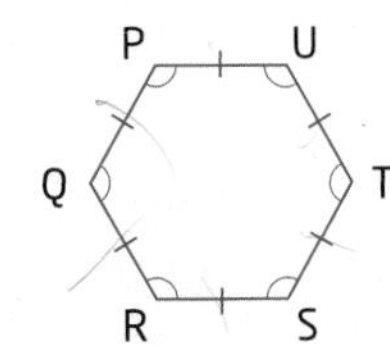

4. Classify each quadrilateral
for your answer.

a) 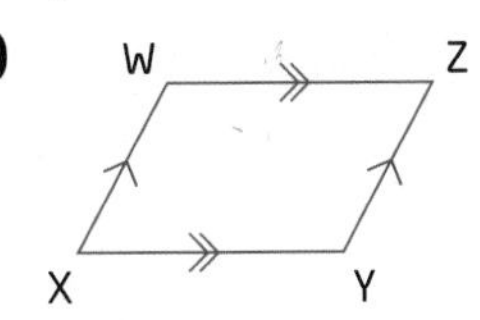

b) 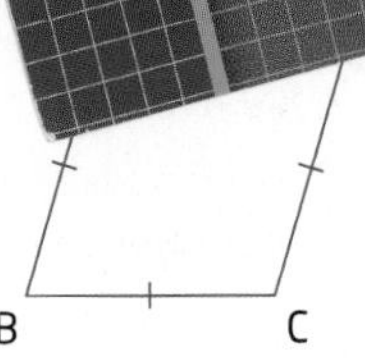

Angle Properties

When two lines intersect, the **opposite angles** are equal.

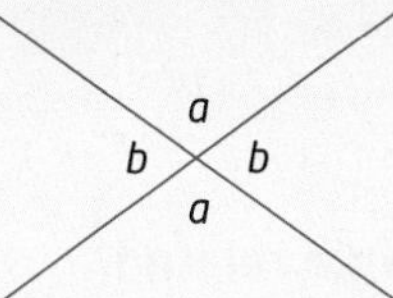

The sum of the interior angles of a triangle is 180°.

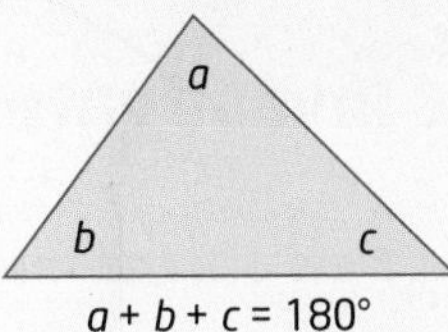

$a + b + c = 180°$

When a transversal crosses parallel lines, many pairs of angles are related.

alternate angles are equal

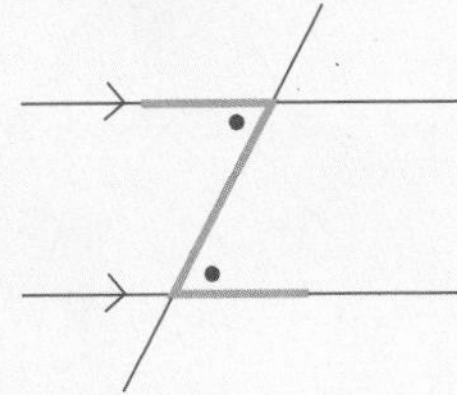

corresponding angles are equal

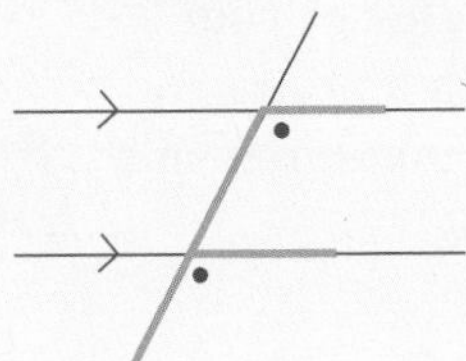

co-interior angles have a sum of 180°

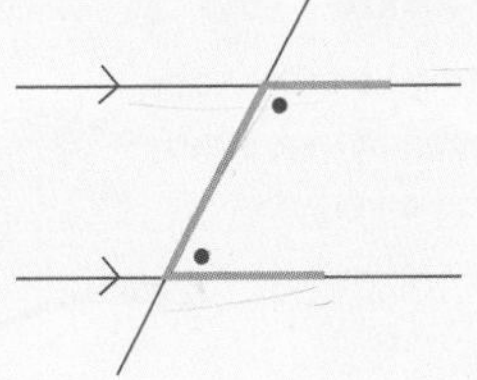

5. Find the measure of the third angle in each triangle.

a) 

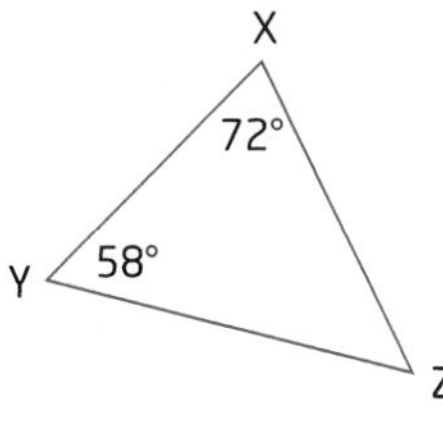

b) 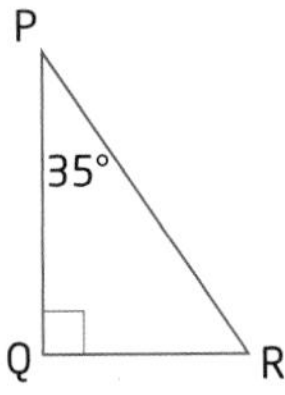

6. Find the measures of the angles a, b, and c. Give reasons for each answer.

a) 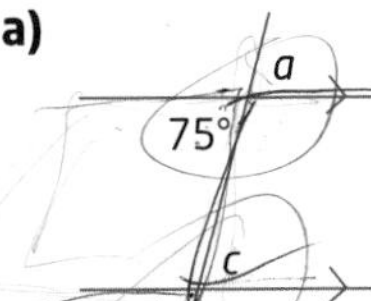

b) 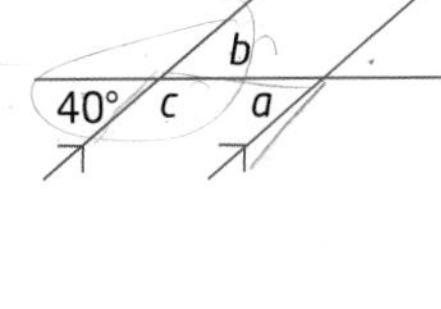

7.1 Angle Relationships in Triangles

The triangle is the simplest type of **polygon**. The structures of buildings and machines often contain triangles. Triangular shapes can be particularly strong and rigid since the shape of a triangle cannot change unless the length of a side changes. In this section, you will learn about some of the other properties of triangles.

polygon

- closed figure made up of line segments

Investigate

Tools

- ruler
- protractor

How are the interior and exterior angles of a triangle related?

Method 1: Use Pencil and Paper

1. Draw a large triangle. Label the first **vertex** A, the second one B, and the third one C.

vertex

- point where two or more sides meet

2. Measure each of the **interior angles** of your triangle with a protractor. Mark these measurements on your diagram.

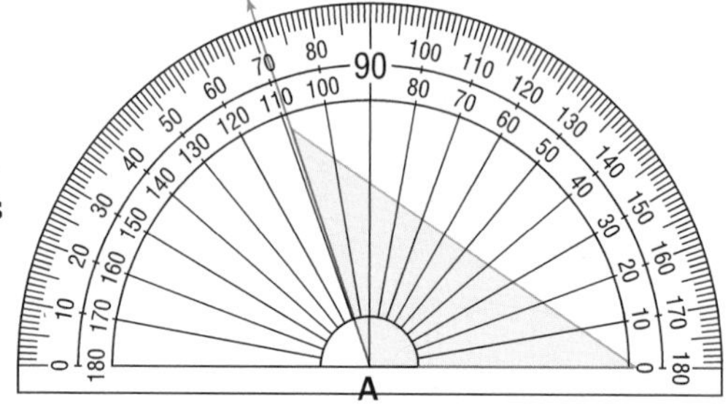

interior angle

- angle formed on the inside of a polygon by two sides meeting at a vertex

3. At each vertex, extend one side of the triangle to form an **exterior angle**. Measure each of these angles, and mark the measurements on your diagram.

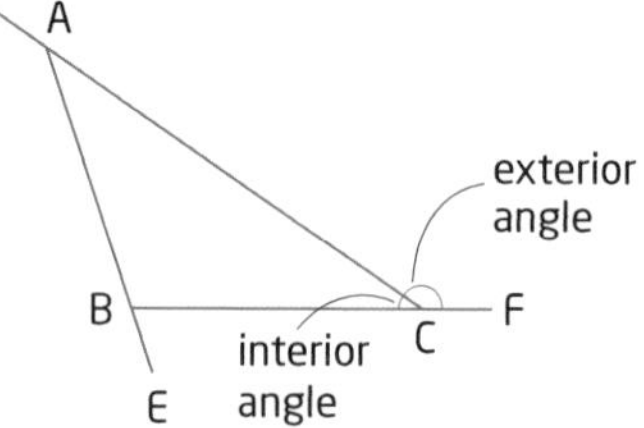

exterior angle

- angle formed on the outside of a geometric shape by extending one of the sides past a vertex

4. Find the sum of the exterior angles. Compare the sum you found to those calculated by your classmates.
5. **Reflect** Do you think the sum of the exterior angles is the same for every triangle? Explain your reasoning.
6. How are the exterior angle and the interior angle at a vertex related?

Literacy Connections

The plural of *vertex* is *vertices*. This plural form comes from Latin.

7. **Reflect**

   a) Describe the relationship between the exterior angle at a vertex of a triangle and the interior angles at the other two vertices.

   b) Will this relationship apply to the exterior angles of all triangles? Explain.

Method 2: Use *The Geometer's Sketchpad®*

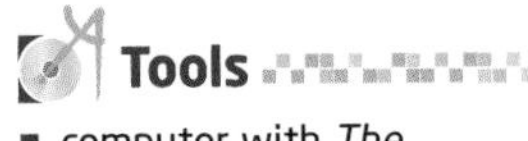

Tools

- computer with *The Geometer's Sketchpad®*

1. Turn on automatic labelling of points. From the **Edit** menu, choose **Preferences**. Click on the **Text** tab, check **For All New Points**, and click on **OK**.

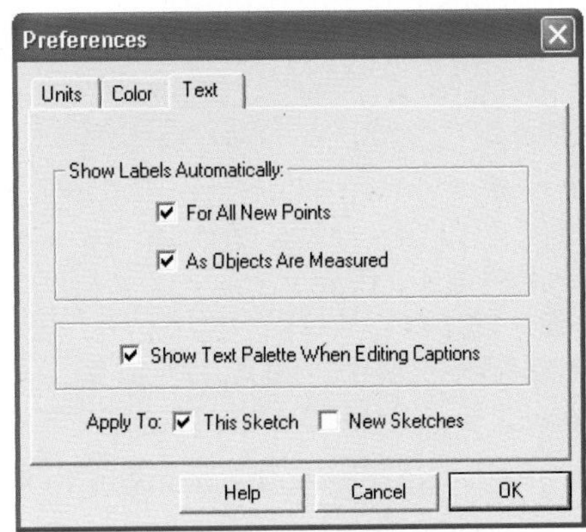

2. Use the **Point Tool** to create three points on the screen.

3. Select point A and point B. From the **Construct** menu, choose **Ray**. Use the same method to construct **rays** from B to C and from C to A.

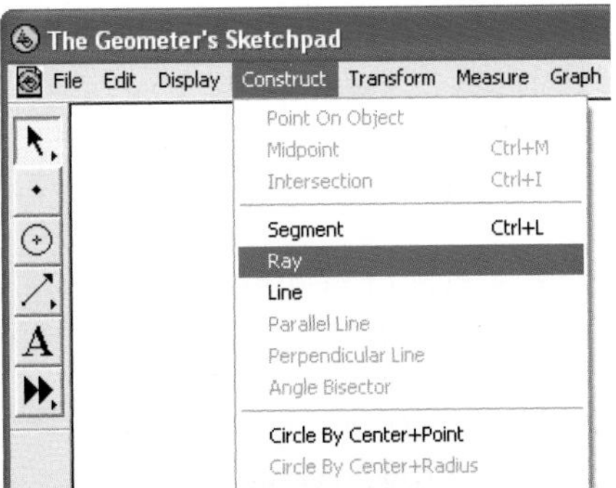

ray

- a part of a line with one endpoint

4. Select the three rays. From the **Construct** menu, choose **Points on Rays**. If necessary, drag each point to a location outside the triangle.

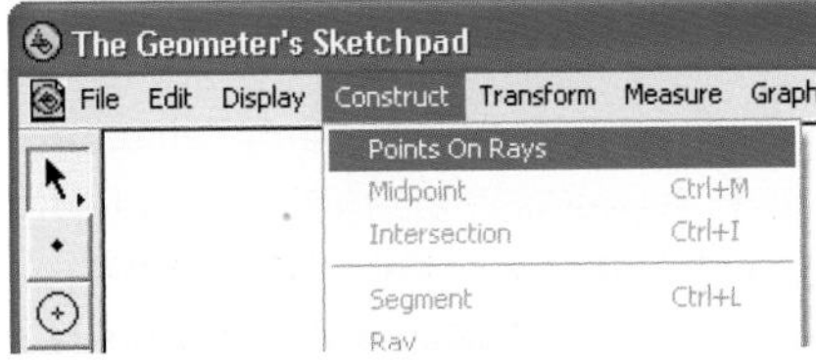

5. To measure ∠FAB, select points F, A, and B in that order. From the **Measure** menu, choose **Angle**. Measure ∠DBC and ∠ECA the same way.

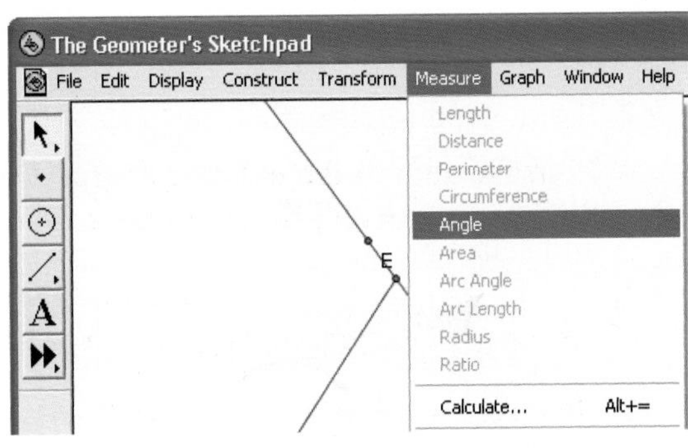

6. From the **Measure** menu, choose **Calculate**. A calculator window will appear. Click on the measure for ∠BAF. The measure will appear in the calculator window. Click (+) on the calculator; then, click on the measure for ∠DBC. Click (+) again, and add the measure of ∠ECA.

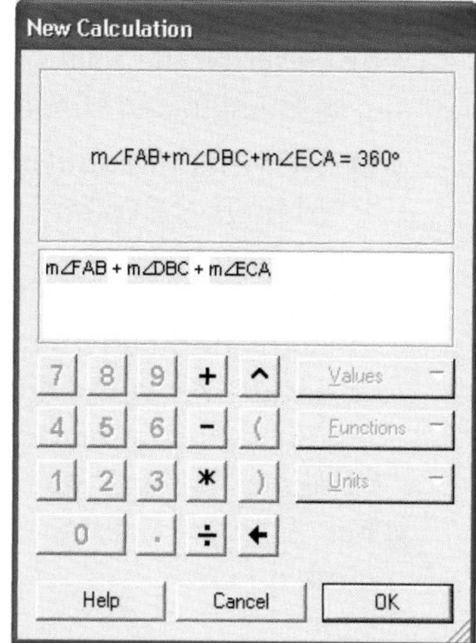

7. How are the exterior angle and the interior angle at a vertex related?

8. Make a hypothesis about the sum of the exterior angles in any triangle.

9. Drag one of the vertices around the screen. What happens to the sum of the exterior angles? Try moving the other two vertices as well.

10. **Reflect** What can you conclude about the sum of the exterior angles of any triangle? Do your observations support your hypothesis? Explain.

11. Make a hypothesis about the relationship between the exterior angle at a vertex of a triangle and the interior angles at the other two vertices.

12. Use the Measure and Calculate tools to test your hypothesis.

13. **Reflect** Is your hypothesis correct? Explain.

Method 3: Use a Graphing Calculator

Tools

- TI-83 Plus or TI-84 graphing calculator

1. Press (APPS) and select **CabriJr**. Press (ENTER) when the title screen appears.

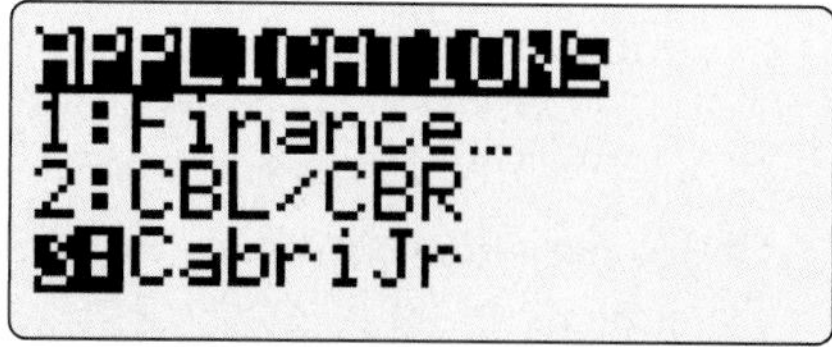

2. If you need to clear the screen, press (Y=) to display the **F1** menu, and select **New**.

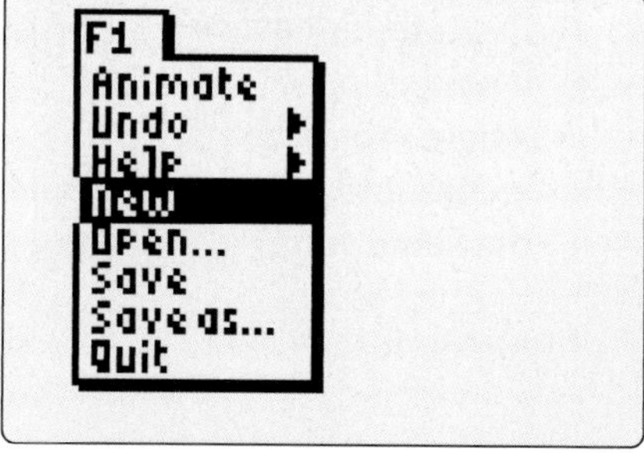

Technology Tip

The position of **CabriJr** on the **APPS** screen depends on what other applications have been installed.

You can download Cabri® Jr. by following the links at www.mcgrawhill.ca/links/principles9.

3. To draw a triangle, press WINDOW to display the **F2** menu, and select **Line**. Move the pencil cursor to where you want the first **vertex** and press ENTER. Move the cursor to the location for the second vertex and press ENTER twice. Position the third vertex in the same way. Then, move the cursor back to the first vertex and press ENTER again.

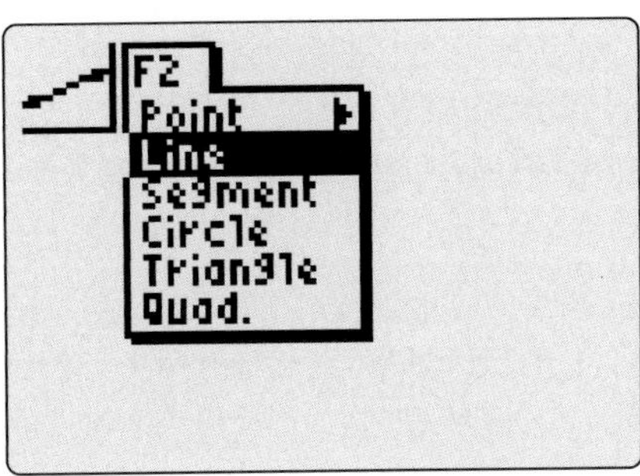

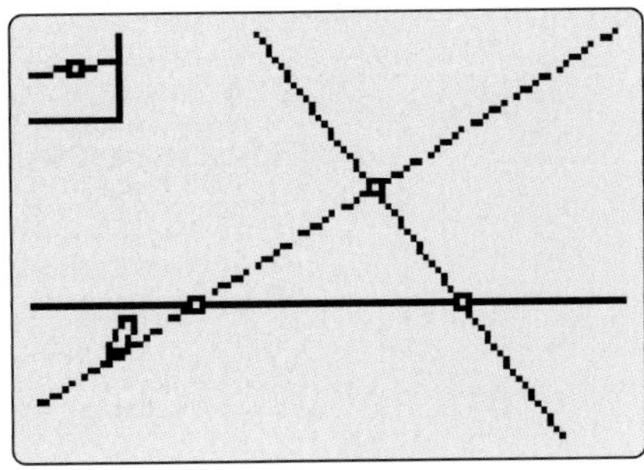

4. Press WINDOW to display the **F2** menu. With the cursor on **Point**, press ▸. Select **Point on** from the submenu. To place a point for an **exterior angle**, move the cursor onto the portion of a line outside the triangle and press ENTER. Place similar points on the other two lines.

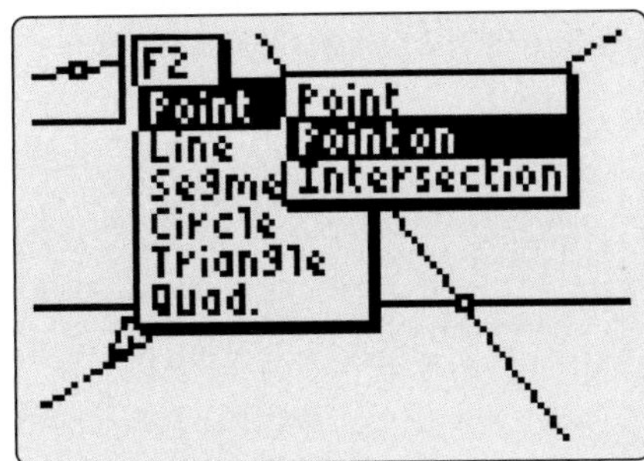

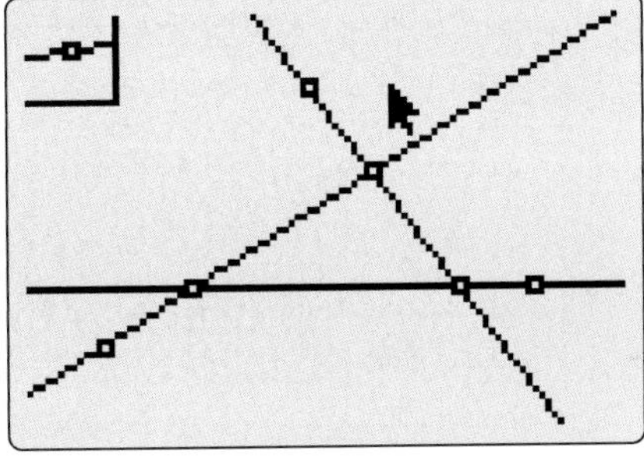

5. Press GRAPH to display the **F5** menu, and select **Alph-Num**. To label a point, move the cursor near the point and press ENTER ALPHA. Press the key for the letter you want; then, press ENTER to lock the label in place. To move the label, press CLEAR, and move the cursor close to the letter until it is underlined. Press ALPHA, use the cursor keys to drag the label to a new location, and press ENTER.

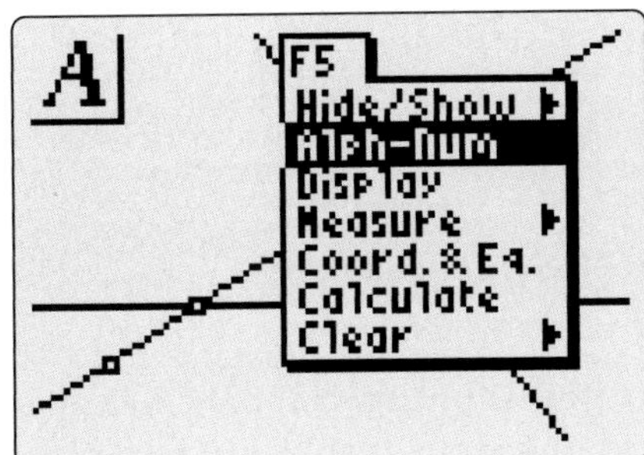

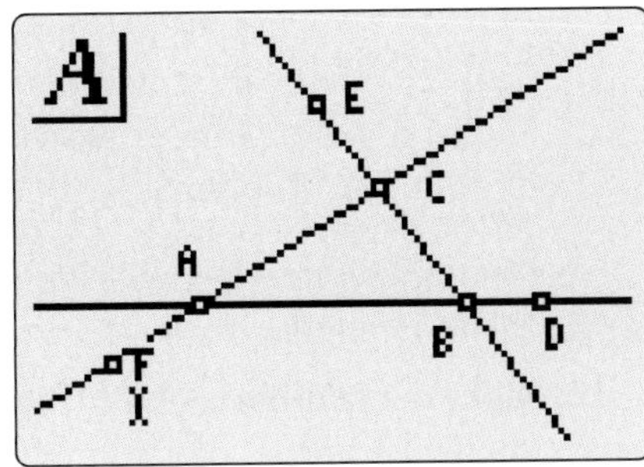

Technology Tip

In Cabri® Jr., you can use the keys directly under the screen as function keys without pressing ALPHA first.

6. To measure angles, press GRAPH to display the **F5** menu, highlight **Measure**, and press ▶. Select **Angle** from the submenu. Select the three points that define the angle in order (the vertex of the angle is the second point). To select each point, move the cursor to it and press ENTER. Use the cursor keys to drag the measurement to a convenient location and press ENTER. Measure the three exterior angles of the triangle.

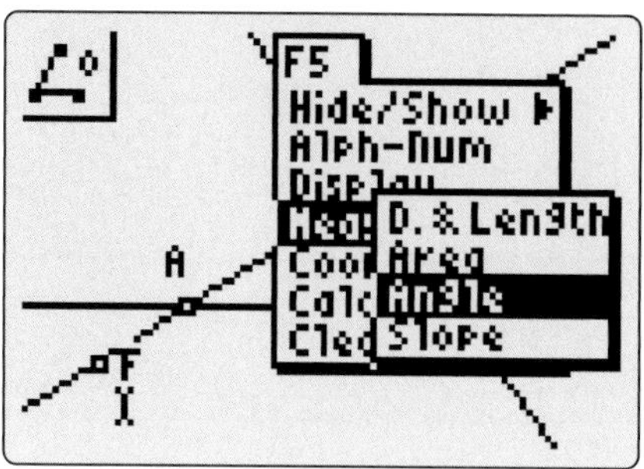

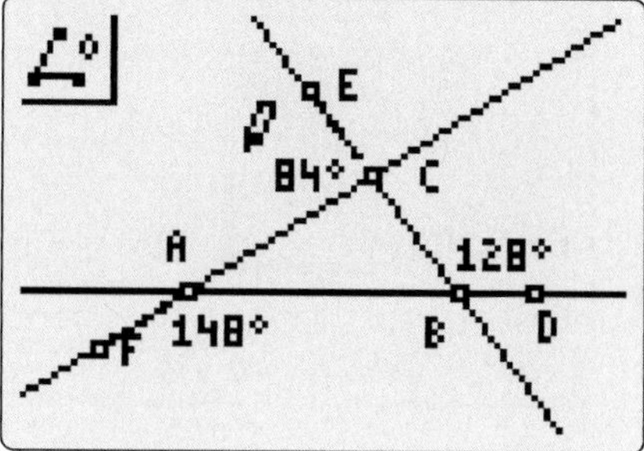

7. Find the sum of the three exterior angles. Press GRAPH to display the **F5** menu and select **Calculate**. Select each measurement by moving the cursor to it and pressing ENTER when the measurement is underlined. Then, press + and drag the total to an empty part of the screen.

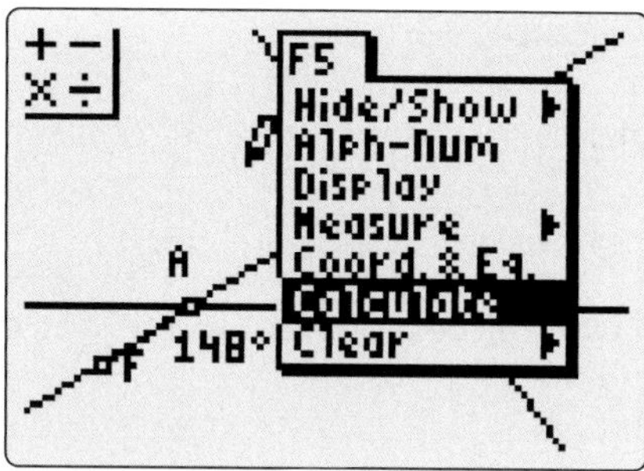

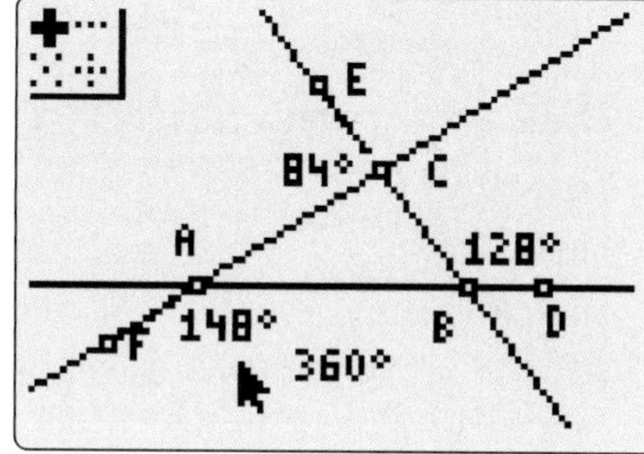

8. Make a hypothesis about the sum of the exterior angles of any triangle.

9. Press CLEAR and move the cursor to one of the vertices. When the vertex starts flashing, press ALPHA. Now, use the cursor keys to drag the vertex to various new locations. Watch the sum of the exterior angles as you move the vertex. Try moving the other two vertices as well.

10. **Reflect** What can you conclude about the sum of the exterior angles of any triangle? Do your observations support your hypothesis? Explain.

11. How are the exterior angle and the interior angle at a vertex related?

12. Make a hypothesis about the relationship between the exterior angle at a vertex of a triangle and the interior angles at the other two vertices.

13. Use Cabri® Jr. to test your hypothesis.

14. **Reflect** Is your hypothesis correct? Explain.

Example 1 Measures of the Exterior Angles of a Triangle

Find the measures of the exterior angles of $\triangle ABC$.

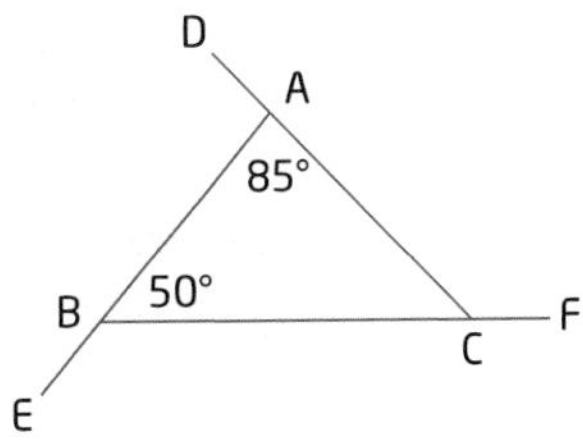

Solution

At vertex A and at vertex B, the interior and exterior angles together form a 180° angle.

$$\angle DAB + \angle CAB = 180°$$
$$\angle DAB = 180° - \angle CAB$$
$$\angle DAB = 180° - 85°$$
$$\angle DAB = 95°$$

$$\angle EBC + \angle ABC = 180°$$
$$\angle EBC = 180° - \angle ABC$$
$$\angle EBC = 180° - 50°$$
$$\angle EBC = 130°$$

There are two ways to use the properties of exterior angles to find the measure of $\angle ACF$.

Method 1

Since the exterior angle at a vertex of a triangle is equal to the sum of the interior angles at the other two vertices,

$$\angle ACF = \angle CAB + \angle ABC$$
$$= 85° + 50°$$
$$= 135°$$

Method 2

Since the sum of the exterior angles of a triangle is 360°,

$$\angle ACF + \angle DAB + \angle EBC = 360°$$
$$\angle ACF = 360° - \angle DAB - \angle EBC$$
$$\angle ACF = 360° - 95° - 130°$$
$$\angle ACF = 135°$$

The measures of the three exterior angles are $\angle DAB = 95°$, $\angle EBC = 130°$, and $\angle ACF = 135°$.

Literacy Connections

In angle names with three letters, the middle letter is always the vertex of the angle.

Example 2 Exterior Angles of an Equilateral Triangle

What is the measure of each exterior angle of an equilateral triangle?

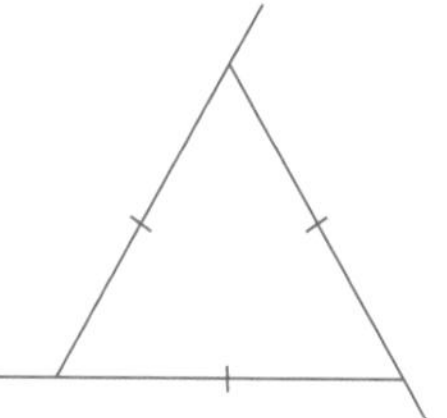

Solution

Method 1: Calculate the Measure of the Interior Angles First

equiangular

- having all angles equal

An equilateral triangle is also **equiangular**. The sum of the interior angles of any triangle is 180°. Since the three interior angles are equal, each one must measure $\frac{180°}{3}$ or 60°.

At each vertex, the interior angle and the exterior angle together make a 180° angle.

Therefore, the measure of each exterior angle is 180° − 60° or 120°.

You get the same result by using the property that each exterior angle is equal to the sum of the interior angles at the other two vertices.

Method 2: Apply the Properties of Exterior Angles

At each vertex, the interior angle and the exterior angle together make a 180° angle. Since the interior angles are equal, the three exterior angles must also be equal.

The sum of the exterior angles is 360°. Therefore, each exterior angle of an equilateral triangle must measure $\frac{360°}{3}$ or 120°.

Key Concepts

- The sum of the exterior angles of a triangle is 360°.

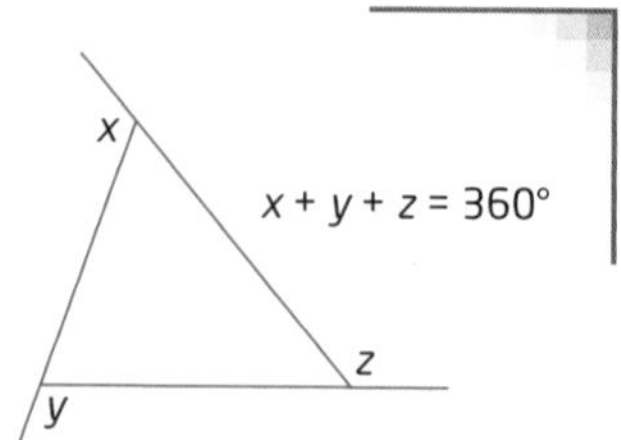

- The exterior angle at each vertex of a triangle is equal to the sum of the interior angles at the other two vertices.

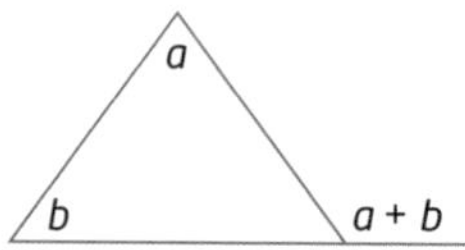

Communicate Your Understanding

C1 Find the measure of the exterior angle at vertex X. Explain your reasoning.

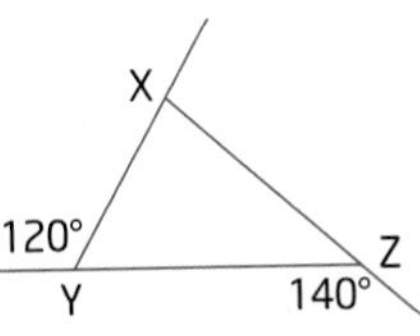

C2 Helena says this exterior angle measures 110°. Is she right? Explain.

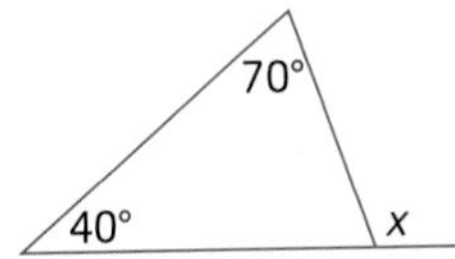

Practise

For help with questions 1 to 3, see Example 1.

1. Find the measure of each exterior angle.

a)

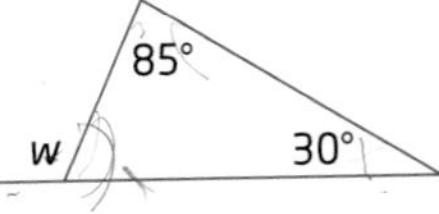

b)

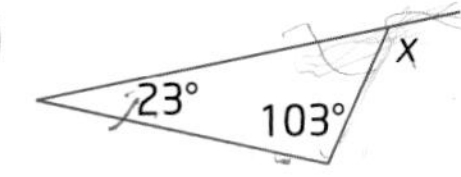

c)

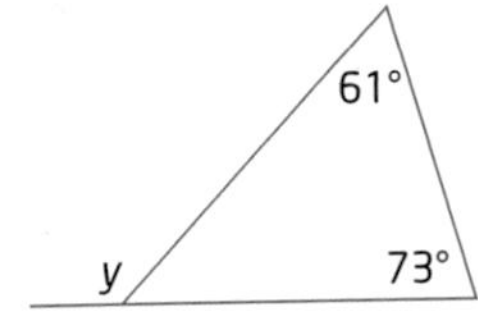

d)

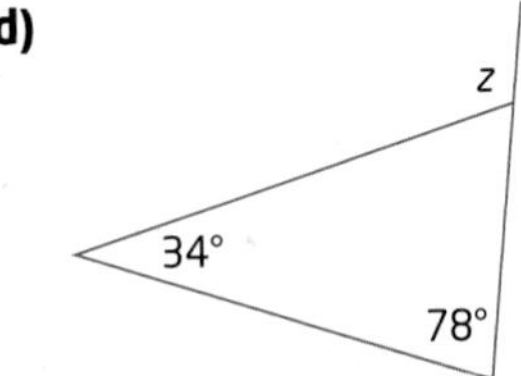

2. Find the measure of each unknown exterior angle.

a)

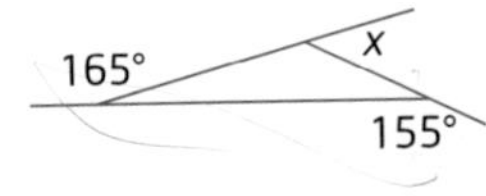

b)

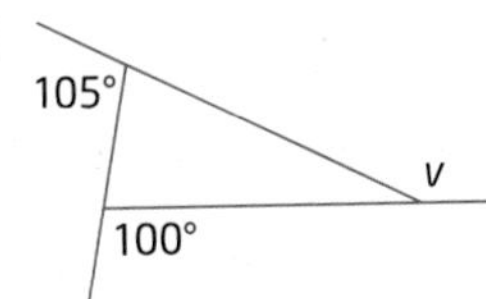

c)

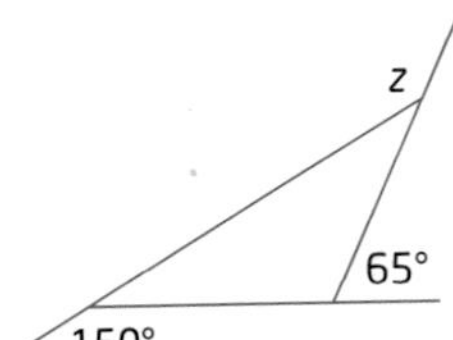

3. If the measures of two of the exterior angles of a triangle are 70° and 120°, the measure of the third exterior angle is

A 10°

B 70°

C 170°

D 190°

Connect and Apply

4. Find the measure of the exterior angle labelled x for each isosceles triangle.

a)

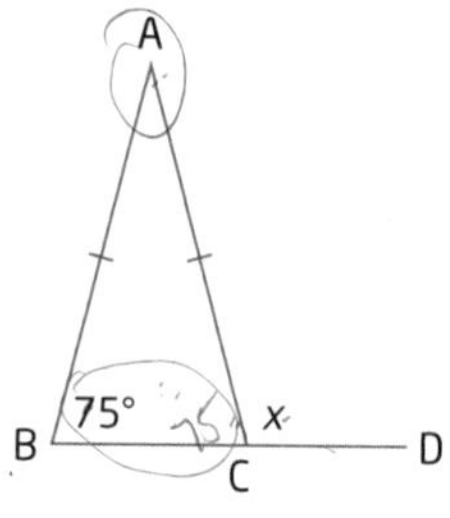

b)

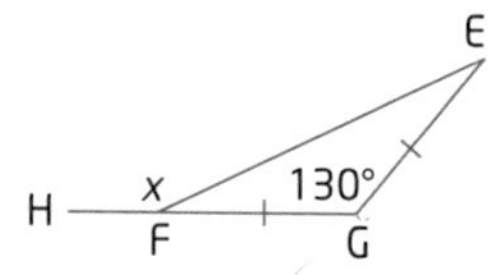

c)

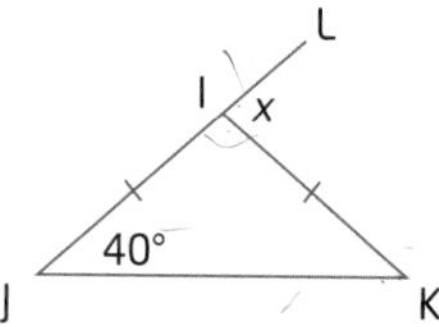

5. Find the measure of each unknown angle.

a)

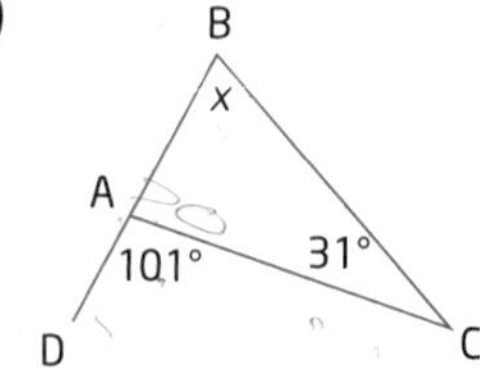

b)

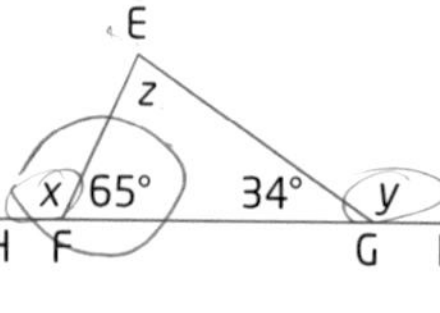

c)

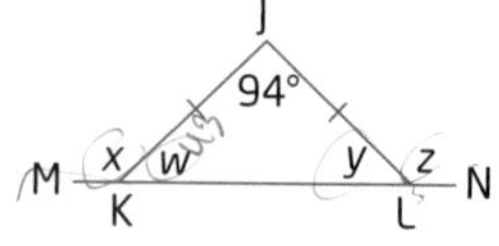

d)

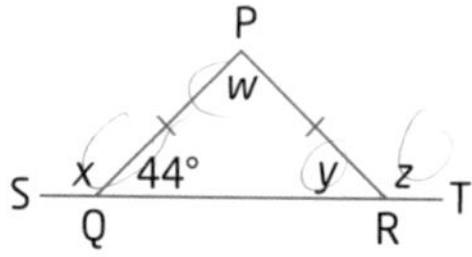

e)

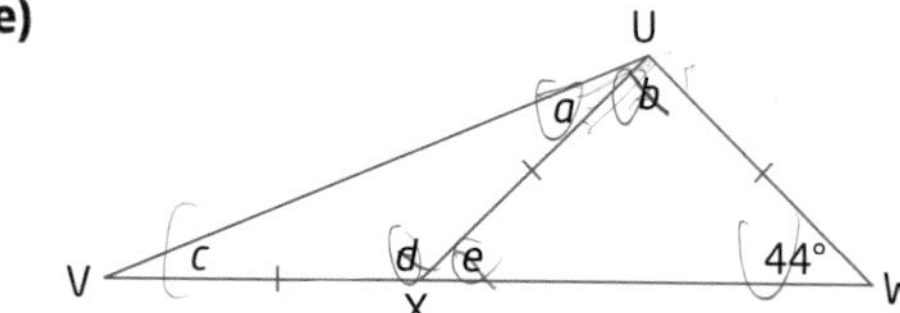

6. One exterior angle of an isosceles triangle measures 140°. Find the possible measures for the other two exterior angles.

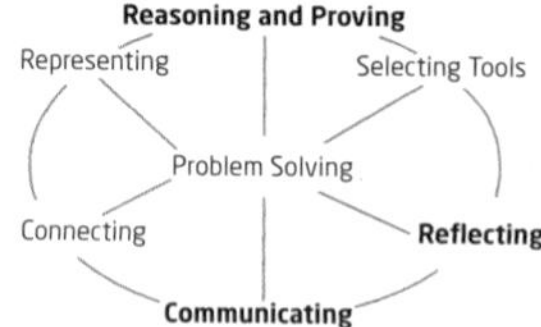

7. Calculate the mean measure of the exterior angles of a triangle.

8. What types of triangles have some exterior angles equal?

9. a) Explain why a triangle cannot have two obtuse interior angles.

b) Can a triangle have three obtuse exterior angles? Justify your answer.

10. A contractor is building a wheelchair ramp. To be safe for all users, the ramp should rise at an angle of about 5°.

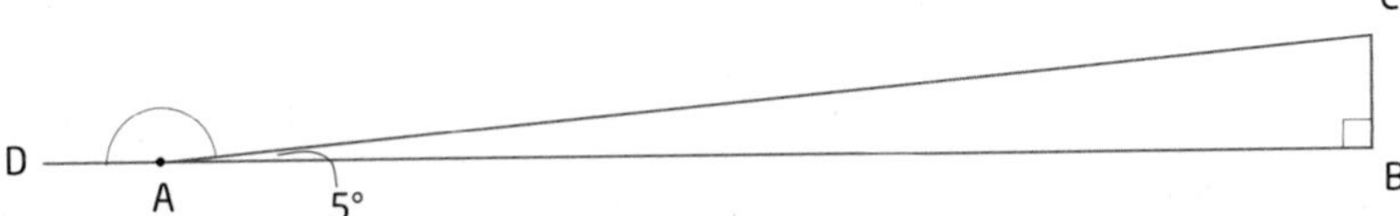

a) To check the slope of the ramp, the contractor measures ∠DAC at the foot of the ramp. What measure should this angle have?

b) Find the measure of the interior and exterior angles at the top of the ramp.

Extend

11. Find the measure of each unknown angle.

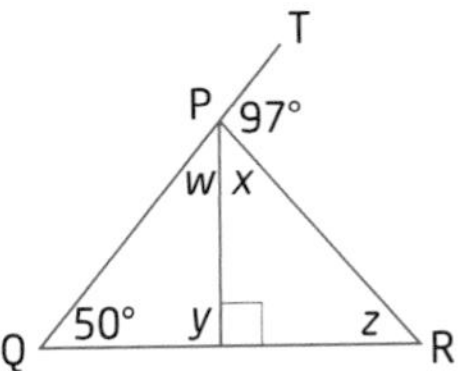

12. Each ratio shows the relationships among the measures of the exterior angles of a triangle. Find the measures of the angles. Then, draw each triangle, or explain why the triangle is not possible.

a) 1:1:1 **b)** 1:2:2 **c)** 1:2:3 **d)** 1:1:2

e) 3:4:5 **f)** 4:5:6 **g)** 3:4:8

13. Do an Internet search for *hexaflexagon*. Then, construct a hexaflexagon using the information you find.

WWW Go to www.mcgrawhill.ca/links/principles9 and follow the links to learn more about hexaflexagons.

14. Math Contest What angle measure does *x* represent?

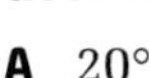

A 20°

B 50°

C 60°

D 100°

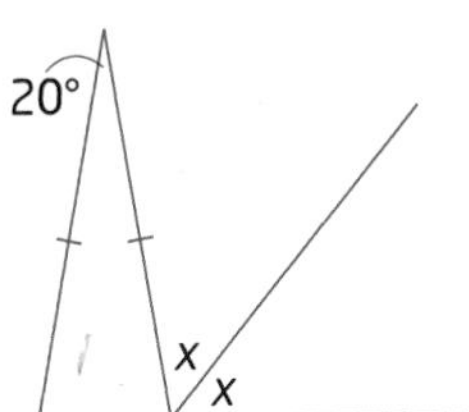

15. Math Contest Calculate the sum of ∠ABC and ∠ADC.

A 60°

B 70°

C 90°

D 100°

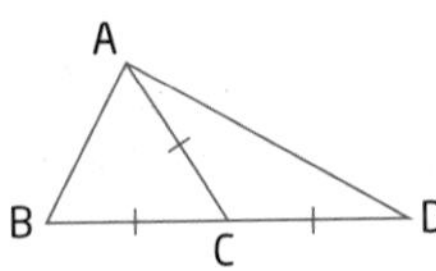

7.2 Angle Relationships in Quadrilaterals

Many quadrilaterals are visible in this photograph of the recent addition to the Ontario College of Art and Design. Quadrilaterals are important shapes in design and construction. Quadrilateral shapes appear in both ordinary and unusual new buildings, as well as in everyday objects all around you.

Investigate

Tools
- ruler
- protractor

How are the interior and exterior angles of a quadrilateral related?

Method 1: Use Pencil and Paper

1. Draw a large quadrilateral. Label the vertices.
2. Use a protractor to measure each of the four interior angles.
3. Find the sum of the four interior angles.
4. Compare your results with those of your classmates.
5. **Reflect** Make a hypothesis about the sum of the interior angles of any quadrilateral. Describe how you can test your hypothesis.
6. Any quadrilateral can be divided into two triangles by constructing a diagonal like line segment AC. How are the angles in the two triangles related to the interior angles of the quadrilateral?

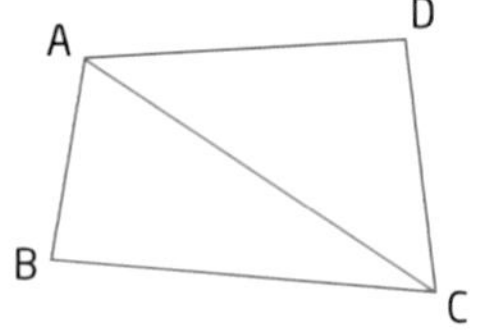

7. **Reflect** Explain how you can show that the sum of the interior angles is the same for all quadrilaterals.
8. Extend one side at each vertex of your quadrilateral to create an exterior angle. Name and measure the four exterior angles. Find the sum of these exterior angles.
9. **Reflect** Make a hypothesis about the sum of the exterior angles of any quadrilateral. Describe how you can test your hypothesis.

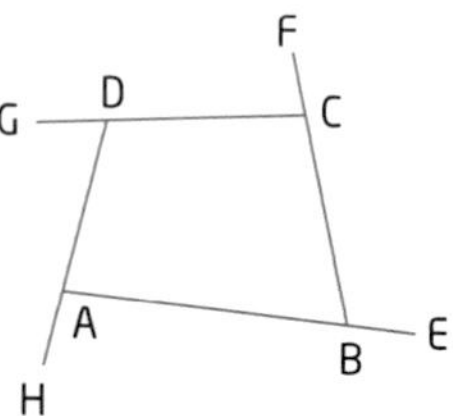

Method 2: Use *The Geometer's Sketchpad®*

1. Turn on automatic labelling of points. From the **Edit** menu, choose **Preferences**, click on the **Text** tab, check **For All New Points**, and click on **OK**.

2. Use the **Point Tool** to create four points on the screen.

3. Select point A and then point B. From the **Construct** menu, choose **Ray**. Use the same method to construct rays from B to C, from C to D, and from D to A.

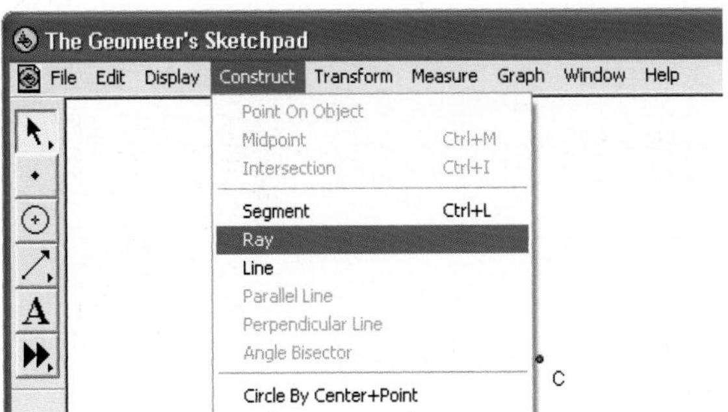

4. To measure ∠DAB, select points D, A, and B in that order. From the **Measure** menu, choose **Angle**. Use the same method to measure the other three interior angles of the quadrilateral.

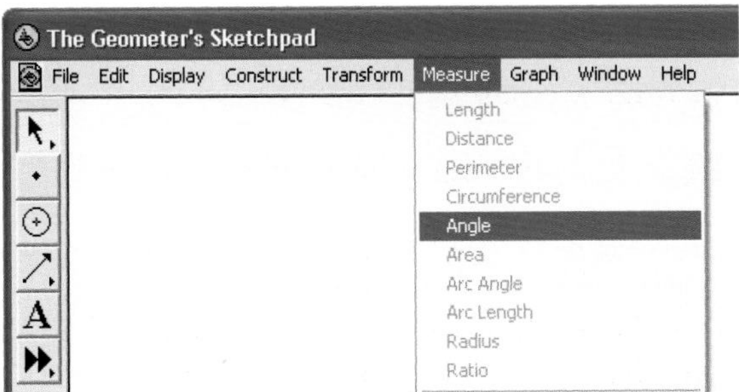

5. From the **Measure** menu, choose **Calculate**. Click on the measure for ∠DAB. Click (+) on the calculator; then, click on the measure for ∠ABC. Add the other two interior angles to the calculation.

6. Make a hypothesis about the sum of the interior angles of any quadrilateral.

7. Drag one of the vertices around the screen. Watch the sum of the interior angles as you move the vertex. Try moving the other vertices as well.

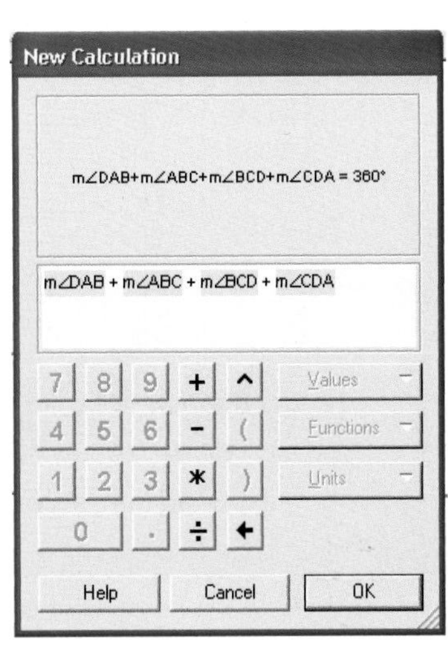

Tools

- computer with *The Geometer's Sketchpad®*

8. **Reflect** What can you conclude about the sum of the interior angles of any quadrilateral? Do your observations support your hypothesis? Explain.

9. Make a hypothesis about the sum of the exterior angles in any quadrilateral.

10. Select the four rays. From the **Construct** menu, choose **Points on Rays**. If necessary, drag each point to a location outside the quadrilateral.

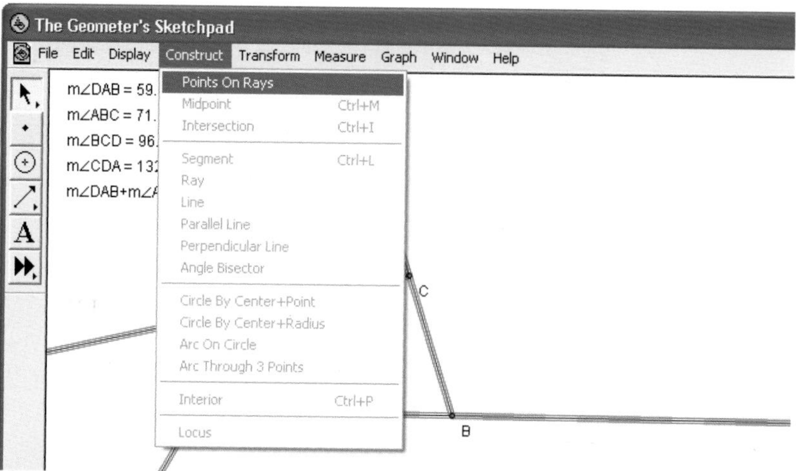

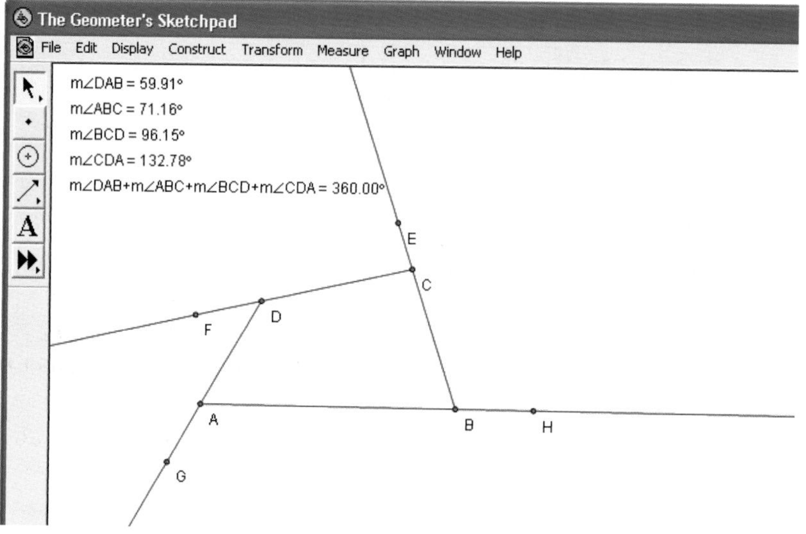

11. Use the Measure and Calculate tools to test your hypothesis about the sum of the exterior angles.

12. **Reflect** Is your hypothesis correct? Explain.

Method 3: Use a Graphing Calculator

1. Press (APPS) and select **CabriJr**. Press (ENTER) when the title screen appears. If you need to clear a previous drawing from the screen, press (Y=) to display the **F1** menu, and select **New**.

2. Press (WINDOW) to display the **F2** menu. Select **Quad.**. Use the cursor keys to move the pencil cursor around the screen. Press (ENTER) to place each vertex of the quadrilateral.

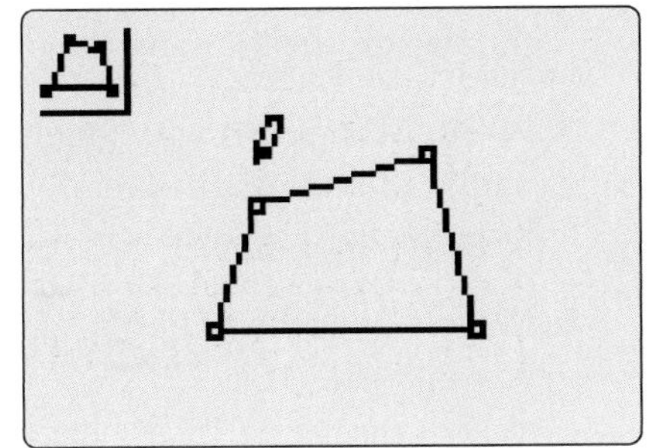

3. To measure angles, press (GRAPH) to display the **F5** menu, highlight **Measure**, and press (▸). Select **Angle** from the submenu. For each angle, select three points that define the angle by pressing (ENTER) at each point. Always select the vertex as the second of the three points. Use the cursor keys to drag the measurement so that it labels the angle clearly; then, press (ENTER). Measure the four interior angles of the quadrilateral.

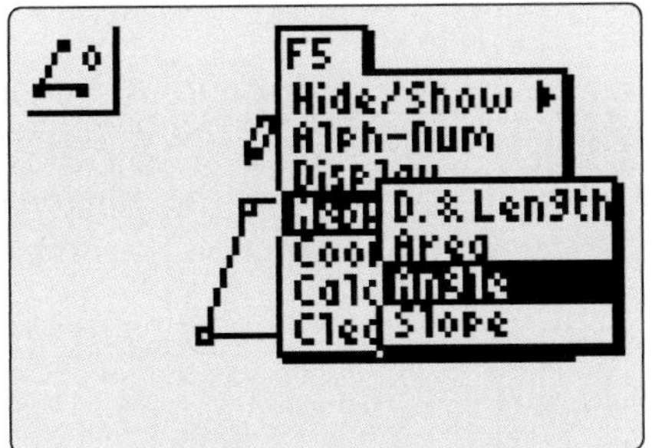

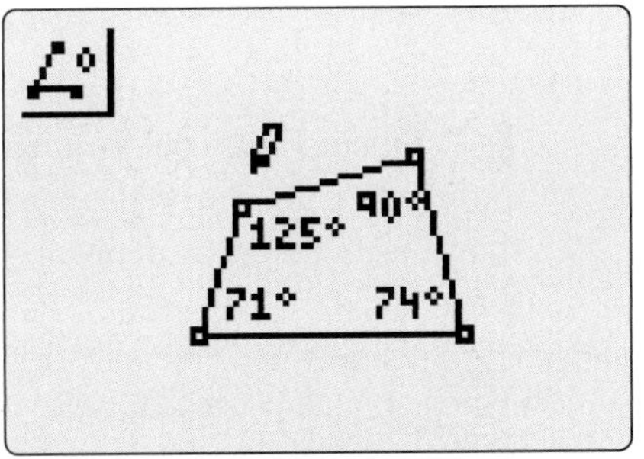

4. Press (GRAPH) to display the **F5** menu, and select **Calculate**. Select three of the angle measures by moving the cursor to each one and pressing (ENTER) when the measurement is underlined. Press (+) and drag the subtotal to an empty part of the screen. Select this subtotal and the fourth angle measure. Now, press (+) to display the sum of all four angles. To avoid confusion, hide the subtotal by dragging the total sum to the same location.

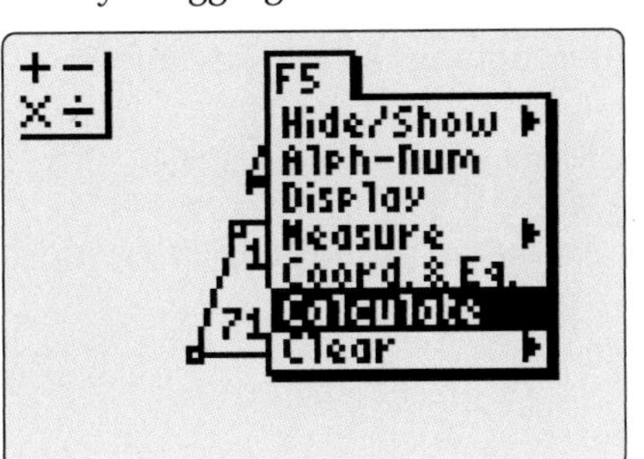

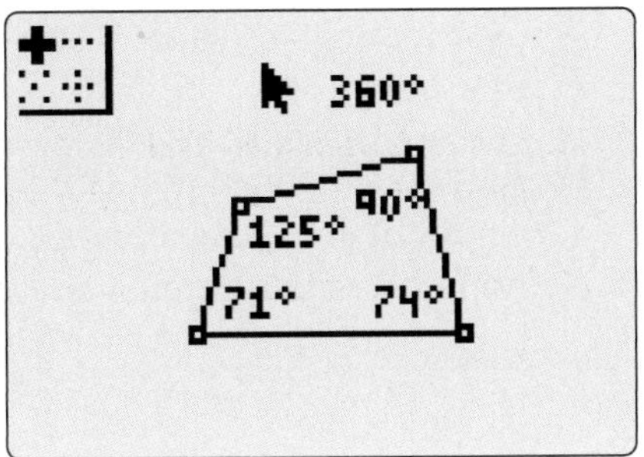

Tools

- TI-83 Plus or TI-84 graphing calculator

Technology Tip

Version 2.00 of Cabri® Jr. can add only three angles at a time. Later versions may let you add all four angles of the quadrilateral in a single operation.

5. **Reflect** Make a hypothesis about the sum of the interior angles of any quadrilateral.

6. Press CLEAR. Move the cursor to one of the vertices and press ALPHA. Now, use the cursor keys to drag the vertex to various new locations. Watch the sum of the interior angles as you move the vertex. Try moving the other vertices as well.

7. **Reflect** What can you conclude about the sum of the interior angles of any quadrilateral? Do your observations support your hypothesis? Explain.

8. Make a hypothesis about the sum of the exterior angles for any quadrilateral.

9. Press WINDOW to display the **F2** menu and select **Line**. Move the cursor to a point on one side of the quadrilateral and press ENTER. Then, move the cursor to another point on the side and press ENTER again. Use the same method to extend the other three sides.

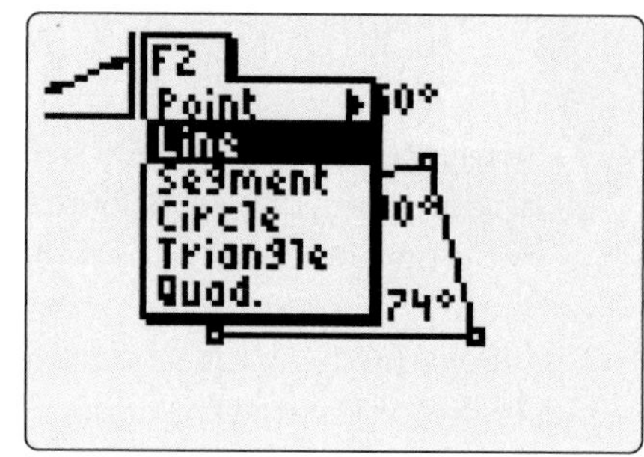

10. Press WINDOW to display the **F2** menu. With the cursor on **Point**, press ▸. Select **Point on** from the submenu. To place a point for an exterior angle, move the cursor onto the portion of a line outside the quadrilateral and press ENTER. Place similar points on the other three lines.

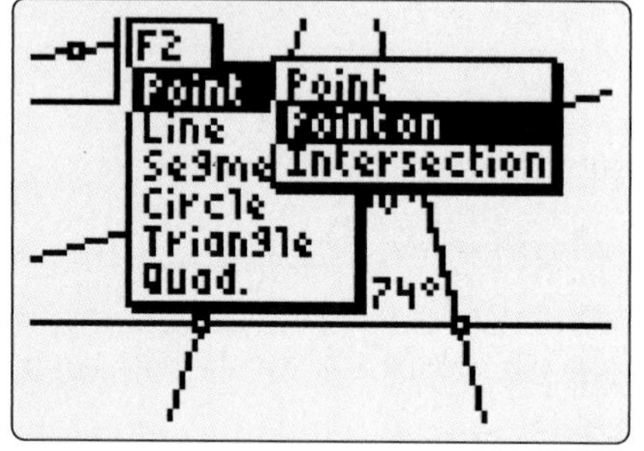

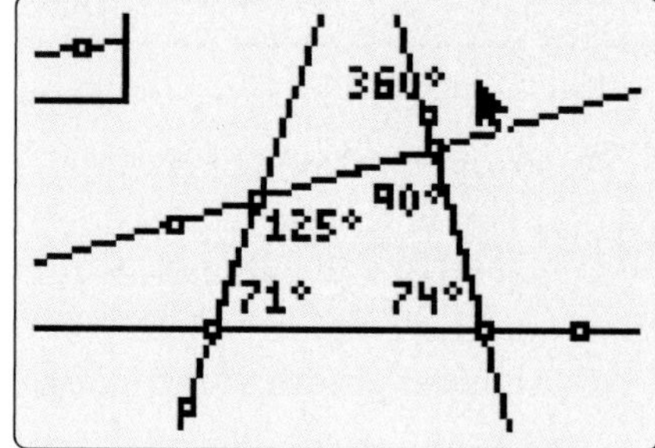

11. Use the **Measure** and **Calculate** functions to find the sum of the exterior angles. Then, test whether moving the vertices affects this sum.

12. **Reflect** What can you conclude about the sum of the exterior angles of any quadrilateral? Do your observations support your hypothesis? Explain.

Example 1 Measures of Angles of a Quadrilateral

Find the measure of the unknown angle in each quadrilateral.

a)

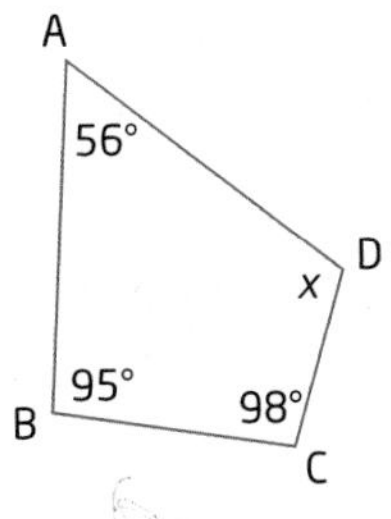

b)

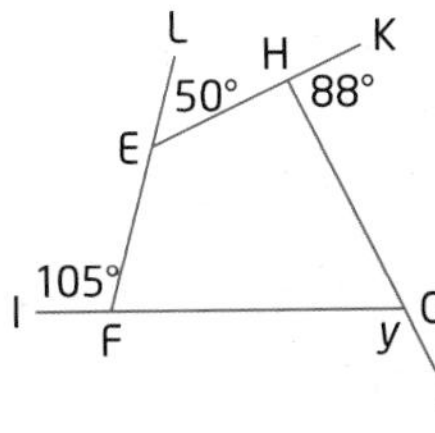

Solution

a) Since the sum of the interior angles of a quadrilateral is 360°,

$$\begin{aligned} \angle A + \angle B + \angle C + \angle D &= 360° \\ 56° + 95° + 98° + x &= 360° \\ 249° + x &= 360° \\ x &= 360° - 249° \\ x &= 111° \end{aligned}$$

b) Since the sum of the exterior angles of a quadrilateral is 360°,

$$\begin{aligned} \angle EFI + \angle LEH + \angle KHG + \angle JGF &= 360° \\ 105° + 50° + 88° + y &= 360° \\ 243° + y &= 360° \\ y &= 360° - 243° \\ y &= 117° \end{aligned}$$

Example 2 Angle Relationships in Parallelograms

Use this diagram to determine two of the angle properties of a parallelogram.

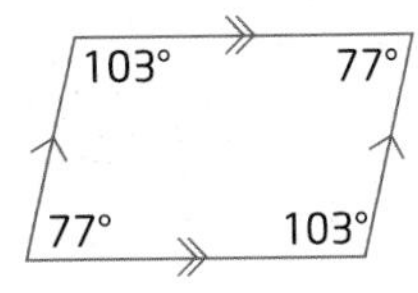

Solution

Examining the measures of the interior angles of this parallelogram shows that

- **adjacent** angles are **supplementary**
- angles at opposite vertices are equal

You can show that these relationships apply to all parallelograms.

Where a **transversal** crosses two parallel lines, angles that form a "C" pattern are supplementary.

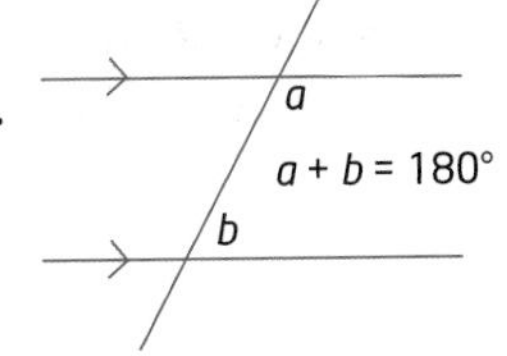

adjacent

- adjoining or next to

supplementary

- adding to 180°

transversal

- line intersecting two or more lines

In any parallelogram ABCD, AD is a transversal between the parallel sides AB and CD. So,

$\angle CDA + \angle DAB = 180°$

Applying the same reasoning to each side gives

$\angle DAB + \angle ABC = 180°$
$\angle ABC + \angle BCD = 180°$
$\angle BCD + \angle CDA = 180°$

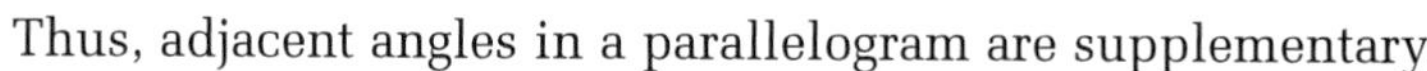

Thus, adjacent angles in a parallelogram are supplementary.

This angle property leads to a relationship between opposite angles.

Since $\angle CDA + \angle DAB = 180°$, $\angle CDA = 180° - \angle DAB$.
Since $\angle DAB + \angle ABC = 180°$, $\angle ABC = 180° - \angle DAB$.
Therefore, $\angle CDA = \angle ABC$.

In the same way, you can show that $\angle BCD = \angle DAB$.

Therefore, opposite angles in a parallelogram are equal.

Key Concepts

- The sum of the interior angles of a quadrilateral is 360°.
- The sum of the exterior angles of a quadrilateral is 360°.

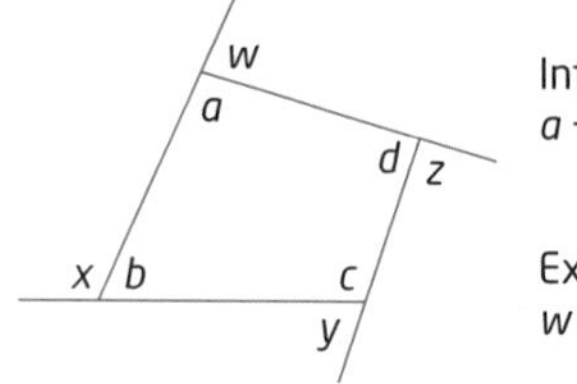

Interior angles:
$a + b + c + d = 360°$

Exterior angles:
$w + x + y + z = 360°$

Communicate Your Understanding

C1 Calculate the measure of $\angle P$. Explain your calculation.

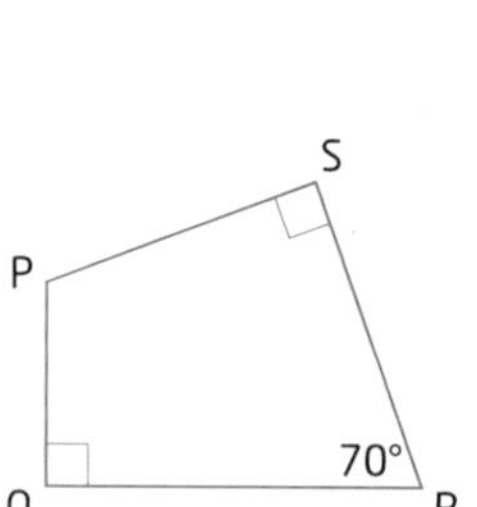

C2 Omar calculates that x represents an angle measure of 50°. Is he correct? How do you know?

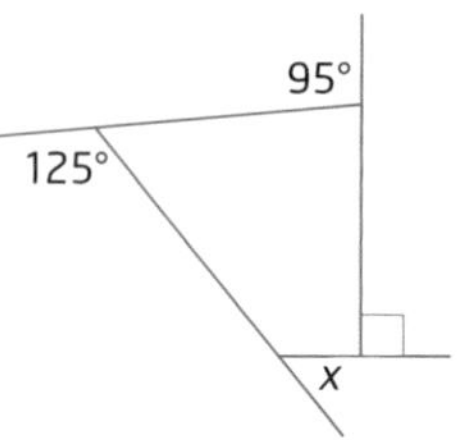

Practise

For help with questions 1 to 4, see Example 1.

1. Find the angle measures w, x, y, and z.

a)

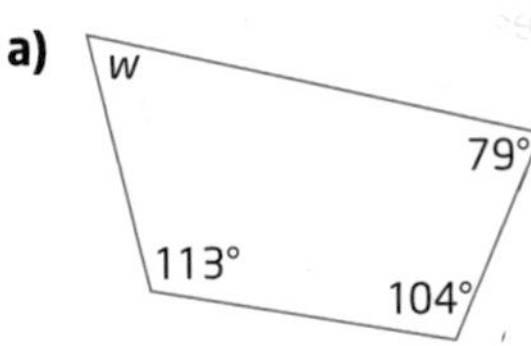

b)

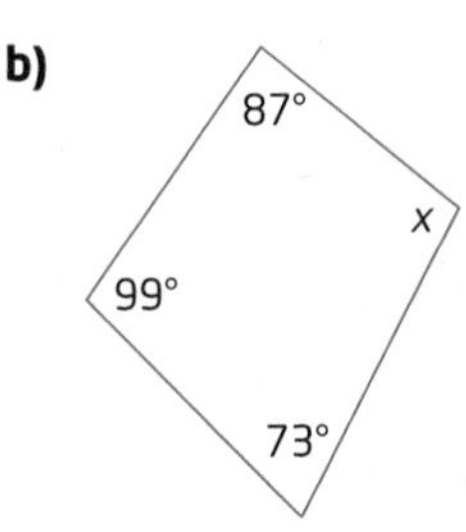

c)

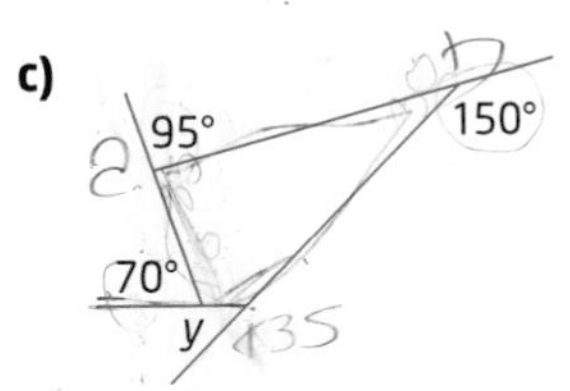

d)

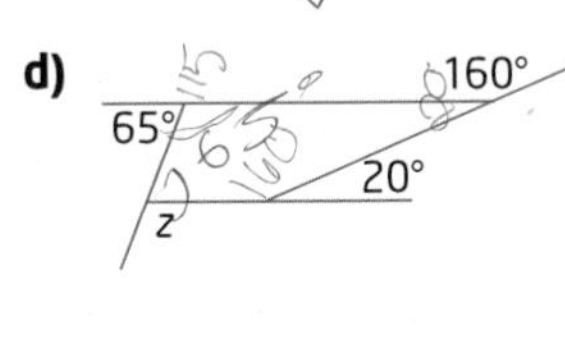

2. The measures of three of the interior angles of a quadrilateral are 40°, 90°, and 120°. The measure of the fourth interior angle is

A 110° **B** 130° **C** 210° **D** 250°

3. The measures of exterior angles at three vertices of a quadrilateral are 80°, 100°, and 120°. The measure of an exterior angle at the fourth vertex is

A 40° **B** 60° **C** 100° **D** 140°

4. Each row of this table lists measures of three interior angles in a quadrilateral. Find the measure of the fourth interior angle in each quadrilateral.

	∠A	∠B	∠C	∠D
a)	100°	75°	50°	unknown
b)	20°	35°	unknown	150°
c)	70°	unknown	70°	70°
d)	unknown	90°	90°	90°

For help with question 5, see Example 2.

5. Find the measure of each unknown angle.

a)

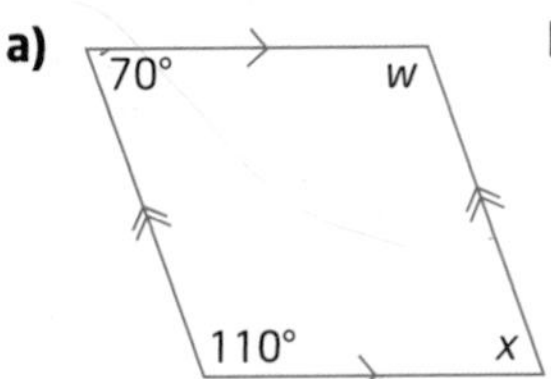

b)

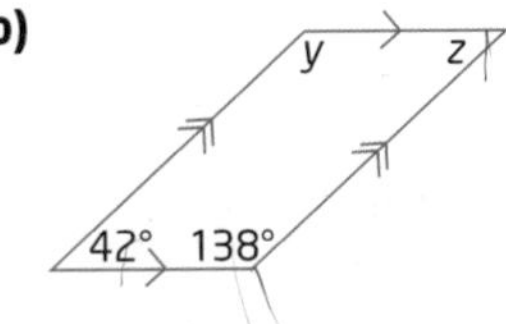

c)

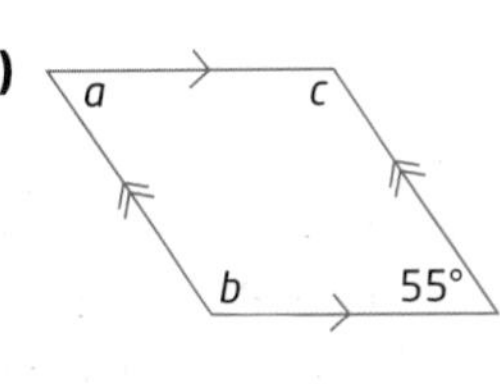

6. What angle property do triangles and quadrilaterals have in common?

Connect and Apply

7. Find the measure of each unknown angle.

a) 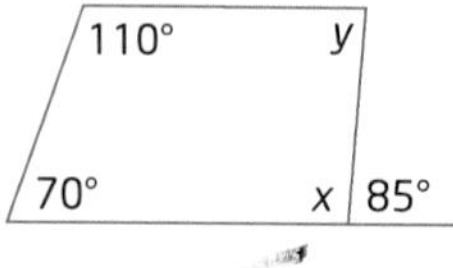

b) 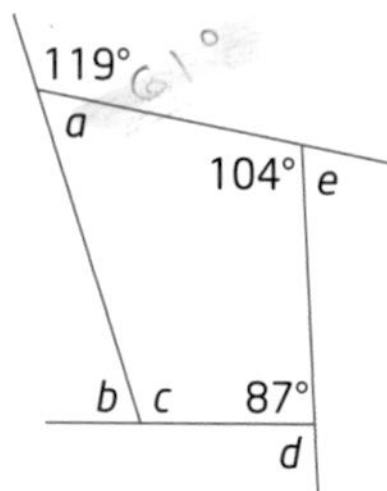

8. What is the minimum number of angles you need to measure to calculate the measure of all of the interior and exterior angles of a quadrilateral? Justify your answer.

9. Draw a quadrilateral with each set of interior angles, or explain why the quadrilateral is not possible. Calculate the measure of the fourth angle where possible.

   a) $\angle A = 170°$, $\angle B = 65°$, and $\angle C = 160°$

   b) $\angle E = 60°$, $\angle F = 75°$, and $\angle G = 120°$

   c) $\angle P = 30°$, $\angle Q = 65°$, and $\angle R = 60°$

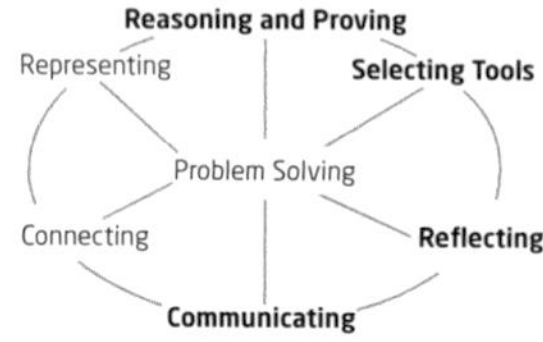

10. Draw an example of a quadrilateral with each set of interior angles, or explain why the quadrilateral is not possible.

    a) four obtuse angles

    b) exactly two obtuse angles

    c) one obtuse angle and three acute angles

    d) one obtuse angle and two right angles

    e) exactly three right angles

11. Calculate the mean measure for the interior angles of a quadrilateral.

12. This diagram shows the structure of a bridge over the river between Ottawa and Gatineau.

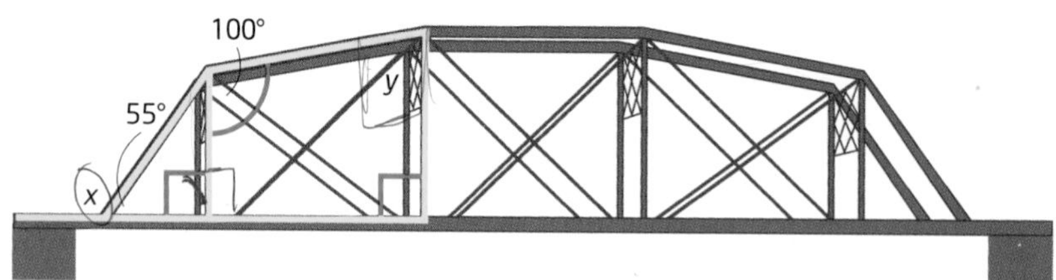

    a) Calculate the measure of the exterior angle between the road and the foot of the triangle at the left end of the bridge.

    b) Calculate the angle at the upper right corner of the quadrilateral on the left side of the bridge.

    c) Why did the bridge's designers use these shapes?

Extend

13. Find the measure of each unknown angle.

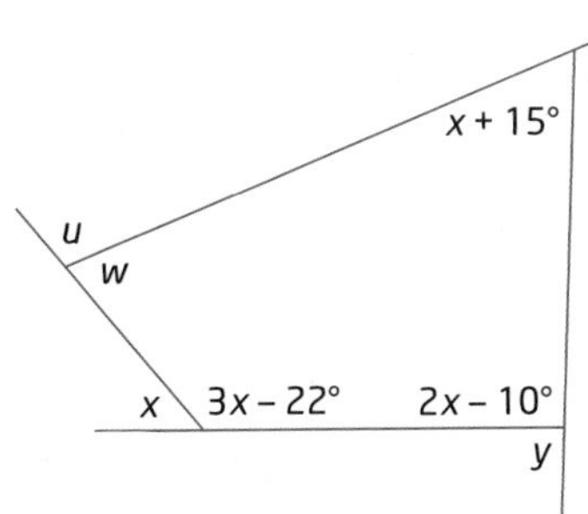

14. Draw a square ABCD and a rectangle PQRS. Construct diagonals AC and PR. Investigate the properties of the two quadrilaterals to answer parts a) to c). Describe how you determined the answer to each question.

a) Does each diagonal divide the quadrilateral into two **congruent** triangles?

b) Is the diagonal a line of symmetry in either of the quadrilaterals?

c) Does the diagonal bisect any angles in the quadrilateral?

congruent

- equal in all respects

15. a) Draw a quadrilateral, and place a point E anywhere inside it. Then, draw a line segment from E to each vertex.

b) Find the sum of the four angles at point E.

c) Find the sum of all of the interior angles of the four triangles inside the quadrilateral.

d) Use your diagram to show that the sum of the interior angles of a quadrilateral is 360°.

16. Find the measures of the interior angles of a quadrilateral so that the measures have each ratio. Then, sketch each quadrilateral.

a) 1:1:1:1 **b)** 1:1:2:2 **c)** 1:2:3:4 **d)** 3:4:5:6

17. Quadrilaterals that can be inscribed in a circle with all four vertices on the circumference of the circle are called *cyclic quadrilaterals.* Investigate angle relationships in cyclic quadrilaterals. Write a brief report of your findings.

18. Math Contest ABCD is a square and $\triangle DCE$ is equilateral. The measure of $\angle CEB$ is

A 10° **B** 15° **C** 20° **D** 30°

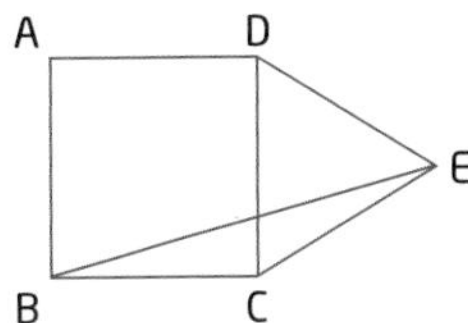

19. Math Contest Given four sides with unequal lengths, how many non-congruent quadrilaterals can you make?

7.3 Angle Relationships in Polygons

Although triangles and quadrilaterals are the most common shapes in construction, you will find many other types of polygons in both natural and manufactured objects.

The investigations in this section deal with **convex polygons**. All the interior angles of these polygons measure less than 180°. A **concave polygon** can have angles greater than 180°.

convex polygon

- a polygon with no part of any line segment joining two points on the polygon outside the polygon

concave polygon

- a polygon with parts of some line segments joining two points on the polygon outside the polygon

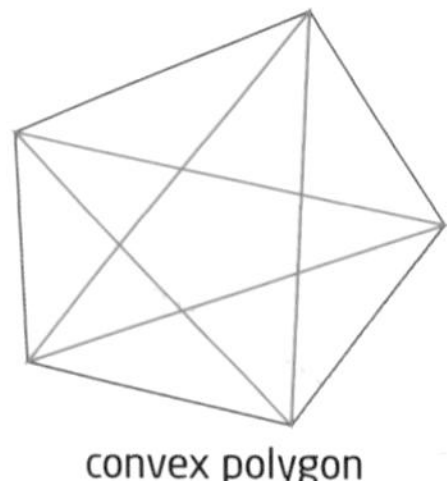

convex polygon

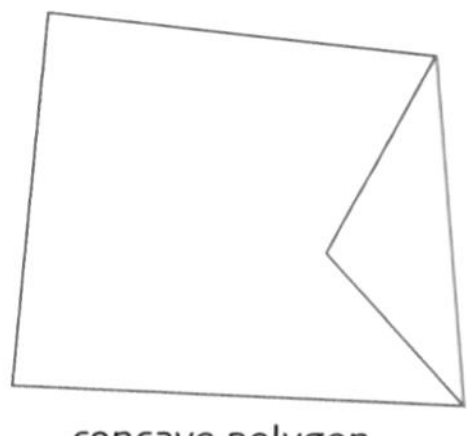

concave polygon

Tools

- ruler
- protractor

pentagon

- a polygon with five sides

Investigate A

How are the angles in a pentagon related?

1. Make a hypothesis about the sum of the interior angles of a **pentagon**.

2. Draw a pentagon. Then, label and measure the five interior angles.

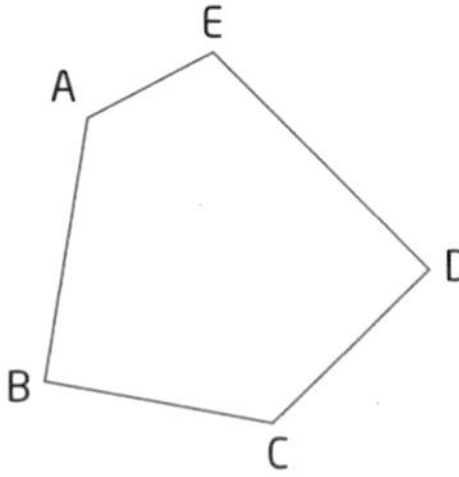

3. Find the sum of the five interior angles. Compare this sum to the sums found by your classmates.

4. **Reflect** Discuss whether the sum of the interior angles is the same for all pentagons.

5. Draw two diagonals from one vertex of your pentagon. How many triangles do these diagonals create?

6. How do the interior angles of the triangles relate to the interior angles of the pentagon? Does the same relationship hold for all pentagons?

7. **Reflect** Does the relationship in step 6 confirm your hypothesis about the sum of the interior angles of the pentagon? Explain.

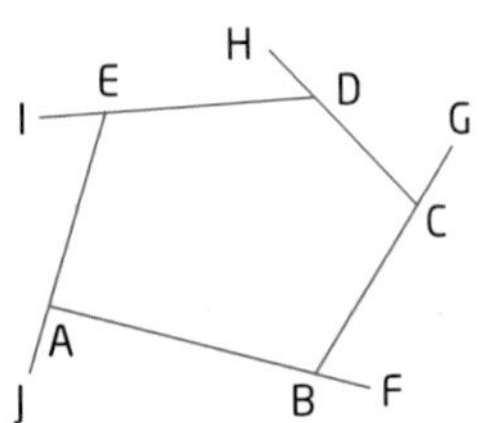

8. Draw another pentagon. Extend one side at each vertex to create an exterior angle. Name and measure the five exterior angles.

9. Find the sum of the exterior angles. Compare this sum to those found by your classmates.

10. **Reflect** Discuss whether the sum of the exterior angles is the same for all pentagons.

Investigate B

Are there patterns in the angles of polygons?

Method 1: Use Pencil and Paper

- ruler
- protractor

1. Set up a table like the one shown. Enter the results of your previous investigations of angles in polygons. Use the table to record your results during this investigation.

Polygon	Number of Sides	Number of Diagonals From One Vertex	Number of Triangles in the Polygon	Sum of Interior Angles	Sum of Exterior Angles
triangle	3	0	1	180°	360°
quadrilateral					
pentagon					

2. Draw a **hexagon**. Label and measure its interior angles. Find the sum of these angles.

hexagon
- a polygon with six sides

3. Extend one side at each vertex to create an exterior angle. Name and measure these exterior angles. Find the sum of the exterior angles.

4. Draw a **heptagon**. Label and measure its interior angles. Find the sum of these angles.

heptagon
- a polygon with seven sides

5. Extend one side at each vertex of your heptagon to create an exterior angle. Name and measure these exterior angles. Find the sum of the exterior angles.

6. **Reflect** Describe any pattern you see for the sum of the exterior angles of a polygon.

WWW Go to www.mcgrawhill.ca/links/principles9 and follow the links to learn more about the names for polygons.

7. How many diagonals can you draw from a vertex in each polygon? How does the number of diagonals relate to the number of sides? Use a scatter plot or first differences to help identify the relationship.

8. How does the number of triangles formed by the diagonals relate to the number of sides?

9. **Reflect** Explain the pattern in the sums of the interior angles of polygons. Write an equation for this pattern. Describe how you can use this equation to find the sum of the interior angles of any polygon.

- computer with *The Geometer's Sketchpad®*

Method 2: Use *The Geometer's Sketchpad®*

1. Set up a table like the one shown. Enter the results of your previous investigations of angles in polygons. Use the table to record your results during this investigation.

Polygon	Number of Sides	Sum of Interior Angles	Sum of Exterior Angles
triangle	3	180°	360°
quadrilateral			
pentagon			

2. Turn on automatic labelling of points. From the **Edit** menu, choose **Preferences**. Click on the **Text** tab, check **For All New Points**, and click on **OK**.

3. Construct a hexagon. Use the **Point Tool** to create six points on the screen. Select point A and then point B. From the **Construct** menu, choose **Ray**. Use the same method to construct rays from B to C, from C to D, from D to E, from E to F, and from F to A.

Technology Tip

You can also do this investigation using Cabri Jr. on a graphing calculator. For step-by-step instructions, follow the links at www.mcgrawhill.ca/links/principles9.

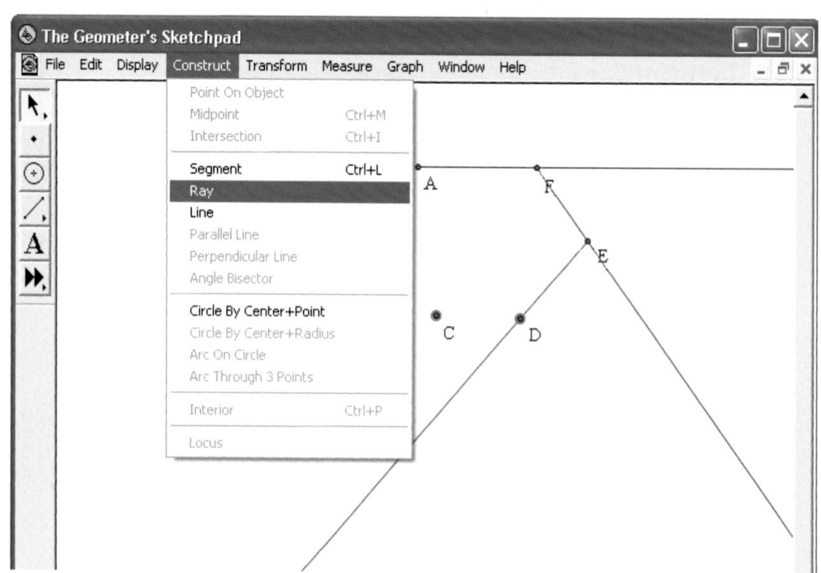

4. To measure ∠FAB, select points F, A, and B, in that order. From the **Measure** menu, choose **Angle**. Use the same method to measure the other five interior angles of the hexagon.

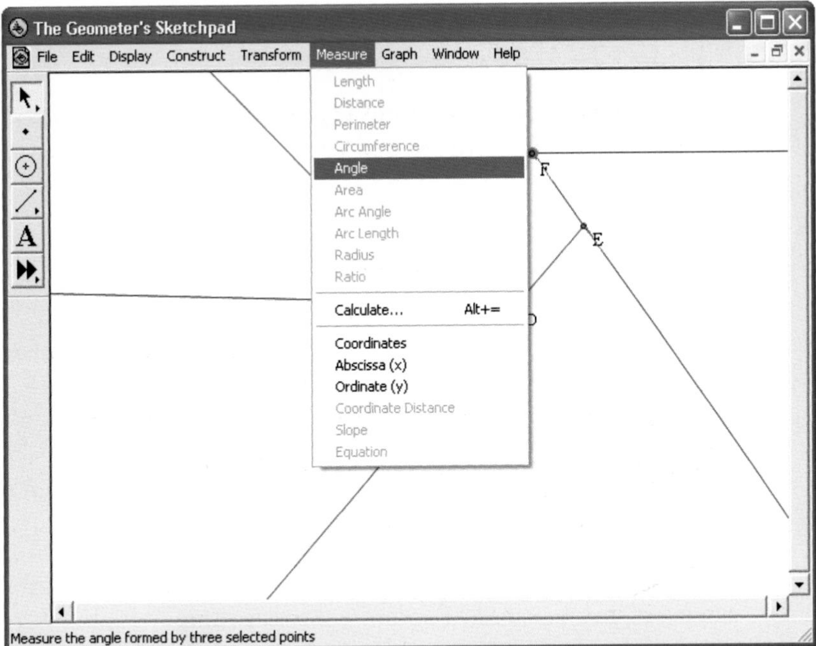

5. From the **Measure** menu, choose **Calculate**. Click on the measure for ∠FAB. Click (+) on the calculator; then, click on the measure for ∠ABC. Add the other four interior angles to the calculation. Check whether moving any of the vertices affects the sum of the interior angles.

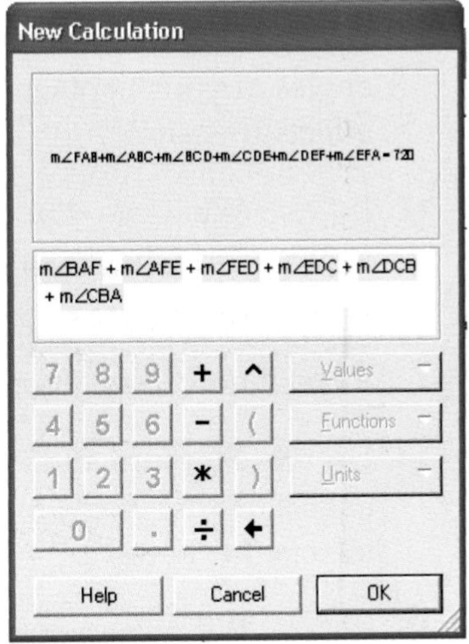

6. **Reflect** What can you conclude about the sum of the interior angles of any hexagon? Explain your reasoning.

7. Select the six rays. From the **Construct** menu, choose **Points on Rays**. If necessary, drag each point to a location outside the hexagon.

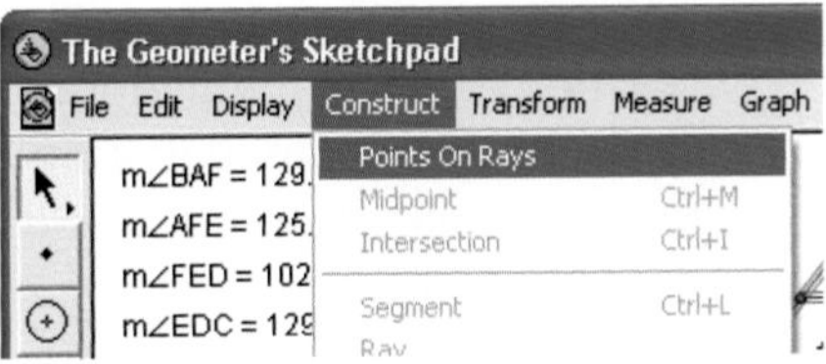

8. Use the Measure and Calculate tools to find the sum of the exterior angles. Check whether moving any of the vertices affects this sum.

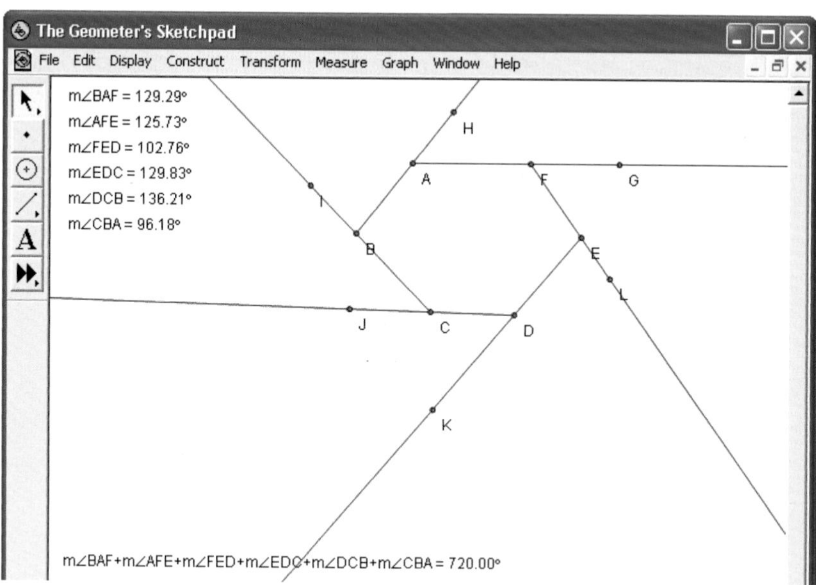

9. **Reflect** What can you conclude about the sum of the exterior angles of any hexagon? Explain your reasoning.

10. Use points and rays to construct a heptagon with exterior angles.

11. Use the Measure and Calculate tools to find the sum of the interior angles of your heptagon. Check whether moving any of the vertices affects this sum.

12. **Reflect** What can you conclude about the sum of the interior angles of any heptagon?

13. Select the seven rays. From the **Construct** menu, choose **Points on Rays**. If necessary, drag each point to a location outside the heptagon.

14. Use the Measure and Calculate tools to find the sum of the exterior angles of your heptagon. Check whether moving any of the vertices affects this sum.

15. **Reflect** What can you conclude about the sum of the exterior angles of any heptagon?

16. **Reflect** Describe any pattern you see for the sums of the exterior angles of polygons.

17. **Reflect** Explain the pattern in the sums of the interior angles of polygons. Write an equation for this pattern. Describe how you can use this equation to find the sum of the interior angles of any polygon.

WWW Go to www.mcgrawhill.ca/links/principles9 and follow the links to learn more about the names for polygons.

Example 1 Interior Angles of an Octagon

Calculate the sum of the interior angles of an **octagon**.

octagon

- a polygon with eight sides

Solution

The equation for the linear relation between the sum of the interior angles of a polygon and its number of sides, n, can be written as

Sum of Interior Angles $= 180(n - 2)$
For an octagon, $n = 8$. So,

$$\begin{aligned}\text{Sum of Interior Angles} &= 180(n - 2)\\ &= 180(8 - 2)\\ &= 180 \times 6\\ &= 1080\end{aligned}$$

The sum of the interior angles of an octagon is 1080°.

Example 2 Interior Angles in a Regular Octagon

Find the measure of each interior angle of a **regular** octagon.

regular polygon

- a polygon with all sides equal and all interior angles equal

Solution

Method 1: Use the Formula

As shown in Example 1, the formula for the sum of the interior angles of a polygon tells you that the sum of the interior angles in an octagon is 1080°. A regular octagon has eight equal interior angles, so the measure of each angle is $\frac{1080°}{8}$ or 135°.

Method 2: Use Supplementary Angles

The sum of the exterior angles of any octagon is 360°. For a regular octagon, these eight angles are equal to each other.

Therefore, the measure of each exterior angle is $\frac{360°}{8}$ or 45°.

At each vertex, the exterior and interior angles sum to 180°. So, the measure of each interior angle is 180° − 45° or 135°.

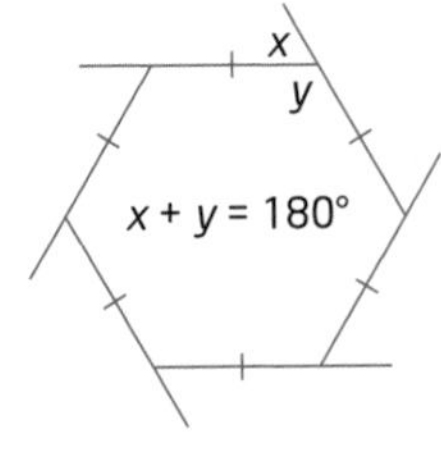

Example 3 Find the Number of Sides

How many sides does a polygon have if each of its interior angles measures 140°?

Solution

An n-sided polygon has n interior angles. If each interior angle measures 140°, their sum, in degrees, is $140n$. The sum of the interior angles, in degrees, of any polygon is $180(n - 2)$. Therefore,

$$180(n - 2) = 140n$$

$$180n - 360 = 140n \quad \text{Expand the left side.}$$

$$40n - 360 = 0 \quad \text{Subtract } 140n \text{ from both sides.}$$

$$40n = 360 \quad \text{Add 360 to both sides.}$$

$$n = 9 \quad \text{Divide both sides by 40.}$$

A polygon with interior angles of 140° has 9 sides.

Literacy Connections

A 9-sided polygon is a nonagon. This name comes from *nonus*, the Latin word for ninth.

Key Concepts

- The sum of the exterior angles of a convex polygon is 360°.
- For a polygon with n sides, the sum of the interior angles, in degrees, is $180(n - 2)$.

Communicate Your Understanding

C1 Describe how you can determine the sum of the interior angles of this polygon.

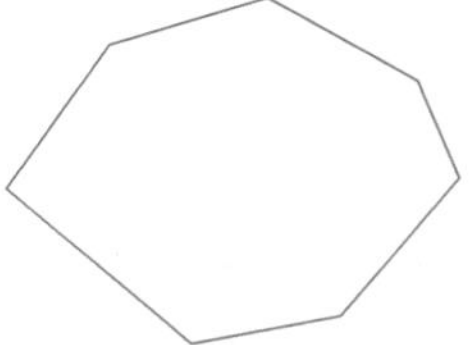

C2 This pentagon has five equal sides. Is it a regular polygon? Why or why not?

Practise

For help with question 1, see Example 1.

1. Find the sum of the interior angles of a polygon with
   - a) 10 sides
   - b) 15 sides
   - c) 20 sides

For help with question 2, see Example 2.

2. Find the measure of each interior angle of a regular polygon with
   - a) 7 sides
   - b) 12 sides

For help with question 3, see Example 3.

3. How many sides does a polygon have if the sum of its interior angles is
   - a) 540°?
   - b) 1800°?
   - c) 3060°?

4. Copy this table and fill in the missing entries.

Polygon	Number of Sides	Number of Diagonals From One Vertex	Number of Triangles in the Polygon	Sum of Interior Angles
quadrilateral	4	1	2	360°
pentagon		2		
decagon	10			
icosagon	20			

5. What properties does a regular polygon have?

Connect and Apply

6. Use the formula for the sum of the interior angles of a polygon to show that each interior angle of a square measures 90°.

7. A furniture-maker is designing a hexagonal table.
   - a) At what angle will the adjacent sides of the table meet if its shape is a regular hexagon?
   - b) Do you think the angles between the adjacent sides of the table will all be equal if one pair of opposite sides are twice as long as the other sides?
   - c) Check your answer to part b) by making a drawing and measuring the angles.

8. a) Draw a nine-sided polygon.
   - b) Calculate how many diagonals you can draw from any one vertex of this polygon. Check your answer by drawing all possible diagonals from one of the vertices.
   - c) Calculate the sum of the interior angles of the polygon. Check your answer by measuring the angles on your drawing.

9. a) Find the measure of each interior angle of a regular 10-sided polygon. Use a second method to check your answer.
   b) Find the measure of each interior angle of a regular 16-sided polygon.
   c) Find the measure of each interior angle of a regular 20-sided polygon.
   d) Write an expression for the measure of each interior angle of a regular polygon with n sides.

10. a) How many sides does a Canadian dollar coin have?
    b) What is the measure of the angle between adjacent sides of the coin?
    c) Suggest reasons why the Royal Canadian Mint chose this shape.

11. Can you determine the number of sides a polygon has from the sum of its exterior angles? Explain your reasoning.

12. Floor tiles are often in the shape of regular polygons. In order to make a pattern without any gaps, such tiles must have interior angles that divide evenly into 360°. Which three regular polygons have this property?

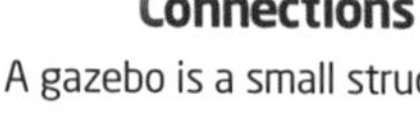

A gazebo is a small structure with open or screened sides that give a wide view.

13. This photograph shows the roof of a gazebo. The sides of this gazebo form a regular polygon.
    a) How many sides does the gazebo have?
    b) Calculate the angle between adjacent sides of the gazebo.
    c) Calculate the angle between adjacent roof supports in the photograph.
    d) Draw a plan of the gazebo.
    e) Calculate the angle between adjacent supports in the roof of a gazebo with six sides.

14. You can draw regular polygons by constructing angles at the centre point of the figure.
    a) Construct a line segment AB with a length of 4 cm. Rotate the segment 72° around point A four times. What shape is formed by joining the endpoints of the rotated segments?
    b) Describe how to use this method to construct a regular octagon.
    c) What angle would you use for a regular 20-sided figure?
    d) Describe how the rotation angle for constructing a regular polygon changes as the number of sides increases.

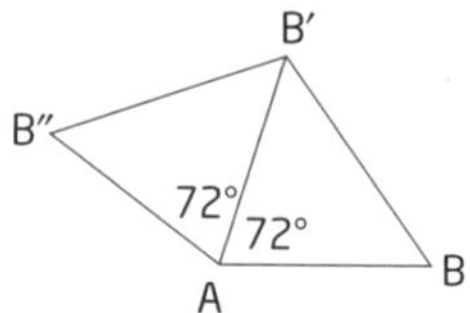

Achievement Check

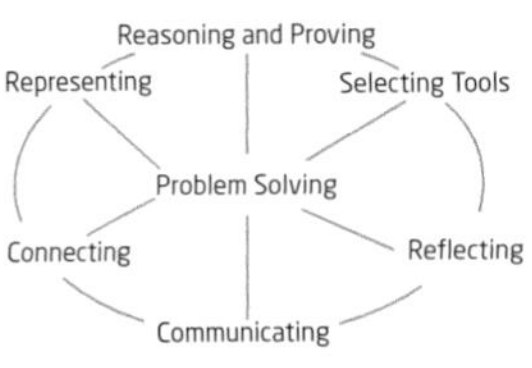

15. Draw and label an example of each shape, or explain why it is not possible.

a) a triangle with one acute exterior angle

b) a triangle with two right angles

c) a quadrilateral with four equal angles

d) a quadrilateral with three obtuse angles

e) a pentagon with two obtuse angles and three acute angles

f) a convex hexagon with five acute angles

Extend

16. Are all regular polygons convex? Justify your answer.

17. Does the formula for the sum of the interior angles apply for concave polygons? Explain your reasoning.

18. Investigate angle relationships in these two diagrams.

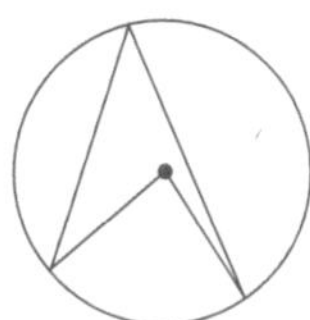

19. Use the Internet or a library to find an image of a famous building. Describe how polygons were used in the construction of the building.

Go to www.mcgrawhill.ca/links/principles9 and follow the links to learn more about famous buildings.

20. Math Contest The measure of $\angle BCA$ is

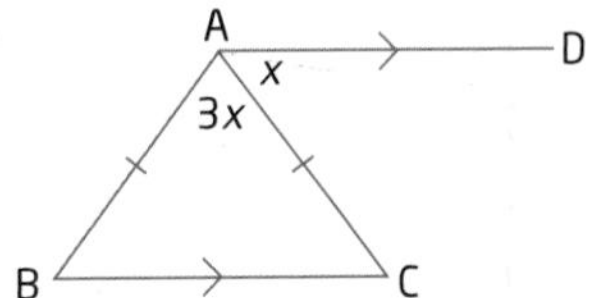

A 30°

B 36°

C 45°

D 60°

21. Math Contest How many diagonals can you draw in a convex 12-sided polygon?

A 54

B 60

C 108

D 120

7.4 Midpoints and Medians in Triangles

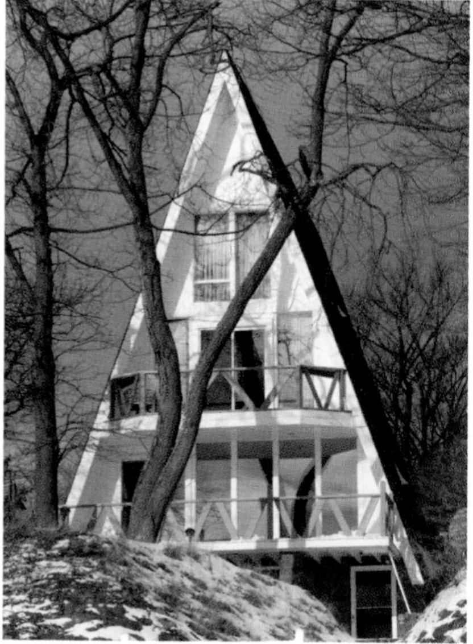

In this section, you will examine the properties of line segments that divide triangles in various ways. These properties are useful in calculations for the design of buildings and machinery.

Investigate

Tools

- ruler
- protractor

midpoint

- the point that divides a line segment into two equal segments

What are the properties of the midpoints of the sides of a triangle?

Method 1: Use Paper and Pencil

1. Draw a large triangle on a sheet of paper. Label the vertices A, B, and C. Then, measure the length of side AB and mark the **midpoint**. Label this point D. Find the midpoint of AC and label it E. Draw a line segment from D to E.

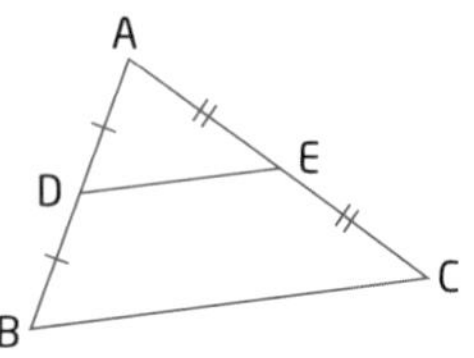

2. Measure the lengths of DE and BC. How are these lengths related?

3. If the co-interior angles formed by a transversal and two line segments are supplementary, the two segments are parallel. Determine whether DE is parallel to BC.

4. Fold your diagram across the line through points D and E. Where does the vertex A touch the lower part of the diagram?

5. What can you conclude about the heights of △ADE and △ABC? How is the height of △ADE related to the height of quadrilateral BCED?

6. Compare your results from steps 2 to 5 with your classmates' results.

7. **Reflect** Do you think your results apply for all triangles? Explain your reasoning.

Method 2: Use *The Geometer's Sketchpad*®

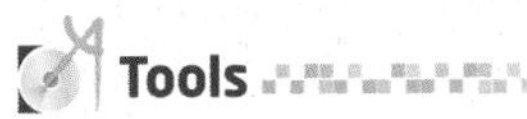

Tools

- computer with *The Geometer's Sketchpad*®

1. Turn on automatic labelling of points. From the **Edit** menu, choose **Preferences**. Click on the **Text** tab, check **For All New Points**, and click on **OK**.

2. Construct a △ABC. To construct the midpoints of AB and AC, select these two sides (but not the vertices), and choose **Midpoints** from the **Construct** menu.

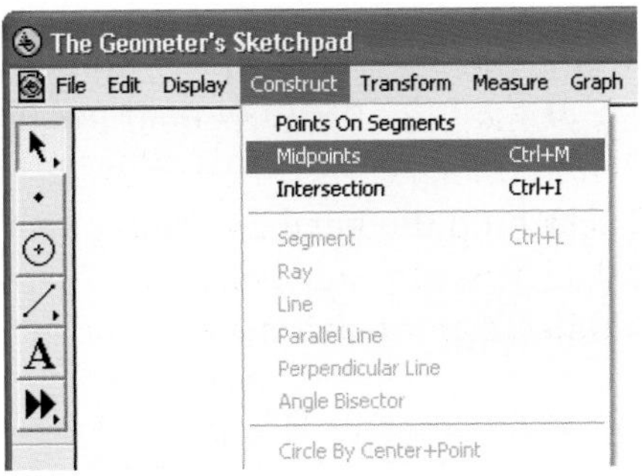

Technology Tip

The keyboard shortcut for choosing **Midpoints** is Ctrl+M.

3. Measure the lengths of DE and BC. How are these lengths related?

4. If the co-interior angles formed by a transversal and two line segments are supplementary, the two segments are parallel. Use the sum of ∠EDB and ∠DBC to determine whether DE is parallel to BC.

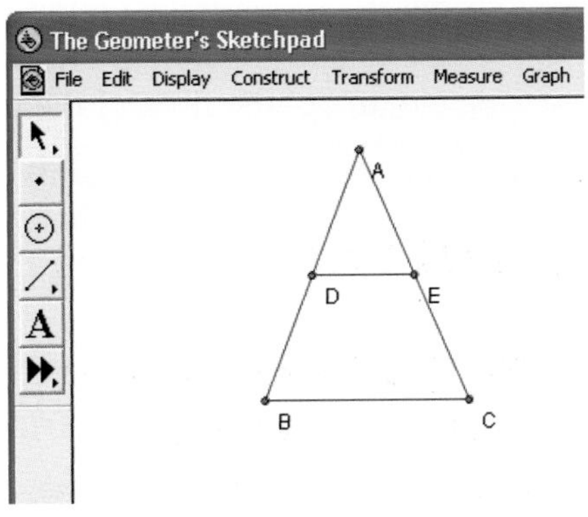

5. Select vertex A and side BC. From the **Construct** menu, choose **Perpendicular Line**. Select the perpendicular line and line segment DE. Then, choose **Intersection** from the **Construct** menu.

6. Compare the height of △ADE to the height of △ABC.

Technology Tip

You can also do this investigation using Cabri Jr. on a graphing calculator. For step-by-step instructions, follow the links at www.mcgrawhill.ca/links/principles9.

7. Compare the height of △ADE to the height of quadrilateral BCED.

8. Watch the length and angle measures as you drag vertex A to various new locations. Do any of the length ratios change? Does the sum of ∠EDB and ∠DBC remain constant? Try dragging vertices B and C around the screen as well.

9. **Reflect** What properties does the line segment joining the midpoints of two sides of a triangle have?

Example 1 A-Frame Construction

In areas that get a lot of snow, cottages are often built with a triangular shape called an A-frame. This shape helps prevent damage from heavy loads of snow on the roof.

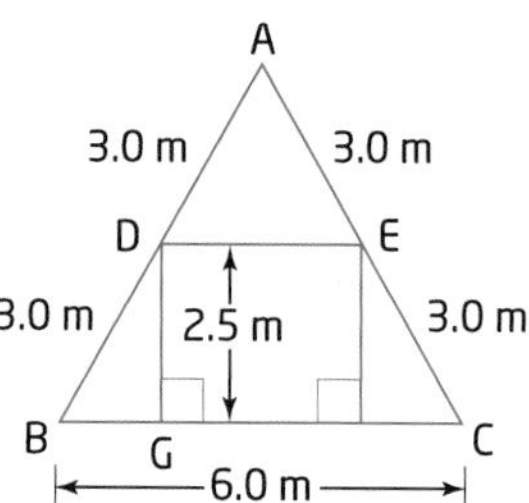

a) Find the width of the floor of the upper room in this cottage.

b) Find the height of the upper room.

Solution

a) Since BD = DA, point D is the midpoint of side AB. Similarly, point E is the midpoint of side AC.

From the properties of midpoints of the sides of a triangle, DE must be half the length of BC. On the drawing, the length of BC is 6.0 m. So, the floor of the upper room is 3.0 m wide.

b) Since D and E are midpoints of two sides of △ABC, the height of △ADE is equal to the height of trapezoid DECB.

The height of the upper room is 2.5 m.

Example 2 Medians of a Triangle

median

- the line segment joining a vertex of a triangle to the midpoint of the opposite side

bisect

- divide into two equal parts

Show that a **median** **bisects** the area of a triangle.

Solution

Method 1: Use the Area Formula

The median AD joins the vertex A to the midpoint of CB. Therefore, CD = BD.

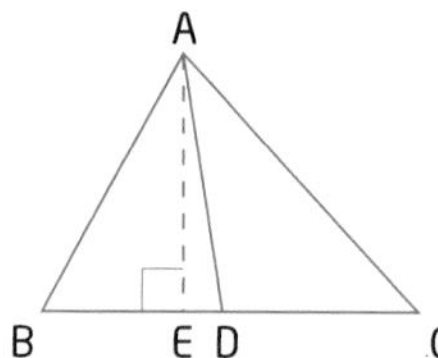

The formula for the area of a triangle is $A = \frac{bh}{2}$.

Since CD = BD, the bases of △ACD and △ADB are equal. These two triangles also have the same height, shown by altitude AE. The areas of the two triangles are equal. Therefore, the median AD divides the area of △ABC into two equal parts.

The same logic applies to a median drawn from any vertex of any triangle. Thus, any median of a triangle bisects its area.

Method 2: Use *The Geometer's Sketchpad®*

Construct any △ABC. Construct the midpoint of side BC by selecting the side and choosing **Midpoints** from the **Construct** menu. Construct a line segment from this midpoint to vertex A. This line segment is a median.

Select points A, B, and D; then, choose **Triangle Interior** from the **Construct** menu. Select points A, D, and C; then, choose **Triangle Interior** from the **Construct** menu again.

Select the interior of △ABD, and choose **Area** from the **Measure** menu. Measure the area of △ACD in the same way. These measures show that the two areas are equal.

Drag any of the vertices A, B, and C around the screen. The software automatically moves point D so that it stays at the midpoint of BC and AD is still a median. The areas of △ACD and △ABD remain equal for all shapes of △ABC.

This relationship shows that a median bisects the area of any triangle.

- computer with *The Geometer's Sketchpad®*

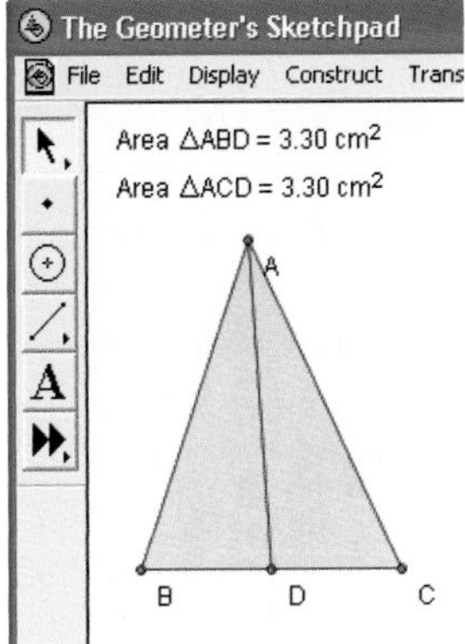

Example 3 Use a Counter-Example

Shivany measured this right triangle and noticed that a median bisects the right angle. She conjectures that a median will bisect the right angle in all right triangles. Is this conjecture correct?

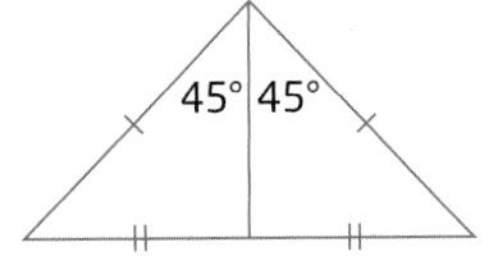

Literacy Connections

A conjecture is an educated guess.

Solution

In this right triangle, ∠ABD and ∠DBC are clearly not equal. Thus, the median does not bisect the right angle.

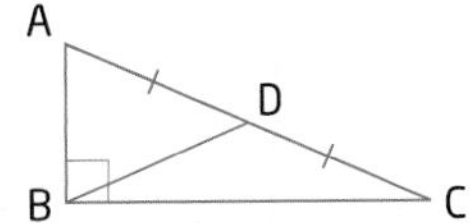

This **counter-example** shows that Shivany's conjecture is incorrect.

Key Concepts

- A line segment joining the midpoints of two sides of a triangle is parallel to the third side and half as long.
- The height of a triangle formed by joining the midpoints of two sides of a triangle is half the height of the original triangle.
- The medians of a triangle bisect its area.
- A counter-example can disprove a conjecture or hypothesis.

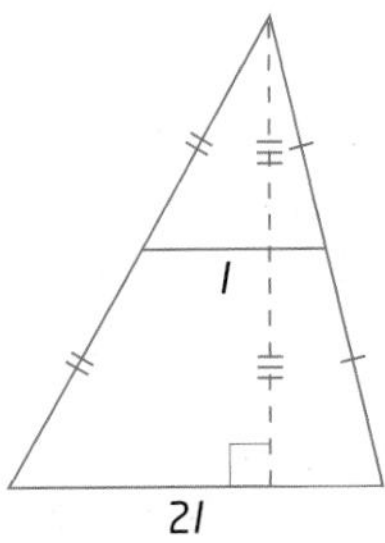

Communicate Your Understanding

C1 Points D, E, and F are the midpoints of the sides of △ABC. Explain how you can show that the area of △DEF is one quarter of the area of △ABC.

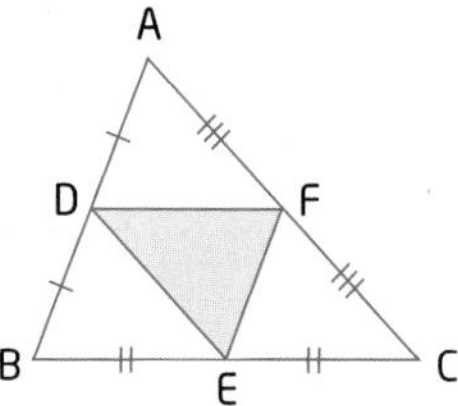

C2 Explain how you could use a counter-example to disprove the hypothesis that all scalene triangles are acute.

Practise

For help with question 1, see Example 1.

1. Calculate the length of line segment XY in each triangle.

a)

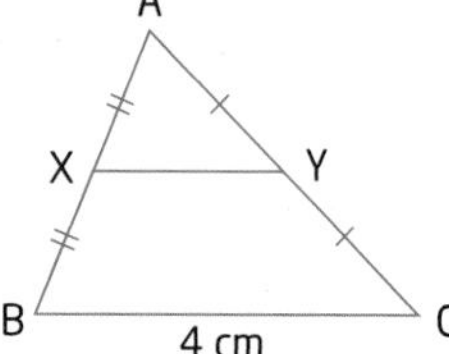

b)

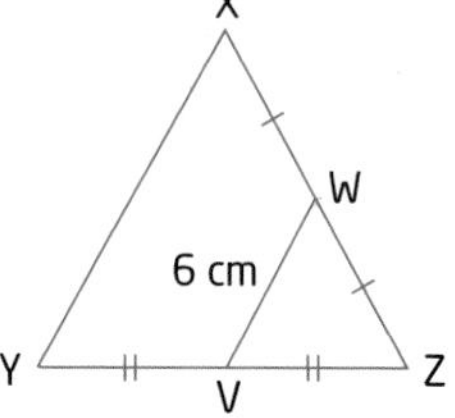

For help with questions 2 and 3, see Example 2.

2. The area of △PQR is 16 cm^2. Calculate the area of

a) △PQS

b) △QSR

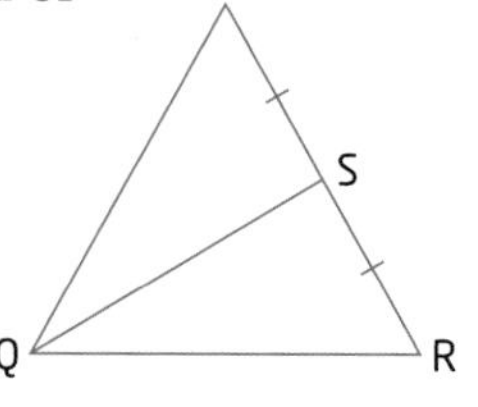

3. The area of △XYZ is 19 cm^2. Calculate the area of

a) △WZY

b) △WXY

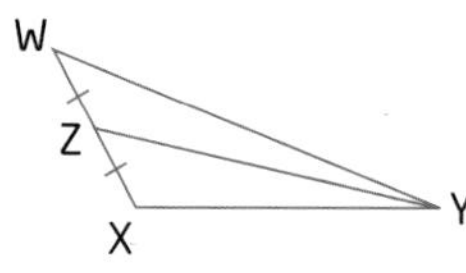

Connect and Apply

Did You Know?

The cross-brace stops the weight of the bridge from bending the sides of the support outward.

4. Calculate the length of the cross-brace AB in this bridge support.

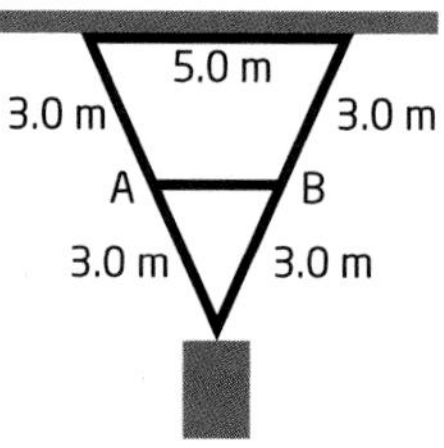

5. **a)** Make a conjecture about whether the median to the vertex opposite the unequal side of an isosceles triangle bisects the angle at the vertex.

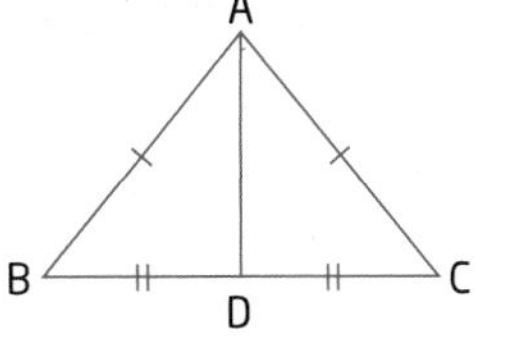

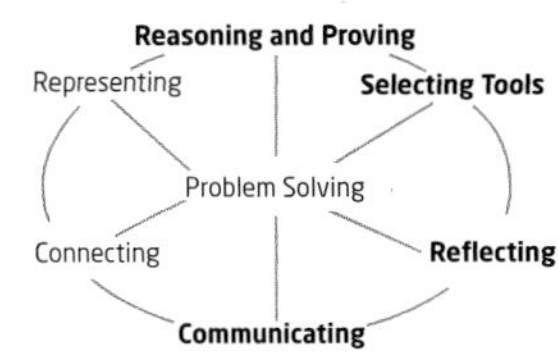

b) Describe how you can see if your conjecture is correct by folding a diagram of an isosceles triangle.

c) Describe how you could use geometry software to see if your conjecture is correct.

d) Use one of the two methods you described to test your conjecture. Describe your results.

6. Raquel conjectures that $\angle ADC$ in this diagram will be acute when point D is located anywhere on side AB. Use a counter-example to show that this conjecture is false.

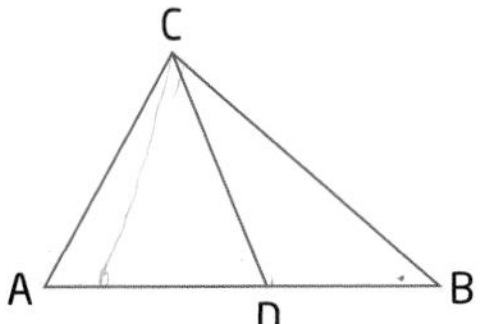

7. Here are three conjectures about scalene triangles with a 60° interior angle. For each conjecture, either draw a counter-example or explain why you think the conjecture is true.

a) The 60° angle is always opposite the shortest side.

b) The 60° angle is always opposite the longest side.

c) The 60° angle is always opposite the second-longest side.

8. Harpreet constructed $\triangle ABC$ with $AB = AC$. He then constructed the midpoint of BC at D and drew a perpendicular line through BC at D. Will this **right bisector** pass through vertex A? Justify your answer.

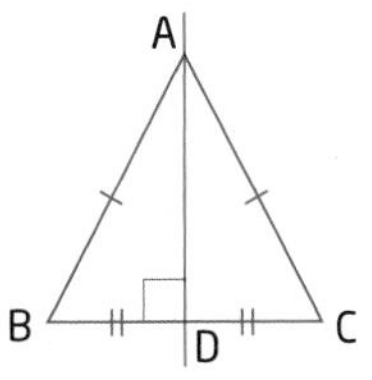

right bisector

- a line perpendicular to a line segment and passing through its midpoint

9. Tori constructed an equilateral $\triangle ABC$ and the right bisector of each side. She found that the three bisectors intersect at point G. Tori conjectured that $\triangle AGC$, $\triangle CGB$, and $\triangle BGA$ are also equilateral triangles. Is she correct? Explain.

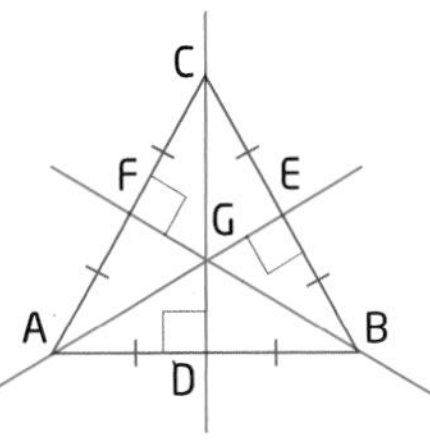

10. **Chapter Problem** Determine whether the three medians of a triangle intersect at a single point.
    - If you are using pencil and paper, draw the medians in at least one example of each type of triangle.
    - If you are using geometry software, construct a triangle and line segments joining each vertex to the midpoint of the opposite side. Drag each vertex to various new locations. Does changing the shape of the triangle affect how the medians intersect?

    Do you think that the medians intersect at a single point in all triangles? Explain your reasoning.

Extend

centroid

- the point where the medians of a triangle intersect

11. The three medians of this triangle intersect at point G. This point is called a **centroid**.

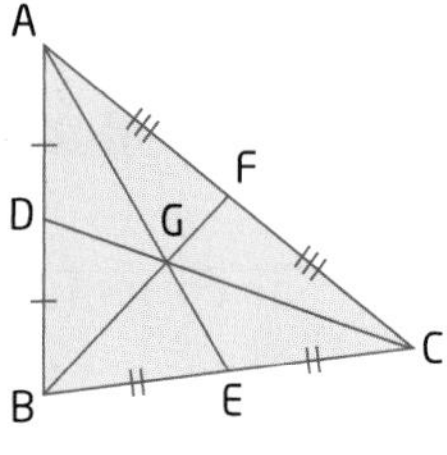

a) Show that △BEG has the same area as △CEG.

b) Can you use your answer to part a) to show that the area of △ADG is equal to the area of △BDG and that the area of △AFG is equal to the area of △CFG? Explain.

c) Show that all six of the triangles in part a) and part b) have the same area.

similar

- having all corresponding sides proportional

Go to www.mcgrawhill.ca/links/principles9 and follow the links to learn more about Sierpinski's triangle.

12. The Polish mathematician Waclaw Sierpinski devised a process for repeatedly dividing a triangle into smaller **similar** triangles. Question C1 on page 398 shows the first step in this process.

a) Use a library or the Internet to learn how to produce Sierpinski's triangle.

b) Conjecture what fraction of the triangle is shaded after each step of the process.

c) Calculate the area that is shaded after four steps.

13. a) Investigate whether the right bisectors of the sides of a triangle always intersect at a single point. Describe your findings.

b) Draw a triangle in which the right bisectors of the sides intersect at a single point. Can you draw a circle that has this point as its centre and intersects the triangle at exactly three points? If so, describe the properties of the circle.

14. a) Investigate whether the lines that bisect the angles of a triangle always intersect at a single point. Describe your findings.

b) Draw a triangle in which the angle bisectors intersect at a single point. Can you draw a circle that has this point as its centre and intersects the triangle at exactly three points? If so, describe the properties of the circle.

15. Math Contest Is the intersection of the right bisectors of the sides of a triangle always inside the triangle? Support your answer with a diagram.

16. Math Contest Which of these ratios cannot represent the relative lengths of the sides of a triangle?

a) 1:1:1 **b)** 1:2:2 **c)** 1:2:3 **d)** 1:1:2

e) 3:4:5 **f)** 3:4:6 **g)** 3:4:8

7.5 Midpoints and Diagonals in Quadrilaterals

Copper sulphate is one of the many minerals and chemical compounds that form crystals with quadrilateral faces. In this section, you will examine the properties of sides and diagonals of quadrilaterals.

Investigate

Tools
- ruler
- protractor

What are the properties of the midpoints of the sides of a quadrilateral?

Method 1: Use Paper and Pencil

1. Draw a large quadrilateral ABCD. Measure the four sides and mark the midpoints, with E the midpoint of AB, F the midpoint of BC, and so on.

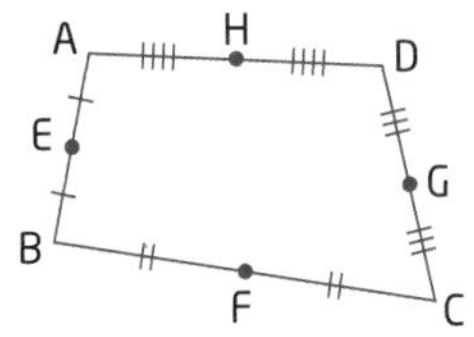

2. Draw line segments joining E to F, F to G, G to H, and H to E. What type of quadrilateral does EFGH appear to be?
3. Measure and compare the line segments in the smaller quadrilateral. What relationships are there among the lengths of these line segments?
4. Measure the interior angles of quadrilateral EFGH with a protractor. Mark these measures on your drawing.
5. If the co-interior angles formed by a transversal and two line segments are supplementary, the two segments are parallel. Are any of the sides of the quadrilateral EFGH parallel?
6. **Reflect** Do your answers to steps 3 to 5 confirm your conjecture in step 2? Explain.
7. Compare your results with those of your classmates.

8. **Reflect** Do you think that joining the midpoints of the sides of any quadrilateral always produces the same type of geometric shape? Explain your reasoning.

Tools

- computer with *The Geometer's Sketchpad®*

Technology Tip

You can also do this investigation using Cabri Jr. on a graphing calculator. For step-by-step instructions, follow the links at www.mcgrawhill.ca/links/principles9.

Method 2: Use *The Geometer's Sketchpad®*

1. Turn on automatic labelling of points. From the **Edit** menu, choose **Preferences**. Click on the **Text** tab, check **For All New Points**, and click on **OK**.

2. Construct any quadrilateral ABCD. Construct the midpoints of the four sides by selecting the sides and then choosing **Midpoints** from the **Construct** menu.

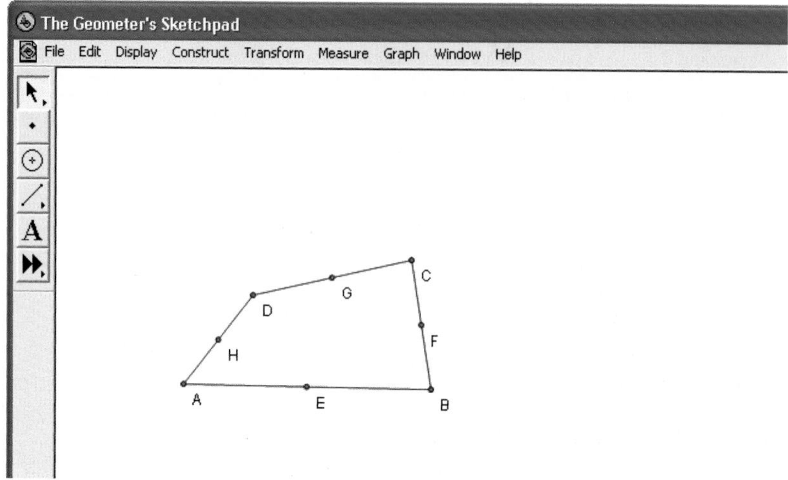

3. Construct line segments EF, FG, GH, and HE. What type of quadrilateral does EFGH appear to be?

4. Measure and compare the sides of the smaller quadrilateral. What relationships are there among these lengths?

5. Do any of these relationships change if you drag any of the vertices of ABCD to a different location?

6. Measure all the interior angles of quadrilateral EFGH.

7. If the co-interior angles formed by a transversal and two line segments are supplementary, the two segments are parallel. Calculate the sums of adjacent interior angles to see if any of the sides of quadrilateral EFGH are parallel. Does moving a vertex of the original quadrilateral ABCD change any of the angle sums?

8. **Reflect** Do your measurements confirm your conjecture in step 3? Do you think that joining the midpoints of the sides of any quadrilateral produces the same type of geometric shape? Explain your reasoning.

Example 1 Diagonals of a Parallelogram

Show that the diagonals of a parallelogram bisect each other.

Solution

Use *The Geometer's Sketchpad*®. Turn on automatic labelling of points.

Construct line segment AB and point C above it. Connect B to C with a line segment.

Select point C and line segment AB. Choose **Parallel Line** from the **Construct** menu.

Select point A and line segment BC. Then, choose **Parallel Line** from the **Construct** menu again.

Select the two lines that you constructed. Then, choose **Intersection** from the **Construct** menu.

Select the two lines again, and choose **Hide Parallel Lines** from the **Display** menu.

Construct line segments from C to D and from D to A. Then, construct diagonals AC and BD. Select the two diagonals and choose **Intersection** from the **Construct** menu.

Measure each line segment from point E to a vertex. These measurements show that EB = DE and AE = CE. The diagonals of this parallelogram bisect each other.

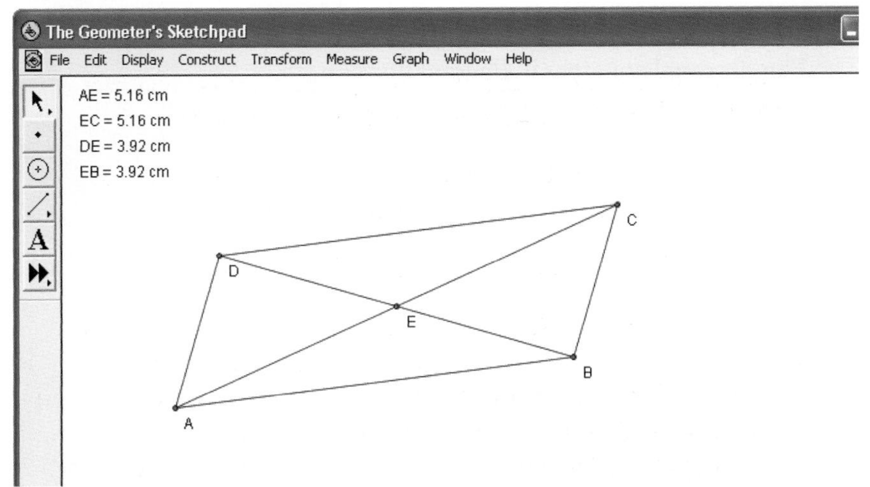

Now, drag each of the vertices to various new locations. ABCD remains a parallelogram, and the lengths of EB and DE remain equal, as do the lengths of AE and CE. Therefore, the diagonals of any parallelogram bisect each other.

Tools

- computer with *The Geometer's Sketchpad*®

Technology Tip

The keyboard shortcut for the Hide option is Ctrl+H.

Example 2 Use a Counter-Example

Jody conjectured that the diagonals of a parallelogram are always perpendicular to each other. Is she correct?

Solution

Draw any parallelogram ABCD that is not a rhombus. Draw the diagonals BD and AC. Then, measure the angles at the point E where the diagonals intersect. None of these angles is a right angle. Since perpendicular lines meet at right angles, the diagonals in this parallelogram are not perpendicular to each other. Therefore, the conjecture that the diagonals of a parallelogram are always perpendicular to each other is incorrect.

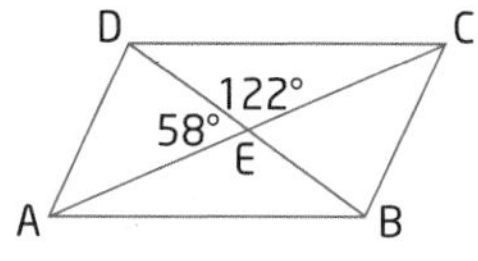

Key Concepts

- Joining the midpoints of the sides of any quadrilateral produces a parallelogram.

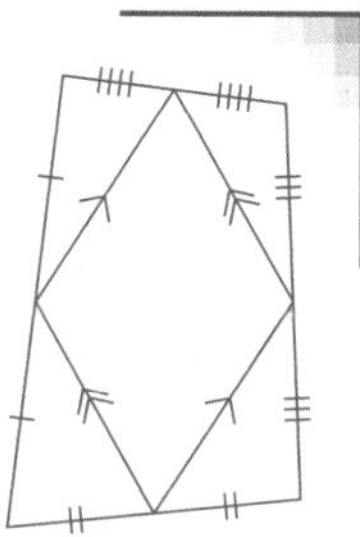

- The diagonals of a parallelogram bisect each other.

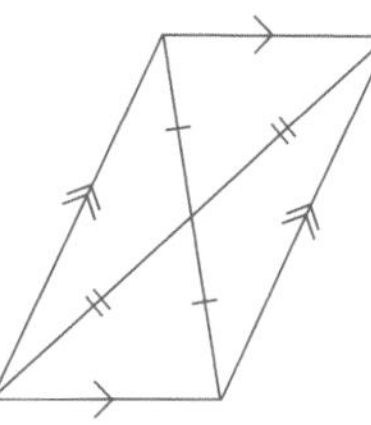

Communicate Your Understanding

C1 Describe how you can tell if two sides of a quadrilateral are parallel.

C2 Describe how you could fold a diagram of a parallelogram to show that its diagonals bisect each other.

Practise

1. Which line segments in this diagram are parallel?

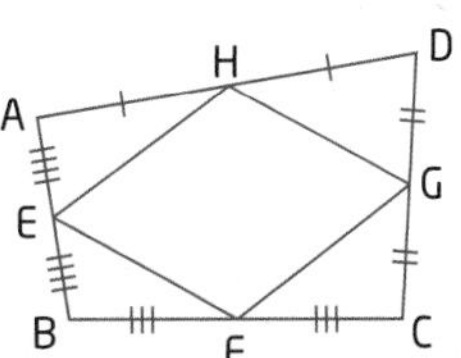

For help with questions 2 and 3, see Example 1.

2. Calculate the lengths of BE, CE, AC, and BD.

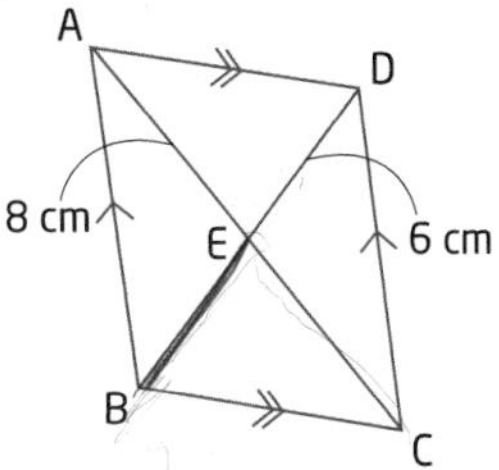

3. Calculate the lengths of PT and ST given that PR measures 14 m and QS measures 10 m.

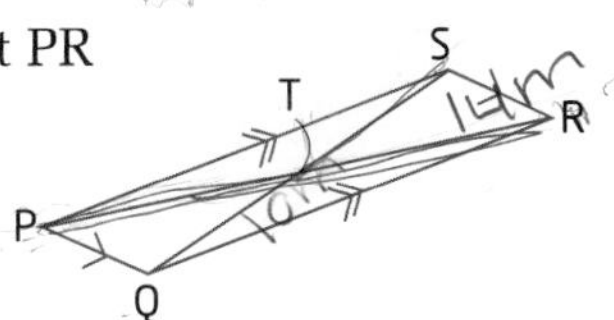

Connect and Apply

4. Drivers often use a scissor jack when changing a tire. The crank turns a threaded shaft that pulls the sides of the hinged parallelogram toward each other, raising the top of the jack. How high will the top of the jack be when the shaft is 20 cm from the base?

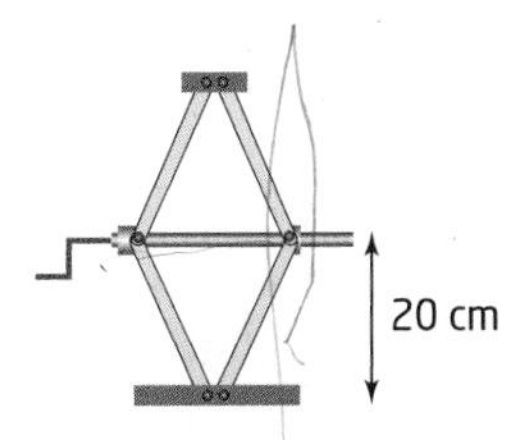

Did You Know?

Multistage scissor mechanisms can raise a platform 15 m or more. These machines are often used in construction and movie-making.

5. Construct a parallelogram, a rectangle, a rhombus, and a square. Draw the diagonals for each quadrilateral. Then, use your drawings to determine in which of the four quadrilaterals the diagonals
   - **a)** bisect each other
   - **b)** have the same length
   - **c)** intersect at 90°
   - **d)** bisect each other at 90°

6. Construct a parallelogram ABCD. Let E be the midpoint of AB, F be the midpoint of BC, G be the midpoint of CD, and H be the midpoint of DA. Connect EF, FG, GH, and HE to form a new parallelogram EFGH. Under what conditions is EFGH a rhombus?

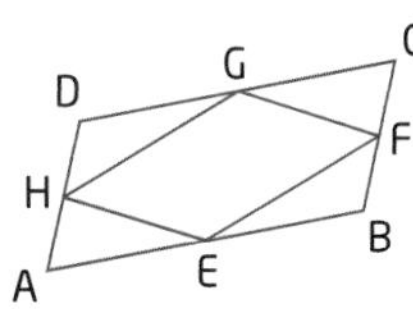

7. For each statement, either explain why it is true or draw a counter-example to show that it is false.
   - **a)** Any diagonal of a quadrilateral bisects its area.
   - **b)** Any line segment joining the midpoints of opposite sides of a parallelogram bisects its area.

8. On grid paper, draw a square PQRS and mark the midpoints of the four sides. Label these midpoints W, X, Y, and Z.

   a) What type of quadrilateral is WXYZ?

   b) How is the area of WXYZ related to the area of PQRS? Explain your reasoning.

   c) What shape will WXYZ become if PQRS is stretched to form a rectangle? Support your answer with a drawing.

   d) Will the relationship between the areas of WXYZ and PQRS change when PQRS is stretched into a rectangle? Explain.

9. a) Draw a quadrilateral ABCD with AB = AD and BC = DC.

   b) At what angle do the diagonals of the quadrilateral intersect?

   c) Join the midpoints of the sides of the quadrilateral to form a smaller quadrilateral EFGH. What type of quadrilateral is EFGH?

   d) Make a conjecture about how the area of EFGH is related to the area of ABCD.

   e) Describe how you can use geometry software to test your conjecture.

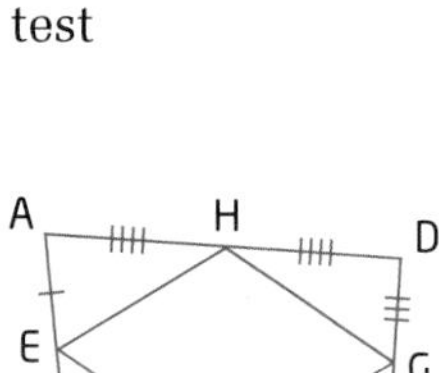

10. In this diagram, line segments joining the midpoints of the four sides of a quadrilateral form a smaller quadrilateral inside the original quadrilateral.

   a) How do you think the area of the smaller quadrilateral compares to the area of the original quadrilateral?

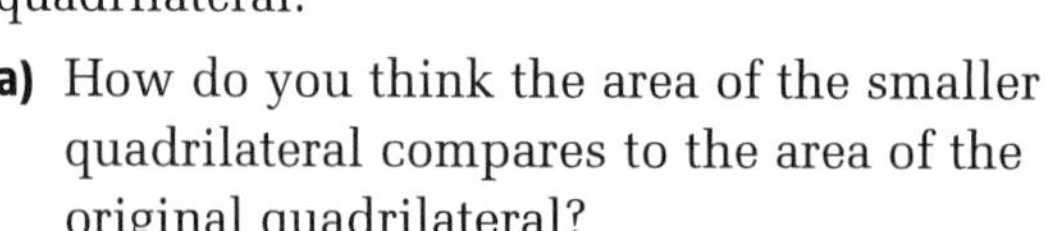

   b) Describe how you could confirm your conjecture.

11. **Use Technology**

   a) Construct ∠ABC with BA = BC. Construct a line perpendicular to AB at point A and a line perpendicular to BC at point C. Label the intersection of these lines D.

   b) Show that AD = CD.

   c) Show that BD bisects ∠ABC.

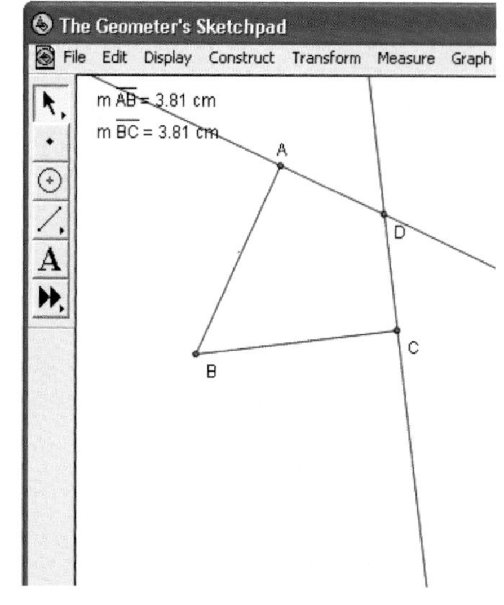

Achievement Check

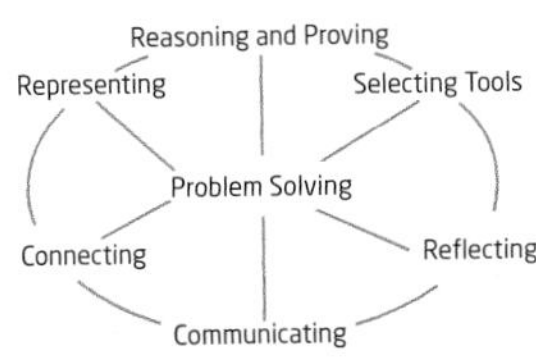

12. While reviewing for a geometry test, two of your friends find that they have different answers for several true/false questions. The two friends ask you to help them decide which answers are right. For each of these statements, either use a diagram to help explain why the statement is true, or draw a counter-example and explain why the statement is false.

a) A line segment joining the midpoints of two sides of a triangle bisects the area of the triangle.

b) Any diagonal of a parallelogram bisects its area.

c) A line segment joining the midpoints of the parallel sides of a trapezoid bisects its area.

d) A line segment joining the midpoints of opposite sides of a quadrilateral bisects its area.

Extend

13. Use congruent triangles to show that the diagonals of a parallelogram bisect each other.

14. a) Draw a quadrilateral ABCD with AB = CD and AD = CB.

b) Show that this quadrilateral must be a parallelogram.

15. This diagram shows all possible diagonals for a regular pentagon ABCDE.

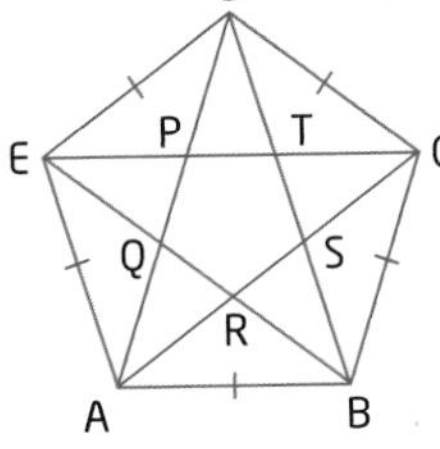

a) Is PQRST a regular polygon? How do you know?

b) Is PQRST similar to ABCDE? Explain.

c) Compare the lengths of the sides of PQRST to those of ABCDE.

d) Make a conjecture about how the ratio of the areas of PQRST and ABCDE is related to the ratio of their side lengths.

e) Use geometry software to test your conjecture. Describe your results.

16. Math Contest

a) How many line segments can be constructed between 10 points in a plane? Assume that no three points are on the same straight line.

b) Twelve people arrive at a meeting, one at a time. Each of these people shakes hands with everyone who is already there. How many handshakes have occurred once the 12th person has finished shaking hands?

17. Math Contest

a) Find a formula for the total number of line segments that can be constructed between n points in a plane if no three points are on the same straight line.

b) Use your answer to part a) to find a formula for the number of diagonals in a polygon with n sides.

Chapter 7 Review

7.1 Angle Relationships in Triangles, pages 364–373

1. Calculate the measure of each unknown angle.

a)

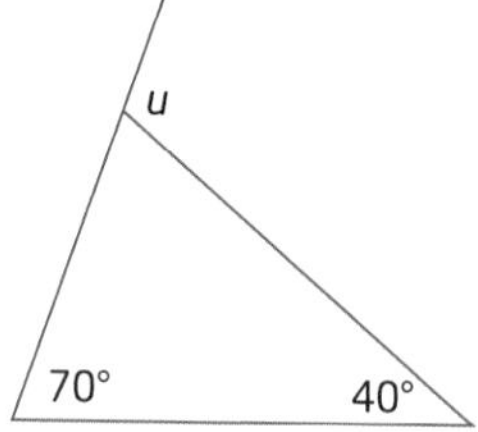

b)

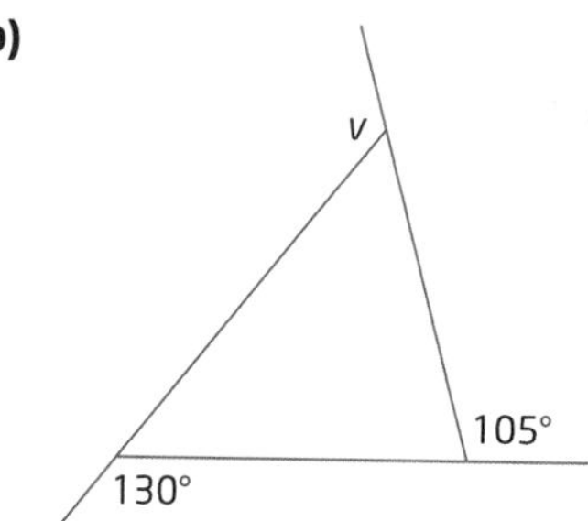

c)

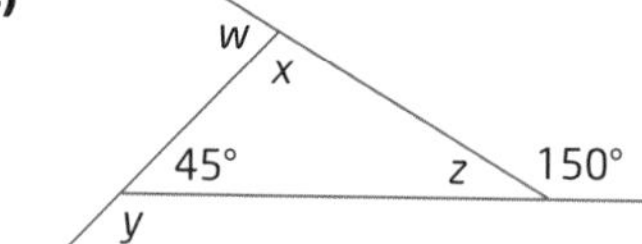

2. Explain why the angle relationships shown are not possible.

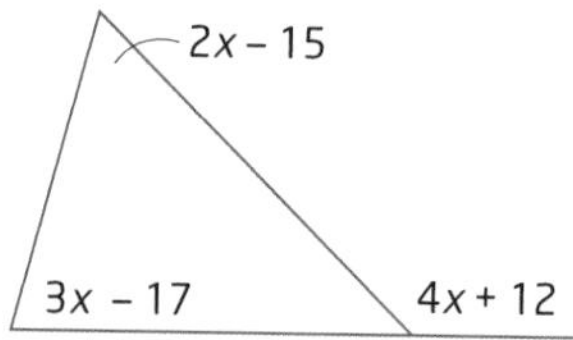

3. For each description, draw an example of the triangle or explain why it cannot exist.

a) a triangle with an acute exterior angle

b) a triangle with two acute exterior angles

c) a triangle with three obtuse exterior angles

d) a triangle with an acute exterior angle, a right exterior angle, and an obtuse exterior angle

7.2 Angle Relationships in Quadrilaterals, pages 374–383

4. Calculate the measure of each unknown angle.

a)

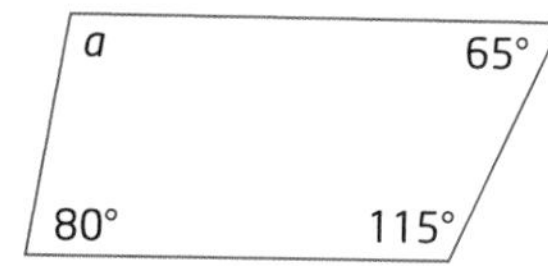

b)

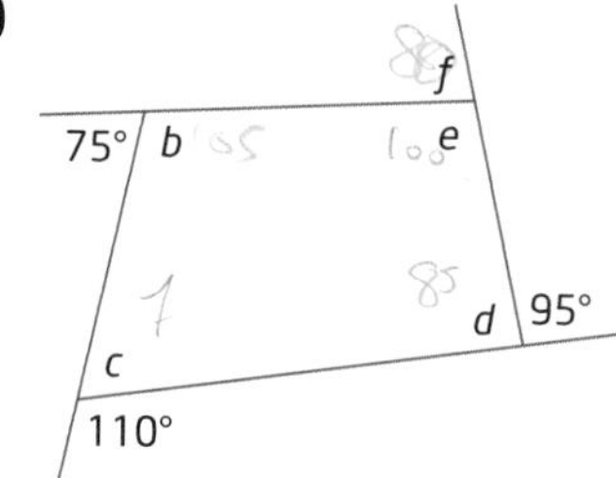

c)

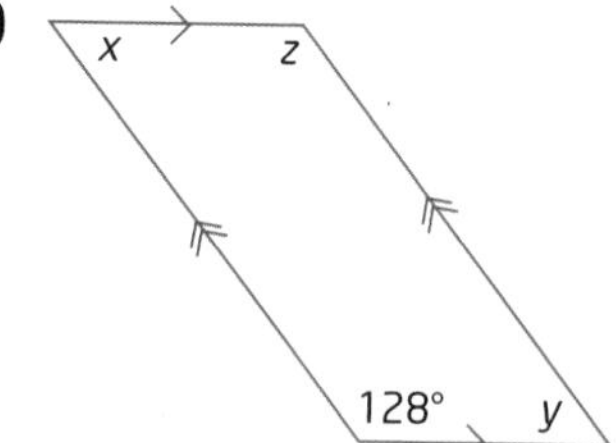

5. For each description, draw an example of the quadrilateral or explain why it cannot exist.

a) a quadrilateral with three obtuse interior angles

b) a quadrilateral with four obtuse interior angles

c) a quadrilateral with three obtuse exterior angles

d) a quadrilateral with four obtuse exterior angles

7.3 Angle Relationships in Polygons, pages 384–393

6. Find the sum of the interior angles of each polygon.

a) hexagon

b) octagon

c) dodecagon (12-sided figure)

7. Find the measure of each interior angle of a regular

a) pentagon

b) nonagon (9-sided figure)

c) hexadecagon (16-sided figure)

8. If each interior angle of a regular polygon measures 168°, how many sides does the polygon have?

9. a) Construct a regular octagon.

b) Describe the method you used.

7.4 Midpoints and Medians in Triangles, pages 394–400

10. Show that the area of $\triangle ADE$ is one quarter of the area of $\triangle ABC$.

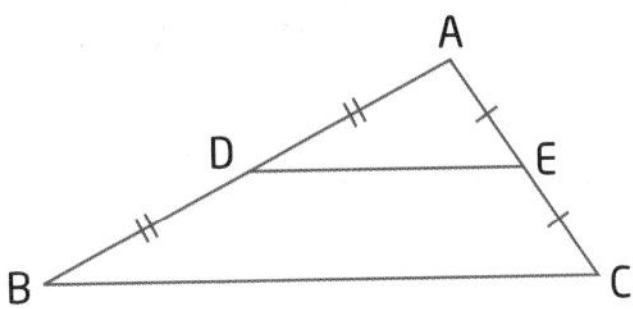

11. For each of these statements, either explain why it is true or draw a counter-example to show that it is false.

a) The medians of an equilateral triangle are equal in length.

b) The medians of a triangle are equal in length.

7.5 Midpoints and Diagonals in Quadrilaterals, pages 401–406

12. Make a conjecture about the diagonals of each type of quadrilateral. Show that each conjecture is true or use a counter-example to disprove it.

a) square

b) rectangle

c) rhombus

d) parallelogram

e) trapezoid

13. Describe how you can use geometry software to determine the types of quadrilaterals in which a line segment joining the midpoints of opposite sides bisects the area.

Chapter 7 Practice Test

Multiple Choice

For questions 1 to 5, select the best answer.

1. If an isosceles triangle has two exterior angles that each measure 110°, the measure of the third exterior angle is

A 70°

B 120°

C 140°

D 250°

2. In △ABC, the interior angle at A is 51° and the exterior angle at B is 119°. The interior angle at C measures

A 51°

B 68°

C 90°

D 39°

3. The sum of the exterior angles of a convex polygon

A is always 180°

B is always 360°

C is always 720°

D depends on the number of sides

4. The area of △ADE is

A half the area of △ABC

B one third the area of △ABC

C half the area of trapezoid DBCE

D one third the area of trapezoid DBCE

5. The diagonals of a rectangle

A are perpendicular to each other

B bisect each other

C bisect each other and are perpendicular to each other

D bisect the interior angles

Short Response

Show all steps to your solutions.

6. Find the measure of each unknown angle in these diagrams.

a)

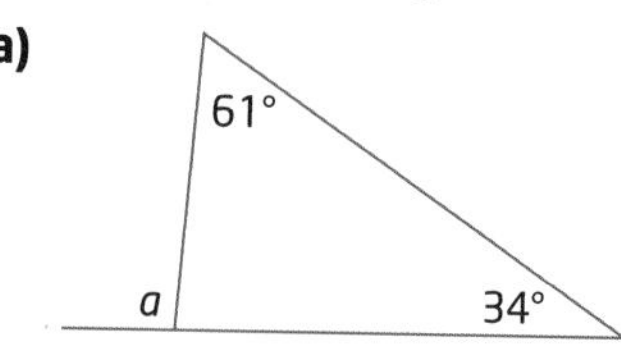

b)

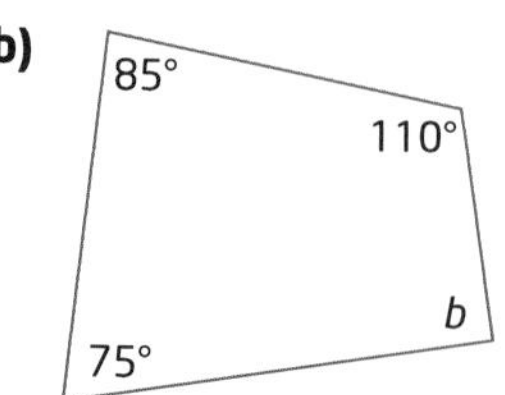

c)

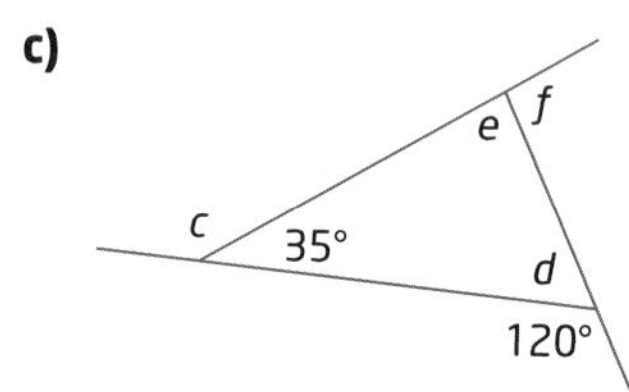

d)

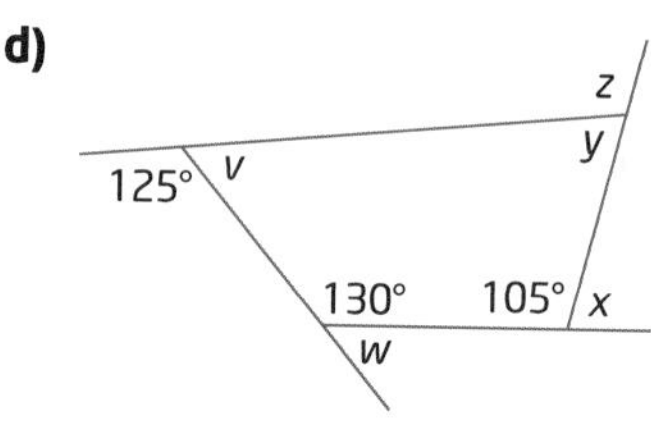

7. a) List three properties of the interior angles of a parallelogram.

b) List two properties of the diagonals of a parallelogram.

8. Draw a counter-example to disprove the hypothesis that all quadrilaterals with a pair of equal opposite angles are parallelograms.

9. Find the sum of the interior angles of a 14-sided polygon.

Extended Response

Provide complete solutions.

10. The sum of the interior angles of a polygon is 2340°. How many sides does the polygon have?

11. A town is building a small park on a triangular lot. The park will have a children's playground and a horseshoe pitch. For safety, a fence will separate the playground from the area where people will be throwing horseshoes. Describe how you could place the fence to divide the park evenly for the two uses.

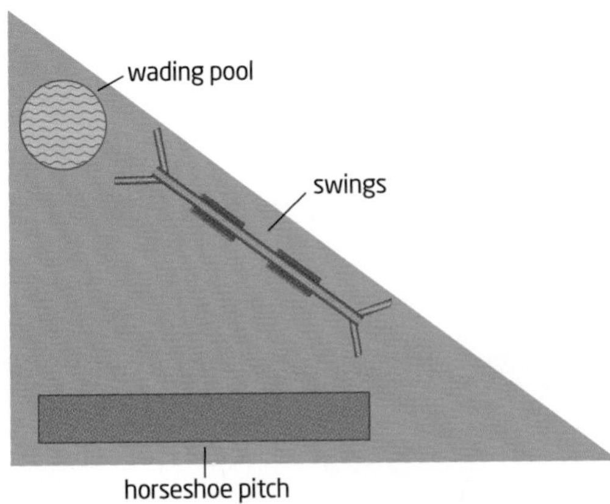

12. Manpreet used geometry software to construct this diagram.

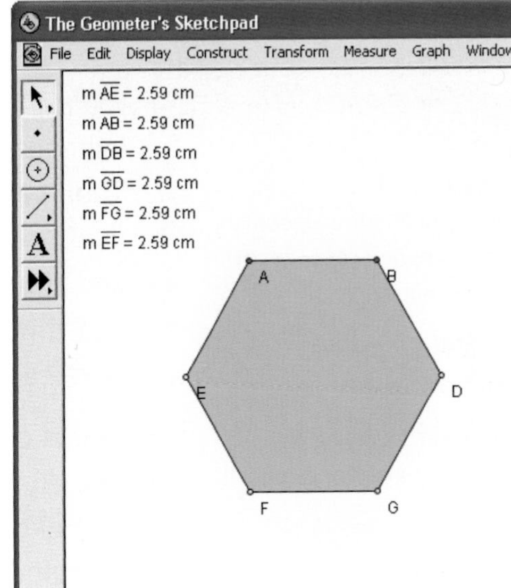

a) Identify the shape that she has constructed.

b) Is the shape regular? Justify your answer.

c) Calculate the measure of each angle in the diagram.

d) If Manpreet wants to change her drawing to a regular octagon, should she increase or decrease the measure of each interior angle? Explain your reasoning.

Chapter Problem Wrap-Up

The centre of mass of an object is the mean position of the mass in the object. The object can balance at this point since the mass in any direction from the centre of mass is matched by mass on the opposite side.

Consider how the mass of a triangular object is distributed on either side of the medians of the triangle. Assume that the triangular cardboard cutout has an even thickness and density.

a) Would the cutout balance if placed with one of its medians along the edge of a metre stick? Explain why or why not.

b) Where is the centre of mass of the triangular cutout? Explain your reasoning.

c) Mark this centre on cutouts of several different triangles. Check your answer to part b) by seeing if each cutout will balance perfectly when you place your finger under the centre point.

CHAPTER

8 Measurement Relationships

Measurement and Geometry

- Relate the geometric representation and the algebraic representation, $a^2 + b^2 = c^2$, of the Pythagorean theorem.
- Solve problems using the Pythagorean theorem.
- Solve problems involving the areas and perimeters of composite shapes.
- Determine, through investigation, the formula for the surface area of a pyramid.
- Develop, through investigation, the formulas for the volume of a pyramid, a cone, and a sphere.
- Solve problems involving the surface areas and volumes of prisms, pyramids, cylinders, cones, and spheres.

Vocabulary

hypotenuse
Pythagorean theorem
surface area
volume
pyramid
lateral faces
cone
sphere

Landscape architects design, plan, and manage land. Their work can be seen in the attractiveness and usefulness of parks, highways, neighbourhoods, gardens, and zoos. Concepts of measurement in two-dimensional and three-dimensional geometry are important in landscape design and construction.

In this chapter, you will solve problems involving two-dimensional and three-dimensional figures. You will also extend your skills with three-dimensional geometry to include pyramids, cones, and spheres.

Chapter Problem

For her summer job, Emily will help her brother with his landscaping business. The company designs and installs patios and gardens and puts the finishing touches around swimming pools. Throughout this chapter, you will apply your skills to help Emily complete her projects.

Get Ready

Calculate Perimeter and Circumference

The perimeter of a shape is the distance around the outside. Circumference is the perimeter of a circle.

$P = 2(l + w)$
$= 2(8.2 + 5.6)$
$= 2(13.8)$
$= 27.6$

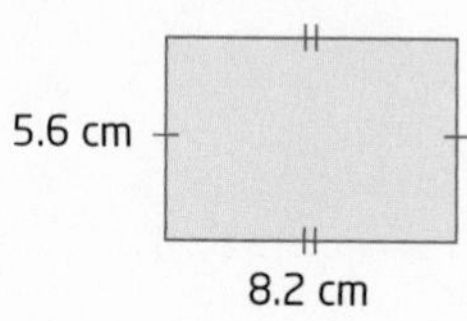

The perimeter of the rectangle is 27.6 cm.

$C = 2\pi r$
$= 2\pi(5.3)$ **Estimate: 2 × 3 × 5 = 30**
$\doteq 33.3$ C 2 × π × 5.3 =

5.3 cm

The circumference of the circle is approximately 33.3 cm.

1. Determine the perimeter of each shape.

a) **b)**

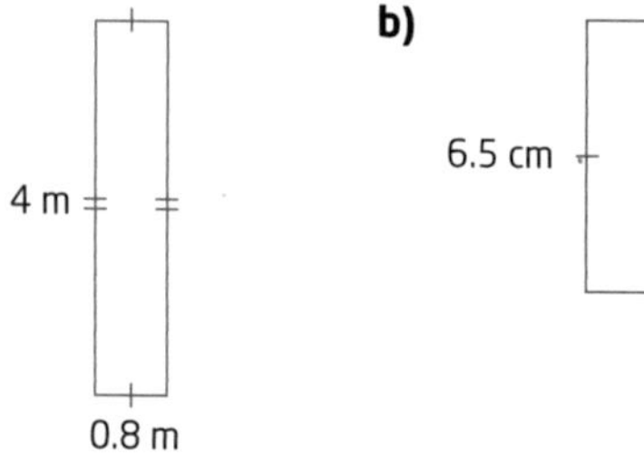

c) **d)**

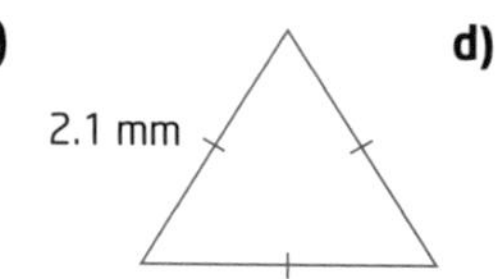

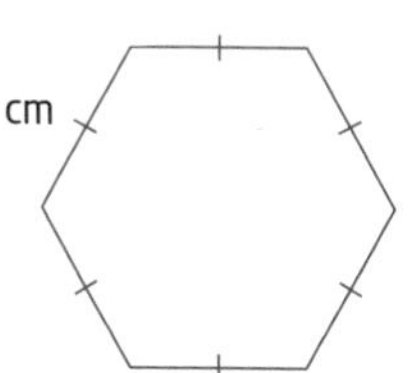

e) **f)**

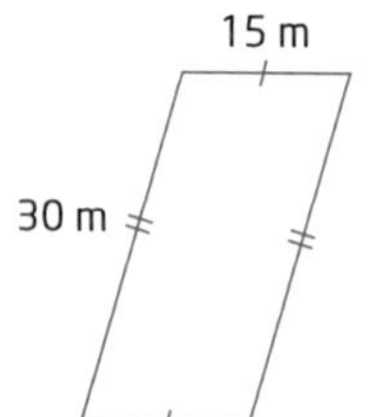

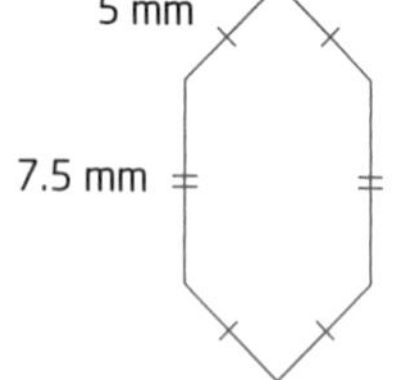

2. Determine the circumference of each circle. Round answers to the nearest tenth of a unit.

a) **b)**

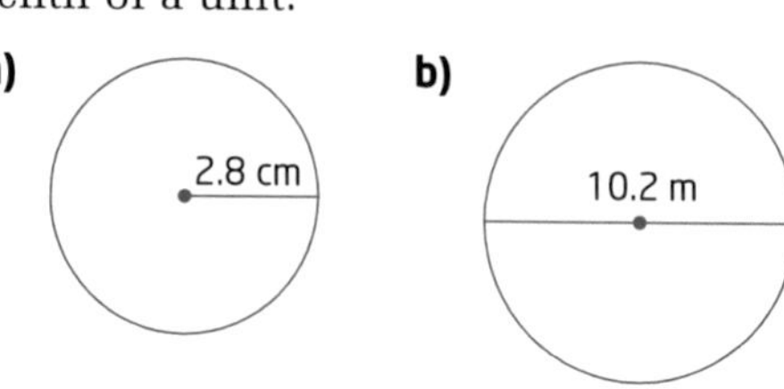

c) **d)**

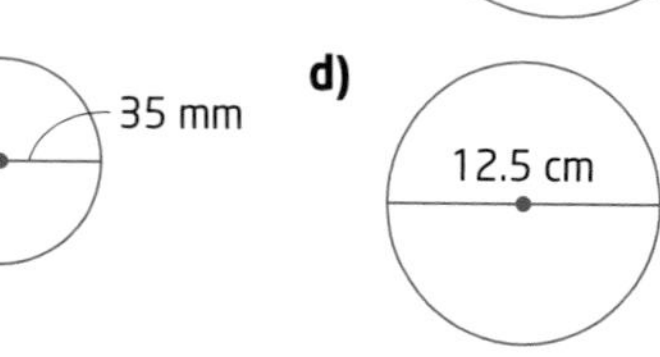

3. A flower bed has the dimensions shown.

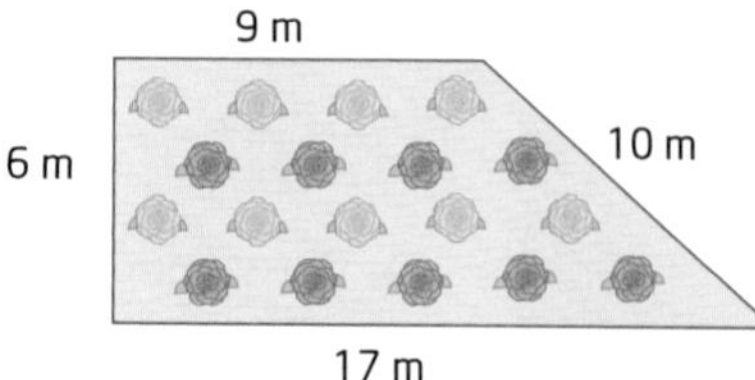

Find the perimeter of the flower bed.

Apply Area Formulas

Area measures how much space a two-dimensional shape covers. It is measured in square units.

The table gives the area formulas for some common shapes.

Shape	Name	Area Formula
l, w	rectangle	$A = lw$
h, b	triangle	$A = \frac{1}{2}bh$
r	circle	$A = \pi r^2$
h, b	parallelogram	$A = bh$
a, h, b	trapezoid	$A = \frac{1}{2}h(a + b)$

Apply the formula for the area of a rectangle. Substitute $l = 6.0$ and $w = 4.5$.

$$
\begin{aligned}
A &= lw \\
&= (6.0)(4.5) \\
&= 27
\end{aligned}
$$

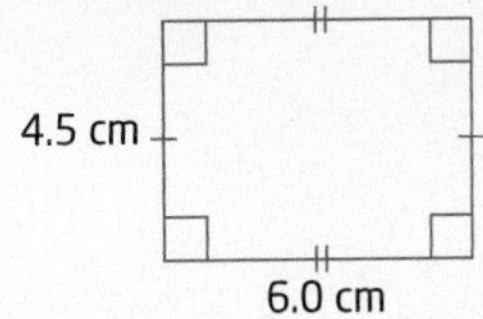

The area of the rectangle is 27 cm^2.

4. Determine the area of each shape. Round answers to the nearest tenth of a square unit.

a)

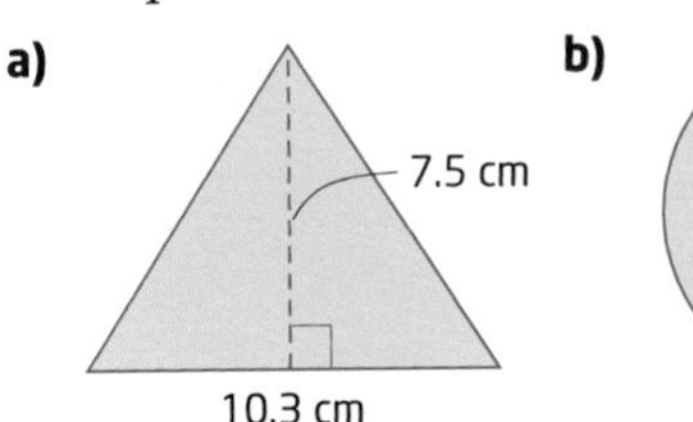

b)

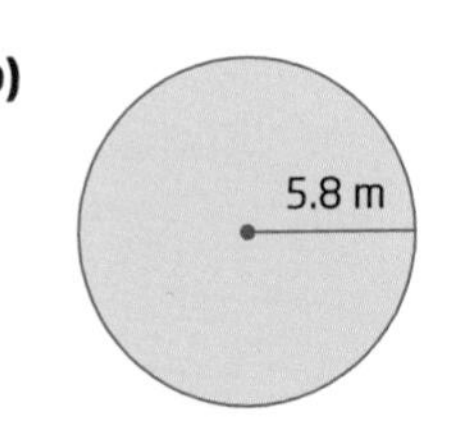

5. Determine the area of each shape.

a) **b)**

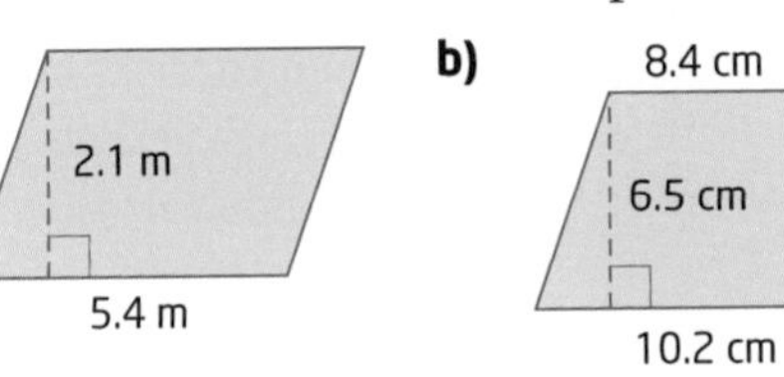

Calculate Surface Area and Volume

A net, which is a flat pattern that can be folded to form a figure, can help you visualize the faces of a three-dimensional figure.

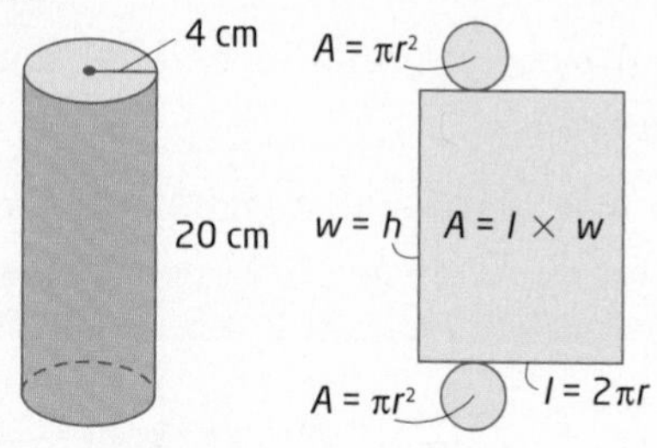

The surface area of the cylinder consists of the top and bottom, which are circles, and the curved surface, which is a rectangle.

Apply the formula for the surface area of a cylinder.

$$\begin{aligned} SA &= 2\pi r^2 + 2\pi rh \\ &= 2\pi(4)^2 + 2\pi(4)(20) \\ &\doteq 603 \end{aligned}$$

C 2 × π × 4 x² + 2 × π × 4 × 20 =

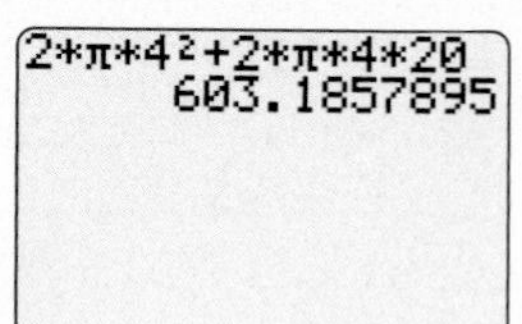

The surface area is approximately 603 cm^2.

My scientific calculator may be different. If these keystrokes don't work on my calculator, I'll look at the manual.

Apply the formula for the volume of a cylinder.

$$\begin{aligned} V &= \text{(area of base)(height)} \\ &= \pi r^2 h \\ &= \pi(4)^2(20) \\ &\doteq 1005 \end{aligned}$$

The volume is approximately 1005 cm^3.

6. Determine the surface area of each three-dimensional figure. If necessary, round answers to the nearest square unit.

a) **b)**

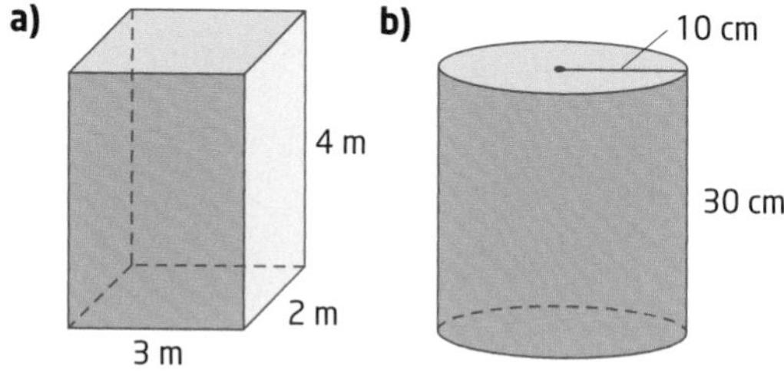

7. Find the volume of each three-dimensional figure in question 6. If necessary, round answers to the nearest cubic unit.

8. a) Draw a net for the triangular prism. What shapes do you need? Label the dimensions on the shapes in your net.

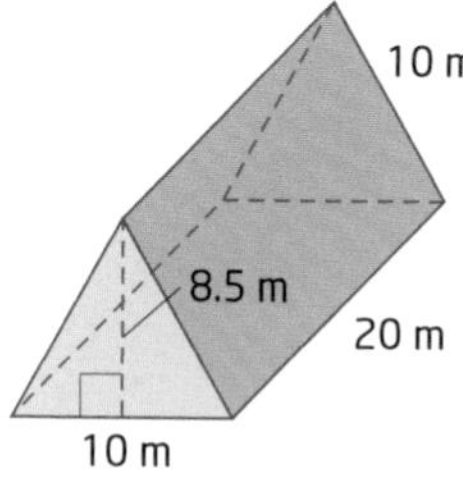

b) Find the surface area of the prism.

c) Find the volume of the prism.

Use *The Geometer's Sketchpad®*

Draw and measure a line segment using *The Geometer's Sketchpad®*.

- Use the **Straightedge Tool** to create a line segment AB.
- Use the **Selection Arrow Tool** to select the line segment.
- From the **Measure** menu, choose **Length**.

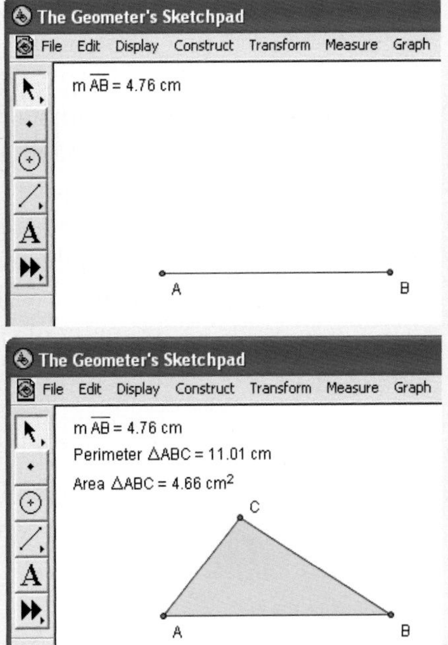

Drag one of the endpoints of line segment AB to change its length. Notice how the measurement on the screen changes as you do this.

Draw and measure the perimeter and area of a triangle using *The Geometer's Sketchpad®*.

- Use the **Straightedge Tool** to create three line segments to form △ABC.
- Use the **Selection Arrow Tool** to select all three vertices.
- From the **Construct** menu, choose **Triangle Interior**.
- From the **Measure** menu, choose **Perimeter** and then **Area**.

Drag one vertex of the triangle to change its shape. Notice how the perimeter and area measurements change as you drag the vertex.

Draw and measure the circumference and area of a circle using *The Geometer's Sketchpad®*.

- Use the **Compass Tool** to create any circle.
- Make sure the circle is selected. Then, from the **Measure** menu, choose **Circumference** and then **Area**.

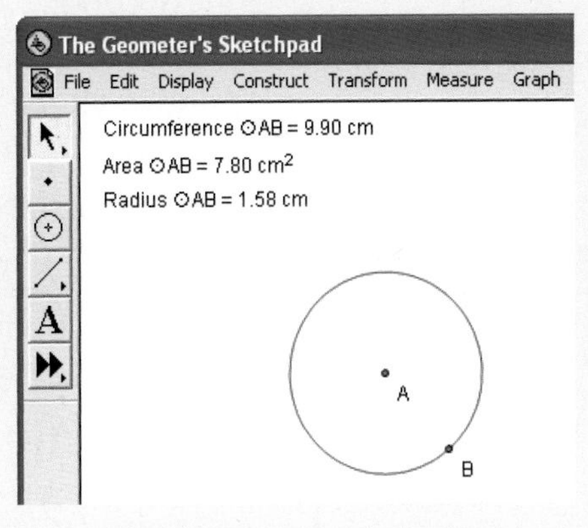

You can also measure the radius.

- Select the circle. From the **Measure** menu, choose **Radius**.

Change the size of the circle and watch the measurements change.

9. Use *The Geometer's Sketchpad®* to create a triangle with each characteristic.

a) a perimeter of 15 cm

b) an area of 10 cm^2

10. Use *The Geometer's Sketchpad®* to create a circle with each characteristic.

a) a circumference of 12 cm

b) an area of 20 cm^2

11. Use *The Geometer's Sketchpad®* to create any circle.

a) Measure its circumference and area.

b) Create a quadrilateral that has the same perimeter. Predict which figure has the greater area.

c) Calculate the area of the quadrilateral. Was your prediction correct?

8.1 Apply the Pythagorean Theorem

The Pythagorean theorem is named after the Greek philosopher and mathematician Pythagoras (580–500 B.C.E.). Although ancient texts indicate that different civilizations understood this property of right triangles, Pythagoras proved that it applies to all right triangles.

If a right triangle is labelled as shown, then the area of the large square drawn on the **hypotenuse** is c^2, while the areas of the other two squares are a^2 and b^2.

hypotenuse
- the longest side of a right triangle
- the side opposite the 90° angle

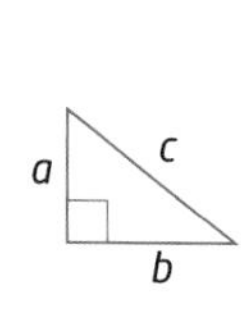

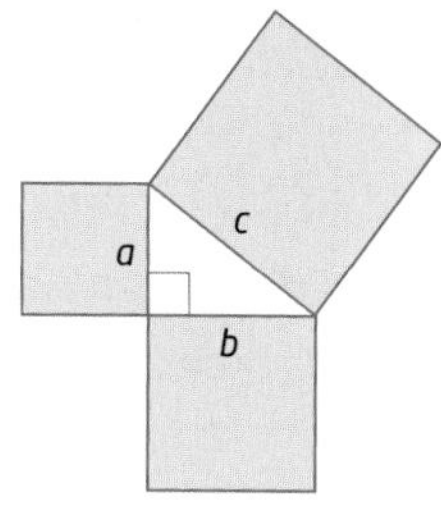

According to the Pythagorean relationship, the area of the square drawn on the hypotenuse is equal to the sum of the areas of the squares drawn on the other two sides.

Therefore, the algebraic model for the Pythagorean relationship is $c^2 = a^2 + b^2$. This is known as the **Pythagorean theorem**.

Pythagorean theorem
- in a right triangle, the square of the length of the hypotenuse is equal to the sum of the squares of the lengths of the two shorter sides

Investigate

How can you illustrate the Pythagorean theorem?

- grid paper
- ruler

Method 1: Use Pencil and Paper

1. Construct any right triangle. Label the sides of your triangle using three different letters.

2. Measure the length of each side of your triangle. Indicate these measures on your diagram.

3. a) Calculate the area of the square on the hypotenuse.

b) Calculate the sum of the areas of the squares on the two shorter sides.

c) Write the Pythagorean theorem using your side labels.

4. **a)** Calculate the square root of your answer to step 3b).

   b) Compare this value to the length of the hypotenuse.

5. Construct any non-right triangle. Does the Pythagorean relationship still hold? Does the relationship from step 4, part b), still hold?

6. **Reflect** Explain how this activity illustrates the Pythagorean theorem.

Method 2: Use *The Geometer's Sketchpad®*

1. From the **Edit** menu, choose **Preferences.** Click on the **Units** tab. Set the precision to tenths for all three boxes. Click on the **Text** tab and check **For All New Points**. Click on **OK**.

2. Use the **Straightedge Tool** to create any △ABC.

3. **a)** To measure ∠ABC, select vertices A, B, and C, in that order. From the **Measure** menu, choose **Angle**.

   b) To measure the length of AB, select line segment AB. From the **Measure** menu, choose **Length**. Repeat for line segments BC and CA.

4. **a)** Drag a vertex of the triangle until ∠ABC measures 90°.

   b) Select the measure $\mathbf{m\overline{CA}}$. From the **Measure** menu, choose **Calculate**. Enter $\mathbf{m\overline{CA}\hat{}2}$, by selecting $\mathbf{m\overline{CA}}$ from the **Values** drop-down menu on the calculator.

   c) Select $\mathbf{m\overline{AB}}$ and $\mathbf{m\overline{BC}}$. From the **Measure** menu, choose **Calculate**. Enter $\mathbf{m\overline{AB}\hat{}2 + m\overline{BC}\hat{}2}$.

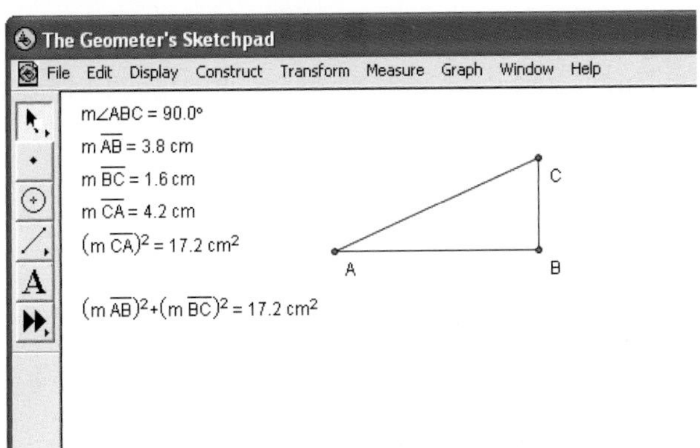

Tools

- computers
- *The Geometer's Sketchpad®* software

Go to www.mcgrawhill.ca/links/principles9 and follow the links to an interactive proof of the Pythagorean theorem.

Did You Know?

To create a right angle for measuring land or building pyramids, the ancient Egyptians tied 12 equally spaced knots in a rope. They then tied the rope into a loop and stretched it to form a triangle with a knot at each vertex. The only way this works is in the ratio 3:4:5, resulting in a right triangle.

5. a) Select $(m\overline{AB}^2)$ and $(m\overline{BC}^2)$. From the **Measure** menu, choose **Calculate**. Evaluate $\sqrt{(m\overline{AB})^2 + (m\overline{BC})^2}$ by choosing **sqrt** from the **Functions** pull-down menu on the calculator.
   b) Compare this value to the length of side CA.

6. Drag a vertex of the triangle so that the measure of ∠ABC is no longer 90°. Does the Pythagorean relationship still hold? Does the relationship from step 5b) still hold?

7. **Reflect** Explain how this activity illustrates the Pythagorean theorem.

Example 1 Find the Hypotenuse

The advertised size of a computer or television screen is actually the length of the diagonal of the screen. A computer screen measures 30 cm by 22.5 cm. Determine the length of its diagonal.

Solution

In the diagram, the diagonal, d, is the hypotenuse.

22.5 cm

d

30 cm

Apply the Pythagorean theorem.

$$d^2 = 30^2 + 22.5^2$$
$$d^2 = 900 + 506.25$$
$$d^2 = 1406.25$$
$$\sqrt{d^2} = \sqrt{1406.25}$$
$$d = 37.5$$

Only the positive square root needs to be used because *d* is a length.

The length of the diagonal of the computer screen is 37.5 cm.

Example 2 Find One of the Shorter Sides

Jenna is changing a light bulb. She rests a 4-m ladder against a vertical wall so that its base is 1.4 m from the wall. How high up the wall does the top of the ladder reach? Round your answer to the nearest tenth of a metre.

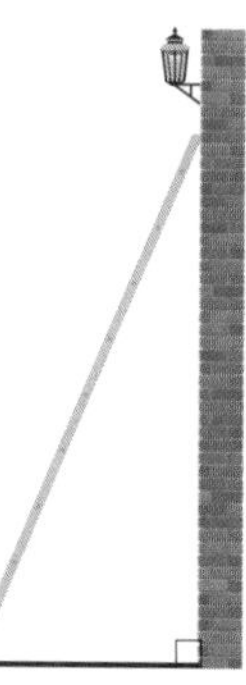

Solution

In this case, the ladder is the hypotenuse, with a length of 4 m. The unknown side length is h.

Apply the Pythagorean theorem.

$$
\begin{aligned}
4^2 &= 1.4^2 + h^2 \\
16 &= 1.96 + h^2 \\
16 - 1.96 &= 1.96 - 1.96 + h^2 && \text{Subtract 1.96 from both sides.} \\
14.04 &= h^2 \\
\sqrt{14.04} &= \sqrt{h^2} && \text{Take the square root of both sides.} \\
3.7 &\doteq h
\end{aligned}
$$

The ladder reaches 3.7 m up the wall, to the nearest tenth of a metre.

Example 3 Calculate the Area of a Right Triangle

Calculate the area of the triangular sail on the toy sailboat.

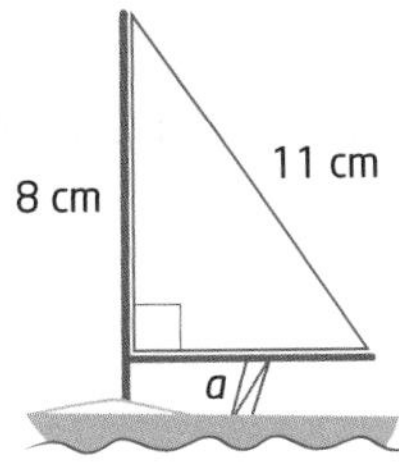

Solution

The formula for the area of a triangle is $A = \frac{1}{2}bh$.

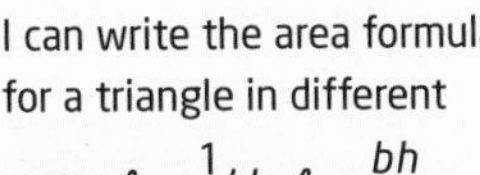

I can write the area formula for a triangle in different ways: $A = \frac{1}{2}bh$, $A = \frac{bh}{2}$, and $A = 0.5bh$.

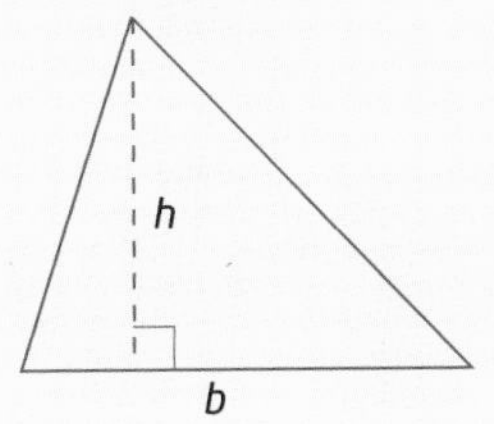

The base, b, and the height, h, must be perpendicular to each other. For a right triangle, the base and the height are the lengths of the two shorter sides.

First, use the Pythagorean theorem to find the length of the unknown side, a.

$$
\begin{aligned}
11^2 &= a^2 + 8^2 \\
121 &= a^2 + 64 \\
121 - 64 &= a^2 + 64 - 64 && \text{Subtract 64 from both sides.} \\
57 &= a^2 \\
\sqrt{57} &= \sqrt{a^2} && \text{Take the square root of both sides.} \\
a &\doteq 7.5
\end{aligned}
$$

The length of side a is approximately 7.5 cm.

Now, apply the formula for the area of a triangle.

$$
\begin{aligned}
A &= \frac{1}{2}bh \\
&= \frac{1}{2}(8)(7.5) \\
&= 30
\end{aligned}
$$

The area of the sail is approximately 30 cm^2.

Literacy Connections

The perpendicular sides of a right triangle are called the legs of the triangle.

Key Concepts

- The longest side of a right triangle is the hypotenuse.
- The Pythagorean theorem states that the square of the length of the hypotenuse is equal to the sum of the squares of the lengths of the two shorter sides.
- An algebraic model representing the Pythagorean theorem is $c^2 = a^2 + b^2$, where c represents the length of the hypotenuse and a and b represent the lengths of the two shorter sides.

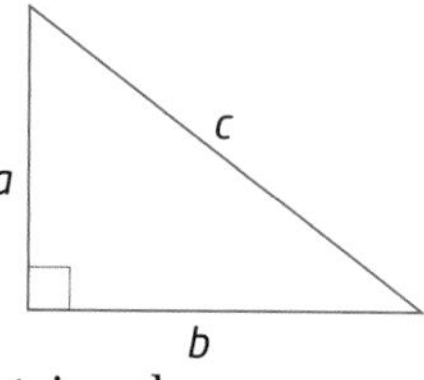

- You can use the Pythagorean theorem to calculate the length of an unknown side of a right triangle.
- You can calculate the area of a right triangle by using the formula $A = \frac{1}{2}bh$, with the lengths of the two shorter sides as the base, b, and the height, h. If one of these dimensions is unknown and you know the hypotenuse, apply the Pythagorean theorem to calculate the length of the unknown side. Then, use the area formula.

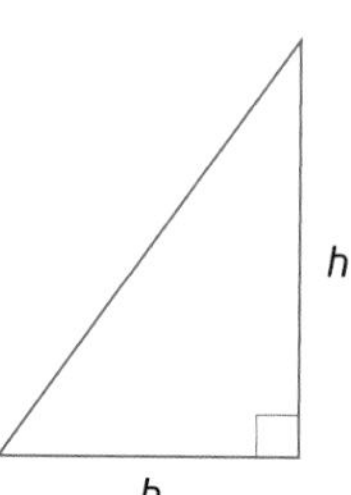

Communicate Your Understanding

C1 Describe how you can use the Pythagorean theorem to determine the length of the diagonal of the square.

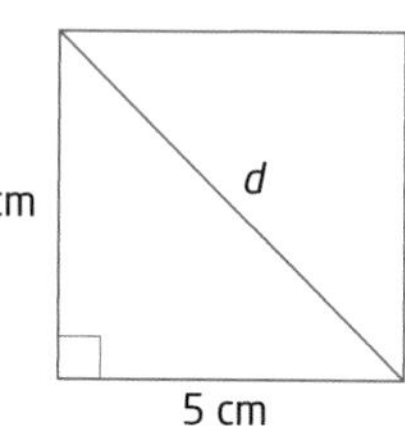

C2 Describe how you can use the Pythagorean theorem to determine the distance between two points on a grid.

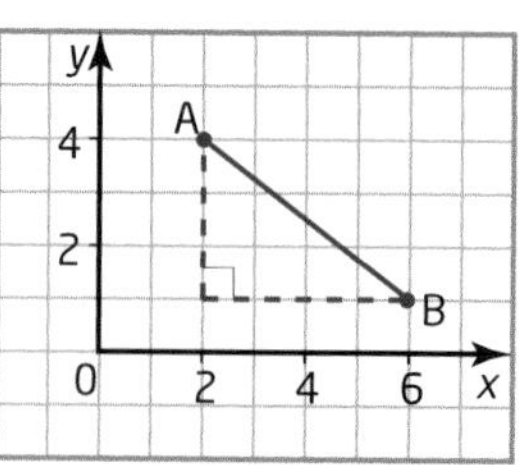

C3 Describe how you would find the area of a right triangle if you knew the lengths of the hypotenuse and one of the other two sides.

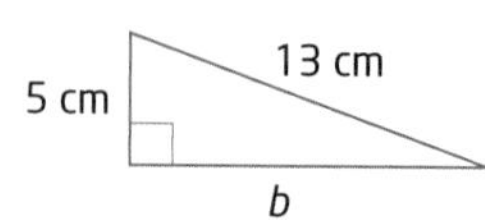

Practise

For help with question 1, see Example 1.

1. Calculate the length of the hypotenuse in each triangle. Round your answers to the nearest tenth of a unit, when necessary.

a)

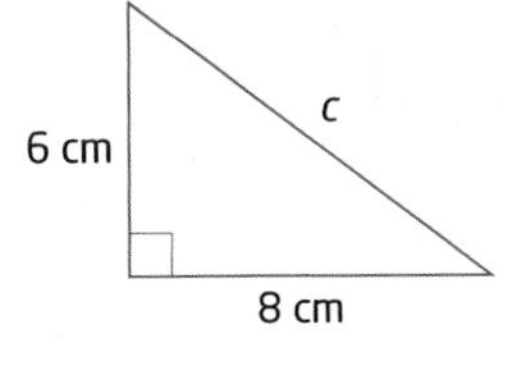

b)

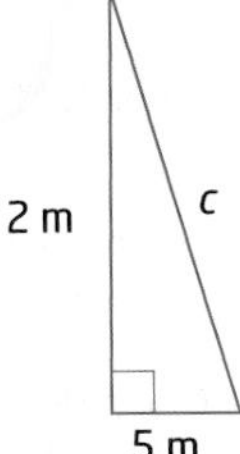

c)

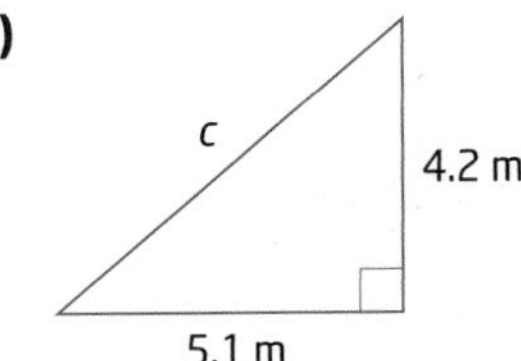

d)

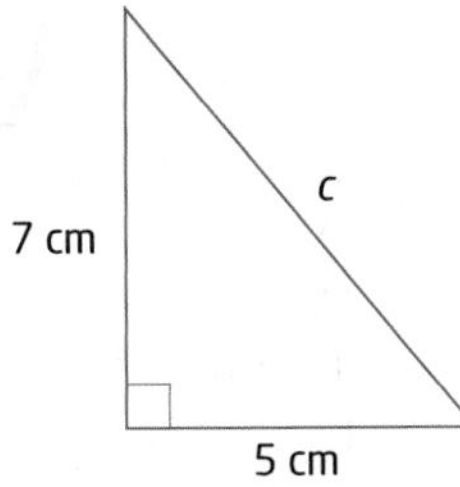

For help with question 2, see Example 2.

2. Calculate the length of the unknown side in each triangle. Round your answers to the nearest tenth of a unit, when necessary.

a)

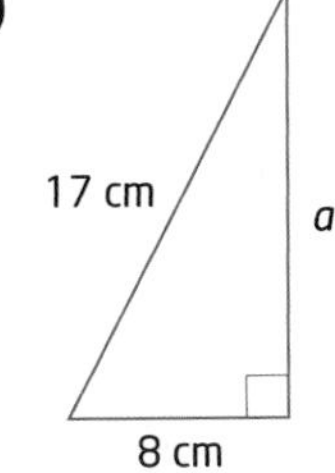

b)

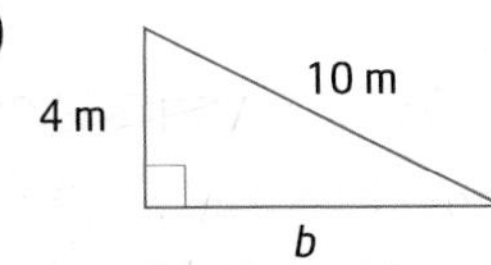

c)

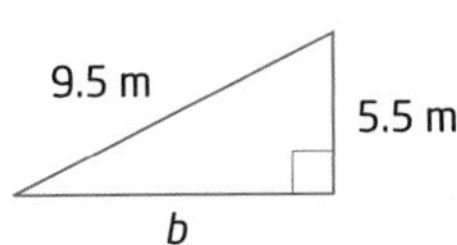

d)

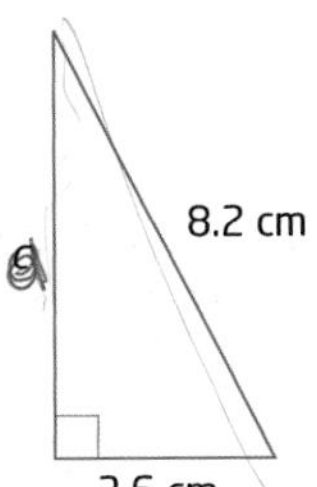

For help with question 3, see Example 3.

3. Determine the area of each right triangle. Round your answers to the nearest tenth of a square unit, when necessary.

a)

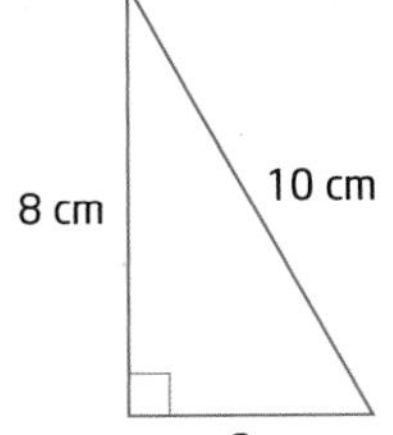

b)

7 m

12 m

a

Connect and Apply

4. Calculate the length of each line segment. Round answers to the nearest tenth of a unit, when necessary.
   a) AB
   b) CD
   c) EF

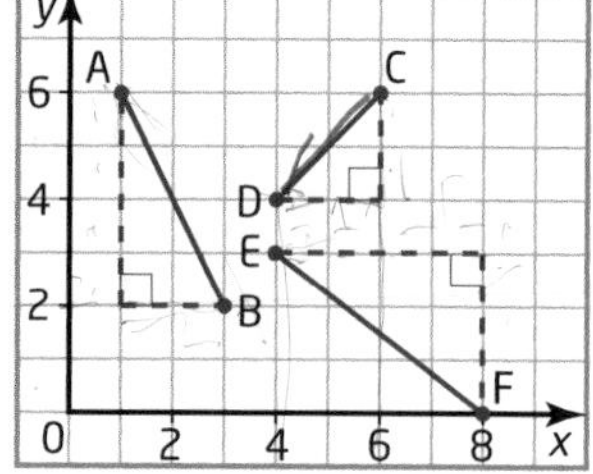

5. What is the length of the diagonal of a computer screen that measures 28 cm by 21 cm?

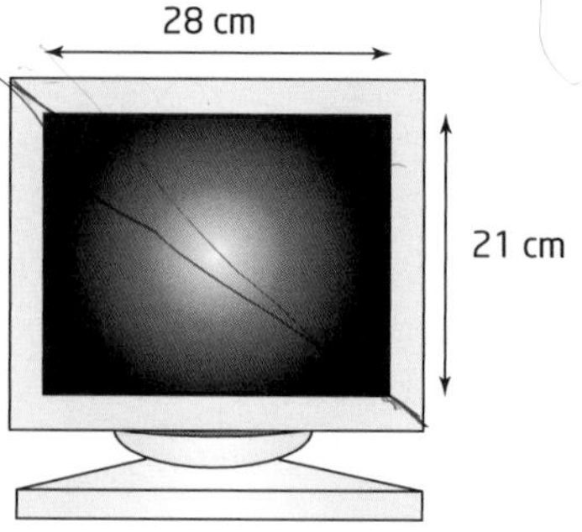

Did You Know?

Baseball was formally introduced as a medal sport at the 1992 Summer Olympics in Barcelona, Spain. Canada made its first appearance in this event in the 2004 Summer Olympics.

6. A baseball diamond is a square with sides that measure about 27 m. How far does the second-base player have to throw the ball to get a runner out at home plate? Round your answer to the nearest metre.

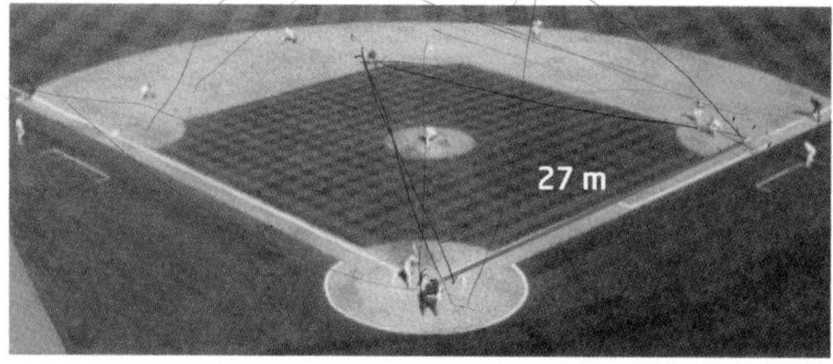

7. A square courtyard has diagonal paths that are each 42 m long. What is the perimeter of the courtyard, to the nearest metre?

8. Brook is flying a kite while standing 50 m from the base of a tree at the park. Her kite is directly above the 10-m tree and the 125-m string is fully extended. Approximately how far above the tree is her kite flying?

9. **Chapter Problem** Emily has designed a triangular flower bed for the corner of her client's rectangular lot. The bed is fenced on two sides and Emily will use border stones for the third side. The bed measures 2 m and 2.5 m along the fenced sides. How many border stones, 30 cm in length, will Emily need to edge the flower bed?

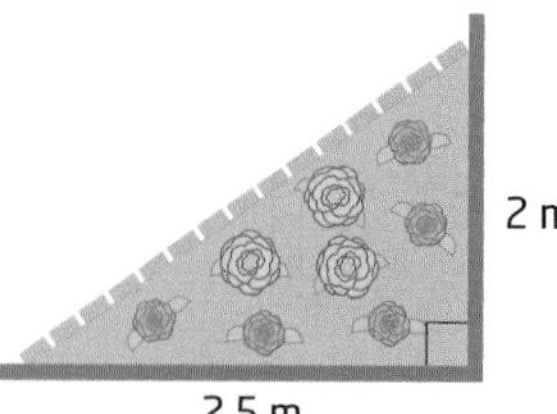

Extend

10. A cardboard box measures 40 cm by 40 cm by 30 cm. Calculate the length of the space diagonal, to the nearest centimetre.

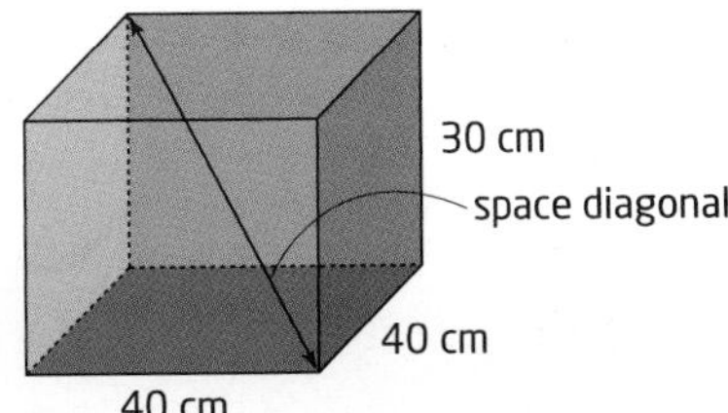

11. The Spider and the Fly Problem is a classic puzzle that originally appeared in an English newspaper in 1903. It was posed by H.E. Dudeney. In a rectangular room with dimensions 30 ft by 12 ft by 12 ft, a spider is located in the middle of one 12 ft by 12 ft wall, 1 ft away from the ceiling. A fly is in the middle of the *opposite* wall 1 ft away from the floor. If the fly does not move, what is the shortest distance that the spider can crawl along the walls, ceiling, and floor to capture the fly?

Hint: Using a net of the room will help you get the answer, which is less than 42 ft!

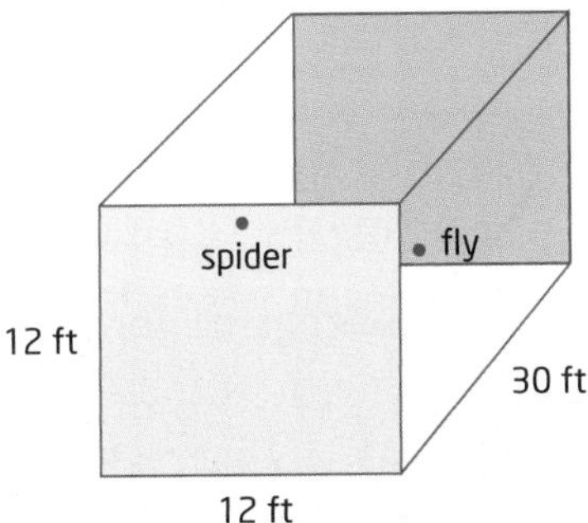

12. A spiral is formed with right triangles, as shown in the diagram.

a) Calculate the length of the hypotenuse of each triangle, leaving your answers in square root form. Describe the pattern that results.

b) Calculate the area of the spiral shown.

c) Describe how the expression for the area would change if the pattern continued.

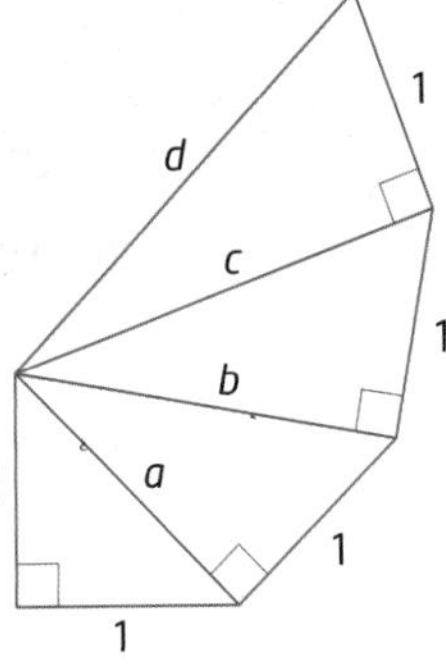

13. Math Contest

a) The set of whole numbers (5, 12, 13) is called a *Pythagorean triple*. Explain why this name is appropriate.

b) The smallest Pythagorean triple is (3, 4, 5). Investigate whether multiples of a Pythagorean triple make Pythagorean triples.

c) Substitute values for m and n to investigate whether triples of the form $(m^2 - n^2, 2mn, m^2 + n^2)$ are Pythagorean triples.

d) What are the restrictions on the values of m and n in part c)?

8.2 Perimeter and Area of Composite Figures

Shapes in everyday life are often made up of several simple shapes. Examples can be seen in logos, architecture, and landscaping. Determining the amount of material needed to construct any of these items may require calculating the perimeter or area of a composite shape.

In this section, you will apply the formulas for the perimeter and area of simple shapes to more complex shapes.

Investigate

How can you apply your knowledge of perimeter and area to a composite figure?

The owners of a restaurant have decided to build an outdoor patio to increase the number of customers that they can serve in the summer. The patio design consists of a rectangle, two right triangles, and a semicircle.

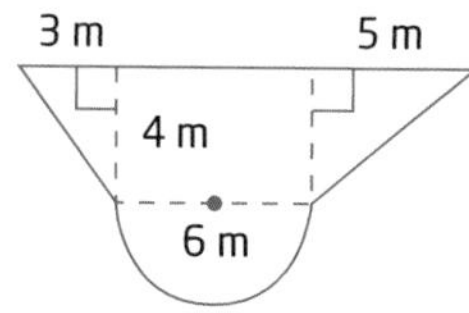

The patio area will be made of interlocking paving stones with different stones along the border. The paving stones cost $52.95/m². The border stones are priced according to the length of the border and cost $15.50/m. How much will the materials for the patio cost, including 8% PST and 7% GST? Allow an additional 10% to account for stones that must be cut for the design.

1. Before making any calculations, estimate the cost of the stones for the patio.
2. To calculate the perimeter of the patio, you will need to determine some of the outside measurements.
   a) Describe how you can calculate the perimeter of the semicircle and the lengths of the two unlabelled sides of the triangles.
   b) Calculate each of the unknown outside measurements.
   c) Calculate the total perimeter. Add 10% for waste due to cuts.

3. Now, consider the area of the patio.
   a) Describe the simple shapes that make up the area.
   b) Describe how you will calculate the area of each shape.
   c) Calculate the total area of the patio. Again, add 10% for waste.

4. a) Calculate the cost of the materials for the patio before taxes.
   b) Calculate the total cost of the materials, including 8% PST and 7% GST.
   c) Compare this answer to your original estimate. How close were you?

5. **Reflect** Describe an advantage to using simple shapes to calculate the perimeter and area of a composite figure.

Example 1 Area and Perimeter of a Composite Figure

a) Determine the area of the stained-glass panel shown.

b) Determine the perimeter. Round to the nearest centimetre.

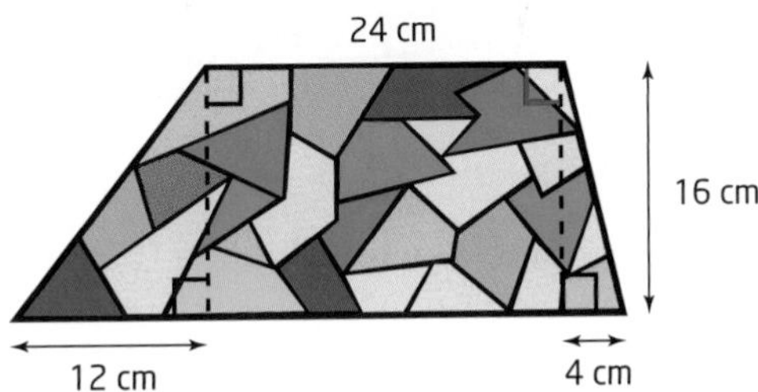

Solution

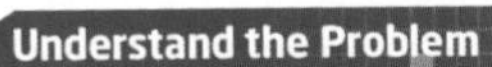

a) The stained-glass panel can be split into a rectangle and two right triangles.

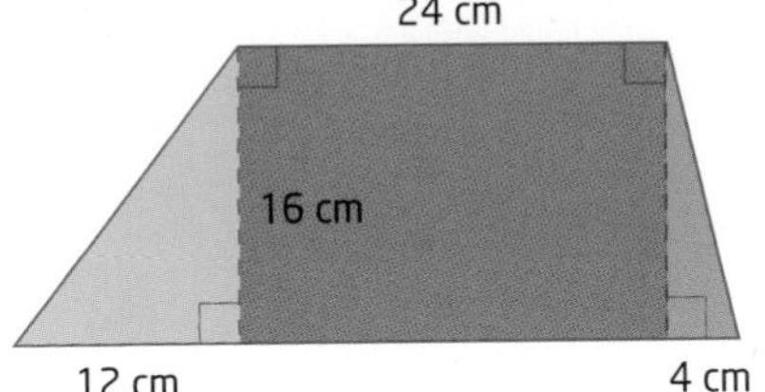

Choose a Strategy

To find the total area of the panel, add the area of the rectangle and the areas of the two right triangles. Use the formulas for the areas of these shapes.

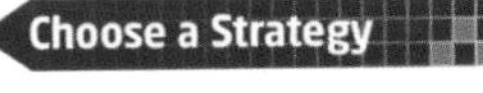

Call the area of the rectangle $A_{\text{rectangle}}$.

$$\begin{aligned} A_{\text{rectangle}} &= lw \\ &= (24)(16) \\ &= 384 \end{aligned}$$

Call the area of the triangle on the left $A_{\text{triangle 1}}$.

$$A_{\text{triangle 1}} = \frac{1}{2}bh$$
$$= \frac{1}{2}(12)(16)$$
$$= 96$$

Call the area of the triangle on the right $A_{\text{triangle 2}}$.

$$A_{\text{triangle 2}} = \frac{1}{2}bh$$
$$= \frac{1}{2}(4)(16)$$
$$= 32$$

Call the total area A_{total}.

$$A_{\text{total}} = A_{\text{rectangle}} + A_{\text{triangle 1}} + A_{\text{triangle 2}}$$
$$= 384 + 96 + 32$$
$$= 512$$

The total area of the stained-glass panel is 512 cm^2.

Reflect

Is there another way to solve the problem?

This stained-glass panel is in the shape of a trapezoid. Another way to calculate the area of this figure is to use the formula for a trapezoid, $A = \frac{1}{2}h(a + b)$ or $A = \frac{h(a + b)}{2}$.

The parallel sides of the trapezoid are the *a* and *b* in the formula. The distance between the parallel sides is the height, *h*.

$$A = \frac{1}{2}h(a + b)$$
$$= \frac{1}{2}(16)(24 + 40)$$
$$= 8(64)$$
$$= 512$$

The longer parallel side is (12 + 24 + 4) or 40 cm.

This gives the same answer as the other method.

Which method was easier?

The area of the stained-glass panel is 512 cm^2.

Understand the Problem

Choose a Strategy

b) The perimeter of the stained-glass panel includes two unknown side lengths.

When the figure is split into a rectangle and two right triangles, each unknown side is in a triangle. Apply the Pythagorean theorem to determine the lengths of the two unknown sides in the perimeter.

Carry Out the Strategy

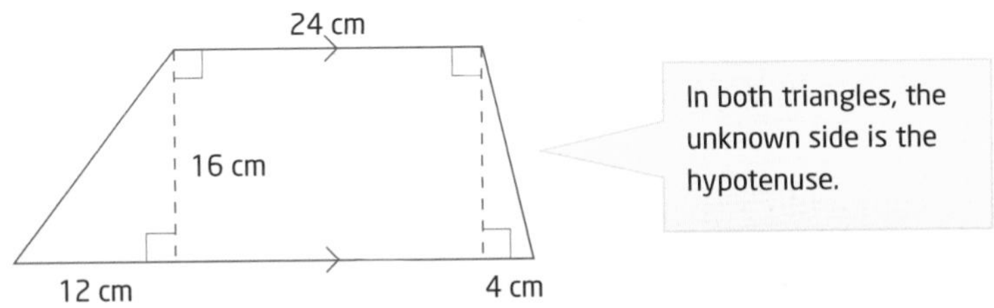

In both triangles, the unknown side is the hypotenuse.

First, find the length of the unknown side on the left. Call it c.

$c^2 = 12^2 + 16^2$
$c^2 = 144 + 256$
$c^2 = 400$
$c = \sqrt{400}$
$c = 20$

Next, find the length of the unknown side on the right. Call it d.

$d^2 = 4^2 + 16^2$
$d^2 = 16 + 256$
$d^2 = 272$
$d = \sqrt{272}$
$d \doteq 16$

Now, find the perimeter by adding the outside measurements.

$P = 24 + 16 + 40 + 20$
$= 100$

The perimeter of the stained-glass panel is approximately 100 cm.

Reflect

The two unknown sides of the trapezoid must each be longer than 16 cm. This means that the total perimeter must be longer than (24 + 16 + 40 + 16) or 96 cm. A perimeter of 100 cm seems reasonable for this stained-glass panel.

Example 2 Area of a Composite Figure, by Subtraction, and Perimeter

A hotel is remodelling its outdoor entrance area. The new design includes a tile walkway leading to a semicircular fountain.

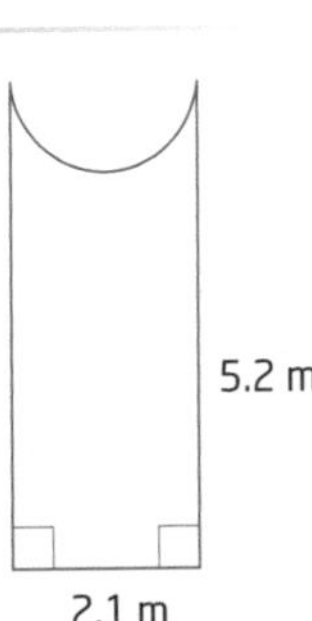

a) Describe the steps you would use to find the area of the walkway.

b) Calculate the area of the walkway. Round to the nearest tenth of a square metre.

c) The walkway will have a border in a different colour of tile. Calculate the perimeter of the walkway. Round to the nearest tenth of a metre.

Solution

a) The walkway is a rectangle with a semicircle cut out of it.

Determine the area of the rectangle minus the area of the semicircle.

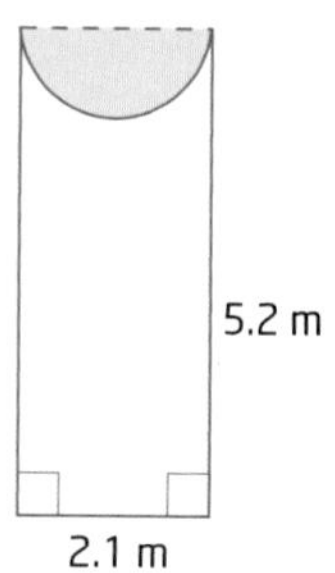

b) $A_{rectangle} = lw$
$= (5.2)(2.1)$
$= 10.92$

Estimate: $5 \times 2 = 10$

The radius, r, is half the diameter.

So, $r = 2.1 \div 2$ or 1.05.

$A_{semicircle} = \frac{1}{2}\pi r^2$

A semicircle is half a circle. So, the area of a semicircle is $\frac{1}{2}$ the area of a circle.

$= \frac{1}{2}\pi(1.05)^2$

Estimate: $0.5 \times 3 \times 1 \times 1 = 1.5$

$\doteq 1.73$

C 1 ÷ 2 × π × 1.05 x² =

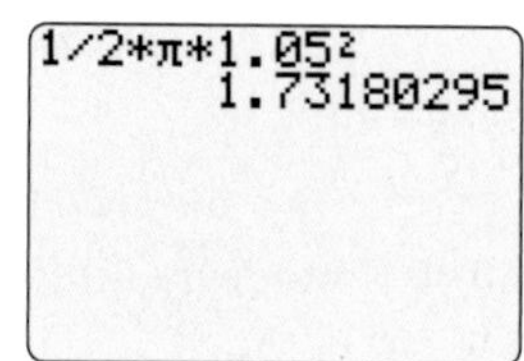

$A_{walkway} = A_{rectangle} - A_{semicircle}$
$= 10.92 - 1.73$
$= 9.19$

The area of the walkway is approximately 9.2 m^2.

c) The perimeter of the walkway consists of the three sides of the rectangular section and the semicircular arc.

First, find the length of the semicircular arc.

$L = \frac{1}{2}(\pi d)$
$= \frac{1}{2}\pi(2.1)$
$\doteq 3.3$

The formula for the circumference of a circle is $C = \pi d$. So, the length of a semicircular arc is half the circumference.

Now, add the distances around the outside of the walkway.

$P_{walkway} = L +$ three sides of rectangle
$= 3.3 + (5.2 + 2.1 + 5.2)$
$= 15.8$

The perimeter of the walkway is about 15.8 m.

Key Concepts

- A composite figure is made up of more than one simple shape.
- To determine the total area of a composite figure, add and/or subtract areas.
- To determine the perimeter of a composite figure, add the distances around the outside of the figure.

Communicate Your Understanding

C1 Refer to the Investigate on pages 426 and 427. The patio was divided into four simple shapes: a rectangle, two triangles, and a semicircle. Describe how to determine the area of the patio by adding the areas of two shapes.

C2 Consider the yard shown.

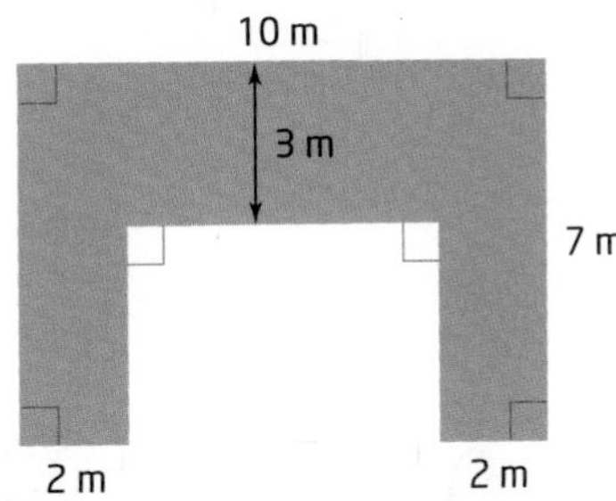

a) Describe how you can determine the unknown lengths.

b) Describe how you can determine the area of the yard by adding the areas of simpler shapes.

c) Describe how you can determine the area by subtracting areas.

C3 **a)** Suppose you need to calculate the perimeter of the yard in question C2. Explain why you cannot simply add the perimeters of the rectangles that make up the composite figure.

b) Without calculating, describe how the perimeter of this yard compares to the perimeter of a rectangular yard that measures 10 m by 7 m.

C4 **a)** How does the perimeter of the yard in question C2 compare to the perimeter of the yard shown, which has been increased by the smaller rectangular section rather than being decreased in size?

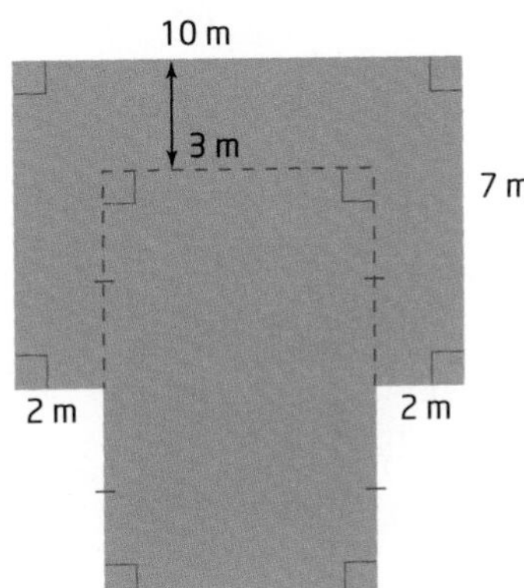

b) Describe how you would determine the area of this yard.

c) How does its area compare to the area of the yard in question C2?

Practise

For help with questions 1 and 2, see Examples 1 and 2.

1. For each composite figure,
   - solve for any unknown lengths
   - determine the perimeter

   Round to the nearest unit, if necessary.

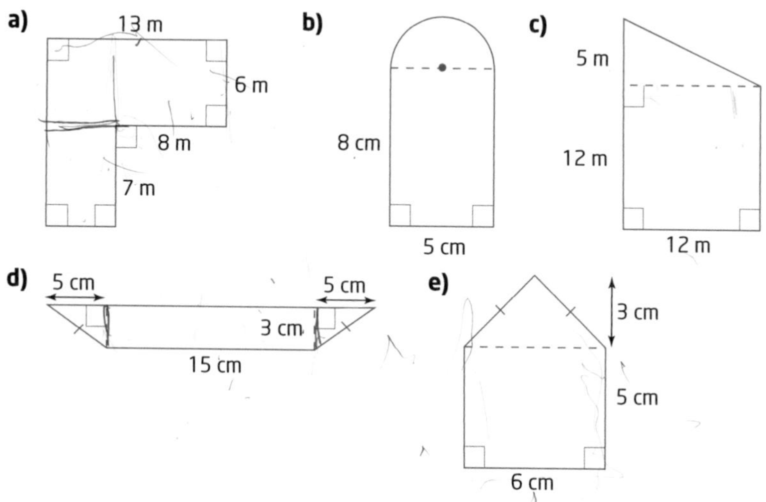

2. Calculate the area of each composite figure. Round to the nearest square unit, if necessary.

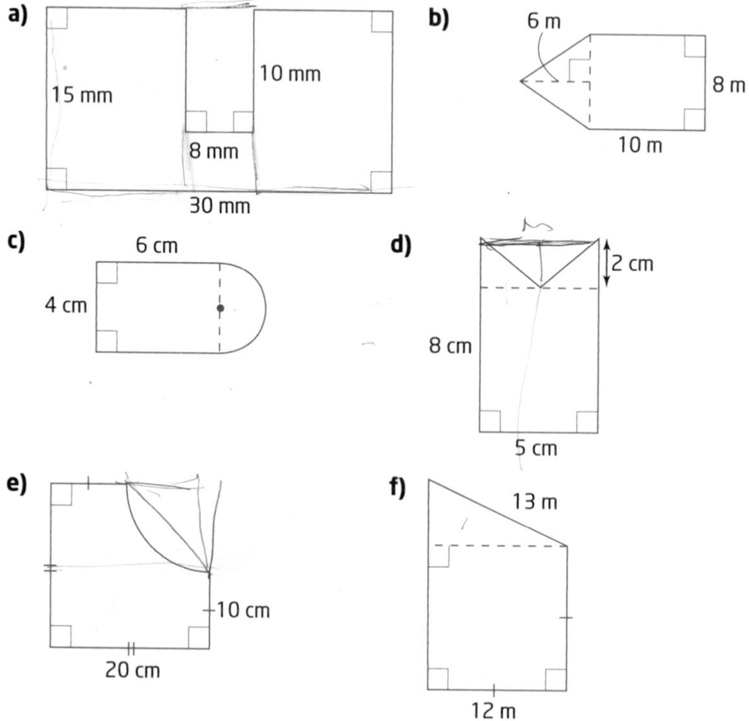

Connect and Apply

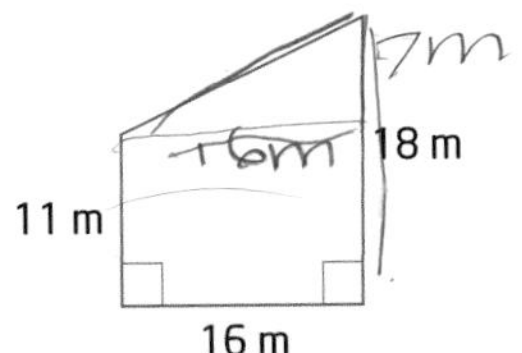

3. a) What length of fencing is needed to surround this yard, to the nearest metre?

   b) What is the area of the yard?

   c) Explain the steps you took to solve this problem.

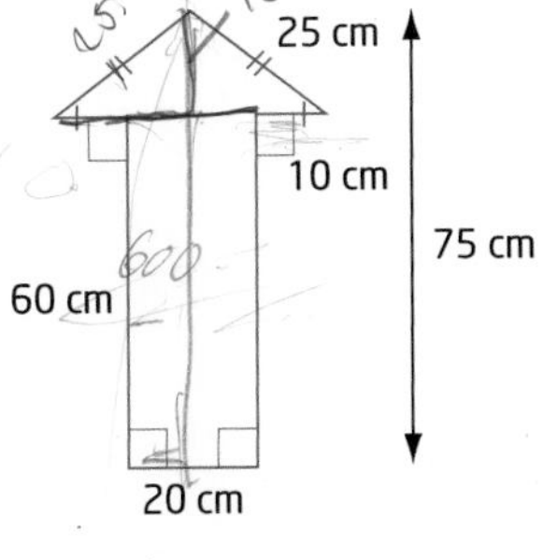

4. Patrick is planning a garage sale. He is painting six arrow signs to direct people to his sale.

   a) Calculate the area of one side of one arrow.

   b) Each can of paint can cover 2 m^2. How many cans of paint will Patrick need to paint all six signs?

   c) If the paint costs \$3.95 per can, plus 8% PST and 7% GST, how much will it cost Patrick to paint the six signs?

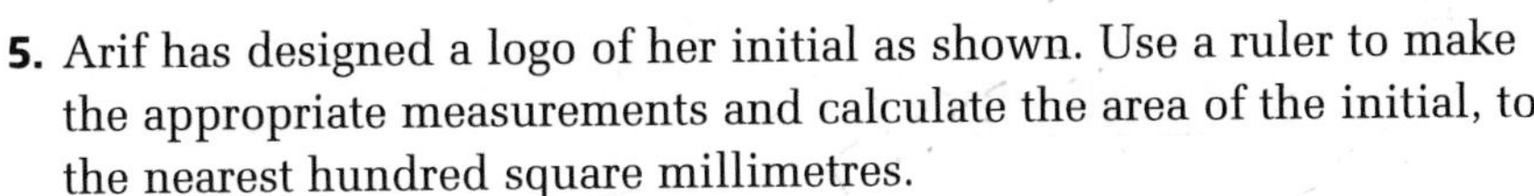

5. Arif has designed a logo of her initial as shown. Use a ruler to make the appropriate measurements and calculate the area of the initial, to the nearest hundred square millimetres.

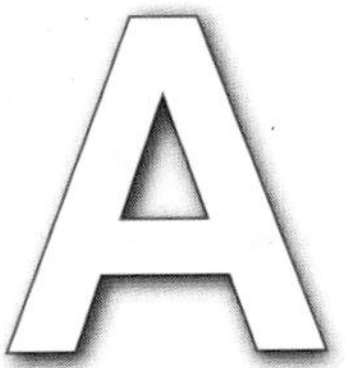

6. Create your own initial logo similar to the one in question 5. Calculate the total area of your logo.

7. **Use Technology**

   a) Use *The Geometer's Sketchpad®* to draw your design from question 6.

   b) Use the measurement feature of *The Geometer's Sketchpad®* to measure the area of your design.

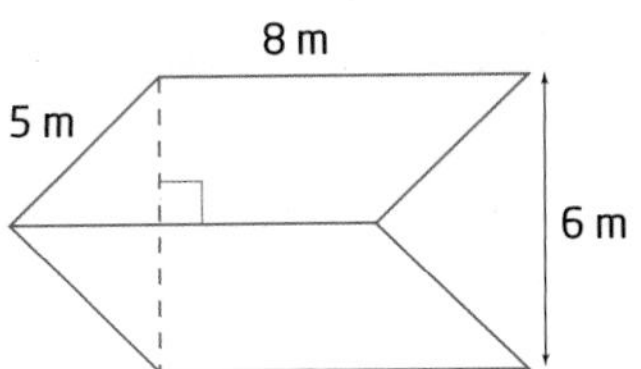

8. **Chapter Problem** One of the gardens Emily is designing is made up of two congruent parallelograms.

   a) A plant is to be placed every 20 cm around the perimeter of the garden. Determine the number of plants Emily needs.

   b) Calculate the area of her garden.

9. **Use Technology** Use *The Geometer's Sketchpad®* to create a composite figure made up of at least three different shapes.

   a) Estimate the perimeter and area of the figure you created.

   b) Determine the area using the measurement feature of *The Geometer's Sketchpad®*. Was your estimate reasonable?

10. An archery target has a diameter of 80 cm. It contains a circle in the centre with a radius of 8 cm and four additional concentric rings each 8 cm wide.

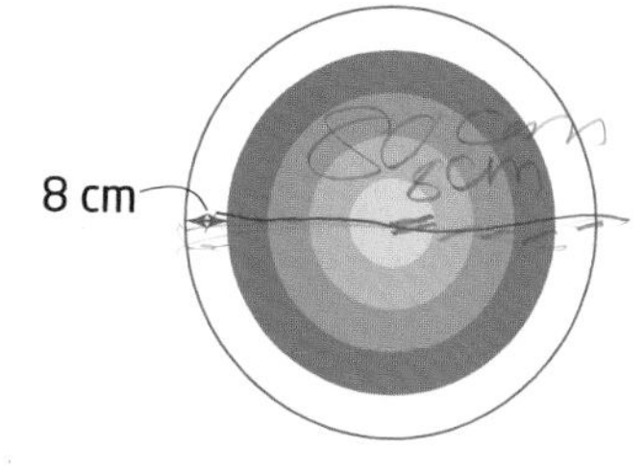

a) Find the area of the outer ring, to the nearest square centimetre.

b) What percent of the total area is the outer ring?

11. The area of a square patio is 5 m^2.

a) Find the length of one of its sides, to the nearest tenth of a metre.

b) Find the perimeter of the patio, to the nearest metre.

12. Brandon works as a carpenter. He is framing a rectangular window that measures 1.5 m by 1 m. The frame is 10 cm wide and is made up of four trapezoids. Find the total area of the frame, to the nearest square centimetre.

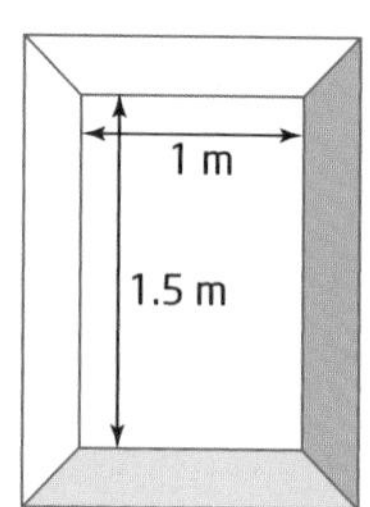

Achievement Check

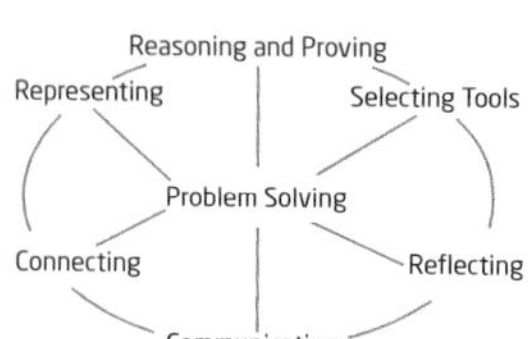

13. Susan is replacing the shingles on her roof. The roof is made up of a horizontal rectangle on top and steeply sloping trapezoids on each side. Each trapezoid has a (slant) height of 4.5 m. The dimensions of the roof are shown in the top view.

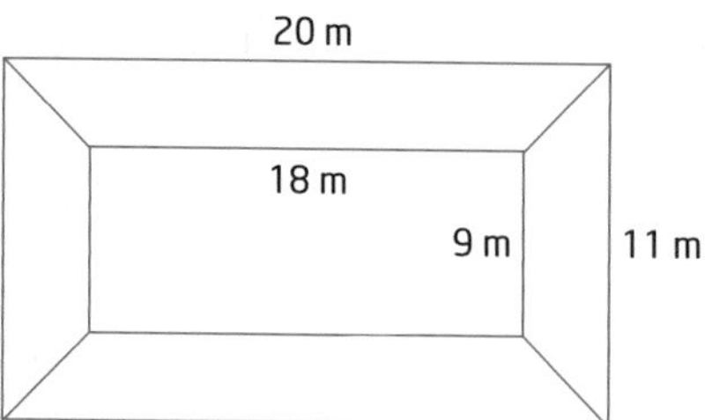

a) Calculate the area of the roof.

b) A package of shingles covers 10 m^2. How many packages will Susan need to shingle the entire roof?

c) Describe an appropriate way to round the number of packages in part b).

Extend

14. Sanjay is designing a square lawn to fit inside a square yard with side length 10 m so that there is a triangular flower bed at each corner.

a) Find the area of Sanjay's lawn.

b) How does the area of the lawn compare to the area of the flower beds?

c) Sanjay's design is an example of a square *inscribed* within a square. The vertices of the inside square touch the sides of the outside square but do not intersect. Will your answer in part b) always be true when a square is inscribed within a square? Explain.

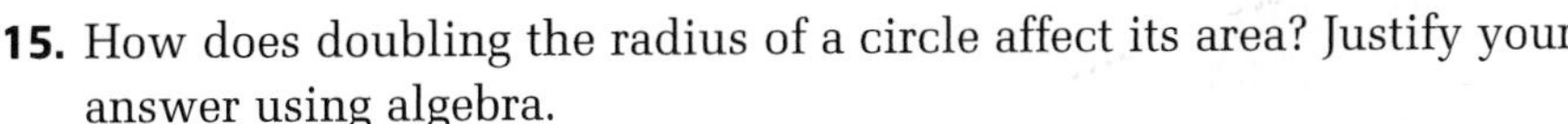

15. How does doubling the radius of a circle affect its area? Justify your answer using algebra.

16. Leonardo of Pisa lived in the 13th century in Pisa, Italy. He was given the nickname Fibonacci because his father's name was Bonacci. Among his mathematical explorations is the sequence of numbers 1, 1, 2, 3, 5, 8, 13, 21, ...

a) Determine the pattern rule for this sequence, and list the next four terms.

b) Construct rectangles using consecutive terms for the sides. The first rectangle is 1 by 1, the second is 1 by 2, the third is 2 by 3, and so on. Find the area of each rectangle.

c) Explore the ratios of the sides of the rectangles. Make conjectures about this ratio.

d) Explore the ratios of the areas of the rectangles. Make conjectures about this ratio.

17. Math Contest Determine the ratio of the perimeter of the smallest square to the perimeter of the largest square.

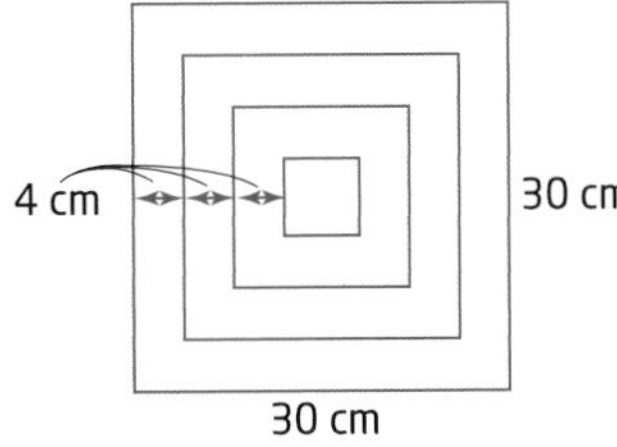

18. Math Contest The midpoints of the sides of a rectangle that measures 10 cm by 8 cm are joined. Determine the area of the shaded region.

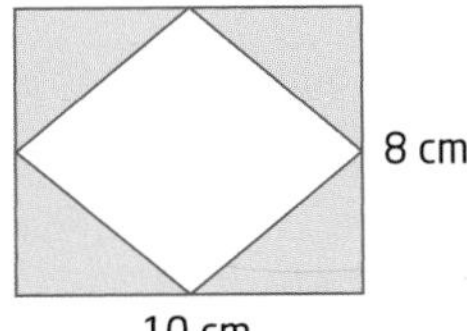

8.3 Surface Area and Volume of Prisms and Pyramids

To package their products economically, manufacturers need to know the amount of material required for the package. To do this, they need to know the **surface area** of the package.

The amount of space a package occupies is the **volume**. Products such as cereal, laundry detergent, and dog food are often sold by mass rather than volume. Why do you think these products are sold by mass?

surface area

- the number of square units needed to cover the surface of a three-dimensional object

volume

- the amount of space that an object occupies, measured in cubic units

pyramid

- a polyhedron whose base is a polygon and whose faces are triangles that meet at a common vertex

lateral faces

- the faces of a prism or pyramid that are not bases

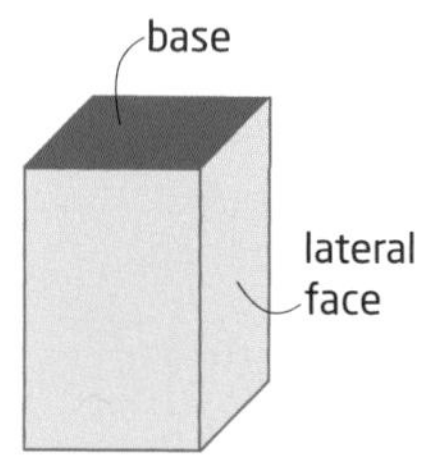

Investigate

How can you model the surface area and volume of a pyramid?

A: Surface Area

1. A square-based **pyramid** and its net are shown.

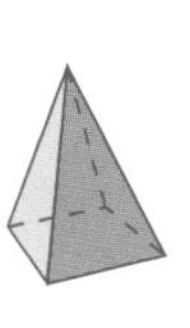

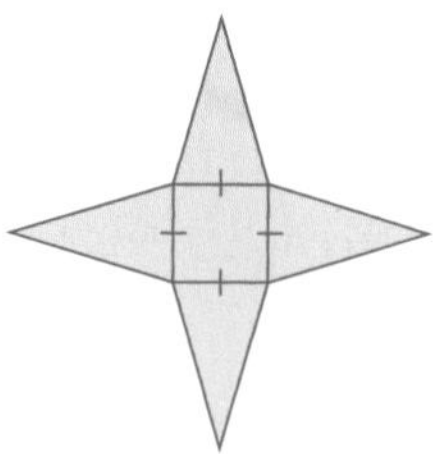

   a) What is the shape of the base? Write a formula for its area.
   b) What is the shape of each **lateral face**? Write a formula for the area of one lateral face.
   c) Write an expression for the surface area of the pyramid. Simplify the expression to give a formula for the surface area of a pyramid.

2. **Reflect** How would the results in step 1 change if you were developing a formula for the surface area of a hexagon-based pyramid? an octagon-based pyramid? Describe how to find the surface area of any pyramid.

B: Volume

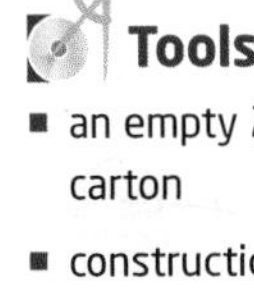

Tools

- an empty 250-mL milk carton
- construction paper
- scissors
- tape
- sand, rice, or another suitable material

Optional

BLM 8.3.1 Net for a Pyramid

BLM 8.3.2 Net for a Prism

1. **a)** Cut the top off the milk carton to form a prism.
   b) On a piece of construction paper, draw a net for a pyramid that has the same base and height as the prism.
   c) Cut out the net and tape it together to form a pyramid.
2. Estimate the ratio of the volume of the prism to the volume of the pyramid.

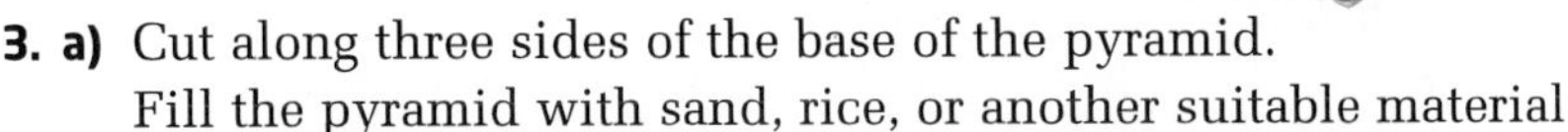

3. **a)** Cut along three sides of the base of the pyramid. Fill the pyramid with sand, rice, or another suitable material.
   b) Pour from the pyramid into the prism. How many pyramids full of material does it take to fill the prism?
   c) What fraction of the volume of the prism is the volume of the pyramid?
4. **Reflect** What conclusion can you draw about the relationship between the volume of a pyramid and the volume of a prism with the same base and height?

Example 1 Surface Area of a Pyramid

A modern example of a pyramid can be found at the Louvre in Paris, France. The glass square-based pyramid was built as an entrance to this famous museum.

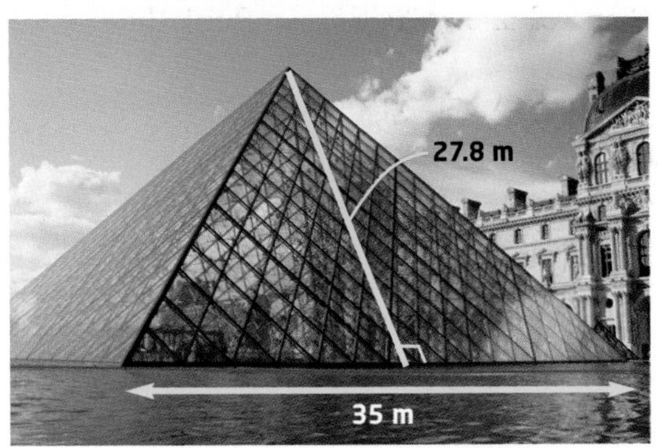

Calculate the surface area of the pyramid, including the base area.

Solution

The surface area consists of the square base and the four congruent triangular faces.

$$SA_{pyramid} = A_{base} + 4A_{triangle}$$
$$= (35)(35) + 4\left[\frac{1}{2}(35)(27.8)\right]$$
$$= 1225 + 1946$$
$$= 3171$$

Each triangle has a base of 35 m and a height of 27.8 m.

The surface area of the pyramid is 3171 m^2.

Example 2 Volume of a Pyramid

a) Determine the volume of the pyramid-shaped container, to the nearest cubic centimetre.

b) Express the capacity, in litres.

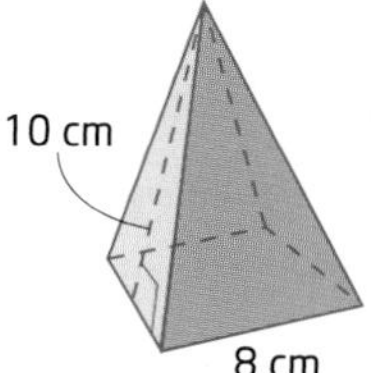

Solution

a) The volume of any pyramid can be determined using the formula $V = \frac{1}{3}$(area of the base)(height).

First, determine the height of the pyramid using the Pythagorean theorem.

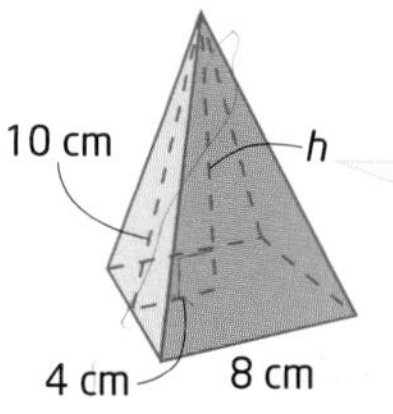

The height of a pyramid is the perpendicular distance from the vertex to the base.

$$h^2 + 4^2 = 10^2$$
$$h^2 + 16 = 100$$
$$h^2 = 84$$
$$h = \sqrt{84}$$
$$h \doteq 9.2$$

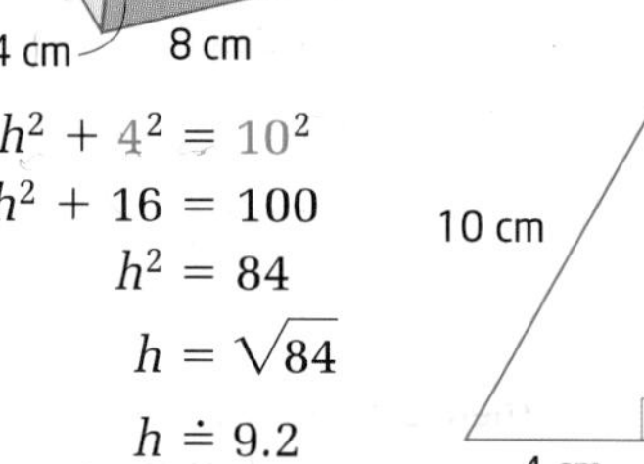

The slant height of 10 cm is the hypotenuse of the triangle. Since this is the longest side of the triangle, this means that the height of the pyramid is less than 10 cm.

Literacy Connections

For a pyramid, the height of a lateral face is called the *slant height*. The slant height of the pyramid in Example 2 is 10 cm.

Now, calculate the volume.

$$V = \frac{1}{3}\text{(area of the base)(height)}$$
$$= \frac{1}{3}(8^2)(9.2)$$
$$\doteq 196$$

The volume of the container is about 196 cm^3.

b) The capacity is the maximum volume that a container will hold. When a product is packaged, the container is usually not filled to capacity. This may be a factor to consider in some problems.

$1 \text{ cm}^3 = 1 \text{ mL}$

The capacity of the container is 196 mL or 0.196 L of liquid.

Example 3 Surface Area and Volume of a Triangular Prism

Chocolate is sometimes packaged in a box that is shaped like a triangular prism.

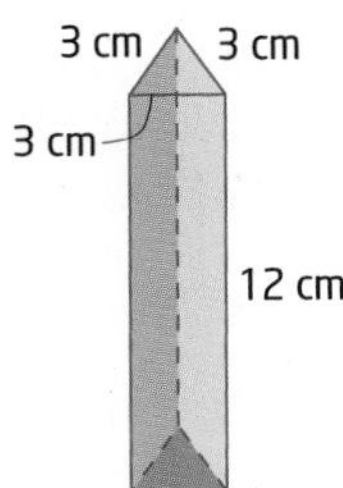

a) Calculate the amount of material required to make this box, to the nearest square centimetre.

b) Calculate the volume of this box, to the nearest cubic centimetre.

Solution

a) The amount of material required is the surface area of the prism. The surface area consists of the top and bottom of the box, which are triangles, and the three faces, which are congruent rectangles.

First, determine the height, h, of each triangle.

Use the Pythagorean theorem.

$h^2 + 1.5^2 = 3^2$

$h^2 + 2.25 = 9$

$h^2 = 6.75$

$h = \sqrt{6.75}$

$h \doteq 2.6$

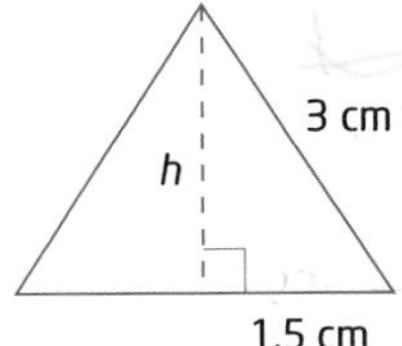

Now, calculate the surface area.

$$\begin{aligned} SA &= 2A_{\text{base}} + 3A_{\text{face}} \\ &= 2\left[\frac{1}{2}(3)(2.6)\right] + 3(3)(12) \\ &= 7.8 + 108 \\ &= 115.8 \end{aligned}$$

There are two bases and three lateral faces.

Approximately 116 cm^2 of material is needed to make the triangular prism box.

b) The volume of any right prism can be found using the formula $V =$ (area of the base)(height).

$$\begin{aligned} V_{\text{triangular prism}} &= \text{(area of the base)(height)} \\ &= (3.9)(12) \\ &= 46.8 \end{aligned}$$

The volume is about 47 cm^3.

Literacy Connections

A right prism has two parallel and congruent bases and lateral faces that are perpendicular to its bases. The triangular prism in Example 3 is a right triangular prism.

Key Concepts

- Surface area is a measure of how much material is required to cover or construct a three-dimensional object. Surface area is expressed in square units.
- The surface area of a prism or pyramid is the sum of the areas of the faces.
- Volume is a measure of how much space a three-dimensional object occupies. Capacity is the maximum volume a container can hold. Volume and capacity are measured in cubic units.
- The litre (L) is a measure of capacity or volume often used for liquids.
  1 L = 1000 cm^3 or 1 mL = 1 cm^3.
- For a prism, Volume = (area of base)(height).

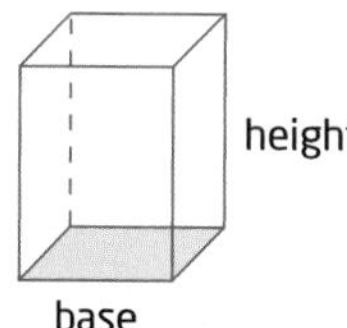

- For a pyramid, Volume = $\frac{1}{3}$(area of base)(height).

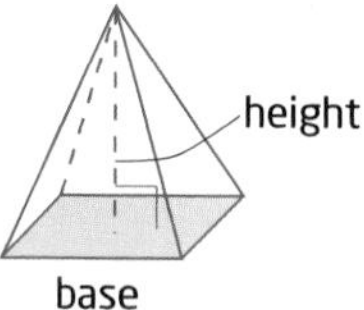

Communicate Your Understanding

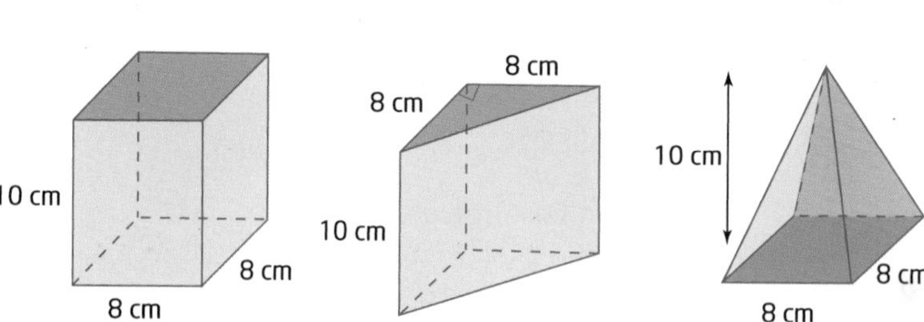

C1 Describe how the shapes are alike. How are they different?

C2 Describe how you would determine the volume of each shape.

C3 Without doing the calculations, predict which shape has the greatest volume. Explain.

C4 Describe how you would determine the surface area of each shape.

C5 What unknown values would you need to find to complete the surface area calculations? Explain how you can determine the unknown values.

Practise

For help with question 1, see Example 1.

1. Determine the surface area of each object.

a)

12.2 cm
8.5 cm
8.5 cm

b)

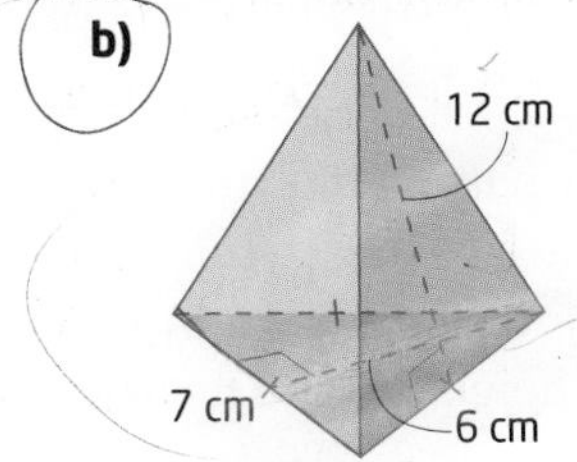

For help with question 2, see Example 2.

2. Determine the volume of each object. Round to the nearest cubic unit, when necessary.

a)

15 mm
20 mm
20 mm

b)

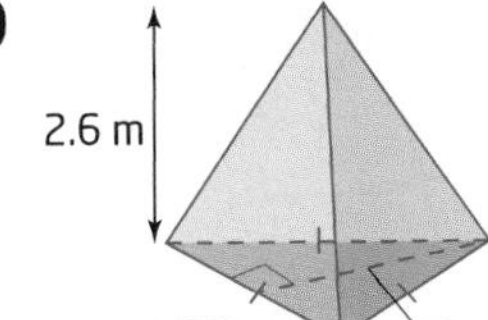

For help with questions 3 to 5, see Example 3.

3. Determine the surface area of each object.

a)

8 mm
10 mm
15 mm

b)

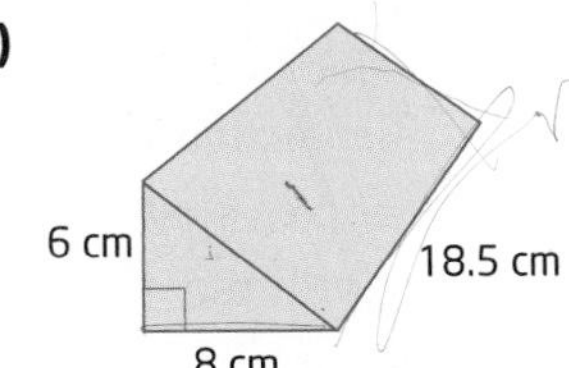

4. Determine the volume of each object.

a)

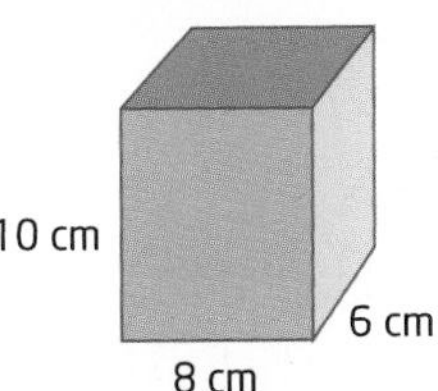

b)

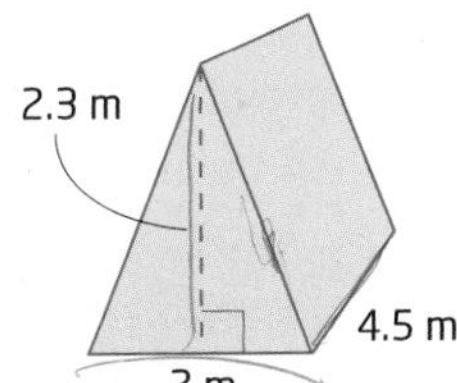

5. A rectangular prism has length 3 m, width 2 m, and height 4 m.
   - **a)** Determine the surface area of the prism.
   - **b)** Determine the volume of the prism.

Connect and Apply

6. A cereal box has a volume of 3000 cm^3. If its length is 20 cm and its width is 5 cm, what is its height?

7. Sneferu's North Pyramid at Dahshur, Egypt, is shown. Its square base has side length 220 m and its height is 105 m.
   a) Determine the volume of this famous pyramid.
   b) Determine its surface area, to the nearest square metre.

8. The Pyramid of Khafre at Giza, Egypt, was built by the Pharaoh Khafre, who ruled Egypt for 26 years. The square base of this pyramid has side length 215 m and its volume is 2 211 096 m^3. Calculate its height, to the nearest tenth of a metre.

9. The milk pitcher shown is a right prism. The base has an area of 40 cm^2 and the height of the pitcher is 26 cm. Will the pitcher hold 1 L of milk?

10. A juice container is a right prism with a base area of 100 cm^2.
    a) If the container can hold 3 L of juice, what is its height?
    b) Describe any assumptions you have made.

11. Adam has built a garden shed in the shape shown.

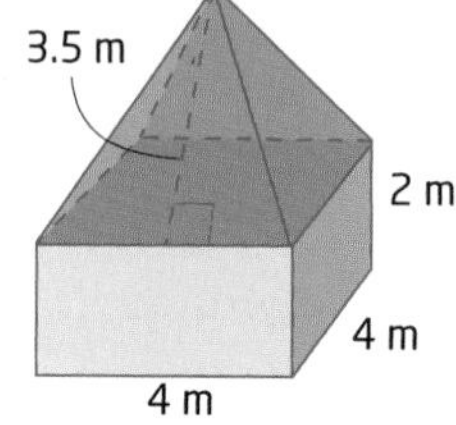

    a) Calculate the volume of the shed, to the nearest cubic metre.
    b) Adam plans to paint the outside of the shed, including the roof but not the floor. One can of paint covers 4 m^2. How many cans of paint will Adam need?
    c) If one can of paint costs \$16.95, what is the total cost, including 7% GST and 8% PST?

12. **Chapter Problem** The diagram shows the side view of the swimming pool in Emily's customer's yard. The pool is 4 m wide.

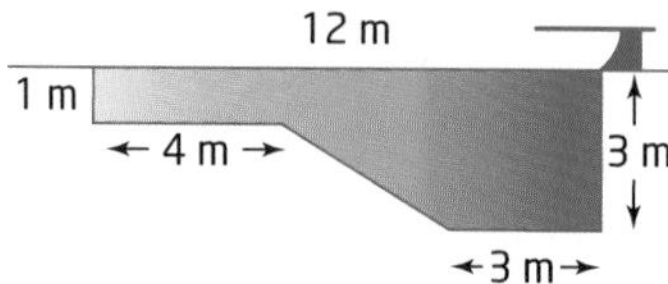

    a) Estimate how many litres of water the pool can hold.
    b) Calculate how many litres of water the pool can hold.
    c) When the pool construction is complete, Emily orders water to fill it up. The water tanker can fill the pool at a rate of 100 L/min. How long will it take to fill the pool at this rate?

13. A triangular prism has a base that is a right triangle with shorter sides that measure 6 cm and 8 cm. The height of the prism is 10 cm.

a) Predict how doubling the height affects the volume of the prism.

b) Check your prediction by calculating the volume of the original prism and the volume of the new prism.

c) Was your prediction accurate?

d) Is this true in general? If so, summarize the result.

Achievement Check

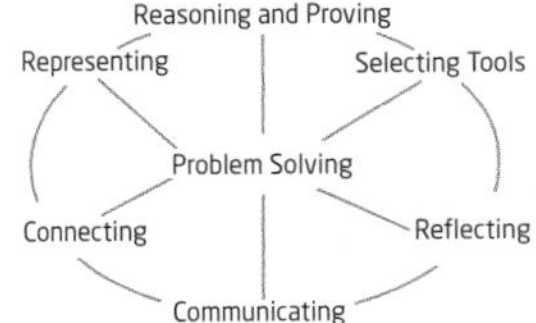

14. a) Design two different containers that hold 8000 cm^3 of rice. One should be a rectangular prism and one should be a cylinder.

b) Determine the surface area of each one, to the nearest square centimetre.

c) Which shape would you recommend to the manufacturer and why?

Extend

15. A pyramid and a prism have congruent square bases. If their volumes are the same, how do their heights compare? Explain.

16. A statue is to be placed on a frustum of a pyramid. The frustum is the part remaining after the top portion has been removed by making a cut parallel to the base of the pyramid.

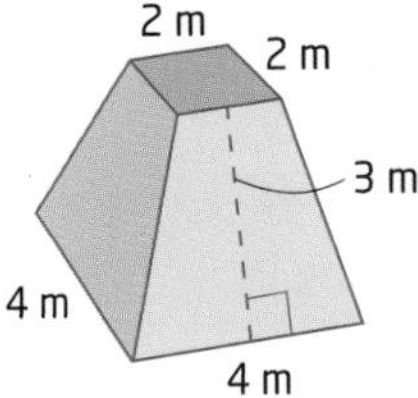

a) Determine the surface area of the frustum.

b) Calculate the cost of painting the frustum with gilt paint that costs \$49.50/m^2. It is not necessary to paint the bottom of the frustum.

17. A formula for the surface area of a rectangular prism is $SA = 2(lw + wh + lh)$.

a) Suppose each of the dimensions is doubled. Show algebraically how the surface area is affected.

b) How is the volume affected if each of the dimensions is doubled? Justify your answer algebraically.

18. **Math Contest** A large wooden cube is made by glueing together 216 small cubes. Cuts are made right through the large cube along the diagonals of three perpendicular faces.

How many of the small cubes remain uncut?

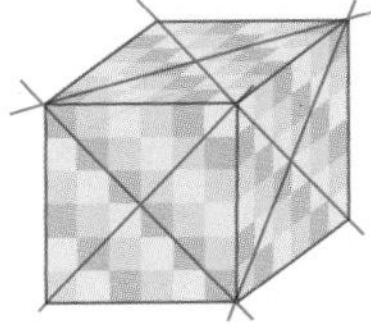

8.4 Surface Area of a Cone

cone

- a three-dimensional object with a circular base and a curved lateral surface that extends from the base to a point called the vertex

A **cone** is a familiar shape to most people. Many of us learn about this shape as children when eating an ice cream cone or snow cone for the first time.

As with a pyramid, the height of a cone is the perpendicular distance from the vertex to the base. The slant height of a cone is the distance from the vertex to a point on the edge of the base.

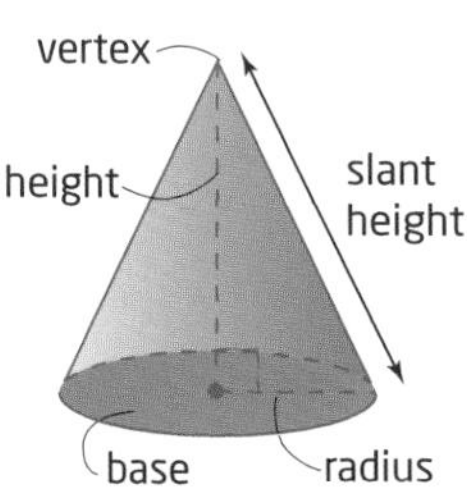

Investigate

Tools

- construction paper
- scissors
- ruler
- compasses
- tape

Literacy Connections

A sector of a circle is a part of the circle bounded by two radii and an arc of the circumference.

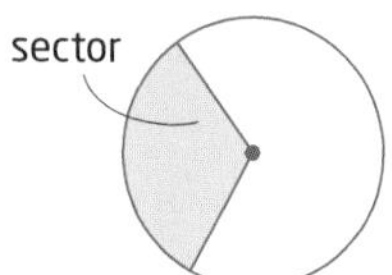

How can you model the lateral area of a cone?

Work with a partner.

1. Construct a circle with a radius of 10 cm.

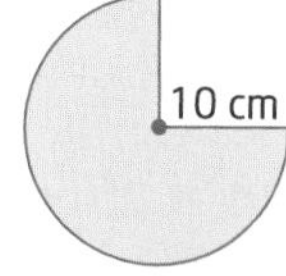

2. Draw two perpendicular radii and cut out and set the smaller sector of the circle aside to use later. What fraction of the circle is the larger piece?

3. Tape the radius edges on the large piece to form a cone. Measure the height, h, of the cone and record it. Measure the radius, r, of the base and record it.

4. Notice that h and r are sides in a right triangle. Calculate the length of the third side, s. How is the length of the third side related to the circle you started with?

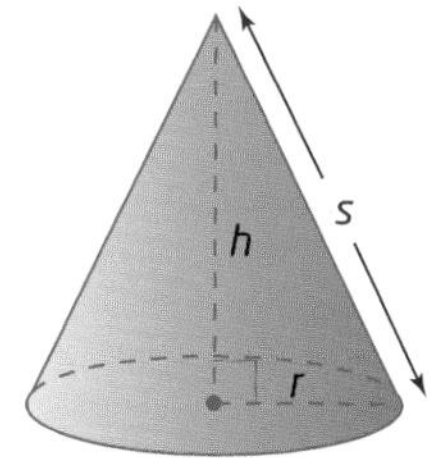

5. Calculate the circumference of the base of your cone. What fraction of the circumference of the original paper circle is this?

6. The curved surface of the cone is called the *lateral area*. What fraction of the area of your original paper circle is the lateral area of the cone?

7. a) Draw and cut out another circle with radius 10 cm. Draw any diameter and cut along the diameter. Construct a cone using the semicircle for the lateral area.

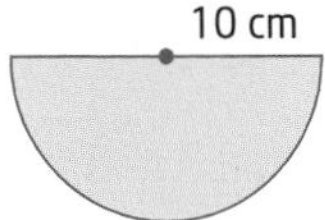

   b) Repeat steps 3 to 6 for this cone.

8. a) Use the smaller sector of the circle you cut out in question 2 to form another cone.

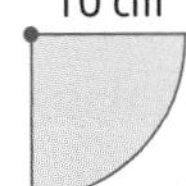

   b) Repeat steps 3 to 6 for this cone.

9. **Reflect** Describe the relationship between the fraction of the circumferences and the fraction of the areas.

You can use proportional reasoning to find the lateral area of a cone. The ratio of the areas is the same as the ratio of the circumferences.

$$\frac{\text{Lateral area of cone}}{\text{Area of circle}} = \frac{\text{Circumference of cone}}{\text{Circumference of circle}}$$

Consider a cone with slant height s and base radius r.

The circumference of the large circle is $2\pi s$ and the circumference of the base of the cone is $2\pi r$.

The area of the large circle is πs^2.

Substitute into the proportion:

$$\frac{\text{Lateral area of cone}}{\text{Area of circle}} = \frac{\text{Circumference of cone}}{\text{Circumference of circle}}$$

$$\frac{\text{Lateral area of cone}}{\pi s^2} = \frac{\cancel{2\pi} r}{\cancel{2\pi} s}$$

$$\frac{\text{Lateral area of cone}}{\pi s^2} = \frac{r}{s}$$

$$\text{Lateral area of cone} = \frac{r}{\cancel{s}_1} \times \pi \cancel{s^2}^{s}$$

$$\text{Lateral area of cone} = \pi rs$$

The lateral area of a cone with radius r and slant height s is πrs.

The base of a cone is a circle with radius r, so its area is πr^2.

The total surface area of a cone is the sum of the areas of the base and the lateral surface.

$SA_{cone} = \pi rs + \pi r^2$

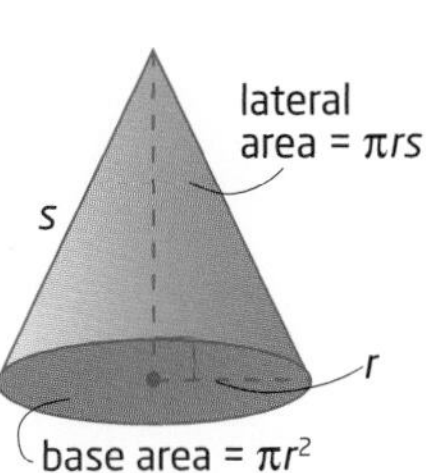

Example Surface Area of a Cone

Calculate the surface area of the cone, to the nearest square centimetre.

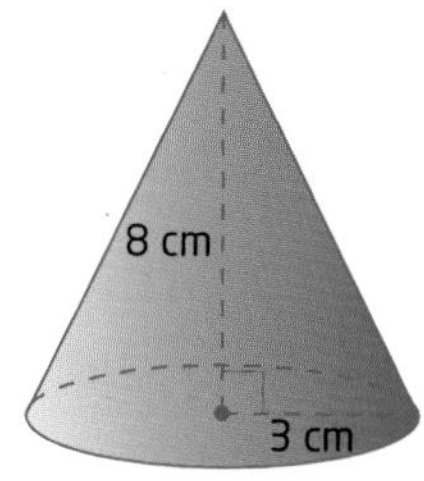

Solution

To use the formula for the surface area of a cone, determine the slant height, s.

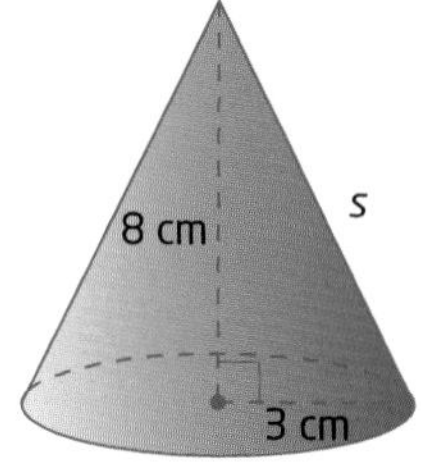

Use the Pythagorean theorem.

$s^2 = h^2 + r^2$

$s^2 = 8^2 + 3^2$

$s^2 = 64 + 9$

$s^2 = 73$

$s = \sqrt{73}$

$s \doteq 8.5$

The slant height of the cone is about 8.5 cm.

Now, use the formula for the surface area of a cone.

$SA_{\text{cone}} = \pi rs + \pi r^2$

$= \pi(3)(8.5) + \pi(3)^2$

$\doteq 108$

C π × 3 × 8.5 + π × 3 x^2 =

```
π*3*8.5+π*3²
        108.3849465
```

The surface area of the cone is approximately 108 cm^2.

Key Concepts

- The surface area of a cone consists of the lateral area and the area of the circular base.
- The lateral area is formed by folding a sector of a circle. The radius of the circle used becomes the slant height, s, of the cone formed. The area of this curved surface is πrs, where r is the radius of the base of the cone.

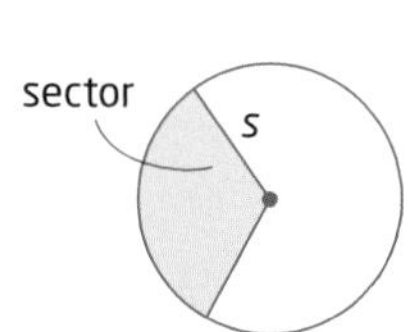

- The area of the circular base is πr^2.
- The formula for the surface area of a cone is $SA_{\text{cone}} = \pi rs + \pi r^2$.
- When you know the radius, r, and height, h, of a cone, you can determine the slant height, s, using the Pythagorean theorem.

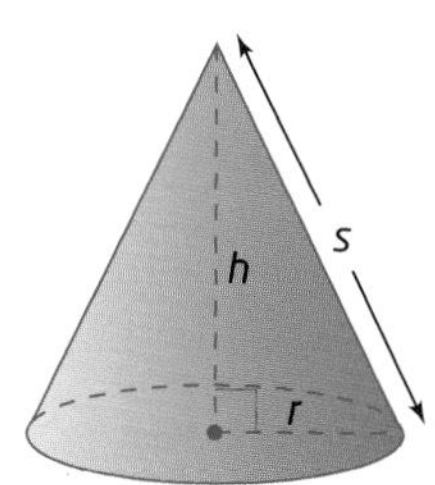

Communicate Your Understanding

C1 A cone is formed from a circle with a 90° sector removed. Another cone is formed from a semicircle with the same radius. How do the two cones differ? How are they the same?

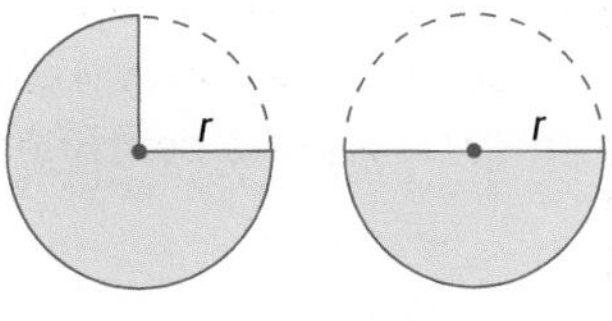

C2 A cone is formed from a circle of radius 10 cm with a 60° sector removed. Another cone is formed from a circle of radius 15 cm with a 60° sector removed. How do the two cones differ? How are they the same?

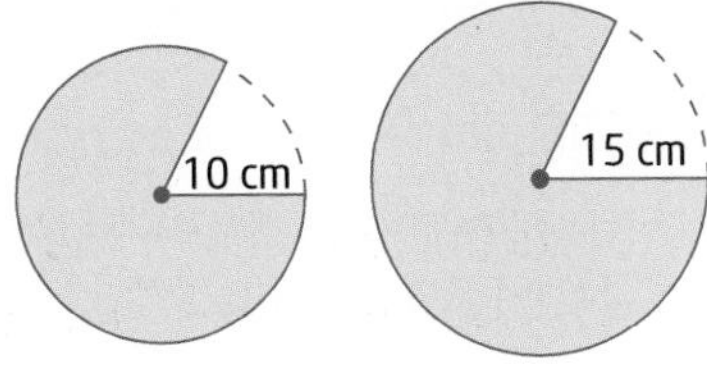

C3 The slant height of a cone is doubled. Does this double the surface area of the cone? Explain your reasoning.

Practise

For help with questions 1 and 2, see the Example.

1. Calculate the surface area of each cone. Round to the nearest square unit.

a) 2 m, 1 m

b) 30 cm, 10 cm

c) 8.4 cm, 3.7 cm

2. a) Find the slant height of the cone.

b) Calculate the surface area of the cone. Round to the nearest square metre.

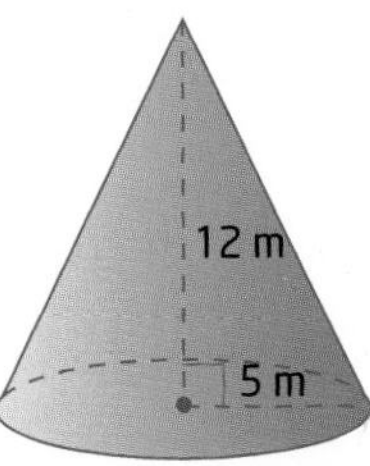

Connect and Apply

3. Some paper cups are shaped like cones.

a) How much paper, to the nearest square centimetre, is needed to make the cup?

b) What assumptions have you made?

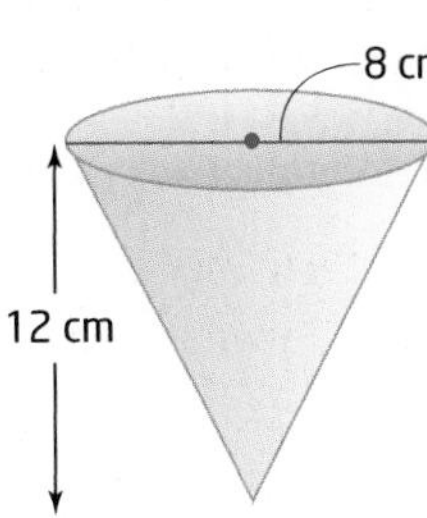

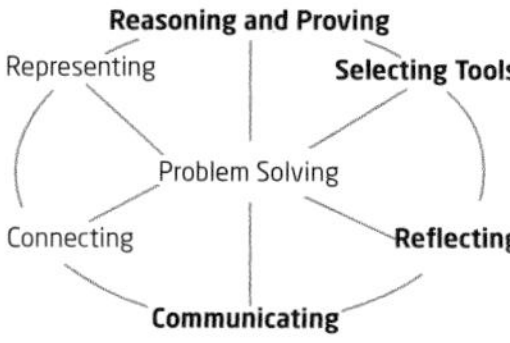

4. One cone has base radius 4 cm and height 6 cm. Another cone has a base radius 6 cm and height 4 cm.

a) Do the cones have the same slant height?

b) Do the cones have the same surface area? If not, predict which cone has the greater surface area. Explain your reasoning.

c) Determine the surface area of each cone to check your prediction. Were you correct?

5. The lateral area of a cone with radius 4 cm is 60 cm^2.

a) Determine the slant height of the cone, to the nearest centimetre.

b) Determine the height of the cone, to the nearest centimetre.

6. The height of a cone is doubled. Does this double the surface area? Justify your answer.

7. The radius of a cone is doubled. Does this double the surface area? Justify your answer.

8. A cube-shaped box has sides 10 cm in length.

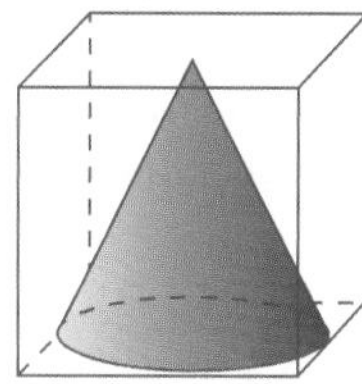

a) What are the dimensions of the largest cone that fits inside this box?

b) What is the surface area of this cone, to the nearest square centimetre?

9. A cone just fits inside a cylinder. The volume of the cylinder is 9425 cm^3. What is the surface area of this cone, to the nearest square centimetre?

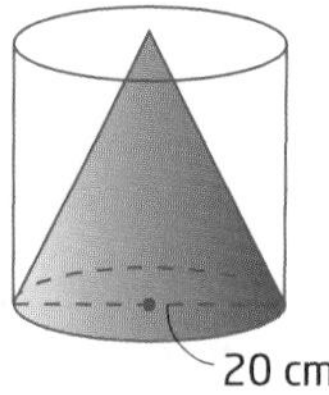

10. The frustum of a cone is the part that remains after the top portion has been removed by making a cut parallel to the base. Calculate the surface area of this frustum, to the nearest square metre.

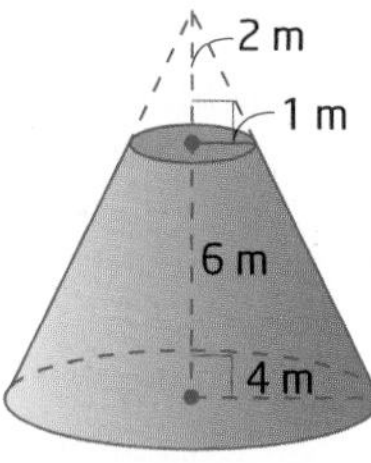

11. **Chapter Problem** Emily has obtained an unfinished ceramic birdbath for one of her customers. She plans to paint it with a special glaze so that it will be weatherproof. The birdbath is constructed of two parts:

- a shallow open-topped cylinder with an outside diameter of 1 m and a depth of 5 cm, with 1-cm-thick walls and base
- a conical frustum on which the cylinder sits

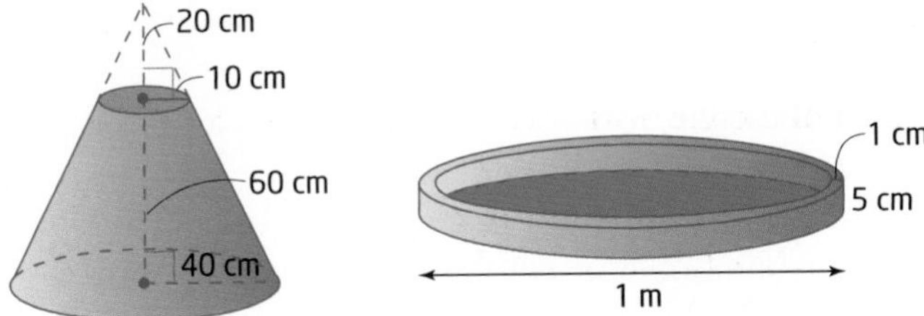

a) Identify the surfaces that are to be painted and describe how to calculate the area.

b) Calculate the surface area to be painted, to the nearest square centimetre.

c) One can of glaze covers 1 m^2. How many cans of glaze will Emily need to cover all surfaces of the birdbath and the frustum?

12. Create a problem involving the surface area of a cone. Solve the problem. Exchange with a classmate.

Extend

13. Suppose the cube in question 8 has sides of length x.

a) Write expressions for the dimensions of the largest cone that fits inside this box.

b) What is a formula for the surface area of this cone?

14. a) Find an expression for the slant height of a cone in terms of its lateral area and its radius.

b) If the lateral area of a cone is 100 cm^2 and its radius is 4 cm, determine its slant height.

15. Located in the Azores Islands off the coast of Portugal, Mt. Pico Volcano stands 2351 m tall. Measure the photo to estimate the radius of the base of the volcano, and then calculate its lateral surface area, to the nearest square metre.

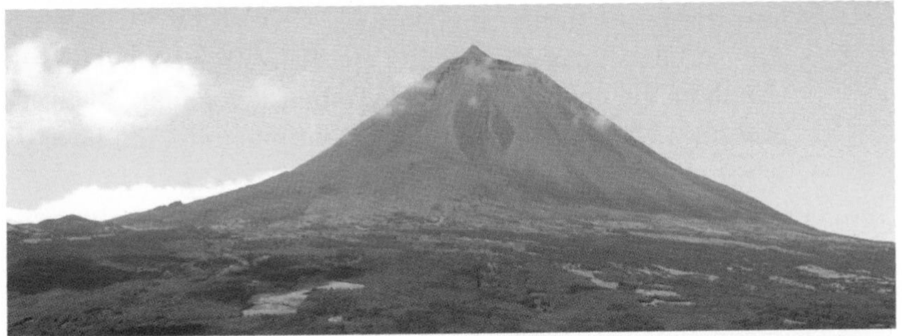

Did You Know?

There are 8000 to 10 000 people of Azorean heritage living in Ontario.

16. Use Technology A cone has a radius of 2 cm.

a) Write an algebraic model for the surface area of this cone in terms of its slant height.

b) Use *The Geometer's Sketchpad®* to investigate how the surface area of a cone changes as the slant height changes. Since *The Geometer's Sketchpad®* cannot easily show three-dimensional objects, represent the cone with a triangle that is a side view of the cone.

- From the **Edit** menu, choose **Preferences**. Click on the **Text** tab. Ensure that **For All New Points** is checked.
- Draw a point A. Select point A. From the **Transform** menu, choose **Translate**. Ensure that the **Polar**, **Fixed Distance**, and **Fixed Angle** radio buttons are on. Change the distance to 2 cm and the angle to 0°. Click on **Translate**. Point A′ will appear 2 cm to the right of point A. Draw another point 2 cm to the left of point A, using an angle of 180°.
- Construct a line segment joining the three points. Select point A and the line segment. From the **Construct** menu, choose **Perpendicular Line** to draw a perpendicular line through point A.
- Draw a point B on the line above point A. Construct line segments to form a triangle. This triangle represents the side view of a cone with a variable height AB and a fixed radius of 2 cm.
- Measure the radius of the cone. Select this measurement. Right click and choose **Label Measurement** from the drop-down menu. Change the label to **r**.
- Measure the slant height of the cone. Change the label to **s**.
- Select **r** and **s**. From the **Measure** menu, choose **Calculate**. Enter the formula π***r**^2+π***r*****s** by selecting π, **r**, and **s** from the **Values** drop-down menu on the calculator. Change the label to **SA**. This is the surface area of the cone. Drag point B back and forth along the line. Watch how the measurements change.

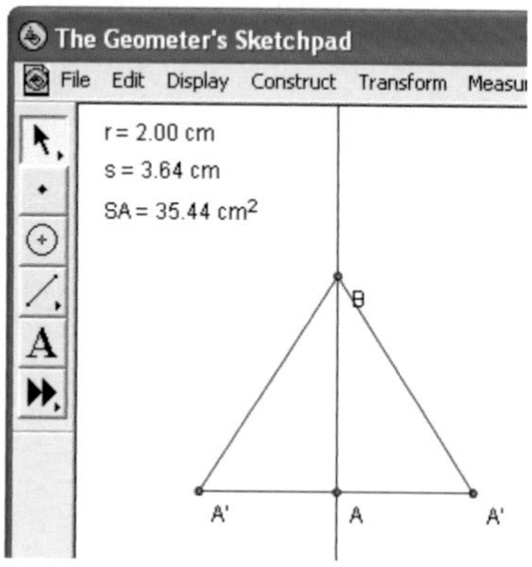

- Select **s** and then **SA**. From the **Graph** menu, choose **Tabulate**. Move the table to a convenient location. Move point B, and note how the values in the table change.
- Adjust the value of **s** to about 3 cm. Select the table. From the **Graph** menu, choose **Add Table Data**. Click on **OK**. Repeat this process with **s** set to about 4 cm. Continue until you have five sets of data.

From the **Graph** menu, choose **Plot Table Data**. You will see a graph of the data that you have collected.

c) Describe the relationship that resulted from this investigation using mathematical terms.

Volume of a Cone

Cone-shaped containers are used in a variety of professions, such as environmental studies, agriculture, and culinary arts.

In this section, you will develop a formula for the volume of any cone.

Investigate

Tools

- empty cylindrical can
- construction paper
- scissors
- tape
- sand, rice, or another suitable material

How can you model the volume of a cone?

Work with a partner.

1. Measure the radius and height of the can.
2. Construct a cone with the same base radius and height as the can.
   a) Use the radius and height to calculate the slant height of the cone.
   b) Construct a circle with a radius equal to the slant height you determined. Make a cut along a radius so that the circle can be formed into a cone.
   c) The cone's circumference should fit the circumference of the can. Tape the seam to form a cone.

3. Fill the cone with sand, rice, or another suitable material. Empty the rice into the can. Repeat until the can is full. How many cones of material does it take to fill the can?
4. a) **Reflect** What conclusion can you draw about the relationship between the volume of a cone and the volume of a cylinder with the same height and radius?
   b) You know the formula for the volume of a cylinder. Use your conclusion from part a) to write a formula for the volume, V, of a cone in terms of the radius, r, of the base and the height, h.

Example 1 Volume of a Frozen Yogurt Treat

Tracy makes her own frozen yogurt treats in cone-shaped paper cups. Determine the volume of the frozen yogurt treat shown, to the nearest cubic centimetre.

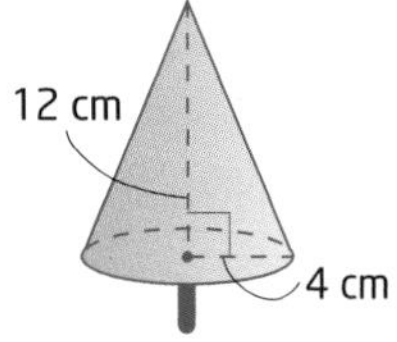

Solution

The volume of a cone is one third the volume of the cylinder with the same base and height.

$$\begin{aligned} V_{cone} &= \frac{1}{3}(\text{volume of a cylinder}) \\ &= \frac{1}{3}\pi r^2 h \\ &= \frac{1}{3}\pi(4)^2(12) \\ &\doteq 201 \end{aligned}$$

Estimate: $\frac{1}{3}(3)(4^2)(12) = (16)(12)$
$= 192$

The volume of the frozen yogurt treat is approximately 201 cm^3.

Example 2 Volume of a Sand Pile

A conical pile of sand has a base diameter of 10 m and a slant height of 8 m. Determine the volume of the sand in the pile, to the nearest cubic metre.

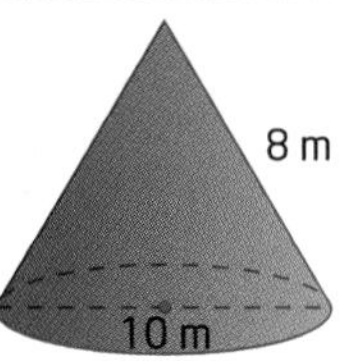

Solution

Since the diameter of the base is 10 m, the radius is 5 m.

To determine the volume of the cone, you need to know the height.

Apply the Pythagorean theorem.

$$\begin{aligned} s^2 &= h^2 + r^2 \\ 8^2 &= h^2 + 5^2 \\ 64 &= h^2 + 25 \\ h^2 &= 64 - 25 \\ h^2 &= 39 \\ h &= \sqrt{39} \\ h &\doteq 6.2 \end{aligned}$$

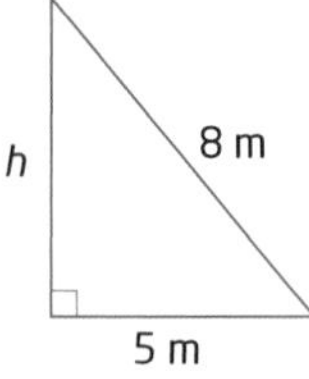

The height of the cone is approximately 6.2 m.

Now, determine the volume.

$$V_{\text{cone}} = \frac{1}{3}\pi r^2 h$$

$$= \frac{1}{3}\pi(5)^2(6.2) \quad \textbf{Estimate: } \frac{1}{3}(3)(5^2)(6) = (25)(6) = 150$$

$$\doteq 162$$

C 1 ÷ 3 × π × 5 x² × 6.2 =

```
1/3*π*5²*6.2
         162.3156204
```

The volume of the sand in the pile is approximately 162 m^3.

Example 3 Find the Height of a Container

A fountain firework is packaged in a conical container. Its volume is 210 cm^3. Its diameter is 8 cm. What is the height of the fountain firework, to the nearest tenth of a centimetre?

Solution

Substitute the given values into the formula for the volume of a cone.

$$V_{\text{cone}} = \frac{1}{3}\pi r^2 h$$

$$210 = \frac{1}{3}\pi(4)^2 h$$

Since the diameter is 8 cm, the radius is 4 cm.

$$210 = \frac{16\pi}{3}h$$

$$210 \times \frac{3}{16\pi} = h$$

To isolate h, I'll divide both sides by 16π and multiply both sides by 3.

$$h \doteq 12.5$$

```
210*3/(16*π)
         12.53345177
```

The height of the conical firework is approximately 12.5 cm.

Key Concepts

- The volume of a cone is one third the volume of a cylinder with the same base radius and height:

$$V_{\text{cone}} = \frac{1}{3}\pi r^2 h$$

- If you know the slant height, s, and base radius, r, of a cone, you can use the Pythagorean theorem to determine the height, h, of the cone.

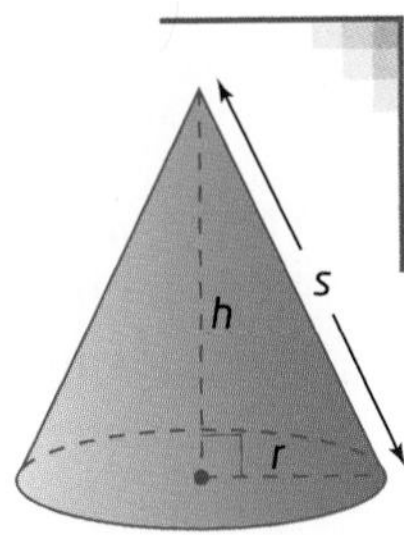

Communicate Your Understanding

C1 A cylindrical container and a conical container have the same radius and height. How are their volumes related? How could you illustrate this relationship for a friend?

C2 Suppose the height of a cone is doubled. How will this affect the volume?

C3 Suppose the radius of a cone is doubled. How will this affect the volume?

Practise

For help with question 1, see Example 1.

1. Determine the volume of each cone. Round to the nearest cubic unit.

a)

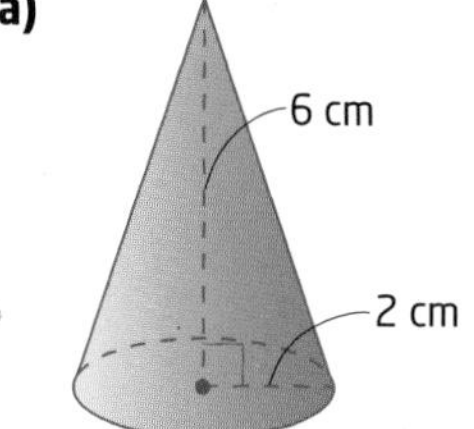

b)

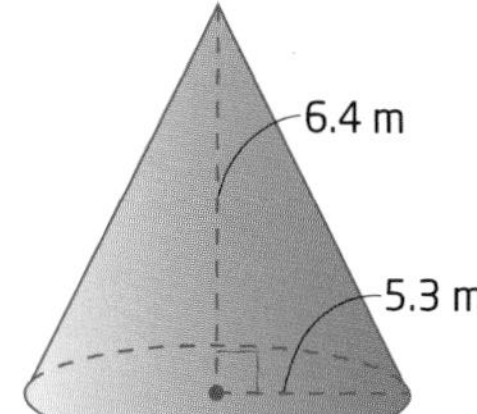

c)

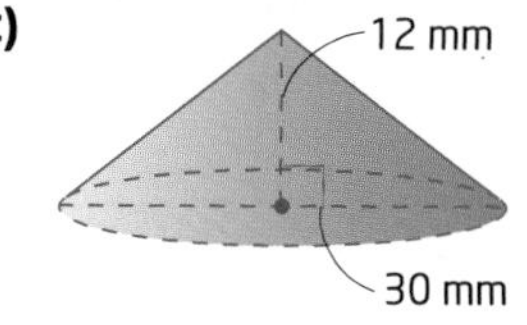

d)

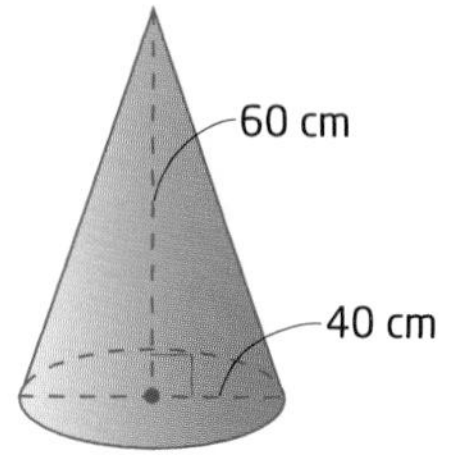

For help with questions 2 and 3, see Example 2.

2. Determine the volume of each cone. Round to the nearest cubic unit.

a)

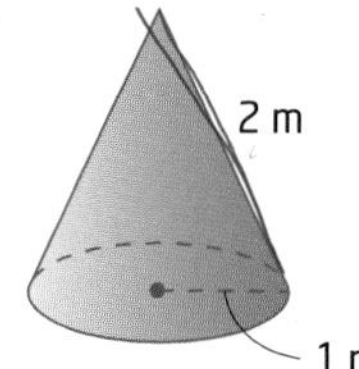

b)

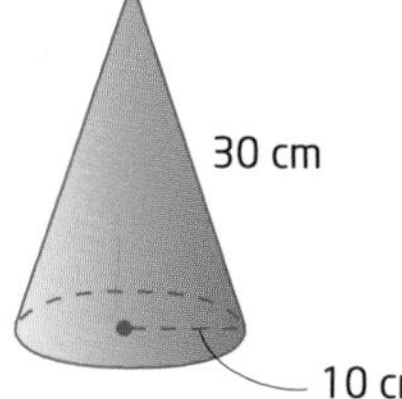

3. Wesley uses a cone-shaped funnel to put oil in a car engine. The funnel has a radius of 5.4 cm and a slant height of 10.2 cm. How much oil can the funnel hold, to the nearest tenth of a cubic centimetre?

5.4 cm

10.2 cm

For help with question 4, see Example 3.

4. A cone-shaped paper cup has a volume of 67 cm^3 and a diameter of 6 cm. What is the height of the paper cup, to the nearest tenth of a centimetre?

Connect and Apply

5. A cone just fits inside a cylinder with volume 300 cm^3. What is the volume of the cone?

6. Create a problem involving the volume of a cone. Solve it. Exchange your problem with a classmate.

7. A cone has a volume of 150 cm^3. What is the volume of a cylinder that just holds the cone?

8. A cone-shaped storage unit at a highway maintenance depot holds 4000 m^3 of sand. The unit has a base radius of 15 m.

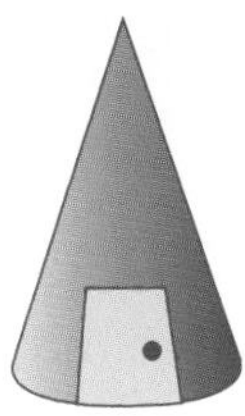

a) Estimate the height of the storage unit.

b) Calculate the height.

c) How close was your estimate?

9. A cone has a height of 4 cm and a base radius of 3 cm. Another cone has a height of 3 cm and a base radius of 4 cm.

a) Predict which cone has the greater volume. Explain your prediction.

b) Calculate the volume of each cone, to the nearest cubic centimetre. Was your prediction correct?

10. Chapter Problem Refer to question 11 in Section 8.4. Determine the volume of concrete in Emily's birdbath. Round your answer to the nearest cubic centimetre.

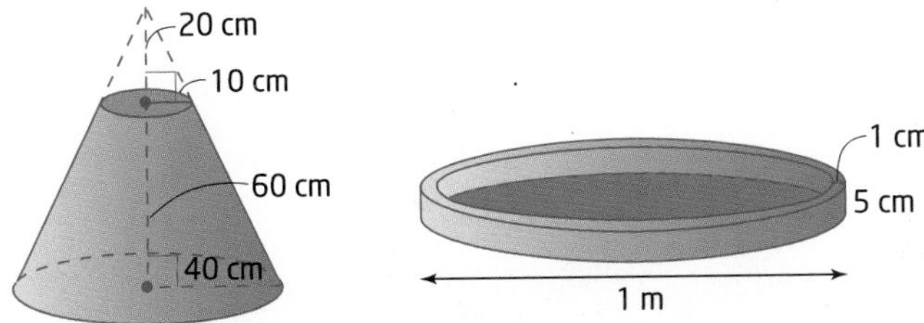

11. a) Express the height of a cone in terms of its volume and its radius.

b) If a cone holds 1 L and its radius is 4 cm, what is its height? Round your answer to the nearest tenth of a centimetre.

12. A cone-shaped funnel holds 120 mL of water. If the height of the funnel is 15 cm, determine the radius, rounded to the nearest tenth of a centimetre.

Extend

13. A cone just fits inside a cube with sides that measure 10 cm.

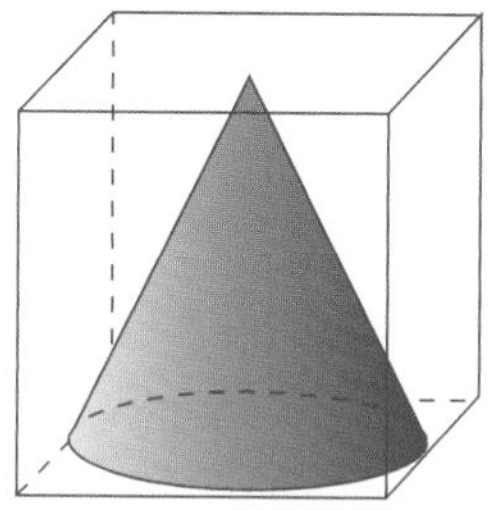

a) What are the dimensions of the largest cone that fits inside this box?

b) Estimate the ratio of the volume of the cone to the volume of the cube.

c) Calculate the volume of the cone, to the nearest cubic centimetre.

d) Calculate the ratio in part b).

e) How close was your estimate?

14. A cone has a height equal to its diameter. If the volume of the cone is 200 m^3, determine the height of the cone, to the nearest tenth of a metre.

15. Use Technology Use a graphing calculator, *The Geometer's Sketchpad®*, or a spreadsheet to investigate how the volume of a cone is affected when its radius is constant and its height changes.

16. Use Technology A cone has a height of 20 cm.

a) Write an algebraic model for the volume of the cone in terms of the radius.

b) Choose a tool for graphing. Graph the volume of the cone versus the radius.

c) Describe the relationship using mathematical terms.

17. Math Contest A cube has side length 6 cm. A square-based pyramid has side length 6 cm and height 12 cm. A cone has diameter 6 cm and height 12 cm. A cylinder has diameter 6 cm and height 6 cm. Order the figures from the least to the greatest volume. Select the correct order.

A cube, pyramid, cone, cylinder

B cylinder, cube, cone, pyramid

C cube, cone, cylinder, pyramid

D cone, pyramid, cylinder, cube

E pyramid, cone, cylinder, cube

8.6 Surface Area of a Sphere

sphere

- a round ball-shaped object
- a set of points in space that are a given distance (radius) from a fixed point (centre)

A **sphere** is a three-dimensional shape that is often seen in sports. Balls of different sizes are used to play basketball, soccer, and volleyball, to name a few.

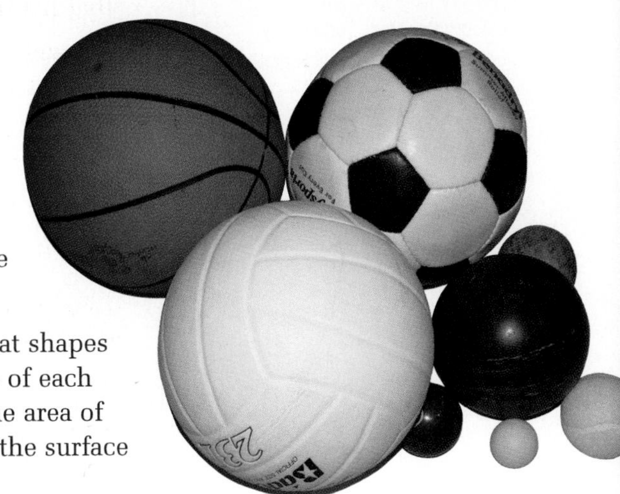

Consider the balls shown. What shapes appear to make up the surface of each sphere? How could you use the area of these shapes to help you find the surface area of a sphere?

Investigate

Tools

- orange
- string
- ruler
- centimetre grid paper

How can you model the surface area of a sphere?

Work with a partner.

1. Choose an orange that is as spherical as possible. Estimate the surface area of the orange, in square centimetres.

2. a) Measure the circumference of the orange. Use a piece of string to go around the outside of the orange. Then, measure the length of the string.

   b) Use the formula for the circumference of a circle, $C = 2\pi r$, to find the radius of the orange.

3. Carefully peel the orange. Flatten the pieces and place them on grid paper. Trace around the pieces. Find the area of the peel by counting squares and partial squares on the grid paper.

4. a) Determine the area of a circle with the same radius as the orange.

   b) What is the approximate ratio of the orange's surface area to the area of the circle?

   c) Describe a possible formula for the surface area of a sphere based on your results.

5. **Reflect** Compare your results with those of your classmates. What do you conclude that the formula for the surface area of a sphere is?

Did You Know?

The first in-socket artificial eyes were made in the 15th century from gold and coloured enamel. Today they are made from a medical grade acrylic plastic.

Example 1 Surface Area of an Eyeball

The dimensions of an adult human eyeball are reasonably constant, varying only by a millimetre or two. The average diameter is about 2.5 cm. Calculate the surface area of the human eyeball, to the nearest tenth of a square centimetre.

Solution

The formula for the surface area of a sphere is $SA_{sphere} = 4\pi r^2$.

The eyeball has a diameter of 2.5 cm, so the radius is 1.25 cm.

$$\begin{aligned} SA_{sphere} &= 4\pi r^2 \\ &= 4\pi(1.25)^2 \quad \text{Estimate: } 4(3)(1)^2 = 12 \\ &\doteq 19.6 \end{aligned}$$

The surface area of the human eyeball is about 19.6 cm^2.

Example 2 Find the Radius of a Baseball

Determine the radius of a baseball that has a surface area of 215 cm^2. Round your answer to the nearest tenth of a centimetre.

Solution

Substitute the values into the formula.

$$\begin{aligned} SA_{sphere} &= 4\pi r^2 \\ 215 &= 4\pi r^2 \\ \frac{215}{4\pi} &= r^2 \\ \sqrt{\frac{215}{4\pi}} &= r \\ r &\doteq 4.1 \end{aligned}$$

C 215 ÷ (4 × π) = √

```
√(215/(4*π))
           4.1363216
```

The radius of the baseball is about 4.1 cm.

Key Concepts

- The formula for the surface area of a sphere with radius r is $SA_{sphere} = 4\pi r^2$.
- If you know the surface area of a sphere, you can determine the radius, r, of the sphere.

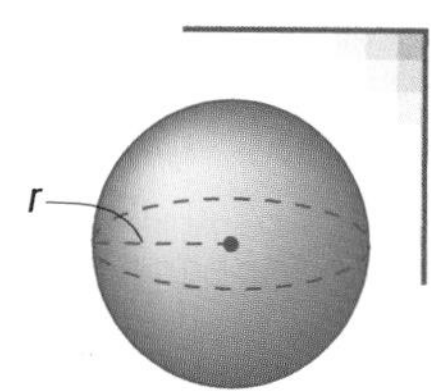

Communicate Your Understanding

C1 Describe how you would determine the amount of leather required to cover a softball.

C2 Does doubling the radius of a sphere double the surface area? Explain your reasoning.

Practise

For help with questions 1 and 2, see Example 1.

1. Determine the surface area of each sphere. Round to the nearest square unit.

a)

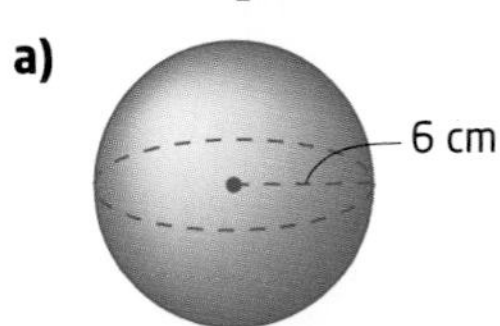

b)

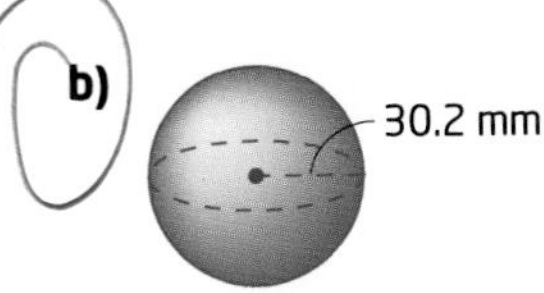

c)

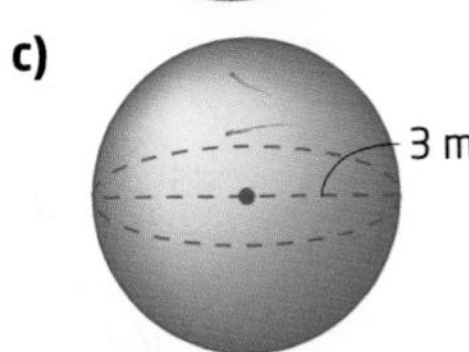

d)

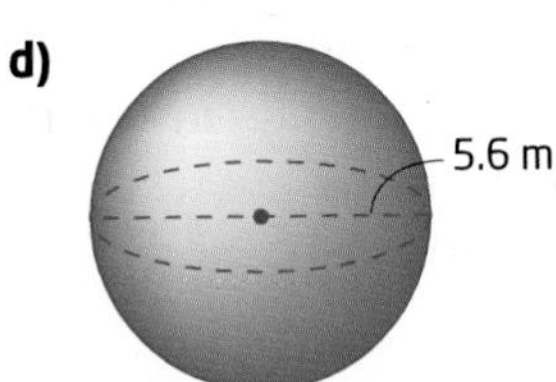

2. A ball used to play table tennis has a diameter of 40 mm.

a) Estimate the surface area of this ball.

b) Calculate the surface area, to the nearest square millimetre. How close was your estimate?

For help with question 3, see Example 2.

3. A sphere has a surface area of 42.5 m^2. Find its radius, to the nearest tenth of a metre.

Connect and Apply

4. A basketball has a diameter of 24.8 cm.

a) How much leather is required to cover this ball, to the nearest tenth of a square centimetre?

b) If the leather costs $\$28/m^2$, what does it cost to cover the basketball?

5. The diameter of Earth is approximately 12 800 km.

a) Calculate the surface area of Earth, to the nearest square kilometre.

b) What assumptions did you make?

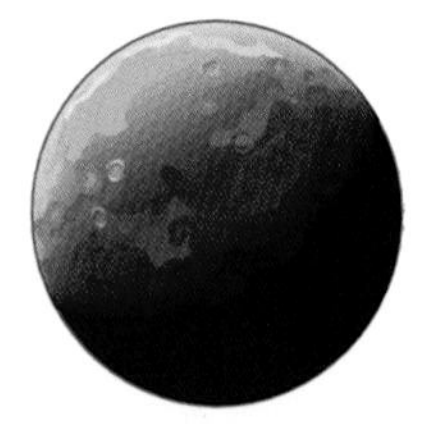

6. a) The diameter of Mars is 6800 km. Calculate its surface area, to the nearest square kilometre.

b) Compare the surface area of Mars to the surface area of Earth from question 5. Approximately how many times greater is the surface area of Earth than the surface area of Mars?

7. Chapter Problem Emily is placing a gazing ball in one of her customer's gardens. The ball has a diameter of 60 cm and will be covered with reflective crystals. One jar of these crystals covers 1 m^2.

a) Estimate the surface area to decide whether one jar of the crystals will cover the ball.

b) Calculate the surface area, to the nearest square centimetre.

c) Was your estimate reasonable? Explain.

8. The radius of a sphere is 15 cm.

a) Predict how much the surface area increases if the radius increases by 2 cm.

b) Calculate the change in the surface area, to the nearest square centimetre.

c) How accurate was your prediction?

9. Use Technology

a) Use a graphing calculator to graph the surface area of a sphere versus its radius by entering the surface area formula.

b) Describe the relationship.

c) Use the TRACE feature to determine
- the surface area of a sphere with radius 5.35 cm
- the radius of a sphere with surface area 80 cm^2

Extend

10. Use Technology

a) Determine an algebraic expression for the radius of a sphere in terms of its surface area.

b) Use your expression from part a) and a graphing calculator to graph the relationship between the radius and the surface area.

c) Describe the relationship.

d) Use the graphing calculator to find the radius of a sphere with surface area 200 cm^2.

11. A spherical balloon is blown up from a diameter of 10 cm to a diameter of 30 cm. By what factor has its surface area increased? Explain your reasoning.

12. Which has the larger surface area: a sphere of radius r or a cube with edges of length $2r$?

13. Use Technology A sphere just fits inside a cube with sides of length 10 cm.

a) Estimate the ratio of the surface area of the sphere to the surface area of the cube.

b) Calculate the surface areas of the sphere and the cube and their ratio.

c) How does your answer compare to your estimate?

d) Use *The Geometer's Sketchpad®* to investigate this relationship for any size of cube with an inscribed sphere. Since *The Geometer's Sketchpad®* cannot easily show three-dimensional objects, represent the cube with a square and the sphere with a circle.

- From the **Edit** menu, choose **Preferences**. Click on the **Text** tab. Ensure that **For All New Points** is checked.
- Select the **Custom Tool**. From the drop-down menu, choose **Polygons** and then **4/Square (By Edge)**. Draw a square ABCD.
- Construct the diagonals of the square. Draw a circle with its centre at E, where the diagonals cross, such that it is inscribed in the square. Draw a radius EF.
- Measure radius EF of the circle. Select this measurement. Right click and choose **Label Measurement** from the drop-down menu. Change the label to **r**.
- Measure side AB of the square. Change the label to **s**.
- Select **s**. From the **Measure** menu, choose **Calculate**. Enter the formula 6***s**^2 by selecting **s** from the **Values** drop-down menu on the calculator. Change the label to **SA of Cube**.
- Select **r**. From the **Measure** menu, choose **Calculate**. Enter the formula 4*π***r**^2 by selecting **r** from the **Values** drop-down menu on the calculator. Change the label to **SA of sphere**.
- Calculate the ratio $\frac{\text{SA of cube}}{\text{SA of sphere}}$.

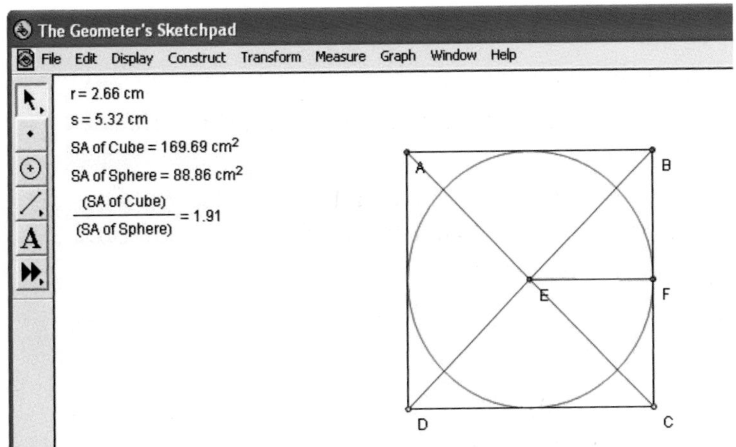

- Drag point A. Watch how the measurements change.

What can you conclude about the ratio of the surface areas of a cube and a sphere inscribed in the cube?

8.7 Volume of a Sphere

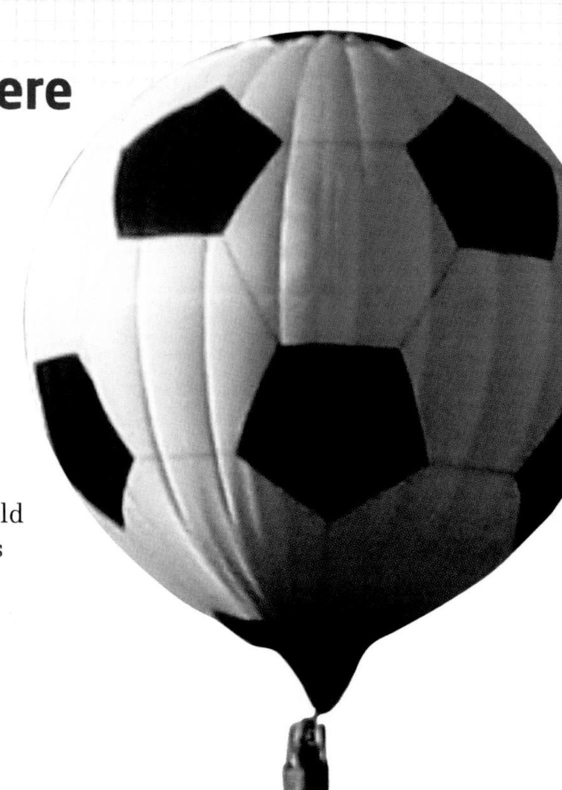

The annual Gatineau Hot Air Balloon Festival has been held since 1988 in Gatineau, Québec. Hot air balloons come in a variety of shapes. One special shape that appeared at the festival was a soccer ball. This soccer ball was about 17.4 m in diameter, and could hold 385 696 ordinary soccer balls inside it.

In this section, you will develop a formula for the volume of any sphere.

Investigate

Tools

- a cylindrical container that just holds three tennis balls
- three old tennis balls
- water
- a container to catch the overflow water

How can you model the volume of a sphere?

Work in small groups.

1. Before you take any measurements, estimate the volume of one tennis ball.

2. a) Measure the diameter of the cylinder. It should be almost the same as the diameter of the tennis ball.

b) Measure the height of the cylinder. It should be almost the same as three times the diameter of the tennis ball.

3. Place the cylinder in the overflow container and fill the cylinder with water.

4. Slowly place the three tennis balls inside the cylinder, one at a time, allowing the water to overflow into the container. Push the balls down to the bottom of the cylinder.

5. Remove the tennis balls from the cylinder, take the can out of the overflow container, and empty the water from the cylinder into the sink. Pour the water from the overflow container back into the cylinder. Measure the depth of the water.

6. What fraction of the cylinder is filled with water? How does the volume of this displaced water compare to the volume of the three tennis balls?

7. If the cylinder were only big enough to hold one tennis ball, what fraction of the can would be filled with water?

8. **Reflect** How does the volume of a sphere compare to the volume of a cylinder? How would you calculate the volume of one tennis ball?

9. Use your method to calculate the volume of one tennis ball. How does your answer compare to your estimate?

Example 1 Volume of Pluto

Pluto is the smallest planet in the solar system. The diameter of Pluto is approximately 2290 km. Calculate the volume of Pluto.

Did You Know?

Jupiter is the largest planet, with an equatorial diameter of 143 884 km. Its diameter is more than 11 times that of Earth.

Solution

The volume of a sphere is two thirds the volume of a cylinder with the same radius and a height equal to the diameter of the sphere. If the sphere has radius r, then the cylinder has a base radius r and height $2r$.

cylinder

r

h = 2r

sphere

r

h = 2r

$$V_{sphere} = \frac{2}{3}(\text{volume of a cylinder})$$
$$= \frac{2}{3}\pi r^2 h$$
$$= \frac{2}{3}\pi(r^2)(2r)$$
$$= \frac{4}{3}\pi r^3$$

The radius is one half the diameter. The radius of Pluto is 1145 km. Use the formula for the volume of a sphere.

$$V_{sphere} = \frac{4}{3}\pi r^3$$
$$= \frac{4}{3}\pi(1145)^3$$
$$\doteq 6\ 300\ 000\ 000$$

```
4/3*π*1145^3
      6287891937
```

The volume of Pluto is approximately 6 300 000 000 km^3.

Example 2 Package a Gemstone

A spherical gemstone just fits inside a plastic cube with edges 10 cm.

a) Calculate the volume of the gemstone, to the nearest cubic centimetre.

b) How much empty space is there?

Solution

a) The diameter of the gemstone is about 10 cm, so its radius is 5 cm.

$$V_{\text{sphere}} = \frac{4}{3}\pi r^3$$
$$= \frac{4}{3}\pi(5)^3$$
$$\doteq 524$$

Estimate: $\frac{4}{3}(3)5^3 = 4(125)$ $= 500$

The volume of the gemstone is about 524 cm^3.

b) Determine the volume of the cube.

$$V_{\text{cube}} = s^3$$
$$= 10^3$$
$$= 1000$$

The empty space is the difference in the volumes of the cube and the gemstone.

$$V_{\text{empty space}} = V_{\text{cube}} - V_{\text{sphere}}$$
$$= 1000 - 524$$
$$= 476$$

There is about 476 cm^3 of empty space in the box.

Did You Know?

Since medieval times quartz crystal balls have been used in attempts to divine the future. Gemstone spheres are thought to have healing powers, with each gemstone having a different therapeutic energy.

Key Concepts

- The volume of a sphere with radius r is given by the formula $V_{\text{sphere}} = \frac{4}{3}\pi r^3$.
- You can calculate the empty space in a container by subtracting the volume of the object from the volume of the container in which it is packaged.

r

Communicate Your Understanding

C1 Describe how you would determine the volume of a sphere if you knew its surface area.

C2 How is the volume of a sphere affected if you double the radius?

Practise

For help with questions 1 to 3, see Example 1.

1. Calculate the volume of each sphere. Round to the nearest cubic unit.

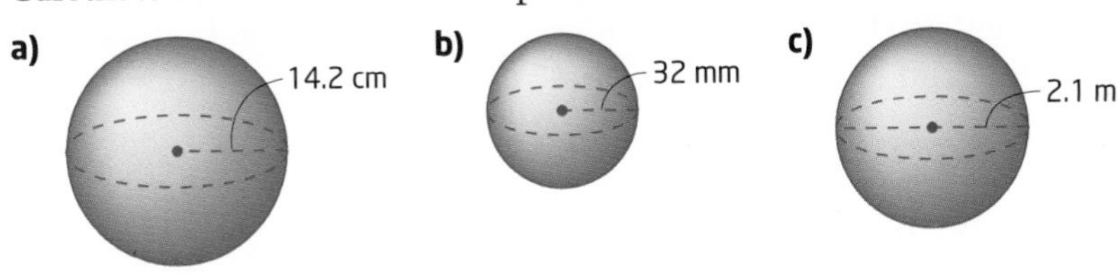

2. A golf ball has a diameter of 4.3 cm. Calculate its volume, to the nearest cubic centimetre.

3. Hailstones thought to be the size of baseballs killed hundreds of people and cattle in the Moradabad and Beheri districts of India in 1888. The hailstones had a reported diameter of 8 cm. What was the volume of each one, to the nearest cubic centimetre?

For help with question 4, see Example 2.

4. A table tennis ball just fits inside a plastic cube with edges 40 mm.

a) Calculate the volume of the table tennis ball, to the nearest cubic millimetre.

b) Calculate the volume of the cube.

c) Determine the amount of empty space.

Connect and Apply

5. The largest lollipop ever made had a diameter of 140.3 cm and was made for a festival in Gränna, Sweden, on July 27, 2003.

a) If a spherical lollipop with diameter 4 cm has a mass of 50 g, what was the mass of this giant lollipop to the nearest kilogram?

b) Describe any assumptions you have made.

6. Chapter Problem Emily orders a spherical gazing ball for one of her customers. It is packaged tightly in a cylindrical container with a base radius of 30 cm and a height of 60 cm.

a) Calculate the volume of the sphere, to the nearest cubic centimetre.

b) Calculate the volume of the cylindrical container, to the nearest cubic centimetre.

c) What is the ratio of the volume of the sphere to the volume of the container?

d) Is this ratio consistent for any sphere that just fits inside a cylinder? Explain your reasoning.

7. Golf balls are stacked three high in a rectangular prism package. The diameter of one ball is 4.3 cm. What is the minimum amount of material needed to make the box?

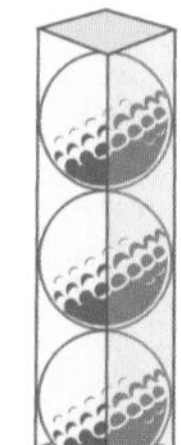

8. A cylindrical silo has a hemispherical top (half of a sphere). The cylinder has a height of 20 m and a base diameter of 6.5 m.

a) Estimate the total volume of the silo.

b) Calculate the total volume, to the nearest cubic metre.

c) The silo should be filled to no more than 80% capacity to allow for air circulation. How much grain can be put in the silo?

d) A truck with a bin measuring 7 m by 3 m by 2.5 m delivers grain to the farm. How many truckloads would fill the silo to its recommended capacity?

9. The tank of a propane tank truck is in the shape of a cylinder with a hemisphere at both ends. The tank has a radius of 2 m and a total length of 10.2 m. Calculate the volume of the tank, to the nearest cubic metre.

10. Estimate how many basketballs would fit into your classroom. Explain your reasoning and estimation techniques and describe any assumptions you have made. Compare your answer with that of a classmate. Are your answers close? If not, whose answer is a more reasonable estimate and why?

Achievement Check

11. The T-Ball company is considering packaging two tennis balls that are 8.5 cm in diameter in a cylinder or in a square-based prism.
    a) What are the dimensions and volumes of the two containers?
    b) How much empty space would there be in each container?
    c) What factors should the T-Ball company consider in choosing the package design? Justify your choices.

Extend

12. Estimate and then calculate the radius of a sphere with a volume of 600 cm^3.

13. **Use Technology** Graph $V = \frac{4}{3}\pi r^3$ using a graphing calculator.
    a) Use the TRACE feature to determine the volume of a sphere with a radius of 6.2 cm.
    b) Check your answer to question 12 by using the TRACE feature to approximate the radius of a sphere with a volume of 600 cm^3.

14. If the surface area of a sphere is doubled from 250 cm^2 to 500 cm^2, by what factor does its volume increase?

15. A sphere just fits inside a cube with sides of length 8 cm.
    a) Estimate the ratio of the volume of the sphere to the volume of the cube.
    b) Calculate the volumes of the sphere and the cube and their ratio.
    c) How does your answer compare to your estimate?

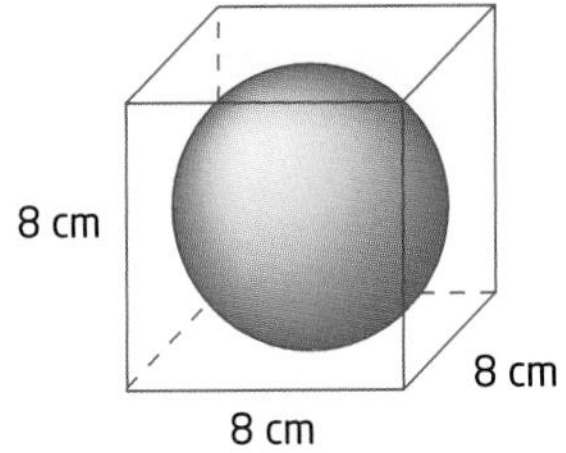

16. Which has the larger volume: a sphere of radius r or a cube with edges of length $2r$?

17. Use Technology Use *The Geometer's Sketchpad®* to investigate how the volume of glass required to make a spherical light bulb of constant thickness 0.2 cm changes as the radius of the light bulb changes. Since *The Geometer's Sketchpad®* cannot easily show three-dimensional objects, represent the spherical light bulb with two concentric circles 0.2 cm apart.

- From the **Edit** menu, choose **Preferences**. Click on the **Text** tab. Ensure that **For All New Points** is checked.
- Draw a point A. Select point A. From the **Transform** menu, choose **Translate**. Ensure that the **Polar**, **Fixed Distance**, and **Fixed Angle** radio buttons are on. Change the distance to 1 cm and the angle to 0°. Click on **Translate**. Point A′ will appear 1 cm to the right of point A. Construct a line through points A and A′.
- Draw a circle with centre A and radius AB such that point B is to the right of A′, and on the line.
- With point B selected, choose **Translate** from the **Transform** menu. Ensure that the **Polar**, **Fixed Distance**, and **Fixed Angle** radio buttons are on. Change the distance to 0.2 cm and the angle to 0°. Click on **Translate**. Point B′ will appear 0.2 cm to the right of point B.
- Draw a circle with centre A and radius AB′.
- Measure the inner radius AB. Select this measurement. Right click and choose **Label Distance Measurement** from the drop-down menu. Change the label to **Inner r**.
- Measure the outer radius AB′. Change the label to **Outer r**.
- Select **Inner r**. From the **Measure** menu, choose **Calculate**. Enter the formula 4÷3*π***Inner r**^3 by selecting **Inner r** from the **Values** drop-down menu on the calculator. Change the label to **Inner V**. This is the volume of the sphere inside the light bulb.
- Select **Outer r**. From the **Measure** menu, choose **Calculate**. Enter the formula 4÷3*π***Outer r**^3 by selecting **Outer r** from the **Values** drop-down menu on the calculator. Change the label to **Outer V**. This is the outer volume of the light bulb.

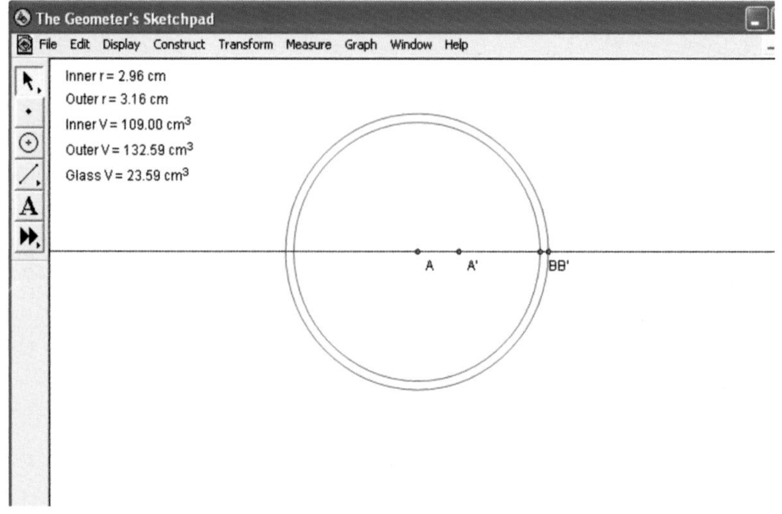

- Calculate the value **Outer V** − **Inner V**. Change the label to **Glass V**. This is the volume of glass required to make the light bulb.
- Select **Outer r** and then **Glass V**. From the **Graph** menu, choose **Tabulate**. Move the table to a convenient location. Move point B, and note how the values in the table change.
- Adjust the value of **Outer r** to about 1 cm. Select the table. From the **Graph** menu, choose **Add Table Data**. Click on **OK**. Adjust **Outer r** to about 2 cm. Choose **Add Table Data** again. Continue until you have five sets of data.
- From the **Graph** menu, choose **Plot Table Data**. You will see a graph of the data that you have collected.

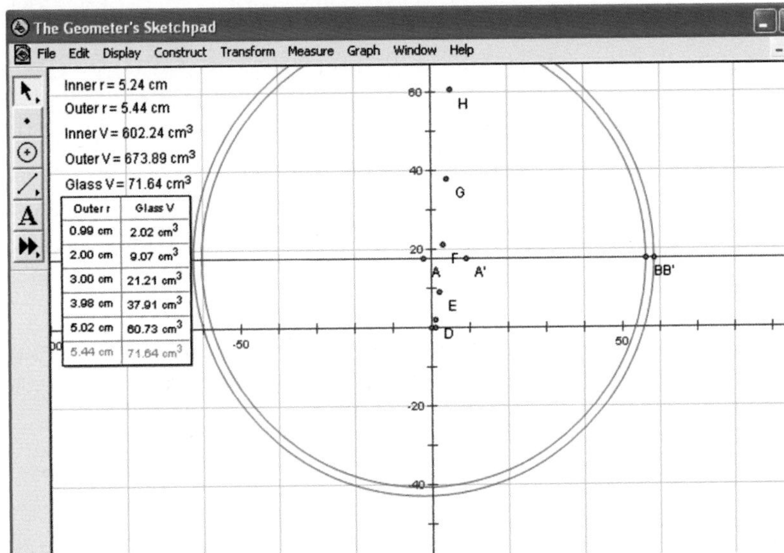

Describe the relationship in mathematical terms.

18. Math Contest A cylinder has radius 6 cm and height 6 cm. A cone has radius 6 cm and height 6 cm. A sphere has radius 6 cm. Order the figures from least volume to greatest volume. Select the correct order.

A cone, sphere, cylinder
B cone, cylinder, sphere
C sphere, cone, cylinder
D cylinder, sphere, cone
E cylinder, cone, sphere

19. Math Contest A dozen of Terry's favourite golf balls are sold in a rectangular box. Each ball has a diameter of 4 cm. Determine the volume of empty space in the box of golf balls.

Chapter 8 Review

8.1 Apply the Pythagorean Theorem, pages 418–425

1. Determine the perimeter and area of each right triangle. Round answers to the nearest tenth of a unit or square unit.

a)

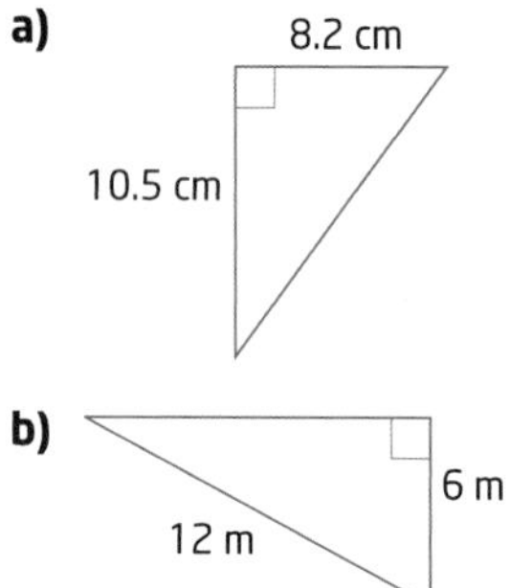

b)

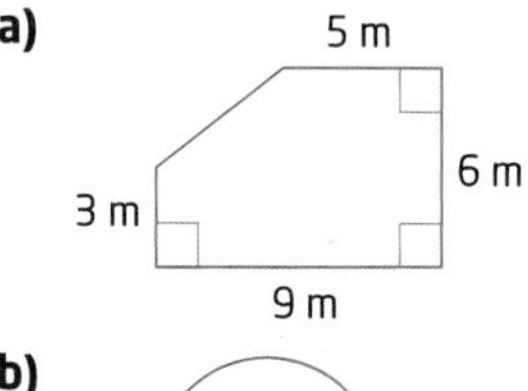

2. A 6-m extension ladder leans against a vertical wall with its base 2 m from the wall. How high up the wall does the top of the ladder reach? Round to the nearest tenth of a metre.

8.2 Perimeter and Area of Composite Figures, pages 426–435

3. Calculate the perimeter and area of each figure. Round answers to the nearest tenth of a unit or square unit, if necessary.

a)

b)

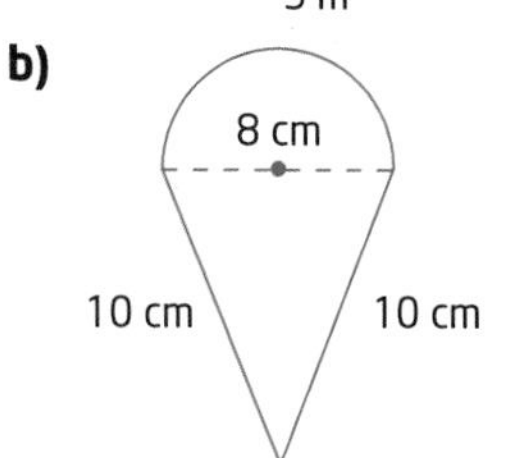

4. The diagram shows a running track at a high school. The track consists of two parallel line segments, with a semicircle at each end. The track is 10 m wide.

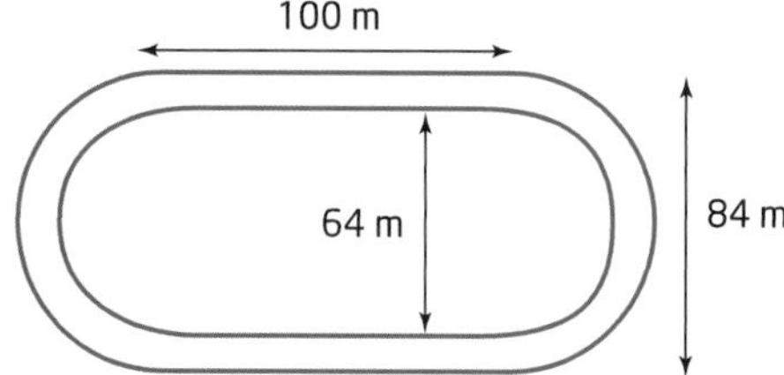

a) Tyler runs on the inner edge of the track. How far does he run in one lap, to the nearest tenth of a metre?

b) Dylan runs on the outer edge. How far does he run in one lap, to the nearest tenth of a metre?

c) Find the difference between the distances run by Tyler and Dylan.

8.3 Surface Area and Volume of Prisms and Pyramids, pages 436–443

5. Calculate the surface area of each object. Round answers to the nearest square unit, if necessary.

a)

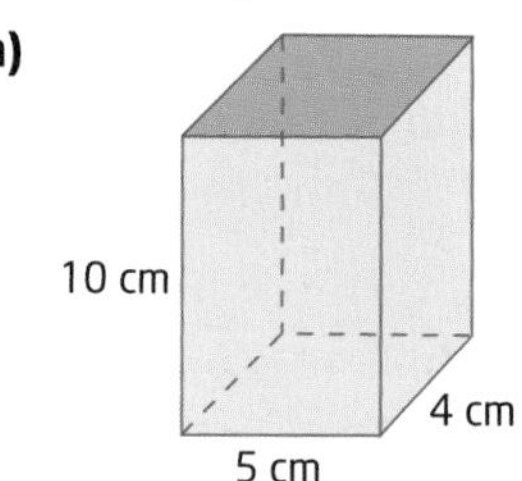

b) the Great Pyramid of Cheops, with a height of about 147 m and a base width of about 230 m

6. a) Calculate the volume of the tent.

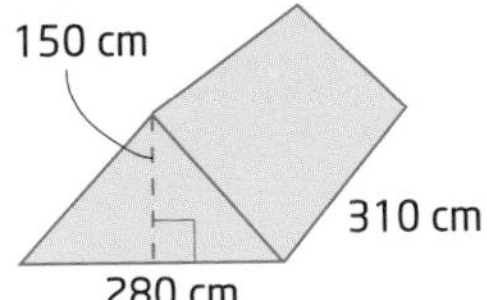

b) How much nylon is required to make this tent?

c) Describe any assumptions you made in part b).

d) How reasonable is your answer in part b)?

7. A cylindrical can holds 500 mL and has a radius of 4 cm. Calculate the height of the can, to the nearest tenth of a centimetre.

8.4 Surface Area of a Cone, pages 444–450

8. Calculate the surface area of a cone with a slant height of 13 cm and a height of 12 cm. Round to the nearest square centimetre.

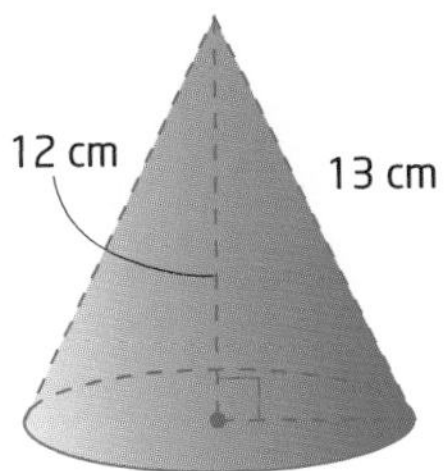

9. The cone portion of a traffic pylon has a diameter of 20 cm and a vertical height of 35 cm. Calculate the surface area of the cone portion of the pylon, to the nearest square centimetre. Assume that the bottom of the cone is complete.

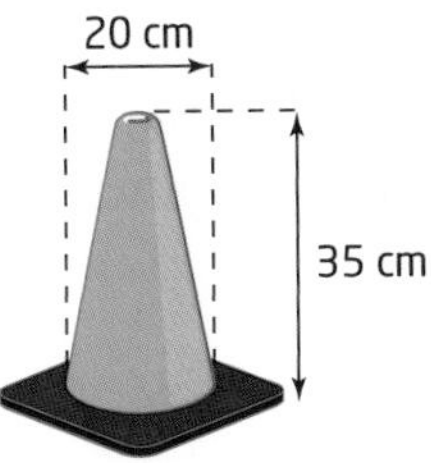

8.5 Volume of a Cone, pages 451–456

10. A conical funnel holds 100 mL. If the height of the funnel is 10 cm, determine its radius, to the nearest tenth of a centimetre.

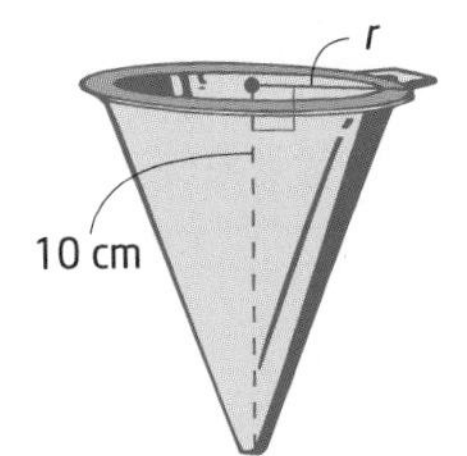

11. Calculate the volume of a cone that just fits inside a cylinder with a base radius of 8 cm and a height of 10 cm. Round to the nearest cubic centimetre. How does the volume of the cone compare to the volume of the cylinder?

8.6 Surface Area of a Sphere, pages 457–461

12. A volleyball has a diameter of 21.8 cm. Calculate the amount of leather required to cover the volleyball, to the nearest tenth of a square centimetre.

13. The diameter of Earth is about 12 800 km.

a) Calculate the area of the Northern Hemisphere, to the nearest square kilometre.

b) What assumptions have you made?

c) Canada's area is 9 970 610 km^2. Estimate the fraction of the Northern Hemisphere that Canada covers.

8.7 Volume of a Sphere, pages 462–469

14. Calculate the volume of a soccer ball with a diameter of 22.3 cm, to the nearest tenth of a cubic centimetre.

15. The soccer ball in question 14 is packaged so that it just fits inside a cube-shaped box.

a) Estimate the amount of empty space inside the box.

b) Calculate the amount of empty space.

c) How close was your estimate?

Chapter 8 Practice Test

Multiple Choice

For questions 1 to 5, select the best answer.

1. A sphere has a radius of 3 cm. What is its volume, to the nearest cubic centimetre?

A 339 cm^3

B 38 cm^3

C 113 cm^3

D 85 cm^3

2. What is the area of the figure, to the nearest square centimetre?

10 cm

7 cm

5 cm

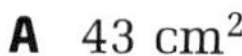

A 43 cm^2

B 54 cm^2

C 62 cm^2

D 73 cm^2

3. A circular swimming pool has a diameter of 7.5 m. It is filled to a depth of 1.4 m. What is the volume of water in the pool, to the nearest litre?

A 61 850 L

B 247 400 L

C 23 561 L

D 47 124 L

4. A conical pile of road salt is 15 m high and has a base diameter of 30 m. How much plastic sheeting is required to cover the pile, to the nearest square metre?

A 414 m^2

B 990 m^2

C 707 m^2

D 999 m^2

5. What is the length of the unknown side of the triangle, to the nearest tenth of a millimetre?

A 2.3 mm

B 5.0 mm

C 6.1 mm

D 7.7 mm

Short Response

Show all steps to your solutions.

6. A candle is in the shape of a square-based pyramid.

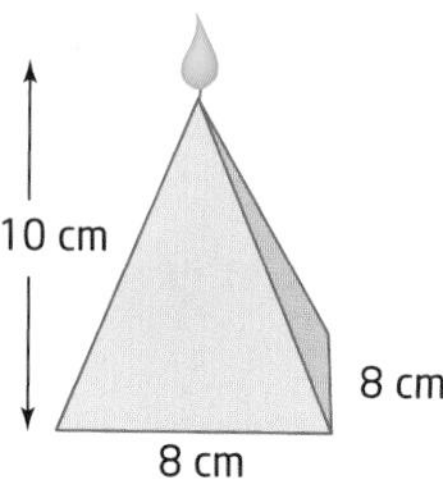

a) How much wax is needed to create the candle, to the nearest cubic centimetre?

b) How much plastic wrap, to the nearest tenth of a square centimetre, would you need to completely cover the candle? What assumptions did you make?

7. A rectangular cardboard carton is designed to hold six rolls of paper towel that are 28 cm high and 10 cm in diameter. Describe how you would calculate the amount of cardboard required to make this carton.

8. Compare the effects of doubling the radius on the volume of a cylinder and a sphere. Justify your answer with numerical examples.

9. Calculate the surface area of the cone that just fits inside a cylinder with a base radius of 8 cm and a height of 10 cm. Round to the nearest square centimetre.

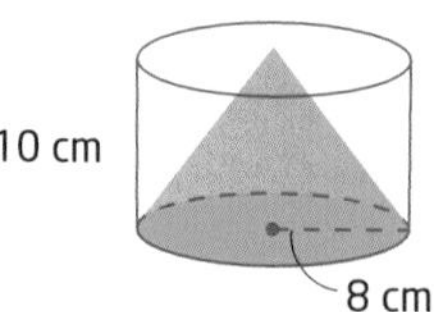

10. Determine the volume of a conical pile of grain that is 10 m high with a base diameter of 20 m. Round to the nearest cubic metre.

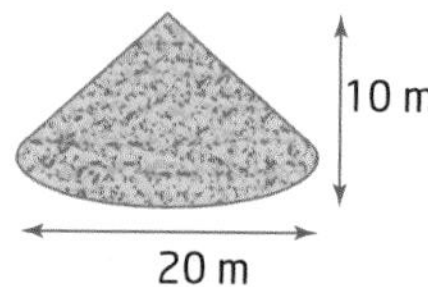

Extended Response

Provide complete solutions.

11. Three tennis balls that measure 8.4 cm in diameter are stacked in a cylindrical can.

a) Determine the minimum volume of the can, to the nearest tenth of a cubic centimetre.

b) Calculate the amount of aluminum required to make the can, including the top and bottom. Round to the nearest square centimetre.

c) The can comes with a plastic lid to be used once the can is opened. Find the amount of plastic required for the lid. Round to the nearest square centimetre.

d) Describe any assumptions you have made.

12. A rectangular carton holds 12 cylindrical cans that each contain three tennis balls, like the ones described in question 11.

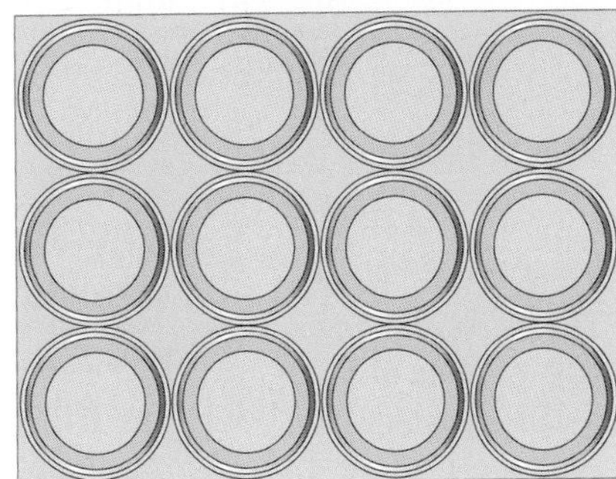

a) How much empty space is in each can of tennis balls, to the nearest tenth of a cubic centimetre?

b) Draw a diagram to show the dimensions of the carton.

c) How much empty space is in the carton and cans once the 12 cans are placed in the carton?

d) What is the minimum amount of cardboard necessary to make this carton?

Chapter Problem Wrap-Up

You are to design a fountain for the garden of one of Emily's customers.

- The fountain will have a cylindrical base with a cone on top.
- The cylindrical base will have a diameter of 1 m.
- The fountain is to be made of concrete.
- The entire fountain is to be coated with protective paint.

a) Make a sketch of your design, showing all dimensions.

b) How much concrete is needed to make the fountain?

c) What is the surface area that needs to be painted?

d) Concrete costs $\$100/\text{m}^3$. Each litre of protective paint costs \$17.50 and covers 5 m^2. Find the total cost of the materials needed to make the fountain.

CHAPTER

9 Optimizing Measurements

Measurement and Geometry

- Determine the maximum area of a rectangle with a given perimeter by constructing a variety of rectangles, using a variety of tools, and examining various values of the area as the side lengths change and the perimeter stays constant.
- Determine the minimum perimeter of a rectangle with a given area by constructing a variety of rectangles, using a variety of tools, and examining various values of the side lengths and the perimeter as the area stays constant.
- Identify, through investigation with a variety of tools, the effect of varying the dimensions on the surface area (or volume) of square-based prisms and cylinders, given a fixed volume (or surface area).
- Explain the significance of optimal area, surface area, or volume in various applications.
- Pose and solve problems involving maximization and minimization of measurements of geometric shapes and figures.

A large amount of our national resources is used to produce packaging materials. Packaging contains a product safely until it reaches our homes, but then these materials usually end up in landfill sites. The amount of packaging in landfill sites can be reduced by recycling, but energy is still wasted and consumers must pay more for overpackaged products.

In this chapter, you will investigate relationships that will allow you to minimize surface area as well as explore other measurement concepts and relationships.

Vocabulary

optimization
maximum
minimum

Chapter Problem

Talia has started a mail-order division in her uncle's computer-supply company. Customers order supplies on the Internet and Talia packages their orders and sends them to the customers by courier. In this chapter, you will apply the mathematical skills you learn to help Talia design packages that suit the product, the consumer, and the environment.

Get Ready

Measurement Concepts: Perimeter, Circumference, Area, Surface Area, and Volume

Perimeter, circumference, and area are measurement concepts that apply to two-dimensional shapes, while surface area and volume apply to three-dimensional figures.

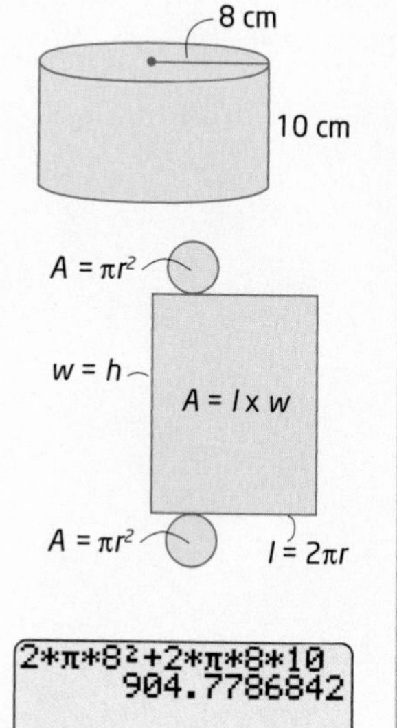

Calculate the volume and the surface area of the cylinder.

Use the formula for the volume of a cylinder.

$$V = \pi r^2 h$$
$$= \pi(8)^2(10)$$
$$\doteq 2011$$

The volume of the cylinder is about 2011 cm^3.

Use the formula for the surface area of a cylinder.

$$SA = 2\pi r^2 + 2\pi rh$$
$$= 2\pi(8)^2 + 2\pi(8)(10)$$

C 2 × π × 8 x² + 2 × π × 8 × 10 =

$$\doteq 905$$

2*π*8²+2*π*8*10
904.7786842

The surface area of the cylinder is about 905 cm^2.

1. Calculate the perimeter and area of each shape.

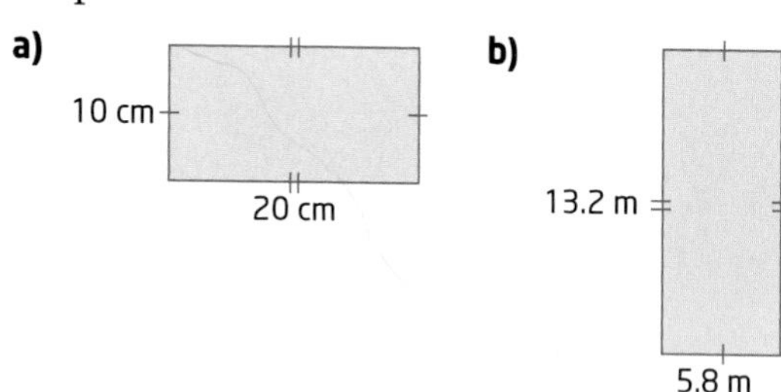

2. Calculate the circumference and area of each circle. Round to the nearest tenth of a unit or square unit.

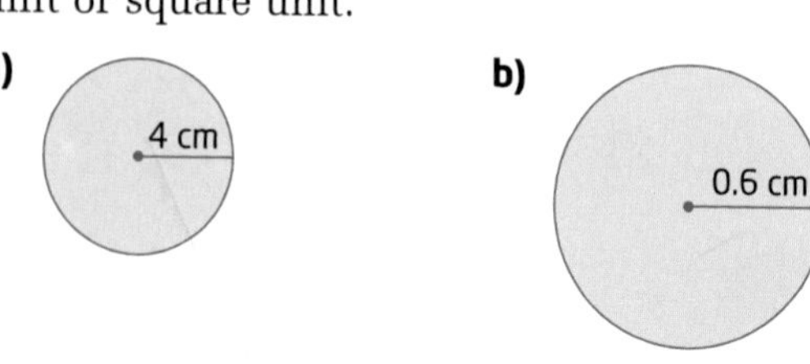

3. Calculate the volume and surface area of each figure.

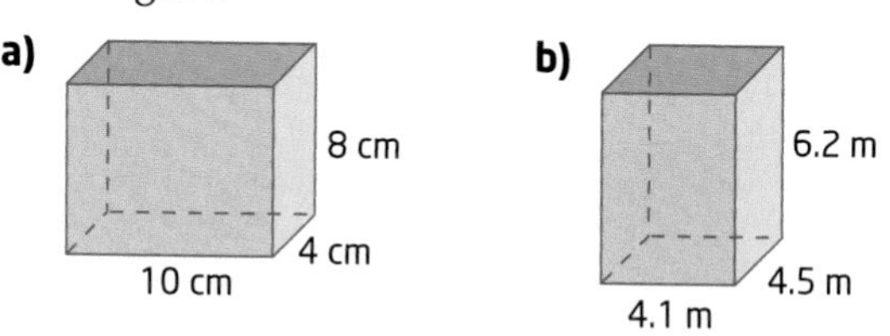

4. Calculate the volume and surface area of each figure. Round to the nearest cubic or square unit.

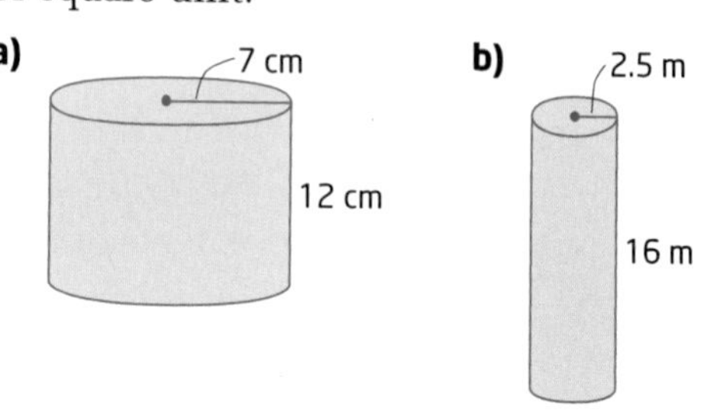

Compare Figures

The Pop-it-up Popcorn company is looking for the best design for an open-topped popcorn container to be used at concession stands.

Compare the volume and surface area of the two containers.

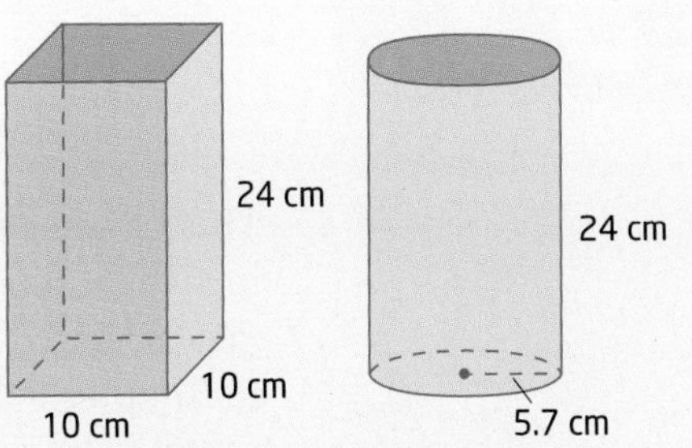

For the square-based prism:

$$\begin{aligned} V &= lwh \\ &= (10)(10)(24) \\ &= 2400 \end{aligned}$$

$$\begin{aligned} SA &= A_{sides} + A_{bottom} \\ &= 4(10)(24) + (10)(10) \\ &= 960 + 100 \\ &= 1060 \end{aligned}$$

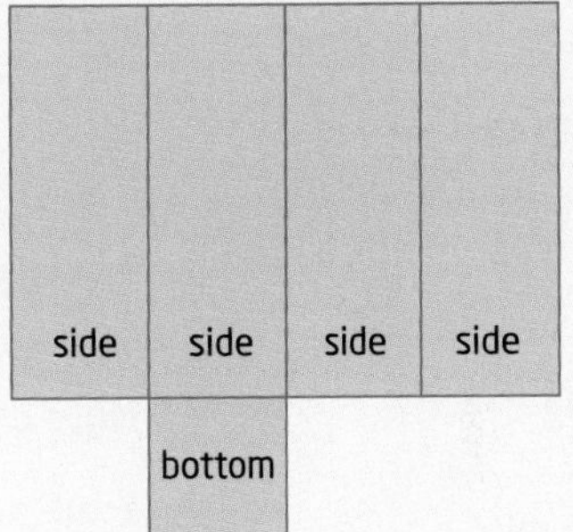

For the cylinder:

$$\begin{aligned} V &= \pi r^2 h \\ &= \pi(5.7)^2(24) \\ &\doteq 2450 \end{aligned}$$

$$\begin{aligned} SA &= A_{bottom} + A_{curved\ surface} \\ &= \pi r^2 + 2\pi rh \\ &= \pi(5.7)^2 + 2\pi(5.7)(24) \\ &\doteq 962 \end{aligned}$$

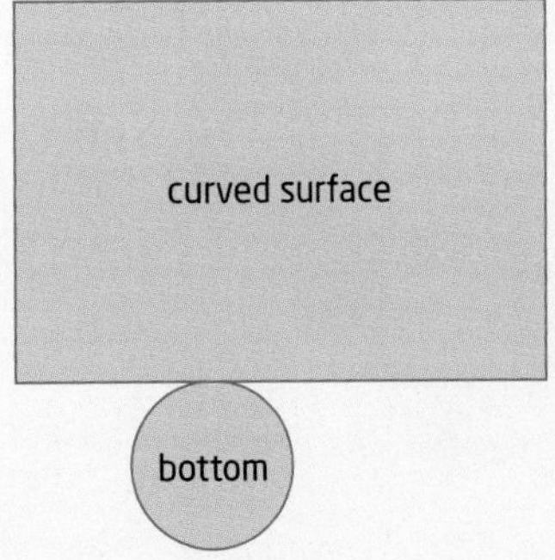

The square-based prism has a volume of 2400 cm^3 and the cylinder has a volume of about 2450 cm^3, so the cylinder has a slightly larger volume.

The square-based prism has a surface area of 1060 cm^2 and the cylinder has a surface area of about 962 cm^2, so the cylinder requires less material to make.

5. a) Calculate the volume and the surface area of the two open-topped containers.

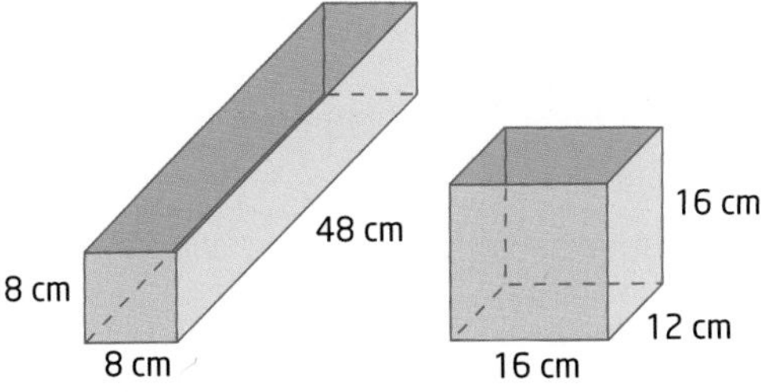

b) How do their volumes compare?

c) Which container requires less material?

6. a) Calculate the volume and the surface area of the two open-topped containers. Round to the nearest cubic or square unit.

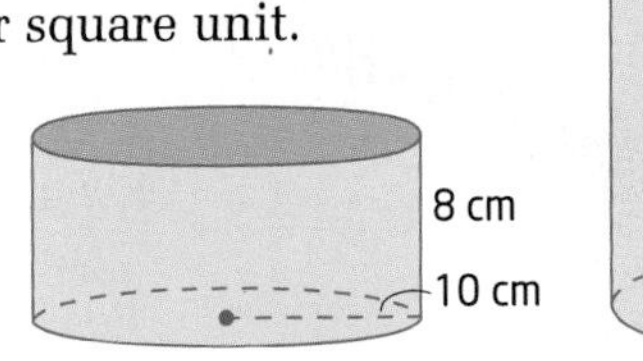

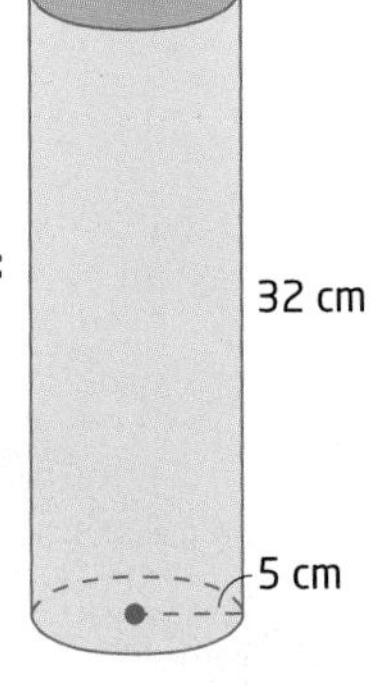

b) How do their volumes compare?

c) Which container requires less material?

9.1

Investigate Measurement Concepts

This chapter includes several investigations involving measurement concepts you studied in Chapter 8. When conducting an investigation, use the problem solving process introduced in Chapter 1.

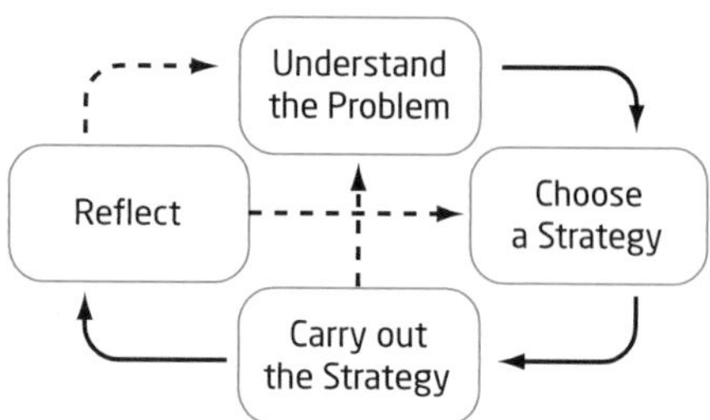

Investigate A

Tools

- geoboard
- elastic bands

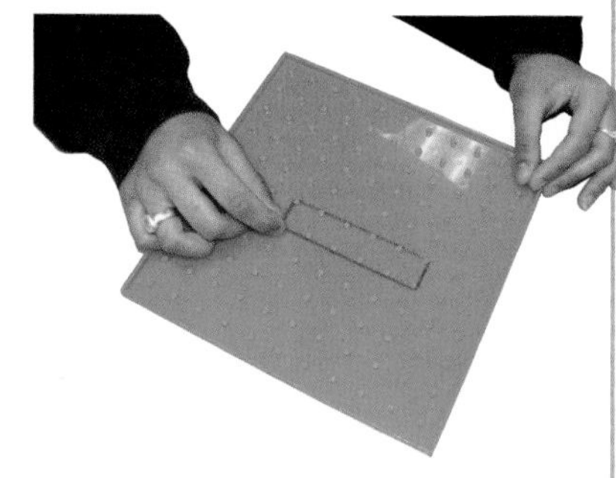

How can you model the areas of rectangles with the same perimeter?

You have 12 m of rope to fence off a rectangular play area at a summer day camp.

Method 1: Use a Geoboard

Use a geoboard to explore the different rectangles that can be formed with a perimeter of 12 m.

1. Let the distance between the pegs on the geoboard represent 1 m.
   a) Use an elastic band to construct a rectangle that represents the play area.
   b) What are the dimensions of the rectangle? Calculate the area. Use a table like this one to record your results.

Rectangle	Width (m)	Length (m)	Perimeter (m)	Area (m^2)
1			12	
2			12	
3			12	

   c) Construct additional rectangles with the same perimeter and record your results. How many different rectangles were you able to create?

2. a) Which rectangle had the least area? What are its dimensions? Describe its shape.
   b) Which rectangle had the greatest area? What are its dimensions? Describe its shape.

3. **Reflect** Which shape would you choose for the play area at the day camp? Give reasons for your choice.

Method 2: Use *The Geometer's Sketchpad®*

Use *The Geometer's Sketchpad®* to investigate the areas of rectangles with a fixed perimeter of 12 m.

1. From the **Edit** menu, choose **Preferences**. Click on the **Text** tab. Ensure that **For All New Points** is checked. Click on **OK**.

2. Construct a slider to control the dimensions of the rectangle.
   - Construct a horizontal line segment AB.
   - Construct a point C on the line between A and B.
   - Select points A, B, and C, in that order. From the **Measure** menu, choose **Ratio**. The ratio AC:AB will appear on the screen.
   - To change the label of AC:AB, select this ratio measurement. Right click and choose **Label Measurement** from the drop-down menu. Change the label to **r**.
   - Drag the point C back and forth. Note how the ratio **r** changes. This forms a slider that can be used to control the dimensions of a rectangle.

3. Select the ratio **r**. From the **Measure** menu, choose **Calculate**. Enter the formula 6***r** by selecting **r** from the **Values** drop-down menu on the calculator. Change the label to **Length**.

4. Select **r** again. From the **Measure** menu, choose **Calculate**. Enter the formula 6*(1 − **r**). Change the label to **Width**.

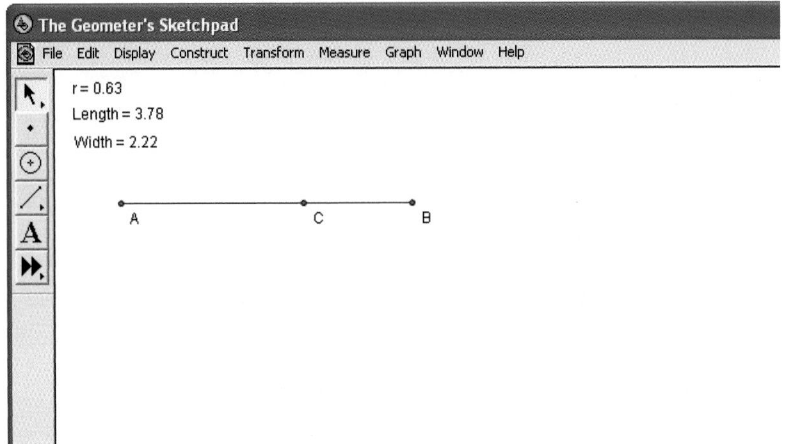

5. Construct a point D in the workspace. Select point D. From the **Measure** menu, choose **Abscissa (x)**. Select point D again. Then, from the **Measure** menu, choose **Ordinate (y)**. These are the coordinates of point D.

6. Select $\mathbf{x_D}$ and **Length**. From the **Measure** menu, choose **Calculate**. Enter the formula $\mathbf{x_D}$ + **Length**.

7. Select $\mathbf{y_D}$ and **Width**. From the **Measure** menu, choose **Calculate**. Enter the formula $\mathbf{y_D}$ + **Width**.

Tools
- *The Geometer's Sketchpad®* software
- computers

8. Plot the remaining three points to form the vertices of a rectangle DEFG.

- Select $\mathbf{x_D}$ and $\mathbf{y_D}$ **+ Width**, in that order. From the **Graph** menu, choose **Plot As (x, y)**. This is point E.
- Select $\mathbf{x_D}$ **+ Length** and $\mathbf{y_D}$ **+ Width**. From the **Graph** menu, choose **Plot As (x, y)**. This is point F.
- Finally, select $\mathbf{x_D}$ **+ Length** and $\mathbf{y_D}$. From the **Graph** menu, choose **Plot As (x, y)**. This is point G.

9. Select points D, E, F, and G, in that order. From the **Construct** menu, choose **Quadrilateral Interior**.

10. Move point C back and forth on the slider. Notice how the dimensions of the rectangle change. If the rectangle goes off your screen, drag the unit point to adjust the scale of your sketch.

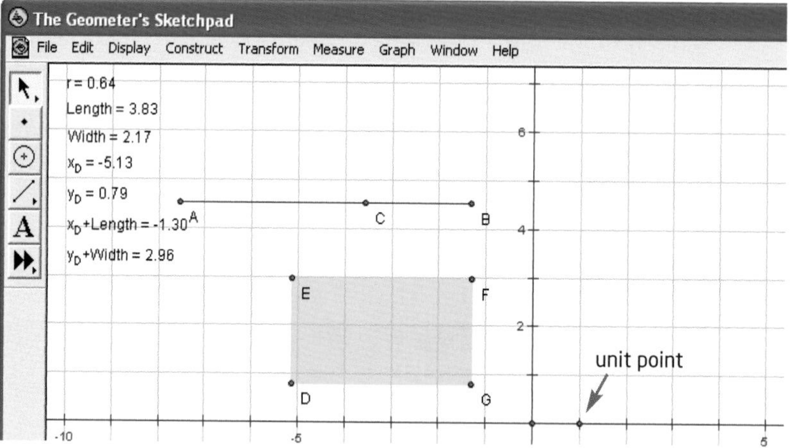

11. Select **Length** and **Width**. From the **Measure** menu, choose **Calculate**. Enter the formula 2*(**Length** + **Width**). Change the label to **Perimeter**.

12. Select **Length** and **Width**. From the **Measure** menu, choose **Calculate**. Enter the formula **Length*Width**. Change the label to **Area**.

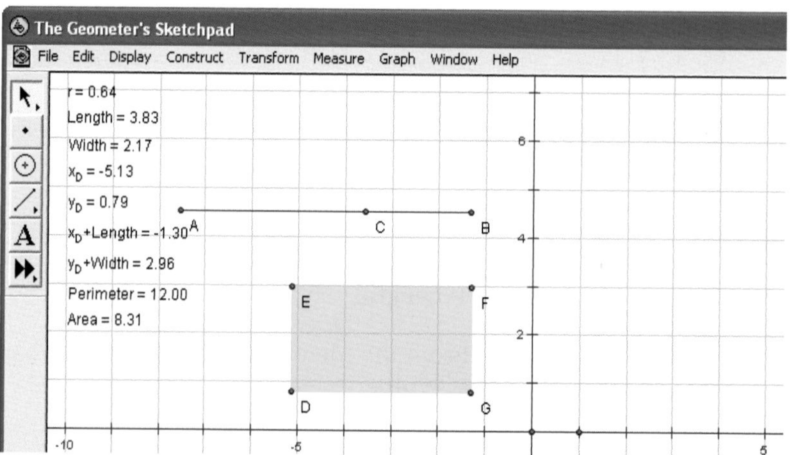

13. Verify that the perimeter remains constant as you move point C on the slider back and forth.

14. Use the slider to experiment with different dimensions for the rectangular play area with a perimeter of 12 m.
    a) Describe the shapes that occur.
    b) Which dimensions create the greatest area? Describe the shape of this play area.

15. **Reflect** Which shape would you choose for the play area? Give reasons for your choice.

16. Save your sketch for use in later investigations.

Investigate B

What is the relationship between the perimeters of rectangles with the same area?

Tools
- grid paper

Optional
- spreadsheet software
- computers

A rectangular pet exercise area is to have an area of 36 m^2.

1. a) Sketch all the rectangles that have whole-number dimensions and an area of 36 m^2.
   b) Copy and complete the table or use a spreadsheet like the one shown.

Rectangle	Width (m)	Length (m)	Perimeter (m)	Area (m^2)
1				36
2				36
3				36

	A	B	C	D	E
1	Rectangle	Width (m)	Length (m)	Perimeter (m)	Area (m^2)
2	1	1	=36/B2	=2*B2+2*C2	36
3	2	=B2+1	=36/B3	=2*B3+2*C3	36
4					

2. a) What dimensions use the least amount of fencing?
   b) What dimensions use the greatest amount of fencing?

3. **Reflect** Which shape would you choose for the pet exercise area? Give reasons for your choice.

Key Concepts

- Use the problem solving process to conduct an investigation.
  - Understand the problem so that you can investigate it properly. Is the perimeter fixed? Is the area fixed?
  - Choose a strategy for the investigation. Use manipulatives, such as toothpicks or geoboards and elastics, or use technology, such as a spreadsheet or *The Geometer's Sketchpad*®, whichever is appropriate for the investigation.
  - Record the results of each investigation so that you can refer back to them later.
  - When drawing conclusions from an investigation, always reflect on your answer. Ask yourself if you need to consider other factors.
- Rectangles with the same perimeter can have different dimensions and contain different areas.
- Rectangles with the same area can have different dimensions and different perimeters.

Communicate Your Understanding

C1 Describe how you could use grid paper to investigate the areas of rectangles with a perimeter of 40 units.

C2 Describe how you could use a geoboard to investigate the perimeters of rectangles with an area of 15 square units.

Practise

1. Explore the different rectangles that you can form with a perimeter of 24 units.

a) What are you to investigate?

b) Choose a strategy that you can carry out on grid paper. Record the areas of five different rectangles.

2. Explore the different rectangles that you can form with a perimeter of 20 units.

a) What are you to investigate?

b) Choose a strategy that you can carry out using toothpicks. Record the areas of three different rectangles.

3. Explore the different rectangles that you can form with an area of 12 square units.

a) What are you to investigate?

b) Choose a strategy that you can carry out using elastics on a geoboard. Record the perimeter of each rectangle.

Connect and Apply

4. You are designing a rectangular shed that has a floor area of 16 m^2. Using a geoboard, let the distance between the pegs represent 1 m.

a) With an elastic, construct different rectangles to represent the shed's floor. Record the dimensions of each rectangle you create in a table. Calculate the perimeter of each rectangle.

Rectangle	Width (m)	Length (m)	Perimeter (m)	Area (m^2)
1				16
2				16
3				16

b) Explain how the perimeter affects the cost of the shed.

c) Which shape would be the most economical for the shed? Why?

d) Is cost the only factor when choosing a shape for the shed? What other factors might you need to consider?

5. Use Technology Padma is making a vegetable garden in her yard. She wants to fence the garden to keep out small animals. She has 16 m of fencing. Use *The Geometer's Sketchpad®* to investigate the dimensions of the rectangular garden with the greatest area that Padma can enclose with this fencing.

6. Colin is enclosing a rectangular area for his dog with 32 m of fencing. Use a table or a spreadsheet to investigate the greatest area that Colin can enclose.

Rectangle	Width (m)	Length (m)	Perimeter (m)	Area (m^2)
1	1	15	32	15
2	2	14	32	28

	A	B	C	D	E
1	Rectangle	Width (m)	Length (m)	Perimeter (m)	Area (m^2)
2	1	1	=16-B2	32	=B2*C2
3	2	=B2+1	=16-B3	32	=B3*C3
4					

Extend

7. What happens to the area when you change the shape of an enclosure? Suppose each toothpick represents a 1-m length of fence.

a) Use 36 toothpicks to build enclosures with the greatest area, using the following shapes:
- triangle
- rectangle
- hexagon
- circle

b) Find the area of each enclosure in part a).

c) Does the shape of the enclosure affect its area? Write a brief report on your findings.

9.2 Perimeter and Area Relationships of a Rectangle

Brandon works during the summers for a fencing company. He has 32 sections of prefabricated fencing, each 1 m in length, to enclose a rectangular area for a customer. The customer wants the enclosure to have the greatest area possible.

Finding the dimensions that will maximize a rectangular area given its perimeter is called *optimizing* the area. The mathematical process used to solve this type of problem is known as **optimization**.

optimization

- the process of finding values that make a given quantity the greatest (or least) possible given certain conditions

Investigate A

- toothpicks or grid paper

How can you model the maximum area of a rectangle with a fixed perimeter?

Brandon needs to find the dimensions that will maximize the rectangular area of an enclosure with a perimeter of 32 m.

Method 1: Use Manipulatives or Diagrams

1. Use 32 toothpicks, each representing a 1-m section of fencing, to create rectangles of different shapes with whole-number dimensions and a perimeter of 32 m. Or, draw different rectangles on grid paper, letting each grid unit represent 1 m of fencing.

2. Copy and complete the table.

Rectangle	Width (m)	Length (m)	Perimeter (m)	Area (m^2)
1	1	15	32	15
2	2	14	32	
3	3	13		

3. a) What are the dimensions of the rectangle with **maximum**, or *optimal*, area?

b) What is the maximum area?

c) Describe the shape of the rectangle.

maximum

- greatest possible

4. Suppose the customer decides to use 40 m of fencing instead.
   a) Predict the dimensions of the rectangle with the maximum area.
   b) Use 40 toothpicks or grid paper to test your hypothesis.
   c) Compare your results with your prediction.

5. **Reflect** How can you predict the dimensions of a rectangle with maximum area if you know the perimeter?

6. a) Use your method to predict the dimensions of a rectangle with maximum area made of 60 toothpicks.
   b) Repeat part a) with 30 toothpicks. Describe any problems in applying your method.

Method 2: Use a Graphing Calculator

- graphing calculators

1. Use your table of results from step 2 of Method 1 to create a scatter plot of area versus width.
   a) Enter the width values in list **L1** and the area values in list **L2**.
   b) Set up the scatter plot using the settings shown.
   c) Press ZOOM and select **9:Zoomstat** to create an appropriate window.

2. Draw a sketch of the scatter plot in your notebook. Circle the region where the area of the garden is the greatest.

3. You can create an algebraic model of this relationship. Look at the columns entitled Width and Length in your table of results. Notice that the length and width values always have a sum of 16.
   a) Consider a rectangle of width x. Explain why the length of the rectangle can be represented by the expression $(16 - x)$.
   b) The area of a rectangle is the product of its length and width. Use the expressions for length and width to create an expression for the area.

4. Press Y=, and then enter $x(16 - x)$. Press GRAPH. How does this graph compare to the scatter plot?

5. Turn off Plot1. Use the TRACE feature on the graphing calculator to trace points on the graph of $y = x(16 - x)$.
   a) Find the point on the graph that represents the rectangle with maximum area. The x-coordinate of this point represents the width of the rectangle and the y-coordinate represents the area of the rectangle.
   b) Record the width and the area of the rectangle. Verify that this is the same rectangle you found in Method 1. Describe the location of this point on the curve.

6. a) How does the algebraic model change if the perimeter of the rectangle is 40 m? Graph the relationship. Locate the point on the graph that represents the rectangle with maximum area.
   b) What are the dimensions of the rectangle with maximum area? Describe the shape of the rectangle. Does this agree with your findings in step 4 of Method 1?

7. Suppose the perimeter of a rectangle is 45 m.
   a) Predict the dimensions of the rectangle with maximum area.
   b) Check your prediction by creating an algebraic model and graphing it. Was your prediction correct?

8. **Reflect** How can you predict the dimensions of a rectangle with maximum area if you know the perimeter?

Investigate B

- toothpicks or grid paper

How can you model the maximum area of a rectangle with a fixed sum of the lengths of three sides?

Brandon's customer decides to use an existing hedge as one of the boundaries for the enclosure. This means that he will only use the prefabricated fencing on three sides of the rectangular enclosure. The client still wants the enclosure to have the greatest area possible.

1. Brandon has 32 m of prefabricated fencing.
   a) Do you think Brandon will be able to enclose more, less, or the same amount of area now that the hedge is being used on one side?
   b) What shape do you think will have the maximum area?
   c) Make a hypothesis about what dimensions will have the maximum area.

2. Use toothpicks or sketch rectangles on grid paper to determine the dimensions of the rectangle that has the maximum area. Record your results in a table.

Rectangle	Width (m)	Length (m)	Sum of Lengths of Three Sides (m)	Area (m^2)
1	1	30	32	30
2	2	28	32	
3	3			

3. a) What are the dimensions of the rectangle with maximum area?
   b) Compare this result with your hypothesis.

c) Compare this result with the maximum area you found in Investigate A. Will the hedge allow Brandon to enclose more, less, or the same amount of area as before?

4. Examine the length and width of the enclosure of maximum area that you found. Describe any relationship that you notice.

5. Suppose Brandon has 40 m of prefabricated fencing to work with.

   a) Predict the dimensions of the rectangle with maximum area.

   b) Test your prediction. Were you correct? Do you need to change your hypothesis?

6. **Reflect** How can you predict the dimensions of a rectangle with maximum area if you know the sum of the lengths of three sides?

Key Concepts

- Optimizing the area of a rectangle means finding the dimensions of the rectangle with maximum area for a given perimeter.
- For a rectangle with a given perimeter, there are dimensions that result in the maximum area.
- The dimensions of a rectangle with optimal area depend on the number of sides to be fenced. If fencing is not required on all sides, a greater area can be enclosed.

Communicate Your Understanding

C1 A farmer wants to fence a rectangular field. Suggest two things that will allow the farmer to maximize the enclosed area.

C2 a) When does a square maximize the enclosed area?

b) When does a square not maximize the enclosed area?

C3 At a lake, a rectangular swimming area is to be roped in on three sides to create the greatest area possible. How will the length and width of this optimal area be related?

Practise

1. What dimensions will provide the maximum area for a rectangle with each perimeter?

   a) 20 m
   b) 36 m
   c) 50 m
   d) 83 m

Connect and Apply

2. To brighten a room, a rectangular window will be built into a wall. To keep the cost as low as possible, the perimeter of the window must be 6.0 m.

a) Sketch three different windows that have a perimeter of 6.0 m. Include dimensions.

b) What window dimensions will allow the maximum amount of light to enter the room?

3. A rectangular enclosure is to be created using 82 m of rope.

a) What are the dimensions of the rectangle of maximum area?

b) Suppose 41 barriers, each 2 m long, are used instead. Can the same area be enclosed? Explain.

c) How much more area can be enclosed if the rope is used instead of the barriers?

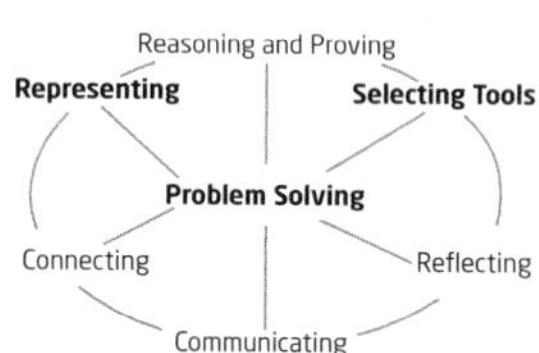

4. A farmer is adding a rectangular corral to the side of a barn. The barn will form one side of the rectangle. The farmer has 16 m of fencing to use. Conduct an investigation to determine the dimensions of the corral with maximum area. Use any tools: toothpicks, geoboards, grid paper, tables, or technology such as spreadsheets, *The Geometer's Sketchpad*®, or a graphing calculator.

5. A fence is to be built with prefabricated sections that are 2.8 m in length. What is the maximum rectangular area that you can enclose with

a) 20 pieces?

b) 40 pieces?

6. A fence is being built using the materials in question 5, but now there is an existing wall that will be used as one of the boundaries. Draw a diagram and label the dimensions of the maximum rectangular area that you can enclose with

a) 20 pieces

b) 40 pieces

For the fence materials in each of parts a) and b), how much additional area does using an existing border provide?

7. Chapter Problem Talia's uncle owns a warehouse and he has given Talia an area in which to store the computer supplies for his company. Her uncle gave Talia 40 m of rope and told her to section off a rectangular area in a corner of the warehouse. Conduct an investigation to determine the greatest area that Talia can rope off.

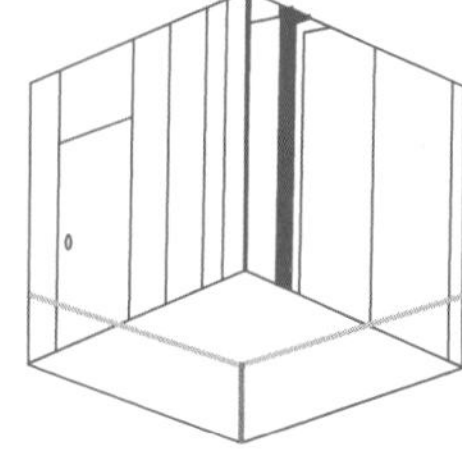

8. Brandon prepares a proposal for his client. In the proposal, he reports how the 32 m of fencing that is available can be used to fence an enclosure on

- four sides
- three sides, using a hedge at the back of the property as the fourth side
- two sides, using the hedge and an existing neighbour's fence on an adjacent side

Draw diagrams for each of the three scenarios in Brandon's proposal and calculate the maximum area that can be enclosed in each case.

9. A contractor is adding a rectangular kindergarten playground to the side of a school. The school will form one side of the rectangle. The area of the playground is to be 72 m^2. One possible rectangle is shown.

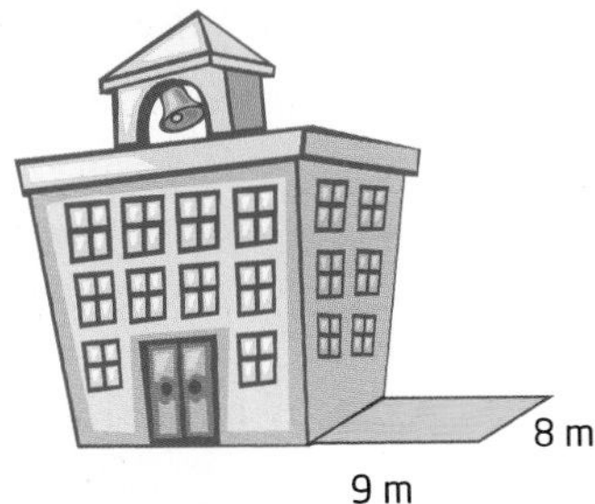

a) Investigate other possible rectangles with an area of 72 m^2. Copy and complete the table or use a spreadsheet like the one shown.

Rectangle	Width (m)	Length (m)	Area (m^2)	Length of Fence Used (m)
1			72	
2			72	
3			72	

	A	B	C	D	E
1	Rectangle	Width (m)	Length (m)	Area (m^2)	Length of Fence Used (m)
2	1	1	=72/B2	72	=C2+2*B2
3	2	=B2+1	=72/B3	72	=C3+2*B3
4					

b) What dimensions use the minimum length of fence to enclose the playground?

c) What is the minimum length of fence that can be used to enclose the playground?

10. Pose a problem involving the relationship between the perimeter and the area of a garden. Solve the problem and then have a classmate solve it.

11. Describe a situation in which it is important to know

a) the minimum perimeter of a rectangle for a given area

b) the maximum area of a rectangle for a given perimeter

Achievement Check

12. A rectangular area is to be enclosed with 12 m of fencing.

a) What is the maximum area that can be enclosed if fencing is used on all four sides? What are the dimensions of this optimal shape?

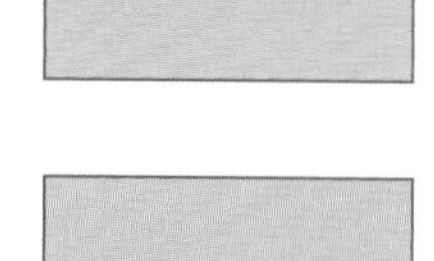

b) Suppose an existing hedge is used to enclose one side. Use diagrams or toothpicks to determine the maximum area that can be enclosed. Record your results in a table. What are the dimensions of this shape?

c) Suppose two perpendicular hedges enclose the area on two sides. What are the dimensions of the maximum area that can be enclosed?

Extend

Did You Know?

According to the Building Code Act of Ontario, a building permit is required for any new building with area greater than 10 m^2.

13. Conduct an investigation to determine the dimensions of the rectangular floor of a toolshed with area 35 m^2 and minimum perimeter.

14. A rectangular yard with an area of 50 m^2 is to be fenced on three sides. Minimizing the perimeter will minimize the cost of the fence. Conduct an investigation to determine the shape of the yard with minimum perimeter.

15. If a triangle is drawn inside a circle so that the three vertices touch but do not intersect the circle boundary, then the triangle is *inscribed* in the circle. Conduct an investigation to find the dimensions of the triangle of maximum area that can be inscribed in a circle with diameter 20 cm.

16. Math Contest Find the dimensions of the rectangle of maximum area that can be inscribed in a circle of radius 10 cm.

17. Math Contest Katrina and Ranjeet have a piece of string 24 cm long and want to determine the maximum area that can be enclosed by the string. Katrina said, "The shape that will give the maximum area is a square. So, the maximum area for a square with sides 6 cm each is 36 cm^2." Ranjeet replied, "I can make a figure with a greater area." Is Ranjeet correct? If so, find the maximum area that can be enclosed with the string.

18. Math Contest A farmer has 500 m of fencing. He wants to construct three adjoining rectangular fields that have the greatest possible area. Determine the dimensions of the three fields.

9.3 Minimize the Surface Area of a Square-Based Prism

The boxes used in packaging come in many shapes and sizes. A package must be suitable for the product, visually appealing, and cost efficient. Many manufacturers and consumers are conscious of our environment and want to conserve materials whenever possible.

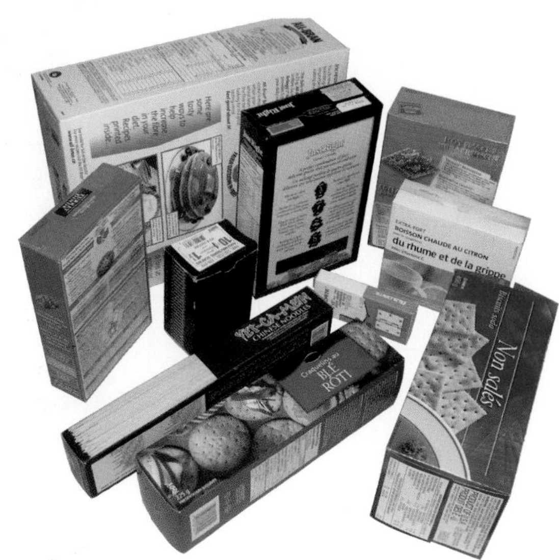

Investigate

How can you compare the surface areas of square-based prisms with the same volume?

Tools

- interlocking cubes

Method 1: Use Manipulatives

1. Use 16 interlocking cubes to build as many different square-based prisms as possible with a volume of 16 cubic units. Calculate the surface area of each prism. Record your results in a table.

Length	Width	Height	Volume	Surface Area
1	1	16	16	

2. Is it possible to build a prism with this volume that has a square base with three cubes on each side? Explain.

minimum

- least possible

3. Which square-based prism has the **minimum**, or optimal, surface area? Describe the shape of this prism compared to the others.

4. **a)** Predict the dimensions of the square-based prism with minimum surface area if you use 64 cubes.

   b) Test your prediction by completing a similar table.

5. Predict the dimensions of the square-based prism with minimum surface area if you use 27 cubes. What about 125 cubes?

6. **Reflect** Summarize your findings. Describe any relationship you notice between the length, width, and height of a square-based prism with minimum surface area for a given volume.

- spreadsheet software
- computers

Method 2: Use a Spreadsheet

1. Set up a spreadsheet to automatically calculate the height and surface area of a square-based prism given the dimensions of the square base and the volume.

	A	B	C	D	E
1	Side Length of Square Base (cm)	Area of Square Base (cm^2)	Height (cm)	Volume (cm^3)	Surface Area (cm^2)
2	1			64	
3	2			64	
4					

2. Enter the formula for the area of the square base.

3. The volume of the prism is always 64 cm^3. Explain why the height can be found using the expression 64/(area of the square base). Enter this expression as a formula in the Height column.

4. The surface area of a square-based prism consists of the two square ends and the four rectangular sides. The surface area can be found using the expression 2*(column B) + 4*(column A)*(column C). Explain why. Enter this expression as a formula in the Surface Area column.

5. Use the spreadsheet to create different square-based prisms with a volume of 64 cm^3. Begin with a prism that has a square base with sides of 1 cm. Next, increase the dimensions of the square base to 2 cm, then 3 cm, and so on. Use **Fill Down** to complete the spreadsheet.

6. Which prism has the least surface area? Describe the shape of this prism.

7. **a)** Predict the dimensions of the square-based prism with minimum surface area if the volume of the prism is 125 cm^3.
   b) Test your prediction using a spreadsheet.

8. **a)** Predict the dimensions of the square-based prism with minimum surface area if the volume is 300 cm^3.
   b) Test your prediction using the spreadsheet. Enter dimensions for the base that are not whole numbers, trying to decrease the surface area with each attempt. What dimensions give the minimum surface area? Describe the shape of this prism.

9. **Reflect** Summarize your findings. Describe any relationship you notice between the length, width, and height of a square-based prism with minimum surface area for a given volume.

10. Save your spreadsheet for future use.

Example 1 Cardboard Box Dimensions

a) The Pop-a-Lot popcorn company ships kernels of popcorn to movie theatres in large cardboard boxes with a volume of 500 000 cm^3. Determine the dimensions of the square-based prism box, to the nearest tenth of a centimetre, that will require the least amount of cardboard.

b) Find the amount of cardboard required to make this box, to the nearest tenth of a square metre. Describe any assumptions you have made.

Solution

a) A square-based prism with a given volume has minimum surface area when it is a cube.

The formula for the volume of a cube is $V = s^3$, where s is the length of a side of the cube.

Substitute the given volume of 500 000 cm^3. Find s.

$500\,000 = s^3$

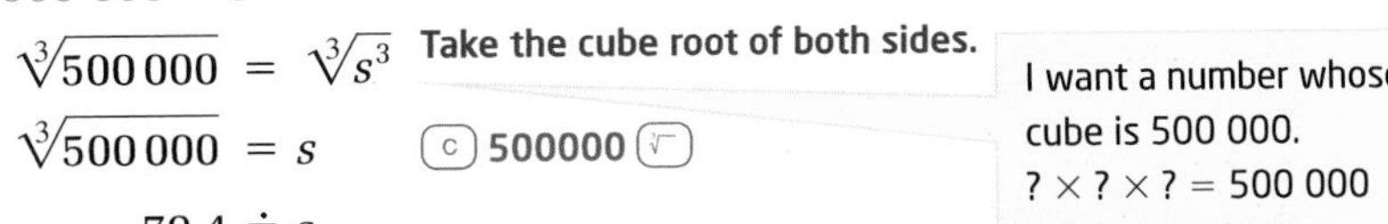

$\sqrt[3]{500\,000} = \sqrt[3]{s^3}$ **Take the cube root of both sides.**

$\sqrt[3]{500\,000} = s$ **(C) 500000 (∛)**

$79.4 \doteq s$

I want a number whose cube is 500 000.
? × ? × ? = 500 000

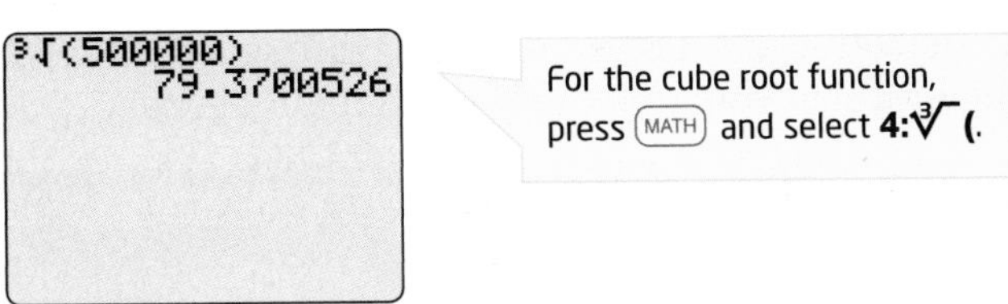

For the cube root function, press (MATH) and select **4:∛(**.

To use the least amount of cardboard, the popcorn should be shipped in a cube-shaped box with side lengths of 79.4 cm.

b) The amount of cardboard needed is the surface area of the box. A cube has six square faces.

$$
\begin{aligned}
SA &= 6s^2 \\
&= 6(79.4)^2 \\
&\doteq 38\,000
\end{aligned}
$$

There are 100 cm in 1 m. So, there are 10 000 cm^2 in 1 m^2.

To express 38 000 cm^2 in square metres, divide by 100^2, or 10 000.

$$\frac{38\,000}{10000} = 3.8$$

It would take about 3.8 m^2 of cardboard to make this box. However, these calculations do not take into account the extra cardboard for the seams or any overlapping flaps.

Literacy Connections

A cube is a number that is the product of three identical factors. Each of the factors is the cube root of the number.

For example, the cube root of eight is two.

$$
\begin{aligned}
2^3 &= 2 \times 2 \times 2 \\
&= 8
\end{aligned}
$$

Example 2 Minimize Heat Loss

Tyler has been asked to design an insulated square-based prism container to transport hot food. When hot food is placed in the container, it loses heat through the container's sides, top, and bottom. To keep heat loss to a minimum, the total surface area must be minimized.

a) Find the interior dimensions of the container with volume 145 000 cm^3 that has minimum heat loss. Round the dimensions to the nearest tenth of a centimetre.

b) What other factors might Tyler consider?

Did You Know?

There are different types of insulators.

- Thermal insulators reduce the flow of heat.
- Electrical insulators reduce the flow of electricity.
- Acoustical insulators reduce the flow of sound.

Solution

a) To minimize heat loss, Tyler must find the optimal surface area for a volume of 145 000 cm^3. The minimum surface area occurs when the container is cube-shaped.

Use the formula for the volume of a cube.

$$V = s^3$$
$$145\ 000 = s^3$$
$$\sqrt[3]{145\ 000} = s \quad \text{Take the cube root of both sides.}$$
$$52.5 \doteq s$$

To minimize heat loss, the container should be cube-shaped with interior side lengths measuring about 52.5 cm.

b) Tyler may decide to design the container with a different shape, even though a cube would be the best for reducing heat loss. The container should also be shaped so that it is easy to carry, visually appealing, and handy to store, and holds the hot food conveniently.

Does a cube satisfy these criteria?

Key Concepts

- Minimizing surface area for a given volume is important when designing packages and containers to save on materials and reduce heat loss.
- For a square-based prism with a given volume, a base length and a height exist that result in the minimum volume.
- For a square-based prism with a given volume, the minimum surface area occurs when the prism is a cube.
- Given a volume, you can find the dimensions of a square-based prism with minimum surface area by solving for s in the formula $V = s^3$, where V is the given volume and s is the length of a side of the cube.

Communicate Your Understanding

C1 Describe a situation when you would need to minimize the surface area for a given volume.

C2 If a cube-shaped box requires the least amount of material to make, why are all boxes not cube-shaped? Give an example of a situation where a cube-shaped box is not the most desirable shape.

Practise

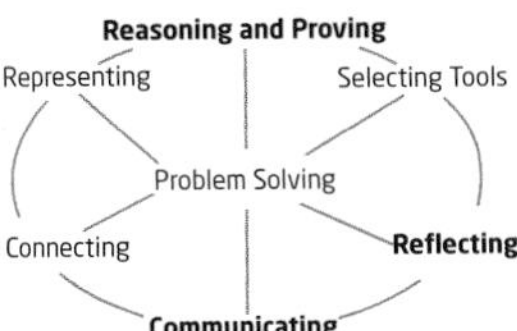

1. These square-based prisms all have the same volume. Rank them in order from least to greatest surface area. Explain your reasoning.

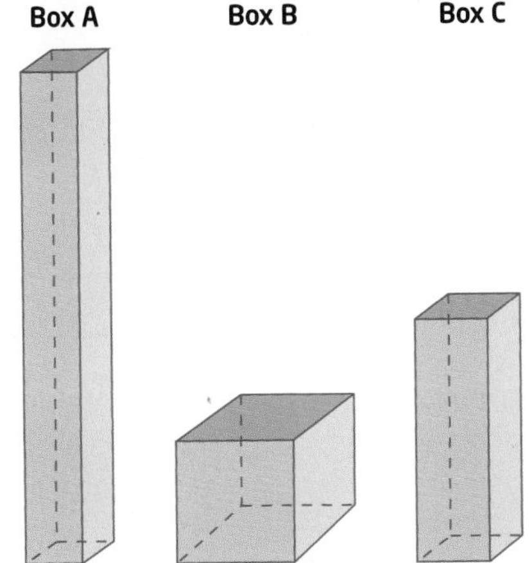

For help with questions 2 and 3, see Example 1.

2. Determine the dimensions of the square-based prism box with each volume that requires the least material to make. Round the dimensions to the nearest tenth of a centimetre, when necessary.

a) 512 cm^3 **b)** 1000 cm^3 **c)** 750 cm^3 **d)** 1200 cm^3

3. Determine the surface area of each prism you found in question 2, to the nearest square centimetre.

For help with question 4, see Example 2.

4. Determine the dimensions of a square-based prism container with volume 3200 cm^3 and minimum heat loss. Round the dimensions to the nearest tenth of a centimetre.

Connect and Apply

5. Laundry detergent is packaged in a square-based prism box.

a) The box contains 4000 cm^3 of detergent. What dimensions for the box require the least amount of cardboard? Round the dimensions to the nearest tenth of a centimetre.

b) Does laundry detergent usually come in a box shaped like the one you found in part a)? Suggest reasons for this.

6. Chapter Problem Talia is shipping USB (universal serial bus) cables in a small cardboard squared-based prism box. The box must have a capacity of 750 cm^3 and Talia wants to use the minimum amount of cardboard when she ships the box.

a) What should the dimensions of the box be, to the nearest hundredth of a centimetre?

b) What is the minimum amount of cardboard that Talia will need, to the nearest tenth of a square centimetre?

7. A movie theatre wants its large box of popcorn to be a square-based prism with a capacity of 2.5 L. Determine the least amount of cardboard required to construct this box, to the nearest square centimetre. Hint: 1 L = 1000 cm^3.

8. Refer to question 7. Usually, when you buy popcorn in a movie theatre, the box does not have a lid.

a) Carry out an investigation to determine the dimensions of a lidless box with minimum surface area and a capacity of 2.5 L.

b) Compare your results to those in question 7. Are the dimensions the same or different?

c) Does the lidless box require more, less, or the same amount of material to construct, compared to the box with a lid?

9. a) Determine the dimensions of a square-based prism juice box that holds 200 mL of juice and requires the least amount of material. Round the dimensions to the nearest tenth of a centimetre. Hint: 1 mL = 1 cm^3.

b) Suggest reasons why juice boxes are not usually manufactured with the dimensions you found in part a).

c) Write a letter to the manufacturer recommending a new design for its juice boxes, keeping your results from parts a) and b) in mind.

10. Create a problem that involves designing a square-based prism with minimum surface area. Solve the problem. Exchange with a classmate.

Extend

11. How would you arrange 100 interlocking cubes in a square-based prism with the smallest surface area possible?

12. A carton must be designed to hold 24 boxes of tissues. Each tissue box has dimensions 12 cm by 8 cm by 24 cm.

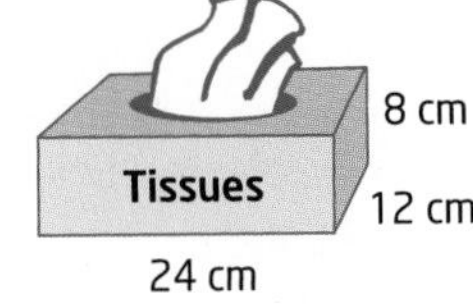

    a) Design the carton so that it requires the least amount of cardboard. Include a diagram showing how the tissue boxes are to be stacked in the carton.
    b) Explain why you think your design is the optimal shape.
    c) Is packaging 24 boxes of tissue per carton the most economical use of cardboard? Explain your reasoning.

13. A warehouse is designed to provide 1000 m^3 of storage space. The surface area of the walls and roof must be kept to a minimum to minimize heat loss. Very little heat is lost through the floor, so you can ignore it. Carry out an investigation to determine the best dimensions for the warehouse.

14. **Math Contest** RiceCo ships long-grain rice in large cardboard boxes that hold 216 000 cm^3. Determine the least amount of cardboard needed for one of these boxes, if an extra 10% is used to join the sides of the boxes.

15. **Math Contest** At the Beautiful Box Company, cardboard boxes must hold 2700 cm^3. Determine the least amount of cardboard needed for one of these boxes if the boxes have right-triangular flaps to fasten the faces together. The triangular flaps are all the same size with one leg equal to one third the length of the box and the other leg equal to one third the width of the box.

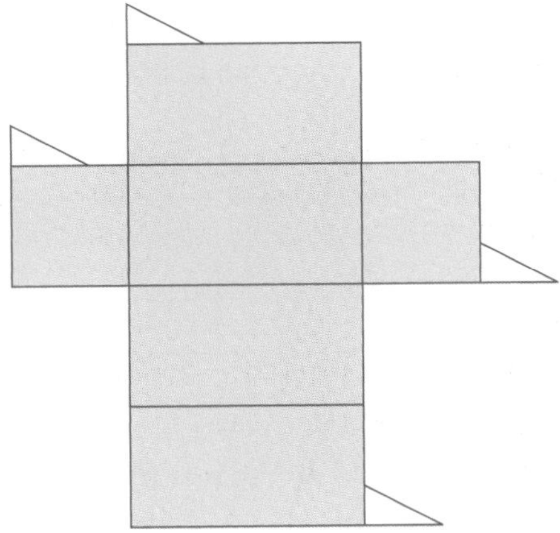

9.4 Maximize the Volume of a Square-Based Prism

Have you ever been restricted by the amount of material you had to finish a job? This may have happened when you were wrapping a gift or packaging food. In the packaging industry, it may be important to make a carton with the greatest possible volume from the cardboard that is available. This involves determining the maximum, or optimal, volume for a given surface area.

Investigate

How can you compare the volumes of square-based prisms with the same surface area?

Method 1: Pencil and Paper

1. Each of the square-based prisms has a surface area of 24 cm^2. Calculate the area of the base and the volume of each prism. Record your data in a table.

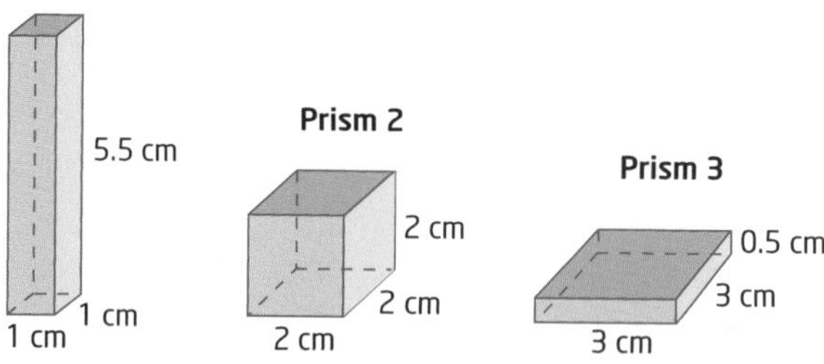

Prism Number	Side Length of Base (cm)	Area of Base (cm^2)	Surface Area (cm^2)	Height (cm)	Volume (cm^3)
1			24		
2			24		
3			24		

2. Which square-based prism has the maximum volume? Describe the shape of this prism compared to the others.

3. Each of the square-based prisms has a surface area of 54 cm^2.

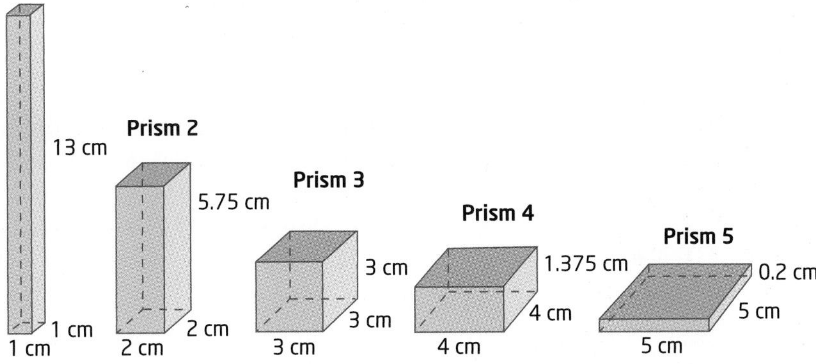

a) Predict the dimensions of the square-based prism with maximum volume if the surface area is 54 cm^2.

b) Test your prediction by completing a similar table to the one in step 1.

4. Repeat step 3 for a square-based prism with surface area 96 cm^2.

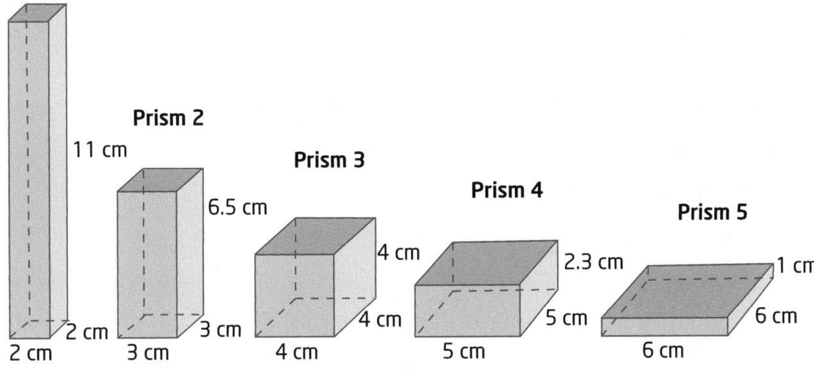

5. **Reflect** What conclusion can you make about the maximum volume of a square-based prism with a given surface area?

Method 2: Use a Spreadsheet

Use a spreadsheet to examine the volume of different square-based prisms with a fixed surface area of 24 cm^2.

1. Create a spreadsheet with formulas as follows.

	A	B	C	D	E
1	Side Length of Base (cm)	Area of Base (cm^2)	Surface Area (cm^2)	Height (cm)	Volume (cm^3)
2	1	=A2^2	24	=(C2-2*B2)/(4*A2)	=B2*D2
3	=A2+1	=A3^2	24	=(C3-2*B3)/(4*A3)	=B3*D3
4					

Tools
- spreadsheet software
- computers

2. You can find the surface area of a square-based prism by calculating 2(area of base) + 4(area of sides). The surface area of the prism is always 24 cm². So, the height can be found using the expression (24 – 2*(area of base))/(4*(side length of base)). Explain why.

3. Use **Fill Down** to complete the spreadsheet. What dimensions result in the greatest volume? Describe the shape of this square-based prism.

4. a) Predict the dimensions of the square-based prism with maximum volume if the surface area is 54 cm².

   b) Check your prediction by changing the surface area value in the spreadsheet.

5. Repeat step 4 for a square-based prism with surface area 96 cm².

6. **Reflect** What conclusion can you make about the maximum volume of a square-based prism with a given surface area?

7. Save your spreadsheet for future use.

Example Maximize the Volume of a Square-Based Prism

a) Determine the dimensions of the square-based prism with maximum volume that can be formed using 5400 cm² of cardboard.

b) What is the volume of the prism?

Solution

a) Given the surface area of a square-based prism, the prism with the maximum volume is in the shape of a cube. This means that the sum of each of the six square faces of the cube must be 5400 cm².

Let s represent the length of each side of the cube.

$$\begin{aligned} SA &= 6s^2 \\ 5400 &= 6s^2 \\ 900 &= s^2 \\ \sqrt{900} &= s \\ 30 &= s \end{aligned}$$

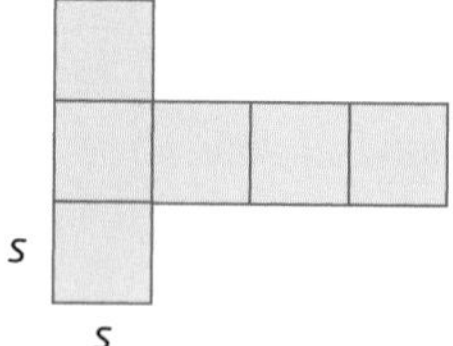

The square-based prism with maximum volume is a cube with side length 30 cm.

b) Use the formula for the volume of a cube.

$$\begin{aligned} V &= s^3 \\ &= (30)^3 \\ &= 27\ 000 \end{aligned}$$

The maximum volume of the square-based prism is 27 000 cm³.

Key Concepts

- For a square-based prism with a given surface area, a base length and a height exist that result in the maximum volume.
- The maximum volume for a given surface area of a square-based prism always occurs when the prism is a cube.
- The surface area of a cube is given by the formula $SA = 6s^2$, where s is the side length of the cube. When you are given the surface area, solve for s to find the dimensions of the square-based prism with maximum volume.

Communicate Your Understanding

C1 Describe a situation where it would be necessary to find the maximum volume of a square-based prism, given its surface area.

C2 These three boxes all have the same surface area. Which box has the greatest volume? Explain how you know.

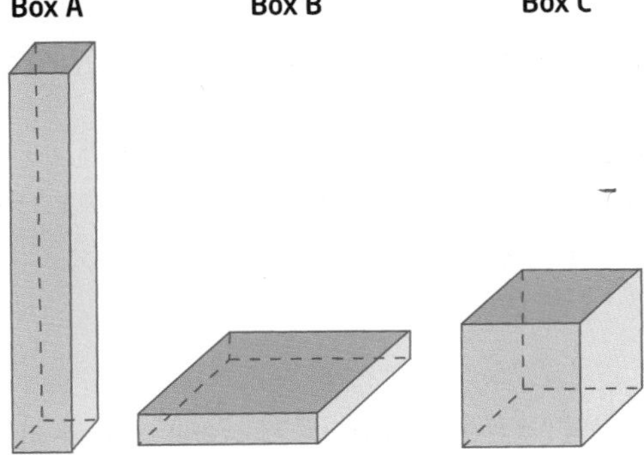

Practise

1. The three square-based prisms have the same surface area. Rank the prisms in order of volume from greatest to least.

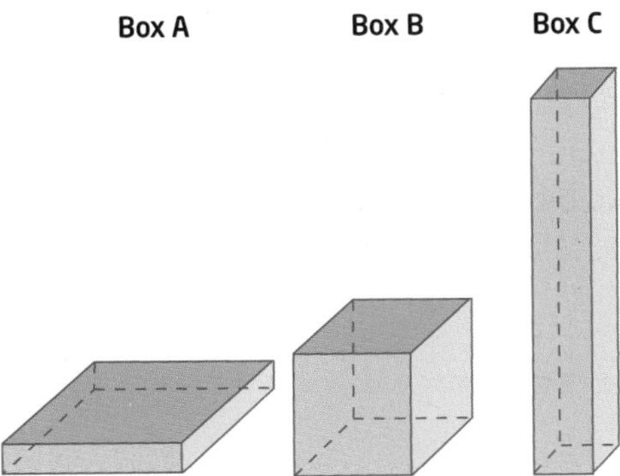

For help with questions 2 and 3, see the Example.

2. Determine the dimensions of the square-based prism with maximum volume for each surface area. Round the dimensions to the nearest tenth of a unit when necessary.

a) 150 cm^2

b) 2400 m^2

c) 750 cm^2

d) 1200 m^2

3. Determine the volume of each prism in question 2, to the nearest cubic unit.

Connect and Apply

4. Use a table or a spreadsheet to conduct an investigation to find the dimensions of the square-based prism box with maximum volume that can be made with 700 cm^2 of cardboard.

5. a) Determine the surface area and the volume of the square-based prism box shown.

b) Determine the dimensions of a square-based prism box with the same surface area but with maximum volume. Round the dimensions to the nearest tenth of a centimetre.

c) Calculate the volume of the box in part b) to verify that it is greater than the volume of the box in part a).

36 cm
12 cm
12 cm

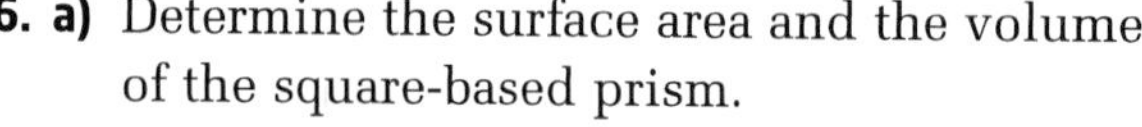

6. a) Determine the surface area and the volume of the square-based prism.

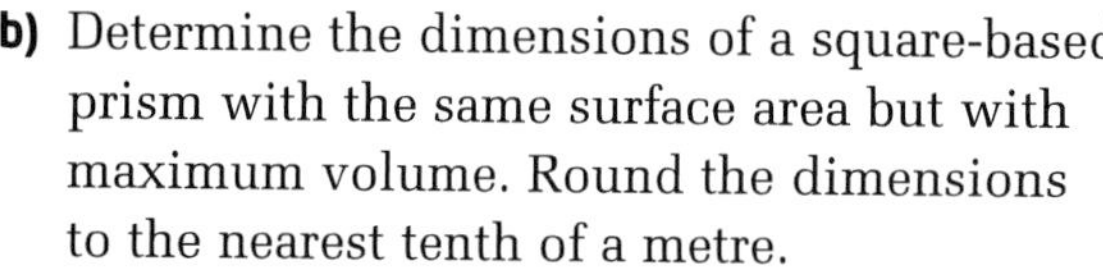

b) Determine the dimensions of a square-based prism with the same surface area but with maximum volume. Round the dimensions to the nearest tenth of a metre.

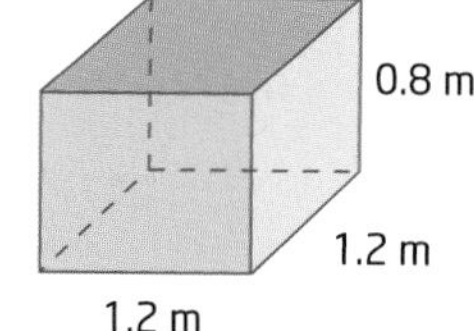

c) Calculate the volume of the prism in part b) to verify that it is greater than the volume of the original square-based prism.

7. Gurjit is building a square-based prism storage bin with a lid to hold swimming pool toys and equipment on her deck. She has 12 m^2 of plywood available.

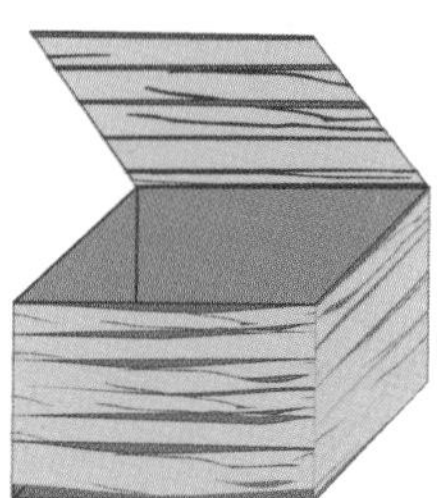

a) Determine the dimensions of the bin with maximum volume, to the nearest tenth of a metre.

b) Determine the volume of Gurjit's bin, to the nearest cubic metre.

8. **Chapter Problem** Talia is packaging a DVD drive to be shipped to one of her customers. She has 2500 cm^2 of cardboard and will put shredded paper around the drive to protect it during shipping.

a) What are the dimensions of the square-based prism box with maximum volume? Round the dimensions to the nearest tenth of a centimetre.

b) What is the volume of this box?

c) If the DVD drive measures 14 cm by 20 cm by 2.5 cm, how much empty space will there be in the box?

d) What assumptions have you made in solving this problem?

Did You Know?

A DVD may have one or two sides, and one or two layers of data per side. The number of sides and layers determines the disc capacity.

Achievement Check

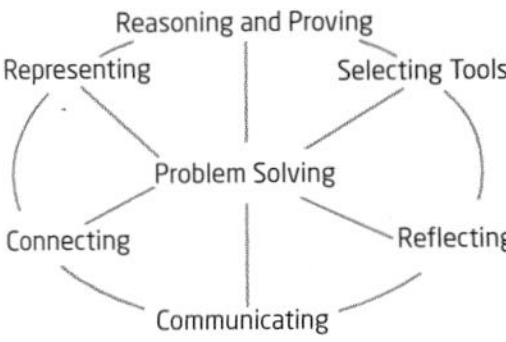

9. Kayla has 1.5 m^2 of sheet metal to build a storage box for firewood.

a) What is the surface area of the metal, in square centimetres?

b) What are the dimensions of the square-based prism box with maximum volume, including a lid?

c) If the box does not have a lid, what are the dimensions of the square-based prism box with maximum volume? Round the dimensions to the nearest tenth of a centimetre. (Hint: Make a table of possible boxes.)

d) What assumptions have you made in solving this problem?

Extend

10. Dylan has a piece of plywood that measures 120 cm by 240 cm. He wants to construct a square-based prism box to hold his sports equipment in the garage. Dylan wants to maximize the volume of the box and to keep the waste of plywood to a minimum.

a) Determine the dimensions of the box with maximum volume that he can construct, including a lid. Round to the nearest tenth of a centimetre.

b) Draw a scale diagram on grid paper to show how Dylan should cut the plywood.

c) Describe any assumptions you have made in solving this problem.

11. Sonia has a piece of stained glass that measures 20 cm by 30 cm. She is cutting the glass to make a small square-based prism box for jewellery. Sonia wants each face of the box to be made from one piece of glass.

a) Draw a scale diagram on grid paper to show how Sonia should cut the stained glass for a box with a lid.

b) Calculate the volume of this box.

c) Draw a similar scale diagram for a lidless box, showing how the glass will be cut.

d) Calculate the volume of this box.

e) Describe any assumptions you have made.

9.5 Maximize the Volume of a Cylinder

The National Packaging Competition is sponsored by the Packaging Association of Canada. This competition is held every 2 years to promote the Canadian packaging and design industries. One of the packaging categories at the competition is rigid and semi-rigid containers. Entries are judged on creativity, effectiveness of communication, originality, environmental considerations, and product suitability.

In Section 9.4, you learned how to maximize the volume of a square-based prism for a given surface area. In this section, you will perform the same investigation for a cylinder.

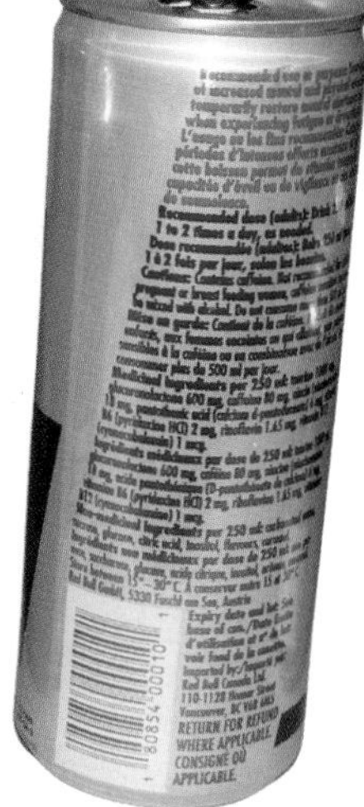

Investigate

How can you compare the volumes of cylinders with the same surface area?

Method 1: Use a Table

Your task is to design a cylindrical juice can that uses no more than 375 cm^2 of aluminum. The can should have the greatest capacity possible.

1. To investigate the volume of the cylinder as its radius changes, you will need an expression for the height in terms of the radius.
   - Start with the formula for the surface area of a cylinder: $SA = 2\pi r^2 + 2\pi rh$.
   - Substitute 375 cm^2 into the formula.
   - Rearrange the formula to express the height, h, in terms of the radius, r.

Copy the steps and write a short explanation beside each. The first has been done for you.

Step	***Explanation***
$SA = 2\pi r^2 + 2\pi rh$	
$375 = 2\pi r^2 + 2\pi rh$	Substitute *SA* = 375.
$375 - 2\pi r^2 = 2\pi r^2 + 2\pi rh - 2\pi r^2$	
$375 - 2\pi r^2 = 2\pi rh$	
$\frac{375 - 2\pi r^2}{2\pi r} = \frac{\overset{1}{\cancel{2\pi r}}h}{\underset{1}{\cancel{2\pi r}}}$	
$h = \frac{375 - 2\pi r^2}{2\pi r}$	

Making Connections

You learned how to rearrange formulas in 4.4 Modelling With Formulas.

2. Let the radius be 1 cm.

a) Determine the height of the can by using the algebraic model you found in step 1.

b) Determine the volume of this can using the formula for the volume of a cylinder: $V = \pi r^2 h$. Record the data in a table.

Radius (cm)	Height (cm)	Volume (cm^3)	Surface Area (cm^2)
1			375
2			375
3			375

3. Repeat step 2, letting the radius take whole-number values from 2 cm to 7 cm.

4. What is the maximum volume for the cans in your table? What are the radius and height of the can with this volume?

5. Reflect Do these dimensions give the optimal volume for the surface area of 375 cm^2? Describe how you could extend your investigation to determine the dimensions of a can with a volume greater than the value in the table.

Method 2: Use a Spreadsheet

Use a spreadsheet to investigate the volume of a cylinder with a surface area of 375 cm^2 as the radius changes. The spreadsheet will let you investigate values for the radius that are not whole numbers.

1. Create a spreadsheet with formulas as follows. Notice that the formulas for height and volume are the same as those used in Method 1.

	A	B	C	D
1	Radius (cm)	Height (cm)	Volume (cm^3)	Surface Area (cm^2)
2	1	=(375-2*PI()*A2^2)/(2*PI()*A2)	=PI()*A2^2*B2	375
3	2	=(375-2*PI()*A3^2)/(2*PI()*A3)	=PI()*A3^2*B3	375

2. Use **Fill Down** to complete the spreadsheet for radius values from 1 cm to 7 cm. What happens when you enter a radius value greater than 7 cm? Explain why this happens.

3. What is the whole-number radius value of the cylinder with the greatest volume? Try entering a radius value 0.1 cm greater than this value. Does the volume increase? If not, try a value 0.1 cm less. Continue investigating until the volume is a maximum for the radius value, to the nearest tenth of a centimetre.

4. Keep refining the radius value to hundredths of a centimetre. The volume should be slightly greater than your last attempt.

5. a) Record the radius and height of the can with the optimal volume.
   b) How do the values of the radius and height of this can compare?
   c) How do the values of the diameter and height of the can compare?

6. Change the formulas in the spreadsheet to investigate the dimensions of a cylinder with maximum volume if the surface area is 500 cm^2. How do the radius and height compare?

7. Repeat step 6 for a cylinder with a surface area of 1000 cm^2.

8. **Reflect**
   a) Describe any relationship you notice between the radius and height of a cylinder with maximum volume for a fixed surface area.
   b) How does this compare to the relationship between the dimensions of a square-based prism?

9. Save this spreadsheet for use in later investigations.

Example Maximize the Volume of a Cylinder

a) Determine the dimensions of the cylinder with maximum volume that can be made with 600 cm^2 of aluminum. Round the dimensions to the nearest hundredth of a centimetre.

b) What is the volume of this cylinder, to the nearest cubic centimetre?

Solution

a) For a given surface area, the cylinder with maximum volume has a height equal to its diameter.

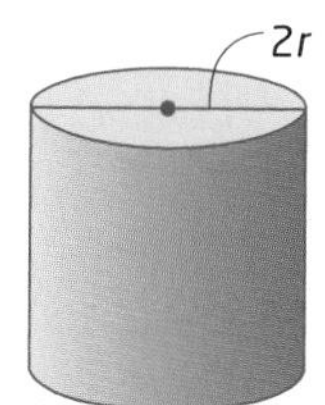

If I look at this cylinder from the front, it looks like a square.

Substitute $h = 2r$ into the formula for the surface area of a cylinder.

$$\begin{aligned} SA &= 2\pi r^2 + 2\pi rh \\ &= 2\pi r^2 + 2\pi r(2r) \\ &= 2\pi r^2 + 4\pi r^2 \\ &= 6\pi r^2 \end{aligned}$$

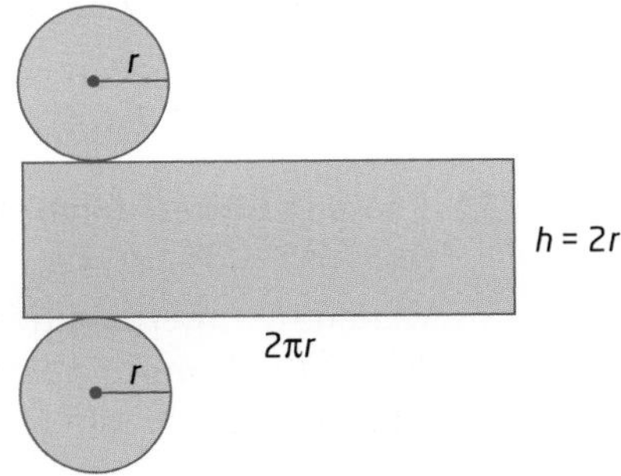

Substitute the surface area of 600 cm² to find the dimensions of the cylinder.

$$600 = 6\pi r^2$$

$$\frac{\overset{100}{\cancel{600}}}{\underset{1}{\cancel{6}\pi}} = \frac{\overset{1}{\cancel{6\pi}}r^2}{\underset{1}{\cancel{6\pi}}}$$ **Divide both sides by 6π.**

$$\frac{100}{\pi} = r^2$$

$$\sqrt{\frac{100}{\pi}} = r$$ **Take the square root of both sides.**

$$5.64 \doteq r$$

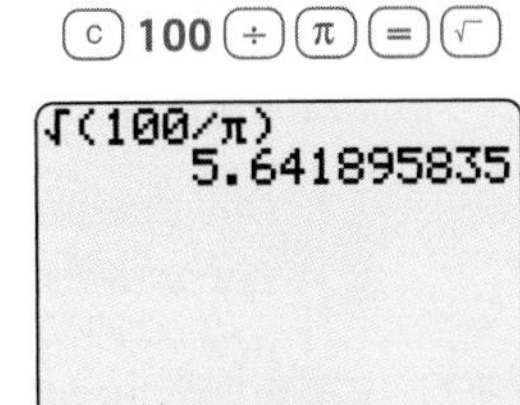

The radius of the cylinder should be 5.64 cm and the height should be twice that, or 11.28 cm.

b) Use the formula for the volume of a cylinder.

$$\begin{aligned} V &= \pi r^2 h \\ &= \pi(5.64)^2(11.28) \\ &\doteq 1127 \end{aligned}$$

Estimate: 3 × 6² × 11 = 1188

The volume of this cylinder is about 1127 cm³.

Key Concepts

- For a cylinder with a given surface area, a radius and a height exist that produce the maximum volume.
- The maximum volume for a given surface area of a cylinder occurs when its height equals its diameter. That is, $h = d$ or $h = 2r$.

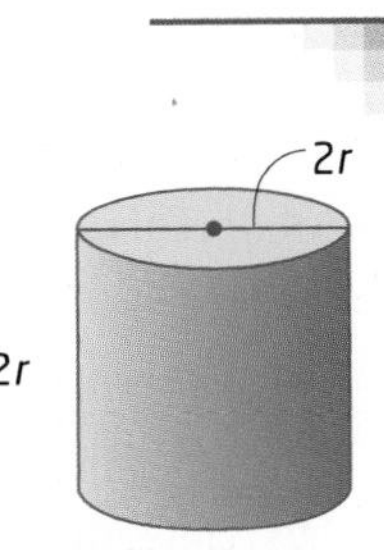

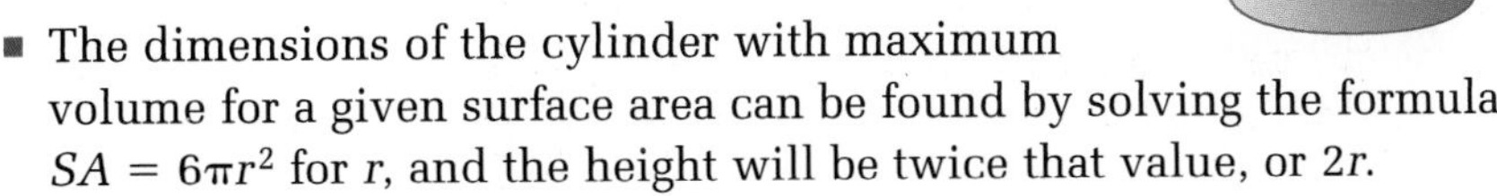

- The dimensions of the cylinder with maximum volume for a given surface area can be found by solving the formula $SA = 6\pi r^2$ for r, and the height will be twice that value, or $2r$.

Communicate Your Understanding

C1 Describe a situation where it would be necessary to find the maximum volume of a cylinder, given its surface area.

C2 These cylinders have the same surface area. Which cylinder has the greatest volume? Explain your answer.

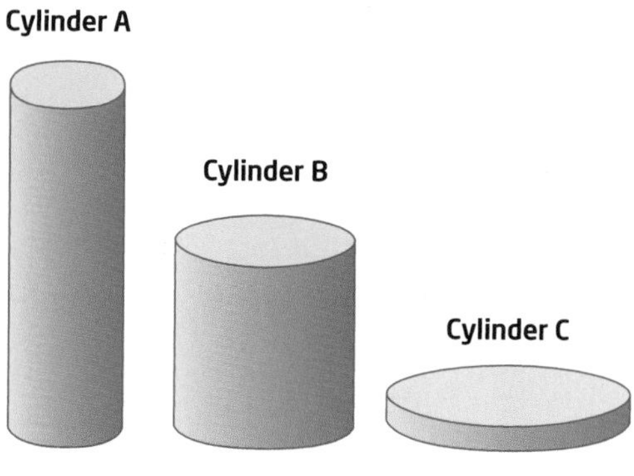

C3 Not all drinking glasses are designed to have the greatest volume for a given surface area. Why might these glasses be designed in other ways?

Practise

For help with questions 1 and 2, see the Example.

1. Determine the dimensions of the cylinder with the maximum volume for each surface area. Round the dimensions to the nearest hundredth of a unit.

a) $1200\ \text{cm}^2$ **b)** $10\ \text{m}^2$

c) $125\ \text{cm}^2$ **d)** $6400\ \text{mm}^2$

2. Determine the volume of each cylinder in question 1. Round to the nearest cubic unit.

Connect and Apply

3. Many European businesses buy aircraft manufactured in North America. To make the flight home across the Atlantic Ocean, extra fuel tanks are often carried in the cabin of the plane. These extra fuel tanks, called ferry tanks, must be as light as possible. A cylindrical ferry tank is to be made from $8\ \text{m}^2$ of aluminum. What is the maximum volume of fuel that it can hold, to the nearest cubic metre?

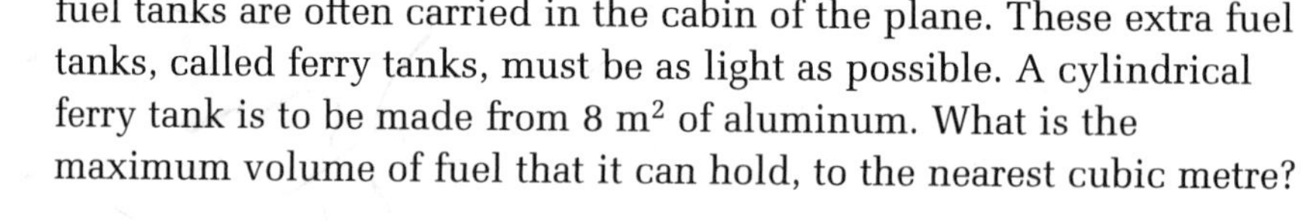

Did You Know?

The first trans-Atlantic crossing by a miniature robotic airplane occurred on August 25, 1998. The unpiloted airplane took 26 h to make the over 3200 km flight, taking off from Bell Island, Newfoundland and Labrador, and landing in the Hebrides Islands of Scotland.

4. A fertilizer company wants to make a cylindrical storage container of sheet metal. $72\ \text{m}^2$ of metal is available.

a) Determine the dimensions of the container with maximum volume. Round the dimensions to the nearest tenth of a metre.

b) Determine how many litres of liquid fertilizer this container can hold. Hint: $1\ \text{m}^3 = 1000\ \text{L}$.

c) Describe any assumptions you have made in solving this problem.

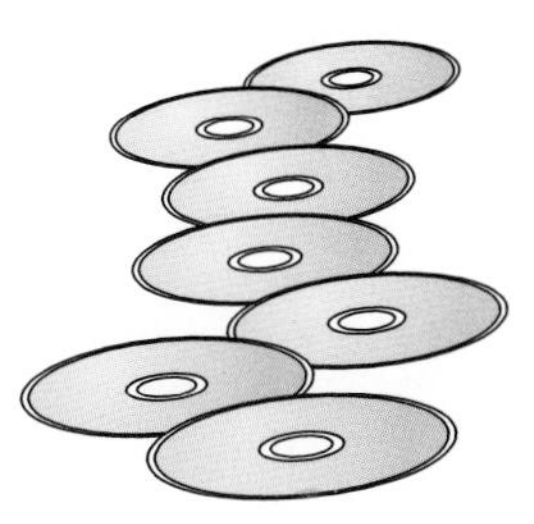

5. **Chapter Problem** Talia ships CDs to her customers in cylindrical plastic containers. The CDs are 12 cm in diameter and 2 mm thick. Talia wants the cylinder to hold as many CDs as possible, but to use as little plastic as possible.

   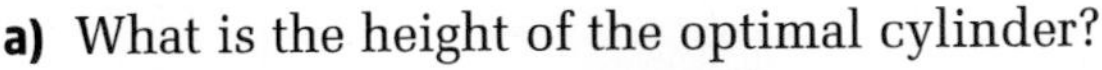

   a) What is the height of the optimal cylinder?

   b) How many CDs will this cylinder hold?

   c) Describe any assumptions you have made.

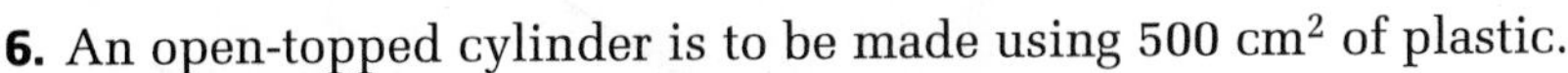

6. An open-topped cylinder is to be made using 500 cm^2 of plastic.

   a) Describe how you would determine the dimensions of the cylinder of maximum volume.

   b) Determine the dimensions of the cylinder with the optimal volume. Round to the nearest tenth of a centimetre.

Extend

7. You have a piece of sheet metal. Your task is to use this material to create a fuel container with maximum volume.

   a) Which shape would have the greatest volume: a square-based prism or a cylinder?

   b) Justify your answer using a fixed surface area of 2400 cm^2.

8. Suppose you have 2000 cm^2 of material to create a three-dimensional figure with the greatest volume. The material can be formed into a square-based prism, a cylinder, or a sphere.

   a) Predict which shape will produce the greatest volume.

   b) Determine the dimensions of each shape so that the volume is maximized.

   c) Determine the volume of each shape.

   d) Was your prediction correct? If not, which of the three shapes has the greatest volume for a given surface area? Will this always be true?

   e) Summarize your findings.

Making Connections

You worked with the volume and surface area formulas for a sphere in Chapter 8: Measurement Relationships:

$V = \frac{4}{3}\pi r^3$ and $SA = 4\pi r^2$

9. **Use Technology** You are to construct a cylinder that has a surface area of 2 m^2. Use a spreadsheet to investigate the dimensions of the cylinder with the greatest volume if

   a) the cylinder has a top and a bottom

   b) the cylinder has no top

10. **Math Contest** Determine the dimensions of the cylinder of maximum volume that can be inscribed in a sphere of radius 8 cm.

9.6

Minimize the Surface Area of a Cylinder

Many products are packaged in cylindrical containers. Consider the food items on the shelves in a grocery store. You can buy fruits, vegetables, soups, dairy products, potato chips, fish, and beverages in cylindrical containers.

Investigate

Tools

- construction paper
- ruler
- scissors
- tape

How can you compare the surface areas of cylinders with the same volume?

Method 1: Build Models

Your task is to construct three different cylinders with a volume of 500 cm^3.

Work with a partner or in a small group.

1. Choose a radius measurement for your cylinder. Calculate the area of the base.
2. Using the formula V_{cylinder} = (area of base)(height), substitute the volume and the area of the base. Solve for the height.
3. Calculate the circumference of the base.
4. Construct the rectangle that forms the lateral surface area of the cylinder. The rectangle should have a length equal to the circumference you determined in step 3 and a width equal to the height you determined in step 2. Tape the rectangle to form the curved surface of the cylinder.

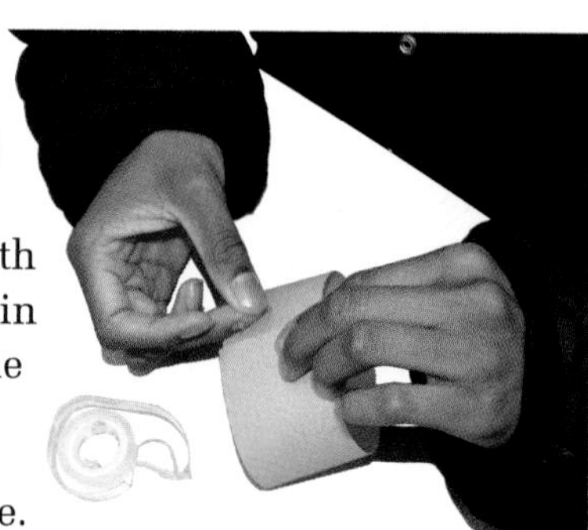

5. **a)** Calculate the area of the rectangle.
   b) Calculate the total surface area of the cylinder, including the base and the top.

6. Record the results for this cylinder in a table.

Cylinder	Radius (cm)	Base Area (cm²)	Height (cm)	Surface Area (cm²)
1				
2				
3				

7. Repeat steps 1 to 6 to create two different cylinders, each with a volume of 500 cm³.

8. Compare the surface areas and dimensions of the cylinders. Choose the cylinder that has the least surface area. How does its height compare to its diameter?

9. **Reflect** Compare your results with those of other groups in the class. Describe the dimensions of the cylinder with the least surface area. Are these dimensions the optimal ones? Explain.

Method 2: Use a Spreadsheet

1. Use a spreadsheet to investigate the surface area of cylinders with different radii that have a volume of 500 cm³. Start with a radius of 1 cm.

	A	B	C	D	E
1	Radius (cm)	Base Area (cm²)	Volume (cm³)	Height (cm)	Surface Area (cm²)
2	1	=PI()*A2^2	500	=C2/B2	=2*B2+2*PI()*A2*D2
3	2	=PI()*A3^2	500	=C3/B3	=2*B3+2*PI()*A3*D3
4					

2. Use **Fill Down** to complete the spreadsheet. What is the whole-number radius value of the cylinder with the least volume? Try entering a radius value 0.1 cm greater than this value. Does the surface area decrease? If not, try a value 0.1 cm less. Continue investigating until the surface area is a minimum for the radius value in tenths of a centimetre.

3. What is the radius of the cylinder with minimum surface area? How does this compare to the height of this cylinder?

4. Change the value of the volume in the spreadsheet to investigate the dimensions of a cylinder with minimum surface area when the volume is 940 cm². How do the radius and height compare?

5. Repeat step 4 for a cylinder with a volume of 1360 cm².

6. **Reflect** Summarize your findings. Describe any relationship you notice between the radius and height of a cylinder with minimum surface area for a given volume.

Example Minimize the Surface Area of a Cylinder

a) Determine the least amount of aluminum required to construct a cylindrical can with a 1-L capacity, to the nearest square centimetre.

b) Describe any assumptions you made.

Solution

a) For a given volume, the cylinder with minimum surface area has a height equal to its diameter.

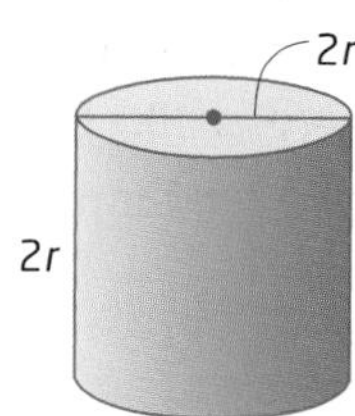

The front view of this cylinder is a square.

Substitute $h = 2r$ into the formula for the volume of a cylinder.

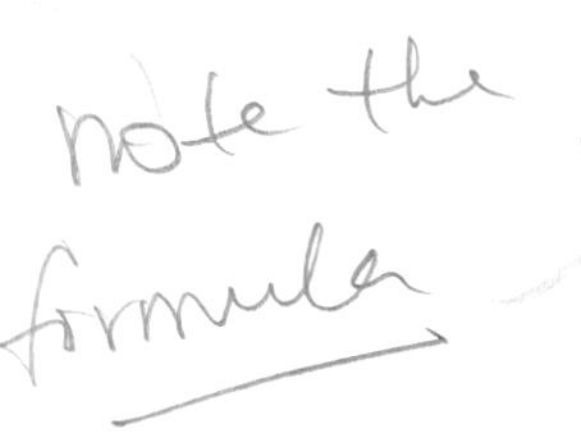

$$V = \pi r^2 h$$
$$= \pi r^2(2r)$$
$$= 2\pi r^3$$

Substitute the volume of 1 L, or 1000 cm^3, to find the dimensions of the cylinder.

$$1000 = 2\pi r^3$$

$$\frac{\overset{500}{\cancel{1000}}}{\underset{1}{2\pi}} = \frac{\overset{1}{\cancel{2\pi}} r^3}{\underset{1}{\cancel{2\pi}}}$$ **Divide both sides by 2π.**

$$\frac{500}{\pi} = r^3$$

$$\sqrt[3]{\frac{500}{\pi}} = r$$ **Take the cube root of both sides.**

$$5.42 \doteq r$$

C 500 ÷ π = ∛

```
³√(500/π)
          5.419260701
```

The radius of the can should be 5.42 cm. The height is twice this value, or 10.84 cm.

To find the amount of aluminum required, calculate the surface area.

$$SA = 2\pi r^2 + 2\pi rh$$
$$= 2\pi(5.42)^2 + 2\pi(5.42)(10.84)$$
$$\doteq 554$$

The least amount of aluminum required to make a cylindrical can that holds 1 L is about 554 cm^2.

b) The calculations in part a) do not take into account the extra aluminum required for the seam along the lateral surface. Also, along the top and bottom edges, there will likely be a rim that requires more aluminum.

Key Concepts

- For a cylinder with a given volume, a radius and a height exist that produce the minimum surface area.
- The minimum surface area for a given volume of a cylinder occurs when its height equals its diameter. That is, $h = d$ or $h = 2r$.
- The dimensions of the cylinder of minimum surface area for a given volume can be found by solving the formula $V = 2\pi r^3$ for r, and the height will be twice that value, or $2r$.

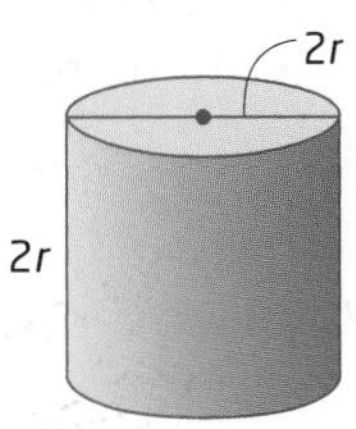

Communicate Your Understanding

C1 Describe a situation where it would be necessary to find the minimum surface area of a cylinder, given its volume.

C2 These cylinders all have the same volume. Which cylinder has the least surface area? Explain your answer.

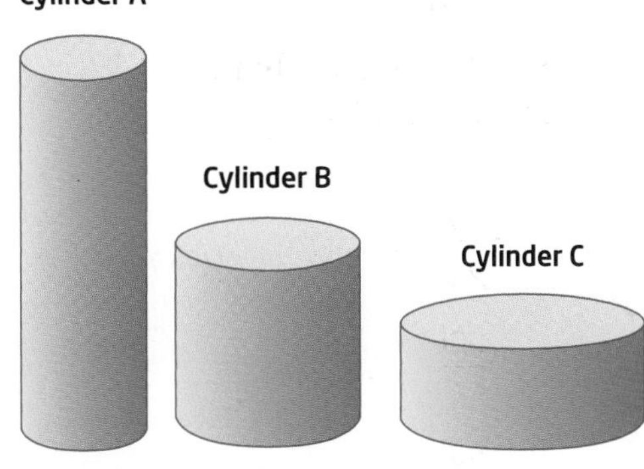

Practise

For help with questions 1 to 3, see the Example.

1. Determine the dimensions of the cylinder with minimum surface area for each volume. Round the dimensions, to the nearest tenth of a unit.

a) 1200 cm^3 **b)** 1 m^3

c) 225 cm^3 **d)** 4 m^3

2. Determine the surface area of each cylinder in question 1 to the nearest square unit.

3. A cylindrical can is to have a volume of 540 cm^3. What should its dimensions be to minimize the amount of material used to make it? Round the dimensions to the nearest tenth of a centimetre.

Connect and Apply

4. A cylindrical gas tank is designed to hold 5 L of gas.

a) Determine the dimensions of the can that requires the least material. Round the dimensions to the nearest tenth of a centimetre.

b) Describe any assumptions you made in solving this problem.

5. Wade has been asked to design an insulated cylindrical container to transport hot beverages. To keep heat loss to a minimum, the total surface area must be minimized. Find the interior dimensions of the container with volume 12 L that has minimum heat loss. Round to the nearest tenth of a centimetre.

6. A cylindrical can must hold 375 mL of juice.

a) Determine the dimensions of the can that requires the least amount of aluminum. Round the dimensions to the nearest tenth of a centimetre.

b) If aluminum costs $0.001/cm^2, find the cost of the aluminum to make 12 cans.

7. Many of the cans found in our homes are not designed to use the least amount of material. Give reasons why the cans might be designed in other ways.

Did You Know?

The design of the USB is standardized by the USB Implementers Forum. The current specification is at version 2.0. This version supports three data-transfer rates: low speed, full speed, and high speed.

8. Chapter Problem Talia is shipping USB (universal serial bus) cables to a customer. She needs a container with a volume of 500 cm^3 that is as cost efficient as possible. Should she use a square-based prism box or a cylinder for the cables? Justify your answer mathematically.

9. A cylindrical building at Laurentian University in Sudbury, Ontario, is shown in the photo. Do you think it was designed to minimize the amount of heat loss? Justify your answer mathematically.

Achievement Check

10. Extra fuel tanks carried in the cabin of a plane are called ferry tanks. These tanks allow a plane to fly greater distances. A cylindrical ferry tank needs to hold 600 L of aircraft fuel.

a) What are the dimensions of two possible cylindrical fuel tanks?

b) What should the dimensions of the tank be to minimize the amount of aluminum used in its construction?

c) How do these dimensions compare to the optimal square-based prism fuel tank?

Extend

11. A movie theatre sells popcorn in an open cylindrical container. The large size holds 1500 cm^3 of popcorn.

a) Determine the dimensions of the container that requires the least amount of cardboard.

b) How much cardboard is required to make one container?

c) Describe any assumptions you have made in solving this problem.

12. a) For a given volume, predict which three-dimensional figure will have the minimum surface area: a cube, a cylinder with height equal to diameter, or a sphere.

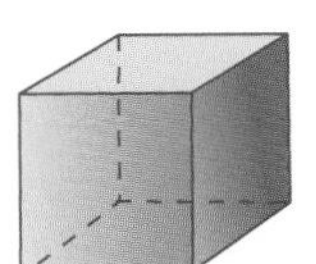

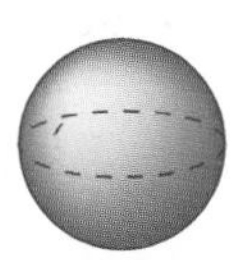

b) Check your prediction using the formulas for volume and surface area and a fixed volume of 1000 cm^3.

13. Math Contest You are to use 3584 cm^2 of newsprint. Determine the greatest volume that can be completely covered by the newsprint.

14. Math Contest Find the dimensions of the square-based prism box with maximum volume that can be enclosed in a cone with base radius 20 cm and height 30 cm.

15. Math Contest Find the dimensions that minimize the surface area for a cone with a volume of 225 cm^3.

16. Math Contest Find the dimensions of a cone with a surface area of 600 cm^2, if the cone has the greatest possible volume.

Chapter 9 Review

9.1 Investigate Measurement Concepts, pages 478–483

1. Derrick is building a rectangular frame for a children's sandbox with 40 m of lumber. Use toothpicks to investigate the greatest area that Derrick can enclose.

a) Let each toothpick represent 1 m of lumber. Construct different rectangles to represent the sandbox's area. Record the dimensions and the area in each case.

Rectangle	Width (m)	Length (m)	Perimeter (m)	Area (m^2)
1			40	
2			40	

b) How many different rectangles are possible?

c) Which shape would you choose for the sandbox? Give reasons for your choice.

2. A rectangular flower garden is to have an area of 16 m^2. Edging bricks will be used to form the perimeter of the garden.

a) On grid paper, sketch all the rectangles with whole-number dimensions and an area of 16 m^2.

b) Record the dimensions and the perimeter in each case.

Rectangle	Width (m)	Length (m)	Perimeter (m)	Area (m^2)
1				16
2				16

c) Which shape would be the most economical for the garden? Why?

9.2 Perimeter and Area Relationships of a Rectangle, pages 484–490

3. A whiteboard is to have an area of 1 m^2. What should the dimensions of the whiteboard be to minimize the amount of framing required to go around the outside?

4. What is the maximum area of a rectangular yard that can be enclosed with 120 m of fencing in each case?

a) The yard is enclosed on all four sides.

b) The yard is enclosed on three sides.

5. A rectangular skating rink is to have an area of 1800 m^2. The rink is surrounded by boards.

a) What are the dimensions of the rink that can be enclosed most economically? Round the dimensions to the nearest tenth of a metre.

b) Give reasons why the rink might not be designed in the most economical shape that you determined in part a).

9.3 Minimize the Surface Area of a Square-Based Prism, pages 491–497

6. Crackers are to be packaged in a square-based prism box with a capacity of 875 cm^3. Use a table like the one shown, or the spreadsheet you created in Section 9.3, to determine the dimensions of the box that requires the least amount of material.

Side Length of Square Base (cm)	Area of Square Base (cm^2)	Height (cm)	Volume (cm^3)	Surface Area (cm^2)
6			875	
7			875	

7. Chicken broth is packaged in a plastic-coated square-based prism box with a capacity of 1 L.

a) Determine the dimensions of the box that requires the minimum amount of material. Round the dimensions to the nearest tenth of a centimetre.

b) Explain why these dimensions might not be the ones the manufacturer chooses.

8. A 3-L box of rice is a square-based prism and is to be made from the minimum amount of cardboard. Determine the minimum amount of cardboard required, to the nearest square centimetre.

9.4 Maximize the Volume of a Square-Based Prism, pages 498–503

9. Use a table like the one shown, or the spreadsheet you created in Section 9.4, to investigate the dimensions of the square-based prism box with maximum volume that can be made from 2 m^2 of cardboard.

Side Length of Base (m)	Area of Base (m^2)	Surface Area (m^2)	Height (m)	Volume (m^3)
1		2		
2		2		

10. What are the dimensions of the square-based prism box with maximum volume that can be made from 1200 cm^2 of cardboard? Round the dimensions to the nearest tenth of a centimetre.

11. Suppose the cardboard in question 10 is a rectangular sheet that measures 60 cm by 20 cm. Explain why it may not be possible to make the shape you determined.

9.5 Maximize the Volume of a Cylinder, pages 504–509

12. Use a table like the one shown, or the spreadsheet you created in Section 9.5, to investigate the dimensions of the cylinder with maximum volume that can be formed using 720 cm^2 of cardboard.

Radius (cm)	Height (cm)	Volume (cm^3)	Surface Area (cm^2)
3			720
4			720

13. Explain how you could change the spreadsheet or table you used in question 12 if the container does not have a lid.

14. A manufacturer is trying to choose the best package for whole-grain cereal. A square-based prism and a cylinder require the same amount of cardboard to make. Which shape should the manufacturer choose? Give reasons for your answer.

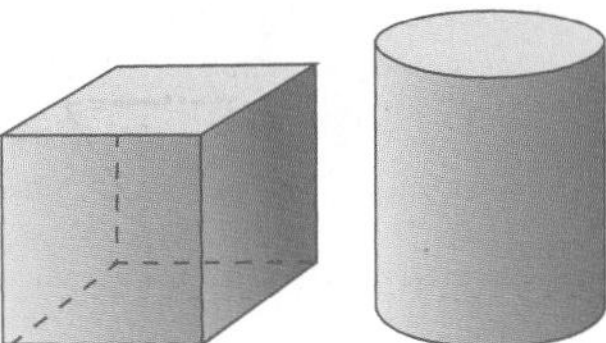

9.6 Minimize the Surface Area of a Cylinder, pages 510–515

15. a) Use a table like the one shown, or the spreadsheet you created in Section 9.6, to determine the minimum amount of aluminum required to make a pop can with a capacity of 400 mL.

Radius (cm)	Base Area (cm^2)	Volume (cm^3)	Height (cm)	Surface Area (cm^2)
1				
2				

b) What assumptions did you make in your solution?

16. CDs are 12 cm in diameter and 2 mm thick. They are to be packaged in a cylindrical container that is 12.2 cm in diameter.

a) Recommend the number of CDs that should be placed in the container to make it cost efficient.

b) Describe any assumptions you have made.

c) Determine the amount of material required to make the container.

Chapter 9 Practice Test

Multiple Choice

For questions 1 to 4, select the best answer.

1. A farmer wants to enclose a rectangular field with an area of 10 000 m^2 using the minimum amount of fencing. What should the dimensions of the field be?

A 250 m by 40 m **B** 100 m by 100 m

C 50 m by 200 m **D** 400 m by 25 m

2. A square-based prism box has a capacity of 8 L. What dimensions produce the minimum surface area?

A 80 cm by 10 cm by 10 cm

B 40 cm by 20 cm by 10 cm

C 25 cm by 16 cm by 20 cm

D 20 cm by 20 cm by 20 cm

3. These cylinders all have the same volume. Which shape requires the least material?

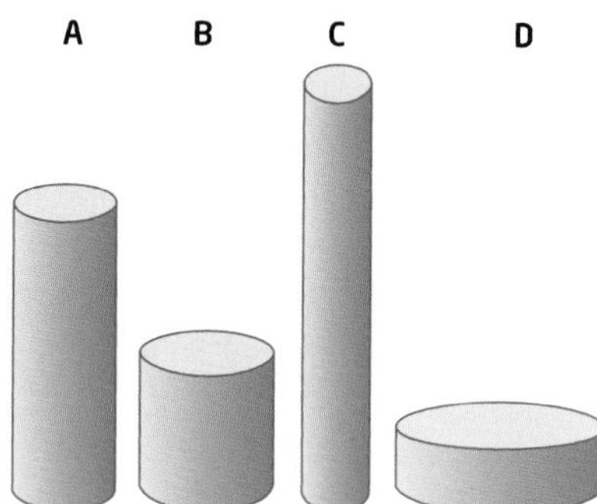

A cylinder A

B cylinder B

C cylinder C

D cylinder D

4. What are the dimensions of the square-based prism box with maximum volume that can be made using 600 cm^2 of cardboard?

A 10 cm by 10 cm by 10 cm

B 4 cm by 4 cm by 35.5 cm

C 12 cm by 12 cm by 6.5 cm

D 8 cm by 8 cm by 14.75 cm

Short Response

Show all steps to your solutions.

5. 200 cm of metal framing is available to surround a child's rectangular blackboard. What should the dimensions be to maximize the area?

6. One container is in the shape of a square-based prism and the other is a cylinder. The containers have bases with the same area and have identical heights. Describe how the volumes of the containers compare. Which container would require less material to make?

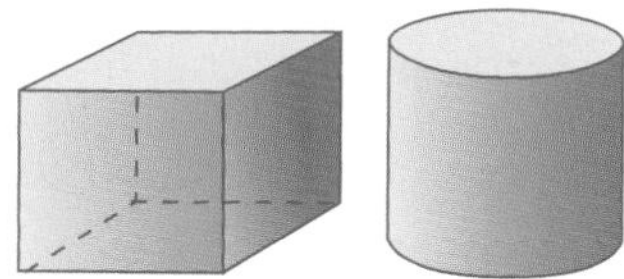

7. A square-based prism box is designed to hold 5 L of detergent.

a) What are the dimensions of the box that requires the least amount of cardboard? Round the dimensions to the nearest tenth of a centimetre.

b) What assumptions have you made?

8. Paulo has 8.64 m^2 of plywood. He wants to use this plywood to construct a square-based prism compost bin with maximum volume. The bin will have a lid.

a) What are the dimensions of the bin with maximum volume?

b) Calculate the volume of this compost bin, ignoring any loss due to cuts.

c) Suppose Paulo constructs three smaller bins with the plywood, making each of them with the same maximum volume. What are the dimensions of each bin?

d) How does the total volume of the three small bins compare to the volume of the large bin?

Extended Response

Provide complete solutions.

9. An architect is designing a new library. The library is to be cylindrical in shape. The architect wants the volume of the library to be about 20 000 m^3. To keep heat loss to a minimum, the architect wants to minimize the surface area. Ignore the heat loss through the floor. Determine the dimensions of the building that will best suit these restrictions. Round the dimensions to the nearest hundredth of a metre.

Library

Volume 20 000 m^3; minimize surface area

10. Minimizing weight is important in constructing light aircraft. The inside of an aircraft cockpit is a square-based prism and will be built using 4 m^2 of aluminum. The cockpit needs a floor, ceiling, and three walls. What dimensions will maximize the volume of the cockpit? Round the dimensions to the nearest tenth of a metre.

Chapter Problem Wrap-Up

One of Talia's customers has placed a large order for mini-CDs. The mini-CDs are 8 cm in diameter and 1 mm thick.

a) Talia wants to package the CDs in a plastic cylindrical container. Determine the dimensions of the cylinder that will require the least material to make.

b) How many CDs will each cylindrical package hold?

c) Several cylinders of CDs are to be packaged in a cardboard square-based prism carton. The customer needs at least 750 CDs. How many cylinders of CDs should Talia suggest for this order?

d) Draw diagrams, with dimensions, of two different cartons that could be used to package the cylinders of CDs.

e) How many CDs should Talia recommend that the customer order next time so that the carton packaging is minimized?

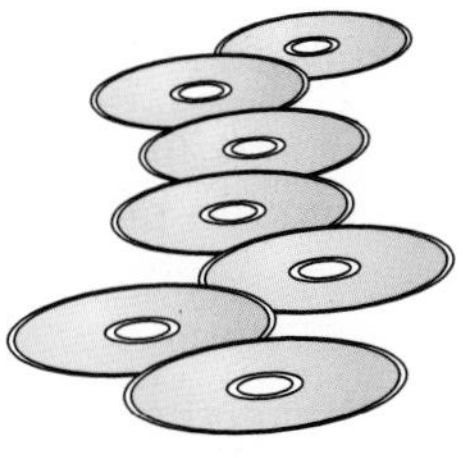

Chapters 7 to 9 Review

Chapter 7 Geometric Relationships

1. Calculate the measure of each unknown angle.

a)

b)

2. Calculate the measure of each unknown angle.

a)

b)

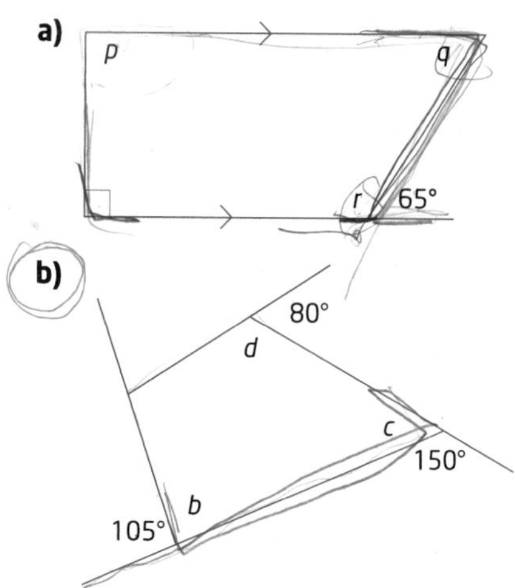

3. For each description, draw an example of the shape or explain why it cannot exist.

a) triangle with one right exterior angle

b) triangle with two right exterior angles

c) quadrilateral with two acute exterior angles

d) quadrilateral with two right interior angles

4. a) If each interior angle of a regular polygon measures 144°, how many sides does the polygon have?

b) What is the sum of the exterior angles of the polygon in part a)?

5. a) Construct a regular hexagon.

b) Describe the method you used.

6. Adam conjectures that the median from the hypotenuse divides the area of a right triangle into two equal parts. Is his conjecture true?

7. For each statement, either explain why it is true or draw a counter-example to show that it is false.

a) The diagonals of a parallelogram are equal in length.

b) The line joining the two midpoints of the two legs of a right triangle is parallel to the hypotenuse.

c) The diagonals of a trapezoid are never equal in length.

Chapter 8 Measurement Relationships

8. Calculate the perimeter and the area of each right triangle. Round your answers to the nearest tenth of a unit.

a)

b)

9. The floor plan of an L-shaped room is shown. Calculate the perimeter and the area of the room.

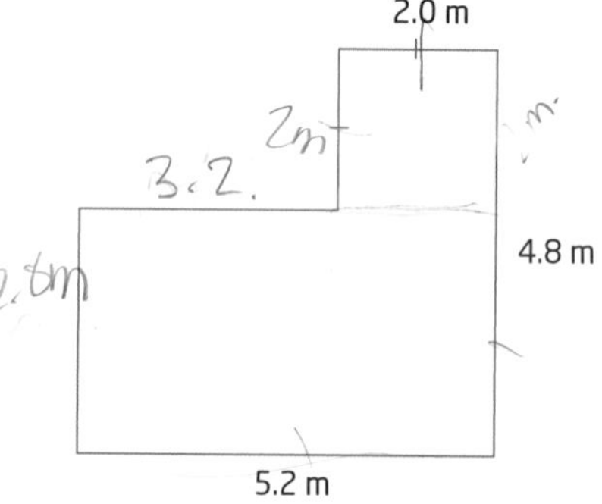

The Ice Rink

The Subzero Community Association is going to build a skating rink in a park. They have thirty 3-m-long sections of board that will be used to contain the rectangular rink.

a) Several different rectangular rinks are possible. Give the dimensions of two possibilities.

b) Is a rink that has a length-to-width ratio of 2:1 possible? Explain.

c) Is a square rink possible? Explain.

d) Which rink has the greatest surface area? Give its dimensions and justify your choice.

e) The ice for the rink you found in part d) is to be 3 cm thick, but it also needs to cover the wading pool that is used during the summer. This circular wading pool has a shallow cone shape with diameter 10 m and depth 30 cm at the centre. How much water will be required to initially flood this rink? Round your answer to the nearest litre.

Packing Compressed Air

Compressair Company provides cylindrical tanks of compressed air for divers. Their standard tank is a cylinder with a volume of 0.015 m^3. Each cylinder is 75 cm long and is designed to fit into a special diver's pack.

a) What is the diameter of the cylinder, to the nearest centimetre?

b) Compressair staff are designing a new cylinder that also has a volume of 0.015 m^3, but uses the least material to make. What are the dimensions of the new cylinder, to the nearest tenth of a centimetre? What is its surface area, to the nearest square centimetre?

c) Compressair plans to ship 20 of its standard 75-cm-long cylinders upright in a closed rectangular reinforced cardboard box. Staff are considering packing the cylinders in identical rows or in staggered rows, as shown below. Which packing arrangement will require the box of least volume and surface area?

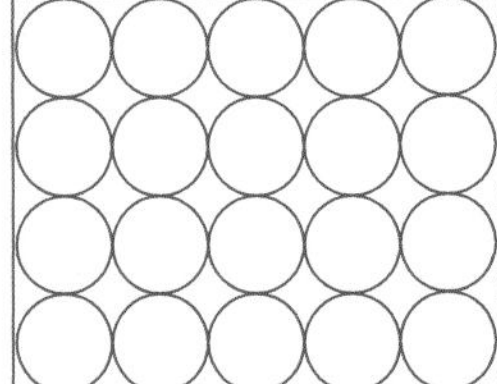

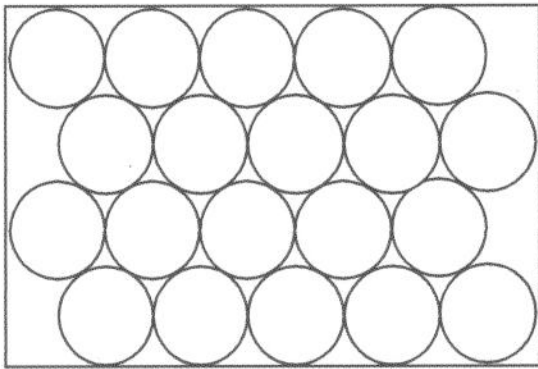

Technology Appendix

CONTENTS

The Geometer's Sketchpad® Geometry Software page

TI-83 Plus and TI-84 Graphing Calculators

The Geometer's Sketchpad® Basics

Menu Bar:

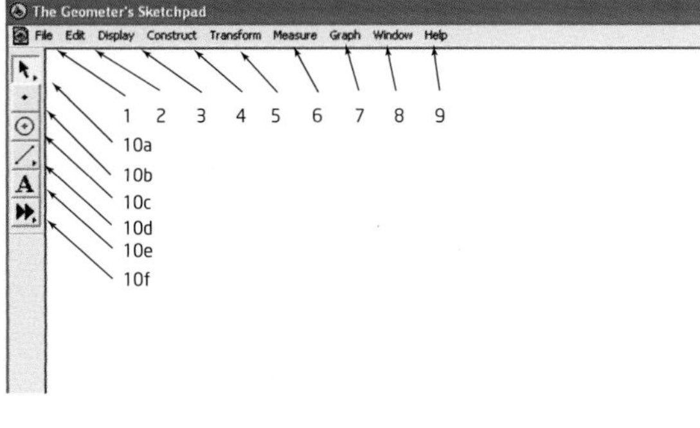

1 **File** menu—open/save/print sketches
2 **Edit** menu—undo/redo/actions/set preferences
3 **Display** menu—control appearance of objects in sketch
4 **Construct** menu—construct new geometric objects based on objects in sketch
5 **Transform** menu—apply geometric transformations to selected objects
6 **Measure** menu—make various measurements on objects in sketch
7 **Graph** menu—create axes and plot measurements and points
8 **Window** menu—manipulate windows
9 **Help** menu—access the help system, an excellent reference guide
10 **Toolbox**—access tools for creating, marking, and transforming points, circles, and straight objects (segments, lines, and rays); also includes text and information tools
10a **Selection Arrow Tool** (Arrow)—select and transform objects
10b **Point Tool** (Dot)—draw points
10c **Compass Tool** (Circle)—draw circles
10d **Straightedge Tool**—draw line segments, rays, and lines
10e **Text Tool** (Letter A)—label points and write text
10f **Custom Tool** (Double Arrow)—create or use special "custom" tools

Creating a Sketch

- Under the **File** menu, choose **New Sketch** to start with a new work area.

Opening an Existing Sketch

- Under the **File** menu, choose **Open…**. The Open dialogue box will appear.
- Choose the sketch you wish to work on. Then, click on Open.

OR

- Type in the name of the sketch in the **File name:** entry box. Then, click on **Open**.

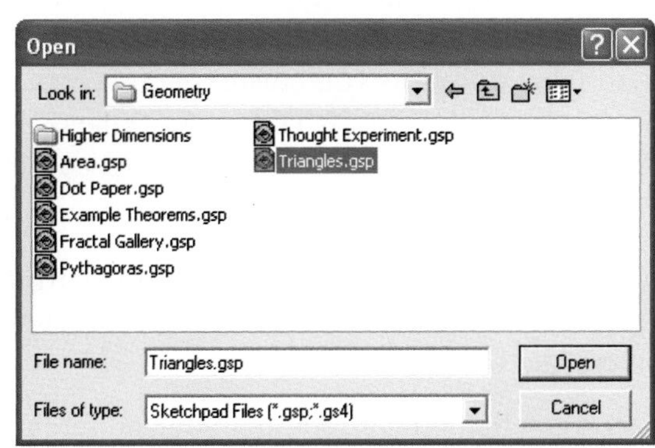

Saving a Sketch

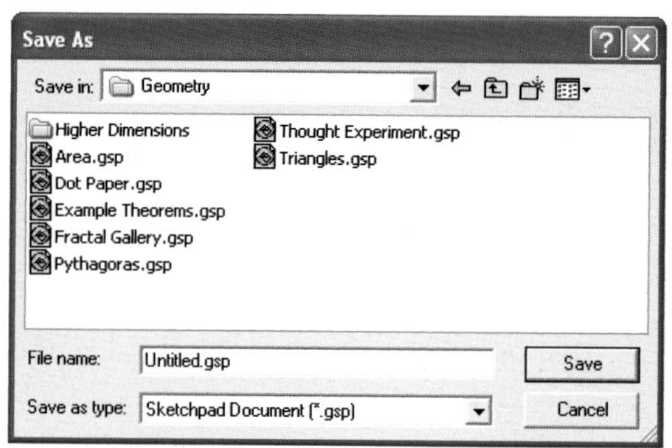

If you are saving for the first time in a new sketch:

- Under the **File** menu, choose **Save As**. The Save As dialogue box will appear.
- You can save the sketch with the name assigned by *The Geometer's Sketchpad*®. Click on **Save**.

OR

- Press the Backspace or Delete key to clear the name.
- Type in whatever you wish to name the sketch file. Click on **Save**.

If you have already given your file a name:

- Select **Save** from under the **File** menu.

Closing a Sketch Without Exiting *The Geometer's Sketchpad*®

- Under the **File** menu, choose **Close**.

Exiting *The Geometer's Sketchpad*®

- Under the **File** menu, choose **Exit**.

Setting Preferences

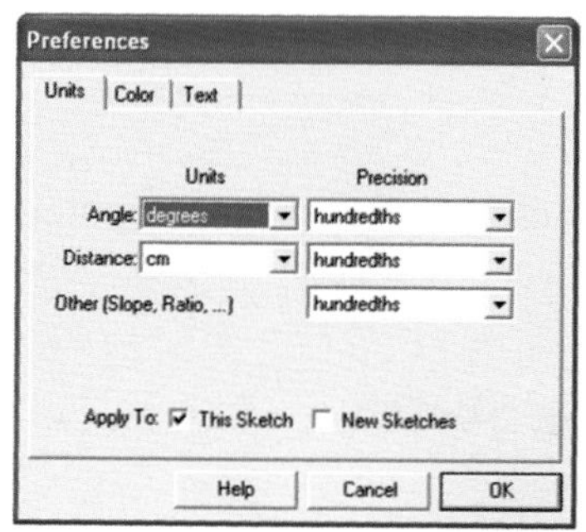

- From the **Edit** menu, choose **Preferences...**.
- Click on the **Units** tab.
- Set the units and precision for angles, distances, and calculate values such as slopes or ratios.

- Click on the **Text** tab.
- If you check the auto-label box **For All New Points**, then *The Geometer's Sketchpad*® will label points as you create them.
- If you check the auto-label box **As Objects Are Measured**, then *The Geometer's Sketchpad*® will label any measurements that you define.

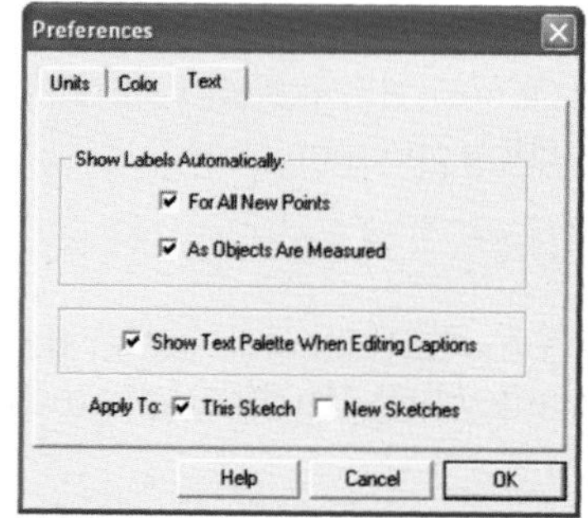

You can also choose whether the auto-labelling functions will apply only to the current sketch, or also to any new sketches that you create.

Be sure to click on **OK** to apply your preferences.

Selecting Points and Objects

- Choose the **Selection Arrow Tool**. The mouse cursor appears as an arrow.

To select a single point:
- Select the point by moving the cursor to the point and clicking on it.

The selected point will now appear as a darker point, similar to a *bull's-eye* ⊙.

To select an object such as a line segment or a circle:
- Move the cursor to a point on the object until it becomes a horizontal arrow.
- Click on the object. The object will change appearance to show it is selected.

To select a number of points or objects:
- Select each object in turn by moving the cursor to the object and clicking on it.

To deselect a point or an object:
- Move the cursor over it, and then click the left mouse button.
- To deselect all selected objects, click in an open area of the workspace.

Constructing Line Segments

- Choose the **Point Tool**. Create two points in the workspace.
- Choose the **Selection Arrow Tool**, and select both points.
- From the **Construct** menu, choose **Segment**.

You can also use the **Straightedge Tool**:
- Choose this tool.
- Move the cursor to the workspace.
- Click and hold the left mouse button.
- Drag the cursor to the desired location.
- Release the mouse button.

Constructing Triangles and Polygons

To construct a triangle:
- Choose the **Point Tool**. Draw three points in the workspace.
- Select the points.
- From the **Construct** menu, choose **Segments**.

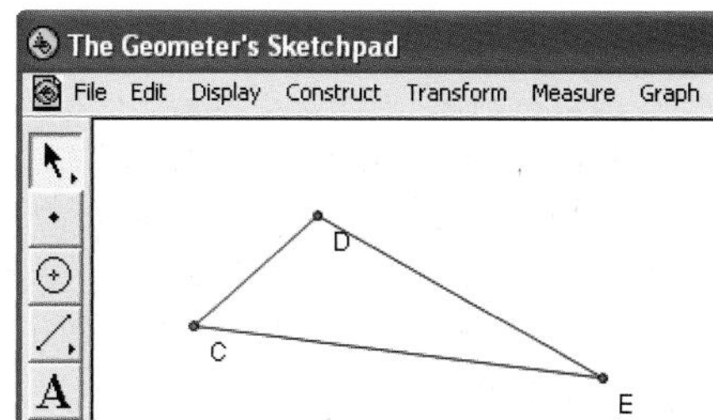

You can construct a polygon with any number of sides.

To construct a quadrilateral:
- Draw four points.
- Deselect all points.
- Select the points in either clockwise or counterclockwise order.
- From the **Construct** menu, choose **Segments**.

Constructing a Circle

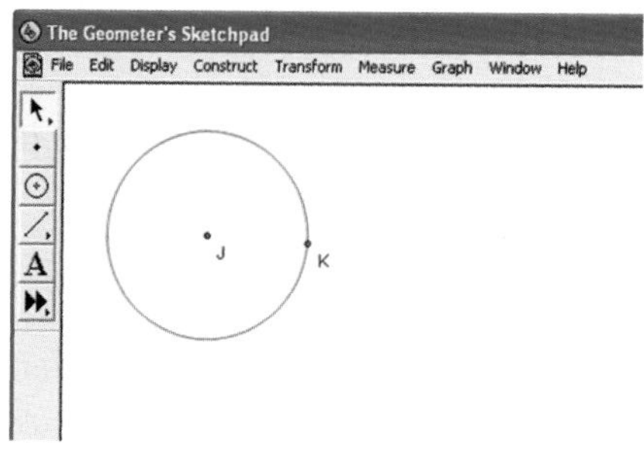

- Select the **Compass Tool**.
- Move the cursor to the point where you want the centre of the circle.
- Click and hold the left mouse button. Drag the cursor to the desired radius.
- Release the mouse button.

Constructing Parallel and Perpendicular Lines

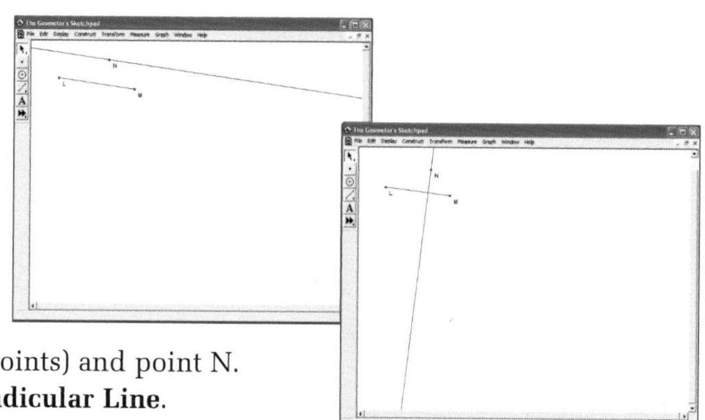

To construct a line parallel to LM, passing through N:
- Select line segment LM (but not the endpoints) and point N.
- From the **Construct** menu, choose **Parallel Line**.

To construct a line perpendicular to LM, passing through N:
- Select line segment LM (but not the endpoints) and point N.
- From the **Construct menu**, choose **Perpendicular Line**.

Constructing Rays

To construct a ray OP:
- Select point O and then point P.
- From the **Construct** menu, choose **Ray**.

OR

- Click and hold on the Straightedge Tool on the left toolbar until a menu appears. Choose the option for a ray.
- Select point O and then point P.

Constructing Midpoints

To construct the midpoint of line segment PQ:
- Select line segment PQ (but not the endpoints).
- From the **Construct** menu, choose **Midpoint**.

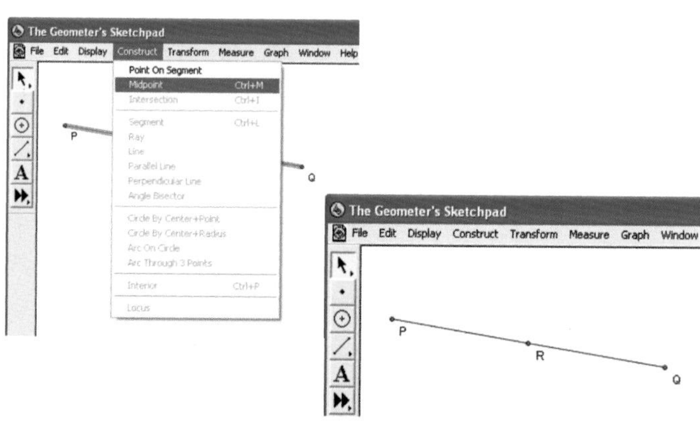

Using the Measure Menu

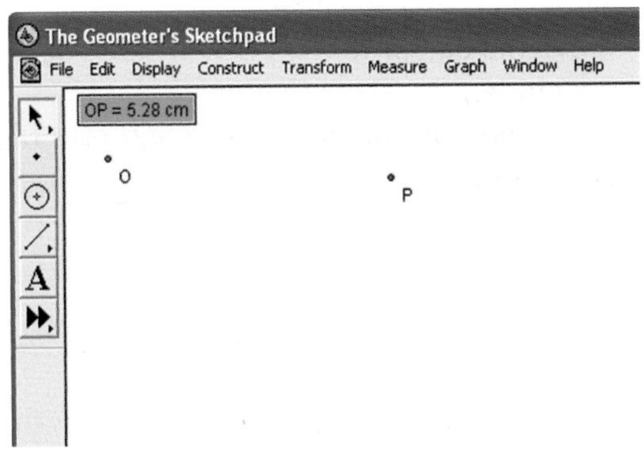

To measure the distance between two points:

- Ensure that nothing is selected.
- Select the two points.
- From the **Measure** menu, choose **Distance**.

The Geometer's Sketchpad® will display the distance between the points, using the units and accuracy selected in **Preferences...** under the **Edit** menu.

To measure the length of a line segment:

- Ensure that nothing is selected.
- Select the line segment (but not the endpoints).
- From the **Measure** menu, choose **Length**.

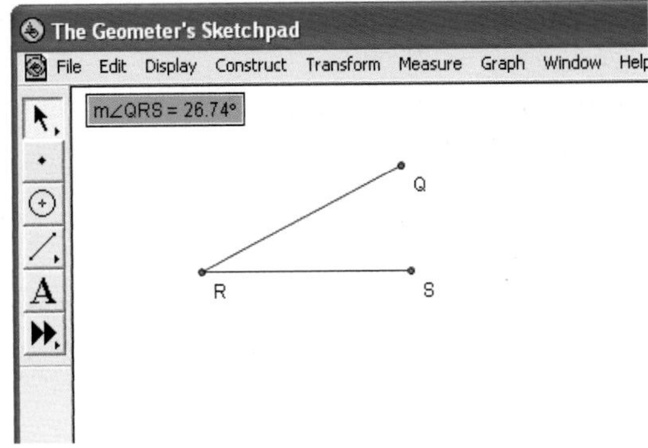

To measure an angle:

- Ensure that nothing is selected.
- Select the three points that define the angle in the order Q, R, S. The second point selected must be the vertex of the angle.
- From the **Measure** menu, choose **Angle**.

To calculate the ratio of two lengths:

- Select the two lengths be compared.
- From the **Measure** menu, choose **Ratio**.

Constructing and Measuring Polygon Interiors

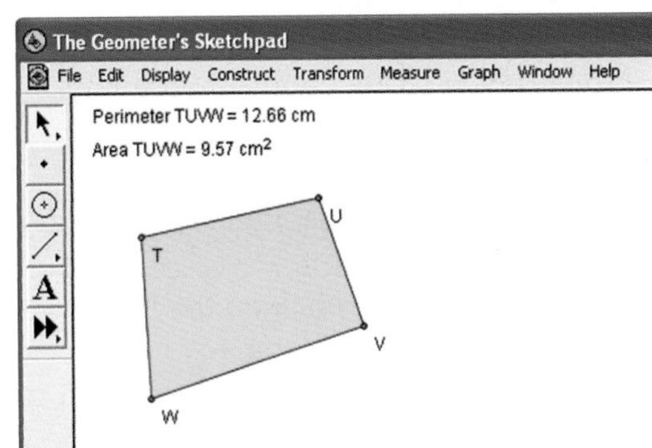

The Geometer's Sketchpad® will measure the perimeter and the area of a polygon. However, you must first construct the interior of the polygon.

To construct the interior of this quadrilateral:

- Choose the four points of the quadrilateral, in either clockwise or counterclockwise order.
- From the **Construct** menu, choose **Quadrilateral Interior**. The interior of the quadrilateral will change colour.

To measure the perimeter:

- Select the interior of the polygon. It will have a cross-hatched appearance when selected.
- From the **Measure** menu, choose **Perimeter**.

The Geometer's Sketchpad® will display the perimeter of the polygon, using the units and accuracy selected in **Preferences...** under the **Edit** menu.

To measure the area:

- Select the interior of the polygon.
- From the **Measure** menu, choose **Area**.

Dilating and Rotating an Object

To dilate an object:

- Select a point to be the centre of the dilatation. Then, from the **Transform** menu, choose **Mark Center**.
- Select the object(s) to be dilated. From the **Transform** menu, choose **Dilate...**.
- In the Dilate dialogue box, enter the Scale Factor by which you want to dilate the object. Make sure that **Fixed Ratio** is selected. Click on **Dilate**.

To rotate an object:

- Select a point to be the centre of rotation. Then, from the **Transform** menu, choose **Mark Center**.
- Select the object(s) to be rotated. From the **Transform** menu, choose **Rotate...**.
- In the Rotate dialogue box, enter the number of degrees you want to rotate the object. Make sure that **Fixed Angle** is selected. Click on **Rotate**.

Changing Labels of Measures

- Right click on the measure and choose **Label Measurement** (or **Label Distance Measurement** depending on the type of measure) from the drop-down menu.
- Type in the new label.
- Click on **OK**.

Using the On-Screen Calculator

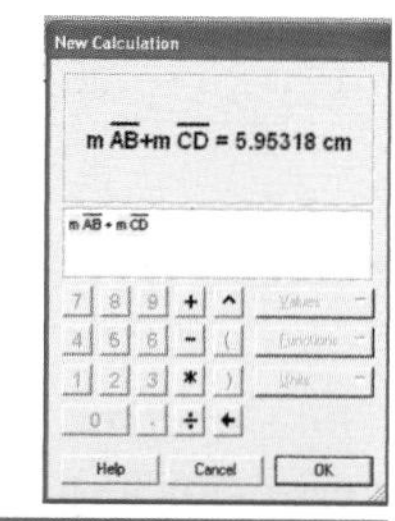

You can use the on-screen calculator to do calculations involving measurements, constants, functions, or other mathematical operations.

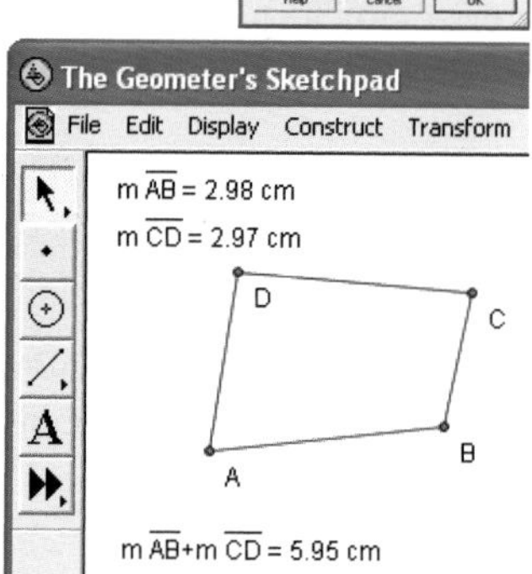

To add two lengths:

- From the **Measure** menu, choose **Calculate**. The on-screen calculator will appear.
- On the workspace, click on the first measure.
- On the keyboard, click on +.
- On the workspace, click on the second measure.
- Click on **OK**.

The sum of the measures will appear in the workspace.

OR

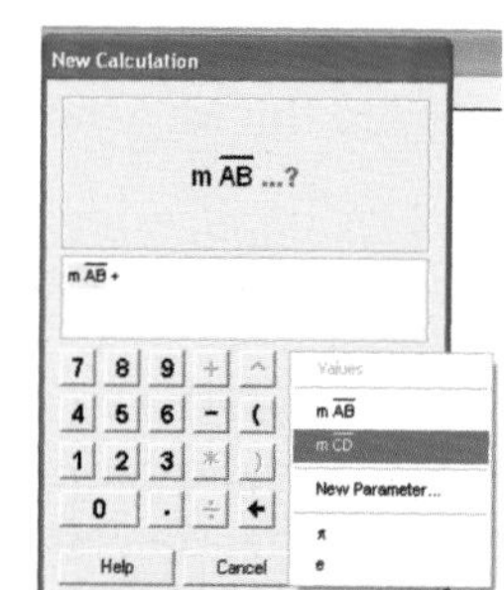

- Select the two measures. Then, choose **Calculate** from the **Measure** menu. This adds the measures to the drop-down list available by clicking on the **Values** button of the on-screen calculator.
- Click on the **Values** button. Select the first measure.
- Click on +.
- Click on the **Values** button. Select the second measure.
- Click on **OK**.

Coordinate System and Axes

The default coordinate system has an origin point in the centre of your screen and a unit point at (1, 0). Drag the origin to relocate the coordinate system and drag the unit point to change its scale.

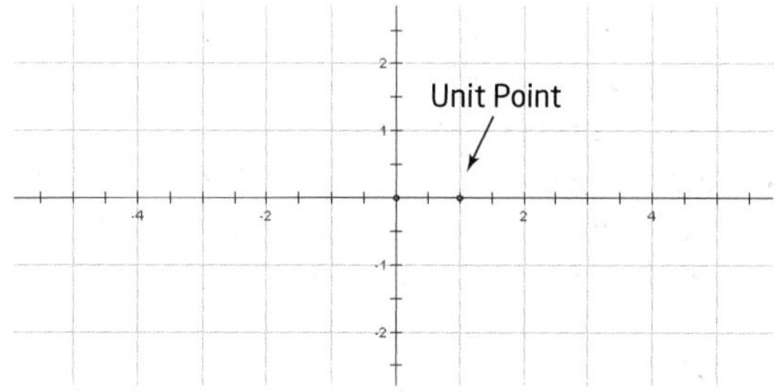

Creating Graphs

To plot a point on an *x*-*y* grid:

- From the **Graph** menu, choose **Plot Points…**.
- Ensure that **Plot As** is set to **Rectangular (x, y)**.
- Enter the *x*- and *y*-coordinates of the point.
- Click on **Plot**. A grid will appear with the plotted point. Click on **Done**.

You can plot additional points once you access the Plot Points dialogue box. Enter the coordinates of the next point and click on **Plot**. When you are finished plotting points, click on **Done**.

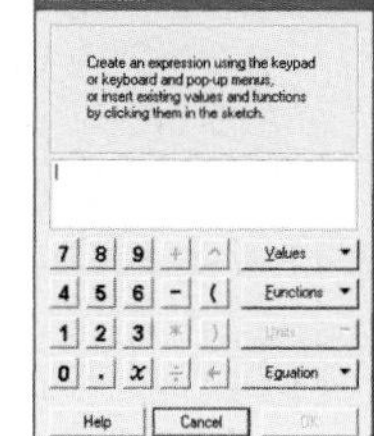

To graph an equation:

- From the **Graph** menu, select **Plot New Function**. A calculator screen with the heading **New Function** will appear.
- Using the calculator interface, enter the equation.
- Click on **OK**.

To plot a table of values:

- Select the table of data.
- From the **Graph** menu, select **Plot Table Data**.

Loading Custom Tools

Before you can use a **Custom Tool**, you must either create your own custom tools, or transfer the sample tools included with *The Geometer's Sketchpad®* program to the **Tool Folder**.

To transfer a sample custom tool:

- Open **Windows® Explorer**, and navigate to the **Sketchpad** directory, or whatever directory was used to install *The Geometer's Sketchpad®*.
- Choose **Samples**, and then **Custom Tools**. You will see a list of the custom tools provided with the program.
- Select the sets of tools you want to use. Then, select **Copy** from the **Edit** menu.
- Move back up two directory levels to the **Sketchpad** directory, and then select **Tool Folder**. Select **Paste** from the **Edit** menu.
- Open *The Geometer's Sketchpad®*. Choose the **Custom Tool**.

You will see the custom tool sets that you copied. Select one of the tool sets, say **Polygons**. You will see a list of the individual tools available.

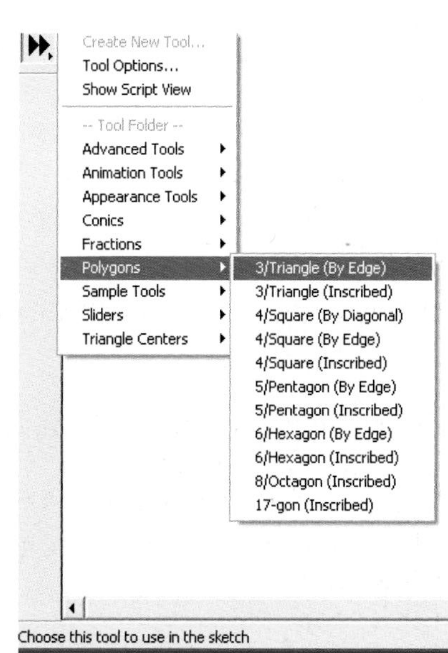

TI-83 PLUS AND TI-84 BASICS

The keys on the TI-83 Plus and TI-84 are colour-coded to help you find the various functions.

- The grey keys include the number keys, decimal point, and negative sign. When entering negative values, use the grey [(−)] key, not the blue [−] key.
- The blue keys on the right side are the math operations.
- The blue keys across the top are used when graphing.
- The primary function of each key is printed on the key, in white.
- The secondary function of each key is printed in yellow and is activated by pressing the yellow [2nd] key. For example, to find the square root of a number, press [2nd] [x^2] for [√].
- The alpha function of each key is printed in green and is activated by pressing the green [ALPHA] key.

Graphing Relations and Equations

- Press [Y=]. Enter the equation.
- To display the graph, press [GRAPH].

For example, enter $y = \frac{3}{5}x - 2$ by pressing

[Y=] [(] 3 [÷] 5 [)] [X,T,θ,n] [−] 2.

Press [GRAPH].

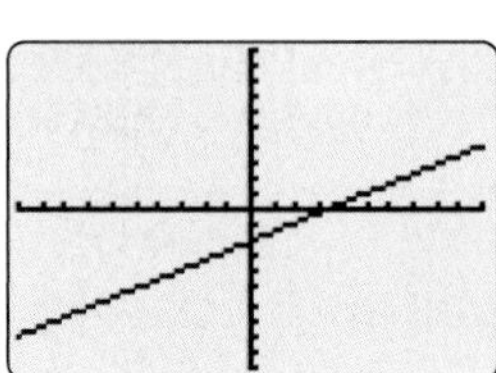

Setting Window Variables

The [WINDOW] key defines the appearance of the graph. The standard (default) window settings are shown.

```
WINDOW
 Xmin=-10
 Xmax=10
 Xscl=1
 Ymin=-10
 Ymax=10
 Yscl=1
 Xres=1
```

To change the window settings:

- Press [WINDOW]. Enter the desired window settings.

In the example shown,

- the minimum x-value is -47
- the maximum x-value is 47
- the scale of the x-axis is 10
- the minimum y-value is -31
- the maximum y-value is 31
- the scale of the y-axis is 10
- the resolution is 1, so equations are graphed at each horizontal pixel

```
WINDOW
 Xmin=-47
 Xmax=47
 Xscl=10
 Ymin=-31
 Ymax=31
 Yscl=10
 Xres=1
```

Tracing a Graph

- Enter a function using Y=.
- Press TRACE.
- Press ◀ and ▶ to move along the graph.

The *x*- and *y*-values are displayed at the bottom of the screen.

If you have more than one graph plotted, use the ▲ and ▼ keys to move the cursor to the graph you wish to trace.

You may want to turn off all STAT PLOTS before you trace a function:
- Press 2nd Y= for [STAT PLOT]. Select **4:PlotsOff**.
- Press ENTER.

Using Zoom

The ZOOM key is used to change the area of the graph that is displayed in the graphing window.

ZOOM MEMORY
1:ZBox
2:Zoom In
3:Zoom Out
4:ZDecimal
5:ZSquare
6:ZStandard
7↓ZTrig

To set the size of the area you want to zoom in on:
- Press ZOOM. Select **1:Zbox**. The graph screen will be displayed, and the cursor will be flashing.
- If you cannot see the cursor, use the ▶, ◀, ▲, and ▼ keys to move the cursor until you see it.
- Move the cursor to an area on the edge of where you would like a closer view. Press ENTER to mark that point as a starting point.
- Press the ◀, ▶, ▲, and ▼ keys as needed to move the sides of the box to enclose the area you want to look at.
- Press ENTER when you are finished. The area will now appear larger.

To zoom in on an area without identifying a boxed-in area:
- Press ZOOM. Select **2:Zoom In**.

To zoom out of an area:
- Press ZOOM. Select **3:Zoom Out**.

To display the viewing area where the origin appears in the centre and the *x*- and *y*-axes intervals are equally spaced:
- Press ZOOM. Select **4:ZDecimal**.

To reset the axes range on your calculator:
- Press ZOOM. Select **6:ZStandard**.

To display all data points in a STAT PLOT:
- Press ZOOM. Select **9:ZoomStat**.

Setting the Format

To define a graph's appearance:
- Press (2nd)(ZOOM) for [FORMAT] to view the choices available.

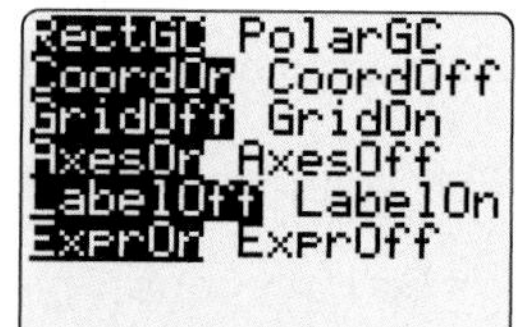

The **Default Settings**, shown here, have all the features on the left "turned on."

To use Grid Off/Grid On:
- Select [FORMAT] by pressing (2nd)(ZOOM). Cursor down and right to **GridOn**. Press (ENTER).
- Press (2nd)(MODE) for [**QUIT**].

Working With Fractions

To display a decimal as a fraction:
- Key in a decimal.
- Press (MATH), and then select **1:▸Frac**. Press (ENTER).

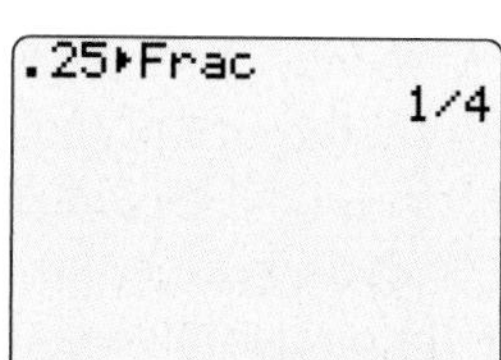

The decimal will be displayed as a fraction.

To enter fractions in calculations:
- Use the division key (÷) to create fractions as you key them in.
- If you want the result displayed as a fraction, Press (MATH), and then select **1:▸Frac**.
- Press (ENTER).

For example, to calculate $\frac{3}{4} - \frac{2}{3}$:

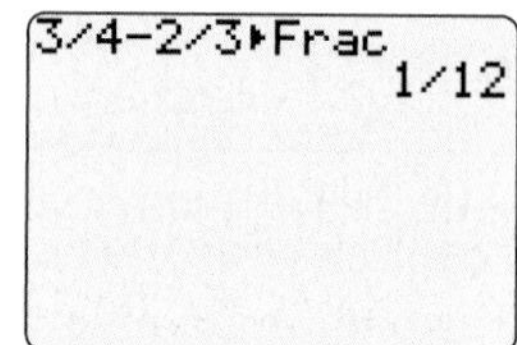

- Press 3(÷)4(−) 2(÷)3.
- Then, press (MATH), select **1:▸Frac**, and then press (ENTER).

The result will be displayed as a fraction.

To calculate with mixed numbers:
- Use the (+) and (÷) keys to enter mixed numbers.
- If you want the result displayed as a fraction, press (MATH), select **1:▸Frac**, and then press (ENTER).

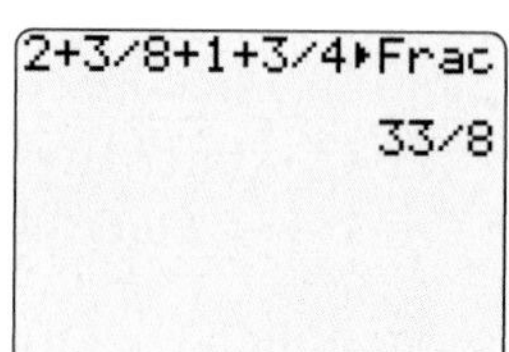

For example, to calculate $2\frac{3}{8} + 1\frac{3}{4}$:
- Press 2(+) 3(÷) 8(+) 1(+) 3(÷) 4.
- Then, press (+), select **1:▸Frac**, and then press (ENTER).

The result will be displayed as a fraction.

Entering Data Into Lists

To enter data:

- Press STAT. The cursor will highlight the **EDIT** menu.
- Press **1** or ENTER to select **1:Edit...**.

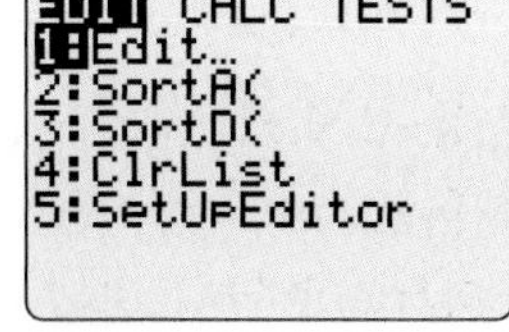

This allows you to enter new data, or edit existing data, in lists **L1** to **L6**.

For example, press STAT, select **1:Edit...**, and then enter six test scores in list **L1**.

- Use the cursor keys to move around the editor screen.
- Complete each data entry by pressing ENTER.
- Press 2nd MODE for [QUIT] to exit the list editor when the data are entered.

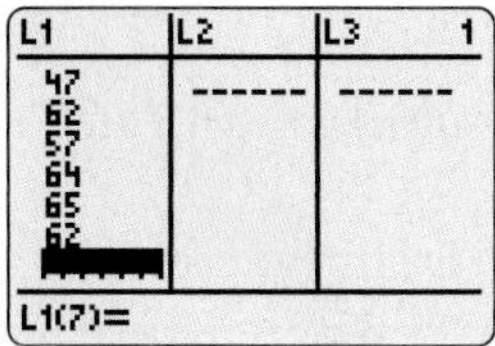

You may need to clear a list before you enter data into it. For example, to clear list **L1**:

- Press STAT and select **4:ClrList**.
- Press 2nd **1** for [L1], and press ENTER.

OR

To clear all lists:

- Press 2nd + for [MEM] to display the **MEMORY** menu.
- Select **4:ClrAllLists**, and then press ENTER.

Creating a Scatter Plot

To create a scatter plot:

- Enter the two data sets in lists **L1** and **L2**.
- Press 2nd Y= for [STAT PLOT].
- Press **1** or ENTER to select **1:Plot1...**.
- Press ENTER to select **On**.
- Cursor down, and then press ENTER to select the top left graphing option, a scatter plot.
- Cursor down and press 2nd **1** for [L1].
- Cursor down and press 2nd **2** for [L2].
- Cursor down and select a mark style by pressing ENTER.
- Press 2nd MODE for [QUIT] to exit the **STAT PLOTS** editor when the data are entered.

To display the scatter plot:

- Press Y= and use the CLEAR key to remove any graphed equations.
- Press 2nd MODE for [QUIT] to exit the **Y=** editor.
- Press ZOOM and select **9:ZoomStat** to display the scatter plot.

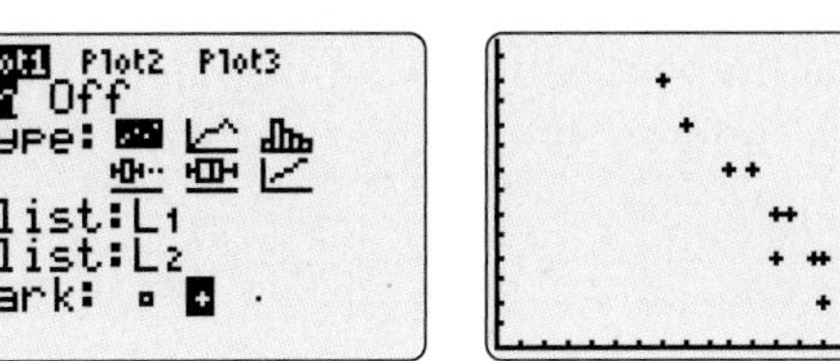

Line of Best Fit

You can add the line of best fit to a scatter plot by using the LinReg function:

- With the scatter plot displayed, press STAT. Cursor over to display the **CALC** menu, and then select **4:LinReg(ax+b)**.
- Press 2nd **1** for [L1], followed by ,.
- Press 2nd **2** for [L2], followed by ,.
- Then, press VARS, cursor over to display the **Y-VARS** menu, select **1:FUNCTION**, and then select **1:Y1**.

- Press ENTER to get the LinReg screen, and then press GRAPH.

The linear regression equation is stored in the **Y=** editor. If you press Y=, you will see the equation generated by the calculator.

Note: If the diagnostic mode is turned on, you will see values for **r** and **r**^{2} displayed on the LinReg screen. To turn the diagnostic mode off:

- Press 2nd **0** for [CATALOG].
- Scroll down to **DiagnosticOff**. Press ENTER to select this option.
- Press ENTER again to turn off the diagnostic mode.

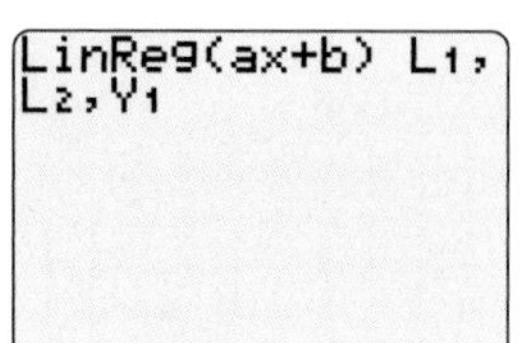

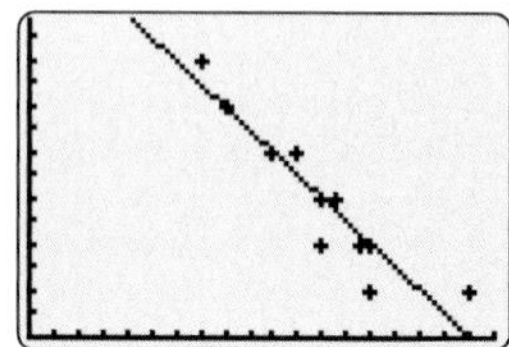

Using the CBR™ (Calculator-Based Ranger)

To access the CBR™ through the TI-83 Plus or TI-84:

- Connect the CBR™ to the TI-83 Plus or TI-84 with the calculator-to-CBR cable.

Make sure both ends of the cable are firmly in place.

- Press APPS. Select **2:CBL/CBR**.
- When the CBL/CBR™ screen is presented, press ENTER.
- To access the programs available, select **3:Ranger**.
- When the **Ranger** menu is presented, press ENTER.

To record data from the CBR™:

- From the MAIN MENU screen, select **1:SETUP/SAMPLE**. All settings, except TIME (S), can be changed by using the cursor keys to position the ▸ beside the current option and pressing ENTER to cycle through the choices.

If the REALTIME option is set to YES, the sampling time is fixed at 15 s. To change the TIME (S) setting, you must first change the REALTIME option to NO, as shown. Then, cursor down to TIME (S), enter the desired value, and then press ENTER.

MAIN MENU ▸START NOW

REALTIME: no
TIME(S): 4
DISPLAY: DIST
BEGIN ON: [ENTER]
SMOOTHING: none
UNITS: METERS

- Move the cursor up to START NOW at the top of the screen, and then press ENTER.

Answers

Chapter 1

Get Ready, pages 4–5

1. a) $1\frac{1}{5}$ **b)** $\frac{5}{8}$ **c)** $\frac{13}{30}$ **d)** $1\frac{17}{45}$

2. a) $\frac{1}{8}$ **b)** $1\frac{1}{8}$ **c)** $18\frac{11}{16}$ **d)** $\frac{7}{72}$

3. $\frac{13}{24}$

4. a) 8 **b)** −5 **c)** −23 **d)** −4
e) −14 **f)** 15 **g)** 4 **h)** −400
i) −49 **j)** 42 **k)** −7 **l)** −4

5. a) 48 **b)** −8 **c)** −23

6. loss of $3570

7. a) −60 **b)** 110 **c)** −1 **d)** −65
e) 6241 **f)** 39

9. net loss $8

10. Answers will vary.

1.1 Focus on Problem Solving, pages 6–9

1. a) 11, 13, 15; add 2 to the previous term
b) 56, 69, 82; add 13 to the previous term
c) 32, 64, 128; multiply the previous term by 2
d) 13, 21, 34; add the two previous terms

2. 11

3. a) $1 \times 1 = 1$
$11 \times 11 = 121$
$111 \times 111 = 12\ 321$
$1111 \times 1111 = 1\ 234\ 321$
b) The digits increase from 1 up to the number of 1s in one of the factors and then decrease to 1 so that the answer is symmetric.
c) There are nine 1s in the first factor, so the product is 12 345 678 987 654 321.

4. a) 407, 814, 1221
b) 1628, 2035, 2442; add 407 to the previous term
c) 99×37 is the eighth term after 11×37, so add 407 eight times to 407 to get 3663.

5. a) $0.\overline{1}$, $0.\overline{2}$, $0.\overline{3}$, …; If the numerator is less than 9, then the decimal will be that digit repeated infinitely after the decimal place.
b) If the numerator is less than 99, then the decimal will be that number written as a two-digit number, repeated infinitely after the decimal place.
c) If the numerator is less than 99 999 then the decmal will be that number written as a five-digit number, repeating infinitely after the decimal point.

6. The middle 3 by 3 square is shown.

2	4	3
9	5	8
1	6	7

7. a) Gina: 22 years, 3 months, and 17 days; Sam: 25 years, 11 months, and 9 days
b) To find the number of years, subtract the birth year from 2019. To find the number of months, subtract the month number from 12. To find the number of days, subtract the birthday number from 31 and add 1.

8. a) 1 **b)** 3 **c)** 6 **d)** 45

9. 7

10.

630	or	860
1766		1788
2396		2648

11.

1	15	14	4
12	6	7	9
8	10	11	5
13	3	2	16

1.2 Focus on Communicating, pages 10–13

1. a) Subtract 5 from the previous term; 0, −5
b) Subtract 4 from the previous term: −18, −22
c) Add $\frac{1}{4}$ to the previous term; 1, $1\frac{1}{4}$
d) Subtract $\frac{2}{5}$ from the previous term; $\frac{6}{5}$, $\frac{4}{5}$
e) Multiply the previous term by −2; 48, −96
f) Divide the previous term by 2; −12, −6
g) Subtract descending multiples of 5, starting with 20, from the previous term; 50, 50
h) Multiply the previous term by 1, 2, 3, 4, …; 360, 2160
i) Multiply the previous term by $\frac{1}{5}$;

𓂋 over 𓆼𓍢𓍢𓎆𓎆𓎆𓎆𓎆 𓂋 over 𓆼𓆼𓆼𓆼𓆼𓆼𓍢𓍢𓎆𓎆𓎆𓎆𓎆

i) Multiply the previous term by 2; 𓂋 over 𓎆𓎆𓎆𓎆𓎆 𓂋 over 𓎆𓎆𓏺𓏺𓏺𓏺𓏺

2. Answers will vary.

3. Yes; the area of the semicircle on the hypotenuse equals the sum of the areas of the semicircles on the other two sides.

4. B; As the wheel moves forward, the height of the light will increase and decrease smoothly.

5. a) The map is divided into sections where time changes by 1-h intervals. Starting at the original time zone, count how many time zones away the other one is using positive integers to the right and negative integers to the left. Add this integer value to the original time.
b) 4:00 P.M. **c)** 4:30 A.M.

6. a) Use the last two rows. In the fraction strip made of $\frac{1}{7}$ pieces, shade three parts. In the fraction strip made of $\frac{1}{8}$ pieces, shade four parts. Compare the shaded parts. $\frac{4}{8} > \frac{3}{7}$ because four pieces of $\frac{1}{8}$ are wider than three pieces of $\frac{1}{7}$.

b) Place the $\frac{1}{2}$ piece and the $\frac{1}{3}$ piece side by side; they will have the same width as a $\frac{5}{6}$ piece.

c) Twelve rows are needed because the lowest common denominator is 12.

d) The dark blue bars are getting smaller. When 1 is divided by larger and larger numbers, the pieces become smaller and smaller. The number of pieces is the denominator of the fraction.

7. a) The rectangle is divided into thirds horizontally and two of these rows are shaded to show $\frac{2}{3}$. Then the rectangle is divided into quarters vertically and three of these columns are shaded to show $\frac{3}{4}$. The overlap of the shading shows the product. Since six parts are double shaded, $\frac{2}{3} \times \frac{3}{4} = \frac{6}{12} = \frac{1}{2}$

b) $3 \times \frac{3}{4} = 2\frac{1}{4}$

8. a) The sum of the first n odd numbers is n^2.

b) fifth diagram: $1 + 3 + 5 + 7 + 9 = 25 = 5^2$; sixth diagram: $1 + 3 + 5 + 7 + 9 + 11 = 36 = 6^2$

c) There are 50 odd numbers from 1 to 99 inclusive. The sum is $50^2 = 2500$.

d) There are 75 odd numbers from 1 to 150. There are 300 odd numbers from 1 to 600. The sum of the odd numbers from 150 to 600 is $300^2 - 75^2 = 84\ 375$.

9.

6	1	9	3	7	8	4	5	2
4	7	5	2	6	9	3	8	1
8	2	3	4	5	1	6	7	9
1	6	7	5	2	3	8	9	4
5	3	8	1	9	4	2	6	7
9	4	2	6	8	7	1	3	5
7	9	1	8	3	2	5	4	6
3	5	4	7	1	6	9	2	8
2	8	6	9	4	5	7	1	3

10. The best location would be 4.5 m from the end of the assembly line toward the middle of the line and a perpendicular distance of 5 m from the line.

1.3 Focus on Connecting, pages 14–18

1. a)

800 m
400 m
200 m
100 m
50 m
25 m

b) 1575 m

c) 525 m

2.

Quarters	Dimes	Nickels	Value ($)
4	0	0	1.00
3	1	0	0.85
3	0	1	0.80
2	2	0	0.70
2	1	1	0.65
2	0	2	0.60
1	3	0	0.55
1	2	1	0.50
1	1	2	0.45
1	0	3	0.40
0	4	0	0.40
0	3	1	0.35
0	2	2	0.30
0	1	3	0.25
0	0	4	0.20

3. Answers will vary depending on the dimensions of the classroom. A possible estimate can be made using this formula: Number of pucks = Volume of classroom ÷ Volume of one puck (108 cm^3).

4. Each day, Honi rides about 16 km to and from school. So, her tires will last about 125 school days which is about 6 months of riding to and from school.

5. Guess and test. Start by guessing that Joe ate 1 slice, then Emily ate 2 slices, Samir ate 3 slices, then Kendra ate 1 slice and Fong ate 5 slices. This works, since $1 + 2 + 3 + 1 + 5 = 12$. Then, rewrite each person's share as a fraction of the pizza.

Emily: $\frac{1}{6}$, Samir: $\frac{1}{4}$, Joe: $\frac{1}{12}$, Kendra: $\frac{1}{12}$, Fong: $\frac{5}{12}$

6. Add up the number of triangles with side lengths 1, 2, 3, and 4; 27

7. Each square has area 0.25 cm^2. The area of the arrow is about 12 squares, or 3 cm^2.

8. The snail will have a net climb of 1 m up per day. But, on the last day, the snail will not slide down. It will reach 3 m above ground by the end of the 23rd day. So, on the 24th day, the snail will reach the top.

9. Answers will vary. Research the average heart rate and lifespan of a cat. Multiply the rate per minute by 525 600 and by the lifespan in years.

10.

9	6	1	7	5	3	2	8	4
2	8	7	6	1	4	5	9	3
4	3	5	8	2	9	6	1	7
1	7	6	4	8	5	9	3	2
3	2	8	9	6	1	4	7	5
5	4	9	2	3	7	1	6	8
7	9	3	1	4	2	8	5	6
8	1	2	5	7	6	3	4	9
6	5	4	3	9	8	7	2	1

11. Answers will vary.

12. 170

1.4 Focus on Representing, pages 19–22

1. 2 km east of the starting point.
2. 4 floors with 27, 18, 12 and 8 apartments on the floors. The maximum is 27 apartments because the next lower floor would have 40.5 apartments, which is not possible.
3. 11
4. 15
5. **a)** The x-coordinate increases by 3 and the y-coordinate increases by 1. D(11, 6), E(14, 7), F(17, 8)
   b) The x-coordinate decreases by 5 and the y-coordinate decreases by 2. S(−14, 0), T(−19, −2), U(−24, −4)
   c) Both the x- and y-coordinates decrease by 3. J(−6, −6), K(−9, −9), L(−12, −12)
6. **a)** $\frac{1}{2} < \frac{2}{3}$ $\frac{1}{2}$ $\frac{2}{3}$
   b) $\frac{2}{3} < \frac{3}{4}$ $\frac{2}{3}$ $\frac{3}{4}$
   c) $\frac{3}{4} < \frac{4}{5}$ $\frac{3}{4}$ $\frac{4}{5}$
   d) $\frac{4}{5} < \frac{5}{6}$ $\frac{4}{5}$ $\frac{5}{6}$
7. **a)** $4\frac{1}{2}$ **b)** $\frac{3}{4}$ **c)** $3\frac{1}{3}$ **d)** $\frac{3}{10}$
8. (1, −2) and (−3, 2); (5, −2) and (1, −6); (−7, 2) and (−3, 6)
9. (−1, 2), (−1, −8), (−7, 2), (−7, −8)
10. The same answers would result. The middle cog does not change the ratio of the driver cog to the driving cog.

1.5 Focus on Selecting Tools and Computational Strategies, pages 23–28

1. **a)** 12 squares divided into 4 columns gives 3 squares in each column.
   b) 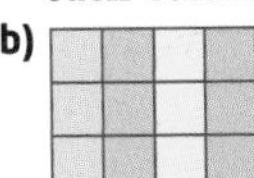 **c)** 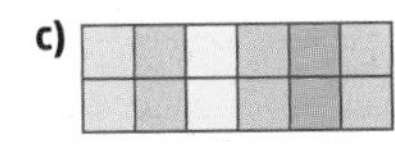
   d) You can never arrange the squares with a width of zero, so the quotient is undefined.
2. **a)** $3 \times \left(-\frac{2}{3}\right)$ means subtracting $\frac{2}{3}$ three times, which will land you at −2.
   b) 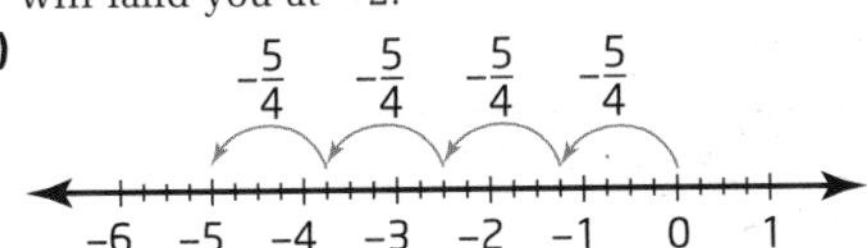

3. **a)** ⊥ **b)** Make a physical model.
   c) Answers will vary.
4. calculator, survey
5. Answers will vary.
   a) for complicated math expressions involving square roots and fractions
   b) to draw a diagram to scale
   c) to solve real life problems
   d) to organize data and generate complicated graphs
6. 39; Answer will vary. Use a calculator.
7. **a)** −57, −63 **b)** 1215, 3645
   c) −4, 2 **d)** −158, −161
   e) −6144, 12 288 **f)** 32, 56
8. **a)** $\frac{1}{3}, \frac{1}{21}, \frac{1}{168}$ **b)** $-\frac{4}{3}, -\frac{5}{3}, -2$
   c) $0, -\frac{1}{4}, -\frac{1}{2}$ **d)** $\frac{1}{3}, \frac{1}{4}, \frac{1}{6}$
9. **a)** −1 **b)** $-1\frac{5}{12}$ **c)** $-\frac{9}{35}$ **d)** $-\frac{7}{24}$
10. **a)** $-\frac{11}{24}$ **b)** $-\frac{1}{6}$ **c)** $-\frac{5}{12}$ **d)** $-\frac{1}{2}$
11. Answers will vary. To multiply rational numbers in fraction form, multiply the numerators and multiply the denominators. To divide rational numbers in fraction form, multiply the dividend by the reciprocal of the divisor.
12. **a)** $-\frac{1}{4}$ **b)** $\frac{3}{35}$ **c)** $-\frac{3}{44}$
    d) $-1\frac{1}{20}$ **e)** $1\frac{1}{9}$ **f)** $-2\frac{4}{5}$
13. **a)** Answers will vary. **b)** 0.16 mm
    c) 83 886.08 mm or 83.886 08 m
    d) 7. As the number of folds increases, the thickness also increases, making it more difficult to fold the paper.
14. Answers will vary.
15.

Length (cm)	Width (cm)	Perimeter (cm)	Area (cm²)
1	9	20	9
2	8	20	16
3	7	20	21
4	6	20	24
5	5	20	25
6	4	20	24
7	3	20	21
8	2	20	16
9	1	20	9

16. **a)** A, B $= \frac{1}{4}$; C, E $= \frac{1}{16}$; D, F, G $= \frac{1}{8}$
    b) i) $\frac{1}{2}$ **ii)** $\frac{3}{16}$ **iii)** $\frac{3}{16}$ **iv)** $\frac{1}{16}$ **v)** $\frac{1}{16}$ **vi)** $-\frac{1}{16}$
17. **a)** F = C + E **b)** B = C + E + F
18. −3951
19. 101st term
20. Answers will vary. Consider the dimensions of a bathtub to find the volume. Then consider the dimensions and volume of a cup. The number of cups required will be the quotient of the two volumes.
21. $2^n + 1$
22. at least 40 m

1.6 Focus on Reasoning and Proving, pages 29–33

1.

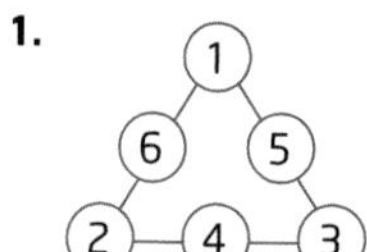

2.

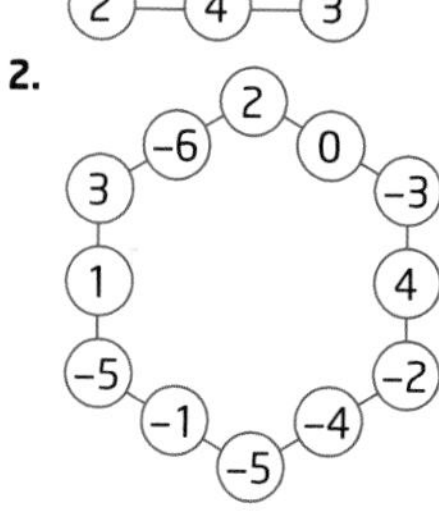

3. Let the consecutive whole numbers be $n - 1$, n, and $n + 1$. Then, the sum is $n - 1 + n + n + 1 = 3n$, which is divisible by 3.

4. Answers may vary. Example: Since a newspaper is made by folding a sheet in half, there will always be an even number of pages because the number of pages equals two times the number of sheets.

5.

Cents	Number of Coins
1	1
2	2
3	3
4	4
5	1
6	2
7	3
8	4
9	5
10	1

Continue this pattern. For example, 14¢, 18¢, 23¢, and 29¢ require five coins each. 24¢, 34¢ and 39¢ each require six coins. As a maximum, 44¢ and 49¢ each require seven coins. Therefore, you only need seven coins to be able to make any amount of money up to 50¢.

6. a) $5 \times 2 + 8 - 3 = 15$ **b)** $25 \div 5 + 11 = 25 - 9$

c) $\frac{1}{2} + \frac{1}{3} = \frac{11}{12} - \frac{1}{12}$ **d)** $\frac{2}{3} \times \left(-\frac{1}{8}\right) = -\frac{1}{12}$

7. a) -36°C **b)** 10.5°C

8. a) 2 is a prime number that is not odd.

b) $4 + (-1) = 3$ is a positive sum, not negative.

c) $\frac{3}{2}$ is a fraction, but is not less than 1.

d) A trapezoid is a quadrilateral, but not a rectangle.

9. Yes.

10. 3 lbs

11. seven $(-1, -3, -4, -5, -7, -8, -9)$

12. Roller Magic: 1, Death Drop: 1, Amazing Loop: 2, Fire Pit: 4

13. Answers will vary. Divide the surface area of each hallway by the surface area of one tile.

14.

5	4	1	6	9	7	8	3	2
2	6	7	5	3	8	1	4	9
8	9	3	2	4	1	5	7	6
9	2	5	3	7	4	6	8	1
4	1	6	8	5	9	7	2	3
7	3	8	1	6	2	9	5	4
6	7	2	4	1	5	3	9	8
1	5	4	9	8	3	2	6	7
3	8	9	7	2	6	4	1	5

15. Answers will vary. Estimate the average mass of a bus and the average mass of a student.

16. a) -10 **b)** -14 **c)** -5 **d)** -35

1.7 Focus on Reflecting, pages 34–36

1. You obtain two double Mobius strips that are looped together.

2. 56

3. $2\frac{2}{3}$

4. Answers will vary. Working backward is very effective.

5. 2520. Find the lowest common multiple of the integers.

6. a)

X	Y	Z
-3	-3	1
-3	-2	0
-3	-1	-1
-3	0	-2
-3	1	-3
-2	-3	0
-2	-2	-1
-2	-1	-2
-2	0	-3
-1	-3	-1
-1	-2	-2
-1	-1	-3
0	-3	-2
0	-2	-3
1	-3	-3

b) organized table and patterning

7. a) 24 **b)** 24 **c)** 120

d) 120 **e)** 840 **f)** 840

g) When you multiply four consecutive natural numbers, the product equals one less than the square of one more than the product of the first and last number.

h) $5 \times 6 \times 7 \times 8 = 41^2 - 1$;
$10 \times 11 \times 12 \times 13 = 131^2 - 1$

8. a) 5 moves

b) $-60 + 90 = 30$; $30 + (-75) = -45$; $-45 + 60 = 15$; $15 + (-45) = -30$; $-30 + 30 = 0$

9. 66; 49 numbers are divisible by 2 and 33 numbers are divisible by 3. However, 16 of these are numbers that are divisible by both 2 and 3. Subtract 16 from 49 + 33 to give 66. You could check by using a hundred chart and circling numbers that are divisible by 2 or 3.

10. **a)** Karen used too much milk and sugar. She used the wrong unit, litres instead of millilitres, for the milk.
b) 3×500 mL $= 1500$ mL or 1.5 L;
3×125 g $= 375$ g or 0.375 kg

11. Answers will vary. Consider the average size and surface area of a pizza, how many pizzas are ordered in a week, and how many pizza restaurants are in Ontario.

12. **a) i)**

2	7	6
9	5	1
4	3	8

ii)

-3	2	1
4	0	-4
-1	-2	3

b) Pair off the least and greatest numbers, moving toward the median. Then, put that single number in the centre square and arrange the pairs around it.

Chapter 1 Review, page 37

1. **a)** 0, −3, −6; subtract 3 from the previous term.
b) 56, 112, 224; multiply the previous term by 2.
c) 15, 20, 26; add consecutive numbers, 1, 2, 3, ..., to the previous term.
d) −19, −27, −36; subtract consecutive numbers, 4, 5, 6, ..., from the previous term.

2. 68; $2(100 \div 5) + 2(70 \div 5)$

3. **a)** Make a table and use patterning.
b)

20s	15s	10s	-5s	Score
3	0	0	0	60
2	1	0	0	55
2	0	1	0	50
2	0	0	1	35
1	2	0	0	50
1	1	1	0	45
1	1	0	1	30
1	0	2	0	40
1	0	1	1	25
1	0	0	2	10
0	3	0	0	45
0	2	1	0	40
0	2	0	1	25
0	1	2	0	35
0	1	1	1	20
0	1	0	2	5
0	0	3	0	30
0	0	2	1	15
0	0	1	2	0
0	0	0	3	-15

4. It cannot be done because one house will always be blocked from one of the services.

5. (−2, 1), (10, 9), (4, −9)

6. 30. Use a table to keep track of the number of squares of each dimension.

7. Dave needs to catch the bus by 6:47 P.M. Calculate the time to travel 20 km, and then subtract this time from 7:30 P.M.

8. **a)** The new area is four times greater.
b) One method is to use the formula for the area of a rectangle, $A = lw$.
New Area $= 2l \times 2w$
$= 4 \times l \times w$
$= 4 \times$ (Old Area)

9. 9; systematic trial

10. −135, −134, −133. Divide 402 by 3 to find the approximate value of each integer. Then, use systematic trial to find the correct three integers.

11. **a)** $-\frac{1}{35}$ **b)** $-\frac{1}{18}$ **c)** $-\frac{1}{6}$ **d)** $-\frac{1}{3}$

12. Answers will vary. Example:
$-\frac{11}{12} + \frac{5}{12} + \left(-\frac{1}{12}\right) = -\frac{7}{12}$,
$\frac{1}{2} + \left(-\frac{3}{4}\right) + \left(-\frac{1}{3}\right) = -\frac{7}{12}$,
$\frac{7}{12} + \left(-\frac{2}{3}\right) + \left(-\frac{1}{2}\right) = -\frac{7}{12}$

13. 3; Make a model or draw a diagram.

Chapter 2

Get Ready, pages 40–41

1. **a)** unemployment rates in 2003
b) Newfoundland and Labrador
c) the prairie provinces since they have the lowest unemployment rates

2. **a)** \$1.16 CDN **b)** May
c) a downward trend overall

3. **a)**

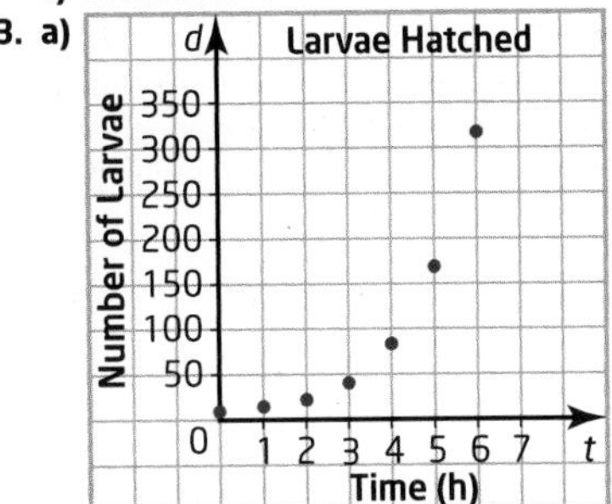

b) about 110

4. **a)** Air Pressure Versus Altitude **b)** about 7.5 kPa

5. **a)** 7 pages/min **b)** \$3/kg **c)** 80 km/h

6. **a)** 0.56¢/g **b)** 20.8 mL/muffin **c)** 130 m/min

2.1 Hypotheses and Sources of Data, pages 42–47

1. **a)** Most people's favourite number is not 7.
   b) Adults do not spend more time listening to classical music than rap. (Alternative: Adults spend either less time or as much time listening to classical music as they spend listening to rap.)
   c) In Ontario, the number of teenagers who join hockey teams is greater than or equal to the number who join soccer teams.
   d) Chocolate is the most popular flavour of ice cream.
2. Answers will vary. Examples:
   a) Hypothesis: Time spent doing homework increases as a student's age increases. Opposite: Time spent doing homework does not increase as a student's age increases.
   b) Hypothesis: Children tend to grow to the same height as their mothers. Opposite: Children do not tend to grow to the same height as their mothers.
   c) Hypothesis: As temperature increases, the crime rate also increases. Opposite: As temperature increases, the crime rate decreases or remains constant.
   d) Hypothesis: As the cost of gasoline increases, the number of people using public transit increases. Opposite: As the cost of gasoline increases, the number of people using public transit decreases or stays the same.
3. **a)** Primary; the office manager gathers the data.
   b) Secondary; the student uses data gathered by Statistics Canada.
   c) Primary; the researcher gathers the data.
   d) Secondary; the researcher uses data gathered by the transit authority.
4. Answers about advantages will vary.
   a) Primary; data are up-to-date
   b) Secondary; Internet search is fast and easy
   c) Primary; getting opinions from customers
   d) Primary; data are up-to-date
5. Answers will vary. Examples:
   a) Most students in the class prefer dogs as pets.
   b) Survey the class. Primary data are best since the population is small and secondary data may not be available.
6. **a)** Primary; Steve gathered the data himself.
   b) Answers will vary. Examples: Brown-eyed students are shorter. Blue is the least common eye colour.
   c) Survey a larger sample.
7. Answers will vary. Examples:
   a) Females make more phone calls than males.
   b) Survey 50 females and 50 males.
   c) Look for data on the Internet or in publications.
   d) Secondary sources using larger samples are more likely to be accurate.
8. Answers will vary. Examples:
   a) Taller people perform better at the high jump.
   b) Heights of the athletes and how high the athletes can jump; primary data for the school team would be easy to collect, but secondary sources could give a larger sample and more accurate results.
9. Answers will vary. Examples:
   a) The faster the computer, the more it will cost.
   c) primary if you collect prices from Web sites for individual suppliers; secondary if you find price surveys with data gathered by someone else
   d) Visit a computer store to research speeds and prices.
10. **a), b)** Answers will vary.
    c) secondary since the data was collected by others
12. Answers will vary. Example:
    a) The greater the latitude of a city, the lower the mean of its daily maximum temperatures in January.
13. Answers will vary.
14. 10

2.2 Sampling Principles, pages 48–55

1. **a)** all children **b)** everyone who wrote the test
   c) all cars **d)** all food stores
2. **a)** age when girls and boys learn to walk; sample
   b) test marks; census
   c) salaries of Canadian employees; sample
   d) people's heights and ages; sample
   e) make of car in school parking lot; census
   f) colour of cars driving by the school; sample
3. Answers will vary. Examples:
   a) Survey every fourth customer who comes into the cafe.
   b) Randomly select 1% of the teenagers in every high school across Ontario.
   c) Use a random number generator to select telephone numbers within Canada, and then survey the people who identify themselves as bilingual.
   d) Select households to survey by any random method, and then ask the people surveyed where they were born.
4. **a)** non-random sample; could be biased since University of Waterloo students may not be representative of all university graduates
   b) simple random sample; could be biased since the sample excludes anyone who does not have a telephone listing
   c) non-random sample; biased because it includes only people who have chosen to spend some of their free time going to a movie
   d) systematic random sampling
5. by age, by grade, by gender
6. **a)** all Ontario farmers
   b) Answers will vary. Example: Randomly select 10% of the farmers in each county.
7. **a)** the company's employees
   b) Randomly select a starting point on an alphabetical list of the employees, and then select every sixth person until you have a total of 50.
8. **a)** members of the school teams
   b) Answers will vary. Example: Write each team member's name on a slip of paper, and then randomly draw 15% of the slips out of a box.
9. grade 9, 41; grade 10, 38; grade 11, 36; grade 12, 35
10. **a)** randInt(12,36,25)
    b) Enter randInt(1,500,40). If any numbers are repeated, change the command to generate more random numbers and use the first 40 that are not duplicates.
    c) Enter randInt(100,1000,75). Increase 75 to 100 or more if some numbers are repeated.

11. a) Students at small schools have a greater chance of being selected than students at large schools.

b) The sample is likely to have a greater proportion of students from small schools than the population does.

12. Answers for sampling methods will vary.

a) students in the school

b) all people in the community

c) all people aged 18 to 30

d) all senior citizens in Ontario

e) all computer printers for sale in Canada

f) gasoline prices at all vendors in the community

13. The sample is representative only of people who browse the site and are willing to fill out the form. The sample excludes anyone who does not have Internet access or the time to complete the survey.

14. a) In the 1920s, many people did not have telephones. Since these people were not included in the surveys, the samples were not representative of the whole population.

b) Answers will vary. Examples: People with more than one telephone number have a greater chance of being selected. People refusing to answer telephone surveys may make the sample unrepresentative of certain groups. Deaf people will be left out of the sample.

15. Answers will vary.

16. Answers will vary.

17. Answers will vary. Examples: Poorly designed questions could influence people's answers. People may give false answers to personal questions.

18. Answers will vary. Examples:

a) Assign each tree a number and use a random number generator to choose 10% of the trees.

b) Divide the park into sections and randomly select 10% from each section.

c) Assign each tree a number. Randomly select a starting point, and then select every tenth number before and after the starting number.

d) Sample the 10% of the trees closest to roads.

Any of the random samples will test trees throughout the park. However, the forester could choose a non-random sample with a larger proportion of the hardwood trees that the beetle attacks most often.

19. a) Answers will vary. Examples: interviewing sports fans at a sports venue, interviewing classmates

b) Convenience samples are not truly random because every member of the population does not have an equal chance of being selected.

20. 120

2.3 Use Scatter Plots to Analyze Data, pages 56–67

1. a) independent: physical fitness; dependent: blood pressure

b) independent: level of education; dependent: income

c) independent: load in an airplane; dependent: length of runway needed for take off

2. a) Put wingspan on the horizontal axis.

b) As the length increases, so does the wingspan.

3. a) independent: number of days absent; dependent: science mark. Marks depend on attendance, rather than attendance depending on marks.

b)

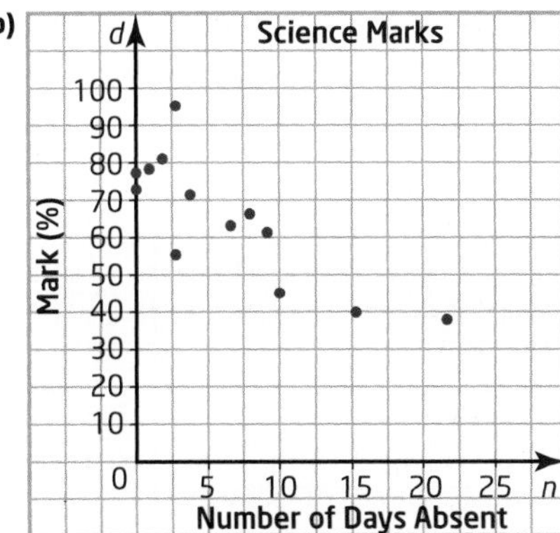

c) As the number of days absent increases, the marks generally decrease.

d) The point (3, 95) lies somewhat apart from the rest of the data.

4. a) independent: initial height; dependent: bounce height

b)

Bounce Heights

d

Bounce Height (m)

2.5
2.0
1.5
1.0
0.5
0

1.0 2.0 3.0 4.0 n

Initial Height (m)

c) As the initial height increases, so does the bounce height.

d) (4.00, 1.62) is an outlier. Discard only for a valid reason, such as a measurement error.

5. a)

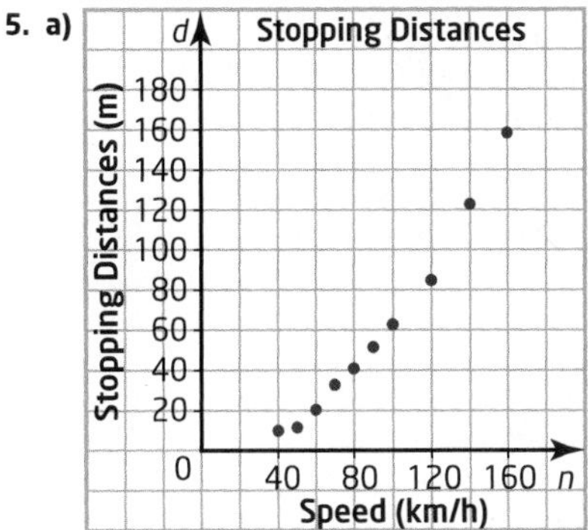

b) As the speed of a car increases, the stopping distance increases; the pattern is non-linear.

c) A car travelling at 85 km/h needs 46 m to stop. The point is not an outlier since it follows the pattern of the other data.

6. Answers will vary. Examples:

a) As person's height increases, so does the shoulder width.

d) Improve accuracy of measurements; use a larger sample.

7. Answers will vary. Examples:

a) Measure each athlete's height and the maximum height they can jump.

b) independent: height; dependent: jump height

c) If the hypothesis is true, then the points should follow a line or curve that rises to the right.

8. a)

Item	Fat (mg/g)	Energy (kJ/g)
Harvey's Original Hamburger	127	2.6
Harvey's Veggie Burger	63	2.2
Mr. Submarine Small Assorted Sub	34	1.6
Mr. Submarine Small Vegetarian Sub	26	1.5
Pizza Pizza Pepperoni Slice (walk-in)	69	2.3
Pizza Pizza Vegetarian Slice (walk-in)	43	1.8
KFC Chicken Breast	118	2.4
KFC Popcorn Chicken	184	3.3
Swiss Chalet Quarter Chicken Breast	75	1.9
Swiss Chalet Garden Salad, undressed	0	0.2
Swiss Chalet Caesar Salad	188	2.1

b) Content of Fast Foods

Energy (kJ/g)

3.5
3.0
2.5
2.0
1.5
1.0
0.5
0
100 200 300
Fat (mg/g)

c) The point for Caesar Salad is an outlier due to its high fat content. Nonetheless, this point represents valid data that should not be discarded.

d) Answers will vary. Example: Fast foods can have a high energy content without a high fat content.

9.

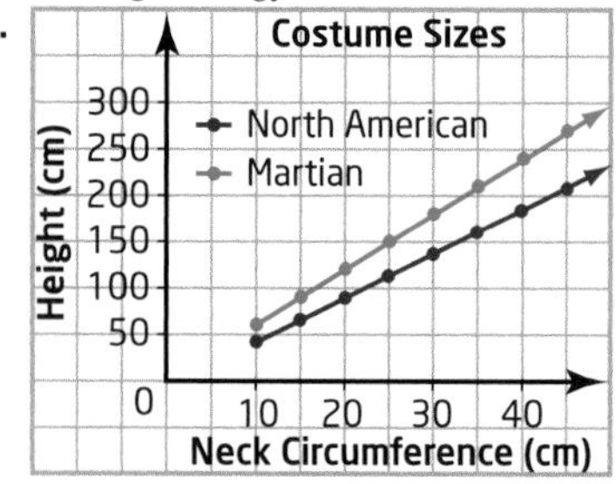

10. a)-c) Graphs will vary.

d) Home runs per at bat seem to increase somewhat as the number of strikeouts per at bat increases. The other two scatter plots do not show any relationship between the variables.

11. $\frac{1}{4} + \frac{2}{5} + \frac{3}{6} = 1\frac{3}{20}$

2.4 Trends, Interpolation, and Extrapolation, pages 68–76

1. a)

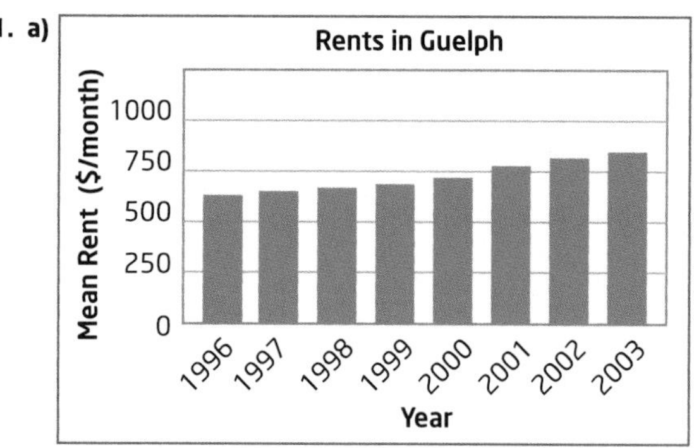

b) Rents increased every year.

c) about $986

2. a)

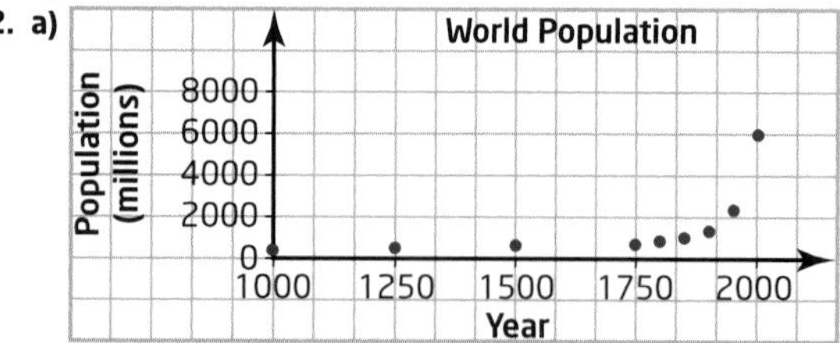

b) The world population is growing much more quickly now than in the past.

c) No; the graph shows an increasing rate of growth.

3. a)

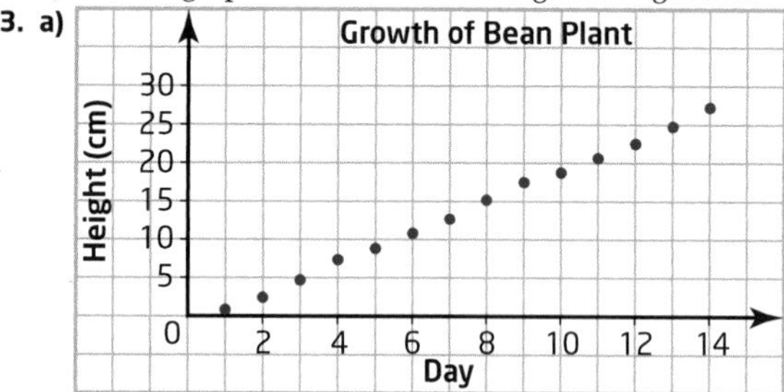

b) The height is increasing at a nearly constant rate.

c) The height will increase at a slower rate as the plant matures.

4. a)

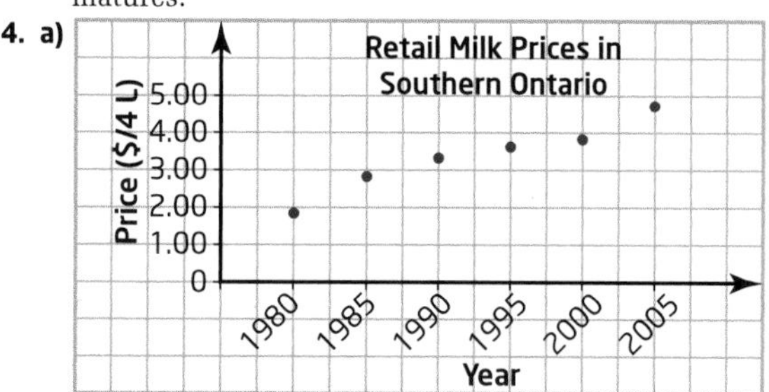

b) Milk prices increased over each 5-year period, but not at a constant rate.

c) about $3.69

d) 2020, assuming prices increase at the same overall rate

5. Bar graphs will vary depending on scale chosen for vertical axis.

a) The donation rate increases up to the 35–44 age group, then decreases somewhat.

b) Donation amounts increase with age up to the 45–54 interval, then decrease somewhat, but increase again for people over 74. Donation amounts are greater for people over 44 than for younger people.

c) Both graphs rise to a maximum for middle-aged people, then decease somewhat. However, the donation amount rises again in the 75+ interval while the donor rate continues to decrease.

6. a)

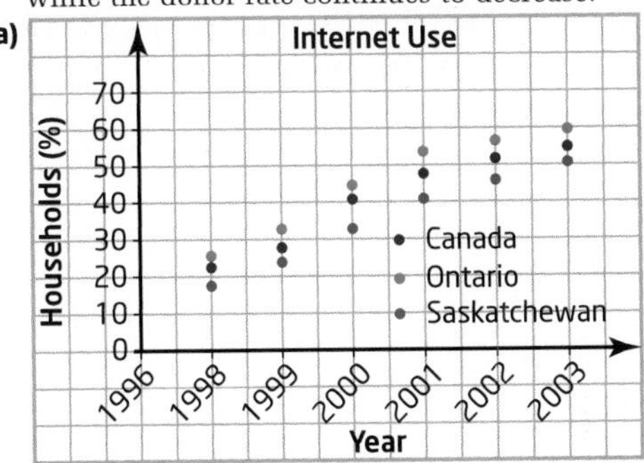

Internet use increased each year, with the national rate being about halfway between the rate in Ontario and the rate in Saskatchewan.

b) about 70%, assuming the rate of increase is constant

7. a)

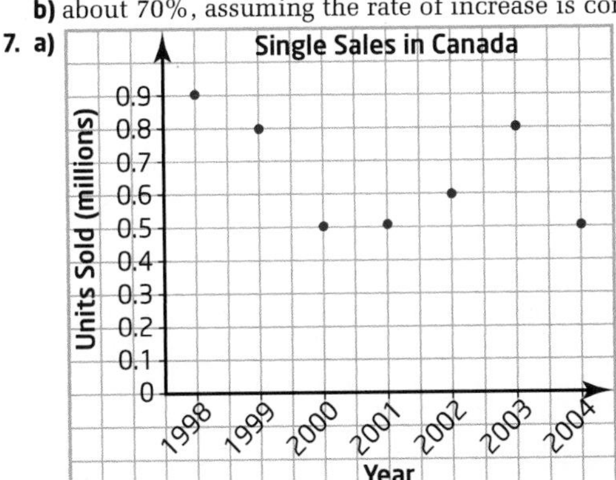

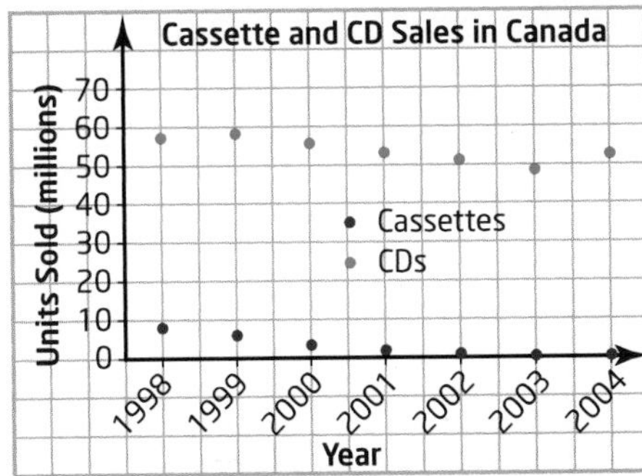

Overall, sales of singles have a downward trend. Sales of cassettes have a clear downward trend, while sales of CDs show a moderate downward trend.

b) Answers will vary. Example: singles, 0.5 million; cassettes, 0.05 million; CDs, 55 million

9. a) The volunteer rate in Ontario is about the same as for all Canadians except in the age group 25–34, when 5% fewer Ontarians volunteer.

b) Ages 45–54; people in this age range may have more free time.

c) As age increases, the hours per volunteer across Canada also increase, especially beyond the age of 65. Most people over 65 are retired and could have more time to volunteer.

10. Answers will vary.

11. B

12. 15 when the first or 100th day is a Saturday.

2.5 Linear and Non-Linear Relations, pages 77–87

1. a) Yes; the points lie close to a straight line.

b) No; the points lie close to a curve.

2. a) Linear; the points lie on a straight line.

b) Non-linear; the points lie on a curve.

3. a) Yes; points are reasonably close to a straight line.

b) No; the points follow a curve.

c) Yes; the points lie close to a straight line.

d) No; there is no apparent pattern.

e) No; there are not enough points to find a good line of best fit.

4. a)

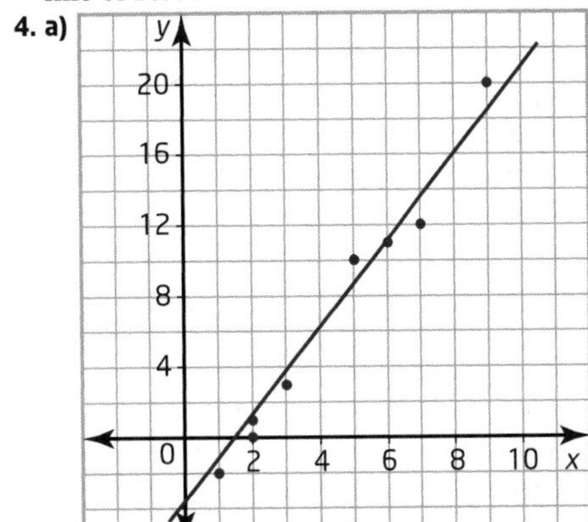

b)

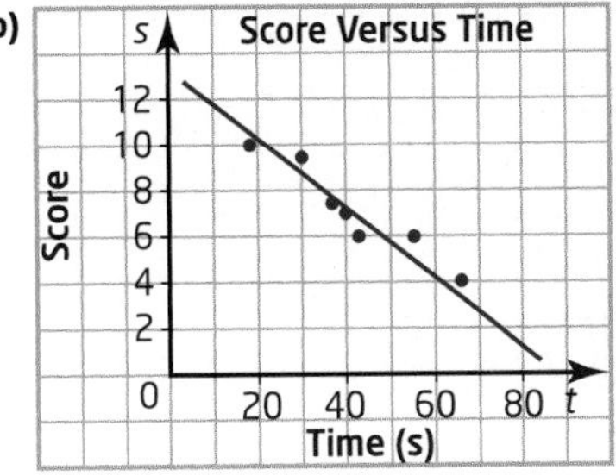

c)

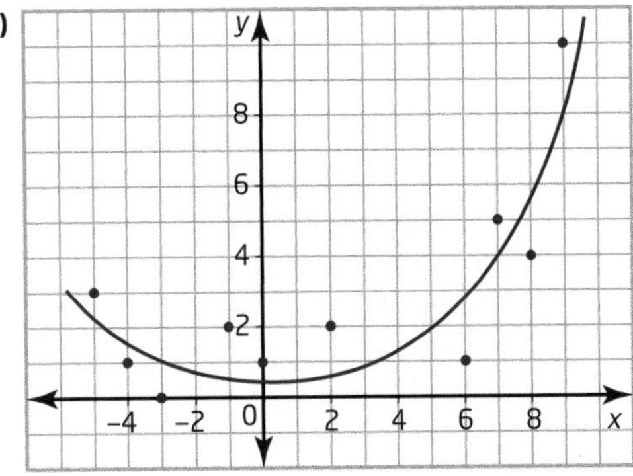

5. **a), b)**

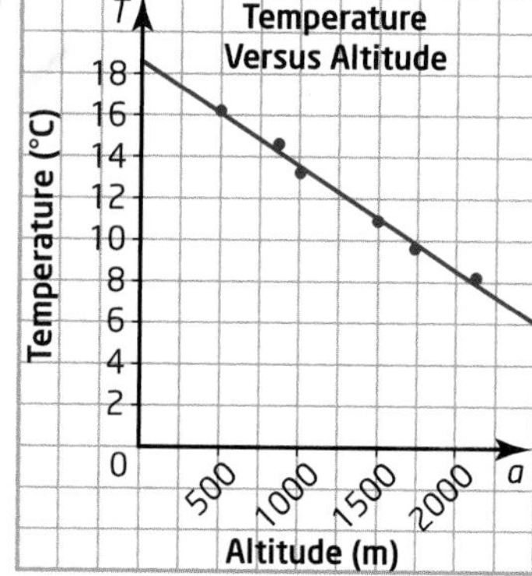

The temperature decreases linearly as the altitude increases.

c) 15.5°C **d)** 6.0°C

6. **a)**

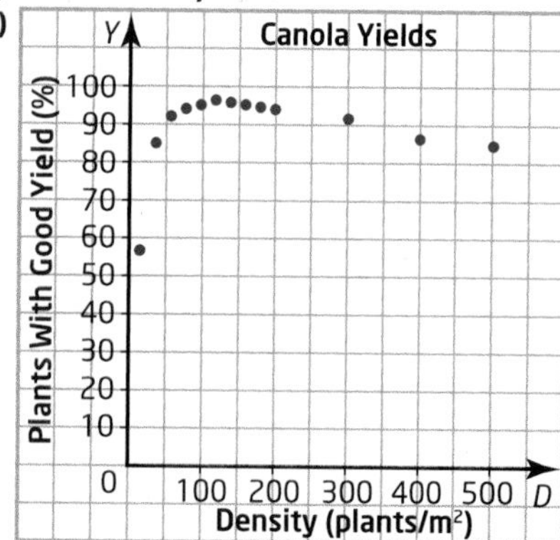

b) The yield rises steeply at first, levels off to a maximum around 120 plants/m^2, and then decreases slowly.

c) No; the points follow a curve.

d) Answers will vary. Examples: crowding out weeds, water and nutrients in the soil, pollination

7. **a), c)**

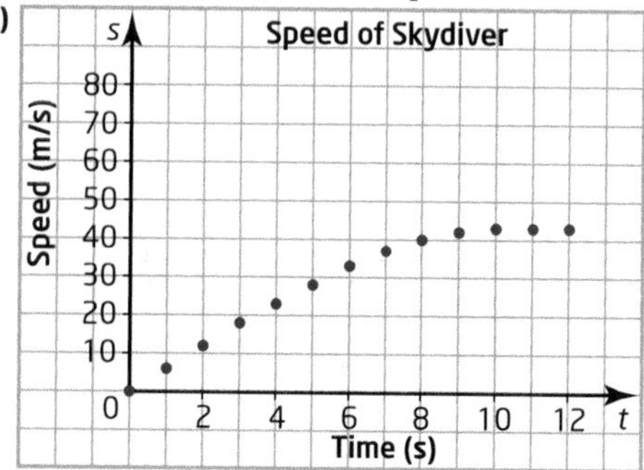

b) about 70 m/s

d) Air resistance increases with speed, so the speed increases only until the air resistance offsets the acceleration due to gravity.

e) The relationship between the variables may change beyond the range of the data.

8. Answers will vary. Examples:
   a) to investigate how a person's heart rate changes immediately after exercise
   b) A person's heart rate will decrease steadily in the time immediately after vigorous exercise.
9. Answers will vary.
11. **a)** Linear; each time t increases by 1, d increases by 5.
   b) Non-linear; h does not change by a constant amount each time t increases by 1.
12. There is a non-linear relation between the gauge reading and the volume of fuel in the tank. The eighths at the low end of the gauge correspond to less fuel than than the eighths at the "full" end of the gauge.
13. D
14. 60

2.6 Distance-Time Graphs, pages 88–94

1. **a)** moving away at constant speed
   b) moving away with increasing speed
   c) no movement
   d) moving closer at constant speed
   e) moving away at increasing speed, then slowing down and stopping
   f) moving away at decreasing speed, stopping for a moment, then coming back with increasing speed
2. Graphs a, c, d; the points lie on a line.
3. **a)** 4 h **b)** 6 km
   c) stopping at the end of the lake
   d) on the way back
4. After starting out, the cyclist increases her speed, then slows down. Then she travels a bit faster than before, then slows down and stops.
5. **a)** Move away from the wall at a constant speed, then walk back toward the wall at the same speed, but stop before you reach your starting position.
   b) The sloped line segments would be steeper.
   c) The sloped line segments would be less steep.
   d) The middle segment would be shorter and the horizontal segment would be higher.
6. Answers will vary.
7.

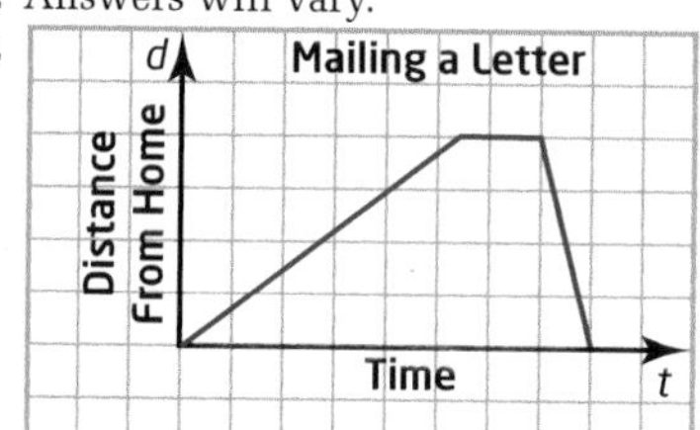

8.

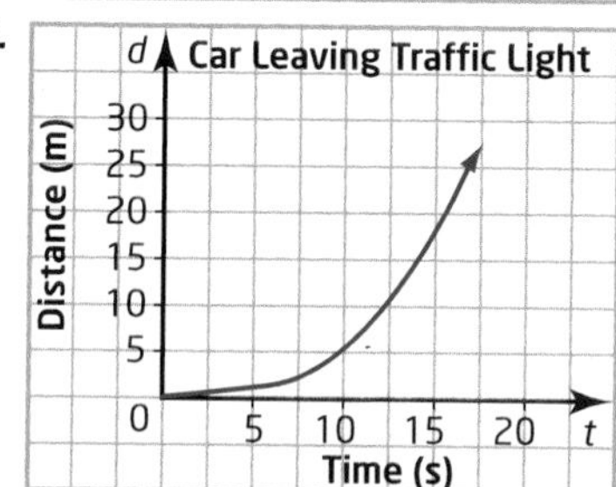

9.

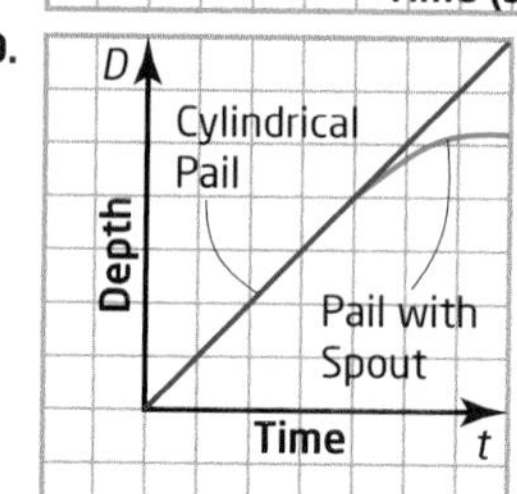

10. Answers will vary.

11. a) 3 km/h, 0 km/h, 4 km/h

b)

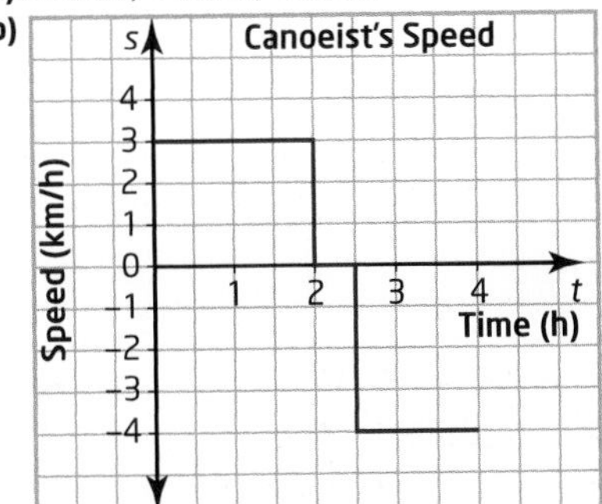

c) The faster the speed, the steeper the slope.

d) rate at which the canoeist moves toward the dock

12. d) horizontal: time; vertical: distance from the CBR™

e) No; the points do not lie close to a line

i) Yes; the points lie close to a line.

13. Answers will vary.

14. 1979

Chapter 2 Review, pages 95–96

1. Answers will vary. Examples:

a) Hypothesis: As the temperature in a town during the summer increases, so does the volume of water used by the town's residents. Opposite: As the temperature in a town during the summer increases, the volume of water used by the town's residents does not increase.

b) Hypothesis: Taller people have higher marks in mathematics. Opposite: Taller people do not have higher marks in mathematics.

2. a) Primary; a survey of students at the school could give more accurate results than secondary data would.

b) Secondary; primary data could take a lot of time to collect.

c) Secondary; the encyclopedia might not give information on bears in a specific province.

d) Secondary; the source of data is convenient, but may not reflect the tastes of students at the school.

3. a) students at the school

b) Answers will vary. Example: Use a graphing calculator to randomly select 25% of the students from the class lists for each grade.

4. a) passengers of the airline

b) Answers will vary. Example: Randomly select one name on a list of the airline's passengers, and then select every hundredth person before and after that name.

5. a) customers of the department store

b) campers at provincial parks

c) students at the school

Answers for survey methods will vary, but the methods should use random samples.

6. a)

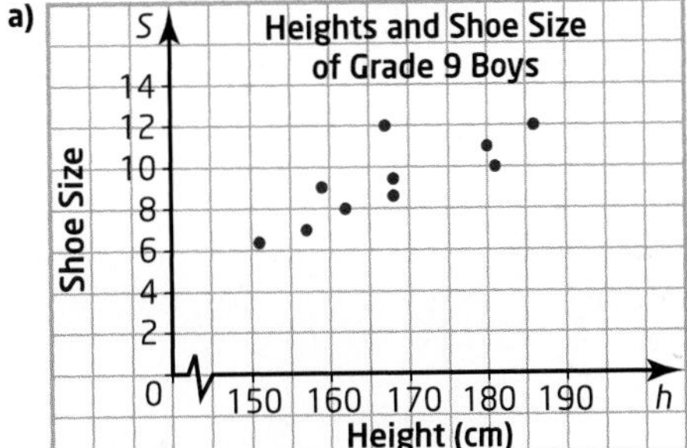

b) As the students' heights increase, so do their shoe sizes.

c) (167, 12) is an outlier, but should not be discarded since it is a valid measurement.

7. a)

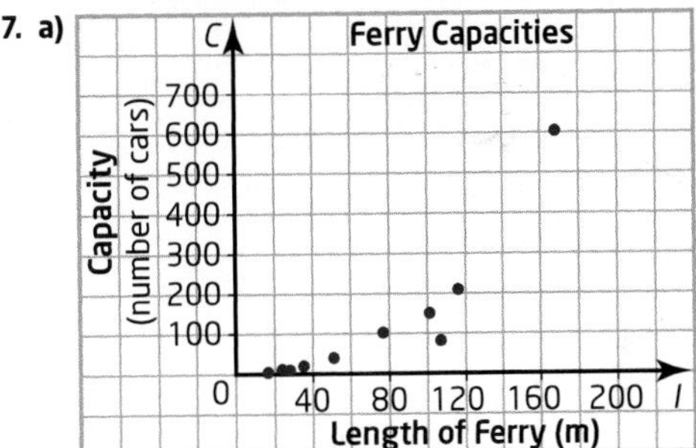

b) As the length of the ferry increases, the capacity also increases. The points follow a curve, so the relationship is non-linear.

c) The point (110.8, 80) is an outlier. Answers about causes may vary. Examples: The ferry might carry cargo as well as cars, or it might carry fewer cars so that it can travel faster.

8. a) Graphs may vary.

b) The population of Canada has grown at an increasing rate since 1861.

c) 20 million **d)** 40 million

9. a)

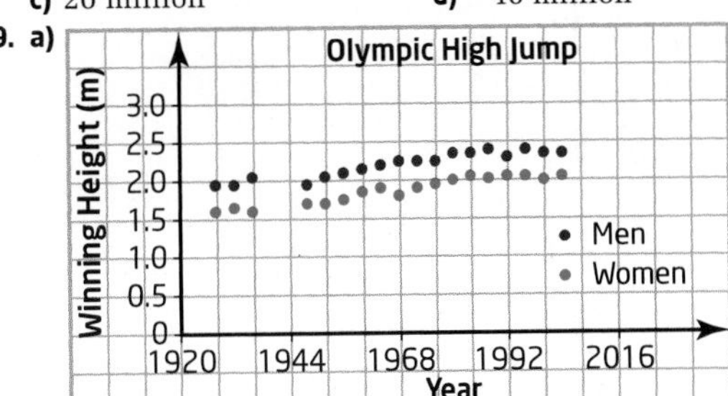

b) Both the men's and women's winning heights are increasing, but the rate of increase has been slower since about 1980.

c) no outliers

d) Answers will vary. Examples: Men's winning height about 2.48 m, women's winning height about 2.15 m

10. a)

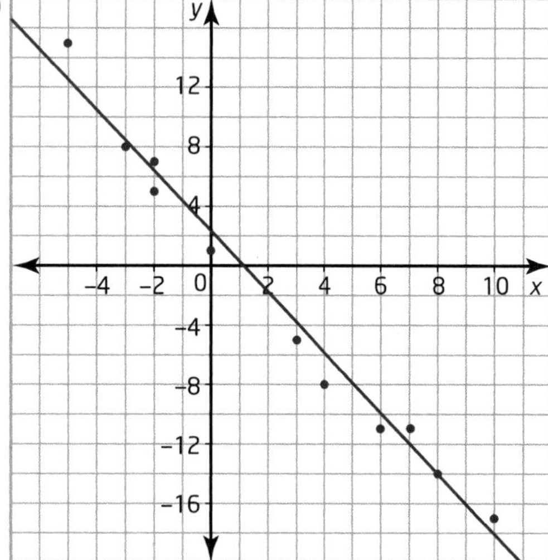

Yes; the points lie close to the line.

b)

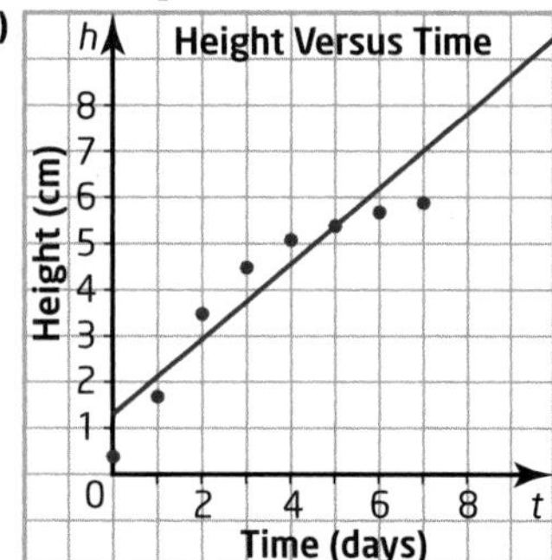

No; the points follow a curve.

11. a)

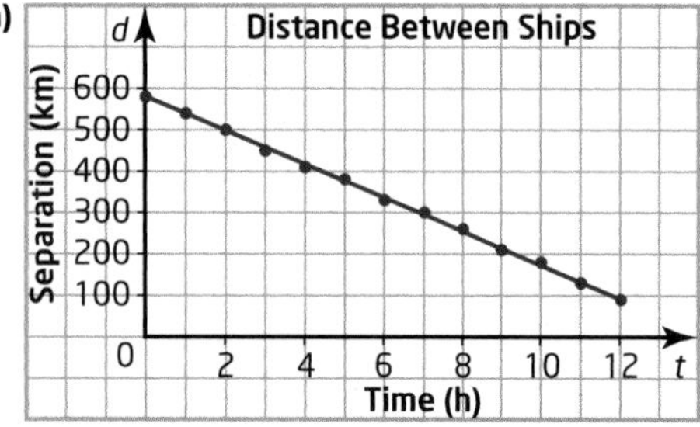

b) As time increases, the distance between the two ships decreases. The relationship is linear.

c) no outliers

d) after 14.3 h

12. Answers will vary. Examples:

a) Marni walks away from her home for 3 min at a constant speed, and then runs in the same direction at a constant speed.

b) John bikes from school to a store, buys something, and then bikes back past the school to home.

c) A car speeds up as it leaves a traffic light, and then slows down and stops at another light.

13. a)

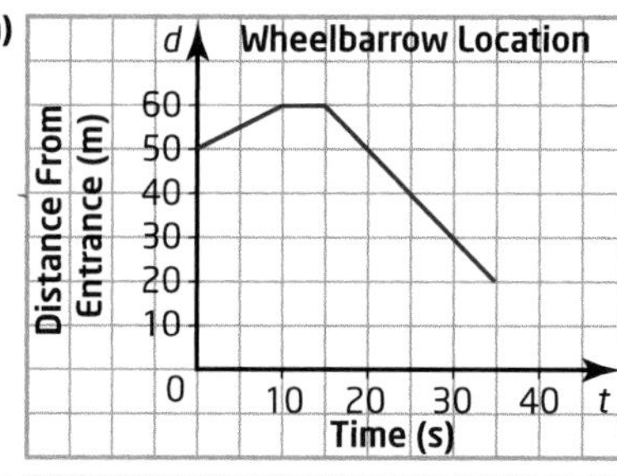

b)

Chapter 2 Test, pages 98–99

1. B
2. C
3. A
4. C
5. **a)** Caffeine cannot affect your sleep.
   b) If you study more, your results on tests either improve or stay the same.
   c) At least half of the students in your school do not have a part-time job.
   d) Cell phone use has not more than doubled in the past 2 years.
6. **a)** teachers working for the school board
   Answers will vary. Examples:
   b) Randomly select 20% of the teachers in each school.
   c) Select a name at random from a list of all of the teachers, and then select every fifth name before and after the first name selected.
   d) Survey all the teachers in the nearest school.
   e) Teachers at the school have the same students and work conditions. These teachers may not have the same concerns and opinions as teachers at other schools.
7. **a)** Non-linear; the points follow a curve.
   b) Linear; the points lie close to a straight line.
8. AB: distance decreasing at a steady rate; BC: distance increasing at a steady rate; CD: no motion; DE: distance increasing at an increasing rate; EF: distance increasing at a decreasing rate.
9. Answers will vary.
10. **a), d)**

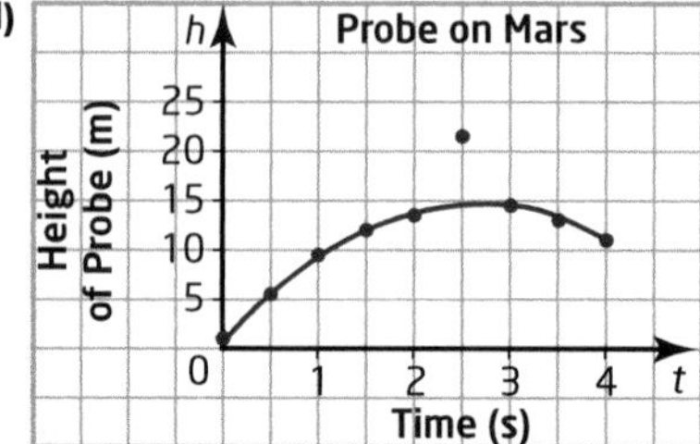

b) Non-linear: As time increases, the height increases and then decreases.
c) (2.5, 21.4) is an outlier. Possible causes include an inaccurate reading or a transmission error.
e) 4.7 m

Chapter 3

Get Ready, pages 102–103

1. a) 12 **b)** 7 **c)** −4 **d)** 9 **e)** 2 **f)** −2 **g)** −14 **h)** 4
2. a) −3 **b)** 13 **c)** 5 **d)** −1 **e)** −15 **f)** 2 **g)** −13 **h)** −1
3. a) −24 **b)** 24 **c)** −32 **d)** 30 **e)** −60 **f)** −40
4. a) −2 **b)** −3 **c)** −2 **d)** 1 **e)** −5 **f)** 9
5. a) $\frac{4}{15}$ **b)** $-\frac{1}{12}$ **c)** $-\frac{2}{15}$ **d)** $\frac{3}{20}$ **e)** $-\frac{3}{10}$ **f)** $-\frac{3}{4}$
6. a) $-\frac{1}{10}$ **b)** $\frac{1}{4}$ **c)** −0.57 **d)** 0.12 **e)** 8.0 **f)** −30.4

3.1 Build Algebraic Models Using Concrete Materials, pages 104–109

1. C
2. a)–d) Tile models may vary.
3. a) $x + 3$ **b)** $x^2 + 2$ **c)** $2x^2 + x + 6$ **d)** $x^2 + 4x + 4$
4. a) 4 km **b)** 7 km **c)** x kilometres **d)** $4x$ kilometres
5. Answers will vary.
6. a)

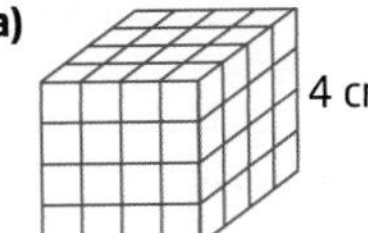

b) 4^3 cm^3
c) $A = 4^2 = 16$; Area = 16 cm^2
7. a) 6 cm **b)** 36 cm^2
8. a) 7 m **b)** 343 m^3
9. a) **b)**

10. 24 cm^2
11. Answers will vary.
12. $1^6 + 5^2 + 4^3 = 90$
13. C
14. Answers will vary.

3.2 Work With Exponents, pages 110–118

1. B
2. C
3. a) $(-5)^3$ **b)** 1.05^6 **c)** $\left(-\frac{3}{5}\right)^3$
4. a) $(-4) \times (-4) \times (-4) = -64$ **b)** $0.8 \times 0.8 = 0.64$
c) $\frac{3}{4} \times \frac{3}{4} \times \frac{3}{4} \times \frac{3}{4} = \frac{81}{256}$
5. a) 729 **b)** 49 **c)** −16 **d)** $\frac{125}{216}$ **e)** $\frac{16}{81}$ **f)** 1.44 **g)** 1 **h)** −1 **i)** 0.125
6. a) 2 **b)** 100 **c)** 1 **d)** 10 **e)** $\frac{1}{6}$ **f)** 734.66
7. a) 150 **b)** 19.6 **c)** 25 **d)** 86.4 **e)** 14.1 **f)** 24
8. a) 4, −8, 16, −32
b) When the exponent is odd, the power is negative, and when the exponent is even, the power is positive.
c) Negative bases will give a positive answer if the exponent is even ($(-1)^2 = -1 \times -1 = 1$) and a negative answer if the exponent is odd ($(-1)^3 = -1 \times -1 \times -1 = -1$).
9. a)

Time (min)	Population of Listeria
0	800
60	1 600
120	3 200
180	6 400
240	12 800

b)

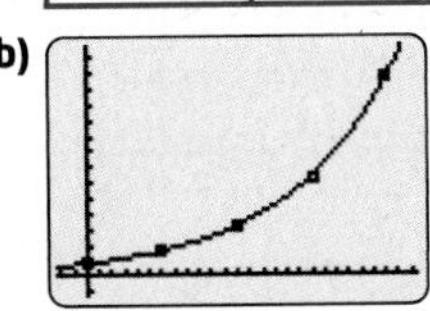

The graph is non-linear. It is increasing, as an upward curve.
c) 800×2^{24}, 800×2^{48}
d) Food poisoning will occur much faster if a large quantity of the bacteria is ingested rather than a smaller quantity because it will take the bacteria longer to multiply to a harmful amount. A faster growth rate of bacteria will cause the food poisoning to begin rapidly while a slower growth rate of bacteria will cause the food poisoning to start at a relatively slower rate.
10. a)

Time (min)	Population of Listeria	Population of E. Coli
0	800	10
20		20
40		40
60	1600	80
80		160
100		320
120	3200	640

b) after 3 h **c)** about 7000

11.

Note	Duration (in beats)	Power Form
whole	1	
half	$\frac{1}{2}$	$\left(\frac{1}{2}\right)^1$
quarter	$\frac{1}{4}$	$\left(\frac{1}{2}\right)^2$
eighth	$\frac{1}{8}$	$\left(\frac{1}{2}\right)^3$
sixteenth	$\frac{1}{16}$	$\left(\frac{1}{2}\right)^4$
thirty-second	$\frac{1}{32}$	$\left(\frac{1}{2}\right)^5$

12. $\left(\frac{1}{2}\right)^0 = 1$. Any base (except 0) to the exponent 0 is equal to 1.

13. a) Let the area of the rectangle be A.
Let the width of the rectangle be w.
Let the height of the rectangle be h.
Then, $A = w \times h$. Since $h = 2w$, $A = 2w^2$.
b) 128 cm^2 c) 12 cm

14. a)

Number of Half-Life Periods	Time (min)	Amount of U-238 Remaining (mg)	Expression
0	0	100	
1	23	50	$100\left(\frac{1}{2}\right)^1$
2	46	25	$100\left(\frac{1}{2}\right)^2$
3	69	12.5	$100\left(\frac{1}{2}\right)^3$
4	92	6.25	$100\left(\frac{1}{2}\right)^4$

b)

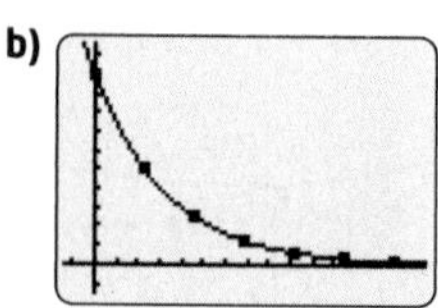

The graph has a decreasing non-linear (curved) trend.
c) 2.69 mg d) 152.8 min
e) $100\left(\frac{1}{2}\right)^0$. Yes, this does make sense.

15. a) 4.5×10^9 b) 1.4×10^{17}
c) 602 200 000 000 000 000 000 000
d) Answers will vary. Very large and very small numbers can be represented using a lot less space. It is also easier to understand scientific notation than trying to count the number of zeros in very large or very small numbers. It also reduces the probability of errors when rewriting these numbers.

16. a) 7, 63 b) 9th day c) $C = 2^n$
d) Answers will vary. Assume that the trend continues without any change.

17. 9

18. C

19. 1, 4, 8, 16, 32, 64, 128, 256, 512, 9, 27, 81, 243, 729, 25, 125, 625, 36, 49, 216, 343, 121, 144, 169, 196, 225, 289, 324, 361, 400, 441, 484, 529, 576, 676, 784, 841, 900, 961

20. Use a table or a spreadsheet to find a pattern.

$x = 1$	$y = 0$
$x = 2$	$y \le 1$ or $y \ge 5$
$x = 3$	$y \le 2$ or $y \ge 4$
$x \ge 4$	$y \le 1$ or $y > x$

3.3 Discover the Exponent Laws, pages 119–129

1. B
2. a) $3^{11} = 177\,147$ b) $2^8 = 256$
c) $(-1)^{11} = -1$ d) $\left(\frac{2}{5}\right)^6 = \frac{64}{15\,625}$
3. D
4. a) $12^6 = 2\,985\,984$ b) $(-6)^1 = -6$
c) $\left(-\frac{3}{4}\right)^3 = -\frac{27}{64}$ d) $(0.1)^0 = 1$
5. A
6. a) $4^4 = 256$ b) $(-3)^6 = 729$
c) $(-0.1)^8 = 0.000\,000\,001$ d) $\left(\frac{3}{2}\right)^6 = \frac{729}{64}$
7. a) $5^1 = 5$ b) $3^3 = 27$
c) $(0.5)^2 = 0.25$ d) $(-2)^0 = 1$
8. a) y^6 b) m^3 c) k^{10}
d) c^{12} e) a^5b^3 f) $8u^3v^6$
g) m^3n^3 h) hk^2 i) a^6b^2
9. a) $3km^3$ b) $-32a^{11}$ c) $-9x^{10}$
d) dw^4 e) $\frac{2}{3}fg$ f) $9a^2$
g) $5cd$ h) $-27xy^3$ i) $4g^2$
10. a) $-\frac{15}{2}$ b) $-\frac{15}{2}$
c) Answers will vary. Substituting values into a simplified expression is much easier than substituting into the original expression. The disadvantage is that it is easy to make a mistake when simplifying the expression.
11. 10 000 m^3
12. a) 6 heads: $\frac{1}{64}$; 12 heads: $\frac{1}{4096}$
b) $\left(\left(\frac{1}{2}\right)^2\right)^3$, $\left(\left(\frac{1}{2}\right)^2\right)^6$
13. a) $\frac{1}{6}$ b) $\frac{1}{1296}$ c) $\frac{1}{3}$ d) $\frac{1}{6561}$
e) $\left(\left(\frac{1}{6}\right)^2\right)^2$, $\left(\left(\frac{1}{3}\right)^4\right)^2$
15. a) $8 \times 10^5 = 800\,000$ b) $9 \times 10^{10} = 90\,000\,000\,000$
c) $4 \times 10^2 = 400$ d) $1.3 \times 10^4 = 13\,000$
16. a) Answers will vary. b) 0.15
17. a) Answers will vary. b) 5.0×10^{15}
18. a) $8 \times 10^{15} = 8\,000\,000\,000\,000\,000$
b) Answers will vary. $(a^x \times 10^y)^z = a^{xz} \times 10^{yz}$
19. The missing entries, from top to bottom, are a^5b^2, $a^{17}b^{14}$, and $a^{11}b^8$.
20. x^3, x^2, x, $\sqrt{x}$, $\frac{1}{x}$

3.4 Communicate With Algebra, pages 130–139

1. a) coefficient: 2, variable: y
b) coefficient: -3, variable: x
c) coefficient: 1, variable: mn
d) coefficient: $\frac{1}{2}$, variable: x^2
e) coefficient: -1, variable: w^2
f) coefficient: -0.4, variable: gh^3

2. C

3. a) monomial **b)** trinomial **c)** binomial **d)** trinomial **e)** binomial **f)** four-term polynomial

4. B

5. a) 2 **b)** 1 **c)** 0 **d)** 6 **e)** 5 **f)** 3

6. a) 1 **b)** 2 **c)** 3 **d)** 7 **e)** 6

7. B

8. a) C, D
b) Yes. C shows a coefficient of 1 and D does not, but $1t = t$.

9. a) 11 **b)** -4 **c)** 11 **d)** -1

10. a) s **b)** $0.37s$ **c)** \$9.62 **d)** \$1575.27

11. a) $5s + 7a$
b)

Term	Variable	Coefficient	Meaning
5*s*	*s*	5	*s*: number of student memberships she sells
7*a*	*a*	7	*a*: number of adult memberships she sells

c) \$130

12. a) $25g + 18r + 15b$
b)

Term	Variable	Coefficient	Meaning
25*g*	*g*	25	*g*: number of gold seats sold
18*r*	*r*	18	*r*: number of red seats sold
15*b*	*b*	15	*b*: number of blue seats sold

c) \$10 000

13. a) $2c - w$ **b)** 27

14. Answers will vary.

15. Answers will vary. Example:
Hello Manuel,
A term is made up of a coefficient (a number) and a variable (e.g., *a*, *x*, *j*), but there are no mathematical operations (addition, subtraction) involved. A polynomial is a set of terms being added or subtracted (e.g., $7x + 5y$).
Jill

16. a) height $= 2w$ **b)** 10 cm **c)** 12.5 cm

18. a) Answers will vary. *s*: swim, *c*: cycle, *r*: run.
b)

Part of the Race	Speed (km/h)	Distance (km)	Time (h)
Swim	1.2	*s*	$\frac{s}{1.2}$
Cycle	25	*c*	$\frac{c}{25}$
Run	10	*r*	$\frac{r}{10}$

c) $\frac{s}{1.2} + \frac{c}{25} + \frac{r}{10}$
d) 3.85 h or 3 h 51 min
e) Answers will vary. It is a reasonable time considering all the things he has to complete in only 3.85 h.

19. a) Answers will vary. Walking is faster.
b) 17.5 s **c)** $\frac{s}{1}$; 26.9 s
d) Walking is faster by 9.4 s.

20. a) Answers will vary.
b) 22.25 s; Walking all the way is faster.
c) Walking all the way takes 17.5 s and it is the fastest way. Find the time for all three ways and compare the times.

21. a) Let an *x*-tile represent $0.1v$, and show one of them.
b) Let a *y*-tile represent $100s$, and show three of them.
c) Let an *x*-tile represent \$100.

d) \$65 500

22. C

23. B

24. $m = 2$. Yes, this expression is true for all values of m.

3.5 Collect Like Terms, pages 144–153

1. B

2. a) like terms **b)** unlike terms **c)** like terms **d)** unlike terms **e)** unlike terms **f)** unlike terms **g)** like terms **h)** like terms

3. $3x^2, 4x^2; -x, 7x; xy, -4xy; 2y^2, y^2; 5x^2y, 3x^2y; -7y, \frac{1}{2}y$

4. Answers will vary.
a) $3m, 9m$ **b)** $4x, -6x$ **c)** $9y^2, 7y^2$ **d)** $-ab, 2ab$

5. a) $9x$
b) The terms cannot be added together because they are not like terms.
c) $15h$ **d)** $12u$

6. a) $2k$ **b)** $7n$ **c)** $-4z$
d) These are not like terms, so it is not possible to simplify.

7. a) $5x + 6$ **b)** $8y + 11$ **c)** $8k + 7m$ **d)** $8u + 2v$ **e)** $5n + 3$ **f)** $3p + 4q$

8. a) $-x - 5$ **b)** $-5y - 16$ **c)** $6x^2 + 8x$ **d)** $7m^2 + 5m$ **e)** $-2k + 4$ **f)** $u^2 - 6$

9. a) $4b^2 + 2ab + 3b + 1$ **b)** $5m^2 + n^2 - 1$

10. a) Claudette: $7t + 100$, Johanna: $7t + 125$, Ming: $7t + 110$
b) Claudette: \$240, Johanna: \$300, Ming: \$299
c) $7t + 335$ **d)** \$839

11. a) Yannick added the constants to the coefficients of the *x*-terms. He did not realize that 4 is an unlike term.
b) Answers will vary. Example: Substitute any value for *x* into the original expression and into the simplified expression.
c) $9x + 4$. Verify by substituting a value for *x* into the expressions.

12. a) $2(w + 3w)$ **b)** 2400 m
c) 200 m wide and 600 m long

13. a) $8x + 5$ **b)** $3y + 1$ **c)** $3y + 10$

14. a) $6w, 7w$ **b)** 70 cm

15. **a)** $3x$

b) The perimeter of the isosceles triangle is $2x + x\sqrt{2}$, which is greater than the perimeter of the equilateral triangle.

16. The area of the isosceles triangle is $\frac{x^2}{2}$, which is greater than the area of the equilateral triangle, which is $\frac{x^2\sqrt{3}}{4}$.

17. D

18. C

3.6 Add and Subtract Polynomials, pages 154–159

1. C

2. **a)** $10x + 9$ **b)** $7y + 5$ **c)** $7m - 9$ **d)** $-2d - 1$ **e)** $10k + 5$ **f)** $3r$

3. A

4. **a)** $x - 3$ **b)** $7s$ **c)** $4m + 3$ **d)** $7v - 17$ **e)** 17 **f)** $10h + 3$

5. **a)** $8x - 13$ **b)** $2y + 3$ **c)** $7c - 13$ **d)** $-2k + 4$ **e)** $12p^2 - 4p$ **f)** $2xy^2 + 12x - 14y$ **g)** $3x + 10$ **h)** $6uv^2 - 4v - 12u$

6. **a)** $8500 + 0.6n$

b) 100 copies: $8560, gold status: $38 500, diamond status: $608 500

c)

Status	Musician
gold	Fredrick
platinum	Fredrick
diamond	Fredrick

d) Answers will vary. Example: **Fixed rate**: If there are few sales, the musician still makes some money. However, if there are lots of sales, the musician does not profit as much as they would with other methods of payment. **Royalty**: The more sales that are made, the more money the musician makes. The musician, however, will make no money if there are no sales. **Combination**: The musician still gets the fixed rate if there are no sales but receives some royalties if there are sales. The downside is that the fixed rate is smaller than if they were just being paid by a fixed rate and the royalties rate is also smaller than if they were just receiving royalties.

7. **a)** $190\ 000 + 100b$ **b)** $198 900

8. **a)** $5x + 7$ **b)** $2y^2 + 5y + 3$ **c)** $4x^2 + 4x + 6y^2$

9. **a)**

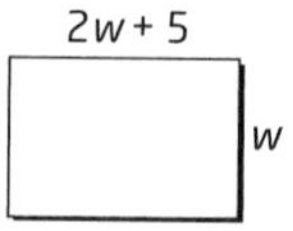

b) $6w + 10$ **c)** 46 m

10. **a)** Answers will vary. **b)** 82 m

11. No. Width = w, Length = $2w + 5$, Perimeter = $2(3w + 5)$. When the width changes, the length and the perimeter also change but not by the same factor. So, the proportions between the three do not change; only their actual values change.

12. **a)** missing expressions: step 1: $-11k$ and $-2p - 2k$; step 2: $-14k + 11p$ and $-2p - 13k$; step 3: $-27k + 9p$.

b) Answers will vary.

3.7 The Distributive Property, pages 160–169

1. D

2. **a)** $2x + 6$ **b)** $x^2 + 4x$ **c)** $5x + 13$

3. **a)** $4x + 8$ **b)** $5k - 15$ **c)** $-2y - 2$ **d)** $8d - 16$ **e)** $10t - 15$ **f)** $-4y + 5$

4. **a)** $y^2 - 4y$ **b)** $r^2 + 5r$ **c)** $2x^2 - 5x$ **d)** $-4q^2 + 8q$ **e)** $-3z^2 + 2z$ **f)** $-m^2 - 5m$

5. **a)** $6b^2 - 10b$ **b)** $24v^2 + 21v$ **c)** $-12w^2 + 4w$ **d)** $6m^2 + 30m$ **e)** $-8q^2 + 6q$ **f)** $3d^2 - 6d$

6. **a)** $4n - 20$ **b)** $18p + 36$ **c)** $-28m - 24$ **d)** $3c^2 + 21c$ **e)** $12w - 6$ **f)** $-12k^2 - 21k$

7. **a)** $2a^2 + 10a + 6$ **b)** $-6n^2 + 24n - 15$ **c)** $4k^3 + 4k^2 - 12k$ **d)** $-15h^3 + 35h^2 + 10h$ **e)** $-3x^2 + 15x - 6$ **f)** $8y^3 + 12y^2 - 4y$

8. **a)** $7x - 14$ **b)** -10 **c)** $-u + 5v$ **d)** -22 **e)** $-5a - b$ **f)** 0

9. **a)** $9x - 24$ **b)** $10y - 25$ **c)** $3k - 6$ **d)** $-4r + 60$ **e)** $-6h + 4$ **f)** $3p - 12$

10. **a)** $50 + 30h$ **b)** $125 **c)** $100 + 60h$

d) $250. Yes, the answer makes sense.

11. Niko is right. The order of operations always apply and if there is no other way to simplify the expression according to the order of operations, then the expression is in simplified form.

12. $A = \frac{ah}{2} + \frac{bh}{2}$

13. **a)** $10x + 2$ **b)** $6x^2 + 2x$

c) $P = 30x + 6$, $A = 54x^2 + 18x$

d) Yes. Triple the old perimeter is $3(10x + 2)$ or $30x + 6$, which is equal to the new perimeter

e) No. Triple the old area is $3(6x^2 + 2x)$ or $18x^2 + 6x$, which is not equal to the new area

14. Yes. Example:

$2(5 - 3)$
$= 2(2)$
$= 4$

$2(5 - 3)$
$= 2 \times 5 - 2 \times 3$
$= 10 - 6$
$= 4$

15. **a)** $5x + 9$ **b)** $k - 14$ **c)** $1.4p^2 - 1.8p$ **d)** $-2h^2 - 11h$ **e)** $3j^2 - 12j$ **f)** $-2w^2 + 0.3w$ **g)** -8 **h)** $k^2 - 6k - 3$

16. **a)** $2a + \frac{1}{6}$ **b)** $-\frac{x}{6}$ **c)** $-4m + \frac{1}{6}$ **d)** $-\frac{23}{5}u + \frac{27}{4}v$

18. **a)** $-4m^2 - 12m$ **b)** $-9p^3 - 24p^2$ **c)** $-2x + 36$ **d)** $-y - 81$

19. **a)** $2x^2 + 4x - 6$. Yes, they are equivalent.

b) Answers will vary.

c) Answers will vary. For example, multiply the first term in the first binomial by each term in the second binomial, and then multiply the second term in the first binomial by each term in the second binomial. Simplify the resulting polynomial by collecting like terms.

20. $k^3 - k^2 - 3k - 1$

21. $x = 6$

Chapter 3 Review, pages 174–175

1. a) 4 **b)** $2x$ **c)** $x + 3$ **d)** $2x$

2. a) 3 cm

b) 27 cm^3; 3^3 cm^3

c) 9 cm^2; 3^2 cm^2

3. a) 1024 **b)** 81 **c)** $\frac{8}{125}$ **d)** 1.4775

4. a) \$133.82 **b)** \$179.08

5. 6%

6. a)

Number of Half-Life Periods	Years	Amount of C-14 Remaining (g)	Expression
0	0	50	
1	5 700	25	$50\left(\frac{1}{2}\right)^1$
2	11 400	12.5	$50\left(\frac{1}{2}\right)^2$
3	17 100	6.25	$50\left(\frac{1}{2}\right)^3$
4	22 800	3.125	$50\left(\frac{1}{2}\right)^4$

b)

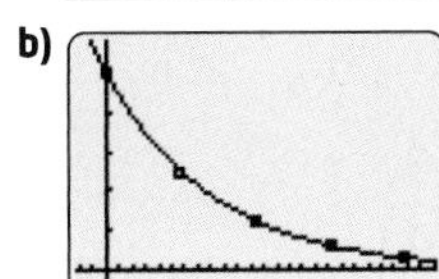

c) Students should use their graphs to interpolate an answer close to about 4.4 g.

d) Students should use their graphs to extrapolate an answer close to about 32 000 years.

7. a) $2^9 = 512$ **b)** $6^2 = 36$

c) $(-4)^6 = 4096$ **d)** $7^1 = 7$

8. a) n^4 **b)** c^5d^5 **c)** $\frac{3}{8}a^2b$

9. a) coefficient: 5, variable: y

b) coefficient: 1, variable: uv

c) coefficient: $\frac{1}{2}$, variable: ab^2

d) coefficient: -1, variable: de^2f

e) coefficient: 8, variable: none

10. a) trinomial **b)** monomial **c)** four-term polynomial

d) monomial **e)** binomial

11. a) $3w + 2o + l$, where w represents a win, o represents an overtime win, and l represents an overtime loss.

b) 16

12. a) 2 **b)** 4 **c)** 0 **d)** 4

13. a) 1 **b)** 2 **c)** 2 **d)** 3

14. a) $2p$, p **b)** $5x^2$, $-5x^2$, $3x^2$

15. a) $10x + 2$ **b)** $6k - m$

c) $3a^2 - 1$ **d)** $6x^2 + 5y^2 - 8$

16. a) $7x + 1$ **b)** $8k - 7$ **c)** $4u - 4$

d) $-y^2 + 2y$ **e)** $a^2 - 4$ **f)** $4v - 6$

17. $10x - 10$

18. a) $3y - 21$ **b)** $-2x - 6$ **c)** $5m^2 - 3m$

d) $-8k^2 - 24k$ **e)** $-5p^2 - 15p + 5$ **f)** $4b^3 - 8b^2 + 20b$

19. a) $14q - 2$ **b)** $4x^2 - 20x - 24$

c) 10 **d)** $d^2 - 3d - 20$

20. a) $6x - 22$ **b)** $-9k - 9$

Chapter 3 Practice Test, pages 176–177

1. D

2. B

3. C

4. D

5. C

6. B

7. D

8. B

9. A

10. a) $(-2)^6 = 64$ **b)** $3^2 = 9$

11. a) k^3n^7 **b)** $-2p^3$ **c)** $-27g^6h^3$

12. a) $7x + 4$ **b)** $-2u - 3$

13. a) $9y$ **b)** $-27b + 7$

14. a) They are both correct. It is possible for the expressions to be equal. Use the distributive property to expand the right side of James's formula.

b) $P = l + l + w + w$, $P = l + w + l + w$; These can both be simplified to Sylvia's formula, which is equivalent to James's formula.

c) Answers will vary.

15. a) 128

b) ninth; I used patterns of powers to determine that 2^n students receive the e-mail on the nth mailing.

c) 1022 **d)** 8

16. a) $5n + 5500$

b) 200 copies: \$6500, 5000 copies: \$30 500

17. a) 2^{63} **b)** $2^{64} - 1$

Chapters 1 to 3 Review, pages 178–179

1. a) 11, 16, 22: add consecutive integers (1, 2, 3, …) to the previous term

b) 25, 36, 49: the sequence shows the number of the term squared (term 2 is 2^2 or 4)

c) -3, -8, -13: subtract 5 from the previous term

d) 30, 42, 56: add consecutive even integers, starting from 4 (4, 6, 8, 10, …), to the previous term

2. A = 2, B = 40, D = $\frac{9}{10}$, E = 20. Strategy: Substitute the given value of 100 for C in equation 2 and solve for A, and then substitute that value for A in equation 1. Solve for B and substitute that value for B in equation 3. Solve for D and substitute the value into equation 4 and solve for E.

3. 14

4. 110 cm

5. a) $\frac{7}{24}$ **b)** $-\frac{1}{24}$ **c)** $\frac{5}{12}$ **d)** $\frac{1}{24}$

6. -3°C

7. 28 **Strategy**: A prime number cannot be a perfect number. Skip all prime numbers. Factor each number and calculate the sum of the factors.

8. Answers will vary. Example: Count how many breaths you take in a minute, multiply by the number of minutes in an hour, hours in a day, and days in a year (number of breaths × 60 × 24 × 365).

9. No. Every odd number can be represented as the sum of an even number and 1. So, let the odd numbers be represented by $a + 1$, $b + 1$, $c + 1$, $d + 1$, and $e + 1$.

Their sum is

$(a + 1) + (b + 1) + (c + 1) + (d + 1) + (e + 1)$
$= a + b + c + d + e + 5$

The sum of even numbers is an even number, so $a + b + c + d + e$ is an even number. The sum of an even number plus an odd number is an odd number, so $a + b + c + d + e + 5$ is an odd number. Thus, five odd numbers cannot have a sum of 50.

Since the sum of five odd numbers must be an odd number, the sum of six odd numbers is an odd number plus an odd number, which gives an even number. So, six odd numbers can have a sum of 50. An example is $3 + 5 + 7 + 9 + 11 + 15 = 50$.

10. a) Answers will vary. Example: $4 + 9 = 13$
b) Answers will vary. Example: $10° + 20° = 30°$
c) Answers will vary. Example: $2 + 7 = 9$

11. a) Answers will vary.
b) Answers will vary. Example: Conduct a stratified random sample survey by grade of your school. This is primary data.

12. a) Answers will vary. Example: A simple random sample of 20% of the grade 9 girls.
b) Answers will vary. Example: Stratified random sample by grade.

13. a)

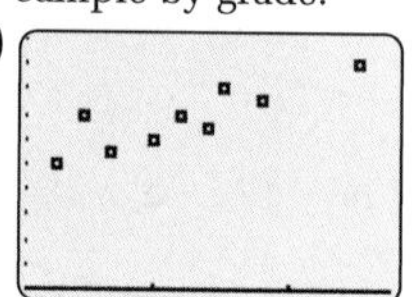

b) The taller the student, the greater the shoe size.
c) There are no outliers. Outliers should not be disregarded unless the data were inaccurate or unrepresentative.

14. a) the 50 employees
b) Answers will vary. He can randomly select 20% of the female employees and 20% of the male employees.

15. a), b)

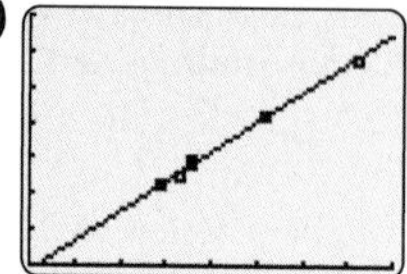

c) The greater the number of storeys, the taller the building.
d) Answers will vary. 160 m

16. Starting at 9:00, Claire ran at 6 km/h until 9:30, then stopped for 15 min, and then ran at a speed of 8 km/h until 10:15 when she stopped again for 15 min. Claire then ran back home at 7 km/h. She got there at 11:30.

17. a) 8 cm **b)** 512 cm^3

18. a) 17 **b)** 16 **c)** 39 **d)** $\frac{2}{5}$

19. a) n^5 **b)** d^6 **c)** a^{12}
d) $12m^3n^4$ **e)** $6kq$

20. a) $10c - 5i$ **b)** 95

21. a) $2m - 2$ **b)** $2x^2 + x - 4$ **c)** $-2h + 13$ **d)** $2t - w$

22. a) $5x + 15$ **b)** $2k^2 - k$ **c)** $18y - 13$
d) $4a + \frac{1}{6}$

23. a) $13n - 21$ **b)** 44

Chapter 4

Get Ready, pages 184–185

1. a) $8x$ **b)** $4y$ **c)** $4m$ **d)** $5n$

2. a) $4v - 2$ **b)** $7x + 3$ **c)** $-3y + 4$ **d)** $-2k - 3$

3. a) $8k - 36$ **b)** $-10m - 12$
c) $18x + 3$ **d)** $-7y + 14$

4. a) $7x + 17$ **b)** $26y - 16$
c) $19n$ **d)** $-11k - 1$

5. a) 60° **b)** 65°

6. a) $x = 70°$, $z = 110°$ **b)** $m = 30°$

7. a) 40 **b)** 18

8. a) 12 **b)** 36

9. a) $\frac{4}{3}$ **b)** $\frac{3}{8}$

10. a) $\frac{31}{24}$ **b)** $\frac{49}{60}$

4.1 Solve Simple Equations, pages 186–195

1. a) $x = 9$ **b)** $m = 3$ **c)** $y = 3$ **d)** $h = 4$

2. a) $x = 7$ **b)** $x = 13$ **c)** $y = 7$ **d)** $y = 6$

3. a) $x = 5$ **b)** $n = 19$ **c)** $y = 3$ **d)** $h = 3$

4. a) $x = 4$ **b)** $y = 4$ **c)** $n = 24$ **d)** $k = -8$

5. a) $z = -6$ **b)** $h = 30$ **c)** $c = 7$ **d)** $u = -5$

6. a) $x = 2$ **b)** $k = 2$ **c)** $p = 7$ **d)** $g = -\frac{11}{4}$

7. a) $k = -5$ **b)** $x = -5$ **c)** $q = 14$
d) $y = 8$ **e)** $w = -5$ **f)** $q = -2$

8. a) $p = -11$ **b)** $x = -7$ **c)** $u = -32$
d) $r = 5$ **e)** $c = -1$ **f)** $v = 5$

9. The variable used may vary.
a) $7p = 84$ **b)** 12 pies

10. The variable used may vary.
a) $50j = 700$ **b)** 14 jerseys

11.

Step	Explanation
$3x - 8 = 7$	Given equation
$3x - 8 + 8 = 7 + 8$	Add 8 to both sides.
$3x = 15$	Simplify by adding integers.
$\frac{3x}{3} = \frac{15}{3}$	Divide both sides by 3.
$x = 5$	Divide integers to give the solution for x.

12. a) $k = -\frac{1}{2}$ **b)** $x = -2$ **c)** $m = \frac{9}{2}$ **d)** $u = -\frac{5}{3}$

13. a) $r = -\frac{27}{16}$ **b)** $h = -\frac{14}{25}$

14. a) $50n = 2000$; $n = 40$
b) In addition to the fee of \$30 per person, there is a \$1000 charge for renting Broadway Nights.
c) $n = 33$
d) Royal James Hall, because, for the same price, seven more contestants can be invited.

15. The variables used may vary.
a) $C = 40n + 75$
b) $n = 15.625$; The team can afford 15 jerseys.

c) Rink Rat, because, for the same price, the team can buy one more jersey.
d) The answers may vary. Example: the quality of the jerseys

16. Without membership pass:

Number of rides $= \frac{40}{1.5} \doteq 26.67$ or 26 rides.

With a membership pass:

Number of rides $= \frac{40 - 5}{1.25} = 28$ rides.

For the same amount of money, with a membership pass, Marcel can go on 28 rides. Therefore, he should buy the membership pass.

18. a) $5000 + 840n = 21\ 800$, where n is the number of litres
b) 20 L

19. a) Yes. When the amount is doubled, the number of people in Royal James Hall will be $\frac{4000}{50}$ or 80. On the other hand, for the same amount, the number of people in Broadway Nights will be $\frac{4000 - 1000}{30}$ or 100.
b) Yes. For a budget of $2500, it does not matter which hall is rented.

20. E

4.2 Solve Multi-Step Equations, pages 196–203

1. a) $m = 2$ b) $y = 5$ c) $w = -4$ d) $d = \frac{8}{3}$

2. a) $x = -1$ b) $u = -1$ c) $y = 2$ d) $m = 3$

3. a) $x = -1$ b) $n = 2$ c) $t = 5$ d) $k = 0$

4. a) $x = -1$ b) $c = -15$ c) $p = -5$ d) $k = 12$

5. a) $x = 6$ b) $y = 3$ c) $c = 2$ d) $t = 4$

6. a) $x + 2x = 180$, $x = 60$; the two angles are 60° and 120°.
b) 30°, 150°

7. 15°, 30°, 45°

8.

Step	Explanation
L.S. = 2[(−3) + 4] + 5	Substitute the root into the left side.
= 2(1) + 5	Simplify the expression inside the brackets.
= 2 + 5	Multiply.
= 7	Add.
L.S. = 6 − [(−3) + 2]	Substitute the root into the right side.
= 6 − (−1)	Simplify the expression inside the brackets.
= 6 + 1	Subtract by adding the opposite.
= 7	Add.

9. a) $x = -\frac{9}{2}$ b) $i = -\frac{7}{2}$ c) $u = -\frac{8}{5}$
d) $k = \frac{10}{3}$ e) $p = -\frac{2}{3}$ f) $x = \frac{4}{3}$

10. a) $x = 8.1$ b) $d = 1.0$

11. b) $5(y - 3) - (y - 2) = 19$
$4y - 13 = 19$
c) The CAS has expanded the brackets on the left side of the equation and collected like terms.
d) $y = 8$

12. a) $q = 3$ b) $u = 0$

13. isosceles triangle: 5, 5, 8; equilateral triangle: 6, 6, 6

14. 90°, 45°, 45°

15. a) 14.7 cm, 14.7 cm, 20.6 cm
b) The perimeter is the sum of the sides and this is to be 50. So, write and solve the equation $1x + 1x + 1.4x = 50$.

16. 386 cm^2

17. a) $x = \frac{22}{7}$ b) $k = -6$

18. a) $x = -2$ b) $x = \frac{6}{11}$

19. E

20. D

21. No. For a triangle to be equilateral, all the sides must be equal. However, no value of x satisfies all three equations.
(1) $2x + 7 = 3x - 4$
$x = 11$
(2) $3x - 4 = 5x - 8$
$x = 2$
(3) $2x + 7 = 5x - 8$
$x = 5$

4.3 Solve Equations Involving Fractions, pages 204–210

1. a) $x = 17$ b) $p = -4$ c) $m = 17$ d) $h = -32$

2. a) $y = -26$ b) $u = -3$ c) $n = \frac{1}{2}$ d) $v = \frac{11}{3}$

3. a) $m = -13$ b) $w = -11$ c) $x = -1$ d) $y = 38$

4. a) $n = \frac{8}{59}$ b) $d = -\frac{13}{63}$ c) $c = -1$ d) $a = \frac{1}{6}$

5. 10 m

6. a) The error is in the second line, $5(x - 3) = 4(x + 1)$. The numerators on each side of the first line were multiplied by their own denominators. The correct step should be to multiply both sides by 20 (the LCD).
b) The third line is incorrect. In the previous line, the denominators and the 12 were eliminated instead of being simplified. The third line should be $4(3y - 2) = 3(y + 3)$.

7. a) $-\frac{35}{9}$°C or approximately −4°C b) 68°F

8. 10 cm

9. 30 m

11. a) $p = 2$ b) $u = -\frac{59}{33}$

12. a) 3, 7 b) 0, 4, −2

13. 84 years old

4.4 Modelling With Formulas, pages 211–219

1. a) $s = \frac{P}{4}$ b) $P = A - I$
c) $r = \frac{C}{2\pi}$ d) $b = y - mx$

2. a) $m = \frac{d - b}{t}$ b) $w = \frac{P - 2l}{2}$ c) $v = at$
d) $t = \frac{d}{v}$ e) $r = \sqrt{\frac{A}{\pi}}$ f) $I = \sqrt{\frac{P}{R}}$

3. a) 15 cm; 90 cm **b)** $I = \frac{C}{2.5}$

c) 30 inches; 40 inches

4. a)

b) Linear. When the equation is graphed, a straight line results.

c) 20 cm; 14 inches

5. Answers may vary.

a) The equation model shows the relation between the two variables in a concise way.

b) The graphical model gives a visual picture of the relationship and you can easily find approximate values from the graph. The disadvantage is that the values obtained by reading the graph may only be approximate.

6. a) $C = 15n + 250$ **b)** \$1000, \$1750

c) $n = \frac{C - 250}{15}$ **d)** 250 people, 116 people

e) the rearranged equation, because the unknown variable is already isolated and so its value can be calculated more easily

f) Linear. For a relation to be non-linear, at least one of the variables must have degree greater than or equal to 2. In this formula, all the variables have degree 1. Hence, it is linear.

7. a) 119 **b)** yes, 9

8. a) $P = \sqrt{16A}$ or $P = 4\sqrt{A}$ **b)** 20 m; 28.3 m

9. a)

b) Non-linear. Since the graph is curved, the relation is non-linear.

c) Answers will vary. Example: The equation is easily simplified to get an answer. The algebraic model is probably faster than graphing.

d) Answers will vary. Example: A graphical model provides a clear visual representation. Any ordered pair can easily be found using tools of the graphing calculator .

10.

Step	Explanation
$E = \frac{1}{2}mv^2$	Start with the original formula.
$2E = mv^2$	Multiply both sides of the equation by 2.
$\frac{2E}{m} = \frac{mv^2}{m}$	Divide both sides of the equation by *m*.
$\frac{2E}{m} = v^2$	Simplify .
$\sqrt{\frac{2E}{m}} = \sqrt{v^2}$	Take the square root of both sides.
$\sqrt{\frac{2E}{m}} = v$	Simplify to isolate *v*.

11. a) Biff; Use the formula from the previous question, $v = \sqrt{\frac{2E}{m}}$, to find each bear's speed. Rocco's speed is 1.3 m/s and Biff's is 1.375 m/s. Since Biff is running faster, he will reach the eucalyptus first.

b) 0.53 J more

12. a) $P = \frac{nRT}{V}$; $V = \frac{nRT}{P}$; $n = \frac{PV}{RT}$; $R = \frac{PV}{nT}$; $T = \frac{PV}{nR}$

b) If you want to calculate one specific unknown value, given the values of the other four variables, you can enter the given values in the appropriate form of the formula and evaluate the answer.

13. a) $l = \sqrt{A}$

b)

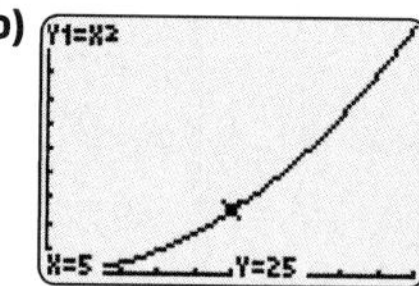

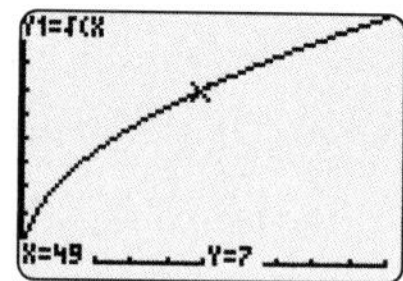

c) Answers will vary. Both the graphs show a non-linear relationship.

d) Answers will vary. In the first graph, $A = l^2$, the curve opens upward. In the second graph, the curve opens to the right.

14. a) $l = \sqrt[3]{V}$

b) Answers will vary.

Graph 1

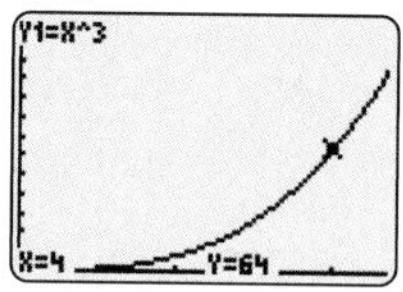

Graph 2

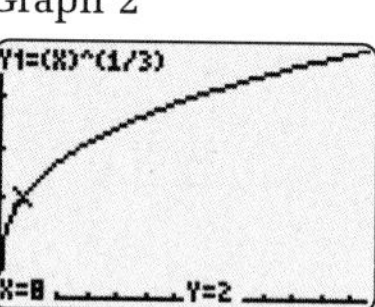

15. a) $v = \frac{d}{t} - \frac{at}{2}$ **b)** 1 m/s

16. a) $a = \frac{2(d - vt)}{t^2}$ **b)** 12.7 m/s^2

17. $e = \frac{w - st}{10}$; 5 errors

18. $L = \frac{gp^2}{4\pi^2}$, 0.248 m

19. a) 11.18 km/s **b)** $M = \frac{rv^2}{2G}$ **c)** 6.36×10^{23} kg

4.5 Modelling With Algebra, pages 220–229

1. The variable used may vary.

a) $3n$ **b)** $n + 4$ **c)** $\frac{1}{2}n$ **d)** $2n - 5$

2. a) $4n = 112$; the variable *n* represents any number.

b) $p + 12 = 56$; the variable *p* represents the perimeter.

c) $3x + 5 = 29$; the variable *x* represents any number.

d) $x + (x + 1) = 63$; the variable *x* represents any number.

3. a) 28; this represents the number that equals 112 when multiplied by 4.

b) 44; this represents the perimeter that when increased by 12 equals 56.

c) 8; this represents the number that, when multiplied by 3, is five less than 29.

d) 31; The sum of this number and the next consecutive number, 32, is 63.

4. Estaban: 16, Raoul: 22

5. Jamal: 1025, Fayth: 1225

6. Natalie: 11, Samara: 22, Chantal: 19

7. \$8350

8. a) $T = 5000m + 2n$ **b)** \$6000 **c)** 29 500 CDs **d)** \$130 000

9. 17, 18, 19

10. −68, −66

11. 8.8 m

12. Answers may vary.

13. a) 50.6 m

b) The cat gets back first. Laurie has to swim 50.6 m, and the cat has to walk 64 m. The speed ratio between Laurie and the cat is 0.75:1. In the time Laurie swims, the cat will be able to walk $\frac{50.6}{0.75}$, or 67.5 m, which is more than the cat needs to get back to the starting point.

14. Answers will vary.

16. 12.5 cm^2

17. a) 1.77 m **b)** Use the Pythagorean theorem.

$2.8^2 = (3x)^2 + (x)^2$

$x \doteq 0.885$

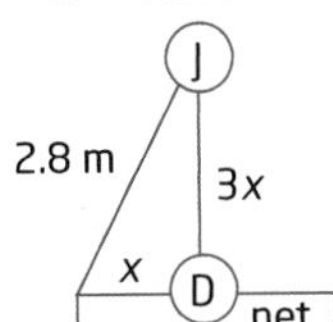

c) Answers will vary. Example: I assumed that the goalie, Dougie, is standing exactly midway between the goalposts and on the goal line.

18.

Planet	Radius of Orbit (AU)	Period of Orbit (Earth Days)	$\frac{(\text{Period})^2}{(\text{Radius})^3}$
Mercury	0.389	87.77	130 870.9915
Venus	0.724	224.70	133 042.5151
Earth	1.0	365.25	133 407.5625
Mars	1.524	686.98	133 331.6600
Jupiter	5.200	4332.62	133 503.0444
Saturn	9.150	10 759.20	151 111.2085

Mean = 135 877.8303

b) $\frac{T^2}{R^3}$ = Kepler's constant **c)** 19.025 AU

d) 60 569.84 Earth days

e) Yes, $\frac{90588^2}{39.5^3}$ = 133 152.7241, which is very close to the actual value.

f) Answers will vary.

19. 72 g

20. D

Chapter 4 Review, pages 230–231

1. a) $m = -10$ **b)** $k = -4$ **c)** $x = 6$ **d)** $h = -20$

2. a) $y = 10$ **b)** $v = -5$ **c)** $x = 5$ **d)** $s = -5$

3. a) $n = 4$ **b)** $r = 9$ **c)** $x = 4$ **d)** $y = 2$

4. a) $0.12c + 0.70 = 2.50$ **b)** $c = 15$

5. a) $m = 2$ **b)** $w = -1$ **c)** $x = -10$ **d)** $w = 1$

6. a) $y = 2$ **b)** $k = 5$ **c)** $w = 1$ **d)** $n = -8$

7. a) $p = 4$ **b)** $h = -2$ **c)** $n = 2$ **d)** $k = \frac{3}{2}$

8. 15°, 45°, 120°

9. a) $x = 13$ **b)** $b = -11$ **c)** $p = 5$ **d)** $x = -5$

10. a) $q = \frac{10}{3}$ **b)** $u = -5$

11. a) $y = -28$ **b)** $w = -58$ **c)** $c = -19$ **d)** $x = 37$

12. a) $a = P - b - c$ **b)** $d = \frac{C}{\pi}$ **c)** $F = am$ **d)** $t = \frac{d - b}{m}$

13. a) 150 W **b)** 125 Ω **c)** 5 A

14. Dina: 9 years, Michelle: 18 years, Juliette: 12 years

15. a) \$32.10 **b)** 129 hamburgers

16. increase by 8 m

17. Answers may vary.

Chapter 4 Practice Test, pages 232–233

1. B

2. D

3. C

4. C

5. a) $y = 9$ **b)** $h = -21$ **c)** $k = 3$ **d)** $x = 5$ **e)** $r = \frac{3}{5}$ **f)** $y = 17$

6. a) $w = -9$ **b)** $a = -\frac{41}{7}$ **c)** $k = 6$

7. a) $b = P - 2a$ **b)** $a = \frac{P - b}{2}$ **c)** 12.5 cm

8. Kristi earns \$550 per week, Charlene earns \$700 per week, and Sacha earns \$800 per week.

9. $p = \frac{11}{3}$

10. a) \$173

b) Murray needs to sell 30 service contracts.

Chapter 5

Get Ready, pages 236–237

1. a) $\frac{-3}{4}$ **b)** $\frac{5}{2}$ **c)** $\frac{-1}{-2}$

2. a) 0.4 **b)** −0.7 **c)** −0.875 **d)** −2.4

3. a) $-\frac{1}{3}$ **b)** $\frac{-3}{2}$ **c)** $\frac{1}{4}$ **d)** $\frac{5}{-2}$

4. a) 1:4 **b)** 1:8 **c)** 6:7 **d)** 4:85

5. 84 people

6. 64 inches

7. Toronto 32.3%, Vancouver 22.6%, Charlottetown 38.7%, St. John's 45.2%

8. a) nitrogen 2.0 kg, phosphorus 0.4 kg, potassium 0.8 kg

b) nitrogen 5.25 kg, phosphorus 1.75 kg, potassium 1.75 kg
c) nitrogen 7.5 kg, phosphorus 2.5 kg, potassium 1.5 kg
d) nitrogen 2.0 kg, phosphorus 1.2 kg, potassium 0.8 kg

5.1 Direct Variation, pages 238–245

1. a) 80 **b)** 7 **c)** 100
2. a) $C = 22.5s$ **b)** the cost of 1 m of sidewalk **c)** $15 750
3. a)

Time, t (h)	Pay, p ($)
0	0
1	8
2	16
3	24

b) Graphs may vary depending on scales used.
c) $p = 8t$
4. a)

Mass of Apples, a (kg)	Cost, c ($)
0	0.00
1	1.50
2	3.00
3	4.50

b) Graphs may vary depending on scales used.
c) $c = 1.5a$
5. a) To get the cost of parking, multiply the time parked, in hours, by $2.75. The cost c, in dollars, of parking, varies directly with the time, t, in hours, for which the car is parked.
b) $c = 2.75t$

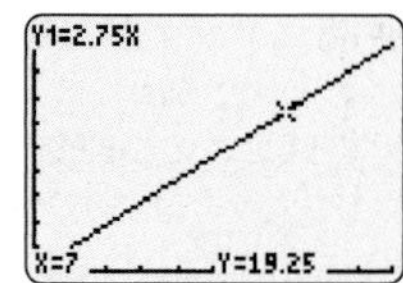

c) Answers will vary. Example: about $20
d) $19.25
6. a) To get the cost C, of oranges, multiply the mass r, in kilograms, of oranges, by $2.25.
b) $C = 2.25r$; the constant of variation represents the constant average cost, $2.25/kg.
c) $67.50
7. a)

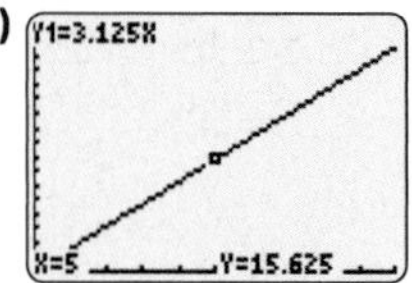

b) $A = 3.125t$ **c)** $75.00
8. a) $P = 9.5h$ **b)** $T = 14.25h$
c) $P = 10h$, $T = 15h$
9. a) This relationship is a direct variation because the price of the sugar varies directly with the amount of sugar that is bought.
b), c) The graph shows that if the price increases to $1.49 for 0.5 kg (or $2.98/kg), the graph becomes steeper.

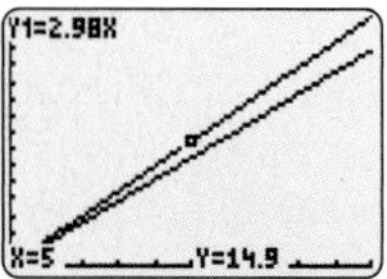

10. a) Answers will vary. Example: Consider the distance, in metres, a cyclists travels in seconds (10 m in 1 s, 20 m in 2 s).
b) Answers will vary. Example: Consider the cost, in dollars, of parking a car for a certain time, in hours, ($2 for 4 h, $4 for 8 h).
11. $d = 171t$

Object	Time (s)	Distance (m)
Tree	0.1	17.1
House	0.25	42.75
Cliff wall	0.04	6.84

12. a) $V = 125t$, where V is the volume of the water, in litres, and t is the time, in minutes. The constant of variation represents the constant average increase in volume, 125 L/min.
b)

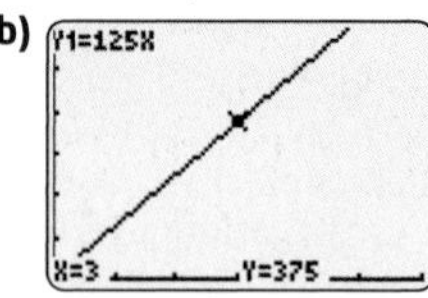

c) 2500 L **d)** 920 min or 15 h 20 min
e) New equation: $V = 100t$. The graph would still increase to the right, but less steeply. It would take longer to fill the pool.
13. a) The freezing point depends on the salt content so the salt content is the independent variable.
b) $F = -0.57s$, where F is the freezing point, in degrees Celsius, and s is the salt content, as a percent.
c) -0.57°C **d)** 5.25%
14. $k = 1.61m$, where k is the number of kilometres and m is the number of miles.
15. Yes, $k = \pi$.
16. From 1 to 100, there are 19 disks that contain a 3: 3, 13, 23, 30, 31, 32, 33, 34, 35, 36, 37, 38, 39, 43, 53, 63, 73, 83, and 93. So, the probability that a disk contains a 3 is $19 \div 100 = 0.19$ or 19%.
17. 41 958

5.2 Partial Variation, pages 246–253

1. a) Direct variation: the equation is of the form $y = kx$.
b) Partial variation: the equation is of the form $y = mx + b$.
c) Partial variation: the equation is of the form $y = mx + b$.
d) Direct variation: the equation is of the form $y = kx$.
2. a)

x	y
0	5
1	10
2	15
3	20
4	25
7	40

b) 5, 5 **c)** $y = 5x + 5$
d) Graphs may vary.
e) The graph is a straight line that intersects the y-axis at (0, 5). The y-values increase by 5 as the x-values increase by 1.

3. a)

x	y
0	-2
1	3
2	8
3	13
4	18
7	33

b) −2, 5 **c)** $y = 5x - 2$
d) Graphs may vary.
e) The graph is a straight line that intersects the *y*-axis at (0, −2). The *y*-values increase by 5 as the *x*-values increase by 1.

4. a) \$7.00, \$1.50 × number of toppings
b) $C = 1.50n + 7.00$ **c)** \$14.50

5. a) \$250, \$4 × number of students
b) $C = 4n + 250$ **c)** \$350

6. a)

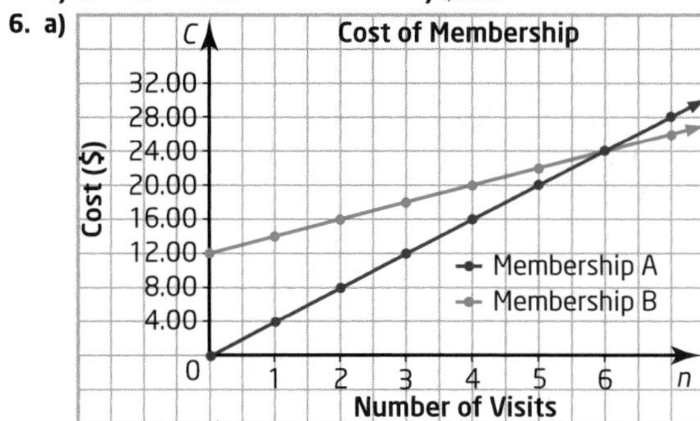

b) A: direct variation; B: partial variation
c) In both cases, *C* represents the cost of membership and *n* represents the number of visits.
A: $C = 4n$; B: $C = 2n + 12$
d) Membership A is cheaper when fewer than six visits are made. Membership B is cheaper when more than six visits are made. They cost the same when six visits are made.

7. a) The fixed cost is \$100 and could represent, for example, the cost of paper, ink, and overhead.
b) From the table, it costs \$20 to print 100 flyers, so the variable cost to print one flyer is \$20 ÷ 100 or \$0.20.
c) $C = 0.2n + 100$
d) \$300 **e)** 900 flyers

8. a) $T = 2n + 1$, where *T* is the number of toothpicks and *n* is the diagram number. This is a partial variation because it is of the form $y = mx + b$.
b) 41 toothpicks

9. a) $P = 10.13d + 102.4$, where *P* is the pressure, in kilopascals, and *d* is the depth below the lake's surface, in metres.
b) 29 m, to the nearest metre

10. Answers will vary. Example: Consider the cost of a plumber repairing a leak. It costs \$30 for a service call and \$10 for each hour after that.

11. a) Graphs may vary. **b)** −250 m/min
c) $H = -250t + 8000$, where *H* is the height above ground, in metres, and *t* is the time, in minutes

13. a) i) 349 m/s **ii)** 313 m/s **b)** 227.5 m

14. a)

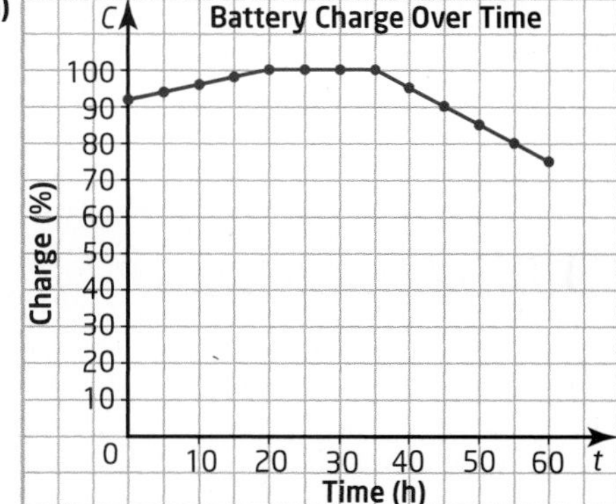

b) In each case, *C* is the charge as a percent and *t* is the time, in hours. From 0 to 20 h, $C = 0.4t + 92$; from 20 to 35 h, $C = 100$; for 35 h and more, $C = -t + 135$.
c) i) 96.8% **ii)** 100% **iii)** 64%

5.3 Slope, pages 254-263

1. a) 0.6 **b)** 1.375
2. 0.02
3. no
4. a) rise 3, run 5, slope 0.6 **b)** rise −3, run 5, slope −0.6
5. a) $\frac{1}{3}$ **b)** 0.5 **c)** −2.5
d) 0 **e)** not possible **f)** −0.4
6. a) b) Answers will vary. For example, B(5, 4).
7. Answers will vary. For example, B(10, −5).
8. a) no **b)** no
9. Answers will vary. Examples:
a) (1, 7) **b)** (1, 3) **c)** (−1, 9)
d) (−1, 2) **e)** (−1, 5) **f)** (−2, 6)
10. 0.6 m, 1.2 m, 1.8 m, 2.4 m
11. a) 4.2% **b)** 18 m
12. a) i) medium **ii)** steep **b)** 2.1 m, to the nearest tenth
13. Yes it does; otherwise the slopes would be different.
14. 1.6, to the nearest tenth
15. minimum 0.84 m, maximum 1.27 m, both to two decimal places
16. The slope is 1.3, to the nearest tenth, so the pyramid is almost twice as steep as a standard staircase.
17. The slope is 0.65, to the nearest hundredth, so the sides of the pavilion are about half as steep as those of the pyramid.
18. more than 111.1 m, easy; from 55.6 m to 111.1 m, intermediate; less than 55.6 m, difficult
19. 0.40, to the nearest hundredth
20. −1.73, to the nearest hundredth
21. a) Answers will vary. Example: one set of stairs has a slope of 0.62 and another has a slope of 0.70. Both sets of stairs are safe, but the set of stairs with the more gradual slope is safer.
b) Answers will vary.
22. Answers will vary. example: 5 switchbacks. There needs to be an odd number of switchbacks for the train to end up going in the correct direction. If the run is 1 km, then the slope of each switchback would be 0.05 or 5% (50 m ÷ 1000 m), which is less than 7%, as required.
23. D

5.4 Slope as a Rate of Change, pages 264-271

1. 7.4 L/min
2. 300 L/h
3. 60 flaps/s
4. a) −3.25 **b)** The height decreases by 3.25 m/s.
5. a) −0.006 **b)** The temperature decreases by 0.006°C/m.
6. 11¢/year
7. 0.23 cm/day, to the nearest hundredth
8. a) Graphs may vary.
b) The slope is about 2571, which means the rate of change is about 2571 downloads/day.
c) Answers will vary. Example: Yes, it is popular, because the number of downloads continues to increase.
9. a) Graphs may vary. **b)** 4 **c)** 4 toothpicks/diagram
10. age 16

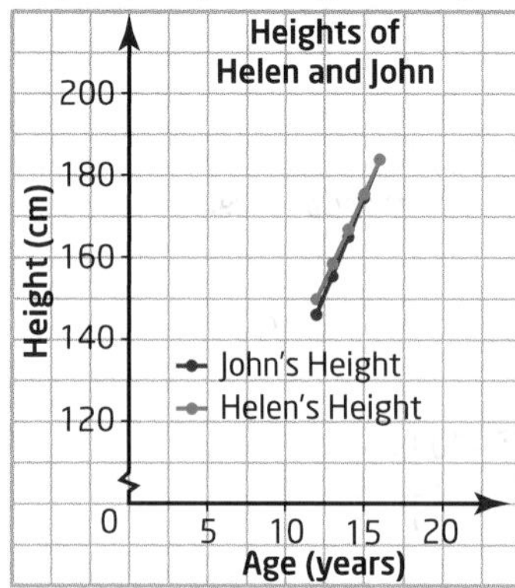

11. a) The graph is a line starting at (0, 0) and passing through (30, 15 000)
b) The slope will become twice as steep.
12. a) Graphs may vary. **b)** 1.56 L/m^2
c) 1.1 min, to the nearest tenth
13. a) The graph is a line starting at (0, 0) and passing through (8, 2.5). **b)** 32 s
14. a) Car B, by 36 km/h
b) It is the time at which they have travelled the same distance. If they are travelling in the same direction, it is the time at which Car B passes Car A.
15. a) Graphs may vary dependng on scales used.
b) from 1990 to 2000
c) from 2000 to 2005; the rate of change increased
16. a) 0.030 m^2 **b)** about 87 min
c) about 43 min **d)** about 17 min
17. a) No
b) Answers will vary. Example: The rates of change are large because the number of jobs increased by about 4300, or 11%, which is a significant amount.
19. a)

Time (h)	Price of Coat ($)
0	190.00
2	180.50
4	171.48
6	162.90
8	154.76
10	147.02
12	139.67
14	132.68
16	126.05

b) Graphs may vary depending on scales chosen.
c) The graph is decreasing and it is curved because the rate of change changes at each interval.

20. From 0 to 100 min, the charge is 35¢/min; from 100 to 200 min, it is 25¢/min; for more than 200 min, it is 20¢/min.

5.5 First Differences, pages 272-278

1. a) linear **b)** linear **c)** non-linear
d) non-linear **e)** linear **f)** non-linear
2. a) 1, 2, 4; non-linear **b)** 3, 3, 3; linear
c) −1, 1, 3; non-linear **d)** −4, −4, −4; linear
3. a) linear **b)** non-linear
4. a) linear, $S = 5h + 1$, 36 segments
b) non-linear, 49 tiles
5. a) linear, $I = 2c - 2$, 12 intersection points
b) non-linear, 35 diagonals
6. a)

Diagram Number	Number of Toothpicks
1	4
2	7
3	10

b) The first differences are the same, 3. The pattern is linear.
c) $T = 3d + 1$ **d)** 31 toothpicks
7. a)

Height (cm)	Wet Area (cm^2)
0	0
1	16
2	32
3	48
4	64
5	80
6	96
7	112
8	128
9	144
10	160

b) linear
c) 800 cm^2
8. a) Example:

Height (cm)	Painted Area (cm^2)
0	0
1	1
2	4
3	9
4	16

b) non-linear
9. non-linear, by first differences and by graph
10. a)

Figure Number	Number of Circles in Pattern
1	1
2	3
3	6
4	10
5	15
6	21
7	28
8	36

b) L3 contains the first differences; $C = 0.5n^2 + 0.5n$

5.6 Connecting Variation, Slope, and First Differences, pages 279-287

1. a) 2.5 **b)** 6 **c)** $y = 2.5x + 6$

2. a) $\frac{4}{3}$ **b)** -1 **c)** $y = \frac{4}{3}x - 1$

3. a) Tables and graphs may vary. Sample tables are shown.

x	y
0	1
1	3
2	5
3	7
4	9

slope 2

b)

x	y
0	4
1	1
2	-2
3	-5
4	-8

slope -3

c)

x	y
0	0.0
1	-1.5
2	-3.0
3	-4.5
4	-6.0

slope $-\frac{3}{2}$

d)

x	y
0	0.2
1	0.7
2	1.2
3	1.7
4	2.2

slope 0.5

4. a) Graphs may vary.
b) Each time the value of x increases by 1, the value of y increases by 3. The graph is a straight line that does not pass through (0, 0). This is a partial variation.
c) $y = 3x + 2$

5. a) Graphs may vary.
b) Each time the value of x increases by 2, the value of y increases by 5. The graph is a straight line that does not pass through (0, 0). This is a partial variation.
c) $y = 2.5x + 16$

6.

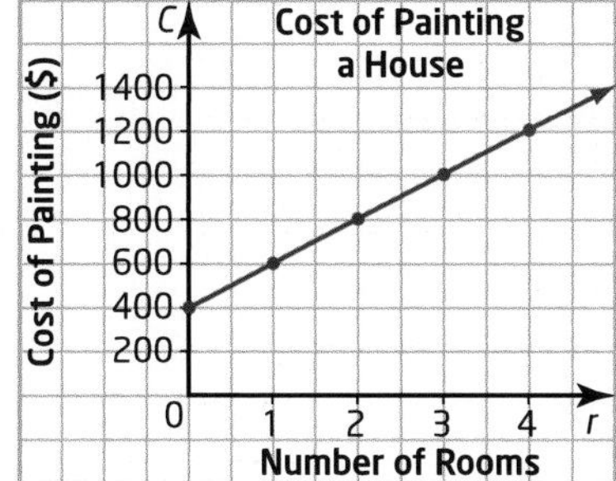

Number of Rooms, r	Cost of Painting, C ($)
0	400
1	600
2	800
3	1000
4	1200

$C = 200r + 400$

7. a) The graph is a line starting at (0, 5) and passing through (1, 6.5) and (2, 8).
b) slope 1.50, cost of travelling 1 km; vertical intercept 5.00, cost of getting cab at start of journey
c) partial variation: graph is a straight line that does not pass through (0, 0).
d) $C = 1.5d + 5.00$

8. Each second, the scuba diver swims 1 m toward the surface of the water. $D = t - 50$

Depth of Scuba Diver

Time (s)

Depth (m)

9. a) 2.25, 0 **b)** $y = 2.25x$ **c)**

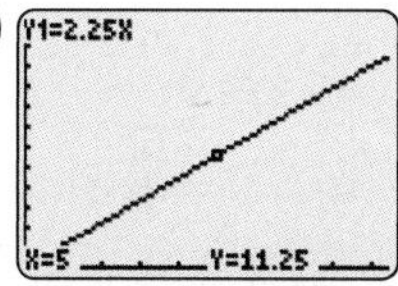

10. a) 0.5, 5 **b)** $y = 0.5x + 5$ **c)**

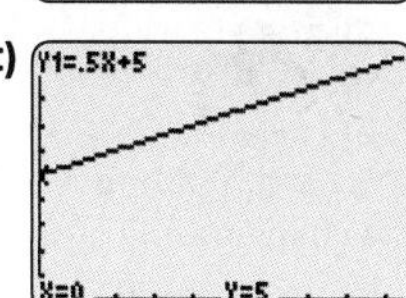

11.

x	y
-6	9
-3	2
0	-5
3	-12

y varies partially with x. As the value of x increases by 3, the value of y decreases by 7.

$y = -\frac{7}{3}x - 5$

12.

Y1=4X-3

X=2 Y=5

x	y
0	-3
1	1
2	5
3	9

y varies partially with x. As the value of x increases by 1, the value of y increases by 4.

13. a) linear
b) Graphs may vary.
c) $-\frac{1}{4}$, -0.25; constant; it represents the fact that 0.25 kL of water drains from the pool every minute.
d) $V = -0.25t + 50$ **e)** 35 kL

15. a) $D = \frac{1}{2}m + 10$ **b)** $D = \frac{11}{20}m + 11$
c)

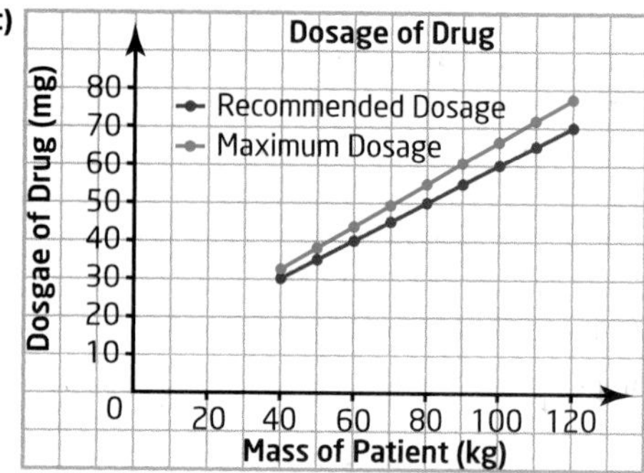

The graph of the maximum dosage has a vertical intercept of 11, which is 1 higher than the vertical intercept of the recommended dosage, 10. The maximum dosage graph rises more steeply.

16. base salary \$1000/month, commission 2%; the percent commission is constant

Chapter 5 Review, pages 288–289

1. Graphs may vary.

Time Worked, t (h)	Pay, P (\$)
0	0
1	9
2	18
3	27

c) $P = 9t$

2. a) $d = 96t$, speed of 96 km/h
b) 3 h 7 min 30 s

3. a) Direct variation: the volume of soup varies directly with the volume of water used to prepare it.
b) The graph is a line starting at (0, 0) and passing through (2.5, 3).
c) The graph will become less steep.

4. a)

x	y
0	4
1	7
2	10
3	13
4	16
7	25

b) 4, 3 **c)** $y = 3x + 4$

d)

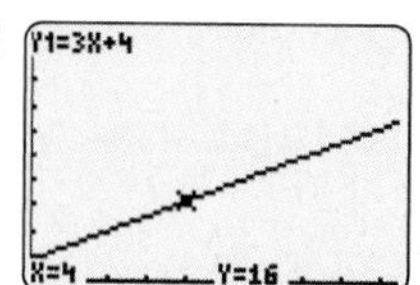

The graph is a straight line that starts at (0, 4) and rises upward to the right with a slope of 3.

5. a) Neither: it is not a straight line.
b) Partial variation: it is a straight line that does not pass through (0, 0).
c) Direct variation: it is straight line that passes through (0, 0).
d) Partial variation: it is a straight line that does not pass through (0, 0).

6. a) 500, $0.15f$ **b)** $C = 0.15f + 500$ **c)** \$575

7. a) 0.13 **b)** 1.406 25

8. a) $\frac{1}{4}$ **b)** $\frac{5}{4}$ **c)** $-\frac{3}{4}$

9. a) Answers will vary. Example: Any horizontal line segment from (3, 5) to another point (x, 5)
b) Answers will vary. Example: Any vertical line segment from (−4, 1) to another point (−4, y)

10. No.

11. walking burns 0.8 kJ/min; swimming burns 1.6 kJ/min; cycling burns 1.2 kJ/min; playing basketball burns 2.8 kJ/min

12. 12.2; hair grows 12.2 cm/year

13. a) linear **b)** non-linear

14. linear

15. a) linear **b)** 3 **c)** $y = 3x + 2$
d)

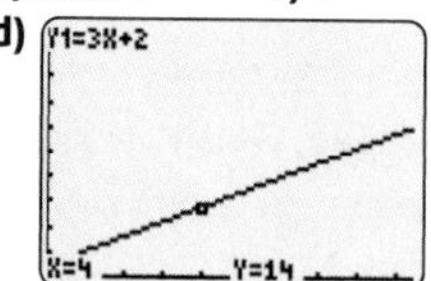

16. a) linear **b)** Graphs may vary.
c) The slope is −0.4 and means that propane is used up at 0.4 kg/h. The vertical intercept is 9.0 and is the initial amount of propane, in kilograms.
d) $M = -0.4t + 9$

Chapter 5 Practice Test, pages 290–291

1. C
2. A
3. C
4. C
5. D

6. a) −1.5 **b)** $y = 1$ **c)** $y = -\frac{3}{2}x + 1$

7. a) $d = 342.5t$
b) The graph is a line starting at (0, 0) and passing through (2, 685).

8. linear: first differences are equal

9. a) $P = 50t + 60$ **b)** \$235 **c)** $P = 45t + 60$

10. a) \$60/page; it is the slope of the graph
b) $C = 60p + 8000$
c) $C = 60p + 9000$; the vertical intercept would be 9000
d) $C = 64.8p + 8000$

Chapter 6

Get Ready, pages 294-295

1. a)

Time Worked (h)	Earnings ($)
3	30
5	50
6	60
9	90

b) The graph crosses the vertical axis at the point (0, 0). This point shows the earnings, \$0, after zero hours.

2. a)

Carlo's Repair Charges

b) A 5-h job would cost \$260.

c) The graph crosses the vertical axis at the point (0, 60). This point shows the repair cost, \$60, for 0 h. It is Carlo's basic charge to make a house call.

3. Answers may vary.
Examples: **a)** 220 m **b)** 540 m

4. Answers may vary.
Examples: **a)** 2 min 15 sec **b)** 7 min

5. a)

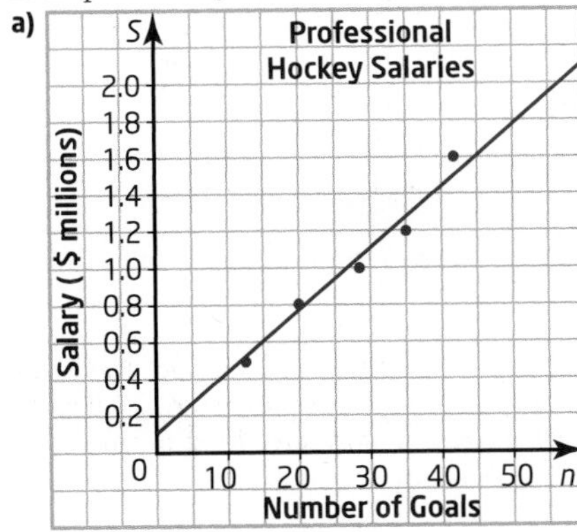

b) \$1.1 million; \$1.8 million **c)** 38 goals; 56 goals

6. a) $\frac{3}{2}$ **b)** -1

7. a)

A Car Trip

b) Answers may vary. (2, 106), (4, 209)

c) The slope is 51.5. This means that the average speed of the car is 51.5 km/h.

6.1 The Equation of a Line in Slope *y*-Intercept Form: *y* = *mx* + *b*, pages 296-307

1.

	Equation	Slope	*y*-intercept
a)	$y = 4x + 1$	4	1
b)	$y = \frac{2}{3}x + 3$	$\frac{2}{3}$	3
c)	$y = x - 2$	1	−2
d)	$y = -\frac{2}{3}x$	$-\frac{2}{3}$	0
e)	$y = 3$	0	3
f)	$y = -x - \frac{1}{2}$	−1	$-\frac{1}{2}$

2. a) slope 3; *y*-intercept −2
b) slope −2; *y*-intercept 3
c) slope $\frac{1}{4}$; *y*-intercept −2
d) slope $-\frac{3}{4}$; *y*-intercept −2

3. a) $y = 3x - 2$ **b)** $y = -2x + 3$
c) $y = \frac{1}{4}x - 2$ **d)** $y = -\frac{3}{4}x - 2$

4. a) $y = 2$; slope 0; *y*-intercept 2
b) $x = -3$; slope undefined; no *y*-intercept
c) $x = 4$; slope undefined; no *y*-intercept
d) $y = 0$; slope 0; *y*-intercept 0

5. *x*-axis

6. a) $y = \frac{2}{3}x + 3$

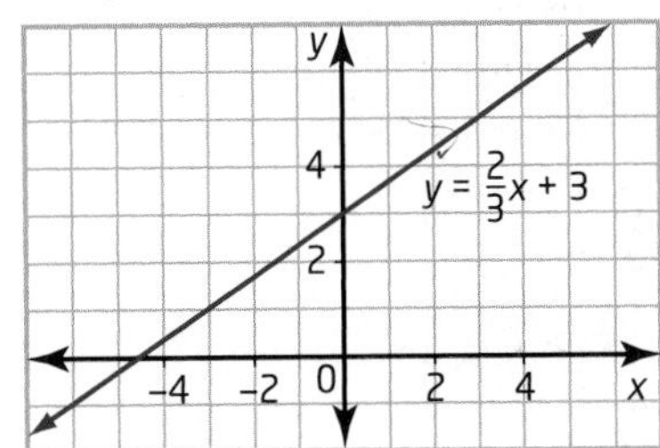

b) $y = -\frac{3}{5}x + 1$

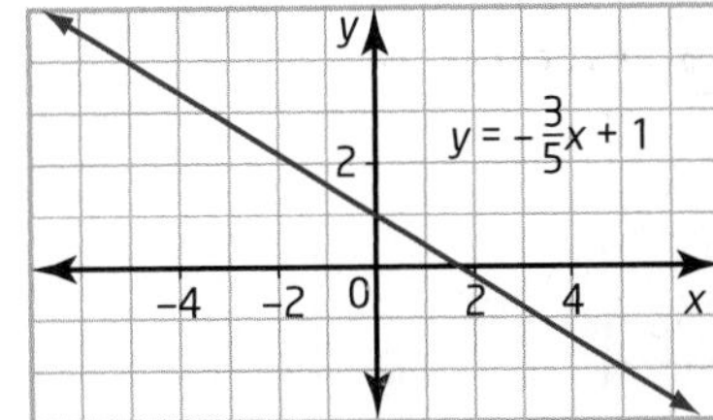

c) $y = -2x$

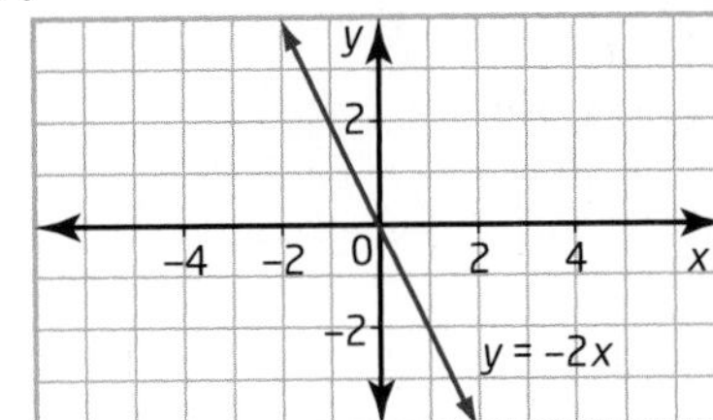

d) $y = \frac{4}{3}x - 4$

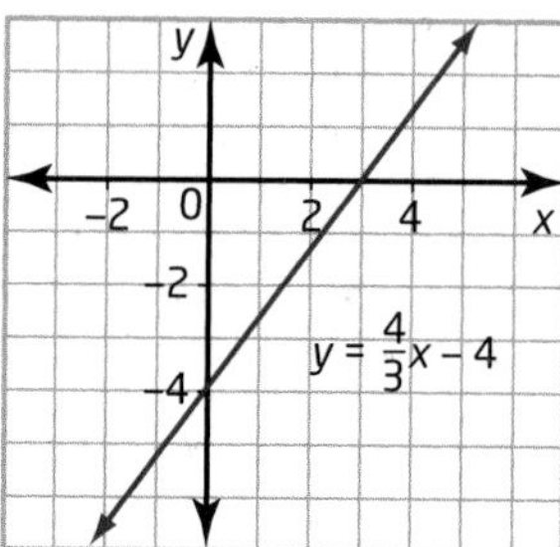

e) $y = -4$

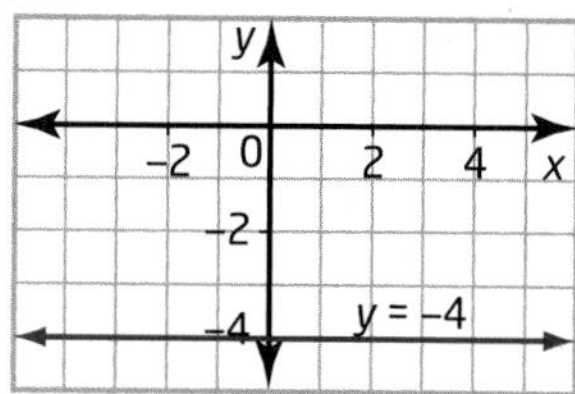

7. a) slope 0; y-intercept -5
b) slope undefined; no y-intercept
c) slope 0; y-intercept $\frac{7}{2}$
d) slope undefined; no y-intercept

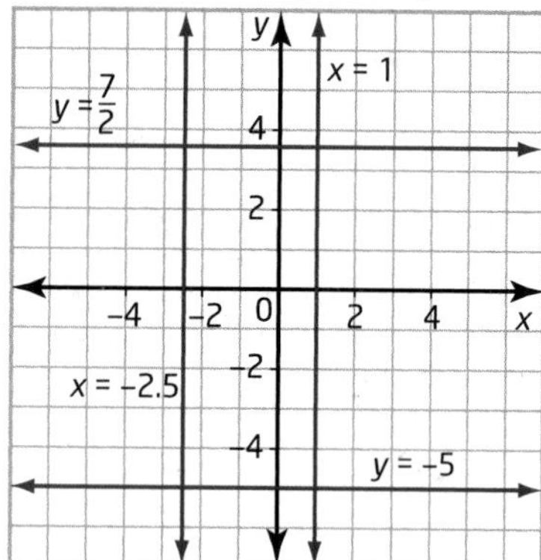

8. a) The person was at an initial distance of 1 m from the sensor.
b) The person was walking at a speed of 0.5 m/s.
c) The person was walking away from the sensor. This is because on the graph, the person's distance from the sensor increases as time goes by.

9. a)

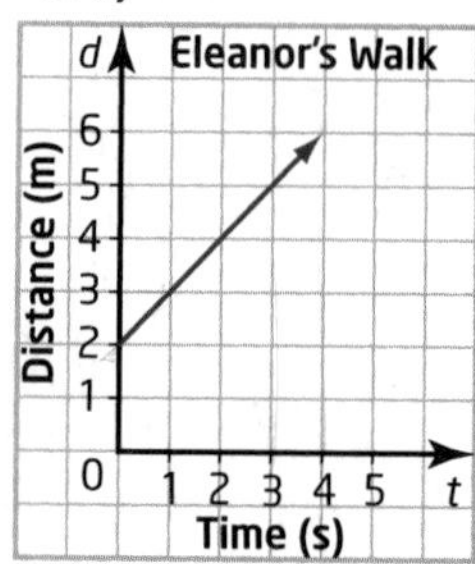

b)

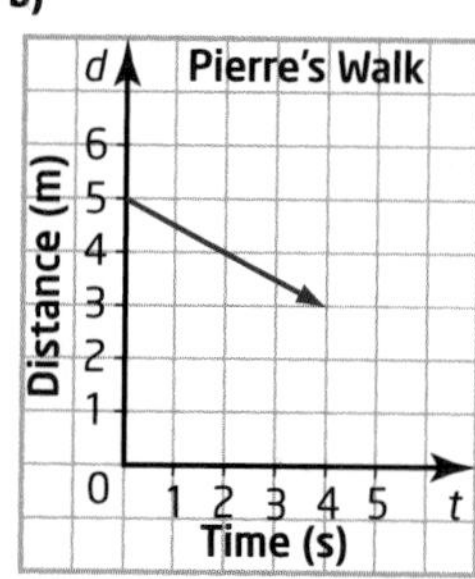

c)

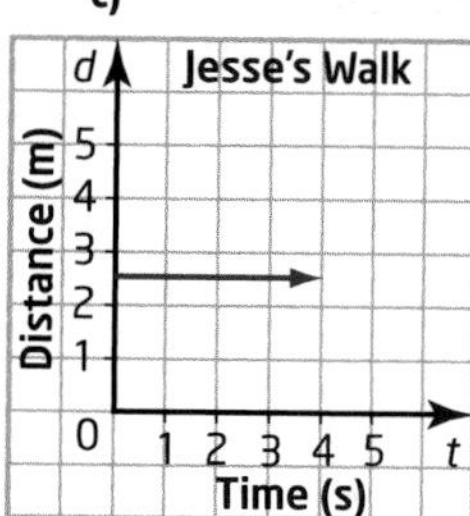

d)

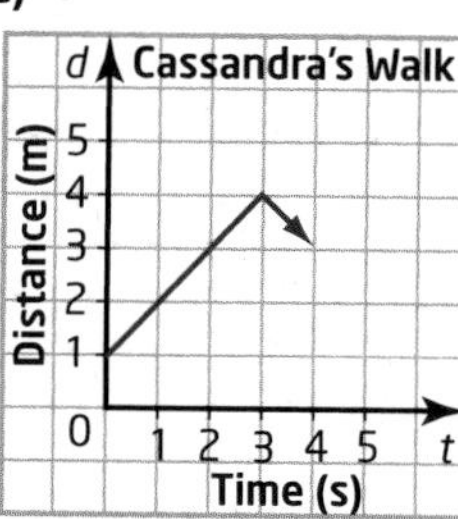

10. a) slope 1; t-intercept 1.5; The slope represents Shannon's walking speed of 1 m/s away from the sensor. The t-intercept represents Shannon's initial distance of 1.5 m away from the sensor; $d = t + 1.5$.
b) slope 3; a-intercept 0; The slope shows that the circumference of the trunk is three times its age. The a-intercept shows that when the tree began to grow from a seed, it had circumference zero. $C = 3a$.

11. 13; 1

12.–14. Answers will vary.

15. a) The value of the y-coordinate for any x-intercept is 0.
b) 2; $-\frac{15}{2}$

16. a) 11 **b)** 23, 35, 47, 59, 71
c) Multiply any whole number by 12 and add 11.

6.2 The Equation of a Line in Standard Form: *Ax + By + C = 0*, pages 308–314

1. a) $y = -x + 3$ **b)** $y = -\frac{2}{3}x - 2$
c) $y = \frac{1}{4}x + 3$ **d)** $y = -\frac{3}{2}x + \frac{5}{2}$

2. a) slope -1; y-intercept 3; the graph is a line crossing the y-axis at 3 and the x-axis at 3.
b) slope $-\frac{2}{3}$; y-intercept -2; the graph is a line crossing the y-axis at -2 and the x-axis at -3.
c) slope $\frac{1}{4}$; y-intercept 3; the graph is a line crssing the y-axis at 3 and passing through (4, 4).
d) slope $-\frac{3}{2}$; y-intercept $\frac{5}{2}$; the graph is a line crossing the y-axis at $2\frac{1}{2}$ and passing through (3, -2).

3. a) slope $-\frac{1}{3}$; y-intercept 1
b) slope $\frac{2}{5}$; y-intercept $\frac{8}{5}$

4. a) $C = 40n + 250$
b) fixed cost $250; variable cost $40 per person

c)

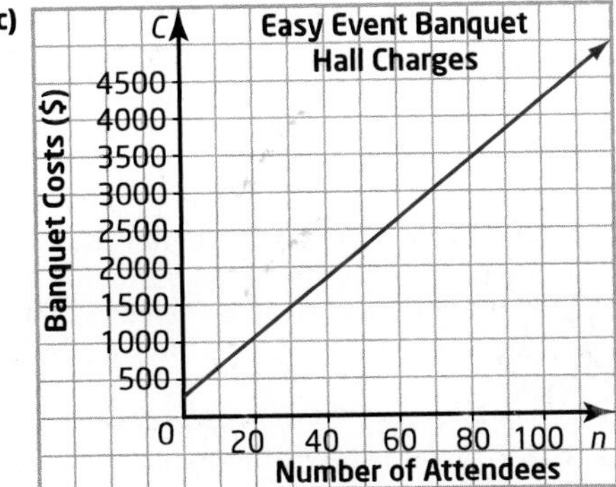

d) \$4250

e) This is not a better deal than Celebrations. Celebrations charges \$3750 for 100 people, whereas Easy Event charges \$4250.

5. If only 50 people attend, then the cost at Celebrations is \$2500 and the cost at Easy Event is \$2250. In this case, Easy Event is a better deal. This is because the lower fixed cost at Easy Event offsets the higher variable cost when there are fewer people at a banquet.

6. \$15; \$20

7. a) $C = \frac{5}{9}F - \frac{160}{9}$

b)

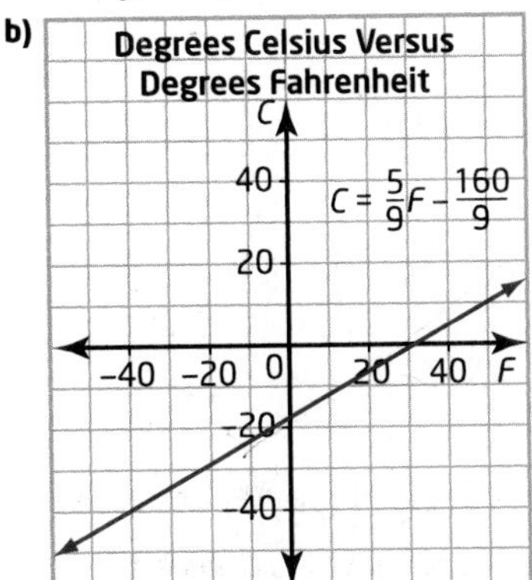

c) The slope is $\frac{5}{9}$ and the C-intercept is $-\frac{160}{9}$. The slope is a multiplication coefficient and the C-intercept is a constant. To change a Fahrenheit temperature to a Celsius temperature, multiply the Fahrenheit temperature by the slope and add the C-intercept.

8. a) $F = \frac{9}{5}C + 32$

b)

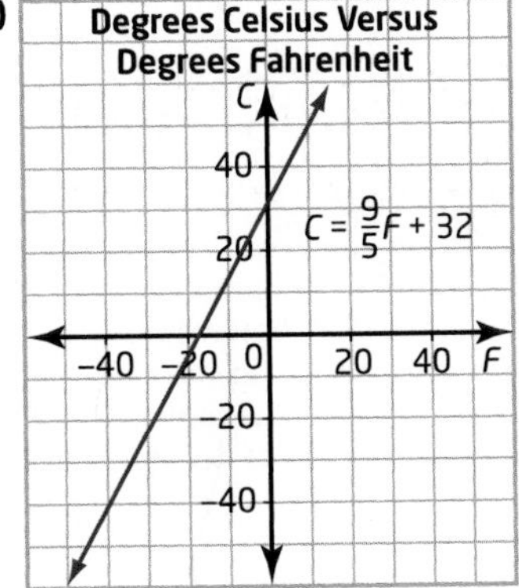

c) The slope is $\frac{9}{5}$ and the F-intercept is 32. The slope is a coefficient and the F-intercept is a constant. To change a Celsius temperature to a Fahrenheit temperature, multiply the Celsius temperature by the slope and add the F-intercept.

9. a) The two graphs are similar in that they both have positive slope. They are different in that one has a positive vertical intercept while the other has a negative vertical intercept.

b) The slopes of the two graphs are reciprocals because $\frac{9}{5} \times \frac{5}{9} = 1$.

11. a) $2x + y - 7 = 0$; $A = 2$, $B = 1$, $C = -7$

b) $x - y - 3 = 0$; $A = 1$, $B = -1$, $C = -3$

c) $3x - 4y - 8 = 0$; $A = 3$, $B = -4$, $C = -8$

12. f) $y = -3x + 8$, $y = \frac{4}{5}x + 4$

6.3 Graph a Line Using Intercepts, pages 315–322

1. a) x-intercept -2; y-intercept 4

b) x-intercept -5; y-intercept 1

c) x-intercept 3; y-intercept $\frac{1}{2}$

d) no x-intercept; y-intercept 3

e) x-intercept -2; no y-intercept

2. a) The graph is a line crossing the x-axis at 2 and the y-axis at 5.

b) The graph is a line crossing the x-axis at -3 and the y-axis at 3.

c) The graph is a line crossing the x-axis at 1.5 and the y-axis at -4.

d) The graph is a horizontal line crossing the y-axis at 6.

e) The graph is a vertical line crossing the x-axis at 4.

3. a) x-intercept 6; y-intercept 4

b) x-intercept 2; y-intercept 6

c) x-intercept 4; y-intercept -1

d) x-intercept -2; y-intercept 5

e) x-intercept 3; no y-intercept

f) no x-intercept, y-intercept -3

g) x-intercept $\frac{3}{2}$; y-intercept 3

h) x-intercept 5; y-intercept $-\frac{5}{3}$

4. a) slope 1

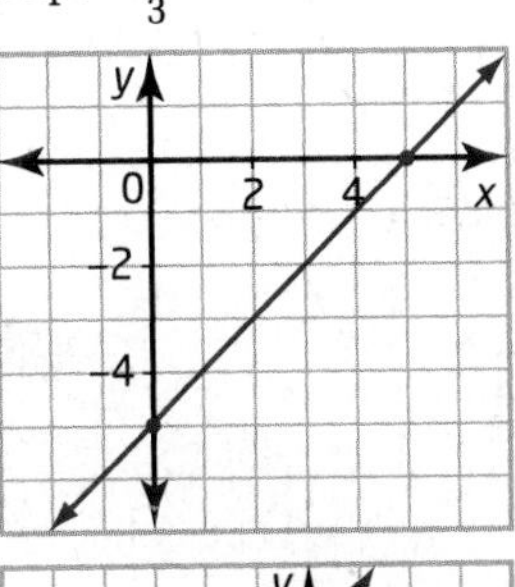

b) slope $\frac{3}{2}$

c) slope undefined

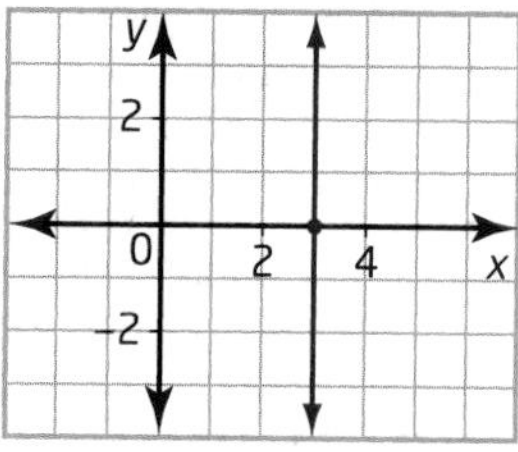

d) slope $\frac{8}{5}$

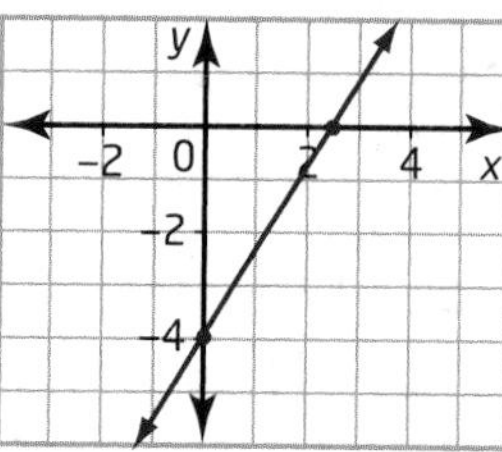

5. a) slope $-\frac{5}{6}$ **b)** slope $\frac{4}{3}$ **c)** slope $\frac{1}{2}$ **d)** slope 0

6. a) The d-intercept, 3.5, represents Carlo's initial distance from the motion sensor because the t-value at the d-intercept is 0.

b) The t-intercept, 7, represents the time at which Carlo's distance from the motion sensor is 0 because the d-value at the t-intercept is 0.

c) Answers will vary. Example: Stand 3.5 m away from the motion sensor and walk at a speed of 0.5 m/s.

7. Answers will vary.

8. a), c)

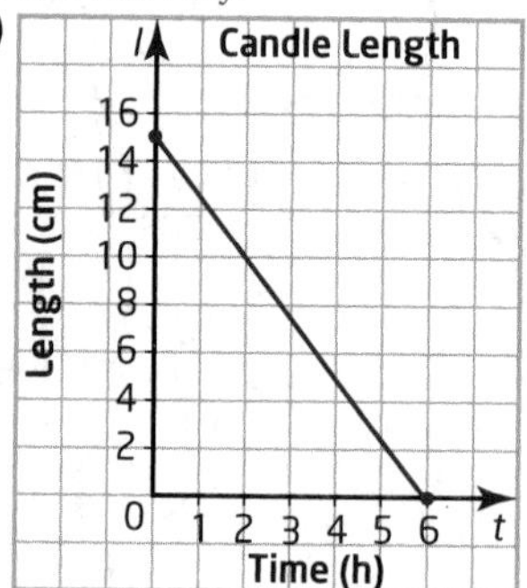

b) The slope should be negative because the candle's length decreases with time.

d) 7.5 cm; 3.75 cm.

e) The t-intercept, 6, represents the time it takes for the candle to burn out completely.

f) The graph has no meaning below the t-axis because a candle cannot have negative length.

9. a) Yes. A horizontal line having y-intercept not equal to 0 has no x-intercept.

b) No. Two distinct lines intersect at one point at most. Considering the x-axis as a line, no other line will cross the axis twice.

c) No. A line can have no x-intercept or no y-intercept, but not both. A line that has no x-intercept is parallel to the x-axis and a line that has no y-intercept is parallel to the y-axis. No line can be parallel to both the x-axis and the y-axis at the same time.

10. b) Answers will vary. Examples:
The x-intercept is increased: The slope decreases.
The x-intercept is decreased: The slope increases.
The y-intercept is increased: The slope increases.
The y-intercept is decreased: The slope decreases.

c) Answers will vary. The increase in the price of comic books means that Joanne will be able to buy fewer comic books. This means that the linear model will have a lower horizontal intercept. Joanne's buying power will be less.

d) Answers will vary. The decrease in the price of novels means that Joanne will be able to buy more novels. This means that the linear model will have a higher vertical intercept. Joanne's buying power will be greater.

11. a) \$1000 **b)** 5 years

c) The slope, −200, shows that the value of the computer decreases by \$200 each year.

12. a)

Time (years)	Computer's Value
0	\$1000.00
1	\$500.00
2	\$250.00
3	\$125.00
4	\$62.50
5	\$31.25

b) non-linear, the points form a curve

A Computer's Value
V
Value (\$)
1000 900 800 700 600 500 400 300 200 100 0
1 2 3 4 5 t
Time (years)

c) Answers will vary. Example: The computer will be worth less than 10% of its value after 3.5 years. It will never be worth \$0 because half of a positive number is always another positive number.

d) No. Answers will vary. Example: It does not exist because the computer's value will never reach 0.

e) Answers will vary. Example: The computer's value depreciates faster in the system where its value is halved each year. This is because half of \$1000 is more than \$200, which is the amount subtracted each year in the other model.

13. a) two x-intercepts; 3 and −3

b) one y-intercept; 9

c)–e) Answers will vary.

14. Answers will vary. Example: Locate B by moving 5 units right, 3 units down, and 1 unit out of the page. Locate C by moving 2 units left, 0 units down, and 4 units out of the page. The resulting figure is a triangle.

15. $y = 3(x - 3)$; The value of a, in this case 6, is the x-intercept. For an equation in the form $y = m(x - a)$, the value of a is the x-intercept of the graph of the line.

Use Technology: Use *The Geometer's Sketchpad®* to Explore Parallel and Perpendicular Lines, pages 323–325

3. b) Answers will vary. In Step 2, the default parameter value for m was left at 1.

4.–6. Answers will vary.

7. 2

9. Answers will vary. Example:

Given Line	Slope of Given Line	Slope of Parallel Line	Slope of Perpendicular Line
$y = -x + 2$	-1	-1	1
$y = \frac{2}{3}x - 4$	$\frac{2}{3}$	$\frac{2}{3}$	$-\frac{3}{2}$
$y = 3x - 3$	3	3	$-\frac{1}{3}$

10. a) They are the same as the original slopes.
b) They are the negative reciprocals of the original slopes.

6.4 Parallel and Perpendicular Lines, pages 326–329

1. a) $\frac{1}{4}$; $\frac{1}{4}$; parallel **b)** 2; 2; parallel
c) -1; 1; perpendicular **d)** $\frac{1}{2}$; $\frac{1}{2}$; parallel

2. a) 0; undefined; perpendicular
b) 0; 1; neither parallel nor perpendicular
c) undefined; undefined; parallel
d) 1; -1; perpendicular

3. a) parallel; $\frac{2}{3}$ and $\frac{4}{6}$ are equivalent
b) perpendicular; $\frac{3}{4}$ and $-\frac{4}{3}$ are negative reciprocals
c) neither; 2 and -2 are unequal and are not negative reciprocals
d) perpendicular; 1 and -1 are negative reciprocals
e) parallel; $\frac{1}{5}$ and 0.2 are equivalent
f) perpendicular; $2\frac{1}{4}$ and $-\frac{4}{9}$ are negative reciprocals

4. a) $\frac{3}{5}$ **b)** -1 **c)** 2
d) $-\frac{4}{3}$ **e)** 0 **f)** undefined

5. a) $-\frac{5}{3}$ **b)** 1 **c)** $-\frac{1}{2}$
d) $\frac{3}{4}$ **e)** undefined **f)** 0

6. Answers will vary. Example: Any two lines with slope $\frac{1}{2}$.

7. Answers will vary. Example: Any two lines with slope $\frac{1}{4}$.

8. a)

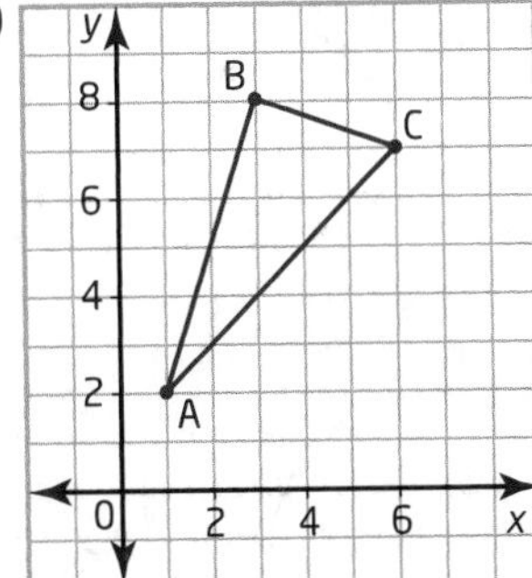

b) The triangle appears to be a right triangle with the right angle at B.
c) slope of AB is 3; slope of AC is 1; slope of BC is $-\frac{1}{3}$
d) The slopes of AB and BC are negative reciprocals. This means that AB and BC are perpendicular. Perpendicular lines meet at right angles so this is a right triangle.

9. a) The slope of AB is $-\frac{4}{3}$. The slope of AC is $-\frac{3}{2}$. The slope of BC is $-\frac{7}{5}$. No two pairs of slopes are negative reciprocals so no two of lines AB, AC, and BC are perpendicular. △ABC is not a right triangle.
b) The slope of PQ is $\frac{1}{2}$. The slope of PR is -2. The slope of QR is $-\frac{4}{7}$. The slopes of lines PQ and PR are negative reciprocals so PQR is a right triangle.

10. a) Possible answers: $(-2, -2)$; $(-6, 3)$; $(3, -1)$; $(8, -5)$; $(-1, -6)$; $(4, -10)$
b) There is more than one solution. Example: the points $(-2, -2)$ and $(-6, 3)$ both produce right triangles.

12. a) $2x + 5y = 10$: x-intercept 5, y-intercept 2; $2x + 5y = -10$: x-intercept -5, y-intercept -2
b) $3x + 4y = 12$: x-intercept 4, y-intercept 3; $3x + 4y = -12$: x-intercept -4, y-intercept -3
c) Answers will vary.

13. a) $3x + 5y = 15$: x-intercept 5, y-intercept 3; $5x - 3y = -15$: x-intercept -3, y-intercept 5
b) $2x + 7y = 14$: x-intercept 7, y-intercept 2; line $7x - 2y = -14$: x-intercept -2, y-intercept 7
c) Answers will vary.

14. a) 7 **b)** 4 **c)** none

6.5 Find an Equation for a Line Given the Slope and a Point, pages 330–337

1. a) $y = x + 2$ **b)** $y = -3x - 4$ **c)** $y = \frac{2}{3}x + \frac{22}{3}$
d) $y = -\frac{1}{2}x + \frac{1}{2}$ **e)** $y = -\frac{4}{5}x$ **f)** $y = 2x - \frac{1}{4}$

2. a) $y = -3x$ **b)** $y = \frac{2}{3}x - \frac{23}{3}$ **c)** $y = -6$
d) $y = \frac{5}{2}x$ **e)** $y = -3$ **f)** $y = -\frac{1}{4}x + \frac{13}{2}$

3. a) $C = 10d + 15$ **b)** \$80

c)

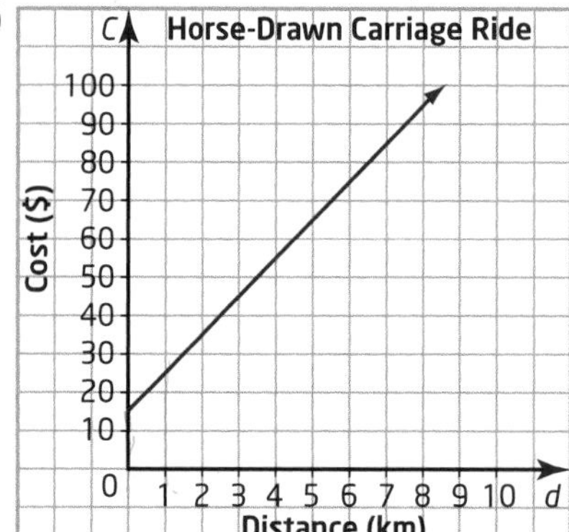

d) \$80

4. a)

Distance (km)	Cost (\$)	First Differences
2.5	40	
3.5	50	10
4.5	60	10
5.5	70	10
6.5	80	10

b) 8.5 km **c)** \$73 **d)** Answers will vary.

5. $y = \frac{2}{3}x - 1$

6. $y = -\frac{5}{4}x - 4$

7. x-intercept 9; y-intercept 8

8. a) Answers will vary. Example: It means that after 3 h of driving toward Ottawa, Aki has 300 km left to drive.

b) This value shows that for each hour that Aki drives, his distance from Ottawa decreases by 80 km. It is negative because it represents a decreasing distance per hour.

c) 540 **d)** $d = -80t + 540$

e) The d-intercept represents Aki's distance from Ottawa just as he started his trip.

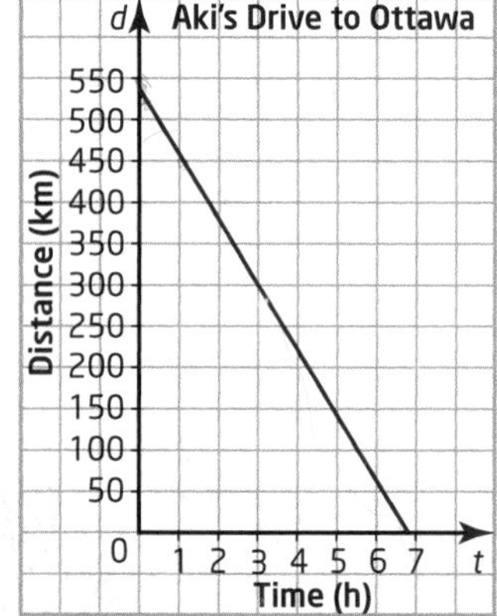

f) $6\frac{3}{4}$ h

g) No. Aki has driven for 3 h at 80 km/h. So, he has driven 240 km. He still has 300 km to drive. At 80 km/h, this will take him another $3\frac{3}{4}$ h.

10. a) 7 **b)** $C = 2.5d + 7$

11. a)

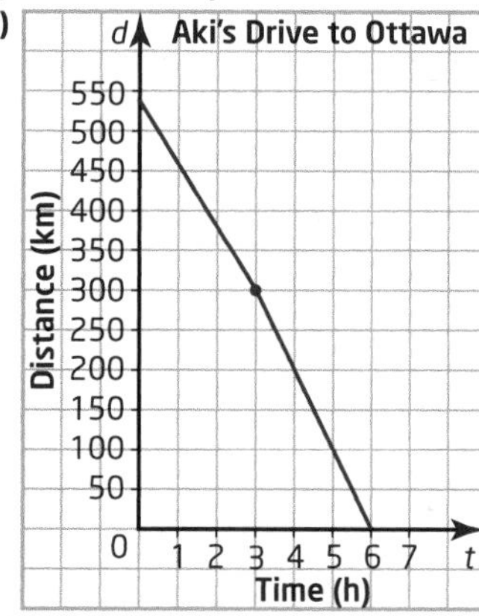

b) Answers will vary. The answer to part f) would change from $6\frac{3}{4}$ h to 6 h, and the answer to part g) would change to yes, because Aki has driven for 3 h up to this point and will drive for exactly another 3 h.

c) Explanations and methods used will vary.

6.6 Find an Equation for a Line Given Two Points, pages 338–343

1. a) $y = x + 1$ **b)** $y = -\frac{3}{2}x + 5$

c) $y = -10x - 26$ **d)** $y = -\frac{5}{3}x + \frac{5}{6}$

2. a) $y = x + 2$ **b)** $y = -\frac{2}{3}x$

3. a) $y = \frac{1}{2}x - 2$ **b)** $y = -x - 5$

4. a) $y = 3$ **b)** $x = -2$

5. a) \$2 per game **b)** $C = 2.00g + 10.50$

c) Graphs will vary depending on scale chosen.

d) \$10.50; It represents the fixed base cost of using the bowling alley.

e) \$50.50 **f)** \$50.50

g) Answers will vary. The graph is inexact. The equation does not give a visual image.

6. a) Fiona is moving away from the sensor because she is farther away from it after 4 s than she was after 2 s.

b) 1.5 m/s **c)** $d = 1.5t - 1.5$

d) The d-intercept, −1.5, means that Fiona's initial position was 1.5 m behind the motion sensor.

7. a) The point (5, 17.25) represents Colette's wage of \$17.25/h with 5 years of experience and the point (1, 14.25) represents Lee's wage of \$14.25/h with 1 year of experience.

b) slope 0.75; w-intercept 13.50; The slope represents the yearly wage increase, and the w-intercept represents the starting wage.

c) $w = 0.75n + 13.50$ **d)** \$18.75

e) \$32.25; Answers will vary.

8. a) 80 km/h **b)** $d = -80t + 240$

c) Yes, with 15 min to spare. It is necessary to assume that the family's driving speed stays at 80 km/h.

9. a) Lucas: $d = -\frac{1}{2}t + 6$; Myrna: $d = \frac{1}{2}t + 2$

b) 4 s **c)** 4 m

d) Answers will vary. Example: Lucas's distance has to equal Myrna's distance, so set the right sides of the equations equal. Then solve for t.

10. a)

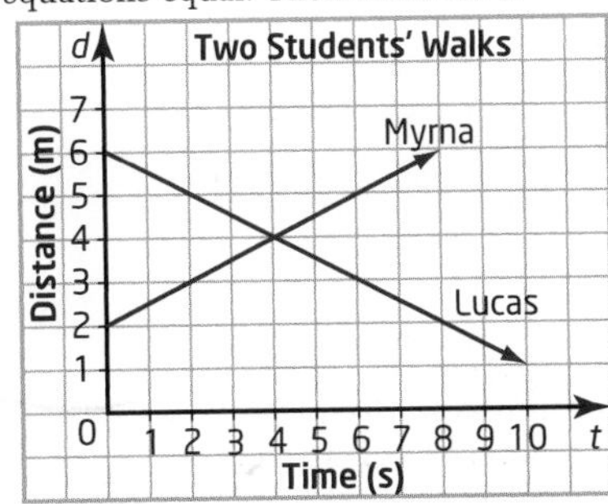

b) (4, 4)

c) Answers will vary. Example: The point of intersection shows that Lucas and Myrna were both 4 m away from the sensor after 4 s. This means that they must have crossed paths at this time and distance from the sensor.

6.7 Linear Systems, pages 344-351

1. a) (3, 1) **b)** (−2, 2)

2. a) (3, −3) **b)** (6, −2)

c) (3, 2) **d)** (3, 3)

3. a) Standard Rate option: $300; Frequent Extremist option: $340

b) The Standard Rate option, because it costs $40 less.

4. a) Standard Rate option: $1000; Frequent Extremist option: $900

b) The Frequent Extremist option, because it costs $100 less.

5. Yes. If Mike went skiing 10 times, then the Standard Rate option would cost 10 × $50, or $500, while the Frequent Extremist option would cost $100 + 10 × $40, or $500. This situation is represented in the graph by the point of intersection (10, 500).

6. Answers will vary. Example: This special may affect the couple's decision because the point of intersection is now (30, 1400). This means that the cost for 30 guests at each hotel is the same. For fewer than 30 guests, the Waverly Inn is cheaper. For more than 30 guests, the Hotel Niagara is cheaper.

7. 2:50 P.M.; 16.6 km

8. (12, 14)

9. a) 100 m **b)** 8 m/s **c)** 6 m/s

d) Cersei will win if the race is longer than 400 m while Tyrion will win if the race is shorter than 400 m. If the race is 400 m, then they will tie.

e) Answers will vary. Example: The solution of this linear system is the point (50, 400). This means that if Cersei gives Tyrion a head start of 100 m, she will catch up with him after she has run 400 m and he has run 300 m. This will occur 50 s after they both start running.

10. a) Answers will vary. Example: If Tyrion's head start is doubled, then his distance-time equation will be $d = 6t + 200$ and the new intersection point will be (100, 800). This means that if the race is less than 800 m, Tyrion will win, and if the race is more than 800 m, Cersei will win. If the race is 800 m exactly, they will tie.

b) Answers will vary. Example: If Tyrion's head start is halved, then his distance-time equation will be $d = 6t + 50$ and the new intersection point will be (25, 200). This means that if the race is less than 200 m, Tyrion will win, and if the race is more than 200 m, Cersei will win. If the race is 200 m exactly, they will tie.

12. a)

Year	Numberton's Population	Decimalville's Population
0	25 000	15 000
1	26 000	16 500
2	27 000	18 150
3	28 000	19 965
4	29 000	21 962
5	30 000	24 158
6	31 000	26 573
7	32 000	29 231
8	33 000	32 154
9	34 000	35 369
10	35 000	38 906
11	36 000	42 797
12	37 000	47 076
13	38 000	51 784
14	39 000	56 962
15	40 000	62 659

b)

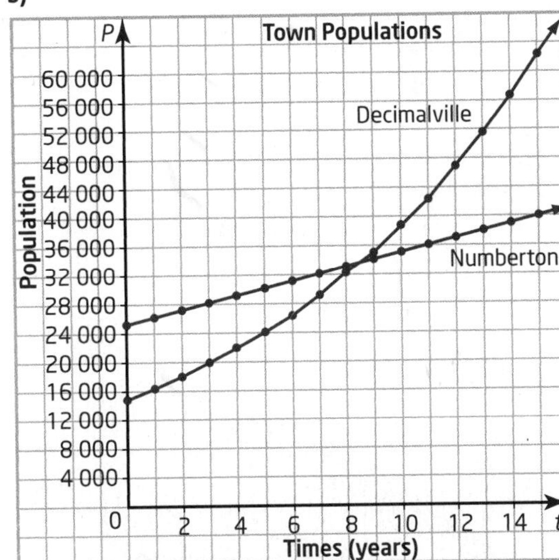

c) Numberton's population growth pattern is linear while Decimalville's population growth pattern is non-linear.

d) The solution to this system occurs some time in the eighth year when both populations number between 33 000 and 34 000. Up to this time, Numberton's population was greater, but after this time, Decimalville's population will be greater.

13. B

14. $y = -\frac{3}{2}x + \frac{3}{2}$

15. a) $(-1, 2)$ **b)** $(-1, 2)$

c) Answers will vary. Example: The point of intersection of several lines whose constants, in standard form, are arithmetic sequences is always $(-1, 2)$.

Chapter 6 Review, pages 352–353

1. a) slope 1; y-intercept 2 **b)** slope -2; y-intercept 0

2. a) slope -3; y-intercept 2 **b)** slope $\frac{3}{5}$; y-intercept -1

3. a) $y = -2x + 3$

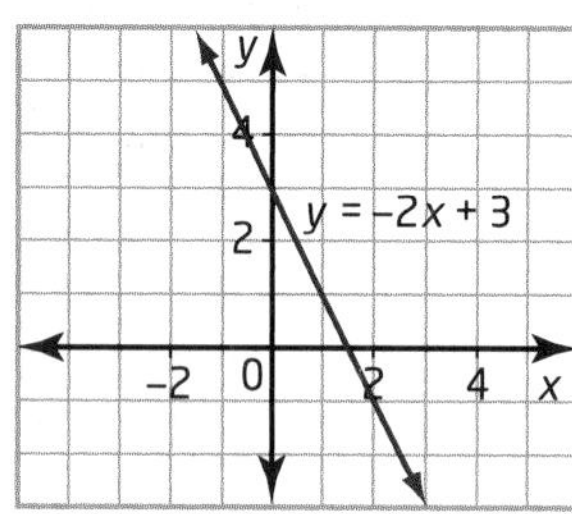

b) $y = \frac{2}{3}x - 4$

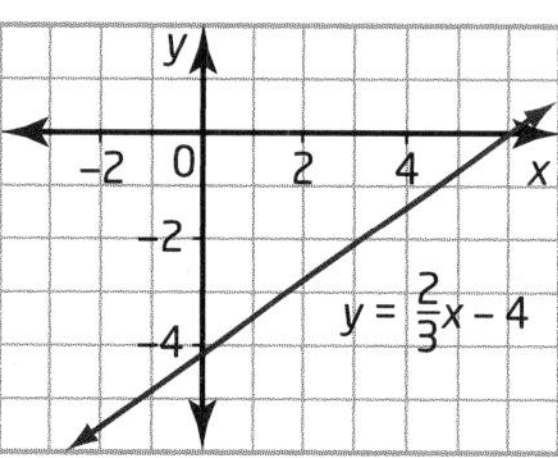

c) $y = 2$

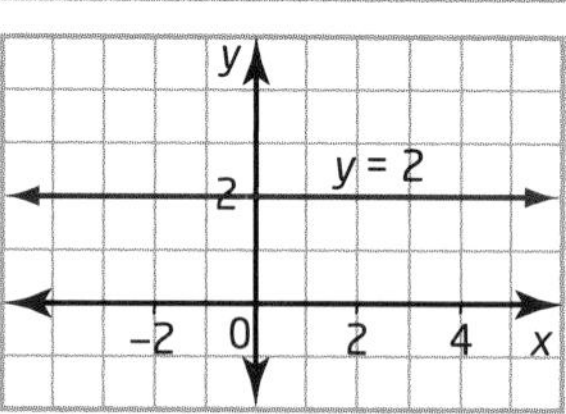

4. a) The slope is 1 and the d-intercept is 2. The slope shows that the person is moving away from the motion sensor at a speed of 1 m/s. The d-intercept shows that the person started 2 m away from the sensor.

b) $d = t + 2$

5. a) $y = -2x + 6$ **b)** $y = -\frac{3}{5}x - 3$

6. a) $C = 60n + 90$

b) The slope is 60 and the C-intercept is 90. The slope represents the dollar amount per hour that the plumber charges. The C-intercept shows that the plumber also charges a base cost of $90.

c) Graphs will vary depending on scale chosen.

d) $270

7. a) x-intercept 4; y-intercept -3

b) x-intercept $\frac{3}{2}$; y-intercept -9

8. a) 6 **b)** 9

c) 2 hamburgers and 6 pops; 4 hamburgers and 3 pops; also, any combination of hamburgers and pops that totals less than $18.

9. The slopes of parallel lines are identical. For example, $y = 3x + 1$ and $y = 3x - 5$ are parallel lines with slope 3.

10. The slopes of perpendicular lines are negative reciprocals. For example, $y = 3x + 1$ and $y = -\frac{1}{3}x$ are perpendicular lines.

11. $y = \frac{2}{3}x - \frac{14}{3}$

12. $y = \frac{3}{4}x - \frac{9}{2}$

13. $y = -\frac{1}{2}x$

14. a) 24 L **b)** $f = 32t + 24$

c) 4 h 15 min **d)** $f = 24t + 24$; 5 h 40 min

15. $y = -2x + 1$

16. a) $d = 0.75t + 1.75$

b) The slope, 0.75, shows that Claudia is walking at a speed of 0.75 m/s away from the motion sensor. The d-intercept, 1.75, shows that she started 1.75 m away from the sensor. **c)** 5.5 m

17. a) $(-3, -3)$

18. a) (4, 160). This means that both tutors charge $160 for 4 h of tutoring.

b) If a student wants to spend as little money as possible, then for less than 4 h the student should hire Mr. Wellington. The student should hire Ms. Tenshu for more than 4 h of tutoring. The assumption is that both tutors are equally helpful.

Chapter 6 Practice Test, pages 354–355

1. C

2. D

3. B

4. B

5. A

6. a) 5 m

b) She was walking toward the sensor, because the distance-time graph has a negative slope.

c) She was walking at a speed of 1 m/s.

d) $d = -t + 5$

7. a) The x-intercept is 2 and the y-intercept is -6.

b)

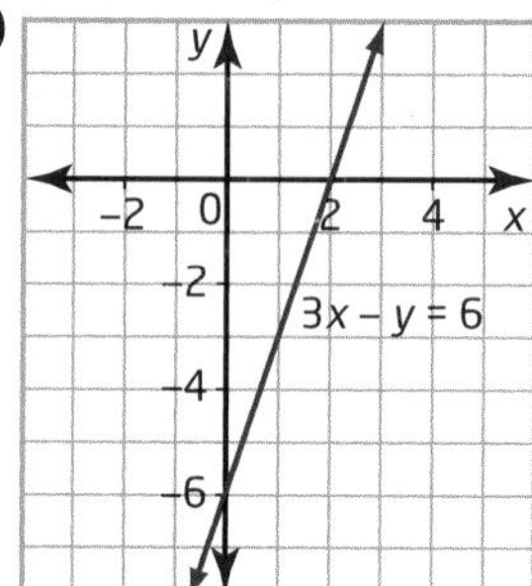

8. a) $C = 75n + 60$

b) The slope, 75, represents the dollar amount per hour that the electrician charges. The y-intercept, 60, represents the fixed dollar amount that the electrician charges on top of the hourly charge.

c) Graphs will vary depending on scale chosen.

d) $210

9. $y = \frac{2}{3}x - \frac{11}{3}$

10. $y = \frac{4}{3}x$

11. a) 1.9 L; 0.45 L **b)** $G = \frac{L}{3.8}$

c) approximately 1.053 gallons; approximately 0.066 gallons

12. $y = -\frac{3}{2}x - \frac{9}{2}$

13. a)

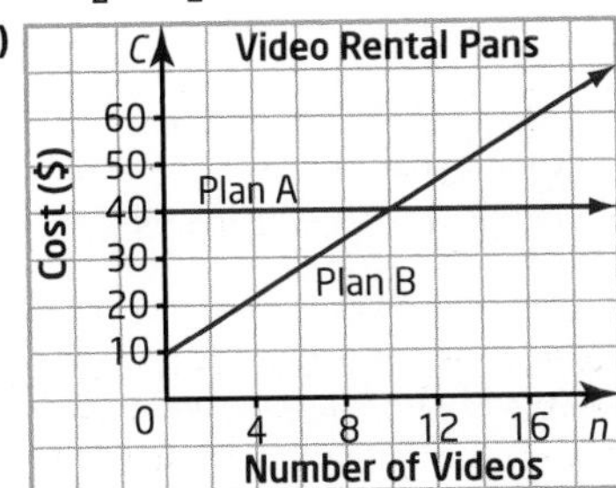

b) If you rent fewer than 10 videos in a month, Plan B is cheaper. If you rent more than 10 videos, Plan A is cheaper. For 10 videos both plans cost the same, \$40.

14. a) 160 km/h **b)** $d = 160t$ **c)** 2:30 P.M.

Chapters 4 to 6 Review, pages 356–357

1. a) $x = -3$ **b)** $y = -42$ **c)** $w = 4$
d) $s = 4$ **e)** $n = 4$ **f)** $r = 6$

2. a) $x = 5$ **b)** $y = -3$ **c)** $w = -2$
d) $s = -1$ **e)** $n = \frac{10}{7}$ **f)** $k = 3$

3. 5, 5, 6

4. a) $x = -16$ **b)** $n = 16$ **c)** $y = -17$ **d)** $k = 19$

5. a) $P = A - I$ **b)** $r = \frac{d}{2}$
c) $a = \frac{v - u}{t}$ **d)** $l = \frac{P}{2} - w$

6. a) width 15 m, length 28 m **b)–c)** Answers will vary.

7. a) Natalie is paid \$9 for each hour that she works.
b) $P = 9t$, where t represents the time, in hours, that Natalie works and P represents the total amount she is paid for this time. The constant of variation represents the dollar amount that Natalie is paid per hour.
c) \$81

8. a) \$50 **b)** \$15 per 100 km
c) $C = 0.15d + 50$ **d)** \$162.50

9. a) $\frac{3}{4}$ **b)** $-\frac{3}{5}$ **c)** 0 **d)** $\frac{4}{3}$

10. a) 1.2 km/min
b)

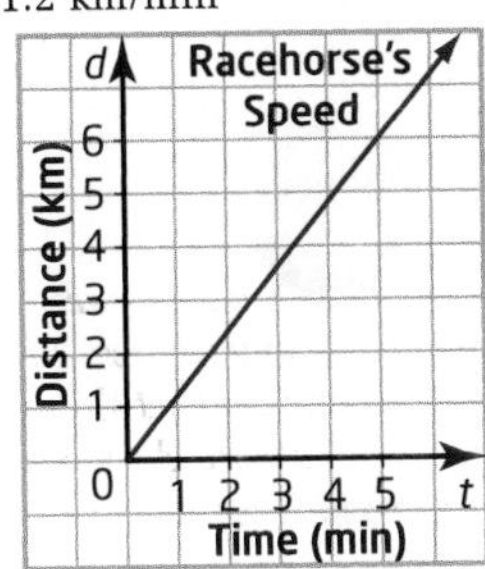

c) The rate of change of the horse's distance is the slope of the line. It shows how quickly the horse's distance changes. It represents average speed: in this case 1.2 km/min or 72 km/h.

11. a) linear

x	y	First Differences
0	5	
1	7	2
2	9	2
3	11	2
4	13	2

b) non-linear

x	y	First Differences
0	−4	
2	−2	2
4	2	4
6	8	6
8	16	8

12. a) Graphs will vary depending on scale chosen.
b) Answers will vary. Multiply any value of x by $\frac{4}{5}$ and add 4 to obtain the corresponding y-value.
c) $y = \frac{4}{5}x + 4$

13. a) slope $\frac{1}{2}$; y-intercept -1; $y = \frac{1}{2}x - 1$
b) slope $-\frac{2}{3}$; y-intercept 4; $y = -\frac{2}{3}x + 4$

14. a) $y = \frac{3}{4}x + 2$
b) The slope is $\frac{3}{4}$ and the y-intercept is 2.
c)

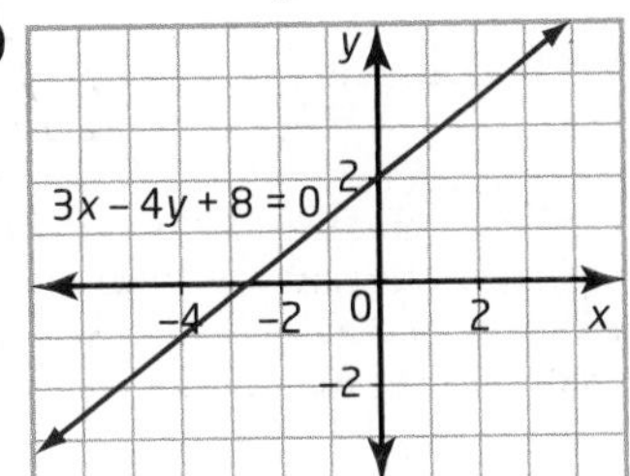

15. a) x-intercept 2; y-intercept -6
b) x-intercept $-\frac{15}{2}$; y-intercept: 3

16. a) The lines are perpendicular because their slopes, 2 and $-\frac{1}{2}$, are negative reciprocals.
b) The lines are parallel because their slopes are both -3.
c) The lines are neither parallel nor perpendicular. Their slopes are $\frac{3}{4}$ and $\frac{4}{3}$, which are neither equal nor negative-reciprocals.
d) The lines are perpendicular because $y = 3$ is a horizontal line and $x = -2$ is a vertical line.

17. a) $y = \frac{1}{3}x + 1$ **b)** $y = -2x - 1$

18. **a)**

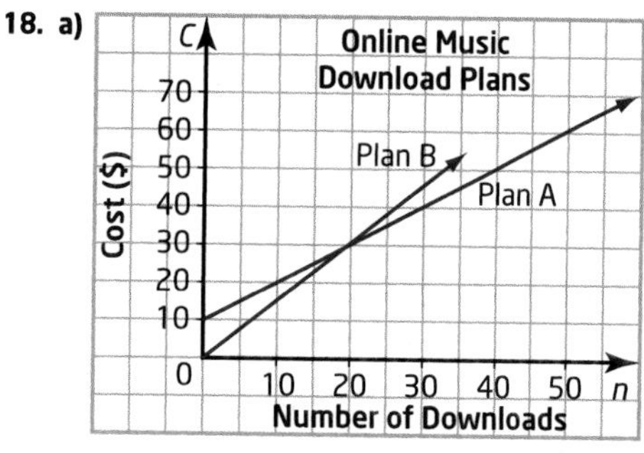

b) If you make fewer than 20 downloads per month, then Plan B is cheaper. If you make more than 20 downloads a month, then Plan A is cheaper.

Chapter 7

Get Ready, pages 362–363

1. **a)** isosceles **b)** scalene
2. **a)** equilateral, acute **b)** isosceles, obtuse
3. **a)** irregular pentagon **b)** regular hexagon
4. **a)** parallelogram; opposite sides are parallel.
   b) rhombus; the four sides are equal
5. **a)** 50° **b)** 55°
6. **a)** $a = 75°$, opposite angles; $b = 75°$, corresponding angles; $c = 75°$, alternate angles.
   b) $a = 40°$, corresponding angles; $b = 40°$, opposite angles; $c = 140°$, supplementary angles (also co-interior with a)

7.1 Angle Relationships in Triangles, pages 364–373

1. **a)** 115° **b)** 126° **c)** 134° **d)** 112°
2. **a)** 40° **b)** 155° **c)** 145°
3. C
4. **a)** 105° **b)** 155° **c)** 80°
5. **a)** 70° **b)** $x = 115°, y = 146°, z = 81°$
   c) $w = 43°, x = 137°, y = 43°, z = 137°$
   d) $w = 92°, x = 136°, y = 44°, z = 136°$
   e) $a = 22°, b = 92°, c = 22°, d = 136°, e = 44°$
6. 140° and 80°, or 110° and 110°
7. 120°
8. isosceles and equilateral
9. **a)** The sum of two obtuse angles is more than 180°.
   b) Yes, any acute triangle has three obtuse exterior angles.
10. **a)** 175°
    b) interior angle, 85°; exterior angle, 95°
11. $w = 40°, x = 43°, y = 90°, z = 47°$
12. **a)** 120°, 120°, 120° **b)** 72°, 144°, 144°
    c) 60°, 120°, 180°, impossible
    d) 90°, 90°, 180°, impossible
    e) 90°, 120°, 150°
    f) 96°, 120°, 144°
    g) 72°, 96°, 192°, impossible; exterior angles must be less than 180°
14. B
15. C

7.2 Angle Relationships in Quadrilaterals, pages 374–383

1. **a)** 64° **b)** 101°
   c) 45° **d)** 115°
2. A
3. B
4. **a)** 135° **b)** 155°
   c) 150° **d)** 90°
5. **a)** $w = 110°, x = 70°$
   b) $y = 138°, z = 42°$
   c) $a = 55°, b = 125°, c = 125°$
6. The sum of the exterior angles is 360°.
7. **a)** $x = 95°, y = 85°$
   b) $a = 61°, b = 72°, c = 108°, d = 93°, e = 76°$
8. Three angles, each at a different vertex; you can use angle relationships to calculate the others.
9. **a)** impossible since $\angle A + \angle B + \angle C = 395°$
   b) fourth angle measures 105°
   c) fourth angle measures 205°
10. **a)** impossible; sum of four obtuse angles is greater than 360°
    b) Example: two 120° angles and two 60° angles
    c) Example: 150° angle and three 70° angles
    d) Example: 120° angle, 60° angle, and two 90° angles
    e) impossible; fourth angle must also be a right angle
11. 90°
12. **a)** 125° **b)** 80°
    c) Answers will vary. Example: Triangles and quadrilaterals are easy to construct; triangles are rigid.
13. $u = 106°, w = 74°, x = 50.5°, y = 89°, z = 114.5°$
14. **a)** Yes.
    b), c) yes for square but not for rectangle
15. **b)** 360° **c)** 720°
    d) The sum of the interior angles of quadrilateral is equal to the sum of the interior angles of the four triangles less the sum of the angles at E.
16. **a)** 90°, 90°, 90°, 90° **b)** 60°, 60°, 120°, 120°
    c) 36°, 72°, 108°, 144° **d)** 60°, 80°, 100°, 120°
17. Answers will vary.
18. B
19. 3 or 0

7.3 Angle Relationships in Polygons, pages 384–393

1. **a)** 1440° **b)** 2340° **c)** 3240°
2. **a)** 128.6° **b)** 150°
3. **a)** 5 sides **b)** 12 sides **c)** 19 sides
4. pentagon: 5, 2, 3, 540°
   decagon: 10, 7, 8, 1440°
   icosagon: 20, 17, 18, 3240°
5. equal interior angles, equal exterior angles, and equal sides
6. Sum of the interior angles is $180°(4 - 2) = 360°$. Since the angles are equal, each one measures $\frac{360°}{4}$ or 90°.
7. **a)** 120° **b)** Answers will vary.
   c) The angles do not change.
8. **b)** 6 **c)** 1260°
9. **a)** 144° **b)** 157.5° **c)** 162°
   d) $\frac{180(n-2)}{n}$

10. **a)** 11 sides **b)** 147.3°
c) Answers will vary. Examples: easier for blind people and vending machines to recognize, harder to forge
11. No; the sum is 360° for all convex polygons.
12. triangles, squares, hexagons
13. **a)** 12 **b)** 150°
c) 30° **e)** 60°
14. **a)** pentagon
b) Rotate a line segment 45° about one endpoint seven times.
c) 18°
d) The angle of rotation is 360° divided by the number of sides.
16. Yes; regular polygons have angles less than 180°.
17. Answers will vary. Example: Yes; an n-sided concave polygon can be divided into $n - 2$ triangles by diagonals from two or more vertices (or use *The Geometer's Sketchpad®* to measure angle sums in various concave polygons).
18. Answers will vary.
19. Answers will vary.
20. B
21. A

7.4 Midpoints and Medians in Triangles, pages 394–400

1. **a)** 2 cm **b)** 12 cm
2. **a)** 8 cm^2 **b)** 8 cm^2
3. **a)** 19 cm^2 **b)** 38 cm^2
4. 2.5 cm
5. **a)** Answers will vary. Examples:
b) Fold along the median and see if the equal sides line up.
c) Construct the isosceles triangle and median, and then measure the angle on either side of the median.
d) The median bisects the angle.
6. ∠ADC is obtuse when D is close to A.
7. **a), b)** Any scalene triangle with a 60° angle is a counter-example.
c) Since the angles sum to 180°, one of the angles must be larger than 60° and the third angle must be smaller. The largest angle is opposite the largest side, and the smallest angle is opposite the smallest side. Therefore, the 60° angle is opposite the second-longest side.
8. Yes; since △ABD and △ACD are congruent (ASA or SAS), the perpendicular at D must pass through A.
9. No; the angles in each triangle are not equal.
10. Medians intersect at one point in all triangles.
11. **a)** △BEG and △CEG have the same area because GE is a median of △BGC.
b) The same logic applies, since DG and GF are also medians.
c) AE is a median, so △ABE has the same area as △ACE. Since the areas of △BEG and △CEG are equal, the areas of △ABG and △ACG are also equal. The areas of the two triangles in △ABG are equal, as are the areas of the two triangles in △ACG. Therefore, △ADG, △BDG, △AFG, and △CFG each have an area equal to half that of △ABG. Comparing △BCF and △BAF shows that △BEG and △CEG also each have an area half that of △ABG.

12. **b)** First step, $\frac{1}{4}$; second step: $\frac{1}{4} + \frac{1}{4}\left(\frac{3}{4}\right)$;
third step: $\frac{1}{4} + \frac{1}{4}\left(\frac{3}{4}\right) + \frac{1}{4}\left(\frac{3}{4}\right)^2$;
nth step $\frac{1}{4} + \frac{1}{4}\left(\frac{3}{4}\right) + \frac{1}{4}\left(\frac{3}{4}\right)^2 + \ldots + \frac{1}{4}\left(\frac{3}{4}\right)^{n-1}$
c) about 0.6836 or 68.36%
13. **a)** The right bisectors of a triangle intersect at a single point.
b) Yes; the circle passes through all three vertices of the triangle.
14. **a)** The angle bisectors of a triangle always intersect at a point.
b) Yes; the circle's radius is the minimum distance from the intersection of the angle bisectors to any side of the triangle.
15. No; for an obtuse triangle the intersection is outside the triangle.
16. c), d), g)

7.5 Midpoints and Diagonals in Quadrilaterals, pages 401–407

1. EF is parallel to HG, EH is parallel to FG
2. BE = 6 cm, CE = 8 cm, AC = 16 cm, BD = 12 cm
3. PT = 7 m, ST = 5 m
4. 40 cm
5. **a)** all four **b)** rectangle, square
c) rhombus, square **d)** rhombus, square
6. when ABCD is a rectangle
7. **a)** False; any quadrilateral with four unequal sides is a counter-example.
b) True; a line segment joining opposite midpoints creates two parallelograms with equal heights and bases.
8. **a)** square
b) The area of WXYZ is half the area of PQRS. The diagonals of WXYZ form four triangles that are congruent to the triangles outside WXYZ.
c) rhombus
d) No; all the triangles are still congruent.
9. **b)** 90° **c)** rectangle
d), e) Answers will vary. Example: The area of EFGH is half the area of ABCD.
10. Answers will vary. Examples:
a) The area of EFGH is half the area of ABCD.
b) Use geometry software to compare the areas.
11. Answers will vary. Example:
b) By the Pythagorean theorem, $AD^2 + AB^2 = BD^2 = CD^2 + AB^2$. So, AD = CD.
c) △ABD is congruent to △CBD (SSS), so ∠ABD equals ∠CBD.
13. In any parallelogram ABCD, △ABC and △CDA are congruent (SSS), as are △ABD and △CDB. Thus, ∠CAB = ∠ACD, ∠CDB = ∠ABD, ∠ACB = ∠DAC, and ∠ADB = ∠CBD. △ABE and △CDE are congruent (ASA), so DE = BE and AE = CE.
14. **b)** △ABC and △CDA are congruent (SSS). So, ∠BCA = ∠CAD. Since ∠BCA, ∠CAB, and ∠ABC sum to 180°, ∠CAD + ∠CAB+ ∠ABC = 180°. Therefore, AD is parallel to BC. Similarly, AB is parallel to CD.

15. Answers will vary. Examples:
   a) The five triangles formed by two adjacent sides of PQRST ($\triangle$ABC, $\triangle$BCD, and so on) are isosceles and congruent (SAS). So, all the acute angles in these triangles are equal. Then, $\triangle$ABR, $\triangle$BCS, $\triangle$CDT, $\triangle$DEP, and $\triangle$EAQ are all congruent (ASA). The obtuse angles of these triangles are opposite to the interior angles of PQRST. Thus, these angles are all equal. $\triangle$DPT, $\triangle$EPQ, $\triangle$AQR, $\triangle$BRS, and $\triangle$CST are all congruent (SAS), so the sides of PQRST are all equal.
   b) Yes; both are regular pentagons.
   c) By measuring the diagram $\frac{AB}{PQ} \doteq 2.7$
   d) Ratio of areas is $\left(\frac{AB}{PQ}\right)^2 \doteq 7.1$.
16. a) 45 b) 66
17. a) $\frac{n(n-1)}{2}$ b) $\frac{n(n-3)}{2}$

Chapter 7 Review, pages 408–409

1. a) 110° b) 125°
   c) $w = 75°$, $x = 105°$, $y = 135°$, $z = 30°$
2. The exterior angle would be greater than 180°.
3. a) any obtuse triangle
   b) impossible; third exterior angle would be greater than 180°
   c) any acute triangle
   d) impossible; sum of exterior angle would be less than 360°
4. a) 100°
   b) $b = 105°$, $c = 70°$, $d = 85°$, $e = 100°$, $f = 80°$
   c) $x = 52°$, $y = 52°$, $z = 128°$
5. a) Example: three 110° angles
   b) impossible; sum of the interior angles would be greater than 360°
   c) Example: three 100° angles
   d) impossible; sum of the exterior angles would be greater than 360°
6. a) 720° b) 1080° c) 1800°
7. a) 108° b) 140° c) 157.5°
8. 30
9. Answers will vary.
10. DE connects the midpoints of AB and AC. Therefore, the base and altitude of $\triangle$ADE are half those of $\triangle$ABC.
11. a) Each median divides the triangle into two triangles. All of these triangles are congruent (SAS). The medians are equal in length since they are sides of the congruent triangles.
   b) False; any scalene triangle is a counter-example.
12.–13. Answers will vary.

Chapter 7 Test, pages 410–411

1. C
2. B
3. B
4. D
5. B
6. a) 95° b) 90°
   c) $c = 145°$, $d = 60°$, $e = 85°$, $f = 95°$
   d) $v = 55°$, $w = 50°$, $x = 75°$, $y = 70°$, $z = 110°$
7. Answers will vary. Examples:
   a) The sum of the interior angles is 360°. Opposite interior angles are equal. Adjacent interior angles are supplementary.
   b) The diagonals bisect each other and bisect the area of the parallelogram.
8. Example: $\angle A = \angle C = 90°$, $\angle B = 60°$, $\angle D = 120°$
9. 2160°
10. 15
11. Answers will vary. Example: Run the fence along the median from the right vertex of the lot.
12. a) hexagon
   b) Yes, the sides are equal, and measuring with a protractor shows that the interior angles are equal.
   c) 120°
   d) For regular polygons, the measure of the interior angles increases as the number of sides increases.

Chapter 8

Get Ready, pages 414–417

1. a) 9.6 m b) 26 cm c) 6.3 mm
   d) 13.2 cm e) 90 m f) 35 mm
2. a) 17.6 cm b) 32.0 m c) 219.9 mm
   d) 39.3 cm
3. 42 m
4. a) 38.6 cm^2 b) 105.7 cm^2
5. a) 11.34 m^2 b) 60.45 cm^2
6. a) 52 m^2 b) 2513 cm^2
7. 24 m^3; 9425 cm^3
8. a)

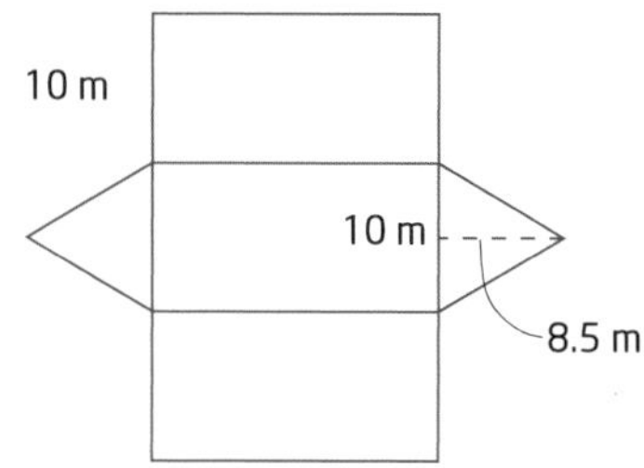

   b) 685 m^2 c) 850 m^3
9.–11. Answers will vary.

8.1 Apply the Pythagorean Theorem, pages 418–425

1. a) 10 cm b) 13 m c) 6.6 m d) 8.6 cm
2. a) 15 cm b) 9.2 m c) 7.7 m d) 7.4 cm
3. a) 24 cm^2 b) 34.1 m^2
4. a) 4.5 units b) 2.8 units c) 5 units
5. 35 cm
6. 38 m
7. 119 m
8. 104.56 m

9. 11 stones
10. 64 cm
11. 40 ft
12. a) $\sqrt{2}$; $\sqrt{3}$; $\sqrt{4}$; $\sqrt{5}$
b) $\frac{\sqrt{1}}{2} + \frac{\sqrt{2}}{2} + \frac{\sqrt{3}}{2} + \frac{\sqrt{4}}{2}$
c) As you add right triangles to the spiral pattern, the area will increase by $\frac{\sqrt{\text{Number of Triangles}}}{2}$.
13. a) This name is appropriate because this set of three whole numbers satisfies the Pythagorean theorem.
b) Yes.
c) Yes, they are Pythagorean triples, with some restrictions on the values of m and n.
d) $m > n > 0$

8.2 Perimeter and Area of Composite Figures, pages 420–435

1. a) 52 m b) 29 cm c) 54 m
d) 52 cm e) 24 cm
2. a) 370 mm^2 b) 104 m^2 c) 30 cm^2
d) 45 cm^2 e) 321 cm^2 f) 174 m^2
3. a) 62 m b) 232 m^2
c) To find the perimeter:
Step 1: Use the Pythagorean theorem to determine the length of the unknown side.
Step 2: Add the dimensions of the outer boundary to determine the perimeter.
To find the area: Use the formula for the area of a trapezoid.
4. a) 1500 cm^2 b) 1 paint can c) $4.54
5. 300 mm^2
6.–7. Answers will vary.
8. a) 180 plants b) 48 m^2
9. Answers will vary.
10. a) 1810 cm^2 b) 36%
11. a) 2.2 m b) 9 m
12. 5400 cm^2
14. a) 50 m^2
b) The area of the lawn is four times the area of one flower bed.
c) It is only true if the vertices of the inscribed square are at the midpoints.
15. Doubling the radius quadruples the area. $\text{Area}_1 = \pi r^2$; $\text{Area}_2 = \pi(2r)^2$ or $4\pi r^2$. So, $\text{Area}_2 = 4 \times \text{Area}_1$.
16. a) 34, 55, 89, 144
b) areas: 1, 2, 6, 15, 40, 104, ...
c)–d) Answers will vary.
17. 1:5
18. 40 cm^2

8.3 Surface Area and Volume of Prisms and Pyramids, pages 436–443

1. a) 279.65 cm^2 b) 147 cm^2
2. a) 2000 mm^3 b) 2 m^3
3. a) 700 mm^2 b) 492 cm^2
4. a) 480 cm^2 b) 10.35 m^2
5. a) 52 m^2 b) 24 m^3
6. 30 cm
7. a) 1 694 000 m^3 b) 115 324 m^2
8. 143.5 m
9. Yes
10. a) 30 cm
b) There are no irregularities (bumps/dimples) on the surface. Also, the top of the juice container is flat and the container is completely full.
11. a) 47 m^3 b) 15 cans c) $292.39
12. a) Answers will vary. Example: 80 m^3
b) 92 000 L
c) 920 min or 15 h and 20 min
13. a) Answers will vary. Example: Double the volume.
b) original prism 240 cm^3; new prism 480 cm^3
c) Answers will vary. Yes.
d) Yes; doubling the height of a triangular prism doubles the volume of the prism.
15. The height of the pyramid is three times the height of the prism.
Volume of pyramid $= \frac{1}{3}lwh$
Volume of prism $= lwh$
If the two volumes are equal, then the height of the pyramid must be three times the height of the prism because w and l are the same for both.
16. a) 56 m^2 b) $1980
17. a)
$$\begin{aligned} \text{SA} &= 2(lw + wh + lh) \\ \text{SA}_{\text{new}} &= 2[(2l \times 2w) + (2w \times 2h) + (2l \times 2h)] \\ &= 2[4lw + 4wh + 4lh] \\ &= 4[2(lw + wh + lh)] \end{aligned}$$
b) The new volume is eight times the old volume.
$$\begin{aligned} \text{Volume}_{\text{old}} &= lwh \\ \text{Volume}_{\text{new}} &= 2l \times 2w \times 2h \\ &= 8lwh \end{aligned}$$
18. 48

8.4 Surface Area of a Cone, pages 444–450

1. a) 9 m^2 b) 1257 cm^2 c) 141 cm^2
2. a) 13 m b) 283 m^2
3. a) 158 cm^2
b) Answers will vary. There is no paper being overlapped.
4. a) Yes.
b) No. The second cone. The slant height is the same for both, but in the expression πrs, the second cone has the greater radius.
c) 141 cm^2; 249 cm^2; yes
5. a) 5 cm b) 3 cm
6. No. Answers will vary. Example: The formula for the surface area of the cone is $\text{SA} = \pi r^2 + \pi rs$. When the height is doubled only the term πrs is changed. The term πr^2 remains unaltered. Hence, doubling the height of a cone does not double the surface area.
7. No. Answers will vary. Example: The formula for the surface area of a cone is $\text{SA} = \pi r^2 + \pi rs$. When the radius is doubled, the term πr^2 will quadruple and the term πrs will more than double. Hence, the surface area of the new cone will be more than double the original cone.
8. a) radius 5 cm, height 10 cm
b) 254 cm^2
9. 1307 cm^2
10. 158 m^2

11. **a)** base of the frustum, lateral area of the frustum, top of the frustum, outer walls of the cylinder, inner walls of the cylinder, the thin strip of the cylinder, the outer part of the base of the cylinder, the inner part of the base of the cylinder
b) 34 382 cm^2 **c)** 4 cans

12. Answers will vary.

13. **a)** radius $= \frac{x}{2}$, height $= x$, slant height $= \frac{\sqrt{5}}{2}x$
b) $SA = \frac{\pi x^2}{4} + \frac{\sqrt{5}}{4}\pi x^2$

14. **a)** $s = \frac{\text{Lateral Area}}{\pi r}$ **b)** $s = 7.96$ cm

15. Answers will vary. about 72 000 000 m^2

16. **a)** $SA = 4\pi + 2\pi s$
b) Graphs will vary. Should be a set points along a straight line.
c) Answers will vary. Example: It is a linear relation.

8.5 Volume of a Cone, pages 451–456

1. **a)** 25 cm^3 **b)** 188 m^3
c) 2827 cm^3 **d)** 25 133 cm^3

2. **a)** 2 m^3 **b)** 2964 cm^3

3. 264.1 cm^3

4. 7.1 cm

5. 100 cm^3

6. Answers will vary.

7. 450 cm^3

8. **a)** Answers will vary. Example: 18 m
b) 16.98 m
c) Answer will vary.

9. **a)** Answers will vary. Example: The cone with base radius of 4 cm has the greater volume. The formula for the volume of a cone contains two factors of r and only one factor of h. Hence, the volume is more dependent on r than on h.
b) Cone (height 4 cm, base radius 3 cm):
Volume = 38 cm^3
Cone (height 3 cm, base radius 4 cm):
Volume = 50 cm^3

10. 141 045 cm^3

11. **a)** $h = \frac{3V}{\pi r^2}$ **b)** 59.7 cm

12. 2.8 cm

13. **a)** radius 5 cm, height 10 cm **b)** Estimates will vary. 1:4
c) 262 cm^3 **d)** 1:3.82 **e)** Answers will vary.

14. 9.1 m

15. Answers will vary. Example: When the radius is constant, a change in height produces a proportional change in volume.

16. **a)** $V = \frac{20}{3}\pi r^2$
b)

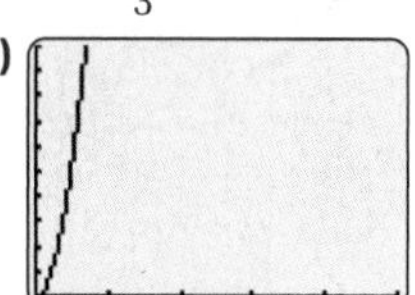

c) Answers will vary. Example: The relation is increasing for all values of r greater than 0 (since the radius cannot be negative). The growth rate is non-linear.

17. D

8.6 Surface Area of a Sphere, pages 457–461

1. **a)** 452 cm^2 **b)** 11 461 mm^2
c) 28 m^2 **d)** 99 m^2

2. **a)** Answers will vary. about 4800 mm^2
b) 5027 mm^2; Answers will vary.

3. 1.8 m

4. **a)** 1932.2 cm^2 **b)** $5.41

5. **a)** 514 718 540 km^2
b) Assumption: Earth is a sphere

6. **a)** 145 267 244 km^2
b) approximately 3.5 times greater

7. **a)** Answers will vary. Example: 10 800 cm^2. No; two jars will be required.
b) 11 310 cm^2
c) Answers will vary. Example: Yes; whether you use the approximate value or the exact value, two jars of reflective crystals are required to cover the gazing ball.

8. **a)** Answers will vary. Example: 750 cm^2
b) 804 cm^2 **c)** Answers will vary.

9. **a)** Y1=4πX²
X=4 Y=201.06193
b) The radius must be greater than 0. As the radius increases, the surface area also increases in a non-linear pattern.
c) 360 cm^2; 2.5 cm

10. **a)** $r = \sqrt{\frac{SA}{4\pi}}$ **b)**

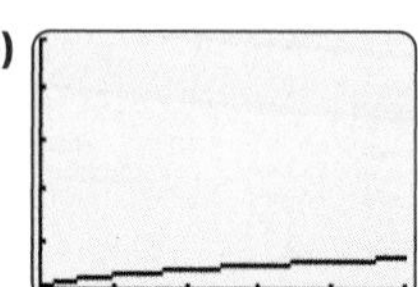

c) The radius and the surface area must be greater than 0. The trend between the two variables is non-linear with the radius increasing as the surface area increases but at a slower rate.
d) 4 cm

11. The surface area has increased by a factor of nine.
$SA_{old} = 4\pi r^2$
$SA_{new} = 4\pi(3r)^2$
$= 4\pi(9r^2)$
$= 9(4\pi r^2)$

12. The cube with edge length $2r$.

13. **a)** Answers will vary. Example: $\frac{1}{2}$
b) surface area of sphere $= 100\pi$;
surface area of cube $= 600$; π:6
c) Answers will vary.
d) 1:1.91

8.7 Volume of a Sphere, pages 462–469

1. a) 11 994 cm^3 b) 137 258 mm^3 c) 5 m^3
2. 42 cm^3
3. 268 cm^3
4. a) 33 510 mm^3 b) 64 000 mm^3 c) 30 490 mm^3
5. a) 70.16 cm
   b) Answers may vary. Example: The largest lollipop had the same mass per cubic centimetre as the small lollipop.
6. a) 113 097 cm^3 b) 169 646 cm^3 c) 2:3
   d) Yes. When the sphere just fits inside the cylinder, $h = 2r$. So,

$$\begin{aligned}\frac{\text{Volume}_{\text{sphere}}}{\text{Volume}_{\text{cylinder}}} &= \frac{\frac{4}{3}\pi r^3}{\pi r^2(2r)}\\ &= \frac{\frac{4}{3}\pi r^3}{2\pi r^3}\\ &= \frac{4}{3} \times \frac{1}{2}\\ &= \frac{2}{3}\end{aligned}$$

7. 258.86 cm^2
8. a) Answers will vary. b) 736 m^3
   c) 588 m^3 d) 12 truckloads
9. 111 m^3
10. Answers will vary.
12. Estimates will vary. Actual radius is 5.23 cm.
13. a) 998.3 cm^3
    b) 5.2 cm
14. by a factor of about 2.83
15. a) Estimates will vary. Example: 1:2
    b) Volume of the sphere = 268 cm^3; Volume of the cube = 512 cm^3; π:6
    c) Answers will vary.
16. the cube
17. Answers will vary.
18. B
19. 365.88 cm^3

Review, pages 470–471

1. a) perimeter 32.0 cm; area 43.1 cm^2
   b) perimeter 28.4 cm; area 31.2 cm^2
2. 5.7 m
3. a) perimeter 28 m; area 48 m^2
   b) perimeter 32.6 cm; area 61.8 cm^2
4. a) 401.1 m b) 463.9 m c) 62.8 m
5. a) 220 cm^2 b) 138 736 m^2
6. a) 6 510 000 cm^3
   b) 256 024 cm^2
   c) Answers will vary. Example: The side walls of the tent are flat.
   d) Answers will vary. Example: The answer is fairly reasonable as when erecting a tent, you want the side walls to be as flat and stretched as possible.
7. 9.9 cm
8. 283 cm^2
9. 1458 cm^2
10. 3.1 cm
11. 670 cm^3; $\text{Volume}_{\text{Cone}} = \frac{1}{3} \times \text{Volume}_{\text{Cylinder}}$
12. 1493.0 cm^2
13. a) 257 359 270 km^2
    b) Earth is a sphere.
    c) Answers will vary. Example: about $\frac{1}{25}$.
14. 5806.5 cm^3
15. a) Answers will vary. Example: about 5200 cm^3
    b) 5283.07 cm^3
    c) Answers will vary.

Practise Test, pages 472–473

1. C
2. A
3. A
4. D
5. B
6. a) 213 cm^3 of wax
   b) 236.3 cm^2; Assumption: No plastic cover is being overlapped.
7. Answers will vary. Example: 5080 cm^2 if the paper towels are stacked in three columns with two rolls in each column.
8. Doubling the radius of a sphere will increase the volume eight times. Doubling the radius of a cylinder will quadruple the volume.
9. 523 cm^2
10. 1047 m^3
11. a) 1396.5 cm^3 b) 776 cm^2 c) 55 cm^2
    d) Answers will vary. Example: The circular lid covers the top of the cylindrical can with no side parts.
12. a) 465.5 cm b)

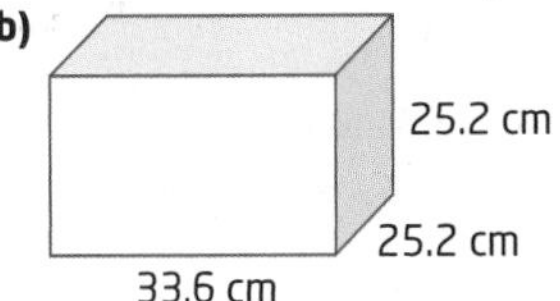

    c) 10 165.3 cm^3 d) 4657 cm^2

Chapter 9

Get Ready, pages 476–477

1. a) 60 cm; 200 cm^2 b) 38 m; 76.56 m^2
2. a) 25.1 cm; 50.3 cm^2 b) 3.8 cm, 1.1 cm^2
3. a) 320 cm^3; 304 cm^2 b) 114.39 m^3; 143.54 m^2
4. a) 1847 cm^3; 836 cm^2 b) 314 m^3; 291 m^2
5. a) i) 3072 cm^3; 1280 cm^2 ii) 3072 cm^3; 1088 cm^2
   b) Their volumes are equal.
   c) The second container requires less material.
6. a) i) 2513 cm^3; 817 cm^2 ii) 2513 cm^3; 1084 cm^2
   b) Their volumes are equal.
   c) The first container requires less material.

9.1 Investigate Measurement Concepts, pages 478–483

1. a) the dimensions of various rectangles with a perimeter of 24 units

b) Answers will vary. Example:

Rectangle	Width (units)	Length (units)	Perimeter (units)	Area (square units)
1	1	11	24	11
2	2	10	24	20
3	3	9	24	27
4	4	8	24	32
5	5	7	24	35

2. a) the dimensions of various rectangles with a perimeter of 20 units using toothpicks

b) Answers will vary. Example: Begin with one toothpick as the width and nine toothpicks as the length. Then increase the width by one toothpick and decrease the length by the same amount to construct a series of rectangles with a perimeter of 20 units.

Rectangle	Width (units)	Length (units)	Perimeter (units)	Area (square units)
1	1	9	20	9
2	2	8	20	16
3	3	7	20	21
4	4	6	20	24
5	5	5	20	25

3. a) the dimensions of various rectangles with an area of 12 square units using a geoboard

b) Answers will vary. Example: Let the space between two pins be 1 unit and use an elastic band to make different rectangles with an area of 12 square units. Start with a width of 1 unit and increase by intervals of one, and find the necessary length.

Rectangle	Width (units)	Length (units)	Area (square units)	Perimeter (units)
1	1	12	12	26
2	2	6	12	16
3	3	4	12	14

4. a)

Rectangle	Width (m)	Length (m)	Perimeter (m)	Area (m²)
1	1	16	34	16
2	2	8	20	16
3	4	4	16	16

b) The greater the perimeter, the more expensive the shed; the smaller the perimeter, the lower the cost.

c) Rectangle 3 (a square) with dimensions 4 m by 4 m will be the most economical.

d) Answers will vary. Example: The quality of the material used to construct the shed and what will be stored in it.

5. A rectangle with dimensions 4 m by 4 m encloses the greatest area for the same amount of fencing.

6. 64 m^2

7. b) triangle: equilateral with each side 12 m, area 62.35 m^2
rectangle: each side 9 m, area 81 m^2
hexagon: each side 6 m, area 93.6 m^2
circle: radius of 5.73 m, area 103.15 m^2

c) Yes. Difference shapes allow for different areas. The greatest area can be achieved by using a circle.

9.2 Perimeter and Area Relationships of a Rectangle, pages 484–490

1. a) 5 m by 5 m **b)** 9 m by 9 m
c) 12.5 m by 12.5 m **d)** 20.75 m by 20.75 m

2. a Answers may vary. Example: 1 m by 2 m, 1.5 m by 1.5 m, 1.4 m by 1.6 m

b) 1.5 m by 1.5 m

3. a) 20.5 m by 20.5 m

b) No. 20.5 m cannot be created using 2-m barriers.

c) 20.25 m^2

4. 8 m by 4 m

5. a) 196 m^2 **b)** 784 m^2

6. a) extra 196 m^2

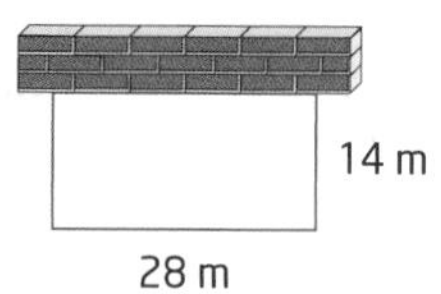

b) extra 789 m^2

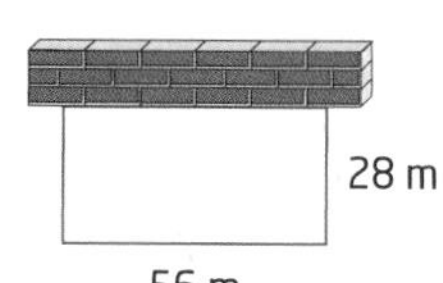

7. The greatest area, 400 m^2, is enclosed when the length and width are each 20 m.

8. 4 sides: a square with sides each 8 m; area 64 m^2
3 sides: a rectangle 8 m by 16 m; area: 128 m^2

8 m
16 m

2 sides: a square with sides 16 m; area: 256 m^2

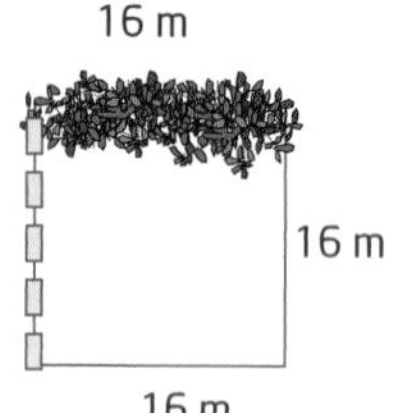

9. a)

Rectangle	Width (m)	Length (m)	Area (m²)	Fence Used (m)
1	1	72	72	74
2	2	36	72	40
3	3	24	72	30
4	4	18	72	26
5	5	14.4	72	24.4
6	6	12	72	24

b) 6 m by 12 m **c)** 24 m

10.–11. Answers will vary.

13. 5.92 m by 5.92 m
14. 5 m by 10 m
15. an equilateral triangle with side length 17.3 cm
16. a square with side length 14.1 cm
17. Yes. A circle has greater area, 45.8 cm^2.
18. Each field is 41.7 m by 62.45 m.

9.3 Minimize the Surface Area of a Square-Based Prism, pages 491–497

1. B, C, A
2. **a)** 8 cm by 8 cm by 8 cm
   b) 10 cm by 10 cm by 10 cm
   c) 9.1 cm by 9.1 cm by 9.1 cm
   d) 10.6 cm × 10.6 cm × 10.6 cm
3. **a)** 384 cm^2 **b)** 600 cm^2 **c)** 497 cm^2 **d)** 674 cm^2
4. cube with side length 14.7 cm
5. **a)** 15.9 cm by 15.9 cm by 15.9 cm
   b) Answers will vary.
6. **a)** 9.09 cm by 9.09 cm by 9.09 cm
   b) 495.8 cm^2
7. 1110 cm^2
8. **a)** 17.1 cm by 17.1 cm by 8.5 cm
   b) different
   c) The lidless box requires less material.
9. **a)** cube with side length 5.8 cm
   b) Answers will vary. Example: Cubical boxes are harder to hold and the cube would be very small.
   c) Answers will vary.
10. Answers will vary.
11. Try to get the square-based prism to be as close to a cube in shape as possible. The dimensions are 5 by 5 by 4.
12. **a)**
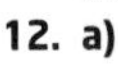
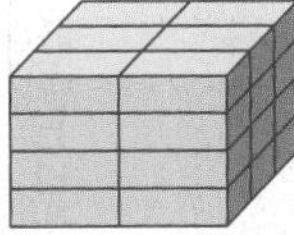
   b) This is the closest that 24 boxes can be stacked to form a cube.
   c) Answers will vary. Example: No. A cube can be created to package 6 tissue boxes: length 1 box (1 × 24 cm), width 2 boxes (2 × 12 cm), and height 3 boxes (3 × 8 cm).
13. 12.6 m by 12.6 m by 6.3 m; surface area 476.22 m^2
14. 23 760 cm^2
15. 1206.7 cm^2

9.4 Maximize the Volume of a Square-Based Prism, pages 498–503

1. B, C, A
2. **a)** 5 cm by 5 cm by 5 cm
   b) 20 m by 20 m by 20 m
   c) 11.2 cm by 11.2 cm by 11.2 cm
   d) 14.1 m by 14.1 m by 14.1 m
3. **a)** 125 cm^3 **b)** 8000 m^3
   c) 1405 cm^3 **d)** 2803 m^3
4. 10.8 cm by 10.8 cm by 10.8 cm
5. **a)** 2016 cm^2; 5184 cm^3
   b) 18.3 cm by 18.3 cm by 18.3 cm
   c) 6128 cm^3
6. **a)** 6.72 m^2; 1.152 m^3
   b) 1.1 m by 1.1 m by 1.1 m
   c) 1.331 m^3
7. **a)** 1.4 m by 1.4 m by 1.4 m **b)** 3 m^3
8. **a)** 20.4 cm by 20.4 cm by 20.4 cm
   b) 8490 cm^3 **c)** 7790 cm^3
   d) Answers will vary. There is no empty space in the box. The DVD would fit into the cube with enough room around the edges for the shredded paper. The shredded paper is tightly packed.
10. **a)** 69.3 cm by 69.3 cm by 69.3 cm
   b)
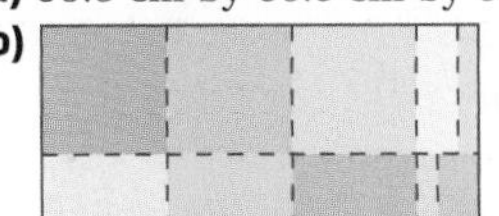
   Diagrams will vary.
   c) Answers will vary. Assume that Dylan cuts the wood carefully to not waste any pieces.
11. **a)**
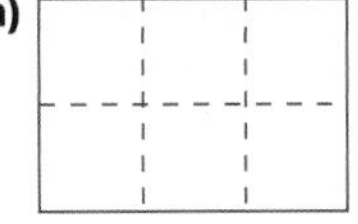
   b) 1000 cm^3
   c) Answers will vary.
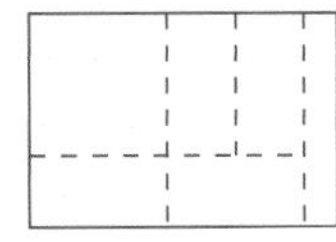
   d) 1185.2 cm^3
   e) Answers will vary. Example: No loss due to cuts.

9.5 Maximize the Volume of a Cylinder, pages 504–509

1. **a)** $h = 15.96$ cm, $r = 7.98$ cm
   b) $h = 1.46$ m, $r = 0.73$ m
   c) $h = 5.16$ cm, $r = 2.58$ cm
   d) $h = 36.86$ mm, $r = 18.43$ mm
2. **a)** 3193 cm^3 **b)** 2 m^3
   c) 108 cm^3 **d)** 39 333 mm^3
3. 2 m^3
4. **a)** $r = 2.0$ m, $h = 4.0$ m **b)** 50 265 L
   c) Answers will vary. Example: no metal will be wasted in the building process, no metal is being overlapped
5. **a)** 12 cm
   b) 60 CDs
   c) Answers will vary. Example: only the dimensions of the CDs need to be considere; no extra space is left for the container's closing mechanism, the plastic container has no thickness.
6. **a)** Answers will vary. Example: Adjust the surface area formula for the new cylinder, isolate the height and run a few trials using a spreadsheet to find the maximum volume.
   b) $h = 7.3$ cm, $r = 7.3$ cm
7. **a)** Answers will vary.
   b) cylinder: $r = 11.28$ cm, volume 9018 cm^3; square-based prism: $s = 20$ cm, volume 8000 cm^3

8. **a)** Answers will vary.
   b) sphere: $r = 12.62$ cm; cylinder: $r = 10.30$ cm, $h = 20.60$ cm, ; square-based prism: $s = 18.26$ cm
   c) sphere 8419.1 cm^3; cylinder 6865.8 cm^3; square-based prism 6088.4 cm^3
   d) The sphere has the greatest volume. Yes, this will always be the case.
   e) For a given surface area:
   volume of a sphere > volume a cylinder > volume of a square-based prism
9. **a)** $r = 0.33$ m, $h = 0.63$ m
   b) $r = 0.46$ m, $h = 0.46$ m
10. $r = 6.53$ cm, $h = 9.24$ cm

9.6 Minimize the Surface Area of a Cylinder, pages 510–515

1. **a)** $r = 5.8$ cm, $h = 11.6$ cm
   b) $r = 0.5$ m, $h = 1.0$ m
   c) $r = 3.3$ cm, $h = 6.6$ cm
   d) $r = 0.9$ cm, $h = 1.8$ cm
2. **a)** 634 cm^2 **b)** 5 m^2
   c) 205 cm^2 **d)** 15 m^2
3. $r = 4.4$ cm, $h = 8.8$ cm
4. **a)** $r = 9.3$ cm, $h = 18.6$ cm
   b) Answers will vary. Example: No extra material will be needed to enclose the volume.
5. $r = 12.4$ cm, $h = 24.8$ cm
6. **a)** $r = 3.9$ cm, $h = 7.8$ cm
   b) $3.44
7. Answers will vary. Example: It is not always practical to use cylinders with the optimum volume. They may be harder to use, to handle, to carry, or to store.
8. A cylinder will have a surface area of 349 cm^2, and a cube will have a surface area of 378 cm^2. A cylinder is more cost efficient.
9. No, because the cylindrical shape is taller than its diameter. However, there is a large glass area which would encourage solar heating.
11. **a)** $r = 7.8$ cm, $h = 7.8$ cm
    b) 576 cm^2
    c) Answers will vary. Example: The only cardboard needed is used to enclose the required volume so there is no wastage.
12. **a)** Answers will vary.
    b) prism 600 cm^2, cylinder 553.7 cm^2, sphere 483.1 cm^2; The sphere has the least surface area.
13. a sphere with volume 20 183 cm^3
14. $s = 26.67$ cm, $h = 10$ cm
15. $r = 4.24$ cm, $h = 11.95$ cm
16. $r = 6.91$ cm, $h = 19.54$ cm

Review, pages 516–517

1. **a)**

Rectangle	Width (m)	Length (m)	Perimeter (m)	Area (m^2)
1	1	19	40	19
2	2	18	40	36
3	3	17	40	51
4	4	16	40	64
5	5	15	40	75
6	6	14	40	84
7	7	13	40	91
8	8	12	40	96
9	9	11	40	99
10	10	10	40	100

   b) 10 possible rectangles when the side measurements are integers
   c) 10 by 10 because it has the greatest area
2. **a)**

   b)

Rectangle	Width (m)	Length (m)	Perimeter (m)	Area (m^2)
1	1	16	34	16
2	2	8	20	16
3	4	4	16	16

   c) 4 m by 4 m because for the same enclosed area, it has the least perimeter. Thus, fewer edging bricks will be required.
3. 1 m by 1 m
4. **a)** 900 m^2 **b)** 1800 m^2
5. **a)** 42.4 m by 42.4 m
   b) Answers will vary. Example: A square ice rink may not be best as people want longer straight paths to gain speed.
6. 9.6 cm by 9.6 cm by 9.6 cm
7. **a)** 10 cm by 10 cm by 10 cm
   b) Answers will vary. Example: The surface area of a cylinder that contains the same volume will be less than the surface area of the box. The manufacturer could save on packaging costs.
8. 1244 cm^2
9. 0.58 m by 0.58 m by 0.58 m
10. 14.1 cm by 14.1 cm by 14.1 cm
11. It is not possible to cut six 14.1 cm by 14.1 cm pieces from a 60 cm by 20 cm piece of cardboard because only four such pieces fit.
12. $r = 6.18$ cm, $h = 12.36$ cm, volume 1483 cm^3

13. Change the formula in the height column from =(D2-2*PI()*A2^2)/(2*PI()*A2) to =(D2-PI()*A2^2)/(2*PI()*A2). The mathematical formula for finding the height changes from $h = \frac{SA - 2\pi r^2}{2\pi r}$ to $h = \frac{SA - \pi r^2}{2\pi r}$.
14. Answers will vary. Example: A cylinder will have a greater volume using the same amount of cardboard but the square-based prism may be easier for customers to store.
15. **a)** 300.53 cm^2, when $r = 3.99$ cm, $h = 8.00$ cm
    b) Answers will vary. Example: There is no waste while making the pop can.
16. **a)** 61 CDs **b)** No extra space is allowed.
    c) 701.4 cm^2

Practice Test, pages 518–519

1. B
2. D
3. B
4. A
5. 50 cm by 50 cm
6. Their volumes are equal but the cylinder requires less material to make.
7. **a)** 17.1 cm by 17.1 cm by 17.1 cm
   b) Answers will vary. Example: No material is overlapped, no extra material is required for sealing purposes.
8. **a)** 1.2 m by 1.2 m by 1.2 m
   b) 1.728 m^3
   c) 0.69 m by 0.69 m by 0.69 m
   d) The three small bins have a total volume of 0.99 m^3, which is less than the one large box.
9. $r = 18.53$ m, $h = 18.54$ m
10. 1.2 m by 1.2 m by 0.5 m

Chapters 7 to 9 Review, pages 520–521

1. **a)** $a = 68°$, $b = 60°$
   b) $x = 45°$, $y = 135°$, $z = 135°$
2. **a)** $p = 90°$, $q = 65°$, $r = 115°$
   b) $b = 75°$, $c = 30°$, $d = 100°$
3. **a)**

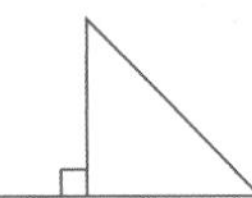

   b) Each exterior angle and its adjacent interior angle have a sum of 180°. Thus an exterior right angle has an adjacent interior right angle. This cannot occur in a triangle because two right interior angles have a sum of 180°, leaving no room for the triangle's third angle.
   c)

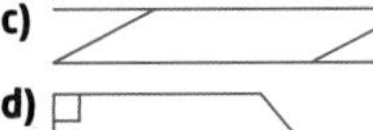

   d)

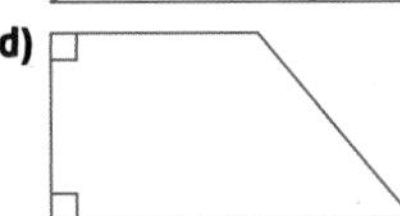

4. **a)** 10 **b)** 360°
5. **a)**
   b) Answers will vary.
6. Yes.
7. **a)** False.

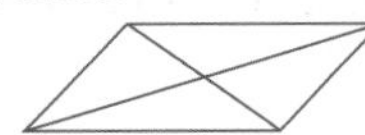

   b) True. The line joining the midpoints of two sides of a triangle is always parallel to the third side.
   c) False.

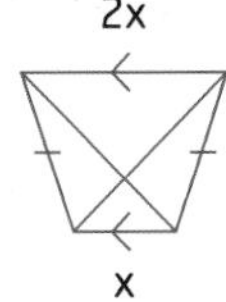

8. **a)** 13.9 m, 8.1 m^2
   b) 60.3 cm, 155.7 cm^2
9. 20 m, 18.56 m^2
10. **a)** 48.3 m^2, 15.6 m^3
    b) 2425 cm^2, 4583.3 cm^3
11. 8.0 cm
12. **a)** 108 cm^2
    b) 75 cm^3
13. **a)** 33 510 mm^3
    b) 5027 mm^2
    c) The entire surface of a golf ball is covered with small indentations (commonly known as dimples). Due to the presence of dimples, the actual surface area of the golf ball is greater and the volume of the golf ball is less than that calculated in parts a) and b).
14. **a)** 6.5 m by 6.5 m
    b) 42.25 m^2
    c) 26 m
15. 2774 cm^2
16. **a)** 5 cm by 5 cm by 5 cm
    b) radius 2.8 cm, height 5.6 cm
17. 293 cm^2

Glossary

A

acute angle An angle whose measure is less than 90°.

acute triangle A triangle in which each of the three interior angles measures less than 90°.

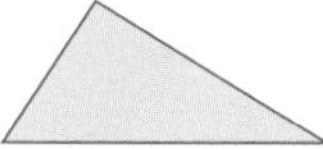

adjacent angles Two angles that share the same vertex and have one side in common.

∠ADB and ∠BDC are adjacent angles.

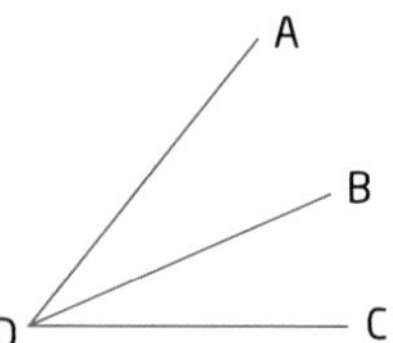

algebra tiles A collection of squares and rectangles, with different coloured sides, that are used to represent units and variables.

algebraic expression A mathematical phrase made up of numbers and variables, connected by addition or subtraction operators.

$x - 3$, $5y$, and $6 + 2k$ are algebraic expressions.

algebraic modelling The process of representing a relationship by an equation or a formula, or representing a pattern of numbers by an algebraic expression.

alternate angles Pairs of equal angles formed on either side of a transversal crossing a pair of parallel lines.

$b = g$

$c = f$

altitude The height of a geometric figure.

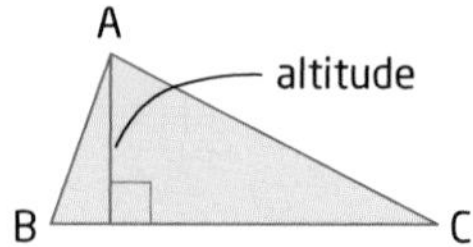

angle bisector A line that divides an angle into two equal parts.

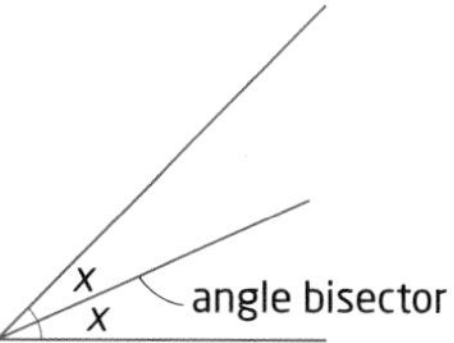

approximate Give a rounded answer or measurement.

area The number of square units contained in a two-dimensional region.

average (also known as the mean) The sum of a set of values divided by the number of values in the set.

The mean of 1, 5, and 6 is $\frac{1 + 5 + 6}{3}$, or 4.

B

bar graph A graph that uses bars to represent data.

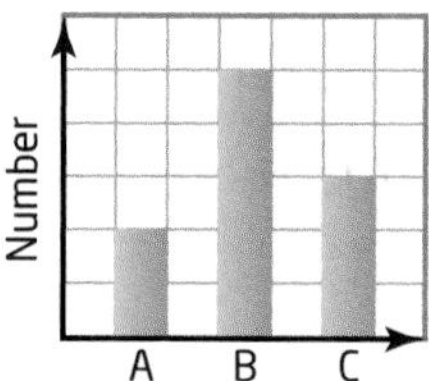

base (of a power) The number used as a factor for repeated multiplication.

In 6^3, the base is 6.

BEDMAS A way of remembering the order of operations. BEDMAS stands for **B**rackets, **E**xponents, **D**ivision, **M**ultiplication, **A**ddition, **S**ubtraction.

bias Error resulting from choosing a sample that is not representative of the whole population.

binomial A polynomial that has two terms.

$3x + 4$ is a binomial.

bisect Divide into two equal parts.

broken-line graph A graph that relates two variables as ordered pairs, with consecutive points joined by line segments.

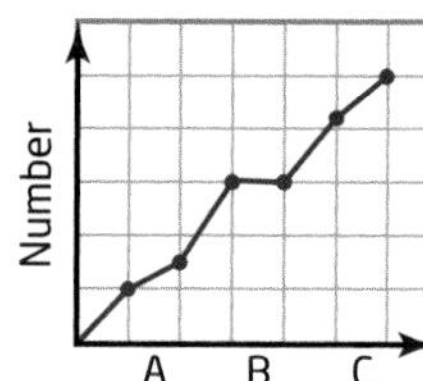

C

Calculator-Based Ranger™ (CBR™) A device that can be attached to a graphing calculator to collect data such as distance and speed.

capacity The greatest volume that a container can hold, usually measured in litres or millilitres.

Cartesian coordinate system The system developed by René Descartes for graphing points as ordered pairs on a grid, using two perpendicular number lines. Also referred to as the Cartesian plane, the coordinate grid, or the *xy*-plane.

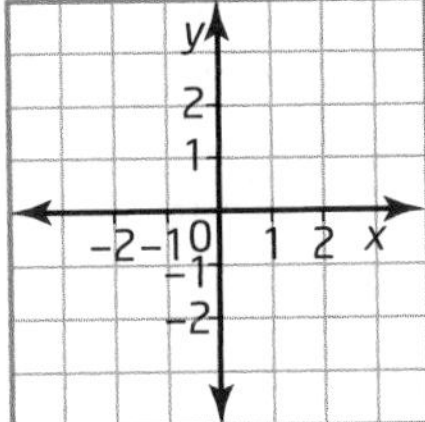

CBR™ See Calculator-Based Ranger.

census A survey of all members of a population.

centroid The point where the three medians of a triangle intersect.

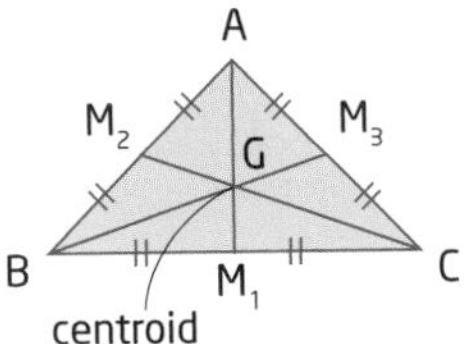

circle The set of all points in the plane that are equidistant from a fixed point called the centre.

circumference The perimeter of a circle.

coefficient The number by which a variable is multiplied.

In the term $8y$, the coefficient is 8.

co-interior angles Pairs of supplementary angles formed between a pair of parallel lines by a transversal.

$b + c = 180°$

$f + g = 180°$

collecting like terms Simplifying an expression containing like terms by adding their coefficients.

commission Pay based on a percent of the amount of sales or business done.

common factor A number that is a factor of (divides evenly into) all the numbers in a set.

3 is a common factor of 6, 12, and 15.

complementary angles Angles whose sum is 90°.

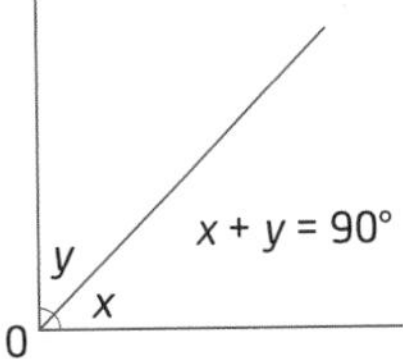

composite figure A figure made up of two or more simple shapes.

composite number A number that has factors other than itself and 1.

$24 = 2 \times 2 \times 2 \times 3$ is a composite number.

concave polygon A polygon in which one or more of the interior angles is greater than 180°.

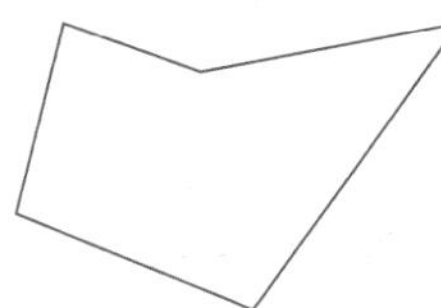

cone A three-dimensional object with a circular base and a curved lateral surface that extends from the base to a point called the vertex.

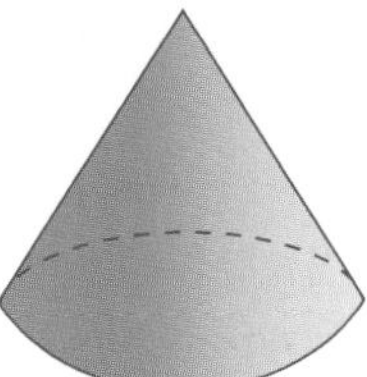

congruent Identical in size and shape.

conjecture A general conclusion drawn from a number of individual facts. It may or may not be true.

constant of variation In a direct variation, the ratio of corresponding values of the variables.

constant term A term that contains no variables. Its value does not change.

In $2x + 5$, the constant term is 5.

convex polygon A polygon in which each interior angle measures less than 180°.

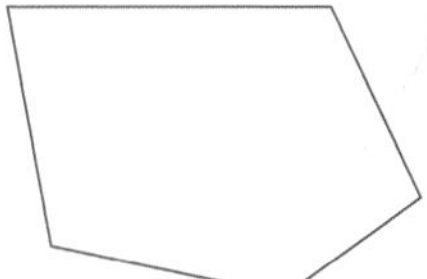

corresponding angles Pairs of equal angles, in corresponding positions, formed by a transversal crossing a pair of parallel lines.

$a = c$

$b = d$

$e = g$

$f = h$

counter-example An example that proves that a hypothesis or conjecture is false.

cube A prism with six congruent square faces.

cube root A number that is multiplied by itself twice to give another number.

$\sqrt[3]{8} = 2$ because $2 \times 2 \times 2 = 8$.

curve of best fit A curve that passes through or as near as possible to the points on a scatter plot.

cylinder A three-dimensional object with two parallel circular bases.

degree (of a polynomial) The degree of the greatest-degree term.

degree (of a term) The sum of the exponents on the variables in a term.

The degree of $5x^2y$ is 3.

denominator The number of equal parts in the whole or the group.

$\frac{3}{4}$ has denominator 4.

dependent variable In a relation, the variable whose value depends on the value of the other variable (the independent variable). On a coordinate grid, the values of the dependent variable are on the vertical axis.

In $d = 85t$, d is the dependent variable.

diagonal A line segment joining two non-adjacent vertices of a polygon.

diameter A line segment, joining two points on the circumference, that passes through the centre of a circle.

direct variation A relationship between two variables in which one variable is a constant multiple of the other.

distance-time graph A graph that plots distance travelled versus time.

distributive property $a(x + y) = ax + ay$

dynamic geometry software Computer software that allows the user to construct two-dimensional shapes, measure them, and transform them by moving their parts.

equation A mathematical statement that says two expressions are equal.

$5k - 2 = 3k + 4$ is an equation.

equiangular Having all angles equal.

equilateral triangle A triangle with all three sides equal.

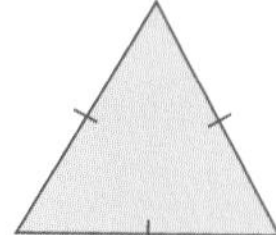

equivalent expressions Algebraic expressions that are equal for all values of the variable.

$7a - 3a$ and $4a$ are equivalent expressions.

equivalent fractions Fractions, such as $\frac{1}{3}$, $\frac{2}{6}$, and $\frac{3}{9}$, that represent the same part of a whole or group.

equivalent rational numbers Numbers, such as $-1\frac{1}{2}$ and -1.5, that represent the same rational number.

equivalent ratios Ratios, such as 1:3, 2:6, and 3:9, that represent the same division of the whole.

estimate A guess at a measurement based on known comparisons, or a rough calculation using approximate numbers.

evaluate To determine a value for an expression or formula.

expand Multiply, often using the distributive property.

expanded form (of a power) The product of like factors that is equivalent to a power.

$2 \times 2 \times 2 \times 2 \times 2$ is the expanded form of 2^5.

exponent A raised number to denote repeated multiplication of a base.

In 3^4, the exponent is 4.

exponent laws A set of rules that can be used to simplify powers. See product rule, quotient rule, and power of a power rule.

exponential form A shorthand method for writing numbers expressed as repeated multiplications.

3^4 is the exponential form for $3 \times 3 \times 3 \times 3$ or 81.

expression A mathematical phrase made up of numbers and variables, connected by operators.

$3x + 2$ is an expression.

exterior angle An angle contained between one side of a polygon and the extension of an adjacent side.

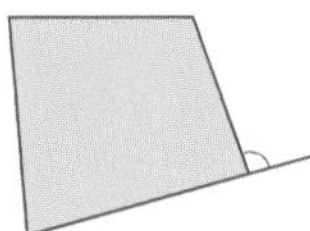

extrapolate Estimate values lying outside the given range of data. To extrapolate from a graph means to estimate coordinates of points beyond those that are plotted.

face A plane surface of a polyhedron.

Fermi problem A problem that requires estimation in its solution. Named after Enrico Fermi.

first differences Differences between consecutive y-values in tables of values with evenly spaced x-values.

formula An algebraic relationship between two or more variables.

frequency The number of times a measure occurs in a data set.

frustum The part that remains after the top portion of a cone or pyramid has been cut off by a plane parallel to the base.

G

graphing calculator A hand-held device capable of a wide range of mathematical operations, including graphing from an equation and constructing a scatter plot and a bar graph. Many graphing calculators attach to scientific probes that can be used to gather data involving physical measurements, such as distance and temperature.

graphing software Computer software that provides features similar to those of a graphing calculator.

greatest common factor (GCF) The greatest number that is a factor of two or more numbers.

The GCF of 12 and 8 is 4.

GST Goods and Services Tax.

heptagon A polygon with seven sides.

hexagon A polygon with six sides.

hypotenuse The longest side of a right triangle.

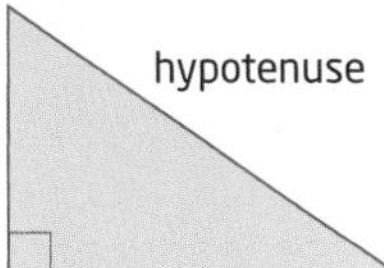

hypothesis A proposed answer to a question or position on an issue that has yet to be tested to see if it is true.

improper fraction A fraction in which the numerator is greater than the denominator, such as $\frac{8}{5}$.

independent variable In a relation, the variable that you need to know first. Its value determines the value of the dependent variable. On a coordinate grid, the values of the independent variable are on the horizontal axis.

In $d = 85t$, t is the independent variable.

inference A conclusion based on reasoning and data.

integer A number in the sequence ..., −3, −2, −1, 0, 1, 2, 3 ...

intercept The distance from the origin of the xy-plane to the point at which a line or curve crosses a given axis.

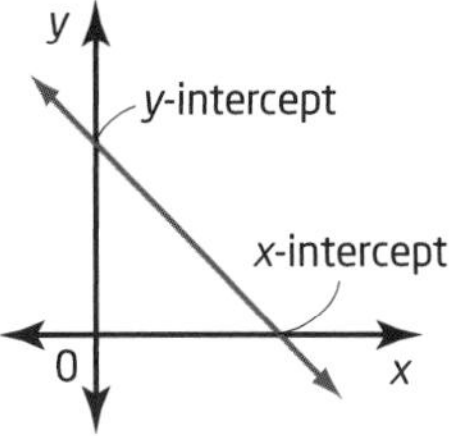

interior angle An angle that is formed inside a polygon by two sides meeting at a vertex.

interpolate To estimate values lying between given data. To interpolate from a graph means to estimate coordinates of points between those that are plotted.

isosceles triangle A triangle with exactly two equal sides.

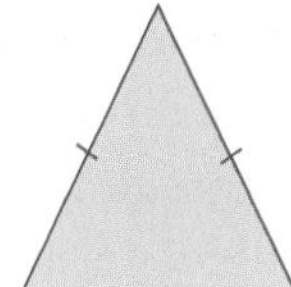

kite A quadrilateral with two pairs of adjacent sides equal.

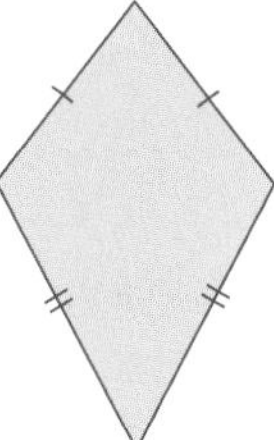

lateral faces The faces of a prism or pyramid that are not bases.

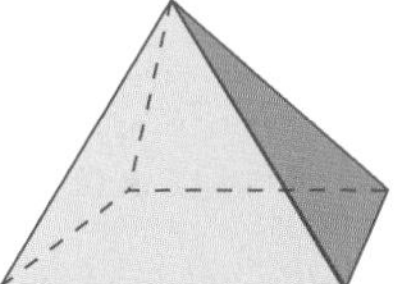

like terms Terms that have the same variable(s) raised to the same exponent(s).

$3xy$, $-xy$, and $2.5xy$ are like terms.

line of best fit The straight line that passes through or as near as possible to the points on a scatter plot.

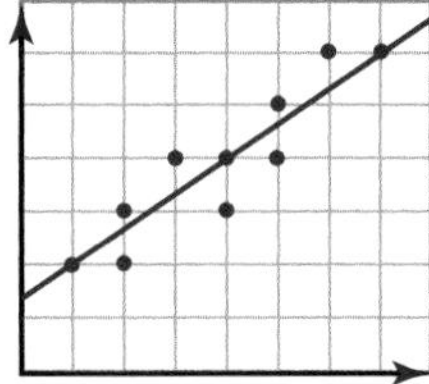

line of symmetry A line that divides a shape into two congruent shapes that are reflections of each other in the line.

line segment The part of a line that joins two points.

linear equation An equation that relates two variables so that ordered pairs satisfying the equation form a straight line pattern on a graph.

linear regression A mathematical process used by graphing calculators and graphing software to find the line of best fit.

linear relation A relation between two variables that appears as a straight line when graphed on the coordinate plane.

linear system A set of two or more linear equations that are considered at the same time.

literal coefficient The variable part of a term.

In $5xy$, the literal coefficient is xy.

lowest common denominator (LCD) The least common multiple of the denominators of two or more rational numbers.

The LCD of $\frac{3}{4}$ and $-\frac{2}{3}$ is 12.

lowest common multiple (LCM) The least multiple that two or more numbers have in common.

The LCM of 5 and 15 is 15.

lowest terms The form in which the numerator and the denominator of a fraction have no common factors other than 1.

$\frac{3}{5}$ is in lowest terms.

mass A measure of the quantity of matter in an object, measured in milligrams, grams, kilograms, or tonnes.

mathematical model A mathematical description of a real situation. The description may be a diagram, a graph, a table of values, an equation, a formula, a physical model, or a computer model.

maximum The greatest value in a set of data.

mean The sum of a set of values divided by the number of values in the set.

The mean of 2, 8, 4, 6, and 10 is $\frac{2 + 8 + 4 + 6 + 10}{5}$, or 6.

measure of central tendency A value that represents the "average" of a set of data. It can be the mean, median, or mode.

median (data) The middle value when data are arranged in order from least to greatest. If there is an even number of pieces of data, then the median is the average of the two middle values.

The median of 1, 1, 3, 5, 6 is 3.

The median of 1, 1, 3, 5 is 2.

median (geometry) A line segment that joins a vertex of a triangle to the midpoint of the opposite side.

BM is a median of $\triangle$ABC.

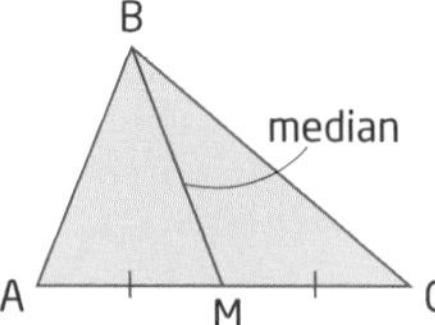

midpoint The point that divides a line segment into two equal segments.

minimum The least value in a set of data.

mixed number A number that is part whole number and part fraction, such as $3\frac{1}{2}$.

mode The value that occurs most frequently in a set of data.

For 1, 2, 3, 3, 8, the mode is 3.

monomial A polynomial with one term, such as $7x$.

N

natural number A number in the sequence 1, 2, 3, 4, ….

negative reciprocals Two numbers whose product is −1.
$\frac{3}{4}$ and $-\frac{4}{3}$ are negative reciprocals.

negative slope The ratio of rise to run of a line that rises to the left.

The line shown has slope −1.

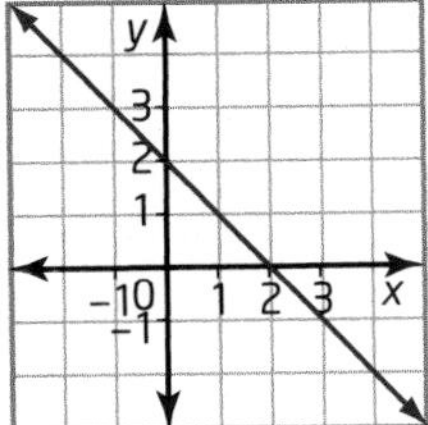

net A two-dimensional (flat) pattern that can be cut out, folded, and taped to form a three-dimensional shape. A net for a cube is shown.

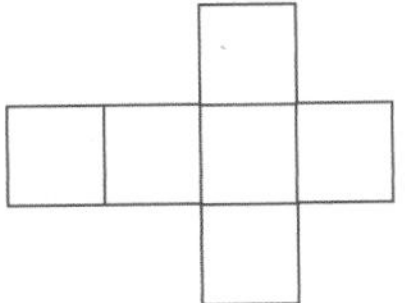

non-linear relation A relationship between two variables that is not a straight line when graphed.

non-random sampling A method of obtaining a sample in which participants volunteer or are selected by convenience.

numerator The number of equal parts being considered in the whole or the group.

$\frac{3}{4}$ has numerator 3.

numerical coefficient The number factor in a term.

In $7x^2$, the numerical coefficient is 7.

O

obtuse angle An angle that measures more than 90° but less than 180°.

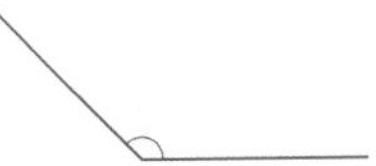

obtuse triangle A triangle containing one obtuse angle.

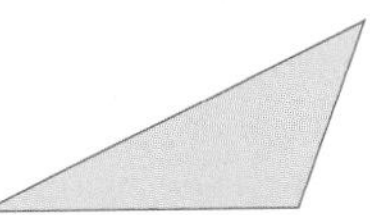

octagon A polygon with eight sides.

opposite angles When two lines cross, the pairs of angles formed on either side.

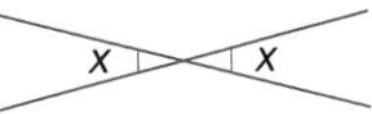

opposite integers Two integers, such as 5 and −5, that are an equal distance either side of 0. Their sum is 0.

optimization The process of finding values that make a given quantity the greatest (or least) possible under certain conditions.

order of operations The convention for evaluating expressions containing several operations: **B**rackets, **E**xponents, **D**ivision, **M**ultiplication, **A**ddition, **S**ubtraction. See BEDMAS.

ordered pair A pair of numbers, such as (2, 5), used to locate a point on the coordinate plane.

origin The point of intersection of the x-axis and the y-axis on a coordinate grid. The point (0, 0).

outlier A data point that does not fit the pattern of the other data.

parallel lines Lines in the same plane that never meet. On a graph, parallel lines have the same slope.

parallelogram A quadrilateral with two pairs of opposite sides that are parallel.

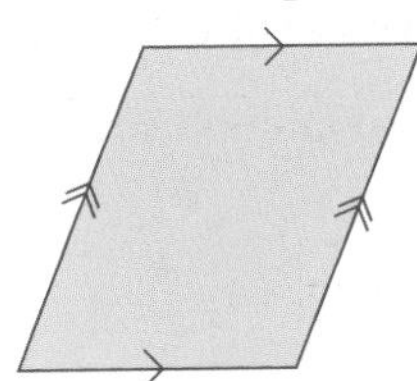

partial variation A relationship between two variables in which one variable equals a constant multiple of the other, plus a constant value.

pentagon A five-sided polygon.

pentomino A shape made of five unit squares in which each of the squares shares at least one side with another of the squares.

percent A fraction whose denominator is 100.

72% means $\frac{72}{100}$.

perfect square A number that can be expressed as the product of two identical factors.

36 is a perfect square, because $36 = 6 \times 6$.

perimeter The distance around the outside of a shape.

perpendicular lines Two lines that cross at 90°. On a graph, perpendicular lines have slopes that are negative reciprocals (their product is -1).

point of intersection The point where two lines cross.

polygon A two-dimensional closed figure whose sides are line segments.

polyhedron A three-dimensional object with faces that are polygons.

polynomial An algebraic expression formed by adding or subtracting terms.

polynomial expression An algebraic expression made up of one or more terms separated by addition or subtraction.

population In data analysis, the entire group that is being studied.

positive slope The ratio of the rise to the run of a line that rises to the right.

The line shown has slope $\frac{2}{3}$.

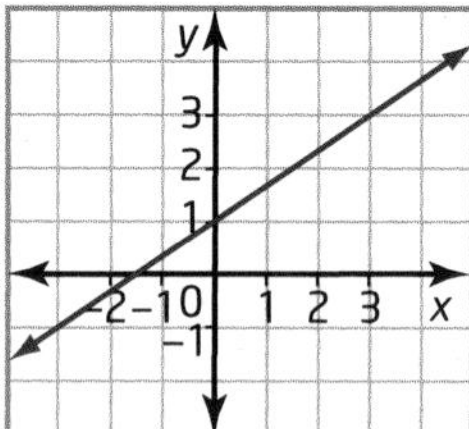

power A short form of writing repeated multiplication of the same number by itself.

5^3, x^2, and 10^7 are powers.

power of a power rule A power of a power can be written as a single power by multiplying the exponents.

$(x^a)^b = x^{ab}$

primary data Use of a survey or an experiment to collect your own data.

prime number A number with exactly two factors—itself and 1.

2, 5, and 13 are prime numbers.

prism A three-dimensional object with two parallel, congruent polygonal bases. A prism is named by the shape of its bases, for example, rectangular prism, triangular prism.

product The result of multiplication.

product rule To multiply powers of the same base, add the exponents.

$x^a \times x^b = x^{a+b}$

proportion A statement that two ratios are equal. Can be written in fraction form or in ratio form.

$\frac{2}{5} = \frac{4}{10}$ or $2{:}5 = 4{:}10$.

PST Provincial Sales Tax.

pyramid A polyhedron whose base is a polygon and other faces are triangles that meet at a common vertex.

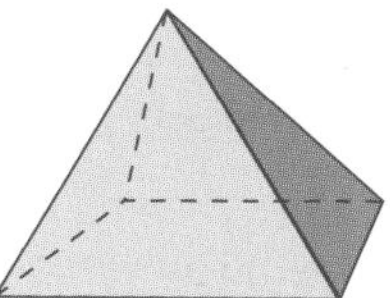

Pythagorean theorem In a right triangle, the square of the length of the hypotenuse is equal to the sum of the squares of the two shorter side lengths.

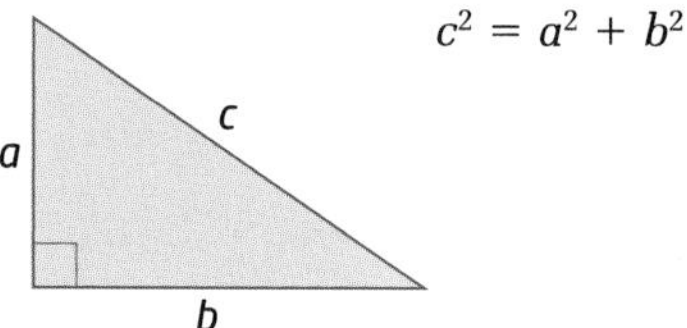

$c^2 = a^2 + b^2$

Q

quadrilateral A polygon that has four sides.

quotient The result of division.

quotient rule To divide powers of the same base, subtract exponents.

$x^a \div x^b = x^{a-b}$

radius A line segment joining the centre of a circle to a point on the circumference, or the length of this line segment.

random sampling A method of choosing a sample in which every member of a population has an equally likely chance of being selected.

rate A comparison of two quantities expressed in different units.

60 km/h and $12.95/kg are rates.

rate of change A change in one quantity relative to the change in another quantity.

ratio A comparison of two quantities with the same units.

rational number A number that can be expressed as the quotient of two integers, where the divisor is not zero.

0.75, $\frac{3}{4}$, and -2 are rational numbers.

ray A part of a line, with one endpoint.

reciprocals Two numbers that have a product of 1.

3 and $\frac{1}{3}$ are reciprocals.

rectangle A quadrilateral with two pairs of equal opposite sides and four right angles.

rectangular prism The mathematical name for a box with six rectangular faces with right angles at every corner.

reflex angle An angle that measures more than 180° but less than 360°.

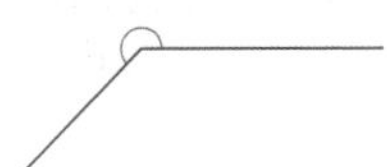

regular polygon A polygon with all sides equal and all interior angles equal.

relation An identified pattern, or relationship, between two variables. It may be expressed as ordered pairs, a table of values, a graph, or an equation.

rhombus A quadrilateral in which the lengths of all four sides are equal.

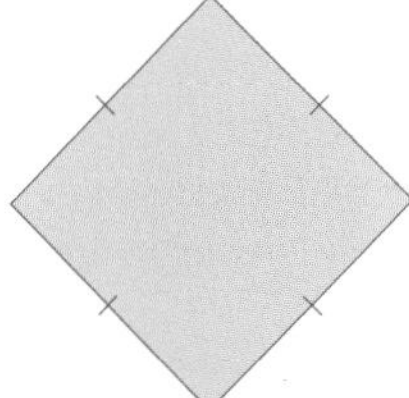

right angle An angle that measures 90°.

right bisector of a line segment A line that is perpendicular to a line segment and divides the line segment into two equal parts. Also called a perpendicular bisector.

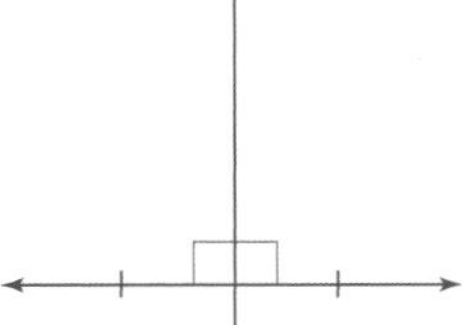

right prism A three-dimensional object with two parallel, congruent polygonal bases and side faces that are perpendicular to the bases.

right triangle A triangle containing a 90° angle.

rise The vertical distance between two points.

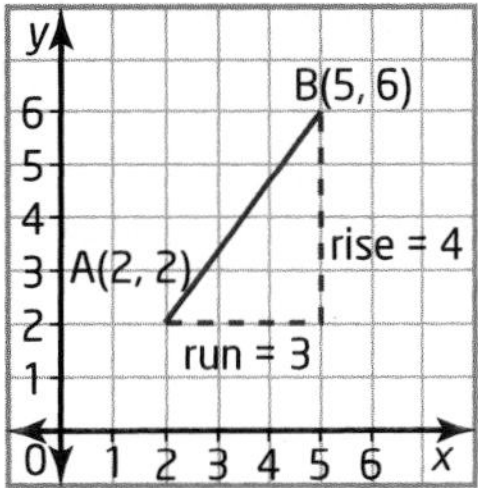

root The value of the variable that makes an equation true. The same as the solution of an equation.

run The horizontal distance between two points. See the diagram above.

S

sample A small group chosen from a population and examined in order to make predictions about the population.

scalene triangle A triangle with no sides equal.

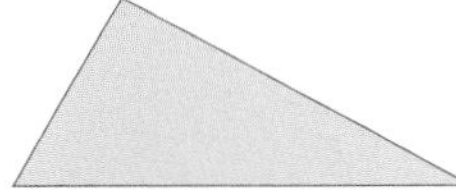

scatter plot A graph showing two-variable data as points plotted on a coordinate grid. See line of best fit.

scientific notation A method of writing large or small numbers that contain many zeros. The decimal is placed to the right of the first non-zero digit and the exponent on the base 10 tells how the decimal point is moved.

$123\ 000 = 1.23 \times 10^5$

$0.000\ 000\ 085 = 8.5 \times 10^{-8}$

secondary data Information that has been collected by someone else.

sector A part of a circle bounded by two radii and an arc of the circumference.

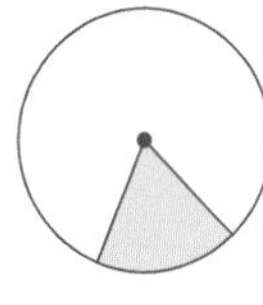

semicircle Half of a circle.

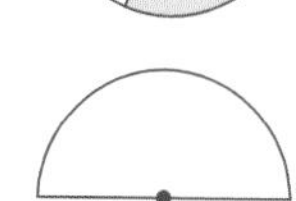

sequence An ordered list of numbers.

similar triangles Triangles in which corresponding side are in proportion.

simple random sampling A method of choosing a specific number of people from a population. Each person has the same chance of being chosen. An example is drawing names from a hat.

simplest form (of a ratio) When the terms of the ratio are whole numbers having no common factors other than 1.

simplest form of an algebraic expression An expression with no like terms. For example, $2x + 7$ is in simplest form, $5x + 1 + 6 - 3x$ is not.

simplify Find a simpler and shorter equivalent expression.

single-variable data Data in which there is just one data list.

slope A measure of the steepness of a line.

$$\text{slope} = \frac{\text{rise}}{\text{run}}$$

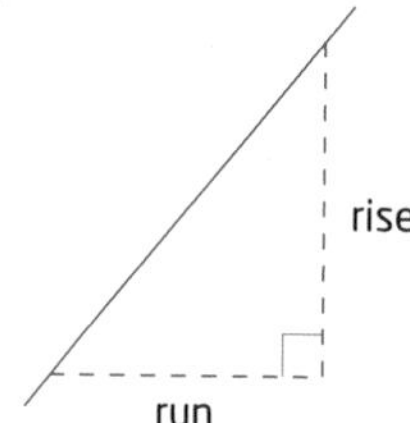

slope formula The slope, m, of a line containing the points $A(x_A, y_A)$ and $B(x_B, y_B)$ is

$$m_{AB} = \frac{\text{vertical change}}{\text{horizontal change}} \text{ or } \frac{\text{rise}}{\text{run}} = \frac{y_B - y_A}{x_B - x_A}, x_B \neq x_A$$

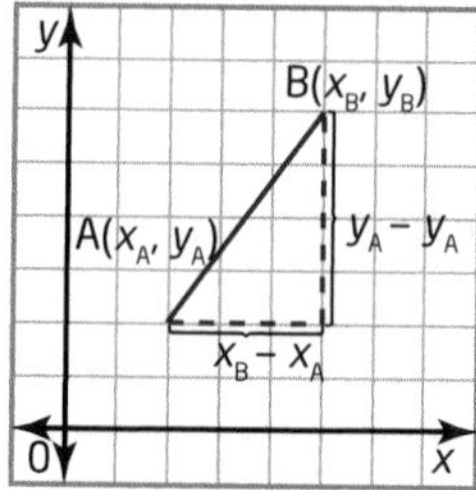

slope *y*-intercept form of a linear equation The equation of a line with slope m and y-intercept b is $y = mx + b$.

solution The value of the variable that makes an equation true.

speed The rate of change in distance compared to change in time. The slope of a distance-time graph.

sphere A round ball-shaped object. All points on its surface are the same distance from a fixed point called the centre.

square A rectangle in which the lengths of all four sides are equal.

square-based prism A prism with two square faces as bases and four rectangular side faces.

square root A number that is multiplied by itself to give another number. For example, $\sqrt{36} = 6$.

standard form of the equation of a line The equation of a line in the form $Ax + By + C = 0$, where A, B, and C are whole numbers, and A and B are not both equal to zero.

statistics Numerical data, or the collection, organization, and analysis of such data.

straight angle An angle that measures 180°.

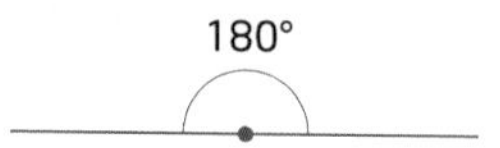

stratified random sampling A method in which a population is divided into groups, and proportional samples are randomly selected from within each group.

substitution Replacing a variable by a value.

supplementary angles Angles whose sum is 180°.

$a + b = 180°$

a b

surface area The number of square units needed to cover the surface of a three-dimensional object.

survey A question or questions asked of a sample of a population.

systematic random sampling A method of choosing, in a pre-determined way, a specified number of people from a population. An example is choosing every 10th person on a list.

table of values A table used to record the coordinates of points in a relation. For example,

$y = x + 3$

x	y
0	3
1	4
2	5

term A number or a variable, or the product of numbers and variables.

The expression $5x + 3$ has two terms: $5x$ and 3.

transversal A line that crosses or intersects two or more lines.

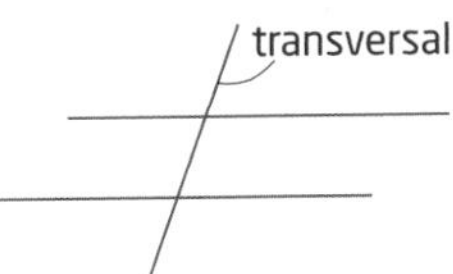

trapezoid A quadrilateral with one pair of parallel sides.

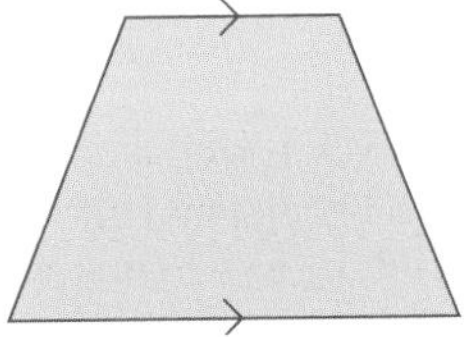

triangle A three-sided polygon.

triangular prism A prism with triangular bases.

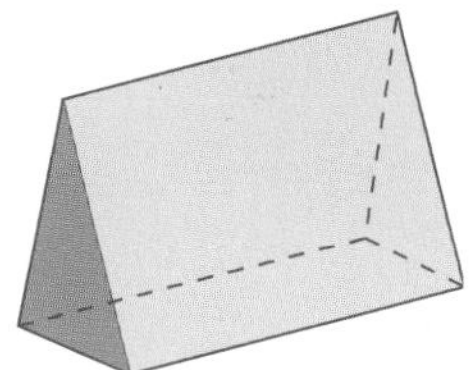

trinomial A polynomial with three terms.

$x^2 + 3x - 1$ is a trinomial.

two-variable data A set of data with two lists of data. Each entry in one list is related in some way to an entry in the other list.

unit price The cost for one item or for one unit of measurement.

unit rate A comparison of two quantities in which the second term is 1. For example, $5 per ticket, or 30 km/h.

unlike terms Terms that have different variables, or the same variable but different exponents.

$2x$, $5y$, and x^2 are unlike terms.

variable A letter used to represent a value that can change or vary. For example, t is the variable in the expression $2t + 3$.

variable term A term that contains a variable. Its value changes when the value of the variable changes.

vertex (plural vertices) A point at which two sides of a polygon meet.

volume The amount of space that an object occupies, measured in cubic units.

whole number A number in the sequence 0, 1, 2, 3, 4, 5, … .

***x*-axis** The horizontal number line in the Cartesian coordinate system.

***x*-coordinate** The first number in the ordered pair describing a point on a Cartesian plane.

The point P(2, 5) has x-coordinate 2.

***x*-intercept** The x-coordinate of the point where a line or curve crosses the x-axis. At this point, $y = 0$.

***xy*-plane** A coordinate system based on the intersection of two perpendicular lines called axes. The horizontal axis is the x-axis, and the vertical axis is the y-axis. The point of intersection of the axes is called the origin.

***y*-axis** The vertical number line in the Cartesian coordinate system.

***y*-coordinate** The second number in the ordered pair describing a point on a Cartesian plane.

The point Q(−3, 4) has y-coordinate 4.

***y*-intercept** The y-coordinate of the point where a line or curve crosses the y-axis. At this point, $x = 0$.

Index

S

T

V

X

Credits

Photo Credits

iv (top) Roland W. Meisel; iv (bottom) Harold V. Green/VALAN PHOTOS; v Roland W. Meisel; vi (top) Bill Ivy/IVY IMAGES; vi (bottom) Hot shots/IVY IMAGES; vii Roland W. Meisel; p2-3 Roland W. Meisel; p14 Roland W. Meisel; p18 Roland W. Meisel; p19 Stephen Frink/CORBIS; p20 Roland W. Meisel; p24 Roland W. Meisel; p29 Roland W. Meisel; p32 Bill Ivy/IVY IMAGES; p38-39 Index Stock/Maxx Images; p42 Roland W. Meisel; p48 Charles Gupton/Getty Images; p50 Sarah Ivy/IVY IMAGES; p55 Creatas/PunchStock; p56 (top) Roland W. Meisel; p56 (bottom) Index Stock/Maxx Images; p60 Hot Shots/IVY IMAGES; p64 Bill Ivy/IVY IMAGES; p68 Ted Streshinsky/CORBIS; p71 Ryan McVay/Getty Images; p74 James W. Porter/CORBIS; p78 Nature's Images/Photo Researchers, Inc.; p87 Bill Ivy/IVY IMAGES; p88 Roland W. Meisel; p92 Bill Ivy/IVY IMAGES; p104 CORBIS; p106 Roland W. Meisel; p109 (top) Roland W. Meisel; p109 Mary Evans Picture Library; p109 Mary Evans Picture Library; p117 B. Lowry/IVY IMAGES; p119 top, CORBIS; p119, left CP/Denis Paquin; p130 Roland W. Meisel; p133 IVY IMAGES; p139 Bettmann CORBIS; p144 Courtesy of Bombardier Recreational Products, Inc.; p154 Roland W. Meisel; p160 Harold V. Green/VALAN PHOTOS; p174 Roland W. Meisel; p180 Roland W. Meisel; p182-183 Bill Ivy/IVY IMAGES; p186 Creatas/Maxx Images; p195 Roland W. Meisel; p196 Roland W. Meisel; p204 F. Staud/www.phototravels.net; p211 Roland W. Meisel; p216 CP/Frank Gunn; p218 Roland W. Meisel; p219 Roland W. Meisel; p220 Roland W. Meisel; p233 CP; p234-235 Roland W. Meisel; p238 McGraw-Hill Companies, Inc./Gary He, photographer; p243 CORBIS; p245 Galen Rowell/CORBIS; p249 D. Trask/IVY IMAGES; p251 Karl Weatherly/Getty Images; p253 NPS/IVY IMAGES; p254 Hot Shots/IVY IMAGES; p261 Roland W. Meisel; p262 Bettmann/CORBIS; p264 CP/Action Press (Von Der Laage); p265 Tom Stewart/CORBIS; p270 Stuart Westmorland/CORBIS; p272 Roland W. Meisel; p279 Roland W. Meisel; p286 Roland W. Meisel; p292-293 Roland W. Meisel; p296 Roland W. Meisel; p307 Roland W. Meisel; p308 Bettmann/CORBIS; p315 Helen King/CORBIS; p326 Roland W. Meisel; p330 Roland W. Meisel; p331 Steve Mason/Getty Images; p336 Roland W. Meisel; p338 David Stoecklein/CORBIS; p344 Mike Chew/CORBIS; p359 O. Bierwagen/IVY IMAGES; p360-361; p364 Roland W. Meisel; p374 Bill Ivy/IVY IMAGES; p384 Roland W. Meisel; p391 Bierwagen/IVY IMAGES; p392 Roland W. Meisel; p394 Roland W. Meisel; p401 Andrew Lambert/Photo Researchers, Inc; p412-413 Roland W. Meisel; p418 Super Stock/Maxx Images; p420 Roland W. Meisel; p426 Eddi Boehnke/zefa/CORBIS; p436 Roland W. Meisel; p437 (top) Roland W. Meisel; p437 (bottom) Andrew Ward/Life File/Getty Images; p442 Sandro Vannini/CORBIS; p444 Roland W. Meisel; p449 Roland W. Meisel; p451 Roland W. Meisel; p457 Roland W. Meisel; p458 Super Stock/Maxx Images; p462 (top) Photo by Lois Siegal; p462 (bottom) Roland W. Meisel; p465 CP/Larry MacDougall; p474-475 Ray Juno/CORBIS; p478 Roland W. Meisel; p484 Roland W. Meisel; p491 Roland W. Meisel; p496 Don Ford; p498 Roland W. Meisel; p504 Roland W. Meisel; p508 Roland W. Meisel; p510 Roland W. Meisel; p514 Roland W. Meisel; p519 Roland W. Meisel

Text Credits

p40 exchange rates: The Bank of Canada; p66 fast food data: www.harveys.ca, www.mrsub.ca, www.pizzapizza.ca, www.kfc.com, and www.swisschalet.ca, Harvey's and Swiss Chalet data courtesy of Cara Operations Limited; p67 baseball statistics, www.mlb.com; p73 world populations: United Nations Population Division; p74 donor data: adapted courtesy of Imagine Canada from "Who Are Canada's Donors?" by Marcus Parmegiani; p75 music sales data: Canadian Recording Industry Association, www.cria.ca/stats.php; p76 volunteer data: adapted courtesy of Imagine Canada from "Who Are Canada's Volunteers?" by Marcus Parmegiani; p78 lizard data: adapted from L.J. Vitt, S.S. Sartorius, and T.C.S. Avila-Pires, *Canadian Journal of Zoology*, Vol 76/9, p1682, 1998, NRC Canada; p85 canola yields, Canola Council of Canada

Illustration Credits

Ben Hodson: p45, 47, 110, 111, 115, 167, 210, 215
www.mikecarterstudio.com: p100-1

Technical Art

Tom Dart, Grey Duhaney, Kim Hutchinson, Nina Obrecht, and Adam Wood/
First Folio Resource Group, Inc.